THE THIRTEENTH
CENTURY

THE
THIRTEENTH
CENTURY

1216–1307

BY

SIR MAURICE POWICKE

FORMERLY REGIUS PROFESSOR OF
MODERN HISTORY IN THE
UNIVERSITY OF OXFORD

SECOND EDITION

Oxford   New York
OXFORD UNIVERSITY PRESS

Oxford University Press, Walton Street, Oxford OX2 6DP

Oxford New York Toronto
Delhi Bombay Calcutta Madras Karachi
Petaling Jaya Singapore Hong Kong Tokyo
Nairobi Dar es Salaam Cape Town
Melbourne Auckland

and associated companies in
Berlin Ibadan

Oxford is a trade mark of Oxford University Press

First edition 1953
Second edition 1962
Published 1963 as volume four of The Oxford History of England

First issued as an Oxford University Press paperback 1991

Reprinted 1992

British Library Cataloguing in Publication Data
Data available
ISBN 0–19–285249–3

Library of Congress Cataloging in Publication Data
Powicke, F. M. (Frederick Maurice), 1879–1963.
The thirteenth century, 1216–1307 / by Sir Maurice Powicke.—2nd ed.
p. cm.
Includes bibliographical references and index.
1. Great Britain—History—13th century. I. Title.
942.03'4—dc20 DA225.P65 1991 91–11658
ISBN 0–19–285249–3 (pbk.)

Printed in Great Britain by
Biddles Ltd.
Guildford and King's Lynn

PREFACE TO SECOND EDITION

IN this edition the pagination of the first edition has been retained. Additions and corrections have been included with slight alterations in the text and notes. A surprising amount of work on the period has been published since 1953, and doubtless more is soon to come; but I have not felt justified as yet in making any major changes in narrative or opinion.

F. M. P.

OXFORD, 1961

PREFACE TO FIRST EDITION

MANY friends have helped me to write this book. I have acknowledged my debt to them in the footnotes and bibliography, but I wish here to give special thanks to Mr. J. C. Trabut-Cussac, who most generously placed at my service his unpublished treatise on Edward I and Gascony, also to Professors T. Jones Pierce and W. C. Dickinson for their guidance on problems of Welsh and Scottish social history and bibliography.

The Bibliography is intended, in part, as a guide, with a running commentary, to the study of matters which I have had to omit or could mention only incidentally in the course of the narrative. References to the more unusual books and articles noticed in the footnotes and bibliography are indexed under the names of their authors, which are printed in italics.

Finally, I beg to thank the Editor of the History and the Secretary and his colleagues at the Clarendon Press for their friendly and helpful interest in a book which departs, more than do previous volumes in the series, from its original plan.

F. M. P.

BALLIOL COLLEGE, OXFORD
February 1953

CONTENTS

LIST OF MAPS   *page* xv
GENEALOGICAL TABLE   xvi–xvii

I. THE MINORITY OF HENRY III

Henry's succession to the throne	1
Regency and council: William the Marshal	2
King John's executors	3
The first confirmation of the Great Charter (1216); its significance	4
On the responsibility of king and magnates to maintain 'the state of the king and of the realm'	5
The nature of the war with Louis of France	8
Resistance to Louis in the south-east; Eustace the Monk	9
The diversion of Louis's forces and their rout at Lincoln (May 1217)	10
First negotiations for peace	12
Sea fight off Sandwich: end of Eustace the Monk	12
The treaty of Kingston (September 1217): the *reversi*	13
The return to normal: Pandulf succeeds Guala as legate	16
Death of William the Marshal (May 1219): Pandulf	17
King Henry's second coronation (May 1220); his character; his majority (1223, 1227)	18
Castles and castellans	20
Archbishop Stephen Langton and the justiciar, Hubert de Burgh	23
The resumption of the royal castles and sheriffdoms	25
The fall of Fawkes de Breauté	26
Financial survey of Henry III's reign	28

II. THE DUTIES OF KINGSHIP

Investigation of rights: the written evidence	38
The position of Richard of Cornwall	40
The lordships of Hubert de Burgh: Wales and the Marches	42
The fall of Hubert de Burgh: his relations with the clergy	45
Peter des Rivaux and the new administration	48
Earl Richard the Marshal's opposition	53
Intervention of the bishops: Edmund of Abingdon	55
King Henry adjusts himself	59
Administrative developments, 1223–41	62
Legislation, 1234–6; a conflict of laws	67
Significance of this period of the reign	72
The king's marriage (1236): trouble at court	73
Plans of reform, 1238–58	75
Additional note on plan ascribed by Matthew Paris to 1244	79

III. FOREIGN RELATIONS, 1216–59

The background: the Crusade   80
An age of truce interrupted by brief periods of war   84
The reconquest of Poitou by Louis VIII of France, 1224   87
The house of Lusignan   89
The statesmanship of Blanche of Castile   91
King Henry and Peter of Dreux   92
The expedition to Brittany, 1230, and the end of the alliance
    with Peter of Dreux   94
King Henry and western politics, 1235–42   97
James of Aragon and Raymond of Toulouse   99
Henry III and the movement against Alphonse of Poitou; the
    expedition of 1242   100
Henry's gradual change of front; the position of Richard of
    Cornwall   104
Simon de Montfort   106
The state of Gascony: Simon de Montfort as lieutenant, 1248–
    52   108
Earl Simon on trial. His outlook   113
Henry III in Gascony, 1253–4. Alfonso of Castile. The estab-
    lishment and marriage of the Lord Edward   115
Henry as a crusader. The Sicilian business and the treaty of
    Paris   119

IV. THE COMMON ENTERPRISE, 1258–62

General considerations. The king and his counsellors   129
The changes of 1258   134
Judicial inquiry. The duties imposed upon the knights of the
    shire   143
The provisions of 1259   146
Baronial households and baronial compacts. Richard of Clare,
    the Lord Edward and Simon de Montfort   151
The crisis of 1260   155
The breach in the community. The papal dispensation. The
    king resumes the initiative in 1261–2   161

V. THE BARONS' WAR AND THE LEGATE'S PEACE

The revival of dissension and the chaos in the Welsh Marches,
    1262–3   170
Simon de Montfort takes the lead   174
The emergence of the Lord Edward. The royalists across the
    Channel   177
King Louis intervenes. The meeting at Boulogne, September–
    October 1263   178
The legation of the cardinal-bishop of Sabina. Deadlock in Eng-
    land. Richard of Cornwall's mediation   180
The Award of Amiens, January 1264   182

War in the Marches and the Severn valley. The Lord Edward's success   184

Fruitless discussions at Oxford. The capture of Northampton by the king and Edward   186

Earl Simon in London. His march south and victory at Lewes, 14 May 1264   187

The 'form of government' of June 1264. Negotiations with King Louis and the legate. The threat of invasion   191

Resistance in the Marches. The pact of Worcester (December 1264). The parliament of 1265   193

Plots and disturbance. Edward's escape from Hereford. Earl Simon's disillusionment. The fight at Evesham   199

The proclamation of peace and the ordinances issued at Winchester and Windsor. The disinherited   203

The Lord Edward and the work of subjugation. The rebels in Axholme, Kenilworth, and the Isle of Ely   206

The legate Ottobuono and the Dictum of Kenilworth   209

The intervention of the Earl of Gloucester and the end of resistance   213

The treaty of Montgomery, September 1267   215

The statute of Marlborough   216

A note on the Charters of Liberties, 1265–1300   217

Ottobuono's work as legate   219

Papal taxation of the clergy to meet the king's debts   220

The subsidy of 1269–70 and its significance. Edward on crusade   221

The dedication of the new church of Westminster Abbey, 13 October 1269   224

The end of the reign and Edward's return and coronation (1270–4)   225

VI. EDWARD I AND HIS TIME

Edward as a man of his age   227

The outlook and plans of Pope Gregory X   231

The age of the *regna*   233

Edward's family connexions in the West   234

Edward and French politics (1272–85). The reign of Philip III

   i. Champagne and Navarre   237

   ii. The disputes about the future succession to Castile   242

   iii. The problem of the kingdom of Arles. Rudolf of Habsburg and Savoy   245

   iv. Peter of Aragon and the Angevins: the Sicilian Vespers and the crusade against Aragon   251

Edward as a peacemaker (1287–91): the treaties of Oloron and Canfran   255

The negotiations about Edward's projected crusade   264

Genealogical table: the marriages of John of Brittany and Edmund of Lancaster   *between* 268–9

VII. THE DUKE OF AQUITAINE

Introductory observations — 270

The French Crown and the succession to the lands of Alphonse of Poitiers — 272

The administration of Gascony as subject to the English Crown: records and personnel — 274

The contributions of Gascony to the needs of the Crown — 280

The Gascon hostages in Aragon, 1288–9 — 283

Gaston de Béarn between 1254 and 1290 — 284

The commission of 1278–9 and the seneschal John de Grilly — 287

The treaties of Amiens (1279) and Paris (1286) — 289

The transfer of the Agenais to Aquitaine (1279) — 292

Edward's periods of residence in Gascony: the surveys of 1273–4 and the ordinances of 1289 — 295

Administrative system of Aquitaine — 300

Finance; coinage; the customs on wine — 304

Social developments: *paréages* and bastides — 307

The problem of appeals — 311

Note on the Channel Islands — 318

VIII. THE PERIOD OF THE STATUTES, 1274–90

The king's household: chamber and wardrobe — 322

Law and prerogative — 324

The central administration: Edward and his servants. The chancellor — 333

Sketch of the life of Robert Burnell — 338

The king's clerks — 340

The king in council in parliament; business and records; petitions — 341

The importance of the *querela* in the judicial and administrative system — 351

The statutes
General observations — 355

The statutes and the commissions of inquiry, 1274–85 — 357

The state trials of 1289–93: — 361
Adam of Stratton — 364

Legislation and the bailiffs of manors and liberties — 365

The statutes as 'new law': their relation to the common law and to the royal prerogative — 368

Quo warranto — 376

IX. WALES

Introduction: Anglo-Welsh relations; the Welsh view — 381

Two impressions of the Welsh — 383

Social and political developments in Wales in the thirteenth century — 384

CONTENTS xi

The religious orders and the Welsh community 389
The episcopate 390
From the Lord Rhys to Llywelyn the Great 391
Llywelyn the Great and Hubert de Burgh 394
The subjection and resistance of David of Snowdonia (1240–6) 398
The treaty of Woodstock (1247). The distribution of power in Wales 400
The rise to power of Llywelyn ap Gruffydd (1255–67). The treaty of Montgomery (1267) 401
The intrigues of prince David and Gruffydd ap Gwenwynwyn (1274); their effect on Llywelyn. The drift to war 406
Eleanor and Amauri de Montfort 408
The war of 1276–7 408
The treaty of Conway (November 1277) 412
The new order and the judicial commissions. The conflict of laws 415
The dispute about Arwystli 417
Prince David's revolt and the war of 1282–3 419
Edward's military plans: the first campaigns and the occupation of Anglesey 422
Archbishop Pecham's intervention 424
The death of Llywelyn (December 1282) 427
The investment of Snowdonia and the capture of prince David 428
The statute of Wales (March 1284) and the settlement 429
    Towns and castles 430
    The Church 433
    Justice and administration 435
The revolt of Rhys ap Mareddud 438
The risings of 1294 and the third war 440
The battle of Maes Moydog (March 1295) 442
Crown and marchers 443

X. THE CLERGY UNDER TWO RULES OF LAW

The ecclesiastical population: seculars and religious 445
The ecclesiastical system: the rectors 447
The Lateran decrees (1215) and the measure of their enforcement 449
Provincial and diocesan constitutions 451
Robert Grosseteste and the *gravamina* 453
The importance of archbishop Boniface's constitutions (1261) 456
High principles and social realities 458
The Church and the Crown 460
    Criminous clerks 462
    Advowsons and tithes 463
    Excommunication 464
    The litigious clerk 467
Archbishop Pecham and his predecessor, Robert Kilwardby 469

The provincial council of Reading, 1279: pluralities   471

The disputes about royal writs of prohibition and the ecclesiastical *gravamina*   477

The discussions in parliament of 1285   480

Trouble in the diocese of Norwich   481

The writ *Circumspecte agatis* (1286) in the setting of the gravamina
(1280–1316)   482

The English bishops in the thirteenth century   485

Pecham and his suffragans: ecclesiastical jurisdiction   490

The province of York: archbishop Romeyn and bishop Antony
Bek   493

The development of convocation and ecclesiastical taxation in
the thirteenth century   496

XI. THE COMMUNITY OF THE REALM AND TAXA-
TION

King Edward in 1289–91 after his return from Gascony   511

The nature of kingship and the plea of necessity. The effect
of events between 1291 and 1307 upon later history   514

War and finance. The taxation of the laity in Edward I's reign   523

The boroughs and the community   529

The knights of the shire and the problem of parliamentary
taxation   535

Knights and lesser landholders in war and defence   540

Developments in military organization in the thirteenth century   542

Money fiefs, the household knights and distraint of knighthood   544

The reduction in the *servitium debitum*: military equipment and
social change. The cavalry of the shires   549

The effect upon the feudal host   554

Scutage   556

XII. IRELAND AND SCOTLAND, 1217–97

Ireland in the thirteenth century: the two races   560

Ireland as a source of economic and military strength   565

The 'land of peace' and the disturbed areas; the causes and
nature of division. Cross currents in the Church   566

The legislation of 1297   569

Comparison between divisions in Ireland and divisions in Scotland   571

The formation of the Scottish state   574

Scotland in the thirteenth century   576

The interlocking of English and Scottish families; tendencies
to union   579

The Scottish Church and the Papacy   583
Anglo-Scottish relations in the reign of Alexander II (1214–49)   585
The Border   588
The minority of Alexander III: the intervention of Henry III   589
The problem of homage, 1212–79   594
The reign of Alexander III (d. 1286)   596
A joint settlement (1286–90). The death of the Maid of
    Norway   598
The problem of the succession   601
The settlement in King Edward's court at Norham and Ber-
    wick. Edward as superior lord   602
The reign of John Baliol, 1292–6   608
The expedition of 1296 and the union of the kingdoms   613

XIII. THE CROWN AND THE MERCHANTS

War economy and the social order   618
Edward and the merchants (1266–74): the 'new aid'   619
The importance of the breach with Flanders: the embargo on
    the export of wool to Flanders. The auditors of disputes   621
The statutes of Acton Burnell and of Merchants, 1284–5. Mer-
    chant law   625
London in royal hands, 1285–98   626
The history of the customs, 1275–1303   628
The coinage of 1279–80: the administration of mints and ex-
    changes   632
Town-planning   634
The Italian merchants in England   637

XIV. THE YEARS OF EMERGENCY

The sailors' war and the breach with France, 1293–4   644
War and truce in Gascony, 1294–1303. The cost of the war   648
The discussions about the status of the duchy of Gascony   650
Naval organization   655
The process of Montreuil-sur-Mer   657
Foreign alliances and the exploitation of the trade in wool   658
The Flemish expedition of 1297. Truce and peace, 1279–1303   666
King Edward and the Church, 1294–8: archbishop Win-
    chelsey   669
The baronial resistance to Edward's war measures   678
The king's surrender to the parliamentary settlement   683
The first stage of Scottish resistance, 1297–8   683
The campaign of Falkirk   689
War and truce in Scotland: the organization of the Borders
    and the Lowlands   692
The parliaments of 1299–1301: the Charters and the Forests   698

Letters to Pope Boniface   705

The isolation of the Scots and the preparations for final con-
    quest, 1302–3   706

The Scottish surrender and the planning of a new Scottish order,
    1303–6   708

The murder of John Comyn   713

King Edward and Robert Bruce: the flight of Bruce   715

The suspension of Archbishop Winchelsey   717

The return of Bruce. Edward's death   718

BIBLIOGRAPHY   720

INDEX   779

LIST OF MAPS

AQUITAINE   *page* 299

WALES   405

ENGLAND, SHOWING KING EDWARD'S MOVEMENTS IN 1289
  and 1290   510

SOUTH SCOTLAND AND THE NORTH OF ENGLAND   691

THE MARRIAGES OF JOHN OF BRITTANY (1260) AND
EDMUND OF LANCASTER (1275)

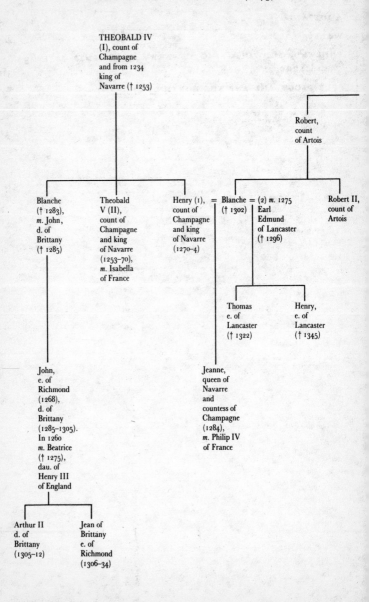

THEOBALD IV (I), count of Champagne and from 1234 king of Navarre († 1253)

Robert, count of Artois

Blanche († 1283), m. John, d. of Brittany († 1285)

Theobald V (II), count of Champagne and king of Navarre (1253–70), m. Isabella of France

Henry (I), count of Champagne and king of Navarre (1270–4)

= Blanche († 1302) = (2) m. 1275 Earl Edmund of Lancaster († 1296)

Robert II, count of Artois

Thomas e. of Lancaster († 1322)

Henry, e. of Lancaster († 1345)

John, e. of Richmond (1268), d. of Brittany (1285–1305). In 1260 m. Beatrice († 1275), dau. of Henry III of England

Jeanne, queen of Navarre and countess of Champagne (1284), m. Philip IV of France

Arthur II d. of Brittany (1305–12)

Jean of Brittany e. of Richmond (1306–34)

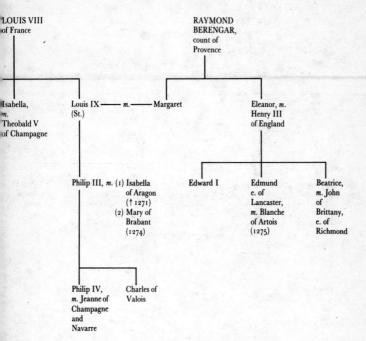

LOUIS VIII
of France

RAYMOND
BERENGAR,
count of
Provence

Isabella,
m.
Theobald V
of Champagne

Louis IX —— *m.*—— Margaret
(St.)

Eleanor, *m.*
Henry III
of England

Philip III, *m.* (1) Isabella
of Aragon
(† 1271)
(2) Mary of
Brabant
(1274)

Edward I

Edmund
e. of
Lancaster,
m. Blanche
of Artois
(1275)

Beatrice,
m. John
of
Brittany,
e. of
Richmond

Philip IV,
m. Jeanne of
Champagne
and
Navarre

Charles of
Valois

I

THE MINORITY OF HENRY III

WHEN King John died his wife and children were in
the south-west of England, probably in Corfe castle.
His elder son Henry, a boy of nine, was brought to Devizes, while the king's executors took his body for burial in the
new choir at Worcester; for John had commended his soul to
God and his body to St. Wulfstan, and the saint's shrine was in
Worcester. The executors went on to the royal castle at Gloucester, the ancient borough in which the Norman kings had been
wont to wear the crown once a year, and here, in the abbey
church, Henry was made king on 28 October 1216. His regnal
year began on this day.

The ceremony was simple, moving, and dignified, but not
splendid. Henry was knighted—he made, we are told, a pretty
little knight. He took the customary oaths. He was crowned by
Peter des Roches, the bishop of Winchester, with a circlet provided by his mother. Stephen Langton, the primate, was in
Rome; the crown, regalia, and jewels were not at hand. There
was no organized government, no exchequer, no royal seal.
London and half the shires of England were held by Louis of
France and the baronial rebels. With the exception of Dover,
the ports of the coast from Portsmouth to the Thames were under their control. The Welsh princes, headed and for the time
mastered by the great Llywelyn ab Iorwerth, prince of north
Wales, were making hay while the sun shone at the expense of
the Marchers. Yet in fact the position of affairs was not so bad
as it looked. The prelates and barons at Gloucester had received
their boy king with emotion. They were united in will and
loyalty. Their leaders were powerful and vigorous men and they
had with them the papal legate, Guala, cardinal priest of St.
Martin, whose sagacity was the more effective because he
brought to their aid the spiritual and moral sanction of the
Church. King John's death and the succession of a helpless
child took the sting out of the forces opposed to them, and gave
the mission of Louis of France the character of a usurpation.

The Welsh, in spite of their keen racial consciousness, were unfitted by their social structure and disinclined by their military habits to indulge in sustained enterprises beyond their borders. Nothing, at first sight, would seem more disastrous than the succession, and especially an unprecedented succession, of a boy of nine in a land divided by civil war, yet Henry's minority was to be, not an episode of troublesome or fitful suspense, but a formative period in the history of English institutions and of the English outlook on political life.

The appointment of regents was the first thing to be done. The authority of the legate was taken for granted. Before he was crowned Henry had done homage to the cardinal, as the pope's representative, for his kingdom of England and his lordship of Ireland. But the legate could not lead an army and do everyday business; indeed this would not have been fitting, for, whatever King John's surrender of his kingdom to the pope had meant, it did not imply the annexation of England by the Papacy. The wish of those gathered together at Gloucester was that the old earl marshal should assume the responsibility for the protection of Henry and his kingdom. The marshal was reluctant. In any case he felt that they should await the coming of Ranulf de Blundevill, earl of Chester, the greatest baron of the realm. Earl Ranulf arrived the next day (29 October). After he and the other barons had done homage to the king, the discussion began in the castle hall. The earl agreed with the others that William the Marshal ought to take the lead, and after some private conference in another room the marshal agreed. In the words of his biographer, he was given the *baillie* of the kingdom. He gave the charge of the king's person to the bishop of Winchester, who during the next few years acted as the boy's guardian and tutor. At first, it would seem, the marshal was regarded as justiciar, and such precedents as there were suggested that the regent should hold this high office; but a justiciar, appointed at Runnymede by King John, already existed in Hubert de Burgh. The marshal became *rector* of king and kingdom. He is so styled a few days later in the first reissue of the Great Charter of liberties.

Although the legate, the marshal, and Peter des Roches took the lead, they did not exercise an autocracy. They led a party firmly held together in face of a great crisis. They were but three of a group of executors appointed by King John from those upon whom he had come especially to rely; and it is likely that this group, which had brought John's body to Worcester and welcomed Henry at Gloucester, was the core of a council, a quasi-executive, quasi-advisory body which in the condition of public affairs during the king's minority was firmly established, to endure from this time as one of the institutions of the realm, whether the king were weak or strong, old or young. We do not know whether Henry's council was formally constituted, or if it was held together by a solemn oath as it was twenty years later, but there is no reason to believe that it did not exist from the first, although its operations are not clearly traceable until England was again at peace. The king's safety depended upon the vassals who were loyal to him; his success would depend on the steady growth of their number; his permanent well-being would require confidence between them and those who conducted his affairs. In other words, the great council which occasionally met implied a small council which was always at hand; and King John's executors were the natural nucleus of the latter. These were the legate, the bishops of Winchester, Chichester, and Worcester, the master of the Temple, the earl marshal, the earls of Chester and Derby, William Brewer, Walter Lacy, John of Monmouth, Fawkes de Breauté, and Savari de Mauléon. The significance of their appointment lay in the responsibility given to them, not in any duty to act together in space and time.[1] As order was restored the council became more official in character, more dependent for its membership upon officers of state and household, more closely in touch with royal judges and the royal exchequer. In the autumn of 1216 the need was for men who would link the will of the dead with the interests of the new king.

The prestige and the local power of these men reflected the state of John's mind and fortunes when death cut short his struggle with Louis of France. For example, the inclusion in the list of Richard le Poor, bishop of Chichester, is noteworthy; for this excellent man was a friend and probably an old pupil of Stephen Langton. Earl Ranulf of Chester held, in addition to

---

[1] Savari de Mauléon was the most loyal and important of the barons of Poitou. He had come to England to serve John and in 1216 was castellan of Bristol. He did not stay long in England. We shall meet with him later in Poitou. The Norman Fawkes de Breauté was settled in England, and there is evidence from a later time that he was regarded as having a special duty to come to the king's court without receiving a summons (*Royal Letters*, i. 226).

his palatinate, the lands of the honours of Lancaster and Richmond. William the Marshal was earl of Pembroke and lord of
Striguil (Chepstow), between the Usk and the Wye, and lord of
Leinster. William Ferrers, earl of Derby, had his feudal centre
at Tutbury in Staffordshire. Walter Lacy, lord of Meath in
Ireland, held Ludlow. John of Monmouth was another lord of
the Marches. William Brewer, a man old in constancy and service, had lands in many shires, but was especially strong in the
west country, in Devon. Each of them had a base in the part of
England unoccupied by Louis of France and some of them had
centres of influence in districts which he held or threatened. In
case of need the marshal could withdraw with the king to hold
out in Ireland. So desperate a move was unnecessary, however,
if Henry's friends could hold the midlands and attract support
by a policy of wise moderation and good intentions. And it was
in the midlands that the soldier Fawkes de Breauté played his
part. His command stretched from Oxford and the middle
Thames over the shires of Buckingham, Hertford, Bedford,
Northampton, and Cambridge. He was castellan throughout
this area of the royal castles and exercised such authority as he
could as sheriff. He was able, energetic, ruthless, and devoted to
the memory of his patron King John.

In November the king's followers gathered together in a great
council at Bristol. The justiciar, Hubert de Burgh, was at last
free to join his colleagues. He had been holding out against
Louis at Dover, but had been able to renew a truce. On 12
November the legate and the rector of the realm attached their
seals to a revised version of the Great Charter of liberties. By this
act they and the prelates and barons who formally attested it
gave to the statement of rights and principles extorted from John
the character of the coronation charter issued by the Conqueror,
by Henry I, and by Stephen. They cut the ground from beneath the feet of the rebels who had called in Louis of France.
They omitted all reference to the baronial committee which had
abused its trust, also clauses of temporary interest, and they reserved some important but doubtful matters for further consideration, but they retained the main fabric of the Charter as
a statement of law and custom and procedure. Whether the
reissue was an act of matured conviction or a piece of expediency we do not know. A record of the discussions which preceded it would be very precious. However the men who met at

Bristol regarded their decision, they undoubtedly made history. They removed the young king from faction and set him squarely and firmly in a legal relation with his subjects. They invested a haphazard statement of rights and regulations with the prestige of a code of social conduct strong enough to survive every time of turmoil and to abate the sting of personal rule. The Charter became a symbol, a rallying point, but those who like to describe it as such sometimes forget that it never became a fetish. Its practical quality gave it the permanence of life. Nowadays it is remembered for a famous clause which gave freemen protection against arbitrary deprivation of life, personal freedom, and goods; but throughout the thirteenth century it affected the relations of men at every turn in their daily lives. It defined a common measure of behaviour which depended for its sanctions on no party and implied allegiance to nothing less than the common well-being. The step taken at Bristol was never retraced. Indeed, the tenacity with which the Charter was maintained gave in the course of time an indestructible fibre to the habitual convictions of English-speaking folk such as could have been derived from no political theory. The promise that the Church in England shall be free has survived all the shocks of later centuries. The jurisprudence of the United States has been shaped in debates and decisions about the meaning of due process of law.

Another act, very significant for the future, may date from this time. Some years later the king's counsellors, in a reply to a petition from the son of the viscount of Limoges, referred to an oath sworn before the legate by the chief men of the realm that until the king came of age they would allow no alienation in perpetuity but would maintain intact all lands held by King John. A similar undertaking against the alienation of royal rights and liberties was included in the later oaths taken by members of the council both in England and in Gascony; and the responsibility of the king's vassals to maintain the 'state' of the Crown, even against the will of the king himself, was frequently expressed in Henry's reign. It underlay the objection to the inclusion among the king's intimates of men who had no standing in the realm, unsubstantial, frivolous, self-seeking persons, aliens, and upstarts. It justified the dislike and suspicion with which Henry's foreign relatives and their protégés were regarded. An escheat, a marriage, a wardship, an office, an annual pension, might be sought after like any other mark of royal favour or gratitude, but to contrive, promote, assist, or use a position of trust to effect or countenance the alienation of the royal domain and the permanent sources of royal revenue was regarded by serious men as an offence. It was a cause of scandal. Minute investigation would no doubt show that this lofty attitude was not generally maintained, and would raise many difficult questions; but the principle was clear. The king, like any husbandman who depended for his existence in well-being upon his 'contenementum', had his 'state' and the maintenance of his state was a matter of common concern. One of the most frequent phrases used in the discussions between the king and the pope, the king and bishops or magnates or towns, was 'the state of the king and of the realm'. When the heir to the Crown was invested in 1254 with Ireland and Gascony he was warned that these lordships were annexed to the Crown and no alienations from them would be tolerated. A new market could not be set up in the country-side until the king was satisfied that its establishment would not be prejudicial either to neighbouring markets or to his own rights.

When we remember the lavish grants of royal domain in the past, notably by King Henry I, the *terrae datae* which had eaten into the *terra regis* of Domesday Book, this assumption of responsibility by the prelates and magnates on the threshold of the new reign is very striking. The idea was not new, but its assertion throughout the century reveals a new coherence in what was called the community of the realm, the baronage regarded as a body. The motive, no doubt, was the desire of decent men to do for the king what a feudal guardian was required to do for his ward, to keep his lands in good order and adequately stocked; but the fact that Henry's interests were protected in this way by decent men gives the lie to the curious view that king and barons were natural enemies. And beneath the surface of their simple creed we can trace the springs of far-reaching political ideas, ranging from the ideal of the kingdom as a spiritual and moral unity to the doctrine that the king should live of his own, or if he cannot, seek the co-operation of a free people. The fact that the king was a child gave free impulse to these hidden doctrines. When he came of age Henry looked at the matter rather differently. As we shall see, he set himself to take stock of his rights. Yet he also shared in the general obligation. Just as he acknowledged the Charter of liberties, as finally reissued in 1225, although it had been published in his name during his minority, so he repudiated alienations of his rights on the ground that at his coronation he had sworn to maintain them unimpaired. He had a duty as a crowned and anointed king to maintain them. In the reign of his son this argument became still more emphatic. Edward appealed to it again and again, and with such energy that in the opinion of at least one historical scholar he must have taken a special oath at his coronation in 1274 in addition to the threefold oath to maintain the honour of the Church, administer justice, and observe only good laws. Indeed it has been suggested that, before his second and more formal coronation in 1220, Henry did the same.[1] Precise evidence in support of this view is wanting and the question remains open; but, whether the traditional form of oath was enlarged or not, the fact remains that both Henry and Edward regarded the maintenance of their rights as a duty implied by it. A London collection of law written early in the thirteenth century and some continental evidence support this interpretation of the coronation oath. The king, in short, had a duty where at first sight he would seem to have asserted a right. He was morally if not legally expected to discuss with his advisers or with his magnates weighty matters which affected the state of the Crown and realm. Edward frequently refused to return an answer until he had referred a question or petition to his council or to his council in parliament. This was a recognition of the nature of kingship, not a reluctant acknowledgement of a limitation upon the power of the Crown. More often than not, perhaps, it was a precaution of prudence, but of a wise prudence deep-seated in a sense of responsibility, just as a wise pope would refuse to proceed with a case until he could have his brothers the cardinals by his side. Such prudence was not regarded as incompatible with but rather as a condition of power. In the thought of the thirteenth century absolutism, in the sense of irresponsibility, was a proof of weakness or of a bad education in kingcraft.

These observations upon the generous spirit in which the

[1] This has been strongly maintained by H. G. Richardson in numerous papers. For the fullest expression of his argument see *Speculum*, xxiv (1949), 44 ff. Now see also E. H. Kantorowicz in *Speculum*, xxix (1954), 488–502 and R. S. Hoyt in *Traditio*, xi (1955), 255.

marshal and his colleagues, with the approval of a papal legate, approached their anxious task have been put in the forefront because they indicate the main theme of this book. They allow us to see in perspective the interplay of mind and character in all sorts and conditions of men, the success and failure of Simon de Montfort, the leadership in his best days of Edward, and the gradual evolution of our institutions, including parliament. Now we may return to the story of Henry's minority.

Warfare in this age was a desultory affair, and tended to die down during the winter months. A resolute and organized campaign like that which ended in the battle of Bouvines was very uncommon. It came of a fierce exaltation engendered by a great emergency; and no passion of this kind inspired the French nobles who had come with Louis or the English barons led by Robert fitzWalter and the earl of Winchester. Families were divided between either side. Personal hostility to King John could no longer sustain the forces of rebellion or encourage the hopes of the invaders. The cause of Louis was upheld in sermons at St. Paul's by a group of able clerics, including the chancellor and acting dean, Gervase Hobregge, Simon Langton, the archbishop's brother, who was Louis's chancellor, and Elias of Dereham, who had served two archbishops of Canterbury; but the eloquence of these sincere and scholarly persons was out of touch with events. Nothing in the ill-assorted alliance could prevent the gradual attrition of forces excommunicated by the Church and now, it would seem, repudiated by Louis's father, King Philip Augustus. The great enterprise had become an adventure, kept alive by the gallantry of the French friends of Louis and his able wife Blanche of Castile, whose descent from Henry II gave him his chief claim to the throne, and by the obstinate hopes of barons who clung to their pleasant headquarters in London.

They had, however, no reason for alarm. Louis held London and controlled the Channel. He could strike here or there as he pleased from interior lines. Like every war, this war was a matter of holding and capturing castles. A castle was not a strategic point in a planned system of fortification, but the military and administrative centre of a district or a barony which provided knights to guard it and means to supply it. The statement that Louis held the south-east of England is a convenient phrase which does not convey an exact impression. His authority was recognized on the whole in the fortified places of the area, but his writs were not obeyed throughout it. When Henry was crowned at Gloucester royalists still held Dover in Kent and castles in East Anglia, areas which generally recognized Louis, and Louis's partisans held Marlborough, a few miles over the downs from Devizes, in the upper valley of the Kennet, and Mountsorel far away in the northern part of Leicestershire. The war was sporadic, even casual. A truce might prevail in one place while fighting went on in another. Thus Hubert de Burgh could leave Dover in peace while Louis was preparing to attack Hertford and other castles in the home counties. While much country was hardly touched by the war, some was at the mercy of both sides. The abbot of St. Albans kept an account of the large sums of money which he spent during this war in order to keep his rich 'liberty' immune from the attentions of Fawkes de Breauté on the one hand and the rebels on the other. According to the Charter of 1215 castellans were required to pay cash down for their requisitions, a hard rule at any time and impossible in times of disturbance, and in the revised Charter of 1216 the marshal and his colleagues allowed three weeks delay. It is unlikely that Fawkes de Breauté was careful to observe either form of obligation. The isolation to which castle warfare condemned particular areas gave opportunities to the ruthless. It also weakened the morale of the defenders. In January 1217 the leading royalists combined in a sworn undertaking to pay the ransoms of those captured in royal castles and with this promise urged the garrison of Bedford to hold out.

Louis made some progress with his piecemeal policy. Hertford, Berkhamsted, Colchester, Orford, Norwich, and Cambridge fell, also the important baronial strongholds at Pleshey and Hedingham in Essex; but he was unable or unwilling to press westwards. One truce followed another until February. Then the marshal concentrated on the Channel and Louis's communications with France. Dover still held out for the king, the Cinque Ports were notoriously unstable, the Weald or upland wooded country north of the coast was admirably suited for guerilla warfare. The royalists found the right man in Philip Daubeny, titular warden of the Channel Islands, and later the king's tutor in the arts and exercises of secular life. He belonged to a great baronial house and was devoted to Henry's service.

As the 'leader of the militia of God' he organized an amphibious effort to control the narrow seas while he remained in touch with the marshal's forces south of the Thames. Rye, which he made his headquarters, then Winchelsea, came over to him, and he gathered a fleet together. Resistance in the Weald was organized by a local man, William of Kensham, who won popular fame and affection under the nickname of Willikin of the Weald. William was a royal bailiff. It was his duty to administer the denns or pastures of the Weald in the hundred of Marden, attached, in accordance with the immemorial practice of husbandry in Kent and Sussex, to the royal manor of Milton, in the north-east of Kent; and for the purposes of war he was given powers to maintain his band from all the seven hundreds of the Weald. The effect of the alliance between Philip Daubeny and the piratical men of the two chief ports and of the co-operation of Willikin was soon felt. Louis, who had been summoned to confer with his father and the French court, had some difficulty in reaching the coast and crossing the Channel. Before his return in April, the marshal had closed in from the north. Waverers began to come over to the king's side and were assured of an easy reception. The marshal himself welcomed his own eldest son and the earl of Salisbury, a natural son of Henry II. For a time the strong points of Surrey, Sussex, and Hampshire, including Winchester, were in his hands. Marlborough fell in the west. The sea was still held by Louis, for he had in his service the most famous sailor adventurer of his time, Eustace, nicknamed the Monk, whose exploits became legendary. Eustace had been at one time in King John's service, and well known in the streets of Winchelsea. Sprung of a good family in the county of Boulogne, he had ultimately taken to the sea. After quarrelling with John he joined Louis and had a command to keep the narrow seas and their coasts safe, and to convey troops and stores. He and his brothers seized the Channel Islands, which they used as an independent base. Philip Daubeny could not master the Monk, but he managed to hold his own in the Channel.

Louis's return checked the marshal's progress in the south. Winchester and other places were reoccupied. Louis decided that Dover must be taken before he resumed his activities in the midlands; but at this point the wishes of the English rebels, who had remained quiescent in London during his absence, prevented a concentration of his strength. News came that the earls of Chester and Derby were likely to force the outlying castle of Mountsorel in Leicestershire to surrender. This place was part of that half of the lands of the last Anglo-Norman earl of Leicester which had come by marriage to Saer de Quincy, earl of Winchester. He insisted that he should be allowed to relieve Mountsorel, and the prospect of a scamper through the midlands appealed to the rebels in London and some of their French allies after the long rest of winter. Louis acquiesced in this division of his forces. While he resumed the siege of Dover, the earl, with Robert fitzWalter, the count of Perche, and others, made a dash to Mountsorel. When they reached the castle the siege had been raised. Then another adventure tempted them. The constable of Arras, one of Louis's captains, had for some time been engaged with a force of northern rebels in the siege of the great castle at Lincoln. He clamoured for aid, and the army from the south slipped through the vale of Belvoir and along the high road to Lincoln.

By this time the legate and the marshal were at Northampton. They heard the news on 12 May 1217, the Friday before Whit-Sunday. They were in royalist country. To the north Nottingham and the episcopal castles at Newark and Sleaford were manned by John's mercenaries. The marshal decided to strike at once. Making a detour from Newark he and his army reached the castle at Lincoln from the north-west early in the morning on 20 May. Lincoln castle formed, as it still forms, the south-west quarter of the old Roman city built on the high plateau to the north of the medieval city. It faces the western front of the cathedral, which with its precincts occupies the south-eastern quarter. In medieval times the Roman walls, with their great northern gateway, still stood to west, north, and east. The open space between cathedral and castle was reached by Steep Street which ascends from the town. Hence the marshal, coming from the north-west, could enter the castle built along the west Roman wall, but not the enclosure which was formed by the rest of the Roman city. He met with no opposition as he came and was soon in touch with the hereditary castellan, a stout-hearted woman, Nicolaa de la Hay. Fawkes de Breauté went to aid the garrison and prepared to attack from the inner or eastern gate of the castle. The bishop of Winchester, after greeting Nicolaa, made a little tour of inspection. He noticed that there was a gateway, then built up but capable of breach, in the wall which continued to the north the west or outer wall of the castle. He reported his discovery and the gateway was opened. The new-comers streamed through. The besiegers of the castle who were massed in the open space between the castle and cathedral were attacked and broken. The young count of Perche was slain, the rest scattered and fled down the steep street into the lower town. The north gate of the city, now between two fires, was carried. Later attempts of the French and barons to regain the high ground were checked and broken. Within a few hours 300 knights, half the total number of knights in the rebel army, had been captured. The rest were dispersed in all directions. The royalists had won this bloodless victory, as in a tournament, with 406 knights, 317 crossbowmen, and their attendant men-at-arms.

The disaster at once led to negotiations for peace. Louis raised the siege of Dover and returned to London. He was isolated. His English allies flocked to change sides. In three months more than 150, who included several of the leading opponents of King John and were all important enough to be named in royal writs, returned to their allegiance to the king of England. It is probable that, before the rout at Lincoln, King Philip of France had begun to work for a settlement and had enlisted the aid of the archbishop of Tyre, who was preaching a crusade in France. At any rate the archbishop, with the abbots of the Cistercian monasteries of Citeaux, Clairvaux, and Pontigny, was in England and wrote a report of the discussions which took place in the first half of June. Terms of peace were defined, but Louis objected to the exclusion from the amnesty of four of his ecclesiastical supporters, the three already mentioned and Robert of St. Germain, a clerk of Alexander, king of the Scots. The legate refused, without reference to the pope, to absolve men who had preached against the validity of the excommunication of Louis and his followers, and Louis would not sacrifice his friends. He preferred to hold out until reinforcements arrived, although the marshal could now march where he wished and Philip Daubeny's strength at sea had become formidable.

In the face of all obstacles Blanche of Castile and Eustace the Monk made one last effort. Volunteers of high rank and knights of Boulogne and Artois, always willing to take pay for a military

adventure, were collected under the leadership of Robert de
Courtenai, a kinsman of Louis who had already served with
him in England. Eustace provided the shipping. The flotilla set
sail on 24 August, St. Bartholomew's day. Seven larger ships
carried about 120 knights, some seventy small craft followed
with stores. The weather was clear, the wind in their favour. As
they made for the Thames, they were met by the ships which
the marshal and Philip Daubeny had collected off Sandwich.
Hubert de Burgh's ship led the line, followed by that of Richard,
a natural son of King John, the large 'cog' of William the
Marshal, who would fain have been on board but had been
dissuaded, and others. They sailed to windward of Eustace the
Monk's ship, which was heavily laden and carried thirty-six
knights. Apparently this vessel lagged somewhat behind the rest
and Robert de Courtenai insisted on engaging Richard's ship.
Too late he discovered the secret of the English manœuvre.
Knights and sailors were incapacitated by powdered lime
thrown from the enemy ships and carried by the wind. Eustace's
ship was boarded and overpowered. The Monk was found below
and beheaded, Robert de Courtenai and his companions were
taken prisoner. While the English made havoc with the little
ships which carried the stores, the other troopships, instead of
sailing on to the Thames, managed to make their way back to
the French coast. The helpless mariners in the store ships were
the real sufferers; the booty captured by the English was great.
Some of it was sold to provide for the building of the hospital of
St. Bartholomew near Sandwich, founded in commemoration
of the victory.

Louis had now to accept with certain changes and additions
the terms which he had refused in June. Peace was made on 12
September on an island in the Thames off Kingston. Although
no authentic instrument has survived, the contents of the treaty
are known from contemporary references and from the text of a
preliminary *forma pacis*, obviously based upon the terms of June.[1]
This was printed in the seventeenth century from a Norman
source. From the English point of view the most important thing
in the treaty was the provision of a general amnesty, restoration
of lands, and freedom from all ransoms except payments still due
of ransoms previously agreed. Clerks, though liable to ecclesiastical penalties, were to recover their lay lands like the laymen.

[1] Kate Norgate, *The Minority of Henry III* (1912), pp. 278–80.

Louis undertook never to resume his co-operation with English rebels, and, according to one chronicler, to try to procure the restoration to King Henry of Normandy and the other fiefs held by King John across the Channel. The brothers of Eustace the Monk were to give up the Channel Islands. The records of chancery and the exchequer in Louis's possession were to be restored. The four ecclesiastics were left to the judgement of the Church. Their exile was not prolonged, nor was their punishment severe. Simon Langton, who had at one time been arch-bishop-elect of York, returned to be a powerful and assertive archdeacon of Canterbury, with a remarkable influence in papal circles. Elias of Dereham, canon of Salisbury, is remembered as a fine craftsman who helped to make the new shrine of St. Thomas at Canterbury and to direct the building of Salisbury cathedral.

The most striking proof of the royalists' desire to get Louis out of England is not to be found in the 'form of peace'. They paid Louis 10,000 marks or nearly £7,000 sterling. This was a large sum, ten times as much as John's annual tribute to the pope and between a fourth and fifth of the normal revenue of the Crown. Most of the money was paid within a year of the treaty, the remainder in February 1221. The royal guarantee was deposited in the Temple at Paris, or, as we should say, with the French king's bankers. The brokers were two merchants of St. Omer. The sum was raised by a levy on knights' fees. The country had obviously not been crippled by the civil war, and could well afford this insurance against further trouble. Years after, when the danger was forgotten, critics who had said little in 1217 raised their voices and worked upon the suspicious nature of the young king. Henry professed the belief that the marshal had betrayed his interest by not fighting Louis to the finish. But the way of generosity had been prudent, even if the motives which directed it had been mixed. Old companions had been reconciled, families reunited, havoc checked. Landholders whose manors were scattered throughout the disturbed shires could resume possession and restore order. The connexions which Louis, with his administrative system and his control of London, had formed in the country were broken. A danger which a year earlier must have seemed wellnigh insuperable was removed for ever. That it had been real and might have been lasting was shown during a riot in London five years later, when the cry of

'Louis of France' was heard in the streets. The treaty of Kingston prepared the way for unity. Shortly afterwards the Great Charter was reissued with the revisions promised in the previous year, and the forest clauses were expanded into a long Charter of the Forest. So moderates on either side could come together on common ground. It is likely enough that personal considerations affected the *rector* and his colleagues. The marshal's eldest son had been a rebel. He himself was a close friend of some of Louis's companions and must have known most of them.[1] He was one of the few vassals of King John who had been allowed to retain their lands in Normandy. On the other hand what helped him might help the king and very many more. Normandy might be restored to its former allegiance to the Angevin house. The lands of the English barons in Normandy, and also the 'lands of the Normans' in England, might revert to their old lords. The community of the realm in England had not yet created a national state.

So Louis was absolved. He was allowed to wear his robe over the woollen garment of the barefooted penitent. The treaty was confirmed, and the legate and marshal saw the invader sail away. All the same, Louis did not forget or forgive his humiliation. England was saved, but Normandy was never returned.

The most troublesome duty imposed by the treaty was the restoration of the *reversi* to their lands, for even in a short war changes occur and interests are created which impede the best-intentioned settlement. Indeed, just because it had been a short war, former claims and suits survived to complicate the problem. The plea rolls of the *curia regis*, both those of the Bench and those of the itinerant justices, show that the war had its aftermath. Yet on the whole the reinstatement was made quickly and smoothly. A man deprived of the possession of lands which he had held at the outbreak of war could apply for a common writ, addressed to the local sheriff, authorizing his resumption in seisin of such lands. This was the 'commune breve de tali saisina habenda', hundreds of which were issued during the years 1217 and 1218. The sheriff summoned a local jury to testify to the claim, and if it was confirmed the applicant was given

---

[1] Notably Peter of Dreux, count of Brittany, who helped to negotiate the peace. Louis had recognized his claim to the honour of Richmond and Peter hoped to get confirmation of his right. See S. Painter's biography of Count Peter, entitled *The Scourge of the Clergy* (1937), pp. 15–17.

possession. This practice was adopted fifty years later to supply defects in the settlement of England after the battle of Evesham, but then it was used to assist royalists rather than rebels. Indeed the change in feudal society between the two civil wars can be seen in the fact that Simon de Montfort and his accomplices (*fautores*), who had fought in the king's name, were described as rebels, while those who fought in the name of Louis and had been excommunicated as the enemies of Church and king in a holy war were considered to have been perverse.

The royalists had fought in the name of the Church. They had worn the badge of a crusader. Pope Honorius III, eager for a crusade against the Saracens in Egypt and Syria, had done all that he could for his boy vassal and for a land, 'especially subject to the Holy See', whose peace and unity were both his immediate concern and a necessary preliminary to his greater task. His correspondence with the legates Guala and Pandulf show that he was kept informed and gave detailed counsel on affairs in England. In England Guala and the marshal continued to work smoothly together until the cardinal left in November 1218. Pandulf, who succeeded him, had the marshal's full confidence until the regent's death in the following May. By this time normal life had been resumed in the land. Peace had been made at Worcester with Llywelyn ab Iorwerth, a friendly understanding reached with Alexander II of Scotland. The exchequer had been reopened on 12 November 1217, a great seal had been made for the king, and in November 1218, the month of Guala's departure, the justices of a general eyre began work in their circuits. The commission of *capitula itineris* given to the justices included the charge to obtain from the local juries a detailed return of the king's rights—the number and nature of serjeanties, lands escheated to the Crown, the names of widows and minors in the king's gift or wardship, royal advowsons, and encroachments on the king's lands. Some of these returns still exist among the records of the exchequer.

The renewal of administrative activity and routine brought to the aid of the king's governors and advisers a group of able men familiar with the methods of government and with the law and custom of the land. The new treasurer Eustace de Fauconberg, afterwards bishop of London, Ralph Nevill, who kept the great seal and supervised the business of the chancery until the death of the chancellor Richard Marsh, bishop of Durham, and in due course succeeded him in office, and the lawyer and judge Martin of Pattishall were the most outstanding of these servants of the Crown. They and their colleagues in the royal household, at the exchequer, or on the judicial bench could continue and adapt a tradition uncongenial to the rough and irresponsible loyalty of King John's mercenary captains, who still held castles and ruled too many shires. Although anxious issues loomed ahead the marshal, as he lay dying at his manor of Caversham, could be satisfied with his work. As his colleagues had written of him in December 1216, he had proved himself in time of need as gold is tried in the furnace. His squire and biographer gives his death the dignity of a fine episode in English history. The prelates and barons waited in suspense at Reading on the other side of the Thames. The old man discussed the future with their leaders. He decided that the king should be entrusted to the legate Pandulf, and when the bishop of Winchester protested, brushed his claim on one side: Pandulf had done well, Peter des Roches had merely acted as the regent's deputy and nominee. He made provision for his sons. Before he said good-bye to his daughters, he bade them sing to him. He took leave of his wife. He fingered his treasures for the last time and disposed of them. In the last days his mind was slightly troubled by a question put to him by one of his knights. In the course of his long life of some eighty years he had taken many men captive, exacted many ransoms, won many splendid horses. Ought he not to make reparation so that the Church might open the gates of heaven to him? He thought of those long-past tournaments. No, it was too late. The clerks asked too much. His friend the master of the Temple intervened to re-assure him that all was well. He had lived and would die a gentleman. So the marshal died. He was buried in the round church of the New Temple in the Strand. Stephen Langton, the archbishop of Canterbury, now home again, spoke about him with dignity and authority, as one great man may speak of another (May 1219).

Until the autumn of 1221 the legate Pandulf took a leading share in the administration. He knew England well, for he had represented Pope Innocent III in John's time, and since 1215 had been bishop-elect of Norwich.[1] His letters reveal a practical

---

[1] The election was confirmed and Pandulf enjoyed the revenues, but he was not consecrated until 1222, after he had left England. The delay was due to the pope's

grasp of details. On the other hand, he did not have the prestige of his distinguished predecessor. He was a papal familiar, a sub-deacon, and in any case lacked Guala's ample opportunities. The return of the archbishop, himself a cardinal, made his position wellnigh impossible. In the archbishop's view it was unnecessary and he procured Pandulf's withdrawal. By this time the king's tutelage had come to an end; the lad himself had become impatient of it, and the growing influence upon him of the justiciar Hubert de Burgh led to friction with the bishop of Winchester. There seems even to have been some talk of declaring Henry of age when in October 1220 he reached the age of thirteen.

A few months earlier, on Whit-Sunday, 17 May, Henry had been crowned by the archbishop in the Confessor's church at Westminster. On this occasion the ceremony was complete in form and splendour. On the previous day he had laid the foundation-stone of a new Lady chapel which the monks had planned to build in the new style of architecture to the east of the primitive Norman choir. The first step in the realization of an ambitious design—the building of a new church for the abbey—was taken under the auspices of a great occasion. We do not know when or under what influence Henry made the Confessor his patron saint. His choice can hardly have been inspired by Peter des Roches; it suggests, rather, a Langtonian desire to tune his mind to English traditions, though in fact it grew into an assiduous cult in which, while it gave pious satisfaction, the king gave expression to his artistic interests and his love of ceremonial. The Confessor's day, 13 October, became for him the great day of the year, and the more so because it comes conveniently a fortnight after Michaelmas, the beginning of the financial year, when the exchequer was busy, Westminster crowded, and a great council or parliament was generally held. On 13 October Henry was wont to gather about him the members of his household in the new robes which he had provided for them, to knight young nobles and protégés, and to hold a great feast. In due course he made himself responsible for the building of the new church.

During the four or five critical years after his second coronation the king was finding his feet and beginning to assert himself.

desire not to have as his legate a suffragan of Canterbury. Pandulf continued to assist English interests until his death. His body was brought to Norwich for burial.

He was intelligent, even precocious, if reports of him sent to Pope Honorius were true. He was well-made, and had the bearing of a prince. His only physical defect was a droop of an eyelid. The 'simplicity' so often mentioned by Matthew Paris and others was a kind of innocence which remained in him throughout his life and explains an attractive quality in him even when he was at his worst. In spite of his faults he was never corrupted. If the child was father to the man, he was an inquisitive boy, observant of men and things about him, appreciative of beauty and form, especially in jewel- and metalwork, attentive to detail in apparel, decoration, and ceremonial. He was affectionate and trustful by nature, but impulsive, easily distracted, and hot-tempered. His suspicion, his brooding memory of injuries long after they were generally forgotten, like his grateful reliance upon the few whom he felt he could really trust, may well have been fostered by his experiences as a boy in a court disturbed by the cross-currents of jealousy, faction, and ambition. He was easily frightened and disposed to swing violently from one side to another. He was not generous, though he was lavish; he was poor in judgement, though quick of perception; he was not magnanimous, though he could be dignified and decorous; he was devout rather than spiritually minded. Yet, when all has been said, Henry remains a decent man, and, in his way, a man to be reckoned with. He had a saving sense of realities which rescued him again and again from disaster. He never went so far that he could not retrace his steps. His experience did not make him cynical. The simplicity which could by turns amuse and madden those who had to do with him maintained him in the end. He got through all his troubles and left England more prosperous, more united, more peaceful, more beautiful than it was when he was a child.

Henry's majority was reached in two stages. At the end of 1223, when he was sixteen, he was given the personal, though limited, use of his seal. Three years later, in January 1227, he declared himself of full age without waiting for any further solution of a problem which had become as unreal as it was tedious. The step taken at the end of 1223 was due to the need to associate him with the resumption by the Crown of the royal castles and of unfettered control over local government.

The war against Louis of France had been won in two sharp and decisive engagements, at Lincoln and off Sandwich; but the royal power had been maintained in England since 1215 by King John's baronial friends and his picked servants in the castles and the shires. These men naturally expected to be rewarded rather than dismissed after the restoration of peace, and for some time they were left undisturbed. It was obvious, however, that normal and responsible administration under the direction of court and exchequer would be impossible if foreign adventurers acquired a prescriptive right to hold royal castles and dug themselves into the shires. Already there were several hereditary castellans and hereditary sheriffs in England. No very long tenure of a castle was required to blur the distinction between its 'royal' and 'private' character. Just as the king had the right to commandeer a private castle, for example Newark or Bedford or Wark, in the interests of the safety of the realm, so his right to regard a castle as his could be forgotten or disputed by men who had held it long enough to feel that they were at home in it. Sometimes it is hard to decide to which category at this time particular castles belonged, for the evidence of records is itself conflicting. Moreover, a relapse to the exercise of 'spheres of local influence' was by no means impossible; it might easily, indeed, give a sinister meaning to the phrase 'the community of the realm'. How could a young king be better served than by faithful men willing to do his work for him in their own areas? Earl Ranulf, entrenched as a watchdog over against his friend Llywelyn ab Iorwerth, at Chester, Shrewsbury, and Bridgnorth, would seem to have felt like this, and Earl Ranulf's loyalty to the king and willingness to act with his fellow barons in the king's interest were undoubted.[1] The justiciar himself, another loyal man, did not distinguish sharply between his official standing as constable of the Tower and various other royal castles and his acquisition of the three castles of Gwent in south Wales and the new castle of Montgomery. He combined his service to the Crown with his desire to build up a great lordship. And the earl of Salisbury, after his return to the royal cause, dreamed of a palatinate in Somerset and Devon.[2]

[1] Ranulf held Shrewsbury and Bridgnorth with the sheriffdom of Shropshire. Moreover, he had been granted the earldom of Lincoln and the custody of the Montfort half of the earldom of Leicester, in addition to the custody of the honours of Richmond and Lancaster. The grant of a charter of liberties to his tenants in Cheshire is an important indication of his outlook.

[2] Whether the jurisdiction claimed (see Bracton's *Note Book*, no. 1235) amounted to this is doubtful.

The danger latent in these tendencies and the difficulty of meeting them became apparent very soon after the departure of Louis. Although the council showed the utmost consideration, it took a long time to persuade Philip Mark, the sheriff of Derby and Nottingham, to remove his deputy from the castles of Newark and Sleaford, which belonged to the bishop of Lincoln. The council indeed was half-hearted and it was not until the archbishop and justiciar had assumed the direction of affairs that firm action was taken. The first sign of a general policy was an oath taken by the barons at Henry's coronation in 1220 that they would surrender royal castles and wardships at the king's will and, if need be, help to put down the recalcitrant. A particularly flagrant case may have led to this concerted action. This was the conduct of William de Forz, the son of a Poitevin follower of King Richard I who had married the heiress of the count of Aumâle. The title of count or earl came to William together with the honours of his mother in England, Holderness, Skipton, Cockermouth, and the widespread manors attached to these northern liberties. In addition William held the royal castles of Sauvey and Rockingham in the midlands. He was a violent and irresponsible young man, but his local power and connexions were so great that his conduct was first tolerated, then, when it could no longer be disregarded, condoned. At one time he was considered for appointment as seneschal of Poitou and Gascony, a suggestion which provoked the earl of Salisbury to an indignant and caustic remonstrance. He interfered with the royal bailiffs, flouted the royal justices on eyre, disregarded the injunctions of the legate. In the years 1219 and 1220 he was twice brought to submission and twice pardoned. Finally at the end of 1220 he withdrew from court and broke into open rebellion. His chief offence was his refusal to surrender, under the conditions of the treaty of Kingston, his castle at Bytham, on the southern borders of Lincolnshire, to his tenant William de Colevill, who had taken part against King John. In other words he refused to obey a decision in the king's court. The justiciar took action. He collected forces in the neighbouring shires, proclaimed William de Forz, and speedily forced Bytham to surrender. The count resisted no longer. His influence was shown to have no substance against a resolute show of force. He fled for sanctuary to Fountains. And this time his submission was lasting. As before, he was absolved and pardoned. He retained his ancestral honours, but he had lost the royal castles and had been forced to receive William de Colevill again as his tenant in Bytham.

The ease with which the justiciar had won this success no doubt encouraged those who saw the need for a definite policy. Yet the problem was by no means a simple one. Since the days in 1215 when the barons had insisted on the expulsion from England of the mercenaries of Touraine, Gerard of Athée, Engelard of Cigogné, Andrew of Chanceaux, Philip Mark, and the rest,[1] the situation had entirely changed. War had made a difference, and the issue now was not whether King John's hated agents should be sent out of the land but whether the men, whatever their origin might be, who had held the royal strongholds against an invader should be required to surrender them. One at least of the men mentioned by name in the Great Charter of 1215 had made good. This was Engelard of Cigogné, whose earlier misdeeds as sheriff of Gloucester were revealed before the itinerant justices in 1221. Engelard's brutal exactions as sheriff belonged to the past; his defence of Odiham and Windsor, the castles which he still held, was known to all men. Moreover, he could claim that he had spent more of his own money on the fortification of Bristol and Hereford than he had wrung out of the tenants and peasantry of Gloucestershire.[2] And what about Fawkes de Breauté, one of King John's executors, and Peter de Mauley, the Poitevin, who had protected the royal family and royal treasure in the castle of Corfe? Indeed, had not the royal castles been entrusted by King John to men whom he trusted, to hold until the young king came of age? Much sympathy was felt for these fine soldiers, and especially by those who, like the earl of Chester, had acted as sheriffs and castellans in the same capacity. Hence, when the legate left England and

[1] The group mentioned in the Charter seems to have consisted of inter-related *routiers* or *ruptarii* from a particular district of Touraine between Loches and Amboise. They were professional mercenaries like the later free companies, not originally men of the type of the Norman Fawkes de Breauté or the Poitevin Peter de Mauley who had entered King John's household and could more easily be absorbed into feudal society. Peter de Mauley's descendants in the male line continued to be an important baronial family in Yorkshire until the reign of Richard II.

[2] Engelard lived till 1244. He had been restored to and was still castellan of Odiham, a very important castle in north-east Hampshire. In view of his 'good and praiseworthy service' to the Crown, his executors were relieved of his obligations to the royal exchequer. Another Engelard of Cigogné was in King Henry's service during and after the Barons' wars.

the justiciar took the lead, grave differences of opinion and personal animosities began for the first time to divide the council. The fury and alarm which followed the removal of Peter de Mauley from Corfe revealed the danger in all its complexity.

In this crisis the justiciar was sustained by a group of able and clear-sighted bishops, under the firm guidance of Stephen Langton. Hubert de Burgh and the archbishop both came from the English country-side, the one from Norfolk, the other from Lincolnshire. They belonged to families of local gentry. They had something in common; but whereas the justiciar had made his way at court, probably through the influence at first of the great family of Warenne, the archbishop had enlarged his patriotism during his long residence in Paris and his struggle with King John. Hubert had served King John as chamberlain, as castellan of Chinon, as sheriff of Norfolk, as justiciar. He was an ambitious man, who had had to win a place for himself. He was self-seeking and tended to take the colour of the baronial society which he desired to enter. His determination to maintain the interests of the Crown and the well-being of England on the basis of a strong centralized administration was not, and could not be divorced from his desire to maintain himself. His marriage in 1221 to Margaret, the sister of the king of the Scots, and his creation as earl of Kent raised him to the level, but did not give him the stability of, the earl of Chester or the earl of Pembroke.[1] He had always to think of his position, and to secure it by the possession of lands and castles, by the choice of friends, the careful selection of his clerks and agents, the cultivation of the good-will of the king. The violence of the storm which broke upon him in 1232 shows how hard his efforts to hold his own must have been. He was not liked, had never been accepted, and nothing was too bad to say about him. The archbishop, on the other hand, was independent. He was a man of principles, derived from reflection and experience. He had about him an unusually coherent body of bishops, some of whom were his close friends, and one or two of whom had probably been his pupils at Paris. He was a cardinal. In England he regarded

[1] Hubert had previously married a daughter of the earl Warenne, and widow of Doon Bardolf. She died in 1214, leaving a son who succeeded in due course to some of his father's manors. Hubert then married Isabella, King John's divorced wife, and the widow of the justiciar Geoffrey fitzPeter. She died in 1217. His third wife, Margaret of Scotland, a daughter of William the Lion, had been chosen, when she was about fourteen, as the future wife of Henry III, then not two years old.

himself as a successor of St. Thomas with a duty to maintain the traditions and customs of the Church in England and, at the same time, to strengthen its liberties and deepen its purposes by informing it with all that was best in the invigorating movements of the age. During the celebrations in Whit week 1220, when he crowned the king, he proclaimed the recent canonization of St. Hugh of Lincoln and preached a crusade to the people. A few weeks later, on 7 July, the body of St. Thomas was at last translated to the new shrine behind the new choir at Canterbury. For most of us perhaps this event is a more or less interesting incident in the history of art; for Archbishop Stephen it was an act of deep spiritual significance. In 1221 he welcomed the first Dominicans to arrive in England. In 1222 he presided over the provincial council at Oxford where, in the spirit of the late Pope Innocent III and in the phrases of the legislation of the oecumenical council of 1215, he issued the canons which expressed the unity of the Western Church in faith, law, discipline, and conduct. At such a time and for such a man it was essential to co-operate in the task of making England a fit home for a new spirit in the Church, of setting the feet of the young king and his advisers in the paths of justice and order. Unity was necessary in any case, for, as restlessness in the Marches and in Poitou showed, King Henry's neighbours were quick to take advantage of enmities and divided counsels in his court.

In April 1223 Pope Honorius was prevailed upon to issue letters which declared the king sufficiently mature in mind and character to have the control of his seal and the 'free and quiet' disposal of his kingdom. In spite of cross-currents which perplexed the pope, the justiciar and archbishop went ahead. Issue was joined in November, when, in the absence of the court, Earl Ranulf of Chester and his allies joined forces with the foreign castellans in a demonstration against the Tower of London. On the king's return with the justiciar, the malcontents withdrew to Waltham. At a conference arranged by the archbishop, the division of parties was clearly revealed. The earl and the bishop of Winchester, whom the justiciar denounced as the chief cause of the trouble, led one party, Hubert de Burgh the other. Under these circumstances the council gave effect to the papal letters. Henry was given the free disposal of his seal, castles, lands, and wardships. The only limitation upon his power was the proviso, originally made in 1218, when the great seal had been made, that no permanent grants could be made under it. (This proviso explains the fact that the charter rolls do not begin again until January 1227, when Henry declared himself to be of full age.) From 10 December 1223 the formula *teste me ipso* appears at the end of his letters. Two days earlier he had begun in his own name to dispose of his castles. Henceforward any man who resisted the king's commands resisted the king himself. The archbishop made full use of his opportunity to bring the earl of Chester and his friends to submission. He explained that the surrender of the royal castles was required in the interests of all. Everybody would be treated alike. This was more than a trial of strength between parties. On 29 December the earl agreed to the change, and by the end of April 1224, when a general reconciliation was formally effected, the crisis was over. All the important royal castles in the land had been surrendered by their castellans, generally into the hands of bishops who acted as temporary wardens. Stephen Langton, who is said to have 'distributed the castles by word of mouth', himself took over the Tower and Canterbury castle from the justiciar, and Windsor and Odiham from Engelard of Cigogné. Fawkes de Breauté no longer ruled in the midlands, nor the earl of Chester by the waters of the Severn.

The subsequent redistribution of shires and castles shows no discrimination against men or parties. Indeed, no permanent cleavage had been made. Party politics could not exist in an age when personal relations and private opinion about details of policy changed like the colours in a kaleidoscope. Yet the change implied the supremacy of the justiciar and a centralized system of administration with the grateful support of the young king. Except in one quarter Hubert de Burgh had to face no serious opposition, though he had to overcome many tiresome difficulties, between the spring of 1224 and the summer of 1232. The exception was the rebellion of Fawkes de Breauté, who fortunately showed his hand at once, while the prestige of Stephen Langton was at its height. King, justiciar, and archbishop combined to deal with Fawkes in the summer of 1224.

In the course of his career Fawkes de Breauté had made many enemies. He had done violent acts against persons who hitherto had not been able to retaliate. In particular he had been guilty of disseisin without lawful warrant. He had dispossessed men of their rights and holdings, and many writs had been issued out of chancery to these men. Actions of this kind quickly accumulated, unless, as the Great Charter prescribed, regular commissions were issued for their trial. Naturally enough, as soon as the dispute about the castles was settled, commissions were issued to deal with such cases, and no doubt some persons had welcomed the surrender of his shires and castles as a signal to initiate proceedings against Fawkes. Greater men also had their grudges or grievances. Some time before, in the spring of 1221, many magnates in Devon and Cornwall had combined against him to hamper his position in the west country, where, as the husband of the countess of Devon, he had established himself at Plympton without regard to the lawful rights of his stepson, the heir. His great castle at Bedford should, in equity if not according to the terms of the treaty of Kingston, have been restored to its hereditary lord, William de Beauchamp, who as a rebel had been deprived of it by King John.[1] The earls of Salisbury and Pembroke had in 1223 been scandalized by Fawkes's contemptuous disregard of royal writs procured against him for disseisin by their friend John Marshal. In Fawkes's view, the legal proceedings instituted against him in the spring of 1224 were merely a form of persecution, the vindictive sequel to the archbishop's deliberate plan to deprive him and others of their sheriffdoms and castles. The complaint which he issued after his fall still survives. It depicts him, sincerely enough, as a deeply wronged man, who had done loyal and strenuous service to King John and his son. Instead of leaving good men alone and concentrating on dangers from without, the justiciar and archbishop and their allies had neglected the true interests of the realm in order to ruin the objects of their dislike. His rebellion was justified. This view of the case had some support. Pope Honorius, as his letters to the archbishop show, was greatly disturbed by what he heard, probably from the bishop of Winchester. The answer to all this was simple and clear. The law of the land must be observed; the king's writs must be respected.

One of the actions against Fawkes was a formal accusation of

[1] Bedford is a good case of the confusion between a royal and private castle. It was regarded in 1217 as a royal castle (above, p. 20), but Fawkes was not required to surrender it in 1223–4, when the other royal castles were redistributed. He had fortified it and made it his centre. He complained later that William Beauchamp had persistently sought to recover it.

felony in the king's court. The facts are not certain and do not much matter. Fawkes failed to appear and made himself liable to a sentence of outlawry. In accordance with the lawful procedure, he was summoned month by month to answer for his disobedience in the shire court of Bedfordshire. It so happened that on the very day, 17 June, on which he should last appear or be outlawed, his brother William kidnapped and took to Bedford one of the justices who had recently been hearing cases of novel disseisin at Dunstable. During Whit week (2–8 June) the justices had given judgement against Fawkes in no fewer than sixteen actions. William de Breauté's violence sealed his brother's fate. Fawkes was solemnly outlawed, and Bedford castle was besieged. The feudal host was summoned, siege-engines were collected, the prelates levied a carucage on their lands, Fawkes and his accomplices were excommunicated. The king and justiciar and many barons moved to Bedford. After a siege of eight weeks, William de Breauté and his garrison of eleven knights and a force of men-at-arms were burnt out and surrendered. They were hanged the next day (15 August), though three knights were cut down before they died and were received by the Templars for service in the Holy Land.

Fawkes had not been in Bedford castle. He had fled to the north-west. He tried in vain to rouse Llywelyn. He rushed for protection to the earl of Chester. Earl Ranulf, while willing to do what he could for him, would give him no military assistance and persuaded him to yield himself to the king's mercy. Neither Llywelyn nor the earl believed that Fawkes had 'schemed any evil against the king' and they told Henry so. In their minds the crime of rebellion was a very different matter from a petulant disregard for the forms of legal procedure. Not Fawkes, but his enemies were the aggressors. Llywelyn went so far as to say that those who counselled the king to disinherit great men without cause were much greater disturbers of the realm, and that if Fawkes defended his inheritance even against the pope he was not excommunicated in God's sight. Yet, after consulting together, the friends of the unhappy man would not fight for him. His past services saved his life, but he lost everything else. He died in exile two years later. The archbishop had vindicated the law of the land, the justiciar had rid himself of a tiresome man who could not adjust himself to the ways of government, and the king had tasted the bitter-sweets of power.

Co-operation between the archbishop and the justiciar had given new stability to English affairs, and was needed in order to maintain it. Hubert de Burgh's natural impulse was to strengthen his own position by encouraging the king to assert his rights, and for a while Henry was grateful to him for the enjoyment of his youthful freedom; but danger lurked here. Even before Henry had been given the use of his seal an investigation into the customs and liberties possessed by King John had caused alarm in the country. In January 1223 the sheriffs had been ordered to inquire of juries in full shire court what these customs had been in 1215, before the outbreak of civil war, and they were empowered to enforce the verdicts. To assign this date and to make no provision for the judicial confirmation of the royal liberties was, to say the least, imprudent. The liberties might be unjust, the purpose of the Charters of liberties might be frustrated. In April the council withdrew the order. The king, it declared, did not intend to allow any evil customs. The archbishop, the chief architect of the Charters, was determined that the king should not forget his sworn obligation to maintain them. They were to be as a lamp to guide his feet. And Langton's anxiety was justified. Some of the old servants of King John who had gladly helped him to bring the minority to an end and to resume control of the castles paid little respect to the Charters. When, after the dispute about the castles had been settled, the archbishop requested the king, now a responsible person, to ratify them afresh, no less a man than William Brewer is said to have ejaculated that they had been extorted by violence. But the archbishop got his way. When taxation became necessary in the following year, the grant of a fifteenth of the value of movables or personal property was accompanied by a solemn reissue, in what proved to be their final and definitive form, of the Charter of Liberties and the Charter of the Forest (11 February 1225). Thus the action of the legate and the marshal in 1216 and 1217 was confirmed, as it was to be confirmed again and again in the years to come, until the Charters were firmly stamped into the law of the land and the observance of them became the test of good intentions.

The confirmation of 1225 contains the significant statement that 'in return for the concession and gift of these liberties' the archbishops, bishops, abbots, priors, earls, barons, knights, free tenants, and all people of the realm had given a fifteenth of their movables. The implications latent in these words are important. They blow away the dust of centuries. In the archbishop's view king and taxpayers had a mutual responsibility. A royal letter to the justices in Kent brushed on one side a plea that those who had taken the cross were exempt from payment of the new tax. 'Make it clear to such persons that, if they withhold their gift, they have no share in the liberty granted to our worthy men by the Charters.' The idea that consent to a tax was a personal affair, that one man could agree and another refuse, was overcome in these years by the conception of action by the community; the definition by the king of his duty to his subjects was linked with the duty of his subjects to come to his aid. This was political thought in the making. Moreover, it involved the use of the feudal framework of society for wider social purposes. The taxation of 1225, as we can now see, meant the acceptance, without elaborate argument or clear intention, of the fact that the great council could, in the name of the people of the realm, grant a tax which every householder in the realm had to pay. Only five years before, in 1220, when the council had levied a carucage, or tax on land under the plough, there had been some resistance. The council which granted the carucage had not comprised all the magnates. The magnates thought that they should have been asked to contribute, if not individually, at least in their districts. The sheriff of Yorkshire had had much discussion on the matter with the stewards of the Yorkshire barons. Now, in 1225, a great feudal gathering spoke for all and granted a non-feudal tax—a very special kind of tax which bore no relation to tenure or services—which was to be paid by all. From one point of view, this grant was a belated application of a famous clause in the Great Charter of 1215, stripped of the details and the suggestion of limitations upon the royal power which had doubtless led to its excision from the later reissues.[1] From another point of view it was the assertion of the duty of the community of the realm, that is to say, of the great ecclesiastics and magnates and other counsellors, to provide aid from all, and of its right to insist in return upon the king's sworn obligations to his subjects. This is the kernel of the later parliamentary

---

[1] In 1215 the barons wished to have a council containing every tenant-in-chief, great or small, to grant scutages and all aids other than the three customary aids. The practice from 1225 was more elastic and opened the way to other kinds of taxation.

system, and it is a feudal kernel. It would be wrong either to limit the range of its significance or to read into it principles of government to which later ages gave assent.[1] In short, the question whether this was or was not true feudalism is unreal. It is doctrinaire, and does not arise. We are watching England become more aware of itself. Lordships and hundreds were used almost indifferently as the bases of assessment and collection. In 1225 a bailiff might assess the chattels on his lord's demesne, but did not collect the tax; in 1232, when a similar tax was granted, he might collect but not assess it. In 1225 knights were elected in the shire courts to take a hand, in 1232 they were not, and the name of each taxpayer was enrolled on the record of each vill under the barony of which he held. The practices incidental to the relations between lord and vassal or tenant, and to the administration of shire and hundred, were alike parts of the law and custom of the land. They were the fabric of the common law and of local custom, and were inextricably involved with each other in the common life.

Hence both the king's council and the great council shared responsibility for the maintenance of the state of the Crown and the realm in accordance with the spirit and letter of the Charters. During the minority the king's council and ministers administered the realm. They co-operated with the judges in the interpretation of the law, and were enlarged into the great council when great issues were at stake or special financial aid was required. Here a tradition was set for the future. It is not to go too far to say that all the tension in Henry's reign was caused by the failure of the king's council to co-operate with the larger body and was relaxed by the renewal of understanding between them. In spite of all the attempts which have been made to define in terms of constitutional law the relations between those who had responsibility, the simple fact remains that peace depended upon wise leadership and an atmosphere of goodwill, and that

[1] It would be wrong to see in the grant of 1225 the formal acceptance of a 'principle of representation'. A clear-cut principle of this kind follows long experience. If it had been held with conscious conviction it would have prevented the very developments, e.g. the gradual association of the knights of the shire with the barons, which make the practice of general grants by the great council so significant. Cf. below, pp. 536–40. Moreover, taxation was still so exceptional a measure that the claim to give individual consent died hard. Yet the evidence, considered as a whole, justifies the generalization that from 1225 lay taxes granted by the great council were not resisted. Delay or evasion of payment was no doubt common enough, but it always is.

discord followed failure to observe these conditions of strong and harmonious government. The history of taxation provides the outstanding example of this fact, and this chapter may be brought to an end with a brief survey of the financial position in Henry's reign.

Taxation should be considered in terms of the social structure. For more than a century, in the form of danegeld, it had been imposed as an annual charge on land. As Henry of Huntingdon said, 'we now pay to our kings by custom what used to be paid to the Danes out of unspeakable terror'. King Henry II had ceased to levy the geld. It had come to bear so little relation to the distribution of cultivated land and was limited by such extensive exemptions that it had lost its national character. The carucages levied by Richard I and by John were attempts to reimpose a land tax on a general basis, but they also were proved to be unsatisfactory. Apart from the tax given by the prelates in 1224, during the rebellion of Fawkes de Breauté, the carucage of 1220 was the last. In 1225, when King Louis VIII of France made his attack upon Poitou and Gascony, the justiciar and his colleagues had recourse to a plan which King John had found successful in 1207. In that year a levy of a thirteenth on personal property and rents had produced no less than £60,000. This tax had not been forgotten, and its nature, copied from ecclesiastical practice, was familiar to the exchequer. The ransom of King Richard and casual expedients, such as the provision for the administration of the Channel Islands, had been based upon the same principle. Yet, in contrast to the feudal aids, taxation of this kind was new. Its levy followed a deliberate and agreed determination to meet a particular emergency. Although it was later to become the normal way of increasing the royal revenue, it was levied only four times from laymen during King Henry's reign, in 1225, 1232, 1237, and, after a gap of thirty-two years, in 1269–70. On three of the occasions of its grant its serious and exceptional character was emphasized by a solemn association with the Charters: in 1225 these were reissued, in 1237 they were confirmed under oath and the sanction of excommunication, in 1270 their confirmation by Pope Innocent IV in 1245 and the sentence of excommunication against those who infringed them were recited at St. Paul's. The proceeds of the fifteenth in 1225, the thirtieth in 1237, the twentieth in 1269–70, if not of the fortieth in 1232, were earmarked for special purposes and kept apart in special places. Indeed, the latest of the four taxes was raised as a contribution towards the crusade of the Lord Edward and his brother Edmund, and was not used to meet royal needs at all. Nor were the other three taxes designed to meet domestic expenditure, although the king might disregard the conditions attached to the grants. The bulk of the fifteenth of 1225, which brought in nearly £58,000, went to pay for Richard of Cornwall's campaigns in Poitou and Gascony.[1] The fortieth of 1232 was required to meet the debts incurred by Henry during his own recent campaign and his obligations to Count Peter of Brittany; it amounted to only £16,475. The thirtieth of 1237, which produced about £22,500, supplemented a feudal aid of 1235 granted to pay for the marriage portion of Henry's sister the empress, and was also needed to meet the expenses of the king's marriage to Eleanor of Provence. In short, during Henry III's reign no taxation granted by the great council was intended as a contribution towards the normal expenses of royal administration.

The same was true of the feudal aids, or taxes on the knight's fee. By law the king had a right to levy such aids of his vassals for his ransom, if he were made prisoner, and the knighting of his eldest son and when his eldest daughter was married. He could also ask for an aid on other occasions. Apart from the aid levied after the treaty of Kingston in 1217 and that granted in 1235 when Henry's sister Isabella was married to the emperor Frederick II, no extraordinary aids were granted in this reign. The king frequently asked for them, but without success. It is significant that the aid granted in 1245 for the marriage of his eldest daughter Margaret was in fact an anticipation, grudgingly conceded. Margaret was not yet five years old and was not married to Alexander III of Scotland till the end of 1251. In 1245 Henry wanted money to pay debts incurred during his unpopular Gascon campaign in 1242, and after much discussion this way out of his difficulties was found. A similar situation led to the grant of an aid in 1253 for the knighting of the Lord Edward. Edward, it is true, was knighted by King Alfonso of Castile in the following year, when he married Eleanor of Castile at Burgos, but Henry's urgency was caused by his Gascon needs. Hence, even those aids to which he had a right took the form of grants made by the great council for special

[1] See assessments in H. Jenkinson, *Palaeography and Court Hand* (Cambridge, 1925).

purposes, and as substitutes for extraordinary aids. In any case, a feudal aid was negligible in value if compared with the proceeds of a general tax on movables. The aid of 1245, twenty shillings on the knight's fee, ought to have produced £6,000, that of 1253, forty shillings on the knight's fee, worked out to a figure of £11,000, but the assessment was arduous, evasions and exceptions were frequent, and it is unlikely that more than half these sums reached the royal exchequer.

The financial levy most frequently made in Henry's reign was scutage, which was not, strictly speaking, a tax at all. Nowadays, though the decision to declare war or make peace may lie with the executive, no decision is more a matter of national concern. On no occasion is it more imperative that the ministers of the Crown should have the support of parliament and people. In the thirteenth century, on the contrary, the social system still implied the duty to give military service in return for the tenure of land. In spite of the social changes to which we shall have to refer later, the English baron was primarily a warrior whose tenants were warriors. When the king ordered the feudal host to come together, it did come together. There might or might not have been discussion, feeling might or might not be in favour of the campaign. If it were a failure, the king might be made to suffer, especially when he sought relief from his debts; but the decision had rested with him, not with his vassals. At the end of the campaign the payment known as scutage was usually authorized, though sometimes after a short expedition it was not levied, and sometimes, in the case of a distant and expensive war, arrangements for the levy had been made earlier. If scutage were 'put in charge', those tenants-in-chief who had joined in the campaign got writs allowing them the payment, generally at the rate of forty shillings on the knight's fee, from their tenants. The king had the scutage on the fees of those tenants-in-chief who did not go. The sheriff supervised and checked and accounted for the money due from knights' fees in his shire, and sometimes collected it himself, whether it was payable to king or tenant-in-chief. King John had developed and exploited a practice of levying fines, when the host first assembled, from those vassals who did not wish to go or had not appeared or were not needed. Not only were these fines often excessive, but there was a tendency to levy scutage in addition at the end of the campaign. The barons had doubtless wished to stop the abuse when in 1215 they required the consent of a duly summoned great council to the levy of a scutage. This clause was omitted in later issues of the Great Charter; but though fines were frequently made between Henry III and his vassals, they would seem in his reign to have become anticipations of scutage, not additions to it, and to have been moderate in amount. Hence fines and scutage were, in practice, a contribution to the cost of a campaign; they were levied on knights' fees, paid by subtenants who did not accompany their lords, and divided between the king and the tenants-in-chief who had done service. The sums raised varied greatly. The total depended on the size of the army and the importance of the occasion. Sometimes no scutage was levied; sometimes, as in 1242, great care was taken to make it complete. The sheriffs and tenants-in-chief never succeeded in raising all of it. Religious houses which owed service frequently compounded for it. Its collection put a considerable strain upon the administrative system, for all over the country the land which had originally represented a knight's service was split up into fractions held by different persons in varying degrees of sub-tenancy. Scutage was simply a charge to which a piece of land was liable. It became a public service as danegeld had been, but differently assessed and capricious in operation. It required for its collection the co-operation of royal bailiffs and the ministers of the greater tenants. Its history both illustrates the welding together of the feudal system of land-tenure and the Anglo-Saxon system of local government, and reflects the influence of social change.

Here we come to another factor in the development of military service. For reasons which must be suggested later, the service due from the baronies had greatly decreased. In practice, which broadened into custom and precedent, the survey of 1166 no longer represented the truth. A great vassal whose wide-flung manors comprised, in parcels or fragments, a hundred knights' fees might owe the service of only three or four knights. If he accompanied the king on an expedition and had his royal writ of scutage he raised a sum which bore no relation at all to his expenses, or at any rate to the service which he had rendered. Owing to the rise in prices and the higher cost of military equipment in horses and armour and maintenance, expenses were certainly growing, but, as most of the charge was borne by the Crown, the king was increasingly reluctant to acquiesce in a financial arrangement which brought so little money into the exchequer. Indeed, by the end of the century the link between the tenants-in-chief, as military leaders, and their tenants had broken.[1] Henry raised no scutages after 1257. So far as he could he returned to the fine for non-service, and his son proceeded to the logical conclusion. Edward levied heavy fines from those tenants-in-chief who did not serve and, rather against their will, encouraged those who did serve to raise forces at his expense. The king succeeded on the whole in preserving the baronial character of a new army raised by new methods of contract and commissions, but the exchequer failed to turn scutage into a tax. By Edward III's time the implications of scutage had become unreal, its assessment was tiresome and intricate, its collection was very difficult. The knight's fee and all that it had meant sank to the level of an antiquarian survival.

The scutages, local or general, raised by Henry III and his barons with the help of the sheriffs and their officers were ten in number, and seven of these belong to the years 1221 to 1232. Five, the scutages of Montgomery (1223), Kerry (1228), Elfael (1232), Gannoc (1246), Wales (1257), followed Welsh campaigns; two, the scutages of Bytham and Bedford, were connected with the rebellions of William de Forz in 1221 and Fawkes de Breauté in 1224. The rest, those of Brittany (1230), Poitou (1231), and Gascony (1242), were put in charge to meet expenses of campaigns across the Channel. The accounts of the most important of these scutages, that of 1242, which were enrolled separately, have not survived, but the others, recorded in the Pipe Rolls of the exchequer, are illuminating. They show that if all the payments charged on these nine scutages had been paid, the sum would not have exceeded £28,000; in fact only a total of about £9,700 was collected during the two years following each levy, and little more was realized later. The highest number of fees taxed was about 3,000 for the scutage of Kerry (a district in Wales) in 1228, when £1,800 out of £3,466 was paid. Although fewer fees, some 2,100, were taxed for the foreign campaign of 1230, more money was raised, about £3,700 out of £8,400, but in this case unusually heavy fines for non-service swelled the total. In no case did the total sum raised by fines, scutage, and tallages on the towns and royal demesne suffice

---

[1] Helena M. Chew, in *History*, xiv (1929), 239. See below, p. 556, for Edward I's scutages.

to pay the full cost of the expedition. As a contribution to the normal needs of the king fines and scutages can be neglected. And even if we assume that the amount raised in 1242 was in the neighbourhood of £5,000 and add this to the total issue of the nine other scutages, the grand total, rather less than £15,000, was less than half the normal annual revenue of the Crown.

In the period of transition (1217-57) England was lightly taxed. The annual revenue of the king consisted of customary payments and the proceeds of judicial amercements. Fines and scutages in time of war did not come in all to more than half this revenue for one year. The total sum raised by the carucage of 1220, the feudal aids of 1235, 1245, and 1253, the fifteenth of 1225, the fortieth of 1232, and the thirtieth of 1237 was probably not more than £112,000, and, as we have seen, every one of these taxes except the carucage of 1220, which produced only some £5,400, was earmarked for a special purpose, the cost of a marriage or the payment of debts incurred in Gascony. How did the king extricate himself from the difficulties in which the frequent refusal of assistance by the great council and his own lavish expenditure involved him? He had the right to tallage the royal towns and demesne but, compared with the rest of the country, the towns were not actually an important source of revenue. It has been estimated that all the tallages levied on the nineteen wealthiest towns of the kingdom, including London, between 1223 and 1235 amounted only to £22,000. Henry also had the Jews at his mercy, and from them he extorted by way of tallage much larger sums, but this source tended to run dry. Occasionally the clergy as such were prevailed upon to come to the king's aid and, since they taxed themselves on their annual revenues, their participation formed a most useful example and doubtless made the exceptional expedient of a tax on the value of movables, including crops, more familiar to the laity. Now and then gifts were requested from religious houses. Somehow or other, in a rich land, Henry managed to live from hand to mouth and, if his needs were urgent, to raise loans. The money was undoubtedly there to be had, growing in the fields and on the backs of sheep, if only he could satisfy his magnates that his needs were their needs also. The trouble was that he could so rarely persuade them that this was the case, and that his demands at last, in 1258, amounted to an invitation to put in the brokers, just as he might himself put an embarrassed abbey under financial control. The prolonged crisis of 1258 to 1265 cleared the air. It re-established the royal authority, but it also showed how necessary continuous co-operation between king and magnates was. The greatness of Edward I lay in the fact that, except in the last ten years of his life, his authority was undisputed, while at the same time he was able to turn the financial expedients of 1225, 1237, and 1269 into a normal way of raising revenue and to tap a source hitherto hardly touched, the growing foreign trade in wool and hides. He realized what the marshal and Stephen Langton and Edmund of Abingdon had realized, that the state of the king was in the end identical with the well-being of the community of the realm, and that a wise and valiant king would increase, not suffer, in might and influence through co-operation with his nobles.

II

THE DUTIES OF KINGSHIP

KING HENRY was nineteen years old when, in January 1227, he declared himself to be of full age. This step released him from the limitation set upon the use of his seal, and he at once began to issue charters and to take stock of his affairs. The investigation into royal resources begun by the general eyre in 1218 was continued, with a more systematic and stringent application to details. Henry wanted to know by what right his vassals claimed lands and the 'liberties' which they enjoyed, and one obvious course to pursue was a scrutiny of their charters followed by confirmation in return for a fine. Thus the tendency to emphasize the formal written record, first as the testimony to and ultimately as the authority for a right, was given fresh impetus. Land was transferred, men and women were given 'seisin' of rights and tenements, by formal and symbolic acts such as the handing over of a sod. The ceremony took place in the presence of witnesses and generally on public occasions, when people were gathered together in shire or hundred courts or in a churchyard. The charter was evidence to the act, not the authority for it, still less the act itself. Probably most of the land of England was held by men who could show no written evidence. Their rights were derived from actual possession confirmed by precedent and public knowledge. Charters and other written evidence, even the records of the king's court of exchequer, might be at variance with the facts, inconsistent with each other, vague, inadequate, forged. A long and wavering process of trial and error lies behind the modern methods of conveyance. Yet, in the nature of the case, charters and final concords, written deeds of all kinds, public records and investigations, were destined to become the source of rights, the basis of discussion about rights. Henry's reign saw a great development in the significance of the charter and in the process of public inquiry. Edward I's famous investigations, after his return from his crusade, both in Gascony and England, were the culmination of a persistent habit of asking questions, and especially the question, 'by what warrant do you claim this right or exercise this privilege?' The customary questions asked by the judges on a general eyre, that is, under a comprehensive commission—questions which increased in number as time went on—were supplemented by special investigations. In Henry's reign an inquest in 1255 was the crowning example. Also, the barons of the exchequer got into the way of dealing judicially with alleged rights, with disputes between the Crown and the tenants about rights, with the interpretation of charters. Business of this kind became so common that special days were set aside for investigation at the exchequer. The exact wording of charters became a matter of great importance. Everything must be defined in clear terms. General clauses, however venerable their antiquity might be, could no longer be invoked in support of particular rights. New and more precise formulae were devised. An abbey or a borough, for example, found that it was well worth its while to pay heavily for a new charter which put the possession of an old right beyond doubt. And in those days, as land changed hands so frequently, was cut up or brought together into new holdings, the private charter, or the 'final concord',[1] became in its turn more precise, a dull but indispensable bit of evidence. When in 1227 the young king began to attach his seal to charters and grants in perpetuity and to ask questions through his justices, he took a hand in a movement of infinite complexity. Parchment, then paper, has testified throughout the centuries to the interplay of social change and law. The struggle for rights, the anxiety to hand them on, the greed for possession, the desire for security, the devices of the strong, the concessions of the helpless, the detection of fraud and error, all the natural passions of man and the remorseless processes of order, lie behind the prolixity which has filled our record offices and muniment rooms. The debris of local and family history bears witness to the things which mortal man has most cared about.

As early as the summer of 1227 Henry and the justiciar were

[1] The final concord settled in court a genuine or fictitious suit. The agreement of the parties was authorized by the royal judges. It was drawn up in triplicate, each copy fitting in to the others. The parties had their copies; the third, or 'foot of the fine' (*pes finis*), was kept in the treasury. These 'feet of fines' are the surviving records of countless agreements. On the more general *dies amoris*, see Josephine W. Bennett, 'The Mediaeval Loveday', in *Speculum*, xxxiii (1958), 351–70.

given a sharp reminder that it is easy to arouse these human passions. The king rewarded one of his father's servants, Waleran the German, who had been castellan of Berkhamsted during the recent war, by giving him a manor. In May Henry's younger brother Richard had returned to England from Gascony. This young man, who was to play a leading part in affairs throughout the reign, was born on 6 January 1209. In February 1225, soon after he reached the age of sixteen, he had been knighted by his brother and given the earldom of Cornwall, then an escheat in royal hands. He was also made count of Poitou and sent, with the earl of Salisbury and Philip Daubeny as his chief advisers, to hold Gascony and what he could of Poitou against Louis, now king of France. On the whole he had been successful. Soon after his return he seems to have ejected Waleran the German from his new manor on the ground that in fact it pertained to the honour of Cornwall. This was an act of disseisin; it was also a slight on his brother, and he was ordered to restore the manor. He was sure of his right and insisted upon a trial by the magnates of the realm. The king in a stormy meeting ordered him to restore the manor or leave the land. Richard refused to do either without the judgement of his peers. A quarrel about a manor, in which technically he was in the wrong, had been given a wider range where he could appear in the right. The justiciar was believed to have advised his arrest in the interests of the peace of the realm, and Richard fled. He came to William the Marshal, the earl of Pembroke, at Marlborough. At once the baronage was up in arms. The earls of Chester, Pembroke, Gloucester, Surrey, Hereford, Derby, and Warwick, with others, met at Stamford. They had their own grievance, for the king had recently been calling in question the verdicts of knights who, after the reissue of the Charters, had 'perambulated' the forests in order to fix their rightful bounds, and he had forced the knights to admit his claims to wider bounds than they had allowed. The earls raised this issue when they rallied in Earl Richard's defence. The king had to submit. He was reconciled to his brother. The storm died away. Richard's lordship in England was richly increased during the next three years. He got the big honours of Berkhamsted and Wallingford in the southern midlands.[1] But Henry had had his first fright and his

---

[1] Wallingford was given to Richard of Cornwall for life in 1231. Berkhamsted, which had been given by King John to his wife Isabella, though it was generally

first serious warning that there were things which he could not do. And Richard had found his feet. He was henceforward a man to be reckoned with. In March 1231 he strengthened his relations with the leading families of the land by his marriage with Isabella, a daughter of the great marshal and the widow of Gilbert the earl of Hertford and Gloucester, head of the house of Clare.

Earl Richard's marriage was more than a private affair. While he was in Gascony he had thought of an alliance with a princess of Spain and had been told that the king and council hoped to arrange for him a more advantageous union. The marriage of an important person, from the king downwards, was a very serious matter, to be carefully discussed. That between William the Marshal the younger and Eleanor the king's sister had been considered for many months in all its aspects, so long, in fact, that the marshal lost patience at last and presented an ultimatum to the council. Eleanor's next marriage, to Simon de Montfort, caused a political crisis. Hubert de Burgh's marriage to Margaret of Scotland gave alarm to the justiciar's detractors. Richard of Cornwall's union with a daughter of the old marshal, however it was brought about, gave him a definite and leading position in a family group which both enhanced its importance by a new alliance with the royal house and made him the spokesman of the marshal tradition.[1] The young marshal, whose independence of mind had caused some anxiety a few years earlier, died shortly after Richard's marriage to his sister. Would Richard maintain the tradition of watchful and critical co-operation with the court, or throw in his lot with his brother the king, or take a moderating course? The interest of the ten years or so after his marriage largely turns on this problem. His character was being shaped, and a new generation of barons was growing up beside him.

administered by royal castellans, came to Richard rather earlier, when the king gave him Isabella's dower lands in England. The two castles with their honours were the mainstay of Richard of Cornwall's power and wealth in the Thames valley and southern midlands.

[1] It is not generally realized that most of the leaders on either side in the political crises of the reign were directly descended either from King John or from William the Marshal. One of them, Henry of Almain, Richard of Cornwall's son, was descended from both. He was the half-brother of Richard de Clare, earl of Gloucester. There was no formal party of barons, as barons, opposed to the Crown, but a movement of fluctuating groups within a large family. The table on p. 42 illustrates this point.

For five years after his brush with Earl Richard and his protectors, Hubert de Burgh held his own. A phrase used in the course of a later lawsuit looks back to this time as that when the justiciar held England in his hand. Events showed that in spite of the tension which often prevailed at court, his weakness lay not in his relations with the great earls, who had served King John and the young king as he had served them, but in the restlessness of Henry himself. His fall was due not to the men who disliked or distrusted him but to the king who had expected more from him than he could give and, at the same time, more freedom of action than an old and wary minister would concede.

If Hubert had a forward policy it was directed towards the west. He wished to link the royal interests with those of his family in Wales and Ireland, to confine Llywelyn ab Iorwerth to his principality in Snowdonia, build up a lordship for himself in the east and south of Wales, and promote the claims of his nephew Richard de Burgh by the conquest of Connaught. Differences of opinion about plans of this kind seem, indeed, to have caused the strong action taken against William the Marshal in 1226, when William was ordered to surrender the custody of the castles of Cardigan and Carmarthen and found it prudent to withdraw from his defence of Aedh, king of Connaught. The

(*Note, p. 41, cont.*)

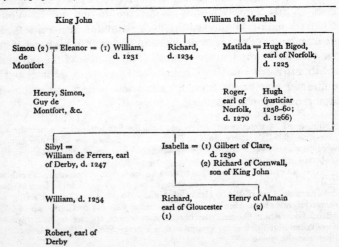

advance in Ireland was, on the whole, successful. Richard de Burgh, who was justiciar in Ireland for four years (1228–32), virtually conquered Connaught by 1235 and made secure on a much wider foundation the position which his father William, Hubert's brother, had established across the Irish Sea. His son Walter was in due course to become earl of Ulster and to add lands in the north to his manors and castles in Munster and Connaught. Hubert de Burgh, until his fall in 1232, had encouraged the advance in Ireland, but his more immediate activity in Wales had not been so successful, or rather, his own success had so far outrun any advantage which it brought to the king as to give him an isolated and perilous eminence. Since the beginning of the reign he had held the three castles in Upper Gwent, between the Usk and the Wye, which were usually described as the 'castles of the justiciar'. These were Grosmont, Skenfrith, and White Castle. In 1223 he had got the castle and honour of Montgomery, which both protected Shropshire and threatened the cantrefs of Powys. In 1229 the important castles of Cardigan, at the mouth of the Teifi, and Carmarthen, farther east on the river Tywi, were made the centres of a great marcher lordship which Hubert held by the service of five knights. Thus the justiciar's castles and honours consolidated a fluctuating frontier in central Wales, in the south-east, and in south Wales. By the summer of 1231 he had acquired a predominant position in the southern marches. The Braose lordship of Gower was subordinated to the honour of Cardigan and Carmarthen. When the earl of Gloucester died in Brittany in 1230, leaving as his heir a boy of eight, Hubert was given the wardship, and so controlled the whole of the earl's marcher lordship in the valleys of Morganwg or Glamorgan. The justiciar and his wife planned a marriage between this lad—the Richard of Clare later so prominent in the baronial movement of 1258—and their daughter Meggotta, a girl of about the same age. If Hubert had been able to maintain his influence, his earldom of Kent and the lands held jointly by him and Margaret of Scotland in England and Wales might have been united to the earldoms of Hertford and Gloucester and the richest lordship in the Marches.[1]

[1] The pathetic story of Meggotta can be read in *E.H.R.* lvi (1941), 539–46. She seems to have been married secretly to Richard of Clare in 1232, when Margaret of Scotland had both children with her in sanctuary at Bury St. Edmunds. Hubert, whose fall from power had just come about, was probably unaware of the marriage, which became known when the desirability of finding a wife for Richard, now the

The splendid prospects opened up by the justiciar's acquisitions were a mirage unless he could justify the king's confidence. Hubert had upset the traditional interests of great families in the Marches. His lordship of Cardigan and Carmarthen and his overlordship of the Gower peninsula encircled the marshal lordship in Pembroke. His position in Glamorgan and Gwent and Montgomery gave him the leadership among all the other marcher lords. His young ward's stepfather, Richard of Cornwall, though he was the king's brother, had no standing in the March. Hubert was an interloper unless, as justiciar, he could use his power to win authority for the king and reduce the Welsh princes to a lasting obedience. And it was just here that he failed. Already in 1228 an impressive campaign from Montgomery into the border district of Cerī or Kerry had been fruitless of result. In 1231 Llywelyn took the offensive and carried everything before him. The English feudal host was summoned, but was kept ineffectively in the district of Elfael, north of the Wye. In November a truce for a year allowed Llywelyn to retain what he had won. It was just about this time that Peter des Roches returned to England and lent a willing ear to the king's fretful story of frustration and waste and incompetence. Henry felt that everything had gone wrong. His rights and liberties were neglected, his treasure was squandered to no purpose, his council had neither unity nor the effective control of affairs; only the justiciar, indifferent to his royal master's interests, seemed to thrive.

Hubert was not entirely to blame for King Henry's disillusionment. The time had not come for a united and strenuous drive against the prince of Snowdonia. That required for its success other conditions in Wales, a firmer grip of the Marches and their lords, and above all a strong, skilful, and determined leader. In 1231 there was no wish to turn border warfare into a national enterprise, even if Hubert himself, as is very unlikely, thought of the Welsh problem in this way. Llywelyn and the other Welsh princes, in spite of their different traditions and environment, lived in constant intercourse with their neighbours, whose castles and lands were, in the east and south, interlocked

king's ward, was discussed in 1236. Meggotta died in November 1237; in the following January Richard de Clare was married to Maud, daughter of John de Lacy, earl of Lincoln. Margaret's action was the cause of Hubert's final downfall in 1236–9.

with their own. Llywelyn himself had married King John's natural daughter, Joan. This lady, after years of helpful agitation in her husband's interests, had recently been discovered in an adulterous intrigue with the lord of Abergavenny, William de Braose. Llywelyn had hanged her lover and imprisoned her, and few had questioned his right to do so. The earl of Chester, indeed, always a friendly neighbour, had upheld Llywelyn's claims to Painscastle in Elfael during the later campaign. In fact, Anglo-Normans and Welsh lived together in turbulent understanding, like quarrelsome neighbours in a back street, conscious of their corporate life. Hubert de Burgh would have to earn his place in such a society; he could not dominate it as a matter of course. Even in Ireland, where racial feeling was stronger and passions more bitter, the situaion was much the same.

Henry had perhaps felt the need for a clearer field of action when he insisted on his Breton expedition. This was in the year after the futile Welsh campaign in Kerry. His discovery at Portsmouth in October 1229 that the force was not in a state of preparation and that the expedition must be deferred produced his first open quarrel with the justiciar. Henry lost his temper. He knew that Hubert was lukewarm in his approval of the adventure and he did not hesitate to accuse him of treachery. As we shall see in the next chapter, the justiciar's hesitations were only too well grounded. Henry's failure to make an impression upon Normandy and Poitou from what had seemed so good a base, followed as it was by the inglorious campaign in Elfael, intensified his suspicions. Hubert was no longer the man for him. A few months later, in the summer of 1232, Peter des Roches was able to effect a dramatic change.

The reason publicly given for Hubert de Burgh's fall was not a cause so much as an excuse. The justiciar was alleged to have connived in a popular movement against the growing practice of providing papal nominees to benefices in England. The pope had complained about the trespasses committed against the Church of Rome and Italian clerks, and on inquiry the king had learned that the justiciar had been responsible for them. So the king's letters patent 'made known to all' in a recital of Hubert's submission and imprisonment. Pope Gregory's indignation had been stirred by the story of a movement led in 1231 by a young Yorkshire landholder, Robert Tweng, who certainly had made a nuisance of himself and had won considerable support at the king's court as well as in the country-side. An alien had been provided to a church to which he had the right of presentation. His protest, deplorable though it was, may have helped to bring about the later exclusion of churches in the gift of laymen from the scope of the practice. Under the name of William Wither he gathered together a band of sympathizers who ranged the country from Yorkshire to Hampshire. They issued manifestoes, warned the bishops not to interfere, ordered those who farmed the lands of churches held by alien absentees to withhold their rents, and molested a few Italians. Beyond emptying barns and distributing grain they did little damage, but their agitation as they moved about, armed and masked, caused some alarm and was doubtless greatly exaggerated by their victims. The movement had died down before the papal expostulation reached England, but it came at a time unfortunate for the justiciar. After his fall, the revenue of some of his lands was used to compensate those who had suffered during the disturbance.

Later in the reign the hostility to papal provisions was to become a major issue at the royal court and in the minds of ecclesiastical reformers. The justiciar may well have expressed approval of the objects, if not of the conduct, of the agitators. His character and outlook are surprisingly elusive, but, so far as inferences from his career are permissible, they suggest that he was an Englishman of the insular type like so many of the gentry and monks and clergy of his time. He had co-operated with the bishops in the past. The intelligent clerks whom he had gathered about him considered that an understanding with the bishops was needed in the interests of all. The bishops were his natural guides and allies, while he could support them in their desire to manage the affairs of the Church in England in accordance with traditional ways and customs. Neither he nor they, for example, wished to see a papal legate in England. When, during the Breton campaign in 1230, King Henry, who seems to have felt rather lonely, begged Pope Gregory to send a legate, the justiciar was much depressed. He was disposed to acquiesce but was roused by one of his clerks to make a fresh effort to dissuade the king. The clerk pointed out that his happy alliance with the bishops might be disturbed, for the English Church would be in subjection. Hubert took action and, to the pope's surprise, the king changed his mind. But in fact the situation was not so simple as Hubert's friends and colleagues imagined. They took no account of the new movement within the Church. They failed to see that Archbishop Stephen's strength had lain not in an appeal to insular prejudice but in his instructed idealism, in his desire to see in England a powerful, well-organized ecclesiastical province able, without constant papal intervention, to express the power of the new life which had directed his teaching in the schools and informed the decrees of the Lateran Council. His political interests were moral, not dictated by convenience; and after his death in 1228 the men of his way of thinking became more sharply divided from the more conventional prelates who were satisfied with things as they were. Men like the new archbishop, Richard Grant, who, unhappily, died in Italy in August 1231, his successor Edmund of Abingdon, and above all Robert Grosseteste, who was raised to the see of Lincoln in 1235, did not share the outlook of the chancellor, Ralph Nevill, the bishop of Chichester, respectable man though he was. They were good and ardent Englishmen, but their horizon was that of the church militant. Archbishop Richard deplored at the papal court the effects in England of the justiciar's domination and was opposed to the participation by the clergy in secular affairs. Edmund of Abingdon exhausted himself in efforts to realize the Langtonian ideal at court, though he robbed his success of much of its effect by that unbridled earnestness which made him one of the most fashionable of saints. Robert Grosseteste raised the issues of the day to still loftier heights—too high, indeed, for others to reach. Yet Grosseteste with his flaming intensity was anything but ineffective.

No longer trusted by the king, deprived of the support of the prelates, looked on askance by the baronial families, Hubert de Burgh, in all his greatness, had become more and more isolated by the end of 1231. His fall was due in the end to the bishop of Winchester, who stood apart alike from king, prelates, and barons. Hitherto Peter des Roches had not played a decisive part in English affairs since King John's death. The legates, the marshal, the archbishop, the justiciar had in turn overshadowed him. His chance had now come. He had left England to go on crusade about the time when King Henry declared himself of age. He returned nearly five years later to find his former pupil in a very different mood, ready to turn for counsel and aid to an old friend of the Angevin house who had no particular respect for English ways and had been consorting on familiar terms with pope and emperor. The bishop was a grand seigneur, a wealthy, independent figure in the great world of the west, outspoken, trenchant, and nimble-witted. He had become a trusted companion of Frederick II in the Holy Land, taken a hand in the treaty with the sultan of Egypt, and played his part in the reconciliation between the emperor and Pope Gregory IX after the treaty of San Germano (July 1230). On his way home from Italy he had negotiated the truce which ended the fighting between the French and the Anglo-Breton alliance. It is significant that a few weeks after he landed in England Henry began to assert himself by the dismissal of Ranulf the Breton, a former chaplain of the justiciar, who, as treasurer of the chamber, had the most responsible office in the royal household.[1]

Little or nothing is known of the personal relations and crosscurrents at court, and, as we cannot be taken behind the scenes, we can only surmise how the bishop of Winchester made his influence felt. He entertained king and justiciar at Winchester on Christmas Day, and although he made no secret of his dissatisfaction with the state of the king's affairs, he did or could do nothing to shake Hubert's position until the summer of 1232. The course of events suggests that important changes at court were deliberately combined with the enhancement of the justiciar's dignity. Thus, between 11 and 28 June, Peter des Rivaux, the man selected to control a new administration, was established as treasurer of the household, granted the custody of the king's small seal for life, and given charge of the Jews, the ports, escheats, wardships, and the mint; but at this very time the justiciar was made justiciar of Ireland for life, with the custody of the royal castles in Ireland and was confirmed in his custody of the Tower of London, Dover, Windsor, and Odiham. Also, his colleagues Walter Mauclerc, bishop of Carlisle, the treasurer, and Ralph Nevill, bishop of Chichester, the chancellor, were granted their offices for life. Nearly all these appointments were ratified by formal royal charters.

Peter des Rivaux was a Poitevin, the son or perhaps the nephew of the bishop of Winchester. He had held office in the royal household for some five years earlier in the reign, but seems to have been deprived and forced to leave England during

[1] The bishop arrived in Winchester on 1 August 1231 and went on to the king in Wales. Ranulf the Breton was dismissed on 12 September. He was ordered to leave the country with his family.

the trouble about the royal castles in 1223-4. He had been allowed to return in 1230, and now in 1232 we find him suddenly exalted to rule the household and control the most fruitful of the incidental resources of the Crown. Moreover, in July he was made sheriff of numerous shires. It looks as though the justiciar and his two colleagues at the exchequer and in the chancery had exacted a heavy price for their acquiescence in this financial reconstruction. They had dug themselves in for life, the justiciar in Ireland, the chancellor and treasurer in their offices. And this view is strengthened by the survival of a very curious series of documents, issued on 2 July at Hubert's manor of Burgh in Norfolk. The king, as was his frequent practice, especially in times of political crisis, was on a tour of pilgrimage to relics and shrines in the eastern counties. On 1 July he was at Bromholm on the Norfolk coast, and the party, which comprised justiciar, treasurer, chancellor, Peter des Rivaux, and the two stewards of the royal household, spent the night at Burgh, a few miles away. Hence it is reasonable to infer that the sworn compacts which were set down in writing at Burgh had been made at Bromholm on the previous day. Henry made an oath on the gospels binding himself and his heirs, with God as his surety, to observe all the charters which he had granted to the justiciar and to Margaret his wife and to the other high officers of the realm and household. On pain of excommunication he submitted himself to the compulsion of the pope in case of any violation of its terms. The justiciar, in his turn, by the king's command, swore to do all in his power to preserve the charters inviolate and to impede any attempt by the king, or any others who might seek to influence the royal will, to violate them. In form this compact, though strongly expressed, was quite normal. Proceedings of this kind, for example, frequently followed a treaty between Welsh princes or between the lords of Poitou and their neighbours. But in content it is extraordinary. It suggests either that, for the time being, King Henry was at the mercy of the justiciar, who, thoroughly alarmed by the designs of the bishop of Winchester and the elevation of Peter des Rivaux, had come to an understanding with his rivals, or that Henry, in one of his moods of pious exaltation, was persuaded to placate his well-tried ministers in this curious way. His later petitions to the pope to be released from an oath which had been extorted from him contrary to his duty to maintain royal rights and liberties points to but does not establish the former explanation. In any case, the incident shows as by a lightning-flash how vain it is to read any later ideas of constitutional law into the minds of this remote age.

The king's mood soon passed. By the end of July, when he was in the other side of the country, he had probably received the papal letters of 9 June about the recent attacks on Italians and these, as we have seen, gave him his opportunity. Hubert de Burgh was ordered to hand over the royal castles in his custody to a new justiciar, Stephen Segrave.[1] A few days later, on 13 August, he was forced to surrender his own castles. The records show that an order of banishment was drawn up, though no action was taken on it. The reign neither of Richard II nor of Henry VIII can show a more dramatic reversal of fortune than the fall of Hubert de Burgh. But at once more prudent and lawful counsels began to prevail. The community of the barons asserted itself, just as it had come to the aid of Richard of Cornwall in 1227. The great earls had no affection for the late justiciar; but like some of the bishops they had, not entirely for selfish reasons, disliked his ascendancy rather than repudiated the traditions for which he had stood. He had been a great servant of the Crown, and as an earl he must be given a formal trial. He was allowed to retire to the priory of Merton, near London, to prepare his defence. The clamour against him, and the fear of an attack by the Londoners, unnerved him. He fled, but was caught at Brentwood in Essex and brought to the Tower. Again the law, this time the law of the Church, was invoked on his behalf, for the steward of the royal household, who had pursued him, had dragged him out of sanctuary. The bishop of London insisted on his restoration to the chapel at Brentwood. He was taken back, the chapel was surrounded by the sheriff and his men, he came out and was taken back to the Tower. Some said that he had been starved out and that his surrender had not been voluntary. Royal commissioners accordingly interviewed him in the Tower and were given, or extorted, a statement that he had left the chapel of his own free will. Now the trial before his peers could proceed. The king's court sat in

[1] Stephen came from Seagrave (in Leicestershire), was a knight who had served John and Henry as justice, and at this time was sheriff of several shires. He and the chancellor had acted as regents during the absence of the king and justiciar in Brittany in 1230. He certainly had much to do with the fall of his colleague before and after he succeeded him as justiciar at the end of July 1232.

Cornhill on 10 November. Hubert's share in the attack on the Italians, and numerous other charges, most of them very fantastic, were pleaded against him. He refused to await judgement and threw himself entirely on the king's mercy. Probably in order to avert scandal, the earls and other magnates arranged a settlement which should take effect after his submission. Four earls, Cornwall, Pembroke, Warenne, and Lincoln,[1] guaranteed his safe keeping, by knights of their choosing, in the castle of Devizes. His private lands were restored to him. His complete submission gave legality to his imprisonment, the suspension of judgement entitled him to retain his lands and dignities as an earl and baron; but he lost all his offices and his Welsh honours, all the royal castles and escheats and wardships which he had held.

The way was now open for the new order, sustained by the bishop of Winchester, directed by Peter des Rivaux and his colleagues. Only the chancellor remained as a link with the past, for in January 1233 the bishop of Carlisle ceased to be treasurer of the exchequer and was succeeded by Peter des Rivaux himself. The result of the change at court was twofold. In the first place, the administrative system was more closely interlocked and the household became the centre not only for the initiation but also for the transaction of business. Peter's base was the royal chamber; he controlled the exchequer through a deputy, and both justiciar and chancellor lost their independent dignity. Secondly, the affairs of the realm were dealt with by a little group of counsellors who were responsible for all the inquiries, stocktaking, revision of technical procedure, which the bishop of Winchester had declared to be necessary if the king was to know where he stood and to be master in his own house. Peter des Rivaux was not a lonely despot. He did not fill the royal household with a crowd of Poitevins. He worked with Stephen Segrave, Robert Passelewe, a king's clerk who at this time came to the front, Brian de Lisle, and a few others, Englishmen as energetic as himself and probably less scrupu-

---

[1] During the events of the autumn Ranulf earl of Chester had died. His last public activity was the exertion of his influence on the side of legality, alongside Richard of Cornwall, Richard the Marshal, and others. His successor as earl of Lincoln was John de Lacy, constable of Chester and lord of Clitheroe and Pontefract, who had married the daughter of one of Ranulf's sisters and co-heiresses. This lady, the countess of Winchester, resigned her claims to the earldom of Lincoln to John de Lacy. So began the Lacy line of earls which ended in 1348.

lous.[1] His own importance was derived from the concentration
in and under him of nearly every office which, in England and
Ireland, collected the royal revenue. He controlled shires,
forests, wardships, escheats, ports, fairs. In addition he, not the
new justiciar, succeeded Hubert de Burgh as castellan of Dover,
also in Cardigan, Carmarthen, and the three 'castles of the
justiciar' in upper Gwent. The object of this monopoly was
not primarily to exalt Peter as a great and responsible minister
but to sweep aside all obstacles to financial reform. When he
fell, he fell as one of a group whose personal disgrace was of
short duration. Indeed, the work went on with Segrave's and
perhaps his own assistance until at least 1241. What this work
was we shall consider later. The storm raised against Peter and
his colleagues was due to the fact that the interests of the community of the realm lay at the mercy of a few men in whom the
masterful spirit of King John seemed to be revived. And the
immediate cause of the revolt of 1233-4 was the disregard of
convention and even of feudal law which such irresponsible
power invited. The outcry against the Poitevins here found such
justification as it had. Some Poitevins were certainly attracted
to England by the dominance of the bishop of Winchester and
his relative. Here and there they picked up some advantage, a
marriage or a wardship, the custody of a castle or a manor.
This was quite enough to arouse indignation and to account for
the passionate cries, repeated by the St. Albans chronicler, that
the rights of the baronage were in jeopardy and that its blood
was being defiled by union with upstart aliens.

At the worst a self-seeking man, after attempting a gangster's
bargain with his rivals, had been overthrown by an irresponsible
group. At the best a powerful but unpopular minister had been
set on one side by an ungrateful king, who wished to manage his
realm like a private estate with the aid of more pliable and more
business-like agents. In either case—and the truth lies some-
where between the worst and the best—Henry, at the instigation

---

[1] Passelewe had been the clerical ally of Fawkes de Breauté and had tried to
persuade the pope to prevent the restoration to the Crown of the royal castles. He
was the most disliked of Henry's busy servants, and later was especially unpopular
for his inquisition into encroachments of the royal forests in 1243-4. Brian de Lisle
(*de Insula*) had been a trusted servant of King John and one of his castellans, notably
at Knaresborough. He had been one of those who resisted the transfer of the castles.
King Henry naturally turned to these and similar men in 1232. They were competent and hated Hubert de Burgh.

of Peter des Roches, had discarded the tradition established by
King John's executors and defined by Stephen Langton. Co-
operation with the community of prelates and barons under the
sanction of the coronation oath and the Charters was incompatible with the rule of Peter des Rivaux and his colleagues.
The magnates were uneasy, and some of them were indignant.

The new earl marshal, Richard, had particular reason to be
on his guard. He had not expected to succeed his brother.
When the younger William died childless in 1231, Richard, in
accordance with arrangements accepted by the kings of France
and England, was settled on his father's lands in Normandy.
Henry and Hubert de Burgh had been reluctant to accept him
as his brother's heir, to see established in the Marches, in Leinster,
and the English manors of this great house a man who had been
a vassal of the French king. Peter des Rivaux's succession to the
justiciar in south Wales, and also his immediate control of the
Irish administration had, from this point of view, peculiar
significance. If trouble came, they invited an alliance between
Earl Richard and Llywelyn and disturbance in Ireland. Trouble
did come and very quickly. It began, as trouble of this kind
usually does, with a trivial incident. Gilbert Basset, lord of
Wycombe in Buckinghamshire and of many manors in the west
country, was disseised 'by the king's will' of a manor in Wiltshire in favour of another claimant, Peter de Mauley, the
former castellan of Corfe. Richard the Marshal upheld the
cause of Gilbert. Before the end of May 1233, just about six
months after Hubert de Burgh had been sent to Devizes, grumbling against the new order of things at court passed into sporadic
but widespread violence. The king had reason to believe that
the guards of the late justiciar, appointed as we have seen by his
brother Richard of Cornwall, the earl marshal, and two other
earls, were not trustworthy. Gilbert Basset, who had at one time
been castellan of Devizes and had land in its neighbourhood,
laid plans to rescue the prisoner. Measures were taken to
strengthen the guard, and about the same time, in the Whitsun
council at Gloucester, a provision for the maintenance of the
peace was made and shortly afterwards was issued to every
sheriff for public proclamation. This provision, explicitly
directed against the spread of disturbance, was the first of those
writs of watch and ward which, repeated in 1242 and 1253,
before the king left England on a Gascon expedition, culminated

in the famous statute of Winchester of 1285, and in this form remained in force for more than three centuries. It ordered the appointment of guards who were to watch every night in every vill until the following Michaelmas, the arrest of strangers who could give no good account of themselves, and restrictions upon hospitality. A fortnight later the leading barons of the March were ordered to give hostages for their loyal service until the realm was safe.

Henry and his advisers must have thought that these and other watchful measures would suffice to keep Earl Richard and his friends in check, for in July they were planning a big military expedition to Ireland. The men of the ports were ordered to collect their ships at Milford Haven and the feudal host was summoned to meet at Gloucester by the end of August. The purpose of the expedition was doubtless the elimination of danger from the marshal on the one hand and Richard de Burgh on the other, to be effected by a strong and united effort to conquer the whole of Connaught for the Crown. The best days of King John must have seemed to his old servants to have come again. The bishop of Winchester knew how to strike. This indeed was business. But more prudent counsels prevailed, especially when Richard de Burgh, no friend to the marshal's influence in Ireland, was found to be loyal and willing to aid the government to conquer Connaught and watch the movements of Earl Richard. It would be wiser to deal at once with the earl in the Marches of Wales. He had formed a confederacy of earls and barons and refused to come to meetings of the great council; his allies, led by Gilbert Basset and his brothers and their kinsman, Richard Siward, were at large to range the southern shires and do havoc on the lands of the king's ministers. The king's brother was known to be inclined to the marshal's cause and others, including the earl of Norfolk, had joined it. So Henry remained in England. Richard of Cornwall, not for the last time, was prevailed upon to throw in his lot with his brother. Pledges of loyalty were taken from suspects, the lands of confederates were seized. In the middle of August a body of Flemish knights and men-at-arms in Henry's pay landed in England under the command of the count of Guisnes. The army at Gloucester had already been moved forward to Hereford. The king formally denounced his feudal obligations to the marshal and laid siege to his castle at Usk. Gilbert Basset and others formally renounced their homage to the king. A state of war prevailed in England and the Marches.

Earl Richard had no personal quarrel with the king. He wanted the correction of abuses, not war. The prelates and other prominent ecclesiastics, in their turn, had already begun to raise warning voices at the king's court. In the previous June the Dominican scholar, Robert Bacon, is said to have told Henry that peace was impossible so long as the bishop of Winchester was in power. For a time both sides shrank from open warfare.[1] The earl agreed to surrender his castle in token of submission, to receive it again after fifteen days, and the king agreed, with the counsel of the bishops, to correct what was amiss. On 8 September Henry declared that the earl had satisfied him, and in due course the earl set out to meet the great council at Westminster; but his suspicions were aroused. His castle was still in the king's hands, he feared treachery and turned back. He recovered Usk, rallied his forces, and came to an understanding with Llywelyn. In a bitter war the March was desolated. The king, though he found some support among the Marchers and had his Flemish mercenaries, got little aid from his vassals. 'He did not dare to meet his enemies', says Roger of Wendover, and when in January the earl and Llywelyn seized Shrewsbury he was inert at Gloucester. He had been able to check a widespread movement among the barons, but he could not stir them to effective action in his cause. In short, he had failed. Opinion was against him.

Just as Archbishop Stephen and his colleagues had intervened in 1223–4, so now bishops with reforming minds, led by Roger Niger, the saintly bishop of London, also some of the Franciscans and Dominicans who had recently begun to influence English society, put an end to the power of Peter des Roches. At the October council, to which Earl Richard had feared to come, they had urged the king to trust to his natural advisers and to proceed against his enemies in accordance with the terms of the Great Charter. It was on this occasion that the bishop of Winchester is said to have made the well-known retort that there were no peers in England. He was doubtless thinking of French provincial practice and the growing importance of the

---

[1] This was a war between the king and the earl, not a military action against a man who had put himself outside the law. Before the battle of Lewes in 1264 declarations of formal repudiation (*diffidatio*) were also exchanged.

'peers of France'.[1] There was nothing comparable to that in this compact, insular land. The gibe was not intended as a piece of political reflection. The splendid prelate, so ambitious for his royal protégé, was stung to anger by what seemed to him an obtuse attack upon his well-meant intentions. The success of the earl marshal in the Marches, and the fall of Shrewsbury, gave the lead to his critics. Henry, after outbursts of impotent anger against the earl and his friends, was reduced to a more submissive mood. For a short time he surrendered to the influence of a finer man than Peter des Roches. This was Edmund of Abingdon, the new archbishop of Canterbury.

The monks of Canterbury had had much difficulty to find an archbishop acceptable to the pope and to those whose advice he sought. They elected the chancellor, Ralph Nevill, but he was rejected as 'illiterate', that is to say, not learned enough for so great an office. They elected their prior, but he was too old and not a man of the world. They elected one of the foremost scholars of the time, John Blund, our first English Aristotelian, but he was suspect as a friend of the bishop of Winchester, as not independent enough to hold his own and take his own course. Then the monks relieved all anxieties by electing Edmund of Abingdon, treasurer of Salisbury, a saintly man of courage and candour, renowned as a scholar and as a former teacher at Oxford. Probably no man since St. Hugh of Lincoln had won such general esteem in the English Church, and, unlike that austere Carthusian, he was a secular priest, in touch with the new movements, and the foremost in the ablest capitular body in the country. His archiepiscopal career, brief and poignant and dramatic, captured the imagination of his contemporaries, and the more quickly because three or four years of success were followed by an equal period of painful disillusionment, by voluntary exile and speedy death. Six years after his death, and only thirteen years after his election, he was a canonized saint. The story of his life and miracles was circulated with a zest only inferior to that of St. Thomas of Canterbury's numerous biographers. Although St. Edmund had lived after his elevation in the thick of controversy, at court, in ecclesiastical circles, and with the monks of his cathedral, his memory was cultivated by friends and foes alike, by kings and friars, rich and poor, seculars and religious. King Henry adjusted his mind to the

[1] See *Cambridge Medieval History*, vi. 326.

canonization with the grace of a convert and visited his shrine
at Pontigny. Richard of Cornwall had peculiar veneration for
him, and his son, named Edmund after him, regarded him as
his patron saint. Scholars treasured the record of his Oxford
days, ecclesiastics the memory of his succession to St. Thomas.
Matthew Paris wrote his life.[1] St. Edmund, indeed, became,
with St. Richard Wych and Robert Grosseteste, an exemplar
cherished by Simon de Montfort and his more serious companions. In 1267 the excommunicated rebels in the Isle of Ely
appealed to him as one of their heroes whose inspiration justified
their contumacy. The impression made by St. Edmund, first in
his lifetime but still more after his death, reminds us of a quality
which is too easily overlooked in the political and social life of
the middle ages, the influence of men of outstanding character
in sustaining the purpose and firing the imagination of men of
action.

The archbishop-elect came to a meeting of the great council
at Westminster in February 1234, when he received the royal
confirmation of his election. He was consecrated on 2 April, and
a week later another meeting of the great council was held. At
the February meeting the king had agreed to consider his relations with his ministers and advisers, and had asked for time.
'He could not change his council so suddenly, before he had
had the account of the money which had been entrusted to
them.' He took the three most important men—the bishop of
Winchester, the justiciar, and Peter des Rivaux—on another
monastic tour in the eastern counties. Presumably he discussed
his and their future with them. On his return the bishops, who
had entered into negotiations with the earl marshal and
Llywelyn, were able to report the terms of a truce which the
king accepted, and a month later, at the April meeting of the
great council, he announced that his counsellors would be removed. The new archbishop himself went to the Marches to join
in the discussion prior to a definite settlement with Llywelyn.

King Henry was deprived of the prospect of an easy and dignified retreat from a difficult position by dreadful news from
Ireland. Not awaiting the issue of the bishops' intervention,
the earl marshal had crossed the Irish Channel to defend his

---

[1] C. H. Lawrence's study, *St. Edmund of Abingdon* (Oxford, 1960), contains a
careful and reliable revision of the extensive literature about the archbishop and his
biographers. He shows, for example, that Matthew Paris's basic source, the life by
Eustace of Faversham, in the St. Edmund chapters, is anything but worthless. Lawrence, it should be added, is sceptical about Edmund's alleged 'voluntary exile'
(pp. 168–76). I agree with him.

lordship and castles in Leinster. The king's partisans had been more active in Ireland than in England. The justiciar of Ireland, Maurice Fitzgerald, Richard de Burgh, and others had carried war into Leinster. After Earl Richard's arrival, a meeting was arranged on 1 April on the Curragh, the meads in Kildare well known in Irish history. When the earl insisted upon a restoration of the castles which had been taken, he was set upon. He was seriously wounded and, on 16 April, he died. Immediately the cry of treachery—that treachery which the earl had feared a year earlier—was raised and spread with all the violence of suspicion which has so often bedevilled the affairs of Ireland. A former justiciar, Geoffrey de Marisco, the leading member of a Somerset family widespread in Ireland, was especially accused, for he had acted as the marshal's friend. He was widely believed to have lured the marshal to his death. He was made the scapegoat, and his infuriated son William began a vendetta which disturbed the peace and affected the peace of mind of the king himself for many years.[1] But the immediate result of the news of the marshal's death was the triumph of the marshal's friends, not in Ireland but in England. Peter des Rivaux, Stephen Segrave, Robert Passelewe, Brian de Lisle were not permitted, as they might have been, to withdraw quietly. Henry denounced and proclaimed them. Special commissions were appointed to investigate their conduct and to hear complaints against them. For a short time, until the bishops intervened in their behalf, they were proscribed and hunted from place to place as traitors. It is impossible to separate Henry's rage against them from a consciousness that he had been tricked, for, at a meeting of the great council at Gloucester in the end of May the archbishop is said to have produced royal letters which suggested that the king himself had aimed at the earl's destruction in Ireland. The whole story is so exaggerated by the St. Albans chronicler, and departs so widely from the impression conveyed by the public records, that it is impossible to be sure of the truth.[2] Henry certainly bore no ill will against the marshal's enemies in Ireland. In England the earl's death does seem, however, to have put him at a disadvantage, and his reaction against his counsellors

[1] See *History*, xxv (1941), 286 ff.; xxvi. 127.
[2] Mr. Hugh Lawrence has pointed out to me that Matthew Paris, in his life of St. Edmund, makes no reference to the incident, although he describes in some detail the archbishop's share in events, nor does he recur to it in his *Historia Anglorum*.

was violent. How violent it was can be seen in a letter written a year later, in April 1235, to the emperor, who had just been affianced to Henry's sister Isabella. By this time Peter des Roches had left the country to give his services to the pope, who was faced by a rebellion in Italy. Henry and his new advisers were afraid that the bishop would give a misleading account of English affairs and begged the emperor to correct any mischief which he might do. The king wrote that he had placed complete confidence in the bishop. As a result he had become alienated from his vassals, had left the paths of justice, and been faithless to the duties of kingship. One may feel that this exposition on kingship, with its luxuriant self-abasement, expresses the mind of Edmund of Abingdon rather than of the young king; but Henry undoubtedly had had a great shock.

His revulsion of feeling was more lasting than any sense of humiliation. He had been put in a false position, and was sorry for himself; but his nature was resilient and his moods of pious exaltation were frequent, seeking divine sanction for his rapid changes. A later chronicler, whose evidence is confirmed by the casual remarks of others, wrote of Henry: 'the less he was clever in his actions within this present world the more he indulged in a display of humility before God. On some days he heard mass three times, and as he longed to hear even more masses, he had them celebrated privately.'[1] His strange compacts with Hubert de Burgh and other officials preliminary to the justiciar's fall, and the arrangements for the dismissal of his new ministers two years later were made, as we have seen, during visitations of East Anglian shrines. In 1233, the year of political independence, he found exultant satisfaction in the voicing of *laudes*, and during the next decade would often order the clerks of his chapel to chant the *Christus vincit* on occasions additional to the great feasts of the liturgical year.[2] King Henry emerged from his difficulties unscathed. All the same, though with no particular sense of gratitude to them, he realized that his episcopal advisers had rescued him from dangerous courses. Henceforward his essays in kingship would be more discreet and be made in safer company, with a decent regard to the customs of the realm.

This was the last political triumph of the English episcopate. The bishops had not sought their own but had intervened, in

---

[1] Quoted from Rishanger by Ernst Kantorowicz, *Laudes regiae* (1946), p. 176.
[2] Ibid., pp. 175-7.

the name of the Great Charter, to save the king. Their spokesmen, the bishops of London, Coventry, and Rochester, later
reinforced and led by the new archbishop, were men in the
Langtonian tradition. Their generation was passing away, new
influences were at work in Church and state alike, and conditions such as those which brought them to the front in 1223 and
1232 did not recur. Neither they nor the earl marshal and his
friends had any subversive ideas. The shock of the marshal's
death brought the king and his vassals together again. The reconciliation at Gloucester in May 1234 was complete. Hubert
de Burgh and his champion, Gilbert Basset, were admitted to
the king's council. The disorder in the southern shires and in the
Marches came to an end. On 21 June the archbishop effected
the truce with Llywelyn at Middle, between Shrewsbury and
Ellesmere. Most important of all, the law of the land was vindicated. In the previous autumn Hubert de Burgh had escaped
from his prison at Devizes and taken sanctuary in the parish
church. He was dragged out and put back in his vaulted cell in
irons. The bishop of Salisbury roused his colleagues to action
and Hubert was restored to the church, which was surrounded.
More fortunate at Devizes than he had been at Brentwood,
Hubert was rescued by Gilbert Basset and Richard Siward, who
hurried him away to the marshal's protection in south Wales.
Hubert and his rescuers were proclaimed in the shire court of
Wiltshire and outlawed. This action was illegal, for the outlawry had not been the outcome of previous judicial proceedings. Outlawry at the king's command was null and void. After
the assembly at Gloucester the sentence was formally reversed.
So also was the arbitrary ejection of Gilbert Basset from the
manor which he had claimed. The details may seem un-
important; but the vindication of the law and custom of the
land was all-important.

Hence, with characteristic resilience, King Henry and his advisers were able to resume their activities. Stephen Segrave, with
some difficulty, was reconciled to the king.[1] The chancellor was
still the bishop of Chichester. A new treasurer, Hugh of Patteshall, was appointed. The effect of the crisis which began with
the fall of Hubert de Burgh was a greater intensity, not a slack-
ening, in the task which had been entrusted to Peter des Rivaux.

[1] The archbishop helped to placate Henry, who for a time was very bitter against
Stephen. Stephen was active, though not as justiciar, from 1236 until his death.

The air had been cleared, and the work went on under more coherent direction. Indeed, Peter and his fellow counsellors had merely given impetus to the activities incident to a centralized administration. Exception was taken to their methods and independence of the community, not to their duties as such. In some respects they carried on the work of Hubert de Burgh, in others they enlarged it. Their successors in office and council continued the tradition, often rather fitfully, into the reign of Edward I. Improvements in technique were accompanied by deliberate legal enactment. The king took the lead in council and in judicial affairs. His desire to have a court of his own may explain the new appearance of two parallel sets of plea rolls, the one of a peripatetic king's bench, the other of a bench of common pleas stationary at Westminster.[1] The household was still the centre of affairs whose clerks, the king's most confidential agents, co-operated with judges, barons of the exchequer, and the clerks of the chancery. At the same time the great council tended to meet more regularly, in those weeks of the year when legal and financial business was greatest and the great feasts were held at court. Criticism was free and outspoken, drastic changes were discussed, the atmosphere was charged with the excitement of personal rivalries, the king and his plans or vagaries were under constant suspicion. The work of government was done under the scrutiny of an impulsive and watchful baronage.

King Henry held his own, and with some splendour, but he never mastered the excitable, closely related society of barons who, during these middle years of his long reign, were young men like himself, in the prime of life. By 1243, the year of Hubert de Burgh's death in melancholy retirement, King John's friends and foes had almost entirely passed away. Magnates, bishops, castellans, sheriffs, civil servants had gone. A new generation had to maintain old traditions in a court to which the Savoyard relations of the queen and the Poitevin kinsfolk of the king were bringing a new and disturbing vitality. The first duty of the historian of this period is to emphasize the coherence of English life beneath its high-spirited turbulence; and if this is not enough, to think of the unrecorded folk, the man at the plough, the shepherd with his flock, the scholar in the schools, the monk in the cloister, the masons, jewellers, tile-makers, and craftsmen of all kinds whose work outlived their casual strife.

[1] On the actual changes in 1234, see G. O. Sayles, *Select Cases in the Court of King's Bench*, iv (Selden Society, lxxiv, 1957), pp. xxx–xxxii and passim.

Recollection of them steadies the mind and deepens one's respect for the routine which kept the land one.

Before Peter des Rivaux was put in charge of the finances, the king's advisers had realized that more than inquiries into royal rights was needed. The system of local administration, its relation to the exchequer, and the practice of the exchequer itself required attention. The sheriffs should be put in their due place. This task was, indeed, a natural sequel to the restoration of the castles to royal control. In fact, in the financial year 1223-4, when the castles were surrendered, the sheriffs were required to pay into the exchequer the profits of their shires in excess of their farms, an obligation which suggests that the inquiries made in 1223 were aimed against the royal sheriffs and bailiffs as well as against the men of the shires.[1] The outcome of this change was a careful scrutiny of the profits and a valuation, finally made by Stephen Segrave in the last year of his life (1241), of their normal proceeds. This, in turn, led in some shires to the exaction of a twofold farm from the sheriff, his old farm and a new and larger farm which covered additional profits. The sheriff, in any case, was from about 1236 a collector of revenue entitled to a salary, not an exploiter of the shire who paid a fixed farm for the privilege of office. King John had dealt with the same problem by exacting heavy increments in addition to the farm. He had associated himself with the sheriffs in the exploitation of the shires—a practice which he had been forced to forbid in the Charter of 1215. The new way of dealing with the sheriffs was a great improvement, for it was based upon investigations into facts and it subordinated the sheriff, as a financial officer, to the exchequer.

The transition, however, from the first reform in 1223 to its logical conclusion in 1236-41 was not an easy matter. It was made possible by the work of Peter des Rivaux. He began his administration in 1232 as the sheriff of twenty-one shires; this meant that he was responsible through his deputies for the local finances in the greater part of England. The sheriffs, so to speak, were shaken out of their ruts. This drastic expedient did not and probably was not intended to last long, but it made it easier for Peter to nominate sheriffs throughout the country, and, when he became treasurer, to institute a survey of local accounts and to deal with defaulters. The memoranda rolls of

[1] Above, p. 28.

the exchequer reveal an unprecedented activity in financial discussion, in the hearing of complaints, and the investigation of irregularities. There had been nothing so thorough since Henry II's inquest of sheriffs more than sixty years before. It caused some anxiety and annoyed some people, but it was not unpopular. The fact that the archbishop and his suffragans softened the fall of the ministers and helped to restore them to royal favour suggests that the outcry against them was not so personal as Henry's anger was. And the speedy renewal of their work is a still more convincing proof that the work was worth doing. The shock was salutary and it was followed by constructive reforms.

Closer control by the exchequer of the profits of the shires was perhaps the most significant but it was by no means the only or most lucrative reform effected in these years. The sheriff, if he did his duty, was a very busy man. The collection of revenue was but one of his functions, yet, if he and his clerks had remained solely responsible, it would have taken up most of his time. Moreover, stricter and more scientific methods of land-management and accounting invited new arrangements. By 1240 the main lines of a specialized financial service become clear. The management of the royal demesne, and the administration of escheats, wardships, and successions, were taken away from the sheriffs; and in course of time other sources of revenue also were separately accounted for at the exchequer. The sheriff, as the chief local officer and as the executor of royal writs, might be ordered to co-operate with the new officers, but the distinction between his accounts and those outside or foreign (*forinseca*) to his immediate purview was made. Apart from some royal manors or lands let out to others whose rents still fell within the farm of the shire,[1] the royal demesne was farmed or managed separately, often by the tenants of the

---

[1] Originally the farm of the shire was derived almost entirely from the proceeds of the royal demesne, but by this time it could be paid and, as we have seen, be increased or supplemented from the 'profits', e.g. fines and amercements levied in shire and hundred courts, sheriff's aid, view of frankpledge, &c. Presumably, if the sheriff had continued to be responsible for the royal manors his farm would have been increased. It should be noted, on the other hand, that the scattered *terra regis*, as distinct from the great manors or the lands attached to a castle like Windsor, for which the sheriff or special bailiffs had accounted separately, had greatly diminished in extent since the early twelfth century. The profits had become more important. The new method of dealing with the demesne was necessary if it was to be increased and the king was to take an active interest in the land-market.

manors themselves. Special wardens of particular lands or of the demesne within a wide range of country begin to appear. The escheats, a more casual but even more important source of revenue, were also given a distinct administration. In the reigns of Henry II and Richard I escheats had received separate attention, and in some shires, if not in all, wardens were appointed in the first years of Henry III's minority, but Hubert de Burgh, shortly before his fall, would seem to have made the first systematic attempt to deal with them. In February 1232 two local men were sworn in by the sheriff in full shire court to be responsible at the exchequer for the proceeds of escheats and wardships in their shire. Later in the year Peter des Rivaux was given the custody of all royal escheats and wardships. After Peter's dismissal in 1234 one of his clerks was made escheator in the southern shires, and a northern escheator is found at work in 1236. Gradually the office of escheator, with its own records and responsibilities, became a most important element in the financial and administrative system of the kingdom. For example, the escheator had to inquire into and 'extend' or describe the lands of a tenant-in-chief after his death, for if there were no heir the lands escheated or fell back into the king's hands, and if there were an heir or heiresses much business had to be done before the lands were given back. The allocation of dower to the widow was in itself a most intricate matter, while if the heir were under age he became the king's ward.

All these developments affected the technical processes, activities, and staff of the exchequer. The stately account roll or Pipe, the two memoranda rolls, the issue and receipt rolls, and the miscellaneous documents such as accumulate in every department were gradually supplemented by a more orderly, though never quite manageable, series of registers and records. For instance, about 1235 the practice began of enrolling the instructions which passed into the exchequer, in the form of royal writs and estreats or extracts from judicial records, because they required financial action or authorized financial action by sheriffs and other persons. It was from this source that the 'summonses' to the sheriffs and bailiffs were issued by the exchequer. Much of the work in the sheriffs' offices was done in obedience to these mandates. The return and checking of them with the money collected under them was an important feature of the account between the exchequer officials and the sheriffs. If it were not carefully made evasion was easy, and in 1230–1 Hubert de Burgh had issued strongly worded injunctions against defaulters. Systematic scrutiny in the exchequer now made it much more difficult for a sheriff to collect miscellaneous charges, payments, and fines in the king's name and to pocket some of the proceeds. Again, the growth of business at the exchequer called for the employment of full-time experts. The exchequer was, as we should say, in close touch with the City. It shared with the king's clerks in negotiations with merchants, Jews, exchangers. The combined mint and exchange by the Tower, though it was a semi-independent institution, was associated with the officials at Westminster. The exchequer, moreover, as the financial aspect of the *curia regis*, was acquiring increasing importance as a centre of jurisdiction. For all these reasons the administration became more professional. After the fall of Peter des Rivaux the court was strengthened by the promotion of several learned clerks to be barons of the exchequer. One of these was Alexander de Swereford, a disciple of William of Ely, King John's competent treasurer. Alexander was the compiler of the famous Red Book, a collection of earlier treatises on the household and exchequer practice, lists of knights' fees, extracts from the Pipe Rolls about scutages, and other miscellaneous items; but the significance of his career lies in the fact that he was a man trained in the affairs of his department, keenly interested in its history, and selected, in a formative period, to be one of its directors. Matthew Paris's interest in the exchequer was enlivened by his friendship with Alexander de Swereford.

Hence the change which followed the dismissal of Hubert de Burgh in 1232 led to much more than a political crisis. It hastened and elaborated in a conscious movement the attempt made in Hubert's time to unify local government under a central system adjusted to the needs of the age and capable of steady development. The brusque energy of Peter des Rivaux and his colleagues and the reforms of 1236–40 defined the course of medieval administration. At the exchequer the technical ordinances of later years, such as the 'Statute of Rhuddlan' in 1284 and the great ordinances of 1323 and 1324, clarified a growing complexity, but comprehended very little which was not foreshadowed at this time. The escheators, wardens of the demesne, and commissions of inquiry prepared the way to a well-informed and better-sustained control of royal interests.

The check given to the king's ill-fated attempt to rule through a small domestic council was followed by a more intelligent co-operation, inspired from the household, between the king's servants and his council. The government of England was carried on by the council, which included a few prelates, barons, judges, and specially important clerks; and the council co-operated day by day with the king's clerks, judges, and the technical advisers of the Crown. The office of justiciar, though restored for seven years (1258–65) never recovered its old predominance; its judicial functions were later divided between the chief justices of the king's bench and the court of common pleas. The keeper of the great seal, for some time after Ralph Nevill's dismissal, might or might not be called a chancellor, and, save as a trusted servant of the king, neither he nor the treasurer had the independent status which the magnates in King Henry's time wished them to possess. The system did not work badly, but it could work really well only under a strong and capable king. It was at its best between 1274, when King Edward returned from his crusade, and 1290, when he was at the height of his power and the troubles in Scotland and Gascony had not begun to impose too great a strain upon it. In King Henry's reign it gradually accumulated trouble, but not so much as a result of its intrinsic weakness as because Henry failed to march in step with his critics. When in 1258 the barons at last took control they were able to correct some abuses, but they soon tired of their own alternative to a political tradition which, after they had turned against each other in fratricidal strife, resumed its course with unimpaired vigour.

At this point it is essential to insist again that the watchfulness of Henry's barons was due not to hostility to the Crown but to the desire to receive recognition of their place in the administrative system. In 1237, when the barons protested against the king's request for taxation, they rose to go apart and confer together. Gilbert Basset, now a member of the king's council, advised the king to send someone to be present at the discussion, and Richard Percy is said to have exclaimed, 'Are we aliens and not also the king's friends?' The nature of English society, and more, the social geography of England itself, implied co-operation between the king and his magnates. Ecclesiastical and lay lords were responsible for the peace and well-being of most of the villages in England. They enjoyed the right, under the supervision of the sheriff, of governing, to their financial advantage, more than half the hundreds in the land.[1] No general tax could be levied without their consent. The scrutiny of their liberties itself welded them more firmly to the central administration. They were the king's companions in war and at the great feasts. They were summoned frequently to meet in great councils or, to use a word soon to be familiar, in parliament. Fresh vigour at court inevitably stirred their lively interest. Hence they were sensitive to any tendency which might raise a barrier between them and the royal household and suspicious of influences alien to their own.

From this point of view later developments become clear. Continental historians like to distinguish a feudal state (*Lehnstaat*) from the more artificial system of bureaucracy and 'estates' (*Ständestaat*) which displaced it. The distinction has no meaning in English history. The 'state of the king and of the realm' implies parliament. 'The community of the realm' points naturally to the comprehension within it of knights and burgesses. The phrases, taken together, suggest an extension of a court centred in the royal household. The periods of sustained administrative activity are also periods of legislative activity. So it was in 1258–60 and in 1274–90, and it was so in 1234–40. Before Peter des Rivaux was dismissed, the attempt to grapple in general ordinances with issues and grievances which administrative activity brings to light had begun; and it began with the grievances of the lesser folk, the element in society which we are usually told became, for the first time, the special concern of the reformers in 1258 and 1259.

At the meeting of the great council in February 1234, when the bishops urged Henry to get rid of his new ministers, an ordinance was issued about 'suit of court', a favourite subject of discussion in 1258–9. The ordinance permitted any free man who owed suit of court in shire, hundred, or private franchise to appoint an attorney to represent him in all cases, and this was done on the ground that rights allowed to the king's tenants were by the Great Charter conceded to all free men. In the following October a clause added to the Great Charter in 1217

[1] At the end of Henry's reign, out of 628 hundreds 270 were royal and 358 were in private hands (Helen Cam, *The Hundred and the Hundred Rolls* (1930), p. 137). The map at the end of Dr. Cam's book conveys an excellent idea of the distribution of hundreds.

(*c.* 42) was interpreted. According to the Charter the sheriff's
tourn, which required the attendance of suitors in a full hundred court, was to be held only twice a year, and in August
1234 this clause was reaffirmed in the misleading form that the
hundred court should meet only twice a year. The ordinance
of October explained that for ordinary business more regular
meetings were necessary and fixed the interval at three weeks.
The occasion and explanation of this order are significant. The
matter had been discussed and settled by the archbishop of
Canterbury and the greater and wiser part of the whole body of
earls and barons after the Great Charter had been read to them.
The decision was justified by the reminder that frequent meetings of the hundred were necessary if the peace was to be kept
and the injuries suffered by rich and poor were to be redressed,
'much though we wish to bear in mind the common convenience
and not to burden the poor'.[1] Regard for the rights of freemen
and the convenience of the poor was as much a royal duty as
was the insistence of the king on the obligations of local officials
and on the maintenance of his rights and liberties. Indeed, the
one was inseparable from the other, and Archbishop Edmund
had reminded Henry of the fact. One remembers how, early in
the reign, the great judge Martin of Patteshall, when he was on
eyre, had suspended his work during harvest so that the villagers could gather in their crops. And the community of the
magnates was concerned no less than the king. Knights, freemen, and villagers were, in their different ways, responsible for
the well-being of shires, hundreds, and villages, which also
were communities. All had a claim upon the attention of the
great council.

In August 1234 a great judicial eyre began, and this produced more legislative activity.[2] It brought the judges to the fore
to raise and suggest to the great council the solution of legal
problems and the removal of anomalies and hardships. At this
time the leader among the judges was the Devonshire man, William Ralegh. He was for some years high in Henry's counsels
and he naturally took the chief part in the decisions made by
the council on some knotty points in the common law. On

[1] The ordinances are in *Close Rolls, 1231–4*, pp. 587–8, 592, 588–9 (in order of
date).
[2] H. G. Richardson in *Law Quarterly Review* (1938), 381 ff.; Powicke, *King
Henry III*, &c., i. 148–52; ii. 769–71.

20 August 1234 a provision was issued to maintain prisoners awaiting trial for serious felonies in the seisin of their lands and chattels. The royal bailiffs were required to make an inventory of the chattels, keep them intact, and provide reasonable maintenance of the prisoner and his family from his resources. More difficult problems than this called for settlement during the following months. In January 1236, shortly after the king's marriage to Eleanor of Provence and the new queen's coronation, the great council met at Merton. The outcome was the first comprehensive statute or series of provisions since the Great Charter. The statute of Merton differed, however, from the Great Charter in circumstance and content. It was not a concession extorted from a reluctant king but a declaration on points of law suggested by experience. On one matter raised in the discussions no agreement was reached because the barons and the king's advisers differed. The king claimed full jurisdiction over refugees and disturbers of the peace in private parks and fisheries, while the barons asserted their right to imprison and deal with convicted offenders.[1] A dispute of this sort, however, might arise at any time. In general the statute declared the law as informed common sense suggested. It gave more definite legal redress to widows, protected successful litigants against further disseisin, forbade the exaction from heirs of the interest on their fathers' debts during their minority, allowed the inclosure of common pastures by the lord where, but only where, the open land was more extensive than was required to meet the customary rights of the tenants. A very slight acquaintance with the plea rolls of cases tried in the royal courts or with the discussions in Bracton's treatise show that it was precisely matters of this kind, and the more technical questions gradually decided by the judges or after consultation with the king in his council, which affected the comfort and safety of the common man or woman. The same or similar issues were raised in 1258 and led to the famous statute of Marlborough nine years later. The legislation of Edward I marked a more elaborate stage in the same process of constant definition. The statute of Merton was indeed a very significant document. At this time, for example, much attention was paid to the necessity to keep Irish feudal practice in line with the English common law. A register

---

[1] The ordinance of watch and ward issued in 1233 (above, p. 53) had ordered the imprisonment of convicted offenders.

of the writs which could be issued from the English chancery to
initiate legal actions was sent to Ireland. Frequent instructions
were sent to the justiciar of Ireland on points of law. And the
proceedings at Merton were carefully reported to the Irish
government. Again, copies of the statute were widely distributed, and were kept for reference by clerks interested in the law.
One of the earliest surviving private collections of ordinances,
which were so common at the end of the century and anticipated
the official statute rolls, dates from this time. It includes the
Great Charters, the statute of Merton, and more incidental provisions. Finally, the statute involved the drafting of new writs.
Some of these writs were worded by William Ralegh himself.

One problem discussed at Merton raised the issue of the divergence between the canon law or common law of the Church
and the common law of England, and brought a very great
man to the fore. The man was the Oxford scholar, Robert
Grosseteste, who in the previous year had been made bishop of
Lincoln. The problem was the legal status of children born before the marriage of their parents. The Church said that a later
marriage legitimated children born out of wedlock. The children
were present at the ceremony and were covered by the nuptial
cloth or mantle. They were 'mantle-children', and henceforth
legitimate children. Since the time of Henry II, if not earlier,
the English law had followed feudal practice and held that such
children were bastards. The question whether a child had or
had not been born before wedlock frequently came up in the
secular courts. The right of succession to land might depend on
the answer; and since 1234 the question in these cases had been
referred to the bishop rather than to a local jury. Presumably
the bishops, who had more trustworthy means of knowing,
had raised no objection or even claimed the right to deal with
this matrimonial inquiry; but when Grosseteste found himself
confronted with the question he was deeply shocked. He believed
and argued earnestly that the Church was right, and, apart
from personal conviction, he held still more strongly that the
law of the Church was of superior validity to the common law.
He refused to answer the question put to him in the king's writ.
He would merely testify to the fact of paternity. He was summoned to account for his contumacy in the royal courts. He was
in a painful dilemma. Accordingly he took the lead in a demand
that the law of England should be changed and brought into

line with the law of the Church. The demand was discussed at Merton and the barons refused to change the law of England. In a report of the discussion sent to Ireland the king added that the bishops had left the matter to the secular law. They washed their hands of it. The writ to the bishop gradually fell into disuse.[1] 'The law of England' was not changed until a few years ago.

This story contains far-reaching implications. It introduces us to the problem of the relations between the secular and ecclesiastical courts, a problem which not only disturbed English life until the Reformation, but also raises the deepest issues of political theory and in one form or another still affects our ideas about the nature of the state. It illustrates the difference between the high churchmen, among whom Grosseteste was the greatest and most thoroughgoing in the later middle ages, and those ecclesiastics who, without committing themselves in any way to the view that the canon law was not common to the whole of western Christendom, were prepared to acquiesce in the observance of local secular variations from the law of the Church. As one reads Grosseteste's passionate appeals to William Ralegh and the archbishop to support him one realizes that Edmund of Abingdon himself, and most certainly the judge, took a more traditional view than he did. Ralegh was a great English lawyer, but he was also a clerk, a friend of the archbishop and the bishop of Lincoln, and a future bishop of Norwich and Winchester. He was prepared on occasion to uphold ecclesiastical liberties. He defended his transference from Norwich to Winchester in the name of the canon law and papal authority against the king and for a time forfeited the royal friendship. On the other hand, he could not share the high church view that ecclesiastics should not take secular office, that the courts spiritual should fight for every jot of their canonical jurisdiction without compromise. As he told Grosseteste, he relied on the issue of bastardy on the opinion of Henry II's justiciar, Richard de Luci; and, apart from this, he followed the dictates of common sense. The community of the realm must have peace and observe the traditions of its secular life. The common law as a whole was consistent with the social ideals which the Church

[1] Apparently the writ fell into disuse, was revived in 1247, and fell into disuse again. The question was put to a local jury, as seems to have been the practice before 1234, not to the bishop.

taught. One could not always be digging into the foundations. Grosseteste did not agree with him. He was prepared to maintain his idea of the Church, centred as it was in the authority of the pope, against the pope himself.

As we survey the course of events and the movements of ideas in Henry's court during the decade after the last great English justiciar was dismissed, we see once more how at every turn, from the technicalities of the exchequer to the nature of kingship and the conflict of laws, the issues which perplexed later generations found conscious expression. Continuity was anything but smooth. It depended on two conditions, the acquiescence of the community of the barons in the growth of a more professional system of administration centred in the royal household, and the king's power to carry the great council with him. Neither condition was easy to maintain. The underlying assumption was that Henry should always be ready in the last resort to 'give himself', in Matthew Paris's phrase, to the counsel of the faithful men of his realm. He did this in 1234 and frequently expressed his desire to do so. He knew quite well that in the end he could do nothing else; but in the vigour of his manhood, when he was at last an independent king, with a wife and family and new kinsfolk about him and able men in his service, he found it very difficult. He was not a big enough man to win the confidence of his barons, and so to give himself that they gave themselves to him. Except in the years between 1245 and 1252 there was frequent friction, a friction which in 1258 led to a temporary subjection, not altogether displeasing to him but very different from the welcome surrender in 1234. Yet somehow or other continuity was preserved. In 1258 it was the turn of the barons to learn their lesson. They discovered that they were royalists at heart. In the end they depended upon the king, just as the king depended on them. They had asked for a power which they did not really want. As Simon de Montfort bitterly remarked, they turned tail, as Englishmen always did.

In 1235 Henry had made a splendid alliance. His sister Isabella had been married to the Emperor Frederick. Frederick had sent to England as his proxy his closest counsellor, Peter de Vinea, and Henry had talked to Peter about his unhappy experience with the bishop of Winchester and doubtless about other affairs. In this year also negotiations began for the marriage between the king and Eleanor of Provence, whose sister

Margaret had recently married the young King Louis of France (May 1234). Several attempts had been made to find Henry a wife. Three had been made in 1225 and 1226. The active hostility of Louis VIII of France at that time prompted the king's council to seek useful alliances, and the archbishop of Cologne, the most powerful statesman in Germany, was anxious to help with suggestions. A marriage with a daughter of Leopold of Austria was considered. A year later the archbishop favoured the idea of a marriage with a daughter of the king of Bohemia. In the meanwhile a proposal for a union with the daughter of the count of Brittany, Peter of Dreux, was rejected, for Peter was not prepared to break with King Louis. In 1231 Henry is said to have fallen in love with a sister of the king of Scots,[1] but his barons, including this same count of Brittany, now his friend and vassal, pointed out that a marriage with the younger sister of the justiciar's wife was quite out of the question. In 1235 Henry was actually married by proxy to Joan, daughter of Simon, count of Ponthieu, but the count failed to get the consent of his lord, the king of France, Louis IX, and the pope released Henry from his vow on the ground of consanguinity.[2] So in January 1236 Henry married the French queen's sister and, through her, formed new connexions which had a deep influence on him during the rest of his life.

The queen undoubtedly had much influence upon Henry. Henry II's wife, Eleanor of Aquitaine, lives in history in her own right, Eleanor of Provence as the companion of her husband. She was a vigorous, incisive, downright woman, less sensitive than he to the general trends of opinion but more clear-sighted in an emergency. Until her death as a nun at Amesbury in 1291 she made England her home. She made herself felt because she was an active woman, always at hand, not, so far as one can see, because she was particularly ambitious or self-assertive. The letters of the Franciscan Adam Marsh, who knew everybody, show that her importance was recognized. She is still better

[1] This was not Isabella, already married to Roger Bigod, the young earl of Norfolk, but Marjorie or Margaret, later the wife of Gilbert the Marshal, earl of Pembroke. She died in 1244. She has sometimes been confused with her elder sister, Margaret, the wife of Hubert de Burgh, who is supposed, quite wrongly, to have got his marriage annulled in 1232. He took preliminary steps but nothing was done. This Margaret lived till 1259.

[2] The count, when he was restored to Ponthieu, had undertaken not to arrange a marriage without the consent of the French king. Joan married the king of Castile, and was the mother of Eleanor, the wife of Edward I.

remembered, however, because her presence in England knit together the courts of the king and the ruling family of Savoy, the mid-Burgundian lands south and south-west of Lake Geneva, with outlying dependencies across the Alpine passes in Piedmont. Eleanor's mother, Beatrice, was a daughter of Thomas, count of Savoy, whose eight adventurous sons 'carried the fame of their house half across Europe'.[1] Friendly relations had begun early in Henry's reign; Eleanor's marriage opened England to the Savoyards. Naturally enough, many Provençals also came north; a long list has been compiled of those who got lands or livings or minor positions in the royal household, or all three together; but the queen, who had no brothers, was more closely in touch with her uncles of Savoy. Two of these, Peter, who in due course became count of Savoy, and Boniface, who succeeded Edmund of Abingdon as archbishop of Canterbury, are inseparable from English history. A third brother, William, bishop-elect of Valence, brought his sister to England and for two years, until he left for Italy, where he died in 1239, was a close friend of the king. Indeed, after the death of Peter des Roches in June 1238, Henry tried hard to persuade the monks of Winchester to elect William of Savoy their bishop. He wished to keep William by him.

The king was rarely allowed to enjoy his high moments to the full. His impulsive welcome of new friends and opportunities, his errors of judgement—in a word his 'simplicity'—constantly provoked comment. Within a few months of his marriage and the council of Merton he began to feel alarm. As he wrote to the pope at the end of May 1236, his royal dignity was threatened. His confidential agents asked Pope Gregory to send a legate, and after some delay a legate was appointed. Otto, cardinal deacon of S. Nicola in Carcere, reached England in the summer of 1237. In the meanwhile baronial criticism had come to a head. It was directed against the king's council, which in April 1236 had been reconstituted under the leadership of William of Savoy.[2] Moreover, the systematic resumption of the inquiries

[1] C. W. Previté-Orton, *The Early History of the House of Savoy* (1912), p. 418. For the lands of Savoy see the sketch-maps inserted in the cover of Previté-Orton's book.

[2] The oath taken by the counsellors at Windsor in April 1236 became the precedent for the later oaths taken by counsellors. The circumstances and precise nature of the oath are not clear. See N. Denholm-Young in *E.H.R.* lviii (1943), 409–14. In his able reconstruction Mr. Denholm-Young takes a more emphatic view than the evidence seems to warrant.

into baronial liberties and local administration, the appointment of many new sheriffs, the activity at the exchequer and of the judges on eyre, all good and proper things in themselves, caused uneasiness. Henry was known to have got papal absolution from the oaths which he had taken in 1232, and apparently on other occasions also, to maintain men in office and in the enjoyment of castles and lands 'contrary to his coronation oath', and the rumour spread that he was trying to repudiate his obligations to observe the Charters. An attempt to follow up his release from his oaths by depriving Ralph Nevill of the chancellorship was certainly most unfortunate. The barons suspected a cleavage between themselves and the royal household, and they ascribed it to William of Savoy. When in January 1237 Henry, using William Ralegh as his spokesman, asked for a general tax to meet the expenses of his sister's and his own marriages, tongues were let loose. The king gave way at once. The poor man may have been foolish, but he had no intention, as a modern scholar suggests, to let bureaucracy loose upon the country. He enlarged his council by the addition of three important barons. He allowed the proceeds of the new tax to be put under baronial control. He confirmed the Great Charters of liberties and the forest and joined in a renewal by the archbishop of the sentences of excommunication against all who infringed them. These were read in the shire courts month by month in March, April, and June. The solemn scene in the chapel of St. Katherine at Westminster Abbey, when the sentences of excommunication were declared and sworn to by all, was not forgotten. It was frequently appealed to in later years and became a landmark in the history of taxation by consent. It rounded off the reconciliation at Gloucester three years before.

The next crisis came in January 1238. This had a more domestic origin, but threatened for a time to be serious. At this time Henry's closest friend among the barons was a young Frenchman, Simon de Montfort, who had come to England in 1231 and been invested as earl of Leicester in virtue of his descent from the Earl Robert who had died in 1190.[1] Simon was a

[1] Robert's daughters Amicia and Margaret married respectively Simon II of Montfort l'Amaury, in France, and Saer de Quincy, afterwards earl of Winchester. On the death of their brother Robert in 1204 these ladies became co-heiresses to the lands of the Leicester honour, and a division was made. Simon II's son Simon, the crusader, died in 1218 and the claim to Amicia's half came to his eldest son

year or so younger than the king. He fell in love with Henry's
sister Eleanor, a young widow in her twenty-third year, whose
husband, William the Marshal the younger, had died, as we
have seen,[1] in the year of Simon's settlement in the country. On
7 January 1238 Simon and Eleanor were married, with the
king's cognizance and approval. It was a secret marriage in the
sense that no discussion with the magnates had preceded it.
There was none of the customary publicity or display. And it
was a sacrilegious marriage, for Eleanor, after her husband's
death, when she was barely sixteen years of age, had taken an
oath of chastity. Her mood did not last. Earl Simon was most
attractive and she broke her vow. Religious opinion was
shocked, the baronage was angry. The archbishop felt a personal grief, for Eleanor is said to have made her vow in his presence. Richard of Cornwall, Eleanor's brother, was greatly
disturbed. He had already shown his displeasure with the influence of aliens at court and now he took the lead in open resistance. He and his allies met together at Kingston. The king,
whose lack of candour had brought this trouble upon him,
took refuge in the Tower of London. The legate advised him to
yield, and on 22 February he accepted a series of provisions.
The legate and the magnates attached their seals to the document. The main ideas of the agreement, which has not survived,
may perhaps be found in a well-known plan of reform inserted
in Matthew Paris's great chronicle under the year 1244. If this
plan does embody the terms accepted by the king in 1238, it
shows how determined the archbishop and magnates were to
safeguard the understandings reached in 1234 and 1237 and
how instinctively the barons in 1258 turned back to ideas which
they and their elders had discussed in their youthful days. The
occasion in 1238, however, was not so serious as it was twenty
years later. As he looked back upon it, even Matthew Paris
revised his earlier judgement and felt that Earl Richard had
been right to withdraw from his rebellious attitude. In his
shorter history he summed up as follows: The realm was vehem-
ently disturbed because, against the wishes of his magnates and
especially of Earl Richard, and in disregard of St. Edmund's
advice, the king arranged the marriage between Eleanor and
Simon. Also he tried to do other important things although

Amaury, who surrendered his rights to his brother Simon, the Simon de Montfort
famous in English history.   [1] Above, p. 41.

he had promised his magnates not to act without them. In the end, however, Earl Richard, the spokesman of all the rest, was pacified. The bitter agitation abated as when cold water has been thrown on a wood fire. The magnates' enterprise happily came to nothing.[1]

Whether the plan of reform preserved in Matthew's greater chronicle goes back to the year 1238 or not,[2] it indicates very clearly how the magnates regarded the royal administration and in what ways they were prepared, if necessary, to remedy its defects. They wished to make sure that the Charters of liberties and the forest should be scrupulously observed, that recent losses in lawful rights and status should be remedied, that the course of justice and the hearing of complainants should be swifter and more impartial, that the king's treasure, especially the proceeds of taxation, should be wisely expended. No doubt they were influenced by personal grievances and grudges. Some were stupid, some perverse, some too hot-tempered, some cynical. They condemned much that was good because they had eyes only for the bad; and later writers have been too ready to endorse their judgement. At the same time they felt that the affairs of the realm were their concern, and they could never know what the king might not do as soon as their backs were turned. They asked for a new charter, and, going further than they had gone since 1215, they required that four 'conservators of liberties' should be added to the king's council. These should be powerful men whose standing and wisdom were assured. Two of them at least should always be in attendance on the king to hear complaints and see that speedy justice was done. They were to be elected by the whole body of the baronage and be irremovable except by the baronage, though if one died the other three should appoint his successor. A justiciar and the chancellor should also be elected by the same body, and be removable only with its consent in a formal and duly consti-tuted meeting. These might be reckoned as two of the con-servators or as additional conservators.[3] The conservators would be sworn to deal faithfully with the affairs of the king and king-dom, to administer justice without favour, and to supervise

---

[1] *Historia Anglorum*, edit. F. Madden, ii (1866), 404–5.
[2] See the additional note at the end of this chapter.
[3] 'Et quia frequenter debent (i.e. the justiciar and chancellor) esse cum domino rege, poterunt esse de numero conservatorum.'

royal expenditure. Presumably, they would act on behalf of the whole body, for it was suggested that they should be responsible for summoning the great council when its presence was required. The plan also provided for the appointment by the great council, which was to be unanimous, of two of the justices of the bench, two barons of the exchequer, and at least one justice of the Jews, though later vacancies in these offices would be filled by the conservators. Writs, that is to say, writs which could be bought in chancery to initiate legal actions, if they were contrary to existing law and custom, were to be revoked. Suspect and useless persons were to be removed from the king's side. The object of these requirements is almost pathetically obvious. The barons wanted to feel safe. They did not wish to do the king's work for him, but to see that he and his council would not stray from the right path. Hence they would place by the king conservators of liberties whom they could trust, men and ministers who would take the lead in his counsels and only trouble them to meet when it was absolutely necessary. The scheme, in its *naïveté*, pays homage to the administrative system which it was designed to improve.

Apart from outspoken criticism in 1242, when taxation was refused on the ground that Henry had never given any account of the thirtieth of 1237 nor observed the obligations imposed upon him, the next attempt to enforce co-operation with the great council was made in 1244 and 1245, in the months to which the plan of reform discussed above is usually ascribed. Again the occasion was Henry's request for a grant, in aid of the king's debts. A discussion in the refectory at Westminster in the autumn of 1244 is notable because the prelates and barons, though they deliberated apart, agreed to act together. Henry hoped to get a grant from the church in England as well as from the laity and prelates as holders of lands in lay fee, and, under Grosseteste's leadership, the clergy refused to be cajoled as a body distinct from the laymen. Prelates and magnates made emphatic reference to the events of 1237, asked for the appointment of a justiciar and chancellor, and combined to elect a committee to report upon a plan of reform. The committee was composed of four bishops, four earls, and four barons, whose report was to be read to the whole body before presentation to the king. Henry, however, was in a stronger position than he had been in 1238 and refused to accept the

proposals. Proceedings were adjourned to the following February, when a feudal aid was granted. Until 1258 the prelates
and barons continued to act together to resist taxation, demand
more independent ministers of the old type, and ventilate particular grievances. In 1253, when another feudal aid was granted,
the Charters were again solemnly confirmed.

Additional Note on the Plan of the Magnates

The baronial provisions described above were inserted in the
definitive copy of the *Chronica Majora* of Matthew Paris in the course
of a confused narrative of the discussions of 1244–5. They may be
found in Luard's edition of the chronicle in volume iv, pp. 366–8.
The rubric prefixed to the text reads: 'Haec providebant magnates
rege consentiente inviolabiliter deinceps observari.' A document with
this title had presumably been inserted in the St. Albans book of
memoranda, which was the chronicler's collection of texts. He did
not always put these documents in their right places when he had
them copied into his chronicle. Its transference from 1244 to 1238
has been urged by N. Denholm-Young in an article contributed to
the *English Historical Review* in 1943 (lviii. 401–23). His argument is
attractive, but not altogether convincing. That the plan was the
work of the committee of twelve appointed in 1244 is improbable, for
the committee included such friends of the king as the archbishop,
Boniface of Savoy, and the earls of Cornwall and Leicester. Matthew
Paris says explicitly that Henry refused to agree to be bound by the
plan proposed, whereas the rubric suggests that he consented to it. In
form, on the other hand, the document is obviously a draft, not a
formally completed text ready for sealing, and, as Professor Cheney
has suggested, probably 'represents what one individual or group
contributed to the committee's discussions' (*E.H.R.* lxv (1950), 216).
For further criticisms see Cheney's paper as a whole (pp. 213–21)
and B. Wilkinson, *The Constitutional History of England, 1216–1399*, i
(1948), 117–30.

III

FOREIGN RELATIONS
1216–59

FREQUENTLY, in the course of the previous chapters, we have had occasion to notice the influence of those moral obligations which were professed, whether by the heart or only with the lips, by men and women conscious of their membership of a universal Church. When we turn to the enlarged relationships which, for the sake of convenience, we call 'foreign affairs', it becomes still more important not to overlook these obligations. The Church was a church militant, and the crusade was still the expression of its holy warfare. Many evaded, but few denied this claim upon them.[1] It added strength, indeed, to the duty of men as Christians to restrain the impulse to decide their disputes with their fellow Christians by force, to their duty to refer them to the courts or to settle them, in or out of court, by agreements ratified by oaths and submitted to ecclesiastical sanctions. Something, therefore, should be said about the mental and spiritual background, revealed by the idea of the crusade and an incessant sequence of truces and treaties, before we deal with King Henry's desire to recover the lost provinces in France and with his activities as a king among the other kings and princes of the west. For he was a ruler in the Christian republic as well as king of England.

It is not too much to say that the recovery of the Holy Land, whether as an ideal, a symbol, or an immediate duty, pervaded the minds of men in the thirteenth century. It was inseparable from the air they breathed. However indifferent or sceptical they might be, they could not escape its influence. 'If I forget thee, O Jerusalem, may my right hand forget her cunning.' It was a constant preoccupation of the papal curia. St. Bernard

---

[1] Among critics of the crusade, though not on pacifist grounds, the English theologian and chronicler Ralph Niger stands out. His work 'De re militari et triplici via peregrinationis Jerosolimitanae', which survives in manuscripts at Lincoln cathedral and Pembroke College, Cambridge (no. 27, formerly at Bury St. Edmunds), contains a searching and thorough deprecation of the third crusade. It has been studied at length with references to other literature by George B. Flahiff in *Mediæval Studies*, ix (1947), 162–88.

had drawn upon the inexhaustible imagery of the theme to colour his picture of human life. The disciples of St. Francis and St. Dominic were made its evangelists. The rescue of the earthly Jerusalem was no independent venture, to be advocated by some and repudiated by others, but was interwoven in men's thoughts with the insistent allegory which made the holy city inseparable from the heavenly Sion, the goal of life's pilgrimage and the object of daily aspiration. A passage to the Holy Land could be an act of penance imposed by authority or the fulfilment of a vow. The hope or the fear of making it might possess anybody; and the crusade was merely a 'great passage'. A man who took the cross was a privileged person, protected by the courts;[1] a man who fulfilled his vow enjoyed plenary indulgence from purgatorial suffering for past sins. The preaching of a crusade was the temporary culmination of an ever-present appeal, a high tide in the perpetual ebb and flow of the spiritual life. The taxation of the clergy which usually accompanied it was a financial drive which supplemented more permanent and exiguous sources of supply, like the rallies which supplement the collections made by a modern missionary society. Legacies, which sometimes went to a local fund, the proceeds of indistinct wills on which no clear decision could be reached by the executors, money commutations of crusading vows or other obligations to go to the Holy Land, were the most fruitful among these contributions from the faithful, and they naturally tended to increase during and after the excitement of a preaching tour. A few surviving records show that careful investigations were made after a crusade had been preached into the fulfilment of vows, and that these applied in particular to the humbler folk, many of whom were too poor to go or to pay because they had not gone. If the call came so near to the common man and woman in the life of every day, the outlook of popes, kings, bishops, and counsellors, and the course of public events were naturally affected by it.

The 'business' (*negotium*) of the Holy Land was a political and economic function of society. The financial administration of a crusade was entirely under the direction of the Holy See and was

---

[1] The plea had to be carefully watched by judges in secular and ecclesiastical courts. Fawkes de Breauté sought protection under it in vain, and in 1225 some Englishmen who had taken the cross claimed to be exempt from payment of the fifteenth, see above, p. 29.

largely responsible for the development, not only of the papal camera and of its local offices, but also of the banking system which was gradually created by the industrial, commercial, and shipping houses of the Italian cities. This system operated throughout Europe and the Mediterranean and only gradually gave way before the advance of the Flemish and German organizations of the later middle ages. Although the days of their brief predominance were passing, the houses and preceptories of the crusading orders were a daily reminder of the activities of Templars and Hospitallers in Acre and in Tyre. The Temple in Paris and the New Temple in London were still safe deposits of the treasure of kings and nobles, neutral and protected ground fit for the transaction of financial business. In papal eyes, the duty of the hierarchy to maintain peace in the west was inseparable from the duty to rally a united Christendom against the infidel. The task was set in the forefront of every conciliar programme, in 1215 at the Lateran, in 1245 and 1274 at Lyons. The conquest of Constantinople in 1204, followed by the establishment of Frankish states in Greece and by the extension of Venetian, Genoese, and Pisan interests in the Levant, had brought Latin feudalism nearer to its outposts in Cyprus and Syria. The immediate enemy was Saladin's successors in Egypt. There lay Babylon, as the Latins named Cairo, which had conquered Jerusalem, as old Babylon had conquered old Jerusalem. There lay the great port of Damietta, where St. Francis went to plead with the Soldan. Symbolism and hard fact were dissolved in each other. In the medieval philosophy of history it is hard to say which is which. The apocalyptic writers who saw looming ahead the crash which was to precede the age of the Spirit tended to locate the conflict on the borders of Christendom. Roger Bacon, for example, thought that Antichrist would come down from the heights of central Asia and urged the Church and the Holy See to be ready with all the contrivances of warfare, all the secret weapons that the skill of men could devise. And when, at the end of Edward I's reign, a Norman publicist Pierre Dubois described in realistic detail the reorganization of Christendom under the leadership of France, he expounded his ideas as a plan for the recovery of the Holy Land.

Dubois dedicated his book to Edward, the last crusader in the medieval tradition, yet in his thought apocalyptic theology had already passed into politics. In his view the crusade was essentially a step towards the advance and settlement of the west in the east. And, as we look back upon the thirteenth century we can see how in all directions the old ideal was losing strength.[1] The great expeditions had failed. The intricate negotiations, the elaborate preparations, the vast expenditure which they had entailed, had been in vain. They had both interfered with and been frustrated by the ambitions of cities and princes. The conception of a Holy War had been perverted to add fervour and give moral justification to civil war between Christians. Every effort of the Papal Curia to maintain its political position and even its spiritual prestige in Europe tended to become a crusade. The financial expedients devised for the rescue and protection of the Holy Places had been used against the Emperor Frederick II and his family. The pope himself was entrammelled in the web of politics. His moral authority as a leader of his Christian subjects was gravely impaired, just when, if they were to be united in a joint endeavour, he needed it most. Other influences, hardly noticeable at the time, but still more effective in the end, were beginning to affect the current conception of the Holy War—a more humane and critical note in theological thought, a preference for evangelical and educational work among the infidels, an interest in the facts of geography and social customs beyond the borders of Christendom, a desire for peace as an opportunity for trade. In due course these movements would come to the aid of the objection to make sacrifices in the interests of the Holy Land and to lose one's life for the sake of one's soul. But, in the period with which we are concerned, the old tradition still prevailed, if only as a habit of life without the vigour of single-minded purpose. Even for those who had the chance to see him as he really was the Saracen was still the monstrous embodiment of everything that Christians hated in themselves, Asia was still the fantastic land of the epic of Alexander the Great, the legend of Prester John, the fable of Gog and Magog. The call to the Crusade still sounded in the ears of men with remorseless iteration, to confuse or inspire the policies of princes. And, as we shall see, it confused no man more than Henry III, and inspired few men more than his son.

[1] See especially P. A. Throop, *Criticism of the Crusade: a Study of Public Opinion and Crusade Propaganda* (Amsterdam, 1940). Cf. his earlier paper in *Speculum*, xiii (1938), 379–412.

When King John died the kings of England and France were bound to each other by the truce of Chinon, made in 1214. Until the treaty of Paris in 1259 they lived almost continuously under the terms of this truce and its numerous successors. In the forty-five years open warfare between them, due to the non-renewal or, in one case, the denunciation of the current truce, existed for only short periods; from the spring of 1224 to the spring of 1227, from August 1229 to the end of June 1231, from June 1242 to April 1243, about six years in all. Fighting, during the six years, was not continuous; indeed, it was desultory. Expensive expeditions were made, but very little happened. From Henry's point of view the results were disappointing, for the French first overran and then consolidated their power in Poitou, from the borders of Brittany to the Gironde.

The series of truces meant that hostilities were merely suspended. The issue between the two kings was not decided until 1259. Henry would not recognize the king of France as duke of Normandy or a French prince as count of Poitou; the French regarded Henry as a usurper in Gascony on the ground that, after the judicial deposition of John, Philip Augustus had recognized Arthur of Brittany and after Arthur's death the duchy, with John's other fiefs, had reverted to the French Crown. The treaty of Paris brought this state of affairs to an end. Henry surrendered his claims to Normandy, Poitou, and other fiefs and did homage to Louis IX for Gascony. When some of his barons expostulated against the recognition of Henry as duke of Gascony, Louis is said to have pointed out that Henry as a vassal of the king of France and as a peer of France would be in a weaker position than he had been as an irresponsible enemy. The answer was shrewd, although future events showed that it was too optimistic. For more than two generations a complicated feudal instrument, involving endless litigation, was the basis of relations between two powerful kingdoms. The treaty of Paris marks an epoch in the history of Europe; in its form and content a dynastic arrangement, it was a formative element in the development of the international system and the diplomatic practice of the west.

All the same, it would be wrong to draw too sharp a distinction between a cessation of hostilities imposed by a series of truces and a state of peace sanctioned by a treaty. Certainly goodwill was not assured and restlessness was not necessarily allayed because a troublesome issue had been settled. Nor was a truce of necessity a fragile affair. A truce defined a certain state of things for a definite period. Its terms might be numerous and elaborate. In form and intention it was but one of the numerous compacts by which sinful and quarrelsome men admitted that they had a moral obligation to live quietly with each other under the rule of law in a Christian commonwealth.

Now it is obvious that this incessant tendency in medieval men or groups of men to come to terms with each other, even for a little while, implied more than a sense of coherence or mutual advantage; it implied a respect for law and a belief in something which could maintain law. The trickiest oath-breaker in Powys or La Marche was paying lip-service to something. In the thirteenth century this 'something' was a common sense of decency, derived from various sources and expressed in the teaching of the Church. It was suffused throughout society, not forcibly imposed. Occasionally we find allusions to the law of nature or even to a law of nations. Henry III in 1264 warned King Louis of France that, if England were invaded, Henry's hostages, his son and nephew, might lawfully be put to death by the barons in accordance with the law of nations. Occasionally also we are made aware of independent criticism, as when Llywelyn the Great protested to King Henry, on behalf of Fawkes de Breauté, that Fawkes's excommunication would be invalid in the sight of God.[1] Reflection was directed by the influence of the law-schools and by the spirit of sophisticated discussion. As the century advanced, the interpretation of treaties and conventions became more and more the province of trained experts and casuists. To suppose that a professional clergy was trying to make lawless laymen see the beauty of peace would be much too simple an explanation of the struggle between self-help and order. The influence of an active hierarchy under a single head was profound, if only because it stood for an ordered way of life, had more than local interests, controlled education, and operated spiritual sanctions; but the hierarchy was an element in a Christian society, not an external missionary force. In the simile of the gospel, the wheat and the tares or, as the great German historian, Otto of Freising, had called them, the 'two cities', were intermingled in clergy and laity alike. Standards of

[1] Above, p. 27. Cf. the well-known words which Dante puts into the mouth of Manfred (*Purgatorio*, iii. 121–45).

decency and habits of self-seeking were diffused in both. The law behind other law and custom was recognized, where it was recognized, by both. The real difference between clergy and laity, in so far as they were conscious of moral obligations, was that, while the good layman normally acted in accordance with them on the level of prudence, the good clerk was more likely— one cannot say more than this—to 'satisfy his desires only so far as their satisfaction was in accordance with the law'.

As soon as we touch medieval social relations, especially beyond the limits of closely organized communities subject to their own courts of law, we make contact with a system charged with moral and religious power. It was a strange system, curiously compromised by worldliness, and directed, in unexpected ways, towards other-worldliness. We may not like it; but it was there. It explains the form and terminology of the treaty, the truce and the diplomatic correspondence of the age—the appeal to high principle, the profession of sincerity, the guarantee given by a solemn oath sworn on the gospels, the submission of the party or parties accused of a breach of faith to the judgement of a group of ecclesiastics or of the pope himself, the invocation of ecclesiastical penalties. It accounts for the frequent and usually ineffective attempt to anticipate legal arguments against the validity of an oath by emphatic assertions that the party had sworn in perfect freedom and would on no account appeal to the spiritual power for dispensation. And it justified the elaborate casuistry by which men satisfied their consciences when they evaded agreements which had ceased to be advantageous to them. We who have had experience in our own time of the attempts to maintain a system of law and order in the world have the least right to scoff at the conception of Christian unity which gave the west many more years of peace than of war, and, in spite of the broken oaths and factious interdicts and excommunications with which its history was littered, only very gradually, and never completely, gave way to the cynical, if more realistic, conception that each state is a law to itself. This medieval experience devised the practices which give scope to international law. When, for example, an English king made a truce with a French king or a Welsh prince, most careful arrangements were made to deal judicially with breaches of its terms by their subjects. Joint boards of arbitrators (*diffini-tores*) were appointed to meet at prescribed places, as occasion required, to investigate in detail the rights and wrongs of every allegation.[1] Cases, especially of violence on the borders or of disputes arising from attacks on ships and the seizure of merchandize at sea, might be discussed for years. These proceedings were the medieval precedents for the numerous arbitrations of later times.

King Philip of France died on 14 July 1223. In 1220 he had renewed until Easter 1224 the truce with Henry III. His successor, Louis VIII, the prince who had invaded England, had nearly a year, therefore, in which to decide what his policy was to be. Pandulf, bishop of Norwich, the late papal legate to England, who was in Paris, is said to have urged Pope Honorius to procure the postponement of Louis's coronation until he had restored Normandy to Henry, while Henry's advisers made arrangements for the collection of ships in the Channel and summoned the barons of Normandy to return to their allegiance. These measures certainly suggest that Louis was under some obligation to give Henry redress;[2] but he had not the slightest intention to do anything of the kind. When an embassy, headed by the archbishop of Canterbury, reached France, the new king was already crowned. He postponed his reply to Henry's demands, renewed truces with the count of La Marche and the viscount of Thouars—the two leading barons of Poitou—and, in answer to a second embassy, maintained, in a great council at Paris, the justice of his retention of the Norman duchy.

At first the crusading ardour of Louis VIII seemed likely to divert him from the attack on Poitou, for it was directed against the heretics of the south and, as contemporaries were not slow to point out, peaceful relations with the king of England as lord of Poitou were necessary to a successful campaign in the Midi. The pope, however, like his great predecessor Innocent III, was not altogether happy about French intervention in the Midi. The crusade which Innocent had let loose had led to more than the slaughter of heretics. It had meant the penetration and perhaps the conquest of the county of Toulouse, whose new lord, Raymond VII, though suspect, was a son of the Church, and it had

---

[1] For example, during the truce of 1220–4 between Henry III and Philip Augustus, charges against the men of the Cinque Ports were heard by commissioners at the Shipway, where the men of the Ports used to meet.

[2] Cf. above, p. 14.

disturbed neighbouring lords and princes on each side of the
Pyrenees. In a word, a holy war had been converted into a
political adventure. That fanatical warrior Simon de Montfort
had already seized for his family and companions baronies
which had become outposts of French influence and French
administration in accordance with the customs of the Île de
France, and Simon's son Amauri, who had found the burden
too much for him, had handed them over to the French Crown.
The pope preferred to work through preachers and inquisitors
and to make his own terms with Count Raymond and his
neighbours. The destruction of a brilliant civilization in the
cause of orthodoxy might be necessary, for the Manichean
heresy was a poisonous thing, but it was not to be regarded with
equanimity. The mind of Honorius III was fixed on a general
crusade to redeem the recent failure at Damietta. He planned to
restore full peace to the west and to join its forces to those of the
young emperor Frederick II, whose restless energy in Italy
might in any case be well diverted to the east. Unfortunately
King Louis was not impressed by this idea. When he found that
the pope was set on a general crusade against the Saracens, he
postponed his southern expedition and decided to invade
Poitou.[1] Negotiations for the renewal of the truce with Henry
came to an end. War was declared on 5 May 1224. Before the
end of the year Poitou had been overrun and the French
king's troops had crossed the Dordogne into Gascony.

Poitou had not been effectively held by its Angevin lord since
the truce of Chinon ten years before. The bases of resistance to
the French king north of the Gironde were Rochelle, the Isle of
Oleron, and the district of Saintonge south of the river Charente. Poitou was a land of semi-independent cities and of fiefs
centred in strong castles. Although many years were to pass before it was firmly consolidated by Louis's brother Alphonse, its
unstable condition, while it provoked efforts to recover it, did
not help King Henry. His resources were not great enough to

---

[1] Honorius, on the other hand, identified himself with Louis's crusade against the
Albigenses in 1226, but after the king's death his widow Blanche of Castile, who
was regent for her young son, reversed her husband's policy. She had her own
difficulties in France, but her inclination was also towards a watchful understanding with Raymond of Toulouse. She was, after all, a princess of Spain and,
like Raymond himself, a grandchild of Henry II of England. On several occasions
she rescued the impulsive and erratic Raymond from his troubles and helped to
maintain on a good footing his uneasy relations with the popes.

enable him to recover it by force and its lords were too wary, self-regarding, and unreliable to be firm allies. His futile expeditions wasted his treasure and confirmed his English barons in their indifference to his claims.

One of Henry's embarrassments was the house of Lusignan, so famous in the history of Syria and Cyprus. The head of this house in the west was the count of La Marche, whose vast lordship sprawled across seven departments of modern France, from the valleys of the Creuse and the Vienne in the east to Lusignan and other castles of Poitou in the west. If the country had been firmly held by a loyal ally, La Marche and the Poitevin homelands could have barred French advance from the north and provided a base for the restoration of the ancestral influence of Henry's family south of the Loire. King John had had this prospect in mind when he betrothed his daughter Joan to Hugh, of Lusignan, and promised to endow her with the city of Saintes and the Isle of Oleron. The prospect seemed still more fair when Queen Isabella left England to return to her old home in Angoulême. But Isabella had her own views. She was a vigorous, passionate, and ambitious woman. Her position as queen mother in England had been negligible and she had no wish to allow her career in Angoulême to be directed by the advisers of her son. She brushed her young daughter aside, turned to Hugh, from whose father, Hugh le Brun, John had snatched her many years before, and married him herself.[1] Joan, after some difficulty—for Isabella and Hugh detained her as a hostage for her dowry—was sent home to become the wife of the king of the Scots, Alexander II. Hugh's marriage with Isabella greatly increased his wealth and importance for it brought with it the consolidation of his scattered fiefs by the addition of the rich county of Angoulême. Why should not he, in his strategic position, play off Henry and the king of France against each other, and become independent of both by selling his help to the highest bidder? The student of English history who remembers how the offspring of this virile pair came in later years with their kinsfolk to increase their fortunes in England, how the boys of La Marche married English heiresses and the girls married

[1] For Hugh le Brun and his son see H. G. Richardson in *E.H.R.* lxi (1946), 296–7. In his essay on *The Lusignans in England, 1247–1258* (University of New Mexico Press, 1950) Harold S. Snellgrove points out that a letter of Gregory IX (1235) clinches the proof that Isabella married the son of her former fiancé: see *Cal. Papal Letters*, i. 146.

English barons, to the enlargement of the royal family circle and the bedevilment of social and political life, should not forget that for more than twenty years Hugh and Isabella had played fast and loose with King Henry, until they over-reached themselves and humiliated him in an impulsive rebellion against King Louis IX. Henry was, so far as he could be, the affectionate son of a self-centred mother, more attached to her second family than to her first.

Hugh of La Marche was able as a rule to work with his neighbours, the lord of Parthenay and the family of Thouars, the most widespread and powerful house in northern Poitou. King John's former friend, Savari de Mauléon, now Henry's seneschal in Poitou, took a more independent line. Savari's lands lay along the west coast of Poitou, from Talmont in the north to the river Charente in the south. They comprised the island of Ré and embraced the port and self-governing commune of La Rochelle. Mauléon, midway between Nantes and Poitiers, was the seat of a brilliant court, a home of troubadours, and Savari was himself no mean poet. After his departure from England,[1] Savari, like several other friends of King John, had joined the crusaders before Damietta. On his return he represented Henry's interests in Poitou, and maintained his own interests against the house of Thouars. There was no coherence in the Poitevin baronage.

Before King Louis left Tours to overrun Poitou in June 1224 he had come to an understanding with Hugh of La Marche. Hugh was promised possession of Saintes and Oleron, claimed by Isabella as her dower lands, and of Bordeaux after its capture. Louis's idea apparently was to conquer Gascony as well as Poitou with the aid of Hugh and his Poitevin friends and possibly to install the count as his vassal in the duchy. His campaign began brilliantly. Poitou was overrun. La Rochelle, to which the seneschal withdrew, surrendered after a siege of three weeks. The seneschal in his turn went over to Louis, and was entrusted with the city and the custody of the coasts. The king of France then returned to the north, leaving Hugh to carry the war into Gascony. Bordeaux, however, stood firm and Hugh was soon brought to a stand. Here we see the limitations which always beset medieval warfare. Expeditions soon exhausted their impetus, and unless their leaders were prepared to

[1] Above, p. 3, n.

settle in the lands which they occupied, they soon had to withdraw. Moreover, settlement was almost impossible if local resistance was obstinate. King Henry's friends in southern Poitou and Gascony were of the opinion that Louis had shot his bolt. They advised him to counter-attack and to send quick aid. The advice was taken. Early in 1225 Henry's brother Richard, a lad of sixteen, was created count of Poitou and sent with the earl of Salisbury, Philip Daubeny, and others to defend Gascony.[1] Troops and stores were dispatched to Bordeaux. Henry proposed to follow himself and to put himself at the head of a concerted anti-French movement in the south. Hugh of La Marche had been checked. Gascony was safe.

Henry's dreams of revenge were disturbed by Louis's departure on crusade against the Albigensians for, as the pope pointed out with energy, he could not attack with impunity a man engaged in the defence of the Christian faith; but they were revived by the news of Louis's death on 8 November 1226. The heir to the French throne, the Saint Louis of history, was only twelve years old. A movement of assertive self-seeking spread rapidly among his vassals and immediately affected the Poitevin lords. Savari de Mauléon returned to his allegiance to Henry, whose advisers also offered tempting terms to the families of La Marche, Thouars, and Parthenay. The young king of France seemed for a time to be in as dangerous a position as Henry himself had been after King John's death. He had not, indeed, to face a rival, but he did incur the danger of submission to a clique and the loss of royal control over some of the provinces which his grandfather Philip Augustus had begun to weld together. He was saved by his mother Blanche of Castile, who now showed that she was one of the great women of history, and a striking contrast to Isabella of Angoulême. Blanche's energy and ability to rally support for her son confounded all the expectations of her rivals. She was the ablest of Henry II's grandchildren. She held her own as regent, restored unity at court, and, early in 1227, reasserted royal authority in the west. Hugh of La Marche was at Thouars with his Poitevin friends and Peter of Dreux, the count of Brittany. The confederates were faced by a powerful French army which had advanced from Tours into northern Poitou. They arranged a truce which on 16 March was converted into a series of treaties at Vendôme.

---

[1] Cf. above, p. 40.

By these important agreements Blanche of Castile destroyed for a time the possibility of a widespread movement in the west, isolated Richard of Cornwall, and turned Hugh and his wife into adherents as well as vassals of France.[1] King Henry had been outwitted. His brother resumed the series of truces with the French king and returned to England.

Henry was deprived for nearly fifteen years of any aid from his mother and stepfather in Angoulême and La Marche. He was also deprived of the prospect of aid from the count of Toulouse. Queen Blanche's sagacious handling of Count Raymond, with whom she made a definitive agreement at Paris in April 1229, diverted him from the traditional policy of co-operation with the duke of Gascony. He preferred to make himself secure by recognizing a French prince as his successor if he died without a male heir. He could not afford to run the risk of another crusade from the north into his embarrassed dominions. Hence Henry, who was as eager as ever to regain his father's lost inheritance, was forced to look elsewhere for help and to find a new base of operations. He turned to Peter of Dreux, styled Mauclerc. Peter was one of three distinguished brothers, descended from an earlier king of France, Louis VI. In 1213 he had been betrothed to Alice, the heiress of Brittany,[2] and he ruled the county until their son John came of age in 1237. The aim of King Philip Augustus in 1213 had been to establish his kinsman as a vassal in Brittany, which, by the marriage between Alice's mother Constance and Henry II's son Geoffrey, had become a fief of the king of England; but after Louis VIII's death in 1226, Peter was quick to realize the possibilities of his strategic position. The diplomatic correspondence of this time shows that various possibilities were discussed at the English court. The feudal geography of the west might be reshaped if Henry and Peter worked together. Brittany would be held of

---

[1] Blanche compensated Hugh and his wife for the loss of Isabella's dower and the recently acquired rights in Bordeaux by a grant of 10,000 pounds of Tours. The money was paid. Saintes and Oleron were to go to one of their daughters if and when she were married to King Louis's brother Alphonse, the future count of Poitou. Their eldest son was to marry one of Louis's sisters. Pope Gregory IX, who was elected on 19 March 1227, later absolved Louis from a sworn undertaking not to make peace with Henry without the consent of the count of La Marche.

[2] Alice was the daughter of Constance of Brittany and her third husband, Guy of Thouars. She was the half-sister of the dead Arthur and his sister Eleanor, who was kept in captivity in England until her death in August 1241. Philip Augustus recognized Alice as the heiress of Brittany, as he could not make use of Eleanor.

Henry. Peter would recover in England the great honour of
Richmond. Henry might weld western Normandy, Poitou, and
Gascony into a new Angevin empire, whose bases would be on
the Atlantic rather than on the Seine. A series of marriages between the royal houses of France and England might even bring
this about without recourse to war. There was, in truth, no substance in these proposals. The French monarchy was much
stronger than it seemed to be. Peter of Dreux was not prepared
to turn his back irrevocably upon his past. The Normans were
not willing to rise. The barons of Poitou found it safer to turn to
France. The English barons had no stomach for the long and
stubborn war which might be necessary to give force and
reality to the dreams of their young king. Hubert de Burgh was
sceptical throughout. Yet for a few years the hopes inspired by
an alliance with Peter of Dreux seem to have dominated Henry's
mind.

Even before the death of Louis VIII Henry and his advisers
had tried to draw Peter of Dreux into the war against France.[1]
The king was to marry Yolande, the daughter of Peter and
Alice of Brittany, and provide a refuge in England if Peter should
lose his lands. After Louis's death Peter came into the open.
He joined the count of La Marche and the other Poitevins. The
scope of the negotiations was enlarged and for a time a general
movement in the west threatened Blanche of Castile. Henry was
soon disillusioned. As we have seen Blanche succeeded in averting this danger, and one of the first to come to terms with her
was Peter of Dreux. At Vendôme in March 1227 Peter arranged
that his daughter should in due course marry Blanche's third
son John who was eight years old. John would become count of
Anjou and Maine, but until he came of age, Peter would rule in
Angers, and afterwards continue to receive its revenues. He was
also to have the ducal castle of Saint James-de-Beuvron (near
the north-western frontier of Normandy) and Bellême in Perche.
Just as Hugh of La Marche was to profit by the French conquest
of Poitou, Peter was to profit by the arrangements for Anjou.
He preferred, it seemed, to lose Richmond and the precarious
benefits of an English alliance if he could increase his wealth
and influence nearer to Brittany. Two years later, however,
Peter was again involved in a widespread disaffection. Early in

---

[1] See S. Painter's biography of Peter (above, p. 15, n. 1) for his political change
(pp. 32–88).

1229 Blanche of Castile and he were at open war. His castle of
Bellême was besieged and lost.[1] By this time he was ready to
join Henry. The truce between the kings would expire in July
and Henry was eager for war if his envoys in Paris were unable
to procure the restoration of Normandy or at the least a satisfactory foothold across the Channel. He was urged to action by
leading men in Gascony, he had reason to think that the Normans would rise, he knew that Peter of Dreux would provide a
base in Brittany. By August he was again in a state of war and
his counsellors and officials were deep in plans for the greatest
military enterprise since that which King John had projected
for the invasion of France in 1205. Peter of Dreux crossed the
Channel and did homage to him for Brittany. In the following
January Peter formally denounced his obligations to Louis IX.
In June he was deprived by the court of the French king of the
right to administer Brittany, and the barons of Brittany were
called upon to withdraw their allegiance to him. But on 2 May
Henry's army had already landed at Saint Gildas, and on the
following day the king himself had landed at Saint Malo.

The preparations for an expedition overseas, as they emerge
from the numerous orders and other entries on the chancery and
exchequer records, are impressive.[2] The king had his own galleys and gathered together the suitable ships of the ports through
the agency of trained officials whose duties and responsibilities
were the equivalent in the thirteenth century to the functions of
a modern board of admiralty, and cut across while they were
interlocked with the administration of the shires and coast towns.
The movements of vessels, the activity of harbours, were controlled in the interests of the great event. Barons and knights
were summoned to meet at the port or ports of sail, stores of all
kinds were bought and collected, crossbowmen and craftsmen
were rounded up. In 1230 about 230 ships sailed from Portsmouth. The picturesque fleet, dancing on the waves of the Channel on a morning in May, was not a massive armament. The
minimum capacity of a requisitioned ship was only sixteen horses,
and even if we suppose that the average capacity was twice as
great, the fleet could not have carried more than the equivalent

---

[1] Painter argues (pp. 131–7) that the siege should be dated in January 1230 but
is not entirely convincing.

[2] The preparations for the expedition of 1230 have been described by E. Berger
in the *Bibliothèque de l'École des Chartes*, liv (1893), 5–44. Cf., for the preparations in
1205, Sidney Smith's introduction to the Pipe Roll for 7 John, published in 1941.

of some 7,500 war-horses in men, horses, equipment, and stores. Yet three or four thousand men, including a few hundred knights, made a respectable feudal army, which might have made much headway from a friendly base if it had been driven on by a sense of resolute purpose under determined leadership; but it could not afford to sit still. This, however, was precisely what it did. Henry came in all the pomp of majesty. He settled at Nantes as though all he had to do was to be recognized, receive oaths of homage, and make treaties. He found some partisans who professed to wish him well but did nothing. The great men of France rallied around the queen mother, who moved to the west to watch events. Henry's mother and her husband renewed their treaty with the French king. Everybody seemed to be content to wait. At last Henry made a move. On 1 July he crossed the Loire. He was allowed to march southwards through western Poitou, to make treaties with the Poitevin barons and cities, and receive oaths of allegiance. He captured a castle north of the Gironde and got as far as Bordeaux. Then early in September he returned to Nantes. He had shown his mother that he was still the lord of Oleron, and had made a demonstration against the king of France; but there had been no drive to the east and only desultory fighting on the Norman marches. At headquarters and throughout the body of the host demoralization prevailed. The great men amused themselves 'as though they were at a Christmas party'; the lesser folk had no money to buy food. The unnatural life bred sickness. Henry himself and his brother Richard fell ill. He decided to go home and leave the knights and about a thousand men at arms to carry on under the leadership of his brother-in-law, the earl marshal. By the end of October he was back in England.

The expedition of 1230 had been a military demonstration. Henry had transferred his court across the sea. He and his counsellors and clerks had been very busy at Nantes in negotiations with the Poitevin barons. As early as 8 June Ralph Fitz-Nicholas, one of the stewards of the household, had anticipated the march through Poitou. So many Poitevin lords were likely to come to Henry's service 'that he could ride in safety through Poitou to Gascony and, if need be, back again'. A more strenuous note was struck by the author of a poem or *sirventés* composed for recital to Henry. If the young king crossed the Channel and acted as a king should, eschewing the soft and frivolous life, he could have at his back the whole south-west. He could take the fortress of Poitiers; the Normans, Bretons, and Angevins, with that model of large-hearted prowess, Peter of Dreux, would rally to him; but he must forsake the men of chicane, lawyers and the like, for the men of war. That was the way to win la Rochelle.[1] The troubadours translated political and social relations into terms of splendid adventure. King Henry may have liked to picture himself in a world of this kind, but he was the last man to follow in the steps of Richard the Lion Heart. He preferred to buy rather than to fight his way, and so did many other princes.

The earl marshal died in April 1231, and the leadership of Henry's forces came to the old earl of Chester, who, when the count of Brittany had been restored to the honour of Richmond in England, had received, in exchange, his hereditary charge, the custody of the castle of St. James de Beuvron, some miles east of Saint Malo. He showed vigour and made a thrust into Anjou; but by the end of June a French army had reached the Breton border. The pope was anxious to bring the two kings to terms, and the bishop of Winchester, on his way back to England, was at hand to mediate. Peter of Dreux and the earl made a truce with the king of France for three years, to end on 24 June 1234, and at the same time Peter undertook not to set his foot in France, east of Mortain and Poitiers, or in the lands of the count of La Marche. After the death of the earl of Chester in the autumn of 1232, Peter was entrusted, as Henry's vassal, with St. James de Beuvron. Throughout the troubles in England between 1232 and 1234, the count of Brittany represented Henry's interests in Brittany and its neighbourhood. As the period of truce drew to an end, and the allies had to choose between its renewal and war, Peter realized that he had chosen the wrong side. His attempt to govern Brittany on Anglo-Norman lines had stirred his vassals to resistance, a French army threatened invasion, and Henry was unable to send adequate help. Peter deserted his lord, surrendered the lands and revenues which he had outside Brittany, and St. James de Beuvron which he held as Henry's castellan. In return he was reconciled with King Louis IX, and allowed to administer Brittany until his son John should come of age. Henceforward Peter Mauclerc

---

[1] A. Jeanroy, 'Un Sirventés politique de 1230', in *Mélanges d'histoire du moyen âge offerts à M. Ferdinand Lot* (Paris, 1925), pp. 275-83.

was an ornament of the French king's circle, the 'good count Peter'. His honour of Richmond in England was granted to Peter of Savoy, the uncle of Queen Eleanor. It was restored in 1268 to Peter Mauclerc's grandson John, who in 1260 had been married to King Henry's daughter Beatrice.

Henry was an adept in the perversion of history to maintain his self-respect. Peter's treacherous desertion shocked him greatly. He explained to Pope Gregory that, from first to last, he had been led on against his better judgement. He had saved Peter from destruction in 1230 and had been prepared to save him again. This view of his relations with the count of Brittany saved his face as he proceeded in the negotiations for a renewal of the truce with Louis. Hugh of La Marche caused some trouble by demanding the restoration of Oleron, as part of Isabella's dower, but he was bought off, and in August 1235 the terms of renewal of the truce, to last for five years, were arranged. So ended the second or Breton phase of Henry's attempt to restore the ancient glories of his house across the Channel.

The third phase was of brief duration and still more inglorious. It was immediately due to Henry's mother Isabella, who dragged her husband into a revolt against Louis IX and Blanche of Castile and induced her son to join them. It led to the depression of the house of La Marche and was so far a blessing in disguise, but also to the migration of a number of Henry's half-brothers and kinsfolk to England, where they were anything but a blessing. The Poitevin expedition of 1242, however, had a much wider significance, for Henry, Hugh of La Marche, and Isabella had really been caught up in a widespread movement in the Midi against French penetration, and this movement, in its turn, had been set going, to a large extent, by the conflict of imperial, papal, and French interests in the valley of the Rhone. The reports which Henry sent to his brother-in-law the emperor were more than friendly attentions to a distinguished relative; they suggest that Henry regarded himself and the emperor as allies in the direction of the affairs of western Christendom. The two men moved in different orbits, but Frederick by precept and example encouraged Henry to assert his own independence of papal policy, both at home and abroad. Frederick created an atmosphere which affected all who breathed it, while Henry, in his turn, was sensitive to the domestic ties between his and the imperial court.

In 1236 issue between pope and emperor was fairly joined. Writing as the lord of Italy rather than of his adjacent kingdom of Germany, Frederick announced his intention to conquer the rebellious Lombards and to resume all lands granted in the past to the Church in Italy. Pope Gregory, in his turn, appealed to the donation of Constantine, stated in uncompromising terms the theory of the translation of the empire from the Greeks to the Germans by the Holy See, and insisted that the right to judge the conduct of emperor and princes remained with the pope. In November 1237 Frederick routed the forces of the Lombard league in the battle of Cortenuova, and, insisting on unconditional surrender, refused the qualified submission of Milan and other cities. His obstinacy was his undoing. Northern Italy became more and more hopelessly divided, the campaigns of 1238 and 1239 were inconclusive, and on 20 March 1239 the pope issued his sentence of excommunication which, renewed by Innocent IV in 1245, destroyed what basis had existed for the hope of a united or, at least, harmonious Christendom in the west under the joint guidance of the spiritual and temporal powers.

Needless to say the verdict of history was not anticipated at the time. Emperors and kings had been excommunicated in the past. That the skilful propaganda which issued from the papal and imperial chanceries involved an appeal to first principles was overlooked by embarrassed princes whose sympathies were divided. Louis of France and Henry of England, loyal sons of the Church though they were, were much too prudent, even if they had had the desire, to treat the most powerful ruler in Europe as an outcast. Henry, indeed, in the previous year (1238) had sent a number of knights under the leadership of Henry de Trubleville, a former seneschal of Gascony, to join the emperor's forces against the rebels in Brescia and Milan; and, after his brother-in-law had been excommunicated, he retained his sympathy for him. He could not anticipate how deeply he would be involved in papal plans after Frederick's death, eleven years later. His wife's uncles also inclined to the imperial side. Frederick's desire to restore imperial control over the lands which comprised the dismembered kingdom of Arles, between the Saône and the sea, would seem to have had their approval. Provence, the most important part of this area, was, it is true, ruled by Henry's father-in-law; and the pope now regarded the count as a 'buckler of the Church'; but none the less the ejection of the French from the Midi might well have followed an imperial victory. If Raymond of Toulouse would stand firm in his co-operation with Frederick, fortune might turn against the ancestral enemy. King James of Aragon might come to recapture the ancestral rights of his house in Languedoc. The French king would be finally ejected from his footing in the Venaissin opposite Avignon[1] on the lower Rhône; his hated officials would be driven out of Carcassonne and his other domains in the county of Toulouse. Then Henry could come to his own again. Such were the dreams which inspired the troubadours of the south and kept alive the consciousness of social and cultural unity on each side of the Pyrenees.

Count Raymond did not, indeed could not, stand firm. For a few years his hopes ran high. The emperor restored the Venaissin to him, the citizens of Marseilles recognized him as their lord. He put forward his claims to the whole of Provence and thought to compensate himself on the east of the Rhône for what he had lost in the west. In 1240 the emperor urged him on to further action; but by this time his bright prospects were clouded. Frederick was under the ban of the Church, a papal legate was actively maintaining the cause of Raymond-Berengar in Provence, King Louis of France had intervened on behalf of his father-in-law. Raymond would himself be excommunicated if he persisted. When the restless expectancy in the Midi came to a head under the exiled viscount of Beziers and Carcassonne, Raymond stood aside and the rising against the French came to nothing. In 1241 he made his peace with the king of France and the count of Provence. The intermediary was James I of Aragon, who, it was widely felt, should have had every inducement to take the lead in a great concerted movement against the French. James was the titular over-lord of Beziers and Carcassonne and many other fiefs in the Midi: he was still in actual possession of Montpellier and other lordships; his aunt Sanchia of Aragon was the wife of Raymond of Toulouse; his father had lost his life fighting against Simon de Montfort at Muret in 1213; but for many years he had devoted himself to the crusade against the Moors and to the enlargement of his kingdom in the Balearic islands and the Spanish peninsula. In 1234 he had made peace with Louis of France, and he preferred to keep it. Moreover, he was the first cousin of Raymond-Berengar.

[1] This was the main achievement of King Louis VIII in 1226.

Provence had for more than a century been ruled by members of the house of Aragon. The tie between Aragon and Provence was very close—many of James's crusaders came to him from their port of sail at Marseilles—and a breach was not to be thought of. Why not try to keep out the French and maintain the Aragonese interests in the Midi by bringing Toulouse and Provence together under the joint auspices of James and the pope? Raymond-Berengar had no son to succeed him, Raymond of Toulouse longed for a son, for only if he had a son could a French succession to Toulouse be evaded.[1] So James of Aragon arranged a settlement. Raymond of Toulouse should have his marriage with Sanchia of Aragon annulled as within the prohibited degrees and get papal consent to a marriage with the heiress of Provence, another Sanchia.[2] The dissolution of the one marriage was effected, and on 11 August 1241 Raymond was bethrothed by proxy to Sanchia of Provence; but a few days later (23 August), before the necessary dispensation for this second marriage was procured, Pope Gregory died. Then Raymond, when it was too late, changed his course. He allowed himself to be caught up in the schemes of Henry III and Hugh of La Marche. The marriage contract was denounced by the count of Provence, and in June 1242 Henry was playing with the idea of a marriage between the count of Toulouse and his half-sister Margaret of Lusignan, a daughter of Hugh and Isabella.

King Henry, like his cousin Raymond and James of Aragon, had stood outside the abortive movement which had disturbed the Midi in 1240 and 1241; but in his case the reason was lack of opportunity rather than deliberate policy. The troubadours could look to him as a saviour with some hope, though hardly with confidence. His return to Gascony in 1242 diverted Raymond from the paths of peace and renewed excitement throughout the south. It was the outcome of the investiture of King Louis's brother Alphonse as count of Poitou (July 1241). The event could have caused no surprise; the career of the young prince as lord of Poitou and prospective successor to Raymond of Toulouse had long been planned; but the ceremony at Poitiers came as a shock to all those who feared the growth of France. Hugh of La Marche in particular was disturbed by the

[1] Above, p. 92.   [2] See the genealogical table opposite.

THE HOUSES OF ARAGON, PROVENCE, AND TOULOUSE

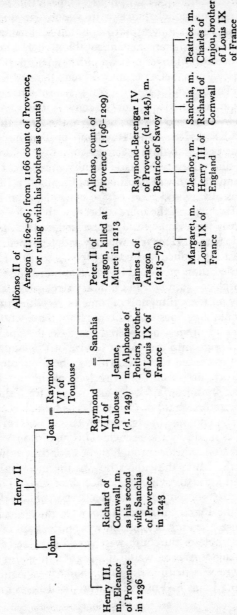

summons to do homage to Alphonse, and Isabella was outraged
by the insolent nonchalance with which the queen mother
received her. The thought that Louis and his brother should be
entertained at Lusignan was unbearable to her. The count and
countess could no longer play an independent part. They must
submit or resist. Isabella persuaded Hugh to resist. He formed a
party in Poitou and entered into a sworn alliance with the
seneschal, cities, and barons of Gascony. A joint attack upon La
Rochelle by land and sea was to reveal the strength of the confederacy. King Henry and Raymond of Toulouse must have
been made parties to this movement sometime before the end of
the year, and efforts were made to enlist the support of James of
Aragon and probably of Ferdinand of Castille. In January 1242
the barons of England received the news of the enterprise with
much disfavour, and the more so because the truce with France
had recently been renewed. They refused, indeed, to have anything to do with it. Henry, however, was determined. He thought
that at last his chance had come. He was told that money was
more needed than men, and he could and did raise money. He
had the right to summon the military strength of England; he
could rely on the willingness of some to go with him to Poitou,
and he could levy fines and scutages from those who did not go.
With this end in view he ordered the most thorough investigation of his reign into the knight service of England.[1] He levied
loans and exploited the Jews. In May he appointed as regent
Walter Gray, archbishop of York, 'one of the last survivors of
King John's ministerial circle, and set sail for Saintonge with
the queen and Richard of Cornwall. His first object was to find
occasion to denounce the truce with King Louis on the ground
of breaches made by the French. This he did on 8 June.

As seen from afar or through the eyes of the exultant troubadours of the Midi, the enterprise was the most serious danger
which had faced the king of France since 1214. The most important barons of southern Poitou had risen at last, the scattered
forces of the Pyrenean malcontents were rallying to Raymond
of Toulouse, the king of England was on the banks of the Charente, the whole of the south-west would soon be in movement
and the king of Aragon would surely come to claim his own. In
truth, there was neither substance nor cohesion in the movement. King Louis had moved in April, and Poitou north of the

[1] *Book of Fees*, pp. 637-9; above, p. 34.

Charente was his. Hugh of La Marche, though disinherited by the French court, had done nothing. The Gascons had not seized La Rochelle, the count of Toulouse was not ready. A news-letter sent to the emperor from Bordeaux in King Henry's name three months later (19 September) describes in terse and vivid sentences how the Poitevins failed to hold the bridge over the Charente at Taillebourg, how on 21 July Henry fell back from Saintes after an engagement; how the count of La Marche and his allies deserted him so that he had been forced to cross the Gironde into Gascony. At Bordeaux, however, an agreement had been reached with Count Raymond. Henry reported that his prospects were fair. The French king had feared to press the siege of Blaye. The emperor should discount irresponsible rumours of disaster.[1] Henry had indeed made a compact with Raymond in August for joint operations against the French, but the prospect was not fair. Louis sent his armies against the count of Toulouse. One of them was commanded by Hugh of La Marche and Peter Mauclerc, the late count of Brittany, surely an ironical turn of affairs. In January 1243, by the peace of Lorris, Raymond, still treated with leniency, agreed to abide by the treaty which he had made at Paris in 1229. In June, after a last desperate demonstration against Provence, he made a truce with Raymond-Berengar, who, in conjunction with the papal legate, brought him to a complete and final submission to the Church. In the meanwhile Henry had renewed the truce with Louis, and in September had returned to England. He had wasted about £40,000 sterling on his ill-considered adventure, and north of the Gironde retained only the island of Oleron and, for a time, of Ré. The success of Louis and Alphonse of Poitiers was complete. The count of La Marche was their sub-missive vassal. Isabella of Angoulême, overwhelmed by igno-miny and scandal, found a refuge with the nuns of Fontevrault where she died three years later (1246). In 1249 Count Ray-mond died and Alphonse ruled in Toulouse.

In the feudal world of the thirteenth century, political rela-tions were more personal, and therefore more resilient, than they are today. Henry had failed and failed miserably. His brother-in-law, Simon de Montfort, who came to join him in Saintonge on his way home from the Holy Land, had been

---

[1] *Close Rolls, 1237–42*, pp. 530–2. This is an admirable example of a thirteenth-century newsletter.

deeply shocked by the incompetence and irresolution which he found at Saintes. He had told the king, in words which Henry never forgot, that he deserved to be shut up like Charles the Simple. The earl hated mismanagement, the king was angered by humiliation; yet neither Henry nor Simon could regard the mishap as more than a mishap. It was a lesson not to break a truce too lightheartedly and a warning not to trust others too easily, not a disaster. Indeed, just as the crises in England between 1233 and 1238 had shown Henry where he stood and how he might safely assert himself, so the Poitevin disillusionment would seem to have enlarged his scope of action as a western king. He disposed himself to a watchful but more friendly rivalry with his cousin of France. He became reconciled to the surrender of his hopes to recover the lost provinces. He renewed the truce with Louis at intervals until the conclusion of peace in 1258-9. The influence of the emperor encouraged him to take a firmer stand, alongside his magnates, against the papal exploitation of his subjects, and the influence of his Savoyard relations certainly helped him to an independent attitude towards the policies of popes and princes; but he was not again led astray in a continental adventure until the pope involved him in the affairs of Sicily. The greatness of King Louis may well have suggested a higher emulation and turned his thoughts to a crusade, the very project which brought him and the papal court together, was perverted to his undoing, and led him at last to seek safety in the friendship and help of his French kinsfolk.

The marriage between Richard of Cornwall and Sanchia of Provence illustrates this resilient quality in feudal society. Before he left England in 1242 King Henry had sent the bishop of Hereford, a Provencal named Peter of Aigueblanche, on a diplomatic journey to seek support. Count Theobald of Champagne, who was king of Navarre, the duke of Burgundy, the count and countess of Provence, the queen's uncles of Savoy were invited to attend to what the bishop should say. It is probable that Henry, aware of the failure of the plan to marry Sanchia to Raymond of Toulouse, had already thought of a marriage between Sanchia and his brother, Richard of Cornwall, for Peter of Aigueblanche was the agent of this alliance, which was finally arranged in the summer of 1243. Any hope which Henry had of rallying the south against Louis had gone, but this did not affect the negotiations for the marriage. Richard would in any case have his own say in the matter. He had become an important person in the world. His outlook had been enlarged. At one time he had been disposed to claim a greater position in England as a landholder and to press his right to Gascony and Poitou, but the birth of Henry's son Edward in 1239, the death of his wife in 1240, and the failure of the Poitevin expedition in 1242 deprived him of his expectations and weakened his close connexion with the English baronage. In 1236, moreover, when a crusade was preached in the west, he had taken the cross and after the troubles of the next three years he had made the passage to the Holy Land. Neither the king nor the pope himself could restrain him. On the way he stayed with the king of France and the count of Provence, on his way back he was the guest of the emperor in Sicily and south Italy. He stood apart from the feuds of the age. In Syria, during his brief visit (October 1240–May 1241), he had brought to a happy conclusion negotiations with the sultan of Egypt, begun a year before by the king of Navarre, and had won the regard of the French by securing the release from captivity of Amauri de Montfort and others who had been taken prisoner in the battle of Gaza (November 1239). He was back in England in time to accompany his brother to Saintonge and, if Matthew Paris can be trusted, to use his influence with the grateful French to rescue him from a difficult position at Taillebourg.

Richard's marriage to Sanchia (23 November 1243), the sister of the queens of France and England, was also a symbol of his position among the princes of Europe. A few days later he formally renounced his rights to Gascony and other claims upon his brother, and took a place by his side as a faithful but independent friend and adviser. He was, it may be added, a very competent man of business who knew how to drive a hard bargain in Henry's frequent times of need. It was Richard who financed the operations required to reform the coinage in 1247 and in return took over the responsibility for the mint and exchange for a half share of the profits. Yet, if we consider the trouble which the king might have had with an able and ambitious brother, we may well feel that Richard's fidelity and counsel deserved any acknowledgement which he wished to demand. From a wider point of view his career shows how unwise it is to separate either domestic or foreign issues, as though they were the expression of consistent principles of policy, from the men who had to deal with them. Richard's marriage to Sanchia, for example, did not mean that he was aligned with the pope against his brother-in-law, the emperor, for he had recently been with Frederick and had tried to reconcile the old pope Gregory to him. Again, when the earl was elected king of Germany, or of the Romans, in 1257, King Henry no doubt welcomed the event as a rebuff to the French ambitions which he had feared, yet all the same it hastened rather than retarded his understanding with King Louis.

Henry's reconciliation with Louis was in a large measure due to the fact that he also had taken the cross. He did this on 6 March 1250. On 14 April 1252 he undertook to start on his journey on 24 June 1256. In 1254, however, Henry accepted the offer made by Pope Innocent IV of the kingdom of Sicily, to be held by his second son Edmund as a fee of the Roman Church, and in the following year the new pope Alexander IV commuted the king's vow to go to the Holy Land into a vow to aid the Church in Sicily, with the permission to use towards this end the papal tax levied in England for the crusade. This in its turn led to the conclusion of a definitive peace with Louis. Baronial feeling here coincided with the drift in Henry's mind towards the family compact which his new interests made advisable. The final ratification of the treaty of Paris in 1259 did not, it is true, open the way to Sicily. The new baronial administration in England had little interest in the adventure. The conclusion of peace, however, did enable Henry to strengthen his friendship with Louis and to turn to him as a mediator between his barons and himself. Many years were to pass by before the kings of France and England were again at war.

Before we deal with the Sicilian adventure and the treaty with France, we must turn to the affairs of Gascony and make the acquaintance of Simon de Montfort. When Henry took the cross in 1250 he was impatiently awaiting the pacification of Gascony by his brother-in-law Simon de Montfort. Simon, like Richard of Cornwall, had found himself since the events of 1238, but, unlike Richard, he had found himself at the cost of his early intimacy with the king. The first quarrel between these incompatible men seems to have come as a surprise to Earl Simon, and can only be ascribed to Henry's resentment against anyone who, however innocently, had put him in a difficulty or caused him humiliation. He had felt like this about Peter des

Roches after his surrender to the bishops in 1234 and he felt like this about Simon after the uproar which followed the earl's marriage to his sister Eleanor in 1238. To all appearance Richard of Cornwall's change of front[1] had restored harmony in the royal family. Simon and the king were on excellent terms. Yet suddenly a storm of passion broke upon the earl and his wife. In August 1239 they left England. Simon returned in 1240, but only to make arrangements for the crusade, for he had taken the cross. Leaving his wife at Brindisi in one of the emperor's castles, he joined Richard of Cornwall in Syria, where he made a great impression upon the barons of the Latin kingdom of Jerusalem. His cousin Philip, the lord of Toron, and other magnates even asked the emperor to appoint the earl as his representative in the kingdom.[2] Simon returned in 1242 and on his way through Burgundy was summoned to join Henry in Saintonge. Here, as we have seen, the state of affairs shocked him, and this time it was his turn to lose his temper and, as he explained long afterwards, to give vent to the anguish of his spirit. He was now a great man, a figure in the world, and he could afford to say what he thought. Perhaps his outburst did good. At any rate the two men became friendly again, though neither of them forgot what he had endured from the other. Simon and his wife settled down in England. Through the good offices of the countess of Provence who brought her daughter Sanchia to England at the end of 1243 to marry Richard of Cornwall, they managed to reach a settlement—inadequate in their view, but still a settlement—about Eleanor's dower. The royal castle of Kenilworth became their home. Simon was regarded by his fellow barons as a king's man. He took no great part in politics, but he was not idle. His alert mind was busy about the problems of Church and state. He became a friend of Adam Marsh, the Oxford Franciscan scholar who, behind the scenes, exercised a good influence in every quarter, and through Adam he fell under the spell of Robert Grosseteste, the bishop of Lincoln. Then he was given a great command. The condition of affairs in Gascony had long

[1] Above, p. 77.
[2] The emperor was king of Jerusalem first in right of his wife Yolande and then, after the birth of his son Conrad (1228), as regent for his son. The imperial rule caused incessant difficulties in the kingdom, and was repudiated after Frederick ceased to be regent on Conrad's coming of age in April 1243. The suggestion of June 1241 that Simon de Montfort should be *bailli* may have been intended to combine allegiance to Conrad with local independence.

caused anxiety and a strong hand was needed to control them. King Henry turned to his brother-in-law and Simon, reluctantly but dutifully, agreed to become his vicegerent as *custos* of the duchy.

Gascony should not be regarded as a part of the English realm. It was the survivor of the bundle of distinct duchies and counties gathered together by Henry II. At the same time it was juridically regarded as, and, with the outlying isle of Oleron, was declared to be, inalienable from the English Crown, when Henry's son Edward was enfeoffed with it in 1254. The idea was to prevent any alienation which might remove it from royal control and allow it to fall under French influence. Henry's feelings on this matter were shared by the Gascon cities and lords, whose strong sense of independence was as firm a guarantee of loyalty as was the more material inducement of a well-established trade between the kingdom and the duchy. Both kingdom and duchy had a highly developed sense of independence. In other respects they differed widely. The political system of the duchy was rather federal than unitary. There was little or no common body of custom, but a variety of jealously guarded local customs. Many of the vassals, especially in the valleys of the Dordogne and Garonne and in the Pyrenean foothills, were semi-independent. The most powerful and troublesome of these, the viscount of Béarn, had his own coinage at Morlaas and his own relations with Aragon and his other neighbours. The cities and towns managed their own affairs and maintained their own cliques and family vendettas. The citizens of Bordeaux, the leading city of the duchy and the chief seat of the ducal administration, did not regard themselves as holding in fee of the duke. They were not vassals but holders of 'allods' which owed no services. They claimed to enjoy of the duke as their lord the use of everything, but not by investiture. They paid a farm and owed military service within the bounds of the diocese for forty days in the year, but their liberties were their own. This extra-feudal tradition was general. Allodial tenure by men of the military class was not uncommon, though it was giving way to the more usual feudal tenure.[1]

---

[1] During the later dispute, between Edward I and King Philip the Fair of France, some English jurists claimed that Gascony as a whole had been an allod before 1259 and still ought to be; that is to say, a free land where the king of England held complete jurisdiction. See below, p. 651.

Government in Gascony was an exercise in the art of persuasion rather than administration along well-defined lines in the name of a common law. The only alternative was brute force. The seneschal and his officials fitted in to the life about them; they did not control it. Rents of domains, farms of cities, and tolls did not meet expenses, for most seneschals seem to have had recourse to loans from the rich wine-growing and shipping or mercantile families or to advances from their own pockets pending the settlement of their accounts. The levy of a hearth-tax as an exceptional measure required the co-operation of those on whose estates it was collected. It was only after 1254, when the Lord Edward became lord, that a separate financial department developed out of the duties of a new official, the constable of Bordeaux. The seneschal was assisted by a small council, and it is significant that in 1245 the persons named were a bishop, an abbot, one or two barons, and the two heads of the rival parties in Bordeaux, Gaillard Colon and Rostein Delsoler. Four courts of justice sat in four centres of ducal administration, at Bordeaux, Bazas, Dax, and Saint-Sever. Here the seneschal dealt with petitions and conducted inquiries or arbitrations, and here the vassals were confirmed in the enjoyment of their liberties and free customs on doing homage. In such a society ducal authority was both hard to maintain and yet always in demand. The land shelved away to a delta fed by streams which ran down from a vast concavity of high ground where no clear boundaries separated the fiefs of the duchy from their neighbours. The cities on plain and seaboard had a keen and independent life. The sense of provincial separatism was strong, but the desire for provincial coherence hardly existed. In the years after the excitement which had swept the Midi and had ended in the futilities of 1242, the turbulence so congenial to the Gascons degenerated into violent disorder. One seneschal after another threw up his task in despair. Theobald, the count of Champagne, who since 1234 had been king of Navarre,[1] had joined with his Gascon neighbours, some of whom he claimed as his vassals, and had ravaged the lands round Bayonne. Gaston of Béarn was a constant nuisance. Bordeaux and other towns were divided by faction. The lords of the north fought with each other.

[1] Theobald IV of Champagne, a great-grandson of Louis VII of France, was the son of Blanche, the heiress of Navarre. Blanche was the sister of Sancho VII of Navarre (d. 1234) and of Berengaria, the wife of Richard I of England.

Earl Simon was asked to pacify Gascony in the spring of 1248. He did not wish to go, for King Louis of France was about to set off on his first crusade and Simon had taken the cross again and had intended to join him with a contingent from England. Jerusalem had been captured in August 1244 by Khorasmians who had come westwards after the Mongols had broken their empire east of the Oxus. They had come at the call of the sultan of Egypt, who was threatened by an alliance between the Syrian Franks and the malik of Damascus. In October this coalition was shattered at Gaza. This victory following the capture of Jerusalem diverted the fears of the west. At one time the Mongols had appeared to be a still greater danger than the Mamluks of Egypt. Their hordes had conquered central Asia and settled west of the Urals in the European steppes. In 1241 they had overcome Hungary and threatened Italy.[1] Now the Mamluks were the more dangerous enemy. In 1245 Pope Innocent IV, at the oecumenical council of Lyons, had called the forces of the west to a general crusade. King Louis had responded, and, as we have seen, Henry III was later to respond. There was a chance, so it seemed, to turn the Asiatic peril to advantage, to convert or at least to use the Mongols and at last to destroy the nearer danger from the sultan of Egypt. King Louis left Paris in June 1248. No wonder that Earl Simon had planned to join him; but a sense of duty had called him elsewhere. Already on 1 May the terms of his commission in Gascony had been defined. When he reached Gascony King Louis was settling down for the winter in Cyprus.

The earl insisted on as independent a position in Gascony as financial reliance upon English resources allowed. He was not to be a removable seneschal but the king's lieutenant for seven

[1] The anxiety caused by reports from Poland, Hungary, and elsewhere must have been felt when the danger had passed. While the danger was imminent, it did not in the least affect, for example, the movements in the Midi between 1239 and 1242; but this is not strange, if one remembers that while the rulers of Silesia and Bohemia were throwing back the invaders, faction continued in Germany. Again, the pope still found it necessary to excommunicate the emperor and to declare him deposed in the council in which he summoned all Christians to the crusade. Matthew Paris notes scandalous rumours current in 1241 and again in 1247 that Frederick, a new Lucifer or Antichrist, was in league with the Tartars for the subversion of the Christian faith (*Chronica Majora,* iv. 119–20, 635). A good way to examine the reaction in the west would be to study the passages in Matthew Paris and the letters collected by him (see Luard's index, op. cit., vii. 521–2). He ascribes the absence in 1238 of the continental herring fleets from their annual visit to English waters to the first alarms caused by the Tartars (iii. 488).

years, to date from Easter 1248. He was to maintain from all
available Gascon revenues the cost of internal war, but to be
repaid by Henry capital expenditure upon the ducal castles.
Henry, if it were necessary, would come to his aid if war should
break out against any of the four neighbouring kings of France,
Navarre, Aragon, and Castile, and would be responsible for any
liabilities not met by the Gascon revenues at the end of the
earl's period of office. Other letters patent, now lost, seem to
have contained agreements about details. In the nature of the
case, Henry and Simon could not anticipate one risk, that they
might not see eye to eye. However independent the earl might
claim to be, he would be helpless if he could not turn to Henry
for help; and however much Henry hoped from Simon, he
could not be expected to give him a free hand and meet his
demands without criticism. In fact, the two men soon ceased to
see eye to eye. The arrangement broke down four years later,
in 1252, after Henry had formally called the earl to defend himself against the complaints of his infuriated vassals in the duchy.

At first all went well. Danger from without was averted by a
renewal of the truce with France and the submission to arbitration of disputes with Theobald of Navarre. Within the duchy
the city of Bordeaux was reduced to order with the aid of the
Colon faction which, rightly or wrongly, Simon maintained
against the rival Delsoler faction. Jurisdiction in the four courts
was upheld and measures were taken to resume and strengthen
ducal power at the expense of the restless barons in the valleys
of the Dordogne and Garonne. Simon was in close touch with
England, which he visited periodically and, although there were
exceptions, Henry on the whole respected the local authority of
his lieutenant and refused to deal with Rostein Delsoler and
other complainants who came to plead their cause against
Simon at the royal court. Simon did not spare himself. He
hired mercenaries in France to fight for him, raised money on
his own account and showed great energy. Henry supported
him, applied the revenues from Ireland for two years to meet
the expenditure on the ducal castles (November 1249) and sent
him friendly advice. Unhappily, Simon's success and Henry's
hopes had no solid foundation. The earl, severe and hasty by
nature, did not know how to manage his temporary subjects.
He overrode unwelcome complaints as factious, took no account
of the cross-currents which disturbed Gascon society, and

regarded its endemic restlessness as a kind of treachery. He
aroused a sense of bitterness and bitterness encouraged a stubborn obstinacy, which soon found vent in armed confederations
against him. He underrated the power of Gaston de Béarn,
with whom he had a private quarrel arising out of disputed
claims to the neighbouring county of Bigorre,[1] and expected
Henry to pay no heed to him, whereas Gaston regarded himself as quite as important a person as the earl was. Simon might
be the king's brother-in-law, but Gaston after all was the queen's
kinsman and could make himself heard.[2] The viscount of Béarn
became the centre of the opposition to Simon in Gascony. He
formed a league against him and complained to Henry of his
unjust conduct.

Early in 1251 Henry sent to Gascony his first commissioners
of inquiry. The king, though disposed by this time to carp at
Simon, was still prepared to stand by him, and was encouraged
by Queen Eleanor herself to hold to his compact with him.
Eleanor thought that the business, once begun, should be pushed
to a conclusion. The fall of the baronial stronghold, Castillon-
sur-Dordogne, at first made an arrangement easier than had
been expected. The king's commissioners were joined with
persons appointed in the four courts to adjudicate upon matters
in dispute and the case put forward by each side; but no decisions seem to have been made, and the prospect of peace grew
worse. After some hesitation Henry took the affair into his own
hands. In January 1252 he summoned the leaders of the opposition to England. Bordeaux and six other towns were asked to
send representatives who, with certain ecclesiastics and barons,
were to state the case of the Gascons before him after Easter.
This communication was taken to Gascony by a second pair of
commissioners, the master of the Temple and Henry of Wingham, one of the king's confidential clerks. It was their duty to
indicate the king's views verbally and to report upon the state
of the duchy. They soon came to the conclusion that concessions

---

[1] The complicated story of the struggle for Bigorre, only ended by its addition to
the French domain in 1307, cannot be told here.

[2] Gaston was count of Béarn from his boyhood in 1229 to 1290. His mother
was Garsenda of Forcalquier whose mother, another Garsenda, had brought this
county to her husband, Alfonso II of Provence, the father of Raymond-Berengar,
who was Queen Eleanor's father. Gaston, therefore, was Raymond-Berengar's
nephew, and the cousin of Queen Eleanor and her sisters. (This corrects the note in
King Henry III and the Lord Edward, i. 223.) Simon complained because Henry
listened to him as a kinsman.

must be made to Gaston of Béarn and his confederates. A truce
must be made, and the parties should meet in England, face to
face. The earl, in other words, was put in the position of a
defendant in the king's court.

The trial opened in the refectory of Westminster Abbey on
9 May 1252. It lasted on and off for about five weeks. The
Franciscan, Adam Marsh, in a letter to Grosseteste, wrote a
vivid, though one-sided account of the proceedings. As the
conflicting evidence was displayed, the general feeling went in
Simon's favour, and those who had stood aloof joined with his
friends in his justification, but no clear issue could be reached
amid the storm of recrimination. The king imposed a truce and
announced his intention to go himself to Gascony or to send his
son Edward early in the next year. The earl left England on
14 June. He had been prepared to resign his office in Gascony,
subject to the settlement of his financial claims, and in the
previous March had made a careful convention with the king by
which he would be relieved (or deprived) of certain castles in
return, after an impartial investigation of his accounts by a
number of *dictatores*, for the money due to him.[1] After his arrival
in Gascony, he persevered in the war. He was determined, if he
could, to restore order. But this was contrary to the truce which
the king had imposed upon the parties. The Gascons were told
that they owed obedience to Henry alone. The earl's position
was an impossible one. He agreed to end his command. Appearances were preserved by his surrender of Gascony to Edward as
its future lord. He was compensated by a gift of 7,000 marks and
allowed his expenses. Then he withdrew to France.

Although the final settlement was friendly, the long debate at
Westminster was a turning-point in the relations between Henry
and Simon. Adam Marsh gives the impression that it was a
dramatic encounter between the two men. The king was greatly
excited and exceeded himself in vituperation, the earl was patient,
self-controlled, and magnanimous. Adam was a friend and
admirer of Simon, and wrote with conscious rhetoric as a partisan, but he was generally trusted and welcomed as a spiritual

[1] *Close Rolls*, *1251–5*, pp. 203–5. The *dictatores* were Henry's half-brother William
of Valence, the king's familiar clerks John Mansel and Peter Chaceporc, with
Simon's friends Peter of Savoy (the queen's uncle), Walter de Cantilupe, bishop of
Worcester, and Peter de Montfort, head of the English and distinct family of
Montfort. Adam Marsh says that these last three stood firmly by the earl during the
later trial.

counsellor, and did not hesitate on occasion to rebuke Simon for his bad temper and angry depression. His picture of Simon, quiet and reasonable, convincing the magnates in the king's court of his honesty, cannot be set altogether on one side. Simon indeed had become one of the most prominent men of his time. His elder brother Amauri, the constable of France, had died on his way home from Syria, after Richard of Cornwall had released him from captivity in Egypt; and Simon was now the outstanding member of the Montfort family in the west as his cousin Philip was in the east. During his Gascon command he had spent much of his spare time in the Île de France and Normandy. He seems to have won the confidence and esteem of those responsible for French affairs during King Louis's absence in Egypt and Syria. After the queen mother's death in November 1252, he is said to have been invited to take charge of the kingdom, bereft as it was of its king and most of the royal family and uncertain if and when Louis would return

Simon's outlook was as wide as his prestige. With all his faults he was sensitive to the issues which disturbed the best thought of his age. His work in Gascony was done during years which seemed more critical than they could ever seem to us. The year 1250, in which King Louis was captured in Egypt in the disastrous battle of Mansourah and King Henry took the cross, and the great emperor died, was a year of jubilee, the close of the twenty-fifth period of fifty years in the era of grace. It was the only one of the twenty-five in which Easter fell on its own proper day, 27 March. 'Many diligent investigators', wrote Matthew Paris, thinking of these things, 'say that more marvels and novelties have happened during the last fifty years than in any of the similar periods preceding it. And greater things than these are to be awaited with dread in the days to come.'[1] Earl Simon did not look on the world with monastic eyes, but he did move among men whose seriousness was mingled with apocalyptic anxieties. It was in this year 1250 that his friend the bishop of Lincoln, nearing the end of his life, faced the pope and cardinals at Lyons with a highly-wrought series of reflections upon the lamentable state of the Christian world and the shortcomings of the Curia. One of the memoranda presented by the bishop was probably the political tract which, as we learn from Adam Marsh,

[1] *Chronica Majora*, v. 191, 197. The chronicler originally ended his work with the year 1250, adding a long list of the chief events during the past fifty years.

the earl desired to see. Simon was a crusader and the son of a crusader. His task in Gascony, as Pope Innocent IV did not fail to point out to the rebellious Gascons, was an interruption, which their behaviour had caused, in a holier duty. In that southern air, with the memory of his father's work among the neighbouring hills in his mind, he may well have faced his enemies with the fierce exaltation of a Christian warrior.

All the same, Simon de Montfort was anything but a saint. Few men of the world have been saints. They see in their fellows, if not in themselves, the 'savage and unreclaimed desires' which lurk in most men, and men of Simon's type are peculiarly open to attack. One of the communities in the Basses-Pyrénées wrote, in its complaint to King Henry: 'We have heard speak of the bad ways of the race of Montfort.' They had indeed, for the ways of the Montforts had long been a by-word in the Midi. They were French ways. They meant the introduction of alien customs and tenures, of fanaticism, pride, and discipline, of self-righteousness put at the service of ambition. Simon was not such a terrible and austere man as his great father, but he was his father's son; and he was much more litigious, querulous, and wayward. His obstinate insistence on his rights was generally justified and indeed required by the moral code of his class, but it fitted ill with his high purpose. He could tire men when he was seeking his own, while he could inspire them when he forgot himself to lead them astray. This fine soldier, shrewd strategist, acute observer of affairs, downright champion of what he had sworn to maintain, who could arouse a legendary devotion in the hearts of the obscure and win the affection of noble men by his grace and dignity and access of Christian humility, lived in a political limbo. Compared with men like Ranulf of Chester or Hugh Bigod, his feet were not firmly planted on the earth. With all his veneration for saintly men, his eyes were not firmly fixed on heaven.

King Henry had two related objects in view when he entrusted the earl of Leicester with the affairs of Gascony. He wished to see the duchy at peace and in accord with its neighbours before he followed the example of Louis of France and went on crusade; and he wished to make provision for his eldest son, Edward. In November 1249 he wrote to Simon that Edward was to have the whole of Gascony. A little more than three months later he took the cross. The outcome of his negotiations

with Pope Innocent, the decision to set out for the Holy Land
in 1256, was announced in 1252 while Simon's critics were on
their way to England. An expedition to Gascony was summoned
immediately after the trial at Westminster, Simon surrendered
his command in the late summer, and Henry left England for
the duchy a year later, on 6 August 1253. In June 1252 Ferdin-
and of Castile had been succeeded by his son Alfonso, the
famous king known in history as the Wise, and Henry had at
once begun or continued negotiations for the marriage of
Edward to Alfonso's half-sister Eleanor. The royal plenipotentiaries, one of whom was Henry's most trusted clerk John
Mansel, were appointed in May, before Henry left England.

King Alfonso's accession caused a stir in Gascony and Navarre. He made it clear that the dormant claim of the kings
of Castile to Gascony was not forgotten. As the descendant of
Henry II he professed to be the lawful successor to Arthur of
Brittany, who had been recognized as duke by Philip Augustus
of France. He welcomed the approaches of Gaston of Béarn,
who in May 1253 appears as his vassal. A few months later,
Alfonso claimed the suzerainty over Navarre after the death of
Theobald IV (July 1253) and drove its young king to seek the
alliance of James of Aragon. When King Henry reached Bordeaux he had to deal with Gaston of Béarn as a vassal in revolt,
not as the friendly kinsman whom he had upheld against Simon
de Montfort. He at once wrote to the queen and Richard of
Cornwall, his regents in England, for help against Gaston.
Rumour, indeed, outran the facts to an extraordinary extent in
the excited south. King Alfonso, Henry was led to believe,
planned a great campaign against Gascony. He would come
after Easter with a host of Christians and Saracens. If he overran
and subdued Gascony, he would try to invade England and
Ireland. Such was the burden of Henry's letters in December.

The regents took prompt action. They summoned the magnates, who, in a parliament at the end of January 1254, promised to cross the sea if the king of Castile should invade
Gascony. The movements of ships from the ports was arrested so
that a fleet might be prepared. A general exodus of the armed
strength of England was planned. The royal writs which were
issued in rapid succession throughout the month of February to
barons, bishops, sheriffs, and others show how the king's counsellors faced the situation. The army was to meet in London

three weeks after Easter (which in this year fell on 20 April) and proceed thence to Portsmouth. The chief difficulty was to rally the knights and those country gentlemen who, having lands of the annual value of twenty pounds or more, ought to be knights. The summons first went out to all such who held of the king in chief or of wards in the king's custody. Then all such in every county were called, without any limitation. Finally, the sheriffs were ordered to collect suitable men, knights and serjeants, explain the king's danger and necessity, and promise adequate wages. As the regents told the king, it was hard to raise these men. They advised new confirmation of the charters of liberties, to be proclaimed in the shires. Money also was needed, and the sheriffs were ordered to arrange for the election of two knights in each shire court who, a fortnight after Easter (a week before the general rally), could agree together on behalf of their shires on a grant in aid. The gossip of the Pyrenees had made a contribution towards the development of the English constitution.[1]

For there was no truth in the report. The quarrel with Navarre may have caused Alfonso to concentrate some forces in the north of Spain, but he himself was far away in the south, busy in preparations for the invasion of Africa which his father had planned. When the magnates met at Westminster, Simon de Montfort, who had arrived from France, was able to assure them that no fear of an invasion of Gascony need be entertained.[2] In

[1] The writ of 14 February (not 11 February, as in the *Select Charters*) orders the sheriff to see that the knights are *coram consilio* to provide aid *cum militibus aliorum comitatum*. They were to appear a fortnight after Easter, whereas the magnates and general body of knights were to come armed a week later (see *Close Rolls, 1252-4*, pp. 111-12, 114-15, 119; M. Paris, *Chronica Majora*, vi (additamenta), 286-7). On the same day the regents wrote to the king that the *alii laici*, i.e. the knights as distinct from the magnates, might refuse an aid unless the charters were again confirmed; and they added that they were to treat with the 'aforesaid clerks and laity' at Westminster a fortnight after Easter. The reference to the clerks is to the lower clergy, for whom the bishops had been unable to answer (*Royal Letters*, ii. 101-2). In other words, the magnates and bishops had consented to help, but the lesser clergy and gentry had to be managed separately. It is not strictly correct, therefore, to say that the knights were summoned to a parliament or great council of prelates and magnates. At the same time, the regents took an important step towards the political recognition of the knights and lower clergy.

[2] It is quite likely that Simon's assurance was unnecessary, for Henry's letters of 8 February about the negotiations with Alfonso (*Chronica Majora*, vi. 284-6) must have reached England long before the great council met after Easter. These letters show that the king did not continue to exploit the scare. The magnates in England had shown a healthy scepticism in spite of their willingness to join the king if he were in personal danger. (Henry of course had taken a considerable number with him when he sailed in August 1253.) On the other hand, the terms of the treaty

the meanwhile King Henry had soon recovered from his alarm. At the very time when the royal messengers were hastening to and fro in the English country-side and the merchants were lamenting the interference with their shipping, the king (8 February) reported that a treaty of friendship with Alfonso was well on the way, while six days later (14 February) he defined the scope of Edward's future establishment   Ireland, with the exception, later revoked, of Dublin and other areas, Chester, Bristol with its castle, lordships in Wales, Stamford, Grantham and the castle of the Peak, the Channel Islands, and the whole of Gascony with the isle of Oleron, a princely estate calculated to bring an annual revenue of 15,000 marks. On 1 April Peter of Aigueblanche, the bishop of Hereford, and John Mansel announced that they had concluded the treaty with Alfonso at Toledo. The terms were those outlined by Henry in February in his letter to the regents. The king of Castile promised to renounce all claims on Gascony. King Henry undertook to help Alfonso against Navarre, and to give consideration to the rights and claims of Gaston of Béarn. In dealing with Gaston and other difficult Gascons Henry would act with Alfonso as a friend with a friend. He would also ask the pope to commute his vow to go to the Holy Land to an obligation to join Alfonso in his expedition against Morocco 'and Africa'.

Edward arrived in Gascony with his mother and Archbishop Boniface of Canterbury a few days before his fifteenth birthday (17 June 1254). The agreements about his marriage were completed by the end of July. He was knighted by Alfonso and wed Alfonso's sister at Burgos at the end of October, and on 1 November the king of Castile issued the splendid document in which he declared his renunciation of all claims to Gascony.[1] Edward gave Eleanor as dower Grantham, Stamford, and the castles of Tickhill and the Peak, and took her back to Gascony.[2] Henceforward Edward had his own household and officials, with chancery and seal and a central exchequer at Bristol for the management of accounts. His enjoyment of Ireland and, for

with Alfonso suggest that Gaston of Béarn, who had been knighted by and done homage to Alfonso, had been in close relations with Castile and that Alfonso had some following in Gascony.

[1] A facsimile may be found in Rymer's *Foedera* (edition of 1816), I. i. 310.

[2] She was still but a child. After she came to England in 1255 she lived mainly at Windsor. Her first child Eleanor was born in June 1264, a month after the battle of Lewes.

the most part, of Gascony was confined to their revenues, but until his return to England in November 1255 he was nominally in control of the duchy.

Although King Henry cannot be said to have reduced Gascony to order, he had appeased the Gascons and done much to restore such harmony as they could tolerate. His new friendship with Alfonso of Castile did not result in the close co-operation foreshadowed in the treaty, still less in the joint aggression against France which the poets and intriguers of Languedoc professed to expect, but it made Alfonso the natural protector of Edward's interests in Gascony and helped to neutralize the turbulent elements in the valleys of the Pyrenees. It survived Alfonso's chagrin when Henry's brother, Richard of Cornwall, became his rival as king of the Romans and emperor-elect by the double election of 1257 to the throne of Germany. Henry himself could start afresh. The nightmare in Gascony was over. His well-loved son was married and endowed. The long entanglement in the affairs of Frederick II was a thing of the past. He was a crusader deeply engaged in the plans of the pope. He decided that he would make the personal acquaintance of King Louis, who was at last back from the east. This was the first step towards the surrender of his rights in Normandy and Poitou, the recognition of accomplished facts, and a peace with France. In November 1254 he travelled north from Gascony to Fontevrault, where he transferred his mother's body to the church. He crossed east to visit Pontigny, where St. Edmund of Canterbury was buried. Thence he made his way to Chartres where he was met by King Louis who brought him to Paris. Louis, in his gracious way, turned the meeting into a family party for Queen Eleanor. The countess dowager of Provence was there with her youngest daughter, the new countess and wife of Charles of Anjou, and so were her other daughters, the queens of France and England and the countess of Cornwall. Henry, who had for some time been rebuilding the church and chapter-house of Westminster Abbey, was able to examine one of his models, the Sainte-Chapelle, which Louis had built a few years before by the royal palace. Henry was very happy. After a few days he left to keep his Christmas feast in England, but the winds were contrary. He crossed the Channel on 27 December and was met by his brother at Dover.

Henry's active and sanguine mind was at work in a changed

world. He saw new horizons. And since the previous spring a
new and exciting adventure had given a definite direction to his
thoughts. The 'Sicilian business' made peace with France inevitable. On 28 June 1257 the king wrote to the pope and cardinals:
'since we have the affair of the kingdom of Sicily much at heart
and wish to see it brought to a happy conclusion, lo, we are
ready, in accordance with your advice, to make peace with the
king of the French'. He asked that a legate should be sent to
further the negotiations with France.[1] The acceptance of the
crown of Sicily for his son Edmund, the treaty of Paris, the
royal surrender to the barons in England, were the results,
inextricably combined, of Henry's understanding with the
papacy.

The king of England had not been quite ingenuous in his
relations with the king of Castile. While his proctors were
settling the terms of the treaty with Alfonso at Toledo, Henry
in March had accepted from the papal legate in France the
grant of the kingdom of Sicily.[2] While they were promising on
his behalf that he would endeavour to join Alfonso in his crusade against the Moors, he was already looking forward to the
mutation of his crusading vow to the conquest of a kingdom for
his son. When, in 1255, Alfonso's ambassador in England was
discussing the action required to give effect to the treaty Henry
was pledged to send troops to Sicily. Henry, in fact, was involved
in the Sicilian business up to the eyes. In 1256 he at last told
King Alfonso that his obligations to Sicily and to the new pope,
Alexander IV, required him to postpone any participation in the
Castilian crusade. What seemed to his English subjects the crowning proof of his simplicity, seemed to him a hopeful transaction,

---

[1] Alexander IV sent a Franciscan, Mansuetus, papal penitentiary, in September
to the French court to make peace, and asked Henry to give credence to him. For
the negotiations see I. J. Sanders in *E.H.R.* lxvi (1951), 81–97, which should be
corrected in the light of P. Chaplais's authoritative study in *E.H.R.* lxvii (1952),
235–53. Chaplais discusses the problem of Gascony's status in a later article, 'Le
Traité de Paris de 1259 et l'inféodation de la Gascogne allodiale', in *Le Moyen Age*,
(1955), 121–37. See below, pp. 313, 651, 654 and notes.

[2] The kingdom of Sicily was the convenient title of the Regnum, that is, the
whole of Italy south of the papal states (the later kingdom of Naples) as well as the
island of Sicily. Pope Alexander excluded only Benevento from his grant. The best
and most convenient summary of Italian affairs after the death of Frederick II in
December 1250 is the careful chapter by C. W. Previté-Orton in the *Cambridge
Medieval History*, vi. 166 ff.

more practicable than a crusade in Africa, more profitable than the passage to the Holy Land, yet still a holy war to be waged with the blessing of the Church. He could send no troops. The vast papal debt (135,541 marks) which he was required to meet under pain of excommunication and the laying of an interdict on England, was nearly twice the amount to be expected from the crusading tenth for five years which could now be devoted to the new enterprise. The child Edmund might distribute estates and titles in his new kingdom to his brother and relatives and his friends at the papal court, but by the end of 1257 the whole of it was in the hands of Manfred, who on 10 August 1258 was crowned king at Palermo. A stronger champion, called in by a stronger pope, was needed to destroy the Hohenstaufen. A Frenchman, Pope Urban IV, determined to bring the French into Italy to oust the 'viper brood'. By the end of 1263 he had convinced King Louis of the righteousness of his cause. In 1264 he negotiated a plan with Louis's brother, Charles of Anjou, who as count of Provence was near at hand and could raise troops and money. Urban's successor, Clement IV, completed the arrangements in April 1265, and Charles was invested as king of Sicily at Rome in June. Yet it required over three anxious years of hard fighting to make the new king the undisputed lord of his kingdom.

When Pope Innocent IV decided in 1252 to bring in a new king he had turned first to Charles of Anjou and to Richard of Cornwall. Richard had looked into the matter and refused. He said that the pope might as well have asked him to climb into the skies and capture the moon. Charles had taken the invitation more seriously and only declined after careful investigation. King Henry had then accepted the kingdom for Edmund. It is but just to Henry to remember that the chance of success in 1254 seemed to be brighter than it was three years later. Pope Innocent had made much headway by his success in fomenting centres of the anti-imperial feeling aroused by the German outlook of Frederick's son Conrad, who had invaded Italy. The death of Conrad from malaria on 21 May 1254 had intensified the factiousness which divided the supporters of the royal house. It is significant that, in a letter to King Henry, written ten days after Conrad's death, the pope advised him not to press for the commutation of his crusading vow on the ground that Conrad's death had removed the main obstacle to success and that from

his future base in Sicily Henry would be in a better position to
help the Holy Land.[1] Innocent, indeed, was at this time so near
a settlement with his divided opponents that he was merely
holding Henry in reserve. He proposed to rule the *Regnum* himself, satisfy Frederick II's natural son Manfred by the restoration of the appanage left to him by his father, and defer the
consideration of the rights of Conrad's son, the child Conradin.
It was only after Manfred had united the forces of resistance and
routed the papal troops in south Italy that Innocent 'coolly
began again to treat with Henry III'. A sick and disillusioned
man, he died on 7 December 1254. His successor, Alexander IV,
immediately clinched the understanding with Henry, commuted his vow, and, as Manfred's power grew, kept him to his
bargain. His obstinacy forced Henry in 1258 to turn to his
barons for support on their own terms.

Henry's prospects, in fact, had been fair until the end of 1254;
at one time so fair that Pope Innocent had decided that he
could get along without him. It is wrong to dismiss the enterprise as doomed from the start. It is wrong also to suppose that
Henry, before he was forced to submit his affairs to his barons,
had not tried to extricate himself from the papal net. When,
in 1257, at Alexander's instance, he opened negotiations for a
treaty with King Louis of France, he was well aware of the
difficulties which loomed ahead. The prospect of ultimate success
was not yet hopeless, for his brother's election as king of Germany meant that pro-papal activity might become more effective in Germany and north Italy, and the house of Savoy was on
his side; but he realized how firm Manfred's hold of south
Italy and Sicily was. He and his council asked Simon de Montfort and Peter of Savoy, then in Paris, to go to the papal court
'with power to settle the whole business'. In case they could not
go, various alternative suggestions were carefully drafted for the
guidance of those who should go. The king, if need be, was prepared to surrender Edmund's rights to Sicily altogether, if the

---

[1] *Foedera*, I. i. 304 (31 May 1254). Similarly, Henry saw no inconsistency between
his obligation to Sicily and the commutation of his vow to the 'passage to Africa'.
On 18 September 1254 he asked Pope Innocent to grant this in order that he might
fulfil the terms of his treaty with Alfonso (ibid., p. 308). He repeated the request
during the negotiations with Alexander IV. Alexander replied on 15 March 1255
that, in the interests of the Holy Land, he could not regard the request with favour.
All the same, only a few weeks later (2 May) he empowered the archbishop of
Canterbury and his nuncio, Master Rostand, to absolve the king from his vow and
to commute it to the execution of the 'business of Sicily' (ibid., p. 319).

pope thought it best and would release him from his financial
obligations and withdraw the spiritual penalties. Various plans
were proposed for the consideration of the Curia, if the pope
should refuse to release him. One of them suggested a composition with Manfred.[1]

Historians of the baronial movement in England have not
always given due weight to the close connexion between the
Sicilian business and the treaty of Paris. It has been supposed
that the treaty was the work of English barons who were determined to have nothing to do with the papal scheme. This view
overlooks the significance of events in 1256, and the measure of
support, however reluctant it may have been, which Henry got
for his adventure. It is true that the baronial government, by
insisting on a drastic relaxation in the conditions, forced Pope
Alexander to face facts and to cancel the grant of Sicily in
December 1258, before the final ratification of the treaty of Paris,
but Henry himself had both sought relaxations and begun
negotiations with France before the barons came into power.
The King decided to treat with France as a necessary means to
an object which he desired to pursue, but knew he could not
attain within the time and subject to the financial conditions
imposed by the pope. Pope Alexander did not close the door
entirely in 1258 and Henry in 1261 and 1262 sought to reopen
the negotiations, but the new pope Urban IV had other plans,
and on 28 July 1263 formally revoked the grant of Sicily. By
this time the friendship with Louis had been found to have its
advantage nearer home, for it gave the king confidence in his
attempt to recover his royal authority in England.

The action of the barons in 1258 will be considered in the next
chapter. Although ratification was delayed until October in
the following year, agreement on the terms of peace with Louis
was reached on 28 May 1258, before the famous parliament at
Oxford in June. It was the outcome of negotiations which had
begun in 1257. The settlement was no doubt hastened by
Henry's surrender to the barons earlier in the year, but it was
made while he was still a free agent, by the men whom he and
his council had chosen. It is probable that the lead had been
taken in 1257 by two men, Peter of Savoy, the ablest of the

---

[1] *Foedera*, i. i. 360. Henry suggested that Edmund might marry Manfred's
daughter. Manfred in 1248 had married a daughter of Amadeus of Savoy, one of
Queen Eleanor's uncles.

queen's uncles, and the earl of Leicester; for both men were busy in Paris in the king's interests and had been selected by Henry as his plenipotentiaries in his attempt to procure better terms from the pope in the Sicilian business.[1] Moreover, the commissioners whom Henry sent to explore the ground in Paris were Hugh Bigod, a political associate of Earl Simon, and two of the earl's closest friends, the bishop of Worcester and the Franciscan, Adam Marsh. They were to co-operate with the earl and Peter of Savoy and to report directly to Richard of Cornwall, recently elected king of the Romans and at this time in Germany. Henry wrote to his brother that nothing would be done without his counsel. The definite settlement in the following May was made, after consultation with Richard, by Earl Simon, Peter of Savoy, Hugh Bigod, and the king's half-brothers Geoffrey and Guy of Lusignan, lords respectively of Jarnac and Cognac, fees held of the count of La Marche.

Now it is clear that the treaty of Paris was made in a domestic gathering. Except Hugh Bigod, every one of the leading negotiators on Henry's side was a member of the royal family, with a personal interest in the transaction. Their consent was necessary to a pact which surrendered royal claims in Normandy and Poitou and affected the future of Saintonge and neighbouring lands. It is also on record that the papal legate in France, Mansuetus, took a most important part in the negotiations. The pope regarded the conclusion of peace as essential to his plans. One of the clauses contains an undertaking by King Louis to pay the cost of 500 knights for two years 'in the service of God and the Church and to the profit of the realm of England'. Pope Alexander himself had put forward this suggestion and had expressed the desire that it might emerge 'from the peace' (*ex illa pace*) as a contribution to the Sicilian enterprise.[2] Thirdly, it is probable, though not quite so clear, that in 1257 the earl of Leicester, closely connected as he was with both the French and the English courts, had formed a working alliance with leading prelates and magnates in England to press on negotiations with Louis, seek a more practical solution of the Sicilian business, and broaden the English administration. He was at this time hand

---

[1] For some reason they were not able to go to the papal court; but the point is that they were asked to go while they were in Paris at the French court.

[2] This is clear from Henry's letters to the pope in August 1258 (*Close Rolls, 1256-9*, p. 326).

in glove with Peter of Savoy and Hugh Bigod. The election of
Richard of Cornwall to the throne of Germany must have
suggested the possibility, later realized at Paris and warmly
acclaimed, of a tripartite pact between the peace-loving King
Louis and the kings of England and Germany, under the
auspices of the pope. If the annalist of Burton can be trusted—
and at this point in his story he writes with an exceptional knowledge of official documents and the course of affairs at the
English court—two reforming bishops, Fulk Basset of London
and Simon's friend Walter de Cantilupe, of Worcester, were
added to the king's council and a far-reaching oath was required
of the members of the council. Finally, as King Henry himself
testified later, Earl Simon had been foremost in the negotiations
for the treaty of Paris.[1] If this reading of the evidence is correct,
the conclusion may be hazarded that Simon, in the spirit of his
master, the late bishop of Lincoln, was possessed for a time by
the dream of a united west, in which England could take a
worthy part, under the direction of the successor to St. Peter.
The pope's refusal to grant adequate relaxations of Henry's
undertaking in Sicily must have come as a shock, but it was
not altogether a disaster. It enabled the barons of England to
take the lead. Then the brothers of Lusignan revolted and were
driven into exile; and the Lord Edward had to be put under
surveillance. Still Simon did not despair. Until the autumn of
1258 he took the lead in representations made to the Curia.
Peace had been made; England, though in danger from malcontents, could look hopefully to the future if only the pope
would come to its aid and send a legate to share in the direction
of its affairs. The pope, however, gave the new order in England
a cool reception. The barons in England longed to be free of the
Sicilian incubus, which, as an isolated venture, made little
appeal to Earl Simon himself. The king of the Romans and
Peter of Savoy had their own, more realistic, points of view.
Simon's dream faded away. For a time he was in despair, and
thought of leaving England for ever. One thing he had—his
rights and his wife's rights. He had never forgotten them even
in his most exalted moods. He would see at least that Eleanor
had her dower.

King Louis very properly required the Countess Eleanor to

---

[1] It should also be noted that a leading negotiator on King Louis's side was
Simon's friend, the Franciscan Odo Rigaud, archbishop of Rouen.

join in the renunciation of any claims which might conflict with the terms of peace. Ratification was put in jeopardy by the insistence of Simon and Eleanor that, as a condition of their concurrence, the countess should be assured of the full enjoyment of her dower. The controversy disturbed the earl's future relations with Henry and his advisers, and, after he had fallen at Evesham, embittered his widow in her exile till the end of her life. Even after King Louis and his queen had patched up the settlement which enabled the treaty to be ratified, it was a *cause célèbre* in the French court. Its tangled history bears testimony to Louis's patient sense of justice and to the friendly consideration which he gave to a great Frenchman, but it lowered Simon's influence as a leading figure in the western world.

While the endless arbitrations about Eleanor's dowry were proceeding in France and England,[1] King Henry was detained in England by the discussions on the baronial settlement. At last, he was free to go. He arrived in Paris on 24 November 1259. In order to secure the adhesion of Simon and Eleanor to the treaty, the king and his new advisers accepted an ingenious compromise. As a pledge of his intention to settle the matter, Henry agreed to the deposit by Louis in the Temple at Paris of 15,000 marks sterling, which were to be deducted from the sum payable to Henry under the terms of peace. Simon and Eleanor then made the renunciations required of them, and on 4 December the treaty was published in the garden of the royal palace. King Henry did homage to Louis for Gascony.

By the treaty Louis got a definite surrender of Henry's claim to Normandy, Maine, Anjou, and Poitou. He in his turn acknowledged Henry's lordship over Gascony—or, so the wording went, Bordeaux, Bayonne, and Gascony—on condition that Henry became his vassal and one of the peers of France.[2] In addition the French king made a generous, but dangerous, concession in acknowledgement of Henry's claims in the extensive region west of the Auvergne, formerly held by his grandfather Henry II and his grandmother Eleanor of Aquitaine. It was impossible to isolate and name particular fiefs affected by this tradition. Hence the three dioceses of Limoges, Perigueux,

[1] The ratifications of 1259 reflect the course of negotiations about Eleanor de Monfort's dower. The final ratification of 13 October omits reference to renunciation by Eleanor, which Louis decided to arrange separately. On all this, with the dates of other renunciations and the story of Henry's new seal and style. see Chaplais, op. cit.   [2] Cf. above, p. 84.

and Cahors were taken as the basis and Louis gave to Henry all his rights in fief and domain within their boundaries, that is to say, between the county of Toulouse and the county of La Marche. In addition a complicated arrangement was made about the future of Saintonge, the Agenais, and lands in Quercy, the province of Cahors. Until its loss in 1242 lower Saintonge had protected Gascony and the isle of Oleron to the north, between the Gironde and the Charente. Louis admitted Henry's interest in this area and made provision for its return to the king of England after the death of his brother Alphonse, the count of Poitou and Toulouse. The Agenais protected Gascony on the north-east. It had come to the counts of Toulouse and had passed to Alphonse after the death of his father-in-law, Raymond VII, but Henry claimed its return as distinct from Toulouse. Louis recognized his rights and promised to pay, until the death of Jeanne, Raymond's daughter and Alphonse's wife, an annual rent equal to the annual value of the county. If it should then escheat to the French Crown, the county was to go to the king of England; if it should pass to another lord, the rent was to continue and the new lord was to hold it of the king of England. Henry also claimed to succeed to Jeanne's lands in Quercy on the ground that they had come to her through her grandmother, a daughter of Henry II. Louis was willing, if it was proved that King Richard I, as lord of Aquitaine, had given these lands to his sister, to allow this claim also and made terms similar to those made about the Agenais.

With the undertaking to pay the cost of 500 knights for two years (a sum reduced by the financial pledge set aside for the settlement of the Countess Eleanor's dower) these were the main articles of the treaty of Paris. The treaty was the work of a wise and noble king, working alongside able men, but at the same time it reveals all the difficulties of peace-making in the middle ages. The only clear-cut provision was the surrender of Normandy. Here the treatment of still outstanding rights and the compensation of landholders who did not wish to settle in the duchy was a comparatively easy problem. It had indeed been anticipated by Louis after Henry's campaign in 1242. The frequent clashes in the Channel between English and Norman sailors gradually became more intense as national feeling drove England and France farther apart, but this was inevitable. Every other provision, even the assessment of the sum owing by

Louis for the 500 knights, bristled with difficulties. His generous gesture in the three dioceses disregarded the wishes of Louis's feudatories, was highly unpopular, and invited incessant litigation in the parliament of Paris until Edward I surrendered his rights twenty years later (1279). The problem of the Agenais and the other neighbours of Gascony led to tiresome negotiations which were complicated by conflicting interests. Above all, the tenure of Gascony by the king of England as a vassal of the king of France exposed the duchy to the perpetual intervention of the French court, just as in Edward I's reign, first Wales and then Scotland was exposed to the interference of the English court. The standing of Gascon appellants to Paris was to become a major issue. The treaty, in short, subjected the two kings and their subjects to all the vexations, delays, intricate legalism, and chicanery of feudal jurisprudence. The royal counsellors in England held in deep suspicion the motives of the French; the parliament of Paris was exasperated by the evasions and delays practised by the government in England and Gascony. The vast dossier of documents relating to disputes about the interpretation of the treaty, to the rights of third parties, to the litigation on appeals, to the details of interference with shipping in the Channel and the Bay of Biscay, required the attention of special clerks under trained specialists. The king of England had to engage the service of famous civilians and French advocates to uphold his interests in the French court. The outcome of all this friction in our period was a series of arbitrations and treaties, a French occupation of Gascony for ten years (1294–1303), the alliance between France and Scotland, and war.

None the less, the treaty of Paris gave King Henry, and King Edward after him, friendship and peace with France for thirty-five years; and during those years the union of king and kingdom, for which Stephen Langton and St. Edmund and Hugh Bigod had striven, was effected on a foundation of law and order strong enough to survive later shocks.

IV

THE COMMON ENTERPRISE
1258–62[1]

THE men who took part in the movement in 1258 or observed it at close quarters were well aware of its importance. 'You know well', said their spokesman to the pope, 'what the condition of affairs in England is, for there has been a new and sudden change.'[2] Even in the early days of unity these men were anxious, and rightly anxious; for before long Englishmen and women in all ranks of society, even in the village communities, were divided against each other. Proclamations, manifestoes, preachings, political songs expressed the ideas which inspired and the propaganda which might explain or excuse or excite the violent actions of groups and parties. Discordant tongues wagged freely in hall and chamber, in monasteries and markets and wayside taverns. Desperate men found refuge in fen and forest. At the sound of the bell the London populace flocked again and again to the cross of St. Paul's to voice what was regarded as the will of the city. After nine incoherent years the turmoil subsided. Moderate counsels prevailed. What was of permanent value in the work of the first years of the movement was re-enacted in a famous statute, with a preamble on the rights and duties of kingship. Three years later the heir to the throne left England on a crusade. He was away for four years. The new peace survived the old king's death and the new king's absence. The new king was strong, and by this time was also wise. His reputation was high at home and abroad. For sixteen years—the years which saw at long last the conquest of Wales—England was united under Edward's rule as it had never been before.

As a young man, between the ages of twenty-four and twenty-six (1263–5), Edward had faced the most terrible of his adver-

---

[1] 'Le conte [the earl of Leicester] dit qu'il n'atret nules genz ne ne fist aliances en contre la fey le roy ne autremant, *fors por la comune emprise*.' From Simon de Montfort's defence in 1260.

[2] 'In quo statu sit regnum Anglie, bene nostis; nam repentinam et novam mutationem recepit' (*Ann. Monast.* i. 465).

saries. He had been defeated and held in thrall by Simon de Montfort. He had escaped and by a sudden change of fortune had overthrown his enemy at Evesham. Then he had a share in doing what the earl had wished to see done, in very different conditions, after the baronial government of 1258 had been established. He helped a papal legate to restore order in England in a spirit of equity. The principle which separated Edward and Simon was simple. At one time, during the negotiations which preceded the campaigns of 1264, it seems to have been narrowed down to a fine point: was the king to be free or not to appoint whom he wished as members of his council? This was the heart of the matter. The highly elaborated theories of the nature of a true commonwealth, the intricate devices which safeguarded baronial control, even the details of the baronial programme, were found to be of secondary importance. King Louis of France, in his award at Amiens in January 1264, expressly affirmed that the king had the power to call to his counsels those who, in his judgement, would be helpful and loyal to him, whether men of the country or aliens (*alienigenas et indigenas*). Earl Simon, while he asserted with fanatical intensity his obligation to maintain the settlement to which all parties had sworn, was ready to consider modifications in the agreements reached at Oxford, but would never give way on this point.

How was it that in England alone, among the monarchies of the west, the right of the king to select his own advisers became a subject of such bitter controversy? Here we must distinguish the position in 1258 from the position five years later, and the sense of expediency from the harsher conviction of necessity. Men so different in temperament and circumstance as Earl Simon, Earl Richard of Gloucester, Peter of Savoy, Hugh Bigod, and their companions did not come together as a revolutionary assembly. They took a mutual oath 'to stand by and help each other, one and all, against all men, to do the right and take nothing that they could not take without doing wrong, saving their fealty to king and crown'.[1] After they had imposed a baronial council upon the king, they described themselves, in Henry's name, as unselfish men, who 'setting our (i.e. the king's)

[1] The original parties to the sworn agreement of 12 April 1258 were the earls of Gloucester, Norfolk, and Leicester, Peter of Savoy, Hugh Bigod, John fitzGeoffrey, and Peter de Montfort. The agreement survives among the archives of the French house of Montfort and is printed in Bémont, *Simon de Montfort* (French edition, 1884), pp. 327–8.

affairs before their own . . . devote their might to our interests
and those of our realm' in the reformation and ordering of the
realm.[1] Writing to the pope in their own names, they explained
that their action was due to the Sicilian business. 'The lord king,
realising the intolerable burden of this business and the feeble
condition of his kingdom, wished and expressly conceded that
the "reformation" should be effected by the counsel of his
magnates, without whom he could neither manage his affairs
nor prosecute the Sicilian business.'[2] He had agreed that twelve
persons chosen by him and twelve acting for the community
(*ex parte communitatis*) should provide for the amelioration and
reform of the realm and matters affecting the realm. These proceedings were grounded in the view that, in a well-ordered
commonwealth, private must give way to public interests. The
expulsion of the king's half brothers, who had tried to persuade
Henry to break his oath and rejected the new order, was justified
by the consideration that the commonwealth (*respublica*) is a
body maintained by reason, and that it is not fitting to allow
in one body discord between its members.[3]

Now it is not hard to trace the origin of the ideas which were
at work in the minds of the confederates. There is nothing
mystical about them. Even the conception of the body politic,
which may have been picked up from a reader of John of
Salisbury, had a very practical bearing, for it was evoked by
the intransigence of the Poitevins. The Savoyard uncle of the
queen, and the French brother-in-law of the king, knew enough
of England to join with the heads of the great houses of Bigod
and Clare in maintaining the duty and right of the *communitas*
to take a responsible part in the affairs of the realm. The history
of John's reign and of King Henry's minority, the events of the
years 1234–8, the repeated requests for the appointment of
responsible officers of state, of justiciar and chancellor and,
later, of treasurer, were well known to all. They were familiar
with the proceedings in frequent parliaments. Moreover, as
political writings were soon to show and as the English jurist
Bracton had already shown, the difference between 'political
rule' and 'royal rule' was a matter of conscious apprehension,

---

[1] *Close Rolls, 1256–9*, p. 328.   [2] *Ann. Monast.* i. 470–4.
[3] Ibid. This is the famous letter to the pope, written in the summer of 1258.
The seals attached to it were those of the original confederates and of the earls of
Hereford and Warwick, the count of Aumale, and James of Audley.

whether these terms were used or not.[1] Both had theological and moral support, and both went beyond the experience and limitations of the feudal state from which they had emerged. Each implied that the king should rule according to law, maintain justice and order, and follow good counsel; each acknowledged, more or less willingly, an ultimate right to resist a tyrant; but, whereas 'royal rule' raised the king above positive law and custom and submitted him to the law of God or nature alone, 'political rule' suggested a more organic political society, maintained by a common regard for positive law and custom, and by a closer co-operation between king and people. England, in the thirteenth century, became in fact an example of 'political rule', in the sense that legislation and taxation and interference with vested interests were subject to the joint control, or rather the united control, of the king and the baronage as the expression of the *communitas*; but it did not become what we call a constitutional monarchy. Edward I worked with and through parliament, but he did not surrender and, by his prudent choice of ministers and counsellors, was not called upon to surrender his executive control. He was king, and at times did not hesitate to appeal from law and custom to a higher law and to considerations of the general well-being and necessary interests of the realm. He had learned much from the lessons given to his father, but he had no use for the Provisions of Oxford which had subjected his father to a baronial committee. In his reign this experiment was completely discredited.

The previous history of Henry III's reign supplies several examples both of the relations between the king and the *communitas* of barons and of the resistance of the king to the suggestion that he should surrender his right to choose his immediate advisers. In his letter to the emperor Frederick in 1235, Henry had expounded the former and bitterly attacked those who had separated him from his natural colleagues. A similar note appears in the denunciation to the pope of the attempt made by

---

[1] St. Thomas Aquinas preferred political, Giles of Rome and Ptolemy of Lucca royal rule; cf. R. W. Carlyle and A. J. Carlyle, *History of Mediaeval Political Theory in the West*, v (1928), 64–85. Fritz Kern, in his *Gottesgnadenthum und Widerstandsrecht* (1914), has discussed the theological basis of royal power (see especially p. 145). A political crisis in Flanders reveals, as early as 1127, the conscious distinction between the two conceptions, though not, of course, in later terms; see an important paper by H. Sproemberg in *L'Organisation corporative du moyen âge* (Louvain, 1939), pp. 33–88, especially pp. 62–63.

the king's half-brothers in 1258 to detach him from his sworn
agreement with the confederated body. In 1245, when king and
baronage were in full accord, Henry welcomed the appointment
of baronial proctors, formally described as agents of the *communitas*, to the papal court at Lyons: indeed he himself gave
procuratorial powers to some of these agents and sent others of
his own choice to join in the protests against papal interventions. The agents sent to the papal court in the summer of 1258
again included men armed with both royal and baronial
authority. Nor had Henry refused on occasion to admit baronial
nominees, or at least barons known to be welcome to the community, to his council. It is possible, indeed, that the council
had been strengthened and subjected to a stringent oath in 1257,
when the consequences of Henry's share in papal policy had
been generally realized and were seen to involve changes at
home and peace with France.

The councillor's oath ascribed by the Burton annalist to this
year was obviously intended to make the council as a body responsible for the prevention of any act or grant which might
cause 'prejudice or injury' to the king or to anybody else (*alteri*);
both king and counsellors were to be apprised of the circumstances, and, in one clause, it is laid down that even if a counsellor prevailed upon the king to make a grant *proprio motu* to
him, he should not accept it without the consent of the whole
council or of the 'greater and saner part' of it.[1] An oath of this
kind certainly suggests that pressure had been brought to bear
upon the king, either by the great council of the magnates or,
as is more likely, by friendly advisers, such as Peter of Savoy and
the earl of Leicester, who desired to avert a crisis.

On the other hand, Henry, since he had declared himself of
age, had never surrendered his right to order his household and
appoint his counsellors as he wished, nor had the barons
pressed him persistently to do so. The attempt in 1238, if it were
made, had been frustrated, the plan ascribed by Matthew Paris
to 1244 had come to nothing.[2] When the joint commission of
1258 imposed a council upon the king, doubts and hesitations
soon began. Fulk Basset, the bishop of London, who had been
added to the council in the previous year, withdrew at once.
During the miserable years 1260-2 Henry, who found strong
sympathizers, gradually succeeded in throwing off the incubus.

[1] *Ann. Monast.* i. 395-7.   [2] Cf. above, pp. 76 ff.

One man, a Frenchman, had watched the process of disintegration with contempt. He had come to feel deep distrust of the king, to loathe the king's counsellors, and to despise the English mentality. He took his stand on his oath, and on the obligations which the baronial council had incurred. He forced the embarrassed barons to choose sides. The result was the barons' war, a war not between king and barons, but between baronial partisans, the king's party, and the party of the Provisions. Simon was a monarchist, and always professed to act on behalf of, and later, when he was in power, in the name of the king; but he insisted that the main principle of the Provisions must be upheld. Here he set himself against the universal practice and theory of royal authority in the west. The only feudal states which were administered by councils of vassals were the small kingdom of Jerusalem and the other Latin states of the east. The only baronies so ruled were the baronies in the kingdom of Jerusalem.[1] Simon is not likely to have been influenced by these examples. He believed in strong rule. What he disliked in England was the lack of purposive action and King Henry's apparent inability to weld his kingdom together in the way to which its peculiar traditions and opportunities seemed to point.[2]

The magnates had never approved Henry's Sicilian adventure. In 1257 they drew up a list of their objections—the distance between England and Sicily, the successes of Manfred, the danger from Wales, the temptations which Henry's commitment to a great military enterprise would suggest to his neighbours, above all, the intolerable cost and probable waste. In April 1258, however, they were faced by the necessity to make a definite choice between helping their king under conditions or seeing him humiliated and excommunicated and the land put under an interdict. Some of their leaders, notably Peter of Savoy and

---

[1] A good account of the 'high court' of the kingdom of Jerusalem may be read in John L. La Monte, *Feudal Monarchy in the Latin Kingdom of Jerusalem, 1100 to 1291* (1932), pp. 87–104. The Provisions of 1259 and 1264 (anticipated in the plan ascribed to 1244) that a certain number of the counsellors appointed by the barons should always be in attendance on the king may possibly have been influenced by the practice in the kingdom of Jerusalem, where, though membership of the High Court depended on the tenure of a fief held of the Crown, the entire body seldom met, and 'two or more liegemen with the president—the king or his representative— were sufficient to make a court' (La Monte, p. 91); but a precaution of this kind would naturally suggest itself.

[2] See above (p. 125) for the influences which affected Earl Simon.

Earl Simon, Henry's foreign relatives, were already committed; none could entirely evade responsibility. In this serious position of affairs, seven men took action.[1] They joined in the sworn compact to which allusion has already been made. On 30 April Hugh Bigod was their spokesman in a painful interview with the king. Henry, probably with some sense of relief, agreed to their demands. Royal letters patent of 2 May defined the settlement.[2] The state of the realm must be reformed and the pope be induced to moderate his terms; in return the barons would try to get a general aid (*commune auxilium*) from the community of the realm (*regni*). The reform of the realm would be made by twelve of the king's council and twelve magnates. This joint committee would set to work at Oxford on 12 June. The result of their deliberations would be issued before Christmas after consultation with the great council and, if he had arrived, with a papal legate. Henry, his son Edward, his Poitevin half-brothers, and others swore to maintain the agreement. The Poitevins, indeed, were chosen by the king as members of the joint committee. Six days later (8 May) two of the four brothers were given powers, with Peter of Savoy, Hugh Bigod, and Earl Simon, to come to terms of peace with King Louis at Paris; and about the same time proctors were assigned to the papal court to press for a revision of the Sicilian agreement and to ask for the dispatch to England of a papal legate. One of these proctors was the Savoyard Henry of Susa, the great canonist,

---

[1] Above, p. 130, n.

[2] It is not easy to distinguish the various sworn obligations undertaken by King Henry between the end of April and the end of July, for the documents in charter form which authenticated them have not survived. According to the annals of Tewkesbury, Henry and Edward swore on the gospels to consent to the plan of 30 April, i.e. the reformation described in the letter patent of 2 May. This action was doubtless recorded in a formal document sealed with the seals of all concerned. The king was, presumably, not required to join in the oaths exacted from the baronial community to maintain the Provisions made in June at Oxford, but after the refusal of his half-brothers to do this and their expulsion, and Edward's reluctant sworn adherence (10 July), a charter, sealed by several of the leading barons and also by Henry and Edward, alluding to a sworn and joint obligation to observe whatever the 'barons' should provide, is said to have been presented at the Gildhall on the morrow of St. Mary Magdalen's day (23 July) to get the seals of the mayor, aldermen, and leading citizens of London (Fitz Thedmar, *Chronicle of Mayor and Sheriffs*, pp. 38–39). Whether this was the agreement of early May or a later document is not clear. Possibly it was a new instrument in solemn form which the leading counsellors considered that the recent division of opinion made necessary. Cf. the observations of V. H. Galbraith, *Studies in the Public Records* (1948), pp. 141–2, where the passage in the London chronicle seems to me to be unduly isolated from the course of events.

now archbishop of Embrun. Nearly twenty years before, when he was a promising young lawyer, the king had employed Henry of Susa in a famous dispute about the succession to the see of Winchester.

It is clear that in May 1258 a comprehensive settlement of foreign and domestic affairs was contemplated, under the auspices of the Holy See. King Henry's co-operation was to be ensured, and the earl of Leicester's idealism might be satisfied[1] by a policy which would be directed to realize the aims of both men. They were soon disillusioned. Pope Alexander was sceptical about the changes in England and unwilling to relax his demands, which even his agent Rostand came to regard as impracticable. In spite of fervent appeals for papal guidance no legate was sent. Towards the end of the year Alexander, seeing no hope of further aid from England, released the Lord Edmund from his obligation and decided to look elsewhere for a king of Sicily. So King Henry lost everything that he had sought to win by his surrender to the barons. For the time being he was in their hands, but he was no longer a willing agent of their reforms. Earl Simon, in his turn, withdrew himself, and paid only brief and disturbing visits to England. At Oxford, and later in the summer of 1258 at the New Temple in London, he had taken the lead in a 'furious' orgy of activity.[2] Now the leadership passed to others, men of steadier judgement, more expert in detail, more moderate in temper, and less willing to compromise their king.

The changes effected by the twenty-four were so drastic and exhilarating that, once made, they were hard to undo; they persisted by their own momentum some time after baronial enthusiasm had waned. Among the first things done at Oxford were the restoration of the office of justiciar, the appointment of a council of fifteen elected by four of the twenty-four, and the

[1] Above, p. 125.

[2] A newsletter written from the king's court ends with the phrases, 'ferociter procedunt barones in agendis suis: utinam bonum finem sortiuntur' (*Ann. Monast.* i. 445). The writer of this important narrative seems to be the most probable source of a series of documents relating to the Sicilian business, the proceedings at Oxford and later in 1258–9, and negotiations with the papal court, copied into the annals of the abbey of Burton-on-Trent. He had access to memoranda which were not published or enrolled, and may have been John Clarel, one of the king's clerks. Clarel's connexions were with the neighbourhood of Burton and he was one of the baronial and royal proctors sent to the papal court in August 1258. His sympathies were at first with the new movement.

distribution of royal castles to new castellans who were sworn not to surrender them for twelve years except by command of this new council. Hugh Bigod was made justiciar, with the custody of the Tower of London, and began at once to hold pleas. The chancellor and treasurer were subjected to the control of the council. Important wardships and escheats could only be granted with the consent of the great council—that is to say, in parliament. Three parliaments were to be held each year, at Michaelmas, Candlemas (2 February), and on 1 June; and in order to secure the fulfilment of this provision a standing legislative commission of twelve, elected by the community of the baronage, was set up to act with the council of fifteen at these times and in such other parliaments as the king and council might summon. While this arrangement relieved the rest of the baronage, it did not imply that the larger body might not be summoned. In fact, the twenty-four placed the whole administrative system firmly under the joint direction of king and barons; both the council of fifteen and the baronial commission of twelve were intended to safeguard this form of government. If it had worked smoothly, the king would have become *primus inter pares*, like the king of Jerusalem.

The changes made by the twenty-four were too novel and too sudden to work smoothly. In August the baronial leaders would seem to have made the danger to unity the most pressing need for the appointment of a papal legate. Already rifts had appeared and self-seeking and intractable men were 'seeking occasions'. Trouble, indeed, serious trouble, had begun at Oxford some weeks earlier. First the lord of Pembroke, William of Valence, one of the king's Poitevin half-brothers, had insisted that the proper business of the king and barons, assembled in parliament, was the prosecution of the Welsh war. William had some justification for this view; for during the previous two years Llywelyn ap Gruffydd, the lord of Snowdonia, had entirely changed the balance of forces west of the Severn. In 1256 he had thrown the English administrators out of the Lord Edward's lands in north Wales and isolated Edward's castles of Diserth and Deganwy. In 1257 he had subdued nearly all the Welsh princes in north, central, and south Wales, secured their allegiance, and inflicted a disastrous defeat upon King Henry's men near the royal stronghold of Carmarthen. In March 1258, in an assembly of princes, he had assumed the title of prince of

Wales. At the same time he had entered into a defensive alliance with the baronial party which had assumed control of affairs in Scotland, where the young king Alexander III, King Henry's son-in-law, was seeking to extricate himself from the trammels of his minority. Llywelyn's successes had aroused a storm of patriotic feeling among the Welsh, and confirmed waverers in their unwilling allegiance. In July 1257 the king had summoned his host to gather in two parts at Chester and Bristol.[1] The men of the Cinque Ports were ordered to send ships to the north Welsh coast. An inglorious campaign of less than a month (17 August to 12 September) had revealed Llywelyn's new strength. A long and tiresome war seemed to have begun. A new campaign was planned in March 1258 and the host was ordered to reassemble at Chester before 17 June. As late as 13 May, eleven days after he had agreed to the terms of the baronial leaders, Henry had written to King Alexander, who was calling for help against the Scottish confederates, that he intended to proceed from the forthcoming parliament at Oxford on his expedition against Llywelyn.[2] It is not surprising, therefore, that William of Valence, one of the chief sufferers at the hands of the prince of Wales, was indignant at Oxford. He learned that Llywelyn's envoys were already on the way to arrange a truce, that the Welsh were to be left at liberty to consolidate their gains at the Lord Edward's and his own and other lords' expense. He entered into a fierce dispute with the earl of Leicester. But King Henry had been persuaded. A truce, to last until 1 August 1259, was made with Llywelyn on 17 June, the very day on which the Welsh campaign had been planned to set out from Chester.

William of Valence did not object merely to the Welsh truce. He and his three brothers, with their brother-in-law, John de Warenne, earl of Surrey,[3] all of them members as royal nominees of the body of twenty-four, were opposed to the Provisions made at Oxford.

---

[1] *Close Rolls, 1256-9*, pp. 139-41.   [2] Ibid., p. 311.

[3] He had been married in 1247 when a minor to the king's half-sister, Alesia de Lusignan, who had come to England with her brothers Guy and William. She had died in 1256, leaving three small children: Alice, who in 1268 married Henry Percy; Isabella, who in 1279 married John Baliol, later king of the Scots; William (1256-86) who was killed in a tournament. Their father, a mainstay of Edward I throughout his reign, lived until 1304, when he was succeeded by William's son John, who in 1306 married Joan of Bar, King Edward's granddaughter.

The breach in the unity of the twenty-four was a disaster. For a time the king was implicated in suspicion aroused by the action of his half-brothers, who did their utmost to persuade him to reject the Provisions. The Lord Edward was easily persuaded. The failure to get papal co-operation confirmed the king's friends in their preference for the old order and their dislike of the new. The work of the twenty-four was first impeded and then arrested. The prospect of general co-operation in the reform of church and state faded away. The movement passed under the control of the council of fifteen, a very mixed body of men, whose resolution was gradually broken by their own incoherence and by the resilient forces of reaction.

King Henry's easy acquiescence in the baronial plans, followed by his rapid repudiation of his half-brothers, had been due to his isolation, not to conviction. It was very significant that the twelve men whom he chose included the unpopular Poitevins and only two other barons, one of whom, John du Plessis, owed his earldom to his marriage. The community of the barons was, for the time being, a reality. It comprehended most of the earls and magnates of England and also the lords of the Welsh March who were in the end to take the lead among the royalists. The nomination of his half-brothers could only be justified by the fact that Henry could find nobody else. They were young, rash, and out of touch with their surroundings. Guy and Geoffrey had no territorial standing in England, where they were but occasional residents. William of Valence,[1] who after his arrival in 1247 had been given in marriage one of the heiresses to the marshal's lands, Joan de Muntchenesy, was a denizen, but he had not yet adapted himself to his new life and had frequently been at loggerheads both with Earl Simon and the queen's Savoyard relatives. Aymer of Lusignan had been forced upon the electors to the bishopric of Winchester in 1250, and though his election had been confirmed by Pope Innocent IV, he was too young to be consecrated and enjoyed rather than ruled his diocese as bishop-elect. All four were vigorous young men; their high spirits and magnificence had strengthened the king's natural affection for them; but their insolence and their irresponsible exploitation of Henry's good nature had

---

[1] William was called 'of Valence' from the name of his birth-place in Saintonge. His wife was the daughter of Warin de Muntchenesy and Joan, fifth daughter of William the Marshal.

made them very unpopular.[1] In 1258 they were suddenly invested, in a grave emergency, with duties which demanded tact and restraint. They found themselves in a company determined to go farther than they had expected. They had taken an oath to abide by the procedure devised in April, and in June they were affronted by the proceedings. The little group of confederates was turned, at Oxford, into a sworn association of the whole baronial body. The oath taken by Earl Richard of Clare, Earl Simon, the Bigods, and Peter of Savoy was taken in an expanded form by the barons who had come in arms to the parliament. The community was bound together in a mutual obligation to maintain the right, not to prejudice the compact by any scramble for lands and goods, and to treat the recalcitrant as public enemies. The instruments of the new peace, justiciar, chancellor, castellans, counsellors, sheriffs, were also sworn to maintain it. There is reason to believe that, in addition, an oath was exacted to maintain the Provisions made by the twenty-four, Provisions which included a resumption of castles and lands recently alienated from the Crown. This was too much for the Poitevins and the Earl Warenne, members of the twenty-four though they were. They left Oxford for the bishop-elect's castle of Wolvesey, by Winchester. King Henry and the barons followed them. During the discussions which ensued, John de Warenne submitted and took the oath to the Provisions, but the barons had no confidence in the Poitevins and, although the king offered to go surety for them, were set on their expulsion from the country. Finally they were told that, if Guy and Geoffrey left, the lord of Pembroke and the bishop-elect, who had extensive lands in England, might remain under custody, or, if they preferred, they might go. The brothers preferred to go together. They left Dover with other Poitevins on 14 July. Their lands and property were given custodians. The Lord Edward then gave way and was placed under the surveillance of four barons who would act as his counsellors. He was at this time just nineteen years of age.

During the next eighteen months the political machinery devised by the twenty-four was in constant motion. Earl Simon

---

[1] A detailed account of the favours granted to the brothers has been given by H. S. Snellgrove in his essay, *The Lusignans in England* (1950). He does not refer to Adam Marsh's encouragement of Aymer to seek the advice and companionship of Bishop Grosseteste (cf. Adam's *Epistolae*, p. 103). The general conclusion that the movement of 1258 was directed against the brothers is not acceptable.

had hoped for a settlement of ecclesiastical problems and the reform of the royal household. Little was done to purge the household and nothing to meet the difficulties of the clergy, who, in a council which met at Merton in Surrey at the same time as the Oxford parliament, had compiled a long and formidable list of their grievances. The barons resumed their old complaints about papal provisions, the pope sent a reasoned reply, and pertinaciously demanded the restoration of Aymer of Lusignan to his diocese. At Oxford a strong baronial committee had been appointed to deal with the financial aid promised to the king, but the deadlock in the negotiations with the pope about the Sicilian business made an aid unnecessary. A good understanding with the baronial caucus in Scotland, a renewal in June 1259 of the truce with Llywelyn, and the ratification of the treaty with King Louis of France left the council free to deal with domestic affairs. After all, the object of the new government was not primarily to control, still less to humiliate the king, but to carry through reforms in the king's name. Since he had thrown himself into the Sicilian business Henry had allowed local government to proceed without the constant supervision which it required. He had worked his officials hard, but with an eye to his financial needs. Without deliberate intent he had drifted dangerously near the rock of isolation from which he had been rescued a quarter of a century before. When the barons met at Oxford in June 1258 they had ready a list of petitions, suggested perhaps by contemporary ecclesiastical practice, and more far-reaching than anything known to historians since the last years of King John's reign. Moreover, since John's time the lesser man, just as had the local clergy, had found means of expression. The community of the barons was aware of a wider community behind them, more assured by long experience in the shires, more vocal than it had been wont to be.

During the scare of 1254, when the knights and men of similar degree were rallied to provide an army for the defence of Gascony against Alfonso of Castile, the barons in parliament refused, it will be remembered,[1] to answer for the knights of the shires as consenting parties to a general aid. The regents told the king that these lesser gentry were restless; they clamoured for a new confirmation of the Charters; they must be dealt with separately. And two knights from each shire were summoned to

[1] Above, p. 117.

appear before the council at Westminster to provide for the king's financial necessity on behalf of 'all and each' of the men of their shires. In the meantime the sheriffs were instructed to explain the need in the shire courts. Now when in April 1258 the barons promised the king that, in return for his agreement to a plan of reform, they would try to obtain a common aid from the community of the realm, they must have had this precedent in mind. A common aid meant a general tax, and a general tax, whether of laity or clergy, required general acquiescence. The idea that the community of the barons could answer for the whole realm had marked a great advance in national coherence earlier in the reign;[1] but although the community of the barons was still usually described as the community of the realm, and for many years to come would speak and act on behalf of the whole realm, the existence of an articulate and larger community of the realm could not be ignored.[2] We no longer think of the Great Charter of 1215 as purely a baronial document concerned with purely baronial grievances, but the petitions of the earls and barons at Oxford in 1258 reveal a more conscious, livelier concern for the interests of lesser folk,[3] as suitors in local courts, as subject to judicial amercements, as the victims of royal officials. Their preoccupation with recent tendencies in the administration of the law affecting their own interests could not be isolated from a regard for more general grievances. The Charters, in letter and spirit, were the safeguard of the well-being of every freeman. More important, however, than any recognition of this kind was the formal and precise determination revealed at Oxford to associate the knights of the shire more closely with local administration and especially to make them responsible for the first hearing and enrolment of popular complaints. Changes in the law would require time; the reform of local administration and justice to the wronged could be undertaken at once. The community of the realm was a vague thing; the community of vill or hundred or shire was a living, actual thing.

[1] Above, p. 29.

[2] Although some of the details are open to question, the best analysis of the phrase, 'community of the realm', can be found in a paper by William A. Morris, 'Magnates and Community of the Realm in Parliament, 1264–1327' in *Medievalia et Humanistica*, fasc. i (Boulder, Colorado, 1943), pp. 58–94, especially pp. 59–73.

[3] As they had shown, probably at the instigation of bishops and judges, during the legislative period 1234–6. Above, pp. 67–68.

THE LOCAL GENTRY   143

'The whole system of royal justice is based upon the plaint.'[1]
The slightest familiarity with medieval books about kingship
brings home the truth of this statement. The story of the emperor Trajan prevailed upon to do justice to an importunate
widow as he was setting out for the wars was as familiar to men
then as the story of King Henry's contemporary, St. Louis,
listening to petitions under an oak at Vincennes is to us. A
study of the plea rolls shows that the oral or written complaint
which, under necessary safeguards, initiated a suit with or without a writ, was almost as common as an action of novel disseisin.
As we read the records on the patent rolls of the commissions
issued to deal with particular cases—commissions which obviously repeat, often in detail, the vivid and artless narratives of
the petitioners—we can well believe an Edwardian writer's
account of the honest and circumspect clerks set aside in the
chancery to examine petitions and plaints and to prescribe the
appropriate way to deal with them. The duty to listen to plaints
was incumbent also upon the local courts, both public and
private. A letter sent in the king's name in March 1255 to the
bailiffs of Archbishop Boniface at Canterbury runs as follows:

Whereas it has hitherto been the law and custom of our realm that
townships (villate) and the communities of vills in our realm have the
power to enter complaints by three or four of their inhabitants in our
courts and in the courts of others, we command you, if the men of our
beloved and faithful Imbert Pugeys, of the township of Siberston,
have any complaints to make or defend on behalf of their community
in the court of your lord in Canterbury, to allow them to enter them
through three or four of their number, so that the said Imbert may
not again be worried in this matter.[2]

At Oxford the barons made this practice, which must so often
have failed to get redress for the sufferers, the basis of an exhaustive inquiry, and they enlisted the services of those administrative maids-of-all-work, the knights of the shires, whom they
associated in a responsible capacity with the new justiciar. At
every meeting of the shire court four knights, elected by the
shire, were to attend to hear and record all complaints of

[1] H. G. Richardson and G. O. Sayles, Select Cases of Procedure without Writ under
Henry III (Selden Society, 1941), p. xxii. This volume has settled once for all the
problem of proceeding by way of petition.
[2] Close Rolls, 1254–6, p. 173. Dr. Helen Cam brought this important bit of
evidence to the notice of the writer.

injuries and trespasses. The parties were to give pledges of appearance before the justiciar and his colleagues as these went their rounds. The records were to be tabulated, according to the hundred to which they belonged, and be submitted to the judges. After the knights had been elected it was decided to enlarge the scope of their duties. They received instructions which in effect made them the agents of the new government in a searching survey of local administration and royal rights. They were required to inquire into the exactions of every kind of local official, sheriffs, bailiffs, coroners, escheators, takers of prise, into the malpractices of Jews, usurers, exchangers, and merchants, and into unauthorized alienations of the royal demesne and royal rights. In writs issued from the chancery on 4 August they were ordered to use other knights of their shires to collect the information and to attend at Westminster a week after Michaelmas with their returns, which were to be sealed with their seals and the seals of their colleagues. They worked so hard that, a month after Michaelmas, the knights of fifteen if not more shires, including the distant Northumberland and Devon, presented themselves 'before the council in parliament'.[1] Nor was this all. At Oxford the barons had provided that there should be a clean sweep of the existing sheriffs. Henceforth a sheriff should be a 'vavassor' of the shire—that is to say, in general a local man of the knightly class, holding land of some barony or baronies, should hold office only for one year, accept no bribes or fees, account for all proceeds, and be rewarded for his work by the Crown. The records show that, after the Michaelmas parliament, this provision was given effect. With three or four exceptions the new sheriffs were local men of the class prescribed, who had not acted as sheriffs before. The knight had indeed come to his own.

No single detail of these measures was novel. Investigation into abuses as well as into the alienation of royal rights had been made before. The articles of the inquiries which the judges on every general eyre had to make included most of the instruc-

---

[1] The sheriffs of their shires were instructed early in November to allow them reasonable expenses of coming and going (*Close Rolls, 1256-67*, pp. 332-3). Helen Cam in 1931 (*E.H.R.* xlvi. 630-1) explained how later historians had been misled by these writs of expenses and concluded that knights of the shire had been summoned to parliament in the previous April. Her paper escaped the attention of Maude V. Clarke, who in 1936, following Pasquet, repeated the error in her *Medieval Representation and Consent*, p. 313.

tions to the knights in 1258. Knights were familiar with the kind
of work now entrusted to them, and had often been called to
appear at the king's court on the business of their shires. What
was new was the systematic use of complaints, investigations,
judicial process, and local appointments in one big coherent
drive to catch up arrears in the correction of malpractice and to
reform local government in the interests and from the point of
view of the people as well as of the king. The knight who in
October 1258 appeared at Westminster 'before the council in
parliament' on business affecting the common well-being of the
'community of his shire' was engaged in a national task as a
chosen representative of his neighbours. He followed instructions issued by the new council, but also, by his association with
it, he acquired new dignity as a public man; and later events
show that he was well aware of his place in the new movement.
It would have been surprising if, before long, his presence in
parliament had not been required. The enthusiasm which gave
zest to the expedients of 1258 did not last and the king recovered control, but after normal conditions had returned the
knights of the shire retained their political significance. The
young Edward was impressed by it at the time. He had also
learned something about social discontents. By the minute
investigations which followed his return from his crusade in
1274 and the attention which he gave, especially in times of
taxation, to the knights of the shire, to burgesses and merchants,
he recognized the interdependence of the maintenance of royal
power, the protection of his people, and the formal association
with his plans of those upon whose service he had to rely. The
evolution of parliament was not mysterious.

The baronial government made its point of view clear during
the October parliament. Two royal proclamations were issued
in Latin, French, and English, and were read aloud in every
shire court. The first, dated 18 October, was drawn up before
the whole council of fifteen, each of whom is named.[1] It declared
the king's will that the things done or to be done to the honour
of God and for the good of the realm by the council elected by

[1] Archbishop Boniface of Canterbury and Peter of Savoy, the queen's uncles, the
earl of Warwick, and John Mansel were present, as members of the council of
fifteen. The earl of Leicester, also present, was not likely to forget the occasion,
when the freemen of the land were associated by royal decree with the baronage in
sworn adhesion to the new order, which was to last 'without end'. He took his stand
on the sanctity of this oath.

the king and the community of the realm,[1] 'should be stedfast and lasting in all things without end'. It then required the whole body of freemen to take the oath already sworn by the community of the barons. The familiar words were recited, ending: 'and if any other one come here against, we will and bid all our true men to hold them deadly foes'. The second proclamation, which was to be read frequently in each year in every shire court, was issued two days later (20 October). Its object was to reassure the folk that the amendment of their wrongs would soon begin. The investigations made by the knights had obviously stirred the king's subjects and there had been some murmuring about the delay in dealing with them. In fact the justiciar and his judicial colleagues, who had not been idle during the summer, began their special eyre at Bermondsey in Surrey in November, after the arduous business of the parliament was concluded. The justiciar spent the greater part of his time until the harvest of 1259 in moving about the south and midlands. His thoroughness, well attested by the records of his court, aroused much enthusiasm, and his tendency to override established rights and even the rules of the common law in the interests of the complainants, also well attested, evoked much criticism and some disturbance.[2] The proclamation of 20 October coupled the hearing of complaints with the changes in the status of the sheriffs and bailiffs. It described in detail the obligations which their new oath of office imposed upon them and pointed out that, as they would henceforth hold office only for one year, the people need 'fear them less' and could 'more surely show their wrong doings'. This pronouncement must have aroused high hopes, and the local support given to Earl Simon between 1263 and 1265 was mainly due to the disillusionment which followed Henry's recovery of power between 1260 and 1263.

The changes in the law suggested by many of the petitions of the barons had probably received some attention in the summer of 1258 and in the October parliament. They were discussed and drafted in the spring of 1259 and were redrafted and embodied in a long series of legislative and administrative provisions issued on St. Edward's day (13 October) in the same

---

[1] The French *commune de nostre reaume* is in English 'loandes folk on ure kuneriche'.

[2] R. F. Treharne has given a masterly analysis of the work of Hugh Bigod and his successor, and of the reasons for its failure, in his *Baronial Plan of Reform* (1932), pp. 144–56, 246–50.

year. The legislative provisions, known as the Provisions of Westminster, but sometimes it would seem, comprehended under the general term for the settlement, 'the Provisions of Oxford', became part of the law of the land. With a few changes they were reissued in 1263, and again in 1267, when they were the substance of the famous statute of Marlborough. The reasons for their endurance are simple. They modified or defined the common law of the land, in the spirit of the Great Charter; they were quite consistent with the return to royal rule; and they were the outcome of deliberation with expert judges, capable draftsmen, who had personal experience of the difficulties which the new provisions were designed to meet. The judges were summoned to meet eight days before parliament 'to consider of what ill laws and need of reformation there were'.[1] What parliament this was is not stated, but the significant thing is that the judges were at work.

The discussions of the council of fifteen and the parliamentary twelve in February and March 1259 were long and sometimes acrimonious. The parliament seems to have met in the New Temple, for one of its pronouncements was published there in March. This dealt with the problem of suit of court and was later revised and included among the provisions of Westminster. Another series of decisions was more controversial. It related to the judicial investigation of grievances in the shires. Although formally issued on 28 March, it had been adopted on 22 February, on which day the earls of Leicester and Gloucester on behalf of the fifteen, two of the twelve on behalf of their colleagues, and two bishops as proctors of the clergy entered into an alliance for the service of the king and the government of the realm.[2] That a compact of this kind was necessary suggests that there had been some difference of opinion; and the combination of the two earls as spokesmen of the council is piquant in the light of the account given by Matthew Paris of a bitter dispute between them on the subject of the Provisions agreed to on the same day. This was the first rift between the leaders of the movement, the original confederates; and it was caused by a very important problem indeed.

[1] From the seventeenth-century abridgement by John Selden of the documents relating to the Provisions of Oxford and subsequent provisions in a manuscript, belonging to Sir Edward Coke, now lost. See H. G. Richardson and G. O. Sayles in the *Bulletin of the John Rylands Library*, July 1933, p. 33 of the off-print.

[2] Richardson and Sayles, op. cit., pp. 12, 33.

The Provisions under discussion were intended to meet serious difficulties which had faced the justiciar and judges when *querelae* or complaints against the bailiffs of baronial franchises were brought to their notice. Hugh Bigod had frequently been met by pleas of exemption based on existing charters and by legal arguments which he did not venture to determine and had referred to the council. Something had to be done to make it clear that the promises to the people of the shires covered grievances against all men, not only against the officers of the Crown. It was ominous, in the light of later disturbances, that the most violent outcry had come from the citizens of London, always so jealous of their liberties; but several great men had also been involved, including the Lord Edward and such prominent members of council as the archbishop of Canterbury, the earl of Gloucester, and Peter of Savoy. They had much to say for themselves, for there was a real danger lest their lawful franchises might be disregarded during the trial of the complaints, and that the normal procedure of the common law, especially in the protection of the free tenement, might be overlooked. Earl Richard of Clare, who afterwards gave active adhesion to the decisions reached in parliament, may well have called attention to possible injustice, and been too hastily attacked by the impulsive Earl Simon. We have no right to assume that Simon's indignation was justified or that Earl Richard was turning his back on his personal obligations. However this may be, the proclamation of 28 March, which was to be read aloud in every shire and hundred court throughout the land, was an unequivocal assertion by the barons of their duty to the community. It naturally insisted that their chartered and prescriptive liberties should be maintained and that suits which by common law required to be opened by appropriate writs should not be pleaded in any other way, but at the same time it admitted their obligation to submit themselves and their bailiffs to the new procedure in the investigation of complaints by knights of the shire and to their trial by the justiciar and other judges. It required every lord of a franchise to take an oath to do or to abstain from doing what the king was expected to do or not to do. It enacted that his bailiffs should take the new oath of office as the king's bailiffs did, in the shire court.

The Provisions read in Westminster Hall on St. Edward's day (13 October) 1259 and put under the solemn sanction of ecclesiastical penalties expressed in more legal form the decisions of the council in parliament on suit of court and the protection of subtenants in manorial and other courts. They dealt also with grievances, which the barons had expounded in their petition, arising out of recent tendencies in the interpretation of the common law of wardship, prise, the law of Englishry, and the like. One provision forbade monastic houses to acquire land without the consent of the lord of whom it was directly held. The general intention of this legislation was to stay sharp practice, abolish unnecessary attendance at courts, and prevent the abuse of distraint, that is to say, the occupation of lands and the seizure of goods by a lord in the course of legal proceedings —in short, to make everyday life easier for all kinds of freemen by protecting them in their free tenements and defining the limits of interference with their freedom. The Provisions did not include the recent promises of the barons, although several of the clauses met in detail the grievances which the sharp practice of their bailiffs had created. Reform of the law was one way to anticipate complaints. On the other hand, the suspicion of baronial good faith, conveyed in this time of parliament by the lesser men to the Lord Edward[1] and the baronial leaders, may have been stirred by the concentration in the Provisions on technical amendments of the common law. A subtenant who had listened to the public recital of the Provisions of Westminster might have wondered what had happened to the proclamation recently read in the shire and hundred courts, for this was *his* charter of liberty; and, as the future was to show, he might well have wondered. All the same, the Provisions of Westminster are of outstanding importance in English social history. They emphasized the subjection of the administration of justice in seignorial courts—the courts of civil jurisdiction best known to the great majority of Englishmen—to rules defined by the law of the land. This was a step towards the unity of England.

Whatever fears may have been felt about the good faith of the magnates may have been allayed by the remarkable administrative actions and injunctions which proceeded from the barons in the October parliament of 1259 and from the council during the next three or four months. A serious attempt was made to enforce reforms by linking members of council with

[1] Below, p. 153.

the judges, the officers of the exchequer, the sheriffs, and the knights. Two or three members of council were chosen to be in constant attendance upon the king between one parliament and the next. A financial committee, the justiciar, the treasurer, a king's clerk, and two judges, Roger of Thurkelby[1] and Henry of Bath, was appointed to inquire into the royal resources with a view to the establishment of a fund to be devoted to the payment of debts and the maintenance of the royal household. This body, with the barons of the exchequer, selected the sheriffs for the year 1259-60 from the vavassors of the shires, and it was decided to choose their successors annually at the exchequer from a group of four elected in a full shire court. The justiciar, Hugh Bigod, who was now in command and seems to have presided over the council of regency appointed to govern England during King Henry's absence in France,[2] summoned all the new sheriffs to come before him on 19 November, with four knights from each shire, to be instructed in their duties under the recent provisions. The four knights sent were probably those who had been elected to register complaints and conduct inquiries, for these were now regarded as permanent watchdogs on the sheriffs. In the same spirit, the barons of the exchequer, the justices at Westminster, and the justices on eyre for the trial of complaints were given baronial assessors. The appointment of judicial assessors made it easier to hasten the hearing of complaints against the bailiffs of the king and of his great tenants-in-chief and others by dividing the land into seven circuits, and to resume work in a systematic way on the morrow of Epiphany (7 January 1260). Sworn men in each hundred were given the

[1] Robert Carpenter, who compiled an important collection of legislative and other material relating to this period, was probably a clerk of Roger Thurkelby, and owed his knowledge of the texts to this connexion; N. Denholm-Young in *E.H.R.* (1935), 22-35; reprinted in his *Collected Papers on Mediaeval Subjects* (1946), pp. 96-110.

[2] The other regents were Archbishop Boniface, the bishop of Worcester, Roger Bigod (the marshal and earl of Norfolk), the earl of Warwick, Roger Mortimer, and Philip Basset. The first five were members of the council of fifteen, Philip Basset was one of the parliamentary twelve. Philip, who now came to the front, was the younger brother of Gilbert Basset and Fulk, bishop of London, and had recently, after the latter's death in May 1259, succeeded to his father's honour of Wycombe. He had joined Gilbert in 1233-4 (above, p. 53) and acted for the barons at Lyons in 1245 (below, p. 499). He had stood by Edward in March 1259 (below, p. 153) and, during the crisis of 1260, was one of the three men—the others being the justiciar and the earl of Gloucester—upon whom the king especially relied. Henceforward he was probably the most steadfast and sanest friend the king had among the barons. He died in 1270.

instructions or 'heads of the inquiry', and were ordered to make their returns to the justices by this day, when also every man who had acted as a royal or baronial bailiff during the last seven years was to appear before the justices. Moreover the justices were to have with them the returns to the great inquiry into royal rights and alienations of demesne made in 1255, so that they might bring them up to date and provide material for the central committee on finance.

Nothing could be more thorough, coherent, and sensible than this activity. Unhappily it lacked driving power. It lost impetus and came to an end, part of it soon, part of it gradually, in the reaction of the next three years. This reaction began even before the king's return from France on 23 April 1260. Reaction was inevitable, if only because nobody at court and in the community of the barons could shed his habitual interests, prejudices, loyalties, and aversions; but the immediate cause of disunion was Simon de Montfort, the man who afterwards tried to revive the ardours of the Oxford movement. To appreciate this, we must glance at certain tendencies in feudal society at this time.

Hugh Bigod was praised because he refused to be moved from the course of justice by pressure from powerful persons. One of the promises made by the barons in March 1259 was that they would not give protection in the courts to men who were not their own; that is to say, they would confine the right and duty to stand by their tenants and those of their household to these and to these alone. And the judges on eyre in 1260 were required to investigate cases since Candlemas 1259 of the reception by any magnate or other person, in return for a gift or rent, of anyone who was not his man, to be under his protection against the king or his neighbour or anybody else. This evidence refers to a tendency, always at work in a feudal society, which had engrafted military tenure on the primitive 'family' with its traditions of corporate self-help and protection and the duty of a man to maintain those in his 'mainpast'[1]—the desire of a lord to

---

[1] A Lincoln case of 1220 puts this point very neatly. Robert de Waville appealed a man for the murder of his (Robert's) lord, William de Tillebroc. Robert said that he was present and saw the crime 'et fuit homo suus de manibus suis et nepos suus et de manupasto suo' (*Curia Regis Rolls*, viii. 381). In a Cornish case of 1214 two men appealed Baldwin Tyrell because he had spoken of the king as having been killed in Wales. 'Illi fuerunt de privata familia domini regis, jurati quod, si illi aliquid audirent quod fuisset contra dominum regem, domino regi illud intimarent' (vii. 170).

seek and give more aid by increasing the number of his adherents. As the cohesion of the lordship was broken, and money became more plentiful, the formation of these associations naturally became more common, especially in times of political strain and disturbance. Richard of Clare, for example, had in his service a large number of 'bachelors', who were closely attached to him but did not necessarily hold lands of him. A well-known knight of Gloucestershire, who at the battle of Lewes fought as an adherent of Simon de Montfort and afterwards was accused of malpractices by the new government, attached himself to the household of Earl Richard's son and successor, Earl Gilbert. The practice became a disease in later times, when it was systematized as 'livery and maintenance'. A closely related practice was the formation of a group of friends and supporters who would stand by each other and, as a group, oppose or make peace with a hostile group.[1] The Lord Edward may be said to have entered political life in this way in 1259 as a consenting party to the Provisions of Oxford. Edward, as a marcher lord in south Wales, was always liable to be embroiled with his neighbours. He had grounds for complaint against the earl of Gloucester, whom he seems to have disliked. He quarrelled with him. Occasion was taken at the parliament in the spring of 1259 to bring the two together in a way which might fully re-establish Edward's enjoyment of his rights and dignities on each side of the Channel. Earl Richard, who was supported by ten important barons as friends and allies, including the earl of Norfolk and his brother Hugh Bigod, undertook to maintain Edward against all men with aid and counsel, and, in particular, to do his utmost to put Edward in possession of his lands and castles. The most interesting part of this agreement—for it was a compact, not a one-sided promise—is the mutual guarantee. Earl Richard had his friends and allies, Edward had his. The two groups swore to aid and maintain each other, doing right. Henry of Almain and the justiciar were appointed as arbitrators in cases of dispute. If peaceful means failed, the aggrieved party had the right, with all his power and effort, to force the other (*justiser*) and distrain him to fulfil his promises, saving the common oath sworn at Oxford to the king and the community.[2]

---

[1] Cf. above, p. 86.
[2] *Hist. MSS. Commission, Report on the Manuscripts of Lord Middleton* (1911), pp. 67-69. Edward's letters of adhesion have not survived.

It is well worth while to look at the names of the 'friends and allies' whom the Lord Edward had gathered about him by this time, 14 March 1259. One of them, Philip Basset, was one of the parliamentary twelve, and another was Robert Walerand, a highly trusted and intimate servant of the king. Both were to take leading parts in the future conflicts. Most of the rest were men nearer to Edward in age—his cousin Henry of Almain, John de Warenne, earl of Surrey, Baldwin de l'Isle, Stephen Longspée, Roger Clifford, Roger Leyburn, John de Vaux, Warin of Bassingburn, Hamo l'Estrange, William la Zuche. In course of time this domestic following suffered changes, but it was the nucleus of the party which led Edward to victory and to the throne, just as his companions on crusade became the core of his strength in the later conquest of Wales. Domestic ties, sworn alliances, tried associations, such as spring from personal rather than political likings, from local rather than national ambitions, are always at work. They maintain the enduring passions. That they did not degenerate in England into blind and factious partisanship was due to four things: the long discipline in what has been called 'self-government by the king's command', for this had given stability and some degree of independence to the knights and other freemen; the widely diffused regard for the common law and for responsible rule; the restraining and, at times, the guiding influence of the Church; and the personality of the Lord Edward. Edward was a wiser man than his father, and he was also a fine soldier, with a passion for tournaments and the chase. He attracted men and knew how to use them. Hence, in his years of maturity, he was able to turn what might have been a curse into a blessing, to build up a state which was directed by, though it might not be based upon, 'friends and allies', chosen, not from a clique, but from the whole community of the realm. He revealed his quickness of perception in the October parliament of 1259, when he replied with sympathetic promises of help to what the Burton annalist describes as the 'community of bachelors', a group of men who had expressed lively fears that the barons did not intend to fulfil their undertakings to their subtenants. The annalist probably picked up the unusual phrase from a Westminster source, but who exactly the bachelors were and from what districts they came is not stated. Most of them probably were knights or other local gentry who were in Westminster in the time of parliament. Some of them may have come in the company of magnates as their bachelors, some on business of their own shires. Others, however, may well have been young men, bachelors in the sense in which Edward himself was a bachelor, as still only his father's son.[1]

More significant at the time was an understanding reached at Westminster on 15 October between Edward, with whom his friends Henry of Almain, John de Warenne, and Roger Leyburn were associated, and Simon de Montfort. Edward swore to give Earl Simon and his heirs aid and counsel against all men, saving their fealty due to the king, to uphold the barons' enterprise to the honour of God, the profit of the king and his heirs and of the kingdom, and not to make war upon any of the confederates.[2] The earl had spent most of the year in France and he returned to the continent immediately after this agreement had been made. His immediate objects, in coming to an understanding with Edward, may have been to strengthen his position at Paris, where the king came a month later to do homage to King Louis,[3] and to bind the restless prince more closely to the 'common enterprise', as he liked to call it; but he soon gave his new alliance a more sinister turn.

No episode in these years is more important, and at the same time more difficult to see in its true perspective. The annalists are meagre and confused. Fortunately, the letters written from France by King Henry are unusually intimate, and a document happily preserved among the archives of the Montfort family in France contains his later charges against Earl Simon. To dismiss this evidence as worthless, one-sided though it is, would be most misleading. Before his departure from England Henry had noticed signs of disunion, and in one of his letters from France he states that the temporary withdrawal of himself and of certain other persons would, he had hoped, extinguish 'the sparks of dissension'. Since he had with him, in addition to John Mansel, three other members of the council, the earl of Gloucester, Peter

---

[1] In the later *Quo Warranto Rolls* King Edward is sometimes described as having been 'commonly called the Lord Edward' during his father's lifetime; but at least twice, in refering to those early years, as a bachelor; e.g. 'dum fuit bachelarius fuit in seisina' (p. 682, cf. 366). I owe this note to the kindness of Mr. Stanley Cohn.

[2] Summarized from the unprinted text or transcript by Bémont, *Simon de Montfort* (Eng. trans.), p. 173 and note. The phrase quoted by Bémont, beginning 'al cuor de Dieu', should obviously read 'al honur de Deu' as in the royal proclamation of October 1258 and the oath of the twenty-four.

[3] Above, p. 126.

of Savoy, and the count of Aumale, and since Earl Simon was already in France, it is reasonable to suppose that he was referring especially to the earl of Gloucester and the ill feeling between him, the Lord Edward, and Earl Simon. Edward's relations with Richard of Clare had not improved, in spite of the compact of March 1259, and as he drew nearer to Earl Simon, his father the king placed increasing confidence in Richard of Clare.

The sparks of dissension were fanned into a flaming fire after Earl Simon's return to England at the end of January 1260. The king delayed his own return, partly because he wished to see a troublesome arbitration about the sum owing to him from Louis under the recent treaty brought to a conclusion, partly because in February he had a bad attack of his annual complaint, a tertian fever, which kept him at St. Omer on his return journey. His absence was disastrous. Llywelyn broke the truce with the king and began a war in Wales. He decided to break down the English barrier to the south, west of the upper Wye, where the Lord Edward held the honour and castle of Builth, with Roger Mortimer of Wigmore, the most powerful of the Marcher lords, as his castellan. Early in January the prince of Wales seized the district, laid siege to the castle, and, without waiting for it to fall, raided south Wales. When the news reached Henry, he wrote on 26 January[1] to the justiciar ordering him to put off the Candlemas parliament indefinitely and to take measures with the council for the relief of the castle and the protection of the Marches. He added that no parliament should meet until his return, which at that time he expected to be not long delayed. This was the position of affairs when Earl Simon returned and rejoined the council. He at once called in question the right of the king to order the suspension of the provision that one of the three annual parliaments must be held on 2 February. Everybody of course had expected that the king would be back in time. The possibility that he might insist on being present, or that the barons might insist on holding parliament in his absence, had not been considered.

The justiciar and his colleagues were in a real difficulty. The relief of Builth became a matter of secondary importance. The justiciar tried to evade the issue by marking time. He postponed

[1] *Close Rolls*, *1259–61*, pp. 267–8; also in *Royal Letters*, ii. 149–50. Internal evidence shows that the date is 26 January, not the 16th.

the parliament week by week in the hope that Henry would return. At this point the Lord Edward began to cause his father anxiety. Disturbing news reached St. Omer. At first Henry was comforted. The bishops of Salisbury and Coventry brought news from the council that the realm 'enjoyed full tranquillity and peace', and Edward sent the royal confessor John of Darlington to allay the king's alarm. Henry, on 1 March, expressed his satisfaction and pressed upon the council his need for money. In a short letter to Edward he said that, while he was delighted by what the confessor had told him, he proposed to send one of his intimates to England 'to see if deeds corresponded to words'.[1] Hardly had the bishops left him when he got news from the earl of Norfolk and other magnates which renewed all his fears. What he was told can only be surmised from later events and from later charges against Earl Simon; probably that the earl was taking a strong line in council, did not wish to send money, was seeking to remove Peter of Savoy, once his close ally, from the council—why, we cannot tell.[2] Henry was certainly informed that a body of armed men with horses was expected to land in Sandwich without royal licence. What had Edward and his dreadful companion in mind to do? During his slow convalescence the king's suspicions must have reached fever heat. Was his son going to betray him and make a bid for the crown? Some people, as we know from the chronicler Wykes, were saying this.

At last on 27 March Henry decided to act, perhaps on advice from home. He sent an order, too secret to be enrolled, to the justiciar. He enclosed a long list of names, of three bishops, two abbots, eight earls, and ninety-nine barons who were all to be summoned, with the service—that is, with the armed following —which they owed to him, to appear in London on 25 April. Henry is said to have been able to remember the names of his barons, and may well have dictated them himself. He omitted the name of Earl Simon.[3] The justiciar received the king's order

[1] *Close Rolls, 1259-61*, pp. 276-7. The count of Aumale had already gone home to the north of England with letters of credence addressed to the principal men in the north (p. 275). The earl of Gloucester returned, probably early in March. He was in correspondence with the king between the end of March and Henry's return a month later. Peter of Savoy also went back.

[2] Relations between Earl Simon and Peter may have become strained after the attempt of the arbitrators (of whom Peter was one) to settle the question of the Countess Eleanor's dower had failed in the previous summer.

[3] This story is revealed by a memorandum entered with the list of names, on the roll of letters close issued from the chancery in England (*Close Rolls, 1259-61*, pp.

at Windsor five days later, on 31 March, the Wednesday before
Easter. The seal used during the king's absence was in the keeping of the king's clerk, Walter de Merton, who was with the
chancery at his manor of Malden in Surrey. Walter got the
justiciar's orders early on Thursday. The chancery clerks worked
on the writs all day. Nothing was done on Good Friday, but on
the Saturday 'immediately after mass and breakfast' the royal
messengers were dispatched. 'Because of the shortness of the
time' the writs were distributed to the sheriffs, who were to send
them on by diverse messengers to their destinations. The schedule
on which the names were written was kept 'in as secret a place
as possible'.

Henry was now well again and according to his letters anxious to return. It cannot have been a coincidence that King
Louis had arrived at St. Omer on a week-end visit to him on the
day during which he sent his mandate to the justiciar. Louis left
him in no doubt that his duty lay at home, and Henry pressed
the justiciar, Richard of Clare, and Philip Basset, the three men
upon whom he especially relied in this crisis, for a report on the
position. With Louis's approval he was collecting a strong body
of hired knights under the lords by the French coast, the count
of St. Pol and others who, as in his father's time and during the
disturbances of 1233, were willing to provide troops. They would
not sail, however, without him. On the other hand, Henry was
waiting for money from England in order to pay his debts and
redeem the crown jewels which he had pawned, and also for an
instalment from King Louis. He was apparently advised to wait.
In the meanwhile he learned that Edward and Earl Simon intended to hold a parliament or *colloquium* in London, and to
take up their quarters in the city while they parleyed with the
earl of Gloucester. He heard also that his brothers of Lusignan
were on the move and were planning to sail from the Breton
coast to the west country with the viscount of Limoges, who
wished to pursue his old claims in that part of England.[1] Earl
Simon, also, was said to have sent for foreign troops from his
friends in France. Edward's friend Roger Leyburn was busy
fortifying his castle in Kent. If all these rumours were true, and
especially if stories about his son Edward were true, England was

157–9). This record was kept concurrently with the rolls of letters issued under the
great seal which the king had with him in France.
    [1] Cf. above, p. 5.

on the eve of a civil war. Henry and the regents took prompt
measures. On 10 April the king ordered the justiciar and
the citizens of London to bar the city against Edward and
other suspect persons. On the following day he wrote to the two
archbishops, the citizens of London and York, and the barons of
the Cinque Ports. In these notable letters he reviewed the whole
situation. Mentioning nobody by name, he recalled the days of
his boyhood when he was mercifully rescued in a time of general
war. Now, again, the kingdom was unreasonably disturbed.
Against his command, armed men were endangering the land
and especially London. They proposed to hold a colloquy in the
city. Their intentions as individuals might be good, but this way
of proceeding would lead not to peace but to the sword. The
sparks of dissension which he had observed before he left threatened to burst into flame. These men were said to have sent for
armed men from abroad. The fire must be stayed. He proposed
to bring an armed force with him to aid in the restoration of
tranquillity. He bade them be steadfast and loyal and confident,
and until he arrived to obey the justiciar as they would obey
himself.[1]

How far Henry's excitement was justified it is hard to say.
Looking back on this time, Thomas Wykes attributed it to the
false rumour that Edward planned to usurp the throne. The
king, he says, was afraid to return until his brother Richard of
Cornwall had sent him letters of assurance sealed with the seals
of Edward and the magnates. This is probably too facile an
impression of the crisis. Strong measures had been taken. The
barons had been summoned secretly to London. The justiciar,
the earl of Gloucester, and Philip Basset had combined to close
the city to Edward and his allies. The king of France and the
duke of Brittany had been warned and urged to prevent the
departure of the king's brothers and others from the Continent.
The archers of the Weald had been rallied to meet the king
when he arrived with his mercenaries. In the face of this demonstration Edward must have paused, however serious his intentions might have been. When his father reached London he
hastened to make his peace with him. At first Henry refused to
see him. He loved him too much, he said, and could not but
embrace him; but he could not give him a free hand in England
after what had occurred. The solace of domestic life meant much

[1] *Close Rolls, 1259–61*, pp. 253-4.

to Henry. Only four months earlier he had told the pope that quite apart from the general determination that his brother, the bishop-elect of Winchester, should not be allowed to return, he himself could not run the risk of the domestic strife which Aymer caused. He had alienated the queen from her husband, and made Edward rebellious against his father.[1] And now, it was suspected, Edward had intrigued with his uncles of Lusignan and perhaps brought them into his unruly alliance with Earl Simon, the man whom Henry most feared. Edward's quarrels with the earl of Gloucester had helped to create discord in England. The young man, it was decided, should leave England for a time. Bristol castle, the seat of his administration, was entrusted to Philip Basset. He himself stayed to take part in the festivities of St. Edward's day (13 October) at Westminster, when the king knighted his new son-in-law, John of Brittany,[2] and eighty other young men, and Edward himself knighted Earl Simon's sons, Henry and Simon. Then he left England with some of the new knights to engage on a jousting tour and after that to settle down in Gascony.

---

[1] Ibid., pp. 264–5 (Saint-Denis, 18 January 1260). It should be remembered that the opposition to the Poitevin relatives of the king was general and at this time transcended any party feeling. In the previous summer, when a papal nuncio, who had been irregularly permitted to land in England, threatened the kingdom with an interdict and the king with excommunication if the bishop-elect were not allowed to return, the prelates, earls, and barons had combined against the papal wishes. Incidentally the royal letters of September 1259 in which this is stated show that a full parliament must have met, probably in June 1259, and that the Provisions of Oxford did not preclude such assemblies (*Close Rolls, 1256–59*, pp. 490–2; and see Treharne, *Baronial Plan of Reform*, pp. 143–4).

[2] John was the son of John the Red, duke of Brittany (d. 1286) and grandson of Peter of Dreux (cf. above, pp. 96–97). Henry and the duke had taken the occasion of the peace with France to settle the duke's claims to the earldom and honour of Richmond on the basis of a family alliance. The duke was to receive Richmond, surrender his claims in the Agenais, and marry his son John to Henry's daughter Beatrice. The marriage took place at Saint-Denis on 22 January 1260. On 9 March Henry, writing from St. Omer, invited the duke to be present at the knighting of his son on St. Edward's day, 'the feast which we have in special veneration among the solemn days of the year'. The transference of Richmond from Peter of Savoy (to whom Henry had given the honour some twenty years earlier) was not immediately effected, for at first, instead of compensating Peter of Savoy, a financial equivalent was granted to the duke (cf. *Cal. Pat. Rolls, 1258–66*, pp. 82, 160, 161). The duke received it in 1268 and transferred it to his son. Peter of Savoy, who died in Savoy in this year, had in 1262 bequeathed with the king's consent the honour and other lands in England to the queen, and her rights to compensation caused some difficulty for a few years longer. The young John became one of Edward's closest friends and allies and continued to be so until he succeeded to his dukedom in 1286. See below, p. 235.

A London chronicler, usually well informed, says that the lead in the prevention of disturbances in London had been taken by Richard of Cornwall,[1] and, as we have seen, Thomas Wykes thought that Richard had been active in smoothing the way for the king's return. The fact that the king of the Romans is not mentioned in the official correspondence about these events does not deprive the stories of credence, for officially Richard was outside the baronial administration. He had not been in England at all during 1258, and when he did return (27 January 1259 to 18 June 1260) he kept himself in the background. The council had insisted, as a condition of his landing, that he should take the oath to respect the Provisions and, to the disgust of his German entourage, had not allowed his royal dignity to give him new weight or prominence as an English earl. He very wisely bided his time, and whatever influence he may have had was exercised behind the scenes. He seems to have withdrawn to Cornwall with his German chancery and his baronial household. His intervention, however, during the crisis of March and April 1260 may well have been important. It would certainly have made an impression on the Lord Edward. Henceforward, with the exception of two brief periods, one between 18 June and 24 October 1260, the other between 21 June 1262 and 10 February 1263, he lived in England and, until open civil war began, was at hand as the sagacious brother, always ready to emerge from Berkhamsted or Wallingford or Beckley or wherever he might be.[2] It was a useful but modest part for a successor of Charlemagne and Frederick Barbarossa.

Henry could not crush the man who in his eyes had been the villain of the piece. He had planned to bring Earl Simon to trial in parliament on 8 July, but powerful influences averted this scandal. A great man reached England on 4 July. This was the

[1] Arnold fitzThedmar, *Chronica majorum et vicecomitum Londoniarum* (in the *Liber de antiquis legibus*, Camden Society, 1846), p. 44. The chronicler appears to confuse the military gathering summoned for 25 April with the *colloquium* which it was designed to frustrate; and he regards Edward and Richard of Clare, then at enmity, as the parties which summoned it. It is possible that Edward and Earl Simon hoped to come to an arrangement with Richard of Clare. Richard of Cornwall is said to have reached Westminster on 11 April. Henry is known to have written two letters to his brother from France. One was a copy of his letter of 26 January (above, p. 155) forbidding a meeting of parliament before his return; the other was to warn him against a landing in Cornwall by his half-brothers and the viscount of Limoges.

[2] Richard's fourth and last visit to Germany was not made until 1268, after the settlement of English affairs. It lasted from 4 August 1268 to 3 August 1269.

Franciscan, Odo Rigaud, archbishop of Rouen, a trusted counsellor of King Louis and a close friend of Simon. The archbishop
had done as much as any man to bring about the treaty of Paris,
and now he arrived, as he says in his own journal, 'on the business of the King of France'. King Louis obviously felt, as Richard
of Cornwall is known to have felt, that peace in England depended upon a good understanding between Henry and his
brother-in-law the earl. He respected Simon and could not forget that he was the most distinguished man in one of the chief
families of the Île de France. So Simon was brought to ask and
King Henry to agree that an episcopal inquiry should precede
any formal trial in the king's council in parliament. Archbishop
Boniface and five of his suffragans should first investigate the
charges against the earl. The council, enlarged by some of the
earl's peers, should then decide, on the evidence of the bishops'
report, if he had done anything which required that amends
should be made. The procedure prevented such unseemly scenes
before the king as had disgraced the trial on the Gascon charges
eight years before. It also extricated Simon's colleagues on the
council from an embarrassing position, for the earl could and
did put up a good defence. He denied every personal charge and
insisted that everything he had said in council was privileged,
in the sense that he had been doing his duty towards the 'common enterprise' as a member of the body which was its instrument. The proceedings were allowed to drop. Unity was restored.
All parties combined in preparations for a campaign against
Llywelyn of Wales. Richard of Clare was chosen to lead one
army from Shrewsbury, Simon de Montfort to lead another
from Chester. Before the armies could start the Welsh truce was
renewed on 22 August at the ford of Montgomery. So peace was
restored. Henry celebrated St. Edward's day in an atmosphere
which seemed to breathe harmony and general goodwill.

   The reality was very different. Earl Simon had broken the
community of the barons. The king had got his way. He now
knew that there were some things which his council would not
do. He had dared, with King Louis's encouragement and the
connivance of the justiciar and the earl of Gloucester and Philip
Basset, to bring foreign knights into the country. He had been
respected as a responsible party to the new order, not humiliated
as its creature. Only the oath stood in the way of its gradual dissolution, that oath with the dreadful clause which made every

opponent of the Provisions a common enemy. As Thomas Wykes says, this clause was the root of the whole trouble, for without it some adjustment might have been reached. The king, as he gained confidence, became determined to extricate himself from the restraints in which he was held. In his view, he ought to be freed from them, for the condition on which he had agreed— the pursuit of the Sicilian business—had not been met. He sought papal absolution from the oath. In the meanwhile he took advantage of the irresolution and cross-currents which had weakened baronial unity. During the crisis the judicial inquiries into which the justiciar had thrown so much energy had been arrested. They were allowed to lapse and a general eyre of the usual kind took their place. They had aroused too many diffi- culties. The new rule that sheriffs should be appointed from a panel of four local men, elected in the shire courts, was circum- vented by the temporary reappointment of the existing sheriffs. The justiciar, who might have stayed the process of dissolution, was either disillusioned by events in the spring or unwilling to resist. He did not seek re-election. The chancellor, Henry of Wingham, now bishop of London, also ceased to hold office. So did the treasurer. Their successors were chosen by five baronial electors. The new justiciar, Hugh le Despenser, and the new chancellor, Nicholas of Ely, were partisans of the Provisions, but they were not men of the calibre of Hugh Bigod and Henry of Wingham. The new treasurer was the abbot of Peterborough. King Henry was irked rather than led by his attendant coun- cillors and ministers. He moved more freely, had more control of his correspondence, could give more scope to his intimates, especially the able clerk John Mansel and his new baronial ally Philip Basset. Without repudiating the Provisions, he could openly regard them as an incubus which he hoped in due time to shake off. Such was the condition of affairs by the spring of 1261, three years after his surrender to the confederates. The change in Henry's position can be measured by the fact that William of Valence was allowed to return to England in the end of March.[1] The king no longer feared embarrassment from the presence of a brother who could add to his strength.

Henry moved quickly in the spring and summer of 1261. On

---

[1] The more troublesome Aymer had died in December 1260, a few months after his consecration as bishop by the pope. Guy and Geoffrey and other Poitevins returned rather later than William.

13 March he issued a proclamation to the shires against his detractors. About the same time he presented a precise and detailed statement to the barons of his objections to the provisions and allowed his case to be submitted to arbitration. He attacked the whole plan, demanded his freedom, and deplored the misgovernment which had resulted from the new order, especially in the shires, so foolishly entrusted to local men who were not fit for their high duties. The barons, in their reply, took the ground that their reforms were in the common interest and, if there had been any failure, it was due to the lack of vigorous and whole-hearted co-operation by the king and his friends. The discussion lost substance when John Mansel, who had been busy at the papal court, arrived in England at the end of May with a bull, dated 14 April, in which Pope Alexander absolved the king from his oath to maintain the Provisions.[1] Henry must have anticipated his release, for during May he had again brought mercenaries into England, established himself in the Tower of London, which was nominally held by the justiciar, Hugh le Despenser, taken Dover and the Cinque Ports out of the control of Hugh Bigod, and summoned the men of Kent, Sussex, and Hampshire to renew their oaths of fealty. On Mansel's arrival he was entrusted with the Tower, while the king took up his quarters and collected his foreign troops at Winchester. Here, at the Whitsun feast (12 June), the papal bull seems to have been proclaimed. Henry then returned to the Tower of London. On or soon after 29 June he wrote to Llywelyn of Wales that he was at last free to discuss terms of peace with him. He had, he wrote, been released from the oath 'by which he had been bound to the leading men of the realm to use their counsel, and had resumed the royal power'.[2] Hugh le Despenser was deprived of his high office about the same time.[3]

Safe in the Tower, with foreign troops to guard him and the faithful Robert Walerand in charge of Kent, Dover, and the Cinque Ports, Henry could now go ahead. He could rely on

[1] The date of Mansel's return is not certain, but if, as would seem to be probable, he brought the papal bull with him, he is unlikely to have reached England from Rome, where the pope was, before the latter part of May.

[2] *Close Rolls, 1259–61*, p. 482. The date on or just before which this letter was written is mentioned in the last sentence of the text. The formal dating clause was not copied on the roll.

[3] Op. cit., p. 402, a writ of 20 June. It is implied in this writ that Hugh was no longer justiciar.

the support of many of the barons, though his recent action and especially his extrication from his oath had brought together the old leaders—the bishop of Worcester, the earls of Leicester and Gloucester, the earl marshal and his brother Hugh Bigod, and also Edward's former companion and future ally the Earl Warenne. Edward himself, who was in England throughout May and June, is said by the St. Albans chronicler to have at first insisted on adhering to the Provisions and even to have joined in a sworn compact against the king's new advisers. If Edward did anything to give rise to this story, his opposition to his father was short-lived, for the record evidence suggests that he was on good terms with Henry. His unobtrusive return to Gascony early in July removed him from the dangerous scene. Earl Simon and his colleagues were in any case anxious for a settlement. They sought to combine the dispute about the Provisions with Simon's more personal grievances in a common plan of arbitration. On 5 July the claims of the earl and countess of Leicester were submitted to four persons, Philip Basset and John Mansel on the king's behalf, the bishop of Worcester and Peter de Montfort on theirs, and the parties also accepted as mediators two Frenchmen, the duke of Burgundy and Peter the chamberlain, who had been sent by King Louis 'touching the matter between the king and his barons, and especially Simon and Eleanor'. From letters written by the bishop of Worcester and the five magnates already mentioned to King Louis on 18 July, we learn that the wider questions at issue between Henry and his barons were also referred to this body, with the king of France as final judge. They besought him to act or induce his envoys to act to prevent irreparable harm. The two Frenchmen had refused to engage upon so difficult a duty. King Henry took an independent course. On 20 July he referred the disputes with Simon and Eleanor to the queen of France.[1] By this time he felt strong enough to deal with the larger problem himself; for between 5 July and the middle of the month he had made a clean sweep of the baronial administration. He dismissed the baronial sheriffs and appointed others, mainly of high rank, to serve during the royal pleasure. He gave to the new sheriffs the custody of royal castles. He politely dismissed the baronial

---

[1] The narrative is deduced from entries in *Cal. Pat. Rolls, 1258–66*, pp. 162, 169, and the barons' letters to King Louis printed in Bémont, *Simon de Montfort* (French edition), pp. 331–2.

chancellor, who on 14 July handed over the great seal to Walter de Merton. A month later, 'for his own preservation, the tranquillity of the realm and for showing justice to all', he made Philip Basset justiciar, with the right to enter the royal castles and to use them as prisons for disturbers of the peace.[1]

The announcement of Philip Basset's appointment and powers was due to the fact that the dismissal of the sheriffs and resumption of his castles had cleared the minds of the opposition and brought the country to the brink of civil war. Even the conscientious waverer, Hugh Bigod, was led to resist. He, with Richard of Clare, had withstood the Lord Edward and Earl Simon in the previous year; he had obeyed Henry's command to give up Dover, the key to England, in the previous May; but now he refused to surrender the castles of Scarborough and Pickering in Yorkshire. On 7 May, in one of his last acts, Pope Alexander had addressed a bull to the archbishop of Canterbury, the bishop of Norwich, and John Mansel designed to secure the effect of a previous bull in which he had released from their oath all who had sworn to maintain the provisions. Anybody who adhered to the plan which, under the pretext of reform, had deprived the king of his full authority was to incur the penalties of excommunication and interdict. This action had broken down every barrier. It was too much. When the abbot of St. Mary's at York, by command of the archbishop, cited Hugh to obey or suffer the consequences, he replied that he had received the castles on oath from the king and his magnates, and to them, and them alone, would he return them.[2] So issue was joined on the oath, and though Hugh Bigod fell away, Earl Simon was later to fight and die for it. In 1261, however, the desire for peace was too strong to allow the crisis to drift into war. Henry could assert with much truth that the community was on his side, that, in possession of the Tower, Dover, and most of his castles, he could face with confidence a few malignants.[3] On 16 August he issued a stirring proclamation to his faithful men throughout the shires. He referred to his folk

[1] *Cal. Pat. Rolls, 1258–66*, p. 172.
[2] The bull is printed in *Foedera*, I. i. 406, the archbishop's injunction and the abbot's report (30 August) on pp. 408, 409.
[3] From an undated letter to the pope, a draft of which is inserted as a schedule in the Close Roll; see *Close Rolls, 1259–61*, pp. 481–2. The letter is mainly concerned to protest against the decrees of the provincial council held by the archbishop in May.

(*populus noster*), whom evil-minded men were seeking to alienate by their lies. He recalled his long and prosperous reign, how justice had been done to all, how all had enjoyed their rights and goods in peace. He had, it was true, been compelled to bring in foreign mercenaries, but he had done this, on the counsel of some of his magnates, in the previous year,[1] and the same good results would follow. Then the king turned to the bad effects of the recent experiment. He defended the appointment of powerful sheriffs. His sole object was the well-being of his people.[2]

Henry had, indeed, again brought in mercenaries from across the Channel, for Earl Simon and his colleagues had been busy in the southern shires and were believed to be trying to find armed aid from the continent themselves. Moreover, they had succeeded in replacing the royal sheriffs in many shires, from Yorkshire to Kent, by their own wardens of the shires, local knights. They summoned a meeting of three knights from each shire to treat with them at St. Albans on 21 September. Henry, or, perhaps we should say, Philip Basset, countered these moves by ordering the sheriffs to send the knights to Windsor on the same day, when the king would discuss terms of peace with the insurgent barons. He also called for more armed aid from France and Gascony and on 18 October summoned about 150 of his tenants-in-chief to appear in London eleven days later with their service of armed knights. As in the previous year, so now, Henry felt that he could rely upon the general obedience. He was justified. At the end of October a long conference began in Kingston between the two parties. A compromise was reached about the sheriffs. The dissidents were divided. Most of them, including Hugh Bigod and, after some difficulty, Richard of Clare, made their peace. Henry ratified the terms of agreement in December and declared an amnesty for all who abode by them. Earl Simon took no part. He felt that he had been deserted and left England in anger.

The compromise was in fact a surrender skilfully prepared under the guidance of the bishops and Richard of Cornwall. The continuance in office of two sets of local officials, of a dual

---

[1] Above, p. 157. The mercenaries had been sent home again, as also were those brought over in May 1261. Henry seems to be referring to contingents which came in August. Others were arranged for in October.

[2] *Foedera*, I. i. 408–9, from the Patent Roll. This interesting manifesto must have been read in English, but no English version has survived.

administration, was obviously impossible; but, until agreement was reached about the appointment of sheriffs, any shire which wished to do so was allowed, in accordance with the method devised by Hugh Bigod and the council at the end of 1259, to elect four knights from whom the king, through the exchequer, should select one as sheriff on 7 January 1262. A board of six arbitrators, three from each side, was to decide how future sheriffs should be appointed, and failing agreement the decision was to be left to Richard of Cornwall. Needless to say the arbitrators did not agree, and Richard decided in favour of the old method of royal appointment. His verdict was given on 20 May 1262, shortly before he left England on his third visit to his neglected kingdom. The most interesting feature in these negotiations is the nature of the baronial arbitrators. Three knights, two of whom were wardens of shires, one of Kent, Surrey, and Sussex, the other of Derby and Nottingham, were selected to meet the justiciar, the chancellor, and the redoubtable Robert Walerand. The baronial supporters of the provisions were doubtless glad to make knights responsible for the defence of their actions, but the fact remains that knights of sufficient standing were ready to maintain the interests of the country gentry in the management of local affairs. The existence of slowly maturing movements is revealed in times of crisis; and in this controversy we see a king appealing to his people against the local leaders whose descendants were to give direction to the people in a national life.

Henry had based his action upon, and, in large measure, owed his success to, the papal bulls. His agents were especially busy at the papal court in these years. As early as March 1261 Edmund had revived his claim to the crown of Sicily. In May the king had been much annoyed by the outspoken and far-reaching decrees of a provincial church council which had originally been summoned to discuss with a papal nuncio the danger from the Tartars,[1] and he had sent proctors to protest against them at Rome. But he had especially been concerned

---

[1] What is known as the Tartar crusade, which carried them to Damascus in 1260, had aroused alarm which can now be seen to have been exaggerated. The short-sighted alliance against them of the Latin princes in Syria with the Mamlūks of Egypt, the alliance so deplored by the Armenians, led to the downfall of the kingdom of Jerusalem thirty years later. For the time being, however, the Tartars were regarded as the chief enemies of Christendom, and Pope Alexander wrote for aid and counsel to the princes and metropolitans of the west.

to be released from his oath to maintain the Provisions of the barons. At the height of his success he heard that Alexander IV had died on 25 May 1261. The news did not divert him from his course, but must have embarrassed him and also encouraged Earl Simon and his friends to renew their efforts, through their own agents at Rome, to save the Provisions and prevent the confirmation of the late pope's action by his successor. The letters of one of Henry's agents at the papal court show that the barons were by no means without influence in papal circles and that he and his colleagues had hard work to repeat John Mansel's success. The new pope, Urban IV, a Frenchman, was elected on 20 August, but it was not until 25 February 1262 that he issued his bull in Henry's favour. Pope Urban, all the more perhaps because he had no intention to have anything more to do with Edmund's claims to Sicily, was to show himself a strong supporter of Henry's royal rights within his own kingdom and to co-operate on his behalf with Louis of France; but, unless Earl Simon was greatly deceived, Urban's decision was not reached without hesitation. Indeed, Simon maintained that the bull was not genuine and, on one of his rapid flights to and from England, embarrassed the council by the production of another document which decided the question in favour of the barons.[1] Henry, however, had his bull. On 2 May 1262 he addressed letters to all the sheriffs on the subject. The charters of liberties were to be enforced, but the ordinances and statutes annulled by the pope were to be publicly denounced. Every opponent of his royal right and everyone who preached against him was to be arrested. He had adhered at Oxford to the baronial plan, but under conditions which had not been observed. This breach of faith and later actions, prejudicial to him and to the realm, had justified his appeal to the pope.[2] At the end of the same month of May in the year 1262 his brother made the award which restored the king's right to appoint his sheriffs.

Henry must have felt more of a king in the summer of 1262 than ever before. It is true that a justiciar was again at the head of the judiciary and the administration, but he was a tried man of the king's own choosing. The chancery and seal were under

---

[1] On St. Edward's day (13 October) 1262 during the feast at Westminster, while the king was in France. The earl certainly came to England at this time. One can only surmise that he had a draft of a bull which the pope had not sanctioned. Simon was neither a liar nor a forger. On the other hand, we have no first-hand evidence about what actually occurred.   [2] *Close Rolls, 1261-4*, p. 123.

the control of one of his best clerks, the exchequer was presided over by an abbot who would cause no trouble. The shires and castles were in safe hands. The Lord Edward was serving his apprenticeship as a ruler in Gascony. The king's half-brothers were again at court. The barons had accepted the return to the old order. Henry decided to make another journey to Paris, where many matters awaited his attention, and not least the affairs of Earl Simon and the Countess Eleanor. If only he could deal with Simon and bring him to reason all would be well.

V

THE BARONS' WAR AND THE LEGATE'S PEACE

IN May 1262 Richard of Cornwall was very busy at his castle of Wallingford. Envoys from Germany had arrived and he was preparing for his departure from England. King Henry begged him to come to the manor of Cippenham near Windsor for a talk. Richard wrote to excuse himself and added: 'If I am wanted about the decision between you and the earl of Leicester, my advice is that, once it is made, you should strictly observe it in every way'.[1] The award was never made, but if King Henry had been more accommodating and then followed his brother's counsel, the Barons' War might have been avoided. Simon had two sides to him and two purposes, the settlement of his wife's claims and his oath to maintain the Provisions. If the arbitrators in England and France had been able to satisfy his first purpose, he would have been more inclined, as the king's brother-in-law and King Louis's friend, to compromise on the second.

Henry left England on 14 July. He seems to have been very confident in the summer of 1262. He had so much business at the French court, where, as a vassal of King Louis, he would be engaged in litigation about the affairs of Gascony and the settlement of matters arising from the treaty of Paris, that he expected to stay until the following Easter. He kept in close touch with the justiciar and counsellors in England, and, with John Mansel in temporary charge of his chancery, conducted his affairs at Saint Maur-des-Fossés, which King Louis had placed at his disposal, just as he would have done at home. He appeared to think that he could deal with Earl Simon in his stride, and was misguided enough to revive old quarrels in the dispute, to broaden, not to narrow the field of controversy. For

---

[1] This letter, 9 May 1262, is dated 1261 in *Royal Letters*, ii. 174–5. It is dated correctly in the *Foedera*, I. i. 420, but the word 'Leicester' is there given wrongly as 'Gloucester'. Reference to the original, now in the Public Record Office (cf. P.R.O. Lists and Indexes, *Ancient Correspondence*, p. 19), shows that, though the manuscript is badly stained, Richard of Cornwall referred to Simon de Montfort, not to Richard of Clare.

example, he summoned to Paris the chief of the party which had been hostile to Simon at Bordeaux twelve years earlier. Gaillard Delsoler was ordered to bring with him those best able to explain the Gascon business 'and the losses which we suffered there on account of Simon de Montfort'. This was provocative. Henry stirred up dust which clouded the prospect of peace. It is not surprising that no progress was made, and that Henry, as he wrote to the justiciar on 8 October, had to abandon as hopeless the way of compromise. Earl Simon, on his side, became convinced that he had to deal with sinister forces behind the king. As late as February 1263 he told King Louis that while he did not doubt Henry's good intentions, he could do no more against the influence of advisers whose intrigues affected his honour. He doubtless referred to Peter of Savoy, William of Valence, and especially John Mansel, the agent of the betrayal of the common enterprise at the papal court. He was in a dangerous mood.

By this time Henry had returned to England, for here also dissension had revived. In September a serious epidemic had spread in Paris. The king's household was decimated, Henry himself, his son Edmund, and John Mansel were seriously ill. Rumours ran in England that he had died. Although he was able by the end of the month to take little walks, he was still far from well when the news from England brought him home. He had to spend Christmas quietly at Canterbury and forgo the usual festivities in Westminster. Deprived of firm guidance from Paris, Philip Basset and his colleagues would seem to have lost grip of affairs at home. Llywelyn of Wales had broken loose again. Henry, in a pathetic letter, turned to his eldest son and urged him to hurry to England. 'This news should give you grave concern. This is no time for laziness and boyish wantonness. . . . I am getting old, you are in the flower of your young manhood.'[1] Edward landed at Dover towards the end of February 1263, with a company of armed knights.

This time Llywelyn had a good excuse for his action. He had won Henry's gratitude for his restraint during the troubles of 1261–2, and in May 1262 had renewed the truce for two years.[2] In the summer, however, the marches of Wales were in a turbulent state. The death on 15 July, the day after Henry sailed for France, of Richard of Clare had removed the greatest man in

---

[1] *Close Rolls, 1261–4*, pp. 272–3, a letter written probably from Canterbury about 24 December 1262.　　[2] *Littere Wallie*, ed. J. G. Edwards, pp. 17–18.

the marches. Unrest was aggravated first by a rumour of Llywelyn's death and then by the news of the king's illness, if not death, in France. Llywelyn had to complain of frequent breaches of the truce. At last his impatience got the better of him, and in November he let himself go in all directions. In the north he attacked the Lord Edward's strongholds at Deganwy and Diserth on the coast, in the south he attacked Abergavenny, held at this time by Edward during the minority of its lord, George Cantilupe. The danger was the more serious because there was no order in the marches. Peter de Montfort, who managed to save Abergavenny, gave sad reports of the lack of cohesion. The lords of the marches were unwilling to join in the defence of Edward's castles. All was at sixes and sevens. Now there is no doubt that the chaos in the marches was largely due to a movement among the younger Marchers which was not directly due to local politics, and had caused Henry much concern some time before the prince of Wales decided to attack Edward's castles. It seems to have originated in a legal proceeding taken by Edward against his companion and steward, Roger Leyburn, who, though he had interests in the southern marches, was a baron in Kent. Edward apparently discovered that Roger had been guilty of peculation in the discharge of his duties, and it is probable that he also had other grounds of complaint against him. During a short visit to England on his domestic affairs he had been egged on by his mother, the queen, to call Roger to account.[1] He left England early in July, before the king left for France, and Roger, not willing to submit to be a broken man, formed one of those confederacies which, as we have seen, were so natural and congenial to the temper of discontented men in a feudal society. He turned especially, though not only, to his neighbours and relatives in the marches, and found a leader for his party in Roger Clifford of Eardisley. The agitation must have spread rapidly. In August a group of young sparks, Roger Clifford, Roger Leyburn, John Giffard of

[1] The story is told by a Kentish chronicler (Gervase of Canterbury, ii. 220–1). That Edward was in England in June 1262 is suggested by an agreement about an exchange of lands with Peter of Savoy made in the king's court (*Close Rolls, 1261–4*, pp. 54, 56; cf. *Royal Letters*, ii. 210–11) and by letters of protection for the Lord Edmund, dated 8 July, where Edmund is said to have gone abroad with Edward the king's son (*Cal. Pat. Rolls, 1258–66*, p. 222). Edward presumably went on to Gascony, while Edmund joined his father in Paris on or soon after the king's arrival. See also above, p. 164, for Edward's visit to England in 1261.

Brimpsfield, Hamo l'Estrange, Peter de Montfort the younger, and others, were organizing tournaments—always a possible source of political action—and had to be restrained by the justiciar. By October the prospect seems to have been so gloomy that Henry, writing from France, took precautions for the safety of the country. He was ill, Edward was in Gascony, anything might happen. He ordered the justiciar, chancellor, and treasurer in England to allow no parliaments, and in case of need to make the Lord Edmund, whom he had sent home for his convalescence, *capitaneus pro parte regis.*[1] This implied a military organization under the control of the next heir but one to the crown.

Two distinct but related features of Roger Leyburn's movement justified the king's fears. Roger had not formed a new band of companions. He had turned to men most of whom had known each other in Edward's household; and gradually the group attracted to itself more important young men, notably Henry of Almain and John de Warenne, who had been Edward's friends. In other words, the nucleus of the party was composed of those who had stood by Edward in 1259 and 1260 after his alliance with the earl of Leicester. Some of them had been with him for a time in France and Gascony. A few months later most of them were to return to Edward's side and to become his champions in the long struggle with the earl in England and on the marches; but for the time being they attracted to themselves the malcontents, mainly young men like themselves, who had not acquiesced, as Hugh Bigod and Richard of Clare had acquiesced, in the annulment of the Provisions of Oxford. Two young northerners, John de Vesci of Alnwick and Robert de Vipont of Appleby, were men of this type; so was the younger Peter de Montfort; and so, most important of all, was Gilbert of Clare, son and heir of the late earl of Gloucester.[2] If Pope Urban

---

[1] *Close Rolls, 1261–4,* p. 162.

[2] The death of a great tenant-in-chief of the Crown always involved the royal escheators and other officials in long and tiresome business, and the heir in delays, before the lands were restored to him. In the case of Richard of Clare, the business was complicated by Henry's conviction that the dead earl's rights to some lands were disputable; and the delay was made more bitter by his discourtesy to Gilbert in Paris in August 1262. The claims of the Clares to Bristol had also to be resisted. It is worth while at this point to add a note on the seven original confederates of April 1258. Richard of Clare was the second to go. The first had been John fitzGeoffrey of Sheen and other places, the son of King John's justiciar, Geoffrey fitzPeter. He had died in November 1258, after a fine career in the royal service

was well informed, even Richard of Cornwall himself was sympathetic, if not active.[1] He must indeed have been annoyed by Henry's failure to come to an agreement with Earl Simon and dismayed by the chaos which he found in England when he returned in February 1263. The second feature of the movement was due to its effect in the shires. It gave a signal to those who had been betrayed, the lesser men who had been sworn to observe the Provisions as valid for all time and to regard objectors as public enemies, the men who had heard proclamations about the redress of their grievances and reforms in local government read in the shire and hundred courts and had put their trust in them. The baronial government, in the king's name, had aroused them, and the king, in his own name, had then dashed their hopes. Public opinion had been stirred in England, public propaganda and popular preachers had excited it, and now an incentive was given both to those who were disappointed and to every disorderly element in the community to rally around a new leader. This new leader was Earl Simon. Roger Clifford and his party called Simon to come over and help them; and at the end of April 1263 he came.

The earl's arrival in England was a turning-point in the history of the movement. It turned a faction born of restlessness and self-interest into a party with a policy. The king and his ministers were taken by surprise. Henry, after his return, had become well aware of the political discontents which had revived around the Marchers and their companions, but his object had been to allay them in order to prepare the way for a campaign against Llywelyn, whom he regarded as the arch-enemy. At the end of January 1263 he reissued the legislative provisions of Westminster, thus removing any doubt whether these had been comprised or not in the papal revocation. Moreover, still hopeful that King Louis would be able to make some settlement with

both in England and Ireland. His son John fitzJohn joined Earl Simon in 1263. Earl Simon and his loyal friend Peter de Montfort were killed at Evesham in 1265. Hugh Bigod, the baronial justiciar, became a royalist and died in the end of 1266. Peter of Savoy, the queen's uncle, who succeeded to the county of Savoy in 1263 and took little part in the wars, died in 1268. Roger Bigod, the marshal, earl of Norfolk, lived until 1270.

[1] On 16 September 1263, naturally too late in the day, the pope exhorted the king of the Romans to consider the tempest stirred up against his kinsman King Henry, which, *if he had not procured, he at least permits*, and to go to that king's defence and assistance (*Cal. Papal Letters*, i. 402). By this time Richard was doing his best to mediate between the hostile parties in England.

Earl Simon, he contemplated further concessions to be drafted by the justiciar, the two Bigods, and Simon himself;[1] but how far he was prepared to go in this direction is not known. In March the magnates, the citizens of London, and the men of the shires were ordered to take an oath of fealty to him and to the Lord Edward as his heir. Gilbert of Clare, who had not yet been given livery of his earldom, is said to have refused to take the oath to Edward, presumably on this technical ground. Finally, as late as 25 May, the king issued writs for a gathering of the feudal host at Worcester on 1 August, to march against the Welsh.

By the end of May, however, Simon was ready to act. The men who had called him to England gathered around him at Oxford, where the famous parliament had met just about five years before. Their demands, under the seal of Roger Clifford, were sent to the king. They required a return to the Provisions and the treatment of all opponents except the king and queen and their children as public enemies. Henry, it is needless to say, refused, and the rebels, as he regarded them, took matters into their own hands. A widespread attack began upon those who had supported the king against the Provisions. Roger Clifford and the Marchers began the pogrom, for so it may be described, in their own country, by the plunder of the manors of the unpopular bishop of Hereford, the Savoyard Peter of Aigueblanche. The bishop was seized and sent to Roger Clifford's castle at Eardisley. They then seized Gloucester, made sure of the passages of the Severn, and, under Earl Simon's command, moved eastwards to Reading. Richard of Cornwall, who was at his manor of Isleworth, came westwards to try what persuasion could do, but the earl disregarded him, and, by a strategic diversion to the south-east, made sure of the Cinque Ports and the men of Kent. The shock of his advance was so unexpected that Henry and his advisers were confounded. John Mansel, his agent in the negotiations with the pope, and Archbishop Boniface, the agent of the papal sentence of excommunication against supporters of the Provisions, left England at once to rally support for the king. In the meanwhile the bishops had

---

[1] This seems to follow from a passage in the London *Chronica majorum et vicecomitum*, p. 53. On 18 January Henry begged Louis to bring the issue with Simon to a conclusion if he could because the earl had been so troublesome a centre of disturbance—an illuminating remark (*Royal Letters*, ii. 234).

been busy. How wide disapproval of the king's desertion of the new order was is shown by the fact that Simon's episcopal ally Walter Cantilupe, the bishop of Worcester, was joined at this time by Henry's kinsman, Roger Longespée, the bishop of Coventry, by Richard Gravesend, the bishop of Lincoln, and by the new bishop of London, Henry of Sandwich. All three went to the king from Earl Simon and Bishop Walter with a 'form of peace'.[1] This was in the end of June, about ten days before Simon reached the south coast. The king was in no position to parley. For the first time the Londoners had risen against him. When the queen, who was with Henry in the Tower, tried to make her way to Edward, who was at Windsor, the mob attacked her barge and forced her to take refuge in the precincts of St. Paul's. The leading citizens, in alarm, told Henry bluntly that he would be well advised to restore the Provisions. On 16 July he announced his acceptance of the terms. He had already authorized Edmund, who was in Dover, to surrender the great castle.

Earl Simon and his companions at once took charge of the Tower of London and the city. Within a week of the king's surrender the conduct of affairs had passed under their control. Hugh le Dispenser was again justiciar, Nicholas of Ely again chancellor. Many royal castles were given new castellans and every shire was given a 'warden of the peace' who, while leaving to the sheriff his financial duties, was to take over the local administration. The feudal host already summoned to be at Worcester on 1 August was ordered to come to the king, ready if necessary to force Edward to surrender Windsor and to drive his mercenaries out of the country. Edward, angry but helpless, surrendered Windsor and disbanded his foreign soldiers without waiting to be attacked.[2] One baron after another, who had been

---

[1] The bishops of Worcester, Lincoln, and Chichester had been present on 27 May at the consecration of the new bishops of London and Salisbury by the bishop of Winchester at Canterbury. They may have come to an understanding with each other on the political situation during the feasts which followed (*Gervase of Cant.* ii. 220). The *forma pacis* was sent to the king on or before 29 June, on which day the bishop of Worcester wrote about it to Walter de Merton (*Foedera*, I. i. 427). The king empowered the three bishops with his confessor, John of Darlington and the judge, William of Wilton, to make peace with the barons. This was on 4 July (*Cal. Pat. Rolls, 1258–66*, p. 268).

[2] Before that he had dashed across to Bristol in June with his mercenaries, in the hope of making a stand there in his own castle, but the townsmen rose against him: see Treharne, *The Baronial Plan of Reform* (1932), p. 310.

despoiled as an opponent of the Provisions, took the oath to maintain them as a condition of regaining possession of his lands.
Commissions of oyer and terminer were issued in August to hear
complaints of trespass, that is, to deal with those who had taken
advantage of the recent drive against the enemies of the Provisions to create disorder, commit thefts and robberies, and
wreak vengeance on their local enemies. Earl Simon's two most
important followers, Henry of Almain and John de Warenne
acted as mediators between the Lord Edward and his former
friends. Roger Leyburn, the leading spirit in the recent movement, was given the important office of steward of the royal
household. Finally on 9 September bishops and magnates met
together in St. Paul's cathedral. The king's adhesion to the
terms of settlement was read, with general assent. Pending the
conclusion of a definitive peace, a brief truce with Llywelyn was
ratified. Within three months Earl Simon seemed to have destroyed the work of three years and to have brought the realm
back to the order of things created in 1258 and 1259.

He had, in fact, done nothing of the sort. He had divided the
land and created a political impasse from which he and the
realm were only extricated by his death at Evesham two years
later. He had done what the king had done, appealed to force
and then thought to create peace and order by proclamation.
The complaints and discord which disturbed his parliament in
September showed that the real work of settlement had hardly
been begun. It was impossible to draw a hard-and-fast line
between the spoliation of the earl's political enemies and unauthorized acts of violence. In the eyes of the victims, whether
they recovered their lands by taking an oath or by seeking redress from the justices, they had all alike been suddenly, wantonly,
and unjustly attacked. Just as there had been innocent men
among the despoiled, so there had been guilty men among the
spoilers. Simon himself admitted this when he procured royal
letters of pardon for acts of violence committed by some of his
adherents, and promised an investigation of grievances against
the spoilers (*spoliatores*) at the ensuing parliament in October.
If the general feeling had swung round again in favour of the
Provisions, difficulties of this kind could no doubt have been
amicably settled, just as, after the still tenser period of bitterness after Evesham, they were settled in 1266 and 1267; but
Simon's dramatic victory did not bring anything like general

acquiescence. The Lord Edward was now a changed man. After his return to England he had been deserted by the Marchers and had had to fight alone in north Wales for the protection of his castles.[1] Then, during the disturbances in London, his mother had been insulted, and after he had withdrawn to Windsor he had been publicly humiliated. Earl Simon may have thought that he had healed all wounds and reconciled Edward; but Edward was henceforward irreconcilable. Simon, indeed, had played into his hands by bringing Henry of Almain, John de Warenne, Roger Leyburn, and others, especially in the Welsh march, back to Edward's side. During the autumn the old confidence between them was restored, never again to be broken. There is a story that, as Simon watched Edward and his army approach Evesham, and saw the good order which they kept, he exclaimed: 'I taught them that.' The story may or may not be literally true, but it points to the truth that Simon himself in 1263 gave shape and coherence to the force which was ultimately to destroy him. And, apart from Edward, Simon had now to deal with active enemies across the Channel. Until his death in January 1265, John Mansel, the ablest of Henry's clerks, was the adviser of a little group of distinguished emigrés, in Boulogne, Montreuil, and other places on or near the coast. The archbishop of Canterbury and, before long, Queen Eleanor were there. Peter of Savoy came from Savoy. The royalists who escaped after the battle of Lewes swelled the number. They were in close touch with King Louis and Queen Margaret of France, with the papal court and the papal legate sent by Pope Urban. Earl Simon had to reckon with them at every turn.

Even before the weaknesses in the position of Simon and his party were fully revealed, steps had been taken to make the cause of the Provisions more secure by using the good offices of King Louis. The bishop of Worcester and Henry of Almain had crossed the Channel to seek an agreement. The king of France was, as always, willing to do his best to bring about a peaceful settlement, but he could not, in face of King Henry's humiliation, regard himself merely as a peacemaker. His attitude is suggested in the terms of a letter which King Henry sent to him on 16 August. Henry informed Louis that he was coming with his

---

[1] Edward had been able to revictual Deganwy and Diserth, with the aid of his mercenaries, in April; but he could do no more, and the castles fell to Llywelyn later in the year.

wife and sons to seek counsel and aid in the amelioration of his
state and to discuss other matters with him as with his lord; he
and the council which was with him waited for the expression
of Louis's wishes, but the magnates desired to be sure of their
king's return by 6 October. Another letter, which was sent with
this, makes it clear that Louis had commanded Henry to come
to him and that his council, while agreeing that Henry should
obey the mandate, was afraid lest he might not return; for he
'wills and requests Louis, if he goes against his promise, to
compel him to fulfil it'.[1] Nothing could illustrate better than
these letters the contrast between the medieval and the modern
outlook. Simon and his allies were in a dilemma. They were and
could only be royalists. Their political thought and intentions
were bounded by their ideas of kingship, its rights and its
duties; but they were also, in a sense, high churchmen who
were prepared, in the interests of the sworn compact which
Henry had made with the community of the barons, to withstand the pope himself, just as their great exemplar Grosseteste
had arraigned the Roman curia in the name of the plenitude of
papal power. Although King Louis's lordship did not extend to
the realm of England, they recognized Henry's peculiar relation
to him and they saw in his intervention the only possible way to
reconciliation on the basis of a revision of the Provisions of
Oxford; and they trusted him to see to it that Henry was not
detained by his friends but would return in time for the October
parliament.

   Louis could certainly be trusted to do this, but he was in the
mood to act as a judge rather than as a friendly intermediary.
When Earl Simon, Peter de Montfort, and other barons arrived
at Boulogne, they found a great gathering. The archbishop of
Canterbury, Peter of Savoy, and the exiles sought instant redress. The baronial proctors replied that 'the barons of England
were not bound to account for their actions in the court of the
French king nor to undergo judgement anywhere save in the
court of the king of England, and this by their peers: and so that
parliament came to an end'.[2] King Henry returned to England

---

   [1] *Foedera*, I. i. 429.
   [2] From the chronicle of Dover; see *Gervase of Canterbury*, ii. 225, note. This statement strengthens the impression which internal evidence suggests that the
important *gravamina* and *petitio* of King Henry which survive in a document
discovered by Professor E. Perroy and edited by Professor R. F. Treharne in his paper
'The Mise of Amiens, 23 January 1264' (*Studies in Medieval History presented to F. M.*

with his sons on 7 October, in time for the parliament in which the future of the country was to be discussed and, it had been hoped, decided. He left the queen behind him with the emigrants.

King Louis and his wife at once informed Pope Urban of their kinsman's plight. On 22 November, the day after he received their letters, the pope appointed Gui, cardinal bishop of Sabina, his legate in England, Wales, and Scotland. The cardinal, a native of Saint-Gilles, was an old friend of Louis and his brothers. His powers were very extensive and included the right to summon princes, prelates, and other persons subject to his legation to come to him even beyond sea. The pope, in letters to King Henry, Queen Eleanor, the Lord Edward, the earls and barons of England, and to Simon himself, 'reported to be the chief disturber of the realm', defined the object of the cardinal's mission to be the restoration of the king and his house to their former position and of the realm to a state of quiet. Although the legate was not allowed to cross the Channel, his presence in the north of France was both an encouragement to Henry and his friends and a warning to their enemies; but he also must have learned a good deal about conditions in England. As Pope Clement IV, after his elevation to the papal throne in succession to Pope Urban (February 1265), he retained a shrewd and friendly interest in the welfare of the king and his realm. His unfailing encouragement strengthened the hands of the new legate, Ottobuono, in his labours for a settlement after the fall of Earl Simon at Evesham.

The parliament which met after the king and Earl Simon returned to England was a fiasco. According to one account, when the council made its proposals, a deadlock was reached at once over the king's right to appoint the members of his household. The discussions were broken off, Edward rushed away to Windsor, and the king, leaving Simon in possession of the Tower, followed his son. Neither side was in a position to fight. Neither side wanted to fight. In a very delicate situation, Henry could not afford to run any risk. If he repudiated his recent undertaking to the earl's party he would at once lose his ability to take

Powicke, Oxford, 1948, pp. 237–9), was presented to King Louis at Boulogne in September 1263, not at Amiens in January 1264. Henry's position as described in the document fits the former date better. Note, for example, the references to the state of the Welsh marches.

a line of his own. He made it quite clear that he 'did not propose in any way to infringe the provisions lately made at Oxford' and on 17 October gave this assurance to a number of barons, including Gilbert of Clare, earl of Gloucester, whom he summoned to Windsor from London.[1] It must have been on this understanding that the parties agreed to the election of Richard of Cornwall and other persons 'as mediators of peace between the king and the nobles of the realm'. From this time we find the king resuming control of the chancery and exchequer, and we may conclude that Richard of Cornwall's intervention had brought this about.[2] Moreover, no doubt also by arrangement, Earl Simon withdrew to Kenilworth. It is hard to imagine that he would have agreed, as he and his allies did, to the *compromissio* reached by the mediators, and to submit the matters at issue to the award of King Louis, if he had not thought that the main point—a form of government consistent with the Provisions of Oxford—was won. He had been put on the defensive, but, after his experience at Boulogne, it is incredible that he was prepared to give King Louis the power to declare the Provisions null and void. At the same time he was not and could never be a dictator. He was a royalist. The king had given assurances that the Provisions would be respected. Richard of Cornwall was working for peace. King Louis was a just man. What could Simon do but agree?

That Henry's calculated adherence to the Provisions was a condition of his success was shown both by the rapid growth of his party at Earl Simon's expense and by the alarm which was created when he began to resume control of the castles and to re-establish his authority in the Kentish ports. An unsuccessful effort to get the castellans of Dover to hand over their charge to him and rumours that he intended to bring mercenary troops into the country[3] brought Earl Simon south at once. The earl entered London with the earl of Derby and their following as Henry approached the city from the coast. The king, writing

[1] *Cal. Pat. Rolls, 1258–66,* p. 290. Gilbert of Clare had been given livery of his earldom in August and at this time was taking a non-committal attitude.

[2] Until 28 October Henry used his smaller seal which he had with him at Boulogne. For the gradual recovery of control over chancery and exchequer and the dismissal of the baronial chancellor see Treharne, pp. 324–5, 330.

[3] According to the king's proclamation of 20 December (see next note) money had been raised, presumably in the areas under Simon's control, to support four or five men from each vill who were to be sent against the mercenaries alleged to be coming from abroad.

from Croydon, scornfully denied the rumours, denounced the disturbers of the peace, and ordered the citizens of London to eject them. Simon and his small force had in fact crossed the Thames and taken up their quarters in Southwark. Four rich Londoners plotted with the king to close London bridge behind the earl, while the king and Edward closed in upon him. This they did on 11 December. The plot was betrayed, the citizens broke down the gates and brought Simon and his men back to safety. The sequel is interesting. Two days later, on 13 December, Earl Simon and his party adhered to the form of compromise (*compromissio*) agreed upon between the mediators and King Louis. On the 16th the king and his party followed suit. On the 20th Henry issued a proclamation in which, after repeating, almost in the same words as he had used to the Londoners, his repudiation of false rumours, and ordering all men to stay quietly in their shires, he made this unequivocal declaration: 'We are and always will be ready firmly to observe the oath made at Oxford to the honour of God, to our fealty and to the well-being of the realm, and to defend and protect you as our good and faithful men in your rights and liberties, against any men whatsoever'.[1] Four days afterwards he appointed wardens of the shires in the parts of England, north, south, and west, no longer controlled by the baronial wardens, and left Windsor for France. He reached Amiens on 12 January 1264. There he was joined by the representatives of what it is convenient, though not quite accurate, to call the baronial party. Their leaders were Peter de Montfort, Earl Simon's son Henry, Humphrey de Bohun the son of the earl of Hereford, and the bishop of Worcester's nephew Thomas de Cantilupe, recently chancellor of the university of Oxford.[2] Simon had unfortunately been thrown from his horse and broken his leg on his way from Kenilworth, and was unable to be present at the conference.[3]

King Louis, by the terms of the agreement of December, was to give his award on the Provisions (*super provisionibus*) and on all outstanding disputes which had arisen by reason of them. It is clear from the documents already mentioned that, up to the

---

[1] *Foedera*, i. i. 433.   [2] The later bishop of Hereford who was canonized.
[3] Simon had turned aside to visit the Cistercian nuns at Catesby in Northamptonshire, a house associated with the memory of St. Edmund of Abingdon. Edmund had placed two of his sisters there, relics bequeathed by him were treasured in a chapel built in his honour, and an annual fair was held in Catesby on the feast of his translation.

eve of his departure for Amiens, King Henry had affirmed his adherence to the Provisions. We know nothing about the discussions between the mediators in England; what is clear is that Simon and his allies felt that Louis, the king of France, as the annalist of Dunstable puts it 'stretched the power granted to him'. Henry's position, on the other hand, is also clear, though he did not reveal it. He was not prepared to maintain his adherence to the Provisions if he could persuade King Louis to annul them and to set him free. He was confident of the issue and, as at Boulogne in September, so at Amiens in January, he was prepared to abide by the French king's decision as though it was a judgement in a court of justice (*ordinacio*), though in form it was sought as the decision of an arbitrator (*arbitrium*). His case is on record. He claimed the right to have his own justiciar, or, if he so desired, no such expensive representative at all while he was in his realm. He asserted that in the name of the Provisions the party hostile to him (*pars adversa*) had deprived him of the right to appoint his ministers, judges, and local officials, and to regulate his own household and control his own castles. He relied on the fact that the pope had already quashed the Provisions and declared those who upheld them to be excommunicate. He declared that concession to the Provisions was contrary to the oath which he had sworn at his coronation[1] and that the maintenance of them by his subjects was contrary to the oath of fealty which they had sworn to him as king.[2] King Louis himself felt no hesitation whatever. He conducted no long or searching inquiry; but on 23 January, within a few days of King Henry's arrival at Amiens, he gave judgement against the barons on every point. Everybody who was a party to the terms of reference was declared to be free from any obligation to maintain the Provisions. They had been annulled by the pope and were of no effect. The claim of the barons to direct Henry's choice of his servants was inconsistent with his customary rights and with the conception of kingship.

The award at first confused the baronial party, and all the more so because news had come of the approach of the papal legate. The emigrants, whatever King Henry might do, now

[1] See above, p. 7.
[2] This is the substance of the *gravamina* and *petitio* referred to above, p. 179, n. These should now be discussed in connexion with the baronial statements in the Archives Nationales in Paris, edited by P. Walne in *E.H.R.* lxix (1954), 418–25. The documents are not precisely dated.

had a clear-cut case. They would hope to invade England, and they would have King Louis and Queen Margaret behind them.[1] King Henry may or may not have hoped that the award would go as far as it did, may or may not have expected it to advance the royal cause, but that he had been well advised to profess his fidelity to the Provisions until the award was made was shown by the widespread disturbances which followed it. The malcontents in London and the shires did not consider that they were bound by it; they had not been parties to it. The expectations aroused by Earl Simon's sudden appearance in the previous summer had been kept alive in the midlands and East Anglia by the baronial wardens and agents and preachers; they were hardened into resolution by the prospect of war and invasion. The general feeling of suspense stirred excitement in quarters where the rights or obligations of king and barons made no appeal. A wave of anti-Semitism devastated the local Jewries. Latent passions were fanned into excitement in some of the boroughs. Throughout the country-side the strong began to spoil the weak. The persistent idea that Simon de Montfort was a democratic leader can be traced to the unrest in England during the barons' war, an unrest sufficient of itself to turn the most outstanding man of his time into a popular saint and hero.

For the time being Earl Simon lay crippled at Kenilworth. In some quarters not very favourable to him it was thought that he might die and that, in the present emergency, a new leader (*capitaneus*) should be found.[2] Gilbert of Clare, for example, the young earl of Gloucester, who had not hitherto been prominent, was a likely man; or there was the young earl of Derby, Robert de Ferrers, the lord of Tutbury, who was showing himself fierce and active. Until Earl Simon, from his base in London, rallied the force which scattered the royalists at Lewes, there was more cohesion in the reaction of the shires against the award of King Louis than in the counsels of the baronial leaders. The Mise of Amiens meant war; King Henry's promise of an amnesty for all who observed it fell on deaf ears; but at first the shock scattered the energies and bewildered the purposes of the opposition. The Lord Edward, on the contrary, struck quickly and hard.

[1] Queen Margaret's efforts in the previous August and September to rouse Alphonse of Poitiers against the baronial party indicate the wide range of danger. Cf. Treharne, p. 338, note.

[2] See a document, likely to have emanated from the circle of Gilbert of Clare, preserved in the annals of Tewkesbury (*Ann. Monast.* i. 179–80).

War began in the Welsh March, where local disputes had been simmering for some time. Here Roger Mortimer, of Wigmore and Radnor, was by far the most powerful enemy of Earl Simon. The earl's sons, Henry and Simon, who acted in co-operation with Llywelyn, planned an attack on the lordship of Radnor. Hearing of this Richard of Cornwall, on 4 February, ordered Roger Clifford, now sheriff of Worcester and Gloucester and castellan of Gloucester, to destroy the bridges over the Severn, except the Gloucester bridge; and he followed up his order by hurrying from Windsor to Worcester and Hereford. He did not stay the movements of the young Montforts, but he prepared the way for Edward, who landed in England with his father about this time and immediately dashed to the west. Edward seized the lands of Humphrey de Bohun the younger in Brecon and forced Henry de Montfort and his brother back to the Severn. Here a stand was made. Henry de Montfort, by means of a ruse, seized the town, though not the castle, of Gloucester, Robert de Ferrers, coming south, had stormed Worcester and prepared to join forces with his allies in Gloucester. It seemed that the first round of the war would be fought out on the Severn. On 5 March Edward was back in Gloucester castle. At this point the weakness in the baronial position—the essential incoherence, from a military point of view, between the desire of its leaders, and especially its episcopal leaders, for peace and the resolute prosecution of war—was seized upon by Edward. He had seized upon it during the lull of the previous year, when he drew John de Warenne, Roger Clifford, Roger Leyburn, and other old friends, finally Henry of Almain himself, back to his side. He was to fasten on it again during the uneasy months before the Evesham campaign. He would keep no faith with these rebels. But he never took more astute advantage of it than at Gloucester in March 1264. Using the bishop of Worcester as mediator he prevailed upon Henry de Montfort to withdraw under the terms of a truce which, he undertook, should be the prelude to a settlement. The Severn valley was lost, the prospects of a Welsh alliance faded, the earl of Derby went back north in anger, Earl Simon chafed and scolded at Kenilworth. Edward in triumph marched away to join the king at Oxford.

King Henry, following his son from Kent more slowly, reached Oxford on 8 March. He lived with the Dominicans in the low ground outside the south-western wall and awaited the coming of his host, which was summoned to meet at Oxford on 30 March. The masters and scholars were dispersed to their homes to be out of the way of the brutal soldiery. The royal standard with the dragon worked on red samite was brought from Westminster. Henry could afford to wait, and hold a parliament, for he had half the baronage of England on his side and the Montfortian bishops were anxious to treat for peace. Four of them, the bishops of Worcester, Winchester, Coventry, and Chichester, did their best in Oxford. Moreover, through the good offices of a French agent, a man well known to both Edward and Simon, plans were made for an arbitration at Brackley —a convenient meeting place, familiar in baronial history. This man was John de Valenciennes, who for four years (1257–61) was lord of Haifa in Syria, and since then had been busy here and there on the affairs of Sicily and in aid of Constantinople, lost by the Franks in 1261, and of Syria, in danger from the Mamlūk sultan, Bibars. At Amiens King Louis had at last come to a financial settlement with King Henry, on condition that Henry contributed 2,000 *livres* in money of Tours to the needs of the Holy Land, and John de Valenciennes was doubtless in England in connexion with this agreement.[1] He wished to prevent the fratricidal strife which he foresaw, and King Henry was willing that he should try what he could do. The king agreed to accept the decision of the bishop of Coventry and the archdeacon of Norfolk after they had heard the case of each side in the presence of and had discussed their verdict with the Frenchman. Whatever was done was inconclusive. In desperation the four bishops at Oxford are alleged to have been ready to accept on the barons' behalf every point in King Louis's award except the king's right to admit aliens to his counsels. All was in vain. The king's army had gathered, the baronial forces were known to be gathering in Northampton from all parts of England. On 3 April Henry and Edward were on the move, on the 6th Edward, with the aid of friends inside the town, broke into Northampton. On the 7th, Passion Sunday, the castle was surrendered. Many prisoners, including Peter de Montfort and the younger Simon, were taken, and much violence was done to the town and townsmen. The important prisoners were taken away by or entrusted to the royalist lords of the Welsh March. The

---

[1] On the day before the battle of Lewes King Henry authorized the French king to pay the £2,000 to John de Valenciennes, from the money due to him.

move against Northampton was later regarded as the beginning of the civil war, though some legalists preferred to date it a few weeks later, from the formal renouncement of homage by each side, on the eve of the battle of Lewes.[1]

Earl Simon had not awaited the outcome of negotiations and was in London when he heard of the threat to Northampton. He moved out to the relief of the town but returned on the news of its capture. If Edward had followed up his victory and kept his knights together the war might have ended almost as soon as it had begun; but, perhaps over-confident, he turned northwards. While the king went by way of Leicester to Nottingham, he harried the earl of Derby's lands in Derbyshire and Staffordshire. Apparently a campaign in the baronial midlands, with the strengthening of friendly and the reduction of hostile castles was in his mind. This diversion gave Earl Simon time to make a new concentration of force in London. Simon could now count on Gilbert of Clare. The young earl had taken no part in the warfare in the Marches and had not been in Northampton. He was at his castle of Tonbridge in Kent, where he could cover Dover and watch his neighbours John de Warenne and Roger Leyburn, who held Rochester for the king. While Henry was spending Passion week in Nottingham, Earl Simon from London and Earl Gilbert from Tonbridge closed in on Rochester. They took the city on Good Friday (18 April) and the outer works of the castle on the following day. Then they settled down to the siege of the great tower of the castle. The king could not afford to lose touch with his friends across the Channel. He hurried south in strength. The two earls withdrew to London. Henry was joined by Edward near Tonbridge, took the castle and secured control of the Cinque Ports. But by this time Earl Simon was ready to join issue with the royalists. Dover still held out against Henry under its castellan, Richard de Grey. The men of the Weald were out on the baronial side. The earl decided to march south. He was still unable to ride, and used a four-wheeled vehicle. He had got as far as Fletching when Henry, on 11 May, reached John de Warenne's little town of Lewes, ten miles or so lower down the valley of the Sussex Ouse.

His control of London and the Tower had given Simon the opportunity to rally his forces. In a few weeks desperation had

[1] See R. F. Treharne on the battle of Northampton in *Northamptonshire Record Society*, ii (1955), 13-30.

given way to confidence. The general feeling in the shires was on
his side. In the city the folk had taken the lead in the previous
summer. It brushed aside the aldermen and their council,
gathered together at the call of the bell of St. Paul's, followed
the guidance of the mayor, Thomas fitzThomas. After the
award of Amiens, the citizens had ordered themselves in armed
array under the direction of a constable and marshal. Before the
king's march on Northampton they had burnt their boats by
attacking Richard of Cornwall's manor of Isleworth and the
lands of other royalists; after the fall of Northampton they had
formed a sworn alliance with the adherents of Earl Simon. They
had found vent for their passion in disgraceful attacks upon the
Jews, and, although the justiciar did his best to check them
and to give the tormented Israelites shelter in the Tower, some
fierce spirits among the baronial leaders were zealous to join the
persecutors. Simon and Gilbert of Clare, in short, were able to
prepare for battle at London and when they moved south an
armed band of citizens went with them.

The highest moments in the history of a cause, as in the life of
a man, transcend time and circumstance. Whatever happened
at Lewes, Simon's dilemma would not be resolved. His cause
was doomed to frustration. Yet a sense of beauty lingers over
those days in May when the great earl waited among the woods
of the Weald. High spirits and anxious forebodings, eager exaltation and solemn resolve had brought bishops, friars, barons,
and Londoners together in a transient mood of high purpose,
giving to our annals a dignity untouched by cause and effect,
or the rights and wrongs of the case. In the words of the St.
Albans chronicler, Earl Simon's followers were united in faith
and will and courage to die for their country. Many of them had
lately been knighted by Simon in London, others were knighted
on the down above Lewes before the battle. Gilbert of Clare,
Robert de Vere the earl of Oxford, John de Burgh the grandson
of the justiciar Hubert, John fitzJohn the grandson of the justiciar Geoffrey fitzPeter were among these young men, caught up
for the moment in fervent devotion to a holy cause. In Earl
Simon's eyes they must have seemed a trusty remnant of the
band which had been with him twelve months before. They had
not been seduced by the Lord Edward. They had been tested
and passed the test like the men of the host of Gideon who had
not knelt down to lap water. Only one who should have been

there was absent, Robert de Ferrers, awaited in vain, a way-ward man.

Two days were spent in an attempt to make peace. Three bishops, Worcester, London, and Chichester, were with Earl Simon at Fletching. With Simon Berksted, bishop of Chichester, a saintly man in the tradition of Grosseteste and St. Richard Wych, the earl was at this time in particularly close converse; and it was he who first went to see King Henry at Lewes. Would the king, to whom the barons were bound in unfailing fidelity, agree to maintain the Provisions subject to changes approved by good and learned men, theologians and canonists of repute? This suggestion gave the policy adopted by Simon in 1263 a sharper edge and put it on a higher plane. It was accompanied by a baronial letter which showed that this time the king must give an unequivocal reply. The barons were determined if neces-sary to use all their strength against the men who were the king's enemies and their own. Their overture was received with much indignation by the royalists. Richard of Cornwall and the Lord Edward responded with a fierce challenge; the king with a for-mal letter of *diffidatio*, of renunciation of homage. Earl Simon prepared for battle. His followers, who are said to have worn the white cross of the crusader, were solemnly absolved by the bishop of Worcester, and on the night of 13 May advanced to-wards Lewes. Superior in number and not expecting such quick action, Henry's army lay in and about the little town, built with its castle and old Cluniac priory—the burying place of the Warennes—in a gap in the South Downs where the valley of the Ouse broadens out in low and, in those days, marshy ground. They neglected to hold the high down which rises rapidly to the north-west and it was on this down that Earl Simon, making a de-tour, deployed his army. When day broke on 14 May he could see Lewes close by, nearly 400 feet below. He placed the Londoners on his left, the eastern slope. The king's forces seem to have been arranged for the ascent in three groups, led by Edward on the right, Henry in the middle, Richard of Cornwall on the left. Where exactly the fight began is not clear, but it can hardly have been far from the town. Edward and his knights broke the Londoners opposed to them, forced them on to the swampy levels, and pursued them ruthlessly about the valley for some hours. When he returned, the battle was over. In the shock of the main fight, Earl Simon won a victory almost as bloodless as that of William the Marshal in the streets of Lincoln thirty-seven years before. The king of the Romans and his son had managed to reach the crest of the down near a windmill, but were taken prisoner in the mill. The centre had been thrown back, scattered, and hunted down. Only a few knights were killed. The slaughter, which was heavy, was confined to men-at-arms and Londoners. The clerks who buried the dead counted 600. The king took refuge in the priory, Edward in the Franciscan friary. William of Valence and his brother Guy de Lusignan, Hugh Bigod, and the Earl Warenne escaped to Pevensey on the coast and thence across the Channel. The earls of Hereford and Arundel, Roger Mortimer and most of the Marcher lords, Philip Basset, and the northerners Robert Bruce, John Baliol, and John Comyn, with many more, were captured.

A form of peace, sealed with the seals of the king and Edward, was drawn up on the day after the battle. The Mise of Lewes, as it is called, has not survived. Its contents are known, but not completely, from other evidence.[1] Edward and Henry of Almain became hostages for the fulfilment of the terms. The castles in royal hands were to be handed over, and orders were sent to their castellans to remain quiet 'for peace has been made and oaths sworn on each side'. The peace, as proclaimed in the shires, stipulated that no indiscriminate attacks were to be made on royalists, no man on either side was to do harm to persons, lands, or chattels. The younger Simon de Montfort, with Peter de Montfort and his two sons, who had been captured at Northampton, were to be released. Provision was made for the exchange of other prisoners taken at Northampton—a provision which later caused endless difficulty. In order to maintain the defence of the marches of Wales, Roger Mortimer, James of Audley, Roger Clifford, and other Marcher lords were allowed to go home, as was John Baliol, who was required to help the cause of peace in the north. This act of confidence in itself justified the confinement of the two princes as hostages. It was done because England depended for order and safety upon a distribution of power, based upon the feudal liberties as well as upon the administrative system of the shires; but it brought about Earl Simon's fall in the end. Simon was too sure that all would now be well. He and his episcopal colleagues made a

---

[1] It should not be confused, as it soon was and still is, with later drafts of settlement; see N. Denholm-Young in *E.H.R.* xlviii (1933), 358–69.

still finer gesture. They agreed to submit certain matters—what they were is not clear—to a number of French prelates, barons, and others named in the Mise, apparently in the hope that the exiles across the Channel might be induced to accept the form of peace. On 25 May a copy of the Mise was sent to King Louis with the request that he would persuade the exiles to fall into line and the arbitrators to act. Earl Simon, however, was not willing to surrender the advantage which his victory had given him. The king's letter to Louis contained the significant proviso: 'If any shorter way of peace, more suitable to us and our realm can be found, we propose to pursue it.'[1]

This letter was sent from Rochester. The earl was taking the king to London. Henry was lodged at St. Paul's. In June the shires were again put under wardens of the peace, some new, some reappointed. The royal castles and the castles of the barons who had fled abroad were distributed among Simon's partisans. A parliament was summoned for 22 June. Roger Mortimer and other Marchers were ordered to appear, and to bring with them the prisoners taken at Northampton. The northern royalists were asked to come south. The place in the movement of the local gentry was recognized by the publication of writs directing the shire courts to elect four knights from each shire to attend this parliament in which the affairs of the realm would be transacted. The Jews were re-established in their homes and facilities for foreign trade were given to merchants.

The prelates and magnates and others present in parliament entrusted the establishment of a provisional administration to the bishop of Chichester and the earls of Leicester and Gloucester. The 'form of government' was ready on 28 June. It was to last until the Mise of Lewes or some other way of settlement had been ratified by all parties concerned. A council of nine, chosen by the three, was to advise the king, and three of these were always to be in attendance upon him. The three electors did not cease to supervise affairs. They were to advise the king on changes in the council of nine and settle matters in dispute between them. The records show that they frequently intervened in public business. They were free, independent, the ultimate authority, responsible to the community of barons and to it alone, for it alone could change the personnel of this triumvirate. It is significant that Earl Simon now relied more upon

[1] *Close Rolls, 1261–4*, pp. 385–6.

Bishop Simon of Chichester than on his old friend Walter, bishop of Worcester. His strongest allies in the council of nine were Peter de Montfort, who was worked hard during the next few months, Humphrey de Bohun the younger, and the bishop of London.[1] The earl exercised a decisive influence in the background while the royal household, the chancery, and exchequer combined to function in the king's name under the direction of the members of the council of nine who were in attendance. Simon's adhesion to the Provisions of Oxford required him to act in this way.[2] He was in his own eyes the faithful vassal entrusted with the obligation to maintain the co-operation, through a council, of king and community. This is the burden of the 'Song of Lewes', a Latin poem written after the victory, perhaps by a Franciscan, to expound the views of the earl's episcopal and clerical friends. At the same time, as the poet explains, the king had had bad advisers, and the Lord Edward was like the leopard, as treacherous as he was brave. The earl could not let go his grip of affairs. The realm was a coherent organized unity like the human body, not, as the royalists urged, an association of barons and freemen, each with his independent rights, and all kept together by a king who obviously was or ought to be as free and independent as they were in the choice of his servants and the performance of his trust. The poet puts the royalist view quite fairly; but in his opinion the *communitas*, of which the king was part, had more authority than the royal will, however wise the king might be.

The concentration of power in a few hands which distinguishes the form of government of June 1264 from the system of 1258 was a military necessity no less than a political expedient. For England was threatened by invasion. Queen Eleanor and the exiles were very busy in the collection of ships and troops. A national rally against the danger was ordered early in July. The feudal host was summoned, the shires and liberties were ordered to gather together knights and freeholders and quotas of men from every vill under the command of local constables. Cities

---

[1] The names are known from a document contained in a Bodleian manuscript (Bodley 91, f. 139ʳ; see *E.H.R.* xlix (1934), 93). In addition to the three given above, they were Adam de Neufmarché, Roger St. John, Ralph Kamoiz, Giles de Argentein, with the chancellor and the treasurer.

[2] When, in the crisis of 1265, Simon felt the need to strengthen his position, he characteristically made inquiries about his rights and functions as steward; cf. L. W. Vernon Harcourt, *His Grace the Steward* (1907), p. 125.

and boroughs sent men. In East Anglia and the southern shires these levies were organized for coast defence; other levies were sent to camps, notably on Barham Down near Canterbury. At this time Walter de Cantilupe and his brother bishops had taken in hand the restoration of order in the Church. During the recent disturbance the cure of souls had been gravely impeded, partly by a tendency among the clergy to take sides, and to desert their parishes for the field, partly by the violence to which the resident clergy were exposed. It was essential to insist on residence and to protect the pastors who remained with their flocks. The canon law forbade the clergy to fight, but in this time of emergency they might be asked to pay. Hence it came about that the only general financial levy raised during the period of baronial rule was a tenth for one year granted by the Montfortian bishops—eight or so in number—in the summer of 1264. There is no doubt that, in spite of some defection and more incompetence, the greater part of the people of England, laity and clergy alike, combined in a vast endeavour, so onerous that the new government, in thanking them for their efforts, promised that the occasion should not be regarded as a precedent.[1] They were roused by the danger from a 'great host of aliens', and until the danger faded away they endured many hardships. 'Our men and especially the barons and pirates of the Cinque Ports', wrote the St. Albans chronicler, 'thirsted for the coming of the enemy.' The men of the Cinque Ports no doubt did; most of the country levies almost certainly did not; but they stood ready behind Earl Simon and his wardens even through the weeks of harvest.

Although King Louis and the exiles had taken no action on the Mise of Lewes, the council did not wait for an invasion before it renewed the efforts for peace. King Henry himself must have desired a settlement, for, as Louis was reminded more than once, the fate of the two royal hostages might depend upon the conduct of the exiles. Their lives would be in jeopardy 'under the law of nations' if Louis encouraged the plan of invasion. Arrangements were made for a conference at Boulogne. King Henry arrived at Canterbury on 12 August, the hostages were

---

[1] The local levies were supported by their communities for forty days, but they were under arms for a longer period than this. Ironically enough, Pope Urban afterwards diverted the uncollected or unspent proceeds of the clerical tenth to meet the losses incurred by the Lord Edward during the barons' war.

brought from Kenilworth, and terms of reference were drawn up
for confirmation by the king and his son. This was the 'peace
of Canterbury', on which negotiations were to be based. The
terms comprised the 'form of government' of the previous June
with the significant preamble that this was to remain in force
throughout King Henry's reign and, until a date to be determined, into Edward's reign—a precaution which gives some
probability to a story that the peace of Canterbury was extorted
from Henry and Edward by threats of deposition and imprisonment. Other clauses dealt with the reform of the Church, freedom of trade, facilities to aliens provided that no aliens were
given office under the Crown or places in the royal household,
and the observance of the Charters of liberties and the Provisions
of Westminster. Under the shadow of invasion and of unrest in
the marches, the peace of Canterbury was stiffer than the Mise
of Lewes. It was given a very cold reception at Boulogne.
Hence, on 9 September new proposals were put forward, and
these in their turn were revised a few days later.[1] In their revised
form they were taken to Boulogne by the bishops of London,
Worcester, and Winchester and Peter de Montfort. The barons'
proposals, it was suggested, should be submitted to arbitration
in England by two Frenchmen and two Englishmen under the
presidency of the legate. If no conclusion were reached the
peace of Canterbury would stand. The arbitrators, two of whom
were to be the justiciar and the bishop of London, should
appoint the king's council provided that this were composed of
Englishmen and denizens. Guarantees against molestation were
to be given to the earls of Leicester and Gloucester and their
adherents, and safeguards imposed upon the two hostages who
would be released after a settlement had been reached and
confirmed. Earl Simon was prepared to go far for the sake of
peace and reunion, even to take the control of the appointments to the king's council out of the hands of the community
of barons; but he would not allow the king unlimited freedom.

---

[1] The board of arbitrators, for example, was to include the archbishop of Rouen,
who in the first draft was suggested as a fifth, to act in case of disagreement. Again,
a stipulation that Earl Simon's dispute with Henry should first be settled was
dropped. It should be noted that King Louis's envoys, the lord of Nesle and Peter
the chamberlain, were at Canterbury, and that Henry of Almain, after the bishops
had gone surety for his return, had been allowed to go to the French court to see
what he could do. The terms of 9 September are in the *Foedera*, I. i. 446; the revised
terms are summarized in the *Cal. Pat. Rolls, 1258–66*, pp. 370, 371.

Any hopes which these proposals may have raised were dispelled by the firmness of the papal legate. The cardinal had been in correspondence with the barons and prelates in England since June. His 'letters of legation' were sent ahead of him at the end of May; but his messengers were deprived of them at Dover and he himself was refused admission to the kingdom. In a reasoned reply to the barons, who had appealed to the ancient privilege that no legate should be sent to England without an invitation, and had desired him to meet their proctors at Boulogne, he reminded them that the pope was not bound by his predecessors and that in fact the presence of a legate had been sought. This was a reference to the urgent request made in 1258.[1] In reply to their demand that he should put an end to the preparations for invasion he said that he had tried to prevent the assembling of knights by the exiles, but he had failed. Now it would be still harder to arrest the movement. The cardinal up to this time (26 July) avoided direct threats. He wished to act independently of the exiles and to be welcomed in England. By 12 August, when he was with King Louis at Boulogne, he changed his tone. He summoned the baronial leaders to admit him before 1 September or to appear to justify their refusal; also, under pain of excommunication and interdict, he fixed a term for the renunciation of the so-called Provisions of Oxford. When the three bishops appointed to bring the baronial proposals arrived with Peter de Montfort and other proctors at Boulogne, the legate ordered them, on their return, to observe the papal sentences pronounced against Earl Simon and his accomplices earlier in the year. They refused. In such an atmosphere negotiation was futile. Earl Simon must now try to unite England without reference to the exiles and, until a settlement was reached, hold by the peace of Canterbury. On 21 October the legate issued formal sentences of excommunication and interdict against the upholders of the Provisions. In December he was recalled to succeed Pope Urban as Clement IV.

The strong rally against the threatened invasion had revealed the range of general feeling behind Earl Simon. The form of government, as confirmed at Canterbury, had defined his position. Hitherto, however, but part of the story has been told.

[1] Above, p. 135. The legate's letter, dated Amiens, 26 July, is preserved in a contemporary register of the dean and chapter of Worcester; see the *Fourteenth Report of the Historical Manuscripts Commission*, Appendix, Part viii (1895), pp. 172–3.

All assured peace was impossible unless the Marcher lords of the west were prepared to observe the conditions on which they had been released. John Baliol and the northern royalists could be left to the attentions of their Montfortian neighbours; but Roger Mortimer and his friends were a real danger. The hard terms of the peace of Canterbury must, indeed, have been regarded as necessary because, while invasion threatened the south, the Marchers in the west were 'digging themselves in'. They did not come to the June parliament. They retained the prisoners taken at Northampton. They took no notice of the summonses sent to them. They held Bristol and other royal castles and plundered their neighbours in the Severn valley. As early as the end of July Earl Simon and Gilbert of Clare were compelled to move against them, to collect local knights and men-at-arms, and to call on the Welsh for aid. The 'peace of Canterbury' was authorized by the two earls from a distance. After a sharp campaign they forced Roger Mortimer, James of Audley, and the other recalcitrants to terms. On 25 August the Marchers agreed at Montgomery to surrender the royal castles and to appear at the king's court with their prisoners. Earl Simon was able to join the court at Canterbury. The failure to come to any agreement at Boulogne revived the defiance of the Marchers. If they had intended to observe the terms of surrender accepted at Montgomery they quickly changed their minds. This time the lead was taken by the Lord Edward's more intimate adherents, who were gathered together at Bristol, under its castellan, the sturdy royalist Robert Walerand. They were a link with the past and the nucleus of the army which, nine months later, was led by Edward at Evesham. Two at least of them, Pain de Chaworth and Robert Tybetot, were later to be leaders in the conquest of Wales. These and other young men in Bristol castle made a quick dash across country to Wallingford, so long the stronghold of Richard of Cornwall, now the prison of the Lord Edward. They failed to rescue him, but their gesture opened the last, the Edwardian, phase of the civil war. It forced Earl Simon to take drastic measures. The Marchers were summoned to attend at Oxford at the end of November. The feudal host was summoned also. The Marchers did not appear. Simon hastened to the Severn and on 12 December forced Roger Mortimer and his fellows to agree to terms at Worcester. A few days later Edward, after a discussion with the three Rogers, Mortimer, Clifford, and Leyburn, accepted the agreement at Simon's castle of Kenilworth.

The covenant of Worcester put the west, from the Mersey to the Severn estuary, under Earl Simon's control. Edward undertook to exchange with him his palatinate county of Chester, his castle and borough of Bristol, and his other lands in the west for lands of the same value elsewhere. The three Rogers and other leading Marchers were to leave their liberties and go to Ireland for a year and a day. In return measures would be taken for Edward's release from captivity. On Christmas eve the tenants of the shire, castle, and honour of Chester were ordered to serve the earl of Leicester as they used to serve the last earl of the old line, Ranulf de Blundeville.[1] At Worcester, the day after the covenant had been accepted, but before Edward had adhered to it, a parliament had been summoned to meet in London on 20 January 1265. Later, after Edward had agreed to the pact, writs to attend this parliament sometimes give as its object the deliverance of the king's son. It is the famous gathering to which, in addition to prelates and barons, and two knights from each shire, two burgesses from York, Lincoln, and other selected boroughs were called. The national rally of the previous summer was given, so to speak, a political character. This is, indeed, suggested by the writs addressed to the barons, for the twenty-three barons first summoned were partisans of Earl Simon. Writs to others, for example John Baliol and the northern royalists, were sent out later. Complaints might be made against them. The settlement which Simon hoped to reach once and for all would necessarily comprise judicial proceedings in this great meeting of the king's court. The policy of the Mise of Lewes had failed. A new start had to be made by the Three and the Nine. All kinds of problems might have to be faced before a peace reached by force could be turned into a real peace.

[1] After Earl Ranulf's death in October 1232 the earldom went to the son of his eldest sister, i.e. John the Scot, earl of Huntingdon, a nephew of King William the Lion. John the Scot died without issue in 1237. The succession raised unprecedented problems. The right to the title and impartible appurtenances of the earl was finally recognized to lie with the elder daughter of John's eldest sister and her husband William de Forz, but whether the lands of the county of Chester went with this right was greatly discussed. Finally the county was declared to be partible like the rest of the inheritance. King Henry bought up all the rights of the co-heiresses, William de Forz and his wife quitclaimed to the king the rights to the title, &c. The shire was kept entire and annexed to the Crown. See R. Stewart-Brown in *E.H.R.* xxxv (1920), 26–53.

The proceedings in parliament began late and continued slowly; but at last a form of peace was agreed on 8 March. It defined the Lord Edward's status and obligations. He was required to adhere under oath to the provisional government of the Three and the Nine, to call in no aliens, and to stay in England for three years from the coming Easter. If he broke these conditions he could be disinherited. His household was to be purged of suspects and subjected to the supervision of the council. The pact of Worcester was restated with ingenious modifications: the castles of Chester, Newcastle-under-Lyme, and the Peak, with the shire and city of Chester, were given in fee to Earl Simon, who was for the time being also to hold Bristol castle. After the transfer had been completed, Bristol was to be restored to Edward with five royal castles—Dover, Scarborough, Bamborough, Nottingham, and Corfe—which the king would give to him; but all these were then to be handed over for five years as hostages for Edward's compliance with the terms of peace. By this expedient Simon held Chester and made sure that strongholds in strategic positions were in safe hands, without depriving either Henry or Edward of their titles and prospective rights. On 10 March Edward and Henry of Almain were surrendered to the king by their guardian Henry de Montfort, who was relieved of responsibility. The king and his son swore to maintain the terms of settlement and to observe the charters of liberties. One of the terms was that they should assure the adherence of Ireland, Gascony, and the king of the Scots 'and other lands subject to the king of England'. On the next day, 11 March, their declarations were proclaimed in Westminster Hall. Nine bishops declared transgressors against the charters and the statutes made in the preceding year to be excommunicated. Every freeman was ordered to renew homage and fealty to the king, saving all the articles of the peace. The council proceeded to tidy up. In February it had appointed a new chancellor, Thomas de Cantilupe, the nephew of the bishop of Worcester. It began to deal with the judicial business which had accumulated during the recent disorders and required the attention of the justiciar and his colleagues.[1] It took steps to re-open the trade in wool with Flanders and issued proclamations

---

[1] Hugh le Despenser was confirmed in office with a stipend of 1,000 marks a year. The assertion of some writers that Earl Simon acted as a second justiciar is due to a misunderstanding.

to the leading exiles in their chief manors to return to answer for their conduct in a new parliament on 1 June. It required the archbishop of Canterbury and the bishop of Hereford to return under stringent conditions.

Yet in this, his greatest hour, Simon's fate was determined. He could hope for no consideration across the Channel. On 19 July Pope Clement, whose news lagged some weeks after events, wrote to the new legate, the Cardinal Ottobuono, warning him 'not to admit a treaty of false peace until the pestilent man, with all his progeny, be plucked out of the realm of England'. Roger Mortimer and the other parties to the pact of Worcester did not go to Ireland. They found one excuse after another, were granted one delay after another, and stayed at home. In February Robert de Ferrers, the earl of Derby, was arrested and imprisoned in the Tower. His wilful trespasses were so patent that he submitted himself wholly to the king's grace. His fall hastened the defection which had already become apparent in the baronial party. Simon's vigorous action had bred jealousy and suspicion. He had seized Chester and Bristol and was trying to make sure of other strongholds. His sons and closest friends had been given key positions. He was believed to be collecting a strong force of paid knights. His wardens governed the shires. His desire to stamp out unauthorized violence and to maintain justice and order threatened leading men who feared the fate of the earl of Derby. A clause in the pact of Worcester requiring the release of the remaining prisoners taken at Northampton without further parley, ransom, or exchange had at once led to private disputes about the ransoms of the prisoners taken at Lewes, for these had no longer to be held for exchange as the Mise of Lewes had stipulated. Probably altercations about prisoners and other grievances had disturbed the proceedings in parliament before the settlement in March. The most serious defection was that of the young earl of Gloucester, one of the triumvirate. Gilbert of Clare had come to hate the younger Montforts and to chafe against the leadership of their father. He showed himself difficult. For example, he would not fulfil an obligation, as surety, to obtain from its castellan the surrender of Bamborough, one of the five royal castles mentioned in the recent terms of peace. He had withdrawn himself and made excuses for staying away from court. With John Giffard of Brimpsfield and others he took cover in the forest of Dean and began to treat with Roger Mortimer. At length, on Gilbert's failure to appear at Northampton, whither the court had moved, Earl Simon again marched to the Severn, taking the king and Edward with him. The armed forces of the shires of Worcester, Gloucester, and Hereford were ordered to attend the king at Gloucester on 3 May to maintain the peace of the realm.

The hopeful scene had changed within a few weeks. Earl Simon must have realized at Gloucester how serious the danger was. The new chancellor withdrew from court at Gloucester and the great seal was entrusted to a layman, a keeper of the royal wardrobe, who used it under the direction of certain members of council. And it was from Gloucester that the earl made his inquiries into his rights as steward. He looked to precedents for support in his isolation. Gilbert of Clare is said by the rhyming chronicler Robert of Gloucester to have encamped on a hill in a wood near the town. His fires lit the country-side by night. He drafted his complaints: the subjection of the king in spite of the peace, the distribution of castles and prisoners, the exaltation of Earl Simon's sons. There were comings and goings at Gloucester and, from 6 May, at Hereford. The bishop of Worcester, the justiciar, and others are said to have arranged a convention between the two earls; but already the men of the marches and the Severn valley were up in arms. Grave news had brought Simon to Hereford. William of Valence and John de Warenne had landed in the lordship of Pembroke. The Cinque Ports were warned on 10 May to be on the alert against other landings, the sheriffs were ordered to arrest preachers of sedition and suppress false rumours. On 20 May the wardens of the peace were instructed to seize the Marchers who had broken their oath to go to Ireland, and to deny the story of discord between Simon and Gilbert. The men of Shrewsbury, Bridgnorth, and Bristol were told to order themselves in constabularies, for a new war was threatened by rebels against the king. On 26 May an emissary of the invaders was told that they must seek justice in the king's court.

Gilbert of Clare must have been a party to the rising. His parleying with Simon was a blind. He was busy in the country-side. 'When one thought he was far, oft he was near.' He was waiting for Edward. His brother Thomas of Clare, who was later to be a close companion and friend of Edward, was at Hereford.

It was his and Henry de Montfort's duty to keep watch over the prince. He slept in Edward's chamber and was in fact one of the plotters. On 28 May, in Whit week, Edward escaped while he was out riding. All had been arranged. He and Thomas of Clare were to make a dash to Roger Mortimer's castle at Wigmore, and thence to Ludlow. There, in Ludlow (the castle of Matilda de Braose and her foreign husband, Geoffrey de Geneville), he was joined by Roger Mortimer and the earl of Gloucester. For some days Earl Simon seems to have been unaware of the range of the conspiracy. He summoned the knight service of England to march by day and night to the Severn, but he did not realize that Edward, Earl Gilbert, and the Marchers were together. When he did a flood of orders and proclamations was let loose over the country. They give the measure of Simon's confidence in the spring, of the bitterness of disillusionment, of the confusion into which a bewildered and unsuspecting land was thrown, of the high-minded folly which let the Marchers go after Lewes and trusted their promises at Montgomery and Worcester.

If Simon had realized how quickly the passages of the Severn would be closed and how demoralized the administration in England would become, he would probably have made for the river at once and tried to join his supporters in and around London. Instead of doing this he ordered his second son, Simon, his warden in Surrey and Sussex, to hurry westwards, while he himself turned for aid to Llywelyn ap Gruffydd. The prince of Wales, who was at Pipton on the upper Wye, on the northern border of medieval Brecon, defined the conditions on which he would accept a treaty, and a treaty was ratified by King Henry three days later (22 June). In return for a fine of 30,000 marks Llywelyn got complete recognition with the right to Montgomery and other conquests which he might win from the rebels on the March. But he made it clear that this must be a firm offer. If the king died or did not accept his existing obligations under the recent peace made in London, his own obligation would cease. In plain words, though he would send aid to Simon, Llywelyn would not commit himself. He would wait and see. A few days later the court moved to Monmouth, from whence Simon presumably intended to attack Earl Gilbert's lands and castles in Glamorgan. This was a mistake. He had been expected to go to the relief of Gloucester castle, which had been besieged by Edward, while the younger Simon came up from the east.

The fall of Gloucester closed the last passage of the Severn. Simon tried to cross the estuary from Newport, and so to reach Bristol, but this way also was barred. He dared wait no longer. He made a detour through the hills back to Hereford and, although Edward with a stronger force was close by at Worcester, contrived on Sunday, 2 August, to cross the Severn, with the barons and knights and Welsh infantry under his command, by a ford to Kempsey, a manor of Bishop Walter. On the night of 3 August he reached Evesham, fourteen miles away. Thence he could strike east towards London, or, if necessary, try to force his way to Kenilworth.

Simon the younger, who ought to have been ready to join his father, had dallied in the south. When he did come west he was probably wise to make for Kenilworth, but he seems to have had no idea of his father's peril and he certainly underrated Edward. When he reached Kenilworth on 31 July he did not enter the castle but stayed the night in the priory. Edward, on the news of his approach, immediately left Worcester to attack him and was able to surprise him outside the castle. Simon the younger escaped into the fortress but most of the barons and knights who were with him were captured. Edward hastened back to Worcester, presumably to prevent the elder Simon's passage of the Severn; but the earl, in his rapid march, reached and crossed the river before he was expected. Edward at once set out again, put himself across the road between Evesham and Kenilworth, and early on 4 August closed in on the town from the north-east. Simon's men were hungry. The king, hurried along as he had been, was tired out. A few hours' rest in Evesham were needed, but the delay forced Simon to fight. Roger Mortimer, who had slipped round the town, was watching the bridge over the Avon; Edward closed the way out on the higher ground to the north. Here the fight was short and fierce. The Welsh foot scattered and were cut down. Simon and his knights fought in a circle round the king. The earl, his son Henry, Hugh Despenser, Peter de Montfort, Ralph Basset of Drayton (the local warden of the shires) were among the slain. Humphrey de Bohun the younger died of his wounds in October in Beeston castle in Cheshire. Guy de Montfort, the earl's third son, was also wounded and captured. The king was rescued from the indiscriminate slaughter by Roger Leyburn. Earl Simon's head was struck off and sent to Roger Mortimer's wife at

Wigmore; his body was buried by the monks of Evesham. His tomb became a place of pilgrimage. In high official circles he was a pestilent fellow, the king's felon; his children were of the race of Ganelon, a treacherous brood; but in many a house of friars and nuns and throughout the country-side he was a popular saint. His legend grew, his miracles were told among the people and collected. Songs were made about him. They lingered in the memories of local singers here and there for many years. In 1323, when Edward II was on progress in the north, he came in August to Whorlton castle in the Cleveland hills, and one evening two women of the neighbourhood sang to him songs about Simon de Montfort.

After his victory Edward hurried north to secure Chester. The king, tired, wounded, and bewildered, was taken to Gloucester, then, three weeks later, to Marlborough for his convalescence. The prelates and magnates of the king's party must have been summoned a few days after the battle to meet at Winchester early in September, for, as early as 13 August, the sheriffs were ordered to hear complaints against and deal with evil-doers who, professing their loyalty, were despoiling clerks and laymen; and to send recalcitrants to Winchester by 9 September. The great seal was entrusted to Walter Giffard, the bishop of Bath and Wells. All over the country resistance crumbled or came to an end. Bristol and Hereford came to terms. Windsor and other royal castles were surrendered. The late justiciar's widow gave up the Tower of London. Indeed, the change of front had begun some weeks before the battle of Evesham. It should be remembered that the king had been in the ascendant fifteen months before, the greater part of England had not been touched by the war, and there was, as there often is in civil war, a majority which waited to see how the fight would go. Earl Simon had had adherents in every shire, but he had also been losing ground and his pact with Llywelyn had not improved his reputation. The war, from both points of view, had been waged by barons to rescue the king from dangerous persons. To the end even the rebels fought in his name.[1]

The natural policy would have combined judicial proceedings against law-breakers with a general amnesty. This was the view

[1] Henry had renounced the rebels by an act of *diffidatio* on the eve of the battle of Lewes, but the victors at once issued writs from chancery in his name. In March 1265 the position was formally regularized by a general oath of allegiance.

of the earl of Norfolk, Philip Basset, and other wise men. It seems to have been the view of Richard of Cornwall, in spite of the fact that he had been immured in Kenilworth. On 6 September Simon de Montfort the younger released the king of the Romans in return for an undertaking that he would be a loyal friend to his sister the Countess Eleanor, her children, and their households, and would do his best to maintain their rights, saving his fealty to the king and Edward. At Winchester a harder spirit prevailed. It is not surprising that Simon was not offered terms lenient enough to bring him to submission and that he continued to resist. It was to be expected that all acts done in the king's name after the battle of Lewes, while he was in Earl Simon's power, should be declared null and void. But an ordinance of 17 September, the day after general peace was proclaimed, prolonged the war, intensified bitterness, and for a time brought England into a state of social chaos. The lands and tenements of every accomplice (*fautor*) of Earl Simon were taken into the king's hands. Any which had already been seized by others—and these were numerous—were to be handed over to the king. Knights were appointed in each shire to co-operate with the sheriff in an extent or survey of the lands. They are described in royal writs as the *saisitores* of the lands and tenements of the accomplices of the late earl of Leicester. If this drastic measure had been the prelude to a systematic policy of settlement with the rebels, much could be said in its favour; it gathered everything into the king's hands and put an end to indiscriminate seizure within and without the franchises by the royalists; but it had been preceded and was followed by an indiscriminate dispersion of the lands and tenements among the king's followers. Moreover, not only were the grants unequally dispersed so that many got too much and others too little in the scramble for the royal favour, but no sure test seems to have applied in the definition of a rebel. The chancery rolls for the next year or so suggest indescribable confusion in the country, and bewildered counsels at court.

One outcome of the confusion was that other and wiser ordinances made at Windsor later in the month could not be properly enforced. One of these measures dealt with robbery and depredation committed since the public proclamation of peace on 16 September. This law (*lex*) was to run until 17 October 1266, but in fact it had to be continued in force after that date. It

THE DISINHERITED 205

provided for trial by the justices with the king on a writ of attachment and imposed penalties of imprisonment and fine (*redemptio*) on the guilty. Another measure, which also had to be renewed and supplemented, brought under review, at the instance of interested parties, transactions in land during the time of war. It enabled any man who had been deprived of his land to summon the existing tenant to show cause in the court *coram rege* why he should not recover. If he had sold it freely he could recover it by repayment to the buyer, for the transaction had been made in time of war. This enactment went far to reinstate loyalists who had lost their lands, but it did not meet all cases; so in the year 1266–7 it was supplemented by the process followed under the writ *talem qualem* after the war of 1215–17. Those who had been faithful to the king—not, as in 1217, all men—were to have such seisin as they had had before the war of lands lost by occupation in time of war. As has been said, it was very hard to put these measures into effect; they imply a state of peace, but rebels whose lands had been seized by the king naturally did not benefit, and by their continued resistance made it harder for loyalists to benefit by them.

All the same the king, his son, and their chosen advisers were in power again during the parliament held in Windsor at Michaelmas. Resistance in London was broken by the fear of a massed attack, and the king was able to celebrate the feast of St. Edward, on 13 October, in Westminster. The city was only gradually allowed its liberties. Although it contained many royalists, it did not escape corporate punishment for the transgressions of the elements which had assumed power, insulted the queen, and despoiled the lands of Richard of Cornwall. Civic administration was entrusted to seneschals who ruled from the Tower. The citizens bought their peace at the price of an enormous fine, 20,000 marks, a liability which continued to cause trouble long after normal life had been resumed, and was not given its final audit at the exchequer until 1301, thirty-five years after its imposition.[1] The fine did not save the known adherents of Earl Simon from the loss of tenements and the ejection of their leaders from the city. As we shall see, their capacity to resist was not destroyed by the submission of their fellows and the rule of the king's agents.

[1] The royal letters remitting Henry's anger and imposing the fine were not issued until January 1266.

The subjection of Simon the younger and of nests of rebels throughout the land was the next task. First of all it was necessary to secure Dover. While the king moved to Canterbury to await the arrival of the queen and the papal legate, Ottobuono Fieschi, Edward went to the south coast. The countess of Leicester was in the castle at Dover. She had already sent her younger sons, Amauri and Richard, across the Channel with a large sum of money and had only her young daughter, Eleanor, with her. She could not resist, for some of the garrison had combined with the prisoners and held the main tower against her. Edward treated her with courtesy and undertook that the members of her household should be restored to their lands and homes. She left England, never to return, on 28 October, a day before the queen and legate arrived. Two or three days earlier, King Henry, at Canterbury, had created his son Edmund earl of Leicester and seneschal of England, endowing him with the lands of the late earl 'our enemy and felon, by whom the war in England was begun'. The feudal host was summoned to meet at Northampton by 13 December for an attack on Kenilworth. Simon did not await the siege. He preferred to join the leaders in resistance who had for some time been making their way, some of them after escaping from their captors, to the Isle of Axholme, in the fens by the lower Trent. Edward, accordingly, diverted the campaign to deal with the rebels in Axholme. About Christmas time he forced them to enter into a mise or convention on Bycarrs Dyke near Haxey. Simon and his companions placed themselves 'at the king's award and ordinance, saving life and limb and prison'. Simon's fate was first decided. He was to leave England on a pension, and to find pledges that he would observe his oath to do nothing to the detriment of the king and the realm. This was at Northampton in January 1266. He was taken by Edward to London, whence, fearing treachery, he managed to escape across the sea. Soon afterwards his brother Guy, who had been taken prisoner at Evesham and had been imprisoned, first at Windsor, then at Dover, also made his escape abroad. England was cleared of the Montforts.

The 'disinherited' remained. Something, it was realized, had to be done about them. Gradually, as passion ceased to inflame greed, more moderate counsels prevailed. Prudence suggested that interests essential to the common well-being, in London, for example, and the Cinque Ports, should be placated. The Lord Edward, more of a statesman than some of his friends, followed up the capture of Sandwich in January and the reduction of Winchelsea in March by a reconciliation with the Portsmen. This wise action cleared the coasts of continual piracy and relieved merchants, both English and aliens, of the dangers which had paralysed trade. Edward, indeed, was established, to his own profit, as the protector of English commerce. He was already warden of the king's exchange in London. He was now made castellan of Dover and warden of the Cinque Ports, with his ablest ally, Roger Leyburn, as his lieutenant. In April he was given control of the foreign merchants. He issued licences to them to trade and gave or withheld permission to them to stay in the country. In return he could levy moderate aids from them over and above the ancient prises which were paid to the Crown. Here, as in other directions, he was, unknown to himself, preparing the way to his future as king and his reliance upon a more methodical system of finance based upon the regulation of trade. He enlarged the range of his personal influence. He did the same when he ran to earth and overcame rebels like Adam Gurdon and then, in due time, turned them into loyal and useful servants. He struck hard, but he knew a good man when he saw him, whether he were friend or foe.

It was the papal legate, however, rather than Edward—though he recognized the prince's high quality—who took the lead in this time of turmoil. Edward's first duty was to fight the rebels; Ottobuono's to bring about a general peace, a lasting settlement. Ottobuono Fieschi was a distinguished man. Since his creation as cardinal in 1252, he had had a hand in most of the important business of the Curia, notably in Sicilian affairs. He was one of the friends at Rome of Richard of Cornwall. He came to England with wide powers, to preach a crusade, order ecclesiastical affairs, deal with the rebels, and bring peace. Himself a future pope, he had in his company two men who were to become two of the most famous popes in history.[1] A month after his arrival he held an ecclesiastical council in London (1 December 1265) where he displayed his credentials and received oaths

---

[1] Ottobuono was pope as Adrian V for only a month in 1276. The others were Tedaldo Visconti, the later Pope Gregory X (1271–6), and Benedict Caetani, later Pope Boniface VIII (Dec. 1294 to 1303).

of obedience. He then proceeded to deal with the bishops who had been most active in their support of the Provisions of Oxford. Earl Simon's oldest friend, the bishop of Worcester, died in February 1266 before the process was concluded; four others, London, Lincoln, Chichester, and Winchester were suspended and ordered to go to the papal court.[1]

The legate's efforts to bring the baronial rebels and their adherents to obedience, and the king's advisers to see reason, were beset by much greater difficulties. At times he was sad and dispirited. The disinherited held out in forests and swamps, and even for a time in a city or a borough. Outbreaks in London were feared. Simon the younger was believed, and rightly, to be planning an invasion from Normandy. The air was full of rumours about royal intentions or royal disasters. Roger Leyburn was able to clean up the south-east, and to break up, though not to destroy, the rebels in Essex. Edward tracked down and captured Adam Gurdon in Hampshire. On 15 May Henry of Almain, John de Warenne, and others surprised the earl of Derby, John d'Eyvill, Henry of Hastings, Baldwin Wake, and others, who had collected together at Chesterfield. The earl of Derby was captured and taken to Windsor; but some of the rest escaped, Henry of Hastings to Kenilworth, others to the woods and ultimately to the Isle of Ely, which became a rallying point and refuge of the disinherited.[2] In the meanwhile preparations for the siege of the strong and well-protected castle at Kenilworth had been completed. Early in June the king and his son arrived in full force with knights, men-at-arms, and engineers, and the business of full investment began; but it was a weary business. The garrison was waiting expectantly for news of invasion and was heartened in August by the seizure of Ely. The besiegers were divided in counsel and eager for the end. So, at long last, the legate got his way. The king agreed to deal with

---

[1] Richard Gravesend of Lincoln got off lightly and was allowed to return (1267). He died in 1279. John Gervais of Winchester died at Viterbo in January 1268. Henry of Sandwich, of London (died 1273), and Stephen Berksted, of Chichester (d. 1287), were pardoned by Pope Gregory X in 1272, and returned after King Henry's death.

[2] Some of them had submitted at Axholme but had either escaped or refused to abide by the terms imposed on them. Robert de Ferrers, earl of Derby, was in an exceptional position. He had been imprisoned in the Tower to await his trial before the fall of Earl Simon and released by the king in December 1265. He was related to the king by marriage, for his wife was a daughter of the count of La Marche, Henry's eldest half-brother. His rebellion cost him dear; see below, p. 212, note 1.

the problem of the disinherited. The procedure approved in parliament at Kenilworth was announced on 31 August. Three bishops and three barons were appointed to co-opt one more bishop and five more barons, who were to be men above suspicion, of most knowledge and weight. The committee of twelve so constituted was to draft a plan which should have the approval of 'the king and the legate, and the legate and Henry of Almain'. The plan was worked out at Coventry. In its first form, as presented for the comments of the legate and Henry of Almain, it gave frank expression to differences of opinion on some points. Decisions on these and other details were pronounced by the two umpires on 31 October and embodied in the final form of what is known as the Dictum of Kenilworth.

The Dictum was included in later collections among the statutes of the realm, between the statute of Merton and the statute of Marlborough. It defined the ways in which the accomplices of Earl Simon might recover the lands seized by the Crown in accordance with the ordinance of Winchester. Its later exaltation has obscured the fact that it implied and did not displace the Winchester ordinance, which remained in force for many years. Lands which had escaped seizure were the object of royal concern after Edward's return from crusade. Proceedings under the Dictum continued much longer. Thorny problems in the redemption of the lands of the rebels engaged the attention of the royal courts until the end of our period. A lucid exposition of the historical setting in which the Dictum operated was made by King Edward in March 1276.[1] He reminded justices in eyre that they must distinguish between offences committed in time of war and offences committed in time of peace. The former if done under guise of war were subject to the rules of the Dictum as interpreted by King Henry's judges. They did not involve the loss of life or limb or perpetual imprisonment. They came under the Dictum and the judges on eyre should have before them a transcript of that document and diligently observe its contents. The war, he continued, began on 4 April 1264, when King Henry went with his army from Oxford to Northampton and ended on 16 September 1265 when peace was proclaimed at Winchester. Two qualifications, however, were attached to this definition. Homicide, robbery, and breaches of the peace committed during the period of war but not under guise of war must

[1] *Cal. Close Rolls, 1272-9*, p. 333.

be regarded as though this had been a period of peace. Secondly, those persons who were in Axholme or at Kenilworth or in the Isle of Ely or at Chesterfield or Southwark (we have yet to mention these last) must be dealt with in accordance with the peace made with them, whether this were the Dictum or special privileges granted to them; the fact that their offences were committed in time of peace, after 16 September 1265, did not affect them for they fell under the terms of the peace made with them. The same principle applied to those who were with the earl of Gloucester during his march from Wales to London and while he was in London; they were protected by the peace made with him. This incident also has yet to be described.

The Dictum, then, defined the way in which the persons, high and low, disinherited under the terms of the ordinance of Winchester as accomplices of Earl Simon, could be restored to their place in society and recover their lands. It arrested, and so far as was possible dissolved the effects of, a social revolution. It is a long document and deals with all sorts of problems; for affairs had not stood still since September 1265 and the situation was complicated. King Henry had not kept the lands of the rebels in his own hands. He had not even regarded them as contingent escheats, like the 'lands of the Normans' seized after the loss of Normandy sixty years before—as lands which, although enjoyed by others, might always be restored to their original tenants or their successors. They had been given away lavishly, hastily, indiscriminately. It is true, on the other hand, that some rebels had made their peace, had redeemed their lands by private arrangements either with the Crown or, with the approval of the royal court, with the new tenants. This process had gone on behind the scenes ever since the battle of Evesham and it continued, to some extent, after the Dictum. The Dictum did not affect settlements of this kind. But it is also true that innocent persons had suffered as rebels or been the victims of local and illegal spoliation. The justices whose duty it was to apply the Dictum had to cope with such cases, and found them more numerous and more difficult than the cases of straightforward redemption, which were in fact generally settled outside court and then submitted for approval, not necessarily to these justices appointed under the Dictum, but often to the king or one of his courts. Gradually—yet on the whole quickly —the disinherited were absorbed. A few cases lingered on into

the next century long after the appointed justices had done their
work, but the great majority were settled before King Henry's
death. Generally the rebels, often after heavy sacrifices, recovered their lands. Minute investigation would show that a
few lost all, and some lost much, but, although the market in
land was busy, the legate and his wiser co-adjutors carried
through a great act of reconciliation.

In 1266 the value of land in England was reckoned as ten
times its annual revenue. This figure was the basis of the plan of
redemption. A man who had taken the field on Earl Simon's
side could be restored fully to the king's peace and recover his
lands if he paid half their market value, or five years' purchase.
This explains the principle underlying the Dictum, not the
usual way of putting it into practice. Sometimes the royal
grantee continued in possession for a term of years until the
'farm' which he owed was equal to the redemption agreed upon
or imposed by the Crown, and this was often less than the
maximum of five years' revenue. Sometimes the rebel was put
in possession and, as the condition of recovering full seisin, paid
the price of redemption in instalments according to the terms
of a contract with the royal grantee. Sometimes the rebel sold
his timber and paid what he got to receivers for whose appointment provision was made in the Dictum. There were all kinds
of expedients and arrangements. We must repeat, however, that
the rebels in this category—the men who had fought at
Northampton, Lewes, Evesham, and Chesterfield or elsewhere
against the king, had taken a willing part in the war, had been
in Kenilworth or as the immediate bailiffs and servants of Earl
Simon had despoiled their neighbours—were the most obvious
offenders, the most numerous, perhaps, but not the most difficult
to deal with.

The Dictum was a great state-paper. Its scope was wide. It
begins with a statement of first principles: the king's subjects
must henceforth settle their affairs according to law in his
courts, and the king should rule through reliable men, in loyal
regard (*pietas*) for his position, and respect the liberties of the
Church and his subjects as defined in the great charters and
later concessions. It continues as an act of oblivion, pardon,
resumption, absolution, and a plea for the settlement of the
affairs of London. It then proceeds to deal with particular
problems in detail. In addition to those landed rebels who had

fought openly on Earl Simon's side,[1] many other delinquents or alleged delinquents had to be restored to the king's peace. Civil war is not a clear-cut affair. The 'disturbance' had been general, the rebels were hardly distinguishable from the large element of 'depredators' with whom official documents frequently identified them. Judicial inquiry into their guilt was no easy matter. The Dictum defined certain principles. Persons who had not personally engaged in the campaigns but had persuaded others to join the earl and his accomplices or dissuaded others from their duty to the king were to redeem their lands for twice their annual value. Landless knights and men-at arms who had taken part on the earl's side, whether independently or as followers of some lord, were to lose a third of such goods as they possessed. Unwilling and helpless people who had been swept into the movement and got out of it as soon as they could were to pay one year's value of their lands. Those who had been in Northampton and, while not resisting the barons, had taken refuge in the churches, were to pay the value of their lands for half a year. Other provisions dealt with banished persons and those who as especially dangerous were left to the king's mercy, with alleged rebels who were abroad and could not immediately make their peace, with the wives and widows of rebels, with the scoundrels who had falsely charged or informed against others as rebels. Obviously these classes of persons and others who might present unforeseen problems could not be dealt with until their cases had been considered, with the aid of local juries, by the justices. The Dictum provided that twelve persons should be appointed to apply its terms. These were the justices commissioned in September 1267[2] to

---

[1] A few persons were dealt with more severely. The future of Earl Simon's sons had already been left to King Louis of France. He did his best for Simon the younger, but no agreement was reached and in due course Simon and Guy joined Charles of Anjou in Italy, and Amauri, the youngest son, went to study in Padua. Robert Ferrers, earl of Derby, Henry of Hastings, the head of the garrison in Kenilworth, and those responsible for the mutilation of a royal messenger were under the Dictum to redeem their lands for seven, not five, times their annual value. At this time the earl of Derby was a close prisoner in Windsor, and may not have been told the terms of the Dictum. However this may have been, he was forced to agree to conditions, as of his own free will, which made it impossible for him to redeem his lands, and prevented him from seeking legal redress after his release. His lands, except Chartley, were given to Edmund of Lancaster, whose grandson Henry of Lancaster was created earl of Derby in 1337.

[2] These commissions seem to have displaced those given to the bishop of St. David's and eleven others, including Bracton, early in the year. The renewal of

traverse the country in four separate circuits. They were required to enforce the Dictum, to inquire into the lands seized under the Winchester ordinance of 1265, and to put a long series of questions to the jurors of each hundred. Unfortunately only a few rolls of their proceedings have survived, and not all of these are complete; but they suffice to give a good idea of the work of the justices in the east midlands and in the southeastern shires south of the Thames.[1]

The Dictum did not satisfy the garrison in Kenilworth and the rebels in the Isle of Ely. England was not at peace after the proclamation on 31 October; and it says much for the determination of the legate and the moderates that the policy worked out at Coventry, in spite of the extremists on both sides, was not allowed to suffer. Patience prevailed. Many of the disinherited made their peace. The defenders of Kenilworth, after a show of bravado, were allowed forty days to await help from the younger Simon de Montfort, and, when no help came, surrendered on 14 December under the protection and also under the obligations of the Dictum. Early in February 1267 a parliament met at Bury St. Edmunds to deal with the situation. The Lord Edward delayed drastic measures against Ely, and long and inconclusive negotiations were conducted from Bury with John d'Eyvill and his companions in the Isle, facts which suggest that the men about the king were divided in purpose, and that the rebels had sympathizers among them. The deadlock was broken by the earl of Gloucester. The king had moved to Cambridge, the legate had returned to the Tower of London, the earl had gone to the west. Earl Gilbert had long been restive, probably since the discussions in Coventry. He was at odds with Roger Mortimer and in close touch with John d'Eyvill. Rather than see the rebels broken and his rivals in the royal councils triumphant, he decided to march on London with his own force of knights and men-at-arms. According to some accounts he was invited to a conference by the legate. He was impelled not merely by fears for himself, but also by the revival of disturbance in many parts of England and by the strong desire of the legate to see a settlement. He reached the outskirts of the city on 8 April and encamped at Southwark on the south bank of

disturbance no doubt prevented this earlier body from acting. In September thirteen, not twelve, justices were appointed.

[1] See the bibliography at the end of this volume.

the Thames. On the next day he settled in the city and talked with Ottobuono in the church of the Holy Trinity, Aldgate. Two days later John d'Eyvill, who had slipped out of Ely with a number of companions, and evaded the efforts of Roger Leyburn to stop his march to the south, arrived at Southwark. The earl's occupation of the city and his union with the king's 'capital enemy' meant war, not peace. The London commune was restored and took control of civic affairs under a chief bailiff chosen by the earl, and for two months London was in the hands of rebels. A ditch was dug around the walls, access from the Tower was cut off, and Southwark was fortified. This was not at all what the legate had expected. He renewed the excommunication of John d'Eyvill and his companions and shut himself up in the Tower. Later he moved to the Cistercian abbey at Stratford Langthorne on the Lea, where on 7 May he was joined by King Henry.

In the meantime the Lord Edward had been very active. His attack on the men in Ely—a most difficult operation—had been deferred, but he and Roger Leyburn and others had held down or subdued the disturbances in much of the country. Edward had gone as far north as Alnwick in Northumberland and reduced its lord, John de Vescy, to submission. He was free to bring considerable forces to London. Roger Leyburn raised mercenaries across the Channel; early in June the counts of Guisnes and St. Pol—always so willing to combine business with adventure—arrived in England with their knights. The sheriffs of the home counties raised local levies and supplies for the siege of London. But a long investment of the chief city of the realm was not to be added to our medieval annals. On the contrary the concentration of political interest in and about London cleared the air. It brought the elusive resistance in the fens and woodlands face to face with realities and it gave the peacemakers their chance. Few wanted a costly and destructive fight to a finish. Discussions, in which Henry of Almain and Philip Basset took a congenial part, were held day by day until, the legate wrote to the pope, reconciliation came from the hand of the Lord. On 18 June the king entered the city. A settlement had been reached and, a few days later, a general peace was proclaimed. The earl of Gloucester gave financial security to maintain it and was reconciled to the resentful and suspicious Edward by the king of the Romans and his son. The disinherited, though separate terms were made with them, were parties to the negotiations. Their intransigence, it is clear, had been due rather to fear of tiresome delays in the operation of the Dictum than to their wordy adherence to principle, and now the timely action of the earl of Gloucester had relieved them from anxiety. John d'Eyvill and his friends were given two assurances: immediate possession of their lands, if they came to the king's peace, and financial aid from a tax recently granted by the clergy towards the costs of redemption. During the next few weeks they availed themselves of these terms. The Lord Edward, informed by some of the rebels who had left the Isle about its approaches, and helped by a dry season, was able in a masterly operation to reduce the remnant of the force in Ely to submission. Except for a few bands who still held out in Sherwood Forest and other districts of the north midlands, the great disturbance was at an end. In September, as we have seen, the justices in eyre whose duty it was to apply the Dictum received their commissions.

The cardinal legate felt a sense of deep relief. He had often been dispirited and unhappy, but now the policy which underlay the Dictum—his policy—had prevailed and he could go on with confidence to other tasks, peace with Llywelyn of Wales, the precise definition of what was constructive and profitable to the realm in the activity of the last nine years, and the restoration of the Londoners to their liberties.

The recent crisis had interrupted plans for negotiation with the Welsh. The parties met at Shrewsbury at the end of August 1267. Llywelyn desired recognition of his title as prince of the whole of Wales outside the marches and of his right to the lands which he had reoccupied during the disturbances. The discussions were long, intricate, and inconclusive; and at last, on 21 September, King Henry entrusted the work of settlement to the legate. Ottobuono settled the terms in four days. The treaty was ratified at Montgomery on 29 September. Llywelyn's title was formally acknowledged and he did homage to the king as prince of Wales. Consideration of the terms of the treaty of Montgomery must await the treatment of Welsh affairs in a later chapter.

The interests of England as a whole next engaged the attention of the legate and king and their expert advisers. These were the theme of a series of provisions issued on 18 November in a great council at Marlborough. The statute of Marlborough is usually described as a reissue, in a revised form, of the legal clauses of the Provisions of Westminster of 1259, to which the king had more than once expressed his adherence. This it certainly was. The greater part of the statute is a careful restatement of the provisions about wardship, suit of court, and other matters contained in the Westminster provisions, or, as they were not unnaturally, though erroneously, described in some quarters, the 'provisions made at Oxford'. Their continuous validity had been hinted at in the Dictum and had presumably been stressed by the earl of Gloucester and other moderates both before and after the publication of the Dictum. They were the most solid achievement of the baronial movement in 1258 and 1259, had been agreed by all parties, and were now put beyond doubt in a permanent enactment. The statute of Marlborough, however, was more than this. Its preamble and first clauses suggest that it was intended to express in a more binding form the hortatory idealism of the Dictum of Kenilworth. It reflects the mind and intention of the papal legate. Its object is stated to be the amelioration of the realm, the removal of dissension, the maintenance of general peace, the better administration of justice 'as belongeth to the office of a king'. It was promulgated in an assembly composed of discreet men chosen from both greater and lesser folk. It puts in the forefront measures to be taken against all those who were taking the law into their own hands during this time of legal settlement. Persons who resorted to private vengeance, and exacted 'redemptions' from their neighbours—the use of this word 'redemptions' is significant—were put in a separate category of offenders. They themselves were liable to the payment of 'redemptions'. In other words, everyone, whether he had been a loyalist or one of the disinherited, must be made to realize that the disturbances were over and that the rule of law prevailed. And, secondly, the Charter must be observed in every detail. Writs were to be issued freely (*gratis*), presumably without fee, against those who were alleged to have infringed the Charter, so that the cases might be tried before the king, in the bench, or by justices in eyre.

This clause is important. It reminds us that the Charter, as issued in 1225, is a precise and detailed document, not a statement of principles. It had, it is true, acquired a unique character as the safeguard and even the symbol of English 'liberties', a statement of the intention shared by king and subjects to maintain the general well-being. It had been read out and confirmed on critical occasions, as in 1237 and 1253, had been confirmed by the pope, and been given the perpetual sanction of ecclesiastical penalties on those who infringed it. Yet, although as an exposition of rules of law it had too often been disregarded, its value in fact depended upon the right of petitioners and litigants to appeal to its wording on this point or that. The difficulty lay in its nature as a body of concessions granted by the king. Some of its clauses, for example, those relating to wardship, dower, procedure, and the like, had, indeed, defined the common law as it was or ought to be applied in the king's courts, and had influenced the wording of writs by which actions could be originated, but more of them defined the way in which the king and his officers, as the source or channels of justice, should act.[1] In some cases, e.g. an unusual distraint on a village community to build a bridge, the denial of justice could hardly give rise to originating writs. Hence the Charter as a whole could only be maintained by constant watchfulness over the conscience of a responsible king.

The statute of Marlborough sought to go much farther. Its authors, knowingly or not, adopted a policy declared by Earl Simon's administration early in 1265: 'it has been provided by the joint counsel of ourselves and the magnates of our realm that the liberties contained in our great charter shall be observed on our part and on the part of others of our realm in every particular.' On this occasion the object was the observance of the provision against the exaction of fines for 'fair pleading'—slips in the technicalities of pleading. This was one of the provisions of 1259, but King Henry was made to invoke as its sanction the great charter of liberties.[2] The provision in the statute of Marlborough that writs against those who committed breaches of the Charter should be freely issued put the Charter in detail

---

[1] One such case, the enforcement, in favour of an abbey, of the clause of the Charter relevant to the case of a deceased person who held in chief of the king only as a tenant of the escheated barony of Boulogne, will be found in *Close Rolls, 1264–8*, pp. 291–2 (Feb. 1267). Examples of the ways in which the Charter was pleaded in the courts may be studied in *Select Cases in the Court of King's Bench under Edward I*, edited G. O. Sayles (Selden Soc.). See the table of statutes cited and the index (s.v. Statutes) in each of the three volumes.

[2] *Close Rolls, 1264–8*, p. 100.

upon the same footing as a statute enforceable by appropriate writs. This provision was not practicable; for, as the *Articuli super cartas* of 1300 pointed out more than thirty years later, parts of the Charter 'had no remedy at the common law'. In that year a very remarkable step was taken with the object of maintaining the observance of the Great Charter and the Charter of the Forest in every point. The community of each shire was to elect three knights or other suitable persons who would be sworn and appointed local justices by royal letters patent 'to hear and determine, without other writ than their common warrant', complaints against any breach of the Charter by the royal officers or others, if these trespasses had no remedy at common law by writ.[1] The barons had never gone so far as this even in 1258 and 1259, though the spirit in which they had acted was very much the same. Needless to say the gesture of 1300 had no permanent effect, but, like the clause in the statute of Marlborough, it shows how firmly the details as well as the principles of the Great Charter were rooted in the consciousness of Englishmen and how hard reformers tried to operate it as a fundamental statute. The Charter was no longer a compact, a series of promises, a gift. It was a daily criterion of sound government. Suitors in the shire courts had long had the opportunity to become familiar with its contents, even though the duty of the sheriff to have it read aloud twice a year is unlikely to have been regularly observed.

The last petition of the framers of the Dictum to be met was the restoration of the Londoners to their normal status and liberties. The legate had been urging this for some time, but the earl of Gloucester's demonstration had caused delay. Government by the 'commune' and the reappearance of the Montfortian partisans could not at once be followed by a return to oligarchic rule free from external direction. A first step was taken in March 1268, and two years later the Lord Edward, then warden of the city, procured the full restoration of its liberties, including the election of mayor and sheriffs.

By this time the legate had left England. He had been a great

---

[1] Cf. W. S. Thomson, *A Lincolnshire Assize Roll for 1298* (1944), pp. cxxi–cxxii. At this time the evolution of the later justices of the peace had begun, but it was not until 1368 that their duty to determine or try cases was established, so that they became *justices* as well as *keepers* of the peace. The early steps in the process are traced by B. H. Putnam in her introduction to *Kent Keepers of the Peace, 1316–1317* (Kent Archaeological Society; *Records*, vol. xiii, 1933).

peace-maker. His legation stands out as the most fruitful and the most beneficent in the list of papal missions to England between the Norman Conquest and the reign of Queen Mary. His work of political reconciliation was but one of his tasks, the means to an end rather than an end in itself. He had been sent to preach a crusade, and this was one of his main preoccupations between the spring of 1267 and his departure in July 1268. The work was carefully planned, well-timed, and had considerable success. The mendicant friars took the greater share, controlled the finances of its operation (for the redemption of the vow to go to the east was more encouraged among lesser folk than its actual observance), and preached assiduously. The legate himself made at least three spectacular interventions, the first during the earl of Gloucester's occupation of London, when he expounded 'the business of the cross' at St. Paul's, the second at Lincoln in October, the third and last at Northampton during the parliament of June 1268, shortly before he left the country. King Henry was already pledged. The fervour of Ottobuono and his preachers provided him with his companions. At Northampton the Lords Edward and Edmund, Henry of Almain, William of Valence, the earls of Gloucester and Surrey, and others took the cross. Not all went, but the crusade was now in the fashion, a spiritual adventure which gave a sense of enlargement after much tribulation. A third duty of the legate had been the reformation and guidance of ecclesiastical affairs in England. Throughout his legation he was busy about this, in full councils and private endeavour. Archbishop Boniface returned to his province, but he was not the man he had been, and in any case he had to give way to the papal representative, who, armed with authority, really governed the Church in England. The legate's labours were brought to their close in a great council in London in April 1268, when his famous constitutions were issued. Altogether Ottobuono did fine work in England. He was one of the big men in the west, and if his later pontificate in 1276 had not been cut short after a few weeks he might well, as Pope Adrian V, have stood out in general as he stands out in English history.

No land in medieval times was at rest during a papal legation. Even if it welcomed one it soon tired of it, for it interfered at every turn with habitual ways of life. A popular legate would have been an anomaly. He would have had to live without reliance on the resources of the province, or, as they were called, on procurations. He would have had to respect interests and susceptibilities which, if he were to fulfil his function, it might be his duty to disregard. He would have been a nonentity. Ottobuono was anything but a nonentity, and, in spite of his services to England, was criticized, at one time or another, from every quarter. Moreover, he had in the last two years of his legation to share with the royal officials the odium caused by heavy taxation of the clergy. During the disturbances the royal revenue had suffered much more than the land as a whole. The domestic economy of the people was, in the main, self-sufficient. There had been no general devastation. Interruption of life in the fields, the workshops, and the ports had been troublesome in some parts, but most of the dwellers in boroughs and villages had gone about their daily tasks very much as usual, except for the inconvenience caused by occasional levies or by the effects of the disturbance on trade and on the disposal of surplus goods and stocks. In later times even the civil wars of the fifteenth and seventeenth centuries do not seem to have prevented economic development; indeed, they provided some fresh opportunities and hastened or created social change. But the bad effect of civil disturbance upon the exchequer was immediate. Half the sheriffs failed to appear at the audits, and the net revenue in cash paid into the treasury of receipt dropped during the years 1264–8 to about one-eighth of the normal. This would not have been so serious if the sheriffs had been able to collect the money due annually from the shires and had paid it, in obedience to royal writs, into the king's chamber or elsewhere; but there is no reason to believe that they could. King Henry and his administration lived on borrowed money and accumulated a load of debt, some of which was still outstanding in the reign of his grandson. Hence the political settlement reached at Coventry and Kenilworth required as its counterpart a financial settlement, and the obvious source of taxation was not the loyalists who had stood by the king nor the disinherited who had nothing to give, but the clergy. King Henry turned to the pope, and not in vain. Clement IV granted a tenth for three years to meet the king's debts incurred by Queen Eleanor on behalf of her husband while she was in France. This was the first mandatory tax levied by the papacy in England for the relief of the king as distinct from the purposes of a crusade. The papal bull was issued before

Kenilworth in August 1266. A new assessment of clerical revenues was to be made under the direction of the legate and the chief collectors.

Apart from such arrears of previous taxation as papal agents had been able to collect, the clergy had paid no tax for nearly ten years. They could not resist the new tax as such, but they resented the new assessment and they resented still more the association of royal agents with the papal machinery of assessment and collection. They showed their hostility at Bury St. Edmunds in February 1267 and continued their opposition in their assemblies and in the dioceses. Yet, although the process of collection was anything but uniform, between £45,000 and £50,000 were raised, much more than the old valuation of Norwich would have produced. Since this was a papal tax its proceeds could not be paid into the exchequer, but since it was intended to meet the king's debts its allocation was naturally made under royal direction. The legate and his collectors worked hand in hand with the king's 'executors'. The latest historian of papal taxation considers that during the last two years of its exaction the tenth 'was practically administered by royal agents'. The clergy did not soon forget this new experience. All the same, they agreed in 1267 to contribute one-twentieth of their revenues for one year to ease the plight of the disinherited. This was the price of peace, arranged by the legate as part of the settlement with the earl of Gloucester and John d'Eyvill.

Ottobuono left behind him a body of men who had taken the cross. The crusade now took the first place in public affairs; and this in its turn involved finance. The king still talked of going to the east himself, but it was generally understood that Edward or Edmund would fulfil his father's vow as well as his own—at the cost of the community. The land was at peace again, the king of France was making his plans, no stringency at home should stand in the way of a sacred obligation so long anticipated and of late so solemnly confirmed. The princes must borrow money and their debts must be discharged from the proceeds of taxation. King Henry met his immediate needs by the levy of a tallage on his demesne and on the cities and boroughs, but the business of the cross required a return, after thirty years, to a general levy. The matter was probably discussed in the council held by the legate in April 1268, for the king is known to have summoned some of his lay vassals to attend at this time, and also to have held a colloquy about the tallage with representatives of twenty-seven cities and boroughs.[1] However the discussions began the outcome was remarkable. After much deliberation a general tax of a twentieth of the value of personal property was agreed in a great Hoketide parliament in April 1270, a parliament to which the king had summoned 'nearly all the bishops, earls, barons, knights and free tenants of the whole of England'. The king and his council had gone cautiously. No incident shows so well how much they had learnt from the disturbances of the past ten years. The ground had first been explored in 1268–9 by forty-five bishops and magnates who would seem to have been elected by groups of shires. When everything was ready, and knights had been appointed to make the assessments, the tax was discussed in parliament in October 1269, after the dedication of the new church of Westminster Abbey. Important boroughs were represented in this parliament. The business still hung 'in suspense' until the Hoketide parliament. After its final ratification nine bishops, following the precedents set in 1239 and 1253, presided over a public recitation at St. Paul's cross of the sentence of excommunication against transgressors of the charters of liberties. The victory of Evesham should be judged in the light of the sequence of events which began with the Dictum of Kenilworth and culminated in this scene at St. Paul's cross.

The higher clergy had from the first consented to the new taxation. The tenants on lands held of them by knight-service were naturally in the same position as the laity. Later, in 1270, the bishops and some of the heads of religious houses agreed to the extension of the levy to their own personal property and that of the free tenants and villeins on their demesne. But the lower clergy, represented in an assembly which met at the time of the October parliament in 1269, had not been so pliable. They refused to be bound by the consent of the bishops. They had recently been subjected to papal taxation in aid of the king's debts. They would not be taxed by the king himself unless the pope willed, for a canon of the Fourth Lateran Council of

[1] The terms of the writ sent to the cities and boroughs suggest financial business as the subject of the colloquy, and also include a reference to the other faithful men summoned to meet 'in the council convoked by the legate'. The writ was discovered by G. O. Sayles and published by him in *E.H.R.* xl (1925), 583–5, with a different interpretation. There had been no general tax on movables since the thirtieth of 1237 (above, p. 31).

1215 forbade them to agree. Behind this argument may have lurked the view that the subvention of a crusade was a matter for the pope, not for a parliament, to decide. Ultimately the diocesan clergy, certainly in the diocese of Canterbury and probably in other dioceses, agreed to a twentieth, to be levied on the recent papal assessment; but whether they paid or not is not known. The stand taken by the parish clergy at this time is significant. They held to the ground which they had won, partly with the help of the bishops, during the first half of the century. As a spiritual order they would not be comprised in the community of the realm, not even in a general act of assistance to the greatest of all spiritual endeavours. Whatever legates and bishops might say, they would grant or withhold aid in their own assemblies. Just as the careful association of the laity with the grant of the twentieth prepared the way for parliamentary taxation, so the insistence of the clergy upon their independence was to give form and meaning to convocation in the days when clerical grants in aid of the Crown had lost any trace of novelty.

The Lord Edward's crusade did little to check the conquests in Syria of the Mamlūks of Egypt. It may well seem in our eyes to have been an ill-considered and wasteful adventure. The story of the last of King Henry's taxes, however, shows that the heir to the throne had contemporary opinion on his side. His dangerous course was anything but a piece of wilfulness. Whatever objections they may have felt the English prelates, barons, and freemen did in 1270 what they had not done since 1239, what they had constantly refused to do, and had only agreed to do in 1258 under conditions which could not be fulfilled; and they did it to finance a crusade. A grant for such a purpose was unprecedented, for hitherto crusades had been financed by papal taxation of the clergy. It was never repeated.[1] But it eased the transition from the haphazard finance of the period of disturbance to the orderly provision for the needs of the realm just because its occasion was removed from recent disputes. Edward's crusade was the expression of a general desire to forget the past, to release the energies of body and spirit in unexceptionable ways, to devote treasure which could still be spared to

---

[1] A 'great passage' to Tunis, still less to the Holy Land, cannot be compared to such a political adventure as the 'crusade' of the bishop of Norwich to Flanders in 1383, although this took advantage of the religious enthusiasm stirred by the papal schism.

an object higher than the domestic needs of the moment. Civil strife was expiated by an attack upon the enemy of Christendom. No serious disturbance shook the peace of the realm during Edward's absence. He succeeded to the throne without the slightest opposition. He returned to a welcoming people, with a new renown, high in the esteem of the whole west, the friend of pope and kings, a man to be reckoned with.

The tax brought in about £30,000. In 1273, when Edward, his vow fulfilled, was on his way home, Pope Gregory X levied on his behalf a tax on the English clergy, a tenth for two years. In 1275, a year after the new king's happy return, some of the proceeds of the first of his many taxes went towards the relief of debts which still remained unpaid. Altogether the expenses of Edward's 'passage' came to two or three times the cost of the new work at Westminster Abbey, his father's greatest achievement.

The spirit of Henry III lingers in the chapter-house in Westminster, in the ambulatory about the high altar, in the choir and the transepts of our most famous church. The new church was dedicated on 13 October 1269, the day of King Henry's patron saint, Edward the Confessor, the founder of the great abbey. The saint's bones were translated to their new shrine which glittered high behind the altar. The work had pre-occupied the king's thoughts for more than twenty years. It had had its own fund and wardens; and upon it the best architects, sculptors, and craftsmen of the time had lavished their skill. The solemn translation of St. Edward was Henry's greatest triumph, the fulfilment of his dearest hopes. He had satisfied his religious and artistic instincts. This was the true end of his long and troubled reign. His last years were passed under a congenial tutelage. The Lord Edward left England with his wife on 20 August 1270 to join King Louis at Aigues Mortes, but he did not leave the kingdom's nor his own interests to chance. Careful provision had been made for the future. The leading spirits in the king's council were the men whom Edward had formally entrusted with the care and custody of his children and his lands. His uncle Richard, or, if Richard should die, Henry of Almain, was to be the guardian of his children. John, his eldest son, who was four years old in 1270, was to come of age when he was twenty. Other potential guardians were the counsellors who had the custody of Edward's lands and castles, Walter

Giffard the archbishop of York, Philip Basset, Roger Mortimer, and Robert Burnell, a favourite clerk who, Edward had hoped, would be the new archbishop of Canterbury.[1] These men had a strenuous life during their lord's absence, and some anxieties, especially on the Welsh border, but, steadied by the growing co-operation of Gilbert of Clare, they directed public affairs without serious hindrance until Edward's return.

The king died on 16 November 1272 in his palace at Westminster. He was buried in the abbey on 20 November, and immediately after the funeral service the magnates, clergy, and people in the church went up to the high altar and took an oath of fealty to Edward. A proclamation in the name of the new king declared that he had succeeded by hereditary right, by the will of the magnates, and their oath of fealty. The earl of Gloucester, who had sworn at King Henry's bedside on the day of his death to guard the kingdom for Edward, was one of the first to take the oath. A few days later news came that Robert Kilwardby had been appointed archbishop of Canterbury by Pope Gregory X. In January 1273 the archbishop-elect held a council of his suffragans at Westminster, while the magnates met in parliament with four knights from each shire and four citizens from each city of the realm. The action of the king's council received a general confirmation when all took the oath of allegiance, and the appointment of Walter de Merton as chancellor was ratified. This quiet, undisputed, and almost instantaneous succession of an absent prince to the English throne was a proof of the unity of the realm and a landmark in the history of the monarchy.

In the meanwhile Edward was in Italy, on his way northwards to greet his friend and fellow crusader, the pope, at Orvieto. He arrived at the papal court on 14 February 1273. One of his objects in making this journey was his desire to avenge a wicked and foolish crime, committed two years before by his cousin Guy de Montfort. This young man, who would seem to have been the ablest of Earl Simon's sons, had risen very high in the service of the king of Sicily, Charles of Anjou. He had won renown in the battle of Alba in August 1268 and had

---

[1] Archbishop Boniface left England for Savoy in 1269 and died there on 18 July 1270. Edward, before he left England, tried in vain to persuade the monks of Canterbury to elect Robert Burnell. The monks elected their prior, who was rejected as unsuitable by Gregory X two years later. The pope chose Robert Kilwardby, the provincial in England of the Dominicans.

shared in the fruits of a victory which had established King
Charles and had ruined the fortunes of the house of the Hohenstaufen. He had been made Charles's vicar in Tuscany and had
married a rich heiress. He stood high in the king's favour.
Hence, when Edward, after he joined the French crusaders in
Tunis, decided to pass the winter of 1270–1 in Sicily before proceeding to Acre, he was in a circle friendly to Guy and his
brothers Simon and Amauri. He entrusted his cousin Henry
of Almain with a mission of reconciliation. Henry arrived at
Viterbo in illustrious company, with the kings of France and
Sicily.[1] Guy de Montfort had ridden into the city with Simon to
meet King Charles. On the following day (13 March 1271)
Guy murdered Henry in a church during mass. He was deprived
of his high office and of Charles's favour, but he was still at
large in southern Tuscany when Edward reached Orvieto nearly
two years later. Edward was not able to hunt Guy down, but his
protestations so far prevailed that Pope Gregory issued a bull
of excommunication of so drastic a nature that the murderer
threw himself upon the mercy of the Church and submitted for
a time to imprisonment.

Edward, by this time, had passed on to Lombardy. He proceeded in leisurely stages by way of Savoy to Paris. At Châlon
he took part in a tournament, probably the last occasion on
which he indulged in this dangerous sport. After doing homage
to Philip III at Paris for the lands which he held of the French
king, he decided to look into his affairs in Gascony. Here he
rejoined his wife Eleanor of Castile, who had travelled from
Italy by way of Spain on a visit to her half-brother, King
Alfonso the Wise.[2] Business kept him in the south until the
early summer of 1274. Then, still in a leisurely way, he came
north again and at last landed at Dover on 2 August. As the
months passed his court had grown. Long before he reached
England he had assumed control of the government of his
realm. He was crowned at Westminster on Sunday, 19 August
1274.

[1] King Philip III of France was taking back the body of his father Saint Louis,
who had died in Tunis.
[2] Alfonso, the third son of Edward and Eleanor, was born on 24 November
1273. The eldest son John had died in 1271 during their absence, the second son
Henry died soon after their return to England in 1274. For ten years, until his death
in August 1284, Alfonso was the heir to the throne. The future Edward II was
born in April 1284.

VI

EDWARD I AND HIS TIME

KING EDWARD I stands apart in our history. We remember him, but not as a living man who stirs the imagination. We think of Alfred and Henry VIII and Elizabeth as persons, and of what they did in terms of them as persons. We remember William the Conqueror and Henry II and Henry V less sharply, it may be, as persons, but we can see them in their works. Edward I may have been as great as any of these, but we think of him in terms of his works. He is the English Justinian, and the Hammer of the Scots. He built most impressive castles in Wales so that he need never have to do over again what he had done there. His records, in more senses than one, are statutes and parliamentary writs about whose significance scholars have never succeeded in coming to complete agreement, except that they can know more about them than they can about the man whose name still gives authority to them. We realize in a dim kind of way that Edward was a figure in the west and even in the middle east. He was acclaimed as a crusader and sought as an arbitrator. He tried to form among the princes in the Low Countries and Germany an alliance against the king of France. His manipulation of the market in wool is a turning-point in what for centuries was our chief export trade and, next to the land, our main source of wealth. We know all this. We are willing to maintain that few rulers of his time stood higher in general esteem than Edward did. Yet his activity across the Channel fails to impress us just because, as we cannot see its effects as we can see the outcome of his domestic energy at Conway or in the statute book, we need to interpret it in the light of Edward himself; and Edward is not there. He stands apart. Is this impression justified? Is it due to us or to him?

It may well be due to us. The chronicles are meagre, it is true; as we are constantly reminded, Edward had no Matthew Paris near by to write down fully what he did and what was said about him; but the records of his reign exceed in number and minuteness of detail the records of any previous reign. The human evidence is considerable and, though some of it may be

doubtful, is consistent. In our desire to avoid credulity we may
have overreached ourselves. We may have set our minds too
firmly upon the things which we are never allowed to forget. King
Edward perhaps was less absorbed than we are in the elucidation of custom in great statutes and in the nature and structure
of parliaments. The conquest of Wales and the temporary subjection of Scotland were such strenuous achievements that they
might have drained the energies and filled the thoughts of a
strong king, but what if, in Edward's eyes, they were troublesome distractions from his main interests? Edward had two
outstanding qualities. He was, both physically and mentally,
a most active man, and he was a consistent and also a very
conventional Christian in his outlook on life. We cannot give
their full significance to these elementary facts unless we try to
forget everything that has happened since 1307 and to look at
the world as he saw it.

If we do this Edward stands out more clearly, more like the
tall, lithe, sinewy creature described by his contemporaries, fine
and attractive, clear and emphatic in speech, uncertain in
temper, reasonable in counsel. The mental and spiritual horizon
which bounded his daily life was the vision of an orderly
Christendom combining its forces in a great crusade, but a
crusade which, though authorized and preached by the pope,
should be led by strong men, and preferably by himself. He enjoyed the pageantry and colour of royalty. His quick response to
every occasion, whether this were a casual difficulty or a public
scandal or emergency, was informed by a sense of obligation. He
hated an untidy situation and resented interference. Yet in
spite of his energy there was a dreamy, slothful strain in him
which may have been derived from his father, who once at least
took him to task for it. His power to concentrate in times of
stress did not inform the whole man. He lacked the continuous
sense of purpose which, for example, drove on his kinsman,
Peter the Great of Aragon, and he was repelled by the fanaticism
which possessed the legists who surrounded Philip the Fair of
France. At times, indeed, he gives the impression that his
heart was not in the business of kingship, and certainly he was
happiest on horseback with his dogs at his side and a hawk on
his wrist.

A much later chronicler preserves a story of him on a Scottish
campaign in the summer of 1300, the year of Jubilee. Pope

Boniface VIII, who at this time felt himself to be the soul of the world, sent the king a command to stop hostilities in a land which belonged to the Holy See. The archbishop of Canterbury, who with some reluctance had brought the papal order, found Edward at Sweetheart Abbey in Galloway. Wishing to curb his anger, he ventured to remind the king of the words of the Psalmist: 'They who trust in the Lord are as mount Zion which cannot be moved. . . . As the mountains are round about Jerusalem, so the Lord is round about his people.' Edward burst out with a quotation from Isaiah: 'By God's blood, "For Zion's sake I will not be silent, and for Jerusalem's sake I will not be at rest", but with all my strength I will defend my right that is known to all the world.' In his own way Edward, no less than Archbishop Winchelsey, was alive to religious symbolism. The archbishop had touched him on the raw. During the years when the prelate had been teaching arts in the university of Paris and theology in the university of Oxford, Edward had been trying to bring peace to the Mediterranean and had planned the great crusade from which the troubles in Scotland and Gascony were to divert him. He could not go to reconquer Jerusalem while his royal rights were flouted. He must finish the task in hand. To us he is an odd mixture. His symbolism seems worldly, his craving for Jerusalem insincere. Even in his own day his ideas about crusades and feudal obligations were becoming old fashioned in some men's eyes. Edward, however, was like this. He was gracious, adroit, busy, and devout, by no means a saint. His intentions were generally good, but he hated to be crossed, and in moods of frustration his impulsive rage could make him overbearing, vindictive, and unjust. His sense of duty could suffer strange degeneration. In his last years he seems to have reverted to his youthful trick of playing with his adversaries; but experience instilled cynicism into all but the very best medieval kings, and if we consider the experience of Edward, we may well marvel that he maintained his poise as well as he did. His outlook on life was a prosaic and faulty version of the idealism of King Louis of France, whom he had known in earlier years. St. Louis's belief in kingship as a trust for which its holder was responsible to God alone, his eagerness to put his skill as an arbitrator at the service of his neighbours, his craving for peace among Christians as the condition of a successful holy war were reflected in the mind of Edward; but while the saint shed radiance and, in his humility, was alive to the perils which beset a king, Edward lived proudly and fiercely in the light of common day.

He was a conventional man in an age of change. Of most of the revolutionary movements at work around him he was, like most people, quite unaware. Their significance in history was hidden from their authors themselves, for they too were men of their own time. Yet what a wonderful time it was. Meister Eckhart, one of the most profound of mystics (1260–1327), Dante (1265–1321), Giotto (1266–1336) were at the height of their powers when Edward died. Roger Bacon wrote his greatest work in the years (1266–8) when Edward was helping to restore England to peace and preparing to join Saint Louis on crusade. St. Thomas Aquinas died in 1274 while the new king was on his leisurely way home to be crowned. In the year of Dante's birth and of the battle of Evesham, Duns Scotus (1265–1308) was born at Maxton near Roxburgh, in the district which was so often to be trampled by Edward's armies. These men opened new vistas in thought and poetry and art. Their work gave new meaning and fresh values to human experience. Edward is unlikely to have known even the names of most of them. The only outcome of their activities which may have attracted his attention was a troublesome dispute at Oxford about the form of the soul. Yet among clergy and laity alike, the faculty of self-criticism, the desire to bring first principles in question, had been awakened. We can never know how far King Edward was aware of the change. We know that he could inspire the planning of towns and fortifications, take pleasure in the decoration of his palaces, turn to advantage the Arthurian romances and the symbolism of the Round Table. We may feel that he was not indifferent to books and illuminations and new styles in architecture and that, whenever he was free to turn aside and observe by the Cheshire woods the slow erection of his new Cistercian abbey, Vale Royal, until he got tired of it, his mind was engaged in more than casual reflection. We may be sure, but we can never know. Only in his concern with the problems of politics can we actually see him at work and dimly trace the interplay of old and new ideas.[1]

[1] See further the discussion and references below, p. 515 and notes, and my paper on Edward I in fact and fiction, in *Fritz Saxl, Memorial Essays* (1957), pp. 120–35.

Hence we should approach a survey of Edward's reign from without and begin with a brief study of his career as a European statesman.

Western Christendom in Edward I's time was passing through the second and formative stage in the crisis which followed the death in 1250 of the Emperor Frederick II. For twenty years King Louis IX of France, by his very presence in the political scene, had done something to fill a vacuum and to ease the passage of his brother, Charles of Anjou, to the throne of Sicily; but when he died in 1270 the restraints which had seemed to give a moral sanction to the new order in western politics went also. For a few years (1271–6) a new pope, Gregory X, strove with some success to maintain a general peace. Tedaldo Visconti had spent many years in the service of the Holy See outside Italy and had earned respect as a humble archdeacon of Liége. The news of his election, which ended a long vacancy in the papal throne, reached him at Acre, four months after his friend Edward had landed in Syria. Pope Gregory's policy was wide and courageous. He realized that the extirpation of the male line of the Hohenstaufen and the emergence of Charles of Anjou, the youngest brother of King Louis, as count of Provence and king of Sicily and south Italy had created a new situation, full of dangerous possibilities in spite of the aid which it could give to the political influence of the Papacy. He now had as his neighbour an ambitious prince tempted to take advantage of his hold on Provence in the northern Mediterranean and eager, from his Sicilian base, to renew traditional enterprises. He was aware of a movement of opinion which would welcome the disappearance for ever of imperial authority in Germany and Italy and a concentration of the Latin world against Constantinople. The death of Richard, king of the Romans and emperor-elect, in April 1272, some months before the death of his brother Henry III of England, and the danger latent in the success of Michael Palaeologus, the new Greek emperor, over the Latins in the east, forced Pope Gregory to define his attitude. He decided to seek reconciliation with the Greeks by a union of the Churches, to urge the German electors to agreement in the choice of a new king and emperor-elect, to summon a general council to co-operate with him in the reform of the Church, and to call on the princes of the west to resume the crusade to which St. Louis's companions had pledged themselves at Trapani in November 1270 after their leader's death. This successor of St. Peter restated the principles of the old in terms which might avert the perils of the new order.

For a short time all went well. The claims of King Richard's rival, King Alfonso of Castile, and the advocates of Philip III, the new king of France, were held in restraint; and the German electors agreed upon a Swabian count, Rudolf of Habsburg, as their new king. Michael Palaeologus welcomed the proposal to unite the Greek and Latin Churches and manipulated support for it in Byzantine circles. The union was solemnly proclaimed at Lyons, where in 1274 the oecumenical council had gathered to accept new canons of reform, based upon a widespread survey of the needs of the Church. And at Lyons Pope Gregory summoned his flock to a new crusade for the reconquest of Jerusalem and the holy places, and, amidst less enthusiasm, arranged for its finance. Yet even before his death two years later the instability of his work was apparent, and during the generation after his death his ideals, however strenuously they might be upheld in words, became little more than pious aspirations.

The crusade was preached again and again, but St. Louis had no successors. The intransigence of Greek monks and the impatience of Latin ecclesiastics broke every attempt to put the union of the Churches into effect. Charles of Anjou became the victim of his own ambitions and left the Mediterranean in east and west a prey to the rivalries which still disturb it. Any hope of return to the policy of Pope Innocent III and of the maintenance, as a restraint upon the bellicose impulses of feudal monarchies, of an understanding between a strong Papacy and an obedient empire was shattered by the fundamental divergence, now fully and consciously exposed, between the political outlooks of the spiritual and secular powers. The noblest attempt to vindicate in this age the conception of the organic unity of the Christian republic was Dante's *Monarchia*, but we should never forget that Dante, just because he was so sensitive to the spiritual beauty and wisdom of God's universe, was concerned, in this book, to maintain the independent validity of imperial power as the unifying principle of an harmonious society of kingdoms and cities. He was always the exile from the city he loved, at home nowhere else. He withstood contemporary tendencies because he craved for the peace without which the best life on earth was impossible, not because he had transcended domestic loyalties. He found no justification for the secular claims of the Papacy, no force in the dialectic which would add a secular content to spiritual authority, and he saw no hope for the world in the independent centres of political egotism; but he was defending a lost cause.

This was the age of the *regna*, not of the *imperium*. Rudolf of Habsburg more or less consciously led the way to a German kingship based on local dynastic sovereignty. The great pope Boniface VIII was forced, like some earlier and most later popes, to compromise with the *regna* in fact if not in theory. The rights of the kings to independent authority had been recognized by some exponents of the civil and canon law for nearly a century, and were to be given a classic justification, after Dante's death, by the great Italian civilians. They lent their authority to accomplished facts which it was useless to deny. The great emperor Frederick II himself had been a herald of the new time, so rich in wealth and opportunity. In Sicily he had built on the work of his Norman predecessors and shown how to reshape a feudal state. He had been a patron of the new learning, the new poetry, and the arts. In the time of his frustration he had tried to rally his fellow princes to unite against the mischievous interventions of the Holy See and had envied the happy autocracy of the Greek emperor in his exile at Nicaea. Only the Italian extremists who clung to the pure teaching of St. Francis, the sectaries and seers, bemoaned, with apocalyptic cries, the miseries latent in the abundant life around them, denounced ecclesiastical and secular rulers alike, and awaited the end of the world.

In the spring of 1273, on his way home from Sicily, Edward had stayed with Pope Gregory X at Orvieto. The pope liked Edward and was solicitous about him. When he heard of Edward's part in the tournament at Châlon he warned him, now that he was a responsible king, to refrain from such exercises, dangerous to both body and soul. He was distressed to hear that Edward's coronation would coincide with the forthcoming Council at Lyons, for he had hoped for his presence and the assistance of a strong delegation from England. Edward postponed the coronation, and the delegation of archbishops, bishops, and proctors went to Lyons, but the king excused himself. He was too busy in Gascony. He had got his hands on the reins of government. He was thirty-five years of age.

Until his death thirty-three years later Edward was involved in the affairs of the west. He was a vassal of the king of France for Gascony and all the lands which, under the terms of the treaty of Paris (1259), he ought to hold of him. One of his first acts after his return was to do homage to his cousin Philip III at Paris (August 1273). The complications in which this relation entangled him were, in later reigns, to change the course of English history; but though never negligible, they were for twenty years (1273–93) one of those irritants which test the skill and endurance of a statesman, not the main preoccupation of his life. Until the king of France, Philip the Fair, decided to force an issue, feudal relations were secondary to the ties of a closer companionship. For Edward was much more than a vassal of his French neighbour. He was a member of his family, a family whose cohesion—remarkable in any age—had been fostered by the influence of King Louis and by the assistance given to Henry III by his French kinsfolk during and after the civil war. The wives of Louis and Henry were sisters and lived for many years after their husbands died. They were powerful behind the scenes. Edward and Philip III were first cousins and were in the same degree of kinship with the sons and daughters of Louis's brother Charles of Anjou, king of Sicily, who had married Beatrice, another daughter of Count Raymond-Berengar of Provence, and after her death in 1267 had continued to rule as count. Queen Margaret of France did not approve of her brother-in-law Charles and his monopoly of power in the land of her birth. She and Eleanor had their own claims on Provence. The two queens looked to Edward to further their rights. Edward had seen a good deal of Charles, both in France and on the way to and from his crusade. He had been his guest in Sicily. He got on well with Charles's children, especially with the younger Charles, Charles of Salerno, or the Lame, his mother's heir in Provence and his father's heir in Sicily. Hence he was a natural mediator in the family disputes. Indeed, one of his first ventures in diplomacy, if such they can be termed, was connected with the Provençal tangle and its implications; but before we examine this we must say something about Edward's other connexions.

Edward was a southerner by blood and, through his dukedom of Aquitaine, by circumstance. His great-grandmother, Eleanor of Aquitaine, his grandmother Isabella of Angoulême, his mother Eleanor of Provence had all come from the land of the troubadours. His wife, Eleanor of Castile, was half a Spaniard, the half-sister of Alfonso the Wise, king of Castile. His youthful marriage had done much, from a Gascon point of view, to ease the constant tension in the Pyrenees, and also had given him a more personal interest in Spanish political problems, in Castile, Aragon, Navarre, and their mutual complexities. But this was not all. Eleanor of Castile had expectations in France. She added another link to the chain of relations which Edward had on the French, Flemish, and Dutch side of the English Channel and to which he was to add other links to the end of his life. Eleanor's mother, Joan, the second wife of Ferdinand III, king of Castile, had succeeded, in right of her mother, to the county of Ponthieu whose chief town was the busy little port of Abbeville in the estuary of the Somme. Queen Joan died early in 1279 and Ponthieu came to Eleanor. Edward at once arranged for her formal succession, sent representatives to Philip III of France, and undertook the administration of the county. A seneschal and exchequer were established at Abbeville. The period of transfer coincided with negotiations with King Philip about the implementation of the treaty of Paris of 1259,[1] and the opportunity was taken to combine the conclusion of a new treaty at Amiens on 23 May with an agreement about Ponthieu. Philip acknowledged Eleanor's rights in the county and received a handsome sum as its relief. Then Edward, before his return to England, spent ten days in his new town of Abbeville.[2]

It is significant that the preliminary negotiations with King Philip about Eleanor's succession to Ponthieu had been entrusted to two important members of the Anglo-French royal circle who for nearly twenty years (1275–94) took a leading part in the maintenance of the friendly and domestic relations which bound the two courts together. One of these was Edward's brother Edmund, earl of Lancaster, the other John of Brittany, earl of Richmond, whose wife Beatrice (d. 1275) had been Edward's sister.[3] The two men knew each other well. They

---

[1] Below, p. 289.

[2] Edward had first taken action in March. For the administration of Ponthieu see *Cal. Pat. Rolls, 1272–81*, pp. 306, 394, 419; and Hilda Johnstone in *E.H.R.* xxix (1914), 435 ff.

[3] John was the grandson of the Peter of Dreux who, as count or duke of Brittany, had tempted Henry III to his first French adventure in 1230 (above, p. 97).

had both been with Edward in Syria, and both were loyal friends of the king.[1] They were further connected by the marriage which made Edmund a vassal of King Philip III. John's mother was the sister of the count of Champagne whose widow, Blanche of Artois—herself a lady of the French royal house—took Edmund of Lancaster as her second husband. France, England, Champagne, Brittany were linked together under the masterful influence of the queen mother of France and her sister the queen mother of England.

The goodwill of St. Louis, displayed during the family gathering in Paris in 1254 and proved so often during the next twenty years, had prepared the conditions favourable to this domestic concord. That friendship between the kings of France and England lasted for forty years is a very remarkable fact in our medieval history. It is, indeed, unique. It does not mean that political considerations were subordinated to personal feeling, still less that matrimonial alliances, so often an occasion of strife, were the guarantee of peace; but it does remind us in an unusually striking way that historians incur grave danger of misconception if they divorce what are called political tendencies from the interplay of personal relations. 'The logic of events' is not derived from concentration upon isolated ideas at work in carefully selected minds. Needless to say, considerations hostile to the good understanding between the two courts found a voice in Edward I's time just as they had found voice between 1254 and the treaty of Paris in 1259. Philip III's son, Philip the Fair, in a few years of incisive endeavour was to give new expression to ambitions which were frequently to recur

John's father, Duke John, had renewed the friendly relations with Henry III which his own father, Peter, had forfeited. Eight years after the younger John was married to Henry III's daughter Beatrice at the abbey of St. Denis near Paris (January 1260) the duke recovered the ancestral English earldom, honour, and castle of Richmond in Yorkshire and handed them over to his son (1268). The connexion with England went back to the days of the Conqueror's companion, Count Alan the Red (d. 1089) whose castle on the river Swale was afterwards called Richmond. The elder John died in 1285. For the date see the *Complete Peerage*, x. 811, note b.

[1] They parted company after the breach between Edward and Philip the Fair in 1294. John's adherence to his suzerain Philip in 1296, with the temporary loss of his English lands, was partly due to the disturbances caused by the forces under Edmund of Lancaster on the Breton coast during their voyage to Gascony. Edmund died at Bayonne during the Gascon war (June 1296) (below, p. 649). John died in 1305. He has sometimes been confused with his younger son, John of Brittany, who was Edward's lieutenant in Gascony and one of his most faithful servants.

in later French history; but his capacity to do this, so far as it went, was derived from the vast acquisitions of his father, whose activities were assisted rather than hindered by his relations with his cousins in England. Indeed, if Philip the Fair had not been induced to break faith with Edward and to make his famous *coup* in Gascony in 1294, it is most improbable that Edward would ever have appeared as the leader of an alliance against France in the north-east, or that we should be told so much about the natural and inevitable rivalry between the two kings. Edward had other duties and aspirations, and in his relations with him Philip was not intransigent.

Philip III's main acquisitions for the French Crown were the wide-flung lands of his uncle, Alphonse, Count of Poitou and Toulouse, the county of Champagne, the richest fief in France, and the kingdom of Navarre, in the Pyrenean district south of Gascony, whose kings were to be so important in later history. Since the year 1234 the counts of Champagne had been kings of Navarre, and it has sometimes been implied, rather than proved, that Edmund of Lancaster's marriage to the widowed countess of Champagne in 1275 was a political move, dictated by Edward's chagrin because he had not secured control of Navarre and by his determination to find a new base nearer to Paris as a northern counterpart to Gascony. How he was able to do this is not explained. In fact the suggestion is unfounded. The political considerations incidental to this family compact were more consistent with mutual goodwill. Edmund's marriage came about indirectly through events in Navarre. Thirty years before, when Theobald IV in the hot days of first manhood had succeeded to the throne of Navarre (1234), he had been a centre of unrest. He was ambitious, proud, and cut a figure in the knightly world as a lover and a poet. In 1235-6 he had joined that assiduous intriguer, Peter of Dreux, still smarting from his failure to establish himself in Brittany and the west, in their last bid for power at the expense of the young king Louis IX. It was then that Peter married his son John to Theobald's daughter Blanche. Theobald agreed that, even if he should have a son, Blanche should succeed him in Navarre. But those wild days were soon over. In 1236 both Theobald and Peter were brought to heel and ceased to trouble the monarchy. The plan for the union of Navarre with Brittany was not pursued. Theobald's son Theobald V, who succeeded to Navarre and Champagne in 1253, was King Louis's son-in-law, went with him on his crusade to Tunis and, like Louis himself, died of the experience (1270). He had no direct heirs and was succeeded by his brother Henry, who the year before had married Louis's niece, Blanche of Artois. The married life of Henry and Blanche was brief and tragic. Their baby son was accidentally tossed by his nurse over the battlements of the Navarrese castle at Estella. Henry himself died in July 1274, leaving a daughter, Jeanne, of eighteen months. What was to happen to Blanche and the infant?

One natural protector would have been King Edward, who had recently been very busy over the border in Gascony coming to a reckoning with his troublesome vassal, Gaston of Béarn, and negotiating with his neighbours. In fact, on 30 November 1273, Henry of Navarre had agreed to a future betrothal and marriage between his baby daughter and Edward's heir, Henry, a child of five.[1] The two kings explained in the treaty that they had a common interest in the suppression of disorders, which had been so frequent. If King Henry had no male heirs when he died, Jeanne would inherit his kingdom of Navarre as well as Champagne and Brie, and on her marriage to the young Henry of England, Gascony would be entrusted to them (just as Edward himself had received Gascony when he married Eleanor of Castile). If the boy died within the seven years before his betrothal his brother Alfonso was to take his place as Jeanne's future husband.[2] The two kings promised to give each other aid against all men except their common lord the king of France, whose consent, it is significant to note, was necessary to the treaty before it could be regarded as binding. But Henry of Navarre's death at Pampeluna in the following July, so far from bringing Edward on the scene, dissolved this pleasant prospect. Edward, who had left Gascony in April, was far off by the English Channel, on his way to be crowned at Westminster. His heir died in October and, in the face of quick-moving events, nothing could be done to keep the arrangement alive. Queen Blanche was faced in Navarre by the pretensions of the

[1] Edward's eldest son John had died in 1271. The agreement is in *Foedera*, i. ii. 508 (30 November). Henry and Edward met at Bonloc, near Bayonne, while the former was on his way to Navarre on what was to be his last visit to his kingdom.

[2] Henry died on 14 October 1274. Alfonso, who was born in Gascony on 24 November 1273, a few days before the treaty was sealed, died on 19 August 1284. See above, p. 226, n. 2.

kings of Castile and Aragon and by civil war. First she favoured the claims of Peter, the son of King James of Aragon, and was even induced to accept him as Jeanne's future husband; then she fled for protection to her cousin Philip III in France. By the treaty of Orléans in May 1275 she entrusted the king with the rule of Navarre until Jeanne should come of age to succeed and promised her in marriage to one of his sons.[1] Hence it was that nine years later (1284) Philip the Fair, in the year before he succeeded his father as king of France, married Jeanne at Estella (16 August) and that Navarre was annexed by the French royal house. The arrangement made at Orléans in 1275 separated Navarre from Champagne, and a second problem, the future of Blanche, had to be solved. Until Jeanne came of age Blanche would rule in Champagne. She would naturally seek a second husband, and he must be a man congenial to the French king, her overlord. The man she chose was Edward I's brother Edmund, earl of Lancaster, formerly in name the king of Sicily, now the greatest landholder in England, with holdings in twenty-five English shires and throughout south Wales, and seneschal of England in right of his earldom of Leicester.[2] Blanche and Edmund were married in December 1275 or in the next month, when Edmund did homage to King Philip for Champagne.

The marriage was not a political transaction, though it was both welcomed and deplored on political grounds. Blanche's brother, Count Robert of Artois, objected to it because, so he is reported to have said, the king of England was known to be hostile to the king of France. Margaret of Provence, the queen mother, furthered it because at this time she was looking to Edward for support in her Provençal plans. Robert of Artois was an ally of his uncle Charles of Anjou, the count of Provence and king of Sicily; Queen Margaret was bitter because she believed that Charles had deprived her of her rights. These family differences were to lead to changes in French policy as the Angevin party grew in influence under the patronage of the new queen, Marie of Brabant, who was married to Philip III in 1274, three years after the death of his first wife Isabella of

---

[1] Before she was three years old the princess was promised in marriage to three princes in succession.

[2] See the life of Edmund, with a description of his lands and honours, by W. E. Rhodes in *E.H.R.* x (1895); especially pp. 29–40, 212–30.

Aragon.[1] The forward movement in which the occupation of Navarre was a step was to become harder and stronger. Yet although Edward I doubtless regarded political activities at the French court with reserve and even suspicion, and the more so because, as we shall see, he wished to settle the ever-pressing difficulties involved in the application of the treaty of Paris, there is no evidence that he saw in his brother's marriage to Blanche of Artois anything more than a new and welcome link with his relatives in France. Certainly Philip III intended that in due course the child Jeanne should bring Champagne as well as Navarre to his son. On the other hand, if Jeanne had died the situation might have become very delicate, and presumably the possibility had not been overlooked either by Edward or at the French court. Edward, for various reasons, was not disinterested in the future of Navarre. It would be interesting to know exactly why Edmund of Lancaster, after he had taken his wife to England in 1276, made a journey to Navarre, just about the time when his brother-in-law, Robert of Artois, was reducing the land to order (September 1276). Blanche's interests had doubtless to be considered, and Edward himself claimed hereditary rights to certain castles, towns, and other lands in Navarre.

An English scholar wrote with much truth more than half a century ago that 'to the Champagnards the rule of the English baron was a sort of foretaste of their incorporation with the monarchy of France and of the loss of that brilliant independent life, centring round the court of their counts, which they had so long enjoyed'.[2] Edmund of Lancaster took only an intermittent part in the administration of this rich and noble land. He was worthy to rule at Provins. He was gracious, cheerful, and munificent, popular with all, a good knightly man, but his interests and duties in the main lay elsewhere. His horizon was bounded not by ambitions in France but by the crusade. During his absences from Champagne the county was administered by a famous Frenchman, John of Brienne or Acre, the butler of France.[3] In 1284, when Jeanne was eleven years old, her

[1] Isabella (the mother of Louis (who died in 1276), Philip IV, and Charles of Valois) died in 1271 in South Italy at Cosenza during the journey home from the Tunisian crusade. For Marie of Brabant and her coterie see Langlois in Lavisse, *Hist. de France*, III. ii. 104–7.   [2] W. E. Rhodes in *E.H.R.* x. 215.

[3] For Champagne during this decade (1274–84) see M. H. D'Arbois de Jubainville, *Histoire des ducs et des comtes de Champagne*, iv (1865), 446–56. The influence of

minority was brought to an end. On 17 May her mother accepted an arrangement. She was to have a large sum down, 70,000 *livres* of Tours, five castles and their estates as her dowry, and her palace in Paris.[1] Later in the year, with due papal dispensations, the younger Philip of France married his cousin Jeanne at Estella, and took over in right of his wife the kingdom of Navarre and the county of Champagne. Blanche survived Edmund for six years in the enjoyment of her double dowry in England and Champagne. She died at Vincennes in May 1302. Through her great-granddaughter, another Blanche, the first wife of John of Gaunt, she became an ancestress of the royal house of Lancaster.

It has been argued that during the critical decade 1275 to 1285 Edward showed himself to be a poor statesman. On the Pyrenees, and in the Rhône valley, if not in the Rhineland, he had opportunities to throw his weight against acquisitive tendencies in French policy and he neglected them. The answer to suggestions of this kind is that Edward did not look at contemporary politics in this way. He may have been tempted and doubtless was frequently advised to justify the suspicions of Robert of Artois and to cause trouble in the family circle to which he belonged; but to do this would have been inconsistent with his position as a liege vassal of the king of France and as a peer of France, liable to be summoned to give military service. He was determined to seek and find a settlement of his differences with his overlord within the framework of the French political system either by formal agreements or by patient pleadings in the Parlement of Paris; and, as the treaties of 1279 and 1286 show, he was not unsuccessful. The legal tussle only later developed into what we may now describe as the 'cold war' conducted by Philip the Fair and his legists. However this may be, Edward in Philip III's time acted with much discretion without loss of dignity or prestige. He respected Philip's rights in the Navarre treaty of 1273. He refused to be diverted by Peter of Aragon[2] and when Alfonso of Castile, his

English practice, it has been suggested, can be seen in the title and form of the survey or *extenta* of the county, now known to date from the years 1276–8, i.e. between Edward I's great inquiries in Gascony and England. See Auguste Longnon, *Documents relatifs au comté de Champagne et de Brie, 1172–1361*, ii (1904), vii–xx; 9–183, the text of the *extenta*; and cf. H. W. C. Davis in *E.H.R.* xx (1905), 782.

[1] The treaty was copied into the Patent Roll; see *Cal. Pat. Rolls, 1282–91*, p. 120.
[2] Cf. below, p. 258. Peter of Aragon surrendered his claims to Navarre during a

brother-in-law, sought his aid in the contest for Navarre, he replied that any help he might give must be subject to his feudal obligations of fealty and homage to the king of France.[1] His letters about an even more serious issue in which the kings of France and Castile nearly went to war reveal Edward's attitude very clearly. About the time when Robert of Artois was restoring order in Navarre and Peter of Aragon succeeded his father in Aragon, that is to say, in the latter half of 1276, King Alfonso was entangled in the disputes about the succession to his throne which worried him and his neighbours till his death in 1284. His heir, Ferdinand de la Cerda, had died in August 1275, and his younger son Sancho was acknowledged by the *cortes* as heir. Alfonso acquiesced, but with some hesitation, for he had regarded as his heirs Ferdinand's young sons, whose mother was a daughter of St. Louis and a sister of King Philip of France. In some respects the difficulty was like that of the succession in England when King John was preferred to Arthur of Brittany. King Philip maintained the rights of his nephews, collected a great army at Sauveterre in Béarn, then ingloriously withdrew (1276–7). During the wrangles which preceded this demonstration of force Edward was expected in some quarters to declare himself on Alfonso's side and, as we have seen, Alfonso had recently sought his aid; but he had other intentions. To a further request by Alfonso for an alliance he replied on 8 January 1277 that the bonds between them were unbreakable, strengthened as they were by his memories of his marriage and knighthood at Burgos, and he sent a copy of the treaty made between Alfonso and his father Henry III, which he would renew on similar lines. He had been willing to come on a mission of peace but King Philip's withdrawal had made this unnecessary.[2] He had indeed been willing, for on 7 November 1276, five days before his formal decision in his great council at Westminster to go upon Llywelyn of Wales as a rebel, he had expressed to King Philip his disappointment at the news brought by the French envoys that peace with Castile had not been made and declared that, in view of the danger to Christendom, he had entrusted operations in Wales and Ireland to others in order to go to

visit to Paris in 1276, before he succeeded as king in July. Alfonso of Castile had come to an understanding about Navarre in the previous November.

[1] *Foedera*, I. ii. 522 (5 May 1275). In this letter Edward reminds King Alfonso of his own hereditary rights to certain unnamed castles, &c., in Navarre.

[2] Ibid. 540–1.

Philip.[1] The fiasco of the expedition of 1276 did not check Philip's determination and throughout 1277 war was still imminent.[2] In this year Edward again excused himself provisionally from personal service. He wrote that his envoys Maurice de Craon and John de Grilly would explain how he was placed. He was detained by the war in Wales and in any event was bound by ties of kinship and friendship to King Alfonso of Castile. He begged, for the sake of Christendom, to be accepted as a peacemaker between the two kings.[3]

Edward, as Philip's vassal and a peer of France, felt bound to make general recognition of his military obligations;[4] yet as an independent king who had pressing business at home and as a friend bound by responsible ties to his brother-in-law of Castile, he would do his best to make peace between Philip and Alfonso. He was so far successful that in the end of November 1279 Alfonso agreed to enter into negotiations for a truce and to entrust Edward with the task of mediating a peace in a formal conference. The truce was made at Paris in the following spring, to last until Martinmas 1282, and Alfonso, in a public announcement in May, referred to Edward's future good offices as peacemaker.[5] Then he suddenly changed his mind. He sent messengers to Charles of Salerno to ask Charles to undertake the task.[6] By this time the problem of the Spanish succession was agitating the whole of western Europe. The pope had intervened in vain.

[1] Champollion-Figeac, *Lettres des rois*, &c. (1839), i. 185. Edward's explicit statement that he would go to Philip if necessary as soon as he had arranged the affairs of his realm ('statu regni nostri cum celeritate qua possumus ordinato') helps to explain why the main effort in Wales was fixed for the following summer. For the disturbances in Ireland in 1276–7 see G. H. Orpen, *Ireland under the Normans*, iv (1920), 17–18.

[2] The letters of the popes John XXI and Nicholas III reveal anxiety. See Langlois, *Philippe le Hardi*, pp. 110–12.

[3] *Foedera*, I. ii. 607, where this letter is printed, I think wrongly, under the year 1282. It seems to belong to the autumn of 1277, during the last stages of the Welsh war. The commission to the two envoys was made before the beginning of October (cf. *Cal. Pat. Rolls*, *1272–81*, p. 231). In his undated letter to Philip, Edward refers to John de Grilly as 'nostre feal', not as seneschal of Gascony, as he was in 1282.

[4] He expressed some doubt and reservation; see below, p. 311 n. He was at least once summoned to attend the Parlement of Paris when a case involving a peer of France, the duke of Burgundy, was under consideration. See his letter of excuse, 11 November 1275, in *Foedera*, I. ii. 530.   [5] Ibid. 576, 580.

[6] In a letter to Edward, written from Paris on 8 July, Charles states that Alfonso's messengers reached him at Aix in Provence on 20 May. The letter is printed by F. Kern, *Acta Imperii, Angliae et Franciae*, *1267–1313* (1911), p. 9, no. 16. The arrangements for a peace conference in Gascony were made in Paris, where Charles of Salerno had gone from Provence.

Peter of Aragon, who tended to the side of Sancho, was actively
interested. Alfonso apparently wished to give a wider setting to
his discussions with the French. His change of mind caused
much comment. Philip III thought that Edward had annoyed
Alfonso because he had not associated him with the negotiations
at Amiens.[1] Queen Margaret, in one of her letters to Edward,
referred to the incident in terms of ironical astonishment.[2]
Edward's agents in Paris, Maurice de Craon and Geoffrey de
Genville, wrote on 3 July that Alfonso had suspicions of Edward
as too close a friend of his cousin the French king, while on the
other hand his agents were spreading malicious reports against
Edward which King Philip refused to believe. Edward, in a
letter to Philip, remarked that Alfonso had, he supposed, relieved him because he considered him 'slothful and sleepy'.
He did not permit himself to be disturbed. While he excused
himself from attending the peace conference with King Philip,
on the grounds that he was about to go to the northern parts of
his kingdom for the first time since his succession to the throne,
and that his magnates were scattered, he did everything that
he could to facilitate the negotiations. He allowed Charles of
Salerno to hold the conference in Gascony (December 1280),
and provided hospitality to his visitors; King Alfonso, whose
large cavalcade caused much alarm to the people of Bayonne,
was made welcome; and later, when the proceedings came to
naught, the king of England offered his services once more. The
seneschal of Gascony wrote to him that 'the kings, princes and
magnates went away well contented with you and yours'.[3]
Edward showed his sympathy with the unhappy Alfonso, shaken
to and fro between the rebellion of Sancho and the champions

---

[1] On the other hand, Edward, just as he reported to Alfonso his negotiations for
marriage alliances with Peter of Aragon, had kept him informed about the negotiations at Amiens. This is clear from a congratulatory letter from Alfonso, who was
especially pleased that the transfer of Ponthieu (above, p. 235) had been satisfactor-
ily arranged: P.R.O. *Ancient Correspondence*, xvi. 12.

[2] Champollion-Figeac, *Lettres des rois*, &c. (1839), i. 253.

[3] The correspondence between Edward, the kings of France, Castile, Charles of
Salerno, and the royal agents in Paris may be studied in the *Foedera*, i. ii. 576,
580–6. It reveals Edward at his best. The reports of Maurice de Craon and
Geoffrey de Genville, Edward's envoys in Paris, about the preliminary negotiations
with Charles of Salerno and the arrangements for the conference in Gascony, and
a long letter from John de Grilly about the early days of the discussions in Gascony
are full of interest. They may be studied in Champollion-Figeac, i. 363–5
(3 July 1280, two letters written on the same day, wrongly ascribed to the year
1289) and in Langlois, *Philippe III le Hardi*, pp. 435–8 (Bayonne, 3 Dec. 1280).

of Sancho's rivals, by subsidizing Gaston of Béarn and other Gascon lords who went to help him in his last years.

With this picture of Edward as a peace-maker in our minds we must turn to his part in more dramatic affairs on a larger stage.

Hitherto we have seen King Edward moving about in a detached, even desultory sort of way in a large family circle. The succession to Navarre and Champagne and the domestic troubles of Alfonso the Wise had not involved these cousins in any major crisis. The houses of France, England, Castile, Aragon, Navarre, Sicily, and Provence were all closely related to each other. The ambitions of the restless Charles of Anjou need not have caused such violent repercussions in European history if the general restraint had been maintained. But since St. Louis's death two dangers, opposed to each other, had appeared. One was the rise to power of Peter the Great, king of Aragon (1276–85), the other the steady formation in the court of Philip III of France of a forward party, cynically hostile to the traditions of King Louis and devoted to the Angevin cause. A French historian once wrote that the alienation of Aragon was the gravest error that it was possible for France to make. This judgement overlooks the consideration that an alliance with Aragon might not have restrained King Peter, who for many years before he succeeded his father, James I, regarded himself as the successor of the Hohenstaufen. It is true, however, that the victory of the Angevin party in the French court changed the whole French outlook. It meant a deliberate return to the days of Philip Augustus and a bellicose revival of the pseudo-Carolingian tradition. It gave to the struggle in the Mediterranean a general impetus which has ever since directed the politics of Europe, and, indirectly, it led to the Hundred Years War and its insidious aftermath. King Edward, living his own life in his own time with his own difficulties, was, it is needless to say, unconscious of all this, and only gradually came to realize the danger in which the new forces at work in Paris would involve himself. He continued to work for peace and the crusade. He held his own in Gascony as a vassal of France; but the days of St. Louis and Margaret of Provence had gone for ever.[1]

The truth is that outside the British Isles and Gascony

---

[1] The most important books and papers in the extensive literature about this period are noted in the Bibliography (below, pp. 743–6). The best and most detailed

Edward could do very little but try to bring his troublesome relations to come to terms with each other. He could not transfer armies at will to the Rhineland or the valley of the Rhône or into Spain, still less to Italy, and he could not have afforded the financial and political risks of doing this even if he had tried. Nothing shows this more clearly than his relations with Rudolf of Habsburg, the emperor-elect, and with his cousins of Savoy. Historians with no sense of reality used to explain that Edward deliberately pursued a policy of encirclement and sought to fulfil a long-treasured Plantagenet plan to stir up and organize enmity to France in the south-east so that the ancestral foe could be attacked in the rear. A study of Edward's correspondence shows, as one would expect, that this view is pure fantasy. What happened was this. Edward was fond of his mother and was very friendly with his aunt Margaret, the queen dowager of France. He sympathized with their desire to get practical recognition of their rights in Provence and the neighbouring county of Forcalquier, rights of which in their view Charles of Anjou had unjustly deprived them. He welcomed a proposal made by Rudolf of Habsburg and his wife that his daughter Joan (a child who had been born at Acre in 1272) should be betrothed to Rudolf's eldest son Hartmann.[1] He had recognized Rudolf after his election as king of the Romans, and the alliance would be gratifying in itself and might ease the friction between Rudolf and the count of Savoy. If it would help his mother and aunt, so much the better.

His ambassadors to the imperial court in 1276 brought the stipulation that suitable provision should be made for Hartmann and Joan, and that Rudolf should try after his coronation as emperor to get his son elected king of the Romans. Rudolf was not crowned by the pope, was not hopeful of getting recognition for his son, and in May 1278, after ratification of the marriage treaty, suggested that the former kingdom of Arles should be revived for Hartmann. Now though this proposal was doubtless pleasing to Queen Margaret, it was very embarrassing to Edward and was not seriously pressed by Rudolf himself. It was

short account for our purpose may be found in Robert Fawtier, *L'Europe occidentale de 1270 à 1380* (Paris, 1940), pp. 261–325, with useful bibliographical notes. I have also been allowed to use an unpublished dissertation by H. Ingram on Edward I as a foreign statesman.

[1] In addition to the texts in the *Foedera* and Champollion-Figeac see those in the *Monumenta Germaniae historica, Constitutiones*, iii. 151–65, nos. 158–78.

embarrassing to Edward because it would arouse instant opposition from Charles of Anjou, whose county of Provence was
historically the richest part of the kingdom of Arles. It was not
pressed by Rudolf, because he was attracted by the idea—which
had been favoured by Pope Gregory X, and was revived in this
year (1278)—of a marriage between his daughter and a grandson of king Charles and the settlement of the kingdom upon *them*.
A settlement between the king of the Germans and the house
of Anjou would resolve many difficulties. Rudolf would be free
to concentrate his attention on the east, Charles and his
successors would hold a firm title to Provence,[1] the scattered
and turbulent Arelate would be reconstituted, a danger to
peace would be checked, the pope would be relieved of the
dread felt since the days of Frederick II lest the empire might
again be a reality in the valley of the Rhône. King Edward,
who had doubtless been made aware of papal hopes and fears
during his talks with his friend Pope Gregory X at Orvieto in
1273 and had a genuine regard for Charles of Salerno, the heir
of his mother in Provence and the future king of Sicily and
Naples, was well able to appreciate the position. If the policy
attributed to him by later historians had possessed his mind,
or even if he had been influenced by Queen Margaret,
he would have bitterly resented Rudolf's action, but he did
nothing. He continued to discuss plans with his future son-in-
law, and after Hartmann was drowned in December 1281 he
maintained friendly relations with the bereaved father, and
showed no concern about the Arelate.

The kingdom of Arles was not restored. What Frederick II
had nearly done, and his son Manfred had planned to do,[2] was
a paper scheme; but the understanding between Rudolf and
Charles of Anjou remained.[3] Charles was able to strengthen his

[1] Margaret and Eleanor claimed parts at least of Provence because their
dowries had not been paid; but in 1274, on the ground that Provence had escheated
to the empire, Margaret persuaded Rudolf to invest her with Provence and Forcalquier (Böhmer, *Regesta Imperii*, vi, *1273–1313*, ed. Redlich (1898), 141).

[2] A prospect envisaged in the undertaking made by Frederick II when a marriage
was arranged in 1247 between Manfred and Beatrice, the daughter of Amadeus of
Savoy, uncle of the queens of France and England, soon after the marriage between
Charles of Anjou and their sister Beatrice.

[3] Edward's mother heard rumours of the negotiations in the spring of 1279 and in
a letter of protest to Edward begged him to get her interests in a 'fourth part' of
Provence recognized. Edward, on 3 April 1279, wrote a vague letter on her behalf to
Rudolf (Kern, op. cit., pp. 6–7, nos. 11, 12). The form of peace between Rudolf and
Charles of Anjou is dated 27 March 1280; it is accompanied by documents giving

hold on Provence, and, as his influence in Paris increased, to take his share in the scramble for influence in the Rhône valley farther north. Tired of fruitless negotiations, Queen Margaret decided to resort to force and, in a letter informing him of her decision, asked Edward to assist her with the troops which he had given her and his mother reason to think would be forthcoming in case of need. She succeeded in gathering her party together. The archbishop of Lyons, the count of Savoy, Edmund of Lancaster as count of Champagne, Duke Robert of Burgundy, Otto, count of the Free County (Rudolf's vassal and enemy), the count of Alençon, and others, endangered or annoyed by Angevin penetration, met in Mâcon in October 1281 and agreed to assemble their forces at Lyons in May 1282.[1] Edward was in a quandary. He longed to see the tiresome affair settled and some justice done to his mother and aunt. He was fond of both of them and was touched by the expressions of the 'special confidence' which they had in him. Always hoping for a peaceful arrangement, he had promised to help them even with armed forces. Now, in November 1281, he replied to Margaret's appeal that he would send his contingent, but he begged her to act prudently and said that he was making another appeal to the king of Sicily. He wrote to the pope, Martin IV, who was a Frenchman committed to a pro-Angevin policy, to Charles of Anjou, and to Charles of Salerno. He urged settlement by arbitration. He explained that his ties with Margaret would compel him to assist her if the issue should be war. He besought King Charles to be generous and humble and to seek a compromise. To his friend and cousin Charles of Salerno he opened his mind, for Charles was less intransigent than his father. 'I am very reluctant in this matter. My heart is not in it, on account of the love between you and me. I pray you, do not take it amiss, for I call God to witness that, if the thing affected me only, I would do nothing against your wishes.'[2] Fortunately, the renewal of the Welsh war in March 1282 spared Edward's con-

---

equivocal assurances on behalf of Margaret of France (*Constitutiones*, iii. 226, 237–41, 245–8) which could have had no effect. A firm understanding seems to have been reached by the spring of 1281. Cf. F. Kern, *Die Anfänge der französischen Ausdehnungspolitik* (1910), pp. 92–94; also, for a discussion of various views, his article on Rudolf's foreign policy in *Mitteilungen des Instituts österreichischer Geschichtsforschung*, xxxi (1910), 54–70, especially the note on pp. 62–63.

[1] Letter from Margaret to Edward, in Champollion-Figeac, i. 265–6.
[2] *Foedera*, I. ii. 600.

science a final decision. He could not send troops, nor would they have been of any service if he had. Charles of Salerno was ready in Provence, and Margaret's allies were not ready. War did not come. But a few weeks before the time when the league of Mâcon was to operate the Sicilians revolted and Charles of Anjou was faced by the last and hardest fight of his life. Peter of Aragon was behind the rebels, and was master of the sea. The 'Sicilian Vespers' gave Queen Margaret what Edward could not give her—the compromise which saved her honour and dignity. In 1283 the parties consented to abide by the decision of Philip III. Philip assigned his mother, if she would renounce her claims to Provence, lands in Anjou to the value of 4,000 *livres* of Tours. His decision, after much delay, was made effective in 1287 by his son and successor, Philip the Fair.

Margaret's political activity in the Rhône valley and relations with King Rudolf had been due entirely to family disputes. Edward's concern to help her was no less domestic. The queen was still powerful at the French court, had her own circle, and wanted Provence. Rudolf, who was at least in name the suzerain of the imperial area east of the Rhône, could be of use to her and Eleanor and she could perhaps be of service to him. She was concerned also to smooth the difficulties of her uncles and cousins in Savoy. In the autumn of 1281, shortly before Hartmann died, she wrote to Edward[1] urging him to further efforts as a peace-maker between Count Philip of Savoy and Rudolf, and suggested that the marriage between Hartmann and Edward's daughter should be deferred until he had succeeded. Edward himself had a still stronger interest in the welfare of his Savoyard relatives. To him, as to every member of the English royal house, his uncle Peter, the late count, had been a familiar figure in England. Peter had been a busy and influential friend of king Henry III for twenty-three years before, in June 1263, he succeeded his nephew Boniface as count of Savoy. His palace on the Strand kept the memory of the Savoyard connexion alive in England for centuries.[2]

---

[1] Champollion-Figeac, i. 209, with wrong date 1278. In this letter Margaret refers to the recent meeting at Mâcon.

[2] For good accounts of Peter see C. L. Kingsford in *D.N.B.*, s.v. Peter of Savoy and *Complete Peerage*, x. 805-9. He was given the honour and castle of Richmond. without the earldom, by Henry III in 1240. By his will he left this escheat to Queen Eleanor (7 May 1268). This is why John of Brittany did not get his estates till 1268 (above, p. 235) and why the queen had to be compensated. Peter's house in the

Edward knew well how delicate and uneasy the relationships
of the counts of Savoy were with the neighbours on every side,
in the Rhône valley, in the Alps, in Vaud and Piedmont, as
they stubbornly maintained their independence in the world.
As count of Savoy Peter had in 1265 become involved in war
with Rudolf of Habsburg, nine or ten years before Rudolf's
exaltation to the German throne. Moreover, the count of Savoy
was Edward's vassal. When Charles of Anjou married Beatrice
of Provence and a new turn was given to political conditions
in the old Arelate, and the English court was moved to indignation by his cool disregard of every right but his wife's in
the succession to Provence, Count Amadeus of Savoy had
made an agreement with King Henry III of a kind familiar in
that part of Europe. In return for a lump sum and an annual
pension the count, in January 1246, a fortnight before Charles's
marriage, surrendered and did homage to Henry for Susa and
other fiefs on either side of the Alps, covering the approaches
to the Great St. Bernard. Edward received the homage of
Count Philip, Peter of Savoy's brother and successor, on his
way home from Italy (June 1273).[1] Although his obligations to
the count were normally confined to an annual payment, both
Edward and his Savoyard vassal found some reality in their
relationship and felt pleasure in it. It helped to keep Savoy
within the domestic circle around the old queens of France and
England. Thus, early in 1282, in response to an appeal from
Philip 'as your man' for help against King Rudolf, who was
preparing to attack him, Edward sent his friend Otto of Granson and the dean of Lichfield to explore every possible way of
peace between the two parties, 'each of which is dear to me'.[2]
Both Philip and his nephews exchanged envoys and letters with
Edward about the affairs of Savoy.[3] The count sought Edward's
advice about the succession, appointed him and his mother

Strand, later called the palace of Savoy, was given to him in 1246. By his will he
left it to the hospice of the Great St. Bernard in Savoy; Queen Eleanor bought it
from the hospice and gave it to Edmund of Lancaster. The property thus passed
into the possession of the duchy of Lancaster.

[1] For these feudal relations see Powicke, *Henry III and the Lord Edward*, i. 365–6;
ii. 612–13. The order of succession in Savoy after the death of Queen Eleanor's
grandfather Thomas I (1233) was Amadeus IV (d. 1253), who was followed by his
son Boniface, a minor (d. 1263); Peter (d. 1268) and Philip (d. 1285), both
brothers of Amadeus IV; Amadeus V (nephew of Philip).

[2] Kern, *Acta*, pp. 19–20, nos. 32–34, letters of 12 February 1282 from Cirencester.

[3] P.R.O. *Anc. Corr.* xx. 126, 128, from Amadeus V.

Eleanor as arbitrators about this, the division of lands, and other disputes, and made them the executors of his will (1284-5). When, after Philip's death, his nephews Amadeus and Louis began to quarrel, the king of England and his mother, associated with the pope and the new king of France, Philip the Fair, acted as arbitrators between them, allotting the county to Amadeus and Vaud as a fief to Louis. Amadeus was grateful to Edward, but as was inevitable it was the king of France who reaped the greater reward of intervention in Savoy.[1] England was far away from Savoy and intercourse derived from personal ties could not endure indefinitely.

In any case Edward, in the years after the fateful year 1285, became involved, as a peace-maker, in the political confusion caused by the war between Charles of Anjou and Peter of Aragon—a war to which Pope Martin IV had given the doubtful prestige of a crusade with Philip III as its executor. Charles of Anjou as king of Sicily was the ally of the Papacy, Pope Martin had emerged as his protector, and the Angevin party prevailed in the French court. The political equilibrium which Pope Gregory X had tried to maintain in Europe had entirely disappeared. Edward alone was the friend of all parties, with no axe to grind. And, for the first time since his coronation, he was free to concentrate on European affairs. Wales had been conquered, the English common law had been revised and defined in his great statutes, his administrative stock-taking had been completed. He could settle for a time in Gascony where there was much to do, and he could plan his crusade. He was at hand in this time of need. In the summer of 1286 he spent two months in Paris.[2] From October in this year until the end of June he was in the south-west, mainly in Gascony, sometimes in Saintonge or the Agenais, never far from the Pyrenees. During these three years the establishment of peace was his main preoccupation; and his efforts now meant more than an agreeable reconciliation of his bellicose relatives, for at last, after many delays and postponements, he fulfilled his engagements to

---

[1] Cf. Fawtier, op. cit., p. 371, note, for a summary of the relations between Amadeus V and Philip the Fair, especially between 1302 and 1308. Amadeus fought for Philip in Flanders. He acquired in 1308 and later an hotel in Paris and other property. On the other hand he always reserved his duty to Edward and supported him in his dealings with Philip. His son Edward, who married a French princess, Blanche, a daughter of Robert II of Burgundy and a sister of two queens of France, was named after the king of England.   [2] Below, p. 255.

Gregory X and his successors. In June 1287 he took the cross. When, in the following October, he received at Bordeaux the emissary of the khan of Persia—the emissary Rabban Cauma was a friend of the Nestorian patriarch—he is reported to have said: 'I have the sign of the cross on my body. This affair is my chief concern.'[1] His hopes were not to be fulfilled.

The crusade of Aragon was over when Edward reached Paris. The stage had been cleared. Charles of Anjou had died on 7 January 1285, Pope Martin IV on 28 March, Philip III on 5 October, Peter of Aragon on 10 November. Charles of Salerno was a prisoner in Aragon. Edward, at the age of forty-seven, was the oldest in a family group of kings. A settlement, one might think, should not have been difficult, but the political network was tangled, and peace was delayed for sixteen years (1302). The trouble was deep-rooted and the Holy See in particular had to be satisfied. Yet Edward achieved a good deal before he withdrew from the scene.

Charles of Anjou had been brought to Italy and Sicily by Pope Urban IV in 1263 to withstand the emperor Frederick II's natural son Manfred, king of Sicily, and to extirpate the influence of the Hohenstaufen. The king of Aragon since the days of Innocent III had been a vassal of the Holy See. But, since Charles of Anjou's marriage to Beatrice of Provence in 1246, there had been a feud between the houses of Aragon and Anjou. The count of Provence, Raymond Berengar, the father of Queen Margaret of France, Queen Eleanor of England, and Beatrice, was head of a younger branch of the house of Aragon and after his death James I, the king of Aragon, had hoped to renew the connexion with the elder branch. Charles of Anjou had prevented this. In the eyes of James and his son Peter he was a French interloper. In 1262 Peter was married to Constance, Manfred's daughter, and henceforward regarded himself as the champion of the Hohenstaufen tradition and of his wife who, if she had her right, should be queen of Sicily. In his father's lifetime, before he succeeded to the throne of Aragon (1276), he and his young son Alfonso spoke and wrote of Constance as a queen. When he was crowned at Saragossa he brushed aside the archbishop of Tarragona and crowned

---

[1] The khan, Arghun, was planning an attack on the sultan of Egypt, and, with the support of the patriarch, sought co-operation with the pope and the western princes.

himself, to show his independence of the papacy. He entered
into relations with the new pope, Nicholas III (1277–81), who
was alarmed by Charles of Anjou's ambitions, and, it is probable, with the Greek emperor Michael. He was privy to the
movement of resistance in the island of Sicily and gave refuge to
its leaders. The 'Sicilian Vespers' of 1282 found him prepared.
His shipyards and armaments had been busy for some time and
an expedition, which aroused the lively anxiety of the French
Pope Martin IV (1281–5) and of the kings of France and Castile
as well as of Charles and his son, was in obvious preparation.
Till the hour of its departure on 7 June from Portfangos, near
the mouth of the Ebro, the sailors did not know its destination.
It was destined for Tunis, 'to fight the enemies of the faith, if
pleasing to the Pope'. So Peter wrote to Edward in July. On 30
August he crossed to Trapani, and on 1 September was crowned
king of Sicily at Palermo. The Angevins were driven out of the
island.[1] Martin IV excommunicated Peter and declared him
deprived of his realm. In February 1284 he entrusted the execution of the sentence to King Philip of France. In June, in a
naval battle off Naples, the Genoese admiral Roger de Loria,
King Peter's right-hand man, took the younger Charles prisoner.
King Charles died at Foggia in the following January.

In general opinion Peter had been stirred by the vengeance
which passed from Queen Constance's heart to his, but what
aroused Catalan enthusiasm in these years was the triumphant
success of the courage and daring of the king. As the chronicler
Muntaner wrote, he fought 'the pope who is over all Christians
and the house of France which is the oldest royal house in
Christendom'. He had shown his hand at a meeting in Toulouse
in 1280, when he met King Philip, James, king of Majorca (his
brother), and Charles of Salerno to discuss the Castilian succession. Peter had a voice in this, for he had given refuge to and
later detained as hostages the two sons of Ferdinand de la Cerda.
At Toulouse he shocked Charles of Salerno by his open hostility
to him, and he alienated Philip of France by reopening the
question which everybody thought had been settled by treaty at
Corbeil more than twenty years before (1258). He demanded

---

[1] For the background, in Aragon, Catalonia, and North Africa, see Ferran
Soldevila, *Història de Catalunya*, i (Barcelona, 1934), 256–75; also Helene Wieruszowski's review of Steven Runciman's *The Sicilian Vespers*, in *Speculum*, xxxiv
(1959), 323–6.

the restitution of the Aragonese lands in the south of France
surrendered by his father. Philip was ready, therefore, in 1283 to
listen to the Angevin party at court, where the queen mother's
opposition to Charles of Anjou had been allayed by his decision
to submit her claims in Provence to arbitration. Negotiations between Pope Martin and the king of France were opened by the
papal legate at Bordeaux.

The occasion was remarkable; for in accordance with a
treaty made on 30 December 1282, Charles of Anjou and Peter
of Aragon had come to Bordeaux to settle the right to Sicily in
personal combat. We are too apt to forget, as we brood over the
political manœuvres of the time, that these kings and barons
lived in the high days of chivalry, though the doings in Bordeaux
may also remind us that its speech and trappings were more impressive than its deeds. King Philip came to Bordeaux and with
him came Charles and the hundred knights who were to take
part with him. Edward was not there; he was busy in north
Wales, rounding up Prince David; but his seneschal in Gascony,
John de Grilly, was present to act as arbiter in the lists.[1] On
31 May Charles duly presented himself, but Peter of Aragon
did not. He feared an ambush. But he was not far away, and
on the next morning, while his enemy still slept, he made the
round of the lists, declared himself victorious and hurried
home.

Naturally enough, King Philip was all the more disposed to
accept the legate's proposals. These were carefully considered
in November in an assembly at Bourges. The prelates and
magnates present stipulated that the war against Peter of
Aragon should be a crusade, subvented by tenths collected from
the clergy throughout Christendom or at least from the ecclesiastical provinces of Gaul.[2] The pope agreed to this and, though
there was some opposition, the venture was approved at Paris
in January 1284. Charles of Valois, the second surviving son of

[1] Pope Martin, in accordance with the canon law, forbade the combat and
absolved Charles of Anjou from his oath to wage it. He asked Edward to prevent it
and to close Gascony to the combatants. Edward, engaged as he was in Wales,
refused to preside at Bordeaux and, famous jouster though he had been, expressed
a preference for peace-making. He would not preside, he said, even to gain the
two kingdoms of Sicily and Aragon (*Foedera*, I. ii. 627; letter from Aberconway,
25 March 1283).

[2] In other words, not only from the French domain but from all the provinces
west of the Rhine and the Alps. The narrative above is based in the main on Fawtier,
op. cit.

Philip III, was accepted as king of Aragon and in March was invested with his new but as yet unconquered kingdom by the legate. Preparations for the crusade were hastened. A great force of men and stores was gathered at Marseilles and Aigues Mortes in January 1285, while Charles of Anjou was dying in Italy. Before the French army reached the frontiers of Catalonia, Pope Martin, the other instigator of the war, was dead also.

King Peter was in much danger. He had been deserted, not without reason, by his brother James, king of Majorca and lord of the border provinces of Cerdagne and Roussillon, whose resources were put at King Philip's disposal. Within the three provinces of his kingdom, Peter could rely only on Catalonia and Valencia. The kingdom of Aragon proper was under the control of a union of barons and towns which in 1283 had forced him to accept an interpretation of Aragonese liberties more onerous and far more crippling than the Provisions of Oxford to which Henry III of England had been subjected in 1258. Even while the French were advancing the union set conditions upon any military service. Moreover, Roger de Loria's fleet had not arrived, while the ships of Provence could keep abreast or ahead of the army of France. Yet King Peter prevailed. His light troops delayed the French in Roussillon and after King Philip had succeeded in forcing his way into the plain in north Catalonia and had laid siege to Gerona, his forces were demoralized by constant attacks, a failure in the commissariat service in the ports, and an epidemic. Then Roger de Loria arrived from Sicily. He broke up the Provençal fleet and occupied the French base at Rosas. King Philip had to retreat. He was ill and had to be carried on a litter. He died at Perpignan on 5 October. King Peter did not long survive his victory, and never knew how great it was. He died on 10 November.

Such was the situation when King Edward came to Paris to do homage to the new king Philip IV in the end of May 1286. He did homage on 5 June and came to an agreement with his overlord about his rights in Quercy, which he sold, and his occupation of southern Saintonge, which he secured. These matters will concern us later. He stayed two months in Paris at the abbey of Saint-Germain-des-Prés, within easy reach of the Louvre by boat. He would not have stayed so long if he had not been on cordial terms with his young cousin. In fact the two kings held

similar views about most matters. Philip, it should be emphasized, had been opposed to his father's crusade. He was instinctively averse from distant enterprises and was as inclined to
compromise as Edward himself. They busied themselves about
a truce, with a view to the release of Charles of Salerno, now his
father's successor, and a treaty of peace between him and the
new king of Aragon, Alfonso. When Edward went south[1] he
seems to have been given a free hand by Philip. At the same
time Philip was not yet ready for a definitive peace. He had to
consider French obligations to James of Majorca and the future
of the Castilian claimants, the sons of Ferdinand de la Cerda
who were still kept in confinement in Aragon, and in the meanwhile he was very willing to receive the papal tenths levied
by the pope to pay for the war.

Edward, after the arrival of the Aragonese envoys in Paris,
had arranged a truce in July, to last until September in the
next year. The new pope, Honorius IV, who, though hostile to
Aragon, was more conciliatory than Martin IV had been, in
due course agreed to the terms and so did James of Majorca.
The position of the latter and of the French vassals who had
lands in Catalonia was safeguarded. Then, although the pope
refused to recognize Alfonso as king of Aragon in spite of his
professions of innocence and obedience, the peace conference
opened at Bordeaux at Christmas time.[2] Little is known about
the discussions at Bordeaux, but Edward must soon have
realized that, in this complicated business, he could not hope for
quick results. The pitiful letters sent to him from Provence in
May 1286 by Charles's little sons—an eloquent cry as from
the lips of orphans who looked to Edward and to him alone to
restore their father to them—could receive no hopeful reply.
The prospect of peace was continually clouded by infractions of
the truce and especially by Aragonese determination to be
revenged on James of Majorca, and to protect Catalonia by the
restoration of the Balearic islands. Still more serious was the
feeling in papal circles against the creation of the island of

[1] He visited Pontigny and Fontevrault on his leisurely way to Saintes from Paris
(29 July to 14 September). After more than a month in Saintonge he went east,
avoiding Bordeaux, and then south to Agen to establish himself personally in the
Agenais, which had been given over by France in 1279.

[2] Most of the voluminous body of documents relating to these and later negotiations are in the *Foedera*. See also L. Klüpfel, *Die äussere Politik Alfonso's III von
Aragonien* (Berlin, 1911–12).

Sicily as an independent kingdom ruled by Alfonso's brother, another James. There was a strong Angevin party among the cardinals and the pope would allow no compromise, such as that James should hold Sicily as a papal fief. Sicily was as important in papal eyes as the Balearic Isles were to the king of Aragon and the seafaring traders of Barcelona and the other ports of Catalonia and Valencia. In March 1287, a month before he died, Pope Honorius made it clear that peace depended upon the restoration of Sicily to the house of Anjou.

In spite of the anxieties which continued to distract him in Aragon after his father's death, King Alfonso was equally stubborn and even raised again the Aragonese claim to Navarre. He probably hoped for more help from Edward than he received, for Edward was an old friend, and Alfonso, whose mother was a Savoyard, had domestic claims upon his goodwill. If a French chronicler can be trusted, Edward was suspected in some quarters in France. He was regarded, we may suppose, as an unreliable person, prepared to work against the royal interests. His disinterested affection for Charles of Salerno, who had been an object of his solicitude ever since the news of his captivity had reached him, was not always taken seriously.[1] Hence Edward may well have been embarrassed by the good relations with Alfonso which should have eased his task as mediator. Here we must turn back a few years.

During his stay in Gascony in 1273, when he negotiated the abortive marriage alliance with the king of Navarre, Edward had met Peter of Aragon, who was not yet king, at St. Jean de Sordes, not far from Bayonne. There they agreed that Peter's eldest son should marry Edward's eldest daughter.[2] Two years later King Peter suggested that, in addition to a marriage between his eldest son Alfonso and Edward's eldest daughter, his eldest daughter Isabella should in due course marry Edward's eldest son.[3] Early in 1282 (15 February), the young princess empowered proctors to conclude the marriage,[4] but now

[1] He had got papal permission to send envoys to Charles in prison before the captive was removed from Sicily to Aragon. The pope forbade people to visit Sicily and threatened to excommunicate those who disobeyed.

[2] *Foedera*, II. ii. 506 (October 1273). No names are mentioned in the treaty. The parties would be the eldest son and daughter surviving 'tempore nuptiarum contrahendarum inter eos'. [3] *Foedera*, I. ii. 521 (March 1275).

[4] This was the time when Antony Bek and John of Vescy were sent to Aragon (cf. below, p. 294). Fritz Kern, who has given the fullest account of these negotiations, suggests that Edward, aware of Peter's designs against Charles of Anjou, was

Edward began to show some hesitation. In view of current rumours he wanted to be sure of Peter's political plans. Peter, on the contrary, after he had embarked on his Sicilian adventure, became more eager to fortify himself by an alliance with Edward. In the summer of 1282, when he announced to Edward his triumphant welcome in Sicily, he also appointed the archbishop of Tarragona and the bishop of Valencia to conclude the marriage. The situation was becoming delicate. On the one hand the Infante Alfonso appealed to Edward for help in case of an attack by France. Edward explained that the Welsh war had prevented him from sending his daughter and that, as he was Philip's vassal, he could not take action against him, but had written to the pope.[1] On the other hand, Pope Martin IV (7 July 1283) expressed astonishment that Edward should offer his daughter to the son of the king of Aragon, whom he had deprived of his kingdom. The marriage, he pointed out, was in any case unlawful, for the parties were within the prohibited degrees.[2] Although Edward temporized and said that he would not be deflected from his purpose by the papal prohibition, which was renewed by Pope Martin's successor in May 1286,[3] he would not take sides. His determination must have been strengthened when his interventions on behalf of peace were repulsed at the papal court. A peacemaker must do nothing to arouse suspicion of his good faith.

Under these circumstances Edward concentrated on the release of Charles of Salerno as the essential preliminary to peace. His own words nearly four years later are precise: taxation in England had been needed to pay the debts which 'the king had

hoping to get his assistance for Queen Margaret's designs against their common enemy. This is not convincing. Edward was working for peace, not for war, between Margaret and Charles (above, p. 246). Kern's article, 'Eduard I von England und Peter von Aragon' was published in the *Mitteilungen des Instituts für österreichische Geschichtsforschung*, xxx (1909), 412–23. He prints the letters about the appointment of the envoys in January 1282 (pp. 421–2). Other documents are printed in the *Foedera*. Cf. above, p. 244, n. 1, and F. D. Swift's article in *E.H.R.* v (1891), 326.

[1] See Kern's article, cited above, p. 422 (12 January 1283).

[2] *Calendar of Papal Letters*, i (1893), 476.

[3] *Foedera*, i. ii. 665. Pope Honorius declared that the dispensation recently granted to Edward allowing him to arrange marriages between his children, nephews, or nieces and their cousins within the fourth degree of affinity or consanguinity was not applicable to the children, &c., of the late Peter of Aragon, or to others not obedient (*indevotis*) to the Church. It was in virtue of this general dispensation that Edward was able to arrange the marriage of his daughters to kinsfolk.

incurred during his absence abroad in effecting the liberation of Charles, king of Sicily, his kinsman, whereby the state of the Holy Land and of the Church was improved and peace secured'.[1] The death of Pope Honorius IV in April 1287 and the period of vacancy in the Holy See which followed would, in any case, have made a more ambitious course impracticable. The cardinals, however, could be asked to agree to a prolongation of the truce made at Paris and the papal envoys in Gascony could give counsel and add authority to discussions about the terms of Charles's release. Terms were agreed at Oloron, in Béarn, on 25 July 1287. King Alfonso's conditions were very stiff, for, once Charles was free and had formally succeeded to his throne, the weaknesses inherent in Alfonso's position would be revealed. Much would depend upon his captive's good intentions. Hence at Oloron Charles was required to surrender two of his sons as hostages before he could be liberated, and to pay 50,000 marks of silver as a pledge of his promise to surrender his eldest son within ten months after his release. (This sum was not a ransom, but a pledge to be repaid when the condition was fulfilled.) Moreover the future of Provence was to depend upon his good faith and success in securing a settlement. The barons, knights, and citizens of Provence were to hand over sixty of their sons, thirty before and thirty after the liberation; and if peace were not made within three years, Charles must either return to captivity or the castellans of Provence were to do homage to Alfonso as their hereditary lord and hold their fortresses at his disposal. To add substance to this condition, Charles was to persuade his allies to grant a further truce for three years before the expiry of the new truce in September 1288. If he failed to do this he was to return to captivity or forfeit the 50,000 marks, his hostages, and his county of Provence. King Edward, in proof of his own earnestness in the matter, made himself responsible for 20,000 of the 50,000 marks. He promised also to seek the consent of the next pope to the marriage between Alfonso and his daughter Eleanor.[2]

[1] *Cal. Pat. Rolls, 1282–91*, p. 419: request in January 1291 to the barons, knights, freemen, and whole community of Wales to grant a fifteenth, as the rest of the realm had done in the previous year. Cf. below, p. 443.

[2] The terms, with documents relating to the extension of the truce between Philip IV and Alfonso, and to completion of the marriage between Eleanor and Alfonso, may be read in the *Foedera*, i. ii. 677–9. In November the cardinals congratulated Edward on his work (ibid. 679).

The new pope, Nicholas IV, was elected in February 1288. He had been master-general of the Franciscans, and was eager for the Crusade; at the same time, while less committed to French influence than his predecessors, he firmly maintained the traditions of the Curia: Aragon was a papal fief, Alfonso a disobedient son, the maintenance of the kingdom of Sicily more important than the personal freedom of its king. By the terms of the treaty of Oloron, Alfonso explicitly required the acquiescence of the Church. Pope Nicholas would not accept this condition. He denounced the treaty of Oloron. The pope's declaration did not, of course, put a stop to the efforts of Charles's friends to set him free—indeed, he strongly urged Edward to maintain his endeavour—but it increased their difficulties. The king of France was unwilling to give facilities for the passage of the Provençal hostages; he was gathering in the papal tenths, his brother Charles of Valois was titular king of Aragon, and he saw no reason why he should make things easy for Alfonso. James of Majorca, whose island kingdom had been reunited with the Crown of Aragon (1286), was a further cause of trouble, and for a time Alfonso threatened to repudiate the treaty unless his uncle was made a party to it. The only course open to Edward was to assume still more responsibility. Edward determined to put the business through. Negotiations were resumed, and on 28 October 1288 another arrangement was sealed at Canfran, in northern Aragon. Gaston of Béarn and the chief Gascon towns with Edward on the one part, certain Spanish towns with Alfonso on the other part, were associated in an elaborate series of guarantees for the fulfilment of the conditions still unfulfilled. As an immediate pledge thirty-six of Edward's English and Aquitanian barons and forty citizens of Gascony and the Agenais were handed over as hostages. Charles's personal obligations to procure a truce for three years or return to captivity remained the same as before.[1] At last Alfonso was satisfied. Charles was released. He returned with Edward to Oloron and assured him that his generous sacrifices would be repaid. He had every reason to be grateful to Edward, and indeed he did not delay. His immediate duty was so far to meet his undertakings to Alfonso as to secure the return of the Gascon hostages. These were released by March

---

[1] For a fuller account of the treaty as it affected Edward in Aquitaine see below, pp. 282–4.

1289. Edward's task was accomplished. He was finally discharged of his obligations in the treaty between Charles and Alfonso of February 1291.

How great the sense of relief was can be seen in a letter written from Agen on 16 March 1289 by a well-known Dominican to his friend Henry Eastry, the prior of Canterbury. The writer, Brother William of Hothum or Hotham, was at this time in close touch with Edward and his court, and during the next ten years was to play an influential part in public affairs. We shall meet him again. He wrote:

> If things had gone smoothly with our lord the king during his stay in Aquitaine I should have written more often; but they were rather bad than good, and I have no wish to be their reporter. So you must excuse my idle pen. The liberation of the prince brought more grief than joy because of our hostages who were in duress on his behalf; but how our happiness has increased, for on 9 March they were restored by the king of Aragon, and soon, I hope, the lord king will be on his way home again. The stay in these parts has seemed too long to both him and his.[1]

Edward, in fact, did reach England in August. The troubles of Charles of Salerno were by no means over, and Edward continued to take a share in the tangled negotiations which fill the next two years; but a start had been made and it was through no fault of his that, in spite of the peace made at Tarascon in February 1291, the early death of King Alfonso of Aragon—he was only twenty-seven years old—gave an entirely new turn to the problem of Sicily. This story does not concern us, but something must be said about Edward's last relations with Alfonso.

Another letter from William of Hotham to his friend the prior provides a starting-point. This was written on 21 October 1289 from Rome, where William had been sent with Otto of Granson by King Edward on an embassy to Pope Nicholas IV. After observing that 'our folk find small favour these days', for the pope is annoyed by the indifference of the king's clerks to his mandates, William goes on to say that King Charles (as he now was), 'for whose release our lord the king laboured so hard', also finds small favour. 'He has little authority in the

---

[1] Hist. MSS. Commission, *Report on Manuscripts in Various Collections*, i (1901), 253. This and other letters, here printed, have escaped the attention of historians. For Hotham see especially Little and Pelster, *Oxford Theology and Theologians, c. 1282–1302* (1934), pp. 82–87.

administration of his kingdom. Whence I fear that we have laboured much in vain in his behalf.'[1] This unequivocal judgement confirms other evidence. The pope had refused to honour Charles's engagements. He had ordered King Alfonso to hand over the young princes and Provençals whom he held as hostages, to repay the money he had received, and to appear in person before him. Charles at last declared that he was returning to captivity, and in accordance with the terms of his treaty with Alfonso would appear at the meeting place which had been arranged in view of such an eventuality on the borders of Catalonia and Roussillon. There Alfonso should hand over the hostages and money and the king of Sicily would surrender himself. This gesture was not free from the fastidious casuistry allowed to chivalrous behaviour. According to Alfonso's account he was taken by surprise, could not ascertain to what particular place Charles was going and missed him. Charles went to the frontier, stayed a day (31 October—1 November) and declared that he had done his part and that Alfonso was a defaulter. He withdrew to Roussillon and argued with Alfonso from Perpignan. Aligning himself with the pope, he demanded the surrender of Sicily, the subjection of Aragon to the Holy See, and the restoration of Majorca to independence. Alfonso told Edward all this and begged him to keep Charles to his engagements. Edward, now very busy in England, had to work from a distance through correspondence and envoys, but his influence upon Alfonso and Charles can be seen in the events of the next twelve months. After a fruitless conference at Perpignan, from which the Aragonese envoys finally withdrew, the two princes came together. They met on the frontier near Junquera in long and private session and departed from each other in good cheer; peace between them was confidently expected.[2] About the same time the kings of France and Castile had met at Bayonne in Gascony and had reached an understanding about the sons of Ferdinand de la Cerda. King Charles, moreover, was in treaty with his cousin Charles of Valois and, in return for the grant of Anjou and Maine, persuaded him to surrender his title to the crown of Aragon. All that was needed

---

[1] Hist. MSS. Commission, op. cit., p. 256.

[2] Letter from William de la Corner, lately made bishop of Salisbury, to the prior of Canterbury (op. cit., pp. 257–8). The bishop wrote early in May 1290, from the neighbourhood of Paris.

was some concession by King Alfonso, and this was forthcoming. As early as 15 June King Charles wrote from Avignon to urge Edward to come south in person to finish the good work he had begun, when 'you proved your sincerity and unloosed my bonds and broke the walls of my prison'. The two cardinals who were with him (one of whom was no less a person than Benedict Gaetani, the future Pope Boniface VIII) agreed emphatically, Charles wrote, that Edward's presence in the negotiations with Alfonso would be decisive. He could name whatever place he preferred for the conference.[1] Edward could not go, but he sent the earl of Lincoln and others who were present at Tarascon when peace was made in February 1291.

Alfonso's concessions were so far-reaching that most Spanish historians have regarded the treaty of Tarascon as humiliating.[2] He agreed to submit himself and his kingdom of Aragon, Valencia, and Catalonia to the mercy of the pope and to be restored to them by the pope. He surrendered the hostages and repaid the money which Charles had sent him. He promised that he would give no aid to his brother James in Sicily and would negotiate the terms of his uncle James's restoration in Majorca. In short, he turned his back upon his father's most cherished hopes. On the other hand, he extricated himself from difficulties and enmities which might well have remained implacable. That he did not regard Edward with a less friendly eye is shown by his arrangements for his marriage, at long last, to Eleanor.[3] Then, suddenly, he died, in the fullness of his youth

---

[1] P.R.O. *Anc. Corr.* xviii. 155. The two cardinals also wrote to Edward; their letter (dated 13 June) has been edited, so far as it is legible, by Robert Weiss with other previously unedited letters of Gaetani, in the *Rivista di storia della Chiesa in Italia*, iii (1949), 160. Both letters were sent by the clerk, Master Stephen of St. George, who had authority to discuss the situation with Edward. Stephen was an interesting man, for he was the clerk of both kings and equally trusted by both. He had recently brought letters from Edward to Charles. He died in the following October (1290). See Weiss, pp. 162–4, who cites the account of him from the necrology of Montecassino, where his brother Peter was a monk: 'obiit Magister Stephanus de sancto Georgio scriptor domini pape et consiliarius et secretarius regum anglie et sicilie.' As long ago as May 1276 Edward had made Peter a royal chaplain in consideration of the services rendered by Stephen to the Crown as a king's clerk (*Cal. Pat. Rolls, 1272–81*, p. 143). Nothing could illustrate better the closely knit nature of diplomatic procedure in western Europe at this time than the appearance of a king's clerk who was also a *scriptor* in the papal chancery and a counsellor of Charles of Salerno (1285–90). See below, p. 421 note.

[2] Ferran Soldevila, op. cit. i. 293, takes a more favourable and sober standpoint.

[3] Cf. the cordial references to Edward and to the advantage to general good relations of the projected marriage in the statement of conditions of peace made by

(18 June 1291). Eleanor and Alfonso were of the same age. In spite of interruptions their betrothal had been under consideration for eighteen years, since they were children of nine. In September 1293, two years after Alfonso's death, Eleanor was married to Henry III, count of Bar.

One of the conditions of Alfonso's reconciliation with the Church had been that he should go on crusade. Edward had already taken the cross in June 1287, some nine months after his arrival in Gascony.[1] His decision, though often deferred, had long been made and was the outcome of the summons to a crusade made in the oecumenical council of Lyons by Pope Gregory in 1274. The clergy throughout the west had been taxed, and the proceeds, carefully kept under papal control, were to be used by any prince who had definitely made his arrangements to depart, and had reached a precise agreement with the pope about the terms of payment. If a prince, intending to go on a crusade, had got the reversion of the tenth paid in his lands, and, having made his plans, received some of the money, he was bound to refund it if he did not fulfil his oath to go. If, with papal approval, he borrowed some of it for current needs— and how tempting were those money-bags stored in the strongrooms of monasteries!—he was under the strictest obligation to repay the loan. Right up to this year 1287 Pope Gregory X and his short-lived successors had been busy on the great enterprise. In 1275 Edward had got the reversion of the tenth in the dioceses of England, Ireland, and Wales and, subject to the consent of the Scottish king, of Scotland, but not of Gascony, for his fief there fell within the metropolitan areas of Gaul. Frequent discussions had been held with the Holy See about the date of his formal reception of the cross. When he took the vow in June 1287, nearly all the papal tenth for six years had been garnered by the papal collectors in the British Isles. The treasure amounted to £130,000 sterling, equal to the normal royal income of some four years. It lay in the great abbeys or was in the hands of the

James of Sicily in 1290–1. This is printed in H. Finke, *Acta Aragonensia*, i (1908), 3–6.

[1] The date is nowhere given precisely, though it was before October 1287 (Lunt, *Financial Relations*, pp. 338–9 note), but it can be established from the place. The place, Blanquefort, near Bordeaux, is mentioned by Nicholas Trevet, whose chronology is not reliable. The king was at Blanquefort in June. According to an agreement with the pope of June 1286 Edward was to take the cross on (or before?) 24 June 1287.

Italian banking houses which operated for the pope in London. And now the time had come to fix the date of his departure and the terms of payment. Pope Honorius IV had already come to a preliminary understanding with Edward, but his death in April, before the king had actually taken the cross, made a more definite settlement necessary with his successor, Nicholas IV.

The new pope, Nicholas IV, who was an Italian Franciscan, had a more measured outlook than his two predecessors. He was fully alive to the urgency of the crusade if the last footholds of the Latin kingdom in Syria were to be maintained as a base for effective co-operation with the khan of Persia and the recapture of Jerusalem and the holy places. His firm dealings with both Charles II and Alfonso of Aragon reveal an independent but not an obstinate mind. King Edward could find in him a man who would hold his own without hindrance to the great cause.[1] Before his return to England, Edward, in May 1289, sent a stately embassy to the pope. It was led by Otto of Granson and was a large company, 'sometimes', to quote the wardrobe accounts, 'with forty seven horses, sometimes with fifty, sometimes with sixty'; but the leading spirit was Brother William of Hotham. The objects of the mission were to procure a dispensation for the marriage proposed between the king's only surviving son Edward, a child aged four, and the little Princess Margaret of Scotland, to settle the problem of arrears in the payment of the annual tribute to the pope, and, most important of all, to make arrangements about King Edward's passage to the Holy Land. The pope seized the opportunity also to discuss with William of Hotham the grievances of the English clergy and the interferences with the exercise of canonical authority, in which he saw the malign influence of the king's clerks, or, as we should say, the civil service.[2] He commissioned Hotham, who returned to England at the end of 1289, to report these frank conversations to the king and in May 1290 he expounded his views in a lengthy exhortation. Just as any monarch would resent interference with his minister in the exercise of his lawful

---

[1] For what follows see especially ibid., pp. 338–65 passim; also the useful biography of William of Hotham in M. H. MacInerny's History of the Irish Dominicans, i (1916), 424–33, 445–6 (based in part on the transcripts of Father Raymond Palmer). Unfortunately the Irish Dominican's narrative is marred by failure to grasp the situation and by his perverse conception of King Edward as a rude, greedy, and treacherous humbug.

[2] Above, p. 261; below, pp. 340, 459–60.

jurisdiction, so, the pope wrote, the Redeemer must be offended by insults to his vicar. They are dictated not by light of reason but by arbitrary will. They are a blemish on Edward's fair fame and an obstacle to the fulfilment of his resolution, as a Christian prince, to go in person to the relief of the Holy Land. Edward's spiritual obligations were linked with the preparations for his passage.

Pope Nicholas, in response to Edward's detailed requests, conveyed by his envoys, had already, in October 1289, laid down the conditions for his crusade and only awaited news of their acceptance before seeking for him the aid of other princes. On 3 February, only a month after Hotham's arrival in England, the king accepted the conditions with certain modifications, to which he sought the pope's consent. So another mission had to go to Rome and the papal instructions had to be revised. The new terms were defined, with unusual speed, in May and were formally accepted by Edward during the important parliament which took place at the royal hunting-lodge at Clipstone on 14 October. The record of the solemn transaction in the king's chamber at Clipstone was drawn up by a papal notary in the presence of an apostolic nuncio. One of the royal clerks and counsellors, William of Greenfield, declared the determination of the king to depart on the appointed date. On 18 March 1291 Pope Nicholas issued the final and authoritative grant and terms in an unconditional form and on the same day ordered his bankers in England, the Riccardi of Lucca, to pay to Edward on 24 June the first half of the crusading tenth which had been collected in the British Isles in accordance with the decision made at Lyons seventeen years before.

This long papal grant, summing up the whole matter, and the outcome of so much deliberation, ratified Edward's determination to fulfil his oath as a crusader. He was to lead a great expedition and to be entrusted with vast funds already collected and to be collected by authority of the vicar of Christ on earth. No series of transactions, not even the release of Charles of Salerno and the succession to Scotland, involved the expenditure of more time and trouble or the use of more ink and parchment. The king was to depart on 24 June 1293. He was to be paid, from the proceeds of Gregory X's taxation, 100,000 marks on 24 June 1291 and the same amount on 24 June 1292. In addition Nicholas IV imposed a further tenth for six years.

Edward, on the date of his departure, would receive as much of this as had been collected. The collectors, who at Edward's request were of native origin, were hard at work on the new valuation and collection throughout 1292 and 1293. Moreover, Edward was to have all obventions (that is to say, all contributions, voluntary or imposed, in addition to the taxes) which had been paid since they had been granted by Honorius IV and all future accumulations of them. Although the pope refused to grant outright the proceeds of the taxes collected in other countries whose rulers did not go on the crusade, he promised adequate help from these continental resources.

If Edward had been ready he would certainly have had companions and financial aid across the Channel; for not long after his arrangement with the pope had been ratified, news spread throughout the west of the fall of Acre, the last Christian stronghold in Syria. The obligation on other kings and princes to follow Edward's example and to take the cross was pressed home. Pope Nicholas, with a united effort in view, appealed to the clergy and ordered their metropolitans to take counsel and submit their conclusions through suitable proctors to the Curia. In obedience to the papal bull of 18 August Archbishop Pecham summoned a council to meet in London in February 1292. There the bishops, abbots, and other prelates drew up a series of articles for consideration in the dioceses. The English view, if the replies which survive were typical, was that there should be a general call for peace; that the additional tenth conceded by Pope Nicholas to Edward for six years should be made general and granted to the kings and princes who were willing to go to the Holy Land; that if these kings and princes were unwilling to go, a single active and powerful leader should be sought; and that if a leader could not be found, the tenths from all lands should be assigned to King Edward, who *was* going.[1]

Edward did not go, and what happened to the proceeds of the papal tenths will concern us later.[2] In October 1290 the king, surrounded by his great men, was at the height of his power, strong and confident. He had accomplished his task in Gascony and peace was in sight; he had reasserted his control of admin-

---

[1] See the papal bull and other documents then in the archives of the cathedral monastery at Norwich and copied by Bartholomew Cotton into his chronicle for the years 1291–8 (*Historia Anglicana*, ed. Luard, pp. 199–210). These include replies from the French clergy and from a council which met at Arles.

[2] Below, p. 500.

istration at home and prepared the way for concentration upon his passage to the east. Protected by papal dispensation he had provided for the future well-being and enlargement of his realm and the settlement of domestic friction. In April his daughter Joan of Acre was married to the earl of Gloucester, one of the most difficult of his subjects. In July his daughter Margaret was married to the heir of Brabant, and his last surviving son, Edward, was betrothed to the Maid of Norway, the little queen of Scotland. Before these unions were made, in a family gathering at the royal convent of Amesbury, where the queen mother, Eleanor of Provence, lived in retirement, he had made an ordinance which regulated the succession to the throne. He had foreseen and tried to meet every contingency. Then, as a crowning act, on 25 October he pronounced his solemn adherence to the plans for his crusade. And suddenly, his world fell into confusion about him. It is possible that even before the ceremony at Clipstone Edward had news of the rumour that Margaret of Scotland had died in the Orkneys.[1] Three weeks later he was summoned to the bedside of his wife, the fair, discreet, devoted Eleanor of Castile, who had been suffering from a slow fever. A week later she died.[2] In the shock of this desolation Edward had to turn his mind to the affairs of Scotland, left without a king, and from this time till his death he was a very busy man, always involved in embarrassing entanglements. The fortunate knight was suddenly dogged by that inscrutable and mysterious enemy which the writers of romances and the troubadours were wont to call mischance, a kind of hound of ill fortune. The arrangements for his passage were never made, and when the date fixed for his departure came and went hardly a thought can have been given to it.

Not everyone forgot it. Among the miscellaneous letters which

---

[1] The bishop of St. Andrews wrote to report the rumour on 7 October, two days before the papal bull confirming the betrothal between Margaret and Edward was brought by the king's clerk, John of Berwick, to Westminster, with a royal order for its enrolment in the exchequer (9 October). On 11 October the bull was read to the prior and convent in the abbey and then brought back to the treasury for deposit (Joseph Bain, *Calendar of Documents relating to Scotland*, ii, no. 460).

[2] Eleanor was not yet forty-five. Of her thirteen children, five daughters and one son survived her. One, Mary, became a nun; she was first promised to the prioress and convent of Fontevrault, but in March 1283 Edward wrote to them that the disposal of her lay with her grandmother, who in the following year procured her reception into Amesbury, at the age of five. She was the only child of Edward and Eleanor who reached the age of fifty.

survive from this period is a request to King Edward from a gentleman of Aragon. He wrote from Saragossa on 5 March 1293 to remind the king how through the mediation of the friars preachers he had often told him of his desire to serve under him with a hundred knights in the army of the Holy Land. He begged Edward to let him know through Brother William of Hotham, the prior provincial of England, what precisely he was to do in the matter, so that at the right time he might be found prepared.[1]

It is a pity that the story compiled in this chapter was not chronicled by a thirteenth-century Froissart. The desultory and incoherent quality of his narrative would in itself have reflected the experience of those who lived not in the glare of trumpeted publicity but, almost casually, from day to day. He would have uncovered so much that is hidden for ever. Every detail of every incident might have to be corrected, and certainly would have to be controlled, in the light of 'public' records, but he would have shown us men and women whose thoughts and behaviour were the expression of the genuine, if fragile, moods of chivalry, where pride and ambition consorted with high purposes, and honest reflection could chasten vindictive impulses, and the quiet pleasures dear to a cultivated spirit could intervene.

[1] *Foedera*, I. ii. 787. Cf. Philip de Castro's letter, dated Paris, 6 December (ibid., p. 793). The writer was 'Petrus Martini de Luna', a member of a distinguished family. His name is third in the list of nobles, knights, and syndics who swore to guarantee King Alfonso's promise to fulfil his obligations under the treaty of Canfran in 1288 (ibid. I. ii. 692).

VII

THE DUKE OF AQUITAINE

AFTER his return to England on 12 August 1289, King Edward only once crossed the Channel again. From the end of August 1297 to the middle of March 1298 he was in Flanders. His other expeditions between 1289 and his death were confined by public business to Wales (December 1294 to July 1295) and to the Scottish border and Scotland. The Scottish business kept him in the north, away from his palaces and hunting-lodges south of the Trent, for close on six and a half years out of the last seventeen years of his life, and throughout these seventeen years was a continuous preoccupation. It could not be localized. All the same Edward, especially during the years 1293 to 1303, was even more preoccupied by his rights and obligations as duke of Aquitaine than he was during the first twenty years of his reign. His anxieties as duke and as the vassal of King Philip of France were intensified by increasing opposition to his formal assumption, with Scottish consent, of the overlordship of Scotland. In 1294 most of Gascony was occupied by the French king and remained in his hands for ten years. During the first three of these years the two kings were at war with each other. In July 1295 an alliance between Philip and John Baliol inaugurated the long series of French understandings, treaties, and interventions which punctuated British history until the union of the crowns of England and Scotland in 1603. In this chapter we shall consider the background to these complications—Edward as duke of Aquitaine, the title under which the king of England expressed his lordship over Gascony and such neighbouring fiefs and cities as later modifications of the treaty of Paris of 1259 brought and left to him.

Apart from the brief period of open hostility—for it was this rather than a state of strenuous warfare—the relations between King Edward and his cousins of France were friendly. Edward, it is true, does not seem to have felt for them, nor they for him, the cordiality which he shared with his aunt Queen Margaret of France and with his cousins of Savoy. He could not with them be conscious of the mutual confidence which informed his relations with Charles of Salerno and even with Peter of Aragon and his successor Alfonso. His feudal obligations to Philip III and his son were fraught with the anxiety of unsettled problems. On the other hand he was, as we have seen, an outstanding member of a family circle and a peer of France. He had no political ambitions dangerous to the continuance of peace and was punctilious in the observance of every feudal duty except the doubtful requirement to provide military service against his friends and relatives in Castile and Aragon. Nor can it be said with justice—though it has often been said—that either Philip III or Philip the Fair was markedly hostile to Edward, still less that either king was moved by a deliberate intention to eject him from Aquitaine. Some elements, represented by Robert of Artois, held him in suspicion, just as, with more reason, some elements had distrusted the good faith of his father King Henry. The royal seneschals and agents in the French domain were naturally prepared to advance the interests of their master, just as the royal court, the *parlement* of Paris, welcomed appeals which emphasized the dependence of Gascony upon the French Crown; but this was implicit in the feudal relationship. If it is true that the legists on whom Philip the Fair relied for guidance were inspired by an uncompromising and conscious 'ideology' in a policy of expansion at Edward's expense, they were not successful in persuading him to give unequivocal expression to it until 1293 nor in holding him to it for very long. Their principles and technique were in any case instruments of alert opportunism, not of a series of vendettas. Moreover, in Aquitaine local loyalties, though they offered openings to French penetration, were more stubborn than they were in what has been described as the vacuum on the west of the Rhine. Gascony was anything but a vacuum and Edward was not, like the counts of Hainault or Bar, a neighbour who was being cajoled to combine a new with an old allegiance and to leave one social orbit for another.

Edward, after his return from the east, found the problems which the treaty of Paris had left for settlement more urgent than they had been in his father's time. The civil disturbances in England had interrupted negotiations on nearly every issue except the terms of St. Louis's financial undertakings, and had in any case made delay, in that unbusinesslike age, less serious just because they had brought the two courts together in ties of closer sympathy. The death of Alphonse of Poitiers at Savona on 21 August 1271, followed on the next day by the death of his wife, Jeanne of Toulouse, changed the situation, for three of the outstanding problems were concerned with the claim of the English king to the Agenais—a matter which had already engaged the attention of Henry III's advisers—and the successions to Quercy and Saintonge; and Alphonse and Jeanne had ruled all three provinces. Since the count of Poitou had left no heir, his enormous apanage fell to the French Crown and was added to the domain of his nephew Philip III. It comprised the seneschalships of Poitou, Saintonge, Toulouse, Quercy, Agenais, Rouergue, the county of Auvergne, and, on the east side of the Rhône, the Venaissin, as the extensive marquisate of Provence, north and east of Avignon, was now known. It encircled 'Aquitaine', from the Bay of Biscay to the Pyrenees and impinged on Edward's fiefs at vital points. Acting with speed and vigour the French administration, within two years, surveyed this enormous area and arranged its transfer to the Crown. In a royal peregrination King Philip III, accompanied by a military force, asserted his authority and brought to heel independent vassals like the count of Foix. This was the greatest addition to the royal domain since the days of Philip Augustus, when the conquest of Normandy, Maine, and Anjou had established the direct authority of the Crown between the Loire and the Channel; and it doubtless facilitated the later absorption of the kingdom of Navarre and the county of Champagne. The *parlement* moreover, in important declarations (*arresta*), upheld the principle that no exceptions could be allowed to the transfer of the escheat. The Countess Jeanne had left to others some of the lands which had accrued to her and not to her husband. The Venaissin, to take the most important district, was not unnaturally left to the count of Provence, Charles of Anjou, her husband's brother, but Philip III gave the *comtat* to the pope and ten years later (1284) the *parlement* finally declared against Charles's rights.[1] Now, unless the duke of Aquitaine could, as

[1] The marquisate of Provence included most of the county of Avignon, but only half of the imperial city of Avignon itself and its district, the other half being held by the count of Provence. Hence, after the death of Jeanne of Toulouse, the city was divided between Philip III, as her successor, and Charles of Anjou, as count of Provence. When in 1290 Charles II gave Anjou and Maine with his daughter Margaret on her marriage to Charles of Valois (above, p. 262) he received the French half of Avignon in compensation. The papacy, already lord of the Venaissin,

a result of the negotiations provided for in the treaty of Paris, secure recognition of his claims to the Agenais, Quercy, and Saintonge, this principle of indivisibility would preclude further resistance to the rights of the French Crown in these border districts. It was essential that Edward should not relax his claims. Here we have the occasion of the busy discussions which ended in the compromises effected by the treaty of Amiens in 1279 and the treaty of Paris in 1286, and the prolonged 'business' of the Agenais, concerned with detailed disputes about such things as the *bastides* built by Alphonse of Poitiers—an affair which agitated official circles in Paris and Westminster for many years after the surrender of the county to Edward in 1279. Edward and his successors had to deal directly with French seneschals and the *parlement* of Paris. They could ring down no iron curtain of separation in those uncertain feudal frontiers, to cut through the tangle of rights and habit and exploitations.

It is natural to deplore the lack of specialized ministries for foreign and Aquitanian affairs, and to ask why some *ad hoc* committee like that which sorted and dealt with petitions in times of parliament was not converted into a permanent department, but this is to neglect the basic distinction between medieval kingship and a government which depends upon the responsibility of ministers, and to forget the perennial tendency in all kinds of government to live from hand to mouth. In fact, Edward I, like his father before him, was not badly served. The large body of king's clerks who transacted the business of the royal household executed special commissions at home and abroad, and provided some of the safest men in the king's council. Probably most of these clerks, though their functions were not rigidly defined, became specialists in one branch or other of the multifarious business of the Crown. But, however responsible their duties, and however valuable their reports might be, their usefulness was necessarily dependent upon the energy and wisdom of the king and his most trusted advisers, and they, in their turn, were limited by distance, difficulties in communication, the procrastination of the papal and other

did not acquire Avignon outright until it was sold to Clement VI by Jeanne, queen of Naples and countess of Provence, for 80,000 golden florins (1348). Until then the popes, from Clement V onwards, had been given asylum in Avignon by the count of Provence. Cf. A. Longnon, *La Formation de l'unité française* (1922), pp. 153–5, 177, 356, 359, 361; G. Mollat, *Les Papes d'Avignon* (new edition, 1949), p. 86.

courts, local rivalries, grievances and passions innumerable, and all the accidents of circumstance.

That politicians had to live from day to day does not mean that their outlook was haphazard, that political aims were not gradually defined, that trained experience was neither acquired nor employed. On the contrary, the administration of Gascony, especially after 1259, and the incessant compulsion of the problems which the wider responsibilities incurred by the treaty of that year aroused in a larger Aquitaine, probably provided the best training ground and the surest tests of fidelity and competence open to the servants of the Crown both high and low. The administration of Gascony under the guidance of Edward and his seneschals brought about a coherence and created a tradition in the local service and a general sense of the value of the connexion between Gascony and England which were to last for two turbulent centuries. Gascony was explicitly and permanently attached by Henry III to the English Crown. How the Gascons valued the union was made clear when Richard II was for a time persuaded to break the connexion in favour of his uncle John of Gaunt.

Union made the Crown responsible for the welfare of the duchy. After the treaty of Paris, King Henry was, as his new seal was inscribed, 'Rex Anglie, Dominus Hybernie, Dux Aquitanie', while Edward continued to use until his accession to the throne the seal which described him simply as 'primogenitus et heres domini regis Anglie'. Edward, so long as his father lived, never bore the title of duke of Aquitaine. Once, but exceptionally and as a flourish, he is described, in November 1254 as 'jam regnans in Vasconia sicut princeps et dominus', but not as duke.[1] His father had granted Gascony and Ireland to him as a source of maintenance (*ad se sustentandum*), not as independent fiefs, and, though he apprenticed his son as an administrator in Gascony, he retained his authority. Only during the last five or six years of Henry's reign did Edward exercise full responsibility in the duchy and its neighbourhood. When, in the generous and angry pride of youth he had compensated his exiled relatives, Geoffrey and Guy de Lusignan,

---

[1] All this has been established by J. C. Trabut-Cussac in his very full and important dissertation on Edward in Gascony. Unfortunately the work is still unpublished, and I am most grateful to the learned author for permission to make use of it, as I have done freely, in this chapter. In my book, *Henry III and the Lord Edward*, i. 231, I erroneously stated that Henry made his son duke of Aquitaine.

by making one the seneschal of Gascony and endowing the other
with the island of Oléron (1258) his action was immediately
repudiated as inconsistent with the terms of his tenure.[1] From
1266, however, Edward made the appointments in Aquitaine.
His friend Roger Leyburn was his lieutenant in Gascony with
power to direct all affairs as fully as he would have done himself.[2] After Leyburn's death in 1271, the prince's representatives in England, who in fact were governing England, appointed
Hugh de Trubleville to succeed him, but as seneschal, not as
lieutenant. Throughout, Gascon affairs were subject to direction
from England.

The outcome was very significant; and, from the standpoint
of the Crown, has never been studied as it deserves to be. A
large and exceedingly turbulent area of administration was not
only disciplined into an uneasy, but on the whole successful,
system of co-operative management—a piece of local history
which lies beyond the range of this book—but was also, so to
speak, thrown open to the royal service. Gascon petitions, for
example, were addressed in great numbers to king and council,
but analysis of the procedure and of the evidence contained in
the Gascon rolls relating to matters referred to England shows
that the king relied especially upon persons conversant with
Gascon affairs or likely to be acquainted with a particular
problem or a particular subject of petition. Decisions might be
taken by the king himself after discussion, or by the council or
left to three or four men or even to one man. In one case the
council in England submitted a treaty between the seneschal,
John de Grilly, and the bishop, chapter, and commune of
Bazas to minute and not very wise criticism, but even this
was probably written by someone who had local knowledge.[3]
Reliance upon such can be traced in the action taken on the
Gascon petitions presented to the king in parliament in 1305.
Moreover the king frequently sent commissioners of high rank
and less exalted agents to Gascony to make investigations or
carry through reforms, and summoned the seneschal and others
to England for the discussion of current problems. At no time

---

[1] See the strongly worded letters in *Close Rolls, 1256–9*, p. 319 (22 July 1258).

[2] The text of Roger Leyburn's nomination (29 November 1269) is to be found
only in Dom P. D. du Buisson, *Historia monasterii S. Severi* (Aire, 1876), i. 246,
noticed by M. Trabut-Cussac.

[3] 'De quibus articulis . . . consilii regis super composicionem Vasatensem.'
P.R.O. Chancery miscellanea 25/1/no. 10 and 24/2/no. 4.

were there no royal agents from England in Gascony and no
Gascons on administrative business in England. This is not
all. Gascons were rewarded by Edward for their help during
the struggle in England against Simon de Montfort. Gascon
troops, mounted crossbow-men in particular, reinforced the
armies which conquered Wales and fought in Scotland.
Gascon merchants grew rich on the vast trade in wine and
contributed the steadiest and largest element in the revenue of
the duchy. The royal household enjoyed the comforts which
the king's right of pre-emption over shipments from Gascony
provided. A merchant of Gascony might be the taker of the
king's wines throughout England, the collector of right prises
on all imported wine, and the inspector of the measure of every
tun which was disembarked in the English ports.[1] Gascons and
English in fact became very well acquainted with each other
in the streets of London and Bordeaux and in the service of
their countries.[2] And the list of well-known English barons,
ecclesiastics, knights, and clerks who were trained in Gascon
affairs in the course of their distinguished careers would be long
indeed. As the range of operations was enlarged and the sessions
of the *parlement* in Paris gradually became, from 1259 onwards,
as busy a scene of activity in Aquitanian affairs as the four
courts of Gascony and the council chambers of the royal
seneschal, the agents of the English king learned, as they had
never learned before, how interwoven their master's interests
were with the incalculable interests of the lords and cities of
south-western France. They had to study currents of opinion
in Paris and the operations and procedure of an unfamiliar
tribunal. They had to deal with men who had the advantage
of working in their own way on their own ground and were often
more able and determined than they were themselves.

The innumerable records of negotiations, treaties, arbitrations, administrative activity, and legal proceedings in the
courts of Paris, Westminster, and Gascony reflect this development.[3] They were not neatly disposed in a single archive, but

[1] Cf. *Cal. Pat. Rolls, 1266–72*, p. 422 (1270).

[2] It is worth remembering that Edward II's favourite, Piers Gaveston, whose
family took its name from Gabaston, near Morlaas in Béarn, was connected 'with
both the urban aristocracy of Bordeaux and the territorial houses of Gascony and
Béarn'. See Tout, *The Place of the Reign of Edward II in English History*, and ed. by
Hilda Johnstone (1936), pp. 11–14.

[3] See George Cuttino in his *English Diplomatic Administration, 1259–1339* (1940),

were to be found in the records of chancery, exchequer, and wardrobe, whether enrolled or copied into registers, and in miscellaneous documents roughly sorted and, as they then were, preserved in bags and chests, stored in the treasury of the exchequer or in other treasuries in Westminster Abbey and the Tower of London. There were records at the papal curia, Bordeaux, and Paris and in every city or fief which had dealings with the popes and the kings of France and England about their local affairs. Although the Public Record Office in England is very rich in these documents, very many known to have existed have been lost, and only fragments, though very valuable fragments, survive in the state archives of France and elsewhere. Some have been published by historical scholars since the eighteenth century, notably by Charles Bémont, but they have only recently been studied as a whole.[1] Just as, in every other field of historical study, we are gradually learning to read the evidence, not as mere information given by unrelated parchments and papers, but from the standpoint of those who originally prompted and authenticated, wrote, stored, and referred to them, so we can now perceive through and behind this particular body of scattered material the working of administrative and legal systems and trace the casual course of specialized interests consciously engaged upon the problems of Aquitaine. In England some progress had been made in the classification of records of this type. The pressure of business and the need for accurate knowledge of historical data gradually produced a series of registers of Aquitanian affairs, not only concerned, as the Gascon rolls mainly were, with the details of Gascon administration, but also with matters which had been discussed at a higher level in England or Gascony or in negotiations with the French court. These were the outcome of concentration upon Aquitanian records in the reign of Edward I.[2]

his edition of *The Gascon Calendar of 1322* (1949) and various articles, e.g. 'An Unidentified Gascon Register', *E.H.R.* liv (1939), 293-9.

[1] Cf. V. H. Galbraith, 'The Tower as an Exchequer Office', in *Essays in Medieval History presented to Thomas Frederick Tout* (1925), pp. 234-8, 247; J. G. Edwards, *Littere Wallie* (1940), pp. xxvii-xxxv.

[2] The first great registers, now known as A and B, were comprehensive collections of documents only partly concerned with Gascony. The work began about 1282: A was finished about 1292, B about 1305. The documents transcribed were papal bulls, treaties, diplomatic documents, and letters relating to European countries, Scotland, and Wales. There were also registers of the feudal survey of Gascony made in 1274 and of documents relating to the restoration of the Agenais and

Indeed it is hardly an exaggeration to say that, within the personnel of trained royal clerks, there began to emerge the nucleus of a foreign office, familiar with the treaties and processes relating to Aquitaine and staffed by a few men who could be trusted to advise the king and his most important envoys and to take a part in negotiations. The first man of this kind to be given precise functions was the king's clerk, Master Philip Martel, a graduate in civil law, and canon of Chichester, who died in September 1306. He was succeeded as keeper of processes by his clerk and helper Elias Joneston. The duties of the keeper were to keep and add to the documents, whether originals or copies, to make them available when required and to examine them for the information of envoys.

We must not suppose that a new department of state was created, nor that the concentration of effort in the reigns of Edward and his son was continued. Our Foreign Office developed centuries later out of the work of the secretariats of state. The Hundred Years War put an end to the period of processes and precedents. Nor were the keepers isolated from the administration as a whole. As the memoranda compiled by Elias Joneston show, his master Philip Martel had established precedents in the handling of documents and the preparation and conduct of cases, but Martel was never withdrawn from the wider tasks in which his proficiency was helpful. He was entrusted with important missions to the papal court and was one of Edward I's intimate advisers. His engagement upon Aquitanian matters was due to the fact that he was well proven in the king's service. Just as in Henry III's time the famous clerk John Mansel, so active everywhere, was recognized as an authority on Spanish affairs, and a group of canon lawyers, employed in many kinds of business, were used especially to further the royal interests in such ecclesiastical business as

related matters (this last is now in the Bodleian Library, Bodley MS. 917, and has been edited by Cuttino, *Le Livre d'Agenais*, Toulouse, 1956, photographed typescript). Before 1320 other registers of Gascon documents were compiled. One at least survives in the Cotton MS. Julius E. 1, of which Dr. Cuttino is preparing an edition. Finally, Walter Stapledon, bishop of Exeter, who was appointed treasurer in 1320, arranged for a complete classification and catalogue of the archives of the exchequer and wardrobe. One result of this famous operation was the Gascon calendar—lists of documents—which has been edited by Cuttino for the Royal Historical Society. It was made by Henry of Canterbury; cf. *E.H.R.* lvii (1942), 298–311. It should be remembered that the documents registered and calendared went far back into British, Aquitanian, and continental history.

episcopal elections, so the men who served Edward in Gascony or on Aquitanian business were more than cabined experts.

King Edward dealt with Gascony with the same elasticity as he dealt with Wales or Scotland. He stretched, so to speak, the activities of his court and household to comprise whatever he might have in hand. Nearly all the men who held the highest office in Gascony or served on special commissions to Aquitaine during Edward's rule were his trusted friends and companions. Roger Leyburn was his first choice as his lieutenant during his absence on crusade. His friend and kinsman Maurice de Craon was left behind as lieutenant when he left Gascony in 1289. When war began with Philip IV of France, Edward sent his nephew, John of Brittany, and his brother, Edmund of Lancaster, to defend his rights. John of St. John, the lord of Halnaker, who had been sent to succeed Maurice of Craon in 1293 and remained as seneschal under John of Brittany and Edmund, had been with Edward in Gascony throughout the long sojourn of 1286–9 and was one of those whom the king liked to have continually with him.[1] John of Hastings, Edward's last lieutenant, one of the claimants to the Scottish throne and the son-in-law of the king's uncle, William of Valence, was a member of the royal circle.

The three outstanding seneschals of the reign, Luke de Tany, John de Grilly or Grelley, and John of Havering, had been trusted administrators. Luke de Tany, seneschal from 1272 to 1278, a landholder in Essex, had served Henry III as constable of Corfe and Edward as constable of Tickhill. He had too heavy a hand, but was a trusty man. John de Grilly, a Savoyard and the most important of all the rulers of Aquitaine, had been Edward's first choice in 1266, when the prince's authority had been enlarged. Later he had controlled Edward's finances as 'purveyor to the king's passage' on his crusade.[2] John of Havering had been entrusted by Edward's council in England, during the prince's absence on crusade, with the administration of some of his lands, and later, in England, Scotland, and Wales, was a responsible agent of the Crown. During the interval between his two periods of service as seneschal (2288–94, 1305 onwards) he was for a time Edward's lieutenant in north Wales

---

[1] He was sent to Gascony as lieutenant in 1293 because he knew the conditions there (*ke conust les countres*).

[2] *Cal. Pat. Rolls, 1272–81*, p. 102. For more about John de Grilly see below, p. 288.

(1295). On a lower level this close relation between Gascon administration and the royal household can be seen in the supervision, at critical times, of Gascon finances, as when the expert, William of Louth, keeper of the king's wardrobe, was made constable of Bordeaux, or when so important an official as Thomas of Sandwich, formerly seneschal of Ponthieu, was given the custody of the mayoralty in the city of Bordeaux.

Edward had served his apprenticeship in Gascony, first after his marriage in 1254-5, when he was under guidance, and again after his conduct in 1260 had for a time grieved his father. He had made good in Gascony during his second period of personal rule in the duchy (1261-3). In 1266 he had taken control of the affairs of Aquitaine as a whole, so far as they were under royal cognizance. A French scholar who has recently given minute attention to his early administrative work has marvelled at the sureness of his touch. He never wished, even if it were possible to do so, to relax his grasp upon the affairs of his distant province. When in 1273 he delayed his arrival in England, postponed his coronation, and sent John of St. John and others to act as his proctors at the Council of Lyons, he acted, as he explained in his letters to his council in England, in the firm belief that his first duty was to Gascony.

Gascony, in spite of the turbulent traditions of its people, was a rich and prosperous land, but if its resources were to be made available, it needed indulgent as well as strong and coherent government. It says much for Edward's administration that on at least three occasions the Gascons, in addition to the assistance which they gave during the Welsh and Scottish wars, rallied with effect to the help of their duke.

Their first opportunity came during the civil war in England after the repudiation by the baronial party of the award of King Louis at Amiens (January 1264). The king of France, while he abstained from active intervention, was willing to finance Queen Eleanor, who with her second son Edmund remained in France. He acquired in return the surrender of all the rights given to the king of England in the three bishoprics of Limoges, Périgueux, and Cahors. The queen, subject to ratification by her husband and his power to repurchase the rights, received 30,000 *livres* in money of Tours.[1] Eleanor was now able to find

---

[1] That Henry's lands in the three bishoprics were in fact held for a time by King Louis in pledge is made clear by a letter sent by Edward in his father's name

allies and collect forces for an invasion of England. One of her recruiting grounds was Gascony, where since 1262 she had enjoyed assignments on the revenues of certain towns and lands; and the scanty evidence suggests that the response to her solicitations was considerable. The sailors of Bayonne were especially active, and heavy losses were suffered by the merchants of Bristol and other English ports as a result of the retention of their ships and merchandise by the men of Bordeaux. Gascony, in short, had a share in the resistance which prevailed so dramatically at Evesham. The victory enabled King Henry to recover his rights, for he had not ratified his wife's agreement with King Louis—the baronial government had seen to that[1]—and Edward was given control of the royal possessions in the three bishoprics, on the usual condition that they should not be separated from the English Crown.[2]

The second occasion on which Edward relied on the resources of Gascony was in 1269 when he was raising money for the expenses of his crusade. King Louis advanced him 70,000 *livres* in money of Tours on the security of the customs of Bordeaux. This large sum was repaid in instalments at the Temple in Paris. Repayment was to begin in March 1274—in fact it did not begin until 1277 and some 4,000 *livres* were still due in June 1289—but the customs, big and little, of Bordeaux did not benefit from the delay. Edward, with the consent of his father and the acquiescence of King Louis, farmed this main source of Gascon revenue to merchant-bankers for the four years 1270–4, so that he could raise further sums in 'the business of the cross which he had taken on his shoulders'.[3] The merchants would advance money on the customs, just as in England they advanced it on the proceeds of the new subsidy.[4] Thus,

to Louis under his own seal, 27 September 1267. (Original letter with seal in Archives nationales at Paris, I. 918, no. 12, noted by Mr. Trabut-Cussac.)

[1] The fine levied on the Londoners provided for some of the money.

[2] The grant was made before 14 February 1266 when the king ratified Edward's nomination of a seneschal in the three dioceses (*Cal. Pat. Rolls, 1258–66*, p. 551).

[3] *Foedera*, I. i. 485. The customs had previously been farmed for one year to merchants of Cahors by the seneschal, John de Grilly, in 1266 (*Cal. Pat. Rolls, 1266–72*, p. 24).

[4] Edward had leased the proceeds of the 'new aid', i.e. the twentieth granted in England (above, p. 224), for one year to Deutautus (of London), the queen's merchant. In August 1270 he arranged an extension of the lease (22 May 1270–end of August) to the firm of Peter Beraldi of Cahors, for 40,000 marks, or close on

with the aid of Jews and merchant-bankers, the vineyards of Gascony and the goods and chattels of Englishmen carried the burden of the vast sums expended on Edward's holy enterprise.

Edward's financial operations in 1269 and 1270 illustrate the value of Gascony to him rather than the alacrity of the Gascons to help him. The wine-growers sold their wine and would not concern themselves with the economic effects of the diversion to foreign purposes of the charges which they paid. A third occasion on which the barons and citizens of the duchy came to Edward's aid gives striking testimony to Edward's hold upon their loyalty. This was in 1288 when Edward required their assistance to meet the conditions on which King Alfonso of Aragon was prepared to release Charles of Salerno from captivity. The response which he received was very notable. The agreement reached at Canfran in north Aragon on 28 October put the whole burden of responsibility for the good faith and competence of Charles of Salerno upon Edward and his vassals. It required the immediate payment in cash of 23,000 marks of silver[1] and the surrender as sworn hostages of thirty-six nobles and barons and forty 'good and sufficient' burgesses as pledges, first, for the fulfilment by Charles of the conditions which he alone could satisfy within the next three months, and secondly, for the payment by Edward of a further sum of 7,000 marks still owing as the residue of the 30,000 marks which he had undertaken to pay in the previous year on behalf of Charles. Further, Edward was liable to pay under various future contingencies sums amounting to no less than 80,000 marks, unless Charles of Salerno, by returning to captivity, released him from all obligations. Gaston of Béarn, his leading vassal, was required under the terms to pledge nearly all his lands in the province of Catalonia as partial security for the payment of the 7,000 marks, and Edward was able to get sworn guarantees from Barcelona, Bayonne, Dax, Condom, Marmande, and other cities, towns, and communities that, to the best of their ability, they would assist their duke to meet the other financial obligations, if the necessity to pay should arise. Edward himself was

£26,000 sterling, 'to be computed to the said Peter against whatever he has lent to the said Edward' (*Foedera*, I. i. 463).

[1] This sum was paid on 28 October in good money of various currencies, at the rate of 13s. 4d. sterling, 54 gross sh. Tours, and 6 gold florins (less 2 small shillings of Tours) to the mark (ibid. I. ii. 691). For the circumstances of this treaty see above, p. 260.

bound under the treaty to associate himself and his realm and other lands in sworn obligation to fulfil its terms and in the meantime not to leave his duchy. If for any good cause he were compelled to depart he was to hand over to Alfonso as pledges four close friends and relatives, namely, Henry, earl of Lincoln, Maurice of Craon, John of Brittany, and Guy de Lusignan. Happily King Alfonso, who had in his turn associated many of his barons and cities with him in a sworn obligation to do his part, was faithful and friendly, while Charles of Salerno, immediately after his release and arrival at Oloron (3 November), made sworn and solemn promises, with financial guarantees from a large number of French and Italian nobles, that Edward should be repaid and suffer no loss.[1] But the whole transaction was burdensome. There must be few parallels in history to this comprehensive gesture by a great king on behalf of a friend.

We can read the story between the lines of the lengthy documents written by Edward's clerk, John of Caen, apostolic notary, and by other scribes. The king and queen arrive at Oloron in Béarn in the middle of October. The seventy-six hostages, including Gaston of Béarn, Otto of Granson, and the three English barons John of St. John, John de Vesci, and Hugh of Audley, are gathered together. At Oloron two young sons of Charles of Salerno are probably waiting with their mother, Mary of Hungary: they are Louis, aged fourteen, the future Franciscan and saint, and Robert, aged ten, the future king of Naples; and they are to be handed over to King Alfonso as hostages for their father.[2] The great cavalcade crosses the Pyrenees to Canfran, where Alfonso awaits it. During the next few days the parchments are sealed, the hostages take their oaths, the money is counted out in gold florins, and sterling silver and money of Tours. Charles of Salerno is set free. The princes say farewell to the children and hostages and return to

---

[1] See the three documents printed in the *Foedera*, i. ii. 694–7. Each was sealed with the impression of Charles's private ring, for he had never had a seal made, and the prince wrote with his own hand the word 'Credatis'. The 30,000 marks paid by Edward were part of the 50,000 marks exacted from Charles as security and were to be repaid by King Alfonso to Charles when he had fulfilled his obligations. At Canfran Edward undertook to pay the other 20,000 marks and also further sums amounting to 60,000 marks under certain eventualities, which, in fact, never occurred, since Charles made peace with Alfonso in February 1291, when the king of Aragon annulled Edward's obligations (*Foedera*, i. ii. 744).

[2] For them see Margaret Toynbee, *Saint Louis of Toulouse* (1929), pp. 52 ff.

Oloron where Charles does his part. Before he goes, Edward lends him 10,000 marks. Then he hurries to Provence to collect the hostages who are to replace the Gascons and to raise the money he so badly needs. The king and queen and their households remain in the Pyrenean foothills, mainly at Bonnegarde, where the Christmas feast is held. All are restless and anxious. The weeks pass, the three months period of grace has expired. How will the hostages be treated? Their freedom to move about and hunt and hawk might now be restricted. The 7,000 marks have been paid, but have the hostages from Provence and Marseilles reached Catalonia? At last the news comes that all is well. King Alfonso is satisfied. On 9 March 1289 the hostages are welcomed at Oloron.

The Gascons had risked much to stand by their duke and save his honour. Their support of Edward in 1288 sets in perspective the disputes and appeals which, when studied in isolation, suggest a less happy relationship between them. The loyalty of Gaston of Béarn is especially significant. His large county controlled the approaches to Spain. He had been a very restless vassal, ambitious, independent, and hot-tempered. In his youth he had imperilled the future of Gascony. He had done homage to Henry III in 1242, and, as a kinsman of the queens of France and England, had expected to exercise a preponderating influence on Gascon affairs. He had been a mainstay of the league against Simon de Montfort and, in spite of King Henry's indulgence, had led the rebellion in favour of King Alfonso of Castile in 1253. The threat from Castile had ended with Edward's marriage and Gaston was reconciled. For nearly twenty years he caused little trouble, and no doubt, during the disturbances in England, was left discreetly alone. In 1269 his connexion with the royal house was strengthened by the marriage of his daughter Constance to Henry of Almain, the son of Richard of Cornwall, king of the Romans, and in the following year Edward made lavish provision for his expenses on the crusade which, in the end, he did not join. He could apparently be trusted to maintain the duke's rights in Gascony and to assert them, as one of the king's proctors, in the royal court at Paris. Then, shortly before the death of King Henry, the council in England appointed a strong but tactless seneschal, an Englishman, Luke de Tany. Edward, on his leisurely way home, arrived in Gascony to find that Gaston, after refusing to

appear to answer for his deeds in the seneschal's court at Saint-
Sever, was bidding defiance in his own town of Orthez. Edward
took swift action. He captured Gaston, and reduced him to
submission. On 6 October 1273 Gaston promised to abide by
the judgement already pronounced against him by the court
of Saint-Sever, to give Edward seisin of all his castles and
goods, and not to leave the king's court without permission;
but he broke his word immediately and again withdrew to
Orthez.

The duel between the two men lasted for five years. It shows
us Edward's way with his vassals. The king did not try to crush
Gaston by force. He summoned at Saint-Sever an assembly of
representatives of the four courts of Gascony, Saint-Sever, Bordeaux, Bazas, and Dax. The assembly was asked to advise
according to law and custom. It answered that Gaston should
be summoned three times to the court of Saint-Sever and, if
he refused to appear, be summoned a fourth time to the court
of Gascony. If he were still recalcitrant, Edward could march
against him. Gaston was obdurate, and Edward occupied his
lands. Again he submitted himself to the king's will, but his
letters of submission were hardly sealed when he appealed to
the court of France. By this action he put himself under the
protection of Edward's suzerain. Edward was ordered to withdraw his troops and became responsible for damages inflicted
upon the population and trade of Béarn. In May 1274 the
king, who was at Limoges, was presented by Gaston's agents
with a long list of grievances suffered by the county. He observed all the rules, agreed to remedy some things, and ordered
an investigation into others; but Gaston was determined to
pursue his appeal, and Edward could no longer delay his own
return to England. Gaston had by this time worked himself
into a state of fury. There were violent scenes at Paris, where
the count called his absent lord a faithless traitor and chal-
lenged him to private combat.[1] Edward urged Philip III to
decide the issue at the Candlemas session of the *parlement* of
Paris in February 1275, where the seneschal of Gascony,

---

[1] Gilles de Noaillan, one of the members of a noble house in Gascony, pleaded
urgently to be allowed to fight in the king's name against Gaston. He implored
Edward to grant the honour to him and not to give the priority to the Frenchman
Érard de Valery (one of Edward's friends who had been on crusade with him).
The letter, misplaced in the *Foedera* (i. ii. 563), shows that Edward had his sym-
pathizers in Paris, as well as in Gascony.

Franciscus Accursius, the famous jurist of Bologna, and others reinforced his permanent proctors, but no judgement was made. Time, indeed, was on Edward's side. More important Pyrenean problems[1] demanded French attention and the troublesome Gaston did not attract sympathy in Paris. King Philip at last sent Gaston to Edward to make what terms he could. Edward received his submission, ordered him back to Paris to withdraw his charges, and on his return imprisoned him. Gaston's constables and ministers in Béarn were ordered to submit to the agents who would take his lands, castles, and towns into the king's hands (6 February 1276). This severity, as Edward wrote later to the king of France, was in strict accordance with the law. Gaston had made an appeal of false judgement and default of right by Edward's court, had withdrawn the appeal and, while a sworn vassal (*lui estant en nostre fei*), 'had said villainous words in your presence against our person'. King Philip felt that the punishment had gone far enough and a year later bade Edward restore Gaston to him with his pardon. Edward released Gaston in April 1277, but, while he remitted his anger, he insisted that there must be an award in the French court and amends to himself. Gaston, he explained, had surrendered himself to Edward's will. Edward, at Philip's request, was passing him on to Paris for mitigation of judgement. This was no submission to an arbitration between one peer and another, but a request for the assessment of damages to be paid by a man who had injured his lord. Nor were Edward's vassals and officials in Gascony involved, for they were not before the French court on appeal and were not subject to the French king's commands.[2] So, in February 1278, the case again came before the *parlement* of Paris. Edward's agents were briefed with the original documents in the case. Gaston realized that his position was hopeless. Queen Margaret begged Edward to be merciful, and Edward was now ready to turn the rebel into a friend. The time had come for discussion and conventions, and in the course of 1278 these were conducted by the king's close friends, the bishop of Bath and Wells and Otto of Granson. The result was formally declared in April 1279. Gaston was restored to all his lands and granted an annual

---

[1] Above, pp. 238 ff.

[2] Letters of November 1277 and February 1278; see *Rôles Gascons*, ii. 161, and *Foedera*, I. ii. 553 (2).

pension from the customs of Bordeaux. He remained faithful till his death in 1290.[1]

This story, though better known than others, is but one of many which illustrate Edward's relations with his troublesome Gascon friends and, it should be added, his firm yet accommodating attitude in the court of France. He was no stranger in Paris. He and his proctors were not faced by a hostile self-contained group of hard-faced lawyers. These legal contests, though they called for incessant vigilance, were waged, not among strangers in an alien land, but in a spacious fluctuating royal court, where friendly discussions behind the scenes were more important than the formal sessions of the *parlement*. And Edward, partly because the transfer of business to Paris was now so easy, learned how to deal with his subjects in Aquitaine as he expected to be dealt with himself in the court of his own lord, and to instil into them the same respect for him as he was prepared to show to the decisions of the *parlement* of Paris. Indeed he succeeded more often than is usually supposed in averting recourse to Paris and in drawing appeals to himself. If his courts were defied he was strong enough, in this atmosphere of general confidence, to impose sanctions which could not be made matters of appeal. Something more will be said later about this, but first we should consider the larger settlements of Aquitanian problems in the treaties of 1279 and 1286.

As we have seen, the conventions with Gaston were made by Bishop Robert Burnell, the chancellor, and Otto of Granson; and if we ask why these important agents were employed, we find that in this year 1278 they were engaged, as lieutenants of the king, upon important missions in Paris and in Gascony. So many attempts to secure the king's rights to the Agenais had failed; this chance must not be lost. Gascony, under the rigid

---

[1] The only serious trouble was caused by the claim of Gaston's daughter Constance, countess of Marsan, the widow of Henry of Almain, to the county of Bigorre, to the east of Béarn. After the death of the count of Bigorre in 1283, Gaston and Constance got control of the county and resisted the attempts of John de Grilly, the seneschal of Gascony, to occupy it. At Dax in October they submitted themselves to the king's judgement, and while Gaston went to fulfil an obligation to help Alfonso of Castile at Edward's cost (cf. above, p. 245) Constance went to England to make her peace. This she did in February 1284 and later at Carnarvon on 29 June. Gaston confirmed her action with reservations at Paris in September 1284. The long story of the succession to Bigorre is very interesting but cannot be told here. An outline may be read in my *Henry III and the Lord Edward*, i. 220-7.

and unsympathetic direction of Luke de Tany, was full of discontents; the seneschal must go and grievances be investigated. The two lieutenants left in February 1278. Their commission, giving them the powers which the king would himself exercise if he were in Gascony, was issued by the king at Dover, a few days before they crossed the Channel. They did their business in Paris, then spent four busy months (May–September) in the duchy. They displaced Luke de Tany and busied themselves from place to place in the restoration of order and confidence. Edward, who had told them not to hurry over their task, was satisfied and, with his usual tact, was careful to write letters of thanks to the Gascon prelates and laymen who had helped them in their work of reconciliation.

Shortly before they left, they appointed John de Grilly as seneschal. The choice was a natural one. The new seneschal had held office before, had local experience, and, though of Savoyard origin, was settled in the duchy. His advancement had probably been due to support given by him to Queen Eleanor in 1265, when, as we have seen, she organized resistance to Simon de Montfort from France and Gascony. In January 1266 Edward, now in the ascendant, gave him and his heirs rich estates in the valley of the Dordogne, including the lordship of Benauges and the land of the viscount of Castillon, except the fiefs and the castle with its demesne, all for the service of two knights' fees. The lordships carried with them the title of viscount of Benauges and Castillon.[1] John de Grilly was a man of great energy; able, as his letters show, to appraise a situation clearly in pithy and vigorous words. He was respected in Savoy, where he held Grilly and other lands of the count, and later, as Edward's agent at the gathering at Mâcon, won the esteem of Queen Margaret of France.[2] His long association with King Edward gave him the right to speak frankly and the confidence to expound his master's views in the French court, where, as seneschal of Gascony, he had to spend much of his time. Unfortunately, in the course of his faithful and arduous service, he did not resist the temptations which beset a man in

[1] This follows from King Henry's confirmation of Edward's grant in *Cal. Pat. Rolls, 1266–72*, pp. 40, 41.
[2] See Bémont's account of his life in *Rôles Gascons*, iii (1906), pp. xxxiii–xlvii. Grilly is in the neighbourhood of Gex, west of the lake of Geneva. For John at Mâcon see Queen Margaret's letters in Champollion-Figeac, *Lettres des rois*, &c., i. 209, 282, written in the autumn of 1281 (for the dates cf. above, p. 249, note 1).

high office. He was left alone too long and in 1287, after the king's arrival in the duchy, was found guilty of peculation. At the time of the examination into his affairs, he was on an important mission to the king of Aragon, but this was his last piece of service to the Crown. He joined a French contingent which went to the defence of Acre during the famous siege of 1290–1, and, after his escape and return, seems to have spent the rest of his life in his native land. He died about the year 1301.

The two lieutenants and the new seneschal resumed in Paris the negotiations preliminary to the meeting in which Edward's rights, under the treaty of Paris, after the deaths of Alphonse of Poitiers and his wife, were to be settled. By February 1279 it was possible to fix the time and place of the conference. The two kings met at Amiens on 23 May.[1] Edward put forward his claims: the transfer of the Agenais, the compensation due to him for the lands of those privileged vassals of the French king in the three dioceses of Limoges, Perigueux, and Quercy whose allegiance could not be transferred to him, and the lands and rights held by Alphonse of Poitiers in the county of Quercy. The Agenais was transferred, an inquiry was arranged about the rights of Quercy, and Edward's claims for compensation in the three dioceses were abandoned, except for the *privilegiati* who since 1259 had recognized him as their lord. King Philip, in his turn, agreed to waive one of the most troublesome conditions of the treaty of Paris; namely, an obligation imposed upon the duke of Aquitaine to extract from his new vassals in Saintonge and the three bishoprics an oath to the king of France that they would oppose the duke if he failed to observe the treaty. Edward had done his best to enforce this oath. His seneschals had been active in the matter in 1275, 1276, and 1277, but all in vain. Persuasion, threats, intimidation had been useless against men who foresaw that, if they took the oath, they might, in case of war, be attacked from both sides, or at least become the victims of a painful dilemma. In the treaty of Amiens King Philip, recognizing that Edward was not at fault, released him from the hopeless task.

Before we proceed to the actual transfer of the Agenais and its inclusion, as a distinct province, within the administrative

---

[1] Here Eleanor of Castile did homage to Philip III for Ponthieu (above, p. 235). For the death of the count and countess of Poitou see above, p. 272.

system of Aquitaine, it will be convenient to describe the next
process of settlement, which was closely linked with the treaty
of Amiens. The treaty involved the necessity for two careful
investigations, the one into the rights of Alphonse of Poitiers in
Quercy, the other into the extent and value of lands in the three
dioceses and Saintonge whose lords, though 'privileged', had
passed to the duke's obedience between 1259 and 1279. As early
as 4 July 1279, John de Grilly, in a letter to Anthony Bek, had
pressed for the appointment of investigators. King Philip, he
said, would take no action until these were known, and time
was passing: unless the inquiry began at once, it would be
difficult to ascertain the facts from witnesses who were growing
old and feeble.[1] However, in spite of various attempts, nothing
effective was done until 1286. King Edward had intended to
cross the Channel in the previous year but delayed his departure. Instead he sent to Gascony one of his most trusted clerks,
frequently employed both at Paris and in the duchy on important missions. This was Master Bonet of Saint Quentin.[2]
The death of the kings of Sicily, France, and Aragon in this
year 1285, the succession of Philip IV in France and of Alfonso
in Aragon, and the obligation to procure, if possible, the release
from captivity of Charles of Salerno, the heir to the throne of
Sicily and Naples, entirely changed the situation of affairs. In
May 1286 Edward arrived in Paris with a large and impressive
following, which included his brother Edmund, the earl of
Lincoln, William of Valence, John of St. John, and the chancellor. He went to do homage to the new king, but he also
intended to settle the affairs outstanding in Quercy, the three
dioceses, and Saintonge. Earlier in the year, Bonet of Saint
Quentin had been sent on another mission, this time to investigate the cases of the 'privileged' who had been subject to
Edward before 1279. Bonet was in Paris, with the results of his
inquiries, by 30 June. Edward had done homage to his new
suzerain on 5 June, 'in the hall near to the king's palace'. In an
opening speech Bishop Burnell, the chancellor, explained that
his royal master's decision to take the oath of homage had not

---

[1] Printed by Langlois, *Le Règne de Philippe III le Hardi* (1887), pp. 433-4.

[2] Master Bonet's career deserves special attention. His executive powers, during
his six months' mission (*per parliamentum Londonie*) in 1285-6 (August to February)
were considerable, and it is possible that he anticipated later legislation. During
Edward's long stay in Gascony (1286-9) Bonet was in receipt of wages and expenses
in officio inquisitoris.

been made lightly; the treaty of 1279 had not been fulfilled and there had been some 'surprises', disturbing incidents in French behaviour. Many members of the king's council would have preferred to have assurances before homage was made, but the king trusted his cousin in France. This homily adds point to the words of the oath which Edward took: 'I become your man for the lands which I hold on this side of the sea according to the form of peace made between our ancestors.' The discussions which began in June ended in a treaty declared by Philip IV in August, after Edward's departure from Paris (29 July). The terms reached were more favourable than might have been expected. Edward's lordship over the 'privileged' in the three dioceses who had been excluded from his surrender in 1279 was confirmed. His position in lower Saintonge was firmly established, in spite of a contrary decision of the *parlement* of Paris in 1281,[1] by the recognition of his lordship over all the lands which Alphonse of Poitiers or his sub-vassals had held south of the river Charente. Alphonso's lands and rights in the county of Quercy were retained by the French Crown but, in return for his renunciation, Edward was granted annual rents to the amount of 3,000 *livres tournois*. Moreover, by a separate and earlier agreement reached in July, the procedure of *parlement* in cases of appeal was defined.[2]

We can now return to Aquitaine and, in the light of the treaties of 1279 and 1286, survey briefly Edward's administration of his duchy. The recovery of the Agenais gave the duke control of the Garonne, on which the city of Agen lies, and of its northern tributary, the Lot, from their emergence from the districts of Toulouse and Quercy. Périgord lies to the north, the combined fiefs of Armagnac and Fezenac, held of the duke, to the south. The most uncertain frontier between Gascony and the outer world was in Périgord, in the valleys of the Dordogne and its tributary the Isle, on which the city of Perigueux lies. Like the Limousin and Quercy, it was a land of interlocking jurisdictions—the famous 'process' of Perigueux, in the reign of King Edward II, was in some ways the expression of this

---

[1] *Olim*, ii. 35. The *parlement* then said that fiefs beyond (i.e. south of) the Charente, if held by lords on the French side of the river, followed the course of their chief lord.

[2] For the ceremony on 5 June and the subsequent agreements see *Foedera*, 1. ii. 665, 673. M. Trabut-Cussac has found a better text of the words of Edward's oath of homage in Brit. Museum. Add. MS. 32085, f. 112ᵛ.

incoherence[1]—dangerously near to the Gascon fortresses on the lower Dordogne, Fronsac, Castillon, and Bergerac. The frontier to the north-west of Périgord was better defined, especially after Edward's lordship of lower Saintonge, between the estuary of the Gironde and the river Charente was fully recognized. The duke could have his seneschals in Saintonge as in the Agenais and even, for a few years (1283–91), in the Pyrenean county of Bigorre; but clear-cut administrations in the three bishoprics were impracticable. Here one seneschal served to collect the ducal revenues and maintain the ducal rights in a block of country which, as Saint Louis had determined, could only be defined vaguely in terms of ecclesiastical geography. Its secular administration was mainly under the control of seneschals and officials responsible to the king of France and other lords, lay and spiritual.

The transfer of the Agenais, the limits of which were those of the diocese of Agen, was begun immediately after the treaty of Amiens had been sealed (May 1279). The task was entrusted to Edward's uncle, William of Valence, but the details seem to have been worked out by John de Grilly, the seneschal of Gascony, and the bishop of Agen. William of Valence was instructed in various letters of credit[2] to give the necessary oaths, on Edward's behalf, to the bishop and people of Agen, to receive oaths of homage and recognition, and to appoint a seneschal. The process of transfer, it was arranged at Paris, should take place in Agen in August. Accordingly, on 9 August the proctors of the two kings met in the cloister of the Friars Preacher at Agen in the presence of a large company of the clergy and lords, and representatives of the towns of the Agenais,

---

[1] See Cuttino, *The Gascon Calendar of 1322*, pp. 62–68, and *English Diplomatic Administration, 1259–1399*, pp. 12–14 and *passim*. The process (1310–11) dealt with all the difficulties in Aquitaine, but especially with disputes which concerned the duke's rights in the three dioceses. The diocese of Perigueux was, like that of Agen, in the ecclesiastical province of Bordeaux, whereas the dioceses of Limoges and Cahors were in the province of Bourges. The dioceses of southern Gascony, Bazas, Dax, Bayonne, Oloron, Aire, Lescar, and Lectoure were within the province of Auch. (The city of Auch was then in the county of Armagnac, south of the Agenais.)

[2] Originally issued between 5 and 8 June 1279; but a month later John de Grilly (in the letter already cited, above, p. 290) noticed that the seals of eleven letters were defective, and a second series was issued in England on 14 July. William's duties comprised the subordination of the revenues of the Agenais, the three bishoprics, and Saintonge, so far as they belonged to the duke, to the constable of Bordeaux.

the counts of Armagnac and Bigorre and other Gascon lords. The transfer was announced. The seneschal of the king of France divested himself of his duties and remitted to the duke the revenues of the Agenais which had accrued since the date of the treaty (23 May). A day was fixed for the settlement of Edward's rights to two bastides whose relations had not been determined. The only jarring note in the general harmony was sounded by the rumour that a Gascon, the lord of Bergerac, was to be appointed seneschal. Because of the clamour and the difficulty of agreement, John de Grilly was appointed seneschal for the time being. On 10 August the seneschal, in the communal house of the city, took in the Gascon tongue the oaths of office in the king's name and his own. Oaths of fealty were sworn. Later, the seneschal appointed a receiver, to be under the authority of the constable of Bordeaux, and a *judex*, responsible to himself. Most of these details are given in a description of the scene written to King Edward by the bishop of Agen. He emphasizes the eager alacrity with which the oaths of fealty were taken. If Edward, he says, could have been present, he would have been filled with joy.[1]

In August Edward appointed John de Grilly seneschal of the three bishoprics and Saintonge as well as of Gascony and the Agenais; so John was the representative of the king throughout Aquitaine. There is some evidence that in 1283, while the succession in Bigorre required attention, he held for a time the higher rank of lieutenant of the king. In this capacity he had in the same year to arrange for and preside over the farcical 'duel of Bordeaux' between Peter of Aragon and Charles of Anjou, and see to the safety of the former.[2] He was, indeed, a very busy man during the troubled years which followed the treaty of Amiens. He was anxious and harassed. Numerous difficult appeals required his watchful attendance in Paris. He felt that he had to be in too many places at once. Endless instructions came from England, but the duke, the seneschal felt, ought to have been on the spot to ease the strain. Edward, in fact, had fully intended to come. The Welsh rebellion put an end to these intentions, and it was only in 1285, after the conquest of Wales and when the Aragonese occupation of Sicily had led to a more general war in the west, that he decided to combine his

---

[1] P.R.O. *Anc. Corresp.* xiv. 136, edited by Trabut-Cussac in his unpublished work.   [2] Above, p. 254.

work as a mediator with the pacification and reorganization of his loyal, but restless, duchy.

How eagerly he had been awaited and how devoted a Gascon family could be, is made clear by letters from two brothers of the house of Ferréol, lords of Tonneins in the valley of the Lot, in northern Agenais. It would seem that the brothers, William and Stephen, had received favours from the king in England and had long wished to visit him; but, Stephen writes, the governors of the Agenais and Lord John de Grilly had thought that they were necessary to them in that land. Then they had decided to join John de Vesci and Anthony Bek, who had come into the Agenais on royal business on their way back from Spain, but in the meantime they had heard of an insurrection against the king—the Welsh war of 1282—and they now put themselves at his service. Here is William's letter, written, like Stephen's, at the end of August or early in September 1282. After greeting Edward as his humble valet (*bailetus*) he proceeds:

My lord, I thank and praise God and you for the marks of your favour and the honour you have done me in England. I have heard, my lord, that there is war in England, wherefore I and my brother Stephen and many others of our lineage and kindred, and especially Amanieu de Madeillan and Amanieu de Fossat, who plan and wish, if it is your pleasure, to join us to your honour and in love for us,[1] are preparing to go to you. We plan to put ourselves and our horses and other gear on a ship at Bordeaux and to board ship there, for we have been told that the king of France would not allow armed men to pass through [his lands] to those parts. And I would have you know, my lord, that I would have gone to you long ago to your great comfort (*comodo*), but there was a rumour and everybody said that you were coming to these parts. And, if it please you, my lord, give us your orders about these and other matters fully pleasing to your will, which we are ready to fulfil to the best of our strength; and, my lord, may the Lord Jesus Christ give you a good long life and preserve my lady to you and all your good household (*societatem*).[2]

Social conditions in the duchy differed from those which

---

[1] The text reads 'qui . . . ad vestrum honorem et amore nostri vobiscum volumus ire', but I suspect that the writer went astray, and meant to write 'nobiscum volunt ire'. It is a true Gascon letter.

[2] The two letters are edited by M. Trabut-Cussac, in his unpublished work, Appendixes xviii, xix, from P.R.O. *Anc. Corr.* xvii, nos. 59, 60. William Ferréol was appointed seneschal of Bigorre by John de Grilly after the occupation of Tarbes in 1284.

Edward had to regard in England; and in dealing with them the duke, living as he did at a great distance, had three bases of activity, Westminster, Bordeaux, and Paris. His administration can best be understood in the light of the measures taken during the two periods of visitation, 1273-4 and 1286-9. In 1273-4 he ordered a thorough survey of his rights in Gascony to be made in cities and fiefs and other communities. The main record of his second visit is the legislation at Condom in western Agenais (1289) about the administrative structure of the duchy as a whole.

The evidence available suggests that Edward, on his way home to England in 1273, had not intended to make a long stay in Gascony; but the revolt of Gaston of Béarn and a dangerous disturbance in the city of Limoges made him decide to go more thoroughly into the affairs of the duchy. It is known that he summoned a general court to meet at Bordeaux on 18 March 1274 for the promulgation of measures affecting Gascony, but what these measures were is not known.[1] Edward, however, had already put his investigations in train, probably as a result of his experience in the joint courts held at St. Sever in the previous autumn. When he took the oaths of homage of his vassals and inquired what their obligations were he found that they seemed to be as ignorant as he was himself about their precise nature. He had to grant a delay of forty days to the hundred persons or so gathered about him, and as he proceeded he met elsewhere with similar uncertainty. The results of his investigations are known as the *recognitiones feodorum*.[2] So far as they go they give a description of tenures and customs in Gascony as valuable as the survey of English conditions contained in the Hundred Rolls compiled after Edward's return

[1] The bishop of Aire-sur-l'Adour (arr. St. Sever), excusing himself, because he had to attend the pope at Lyons, thus describes the court and its business. He is obviously using the words of the writ. His letter (*Foedera*, I. ii. 500) is dated 1273 but this is the old style. The reference to Lyons shows in any case that it was written in March 1273-4.

[2] Ch. Bémont, *Recueil d'actes relatifs à l'administration des rois d'Angleterre en Guyenne au xiiie siècle* (*Recogniciones feodorum in Aquitania*) in 'Doc. inédits sur l'histoire de France', 1914. This volume contains the text of the recognitions in a Gascon register, which was later taken to the Chambre des Comptes in Paris (probably at the end of the sixteenth century) and later passed to the Wolfenbüttel library in Germany. It is now in Paris. This is not a complete record of the inquiries of 1273-4, as Bémont supposed. Other material, which is does not contain, was in at least two other registers, now lost, some of whose contents can be traced. The process of settlement with the vassals was long and diffused.

to England, a year or so later. Their value both to contemporary administrators and to the historian is primarily social; Edward's intention was to provide, at last, a sure basis of information formally recognized by the cities, landholders, and local communities. He wanted to know where he stood as lord and what his rights and obligations were. It would be wrong to regard the recognitions as financial documents, prepared for the use of the constable and his clerks in Bordeaux, though they were doubtless of service to them. The revenues of the duchy were derived in the main from the customs of Bordeaux, from the rents of the ducal domain and other dues farmed out to bailiffs and provosts, from the proceeds of saltworks and forests and local tolls or *péages*. Feudal aids and dues were insignificant in a land which had never known the imposition from above of a tenurial system of knight service, a land which was still partly composed of allods or free tenements. Rents and services to the duke were generally slight and in any case varied in their nature and origin. Land tenure could not be generally expressed in terms of knight's fees, even though most land was held by military service. No surveys in Gascony correspond to the lists of knight's fees compiled in England and Normandy in the twelfth century and to the returns of thirteenth-century inquiries copied into the famous Book of Fees. Feudal relationships were the outcome of local adjustments and separate contractual arrangements.[1]

Until French scholars have done more than they have at present to describe Gascony and the other parts of the duchy of Aquitaine in the light of the local evidence and of the English, French, and Gascon records, it is hazardous to venture even on the generalizations which are relevant to a study of English history and of Edward I as an administrator. It may be suggested, however, that the conditions peculiar to this part of Europe explain the local character of Edward's relations with his Gascon subjects. Gascon society was loose in general texture but very knotty indeed in its centres of urban and feudal life. In both city and castle the family was politically more important than it was in England, so that the habits of family

[1] The inquiry of 1273-4 was, of course, not the only attempt at a Gascon survey. Henry III had ordered one in 1259—this did not take effect—and Edward ordered one in the three dioceses (1276) and the Agenais (1286). The Black Prince instituted similar inquiries in 1363.

alliances and feuds might easily find expression in local resistance to authority. Local traditions and customs were more powerful than any body of common law, which, in the English sense of the term, hardly existed. Racial, provincial, and local feeling could be aroused, but provincial more easily than racial and local more easily then provincial feeling. Occasional great councils or parliaments—best described as 'general courts'— were summoned by the dukes or their lieutenants, but there was no continuous corporate activity such as King Edward could describe in his references to the English magnates 'by whose council the affairs of this kingdom are, for the most part, directed', nor was there any institution similar to the shire court in which royal officials co-operated with the men of the shire. It is significant that the combined meetings in a ducal court of the four courts of the duchy (Bordeaux, Bazas, Dax, and St. Sever) held by Edward in 1273 seem to have been the last of their kind.[1] In such a social atmosphere as this, local resistance, so quickly stirred in the excitable Gascons, could easily result in appeals to Paris, if only to neutralize the ducal officials and to delay proceedings. Moreover, if discontent in the localities were widespread under a strong seneschal whose methods were too reminiscent of Simon de Montfort's, unrest might easily become general. This happened in 1278 when, as we have seen, Edward had to send two of his closest advisers, Otto of Granson and his chancellor, Robert Burnell, to get rid of Luke de Tany and hold a parliament in Bordeaux, and soothe local passions. Misunderstandings were sudden, capricious, incalculable. The arrangements for a public utility like a bastide could create all kinds of unexpected difficulties. The 'recognitions' of 1273 had caused much heart-burning. On the other hand, Gascon fury could easily be appeased if it were met with firm and tactful understanding.

Here we can find the explanation of Edward's twofold policy—his reliance on an articulated bureaucracy on the one hand, and his vigilant recourse to local compromises on the other. The two tendencies were combined in the process of social betterment, notably in the local compacts which preceded the creation of bastides. They can be traced in the realistic attitude of the duke to the allods. According to the

---

[1] The words 'court of Gascony' were retained on the seals of contracts, which bore the inscription *sigillum curie Vasconie*.

orthodox view, the rule of the Plantagenets in Gascony destroyed the allods; but, as a recent writer has shown, this is not
the case. Neither Henry III nor his son had entertained dark
designs against the free tenements. They wished to be sure of
the facts, to protect established customs against tyrannical
intervention and to restrain them from encroachment on ducal
and other rights. Henry III's investigation in 1237 into the
privileges of the inhabitants of the district known as Entre-
deux-mers, the general inquiries of 1274, and an investigation into
local encroachments of 1309 revealed facts and directed policy.
The holders of allods must not escape public charges nor shirk
their responsibilities as subjects of their duke; but their status
is a fact to be respected, and when a change to feudal tenure is
made it must be made by agreement, to the advantage of both
lord and vassal. 'This policy is of great interest to the historian;
in a particular case it allows him to see the sovereign disengag-
ing himself from the suzerain.'[1] The same political approach
can be seen in Edward's care to anticipate or adjust appeals to
the *parlement* of Paris, and to make appeals less fashionable.
Edward's quick-tempered spirit must often have been sorely
tried, his tidy mind often affronted; but he got his reward in
the devotion of some and the confidence of many and, above
all, in an habitual loyalty to the union with the English Crown.

The great ordinances issued by Edward in May and June
1289 give a clear description of the administrative system of
Aquitaine. Edward had been nearly three years in the south.
He had become familiar with every part of the duchy. His
investigator Master Bonet of Saint Quentin and others had
kept him informed. His English constable had controlled the
financial department in the castle of Bordeaux. Early in May
1289, at Condom, the king approved an ordinance about the
government of Gascony, Saintonge, and his lands in the three
dioceses of Limoges, Perigueux, and Cahors. This was followed,
a few weeks later, while he was waiting for his departure at
Condat, near Libourne, by an ordinance about the Agenais.[2]

---

[1] Robert Boutruche, *Une Société provinciale en lutte contre le régime féodal* (Rodez,
1947), p. 116. The whole chapter (pp. 109-31) is important from our point of
view.

[2] The ordinances were transcribed in a Gascon register, A, a copy of which survives in the Cottonian MS. Julius E. 1 (cf. above, p. 278, n.). M. Trabut-Cussac has
edited the texts as his Appendixes xxiv, xxv, and has shown that the ordinances
were issued at Condom and Condat. Condom, which was made the seat of a

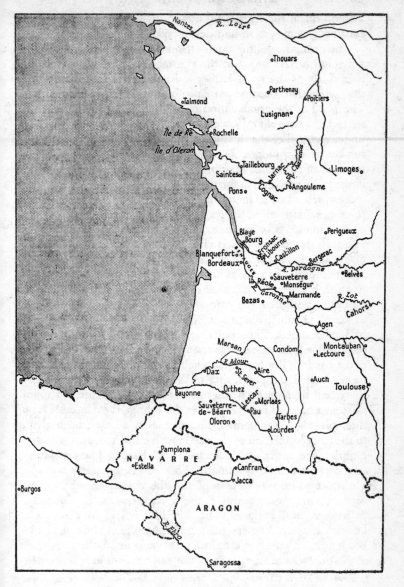

AQUITAINE

The object of the legislation was to define and strengthen the existing system, which had developed since 1254.[1]

The ordinance of the duchy (*terra ducatus*) is addressed to the seneschal of Gascony and the constable of Bordeaux. Nothing is said about the seneschal's council and it is significant that this, which had become more professional, is taken for granted. The head of the organization of the duchy as a whole was the seneschal (*senescallus Vasconie principalis*) who was to appoint, under the seal of the duchy, and throughout the whole duchy, sub-seneschals, judges, *defensores*, auditors of causes, keepers of the seals of contracts, proctors, and advocates in business of the king; to be responsible for them and to allot them the fees and wages prescribed in the ordinance (c. 21). On the other hand, the seneschal is to be paid a fixed stipend of 2,000 pounds per annum in money of Bordeaux, to be received from the constable in quarterly instalments. He is forbidden to receive any money of the king from any officer (*bajulus*) of the king save by the will and mandate of the constable. The intention here was to distinguish between his personal stipend and any payments which he might authorize the constable to make, and thus to avoid, so far as possible, malpractices to which even John de Grilly had succumbed. The constable, appointed by the duke, was responsible for finance. This change in the position of the keeper of the castle of Bordeaux had begun long ago, after Edward had been granted the perquisites of the duchy in 1254. Previously there had been an exchequer at Bordeaux under the control of the seneschal and receivers. After the change the constable took their place and the name exchequer seems to have been given to the area in the hall of the castle where the accounts with the bailiffs were made at Michaelmas and Easter. The constable-ship became primarily a financial office. The constable was still a constable: he was responsible for the visitation, supervision, repairs, and equipment of the ducal castles in Gascony, Saintonge, and Périgord, but this duty fell to him not as a military but as a financial officer. He had often to be away from Bordeaux, either in Westminster or Paris or in the provinces of the duchy, and from 1283, if not earlier, he had a lieutenant

bishopric in Edward II's reign, is in the western Agenais. Edward's court was there from 1 April to 5 May 1289, and at Condat from 20 May to 13 June 1289.

[1] See especially P. Chaplais on the 'Chancery of Guyenne, 1289-1453', in *Studies presented to Sir Hilary Jenkinson* (1957), pp. 61-96.

—described in the ordinance of 1289 as a discreet and well-informed clerk—who worked with him and took his place during his absence. The constable, moreover, was keeper of the archives in the castle of Bordeaux.

The seneschal and constable administered a ducal domain which, especially in the south of Gascony, was distributed in a land of lay and ecclesiastical lordships partly or totally distinct from it and subject only to the courts of Dax and Saint Sever. Gascony proper was divided for administrative purposes into the Bordelais, the Bazais, and the Landes or, more correctly, the areas of Bayonne, Dax, and Saint Sever 'ultra Landas'. In this last area the seneschal was required, according to the ordinance of 1289, to appoint a sub-lieutenant. The local officers were provosts, mainly in the towns, or bailiffs or castellans; however they were called their duties within their areas were the same.[1] The seneschal was required in person to hold assizes in each of the four courts of the duchy—in Bordeaux, Bazas, Dax, and Saint Sever—four times a year, for cases affecting the rights and domains of the duke, barons, and magnates of those parts; and to visit each *seneschalcia* in Aquitaine and to attend an assize of the sub-seneschal at least once a year. He was also required to visit every *balliva* or local unit of administration in Gascony at least once a year and to correct any abuses. Wherever he went he was to have with him, as an adviser, a skilled lawyer who knew the customs of the land.

The lands held by the duke in Saintonge were ruled by a sub-seneschal, the lands in the three dioceses of Limoges, Périgord, and Quercy by another. Both of them were subject to the seneschal of Gascony and, financially, to the constable. The seat of the one was the castle of Saintes, of the other the castle of Villefranche-de-Belvès in southern Périgord. They rendered their accounts twice a year at Bordeaux and held assizes. The chief colleague of the seneschal of Périgord (as we may briefly describe him) was a *judex* who could take his place whenever it was necessary to attend the assizes of the seneschal of the king of France in Périgord. The government of the Agenais was rather different and reflected both the independent

---

[1] Thus in the Bordelais, at the end of Edward's reign, there were eight provosts and four castellans; in the Bazadais three provosts, five bailiffs, and one castellan; in the Landes, three provosts (of Bayonne, Dax, and Saint Sever), sixteen bailiffs, and the castellans of Bayonne and Dax.

and more coherent traditions of this wealthy district and its importance in Edward's eyes. The Agenais, until its reunion with the duchy of Aquitaine in 1279, had been in other allegiance since King Richard I had given it as a marriage portion to his sister Joan, the wife of Raymond VI of Toulouse. It had its own customs which the duke was sworn to observe. Edward, while paying due regard to the susceptibilities of his new subjects, gathered his rights and revenues together with such success that when he died the three districts of the Agenais, south of the Garonne, between Lot and Garonne and beyond the Lot, contained forty-two *bailliae* instead of the thirteen of 1279. The administration was in fact a replica of that of Gascony. The sub-seneschal (whose jurisdiction extended over the duke's lands in the diocese of Auch) had as a colleague a receiver whose duties were like those of the constable of Bordeaux. It was the receiver, not the seneschal, who rendered the accounts. He kept his own archives in the important castle of Marmande, on the Garonne near the Gascon border. His *receptoria* comprised, in addition to the Agenais, the dioceses of Lectoure, Auch, and Cahors (financially the last named was withdrawn from the view of the sub-seneschal of Périgord). He visited, repaired, and furnished with armaments the castles throughout his *receptoria*. For the greater security of the duchy his *receptoria* further comprised the seat of the sub-seneschal of Périgord, the bastide of Villefranche de Belvès.

In other respects the special ordinance for the Agenais reveals a more intricate organization than was possible in Périgord and the Limousin, or was necessary in Saintonge. The sub-seneschal and a judge were to hold assizes in the customary places month by month. The northern part of the county, beyond the Garonne, was to have its own *judex ordinarius*, who was to hold assizes every three weeks at Agen and other places prescribed in the ordinance, and also to keep and administer the seal of contracts throughout his *judicatura*. Another *judex ordinarius* was given similar duties on the other side of the Garonne (*citra Garonam*) and in the dioceses of Lectoure and Auch. The last clause in the ordinance is of special interest to the student of English judicial institutions in the thirteenth century:

The judges in ordinary aforesaid, each in his own *judicatura*, at his last assizes at the end of the year, shall investigate carefully the behaviour in their offices of all our bailiffs and hear every one who has a complaint against the same and do swift justice beyond the usual process (*extra viam ordinariam*) to the complainants. A bailiff guilty of a minor offence shall be condemned to make good to the injured party and to pay to us one hundred shillings in money of Tours. The judges (or one of them) shall assess the punishment for a greater offence according to its measure.

In three other ways the two ordinances of 1289 show how the duchy as a whole was knit together.

(i) The defences of the duchy were controlled by two officers, who presumably worked under the direction of the constable of Bordeaux and the receiver of the Agenais. They were appointed to supervise and stock all the castles and fortified places throughout the duchy. One, called a *bachinator*,[1] was the inspector, the other, called the *atillator*,[2] made the siege engines, quarrels, bows, arrows, lances, pikes, and other weapons required by the garrisons and, in periodic visits, acquainted himself with their needs.

(ii) The duke, in 1289, declared that a new officer, the *defensor* of the ducal rights, acquainted with the law and customs of his district, should be appointed in each administrative area, one for each of the three parts of Gascony, and one for Saintonge. The *defensor* in Saintonge was also to be the assessor and counsellor of the sub-seneschal and attend his assizes. A similar officer, elsewhere called controller, was to maintain the ducal rights in the court of the mayor of Bordeaux. In the Agenais each of the two judicial districts (*judicaturae*) was to have a *defensor*. A *defensor* was to attend the sub-seneschal's assizes in the dioceses of Perigueux and Cahors and also the assizes of the French seneschal, and yet another to do the same in the diocese of Limoges. The *defensor* was appointed to watch the duke's interests in cases which might lead to an appeal to Paris, but, in Gascony and the Agenais especially, his appointment was required also to supply defects in a social organization which did not contain the closely-knit system familiar in England, where sheriffs, coroners, wardens of forests, itinerant justices, the court of the exchequer, and the royal clerks were

---

[1] So also in Ducange who refers to a register of the constable and, as M. Trabut-Cussac points out, must have studied the Register (see above, p. 298 n.) in the Chambre des Comptes.

[2] Cited by Ducange, s.v. artillator.

always available to guard royal interests. The judicial element was further enforced by a skilled and learned judge of appeals who was to live continuously in Bordeaux and to be always *de consilio senescalli Vasconie*; also of an auditor of causes for Bordeaux who was appointed by the seneschal. Finally, the ordinance of Gascony defined the position of the provost of Ombrière, near to Bordeaux, whose duty it had been to have cognizance of strangers (*extranei*) and, by custom, of certain other sorts of person. This officer was to have eight sworn serjeants to make attachments 'and carry out other mandates of the seneschal of Gascony, the constable, the judge of appeals, the auditor of causes, within and without the city'. Bordeaux was a rendezvous of foreigners, especially of merchants.

(iii) As we have seen the constable was a very important person. In some respects he was in closer touch with the royal government in England than the seneschal himself. He had under his eye in Bordeaux the administration of the *custuma*, the richest source of ducal revenues, a guarantee of credit, a reservoir of annual pensions, extraordinary expenses and casual favours, and, as the department which controlled the trade in wine, a link with the outside world. The chief officers of the constable in the castle of Bordeaux were the controller and the clerk (*transrotulator*) who, with other clerks, transcribed the accounts of the customs and of the bailiffs of the duchy. Some day a big volume, we may hope, will be compiled about the revenues of Gascony and in particular about the great *custuma* and the other customs at Bordeaux, at Marmande, and elsewhere. The evidence is considerable and could be used to give a lively picture of social and economic life in Aquitaine and more particularly in Bordeaux and the vine-growing area. Here only a few points can be emphasized.

In the last year of Edward I the annual revenue of Aquitaine was rather more than 84,000 *livres* of Bordeaux, or, at the rate fixed in 1282, about £17,000 sterling. The Bordelais, including the customs, accounted for nearly half of this sum. As we have seen, the duke, in times of exceptional expenditure, anticipated the revenue by loans, usually on the security of the customs. The Italian merchant-bankers who made the advances became so useful that they were at last given a permanent share in the Gascon administration. They were no longer employed to farm the customs, as the merchants of Cahors had done in 1266-7, but were collectors who accounted to the constable of Bordeaux. They paid out sums from the proceeds of the customs at the constable's direction, and accounted for the balance, which might be slight. The controller, or in his absence a qualified clerk, kept his own counter-roll of the customs in the castle.[1]

The provincial debt of Gascony, as it would be called nowadays, had reached a high figure by the time of Edward's return to England in 1289. The normal annual issues of the constable—stipends, wages, pensions, expenditure on castles, and so on—had been swollen by the periodic repayments of the great loan made by St. Louis in 1269, by the heavy damages assessed by the *parlement* of Paris in the case of the viscountess of Limoges (February 1275),[2] and by the annual payments made to Eleanor the queen dowager in lieu of her rights in the Agenais. The lavish expenditure of the royal court during the residence of Edward in the duchy, especially when he entertained King Alfonso of Aragon at Oloron in 1287, was too great to be borne by the current revenue. Edward was forced to have recourse to the merchant family of the Pozzi of Lucca, which was already collecting the customs as the king's bankers. In the spring of 1289, for example, this house lent him 40,000 *livres* in money of Tours, and itself had to draw, for part of the sum, upon merchants in Nîmes and Montpellier. After his return to England the king recognized a total debt to the Pozzi of no less than £107,725 sterling and gave his creditors control of the revenue of the duchy until the debt had been paid, or, in other words, the right to take what they could after the needs of the constable had been met. It is no wonder that while he was in Gascony Edward had put the keeper of his wardrobe, William of Louth, in charge of the finances in the castle at Bordeaux and had required him to draw up a full statement of the financial position. From this time the connexion between

---

[1] This dual system may explain the terms in which the duties of the controller's clerk were described in the ordinance of 1289: 'qui intromittat se de exitubus custumarum Burdegale contra rotulendis [et] petendis'.

[2] For Louis's loan of 70,000 *livres* in money of Tours see above, p. 281. The damages in the Limoges case were assessed at 22,613 *livres* in money of Tours. Edward's intervention (1273–4) in the dispute between the city and viscountess of Limoges had led to war and, though probably justified, was one of his most unfortunate enterprises. He complained in 1298 that the castle of Limoges had been retained by the king of France: *E.H.R.* xlii (1927), 580, § 7. For the details of this controversy and the sentence of the *parlement* of Paris (September 1274) see Langlois, *Philippe III le Hardi*, pp. 73–76, 420–2.

the constable of Bordeaux and the exchequer at Westminster tended to become closer. In 1293 the constable was ordered by the king in parliament to present himself once a year at the exchequer in England with his account.[1] This obligation was, of course, in addition to his annual and great final audits in Bordeaux. After the war and restoration of the duchy, a statement of the accounts was sent each year to Westminster. But, after all, it is policy that matters; and a far-sighted financial policy was almost impossible in those days of living from hand to mouth. The financial strain was eased to some extent by the indirect results of social developments—the results of peace, orderly administration, concessions to traders, better coinage, the exploitation of lands and forests, and the encouragement of new industries.

Many kinds of money[2] circulated in Gascony. Sterling and money of Tours were in general use. The administration for internal purposes used money of Bordeaux and, less confidently, of Poitou. There were also local currencies such as the money of Morlaas, in Béarn. The instability of the exchanges between 1252 and 1307 was great, and was only partially checked by the new coinage of money of Bordeaux issued in 1253, and reformed, after deterioration, in 1261 and 1283, and by another new coinage in 1305. The ratio of exchange was kept, so far as possible, at 5 to 4, as between money of Bordeaux and Tours, with a shilling of Tours worth three pennies sterling, but it was hard to maintain this standard. Fluctuation naturally affected the annual rate of the customs, although the quality and size of the grape crop was the ruling factor.

Here we come to one of those developments which helped to steady and probably to expand revenue. Sudden increases in the duty charged on the tun of wine caused protests from the wine merchants in Toulouse, Montauban, Moissac, and Rabastans, whose merchants appealed to the *parlement* of Paris. Edward wisely ordered the seneschal to come to terms, and in 1284 John de Grilly arranged an economic treaty which was ratified by the king in 1285. Gradually the merchants of other towns, including Paris (1293), availed themselves of the

[1] *Rotuli parliamentorum*, i. 98. The treasurer of Ireland was also to attend. The final audit in Bordeaux was a serious affair, generally conducted under the supervision of a royal commission.

[2] Cf. T. N. Bisson in *Speculum*, xxxii (1957), 443-69.

privilege, and in 1305 the seneschal and constable were given power to grant extensions at their discretion. The privileged merchants paid a fixed duty on the tun of 5s. 6d. in money of Tours if the wine was exported or sold outside the banlieu of Bordeaux. If they sold wine in the city and banlieu they paid in addition the duty known as issac, levied on all wine sold there by growers and merchants who were not citizens.[1] By the end of Edward's reign the greater part of the wine brought into the port for export or sold in the city was charged at the rate fixed by the agreement with the 'privileged'. Bordeaux became the centre not only of the local growers but also of a trade in wine operated by merchants in a great part of France. Thus in 1305–6, when the proceeds of the great custom were 32,000 *livres bordelais*, 58,000 tuns of wine were charged according to the tariff of the privileged, and only 18,000 at the current rate. By this time the privileged sold most of the wine consumed in the city of Bordeaux, for while 1,458 tuns paid the issac at the current rate, 19,800 tuns paid the 2s. 8d. in money of Tours fixed by the treaty twenty years earlier. It is obvious that the financial system of Gascony must have been steadied by a trading connexion with so wide an area in so sensitive a product as wine. The political result of the connexion must also have been considerable, for the merchants of Gascony and south-western France, paying customs at a fixed rate, helped to stabilize the relations between the duchy and its best customer, England. Their trade would be strengthened by habit.

Nothing is easier than to write a one-sided story of the administration of Gascony. The facts, if we chose to isolate some and neglect others, can be made to convey a suggestion of ceaseless tumult, endless appeals to England and Paris, bishops fighting for their rights, cities in riot and revolt, liberties withdrawn, local mayors displaced by English wardens, wages and debts unpaid, bailiffs corrupted by office. If the incidents are examined in detail and circumstances we get a different impression. The flood of petitions which poured in to Edward after his arrival in France in 1286, the intense activity reflected in the Gascon rolls before and after his departure in 1289, the

---

[1] Citizens of Bordeaux were exempt from the great custom and issac on all wines from their vineyards in the diocese of Bordeaux, but paid the former if they bought and sold wine from the vineyards of non-citizens. Many growers, especially religious houses, were also exempted by special grants.

'very strong committee for Gascon affairs', composed mainly of local experts, which dealt with petitions in the parliament of 1305, the arrangements made during the session of this same parliament for the administration of Aquitaine after the restoration to Edward of his duchy—'many feet of Gascon roll are filled with the writs'[1]—all this material shows us Edward as the trusted source of order and justice, a protector to be sought, not an exploiter to be feared. And so he appears, firm, patient, conciliatory in his dealings, in times of trouble, with the communities of Bordeaux, Bayonne, Bazas, and Dax. It is true that the sword of Damocles hung over him, for Aquitaine was not an island owing no external allegiance; but there is little or no evidence that he ever wilfully withheld a right or disregarded an accepted custom.

Perhaps the best way to see how the duties of government, the increase in revenue from an enlarged domain, and the economic well-being of the Gascons were reconciled is to study the numerous agreements or *paréages* with barons, bishops, monasteries, and rural communities, the process which lies behind the establishment of the bastides.[2] The object of these agreements, especially if no new settlement on the land was planned, was to provide adequate authority in the exercise of jurisdiction, or, as it has been described, 'equilibrium favourable to sound administration'. If a bastide was planned, the main purpose was the increase of agriculture and local trade. An abbey 'set in the midst of a perverse people' sought protection and found it in the division of jurisdiction between convent and duke, as at Saint-Sever in 1270 or at Condom in 1283–5. In one place the local abbey as lord might retain jurisdiction over the inhabitants, while the duke had it over strangers; in another it might retain its rights of jurisdiction altogether, but grant land for a new town, a bastide. These *paréages*, indeed, are most interesting when they established a new community. Land and amenities were provided by one party, the protection of ducal bailiffs by the other. Administration was more unified, protection was afforded, ducal rights were extended. Then, as a

---

[1] *Memoranda de Parliamento* (1305), ed. F. W. Maitland (1893), pp. lviii, lx, 3–4, 328–38.

[2] Cf. J. C. Trabut-Cussac, 'Bastides ou forteresses?' in *Le Moyen Age* (1954), pp. 81–135; and an anonymous article 'Medieval "New Towns" in France', in *The Times*, 21 Sept. 1957. The discussion on bastides still continues.

next step, the new community might be given independence
with its own customs and privileges, or an older community,
when it received new inhabitants who paid a fixed rent (half of
which might go to the duke), would be granted the customs of
some other place. Many of Edward's charters are to this effect.
The diffusion of customs, partly as a result of the creation of
bastides, is illustrated by an act of 1262, when the consuls of the
city of Périgueux were empowered to adopt such customs as
they might choose from those granted by Alphonse of Poitiers
in the bastides which he had established. The new customs,
hitherto unknown in Gascon charters, granted by Queen Eleanor
of Provence to Monségur in 1265 were the source of the customs
granted to the bastides built by the seneschal Luke de Tany in
1276. When the bastide of Sauveterre was founded in 1281 the
'liberties already conceded to the bastide or population of
Monségur' were prescribed as the model for those of the new
construction.[1] Lastly, as the bastides increased in number and
prosperity, the more important of them were often made the
centres of new administrative areas or balliages, the seats of
ducal bailiffs. In 1290 Edward gave instructions that as there
was no suitable place available in Quercy where judicial assizes
could be held, some castle or fortified place should be bought
where a bastide could be built in which assizes could be held.

About 140 bastides, some few of which did not come to frui-
tion, can be traced among the public works of Edward I's time.
Nearly a hundred of these, including transformations of old
into new settlements, were built by the seneschals from Luke
de Tany to John of Havering. John de Grilly was particularly
active, as he was in other kinds of public works and clearings.
The duke himself was responsible for only two bastides, both
near Bordeaux. One, Baa,[2] designed in 1287 to assist the more

[1] This is an especially interesting case. On behalf of King Edward the abbot of
Saint Ferme came to an agreement with two local lords. On 9 April these conceded
their jurisdictional rights in the castle and locality of Sauveterre, also such land as
was necessary for the building of a bastide in a suitable place, on condition that
this was built before Martinmas (11 November). The bastide caused much local
opposition and trouble. In 1282 the king's clerk, Adam of Norfolk, was ordered to
investigate the grievances of the promoters, inhabitants, and others. See especially
J. C. Trabut-Cussac, 'La Fondation de Sauveterre-de-Guyenne (1281–1283)' in
Rev. hist. de Bordeaux et du département de la Gironde (1953), 181–217.

[2] Probably as a compliment to Robert Burnell, the chancellor, bishop of Bath
(*Baa*) and Wells.

rapid clearing of the ducal forest, was known later as the castle of Thouars. The other, 'Burgum Regine', was under construction in 1288 on the banks of the Gironde near Bourg-sur-Mer.[1] It must not be supposed that the bastides were powerful fortressed towns, though some became such or were protected by a local castle. To generalize from the liberties of Monségur, they were settlements of houses laid out in plots of fixed length and breadth, arranged in streets, and surrounded by ditch and earthen walls, rapidly constructed. The settlers had facilities for cutting wood, a market, assigned weights, measures, and currency, a governing body of elected jurats, and a scribe (*scriptor*). Most of them were not near the frontiers but on land suitable for exploitation or rich in economic possibilities, as in the western parts of the Agenais. They were intended not to defend the country but to develop it. The settlers were frequently granted exemption from military service for a term of years. When the first burgesses of Sauveterre were in peril from local opposition—and the erection of a bastide often led to an interference with local rights, e.g. if a road were built across a vineyard, or the attraction of the place brought loss of workers to a neighbouring lordship—the burgesses, supported by the abbot of Saint-Ferme, justified an appeal to Edward for help entirely on economic grounds—the potential importance of lands, meadows, and vineyards, which provided nearly all the things necessary to a self-sufficient life.

Edward's relations with prelates, barons, and towns were, in general, conducted in the accommodating spirit which directed his policy of local exploitation. He was a southerner and others, like Alphonse of Poitiers, had already led the way in the south; but the duke of Aquitaine was less masterful than the Frenchman. He does not seem ever to have thought of organizing his lands in Aquitaine on military lines. Only once, so far as the evidence goes, did he deliberately anticipate the danger of war. This was early in 1279, when the dispute between Philip III and Alfonso of Castile was acute, and the negotiations for the succession of Eleanor of Castile to Ponthieu and for the transfer of the Agenais dragged on too slowly. Edward wrote in February to John de Grilly, who was in Paris: 'When the Parlement has ended, we desire you to return to your seneschalship in

[1] Edward and the queen stayed there in May 1288.

Gascony and to guard our land with care. Make such repairs and reconstructions in our castles there as is necessary, but with the utmost secrecy and with as little disturbance as possible.'[1] The danger passed; Ponthieu was secured, the treaty of Amiens concluded, and the kings of France and Castile agreed to arbitrate.[2] Edward, indeed, was clearly determined to recognize the relationship defined in the treaty of Paris and to maintain his causes in the court of Paris by peaceful means, always with vigour and finesse, but never with threats. Philip III and his son Philip the Fair in their turn were not intransigent. They did not, for example, press Edward's obligation to provide military service, although they sought it; and Edward, while he pointed out that in the peace no certain obligation could be found, was ready to give vague undertakings to come to his suzerain's aid.[3] Again, at one time the court of Paris made a great fuss about the style used in dating Gascon charters. It objected to the omission of any reference to the king of France and to the words 'regnante Edwardo rege Anglie'. It refused to recognize documentary evidence in which the objectionable style was used and even summoned to Paris some notaries of the Agenais who had used it. After much discussion with John de Grilly, conducted by the abbot of Saint-Denis, it would go only so far as to concede the style, 'actum fuit regnante Philippo rege Francie, Edwardo rege Anglie tenente ducatum Aquitanie'.[4] But, certainly in his own acts, Edward made no concession to this requirement, and Gascons addressed him as king and duke, with no reference to his overlord.

In spite of the strong sense of grievance created by the practice of the *parlement* of Paris, this unwillingness to push matters to their logical conclusion can be seen in the course of appeals. The process of law was softened by more friendly intervention or averted, without effective protests, by administrative action. Thus a long dispute between Edward and the viscount of Fronsac, which was taken to the *parlement* of Paris by the viscount in 1271 and was finally settled in 1285, was punctuated by the remission of the affair by Edward to

---

[1] *Rôles Gascons*, ii. 197. [2] Above, pp. 235, 243.
[3] Cf. his letter from Rhuddlan in July 1282 to the seneschal: if there should be talk of the service which they require, John de Grilly is to reply, 'quod in pace, inde inita, nondum referitur dicti servicii certitudo', but that he is ready to give such aid as Edward may explicitly (*specialiter*) command. *Foedera*, I. ii. 612.
[4] See John de Grilly's interesting letter in *Foedera*, I. ii. 602–3 (1282).

Philip III and Érard de Valéry (1276) and by accords between Edward and the viscount, and was finally settled, on
the question of damages, by Queen Eleanor of Castile (1285). The
viscount got his castle, but Edward retained the homage and
having obtained from the *parlement* a judgement which moder-
ated the financial claim, left the assessment to his wife, apparently with the consent of all concerned. Again, in 1289 a group
of citizens of Bordeaux appealed to the *parlement* because the
new seneschal, John of Havering, had carelessly begun to
exercise his authority before he had taken the oath to maintain
the liberties of the city. They proceeded to depose their English
mayor and to appoint jurats and a governor to administer the
city under the guardian appointed by the French king to protect the appellants. Edward, in return, seized and confiscated
the wine of the merchants, and awaited the outcome. The loyal
element was soon found to be in the majority and in 1291 the
appellants submitted.[1]

During the thirty-five years of peace which preceded the
sudden and violent outbreak of hostilities in 1293–4, the activity
of the *parlement* of Paris must have become in English eyes a
normal, though tiresome, factor in the administration of the
duchy. It led to the establishment in Paris of a little department
of royal proctors, a fluctuating body of jurists and clerks,
reinforced from time to time by the seneschal and constable
from Gascony and important persons from England. This
development is reflected in the last clause of the Gascon
ordinance of 1289, which provides that the seneschals of
Gascony, the Agenais, Périgord, and Saintonge shall each send
one discreet proctor 'to all the parliaments at Paris to the
council of the king [of England] there established'.[2] The proctors
are to be competent 'to inform and answer (*contra respondere*)
about all the affairs of the king in the said lands and in particular about injuries done by the men of the king of France to
the lord king in their seneschalcies, whereby the cases in dispute
may be more fully declared. Their expenses shall be met by the
constable of Bordeaux and the receiver of the Agenais.' Here
we have a group of four experts who, though they travelled to
and fro, were in regular touch with the royal agents who

[1] M. Trabut-Cussac has collected a list of licences to export wine issued by the
seneschal, constable, and others to merchants who had not joined the appellants.
[2] 'ad omnia parliamenta Parisius ad consilium regis ibidem existens.'

formed a royal council in Paris. The king had settled down to accept the obligations incident to his feudal position. He did not enjoy the acquiescence of all his advisers in England nor did everybody feel his confidence. John de Grilly always inclined to a gloomy view about the frequent appeals. As we have seen,[1] Edward himself, through his chancellor, protested when he did homage to the young Philip IV in 1286 against the 'surprises' to which his administration had been subjected by the French and referred to the hesitations of some of his advisers, who thought that he should insist upon redress before he did homage.

It may have been about this very time that somebody prepared a note in which it was argued that Gascony was not part of the realm of France at all. Gascony was an *allod*. The words in the treaty of Paris describing King Henry III as peer of France were void in law and fact. They assimilated the king of England to the 'peers' who held their lands under conditions of service; but *their* standing and services were established in their investiture with their lands, which 'moved' of the realm of France. The duchy of Aquitaine did not 'move' in this way nor did the king of France invest the duke with it. It was an *allod* and free.[2] Edward did not seek to maintain this argument, though later it was modified to read that until the treaty of 1259 Gascony was held *de allodio regis Anglie*, so that the treaty and homage did not transfer any *proprietas* to the king of France nor turn it into a *feudum*. His case against King Philip, probably prepared by Philip Martel during the negotiations for peace in 1298, was mainly based, as we shall see, on other grounds. It began with this point, but proceeded, without prejudice to its validity, to assume a feudal relation between the duchy and the realm of France and alleged the failure of the French king to observe the rules of law and to fulfil his obligations as lord. It appealed to the law derived by jurists from the Lombard *Libri feudorum*, and argued that Philip had forfeited his rights.[3]

These interesting contentions, however, were devised after the king of France had seized the duchy and while Pope

---

[1] Above, p. 291.

[2] This document has been edited by Pierre Chaplais from P.R.O. Diplomatic Documents, Chancery, 27/5/19, in the *Bulletin of the Institute of Historical Research*, (1948), pp. 211–12.

[3] See the document edited by H. Rothwell in *E.H.R.* xlii (1927), 578. Cf. below, pp. 650–3.

Boniface VIII was trying to bring about a settlement. Until 1293 Edward used other ways to ease the strain of the appeals to Paris. He sought, on the one hand, a clarification in his favour of the rules of the *parlement* of Paris in cases of appeal from his courts, while, on the other hand, he tried to make appeals to himself or his representatives more congenial to Gascon litigants, so that they should prefer to turn to him.

King Philip III had sought to restrain the hearing of appeals by his vassals. In 1277 he had instructed his bailiffs and seneschals not to authorize the appointment by his vassals in Languedoc of judges of appeal. His son opposed all seignorial jurisdiction over appeals except in cases consecrated by ancient custom. In 1285 Philip the Fair attempted to apply rules of this kind to Aquitaine. *Parlement* expressed the opinion that appeals could be made direct to Paris from any person exercising jurisdiction in the name of the duke. The abbot of Saint Denis explained that this opinion was not intended to cover appeals from any local bailiff or provost, but it did apply to appeals from any judge. In reply to Edward's request for a more definite statement, the *parlement* of Paris in 1286 made two formal decisions. It allowed one appeal from an inferior judge in the *pays de droit écrit* to the lieutenant or seneschal of Gascony or his judge of appeals, but it insisted that appeals from these judges should be made to the court of the king of France, and that in districts subject to customary and not to written law, appeals from any inferior judge should be made directly to Paris if this practice had been customary.[1] Edward, during his visit to Paris in this year (1286), had discussed these points; he also obtained from his young cousin assurances which did something to safeguard his independence and rights, at least during his lifetime. Neither he nor his seneschals nor their lieutenants should suffer pains and penalties by reason of any default or error of justice adjudged on appeal in the court of France, nor was he to lose any rights as lord of the appellants in consequence of the latter's forfeiture or other penalties

---

[1] For the discussions of 1285 and the *arresta* of 1286 see Ch. V. Langlois, *Textes relatifs à l'histoire du Parlement* (1888), pp. 121, 133-9, 140-1. The reference to the seneschal's judge of appeals, three years before the ordinance of Condom (above, p. 304), should be noted. The distinction between the areas of written law and those of customary law would apply especially to the parts of Aquitaine, outside Gascony, now subject to Edward. The *arresta* deal in detail with several matters of procedure, the status of the French seneschals, &c.

imposed upon them. Moreover, King Philip declared, appellants would be sent back for amendment of justice and to have right done to them if there had been default of justice, provided that this were done within three months. If this were not done within the prescribed term and the party returned to the French court, the case would be concluded there.[1]

The creation of a judge of appeal who sat in Bordeaux and the appointment of local judges and of *defensores* of ducal rights in the various divisions of Aquitaine[2] show how Edward responded to the challenge of the court of France. It was essential that justice in Aquitaine should be speedy, open to all, and respected, if appeal to the *parlement* of Paris was not to become the normal practice of dissatisfied or crafty litigants. But Edward went much farther than this. He was the duke. His officials were on the spot, in charge of affairs. The duchy was inalienable from the Crown of England, and whatever the king of France might think about this as a question of law, he had acquiesced in its consequences in fact. Appeals to Paris could be anticipated by judicial and other means. Alternative ways of doing justice, more natural to the instincts of his subjects, might be open to them. Edward, indeed, was in a strong position, and he took advantage of it. He was careful to respect the implications of the relationship created by the treaty of Paris. He does not seem to have given any encouragement to a tendency, natural enough in his father's time, towards the infiltration into Gascony of English legal forms and practices unknown to local custom.[3] He preferred to use the influence of his local agents to ease local disputes by persuasion, privileges, compositions, or arbitration, when such courses were possible, and at the same time to encourage his subjects to turn to him as the fountain of justice. Not only during his long stay in Aquitaine from 1286 to 1289, but all the time, wherever he was, petitions from the duchy poured in upon him, petitions with which he dealt as he dealt with petitions from his subjects in England. Some obstinate cases had to be decided in England, but usually the petitions were transferred with instructions to seneschal or

---

[1] Ibid., pp. 130–3; and *Foedera*, i. ii. 665–6.   [2] Above, p. 303.

[3] M. Pierre Chaplais has noticed in writs sent to Gascony in Henry III's time such phrases as *quo warranto*, *habeas corpus*, attachment and appeal (in the English sense of initiating a process by an *appellum*). M. Chaplais, who is preparing a dissertation on the subject of judicial relations between Edward and the Gascons has kindly placed notes at my disposal.

constable or other official to arrange the matters at issue. Two
cases dealt with by chancery warrants—that is, instructions to
the chancellor for action under the great seal—illustrate these
ways of procedure. A dispute about succession begun in the
court of the mayor of Bayonne had gone on appeal first to the
judge of appeals, then to the lieutenants of the king appointed
as supreme judges in Gascony. One of the parties appealed to
the king, who sent for the documents in the process. Edward
received the letters at Berwick, and as he could not deal with
them himself ordered the chancellor, on 13 July 1301, to
assemble the justices and other counsellors of the king, both
clerks and laymen, at York. This council was to examine the
case, decide it, or at least do what seemed best, and to signify
to the people of Bayonne what should be done.[1] In a later case,
still proceeding in 1309 after Edward's death, the appellant
was a yeoman of the count of Foix. He had appealed from the
court of Constance of Béarn, viscountess of Marsan, to the
seneschal, and thence to the king. His petition for the appointment of a commissioner to take the appeal in Gascony was sent
to the chancellor with instructions (15 July 1309) to make by
letters under the great seal such remedy as he could, without
offending right, and according to the liberties and customs of
Gascony.[2]

This last case suggests the difficulty of deciding Gascon cases
in England, however eager litigants in Gascony might be to
appeal to the king. It points to the way in which Edward I had
tried to meet the difficulty, a way which had been familiar for
a long time to litigants at the papal court and to vassals of the
king of France and, in some measure, to Edward's subjects in
England. This was the appointment of commissioners with
general powers to act as supreme courts of appeal or with
instructions to decide a particular case. Another and very
important reason for the use of this method was the fact that
many towns in Gascony and the Agenais and elsewhere, like
many communities subject to the king of France, had been
granted the privilege to have all cases in which they and their
inhabitants were concerned decided within their neighbourhood. The privilege was precious and jealously maintained.
Its possession might, and in some cases did, check any tendency

---

[1] *Calendar of Chancery Warrants*, p. 129. The previous history of the case has been
traced by M. Chaplais.   [2] Ibid., p. 292.

to appeal to the court of France; but it could turn to the duke's advantage only if he himself took steps to maintain it by the appointment of persons who could give final decisions on the spot. Parties might be willing enough to appeal to Edward for justice but they did not wish, and generally could not arrange, to plead their cause in England. Protestations to this effect were not confined to the privileged communities.

In the earlier years of his reign Edward, as we have seen, occasionally sent important commissioners to tidy up affairs in the duchy. As the judicial organization of the duchy was developed, and especially after his return to England in 1289, he tried to round off the system by giving supreme judicial powers to his lieutenants. Thus in July 1289 Maurice de Craon was empowered to receive and deal with all complaints against the seneschal and ministers of the king in the duchy, because 'it is difficult for our subjects to come to us daily in England'. During the French occupation of the greater part of the duchy, when Bayonne and Blaye were the mainstay of ducal authority, and when communications with England were more hazardous, the appointment of special judicial lieutenants with permanent powers as a final court of appeal was almost a necessity. A letter addressed to Edward about the year 1300 by the mayor and jurats of Bayonne describes an agreement which had been made in 1298 between the king's lieutenant, Gui Ferre, and the mayor, jurats, and good men of the town. They had established a rule that appeals allowable from the mayor's court should go first to the seneschal's judge of appeals, then to the royal commissioners Bonet de Pis and Pierre Arnaud de Vicq, the supreme judges in Gascony, but no further. If an appeal were made to the king it should be disregarded and the mayor would execute the decision of the commissioners. This decision was reached, so the writers of the letter explain, to spare the men of Bayonne the expense and danger of the journey to England, for otherwise poor and impotent persons could not obtain justice.[1]

The men of Bayonne had hoped to prevent appeals to England. They relied on the Gascon ladder of justice. Their

---

[1] P.R.O. *Anc. Corresp.* xxxiii. 20. It will be noticed that by 1298 the judicial lieutenants or supreme judges were distinct from the king's highest representative in the duchy, the lieutenant proper, yet were independent of the seneschal and superior to him in judicial matters.

hopes were not fulfilled. There were always persons in Gascony who, in their litigiousness, insisted on turning to England; and, if they were to be restrained from turning to Paris, Edward could not afford to close his ears to them, though he did his best to get a settlement within the duchy in accordance with Gascon customs. His dilemma is perhaps as good testimony as we could have to the strength of the tie between the Crown and the duchy.

Note on the Channel Islands

From 1204 the king of England, as titular duke of Normandy, retained the lordship of the Channel Islands, Jersey, Guernsey, Alderney, Sark. They were ruled by wardens, one of whom, Henry de Trubleville, was in 1234 made lord of the Islands, which he retained until his death in December 1239. In 1254 the Islands were granted in fee to the Lord Edward on the conditions attaching to the grant of Gascony and other lands, that they should never be separated from the English Crown, but should 'remain wholly to the kings of England for ever'. Hence, although the islanders vigorously maintain the recollection of their Norman connexion, their status was not affected by the change of style in 1259, when Henry III ceased to call himself duke of Normandy.[1]

The Islands geographically were a useful link between the ports of Gascony and of England. They were brought into close economic and, to some extent, into social relations with Gascony in an age when the ships of Bayonne and Bordeaux 'steered from headland to headland'. St. Peter Port in Guernsey was a natural port of call, especially in times of storm and danger.[2] On one occasion (1271), during Edward's absence on crusade, his lieutenants in England appointed a well-known citizen and merchant of Bayonne, Arnold son of John de Contis, as bailiff or warden of the Islands. Indeed their economic and strategic importance ensured the constant vigilance of the Crown and explains the particular mingling of supervision with respect for local rights and customs which gives peculiar interest to their history.

In some ways the Islands were like a sub-district of Gascony. They were privileged communities which had to be humoured, for, although they could not appeal to the court of the French king, France was very near, and their traditions were Norman, not English. They were ecclesiastically part of the diocese of Coutances.

[1] This section is based upon J. H. le Patourel, *The Medieval Administration of the Channel Islands, 1199–1399* (1937).

[2] See especially J. H. le Patourel, 'The Early History of St. Peter Port', in the Transactions of *La Société Guernesiaise* (1934), pp. 171–205.

Their legal customs and administrative system can best be understood in the light of Norman law books, just as the customs of Gascon
cities and districts have to be related to the social life of the Midi. On
the other hand, their social structure was simpler and more uniform
than that of Gascony. Only one or two seigneurs had lands by tenure
of more than half a knight's fee. Their fiefs were 'dismembered fragments' with no military value, paid no scutage, and though 'noble'
in status, owing homage and relief and liable to wardship and escheat,
were held by rent or petty serjeanty or no services at all. The bulk of
the population consisted of king's tenants who owed the king's farm,
either at a higher rate in lieu of all but occasional services, as in
Jersey, or at a lower rate, as in Guernsey, where other rents, dues, or
services of various kinds and incidence were also paid.[1] These communities of agriculturists, fisher folk, and craftsmen were, in fact,
like seignorial estates. The king or lord was the landlord; the holders
of fiefs were his chief tenants but with few interests outside those of
the island communities; there was little or no demesne farming, but
a multitude of royal rights, dues, and perquisities. Apart from the
constables of the two castles, Castle Cornet in Guernsey and Castle
Gorey in Jersey, the royal officials administered large manorial establishments; the accounts of the warden were like those of a sheriff or
a steward.

Communities of this kind, isolated and self-contained, can easily
become the victims of brutal exploitation, and at one time the
Channel Islands did not escape the danger. It came while Edward's
confidential companion Otto of Granson was in possession as lord.
In November 1275 Otto was granted the Islands in return for a
farm, first from January 1277 to June 1294 and again from April
1298 until his death in 1328.[2] He was lord, with the enjoyment of the
revenues, though on a tenure which would revert to the Crown and
did not preclude the intervention of the Crown. Otto was given the
Islands in recognition and reward of his manifold services to the king
and was an absentee lord, represented by a series of sub-stewards.
The result of the maladministration which naturally ensued was
twofold. It emphasized the necessity of royal supervision in the interests of peace and justice, and it gave an impetus to the direction of
local affairs and jurisdiction by the islanders themselves.

In the reigns of John and Henry III the customary law and

[1] The king's tenants, it has been suggested, owed their position to arrangements
made with settlers after the devastation of the Northmen. Their customs go back
in some form to the eleventh century. See J. H. le Patourel, op. cit., pp. 76–80,
107–9.

[2] The resumption of direct control by the Crown during the years 1294–8 was
due to the war with France. We may compare Edward's action in the Isle of Man;
see below, p. 596, note.

judicial institutions of the Islands had been frequently confirmed, and various inquiries (1230, 1233, 1247–8) had been made into the customs of the islanders. In 1274 King Edward had appointed two commissioners to make extents of the islands, like the extents made in England and Gascony, to inquire into the conduct of the administration and to hear and determine the islanders' complaints. This investigation established the rights both of the Crown and of its subjects, and was followed in Otto of Granson's time by other commissions, some of inquiry, others of assizes and all other pleas in the islands. The appointment of English commissioners (even though they were officials in the Islands) to hold assizes was a new departure, for, until 1275, the assizes and all pleas had been held by the bailiff or warden of the Islands in accordance with traditional Norman practice.[1] The next step was taken in 1299, when the duties of these various commissions of inquiry and justice were comprehended in a single commission equivalent to that of the great eyre in England. Moreover, in order to meet the complaints of the islanders and to make sure that the judges were acquainted with the laws and customs which it was their duty to observe, the men of Jersey and Guernsey were ordered to set these laws and customs down in writing. Although the practice of sending justices in eyre did not endure for more than a few decades, it secured the right of the islanders to enjoy their customs and the trial of pleas of the Crown under the immediate authority of the Crown.

In the meanwhile the normal administration of the four islands, which during the greater part of the thirteenth century was under the direction of the bailiff or warden (the two titles seem to have been used indiscriminately) was becoming differentiated under the guidance of local bailiffs in Jersey and Guernsey and *prévots* in Alderney and Sark. The separate bailiffs can be traced in the last quarter of the century. The royal seal of the Islands, first granted in 1279, was replaced early in the next century (*c.* 1304) by seals for Jersey and Guernsey kept by the bailiffs. The bailiffs were empowered to seal writs heretofore obtained in chancery[2] and contracts which previously had been made only by word of mouth. Since most of the judicial business of the Islands had been and continued to be transacted in the ordinary courts without writ, the seals in fact seem to have become seals of contract, and to have authenticated forms of

[1] For Normandy see J. B. Strayer, *The Administration of Normandy under Saint Louis* (1932), pp. 11, 19–24.

[2] The letters of 1279 (see Le Patourel, p. 97 and note) are summarized in *Cal. Pat. Rolls, 1272–81*, p. 337. They refer to an 'old register' of writs in the possession of the bailiffs, and ordered a transcript to be sent to England. This would suggest that previously writs framed in accordance with the models in the register had been sought in chancery, but the subject is very obscure.

agreements similar to those familiar in the courts of Normandy and Gascony.

It was, indeed, in the courts that the communal life and gradually the communal independence of the islanders found lively expression. Their mainstay, as popular courts of free suitors, was the bench of *jurats*, who seem to be first mentioned in the inquiry of 1248. Here they are described as sworn coroners instituted by King John to keep the pleas and rights of the Crown; but they were much more than coroners, though they may have assisted in preparing the cases reserved for the assizes, which, until 1275, were held by the warden to deal with more important pleas. When they appear in the full light of history they are judges in the island courts, elected by the greater men, or seigneurs; they fix amercements; they claim and receive the right to sit with the judges in the assizes of the eyre, they have cognizance of all cases. It is hard to resist the conclusion that they derive from an early popular element in the social structure of the Islands. They survived, in ways now untraceable, to become the backbone of resistance to interference with the customs of the islanders. Gradually the courts of bailiff, jurats, and suitors emerged to express the social consciousness of the community. The complaints which led to the Edwardian inquiries and the eyres in the time of Otto of Granson's lordship came from this quarter. After our period, the insular courts resumed jurisdiction over all pleas and were able to become independent of the courts at Westminster. The bailiff 'took an oath in the presence of the jurats and of the community that he would observe and maintain the law of the Island'. Like the comital bailiffs in Flanders he issued summonses, ordered arrests, directed procedure, pronounced and executed the judgements 'found' by the jurats after the 'proof'. The jurats, like the *échevins* of older times in the Low Countries, 'declared and interpreted the customary law; indeed their judgements were making law. . . . The law, however, ultimately resided in the community, which might refuse to sanction any innovations in its interpretation or application introduced by the jurats. . . . The earliest local legislation takes the form of a petition to the king in the name of the bailiff and jurats and the community of the island. Royal assent was expressed in letters patent.'[1] In due course the courts, afforced by other elements, became deliberative and legislative assemblies, known in Jersey and Guernsey as 'states'. Government in the Channel Islands 'sprang from jurisdiction', and its acts are still registered, in a living and growing record office, with the muniments of a medieval court.

[1] Le Patourel, op. cit., pp. 89–92 *passim*. See also the discussion of the origin of the jurats, pp. 113–17.

VIII

THE PERIOD OF THE STATUTES
1274-90

I N the two previous chapters about Edward I as an arbitrator and as duke of Aquitaine, some things have been said incidentally on the king's administration in England. The famous statute of Wales (1284), compared with the later ordinances for Gascony and the Agenais, was a drastic and revolutionary document, for it was concerned with a conquered land, but it reflects the same mind. It was part of the most thorough process of stock-taking to which England had been subjected since the days of the Conqueror, a process which began with a comprehensive survey, comparable to those made in Gascony, the Channel Islands, and Champagne, and ended with the commission of inquiry into complaints against the king's servants, including his judges, after his absence in Gascony. This inquiry lasted for three or four years (1289–93) and can be compared with the minute audit of John de Grilly's accounts after the king's arrival in Gascony (1287). In the interval between these investigations, a series of statutes had defined and revised many sections of the common law and taken into consideration the peculiar status of the foreign merchants who were now inseparable from the economic life of the community and had become the chief financial agents of the Crown. The anomalous position of the Jewish community was emphasized by these developments. In 1275 Edward issued a statute which forbade the Jews to lend money at interest and in return encouraged them to become traders, artisans, and even agriculturists; but this half-hearted recognition of their human rights was quite ineffective, and in 1290 they were expelled from the country.

The administrative methods by which large-scale inquiries were made, the results of experience and reflection were brought to an issue in statutes, armies were raised and equipped, Wales was conquered and organized, have been described in good books.[1] The details need not detain us. The king had his private

---

[1] T. F. Tout, *Chapters in the Administrative History of Medieval England*, ii (1920),

apartments or chamber, wherever he might be, so private that in Edward's reign they still do not appear in the light of history. Only occasionally do we get glimpses of men doing business in the chamber where, protected by his ushers, the king talked with his closest friends and advisers. The principal steward of the household—from 1293, if not earlier, the only steward— was a layman, a knight of social standing, and a sworn counsellor. He was always close to the king, an intimate whose political significance cannot be known. Outside the chamber he was a familiar figure. He was judge over the members of the household and of offences committed within the 'verge' or limits of the court. Every evening he or his colleague met with the treasurer of the household (or, as he was described, the keeper of the wardrobe) to check the daily accounts of those responsible for the expenses of the household. A man like Hugh fitz Otto, who for a short time after the battle of Evesham had been given the custody of the Tower and the city of London, had been with Edward as steward on his crusade, and before the king's return to England in 1274 had proceeded to the stewardship of the royal household, was no nonentity. He and his junior colleague and successor, Robert fitz John, who was with Edward in Gascony during the years 1286–9, must have been links between the official life of the court and those baronial and clerical fellow workers of the king, who were the core of the magnates 'by whose counsel in general the business of the kingdom was done'.[1]

The department of the household in which business was done, the wardrobe, with its treasurer or keeper, controller and cofferer and all its clerks, was politically the central office of affairs, not, so to speak, in its own right, but because it expressed the will of the king in council. It is true, of course, that as a rule these officers of the wardrobe were able and important persons. Many of them rose high in church and state, to become chancellors, or treasurers of the exchequer, or bishops. They were allowed much initiative, whether in the drafting of letters under the king's privy seal or in the management of daily affairs; but their importance was the measure of the confidence

1–163; Helen Cam, *Studies in the Hundred Rolls* (1921) and *The Hundred and the Hundred Rolls* (1930); J. E. Morris, *The Welsh wars of Edward the First* (1901); T. F. T. Plucknett, *Legislation of Edward I* (1949); and the works of Maitland, Richardson, and Sayles, noted below.   [1] *Foedera* i. ii. 585.

of the king and of their value in counsel. If we ask why, in periods of emergency, the wardrobe accounts were swollen to embrace the financial operations of a kingdom at war, we are driven back to the king in council. If we seek the origin of a vital writ of privy seal, or letter of instruction to the chancellor or the treasurer of the exchequer, we must find it in some discussion in the king's chamber. The authority is always the king or somebody who enjoys the king's trust and is ready to take the responsibility. And the test of ability in a king was his capacity to distinguish between those innumerable decisions which he could make alone or with one or two officials or intimates whom he liked to describe as his secretaries, because they had his closest confidence, and the decisions which required deliberation in council with the great officers of state, with judges, with magnates, or decisions which were most suitably made with the public knowledge, if not the active concurrence, of those wider gatherings known as the king in council in parliament. A king who could not or would not draw this distinction ran the risk of alienation from his people. As soon as men began to murmur that matters affecting the state of the realm or Crown were being settled without due counsel, that the normal processes of co-operation were neglected, so that, for example, writs of privy seal were being sent irresponsibly to all and sundry, the king was in danger. This happened in the reign of Edward I's successor when the gossips began to say that the Gascon favourite, Piers Gaveston, was trying to keep persons, who had a claim to audience, out of the king's chamber.

It will be helpful to approach our subject by way of the king's prerogative. The word 'prerogative', as it was used in Edward I's time, referred especially to the rules which constituted the privileges of the king as a feudal overlord, such as the rule which limited the powers of a tenant-in-chief to alienate his lands,[1] or which gave the Crown the wardship of all the lands of a man, of whomsoever he held them, if he also held land by military service directly of the king; or, again, the rule that if the king granted away a manor with its appurtenances, he reserved to

[1] Cf. the pleading in a case in 1279: 'the lord king has a special prerogative attached to his crown, namely, that it is not lawful for anyone to alienate his fee without his special licence' (G. O. Sayles, *Select Cases in the Court of King's Bench*, i. 48). This prerogative is believed to have derived from an order of 1256 (see Plucknett, op. cit., p. 9).

himself the knight's fees, advowsons, and reversion of dowries unless he expressly included them in the grant.[1] The king also had prerogative in many matters, for example, the right of pre-emption of wines, and of prises in general in order to feed his household and armies, and in the legal process, of distraint or distress, where 'he had the same rights as other people but could exercise them with numerous modifications of detail, all of them to the advantage of the crown'.[2] A new statute might have the effect of extending the prerogative. This was the effect of the statute of mortmain (1279) which made illegal the passing of lands into the hands of monastic and similar religious bodies and persons to the loss by lords of services and escheats, even if all the superior lords agreed. This came to imply that only the king could issue licences to alienate into mortmain, and, as is well known, licences soon became frequent: 'By a single stroke Edward I assumed the sole prerogative of amortization, a position which his brother kings in France only achieved by cautious stages.'[3] The courts might help the king to enlarge and define his prerogative. In Edward's time, for example, the right of the king to present clergy to livings under certain circumstances was enforced to stay the operation of papal provisions to the benefices concerned, as well as the rights of the patrons. By the year 1343 his grandson, Edward III, could be described as the supreme patron, who in such cases might exercise his right to provide, *ex plenitudine potestatis suae*.[4]

Little or nothing was said in responsible quarters in Edward I's reign about a royal plenitude of power, but much was said in the courts about the nature and implications of the fact that the king is the chief magistrate (*summus judex*) and has no peer within his lands. Pleaders certainly were ready, in their eagerness to win their case, to make wild claims.[5] The opinion of his

[1] This last case comes in the so-called statute *de prerogativa regis*, which is a statement of law (*Statutes of the Realm*, i. 227).

[2] Plucknett, op. cit., p. 60. The king waived some of his prerogative in a statute of 1275, known as *Districciones Scaccarii*.

[3] Ibid., p. 99. Cf. the more deliberate exclusion of the rights of 'such as pretend to be founders, patrons and donors' of the monastic lands seized in 1536 under the statute 27 Henry VIII, c. 28.

[4] In the judgement in the case of the advowson of the deanery of York, *Year Books 17 Ed. III* (Rolls Series), p. 541, note 3. I owe this reference to Mr. Roger Highfield.

[5] e.g. the argument used by Roger Mortimer's widow, and the plea of the prior of Ely, in Sayles, op. cit. ii. 58; iii. 198–204.

judges was that when it was his pleasure, the king had the power to correct the neglects, defects, and errors of his servants, whoever they were. There were no limits to his right to see that justice was done.[1]

The royal prerogative was either an instrument of justice or a body of privileges which were recognized by the courts and, if raised in court, had to be met and answered. If the king was concerned, as when a royal charter was under discussion, the matter might have to be referred to the king himself. In difficult cases the decision might be referred to him and he might refer it to his council composed of high officials, judges, and 'others of the council who should be called'—a phrase frequently used in the chancery warrants to describe persons fit to deal with the matter in hand—or he might defer it until he and his council could deal with it.[2] In some cases we may see pleaders and judges discussing points of prerogative. In 1292 a great lady of Shropshire, the widow of the still greater lord of Powys, petitions the king about her dower, and the petition is referred to the justices *coram rege*. The king's attorney, who is faced with a charter of King Henry III confirming the husband's deed of dower in Shropshire, argues that the deed infringed Magna Carta, was entirely contrary to common law and was void, wherefore the royal charter confirming it should be regarded as invalid, 'especially as the lord king had no wish by that grant to change the common law of the realm'. The lady urges that the king himself is above all law, but ultimately she withdraws from her petition.[3] She was doubtless treated hardly. When she married she could not—at least it was said—be endowed in Wales, so her husband had given her all his land in Derbyshire, the manor of Ashford; but, according to Magna Carta, she should only have got a third of the manor.

---

[1] Sayles, op. cit. iii. 58. In general, the passages indexed in the three volumes under King, King in Council, Prerogative, repay careful attention.

[2] See, for example, the action taken on the claim of the bishop of Chichester to jurisdiction over the king's chapel in the castle of Hastings: Sayles, op. cit. iii. 183, in a long review of the earlier proceedings made in 1307 (pp. 180-90). This explains a reference to the bishop's petition enclosed in a chancery warrant of February 1302 (*Cal. Chancery Warrants*, p. 160). The case was more than once brought up in parliament, e.g. *Memoranda de Parliamento* (1305), pp. 127-8.

[3] Sayles, op. cit. ii. 67-68. Hawise Lestrange had married Gruffydd ap Gwenwynwyn in 1242, fifty years before her petition. Her husband died in 1291. The case has also been discussed by Faith Thompson, *Magna Carta: its Role in the Making of the English Constitution, 1300-1629* (1948), pp. 53-54.

Edward preferred to act with his judges. He might be above the law, but he rarely asserted his rights. As John Baliol argued in his claim to the throne of Scotland, usage and custom were to be preferred to the 'natural law' on which his rival, Robert Bruce the elder, relied. The king, he added, 'did not by the exercise of his will oust any tenant who had encroached on his demesne; he sued a writ out of his own chancery, like anybody else, and awaited the judgement of his court'. Again, if the king had occasion to issue a special kind of writ to meet a special kind of case, he sought the approval of his council. This fact appears clearly in the record of a complicated case, which involved many arguments and much searching of rolls in the year 1279. King Edward had required Gilbert of Clare, earl of Gloucester to restore the manors of Portland and Hampton Wyck in Dorset, which had been given in custody to his father Richard of Clare, after the expulsion of Aymer, bishop of Winchester, in 1258. The king's attorneys let themselves go freely on the right of the king in council to frame writs. One asserted that, ten years earlier (1269), Gilbert had taken exception in vain to an identical writ of Henry III, a writ framed by the advice of the magnates and those learned in law who were of the royal council. The attorney was bold enough to add that 'there are not now in the kingdom any men of such outstanding diligence or wisdom as were those who framed that writ'. Another attorney enlarged upon the distinction between common original writs established for all and sundry and a writ which the king, when he finds it necessary to implead someone, can lawfully frame with the aid of his council, provided that it is consonant with right. The royal power ought not to be limited in these things or in others. Moreover the lord king demanded the manors 'in order that they may be restored to him for his use, not in order that he may retain them in his own demesne, but so that he can show justice thereupon to every one'.[1]

These last words were not empty verbiage. The *coram rege* rolls show abundantly that in the reigns of Henry III and his son the council was a court, establishing itself in relation to the other courts of the realm. It decided upon knotty points in the law and, if the rules and customs of common law were not

---

[1] Ibid. i. 55, 57–58. In effect the king was acting in the interests of the lord of the manors, the bishop of Winchester.

applicable, it devised other remedies. With the king it determined the meaning of royal charters, sometimes in favour of
baronial claims. What, for example, was the exact intention or
rather the just interpretation of the liberty enjoyed by the
houses of the order of Sempringham to be impleaded only
before the king or his chief justice or the justices in eyre? This
point was raised in 1284 in the case of *Agnes of Vescy* v. *The prior
of Malton*. 'And it seemed to the king and his council that the
liberty in the aforesaid clause contained in the king's charter
was not to the prejudice of any earl or baron with regard to
losing any plea from their court.' The liberty referred to such
courts as shire courts, hundred courts, wapentakes, and other
similar courts of the lord king. It meant that the king's justices
should do speedy justice on the charter or any similar charter
when it happened to come before them. The liberty contained
in the charter ought not to apply to courts baron when the
prior had been impleaded outside the king's court.[1] Now it has
been said that Edward's outlook was strictly and technically
legal, that, though just, he believed in the 'rigour of the game'
and that equity lay far in the future; but in the lay mind this
important decision strikes an equitable note. The king in council,
or council alone, was not a court of equity in the sense in which
we speak of the later equitable jurisdiction of the chancellor,
but this highest court was certainly expected to 'do what seemed
best'. As Maitland said about the king in his council in his
parliaments: 'we must not miss the equitableness of this
tribunal.'[2]

Edward enjoyed co-operation with his council, and realized
that his strength lay in this form of government, for it released
him from the irksome obligation to be always holding his own
against criticism and it enabled him to face difficulties with
confidence and a sense of support. Now and then we are allowed
to hear a discussion in council.[3]

Important affairs, mingling law and politics, should be con-

[1] Sayles, op. cit. i. 132-3.
[2] *Memoranda de Parliamento, 1305*, p. lxxxv. In this sense the court of king's bench,
and *a fortiori* the king in council, certainly was a court of equity. The word is
used more than once. See Sayles, op. cit. ii, pp. cvi, cvii; and cf. the statute of
Gloucester (1278) at the end of c. 11, referring to justice to be done to the 'termor'
who is the victim in any collusive action in the court of the mayor of London.
[3] e.g. on the way to avoid hardship (*duricia*) to either party, in the case (1280)
of *Lovel* v. *The prior of Montacute* (Sayles, op. cit. i. 71-72).

sidered in the light of this coherence between the king and his advisers, before we dismiss them as pieces of royal sharp practice. One of the urgent problems which remained after the destruction of the Welsh princes of Snowdonia was that of the relations between the Crown and the lords of the Marches, who, from their privileged retreats had for so long been so prominent and influential in the political life of the realm. Their *raison d'être* as containers of the Welsh princes had lost most of its force. Were they to continue to enjoy in undisciplined freedom the liberties which they claimed to hold by right of conquest in a distant past? If private war broke out between them, it was of little use to try to restore the king's peace by serving common-law writs, even if they had run in the Marches. Soon after his return from Gascony in 1289 Edward tried to anticipate trouble of this kind by a proclamation (January 1290) forbidding private warfare. In the following May Gilbert of Clare, earl of Gloucester and Hertford, and the greatest of the Marcher lords in south Wales, married Joan of Acre, the king's daughter. As part of a general family settlement, Gilbert surrendered his lands and received them back in his wife's name as well as his own, to go to heirs of his body by the marriage. Gilbert's sense of independence was inflamed rather than restrained by this advancement. Throughout the year he disregarded the proclamation and engaged in war with his northern neighbour, Humphrey de Bohun, earl of Hereford, who was lord of Breck-nock. Humphrey, as had so often happened in times of similar disturbance, appealed to the king, and Edward decided to act. He appointed a commission which was to inquire through a jury of magnates and others in the March into acts done to the prejudice of the royal dignity and against the king's peace. The findings of the judges were considered in parliament at Aber-gavenny in October 1291. In the following January in full parliament, 'by the counsel and judgement of the archbishops, bishops, earls, barons and all the king's council', the two earls were condemned to imprisonment and deprivation of their liberties of Glamorgan and Brecknock. They were soon set free and allowed to make fines for their lands; but an example had been made. Now the really interesting thing in these proceed-ings was the reply of the judges of the preliminary inquiry when the magnates of the March refused to take the oath as jurors. The magnates, recollecting Magna Carta, said that they acknowledged only one kind of writ, and that was one which ordered matters affecting the March to be settled according to the uses and customs of those parts. The judges replied that by his prerogative the king, in the common interest (*pro communi utilitate*), was in many cases above the laws and customs used in his realm. And when further objection was taken to the writ at Abergavenny, the council ruled that the king from whom all ministers subject to him have record is a superior and much more compelling record, excelling all his ministers and the processes and records of their rolls.[1] On occasion, the council in parliament, the highest upholder of the common law, was prepared to go very far indeed in the interests of all.

The finest of all the royal prerogatives is the prerogative of mercy. It may be abused but essentially it is an instrument of equity. In the thirteenth century, as always, it affected all men and women, high and low. One day, towards the end of Edward's reign, a certain Richard Squibes was sitting with Thomas Smel in a tavern in a Hampshire village. They were drinking and contending together. Thomas drew his knife and chased Richard first out of the tavern, then back again. Richard was literally cornered—the jury, when questioned later, said that there was no opening in the corner by which he might have escaped—and in fear of death he drew his own knife and killed Thomas. The judges of jail delivery at Winchester sent a report to the king, as they were required by statute to do in such cases, and the king sent it on to chancery with a mandate that letters of pardon should be issued.[2] Let us see how Edward dealt with greater men.

We know how he treated Gaston de Béarn in 1278 and the earls of Gloucester and Hereford in 1292; in these cases he had good reason for clemency. It must have cost him an effort to release Amauri de Montfort in 1282. This able man, a graduate of Padua and a papal chaplain, was the youngest son of the great Earl Simon. He was the brother of Guy, the murderer of Henry of Almain and Guy was the one man for whom Edward, in spite of frequent appeals from Charles of Salerno

---

[1] The proceedings are entered on the Welsh Roll summarized in *Cal. Chancery Rolls, Various*, pp. 334-49. A full account of the whole incident may be read in J. E. Morris, *The Welsh Wars of Edward I*, pp. 220-39.

[2] *Cal. Chancery Warrants*, pp. 254-5. This is an example of the procedure defined in the statute of Gloucester (1278), c. 9. See below, p. 372, n. It was intended to secure trial before pardon.

and others, would never raise a finger in aid. Amauri was one
of the traitor brood, a litigious man with a vitriolic tongue. At
the end of 1275 he was captured off the coast of Glamorgan
while he was bringing his sister Eleanor to marry Llywelyn,
the prince of Wales. He was sent first to Corfe castle, but later
the archbishop of Canterbury was allowed to be his warden,
responsible for his safe-keeping.[1] One pope after another begged
Edward to release him. Archbishop Pecham pleaded for him,
but neither the king nor his counsellors considered it prudent to
let him go. At length the archbishop, in a personal interview in
the castle of Devizes, in April 1282, got Edward's consent to
Amauri's departure from the country. As the archbishop observed in a report to Pope Martin IV, the time had not been
propitious. War in Wales had recently begun again. Llywelyn
and his brother David were in revolt, news which, in the common opinion, suggested the detention rather than the release of
Amauri; but the king had been merciful, although in a large
assembly of magnates of the realm, who had been consulted,
'the wishes (vota) and counsel of no few had been to the contrary'.[2]

Another act of clemency followed hard on a trial in the first
parliament of 1305. This was the famous case of Nicholas
Segrave, a unique and dramatic case which caused much
excitement, as well it might. Nicholas was the second of three
brothers who were active in the king's service, and inclined to
be violent and touchy in the pursuit of their own affairs. They
were very important people.[3] Their great grandfather was that
Stephen Segrave who had been Henry III's justiciar; their
father was Nicholas Segrave, a disinherited Montfortian who
had held out in the isle of Ely, had been allowed to redeem his
lands on favourable terms, and had seen much service in the

---

[1] In an interesting letter of 14 February 1282 the bishop of London reported
to the archbishop that, in an interview at Bibury, he had presented to the king
letters from Pecham and a transcript of papal letters on behalf of Amauri. After
deliberating with his council, Edward repudiated a suggestion in the papal letters
that Amauri had been handed over to the archbishop by order of the pope. He
insisted that the transfer had been done with the counsel of the barons, at the
instance of the bishops, and that further action could not properly be taken without consulting the barons; and he stated that he intended to discuss the matter in
the forthcoming parliament (Registrum epistolarum J. Peckham (R.S.), i. 208).

[2] Ibid. i. 325–7.

[3] For the family and its connexions see The Complete Peerage, vol. xi, especially
pp. 601–7.

Welsh wars. The eldest brother John who succeeded his father in 1295 was in this very year 1305 the warden of Scotland south of the Forth; and in August was to be one of the judges of William Wallace. A siege-engine used in the Scottish wars was nicknamed 'Segrave'.[1] The warden's brother Nicholas, while on military service in Scotland, quarrelled violently with a fellow soldier, John Cromwell, taxed him with iniquities and offered him wager of battle. Cromwell was provoked, in his turn, to pledge his faith that he would defend himself in the king's court with his body or in such other way as the court might decide. The subsequent withdrawal of the adversaries and their men from the army made Nicholas, as the aggressor, guilty of contempt; so far as was in his power he had exposed the king to danger from his enemies. We can imagine the sensation when it was known that he had added to this offence by 'adjourning' Cromwell to defend himself in the court of the king of France, thus, so far as he could, subjecting the lordship (*dominium*) of the king and his realm to the lordship of the king of France. He disregarded the refusal of the constable of Dover to permit him to leave the country in contravention of the mandate which forbade the passage of men with horses and arms in time of war, and secretly slipped over the Channel from an unauthorized port. The king ordered the constable to arrest him if he should return. He did return and was imprisoned. He escaped and made his way to his manor of Stowe in Northamptonshire. Here the sheriff, in obedience to a royal mandate, summoned him in person to appear before the king in the next parliament at Westminster. If the record can be taken literally the trial began on Sunday, 28 February, the day on which parliament was opened. The case against Nicholas was stated. Nicholas admitted his guilt and submitted himself to the king's will 'in full parliament in the presence of the lord king, the archbishop of Canterbury and many bishops, earls, barons and others of the king's council there present'. The lay magnates and counsellors were enjoined by the king to say what the punishment should be, and in the meanwhile Nicholas was imprisoned in the Tower. After diligent consideration, the magnates gave judgement that a deed of this kind deserved the penalty of death. Then the king, of his special grace and moved by compassion, preferring the life to the death of those who

[1] Bain, *Cal. Doc. relating to Scotland*, ii, nos. 1500, 1599.

submitted to his will, remitted the judgement of life and limb, and conceded that Nicholas should find seven good and sufficient manucaptors who would undertake that he would render himself to prison and be responsible for the surrender of all his lands at the king's will. The men were found and executed their bond on the last day of March.[1] Nicholas also gave his written undertaking.

So far the record; but we hardly require the highly coloured gossip of the local Westminster chronicler to assure us that more than this occurred. The magnates are said to have discussed the fate of Nicholas for three days and to have added to their decision a reminder that the king could show mercy. Edward is said to have declared that he would show no more mercy to him to please them than he would to a dog. Nicholas, who was no stripling, had wounded Edward to the quick by his attempt to seek justice at the French king's court. On the other hand, he was a useful and had shown himself a loyal if a foolish and headstrong person. He had friends and patrons who were doubtless ready to intercede for him. It is significant that in letters under his privy seal Edward II, after his father's death, released Nicholas from his written obligation to return to prison, alleging as his reason Nicholas's good service done and to be done to him.[2]

Nicholas Segrave's impetuosity has detained us longer than it deserves, but his case gives a picture of high life in England. It is a good example of a state trial in time of parliament and shows us what trouble a baronial family might cause the king and his government. It shows also that, in his most arbitrary period Edward was essentially the same man as he had been earlier in his reign, a man of common sense and compassion as he sat with his magnates and judges. Indeed his recovery from his hasty passion could be too confiding, as happened at this very time and as he was to learn very soon in Scotland. William Wallace himself, who suffered a horrible end in August, might have made his peace if he had wished. Moreover, the Segrave case admits us to a *placitum* in parliament and brings us back to the administrative system. The record and all the documents in the case were handed by one of Edward's

---

[1] *Memoranda de Parliamento*, pp. 255–62; cf. the Introduction, pp. lxxvi–lxxvii; also the *History of English Law*, ii. 508, and Plucknett, op. cit., p. 25.

[2] *Memoranda*, &c., p. 263 (Feb. 1308).

judges, Gilbert of Rothbury, who was the clerk of parliament, to be kept in the king's wardrobe, but copies were sent also to the chancery, the judges of king's bench and common pleas, and the exchequer. They were written on the roll of parliament, on the close roll in chancery, and on the *coram rege* roll. The *coram rege* roll is the record of the court of king's bench, of the judges still described as 'in the presence of the king'. It will have been noticed that our references to cases discussed in council have been to this judicial record. We have described the council as a court, and court it was in the sense that it might deal with and conclude cases as well as debate knotty points and give directions;[1] but it was not in itself a court of record, for, from this point of view, it was a less professional and more final extension of the court *coram rege*. Except in parliament, when the king was in council with his people, in solemn proceedings which demanded their own record, there could hardly be a court of record or a kind of record higher than one of proceedings 'before the king'. These judges *coram rege* had not gone 'out of court', in the sense that they were no longer familiar figures in the royal household. True, they conducted their normal everyday business apart in their own place, but they were still at the king's service wherever he might be, if he wished to have them or some of them by him. Just as others, though not justices, might sit with them and utter opinions in their court, the court of king's bench,[2] so they, or some of them, sat with the king and his great council in parliament, and shared in judicial business in the king's council when some difficulty or error was brought before it. It is not always easy to be sure whether the judges joined in a decision in the council itself or made judgement in their own court after hearing the opinion of the king in council.

What is clear is that they were not removed from the central administration. Nor were the great officials of chancery and exchequer, though they, like the judges, did most of their business 'out of court' in their own departments. These great persons, chancellor, treasurer, some judges, with the magnates and king's clerks who were the king's *secretarii*, formed the core

[1] The rolls of proceedings *coram rege* contain many pleas transferred to council from the king's bench and other courts; cf. a case of 1276 under the Dictum of Kenilworth (Sayles, i. 21) and a plea decided before king in council after a search for records going back to 1221 (p. 148); also judgements on pp. 32, 33, 50, 64.

[2] Sayles, op. cit. i. 109, where such persons suddenly intervene in a case.

of the council and could constitute a full council. Until the later years of the reign, when Walter Langton the treasurer took the lead, the chancellor was, next to the king himself, the chief figure in the political life of the realm, and, as he was normally at court, was a peripatetic clearing house of public business. On at least one occasion Burnell presided over the council when it gave judgement on a point of law.[1] He and his clerks, day by day, composed the letters under the great seal, which issued in accordance with the king's mandate, whether verbal or conveyed in letters of privy seal; but he was also, as chancellor, entrusted, like his predecessors,[2] with the expedition of business, in touch with all who wanted something done and were intimate enough with administrative processes to seek his advice or his authority. For example, this is how the judges in eyre in Devon wrote to Robert Burnell the chancellor in the spring of 1281:

Since we fully intend to finish the present eyre in Devon before Easter (13 April) we beg you to tell us as quickly as you can into what shire we should adjourn after Easter and to what date, and whether we must all come to parliament. Please note that, if we must all come, the shire of Cornwall cannot be summoned before the week or fortnight after Trinity (8 June) for the time between Easter week and the parliament is short and it is a long journey from London to Cornwall, and, as you know, parliament involves much delay. If you were willing to prorogue the eyre until after Michaelmas, you would do much service both to the whole shire and to us, for corn has failed there this year and if we go there in the summer we shall bring back meagre cheeks. Please let us know your good pleasure by the bearer. May your reverend lordship ever prosper.[3]

Burnell and his deputy John Kirkby, a royal counsellor who in 1284 became treasurer, received many letters of this kind from all sorts of people. If the king had made a promise or issued a mandate which had not been executed, the chancellor was begged to put the matter through. A man who had fulfilled his military service is being distrained for scutage, another is declared by the earl of Gloucester to be exempted from a tax like the rest who have been constantly in the king's army, a Welsh prince's men in a Gloucestershire manor are being

---

[1] At Shrewsbury in 1285; see Sayles, op. cit. i. 144.
[2] Notably Henry III's Chancellor, Ralph Neville (1222–44).
[3] Sayles, op. cit. i, pp. cxli–cxliii, from *Anc. Corresp.* xxiv, no. 74.

molested, the queen mother has not been paid money assigned to her for payment of her debts to her merchants. Reginald de Grey prays the chancellor, 'upon whose friendship he entirely relies', to let him have a charter of which the king has informed him and adds that he is writing at the king's suggestion.[1] And letters about more important and complicated matters, upon which we cannot dwell, show how intimately the chancellor was involved in the daily problems of feudal society, and how well the magnates understood and co-operated in the mechanism of government.

Burnell was a strong chancellor and enjoyed the special friendship of the king, but it would be hard to discover in the records evidence that the co-operation of chancellor, judges, and the officials and clerks of the wardrobe in the royal household changed after his death. We know from the *articuli super cartas* of 1300 that some later tendencies were regarded with suspicion as dangerous innovations. The king was required, for example, to keep the chancery and the judges of the king's bench beside him so that he should always have with him men learned in the law, and be less tempted to issue writs at common law under the privy seal instead of through the chancery under the great seal, the use of which was hedged about by more authoritative experience and procedure; but we do not know whether the irregularities which this conservatism was intended to remove were serious, or even avoidable. They were a natural result of the Scottish wars, and, however inconvenient, might not have been noticed if relations between the hard-driven king and his magnates had not been strained. However this may be, the more frequent separation of the king from his great seal enables us to see more clearly how the normal system worked. The writs sent to the chancellor under the king's privy seal enhance our sense of the natural co-operation between Edward and his ministers. Thus. writing from Darlington in March 1302, the king returns the draft of certain letters to the pope. They please him well; the chancellor can go ahead, and hand them as soon as he can to the messenger of the bishop of Chester, one of the envoys to the court of Rome. As for the form which the chancellor has ordained about the Scottish business to be

---

[1] These instances have been taken, at random, from the *Calendar of Ancient Correspondence concerning Wales*, edited by J. G. Edwards (1935). They have no peculiar significance.

done by the bishop with the pope, the king, in view of the advice of the council, conveyed to him in a letter from his clerk John of Banstead, does not wish to proceed with it.[1] On another occasion Edward was so pleased with the draft of an important letter which had been submitted to him that, when he confirmed it, he declared that he held the treasurer and chancellor for prophets. They had ordered the thing as well as if St. John with the golden mouth (Chrysostom) had spoken. Things could not have been better done.[2]

So far as the general business of the realm was concerned, Edward, to the last days of his life, neither lost grip and interest nor made any change in his ways of co-operation with his counsellors, judges, and ministers.

It is, indeed, unsafe to identify the activities of the chancellor and the use of the great seal too closely with the chancery. Certainly the official home of the chancellor was the chancery. The annalist of Waverley tells how, after spending Christmas in 1279 with the chancellor at Winchester, Edward went off to hunt while Burnell returned to London 'as to the fixed place where those who seek writs and pursue their rights might find the appropriate remedy'.[3] When he was not on a political mission or visiting his diocese or on vacation in Acton Burnell, the great chancellor was at court, and to be at court meant to be with his clerical staff in chancery, generally near the king if not actually at his side. In his time royal letters, it is true, were enrolled in the wardrobe just as the letters under the great seal were enrolled in the chancery, but that the wardrobe had its own records (other than the rolls of household accounts) does not imply that the chancellor was any the less the king's chief minister. Some business was so secret that, though it required the issue of documents under the great seal, these were not enrolled on the chancery rolls but in the wardrobe; some were

---

[1] *Cal. Chancery Warrants, 1244–1326*, pp. 160–1.

[2] Ibid., p. 255, 28 July 1306, from Thirsk. The letter, as finally delivered, survives—and may be read in the *Foedera*, 1. ii. 991. The vice-chancellor of the Church of Rome had pleaded for certain burgesses of Bayonne who were in an English prison. He had apparently suggested that they should be sent to Gascony through France; this, says the letter, would be unsafe 'nor would our *consilium* persuade us to do it'. Note that the letter, as sent, was dated Thirsk, 28 July, the day and place of authorization under privy seal. This was the practice and reminds us that a royal letter was not necessarily written or dispatched from the place or on the day stated.

[3] *Ann. monastici*, ii. 393.

so secret that even the chancery clerks could not be allowed to know what the documents contained.[1]

Burnell was a great man, so trusted with the cognizance of affairs that even in the transaction of chancery business he might naturally revert to the original function of the chancellor as a personal secretary of the king; but also so close to the king that he, like his less important successors, was Edward's servant rather than the head of a 'constitutional' department of state. We are far removed from the atmosphere of the Provisions of Oxford. It may be true that 'we can trace the removal of Burnell's influence in the more peremptory attitude which the king assumed after his death', but 'the removal of the minister only sharpens the edge of the king's zeal'. His 'continual intelligent supervision' was his own; it directed Burnell's labours and did not vacillate nor change its course after his death.[2]

Burnell was neither a Wolsey nor a Walpole, but he was Edward's best-loved servant, as Otto of Granson was his most trusted friend. In a long and encouraging letter to these two men during their mission to France and Gascony in 1278, the king declared that he had no one about him who understood or could do his will better and to greater advantage than they, not even if he were to attend in person to the matters entrusted to them. He bids them show the faith of St. Mary, the Lord's mother, rather than the hesitation of St. Thomas the Apostle; for he would never for any cause wish to change what they did; he will see to it that their deeds are firmly held, for he deems them to be his own rather than theirs.[3] However resolute, however determined to go through to the end Edward might be, he could never again feel so safe as he felt during the long companionship with Burnell.

The future bishop and chancellor was born at Acton Burnell in Shropshire, a manor held of the Corbet barony by a senior branch of his family. The younger branch to which he belonged seems also to have had lands there. His parentage, the date of his birth, and the kind of education which he had are all obscure. He was a self-made man who, like Geoffrey, the first Scrope of Masham in the next century, and many more, built up a wide-

---

[1] Tout, op. cit. ii. 79-80 and note; and the secret injunctions, dated 15 December 1291, in *Cal. Chancery Warrants, 1244-1326*, p. 31.

[2] Stubbs, *Const. Hist.* ii. 309.   [3] *Cal. Close Rolls, 1272-9*, p. 493.

spread complex of landed property by purchase, exchange, the conversion of loans, and other ways in the course of a prosperous career. He may have entered the Lord Edward's service when the prince's household was given an independent status in 1254. He was certainly one of his clerks in 1260 when he went with him to Gascony. By 1266 he had acquired the manor of Acton Burnell, which henceforward became his chief seat where he built a manor house with a noble hall, not unlike the hall he built as bishop at Wells. He was allowed to have his fair and market and to enclose a large park. When he died he had lands in fifteen English shires, in London, and in Ireland, and the acquisition before 1284 of the barony of Castle Holgate on the other side of Wenlock Edge enabled him to pass on his estates as a barony to his nephew Philip.[1] Other centres of well-furnished domesticity were Condover, Wolverhampton, and, especially, Boreham in Essex, which he had got by 1278. He preferred to found a family by investments in land rather than to amass wealth, as Henry III's famous clerk, John Mansel, had done, by the accumulation of prebends and other benefices. He was a shrewd business man, perhaps not over scrupulous, a man of fine intelligence though of no great learning, and he certainly earned, by his services to the Crown, all that he got. He was not the type of ecclesiastic whom popes were willing to accept as an archbishop of Canterbury and, to Edward's chagrin though not, it would seem, to his surprise, papal confirmation of this high office was twice refused him; but he was a competent, though masterful, bishop of Bath and Wells (1275–92), and he had the confidence and esteem of most men. As one of Edward's proctors or trustees he looked after his lord's interests and helped to rule the country during his absence on crusade, he took his part in securing the quiet passage of the crown after King Henry's death, and, when the new king arrived in 1274, he was made chancellor. We have already seen something of his influence in this capacity, and of his activity in the affairs of state, both in England and in France and Gascony. And, as we turn to the achievements of Edward as a legislator and administrator and conquerer, we should never forget that, at every step, he had Burnell at his side.

[1] The barony became extinct in 1420. The story of Burnell's personal, as distinct from his official, career has been told, in an unpublished dissertation, by Ursula W. Hughes.

In the years before the Hundred Years War, clerical advisers and agents whose memories went back to the time of Edward I looked back to it 'as the one understandable period in their official careers', when plans could be made effective and things could be done.[1] They doubtless had too rosy a view, but in the main they were right. King Edward was well served, and especially happy in his relations with his servants during the sixteen years after his coronation when Burnell was chancellor, and the class of 'king's clerks', to which Burnell belonged, was busy in all sorts of ways and even conscious of itself as the *élite* element in the personnel of royal administration. These men regarded themselves as the mainstay of a commonwealth in which the interests of Church and king were combined, and at least one pope saw in them the chief cause of indifference to his demand that more respect should be paid to ecclesiastical liberties.[2] Their importance in the royal household becomes very clear in Henry III's reign and many of them continued to serve his son, though Edward seems to have relied especially upon those who had acquired experience in his own household. They were recruited in various ways, some from the royal demesne, others from the households of prelates and barons, others, whose services might be intermittent rather than continuous, because they had attracted the casual notice of the king. Some of them were graduates of the universities and other schools, notably of the canon and civil law, and owed their start in administrative life to the recommendation of patrons; but it would be impossible to divide the king's clerks into distinct groups. They were members of a closely knit society of clerics and laymen, had local attachments as landholders and incumbents, passed from department to department, formed their own circles of influential friends and useful adherents and, according to their capacity, did all kinds of work in the royal service. Some rose very high, others remained obscure. During Edward's reign some fifty prelates were consecrated as bishops

[1] Cuttino has compiled from the *Calendar of Chancery Warrants* a list of 135 king's clerks in Edward's reign who were both men of substance and entrusted with significant business. See 'The King's Clerks and the Community of the Realm' in *Speculum*, xxix (1954), 395-409.

[2] See *Henry III and the Lord Edward*, ii. 715-16, and William of Hotham's remarks on the opinion of Pope Nicholas IV in his letter to Prior Eastry of Canterbury in October 1289: 'Dominus papa conqueritur de clericis regis nostri quod suis non obtemperant mandatis' (*Hist. MSS. Com., Report on Various Collections*, i (1901), 256). Cf. above, p. 261.

of English and Welsh sees, and of these seven or eight had been king's clerks. Five of the fifteen men who sat at some time or other in the king's bench as judges and counsellors first appear on the records as king's clerks.[1] In short, the body of royal clerks, so far as the term 'body' is applicable, was just a responsible element (distinguished from the host of clerks in the administrative service of king, prelates, magnates, central and local officials, boroughs, and merchants) in the higher service of the Crown. What was true of the king's clerk is true also of judges and of the king's more intimate advisers and companions among the laity. The judges of the king's bench had reached the top of the legal profession, but not one of them 'was allowed to concentrate his undivided attention upon the work for which he was nominally paid or even upon judicial business in general'.[2] He might be called upon to assess and collect subsidies, act as a commissioner of array, fix boundaries, and inspect rivers, as well as attend parliament, administer Scotland, or go abroad on a diplomatic mission, just as a king's clerk might be the companion of a great baron on embassy to the papal court or a tour of inspection in Gascony. And this disregard of specialization was as natural in war as in peace. The distribution of emphasis was different in war, but from the administrative standpoint the conquest of Wales or Scotland was a particularly strenuous and closely combined activity of the multifarious royal household.

Edward found much to do in England after his return and coronation. He worked with a keen and expectant body of men. The core of his administrative service was composed of those who, headed by the new chancellor, had maintained his interests at home and those whose loyalty had been strengthened in companionship with him on his pilgrimage. From the first he sought in parliament the scene and sanction of his activities.

Sixteen or seventeen assemblies which can be described as parliaments had been gathered together in England between the battle of Evesham and the death of Henry III. Until the summer of 1270 these had been concerned with problems of settlement, the legislation at Marlborough in 1267, the incidence of the twentieth (the first general subsidy since the year

---

[1] Sayles, op. cit. i, p. lxiii, and the biographical notices which precede. Eight of the fifteen were laymen, seven were clerks.
[2] Ibid., p. lxv. The whole passage (pp. lxv–lxvii) is illuminating.

1237), and the departure of Edward on crusade. They had met in various places and at various times of year, only latterly in London; but the fact that, in the three last years of the reign (1270-2), a Michaelmas parliament had met at Westminster suggests a return to an earlier tendency. King Edward summoned parliaments, almost certainly with deliberate intention, to meet after Easter and Michaelmas in nearly every year between 1274 and 1286.[1] The practice was resumed in 1290, after his return from Gascony. The routine of parliament twice a year in the late spring and late autumn, in rhythm with the busiest periods of the financial year, was interrupted after 1294, but, beneath the irregularities of times and places, its tenacity can be observed in the later middle ages, notably in the reigns of Edward II and Richard II. On the other hand, it is unwise to turn what had begun as a convenient practice in the middle of the thirteenth century into a principle. It prevailed regularly only for a few years in the reign of Edward I and its regularity in these years was probably due more to the king's orderly mind than to any other cause.[2]

This is more than a surmise suggested by the facts, for Edward revealed something of his mind in a letter to Pope Gregory X written in June 1275, after his first parliament had dispersed. The pope had demanded payment of arrears of the *census* or annual payment promised by King John, and had been told

[1] The assembly which met at Westminster on 13 January 1273, not long after King Henry's death, was summoned to give formal and public adhesion to the new king, and is mentioned only by the annalist of Winchester (*Ann. monast.* ii. 113). It consisted of magnates and representatives of shires and cities. The bishops met separately in council with the new archbishop, Kilwardby. The first parliament of Edward I met after Easter in 1275.

[2] The phrases 'Easter parliament' and 'Michaelmas parliament' should not be interpreted literally. They refer to terms rather than precise dates. Even when we know that a parliament was summoned to begin three weeks after Easter it should not be assumed that it actually began on that day. Thus the Easter parliament of 1290 was to have met on 22 April, three weeks after Easter, but it certainly did not open before 28 April, after the King's return to Westminster. It was in session on 10 May (cf. the reference to the vigil of the Ascension in *Rotuli Parliamentorum*, i. 32) and right through to 8 July, on which day, 'in parliamento . . . post Pascha', the statute of *Quia Emptores* was conceded. It continued still longer, probably to receive the knights of the shire summoned for 15 July (see Richardson and Sayles in *Bull. of Inst. of Hist. Research*, v. 144). Hence the view that there was a parliament at Easter followed by another at Whitsuntide and yet another in July is an illusion (cf. below, p. 379). This 'Easter parliament' began shortly before Ascension Day and lasted till the seventh Sunday after Trinity, 16 July, if not longer. The King left Westminster on 21 July. Stubbs, it should be added, saw part of the truth, but not the whole (*Constitutional History*, ii. 126); cf. *E.H.R.* lxv (1951), 109.

that, as the king had but recently undertaken the government of his realm he would reserve consideration of the papal request until the council of the great men (*proceres*) in parliament 'which is usually celebrated in England about the octaves of the Resurrection' (i.e. a week after Easter Sunday). In the letter of June 1275 Edward explains that parliament had met and that he had dealt during its sessions with many matters which concerned the amelioration of the state of the English Church and the reform of the realm, but that, before the matter of the *census* could be decided, illness had compelled him to dissolve it. He would certainly take counsel with the prelates and magnates concerning the papal petition in the next parliament which he intended to celebrate before Michaelmas. The promise does not express an intention to hold two annual parliaments, but the previous reference to a customary parliament after Easter seems to imply such an intention. Moreover, in the letter, Edward defined his relation to parliament. Without the counsel of the prelates and magnates, he wrote, he could not give the pope an answer, for he was bound by his coronation oath to preserve uninjured the rights of the realm and, without such counsel, to do nothing which affected the crown of the realm.[1] This statement does not stand alone and should be accepted as an expression of Edward's sense of his royal obligations.

Edward's first parliament (April 1275) was officially described as a 'general' parliament, for it comprised representatives of shires and other communities.[2] This implication of the term 'general' was not made clear until 1910 when some writs and returns were discovered. Similarly only a single writ, addressed to the sheriff of Kent, shows that the second parliament of the year was also a general parliament; indeed the grant of a fifteenth of all movable goods by prelates, barons, 'and others of the realm'—the first parliamentary tax of the reign—suggests that this was the case.[3] The scarcity of evidence,

[1] The letter is printed in *Parliamentary Writs*, i. 381, from the Patent Roll. See *Cal. Pat. Rolls (1272–81)*, pp. 197–8. Although Edward refers to the coming parliament as before Michaelmas, it had already been fixed for the fortnight after Michaelmas (cf. *Cal. Close Rolls (1272–9)*, p. 167).

[2] The first intention had been to hold this parliament a fortnight after the feast of the Purification of the Virgin (i.e. 16 February) with prelates and magnates, but it was postponed, probably because of the decision to summon knights and burgesses.

[3] H. Jenkinson in *E.H.R.* xxv (1910), 231 ff.; Stubbs, *Const. Hist.* ii. 235; for the fifteenth, *Cal. Close Rolls (1272–9)*, pp. 250–1. On the whole subject of Edward's

the various expedients adopted to raise money, and the laxity with which the term parliament was used make it advisable to postpone to a later chapter consideration of the part of the commons in these assemblies and of the connexion between finance and the development of parliament. In the period with which we are concerned only three taxes were granted, the fifteenth of 1275, a thirtieth granted in the anomalous provincial assemblies at York and Northampton early in 1283, and a fifteenth in 1290. The first and third were required to help to meet the debts incurred by the king during his absences abroad, the second to contribute to the extraordinary expenditure caused by the war in Wales. Each was granted in the presence of commons as well as magnates. It would be rash to assume that knights and burgesses were absent from other parliaments of which only scanty evidence survives. They were present in the first parliament of 1275, though no tax was granted, and in the parliament at Shrewsbury on 30 September 1283 to be spectators of the grim fate of David of Wales. All the same, they were not yet by any means an essential element in the assemblies which met so regularly for the transaction of public business and the consent to legislative acts.

Parliament is a general word, used throughout western Europe in a diversity of context. In England it had come to mean the king in council in a gathering of wider scope. It implied the presence of the king and we may assume that any parliament held in the king's absence would be held only by his command.[1] It implied also the presence of council and especially of the judicial element without which business in council could hardly be done. It invested time and place with a sanctity greater than that of the special peace which prevailed within the verge of the king's court. By the middle of Edward's reign obligations which in course of time were to grow into the

parliaments see H. G. Richardson and G. Sayles in the *Bulletin of Inst. of Hist. Research*, v (1928), 129 ff. They incline to the interpretation of the word 'general' adopted above in the text.

[1] During Edward's absence in 1286-9 only one parliament, that of Easter 1289, is known to have been held, but the king's lieutenant, Edmund of Cornwall, sat regularly at Westminster, with other members of the council, in the regular law terms and dealt with matters which might normally have come before parliament (Richardson and Sayles, op. cit., pp. 141-2). Since during these years cases were often deferred till the next parliament, I am inclined to think, in view of the poverty of evidence in this period, that the parliament of 1289 was not 'quite exceptional'.

'privileges of parliament' were well established. Persons who came to parliament were to come unarmed: they were there on the king's business no less than on their own; hence they were under special protection, and were immune. An officer of the law who served a writ upon them did so at his peril. These characteristics point to the fact that parliament developed from the solemn activities of the king in council, and the earliest records of proceedings in parliament show that the activities were, in the main, of a judicial nature. From this point of view, the grant of a tax, or the promulgation of a statute, or the discussion of a political issue was not essential to a parliament. The king in council in times of parliament dealt with matters which had been reserved for consideration there because for some reason they required the personal cognizance of the king, or because the king wished to have at his side responsible advisers in strength or had been too busy or occupied to deal with them earlier and had postponed them to a period of clearance when he would be free.

We may recognize the truth of all this and yet feel that we might easily take too rigid and pedantic an attitude to parliament. Edward and his advisers entered quite naturally into a traditional inheritance of loose texture. As we have seen he regarded his first parliament and looked forward to his second as an opportunity for the settlement of important public matters, as well as an occasion when judicial difficulties could be resolved and petitioners be satisfied. We may well believe that the request for his first subsidy was in his mind the most important business in his second parliament. We may be sure, that when a third parliament was interposed at Gloucester in 1278 between the Easter and Michaelmas parliaments at Westminster for the consideration of an important statute, there was some good reason for the decision, though we may not be able to see 'why the business was not allowed to come before the Michaelmas parliament'. Contemporaries do not appear to have used the word parliament with a regard for technical niceties, just as sometimes they regarded an undoubted parliament as significant because something was done then which did not loom large in the actual proceedings. The one thing done in the Lent parliament of 1305 'that all the chroniclers have thought worthy of note' was an ordinance of trailbaston. 'Indeed a certain annalist speaks of this year as the year of trailbaston.' This measure against felons and trespassers, however drastic, was taken by the king in virtue of his ordinary powers. It was a judicial commission instructed to deal with the scoundrels who had disturbed the land in an anxious time.[1] The men of the shires and boroughs and the gossips who talked to annalists interpreted what they had heard in the light of what they saw. Moreover, any large and impressive assembly which met under royal authority could be a parliament to them, though it might meet in a strange place at an odd time for unusual business. And, at the other end of the scale, royal officials were not fastidious. A deputy justice in north Wales quite naturally refers to the great council summoned by the king in 1291 to deal with the earls of Gloucester and Hereford as the parliament at Abergavenny.[2] He was concerned with other business which had been done there, the time was three weeks after Michaelmas, the occasion highly judicial; what else could it be but a parliament?

Much of the business done in parliament is indistinguishable from that which, as we have already seen, was done or at least discussed by the king in council. The earliest records of parliament are very like the few memoranda which survive earlier of proceedings in council, though these are more appropriately described as *agenda* than as *acta*.[3] The significance of parliament lay not so much in the particular acts as in the concentration of them in a formal and public occasion. These periodical stock-takings were expressions of the cohesion between king, prelates, barons, ministers of state, judges, and, when they were represented, the local communities. They had within them the promise of development. One thing could lead to another; a single problem might suggest a general order and lead to a statute. Foreigners and Englishmen came together in a common forum. As we try to recapture the atmosphere of these gatherings,

---

[1] Maitland, *Memoranda de Parliamento*, p. liii. On the commissions of trailbaston see Helen Cam, *Studies in the Hundred Rolls* (1921), pp. 73–79. G. O. Sayles sees a 'change in social attitudes' between 1286 and 1304 for which he blames the indifference of the king: *Select Cases in the Court of King's Bench*, iv (Selden Society, lxxiv, 1957), pp. lii–lvii.

[2] *Calendar of Ancient Correspondence concerning Wales*, edited by J. G. Edwards, p. 134.

[3] Cf. Treharne, *The Baronial Plan of Reform*, pp. 407–11 (1262); Sayles in *E.H.R.* xl (1925), 583–5, of the year 1268, discussed in *King Henry III and the Lord Edward*, ii. 563 note; Cole, *Documents illustrative of English History*, pp. 358–60, drafts of instructions for the proctors going to the general council at Lyons, and cognate matters.

the details become more real in their casual context. The background is not a scene of conscious struggle so much as a crowded canvas of men and women depicted in their relations with the Crown. Let us look, for example, at the memoranda of the Easter parliament of 1279, the earliest surviving record of its kind.[1]

By the king's special grace the men of Douai are allowed to trade their cloth freely in the fairs of Boston and St. Ives. The concession leads to a unanimous agreement (*unanimiter concordatum fuu*) in parliament about the lawful measures of foreign cloth. An inquiry is ordered into the alleged duty of German merchants in London to contribute towards the upkeep of the city walls. The justices on eyre in Kent are given an additional colleague and the king orders that the itinerant justices in general should be paid their stipends. The king's brother, Edmund of Lancaster, testifies that a landholder, who presumably had seen service in Wales, ought to be allowed his scutage, and it is allowed. Four suits (*loquelae*) affecting the master of the Temple, then before the famous judge, Ralph de Hengham, are postponed for consideration in the Michaelmas parliament; here we have parliament as the highest expression of royal justice. The prior of the cathedral convent of Carlisle appears; he and the canons have been guilty of an enormity which they had regarded too lightly, and they were to be thoroughly frightened; the damages to the king were estimated at the fantastic total of one hundred thousand pounds. They had elected a bishop after seeking and receiving the royal licence to elect, but their choice, the dean of York, had declined the dignity, and without seeking a fresh licence they had first elected another man, and then, in spite of the royal prohibition conveyed to them by two royal judges, they had re-elected him They were guilty of a contempt which, if it were not corrected, might have very serious consequences, obvious enough in royal circles if not at Carlisle. So the prior appears and submits himself to the king's will. He and the convent, he says, believe that legally, after the dean had refused, matters stood where they were—in technical language *res integra fuit*—

---

[1] First printed by E. F. Jacob, with a commentary, at the end of his paper on the reign of Henry III in the *Trans. R. Hist. Soc.*, 4th series, x (1928), 48–53; again edited by Richardson and Sayles in their *Rotuli Parliamentorum Angliae hactenus inediti* (Camden Soc., 1935), pp. 1–7. This volume contains an account of the development of the memoranda of parliamentary business.

but if they had been guilty of contempt, he submits. The new archbishop-elect of Dublin, the famous Dominican John of Darlington, formerly Henry III's confessor and long well known to King Edward, appears to swear fealty to the king— the terms of the oath are copied into our record—and in return receives his temporalities from the king. This was on 27 April, and one entry shows the king's council still tidying up the business of parliament after the king had left England on his short visit to Amiens and Ponthieu in the middle of May. In the interval Edward and his advisers had dealt at length, as they often had to deal, with the troublesome quarrels between the merchants of Holland and the English.

Edward, like his father and grandfather before him, took a lively interest in all legal and administrative matters, and, unlike them, enjoyed more confidence. What share the prelates and barons took in these proceedings it is harder to say. The record refers to unanimous decisions in parliament but does not say who made them. We do not know what full assemblies were held with the magnates nor the extent to which they were responsible for the distribution of business among judges and commissioners and others, while we may be sure that the king's ministers and intimate counsellors and judges took a hand.[1] Yet the concentration in one place and at one time of vigorous persons who were not wont to remain dumb or afraid to speak their minds must gradually have developed a greater sense of solidarity among them and prepared the way for the later house of peers with judicial and other rights of its own.[2]

Some of the entries on the two membranes of parchment which contain the notes of proceedings in the Easter parliament of 1279 are concerned with petitions, but they cannot have been all the petitions presented in this parliament. The number of petitions which poured in was already so embarrassing that in the next year the king provided a remedy for the 'frequent delays and disturbances' which they caused the persons who came to parliament. Henceforth only those petitions which could not be answered without the king were to be brought by the chancellor and other high officers before king and council: 'So the king and his council can attend to the great business

---

[1] For this indispensable element in parliament see Richardson and Sayles, 'The King's Ministers in Parliament, 1272-1377', in *E.H.R.* xlvi (1931), 529-50.

[2] Cf. Barnaby C. Keeney, *Judgment by Peers* (1949), pp. 81-97 *passim*.

(*busoignes*) of his realm and of his outlying (*foreines*) lands and not be burdened by other business.' Here the king reasserts his view that the settlement of public business is his most important function in council in parliament. None the less, the hearing of petitions continued to take up much, if not most, of his time. The memoranda of the Lent parliament of 1305 make this clear. Batches of petitions were brought before him. As each was considered, a note of the decision was made on its back. Later the substance of the petition and a statement of the action taken or to be taken was written on the memoranda or parliament roll. An original petition which has survived, one of a batch of thirty-two, is also endorsed: 'These thirty-two were expedited before the king on the first Sunday in Lent.'[1] In the meanwhile panels of 'triers' were at work on other bundles of petitions which had been sorted before parliament opened into their classes, Gascon, Scottish, Irish, and English. If an ordinance of 1293 was still in force the last class was subdivided for the consideration of chancery, exchequer, and the justices, but on this matter no information is given. It is probable that from about 1290 each panel of triers compiled its own roll. The clerk of parliament kept a roll, more complete than the casual memoranda of earlier years, of other proceedings before the council in parliament. This roll recorded 'pleas', for parliament was a court and a great deal of administrative business arose from judicial proceedings and from the consideration of legal problems. As they get larger, the rolls of parliament tend to become more formal than the earlier agenda and acta of council. For 'big business' such as statutes, taxation, treaties, and the like, we have as a rule to look elsewhere. Records of these matters were doubtless kept, but they 'were never put together on a single roll'.[2]

---

[1] *Memoranda de Parl.* (1305), p. 48. It should be emphasized that this parliament roll (no. 12), now so well known in Maitland's brilliant edition, does not contain all the proceedings in parliament nor has it always been in its present form. It describes action on petitions brought before the king in council, and pleas. Stray membranes from other rolls relating to petitions, considered by, for example, triers of Scottish petitions, have been inserted in it in modern times. See Richardson and Sayles in *Bulletin of Institute of Hist. Research*, vi (1929), 149–50.

[2] *Bulletin*, op. cit., p. 143. The 'statute roll', for example, took definite shape in 1299. It is worth the student's while to study the masterly pages in Stubbs, *Const. Hist.* ii. 275–9, and Maitland's introduction to the *Memoranda* of 1305, and then to proceed to the papers of Richardson and Sayles. Cf. also the work of L. Ehrlich, *Proceedings against the Crown* (1921), especially pp. 83–110. Ehrlich's

The gradual but steady emergence of the multifarious records of parliament in Edward's reign and the regulation of petitions should not lead us to isolate developments either in place or time, nor to interpret them only in the light of a future known to us but not to the participants in all this activity. The view, for example, that petitions were brought to parliament by knights and burgesses and that the presence of these elements, when they were present, was primarily due to the king's desire to concentrate study of the grievances of his subjects so that he could survey the social situation of his realm is entirely discredited.[1] Petitions were made by all sorts of people and communities and about all sorts of things, big and little, trivial and serious, in error and misapprehension and in the stress of urgent need. They were not encouraged by the Crown but by the fact that at certain times of the year it was convenient to hold a parliament. When, three weeks before parliament met on 28 February 1305, the king ordered a proclamation to be made in the Great Hall of Westminster and in four other places in London about the deliverance of petitions and to whom they should be delivered, he was seeking to anticipate and canalize the flood of grievances, not to incite it. Common petitions, of the type of the baronial articles of 1258 and the petitions of grievances by the clergy, were few in Edward's reign, and precedents for the petitions of the 'commons' in parliament— the petitions which later were to lead to the process of parliamentary legislation by bill—are negligible. The rise of the house of commons was hastened by this later practice but did not originate in it.

Legislation in Edward I's time, indeed, was largely influenced by complaints, and a petition in parliament might lead to an ordinance of general import,[2] but this relation between grievance and statute, as will be shown, must be traced on the whole in the experience of judges and in the records of investigation into particular kinds of plaints by special commissions of

contention that an entirely new development in the history of petitions began in 1274 should be approached with caution.

[1] G. L. Haskins, 'The Petitions of Representatives in the Parliaments of Edward I', in *E.H.R.* liii (1938), 1-20.

[2] Below, p. 370. Cf. the reply to the petition of the warden of Jersey and Guernsey in 1305 on behalf of the men of the Channel Islands, who were being summoned to appear before ecclesiastical courts in Normandy by the bishop of Coutances (in whose diocese the islands lay): 'Coram rege. Responsum est quod fiat prohibicio regia in generali', &c. (*Rotuli inediti*, pp. 53, 54).

inquiry, notably those of 1274. In short, the careful regard to and regulation of petitions in Edward I's parliaments must be considered as part of the impressive attack made by the king and his advisers upon problems of administration, not as something new and strange. A young and vigorous prince returned after a long absence to a realm which still bore the scars of civil strife. His trusty caretakers had eagerly awaited his arrival. He had already made a start in Gascony and heavy tasks must now be faced in England. He had seen much in the east and had spent many weeks as the guest of Charles of Anjou and Pope Gregory X. He was an observant man, and, for all we know, had talked about the ways in which things were done in other lands, the way, for example, in which petitions were regulated at the papal court and in the Sicilian kingdom;[1] but, none the less, he came back to old and familiar things.

The plaint was perhaps the oldest and most familiar of all, for to seek justice at the source of justice is natural to man in human society. The provision of legal remedies can never satisfy this need; the law always lags behind. Edward himself was never entirely free of the simplest of all plaints, the oral petition of one man to another. The investigation into grievances implies recognition of this fact, as the process of 'appeal' in criminal cases implies it. A local jury collects evidence from injured parties or the protector of a wounded man 'appeals' on his behalf to the coroners in the county court;[2] neither kind of procedure differs at bottom from the case of the bewildered victim of circumstance who somehow finds a good Samaritan to get his petition through to the king, so that it may be examined, or 'tried' in time of parliament, and some form of dealing with it may be ordered. Many victims of injustice or tyranny doubtless never got relief; many of the clamours were doubtless fraudulent; but in one form or another the plaint can be found in our thirteenth-century courts, local and central, private and royal. Some were caught up into the technicalities of common-law procedure 'without writ'.[3] These for the most

---

[1] Ehrlich (op. cit., pp. 92–94) calls attention to the careful regulation of procedure on petitions in Hungary, Sicily, and, as the exemplar, the papal court, in the time of our Henry III.

[2] Cf. Helen Cam on the plaint before the coroner in the county court, *The Hundred and the Hundred Rolls* (1930), p. 114.

[3] See Richardson and Sayles, *Select Cases of Procedure without Writ under Henry III* (Selden Society, 1941).

part were probably oral plaints, but, in a land where the written *libellus* of the canon-law procedure was widely understood, it is likely that many were written. Other forms of plaint were encouraged by the investigation in 1258-60 into plaints of local grievances against sheriffs, bailiffs, and other royal and baronial officials, though the novelty of this famous reform lay rather in its comprehensiveness than in its resort to new expedients. It was a natural development of a movement expressed in the *capitula* of the general eyre of 1254.[1] The importance of the *querela* or complaint as a source of evidence has been overshadowed by an unreal debate on the origin of the written petition. Attention has been concentrated so much on the appearance in large numbers of the bill or written petition that the existence of petitions in earlier times has even been denied.

The 'critical and reforming impulse' which can be traced in England from the days of Henry III's minority and came to a head in the years 1254-60 was bound to find expression during the years of the chaotic aftermath of war when the cardinal-legate Ottobuono and all the forces of statesmanship and good-will were trying to restore the realm to conditions of unity, order, and peace. The task was twofold, the maintenance of royal rights and the suppression of abuses. During the four or five years (1274-9) after Edward's return to England the king and his ministers were intensely active; but they were active in well-known ways.

We may take as a starting-point a royal proclamation of the duties of the justices in eyre after the parliament of Gloucester in the summer of 1278:

We have appointed these our justices to hear and determine pleas of liberties in accordance with the provision and ordinances made thereon; and, according to the law and custom of the realm and the ordinance which we have made and our statutes and the articles delivered and enjoined upon them (the justices), to hear and fittingly amend the complaints (*querelae*) of all complainants and of those who wish to complain both against our ministers and bailiffs whosoever they may be, and against the ministers and bailiffs of others and against others whosoever they may be, also complaints of any kind.[2]

This statement links recent action with past practice. The

[1] Cam, *Studies in the Hundred Rolls* (1921), pp. 22-25.

[2] Translated from the writ publicly announcing the commission to the men of the shires, printed by Cam (*Studies*, p. 57) from the Patent Roll, in this case to the three northern shires.

'pleas of liberties' or investigations into franchises had just been prescribed in the first part of the statutes of Gloucester, and will require our attention in due course. The abuse of franchises and the right to enjoy them had been one of the objects of inquiry into facts in 1274-5, and had already been the object of inquiry in 1255;[1] in a less systematic way than the new statutes intended the exchequer and justices had been familiar with these matters judicially since the days of Henry III's minority. The proclamation of 1278 then deals with the *querelae* or complaints made in reply to the rest of the investigation in 1274-5. In hearing these the justices in eyre were to have regard not only to the returns to the inquiry (which they had with them) but to an ordinance, statutes, and to the articles of the eyre which had been enjoined upon them. The statutes were primarily those comprised in the long statute of Westminster of Easter 1275. Many of these were drafted with the terms of the inquiry in mind and in the light, we may believe, of the reports of the commissioners. The royal ordinance was almost certainly the so-called statute *de justiciis assignatis*, in fact an administrative order of uncertain date for the appointment of justices to hear and determine complaints against the king's officials and others of offences committed during the twenty-five years prior to Michaelmas 1276. The date suggests that, if the Welsh war had not intervened, general judicial proceedings upon the inquiry of 1274 and the statutes of 1275 would have begun in 1276 rather than two years later, and an injunction to justices contained in the statute of Gloucester goes to confirm this conclusion.[2]

Next we come to the articles of the eyre, that is to say, the long list of questions which local juries had to answer or try to answer. We may safely ascribe to this time the addition of two long series of articles to those which had been in use since 1254. Hence the distinction which was made from this time between the *vetera capitula*, about seventy in number, and the *nova capitula*. The latter, about seventy-five in all, comprised the articles of the inquiry of 1274 and a series of articles 'upon the statute', derived from the statute of Westminster of 1275. The intention

---

[1] Inserted in the annals of Burton (*Annales monastici*, i. 337; Cam, *Studies*, p. 13).

[2] Complaints against the king's bailiffs and bailiffs of others are to be dealt with according to the ordinance *before made* and according to the inquests *before taken*. The reference is clearly to *de justiciis assignatis* and to the returns to the inquest of 1274.

was to bring the articles of the eyre up to date and to ensure that the returns to the inquiry of 1274 and under the statute of Westminster should be followed up in subsequent judicial proceedings.[1] It was a clumsy device and involved some repetition, but the historian can learn from it what a logical and orderly conflation of the old and the new *capitula* might have obscured, namely, that Edward and his legal advisers were repeating in 1274-8 what Henry III and his legal advisers had done in 1254. Henry had driven his subjects hard in the year of the Gascon scare and of Edward's marriage and settlement, and in return had added to the *capitula* of this year 1254 a series of articles directed against official corruption. This fact clearly emerges from a comparison between the articles of previous eyres and the *capitula* of 1254. The reformers of 1258-60 carried the campaign farther. The new king carried it farther still and made it permanent by giving it statutory obligations. The general eyres, before they ceased to be, were supplemented by commissions of assize with more elastic powers, and by more frequent commissions of gaol delivery, oyer et terminer, trailbaston. The sheriffs and other local officials lost much of their power when, as in 1277, during the king's absence in Wales, and in 1286, when the king went abroad, elected keepers of the peace were established in numerous shires to assist in the maintenance of order, and when the successors of these *custodes pacis*, the justices of the peace, were given local judicial authority; but whoever sought out criminals or administered the law, the authority of the statutes, increasing in number, remained to give authority and to adjust the common law to new problems.[2]

Lastly, the instructions to the justices of 1278-80 enable us to

---

[1] In 1279 another important article, *de mutuis sacramentis*, was added. It had been discovered that malicious persons in many shires were conspiring to defeat the ends of justice, as well they might. The royal writ which led to this article anticipated a famous statute or ordinance about conspiracy (1305) which opens a vital chapter in our political as well as in our legal history. Cam, op. cit., pp. 58-59. A writ of conspiracy did not lie at common law before it was authorized by ordinance in 1293; see Sayles, *Select Cases in the Court of King's Bench*, vol. iii, pp. lvii ff., referring to *Rot. Parl.* i. 96.

[2] On the later developments until the middle of the fourteenth century see the interesting section in Cam, op. cit., pp. 72-83. The author points out (p. 81) that an important petition of the commons in parliament in 1362 includes a request that the articles of the eyre should be delivered to the justices of the peace in every county for publication to the local communities. The commons, though opposed to the general eyre, wished to maintain the tradition.

trace the transition from the unregulated *querela* of the previous
period to the written bill or petition presented to commissions,
the justices of the eyre, and the king in parliament. The
justices, we are told, were to hear and determine all kinds of
complaint (*quascunque querimonias*). They had long been wont
to listen to complaints and, at some stage in the hearing, oral
complaints must have been recorded. Hence, when they were
given a general instruction to hear them, it was a simple step
to require that they should be presented in writing. Complainants against the judges and other ministers of the Crown during
the investigations of 1289–93, after Edward's return from
Gascony, were explicitly instructed to come before the auditors
of plaints in the king's great chamber and to bring their
querelae in writing. A clerk was appointed to write bills for
complainants. By this time the presentation of 'bills in eyre'
seems to have been well established;[1] and, as we have already
seen, written petitions to the king in times of parliament had
become so numerous as to require regulation.[2]

Inquests into rights and grievances, replies to the articles of
the eyre, and the 'trial' of petitions in parliament sharpened the
awareness of councillors and judges to the legal, social, and
economic problems which were faced in the Edwardian
statutes. They help the historian to see the background of
parliament, to breathe the air in times of parliament, and to
appreciate the elasticity of mind in legal and administrative
circles. The statutes were not the outcome of systematic reflection about first principles, pursued in learned ease. They were
intended to meet practical difficulties within the ambit of the
common law. They reflect the experience of their begetters. A
brief study of their careers and of their relations with other
men of the world would show the judges to have been as much
at home with squires and bailiffs in the country-side, and with
merchants and foreign bankers in ports and cities, as they were
in the king's chamber and their own courts. In parliament they
met, as men of experience in public affairs, with other councillors, prelates, magnates, and royal clerks; but they were

---

[1] See Richardson and Sayles, *Select Cases of Procedure without Writ*, pp. xlv–lxviii,
on the history of the written plaint; and W. C. Bolland, *Select Bills in Eyre*, on the
procedure in dealing with such bills; also Helen Cam, *Studies*, pp. 133–8, on the
importance of the instructions to the justices in 1278.

[2] Above, p. 348.

there also as experts, with a special duty to give advice on the matters reserved for the king's decision; and when they helped to draft statutes, they gave the highest expression to the king's will as the source of justice.[1] The promulgation of statutes in parliament was, in fact if not in theory, a judicial act, the outcome of garnered experience. It was a generalization of the peculiar functions of the king in council in parliament as a court of law, where, in the words of the contemporary law book, 'judicial doubts are determined, new remedies are prescribed for new injuries, and justice is done to everyone according to his deserts.'[2] It was no accident that the first clerk of the parliament, Gilbert of Rothbury, was a judge.[3]

The Edwardian statutes, therefore, should be considered from two related points of view, first in the light of the circumstances which led to them, secondly as a body of legal material, the expression of a changing attitude to law. Both points of view are suggested by a brief analysis of the external relations between the statutes, as distinct from their contents. For example, legislation about distraint or the right of distress in the statute of Westminster in 1275 resumes a matter which looms large in the statute of Marlborough (1267) and leads us on, by way of the statute known as 'distresses of the exchequer' (Michaelmas 1275), to the treatment of distraint in the second statute of Westminster (1285). The legislation about debts in the first statute of Westminster was followed up in the so-called 'statute' of Rhuddlan (1284), also, in the interests of merchants, in the statute of Acton Burnell (Michaelmas 1283) and the statute of merchants of 1285, which is explicitly said to be a clarification of the statute of Acton Burnell. The first part of

[1] Cf. above, p. 334. Ralph de Hengham, who began his career as clerk to one of Henry III's judges, was a writer of tracts on procedure. A professional lawyer, he was at the same time the greatest and most forthright of Edward's judges. He was a well-known pluralist, and caused the ecclesiastics of the diocese of Worcester much concern when his pluralism was discussed before the bishop of Worcester in his council at Hartlebury in December 1303. It was decided that it would be inexpedient to proceed against him, for he was a member of the king's council. See Sayles, *Select Cases in the Court of King's Bench*, vol. i, pp. lxxiv–lxxv.

[2] This passage from *Fleta* may be compared with the second statute of Westminster (1285), c. 24, on writs *in consimili casu*. If N. Denholm-Young's attractive identification of the author of *Fleta* is correct, the book was written in the Fleet prison between 1290 and 1292 by the lawyer Matthew de Scaccario (*Collected Papers on Medieval Subjects*, pp. 68–79).

[3] Sayles, op. cit., vol. i, p. lxi. Gilbert was appointed in 1290 and still held office in 1307. From 1290 to 1295 he was also clerk of the king's council.

the statute of Gloucester (1278), on the claims to franchises, was a natural consequence of the events of 1274–5, and the uncertainty which it produced was met by the statute of *Quo Warranto* (1290). The provisions in the second statute of Westminster in 1285 are said in their preamble to be a continuation of the statute of Gloucester, that is, of the discursive decrees which follow the part about franchises; while the statute *Quia Emptores* (July 1290), issued at the instance of the magnates, may be regarded as a belated hang-over from the same period of legislative activity. Indeed, it is probable that, but for the Welsh wars and Edward's long absence in Gascony, the statutes issued between the years 1275 and 1290 would all have been crowded into five and not distributed over fifteen years. The one exception is the series of police regulations known as the statute of Winchester (Michaelmas 1285), which was clearly connected with Edward's intention, announced in the previous Easter parliament, to go abroad on Gascon and other business.[1] Finally, it is significant of the unity ascribed to this body of material that in September of the same year the statutes of Westminster of 1275 and 1285, the statute of Gloucester, and the statute of merchants were sent together to the justiciar of Ireland, where they were to be proclaimed and observed.[2]

The starting-point of all this legislation was the inquest of 1274, closely followed by the general parliament in Easter 1275. Edward does not appear to have had more in mind at first than a resumption of the general eyre and an inquiry into his liberties and rights lost from his demesne,[3] but, if this were so,

[1] Above, p. 290.

[2] *Statutes and Ordinances and Acts of the Parliament of Ireland*, edit. H. F. Berry (Rolls Series, 1907), p. 47. The statute of Winchester was sent with police regulations for Ireland, in June 1308 (pp. 245–53). Except the statute of merchants the statutes sent in 1285 were copied into the Red Book of the Irish Exchequer, as also were the statute of mortmain or *de religiosis* (1279) (which may be regarded as an addition to the clauses about monasteries and their patrons in the first series of Westminster statutes), and the 'statute' of Rhuddlan, an ordinance for the exchequer not issued in a parliament. The texts in the Red Book are printed by Berry, and in the absence of a handy and critical edition of the statutes will be found convenient by students who have not ready access to the folio *Statutes of the Realm*, vol. i (1810).

[3] Proceedings in the name of Henry III stopped on his death, and as new writs were not issued in Edward's name to justices in eyre, the general eyre in progress came to an end. An undated schedule stitched into the Close Roll (membrane 7ᵈ, containing letters close of June and July 1273: *Cal. Close Rolls, 1272–9*, p. 52) gives a list of justices appointed in the English shires. This suggests that a resumption of the eyre was contemplated; but except in Worcestershire, Middlesex, and

he very soon enlarged his purposes and decided to overhaul the local administration and to explore to the full the extent to which his tenants-in-chief and others had usurped liberties, appropriated suits and services, and abused their rights. He had been touched by his welcome, shocked by the complaints of misgovernment and crime, and angered by the state of his finances. Hence any idea of restoring a general eyre was postponed, pending the outcome of an inquest and a practical demonstration to his subjects of his 'desire to redress the state of his realm'.

The commissions of inquiry were issued on 10–11 October 1274, one series for England, another for the Channel Islands.[1] The commissioners, men of standing and sometimes with local knowledge, worked from November to May 1275. The articles of the inquest were put as questions to juries of hundreds, boroughs, and numerous liberties. Many of the returns survive, some in their original form with the strips of parchment, to which the seals of the jurors were attached, hanging from them. These returns were nicknamed 'Ragman rolls', in allusion to their ragged appearance, and so gave currency to an epithet, later frequently applied to similar documents; and by association to the statute *de justiciis assignatis*, to which reference has already been made,[2] and to the pleadings based on the returns. In spite of the speed with which the returns were made they were remarkably thorough, and contained a body of information which was used by the justices, on and off, for ten years or so after the general eyre was resumed in 1278.

This inquest of 1274 was by no means the only one. Indirectly, through the statutes suggested by its articles and the returns, it produced others. In March 1279, for example, the king and his advisers, in their desire for information, appointed some twenty-five panels of commissioners to make the most intensive investigation into tenements and liberties of every kind that had been attempted since the Domesday Survey. If the

London no eyres were held till the end of 1278. For earlier commissions of inquiry issued on 28 January 1274 to two judges see *Cal. Pat. Rolls, 1272–81*, p. 65; and Cam, *Studies*, pp. 123–4.

[1] *Cal. Pat. Rolls, 1272–81*, pp. 59, 70. For the inquiry in the Channel Islands see above, p. 320. The articles of the English inquiry, with an English translation, can be read in Cam, *The Hundred*, pp. 248–57. Many returns are printed in the *Rotuli Hundredorum*, vol. i (1812), and vol. ii (1818), pp. 1–320.

[2] Above, p. 353. For the nickname see Cam, *Studies*, pp. 41–56.

returns to this inquiry had survived for the whole of England and not merely from a few shires and had been as full as they are for two or three shires, they would have given us a combined gazetteer, terrier, and at least rural census of tenants for the whole of the country. Moreover this inquest was combined with another into the execution by the sheriffs of their duty to distrain to knighthood all who had land to the annual value of twenty pounds. The commissioners were instructed to enforce the royal mandate and to impose heavy amercements on those who had evaded their obligation to receive knighthood.[1] The object of the main inquest was clearly to have, as a check upon land-holders, sheriffs, and bailiffs, a survey of all the land and land-holders with their rights, dues, and services, from the barons to the serfs: also to provide a more reliable list of rights in private hands than the returns of 1274-5 contained. It was a natural sequel to the statute of Gloucester, but how far it assisted the exchequer and the justices on eyre we cannot tell. The next big inquest was less ambitious and probably more useful to the exchequer. It was undertaken by the new treasurer, John Kirk-by, formerly Burnell's deputy in the chancery, early in 1285 and is known as 'Kirkby's quest'. He and his colleagues were re-quired to report for current use upon knights' fees held of the Crown, and to gather information about the relations between the local officials and the exchequer. Complainants were invited to appear before them with their grievances against sheriffs and bailiffs. This inquiry was related to the problem of corruption in the administration of debts owed by persons in the shires to the Crown and was a practical outcome of the legislation on this matter at Westminster in 1275 (c. 19) and in the 'statute' of Rhuddlan of 1284. Indeed the statute provides for the appoint-ment of a commission and this must have been that headed by the treasurer. One result of Kirkby's quest was the so-called statute of Exeter, dealing with inquiries into the offences of

---

[1] *Cal. Pat. Rolls, 1272-81*, pp. 342, 343. The writ for the main inquiry of 1279, with the form of oath administered to the inquisitors, is printed in the *Rotuli Hundredorum*, ii (1818), p. ix. The returns known in 1818 are printed on pp. 321-877; those of Cambridgeshire, Huntingdonshire, and Oxfordshire fill pp. 356-877. The returns of the jurors to the articles of inquiry were classified by the commis-sioners, not left in their original form as the returns of 1274-5 had been. R. H. Hilton has analysed the Warwickshire return, not printed in the Hundred Rolls, from a contemporary copy in the Public Record Office: 'Social Structure of Rural Warwickshire in the Middle Ages', *Dugdale Society Occasional Papers*, no. 9 (1950).

coroners. This was issued at Exeter in 1286. It was not made in parliament.[1]

No doubt some good result came of these investigations. Articles and instructions based upon them were transmitted to the justices, petitioners were encouraged to air their grievances, statutes were published throughout the land. After what must have been an exciting time in Edward's first parliament, the 'new provisions and statutes . . . ordained for the good of the realm and for the relief of the people' were sent to the sheriffs (May 1275) to be proclaimed in every hundred, city, borough, market town, and other places for general knowledge and observance. Copies were made to be kept in every shire by knights selected with the assent of the community. The hearing and determination by royal justices of cases revealed by the inquest of 1274 must have been salutary. Local bailiffs would be less likely to cheat the king's debtors. Yet these manifestations of royal power were too clumsy and, after the first rapid outburst, too slow to satisfy the victims or disturb the corrupt. 'The king', wrote the Dunstable annalist, 'sent his commissioners everywhere to inquire how his sheriffs and bailiffs had conducted themselves; but no good came of it.'[2]

One obvious cause of frustration was the long delay between the date of the charge and the trial of it by the justices. A general eyre was unpopular in any case, for it involved social dislocation in its neighbourhood and much opportunity to make unexpected amercements of jurors and others; but its worst defect was that, when it was held, the parties might be dead, or, as feeling and memory became dim, bribery and intrigue might have been at work. The administration was well aware of the dangers and injustice of judicial delays. The statute of Westminster in 1275, for example, dealt with the

[1] On 'Kirkby's quest' see *Inquisitions and Assessments relating to Feudal Aids, 1284-1431*, vol. i (Rec. Comm., 1899), pp. viii-xxii. (This series is generally known and cited as *Feudal Aids*.) The *capitula* of the inquiry are printed on pp. xii-xiii, and such of them as were put to and answered by the jurors of a Buckinghamshire hundred on pp. 86-90. Most of the surviving returns are in the form of extracts. For the 'statute' of Exeter (*Statutes of the Realm*, i. 210-12), which is definitely ascribed to 14 Ed. I in a collection made *c.* 1286, now Huntington Library MS. 25782, see the views of V. H. Galbraith in *The Huntington Library Quarterly*, xxxii (1959), 148-151.

[2] *Annales monastici*, iii. 263. For a commentary on the returns on the Ragman or Hundred Rolls of 1274-5, see H. Cam, *Studies*, pp. 142-92; *The Hundred and the Hundred Rolls*, pp. 67-194 *passim*.

temptation opened to those in charge of jails to make profit out of prisoners awaiting trial (c. 15). They let some out on bail whose alleged offences were not bailable, and detained others who had the right to bail. The frequent commissions of jail delivery in which knights of the shire took a hand did not, it would seem, meet the danger.[1] Delays in the trial of civil cases were avoided, to the benefit of the class of small freeholders, by a provision in 1285 which enlarged the scope of the writ of novel disseisin. 'No chancery writ provides quicker relief to complainants than the writ of novel disseisin', wherefore the king, in his desire that justice should be speedy, 'grants that this writ shall apply (*locum habeat*) in more cases than it has hitherto done'.[2] Or again, the king, as the source of justice, might entrust to a special commission any case for which no chancery writ was available: the 'trial' of petitions in parliament seems to have led to an increase in the number of *ad hoc* commissions of this kind. The cases revealed by the inquest of 1274–5, however, had to await the sessions of the general eyre, for they had, so to speak, been subordinated to royal policy: permanence was given to the articles of inquiry by converting them into *capitula* of the eyre.

Edward and his advisers did not develop this policy. In his last great drive against official corruption in 1289, the king issued no articles, ordered no inquest. He called for complaints and appointed commissioners to hear and determine them.[3]

This famous process began soon after Edward's return from his long absence in Gascony. He landed in August, made a visitation of shrines in the eastern counties, and reached Westminster in October. He had found much discontent. 'A very real oppression had lain upon the country' while he was away, due to laxity in high quarters rather than to the orgy of corruption implied by the chroniclers, but notorious enough to

[1] On jail delivery see Pollock and Maitland, *Hist. English Law*, i. 200; ii. 645.

[2] Stat. Westminster II, c. 25. The principles underlying this use of the writ are discussed by Plucknett, op. cit., pp. 20–27, 82, 85–87. The 'possessory' assizes of novel disseisin, mort d'ancestor, and darrein presentment were constantly taken. In Edward's first year some two thousand commissions were issued (*Hist. English Law*, i. 201). The statute of 1275 (c. 51) ends with a request to the bishops to co-operate in allowing the assizes to be taken in Advent, Septuagesima, and Lent.

[3] *State Trials of the Reign of Edward I, 1289–93*, edit. T. F. Tout and Hilda Johnstone (Camden Society, 1906).

infuriate the tidy-minded king. He struck hard, at high and low. No judicial inquiry in the strict sense would serve his purpose, for the justices were implicated. He turned to the men who had been with him in Gascony, men whom he had tested and used during three arduous years in different ways. He chose as auditors to receive and determine complaints John de Pontissara, bishop of Winchester, who had been trained in civil law and was in high favour at the papal court as well as with the king;[1] also his chancellor, Robert Burnell and three laymen, the earl of Lincoln, John of St. John, and William Latimer,[2] all tried members of his household; and to these he added two high officials of his wardrobe, William of Louth the keeper, who had been his chief financial expert in Gascony, and William Marsh the controller, soon to be made treasurer of the exchequer. During the years of the trials, some of these were displaced by others. The prestige of this formidable tribunal was, in general esteem, greater than that of the judiciary itself. Though in fact its decisions were made liable to revision by the justices *coram rege*, that is, of the king's bench, they should, it was sometimes argued, be subject only to the cognizance of the king in parliament.[3]

Proclamations in the shire court invited all persons who since the king's departure in 1286 had been aggrieved by any royal officer to present their *querelae* to the auditors in Westminster. The record of subsequent proceedings before the auditors fills two long rolls. The business, in its early stages, caused much excitement. Edward was compared to the lord in the parable who had gone into a far country and had returned to avenge himself on the labourers in his vineyard; and a sharper point is given to this analogy if we remember that probably all the auditors had been present at Condom when, a

---

[1] The bishop's letters show that he was in Gascony on the king's business during most of 1287 and 1289. In 1288 he was mainly in Paris or its neighbourhood. See the itinerary compiled from the register in his *Registrum* (Canterbury and York Society, 1915 and 1924), ii. 840-1. The letter from Poissy, dated 29 March 1287 by the editors, should be dated 20 March 1288. For the bishop's friendly relations with the king cf. i. 333.

[2] This 'bachelor' and household knight was the son of a well-known sheriff of York (d. 1268) and had been in Edward's service from early days. He took the cross with Edward. He had lands in Yorkshire (Vale of Pickering) and many other shires.

[3] See the case of the complaint of the prior of Butley against John de Luvetot, as continued on the king's authority in the king's bench; printed by Sayles, op. cit. ii. 86-97, especially pp. 86-87, 95; also the editor's comments, pp. xlix-l.

few months before, the great ordinance on the government of Gascony had been issued. The implication in the scandal of many of the judges, including the chief justices of the two benches, intensified the dramatic effect. A contemporary squib, known as the *Passio* or sufferings of the judges, satirized their fall in a ribald travesty of biblical texts.[1] Careful scrutiny of the evidence shows, it is true, that, with two or three exceptions, the judges who were dismissed, imprisoned, and subjected to heavy fines, some ten in number, were by no means the most flagrant offenders, and, it should be remembered, some were not touched at all. The great Ralph de Hengham, chief justice of the king's bench, who was amerced the most heavily of them all, had much to say for himself. Indeed he probably increased the king's animosity by saying it.[2] All the same, the news that so many ornaments of the legal profession had lost their positions and were lying in the Tower and other prisons was very exciting, and the story of their fate lost nothing in the telling. Henry of Bray, justice of the Jews and the king's chief escheator, who was especially hated, was so overwhelmed by grief that he tried to drown himself as he was being conveyed by boat to the Tower, and later sought to dash out his brains against the wall of his prison. The story of the most notorious offender among the judges, Thomas of Wayland or Weyland, the chief justice of the bench of common pleas, had given edge and impetus to popular expectancy even before the auditors had been appointed. The king had dismissed him and seized his lands in September. He fled to sanctuary with the Franciscan friars at Babwell, close to Bury St. Edmunds. He was starved out and taken to the Tower. There he was given the choice between trial, imprisonment, and abjuration of the land. He chose to abjure the land. He was a felon, self-confessed. Another man sat in his place. He was a sorry sight as, in March 1290, holding a cross, he made his painful way on foot to Dover and crossed the Channel, to be heard of no more.

The other victims of Edward's investigation belonged, in the

---

[1] Edited in *State Trials*, pp. 95–99.

[2] Sayles, op. cit., vol. i, pp. lxvii–lxix. Hengham was pardoned in February 1291 but was not restored to public life until 1299. In September 1301 he was reappointed chief justice of the king's bench. He died in May 1311. By Michaelmas 1293 he had paid most of his fine of 8,000 marks, more than a fourth part of the total paid by his fellow judges (*State Trials*, p. xxxviii). For details of his dismissal see W. H. Dunham in *E.H.R.* xlvii (1932), 88–93.

main, to the class of bailiffs and financiers. The irreverent satirist
pictures the arrival of the king in London, where the people welcomed him as a deliverer from the yoke of the Egyptians, and
how the king, going through the midst of them, entered his
paradise to seek the man whom he had created, and called 'Adam,
Adam, where art thou?' This was a reference to Adam de
Stratton, the Wiltshire clerk who had acquired for himself a
profitable but nefarious importance in the city of London as a
Christian usurer and agent.[1] He seems to have found his feet in
the household of the earl of Devon, but as early as 1256 he was
a clerk in the exchequer. He owed his advancement to the favour
of King Henry and of the earl of Devon's sister Isabella, that
great lady who became countess of Aumâle, and for so many years
held masterful and quarrelsome sway in the Isle of Wight, Holderness, Skipton, and Cockermouth. In 1263 he became master of
the king's works at Westminster and Isabella's deputy as a
chamberlain of the exchequer, a post with which she afterwards
enfeoffed him (1276). The enfeoffment brought with it the rich
manors in Wiltshire appurtenant to the office and increased
Adam's importance as a man of property. During the next ten
years or so, in spite of one narrow escape from disaster, he was,
behind the scenes, the most insidious financial adventurer in
England. He was not a creature of the Countess Isabella, but her
confidential man of business, an able friend and adviser who
appealed to her bold acquisitive nature. At the same time he was
a powerful man in the royal service, with the privileges though
not the status of a baron of the exchequer, and a king's clerk.
In his headquarters in Smalelane, near the Fleet prison, he made
a fortune as a money-lender, mainly in petty transactions with
the needy. He bought up debts owing to Jews, and caught
confiding abbots in his toils, while he was reorganizing the management of Isabella's estates and controlling the distribution of
their cash surpluses. He was a very wealthy man. According to
the Norwich chronicler the value of his lands and other temporalities amounted to £50,000, while his ecclesiastical rents came
to £1,000 a year. After his fall, no less than £12,666. 17s. 7d., of
which over £11,000 was in new money, was found in cash in his
house.

As a rich man Adam was an object of envy and scandal, but

[1] The best account of Adam is in N. Denholm-Young, *Seignorial Administration
in England* (1937), pp. 77–84.

was also able to protect himself. His fall was due to his follies of violence, chicanery, and tampering with seals and charters, for these made him a felon, if not a traitor. He was in trouble twice, first in 1279, when he succeeded in clearing himself, or, as the general belief was, in buying himself off,[1] then in 1290–2 when he was ruined. On both occasions his exposure was primarily due to charges brought by a religious house. And in both inquiries complaints were of official as well as private malpractices. In 1279 the abbot of Quarr in the Isle of Wight accused him of tampering with a charter in the course of a long and bitter dispute about suits of courts between the abbey and the countess. The case led to an inquiry into his affairs which was in form an anticipation of the great inquiry of 1289. All who had suffered from Adam, whether as chamberlain or as keeper of the king's works, or indeed as a private person, were invited to present *querelae* before the barons of the exchequer and other commissioners. He managed in the end to satisfy the king and was restored to office at the exchequer. Ten years later he had become a public scandal. The king had heard of the scandal in Gascony, and in January 1290 he was deprived of his office and all his lands and imprisoned. Again he succeeded for a time in making his peace with the king, but this time he had had to face the auditors and his pardon was bought by confession, a fine of 500 marks, and the loss of his confiscated property, though he was allowed to retain his ecclesiastical revenues (June 1291). The relief was temporary. How and why the settlement failed is not clear, but Adam's behaviour as the creditor of the prior of Bermondsey seems to have been too flagrant to overlook. Adam's grip on this Cluniac house had steadily tightened since 1272. By 1288, so the king had heard in Gascony, the usurer had got half its substance and was demanding a capital sum of £6,000.[2] He was accused of forging a deed. This was his undoing. He was imprisoned in the Tower as a felon in 1292 and died not long afterwards.

Apart from his crimes, the career of Adam of Stratton deserves our attention as a striking example of the interplay of public and private, local and central, royal and baronial, financial and administrative activities in social life. It warns us that the class of

---

[1] The letters of pardon, 10 November 1279, state that he had proved his innocence before king and council (*Cal. Pat. Rolls, 1272–81*, p. 335).

[2] Rose Graham, *English Ecclesiastical Studies* (1929), p. 104, in her essay on the priory.

bailiffs was much more than a professional body of experts in estate management, or in public service, each of whom had only one master and closely defined duties. Adam moved in high circles, but, if we could see the bailiffs of hundreds and manors as clearly as we can see him, we should almost certainly find that they also lived in a little world of intricate relationships. Moreover, no sharp distinction separated royal from other bailiffs; the inquiries of 1274 treated all alike. Any hard-and-fast distinction was impossible in a land where, out of 628 hundreds, no less than 358 were in private hands. When John Baliol's seneschal and the mayor of Wallingford pleaded that the auditors of 1289 were empowered only to try ministers of the king, and that they were not sworn to the royal service, the reply was that they executed royal writs. Their work affected the king's interests. Public policy as well as the interests of the lord, for example, dictated the provision in 1285 (Westminster II, c. 11) that the auditors of a lord's account shall commit defaulting bailiffs to the nearest royal prison. 'They shall be received by the sheriff or keeper of the gaol and held in safe keeping in irons and shall remain in that prison at their own cost until they have fully satisfied their lords of the arrears.' They now come under the cognizance of the Crown. If a person so imprisoned complains that the auditors have been unjust and can find friends who will mainprise him and be responsible for his appearance before the barons of the exchequer, he is to be handed over to them. The case will be heard in the exchequer, by the barons or such persons as they may appoint. If the auditors are justified the bailiff will be sent to the Fleet prison. If he should abscond he will be outlawed in the customary way after proclamations in the shire court.[1]

Much social history lies behind this drastic piece of legislation. The summary committal of the defaulter to a royal prison saved the lord much tiresome litigation under which an astute offender might long take cover. A man habituated to a life of easy peculation might well pause in his misdoing, for he ran the risk of detention in irons.[2] Careful auditors were protected, careless auditors corrected by the exchequer. But the statute did more than this. It related the lord's interests with those of the Crown,

[1] On Westminster II, c. 11 and its setting see Plucknett, op. cit., pp. 150-6, also Denholm-Young, op. cit., pp. 154 ff., where cases under the statute are discussed.

[2] Denholm-Young has noted a treatise by Robert Carpenter which 'gives explicit and illuminating instruction for cooking accounts' (*Collected Papers*, p. 100).

and implied that the business of a landholder, though privileged, was as much a matter of royal concern as the business of a merchant. It is not merely a coincidence that in the same parliament of Easter 1285 the statute of merchants orders the imprisonment of the defaulting debtor until his debts are paid, while 'his sacred freehold passes into the profane hands of the merchant'.[1] The royal desire to assist a powerful class against its own agents was quite natural. Estate-management had become a professional business in the social economy. It needed a staff of reeves, bailiffs, seneschals, and auditors. Many great lords, whose estates were numerous and wide-spread, had a council to which important matters could be referred. The view of accounts was a quasi-judicial process, and the auditors possessed disciplinary powers which, though they were recognized, were necessarily exercised within the limitations of the common law. If a tenant could seek protection against unlawful distraint, and a bailiff arm himself with royal writs, a lord might well demand a statute to strengthen the hands of his auditors. The recognition of his need was in itself a proof of the interdependence of social relations from top to bottom, from the king in parliament, through exchequer, chancery, and judges, down to the humblest manor in the land. The days when a baron lived with his warriors on a mound overlooking a ditch lay far behind. Now he was a country gentleman, passed from one house to another, and enjoyed the amenities of parks and fish-ponds. He was involved in an intricate social system, a subject as well as a vassal of the Crown. The statutes make clear a fact which is implicit in Magna Carta itself: 'that from the early years of the thirteenth century feudal institutions were no longer capable of running under their own power; lords found it useful, if not necessary, to obtain royal assistance'.[2]

This social order was not sedate. It had to be watched. Enclosed private fish-ponds and parks, for example, were more than amenities; they could be centres of disturbance. Trespassers upon them were not only casual poachers; they might be a menace to the king's peace. In 1236 Henry III, remembering recent events, had refused to allow lords to detain in private prisons malefactors who had invaded their parks. In 1275 Edward I, mindful of the baronial wars, ordered them to be imprisoned for three years—one of the few instances of imprisonment as a punishment—and

[1] Plucknett, op. cit., p. 141; and see below, p. 625.   [2] Plucknett, op. cit., p. 77.

then, if they could not pay their fines, to abjure the realm (Westminster I, c. 20). Edward, moreover, had vivid memories, some of them recent Gascon memories, of the temptation latent in the possession of castles and other fortified places to resist officers of the law. When, on his return to England in 1274, he heard complaints about the abuse by lords of the legal weapon of distress, his reaction was fierce. The right of a lord to enforce upon his tenant an obligation, such as rent or services or suit of court, by seizing his chattels had been limited by the statute of Marlborough in 1267, and by common law the tenant, if he denied the obligation, could replevin, or get back the distrained goods under pledge; but this process meant legal action and the intervention of the sheriff or some other bailiff of the king. Suppose that the lord or his bailiff had seized a tenant's beasts, required for ploughing and carrying, and had driven them into his castle and refused to release them. The first statute of Westminster (c. 17) enacted that in the last resort, after due warning, the castle or fortified place should be battered down beyond repair. But suppose that this act of despite and trespass has occurred in the March of Wales or in another place where the king's writ does not run? Why then, 'the king, who is sovereign there, shall do right to those who may wish to make complaint'. Edward knew the March of Wales; he realized at once the danger latent in the practice of distress if it got beyond restraint; and in the first statutes of his reign he made his position clear. He would show that he was sovereign in the March. And, as we have seen, he did show this after his second absence, when he brought the earls of Gloucester and Hereford to submission.[1]

So far we have discussed the statutes as expressions of the king's will in parliament in the course of a sustained and vigorous, but day-to-day effort, often haphazard and interrupted, to deal with the administrative problems of his time; as an outcome of corporate activity which laid bare and responded to the hardships and embarrassments of his subjects, and which reflected the experience and counsel of his ministers. In retrospect the statutes are much more impressive; they stand out like a range of hills in a misty landscape. The time has come to ask and try to answer a few questions suggested by this distant view. Were Englishmen in Edward's reign aware of them as the monuments of a new and

[1] Above, p. 329.

significant development? How did the statutes, as formal and solemn acts of state, affect the royal power which gave them authority and influence proceedings in the royal courts? To what extent did they impose a new body of law superior to the common law?[1] These questions are closely connected with each other, and consideration of the first two prepares the way for the answer to the third.

There is no doubt that the ordinary Englishman, however ignorant he might be about their content, was aware of the making of 'new laws'. The Norwich chronicler puts the legislation of 1285 in its context:

King Edward reached London on his return after Easter from the subjugation of Wales on the vigil of the Ascension and on the following Friday (4 May) went in solemn procession on foot from the Tower of London to Westminster, with Queen Eleanor, all the magnates of the realm and fourteen bishops. John Pecham, the archbishop of Canterbury, carried the cross which the king had captured in Wales. On that day the king opened his parliament at Westminster; it lasted seven weeks and in it the king established very many new laws, knighted very many sons of magnates and confirmed many charters of his ancestors who were kings of England. Again in that year he published new statutes at Winchester against thieves, road brigands, receivers and concealers of malefactors, about setting watches in the country and townships and cities and the cutting away of woods by the king's highways. He also forbade the holding of pleas henceforth on Sundays, and of fairs and markets in the burial grounds of churches.[2]

The chronicler, if he had ever heard the statutes of Westminster read, made nothing of them, but he could summarize the statutes of Winchester. All were 'new laws'; yet it is unlikely that he would distinguish clearly between statutes and other royal orders proclaimed in the shire courts, though he would know that the Great Charter and the Charter of the Forests had especial significance. It was the judges, pleaders, and legal advisers of litigants who had occasion to know and appraise the statutes; for they were available and often days were fixed from which they came into force. They were quickly cited in the courts, and their

[1] In addition to Plucknett's book, see especially the valuable discussion in Sayles, *Select Cases in the Court of King's Bench*, vol. iii, pp. xi–xlii.

[2] *Bartholomaei de Cotton Historia Anglicana* (ed. Luard, 1859), p. 166. The annalist is curiously vague about Edward's movements after he left south Wales in December 1284, for the king had actually spent Easter (25 March 1285) at Burgh in Norfolk, during a pilgrimage to shrines. He reached Westminster on 29 April.

bearing in outstanding cases which had begun before they were published was frequently argued. One statute was almost certainly drafted in 1285 with a troublesome and doubtful case in mind, and the case was finally decided before the king in accordance with this 'special act of the lord king and his council'.[1]

Now, as we have seen already,[2] Edward's statutes were related to each other both in matter and intention; and, although each clause might be regarded as a 'special act' or statute and be selected as such for reference in the courts because it was relevant to a particular case, lawyers soon came to regard the statutes issued together in a parliament as a single statute divided into clauses or chapters, and then to regard the statutes as forming a whole; not, it should be added, as a distinct *corpus*, like the *Corpus Juris* of Roman law, but as a matter of practical convenience. They began to collect them together in handbooks for their own use, just as an unknown chancery clerk had collected the provisions of the years 1233-6 as an appendix to the text of Glanvil and of the Charters of liberties; or as the estate-agent Robert Carpenter had added the Provisions of Westminster of 1259 and related documents to very much the same material.[3] Much of the legislation of Henry III was forgotten, and what survived from the baronial wars was only what was recast in the statute of Marlborough (1267). The Edwardian lawyers knew only the Charters of Liberties, a compilation described, from its main ingredients, as the statute of Merton (1236), the Dictum of Kenilworth, and the statute of Marlborough; but, when they collected and added to these the statutes of their own time, they had to include nearly everything, for these statutes were constantly cited in the courts, and had been accepted as law by the judges. The numerous compilations, in short, reveal a realization that there was a new body of law, so comprehensive in range and so rapidly conceived that its impact could not be evaded. The professional handbooks led to an official enrolment of statutes, which began in 1299 and, after various vicissitudes, the practice became regular in the middle of the fourteenth century.

[1] Sayles, op. cit. i. 160. The enactment (statute of Westminster II, c. 16) decided where the right of marriage lay when the infant had several lords. See Plucknett, pp. 112-13.   [2] Above, p. 356.

[3] See Richardson and Sayles, 'The Early Statutes', reprinted from the *Law Quarterly Review* for 1934; Richardson in the same review for 1938, pp. 381 ff.; Denholm-Young, *Collected Papers*, pp. 96-110. On Robert Carpenter of Hareslade see now C. A. F. Meekings in *E.H.R.* lxxii (1957), 260-9.

The development inevitably led to a conscious distinction between the new material and the common law. Occasionally the distinction is suggested in the statutes themselves.[1] Statutes did not merely affirm the common law. In a judgement already noted, where a plaintiff lost his case under a new statute which had come into force since he had first obtained his writ, he was freed from amercement because 'this was not formerly common law, but is the special act of the lord king and his council'.[2] Yet the words 'non fuit *prius* jus commune' preclude the conclusion that a new kind of law was appearing. What had not previously been common law would henceforward be common law. The idea that statute law was a separate body of written law, not customary, but capable of gloss and interpretation in its own right, so to speak, lay far in the future, and has never implied a superiority which requires no accommodation to the common law. To this day it is debated whether what has been legalized by statute can still be regarded as a crime at common law as working public mischief. In Edward I's time a statute was regarded as 'a detail in the mass of custom', an act of change in a body of common law which itself was always changing, an adaptation to meet new forces at work in society, a remedy of something gone wrong. It was often long overdue. It might clarify a previous statute or try to straighten out a tangle in the law of distress or succession. It was on the whole private law, in the sense that the common law was private law, not public law in the sense that it implied a political theory of legislative sovereignty. If it were too clever or introduced from civil law ideas alien to the common law, such as bona fides or the doctrine of use, it might fail in effect and be forgotten. It might be obscure or produce unexpected consequences, which led to petition for its amendment; indeed, such defects were a cause of the later common petitions or bills which gave parliament some initiative in making the law. It was not sacrosanct; one statute, limited in its intention, might gradually be given a wider application in the courts so that it put a later statute in the shade.[3] In view of

---

[1] e.g. Westminster I, c. 20, on the operation of the common law against robbers in private parks 'as upon him who is attainted of open robbery'.

[2] Sayles, i. 160 (cf. above, p. 370); also vol. iii, p. xxxvi.

[3] See Plucknett's long analysis (pp. 63–75) of the way in which c. 9 of the statute of Marlborough (on suit of court) was given general effect and 'undid' Westminster II, c. 2. In 1304 Hengham asked the king's proctor, 'How will you aid yourself for the king, by the common law or by Statute?' *Year Books, Edward I, 32–33*, p. 37.

all this, we should expect the statutes to be related to the king's will and to his customary prerogatives very much as the rest of the common law was; and this was the case.

The solemn words in which they were promulgated in the king's name as expressions of his wish to relieve the distresses of his people or to establish the welfare of Crown and realm convey the royal intention in regard to them. Thus, when an ordinance of 1290 that pleas of *quo warranto* were to be held only before justices in eyre was disregarded in 1298 and the matter came to the king's attention, he wrote to the clerk of parliament for a copy of the ordinance. Gilbert of Rothbury sent it together with the unanimous opinion of the judges of the king's bench that it should be observed, adding: 'And it is good that the king should keep the grace conceded and promise made to his people. This is our advice.' The king accordingly sent a mandate to this effect to the justices of the bench of common pleas before whom a case had been brought.[1] Again, in the statute *Districciones Scaccarii* (1275), the king took the lead in the legal campaign against unreasonable distresses; the Crown would not exercise its prerogative of selling a distress until fifteen days had elapsed after it had been made, and the royal officials were forbidden to distrain beasts essential to agricultural work, and sheep also, unless no other chattels were available.[2] On the other hand, there is no suggestion that any peculiar restraint could be imposed by statute upon the king as the source of justice. He stood where he did. Indeed, a statute may emphasize his prerogative,[3] and on its application the statute of mortmain (*De religiosis*, 1279) increased the prerogative by making the Crown the only authority which could grant dispensation from the statute.

The far-reaching effects of the statute of mortmain are a good illustration of the delicate problem posed by our third question —to what extent did the Edwardian statutes contain new law?

[1] Sayles, op. cit., vol. ii, p. lviii.

[2] Plucknett, p. 60; earlier in the year the first statute of Westminster had re-enacted the limitations imposed upon distress by the statute of Marlborough, and had dealt with the detention of distrained beasts in castles (above, p. 368). Sheep, whose inclusion in the *Districciones* puzzles Plucknett, assisted agriculture by providing manure.

[3] The statute of Gloucester, c. 9, emphasizes the prerogative of mercy in cases of homicide by misadventure, or in self-defence, by forbidding the issue out of chancery of writs of inquiry; the accused, if he is in prison, must await his trial before the justices; if he is exonerated by the jury, the king can grant him his grace. Cf. above, p. 330.

—for, though statutes dealt with old difficulties and current grievances in the spirit of the common law, they made an unprecedented impression simply because they were 'new laws' which had to be digested into the mass of the common law. They were the outcome of the conscious reflection of minds trained in the law. The legislation of 1285, for example, was directed by the penetrating intelligence of Ralph de Hengham, who seems to have been regarded in his and the next generation as the best lawyer of his time. He was in a position to say what a statute's intention was and how it should be applied; for much of the new legislation, while it might sweep aside dilatory processes or meet new occasions by new writs, affirmed the common law, and was to be liberally construed. The courts took some time to become familiar with it. Yet it was undoubtedly new law which had to be enforced, and frequently it dealt with such thorny matters that, in the absence of the desire or intelligence to amend it, it might in time give rise to abuses worse than those which it was intended to remedy.[1] A judge, Chief Justice Bereford, in the next reign said of a statutory procedure in the legislation about reversion to the main lord in cases of dower and cognate cases that 'it was very mischievous; but since the law is such, one cannot avoid the mischief'. Hengham and his fellow draftsmen did their best to find solutions in the light of broad general principles, such as the right of a lord to the tenement of a holder who persistently refuses his services, or the obligation of the courts to protect reversioners against subtle devices, or the maintenance of the will of the donor manifestly expressed in the charter of gift.

These men held dynastic views about tenure and the family, but they also had to recognize changing situations and protect freeholders against exploitation. The results of their work needed the most careful supervision. The famous first chapter of Westminster II, for example, later known as *de donis*, was so drafted, as it has come down to us—perhaps it was revised later —that, even in Edward I's time, Hengham's intention was frustrated, and in the next reign Bereford insisted on applying it as 'he that made the statute intended'. Hengham himself, in the trial of a case in 1303, explained the intention of another clause of Westminster II (c. 18) which gave a creditor the right, under certain eventualities, to hold half the lands of the debtor

[1] This paragraph is based upon Plucknett, *passim*.

until the debt was paid; he recalled that 'this statute was laid before the king and council, and they agreed that any time that the debtor came ready with the debt, his lands should be restored to him'; hence the creditor under the statute had no claim to hold on to his tenancy of the debtor's lands, nor to damages and expenses.[1]

The statement of first principles in statutes primarily intended to solve difficulties which could not be met by existing writs would seem to imply political theory and a system of jurisprudence more coherent than the wisdom acquired in the practice of a living and changing body of customary law. The implication is misleading. From one point of view the Edwardian statutes were a practical expression of the spirit which informs the treatise of Bracton, but this great work was itself an exposition of the law and custom of England, influenced but not directed by the author's humane alertness to legal principles. In Edward's time we can trace in the process of legislation and the practice of the courts the thoughtful opportunism which was to be the characteristic of English law, at once its glory and its shame.

The king in council intervenes with a new purposiveness to revise a mass of law and custom of which he is a part. He emphasizes, with much effect, a sovereignty over a tangled system which he has solemnly sworn to maintain, and fulfils this obligation while he saves his rights and dignity. He is not averse to new law. The statute of Winchester, for example, imposes a joint penalty for the concealment of felonies which, when his father had sought to impose it, had been decried as an innovation from Savoy. The king had determined to make the presentation of offenders a reality in hundreds and franchises: but as the jurors will not indict and neither they nor the district (*pays*) are under oath of responsibility for damages, and incur no penalty for concealment, the statute requires the whole hundred or hundreds concerned, including the franchises, to give satisfaction for the robbery within forty days, or to answer for the

---

[1] Plucknett, op. cit., p. 150. The point in this case seems to be that the creditor could expect five more years of tenure of the lands at the existing rate of payment; but the debtor was ready to pay the balance at once. The statute had given the creditor the right, if he wished, to execute the debt by seizure of chattels and possession of half the lands of the debtor under a new writ, *elegit*. It was intended 'to be firm without being harsh'. It was too brief and required Hengham's elucidation eighteen years later.

bodies of the malefactors. The king, adds the statute, is willing to postpone until Easter the date from which this penalty, which may seem hard, shall be imposed, and will note the outcome in the interval, but let all be assured that the penalty will run everywhere from the time prescribed. Here the same vigorous mind is at work that, ten years earlier, had inspired so much of the statute of Westminster I. The king protects the stranger against assault and robbery, however indifferent the country-side may be, just as he will storm a castle to secure the replevin of cattle, or prevent his officers from conniving with dangerous men in jails, or restrain the right to vessels wrecked on shore if a man or a dog or a cat survives. The opening chapter of the statute of Westminster I, a lengthy prohibition of the abuse of monastic hospitality by all and sundry, was obviously the result of his visits to abbeys after his return to England.

This aspect of Edward's legal activity is a simple assertion of his love of decency and order. He did not fling himself about as a legislator. During these years he was a very busy man, and his interests were as manifold as his duties. He did everything intensely, and, even if he had wished, could not concentrate continuously on the law; he had not the time to do so, and the law was a technical and uneasy reflection of the workings of a complicated society. Perhaps the most remarkable thing in Edward was his readiness, amid all his distractions, to discuss knotty legal details, as they arose, with his advisers. He was the last medieval king of this receptive, ready, and assiduous type. He possessed mental energy, a determination to maintain control, and the good sense which made him willing to trust his expert advisers and, so long as he trusted them, to co-operate with them. The hearing of a difficult case or petition reserved for talk with the king would suggest a general provision, or the need for careful reflection by a judge or two, in the light of their peculiar experience. In course of time a series of drafts would be ready for consideration, as chapters of a rather haphazard statute, which could be promulgated as a whole. The statute of Westminster II was prepared in some such way as this, in continuation of the statute of Gloucester. Some statutes had a more spectacular origin. The statute of Acton Burnell (1283) was devised to meet the grievances of merchants, especially foreign merchants who found difficulty in collecting their debts and whose confidence it was a royal interest to retain; and the statute of Merchants was issued two years later to meet their complaints that the sheriffs were delaying the execution of the statute of Acton Burnell. The immediate occasion of the statute of mortmain (1279), though it dealt with an old problem, was believed to be Edward's desire to punish the indiscretions of an over-zealous archbishop. The statute *Quia Emptores* (1290), which was overdue, was promulgated at the request of the magnates and lesser lords of the realm. The statute of Gloucester (1278) was due to the king's desire to resume the investigation into franchises and also to make various changes in the law after the close of the first Welsh war. 'The law has failed in many cases: divers additions to it and new provisions are needed to avoid grievous damage and disherisons.' Edward was often most active after his return home from some big enterprise.

The treatment of franchises provides a very good example of the nature and significance of statutory legislation. It began in 1274 with an inquiry into usurpations and abuses of royal rights by the lords of manors and baronies and developed into a searching survey of all franchises and of the titles by which they were claimed. Edward did not seek the abolition of private liberties, as such. He wished to ascertain what liberties were enjoyed and by what warrant their holders claimed the right to enjoy them. Our safest course is to regard his action as due not to his desire to recover lost rights (though this was strong in him) but to the necessity to remove the administrative uncertainties and abuses which were the aftermath of civil disorder. The local administration had tended to degenerate into a tangle of authorities; uncertainty bred usurpations and corrupt practices in royal and seignorial officials alike; each type of franchise produced 'its own particular problems, procedural or financial'. It was high time to clarify the situation and the only way to do this was by legislation. A solution was sought in two ways, first, by the clear assertion of the royal right to intervene, in the interests of justice, so that, not in dramatic acts but in everyday practice, the lords of private hundreds and the holders of immunities everywhere should be kept under control as they took their privileged part in local administration; and secondly by an effort to examine by judicial inquiry every claim to exercise a franchise, to authenticate rightful titles and abolish those which could not be established. The inquiry was made by proceedings under writs of *quo warranto.* 'The judicial proceedings thus initiated went on all through the reign of Edward I and into those of his son and grandson, so long as the general eyres continued, and the records of such proceedings are to be found in the eight hundred and odd pages of the *Placita de Quo Warranto* published by the Record Commission in 1818.'[1]

The proceedings *quo warranto* should not be considered in isolation from the Edwardian statutes, nor regarded as new in principle. Both the right to and use of franchises had frequently engaged the attention of Henry III and his ministers, from the days of his minority onwards. In the middle of the century there had been much investigation into titles, especially into the meaning of royal charters and into the reliance of those who held these deeds upon vague and obsolete phrases as title to liberties which they might or might not validate. What, for example, was covered by the grant of a manor with its 'appurtenances' or 'liberties'? Many religious houses and boroughs had found it worth while to buy a new and more explicit charter as a warrant of their liberties.[2] The justices in eyre had sometimes investigated claims to liberties some years before the duty to inquire into unwarranted liberties was permanently enshrined in the *capitula itineris* (1254). Writs containing the words *quo warranto*, requiring the production of evidences, had been issued in cases between parties since the end of the twelfth century, and had occasionally been used by the king to test the claim to liberties. When the results of the inquiries of 1274 were available, it was obvious that more systematic action was required, but it was generalized not novel action. It was action which could be given permanent statutory authority. Thus in the legislation of 1275 (c. 17) royal bailiffs were instructed to execute writs of replevin even in liberties, if the bailiffs of the liberties had refused to act, and in 1285 (Westminster II, c. 39) a long statute was devoted to the iniquities of sheriffs who made false returns to the king's writs or failed to see that they were returned by bailiffs whose lords had the highly treasured privilege of the return of writs, or asserted

---

[1] Helen Cam, 'The Quo Warranto proceedings under Edward I' (in *History*, 1926), reprinted in her *Liberties and Communities in Medieval England* (1944), p. 172. On the legal principles involved see Plucknett, pp. 29–50. The *Placita*, needless to say, do not contain all the evidence and do not reproduce a particular kind of record. They are extracted from plea rolls and are arranged geographically. From the tenth year of Edward III such pleas were heard in the king's bench or the exchequer.   [2] Powicke, *King Henry III and the Lord Edward*, i. 326–31.

that the privilege, and therefore the responsibility, of returning writs existed where it did not. The social history revealed by legislation of this kind explains why new forms of procedure were required in justice to all concerned, king, lords, sheriffs, and bailiffs and, above all, the parties to legal proceedings. The king and exchequer must know what lords had a privilege; so the exchequer was to keep a roll, and the lord was given the right to a writ in answer to the sheriff's assertions. The writ *quo warranto* itself gave an opportunity to the tenant of a franchise: he could prove his claim and reply to the challenge which the royal writ contained. Indeed, it came to be regarded as a writ of right. In course of time it was held that a judgement in favour of the defendant foreclosed the Crown for ever.

A statement inserted in the preamble to the statute of Gloucester in August 1278 suggests that Edward's plans did not work out quite as he had expected. It seems to imply a rapid preliminary survey of all franchises by justices, to be followed by the issue of writs to all holders who appeared before him and could show that they had succeeded to their liberties and had not recently usurped them, or whose cases were not already under judicial consideration. Proceedings under the writs would follow before the king himself in the shires, or if he had not tarried, before the justices in eyre, who, as we know, were appointed in this year. In fact the cases dragged on before the justices from year to year and raised issues of principle which were only decided by the 'statute' of *Quo Warranto* in 1290. On one essential point, which had been raised in 1279 by Gilbert of Clare, earl of Gloucester, the king's council ruled at once: the writs, as issued, were in accordance with precedent and not, as the earl objected, 'contrary to the law of the land'. On a further point, that the king should be named as a party, the justices of the two benches held that, if the writ included a claim by the king, it would seem to admit that a liberty might exist which could not belong to the king. 'Every liberty is royal and belongs to the crown, unless he who has it has sufficient warrant either by charter or from time immemorial.'[1]

In other respects the pleas before the justices were not so satisfactory. The arguments were often extreme, the decisions sometimes tentative; much pressure was brought to bear by

---

[1] Cam, *Liberties and Communities*, pp. 178-82. The texts come from memoranda at the ends of two manuscripts of Bracton's treatise.

defendants upon officials and jurors; much money passed. 'Slowly the impression gained ground that the whole wretched affair was nothing but a vast royal blackmail'.[1] One obvious difficulty was the meaning to be attached to prescriptive right to enjoy a toll or a warren or the return of writs or whatever the liberty might be, in the absence of an unimpeachable charter. Could time run against the Crown? Ought the enjoyment of every liberty to be dependent on a definite royal grant? There is some evidence of a tendency to apply a term to prescriptive right and to fix the accession of Richard I as the limit of legal memory, as it had been fixed, under another context, in the statute of Westminster I, c. 39. Finally this date was adopted in a clarifying order issued in 1290 after Edward's return from Gascony.[2]

To conclude, an examination of Edward's activity as a law-maker shows that the purpose of his statutes was to clarify or amend the common law or, if the law had failed, to make new law. Every clause had its occasion in some grievance or suffering or inadequacy. The preparation and enforcement of so unprecedented a body of new material worked a silent revolution in the attitude to law; but this was not always a happy change, for the mood of watchful accommodation of law to circumstance did not endure. A statute might raise unforeseen difficulties and, in the course of application, create new problems. The statute *Quia Emptores*, for example, had unexpected results. It generalized a condition frequently inserted in private deeds, that the new tenant should be responsible for the services of the mesne tenant from whom he had acquired his tenement: and it did this by abolishing the mesne tenure altogether;[3] but the effect was not, as had been intended, to preserve the rights of lords, great or small, who had suffered from sub-infeudation. It

[1] Plucknett, p. 45.
[2] Plucknett's argument (pp. 49–50) that there were two 'statutes' of *Quo Warranto* the second of which (Whitsun) weakened the force of the first (Easter), is untenable. The so-called Easter parliament of 1290 actually met in or shortly before Whit-week. See above, p. 342, note 2.
[3] See my paper on the English freeholder in *Wirtschaft und Kultur: Festschrift zum 70. Geburtstag von Alfons Dopsch* (1938), pp. 382–93. Probably the overlord had had some influence over these freeholders of Wotton Underwood. In 1260 a tentative anticipation of *Quia Emptores* had been ordered in the county court of Chester, in Edward's own earldom (Plucknett, pp. 105–6, 108–9). The problem of services and the mesne tenant had, in another context, received careful attention in Westminster II, c. 9; op. cit., pp. 93–94.

prevented new grants of tenure by knight service, except by the king, and grants of demesne by the lord of a manor to be held in fee of the manor. It 'slowly dissolved the nexus of tenure which constituted a manor'. The relationship of lord and man was gradually deprived of a tenurial basis. It had to clothe itself in new forms, with very serious results. King Edward had certainly not intended anything of this kind; he had wished to give every man his due.[1]

---

[1] Op. cit., pp. 106–8.

IX

WALES

THE relations between England and the rest of the British Isles must be considered in the light of the administrative system described in the last chapter, without regard to the enlightened principles which inspired the great statute of Westminster in our own time, and gave legal definition to the companionship of free peoples in a British Commonwealth. King Edward and his council would certainly have agreed with the realists of their own age who, in France and Naples, were busily emphasizing the doctrine that a king had the same rights in his kingdom as the emperor had in his;[1] but they would not admit that Ireland or Scotland or Wales could benefit from it. At one stage in the course of Anglo-French disputes, they may have toyed half-heartedly with the suggestion that Aquitaine should be entirely separated from France and held in fee of the Roman Church, but they would never have surrendered the settlement by which it was inalienably attached to the English Crown. In the kingdom of Scotland, where their successors were forced to give way, they insisted on the maintenance of the lordship implicit in the formal 'conjuncture' of the two kingdoms in the middle of 1291, and after John Baliol's election as king, on a relationship based on feudal custom. The establishment in Scotland of a monarchy responsible to the king of England as 'sovereign lord and emperor' under the guidance of 'natural law' would have opened the way to the claim that the king of the Scots had the same rights in Scotland as his 'emperor' had in England. They rejected a like claim by Llywelyn, prince of Wales, to rule his lands according to Welsh law under a sovereign whose power depended, not on feudal, but on a higher, imperial, kind of right, for this would have led to the same contention that the prince was sovereign within his borders. King Edward, of course, did not deny that local law and customs should be maintained. He had

---

[1] See the excellent account by Walter Ullmann in *E.H.R.* lxiv (1949), especially pp. 16–25.

sworn to maintain English custom and in 1280 he had sworn to
maintain the customs of the Agenais. After the conquest of
Wales he submitted the Welsh codes to scrutiny, but he never
denied that Welsh law should be respected where it was consonant with higher law, and by higher law he did not mean the
English common law;[1] but he could not contemplate the possibility of a tribunal, like the judicial committee of the privy council
in our day, for the administration of various kinds of law. The
king in council in parliament satisfied him. There he dealt with
Gascon petitions, Irish petitions, and, later in his reign, Scottish
petitions, and there he would deal with Welsh petitions, with
due regard to local customs and conditions. As he wrote to
Llywelyn on 18 July 1280, he would always 'according to God
and justice, do what the prelates and magnates of his realm
shall advise, especially as no one supposes that such prudent
men will give the king advice dissonant with or contrary to
reason'.[2]

The prince of Wales, in his turn, did not deny his dependence
on the king of England, to whom he, like other Welsh princes,
was on occasion ready enough to appeal for justice and protection. His view was that he held his principality under Edward's royal power but that its rights 'were entirely separate
from the rights' of England.[3] He was not subject to the limitations which prevailed in an English barony. He could receive
fugitives, build castles, and create markets without prohibition
or licence. He should be at liberty to deal with his vassals
according to Welsh law without interference. If any disputes
arose between him and his overlord they should be decided on
the borders by arbitrators appointed by each side, and in
accordance with Welsh or Marcher law, as the case might be.
He took the position taken by Edward's ancestors as dukes of
Normandy; these had done homage to the king of France on the
Norman March just as Llywelyn wished to do homage at the
ford of Montgomery.[4] Hence Llywelyn was intensely suspicious

[1] His father, Henry III, had written in 1244, protesting against the suspicion that
he had ever had the intention to introduce new laws and customs into the land of
his ally, Gruffydd ap Madog of Bromfield, in north Powys (*Cal. Pat. Rolls, 1232–47*,
p. 430).
[2] J. G. Edwards, *Calendar of Ancient Correspondence concerning Wales*, pp. 59–60.
[3] Ibid., p. 86 (letter of July 1273).
[4] J. F. Lemarignier, *Recherches sur l'hommage en marche et les frontières féodales* (1945).
Cf. P. Grierson in *E.H.R.* lxiii (1948), 398: 'There was good Norman tradition behind the plea of Robert of Torigny that the duke owed homage and fealty to the

of any tendency in the English administration to disregard traditional practice or to apply English rules to Welsh affairs. He must have been well aware that there were many deplorable precedents for tendencies of this kind; but ever since the cardinal Ottobuono had arranged the treaty of Montgomery in 1267, he had been a new man. King Henry had acknowledged his title, 'prince of Wales', which he had assumed some years before in place of the former title, 'prince of Aberffraw and North Wales'. His 'personage' (*persona*) had been explicitly enhanced, his rights in an enlarged principality had been recognized by the papal legate; and he had paid a great price. Hence, when, in the years before Edward's return to England, he had been confronted with commissions of judges and barons appointed by the English government, had been forbidden to build a castle over against Montgomery, had been pressed like a fraudulent debtor for instalments of his fine, while Marcher lords were intruding on the rights for which he was paying it, and had been summoned to do homage at Chester to a new king who had not yet arrived, he was, naturally enough, stirred to a state of angry alarm.

Racial, and even provincial and local, prejudices are so strong in men that they are generally immune against and can be strengthened by contact with the objects of their dislike. It has been noticed, for example, that crusaders and pilgrims rarely changed their traditional views about 'Saracens', however absurd these might be; they could not and did not wish to understand differences in behaviour. So the English regarded the Welsh. In spite of the intermarriages between princely Welsh families and Marcher families, tending to the formation of an Anglo-Welsh society, the ordinary Welshman was a barbarian in English eyes. A fragmentary history which was compiled about 1282, possibly by a clerk in Archbishop Pecham's circle, describes the Welsh as a Trojan debris swept into the wooded savagery of Cambria under the guidance of the devil. Their detestable sexual promiscuity played havoc with the laws of God and the principles of hereditary succession. Their lives were spent in theft and rapine or in slothful ease; only a few villeins, who tilled the lands for them as best they could, were exceptions to their depraved way of existence. If it

king [of France] *de sua vita et de suarum rerum honore*, but that Normandy was not a fief, and no *servitium de terra Normanniae* was due to the king.'

were asked why the English had not long ago blotted out the memory of this disagreeable people from the earth, the answer should be sought in the mild forbearance of the English kings who on frequent expeditions had too often allowed themselves to be affected by a show of Welsh penitence.[1] Such was the common opinion in England about the Welsh. A Flemish observer who studied the habits of the Welsh soldiers in Edward's army during the expedition of 1297 was more friendly and realistic. Their camp was in the village of Saint-Pierre near Ghent:

There you saw the peculiar habits of the Welsh. In the very depth of winter they were running about bare-legged. They wore a red robe. They could not have been warm. The money they received from the king was spent in milk and butter. They would eat and drink anywhere. I never saw them wearing armour. I studied them very closely and walked among them to find out what defensive armour they carried when going into battle. Their weapons were bows, arrows and swords. They had also javelins. They wore linen clothing. They were great drinkers. They endamaged the Flemings very much. Their pay was too small and so it came about that they took what did not belong to them.[2]

This impressionistic sketch, though slight, is consistent with the evidence of Welsh sources.[3] The Welsh were, in the main, a pastoral people, hardy, frugal, and lightsome in body and spirit. Their family ties gave them a sense of security, but did not pin them down so closely to the land that they could not move freely. They could pack their goods in wagons or on horses, and leave their rudely fashioned huts in a few hours.[4]

[1] The text is in the Hist. MSS. Commission's *Report on MSS. in Various Collections*, i (1901), 246–50. This view of the Welsh should be contrasted with Gerald of Wales's opinion of the English a hundred years earlier. They were a people born to slavery and in Wales were neatherds and craftsmen, plebeians of the rankest kind. The noble Norman and the freeborn, fearless Welshman were the admirable types (Lloyd, *History of Wales*, ii. 555). In Pecham's time the difference between Normans and English was less apparent.

[2] Lodewyk van Veltheam, *Voortzetting van den Spiegel Historiael* (1248–1316), ii (1931), 229; the translation is from *Trans. of Cymmrodorion Soc.* (1925–6), 46, note. The leaders of this force of Welshmen were three Welsh lords who had been deprived of their lands for taking part in the Welsh rising in 1282.

[3] In what follows I have made free use of the chapter in *King Henry III and the Lord Edward*, pp. 618 ff., which is based mainly on the work of J. E. Lloyd, J. G. Edwards, and Conway Davies; also of notes kindly supplied by Professor T. Jones Pierce.

[4] This applies especially to the busy life in summer on the upland pastures, where the lightly constructed *hafod* or hut was built. The old house or *hendref* in the

Their laws gave their princes the right to the service of the free men on expeditions of war and pillage for six weeks every year. The Welsh travelled light, and could move rapidly in every direction, along lateral ridgeways as easily as up and down the valleys. Their tenacious traditions were racial rather than national, their loyalties personal and local rather than centralized. Their nimble way of life gave free play to their vices as well as to their virtues, so that they seemed to be especially thievish, treacherous, vindictive, and volatile, in comparison with people of more settled habits. Moreover, they spoke a strange tongue and held to peculiar customs. Wales and England were foreign to each other.

Though these generalizations are true, they do not penetrate very far. They do not explain how the social system of Wales was affected by new influences in the course of the thirteenth century nor the extent to which the two Llywelyns of Snowdonia responded to the need to strengthen their administration and to give a national body to racial self-consciousness. What tendencies of this kind were at work in Wales when the end came?

The answer to this question takes us back to the days of King Henry II, when the Lord Rhys ruled so splendidly in south Wales until his death in 1197. Welsh aspirations were then, for the first time, compatible with acquiescence in Anglo-Norman lordship. The Lord Rhys was the king's friend and ally; the king cherished his vassal with the prudence of a statesman. The patriotic ardour of their contemporary, Gerald of Wales, was the more confident because the bounds of his political horizon were the bounds of the Angevin empire, of which Wales was a part. In May 1177 Rhys and David, the prince of Snowdonia, headed a group of Welsh rulers who gathered about the king at Oxford. The change of outlook is reflected in changes of nomenclature. The old royal style, *rex* or *brenin*, disappeared, to be replaced by the style, *dominus* or *arglwydd*, previously borne by minor rulers. The traditional sense of unity with the Britons, which underlies the word *cenhedloedd*, or union of tribes, faded away, to be replaced by the conception of Welsh coherence in the phrase *cenedl y Cymry*. The history of Wales in the thirteenth

valley was of more substantial build. J. E. Lloyd notes that the *hafod* produced a word *hafota*, which means to work hard, while the *hendref* led to *hendrefa*, meaning to rest (*Bull. of Board of Celtic Studies*, iv, pt. iii (1929), 224).

century turns on the inner conflict which ensued. On the one hand was the tribal and pastoral life within the borders of well-established and fiercely treasured lordships, centres of Welsh particularism. On the other was the movement towards the union of the tribal *patriae* under the primacy of the prince of Snowdonia, or Gwynedd, a tendency hastened by the rapid dissolution of the old kingdom of Deheubarth in the south where the Lord Rhys had seemed so secure. Most Welsh lawyers and many poets sought to give a concrete shape to the ideal of Gerald of Wales. The prince of Gwynedd was to be the keystone in an arch of kings. To the poet Dafydd Benfras, Llywelyn the Great was 'the great chief of fair Wales, our common leader'. Encouraged by the skill of lawyers and the poetry of the bards, the rulers of Snowdonia began gradually to extend their demesne and to adjust the law and institutions of their fathers to meet the needs which hampered the fulfilment of their ambition. The process was slow and far from complete when the last, who was also the first, native prince of Wales was killed in battle in 1282, but the changes revealed by recent Welsh scholarship are considerable. They prepared the way for the hybrid Edwardian settlement and, though the dream of a united self-contained Welsh principality was not realized, the spirit which inspired it helped to maintain Welsh nationalism. The words spoken to King Henry II by an old Welshman in 1163 still had their old force: 'I am persuaded that no other race than this and no other tongue than this of Wales, happen what may, will answer in the great day of judgement for this little corner of the earth.'

The tribal organization of Wales was affected by non-tribal changes and by changes within it. On the whole, feudal influences, even upon the relations between the prince and the other Welsh lords, were slight. Welsh neighbours and vassals of the Marcher lords tended to become more feudalized, and there was some penetration of the manorial form of economy into the purely Welsh districts; but the increasing power of the prince was due to the extension and exploitation of his demesne, the building of castles and towns, the encouragement of a military class, and recourse to taxation. The court of the prince, which in the thirteenth century became, in spite of its traditional structure, more and more like that of royal and baronial households in the west of Europe, depended for its maintenance upon the demesne.

Just as the military aid of the other lords was capricious and incalculable, so the prince could not look to them for financial support. He had to meet his household expenses, build his castles, provide his military forces, and organize his commissariat from his own lands. Hence we find a development of non-tribal expedients. Welsh law put at the disposal of the prince the sons of freemen from the ages of fourteen to twenty-one. He trained them for war and maintained them as his retainers. 'The motley crew who composed the royal body-guard (*teulu*) was made up of these young conscripts.' But more than this was needed. 'An attempt was made to bind certain prominent tribesmen, and through them, no doubt, the mass of their kinsmen, more closely to the cause of the house of Aberffraw. Considerable territorial grants—usually of bond-townships—were made to leading tribesmen, comprising jurisdictional immunity and freedom from all services.' In return those who entered into contracts of this kind were required to give more continuous military service. Prolonged operations beyond the borders of Gwynedd rather than brief annual raids were made possible. We are told that the principal military lieutenants of the two Llywelyns were drawn from these picked men.[1] Again, the duties of the bond-men (a small minority of the population) to maintain food-supplies on the demesne-manors, and give transport and building services, were supplemented by rents from the free, extra-tribal settlers in the boroughs. A modest change to a money economy occurred in small market towns modelled on those in the Marches. It is significant that Llywelyn ap Gruffydd's last foundation, at Abermoyl, was created when he built his neighbouring castle of Dolforwyn on the Severn, foundations which alarmed the royal council and the townsmen of Montgomery in 1272–3.[2] Dolforwyn was intended as part of the most southern line of defence of Snowdonia between the Severn and the sea; and the town would help to maintain it. The first general tax on movables and the commutation of tribute in kind for money-rents from the rural districts adjacent to the new towns were further steps towards the substitution of the individual for clan-co-operation in relations with the prince. King Edward later developed these tendencies on an elaborate scale, but, in a small way,

---

[1] Here, as elsewhere in this section, I make use of the notes of Professor Jones Pierce. Cf. his summary in the article on Wales in the new *Chambers's Encyclopaedia*.
[2] Cf. *King Henry III and the Lord Edward*, ii. 621–2.

they had begun before his heavier hand was laid upon the country.

Settlement was assisted by changes which are now perceptible in social life. The network of clan-relationships had begun before 1282 to give way to individual responsibility and a personal control of land which made for order and stability. How far change of this kind was due to such economic and social influences as greater pressure from without and the growth of population within the clan system, or to the policy of the princes, it would be hard to say; but there seems to be no doubt that from the later years of the twelfth century a legal renaissance, which would both reflect and define the attitude of the prince and his advisers, was at work among the jurists. The so-called laws of Hywel Dda should not be regarded as a fixed and untouchable code dating from the tenth century.[1] Revised editions had appeared and the glosses added by the editors show that a living jurisprudence was applied to the study of primitive usage:

Territorial principles now tended to transcend the purely tribal relationship. There could be no land without a lord; actions concerned with land were framed as suits between individual parties; incidents on land were of a feudal order. Though homage was personal, the oath being taken by a tribesman at the age of fourteen, it was fused with the proprietary principle when the son ascended to his father's status on the latter's death and was invested by the lord with a share of the family property.[2]

These changes did not transform the tribal and pastoral system of the tribal group (*llwyth*) in occupation of a free rural township within fixed boundaries, nor of the constituent clans or *gwelys* which had originated in the division of the township between the sons of the founder of a tribe, nor of the family group of co-heirs with its patrimony of scattered plots intermingled with the plots of fellow-tribesmen in dispersed hamlets. Co-operation in agriculture within the *gwely* and common responsibility for the payment of tribute in kind and entertainment of the prince as a burden on the *gwely* were still the marks of the Welsh rural economy. The rules of agnatic succession, within the fourth degree on the father's side, with the hiving-off of new clan-settlements, when individual holdings became too small, on the pastures and mountain slopes common to the

[1] See J. G. Edwards, *Hywel Dda and the Welsh Lawbooks* (Bangor, 1929).
[2] Professor Jones Pierce.

township, still continued. Yet the beginning of a gradual dissolution is apparent, a change to a more intensive agriculture—commutation of services to rents paid by the individual tenant, more give-and-take between the rural pastoral community and the market towns—and, in general, to the Welsh freeman's personal responsibility as a subject of the prince.[1] In one respect the law had gone further in this last direction than it had in modifying the clan system of tenure and succession; for before the conquest of Wales it had made a breach in the distinct and parallel organization of the *ceraint* or group of kindred responsible to the ninth degree for the payment or receipt of wergeld (*galanas*). Murder and homicide were distinguished, so that while the latter, as giving rise to a civil action, was a wrong for which compensation could be made by the *galanas* group, the former became a crime for which the murderer had to pay the penalty.

These tendencies in the administration and social life of north Wales illustrate the activity of the greater princes of Snowdonia as strong rulers at work with lawyers and stimulated by bards. The prince could also rely on the support of the monastic orders. The Cistercian way of life in particular was congenial to the Welsh, and the monks responded to local acceptance with an almost domestic loyalty to the princes who gave them a home in the secluded valleys and the run of the silent pastures on vast mountain slopes. 'The Cistercian abbot', Lloyd writes, 'was a St. David or a St. Teilo restored to life.' The first foundation, Whitland, on the river Taf in the south, was, it is true, the work of a Norman who welcomed disciples of St. Bernard from Clairvaux; but after it had passed under the jurisdiction of the Lord Rhys, it became Welsh, and its daughters and granddaughters, notably Strata Florida in Ceredigion, Aberconway at the mouth of the Conway river, Cymer in Merioneth, Valle Crucis in northern Powys, became centres of national feeling, independent of episcopal control and impatient of any restraint upon their devotion to their princely benefactors.

How closely intertwined the Cistercian houses were with the deepest and fiercest feelings of the men of Gwynedd was shown when the abbots of Strata Florida and Aberconway were allowed by King Henry in 1248 to bring to Conway the remains

---

[1] See T. Jones Pierce, 'The Growth of Commutation in Gwynedd during the Thirteenth Century', in *Bulletin of the Board of Celtic Studies*, x, pt. iv (1941), 309–32.

of Gruffydd the son of Llywelyn the Great, who four years before had been killed on St. David's day, when he was trying to escape from the Tower of London. He was buried in the family sepulchre in the abbey beside his father and his brother David. The kindly abbot, sang the bard Dafyd Benfras, brought him to the land of the Britons for his interment:

> Where run the white-rolling waves,
> Where meets the sea the mighty river,
> In cruel tombs at Aberconwy
> God has caused their dire concealment from us,
> The red-speared warriors, their nation's illustrious sons.[1]

The canons regular and the friars also tended to identify themselves with the aspirations of the two Llywelyns. The friars were always prone to take an independent line, and the Augustinian canons, who sometimes were entrusted with the reorganization of ancient monastic foundations, were, through their obligations to minister to laymen, perhaps used to revive the spirit of the old Celtic *clas* or mother church with its cluster of chapelries.[2] The bishops of north Wales, on the other hand, were in a more equivocal position between the claims of Canterbury and of the princes.[3] As suffragans of the archbishop they were required to maintain the particular rights of their churches and to reform diocesan administration in accordance with the decrees of oecumenical and legatine councils. As advisers of the prince they were expected to acquiesce in the subjection to the revised laws of Hywel Dda of age-long immunities and to approve of practices which, according to the 'law of the synod', should be the object of ecclesiastical censure. On the whole the four north Welsh bishops of our period, Richard and Anian of Bangor, Anian I and Anian II of St. Asaph, were accommodating. Richard of Bangor, before his

---

[1] J. Lloyd-Jones, 'The Court Poets of the Welsh Princes', in *Proc. of the British Academy*, xxxiv (1948), on p. 20 of the separate print. For the Cistercians see Lloyd, ii. 593–603. Cf. J. F. O'Sullivan, *Cistercian Settlements in Wales and Monmouthshire* (New York, 1947).

[2] When the Lord Rhys established Premonstratensian canons at Talley, near his royal seat at Dinefwr on the Tywi, the old mother church of the district, with twenty chapelries, was put under their jurisdiction.

[3] The dioceses, like the archdeaconries and rural deaneries, corresponded in the main to old Welsh divisions. See the introduction to J. Conway Davies, *Episcopal Acts relating to Welsh Dioceses, 1066–1272*, vol. i (1946), and cf. A. Hamilton Thompson on the dioceses in the *Journal of the Historical Society of the Church in Wales*, i (1947), 91–111.

retirement in 1267, and Anian II of St. Asaph, a Dominican who succeeded the more pliable Anian I in 1268, were strong champions of the rights of their sees, but it was always possible to compromise about claims to immunities; whereas, to judge from Archbishop Pecham's later reports, the Welsh bishops had not shown conspicuous vigour in the more hazardous role of disciplinarian. One cannot but sympathize with them. They were loyal Welshmen, the natural colleagues at court of the great lay advisers, Ednyfed Fychan (d. 1246) and his two sons and successors as seneschal, Goronwy (d. 1268)[1] and Tudur. The bishop of Bangor could least of all be expected to isolate his ecclesiastical from his political sympathies. His colleagues of St. David's and Llandaff were rarely of Welsh origin and ruled within the area of Marcher influence. The bishop of St. Asaph himself was constantly involved in local politics in the north-eastern marches and during some periods his diocese was largely withdrawn from Snowdonia and attached to the English Crown. The bishop of Bangor was perforce the spiritual leader of a society increasingly conscious of its mission to maintain Welsh traditions and Welsh independence.

Such was the social background in the century before the treaty of Montgomery in 1267. The period begins in 1165 with Henry II's last disastrous attempt to conquer Wales. The strength of Snowdonia in the north and of Deheubarth in the south had been consolidated by Owain Gwynedd and the Lord Rhys. The death of Owain (1170) left the Lord Rhys the leader of the Welsh princes. Then came the period of mutual under-standing between the king and the princes under the skilful and friendly guidance of Rhys from Dinefwr. The gradual assimi-lation of Welsh to Marcher lordships under the overlordship of the English king seemed to be merely a matter of time. The death of Rhys in 1197 and the passage of the hegemony in Wales to Owain's grandson, Llywelyn the Great, wrought a complete change. The prospect of a pleasant companion-ship preserved from sloth and decay by periodic forays and local vendettas gradually gave way to a sterner outlook. Llywelyn the Great certainly possessed some of the rich quality of the Lord Rhys. He married the natural daughter of King John and his own daughters were married to Marcher lords; he was on terms of cordial friendship with his most powerful

[1] The ancestor of Owen Tudor and the Tudor kings and queens of England.

neighbour, the earl of Chester; in spite of frequent disputes he was able, without much difficulty, both to extend his influence over the rest of Welsh Wales and to exploit such advantages as his feudal dependence upon the young king of England possessed; but the Wales of 1240, when he died, was not the Wales of the Lord Rhys. We see instead, behind the bastions of Snowdonia, an intensely Welsh court, whose modifications only emphasized its continuity with the past.[1] Life on the demesne of the prince continued in the old way. The oblong wooden hall or *neuadd* and its simple offices, maintained by the produce of the neighbouring country, still conformed to the traditional type;[2] but now the prince had his chancellor and chancery and clerks, and authenticated his acts by his great and privy seals. He had his treasurer. His 'high court' became more centralized under a single justice, rather than a peripatetic affair, which administered judicial business commote by commote. This high court, which heard appeals from the commotes, became the seat of government, to which, after the second Llywelyn became the 'prince of Wales' and received the formal submission of other princes, the lords of Wales could be summoned or bring their disputes, and in which all sorts of public business was done in co-operation with the seneschal, bishops, high officials and clerics, the prince's near kinsmen and advisers, and the lesser lords of the principality, and from which missions to the papal and other courts could be sent. The spirit which prevailed, however, was anything but Anglo-Norman; it was Welsh, expressed in traditional ways, in the learning of a live Welsh law, and in the ancient erudite forms of a poetry, whose artifice and obscurities did not preclude the elaboration of new modes, nor fail to convey an intense appreciation of the beauties of nature and of the changing fortunes of man. The soul of Wales lay here.

The changes which renovated the old Wales are all apparent in the reign of Llywelyn ab Iorwerth, the Great. As though to

[1] It is significant that Owain Gwynedd, though he gave up, as Henry II's vassal, the title of *rex* or *brenin*, refused to adopt, as the other princes did, the feudal title of *dominus* or *arglwydd*. He assumed the title of *princeps* or *tywysog*, hitherto a generic term used for members of the ruling class, without constitutional significance.

[2] See Lloyd, i. 313–14; and, for Aberffraw in Anglesey, the description in F. Seebohm, *Tribal System in Wales* (1904), pp. 5–21, with the map. The repairs made in 1306 at Nefyn, the chief residence of the prince in Lleyn, suggest that it survived the conquest unchanged; see T. Jones Pierce in *Bull. of Board of Celtic Studies*, v, pt. ii (1930), 142 ff.

emphasize the power and dignity of his court and the command-
ing outlook from his hills he changed his style from 'the prince
of Gwynedd' to the prince of Aberffraw and lord of Snowdon.
Disregarding the custom of Wales, he declared his son by his
wife Joan, the daughter of King John, his sole heir (1220),
disinherited, with papal approval, his natural son Gruffydd,
and in 1238, at Strata Florida, is said to have secured sworn
recognition of the succession from the other Welsh lords,
whether these were vassals of King Henry or not.[1] In 1216, in
what has been described as the first Welsh parliament, he had
divided the principality of Deheubarth among the heirs of the
Lord Rhys. He was for many years as powerful in south Wales
as he was in Powys, and at one time seemed likely to bring even
the Marcher lords within the ambit of his influence; yet he
never allowed a state of war to develop into a life-or-death
struggle for his independence. He was well aware of the advantages of a relationship which could give him, at need, the
support of the English Crown or make him the trusted agent of
royal policy in dealings with the other princes.

Certainly the turbulence was great and in times of open
warfare ferocious and devastating. During the campaign of Elfael
in 1231, for example, Llywelyn was solemnly excommunicated
for his crimes by the English bishops. The prince's power outside Snowdonia, though always considerable, waxed and
waned. During the war between King John and his rebellious
barons, Llywelyn won control of nearly the whole country. By
the treaty of Worcester, arranged by the legate Guala in 1218,
he retained, as the young King Henry's lieutenant during the
minority, the royal castles and honours of Carmarthen and
Cardigan, and the wardship of the heir of southern Powys. This
co-operation did not last long. After the death of the *rector regni*

---

[1] Earlier in the year Llywelyn had desired the Welsh magnates to do homage to
David as their future lord. King Henry had strongly objected and ordered David to
receive no homage from the magnates of North Wales and Powys until he had done
homage to himself. He pointed out, also, that some of these magnates were his men
and owed homage to him (*Close Rolls, 1237–42*, pp. 123–5). These letters show that
the homage done by David in 1228 for all lands and rights which would accrue to
him on his father's death (Lloyd, ii. 669) was not regarded as covering the case. In
1222 Pope Honorius III confirmed an ordinance made by Llywelyn with King
Henry's consent and by authority of Archbishop Stephen and the legate Pandulf,
to the effect that David should succeed him, and in 1226 the same pope declared
Joan, David's mother, legitimate (without prejudice to the king or realm of
England), and promoted the observance of an oath of fealty taken to David by the
magnates of Wales by command of King Henry (*Cal. Papal Letters*, i. 87, 109).

William the Marshal, Llywelyn attacked and ravaged the earl's honour of Pembroke, in retaliation for local inroads on the neighbouring Welsh. In 1223 the new earl marshal, another William, took his revenge; he crossed the sea from his Irish lands, seized the castles of Carmarthen and Cardigan and set about the restoration of Marcher power in the south. So far we have the familiar story of local warfare between Welsh and Marcher lords, with its usual incoherence and cross-purposes; but from this time a change began. As the king grew older and the justiciar, Hubert de Burgh, took more control of affairs in his name, the danger of Llywelyn's hold on Wales was realized, while the justiciar, in his turn, saw the possibility of reshaping the Anglo-Norman power in the Marches on firmer foundations. The lords Marcher in the south were not united and, as the old generation died out, were embarrassed by quick successions or the prospect of divisions of their lands among co-heiresses. Strong centres of royal control at strategic points were needed— at Cardigan to secure the half-Welsh, half-Norman lordships in the northern parts of Dyved, south of the Teifi, and to weaken Welsh hold south of Aberystwyth; at Carmarthen to defend the valley of the Tywi and the way to the Bristol Channel; at Builth to hold the frontier against Snowdonia and guard the vital valley of the Wye; and at Montgomery to give more unity to the eastern Marches, expose the prince's flank, and close the way to Shrewsbury.

The danger to Builth in the Welsh campaign which followed the new earl marshal's capture of Cardigan and Carmarthen roused the justiciar to action. Hitherto, and partly for personal reasons, support of the marshal had been half-hearted, but from 1223 the lead was taken and held by Hubert de Burgh. He had also been roused by an attack on the Shropshire March from which Llywelyn had been diverted by the landing of the marshal. A royal army was assembled at Hereford, Builth was relieved, and Hubert went on to Montgomery through the districts of Maelienydd and Kerry (*Ceri*). The rocky site was now definitely occupied, and here the new castle of Montgomery was built. Llywelyn submitted. The earl marshal retained Cardigan and Carmarthen as hereditary castellan. Builth was held by its lord, Reginald de Braose, Llywelyn's son-in-law and his former ally in King John's days. Work on the new castle of Montgomery continued.

Montgomery was especially dangerous to Llywelyn, for it threatened his home lands, and the justiciar had ambitious plans. In April 1228 Hubert was granted the castle and lord-ship. He at once set about the clearing of the forests which protected the Welsh commote of Kerry and prepared to push the frontier into this important district. The royal host was summoned, Kerry was invaded, and work began on a second castle, probably at a place now called Pen y Castell. Hubert, how-ever, had been too hasty. The Welsh country-side was roused, his commissariat was inadequate, his fellow barons indifferent. The Kerry campaign was a disastrous failure and the unfinished castle was razed to the ground. Llywelyn in return undertook to pay £2,000 in compensation, but this sum was balanced by the ransom which he exacted for the release of one of his prisoners, William de Braose, who in 1227 had succeeded his father Reginald as lord of Abergavenny and Builth and other Marcher lordships and castles. During his brief captivity William had agreed to give Builth as a marriage portion with his daughter Isabella, who was to wed David, the prince's son and heir. He had also been so mad as to have an intrigue with the prince's wife, Joan, the mother of his young stepmother Gwladus Ddu.[1] A year after his release, while William was on a visit at Easter (1230), Llywelyn discovered his domestic treachery and, sup-ported by general clamour for his death, had him publicly hanged. In letters to William's widow Eva and to her brother the earl marshal, Llywelyn declared that it was the magnates of his land who had given judgement on him for his behaviour. The prince made no excuses for them and expressed no regret, but he assured the earl and his sister that he desired the compact of marriage between his son and William's daughter to stand. He sought their consent and, in a postcript to his letter to the earl, declared that their friendship, so far as he was concerned, would remain firm and inviolable. Neither the king nor any-thing else in the world could affect that.[2] His protestations are

---

[1] William's mother was Reginald's first wife, Graeca, the daughter of William Brewer. In some genealogical tables he is made the son of Reginald and Gwladus Ddu, and so the paramour of his grandmother. He left three other daughters, who brought his lordships to Bohuns (Brecon), Cantilupes (Abergavenny), and Mortimers (Radnor).

[2] Shirley, *Royal Letters*, i. 368–9. Note that Llywelyn sealed his letter to the earl with his secret seal, because his great seal was not with him. He had his constable in Builth a few weeks later, if not already (ibid. ii. 5).

understandable, for the possession of Builth was at stake. The marriage took place and Builth remained in Llywelyn's hands, as Isabella's *maritagium*. The compact was, naturally enough, distasteful to the king. In 1241, after Llywelyn's death, Builth was seized by the Crown.

Llywelyn's letter to his former enemy, the earl marshal, is significant. The prince knew how he stood with the Marcher lords. He lived and fought with them as one great baron with another; but, even while he made truce after truce and begged for a firm peace, he was conscious of a change in England. The justiciar's failure in Kerry had stimulated him and the young king to further action. In 1229 Cardigan and Carmarthen, which in 1226 had been taken into the king's hands, were turned into a new lordship, held by the service of five knights, for Hubert de Burgh. In 1230-1 Hubert was made master in the southern Marches: the peninsula of Gower, the lordship of John de Braose, was subordinated to the lordship of Carmarthen,[1] and after the death of Earl Gilbert of Gloucester in Brittany, the great Anglo-Welsh lordship of Glamorgan was entrusted to him as guardian of the heir, a boy of eight. Finally, on the sudden death of the earl marshal in April 1231, the custody of the lands of William of Braose—the lordships of Brecon, Abergavenny, Radnor, and other castles, now in process of division between his co-heiresses, nieces of the marshal—was transferred from this close relative to the upstart justiciar. As, since 1219, Hubert had held 'the three castles of the justiciar', Grosmont, Skenfrith, and White Castle, in Upper Gwent, north-east of Abergavenny, his control stretched from Cardigan Bay to the Wye.

Llywelyn was in less danger than a study of the map suggests, but he was sufficiently angry and alarmed to begin war on a large scale. Indeed, the transfer of the Braose lands to Hubert in May 1231 may well have been the immediate cause of Llywelyn's violence, for it was a reply to his own movements against them, movements which had brought the English king as far as Hereford and were the subject of negotiations at this very time. Early in June Llywelyn suddenly broke loose. He

[1] John, son and heir of William *junior*, the eldest son of the great William de Braose, had Gower and the *caput* of the Braose lands, Bramber in Sussex. He was, like his uncle Reginald, a son-in-law of Llywelyn. He continued to hold Gower after it was sub-infeudated to Hubert de Burgh. In 1232 he was killed by falling from his horse at Bramber.

carried devastation from the town of Montgomery to Radnor, Brecon, Caerleon, and thence to the south-west, ending with a triumphant attack upon the castle of Cardigan. The result was King Henry's campaign in Elfael, a district of the Braose inheritance, lying to the east of the district of Builth. It would seem that the justiciar had planned a formidable attack on central Wales by way of Builth. His preparations were impressive.[1] That a strenuous campaign was intended is implied in a letter to the justiciar of Ireland, dated 25 June, in which any men in Ireland who might wish to acquire lands in Wales were invited to come and to keep whatever they might acquire. Yet the campaign of Elfael was almost as great a fiasco as the campaign in Kerry had been. The host lingered for months at Painscastle while a stone fortress was built in place of the former Braose castle. The decision to rebuild was sound, for Painscastle lay on one of the few open routes from Wales to Hereford, whether from the north through Builth or along the ancient ridgeway on the mountain of Eppynt from the west;[2] but it is hard to see why the whole of the king's army was arrested, and Llywelyn left free to destroy ten castles while Henry built one. Provisions began to fail. In November Henry made a truce with Llywelyn. When the prince next went to war, to join forces with Richard the Marshal, he was able to follow up his advantage, and to retain Cardigan and Builth. From the truce made in July 1234 at the place called Middle, half-way between Ellesmere and Shrewsbury, until his death in 1240, Llywelyn ruled in peace.[3]

The campaign of Elfael put an end to the justiciar's attempt to take the lead in the Marches and to confine Llywelyn to his mountain fastnesses. His failure led immediately to his fall from power; but, here as elsewhere, his ideas bore fruit. In 1241 Cardigan and Builth were retaken, to be retained, like Carmarthen and Montgomery, as royal fortresses. Cardigan and Carmarthen became the centres of gradually widened areas of administration, to which, from 1241 if not earlier, the same of 'shire' was generally given. They had their county courts and bounds, and in due course were fitted into the shire-system

---

[1] Mr. R. F. Walker is engaged upon a study of this and other Welsh campaigns between 1218 and 1267.

[2] See *King Henry III and the Lord Edward*, ii. 624–5.

[3] Above, p. 60.

established by Edward I in Snowdonia.[1] For the rest, the Elfael
campaign illustrates the difficulty of a sustained effort amidst
the social cross-currents and in the geographical conditions of
a land like Wales. These enterprises had no drive behind them;
and in 1231 the only man with purpose was a desperate man,
harassed by the feeling which his ambition had aroused. Henry
was in a very strange state of mind during these years. When
Llywelyn died he had recovered himself, was a married man
and a father, and had new friends about him.

The change was seen at once when David, after his father's
death, came to King Henry at Gloucester, where he was
knighted and did homage for north Wales. It had long been
clear that the main cause of unrest was the equivocal position
of the other Welsh princes, or, as they were now styled in the
royal chancery, the barons of Wales, in Powys and Ceredigion
and in the lands once ruled by the Lord Rhys. Both they and
the Welsh sub-vassals were an uncertain quantity unless the
prince of north Wales was confined within definite boundaries
and their own position as vassals of the king or the marchers
was put beyond dispute. Hence King Henry at once took
advantage of David's succession, arranged by his father with
royal and papal approval in disregard of Welsh custom, to
insist on a settlement. By the terms of the peace made at
Gloucester on 15 May 1240, 'all the homages of the barons of
Wales' were to be enjoyed by the king and his heirs without
question and the rights to lands claimed by Gruffydd ap
Gwenwynwyn, the greatest lord in south Powys, and by other
lords of Powys and the Marches, were to be submitted to the
arbitration of the papal legate Otto, and of leading men in
England and Wales. David's subsequent failures to appear before
the arbitrators enabled the king, after the legate's departure
from England, to transfer the investigation to a royal commission, and, when the prince resisted, to overrun north Wales
as far as the prince's castle of Degannwy (or Gannoc), east of
the estuary of the river Conway.

Henry also took up the cause of David's elder and illegitimate
brother Gruffydd, whom David had kept in captivity. By a
treaty made near St. Asaph in August 1241, afterwards con-

[1] For details of the composition and administration of these shires see J. G.
Edwards in *E.H.R.* xxxi (1916), 90–98, with a useful map. Cf. J. E. Lloyd, *The
Story of Ceredigion, 400–1277* (Cardiff, 1938).

firmed and enlarged at London in October, the prince undertook
to release his brother and to submit to the decision of the king's
court, either in accordance with Welsh customs or by rules of
law (*jus*), on the lands to be allotted to Gruffydd, who was to
hold these lands in chief of the Crown. He gave up Degannwy,
Ellesmere in Englefield, and also Mold which had been in
dispute, promised to indemnify the king for expenses and
damages, and remitted to him the homages of all noble Welshmen. At London, in October 1241, Henry went farther, indeed
too far; for, in a separate agreement, he was accepted by David
as his heir in north Wales if the prince should die without
lawful issue.[1] Gruffydd's rights, though they were reasserted in
the main treaty, were not given effect. He was kept in honourable captivity in the Tower of London, probably because his
detention was now convenient to both parties. In 1244 (on St.
Davids' day) he tried to escape by means of an improvised rope.
The rope broke and he was killed. His death made him a Welsh
hero, a worthy father of the second Llywelyn. It also freed
David from his greatest fear. In the summer the prince repudiated the treaty, appealed to the pope and revolted, this
time with the support of the Welsh lords. There is evidence that
he even assumed the title prince of Wales.

Henry had to start over again. This time he could use the
base which he had aquired in north Wales, and follow what
was to become a familiar route in Welsh wars. He did not
gather his army until the summer of 1245, but his plan of
campaign was extensive and included the passage of provisions
and troops from Ireland. He had already built a castle on a rock
near Rhuddlan to take the place of the castle there. This was
the castle of Diserth; and in addition he decided to rebuild the
castle at Gannoc or Degannwy, farther to the west. The campaign of Gannoc, like the campaigns in Kerry and Elfael, was
ferocious but short-lived. David held firm behind the Conway
river. A letter from Degannwy, preserved by Matthew Paris,
gives a vivid picture of hardships and lack of food. Prisoners
were slaughtered on both sides; heads of Welshmen were
brought back as trophies after every English success. A force
from Ireland ravaged Anglesey. Yet once again Henry had to

---

[1] The various treaties and other documents are in J. G. Edwards, *Littere Wallie*
(1940), from the register in the P.R.O. known as Liber A. See nos. 2, 4, 6, 5, 23, in
this order.

break off operations. Before he could renew them, David died (February 1246). He left no son, but Gruffydd's second son Llywelyn had been active on his side, and Owain, Llywelyn's elder brother, at once fled from Henry's protection near Chester to join him in the claim for the inheritance. For the time being, the two brothers were persuaded to divide the commotes of north Wales between them and to rule together. The war continued, but as imports were cut off, and Wales to the south was held, and the new castle at Degannwy now threatened the approaches to Snowdonia, the two young princes at last agreed to pay the price of recognition. By the peace of Woodstock, where they met the king in April 1247, they surrendered the whole area between the county of Chester and the Conway valley, that is, the four cantrefs of Perfeddwlad, and agreed to hold north Wales of the king by military service, while Henry retained in perpetuity 'the homages and services of all barons and nobles of Wales'.[1] Thus the principality of Aberffraw and Snowdonia was restricted within narrower limits than it had had since the rise to power of Llywelyn the Great; its swift-footed warriors were liable to royal service within Wales and without. The English king held, as the hinterland to the palatinate of Chester, a broad stretch of country along the coast to the Conway valley with its two new fortresses of Diserth and Degannwy. All the rest of Wales was held of him by Marcher and native lords, or ruled from royal castles.

The story of the recovery of power by Llywelyn ap Gruffydd is almost as much a part of the history of England as it is of Wales itself,[2] for it was made possible by the distracted condition of English affairs during the decade 1257-67. It begins in 1255 with a civil war in the western passes, after a quarrel between Llywelyn and his brother Owain, who was apparently supporting the claims to lands of a younger brother David. Owain and David were defeated and imprisoned, and from this time Llywelyn ruled alone. He immediately turned his attention to the four cantrefs of Perfeddwlad in the north and to the shires of Cardigan and Carmarthen in the south, where King Henry

---

[1] The text of the treaty of Woodstock is in *Littere Wallie*, no. 3, pp. 7–8. For the origin and limits of the four cantrefs, Rhos, Rhuvoniog, Dyffryn Clwyd, and Englefield (or Tegeingl), see Lloyd, i. 239–42. A sketch-map of Wales at the time of the treaty will be found in T. F. Tout's very important paper, 'Wales and the March in the Barons' Wars', reprinted in his *Collected Papers*, ii (1934), 46.

[2] Cf. above, pp. 137–8, 171–2, 201–2, 215.

had made a large and sweeping return, this time under royal auspices, to the policy of Hubert de Burgh. In 1254 the king's eldest son, Edward, had been given his start in political life, and, as part of the great establishment which had its administrative centre in Bristol castle,[1] was endowed with Chester and its palatinate shire, the Four Cantrefs as appurtenant to Chester (and, like it, inalienable from the English Crown), Montgomery and its honour, Builth and its district, the three castles of Upper Gwent, Cardigan, and Carmarthen and their shires, and part of Ceredigion to the north of Cardigan. Not unnaturally, the officials set in charge of these areas regarded themselves as the administrative and financial agents of the young prince with whose interests they were entrusted, rather than as royal officials, as they also were, responsible for the well-being of the inhabitants.[2] They did not possess the tact and experience which had made such Marcher lords as the marshals sensitive to the danger of submitting their Welsh tenants to the control of aliens. Their indifference to Welsh customs and Welsh feeling provided Llywelyn with occasions. He saw that he could appear as a champion of the distressed, and that the Marcher lords were resentful and suspicious of the new order, and he struck. His assumption in 1258 of the title 'Prince of Wales' was more than a gesture; it was both the answer to a challenge and a declaration of purpose.

He had, indeed, reason to feel confident. As early as the spring of 1257 he could claim that his attack had the support of all the magnates of Wales.[3] His success in welding together north and south in an indissoluble union 'such as previously had never been seen' stirred the admiration of Matthew Paris, who saw in his success a timely example to the English. His energy was informed by intelligence. In this war he had bodies of heavily armed horse-soldiers to supplement his footmen, used siege-engines, and protected the Welsh coasts against possible inroads from Ireland or elsewhere by the collection of a small

[1] Above, p. 118.

[2] Geoffrey of Langley, Edward's chief bailiff, is said to have boasted to the king and queen that he had the Welsh in the palm of his hand. See the interesting passage in the annals of Dunstable (*Ann. monast.* iii. 200–1). Cf., for the administration of the Four Cantrefs, A. J. Roderick in *Bull. of Board of Celtic Studies*, x, pt. iii (1940), 246–56.

[3] In the very interesting letter to Richard of Cornwall (*Royal Letters*, ii. 312–13), wrongly dated 1267 by Shirley; cf. Lloyd, ii. 720, note 21. Richard had sent Dominicans to Llywelyn to urge him to restore the Four Cantrefs.

fleet. Between his sudden attack on the Four Cantrefs in November 1256, when he overran them in a week, and the destruction of the castle at Diserth and the recovery of Degannwy in August and September 1263, he established his authority over Powys and the lands held by the descendants of the Lord Rhys, captured Builth, pushed far into the lordships of Roger Mortimer and of the successors of William de Braose, and, in short, went far to justify his new title as prince of Wales. On the king's side, after the failure of Henry's campaign in 1257, resistance had been local and disconnected, weakened by suspicion and divided interests, so that the Marches had become thoroughly demoralized. Peter de Montfort's defence of Abergavenny against the south Welsh princes led by Llywelyn's seneschal in the spring of 1263 is the finest incident in this melancholy record of English indecision.[1]

The story of Llywelyn's achievements and of the breakdown in the Marches should be sought elsewhere; its significance depends on details of incidents and personal relationships.[2] Until the outbreak of war in England in May 1263, Llywelyn tried to consolidate his gains by frequent negotiations for a firm peace or, failing this, the conclusion of truces. Indeed, a state of truce existed throughout this period. The prince broke it twice. The truce arranged at Oxford in June 1258 was renewed at the ford of Montgomery a year later to last till 1 August 1260. Llywelyn, while the king was in France and political tension in England was becoming more acute, made prolonged attacks on Builth and the Marcher lands in the east. The English government planned a united campaign; but before this could begin the truce was renewed to last until June 1262, and in May 1262 was renewed for another two years.[3] When Llywelyn attacked Mortimer (November 1262), devastated his lands and overran Brecon, King Henry tried to organize another campaign, but his hopes were dashed by the explosion of war in England. This was Llywelyn's great year; the Welsh tenants of the Marchers revolted, the Welsh lords of the south were united on his side,

---

[1] Peter's letters and those of John de Grey to the king and his council show that the Welsh lords in the south had combined and that the Welsh tenants of the lords Marcher had deserted to them. See *Royal Letters*, ii. 219–21, 230–1, and J. G. Edwards, *Cal. of Anc. Corresp.*, pp. 17–19, 30, 52–53, 175. Abergavenny was held for the Lord Edward as guardian of the heir, George de Cantilupe. For the dates of these letters see Tout, *Collected Papers*, ii. 64–65, and Edwards's notes.

[2] The best account is in Tout, op. cit. ii. 47–100, where the story is carried to 1267.   [3] *Littere Wallie*, pp. 17, 18.

Edward's castles in north Wales were conquered; even Gruffydd ap Gwenwynwyn of Powys returned to his allegiance and joined with the prince in extending Welsh control at the expense of the Marcher lords west of the Severn.

Llywelyn's success was not due to deep calculation, but rather to the mingling of passion with a quick sense of opportunity. He knew that his position was precarious, that his relations with the southern princes were anything but 'indissoluble', and that he must win for his rapid gains the ratification of a firm peace. He had been stirred to action by the use which the king had made of the advantage given to the Crown in the treaty of Woodstock, and only the king could confirm his encroachments. Hence, when Simon de Montfort sought his aid in 1264-5, he insisted that the new government in England should recognize his title, his lordship over the magnates of Wales, and his gains; and for this he was ready to pay a large sum, 30,000 marks in ten annual instalments; and he made it clear in letters patent that the treaty (Pipton, June 1265) was dependent upon the maintenance by the king of his adherence to the recent settlement in England. If the king defaulted or was denounced to the prince by his council as a defaulter, the prince's obligation to obey him as lord and to pay the price of the treaty would lapse, until he had reconciled himself with the magnates. In supplementary letters, which reflect Simon's view of the treaty, Llywelyn declared that, if the king died or defaulted, payments would continue to his heir or successor willing to observe the ordinance of London, or, alternatively, as the magnates who adhered to it might decide.[1] Llywelyn, in these declarations, was not concerned to profess his own adhesion to the English settlement but to make sure that his position would be respected if Simon and his adherents should win the day; and, after the battle of Evesham two months later, he pursued his object with the triumphant Edward. This was a

---

[1] *Royal Letters*, ii. 284-7. For the English settlement in parliament and the treaty of Pipton see above, pp. 198, 201. Apart from his dependence on the Crown, Llywelyn had to consider the family relations of the chief Welsh princes of Powys and the south with Marcher lords, just as the king had to remember the Welsh connexions of Marcher lords. Thus Gruffydd ap Gwenwynwyn of south Powys was married to a Lestrange, and Roger Mortimer was the son of Gwladus Dda, the daughter of Llywelyn the Great. The desertion of his brother David at the end of 1263 was also a danger to Llywelyn. It is worth noting that two important castles, Diserth in 1256 and Builth in 1260, were razed after capture, not retained by the prince. The royal castle of Rhuddlan later succeeded Diserth, and Builth was rebuilt by Edward in 1277.

very difficult moment in his life, but his pertinacity and insight were rewarded. King Henry was in no position to renew the conflict, the papal legate and the moderate element among his advisers were determined on peace, and, after much vain negotiation, the legate himself brought the matter to a conclusion in the treaty of Montgomery (1267), twenty years after the treaty of Woodstock.

On the other hand, Llywelyn's successes after his unexpected revival of the prestige of Snowdonia in 1256 had done more than anything else to establish the position of the Lord Edward. Edward had been humiliated. Llywelyn had overrun his lands in north Wales and devastated his lordships in the south. Every attempt to organize a Welsh campaign had failed. During his brief alliance with his uncle Simon de Montfort, to whom he had turned in 1259-60, he had lost his castle and lands in Builth.[1] In his efforts to relieve his castles of Diserth and Degannwy, which still held out on the Welsh coast, he had had to rely on his own mercenaries, while the Marches were crumbling away. The events of 1262-3, however, ended the vacillations of the Marcher lords, who from this time rallied to Edward and put behind them their previous suspicions of royal penetration into Wales. With a few exceptions they fought on the royalist side at Lewes and they were the driving force in the royalist triumph in 1265. In this new generation the Marchers found a fierce and vigorous leader in Roger Mortimer, the lord of Wigmore and Weobley and, through his wife, of the old Braose lordship in Radnor. Roger had borne the brunt of Llywelyn's attack on the wild frontier lands east of Builth, and now he gradually acquired a predominance in the eastern Marches of the Severn and the Wye which was to give his family a notable part in the later history of England. He, more than any other man, broke the fortunes of Earl Simon and, by rallying the Marches sustained Edward's independence as heir to the throne, and later as king. Llywelyn had to deal with a new spirit in the Marches after the barons' wars. The treaty of Montgomery, it is true, put the seal of royal acquiescence on his principality, but it did not give him the freedom to consolidate, still less to extend it.

The treaty[2] acknowledged Llywelyn as prince of Wales and

---

[1] For a time Roger Mortimer, to whom the castle had been entrusted, was under grave suspicion of betraying Builth.

[2] The text of the treaty is in *Littere Wallie*, pp. 1–4. For a more detailed study of

1 Gwynedd or Snowdonia
2 Perfeddwlad
3 Powys Faedog
4 South Powys
5 Rhwng gwy a Hafren
6 Ceredigion
7 Dyfed ⎫ Deheubarth
8 Ystrad Tywi ⎭
9 Morgannwg
10 Brycheiniog

WALES

lord of all the Welsh princes except the unstable Mareddud of Dryslwyn on the Tywi, whose homage he afterwards was allowed to buy. It retained the prince's direct lordship over Builth, the Bohun inheritance in Brecon, and the district of Gwerthrynion, between Builth and Roger Mortimer's lands. Although Elfael, conquered in 1264, was not granted, Llywelyn kept his hold there till 1276. He ruled from the upper waters of the Taff, south of Brecon, to Anglesey. Pope Gregory X 'recognized his exceptional position in the English realm' by allowing ecclesiastical citations to the court of Canterbury to be tried by commissioners sent to Wales. On the other hand, Cardigan and Carmarthen, which in December 1265 had been entrusted to Edward's brother Edmund, maintained royal interests in the south-west, while William de Valence as lord of Pembroke[1] and Gilbert of Clare, earl of Gloucester, as lord of Glamorgan, buttressed the hold of the lesser Marcher lords of the south and linked them with the powerful Roger Mortimer and his colleagues in the east. Gilbert of Clare, now more at liberty to resume his ancestral leadership in the south, showed his appreciation of Llywelyn's penetration to the Taff and his claim to the district of Senghenydd, between the Taff and the Rhymni, by the erection at Caerphilly of the greatest fortress yet built in Wales, and this in spite of Llywelyn's violent intervention (1268-71). The interpretation of the terms of the treaty provided local disputes, especially in Brecon and in Mortimer's lands in Maelienydd; and when, after King Henry's death, the rulers of England summoned Llywelyn to do homage to the absent king and tried to prevent him from building a new castle at Dolforwyn, near Montgomery, the prince became still more restive. He slackened his payment, hitherto punctual, of the big fine of 20,000 marks for which he had bought his recognition as prince and intensified his protests against alleged infringements of the treaty. The situation became critical when early in 1274 his brother David, who had been restored to his lands and status in Wales, conspired with Gruffydd ap Gwenwynwyn of south Powys. According to the story, David's daughter was to marry Gruffydd's son, David was to displace his brother as prince of Wales, and the power of

the events between 1267 and 1274, summarized in this paragraph, see Lloyd, ii. 747-54, and Powicke, *King Henry III and the Lord Edward*, ii. 577-82, 637-45.

[1] William de Valence, the eldest of Henry III's half-brothers of the house of Lusignan, got Pembroke, but not the earldom, as the husband of a granddaughter of the great William the Marshal.

Gruffydd was to be greatly enlarged. Llywelyn seized Gruffydd's lordship, David and Gruffydd fled, and in 1275, from his head-quarters in Shrewsbury, the exiled lord of south Powys made numerous forays into central Wales. In the meanwhile King Edward had returned to England, and had been crowned at Westminster.

There can be no doubt that David's treachery and flight to England was the immediate cause of the Welsh war which began in 1276. Llywelyn had received his brother back to favour in 1267, and the discovery of the plot against him, whatever the real truth of the matter was, came as a shock to the prince. The Welsh chronicle states explicitly that the barons of Wales, met together in assembly, advised Llywelyn not to go to do homage to Edward because the king was maintaining David and his ac-complice Gruffydd ap Gwenwynwyn. The king could not accept this point of view. He had returned to England after a long absence. He knew that the prince of Wales had refused to do homage to him before he did return. One of his first acts had been to see the prince's envoys and to fix a date, 25 November 1274, when he would receive Llywelyn and his homage at Shrewsbury. An attack of illness forced him to postpone the meeting; and later he arranged a meeting at Chester (August 1275). In a letter to the pope he afterwards stated that this Chester meeting was arranged at Llywelyn's own request.[1] In the interval Llywelyn had discovered the plot against him, David and the lord of south Powys had fled, and the latter had begun a little war from the security of Shrewsbury, where he was under royal protection. Edward does not seem to have regarded the incident very seriously; he could remember too many Welsh domestic crises to suppose that this could not be settled with all the other difficulties then under the consideration of commissioners of inquiry; but here he was wrong. Llywelyn now would only do homage under conditions; Edward would only do justice after Llywelyn had regularized his position by becoming his vassal. The king went to Chester, Llywelyn did

[1] *Calendar of Ancient Correspondence concerning Wales*, pp. 64–65 (probably Sept.–Oct. 1276). This letter to Pope Gregory was sent to rebut the prince's agents at the papal court. It emphasizes Llywelyn's refusal to appear and the failure of the arch-bishop's attempt at mediation. Other evidence suggests (cf. above, p. 243) that Edward regarded himself as at war with Llywelyn before the final decision in November. There is no evidence, however, that he returned to England with any intention to go to war. Indeed, he showed much patience.

not appear. After consultation with his magnates, Edward formally summoned the prince three times, with due punctilio, to
appear at court; the prince sent envoys and argued but never
came. Even after his last default (26 April 1276) Edward, on
the solicitation of the prelates and barons in parliament, allowed
a final effort to be made through Archbishop Kilwardby, who
chose the archdeacon of Canterbury, a trained diplomat and
canonist, to go to Wales as mediator; but Llywelyn insisted that
the place of homage must be Oswestry or Montgomery and that
his grievances under the treaty should first be met. He had
already appealed to the pope and complained that he had been
summoned to an unsafe place. As the tension grew he thought
of the fate of his father Gruffydd thirty years before, when
King Henry had conspired with another David. Edward determined to bring the long-drawn dispute to an end. On 12 November, with his prelates and magnates about him and on their
judgement, he rejected Llywelyn's last offer and decided to 'go
upon him as a rebel and a disturber of his peace'.

Another incident had exacerbated feeling on both sides. At
the end of 1275, Amauri, the youngest son of Simon de Montfort, attempted to bring over to Wales his sister Eleanor, who,
during the time of her father's ascendancy in England ten years
before, had been betrothed to Llywelyn: whether the arrival of
Amauri and Eleanor was connected with current events in
Wales or was a coincidence is not known, but in any case it was
not timely. Their ship was captured in the Bristol Channel,
Amauri was imprisoned and Eleanor was taken to Windsor.
Edward, who only two years before had been restrained with
difficulty from trying to hunt down their brother Guy in south
Tuscany and had no confidence in Amauri, was not in the mood
to give Llywelyn facilities for a marriage with a lady who, while
she could claim his protection as his cousin, was also the sister of
Henry of Almain's murderer.[1] He detained Eleanor as a kind of
hostage and paid no heed to Llywelyn's demands that she
should be allowed to join him. The marriage could not be allowed before his submission.

The feudal host was summoned to meet at Worcester by 24
June 1277, but the war began at once. It is here that we can see

---

[1] See *King Henry III and the Lord Edward*, ii. 606–12; and, for Amauri in England,
above, pp. 330–1. The view that Llywelyn was deliberately appealing to old
baronial animosities by sending for Eleanor at this time is, I think, far-fetched.

the contrast between Henry III's and Edward's campaigns against the Welsh. In substance the arrangements were the same—the dispatch of paid forces under household knights, the marshalling of local shire levies by the sheriffs, the impressment of woodsmen, carpenters, and diggers, the concentration of supplies from quarters far and near, the activity at the castle of St. Briavell, a border-fortress by the forest of Dean and the chief factory of cross-bow bolts, the gathering of ships from the Cinque Ports and other ports, all these and other measures are familiar. What was new was the intelligence and energy which directed their use, so that the war had been half won before the main army began to move. Llywelyn's impressive principality from north Powys to Ceredigion had crumbled rapidly away. The king had thought out his plan of campaign and gone into action when war was declared in the previous November.[1] Three military commands or captaincies were created; one, under the king's close friend, William Beauchamp, earl of Warwick, in Chester and Lancaster; the second, under Roger Mortimer, in the shires of Shrewsbury, Stafford, and Hereford; the third, in west Wales, under Pain de Chaworth (de Cadurcis)[2] until in April 1277 the earl of Lancaster arrived to take control. The three captains had to restore the defences (municio), take command of troops sent to aid them and of the local militia, and enlist the Welsh. In order to fulfil this last duty, they had power to make terms with local Welsh lords and to organize bands of Welsh footmen. They acted with vigour, not confining themselves to defence; and with such success that by the spring of 1277 they had recovered all the lands which Llywelyn had conquered in the Marches from the Cheshire border to Cardigan Bay.

Humphrey de Bohun, since 1275 earl of Hereford and a Marcher lord, recovered his lands in Brecon, and the earl of Lincoln, in command of a paid force of barons and knights, captured Dolforwyn and re-occupied Builth. In the north the most notable advance was in north Powys, where two of the sons and heirs of Gruffydd ap Madog (d. 1269) at once came to terms and were promised that, if the king were reconciled to Llywelyn, their homage should be retained by the king. This

---

[1] *Cal. Pat. Rolls, 1272–81*, p. 171, and *Cal. Close Rolls, 1272–9*, pp. 358–61. For the campaign see Morris, *The Welsh Wars*, ch. 3.

[2] The lord of Kidwelly on the coast, one of the most important Marches and castles of south Wales.

submission opened Maelor or Bromfield, north of the Dee, and the cantref of Nanheudy, south of the Dee, to the royal forces.[1] In the south Pain de Chaworth had a still more striking success in the valley of the Tywi, where he brought to submission Rhys ap Maredudd, lord of Dryslwyn. Rhys agreed to put his castle and lands at the king's disposal and received the usual promise that the king would retain his homage. He also was assured that if the ancestral castle of Dinefwr, a few miles away, came into the king's hands, his rights to it should be given judicial consideration.[2] He did not succeed in uniting the two castles. Dinefwr, held by another descendant of the great Rhys, fell in June, as also did Carreg Cennen to the east of it and Llandovery, farther up the river. Its lord, Rhys Wyndod, lost his lands and Dinefwr became the centre, like Cardigan and Carmarthen, of an important royal administration. These successes in the valley of the Tywi enabled Edmund of Lancaster, now in command, to penetrate farther north. At the end of July, ten days or so after the king came to his base at Chester, his brother occupied Aberystwyth.

Here we may anticipate a little to emphasize the importance of the conquests in the ancient kingdom of Deheubarth. For the first time the royal power was firmly established in the lands which had been so hotly contested between the heirs of the Lord Rhys, whose fitful loyalties had now enlarged and now embarrassed the authority of the prince of Wales in his endeavours to unite the Welsh princes. Cardigan, Carmarthen, and Kidwelly were henceforth rear defences. The key fortresses lay to the north of them, in an irregular arc round Plinlimmon and the central hills. Much work was done on castles between 1277 and 1280 in central Wales, as it was in the north before and after the war of 1282–3—at Aberystwyth, where the new castle of Llanbadarn became the centre of administration in Ceredigion; in Ystrad Tywi, where the castles at Dinefwr, Carreg Cennen, and Llandovery were strengthened or repaired, and at Builth, where

[1] Gruffydd ap Madog had for ten years before his death been a staunch vassal of Llywelyn, though his wife was an Audley of the neighbouring March. He was buried in the family abbey of Valle Crucis. The division of his lordship and the submission of his sons was followed by the occupation of Dinas Bran on the upper Dee, which was held for a time as a royal castle, and later granted with Bromfield and Yale (Ial) to John de Warenne, earl of Surrey.

[2] See, in correction of Morris on this point, *King Henry III and the Lord Edward*, ii. 652 n., 653. Rhys ap Maredudd quitclaimed the castle of Dinefwr to the king in 1283 (*Littere Wallie*, p. 122).

a strong fortress, which it took four years to build, replaced the castle razed in 1260 by Rhys Fychan of Dinefwr.[1] After its occupation by the earl of Lincoln, Builth and its district had in 1277 been entrusted by the king to Hywel ap Meurig, a Welshman who had been steward of the earl of Hereford in the Brecon march and of Roger Mortimer in the Radnor march, and commander of the Welsh foot-soldiers in these districts. He and his successors as constables of Builth were responsible directly to the Crown, for Builth was a royal march in front of marchlands, of peculiar importance.

We may now return to Edward. When he arrived at Chester he knew that, thanks to Roger Mortimer and his associates, he had to deal with Llywelyn alone, in the Four Cantrefs, Snowdonia, Anglesey, and the district of Merioneth. Every centre of possible unrest in Powys, Builth, the valley of the Tywi, and Ceredigion had been cleared. His captains with their battalions of paid cavalry carefully raised and combined from England by the earl of Lincoln and other leaders, the Marcher lords doing willing service, the infantry, drawn from the neighbouring shires and from the Welsh 'friendlies' of the south, and marshalled under their millenars and centenars in bodies of thousands and hundreds, were free to co-operate with him and his feudal levy of some 800 cavalry as he might direct. A fleet of some thirty ships arrived in the estuary of the Dee under the command of the warden of the Cinque Ports. A skilled corps of 270 crossbowmen and 100 picked archers from the forest of Macclesfield, and large numbers of woodsmen and diggers had been collected. A medieval army, even though it contained a large proportion of paid men, was a fluctuating thing. Men came and went as their term of service began or expired, or as the needs of the moment required. That, at the end of August, Edward had 15,640 foot-soldiers, including about 9,000 Welsh friendlies, in his pay does not mean that he could dispose continuously of such a number, nor that it was convenient to do so. The labourers who cut through the woods and made the roads tended to disappear and had to be as carefully guarded against desertions as against an agile enemy. Yet it is probable that this army was the best controlled, as it was the best led, that had been gathered in Britain since the Norman Conquest.

[1] Morris gives a vivid description, based on the surviving Exchequer Accounts, of the building of this new castle, p. 148.

Edward established his headquarters three miles from Basing-werk, where there was a Cistercian abbey. Here, on a rocky platform jutting out into the Dee, known as 'the Flynt', he had already (17 July) set to work on a new fortress. This was the historical beginning of the castle and town of Flint.[1] After a brief tour in Cheshire, where on 13 August he and the queen and other friends laid the foundation-stones of his new abbey of Vale Royal,[2] he returned to his base, came to an understanding with prince David about the future of north Wales, and thence moved on, first to Rhuddlan, then to Degannwy and the Con-way river (29 August). In the meanwhile forces had been landed in Anglesey and, during the first fortnight of September, the crops so essential to support the Welsh of the mainland during the winter, were harvested by the English. Step by step the coast-line as far as the Conway had been cleared, castle-building had been planned at Flint and Rhuddlan, and Anglesey had been secured; but the fastnesses of Snowdonia were not yet to be overrun. Llywelyn suddenly sought terms, and the king con-sented to treat with him. The treaty of Conway was concluded, after negotiations between assigned persons on both sides, early in November.[3]

Llywelyn was reduced to the position from which his brother Owain and he had started under the terms of the treaty of Wood-stock thirty years before. Indeed the conditions in 1277 were more humiliating. He was an excommunicated person and his lands had been laid under an interdict. After absolution he took the oath of fealty to Edward at Rhuddlan, and at Christmas he did homage at Westminster, having surrendered hostages as security that he would come. He gave up all claims to the Four Cantrefs and to other lands conquered by the king in Wales (this would cover castles in south and north Powys, Aberyst-wyth, the valley of the Tywi, Builth) and promised to pay 500 marks annually at the king's exchequer in Chester until the money still owing (i.e. under the treaty of Montgomery) had been paid; in return for which he was to be reinstated in Angle-sey, but only for life, unless he should leave heirs of his body. David was to be provided for outside Snowdonia. According to the treaty, Llywelyn was also to pay a rent of 1,000 marks a

---

[1] See J. G. Edwards, 'The Name of Flint Castle', in *E.H.R.* xxix (1914), 315-17.
[2] *King Henry III and the Lord Edward*, ii. 722-3.
[3] *Littere Wallie*, nos. 205, 207-11, 279 on pp. 113-14, 116-22, 157.

year for Anglesey, but this was at once remitted, as also was the large and crippling fine of £50,000 formally imposed in return for his restoration to the king's favour. This remission was gracious as well as prudent, for the operations against Llywelyn had cost about half the fine. The clause of the treaty which later caused most trouble related to the lands seized by others than the king outside the Four Cantrefs; for Edward undertook to do full justice in any claims according to the law of the district in which the land in question might lie. Another possible claimant, but against Llywelyn himself, was his elder brother Owain, who had been imprisoned since 1255 and was now released and given a choice between an agreement with Llywelyn or a trial 'in the place of his transgression' according to the laws and customs of Wales. If he were released after trial, he might, if he wished, seek his rights. Naturally enough, the unhappy man preferred a reconciliation and was settled by Llywelyn in the Lleyn peninsula, in the extreme west of north Wales. Finally, elaborate obligations to safeguard the observance of the treaty were imposed upon the men of each cantref which remained in the prince's hand.[1]

At the outset of his advance from his camp at Flint Edward had shown that he was determined, if necessary, to destroy Llywelyn, for he undertook, in that event, to divide Snowdonia between the two brothers, Owain and David, and himself; but, as his agreements about homage with other Welshmen show, he had always contemplated a reconciliation. Owain and David would have held as barons, and have been required, if summoned, to attend parliament. Llywelyn, after the treaty of Conway, was still entitled 'prince of Wales' and—apart from the safeguarding clause—retained his independence under the laws and customs of Wales, within his restricted frontiers. The prince showed every sign of desire to keep the king's favour. In September 1278 he had a cordial meeting with him at Rhuddlan, where a royal castle was in course of erection, and on 13 October, the day of St. Edward the Confessor, after whom

[1] The northern principality, as defined in the letters patent of August 1277, containing the king's agreement with David, included Merioneth (as *pars Snoudon*') and Penlynn, the most westerly cantref of north Powys. To these Edward added Edeyrnion, another cantref of north Powys, but, like Anglesey, only during Llywelyn's lifetime. Four of Llywelyn's five vassals outside Snowdonia proper (the fifth was a former lord in Ceredigion, now settled on the other side of the Dyfi in Merioneth) ruled in Edeyrnion.

Henry III had named his son, he was married to Eleanor de Montfort at Worcester with much ceremony and at Edward's expense. The king was kind and gracious as patron of the wedding-feast on this happy day. Though many occasions for bitterness lay ahead, the prospect seemed bright. There were, however, two dangers. Would the Welsh in the Four Cantrefs and in Ceredigion adjust themselves to English rule, and would David be content with the provision made for him in two of the four cantrefs, Dyffryn and Rhuvoniog? The two questions became one, and the answer was in the negative. The recent war had been precipitated by David, who, after his flight into Cheshire, had asked Edward how he could best 'aggrieve' his brother. The renewal of war in 1282 was due to David; he made himself the champion of every Welshman with a grievance against the Crown, just as his former accomplice, Gruffydd ap Gwenwynwyn, now an ardent and voluble exponent of royal authority in his prolonged lawsuit with Llywelyn, did more than anyone to exasperate his former suzerain and put him in the dilemma in which he found himself when David revolted.

It must be admitted that David had ample material to work on and, when he decided to strike, could rely upon the support of many Welsh lords in north and west Wales. The settlement of Wales, if so it can be called, presents a picture of intense administrative and judicial activity during the years between the wars. By January 1278 the king had his bailiffs in every cantref and march where he had immediate control, in Rhos and Tegeingl (Englefield), Bromfield, Montgomery, Kerry, Cydewain, Dolforwyn, Builth, Llanbadarn, Carreg Cennen, Dinefwr, Llandovery. David had his bailiffs in Duffryn Clwyd and Rhuvoniog. Three of these bailiwicks were given to Roger Mortimer, Dolforwyn with Llywelyn's castle and, later, the cantrefs of Kerry and Cydewain in south Powys, but for a time Edward kept them in his own hands. The bailiffs of Rhos and Tegeingl, the two cantrefs on the coast kept by the king, were at first Welshmen who were responsible to the justice and exchequer of Chester. The bailiffs in Llanbadarn and the castles on or near the Tywi were within the jurisdiction of a justice of south Wales, for Edmund of Lancaster, the king's brother, who was compensated in England, surrendered his lordships of Cardigan and Carmarthen, and west Wales was henceforward under royal administration. In June 1280 Bogo de Knoville, formerly active as sheriff of Shropshire, was made justiciar of west Wales. He was a strong man, but neither tactful nor sympathetic, and before he was succeeded by the king's close friend and fellow crusader, Robert Tybetot (1281), made himself very unpopular.

Within this framework, the local courts were very busy, for the recent disturbances had left or aroused innumerable disputes, in which all kinds of men were involved. At the outset, in January 1278, two judicial commissions had been appointed, one for the north and east, including the Four Cantrefs, Montgomery, Builth, and the royal cantrefs in north and south Powys, the other for west Wales and the lands of Welsh and Marcher lords in the south-west. The first, whose presidency soon came to the English judge Walter de Hopton, was a joint commission of English and Welsh, including Hywel ap Meurig, the constable of Builth, and distinguished Welshmen more friendly to Llywelyn; the other consisted of Payn de Chaworth of Kidwelly and Master Henry de Bray, a king's clerk.[1] They were given the duty to hear and determine, in the king's place, all suits and pleas of lands, trespasses and wrongs in the Marches and in Wales and to do justice therein in accordance with the laws and customs where the lands lay or in which the offences had been committed. Men from each bailiwick who knew the truth were to appear before the judges to give evidence and act as indictors. Snowdonia was, of course, excluded from the scope of the commission in the north, as were Brecon and Glamorgan in the south; but the prince was required to plead before the judges in those cases which concerned him as plaintiff or defendant, that is to say, which fell within the scope of the provisions of the treaty of Conway. The roll of the Hopton commission is the main authority for the study of the causes of the bitterness and unrest which provided the material for David's revolt.[2] Its evidence helps us to understand the background to the lists of grievances presented by Llywelyn and his brother during the abortive attempts of Archbishop Pecham to bring them to voluntary submission before Llywelyn was killed and David was hunted down in Snowdonia.

[1] Payn de Chaworth died in 1278, and this southern commission seems to have been replaced by various local commissions, or left to the justice of west Wales.

[2] See especially J. Conway Davies, *The Welsh Assize Roll, 1277–1284* (1940), the most thorough survey of the commissions, justices, and cases, though strongly critical of Edward. For general accounts see J. G. Edwards, *Littere Wallie*, pp. lxi–lxix; and Powicke, *King Henry III and the Lord Edward*, ii. 652–78.

It is not possible in a book of this scope to summarize and discuss these grievances, still less to survey the work of the Hopton commission.[1] Discussion is not likely to issue in agreement or to be allowed to rest until, if ever, it ceases to be centred in the problem of King Edward's good faith. Edward did not *seek* trouble where so much occasion of trouble already existed; he was too busy elsewhere; but he looked for orderly acquiescence from an incoherent society in a judicial system alien to its traditions and provocative of vexatious delays and appeals. Llywelyn, so long accustomed to freedom of movement within Wales, to the exaltation of his power by bards, to brisk little wars and forays, and bargaining with Marcher relatives and changeable Welsh princes, felt that he was cooped up in Snowdonia, subjected to interference within his borders and harassed outside them by officials who had little respect for his dignity and position. The Welsh lords and freemen in the cantrefs of Rhos and Tegeingl and in west Wales discovered, if they were self-seeking, that their litigious efforts to play off one kind of law against another brought little reward, or, if they wished to make the best of new conditions, that rising discontent was fostered by what seemed to them to be heartless and unnecessary delays. This was why the best of them, Goronwy ap Heilyn, a member of the judicial commission and bailiff of Rhos, who was a friend of both sides, joined David in 1282 and served him as his seneschal to the end. On paper Edward's settlement reads well: it seems to provide for every contingency and it makes use of Welsh and English alike. In practice it worked badly. In particular the justices were constantly faced by the doubt, natural enough in this age of change, whether a certain bit of land was under Welsh or Marcher law. In October 1278 two very competent men, Reginald de Grey, one of the Cheshire barons, who in 1281 became justice of Chester, and William Hamilton, a king's clerk who later rose to be Edward's chancellor, had investigated at Oswestry, with the aid of a jury, the application of Welsh and Marcher law and had reported that the law of Hywel Dda, or Welsh law, had always prevailed in disputes between Welshmen: in such cases English justices had not intervened. The treaty of Conway, however, had made the king responsible for justice outside Snowdonia, and the judicial

[1] Conway Davies, pp. 16, 17. It is significant that this commission was appointed on Llywelyn's wedding day.

commission, sitting at fixed places in formal sessions, had to concern itself with cases in which the pleading was often contradic-
tory on this question of law. Moreover Edward's predominance
outside Snowdonia implied an unlimited development of the
appeals which discontented princes had not hesitated to make to
the Crown.

The problem, in all its complexity and with all its implications, came to a head over Llywelyn's claim to the district or
cantref of Arwystli, in the west of southern Powys, where the
ancient seats of the earlier princes of Powys lay among the hills
in the upper reaches of the Severn. The historian may well
regret that the status of Arwystli had not been defined, once for
all, in the treaty of Conway. Gruffydd ap Gwenwynwyn and
his ancestors had held it, but not continuously. It had never
been regarded as anything but Welsh and, as a link between
Merioneth and Builth, was by nature connected with Snowdonia. Llywelyn, after Gruffydd's treachery in 1274, had annexed it, but, as traditionally part of Powys it was not included
by Edward in his definition of Snowdonia. Llywelyn, in virtue of
his right under the treaty to claim lands which others than the
king had seized, put in his claim at the first meeting of the judicial commission in 1278. The king was pleased that the prince
had so quickly shown his acceptance of the new order by the
submission of his suit; but his gratification must have been short
lived. Llywelyn argued that the case should be tried by Welsh
law in Arwystli and not on the March, Gruffydd claimed the
cantref as a barony held by him, as a Marcher lord, of the
Crown. The king ruled that actions between tenants-in-chief
should be tried on the March.

An attempt at arbitration, entrusted to Goronwy ap Heilyn,
seems to have come to nothing. A hearing before the king himself at a friendly meeting at Rhuddlan did not lead to a decision.
The case was resumed before the commissioners at Oswestry,
but the issues raised were of such high importance that the
judges felt it was beyond their competence; and it was referred
to the king in parliament. A first hearing, in the Michaelmas
parliament of 1279, was adjourned because Llywelyn's attorneys
were not armed with full powers to act for him, and the prince
was commanded to send to the parliament after Easter, in May
1280, attorneys with full powers and fully versed in the two
kinds of law preferred by the two parties, so that there might be

no further delay and justice might be done. In this parliament it would seem that the wider problem of the recognition of Welsh law as such was raised, and the need for some clarification of the terms of peace was felt. Probably the prince's attorneys had repeated the plea used at Oswestry that Wales should be treated as a province, distinct from England, under its own laws and customs. At any rate Edward and Archbishop Pecham, who felt more strongly than the king did about the inferiority of Welsh law, argued the point in letters to Llywelyn. The king wrote as a responsible ruler who had sworn obligations to observe well-established practices, but also had the duty to root out bad laws. He must know the facts, and was acting in his parliaments with the best advice that he could find. He must act with his prelates and magnates in the traditional manner.

Accordingly, it was decided in parliament in May to search the rolls in the treasury for precedents; and later in the year (December 1280) another commission was appointed, consisting of the bishop of St. David's, Reginald de Grey, and the judge Walter de Hopton, to inquire locally 'by what laws and customs the king's ancestors were wont to rule and justice a prince of Wales and a Welsh baron of Wales and their peers and other their inferiors and their peers'. This commission sat in various places; evidence was heard at Chester, Rhuddlan, Oswestry, Montgomery, and Llanbadarn (Aberystwyth). It cannot be said that the results either of the search into the assize rolls or of the local inquiry were satisfactory, and it is not clear by what law the Arwystli case was to be tried; but in June 1281 Llywelyn was informed that he could proceed with his plea before the judicial commissioners.[1] The reports and records had been recited before king, prelates, barons, and council, and justice would be done in accordance with the findings. Llywelyn pursued his case, but when his attorney appeared at Montgomery in October 1281, Gruffydd ap Gwenwynwyn pleaded that, as each party was a baron, he must answer to a writ. The original writ, alleged by Llywelyn to have been produced when the proceedings first began three and a half years before, could not be found. Llywelyn expostulated to Edward in a good-humoured way. Edward replied, with professions of goodwill, that Llywelyn

[1] Llywelyn's letter of 2 February 1282 (the most likely year) suggests that the proceedings at Montgomery were to be 'according to the laws of Wales'. See *Cal. Anc. Corr.*, p. 90.

must get a new writ: there was nothing else to be done. Before the case could proceed, the prince had been drawn into David's rebellion.[1]

The English plea rolls record innumerable adjournments and delays, many quite as vexatious and prolonged as those in the Arwystli case; but Llywelyn, and David also—for he had had his legal difficulties—could not be expected to accept the situation with the grumbling acquiescence of an English suitor. As he said in what may have been his last letter to Edward, he felt the humiliation far more than any possible loss of or profit from the lands of Arwystli. This was but one of many cases. Just when he thought that things were going well, he was always being aggrieved more harshly by other things.[2] All the same David's sudden outburst seems to have been as unexpected by him as it was by the English government. He had no choice, for he could not incur everlasting ignominy by joining in the resistance to his own brother, treacherous creature though he had been, nor by standing apart while the Welsh rose on every side. He could not refuse 'his assent to those who began the war'.

David began his revolt on 21 March 1282 with a sudden night-attack on the castle at Hawarden, then held for its heir by Roger Clifford, who was captured. Within a few days the Four Cantrefs had risen. Flint and Rhuddlan were besieged without success; but Ruthin was lost, also Hope to the east, and Dinas Bran on the Dee to the south. A Welsh 'parliament' at Denbigh committed the Welsh to war. Before the end of the month David had rushed to the south to raise the Welsh in the Tywi valley and in Ceredigion. The castles at Llandovery, Carreg Cennen, and Llanbadarn (Aberystwyth) were seized and destroyed. With the exception of Rhys ap Mareddud at Dryslwyn, the descendants of the great Rhys joined in the insurrection. Montgomery, Builth, Dinefwr, and Cardigan and the Marcher castles in Radnor and Brecon were held, but the Welsh rose in large numbers in the districts about them. David had achieved his purpose and could leave to organize resistance in the north. For a time, while Edward's plans were maturing, the outlook in the south was hopeful for the Welsh princes. As late as 17 June

---

[1] For all this see Conway Davies's introduction. The chief references to this and to other sources will be found in *King Henry III and the Lord Edward*, ii. 663–4, 667–8, 670–6.   [2] *Cal. Anc. Corr.*, p. 91.

Gilbert de Clare, the earl of Gloucester, who was in command of all the royal forces in south Wales, was badly defeated on his return to Dinefwr from a raid. He had taken no precautions and was surprised by a Welsh attack from the hills at Llandeilo Fawr, in whose neighbourhood King John's captains had won a victory in 1213. The confusion which followed this disaster gave Llywelyn himself the chance to make one of his swift and mysterious appearances. His guerilla warfare kept the royal leaders in the south busy until the autumn; but by then the administration of better men than the discredited Gilbert of Clare had prevailed, and in any case the advance of Edward in the Four Cantrefs compelled Llywelyn's return.

The revolt had taken Edward completely by surprise. From his point of view affairs had been going smoothly in Wales, in spite of the troublesome legal disputes. He was on friendly terms with Llywelyn and David and wished to hold the scales of justice even in these debates about jurisdiction. Some of his administrators were good Welshmen. The last thing that he wanted in 1282 was trouble in Wales. The pope was urging him to take the cross and fix a date for his passage. King Philip of France, King Alfonso of Castile, King Peter of Aragon, Margaret of France, and Charles of Salerno were all seeking his good offices. (It is worth noting that the great rising in Sicily began on 30 March 1282, a few days after the Welsh troubles began.) The seneschal and lords of Gascony and the Agenais expected to hear at any time that Edward was coming to the south, where his presence was urgently needed.[1] Wales and its affairs were a domestic matter, only one of the problems which daily called for the attention of a busy king. Indeed, Edward was more concerned at this time with Scotland than with Wales. The news that David, the man whom he had especially cherished, had struck at Roger Clifford and that rebels and malefactors were disturbing the peace in Wales shocked and infuriated him. Since the treaty of Conway he had regarded Wales as a group of royal castellanies and baronies, among which Snowdonia had a privileged position, ruled by a prince whose dignity was adequately recognized. And now everything else had to take second place while he coped with this treacherous people. One of his first acts was to beg the archbishop to put every disturber of the peace under sentence of excommunication, and it is significant

[1] Above, pp. 293–4.

that Pecham did this under the authority of the council of
Oxford in 1222, when Archbishop Stephen had declared excommunicate all who unjustly disturbed the peace of the king
and his realm and withheld his rights.[1]

Neither the king nor his subjects in England and Gascony
underrated the gravity of the revolt. It stirred general reproba-
tion and was suppressed with general approval.[2] In 1277
Llywelyn had submitted as a contumacious vassal who had incurred the condemnation of the king in his court; he had been
generously treated and had agreed to the settlement which his
and the royal advisers had made. In 1282 he was a wanton
aggressor, seeking to spread disaffection everywhere. Such was
the contemporary view of the last serious struggle for Welsh independence. Events showed that outside Snowdonia the danger
was not so great as had perhaps been feared. Sustained resistance
was not possible in the Marches or in south and west Wales.
The lord of south Powys at Pool had become a baron of the
king, more English in sentiment than his neighbours. The lord
of Dryslwyn behaved like a lord of the Marches, and his cousins
in the vale of Tywi and Ceredigion did not long maintain their
attitude of cohesion with the prince of Wales. The Welsh freemen who rose in Builth and the Marches gradually returned to
the king's peace, just as they had been wont to rise and return in
the past; and Welsh 'friendlies', where they were not enlisted in
the royal forces, were useful as spies and informers. All the same,
Edward never acted more quickly and strenuously than he did
when he heard of the rebellion. He could not gauge the extent of
the danger, for he could not, as in 1276–7, methodically prepare

[1] *Foedera*, I. ii. 603 (Devizes, 28 March); Pecham, *Epistolae*, ii. 403–4. In September the archbishop sent a Dominican friar to absolve those who had been received again into the king's peace. Two original documents with remnants of
numerous seals show how leading Welsh freemen were gathered together by Henry
Lacy, earl of Lincoln, to enter into bonds to keep the peace after the wars of 1283
and 1295, in the earl's cantrefs of Rhos and Rufoniog. The former contains 46
names, the latter 57. The documents survive among the Duchy of Lancaster records,
owing to the transfer to the honour of Lancaster of the honour of Denbigh, through
the marriage of the earl's daughter to Thomas of Lancaster. See Francis Jones in
Bull. of Board of Celtic Studies, xiii, pt. iii (1949), 142–4.

[2] For Gascon reactions see above, p. 294; and Gaston of Béarn's letter in *Foedera*,
I. ii. 611; for Gascon contingents in Wales see Morris, op. cit., pp. 186–9. For suf-
frages of masses and chanting of psalms cf. letter from Bury St. Edmunds, *Foedera*,
p. 604; and for a greeting to the king after his victory by his clerk, Stephen of
St. George, E. Kantorowicz in *Laudes Regiae*, p. 30, and on Stephen in *Speculum*,
xxxii (1957), 237–47, where, on p. 240, the text of his encomium is given.

the way for his main attack. He had been taken by surprise and would run no risks and brook no delays.

From the first he decided, so far as possible, to act with paid levies, not only of household troops, crossbowmen, and archers,[1] and of paid companies raised by individual barons by agreement with the Crown, but also of the feudal host. In the summons to 158 vassals issued from Devizes on 6 April 1282 he used the words 'at our wages' (*ad vadia nostra*);[2] and though, partly for political reasons, he later summoned prelates and barons to do service in the ordinary way, the tendency to put warfare on a paid basis is marked in this war, which, in addition to the heavy expenditure on his new castles, cost over £60,000, more than twice as much as the operations in 1276–7. The chancery rolls and exchequer accounts reveal intense activity. Sixty ships of the Cinque Ports were brought round to lie off Neston in the Dee estuary, and in July at Rhuddlan crossbowmen and archers (350 in number) were drafted from the army to go on board them as marines. This fleet was especially needed for the occupation of Anglesey. Bristol was a base from which troops from the south-west of England and vast quantities of ammunition for the little companies of crossbowmen could be sent north or shipped to south or west Wales. The king's vassals in Ireland were asked to provide loans of money. While the main host was gathering at Chester, to move on to Flint and Rhuddlan in June and July, the defence of the central Marches and the west was maintained by Roger Mortimer at Montgomery, Roger Lestrange at Builth, and Robert Tybetot, the justiciar of west Wales. The military command in south and west was given, after the earl of Gloucester's defeat at Llandeilo, to the king's uncle William de Valence, lord of Pembroke; but the organization of victory was due in the main to the justiciar, the king's

[1] Crossbowmen were select highly paid troops, some mounted, more on foot, grouped in small companies and especially used in castle defence. The large Gascon contingent, which in January 1283 reached its peak of 210 horse and 1,313 foot was largely composed of crossbowmen. Archers in 1277 were, apart from the Macclesfield contingent, also armed with the spear. In 1282–3 *sagittarii* proper were more numerous: thus 2,500 were at Hope, protecting the rebuilding operations at the castle, in June 1282. The development of reliance upon English archers in battle was slow. In the Scottish wars Edward's archers were mainly Welsh. In 1266 Roger Leyburn had many archers from the Weald during his clearing up operations in Kent and Essex (see Alun Lewis in *E.H.R.* liv (1939), 203 *passim*) and archers were very effective in the fight at Orewin Bridge in December 1282. The victory at Maes Moydog in 1295 is a turning-point. See Morris, op. cit., 99–104, 160–1, 183, 188–9 (for Gascon crossbowmen), and below, p. 443.   [2] *Foedera*, i. ii. 603–4.

friend and companion in his crusading days. As we have seen, the control of the south and west from Carmarthen to Llanbadarn was regained by the autumn, and Edward could proceed with more assurance in the north.

Edward was ready to begin his main operations in August. By this time his paid forces were absorbed into the feudal host which had been summoned in May and was marshalled at Rhuddlan by the earl of Norfolk as marshal and John de Bohun, the uncle of the constable, the earl of Hereford, who was holding his Marcher lordship in Brecon. The total force at Rhuddlan comprised about 750 heavy cavalry and about 8,000 foot with a corps of 1,000 archers, available for service in the various armies. Edward's plan was first to use his fleet for the occupation of Anglesey and then to conquer the Four Cantrefs, still mainly held by David, before he attacked Snowdonia from two sides. The operation of Anglesey was entrusted to the former seneschal of Gascony, Luke de Tany. The island was occupied and by the end of September a bridge of boats had been built over the Menai strait to Bangor. Luke de Tany had strict instructions not to cross to the mainland until the king was ready to approach by land from Conway. Past experience had shown how fatal it was to march along the coast to the Conway river and attack Snowdonia while the valleys of the Clwyd and Conway rivers were in the control of the enemy. Edward was determined to avoid any danger of this kind.[1] He moved with the earl of Lincoln up the Clwyd valley, while Reginald de Grey, the justice of Chester, advanced from Hope and the Earl Warenne along the middle Dee, farther south. The operations were successful; the lands and castles north of the Dee were won. The fall of Denbigh, the centre of David's barony, in the middle of October, brought the campaign to a triumphant close. The king decided not to reincorporate the Four Cantrefs in his domain nor to retain the lands of north Powys whose lords had revolted with David. With the exception of the fortresses of Degannwy and Rhuddlan, the strip of coast between them, and two or three

[1] It was idle to attempt an invasion from the south-east. As late as November, after the cantrefs had been conquered, Roger Lestrange, Mortimer's successor at Montgomery, wrote to the king that he could not imperil his forces by a north-westerly march over the mountains of Berwyn and Morugge. 'The greatest damage that can be done to them (the Welsh) from this time onwards is to guard the March carefully so that supplies do not pass to them . . . for much supplies enter the land without any one's knowledge' (*Cal. Anc. Corr.*, p. 84).

other areas, he turned the whole district into marcher lordships for the three men who had helped him to conquer it. His devoted follower Henry de Lacy, the young earl of Lincoln, was given Rhos and Rhufoniog (the later honour of Denbigh), his lifelong ally the Earl Warenne Bromfield and Yale, the districts of north Powys, with the castle of Dinas Bran, and Reginald of Grey Duffryn Clwyd (the later barony of Ruthin). Part of the lands previously held by the family of north Powys south of the Dee went to swell Roger Mortimer's new lordship of Chirk, and the rest were given to the queen.[1] Only one of the four sons of Gruffydd ap Madog managed to survive the family disaster; this was the former lord of Yale, another Gruffydd, who, through the favour of the Earl Warenne, was, in February 1283, granted the land of Glyn Dyfrdwy, in the cantref of Edeyrnion, to be held at the king's will. He should be mentioned, for he was the ancestor of Owen Glendower, whose name was derived from the new lordship.[2]

Edward was now free to move westwards and to co-operate with the forces in Anglesey; but for some weeks his mind was diverted by the unwelcome intervention of Archbishop Pecham, who, solicitous for his Welsh flock, decided at this juncture to try to bring Llywelyn to reason. In October he hurried to Hereford, and thence through the border shires by Chester to the king's headquarters at Rhuddlan, which he reached at the end of the month. On his way (21 October) he had sent to the prince in advance a distinguished Franciscan theologian, John of Wales.[3] The seventeen articles, taken in writing to Llywelyn and the Welsh, are a mixture of supplications, exhortations, accusations, and warnings. One, however, in which the archbishop asked how in their view concord might be established, offered a loophole to argument; while his statement that his arrival in Wales had greatly displeased the king suggested that in him the Welsh might find a friendly advocate. Llywelyn,

[1] These lordships composed the greater part of the later shire of Denbigh (1536).
[2] After a period of probation, Gruffydd's tenure at will was converted into a tenure by barony. See J. E. Lloyd, *Owen Glendower* (1931), pp. 10-12.
[3] Since the archbishop was at Chester on the 26th and one of his letters is dated from Rhuddlan on 28 October, he presumably arrived at the king's headquarters on 27 October. John of Wales was probably waiting for him with the documents, for on 31 October Pecham decided to go to see Llywelyn himself. He was back again by 6 November. In view of the risks which he ran he made the chancellor, Burnell, his vicar during his absence. For John of Wales see A. G. Little, *Studies in English Franciscan History* (1917), pp. 174-92.

David, and their counsellors seized the opportunity. They rebutted the charges made against them, set out their case, and compiled, on a long series of parchments (*rotuli*), a list of the wrongs done to them and of the engagements which had been broken. Copies of these documents, which were brought to Rhuddlan, presumably by John of Wales, survive in Pecham's register.[1]

The archbishop was obviously impressed by the allegations. He begged Edward to give them judicial correction or at least, in view of them, to hold the Welsh excused for their excesses.[2] Edward was never responsive to petitions of this kind. He replied that the Welsh excesses were inexcusable just because he was always prepared to do justice to every suppliant for it. The archbishop then begged him to allow the Welsh to have free access and return for the purpose of expounding their grievances to him. The king replied that they could have access and could freely depart if they justly deserved to have the right to do so. This reply determined Pecham to go into Snowdonia himself. He would seek to incline the minds of the Welsh to such humility as would justify him, as their messenger (*quasi ipsorum nuncius*) in trying 'to induce the royal clemency to admit them to his grace'. He had several discussions with the prince and his counsellors and with David. Llywelyn consented to submit himself to the royal will, saving his responsibility to his people and his dignity as a prince. The archbishop returned to report to the king. The king replied that he would have no treaty with the prince and the Welsh unless they submitted themselves entirely to his will. Even then the archbishop would not give up hope. He realized that, unless the Welsh were given acceptable terms of surrender, they would not submit; he succeeded in getting Edward's permission to draw up such terms with the magnates who were present. Agreement was reached and the terms were taken to Llywelyn by John of Wales about 6 November. Some were for the consideration of the prince in council, others were secret.

The conditions, though friendly in tone, reveal no appreciation of the Welsh sense of tradition and the love which the Welsh of Snowdonia had for what they described as their sterile and uncultivated land. Discussion about Anglesey and the Four Cantrefs 'and the lands given by the king to his magnates' was

---

[1] *Epistolae*, ii. 440–65.
[2] See the narrative inserted in the Register (ibid., 465).

ruled out. Their tenants, if they came to the king's peace, would be treated justly. Llywelyn must submit unconditionally to the king's will, but the archbishop and other friends (*cum ceteris amicis*) would do their utmost, and, he was sure, with success, to obtain merciful treatment for him and his subjects. What this meant is revealed in the secret proposals: Llywelyn was offered an English domicile, apparently an earldom with lands to the value of a thousand pounds, in return for the perpetual cession of Snowdonia. David was promised honourable provision, suitable to his state, on condition that he went on crusade and did not return unless recalled by the king's clemency. The archbishop would ask for provision for his children. In their replies (11 November) the prince and his council, it is unnecessary to say, made no distinction between the open and secret conditions. Llywelyn, in a brief and dignified letter, dismissed the 'form' of submission as neither safe nor honourable and said that it had been heard with astonishment by all in council. No subjects of his, noble or freeman, would allow him, even if he wished, to consent to it. He beseeched the archbishop to continue his arduous labours in the cause of peace. The reply on David's behalf referred ironically to his suggested pilgrimage. He would go, when he wished to go, of his own freewill; and for God, who takes no pleasure in forced service, not for man. The reply then diverged into recriminations and, as was more natural in David's case, laid stress on the difference between the mercy shown to other English barons who offended the king and his unjust disinheritance. The reply of the Welsh was based upon an appeal to history and right. Their prince ruled as a descendant of Brutus and his inheritance had been confirmed by Ottobuono, cardinal legate of the Holy See, with the consent of the lord king and his father. They repudiated the English offer of lands in England, for it came from men set on the prince's disinheritance, so that they might have his lands in Wales. They would in no case recognize the exchange of Snowdon for land in England, a bargain which would require them to do homage to a stranger, of whose speech, manners, and laws they were entirely ignorant.[1]

The Welsh could reply with the more confidence because, on 6 November, perhaps on the very day on which the conditions of surrender were defined at Rhuddlan, Luke de Tany, who had

---

[1] *Epistolae*, ii. 466–73. Pecham's long reply to Llywelyn, dated Rhuddlan, 14 November, closes the correspondence (pp. 473–7). It reverts to his worst manner.

lost patience in Anglesey and had crossed into Snowdonia without authority, was routed and driven back. He himself was drowned in the Menai strait.[1] The disaster upset the king's plans but hardened his resolution. He reinforced and reorganized the Anglesey command under Otto of Granson, brought up the Gascons to his army, and on 6 December announced his intention to proceed in a winter campaign. A few days later he heard that Llywelyn had been killed on 11 December, exactly a month after his refusal to accept the terms of surrender.

Llywelyn had seized the chance to revive Welsh resistance in the south and had invaded Builth. His choice of ground was doubtless assisted by the recent death (26 October) of his kinsman Roger Mortimer who held the neighbouring Marches and was in charge of military operations in the 'parts of Montgomery'. Mortimer's death meant changes, during which the prince might reap advantage. Indeed he, who was himself never free from the danger of treachery, may have had hopes from treachery in the March.[2] Roger Lestrange had succeeded Mortimer in the command at Montgomery and as soon as he

[1] Morris (pp. 179–80) corrects the dramatic story in the Guisborough chronicle. The suggestion of Wykes (*Ann. monast.* iv. 290) that Luke treacherously desired to upset the peace negotiations may well be true. His attack synchronized with Pecham's three days' stay in Snowdonia.

[2] The evidence is obscure. It turns on two letters from Pecham, who was in Herefordshire, one to the king, the other to the chancellor (17 December, *Epistolae*, ii. 489–91). In the latter the archbishop enclosed a copy, now lost, of a document found on Llywelyn's body, together with his privy seal, after his death. This document, which was in the custody of Edmund Mortimer, suggested disloyalty in the March, though the names given were fictitious.[1] Again, the sheriff of Shropshire, before Edmund was given seisin of them (24 November) had taken over Roger Mortimer's lands and castles and on a tour early in November had found the tenants 'haughty and fickle' (*Cal. Anc. Corr.*, pp. 130–1). Llywelyn may have been in touch with or hoped for something from these men. Pecham refers to them, however, as magnates and the document may be connected with the Welsh story that Llywelyn was treacherously lured by the young Mortimers into danger. There were cross-currents in Marcher society, and Llywelyn may well have overrated their significance. In the previous autumn (9 October 1281, *Littere Wallie*, p. 99) he had publicly entered into a sworn alliance with his cousin Roger Mortimer; the two men had promised to stand together in peace *or war*, saving in all things their fealty to the king. I suspect that their common enemy was Gruffydd ap Gwenwynwyn, some of whose lands, seized by Gruffydd in 1274, had been granted by the king to Roger (*Cal. Anc. Corr.*, pp. 79, 122, 125). In any case Llywelyn's hope of support in the Marches, if he entertained it, was a delusion.

As for the danger of treachery to Llywellyn himself, the continuation of the Welsh chronicle, *Brut y Tywysogion* (in the Peniarth MS. 20) states that, before he left Snowdonia, an attempt upon him was made by some of his own men in the belfry of Bangor cathedral.

heard of Llywelyn's arrival in the neighbourhood, in the lands
of Gruffydd ap Gwenwynwyn, he went to attack him. The prince
moved on south into the land of Builth, where John Giffard
had succeeded Lestrange as castellan. Roger Mortimer's sons,
Edmund and Roger, were also with the royal forces. Llywelyn
kept to high ground, where, on 11 December, while he was
for the time away from them, his men were surprised above
the river Yrfon, near Orewin bridge. They were shaken by the
archers who 'were interlaced with the heavy cavalry' (this is the
first account in these wars of the value of archers in open fighting), and, when they were attacked by another troop of cavalry
in the rear, they broke and fled. Llywelyn, as he hurried back,
was run through the body by a Shropshire man, Stephen of
Frankton, who did not know who he was. Roger Lestrange sent
the news to the king: his troop had fought with Llywelyn ap
Gruffydd in the land of Builth on the Friday after the feast of St.
Nicholas; Llywelyn was dead, his army defeated, the flower of
his army dead, as the bearer of the letter would tell.[1] Llywelyn's
body was buried by the monks of the Cistercian abbey of Cwm
Hir in Maelienydd. The head had been struck off and was
ultimately exposed on a lance on the Tower of London.[2]

David carried on, but events showed that the loss of their great
prince had dispirited the Welsh. Edward did not attempt to
force the Conway estuary. His control of the interior enabled
him to cross to the upper valley of the river and follow it on the
south-east of the mountains to the old Welsh stronghold at
Dolwyddelan, which fell on the 18th of January. Then he advanced his base from Rhuddlan to Aberconway and contained
the Welsh behind the lower valley of the river. The forces under
Otto of Granson in Anglesey were strong enough to close in on
Snowdonia from Bangor to the south-west. They occupied

[1] *E.H.R.* xiv (1899), 507; calendared, with an earlier letter from Roger Lestrange, in *Cal. Anc. Corr.*, pp. 83–84. Morris (pp. 182–3) without any evidence gave
the credit for the skilful use of archers to John Giffard of Brimsfield, now a Marcher
lord at Clifford and Llandovery in right of his wife, and later made lord of Builth
where he had succeeded Lestrange as royal castellan. For him and his importance
during the barons' wars see above, pp. 172, 199. His wife, Maud, the daughter of
Walter Clifford by a daughter of Llywelyn the Great, was a very important lady,
whose first husband had been William Longspée the third (d. 1256). She interceded
with Pecham to secure Christian burial for her cousin, the prince of Wales (Pecham,
Epistolae, ii. 489). The prince was said to have lived long enough after his wound to
ask for a priest.

[2] J. E. Lloyd pieced together the evidence about the last days of Llywelyn in the
Bull. of the Board of Celtic Studies, v, pt. iii (1931), 349–53.

Caernarvon and Harlech. One outlet was left to David, the region of Cader Idris in Merioneth, where the castle of Bere was still safe in Welsh hands. Here, in wild country, more open than Snowdonia proper, a strong man with a devoted following might hold out for a long time. David made Bere his head-quarters, but again he was not strong enough to hold the country to south and east or to prevent contact between Otto of Granson in Harlech and the forces which came with Roger Lestrange from Montgomery and with William of Valence from Llan-badarn. The castle was besieged by a joint army of 3,600 men, mostly foot, and the Welsh garrison surrendered on 25 April 1283. David, who had remained in the hills, was powerless; the whole country-side was overrun and secured by the English. The Welsh surrendered freely, Welsh bands were sent out to join in the hunt for their prince, and in June David was taken and handed over 'by men of his own tongue'.[1] On 28 June the king issued writs from Rhuddlan to individual barons, to the city of London and twenty of the principal cities and boroughs, and to the sheriffs. He described at length the mischief which the rebels had done. The barons, two of the wiser men of each town, and two knights from each shire were ordered to be at Shrewsbury on the morrow of Michaelmas to consider what action should be taken about Wales.[2] The main action taken in parliament at Shrewsbury was the judicial condemnation of David by the magnates on 2 October. He was dragged by horses to be hanged, his body was quartered and distributed to four parts of the kingdom, his head was placed by his brother's on the Tower of London.

The king passed most of the next year in Wales. On 19 March 1284 he issued from Rhuddlan his long statute of Wales for the future administration of the country. In April, Queen Eleanor gave birth at Caernarvon to a son, named Edward, who, after the death of his brother Alfonso in the following August, be-came heir to the throne. Great festivities and a famous tourna-ment or round table followed at Nefyn in July.[3] Between

---

[1] On 2 May he was at Llanberis with some followers, including his seneschal, Goronwy ap Heilyn, and used his seal. See a charter and the letters patent, which make John ap David his representative in Builth, Brecon, and adjacent parts (*Littere Wallie*, pp. 74–75, 77).   [2] *Foedera*, i. ii. 630–1.

[3] See especially N. Denholm-Young in *Studies in Medieval History presented to F. M. Powicke* (1948), pp. 265–6 and notes. A Welsh national treasure, the crown of King Arthur, was found about this time and was presented to Edward.

September and Christmas the king completed his administrative arrangements in the course of his first tour of Wales as a whole. He held the Christmas feast at Bristol, and this was followed by a parliament of magnates. 'No king of England had ever been for one of the principal feasts at Bristol nor, in living memory, had a parliament been held there before.'[1] The archbishop of Canterbury also had found time to return to Wales, where, between May and August, he made a visitation of the four dioceses, issued injunctions, and discussed Welsh problems with the king.

The political settlement was the logical completion of the system of defence and administration which had been developed in King Henry's reign after the death of Llywelyn the Great in 1240, and had been defined by Edward in 1277.[2] Castles were built, towns founded, and an administration similar to that which prevailed in the county of Chester was extended to cover the conquered lands.

Castle-building had proceeded continuously since 1277, and continued with energy after the conquest of Snowdonia. The new castles at Flint, Rhuddlan, Builth, Llanbadarn, and the work on older Welsh castles in the district of Ystrad Tywi, had been needed to protect the Four Cantrefs and mid-Wales. The fortresses of Snowdonia—Conway, Caernarvon, Criccieth, and Harlech, followed in 1295 by Beaumaris—were in general, on a larger scale, the counterpart to the earl of Gloucester's castle of Caerphilly in the south. The damage done to Llanbadarn and the ease with which it was taken by the Welsh in 1282 showed the need for operations there. In 1282 work had been begun by the king at Denbigh, which was to become the centre of the earl of Lincoln's new lordship, and Reginald de Grey was apparently

---

[1] *Ann. monast.* iv. 300.

[2] Morris, op. cit., pp. 198–204; W. H. Waters, *The Edwardian Settlement of North Wales* (1934); A. H. Williams, *An Introduction to the History of Wales*, ii (1948), 131–75; E. A. Lewis, *Mediaeval Boroughs of Snowdonia* (1912). On the castles see J. G. Edwards, 'Edward I's Castle-building in Wales', in *Proceedings of the British Academy*, xxxii (1946, published 1951), 15–81; A. J. Taylor, 'Master James of St. George', in *E.H.R.* lxv (1950), 433–57; also his *Caernarvon Castle and Town Walls* (H.M. Stationery Office, 1953); D. Knoop and G. P. Jones, 'Castle Building at Beaumaris and Caernarvon in the Early Fourteenth Century', in the *Transactions of the Quatuor Coronati Lodge*, xlv (1932). For ecclesiastical documents see Pecham's *Epistolae*, and Haddan and Stubbs, *Councils and Ecclesiastical Documents relating to Great Britain and Ireland*, i (1869), especially pp. 546–83. Cf. J. W. Willis-Bund in *Transactions* of the Cymmrodorion Society for 1900–1 (1902), pp. 53–86, and J. A. Price on the Church of Wales in *Y Cymmrodor*, xxvi (1916), 191–214.

busy in his new lordship at Ruthin. The destruction done at Caernarvon in the last Welsh rising in 1294 necessitated extensive reconstruction. Throughout this period, from 1277 to 1298, the king's right-hand man in north Wales was Master James of St. George. He is known to have been responsible for the work at Flint and Rhuddlan. In 1286, in the accounts of expenses incurred at Caernarvon, Conway, Criccieth, and Harlech, he is styled 'the master of the king's works in Wales', and from 1295 he was master of the works at the new castle of Beaumaris. He has been identified, with much probability, as the Master James the mason (*lathomus*) who worked in Savoy, first with his father and then alone, from 1261 to 1275. James had got his experience in the service of Peter of Savoy and his successors and had attracted Edward's attention when the king stayed at Saint-Georges-d'Espéranche and received the homage of his cousin Count Philip in June 1273, on his way home.[1] The splendid castles at Conway and Beaumaris, if this identification is correct, express the genius of a Savoyard who had helped to build Peter of Savoy's castle and town at Yverdon, on Lake Neuchâtel, twenty or thirty years before. The resemblance in design and treatment between Yverdon and the north Welsh castles has been described as 'striking'; moreover, at Yverdon Master James had become familiar with the linking of a new town and a new castle in a single architectural achievement, as they were integrated at Aberystwyth, Flint, Rhuddlan, Conway, and Caernarvon.[2]

Master James was not the only fine craftsman in the king's service in Wales. Another outstanding builder, Walter of Hereford, was the master of works at Caernarvon in 1295 during the second stage of the operations there; but no master-mason was more honoured by Edward than was James, or received so high a wage as three shillings a day. He was obviously a man of administrative as well as of technical ability. The king had him by his side in Gascony and later in Scotland, where he was responsible for the Edwardian work in Linlithgow castle. For a

[1] Above, p. 226; Taylor, op. cit., pp. 451–7. Edward's clerk, Master Stephen of St. George, who first appears in the English records in 1274, was possibly a relative of Master James.

[2] The town fortifications at Conway and Caernarvon 'were so elaborate and massive that they have defied the vicissitudes of time' (J. G. Edwards, op. cit., p. 15). Although King Edward's familiarity with the bastides of Gascony and southern France doubtless influenced his planning, it should be remembered that most of these were towns with no castles (above, pp. 308–10). Indeed, the Welsh castles may well have influenced work in Gascony. See also note below, p. 444.

time (1290–3) he combined the constableship of Harlech with the position of master of works, and received 100 marks a year. He ruled in a fortress which he had built. His career, indeed, reminds us that the building of castles, cathedrals, and abbeys implied an elaborate administrative organization, and the expert handling of vast sums of money. The accounts of the building of Vale Royal abbey during the first three years of its construction (1278–80) and the evidence of the exchequer records about the expenses on the five castles of Snowdonia (Conway, Caernarvon, Criccieth, Harlech, and Beaumaris)[1] convey a vivid picture of the concentration from far and near of masons, carpenters, quarrymen, diggers, smiths, and carters, of the transport of material, the progress of the works, the hierarchy of officials, the building and equipment of the masons' dwellings and of the wooden lodges in which the masons did much of their work. Letters written to the exchequer in February 1296 about the operations at Caernarvon and Beaumaris show the speed and zest of all this activity. The constable of the castle and Master James report that they had incurred a cost of £250 every week at Beaumaris, where 400 masons were at work. They beg for money, lest all that had been done on walls, towers, and gates should be wasted for lack of completion. The revolt of 1295 had been crushed, but if the wars in France and Scotland continue, there may be more trouble. 'As you know well', they say, 'Welshmen are Welshmen.'[2] The total expenditure on the five castles up to the end of the century was at least £50,000. In addition, over £22,000 was spent on Builth and the castles and towns of Flint, Rhuddlan, and Aberystwyth. When everything has been taken into account 'we may almost certainly take £80,000 as a safe notional figure for the total sum expended by Edward I on his castle-building in Wales'.[3]

At Flint, Rhuddlan, and by each of his new royal castles of Snowdonia, Edward, in the course of his stately progress through Wales, founded a free borough, whether the town walls were integrated with the fortress or not.[4] Beaumaris was made a

---

[1] Bere was strengthened in 1283–4, but neither the castle nor the new borough there was of lasting importance.

[2] Summarized in Morris, pp. 268–9; edited by Edwards, pp. 80–81. For expenditure on the castles see Edwards, pp. 61–67; for Vale Royal see the evidence referred to in *King Henry III and the Lord Edward*, pp. 723–4 and notes.

[3] Edwards, p. 62.

[4] Rhuddlan was a refoundation; its first borough charter was given in 1278.

borough in 1296. A borough had existed at Aberystwyth or Llanbadarn since 1277, at Builth since 1278, while Abergavenny, Cardigan, and Carmarthen had been boroughs for a long time. The new castle boroughs were generally given the liberties of Hereford. The burgesses were Englishmen, the mayor, as at Conway, might be the constable of the castle. Two other boroughs, not connected with castles, were founded: one at Caerwys in Flintshire in 1290, the other at Newborough (now Newport) in Anglesey, created by Edward of Caernarvon in 1303. The Edwardian boroughs of Snowdonia, except at Conway, Harlech, and Newborough, had been preceded by a Welsh town. To what extent the Welsh penetrated into the royal boroughs, unless as vendors and buyers, is not clear. They would presumably have more freedom in the old boroughs founded in the Marches, generally in the twelfth century, round from Oswestry to Pembroke and Haverfordwest; and of course in Welshpool (1282) and Llanfyllin, founded the one by Gruffydd ap Gwenwynwyn and the other by his son Llywelyn (1286). Archbishop Pecham, who was concerned about the morals of the Welsh, urged that they should be encouraged to settle in boroughs and to send their children to be educated in England;[1] but he was inclined to be impulsive and impractical in his attitude to the Welshmen.

The archbishop had feared for the fate of the Welsh clergy in Snowdonia, and, in his letter about Llywelyn's death, suggested to the king that they should be saved and sent to France after the conquest was completed. At the same time he respected Welsh traditions consonant with social and religious well-being and, while he urged upon the bishops the reform of dangerous practices, notably the abuse of the penitential system by the excessive infliction of money fines, he was determined to protect the rights and liberties of the Church in Wales, now, for the first time, in full communion with the rest of his ecclesiastical province.

Their official records and letters show king and archbishop, with the co-operation of the chancellor, combining to restore

Between 1277 and 1280, £755 was spent on the *fossa maris*, required by the formation of a port at Rhuddlan on the tidal river Clwyd (Edwards, pp. 32, 69).

[1] *Epistolae*, iii. 777 (Newport, 8 July 1284, not 4 July, as Shirley gives; the reference is to the morrow of St. Thomas of Canterbury, not of the Apostle). The Roman emperors, he recollects, had made the Burgundians do this (*habiter en borgs*); that is why they are called Burgundians.

Wales after the destruction and violence of war. Pecham, indeed, sought to do what the legate Ottobuono had done in England after the barons' wars, and it is significant that, at the king's request, Pope Martin IV, in May 1284, granted a general absolution for acts of sacrilege and spoliation to all who had been concerned in the conflicts with Simon de Montfort and in the recent Welsh wars.[1] Edward also, after taking counsel with his advisers, ordered special inquiry to be made into the losses of the clergy and restitution for the same. In June the archbishop nominated the commission of inquiry and considerable restitution was made.[2] Although the English clergy protested in 1285 that the rights and liberties of the church in Wales had not been adequately protected, as the archbishop had required of the king, Edward probably had some justification for his reply that the church had now more freedom than it had had before.

Indeed, he and Pecham had co-operated since 1278, when the king had intervened on behalf of the bishop of Bangor, and had confirmed the liberties of his diocese as he had previously confirmed those of the diocese of St. Asaph (1275). Strongly supported by Bishop Anian he begged the pope in 1281 to permit the transfer of the cathedral of St. Asaph from its exposed and solitary site to the new town of Rhuddlan, where it might have a more dignified and accessible location, protected by the new castle. This plan came to nothing, but another plan, to transfer the Cistercian abbey of Aberconway to Maenan in the same diocese, was put through in 1284, when Edward required the former site of the abbey for his new castle of Conway. The archbishop, though he disliked the removal to Maenan, helped the king in this complicated transfer, and persuaded the bishop to agree to it.[3] Bishop Anian had been in trouble; his loyalty had been suspected; he had had to leave his diocese and take refuge in England; he had delayed to issue the archiepiscopal letters of excommunication of the king's enemies after the outbreak of war in April 1282; indeed, when the English burnt his exposed

---

[1] Haddan and Stubbs, i. 554–5.

[2] See the long series of acknowledgements in November, *Littere Wallie*, pp. 59–76 *passim*.

[3] *Epistolae*, ii. 729–31; cf. *Littere Wallie*, pp. 46–47, for the arrangements. Pecham would have preferred to remove the abbey into another part of the diocese of Bangor, for there were already four Cistercian houses in the diocese of St. Asaph. The Cistercians, he wrote to Edward (*Epistolae*, ii. 726), are the hardest neighbours that prelates and parsons can have.

cathedral shortly afterwards, he was more eager to excommunicate the royal soldiery. A Welsh bishop of a mixed flock, in a disturbed diocese, partly in Wales, partly in the Marches, had no easy life in time of war. Pecham handled Anian with sympathy and frankness. He begged him to be conciliatory about the removal of the abbey to Maenan. The bishop's presence was necessary in his diocese during and after the archbishop's visitation, and Pecham assured the king that Anian had not been disloyal.

Pecham's difficulties were with his own countrymen as much as with the Welsh. The royal officials were slow in their regard for ecclesiastical liberties, especially those, such as the judicial control of patronage, which happened to be more canonical than they were in England. During his visitation the only serious opposition which the archbishop met was from the former royal clerk and minister, Thomas Bek, who since 1280 had been bishop of St. David's. Bek, recalling the claims of his predecessors in Hubert Walter's time, refused to recognize the metropolitan rights of the archbishop in Wales. He made 'the last expiring remonstrance on behalf of the ancient independence of the Welsh Church'.[1] He was reminded that he had himself made the usual profession of obedience before his consecration, and he gave way.

The operation of the administrative settlement of Wales, as defined in the statute of Wales, can best be traced in the records of the fourteenth century, after it had become a matter of course.[2] Here it need only be said that the statute extended to Snowdonia and developed the organization which had existed for some time in west Wales. The Four Cantrefs continued to be an extension of the county of Chester, but only part of them in the east was made into a shire, the county of Flint, whose sheriff was subject to the justice of Chester. The greater part of the district, as we have seen, was composed of lordships. Snowdonia proper was divided into the three shires of Anglesey, Caernarvon, and Merioneth, whose sheriffs were subordinate to a justice of north Wales. Otto of Granson, who had commanded the forces in Anglesey, was left 'to guard the land', as the king had verbally

---

[1] Editorial comment in Haddan and Stubbs, i. 528. See the *relatio* from Pecham's Register, in the same work, pp. 577–9.

[2] For the earlier records see the bibliography in Waters, *The Edwardian Settlement*, and add Myvanwy Rhys, *Ministers' Accounts for West Wales, 1277–1306*, i, Text and Translation (Cymmrodorion Soc. Record Series, no. 13, 1936).

instructed him, and was titular justice of it till 1295, but, of course, as the king's most intimate counsellor, he did not continue to reside, nor did the king cease to issue direct orders to his deputies in the castle at Caernarvon, where the administration, with an exchequer under a chamberlain or treasurer, was centred. The exchequer was subject to the exchequer in Westminster. The royal administration in Wales, like that in Gascony, was under the constant supervision of the Crown and was directed by very much the same group of men as was concerned with Gascon and later with Scottish affairs. Otto of Granson's first deputy, John Havering, who later became justice in 1295, passed from Wales to Gascony and back again. Similarly, west Wales, the administration of which was centred at Carmarthen, was left in the control of Robert Tybetot, who had been justiciar since 1281, and had long been another trusted companion of the king. Here the texture of local government was looser than in Snowdonia. The justiciar had advanced much money in Edward's service; he was indispensable in more senses than one; and in November 1284 the king entered into a compact with him whereby he enjoyed the revenues in return for his duty to keep the castles in sound condition. The shires of Cardigan and Carmarthen were extended and defined, but the two northern parts of the former, and Cantref Mawr north of the Tywi river in the latter, became stewardships, apparently independent of the sheriffs, whose duties were confined to the cantrefs in which the two castles of Cardigan and Carmarthen lay.

Tybetot, after ten years further service as justiciar of west Wales, was sent to Gascony when the French war began in 1294, and returned to Wales to die in 1298. In 1300 John Havering was made justice of all Wales, thus preparing the way for the transfer of Wales and Chester to the king's heir, Edward of Caernarvon, in the following year. The creation of a new princedom of Wales marked the end of the first and most critical stage of settlement. The young prince, though subject to his father's intervention, ruled a more compact and more localized dominion outside the Marches. At the same time Reginald de Grey closed his long administration at Chester. In 1297, when the king went to Flanders and left his son as regent in England, Grey was attached to him as military adviser, and when he was required for the Scottish campaign he ceased to be justiciar of Chester.

The creation of Edward of Caernarvon as prince of Wales

caused pleasure in Wales. He had been born in Wales, and a new, more peaceful period had begun. The early years of settlement had been disturbed by two rebellions, one in 1287, during the king's absence in Gascony, the other in 1294-5, while he was busy with his plans for his operations against King Philip IV of France in the duchy. The risings revealed, in different ways, the strain of a new discipline upon the Welsh rather than any sense of intolerable oppression. The statute of Wales imposed a system of order and justice which was wise and equitable. After the conquest King Edward maintained the principles which he had expounded in 1277 and had elaborated during the period between the wars, and which, as modern investigation has shown, were in closer accord with previous tendencies in Welsh law and government than national feeling in Wales has usually realized. Welsh law and custom were in general to be maintained, bad customs were to be abolished, outmoded practices were to be revised. The Welsh local unit of justice or commote was retained as the hundred and in fact rapidly became the most active centre of justice and administration. Criminal law was definitely anglicized, civil law remained essentially Welsh; Welsh local officials continued to function under the direction of sheriffs and bailiffs; and the Welsh freemen found scope for their way of life and their litigious habits. It would seem, indeed, that life within the areas of royal administration, new and strange though it might feel, became more congenial to the Welsh tenant than life in the more anglicized march-lands of the south.[1] It is unwise to isolate Welsh complaints and charges, or to take literally the words in which the king, after the rebellion of 1295, ordered an investigation into incessant extortion, oppression, and damages alleged to have been inflicted by all officials in north Wales 'since that land came into our hands'.[2] Sweeping generalizations of this kind are familiar to every student of medieval administration. If the proclamations of 1274-5 and the phrases of some of the statutes were precise expressions of undoubted truth, England in Edward I's reign was in a more abject state of subjection to local tyranny than Wales ever was. The roots of Welsh disaffection lay deeper than any

[1] When Edward came to Gower in December 1284 he found a dispute raging about the Welsh tenants of the barony who had migrated in 1283 to the royal lands of Carreg Cennen, and declared that they would live under a king rather than under a lord marcher. Cf. Morris, p. 201.

[2] See the writ cited by Morris, p. 266.

discomforts of the day, and came to flower in the hearts of men who had vivid memories of old days and saw the ancient heritage of their princes encircled by great fortresses whose walls and towers were rising in arrogant intrusion on historic ground; and still more in the hearts of those who were frustrated and disillusioned in spite of their services to the Crown.

Such a man was Rhys ap Maredudd, the only descendant of the Lord Rhys who, since 1277, had been faithful to the king. Through his mother he was related to three English earls, Gloucester, Warenne, and Norfolk.[1] His lordship of Dryslwyn had been enlarged, in recognition of singular services to the Crown in 1282, by the lands of his rebellious cousin, Rhys Wyndod, in Cantref Mawr. In 1285 he had married Ada, a sister of John Hastings, whose father had succeeded by marriage to the old Braose lands in Abergavenny, the march of Cilgerran and Emlyn near Cardigan. With Ada, Rhys had acquired rights in Emlyn and other lands. His position as a baron of Wales seemed as firm in the Tywi valley as that of the lord of Pool in south Powys; yet he was restless and unhappy. He had expected, as a lord marcher, to be as independent as his ancestors had been as Welsh princes, and from the first he found that this was not the case. He had had to surrender all claim to the family fortress at Dinefwr. When he entered upon his new lands in 1282 he was sharply called to order by King Edward because he had neglected to receive investiture in the legal manner, and, though he was at once restored to the lands and the royal favour, he had been humiliated.[2] Since 1282 he had had disputes with his powerful neighbour, John Giffard, lord of Builth and now of the district of Isgenen, which marched with his lands and with Brecon, and by 1287 he seems to have been at feud with him. Finally, and worst of all, in the spring of 1287 he refused to appear in the shire court of Carmarthen, where he had a suit, and the justiciar, Robert Tybetot, proposed to proceed to outlaw him. Rhys submitted a record of the process and complaints against Tybetot to Edward at Bordeaux, whence the king ordered forbearance and delay while Ralph Hengham and other justices were sent to investigate the matter at Carmarthen. The justices found no error and Rhys did not appear; but Edward had given

[1] *Cal. Anc. Corr.*, p. 139.
[2] See the interesting letter issued by Edward at Acton Burnell on 20 October 1283, relating the proceedings in parliament there (*Littere Wallie*, pp. 159–60).

instructions that, whatever their judgement might be, Rhys was not to be molested for the present, and Tybetot arranged to go to London in May for consultation with the regent, Edmund of Cornwall.[1] On 8 June Rhys revolted.

The local castles were weakly manned by their castellans, contrary to the wishes of the regent,[2] and Rhys at first carried all before him; he captured Dinefwr, Carreg Cennen, and Llandovery, and ravaged freely in all directions as far as Swansea in the south, Llanbadarn in the north, and the district of Brecon to the east. His success was brief, and from a military standpoint the story of his rebellion is remarkable as a proof of the ease with which troops and equipment were directed from every part of Wales and the shires on the border in well-ordered combination. By the middle of August the regent, who took supreme command, had 10,600 foot and about 600 horse about him for the siege of Dryslwyn, to which the way had been cleared by the lords of the Marches who, under the earl of Gloucester, had rapidly concentrated in the March of Brecon a force of 12,500 men. The regent's army was drawn from Cheshire and the border counties, which provided some 4,000 men, and from the Marches, Snowdonia, and west Wales, whose contingents, over 6,000 in all, were almost entirely Welsh. North Wales sent 2,600 Welsh. There had never before been so rapid and well planned a concentration of Welshmen in such a large army, nor such a united demonstration by the lords of the Marches. And these forces were marshalled as paid armies, under the direction of the regent, Tybetot, the earl of Gloucester and his fellow Marchers, while the local officials, in their various bases, organized enlistment and sent supplies, including a great siege-engine from Snowdonia. Rhys ap Maredudd could rely only upon the Welsh of his own neighbourhood in Cantref

[1] See letters in *Cal. Anc. Corr.*, pp. 166–9. It should be noted that the neighbouring lords marcher, though their lands were not all within the shire, owed suit at the shire court. Rhys seems to have been engaged in a process concerning the rights of the king and then failed to obey the justiciar's summonses, so making himself liable to outlawry. The Osney-Wykes annals describe his grievance neatly; the Lord Robert Tybetot harassed him, contrary to the liberty granted to him by the king, 'ad leges et consuetudines Anglicanas observandas' (*Ann. monast.* iv. 310).

[2] A letter written by a confidential clerk sent by the regent to the king at Bordeaux (13 December 1287) shows that Edward had been greatly disturbed by the success of Rhys. The writer says that he was able to exonerate Edmund and to explain that the castellans were to blame for their failure to hold the castles (op. cit., pp. 174–5).

Mawr and Isgenen. He got no national response, while the government had no difficulty in raising Welsh freemen to fight under English commanders. These facts go to show why the much more serious rebellion in 1294–5 so soon collapsed.

Dryslwyn fell, after a strong and fierce resistance, on 5 September. Dinefwr and the other castles captured by Rhys were retaken and the country-side reduced to order. The armies were dispersed. Then, in November, Rhys broke out again, this time in the Cardigan area, and seized the 'new castle' of Emlyn, which he claimed as part of his wife's marriage portion. The task of recapturing it and ending the war was left to Tybetot the justiciar. The big siege-engine was dragged from Dryslwyn to Emlyn. The castle was taken in January 1288 and retained by the Crown as a conquest in war. Rhys took to the forests and was at large till 1292. On 2 June he was tried at York by a special royal commission and hanged. Dryslwyn received a royal castellan and his six commotes in Cantref Mawr were added to the shire of Carmarthen.

The next and last revolt was premeditated and planned, for it broke out in all parts of Wales and spread even to Glamorgan, where 'a certain Morgan, whose ancestors had been dispossessed by the Clares' revolted against the earl of Gloucester and for a time with some success.[1] In west Wales, around Cardigan, a young man called Maelgwn took the lead; in the districts of Brecon and Builth a certain Cynan. The danger was most serious in north Wales, where the instigating spirit was Madog ap Llywelyn, whose father, having been ejected by Llywelyn from Merioneth in 1256, had become a royal pensioner. Madog, who claimed 'the whole land of Meirionydd' before the Hopton commission in 1278, had also received favour of a more casual kind from the Crown. His ancestors had been Welsh princes and he was doubtless dissatisfied with his lot as the son of a former royalist, who, preferring his fealty to unfaithfulness, had suffered exile, had spent all that he had, and had been killed in battle in the service of the king.[2] Other Welshmen, whose fathers had

---

[1] On his relations with the famous traitor, Thomas Turberville, see J. G. Edwards in *Studies in Medieval History presented to F. M. Powicke* (1948), pp. 298–304.

[2] See Shirley, *Royal Letters*, ii. 123–4, Llywelyn ap Maredudd's petition to King Henry for sustenance. He was killed in 1263. J. G. Edwards, in *Bulletin of the Board of Celtic Studies*, xiii (1950), 207–10, has shown that it was his son Madog who led the revolt in 1294–5, not an illegitimate son of the late prince, Llywelyn ap Gruffydd.

served the prince of Wales and were less highly born than he, had made their way in the king's service—men like Gruffydd ap Tudor, the son of the prince's steward, and young Gruffydd ap Rhys of Tregarnedd in Anglesey.[1] It would seem that Madog and his fellow rebels were, whether in discontent or patriotism, driven by a contrary impulse, as they saw all the arrangements made by the English government for the expedition to Gascony in 1294, the levies of Welsh from north Wales to fight abroad, the departure of the justiciar of west Wales, the signs of unrest and reluctance among the people. Anyhow, on 30 September 1294, the day on which the Welsh levies had been ordered to be at Shrewsbury, the rebellion began. The weakened castles, some left without their castellans or lords, were suddenly attacked, at Cardigan, Builth, Bere, Denbigh, and notably at Caernarvon, where the sheriff was killed and the castle partially destroyed.

Once again, as in 1282, King Edward had to throw off every other commitment and bend his mind to a Welsh war. The speed with which he concentrated an army, writes Morris, 'is as noticeable as the lightning-like fury of the Welsh outburst'. Indeed, so great was his hold on England that in a few weeks he had three armies, comprising in all more than 31,000 foot-soldiers. William of Valence, reinforced by the earl of Norfolk, held on in the south and Llanbadarn, the earl of Hereford and John Giffard in Brecon and Builth, the justiciar of north Wales in Merioneth, the earl of Lincoln and Reginald Grey in the Four Cantrefs. Edward gathered together at Worcester some 250 lances from the musters in London and Portsmouth which had not yet sailed to Gascony, and concentrated the foot-soldiers of the northern, western, and south-western shires at Chester, Montgomery, and Gloucester. When he reached Chester with his cavalry on 5 December, he found 16,000 foot and also a force based on Rhuddlan. There were 11,460 men at Montgomery, and 4,000 on their way from Gloucester to Cardiff. Leaving Chester on 7 December, he made a detour through Wrexham to crush the rebels in Ruthin and Denbigh, and arrived on the coast shortly before Christmas. Then with the bulk of his foot, which had come from Chester by way of

---

[1] Gruffydd ap Tudor was trusted enough in 1282 to be given the charge of the castle at Dolwyddelan after its capture. For Gruffydd ap Rhys see the story of his career and fame by J. G. Edwards, 'Sir Gruffydd Llwyd' in *E.H.R.* xxx (1915), 589-601.

Rhuddlan, he went on to hold the feast at Conway. In his eagerness and confidence, the king risked an advance with part of his army to Bangor (7–8 January 1295), a temptation which he had been careful to avoid in the past. Immediately the Welsh rushed down, captured his baggage-train, and forced him to turn back to Conway. He succeeded in extricating himself from the enemy and, back in his new fortress, was safe enough, but the setback was serious. Madog had forced him to give up all ideas of a winter campaign. He called for volunteers from the gentry of the shires, and kept his army supplied, while the justiciar, John de Havering, held on as best he could in the outskirts of Snowdonia. In this period of suspense, sea-power was all-important. Two Bristol ships plied between Bristol, Dublin, and Conway with cargoes of wine and oats and other necessaries. Fourteen ships of Bayonne were licensed as privateers to plunder the king's enemies. The castles of Llanbadarn, Harlech, and Criccieth, cut off from support by land, were kept in supply of food and munitions by sea. The constable of Bristol was ordered to relieve Llanbadarn, where Roger de Molis, the marshal of the southern forces, was isolated. An Irish ship, the *Godyer*, of Rosponte in county Wexford, provisioned Harlech and Criccieth.[1]

The end really came before Edward was ready to move in strength; for at the end of February Madog ap Llywelyn, who had wisely left Edward alone in Conway, anticipated attack by an expedition into Powys, and there he met disaster. By this time William Beauchamp, earl of Warwick, had at Montgomery a force reduced to about 3,000 foot, but he also had 119 lances, 13 expert crossbowmen, and a body of archers under his command. Some of the foot also were armed with bows. He marched out and surprised Madog in an open valley at Maes Moydog, some ten miles from Montgomery.[2] This was on 5 March 1295. Warwick attacked by night. He encircled the Welsh with

[1] Two of the exchequer records which give details (cf. Morris, pp. 259–60) have been printed by J. Griffiths in the *Bulletin of the Board of Celtic Studies*, viii (1937), 147–59. They relate to the relief of the small garrison at Harlech and are of much interest. Over £1,000 must have been spent on these relief expeditions from Ireland and Bristol.

[2] Here the fine papers of J. G. Edwards in *E.H.R.* xxxix (1924), 1–12, and xlvi (1931), 262–5, displace the account in Morris's book (pp. 255–8). Morris was misled into thinking that the fight so graphically described by Trevet occurred in January near Conway and relieved Edward. He overlooked an entry in the Worcester annals (*Ann. Monast.* iv. 519) and the pay-rolls.

cavalry interlinked by crossbowmen and archers. 'The Welsh planted the butts of their spears in the ground and turned the points against the charge'; but, before the charge came, the bolts and arrows played havoc, and then the horse scattered them with great slaughter. Similiar tactics were used at Falkirk three and a half years later. Madog escaped, but his cause was ruined. In April the king again moved on to Bangor. He occupied Anglesey and ordered the construction of a new castle at Beaumaris. In the course of the next few weeks, as he made a military circuit of Wales with a force of 94 crossbowmen and 2,350 foot, all resistance crumbled away and the Welsh returned to his peace.[1] By August he was back in Westminster. Madog ap Llywelyn with his household (*familia*) came to terms with the justiciar of north Wales on 31 July, and on the next day was sent to Edward in London.[2]

Since 1284 the fortunes of the lords of the Marches, both English and Welsh, had become inextricably involved with those of the Crown. The rapid and massive demonstration of royal power in 1294 both furthered and demonstrated this development. We have already seen how King Edward had humbled, even while he had exalted, the earl of Gloucester in 1290–1;[3] and it is significant that in 1295 he himself received the submission of the rebels in Glamorgan and for a time took the lordship into his own hands. Early in 1291 he had asked the Marchers to contribute to the subsidy granted in 1290 in parliament in aid of the expense he had incurred during his negotiations for the release of Charles of Salerno,[4] and in 1292 they acceded to this request. They gave a fifteenth from their lands in Wales, and at the same time the good men and *communitas* of Chester and the royal demesne in Wales were subjected to the tax.[5] Power in the Marches might be consolidated as the result of royal favour, but it might also be

---

[1] Morris, pp. 263–5. The king's last concern was to revisit Caernarvon and Beaumaris to make sure that the castle-building was in train. On the rapid, almost feverish, activity at Beaumaris see the letter of 28 February 1296 (above, p. 432). For the method of bringing the Welsh freemen to the king's peace see above, p. 421, n. 1.

[2] *Annales Cestrienses*, ed. R. C. Christie (1887), p. 118; *Ann. Monast.* iv. 522.

[3] Above, pp. 329–30.   [4] Above, p. 259; below, p. 560.

[5] *Parl. Writs*, i. 390, 391. See Francis Jones in *Bull. of Board of Celtic Studies*, xiii, pt. iv (1950), 210–30, for the list of taxers and jurors in the Marches and the text of the assessments in the lordships of Abergavenny and Cilgerran. An assessment of part of Lleyn in Caernarvonshire is printed in the same periodical, v, pt. ii (1930), 54–71.

broken on the stony administration which now encircled it. Roger Mortimer, the paramour of Queen Isabella, and the first earl of March, owed his influence to his strength in the Marches, but his fall was largely due to the strength and loyalty of the royal administration in Wales. Owen Glendower sought to profit from the complexities of royal and Marcher politics. The fratricidal strife between the houses of Lancaster and York and the rise of the Tudor dynasty began here. So Llywelyn ap Gruffydd was avenged.

Additional Note (see above, p. 431, note 2). Mr. Taylor has pointed out to me that Pope Clement V's castle of Villandraut (Gironde) may show the influence of earlier work in Conway and elsewhere in north Wales. It dates from *c.* 1308. The future pope was at Conway in 1295 and had in his household a Bertrand of St. George who may have been a relative of James of St. George. Later in the fourteenth century a Bernard of St. George was master mason of Bordeaux cathedral.

X

THE CLERGY UNDER TWO RULES OF LAW

AT the end of the thirteenth century England was divided into seventeen dioceses and about forty archdeaconries. The archdeaconries, except in the midlands, only roughly corresponded to the shires; just as, except in the east and north-east, there was a curious lack of relation between the boundaries of the hundreds or wapentakes and the boundaries of the rural deaneries.[1] It has been estimated that these ecclesiastical divisions comprehended some 9,500 parishes. Some of these, especially in the north, were of great extent, once the areas served by the Anglo-Saxon minster or central church; many were co-terminous with rural vills, others with rural manors; about 500 were crowded into a few towns, such as the hundred parishes of London, the forty of York, the twenty of Stamford or Bristol.

Scholars have given a good deal of attention to the number of clergy in England; one writer has estimated that in the later thirteenth century there were 40,000 ordained men, from acolytes upwards, in England and Wales at any one time; whereas another says that in 1377, after the visitations of plague, there were 8,100 beneficed and 16,000 unbeneficed clerks, or 24,100 in all. Adam Marsh once exclaimed in a letter to Grosseteste: 'What can be sadder in these evil days than that, though the world is full of the clerical profession, it is so hard to find a tolerable man for the cure of souls?'[2] Yet, if we reduce the estimate of 40,000 by a fourth, the number of clerks would comprise only about one per cent. of the population of thirteenth-century England, or about as many in number as the foot-soldiers collected on the Welsh border by King Edward in 1294 from the northern and western shires. While, however, the pay rolls enable us to know

---

[1] For what follows see A. Hamilton Thompson, 'Diocesan Organisation in the Middle Ages: Archdeacons and Rural Deans', in *Proc. of British Academy*, xxix (1943), 164–91; J. C. Russell, 'The Clerical Population of Medieval England', in *Traditio*, ii (New York, 1944), 177–212; J. R. H. Moorman, *Church Life in England in the Thirteenth Century* (1945), pp. 4–5, 52–55, 403–12.

[2] *Monumenta Franciscana*, ed. J. S. Brewer (1858), p. 144. On the *clericus* in legal administration see F. Pegues in *E.H.R.* lxxxi (1956), 529–59.

exactly the size of an Edwardian army at a given time, the number of clerks can only be roughly estimated from casual material by a precarious recourse to averages.

The number of regular clergy, that is to say, the monks, canons, and friars living under conventual rules, has been estimated at 16,500–17,000 by one writer, at 13,600 by another; the number of nuns at 7,000 at the most. In addition perhaps 1,500 men and women were living under vows in hospitals or as recluses. If these figures are near the truth, from 20,000 to 25,000 persons out of a population of three millions or so were dedicated to the 'religious' life. They were, for the most part, distributed very unevenly among some 780 houses, of which about 530 were major establishments of monks, canons, friars, and nuns. Most of the other 250 had a filial relation to houses at home or abroad, or were very small monasteries and cells. Needless to say, these figures conceal a variety and complexity of the religious life to which the monastic movement owed its social and spiritual influence. They convey no impression of the difference between a great baronial establishment like St. Albans, with its hundred monks or so, and the active houses of the Dominicans and Franciscans in the towns, or the obscurity of a small nunnery in the fens. Even a study of the maps can merely suggest the social significance of geographical distribution—of the Benedictine galaxy between the Welsh border and the coasts of East Anglia, or of the clusters of Augustinian and other canons between their base on the Thames valley and their apex in the North Riding of Yorkshire. Indeed, a human analysis might show that there is no significance in generalizations of this kind. What matters is the way in which the groups and individuals in these variegated and colourful societies of clerks and religious persons lived; and, while it is useful to know that the whole clerical body, secular and religious, did not comprise more than two per cent. of the scattered population of England, it is much more important to remember that a great scholar-bishop like Grosseteste, a saintly and popular busy-body like Adam Marsh, and a powerful king's clerk like John Mansel or Robert Burnell might have a driving force or a conciliating influence, in the peculiarly constituted life of a medieval kingdom, greater than that of any normal community of city or shire, and much greater than that of an ordinary cathedral chapter or of a dozen monastic cloisters.

All the same, whatever the exact number of clerks alive at any one time may have been, it was large enough to make their discipline a hard and perplexing problem. The clerks were a privileged class, whose conduct and behaviour were subject to the control of their superiors and to them alone. Of course in civil matters a clerk who had a dispute with a lay or clerical neighbour and 'went to law' had usually to go to the secular courts, and if he were assaulted the secular authorities were expected to vindicate the breach of the king's peace; but a criminous clerk could be claimed by his bishop to be dealt with. The clerical body, so far as it was composed of persons with the cure of souls, was responsible for its flocks and needed all the encouragement which its spiritual leaders could give. A parson in the thirteenth century, which in our consideration of the clergy may be said with much truth to begin with the fourth Lateran council of 1215, was a member of a vast organization under the authority of pope, archbishops, bishops, archdeacons. He was under a jurisdiction defined by the canon law, or common law of the Church. The tendency, latent in the development of lay patronage, to emphasize his local position and turn him into the paid chaplain of the lord who had appointed him had been checked. He was instituted after examination by his bishop and inducted by episcopal authority conferred upon an archdeacon or rural dean or other commissary. His right to his tithe was carefully defined. He was required to attend episcopal synods and archidiaconal chapters, and expected to possess a copy of the episcopal constitutions which explained for his guidance, under duty of his obedience, the law of the Church so far as it immediately concerned him. While on the one hand his 'benefice' was becoming a kind of freehold of which (once his position was recognized as valid) he could only be deprived by the law of the Church, he was not free to take advantage of his security. In some quarters rectors, in the first half of the century, were inclined to assert that in penitential matters they had no superiors and, if they made confession at all, could go to unauthorized persons; they were reminded that they must subject themselves to the suitable and learned priests appointed in each archdeaconry to hear the confessions of rectors and clergy in holy orders.[1]

[1] Bodley MS. 843, ff. 122–5 (c. 34)—a form of the so-called *Legenda* or collection of material suitable to be recited in a diocesan synod. See C. R. Cheney, *E.H.R.* l (1935), 395–8. Professor Cheney kindly lent me a transcript of the Bodley text.

The history of the Church would be much simpler than it is if we could stop here and define clerical organization as a clear-cut system of residential parsons or rectors whose cure of souls was exercised within fixed boundaries subject to the supervision of bishop and archdeacon; but just as we can rarely regard the knight of the shire as resident in one fixed place within a neat area of a knight's fee, held of a local baron, so we cannot picture the rector as his ecclesiastical counterpart in a neat topographical arrangement of parishes. It is true that the rectors were regarded as the substantial element, the 'greater and saner part' of the local clergy, but, even if they had all resided in their parishes, it was not easy to collect them together and to instil into them a corporate sense.[1] Only once, when Pope Innocent IV asked for clerical subsidies against the emperor, Frederick II (1239–44), do local assemblies of rectors, vicars, and rural deans seem to have found political voice.[2] In a document which was preserved by Matthew Paris and is said to have been presented to the legate Otto by the rectors of the archdeaconry of Berkshire in 1240, the opposition to a subsidy is supported by a remarkable argument. The papal lordship of ecclesiastical goods extends, said the rectors, only to care and concern and is in no way proprietary; the king and magnates of England, by hereditary right and good and approved custom, have the right of patronage of churches in England; hence the rectors had no obligation to contribute to papal needs, nor could they do so, without consultation with their patrons, whose intentions might be frustrated by such exactions. Unfortunately, the source of this document, which obviously reflects widespread discussion in legal and academic circles, is not known, but there is no reason to doubt that its contents were approved by groups of local clergy duly assembled. Here, on the one occasion when the rectors of churches are said to have expressed a corporate opinion, they were concerned to maintain the inviolability of their benefices against papal demands for money and their dependence upon their lay patrons. They emphasize their position as

---

[1] See the interesting letter from Bishop Herbert of Salisbury to Archbishop Hubert Walter in Hist. MSS. Com., *Report on MSS. in Various Collections*, i (1901), 233–4.

[2] *Chron. majora*, iv. 38–43. The document in its essentials was also preserved by the monks of Burton-on-Trent as an expression of the views of all the rectors of England (*Ann. Monast.* i. 265–7, under the year 1244). For the circumstances see W. E. Lunt, *Financial Relations of the Papacy with England to 1327* (1939), pp. 199–202.

possessors of lands and tithes, with obligations to nourish the poor, not as soldiers in the militia of Christ. Their protest reminds us that secular and ecclesiastical activities were very closely intertwined in English society. There was no coherent body of parish clergy in England, just as there were no 'movements' among the clergy in the sense in which we speak of the evangelical or the Oxford Movement in later times.

The ideal expounded in the councils of the Church and in the exhortations of reformers was precise. Its highest and most comprehensive expression in our period is to be found in the canons of the twelfth oecumenical or fourth Lateran council summoned by Pope Innocent III in 1215. These canons, most of which passed into the body of common law comprised in the authoritative Decretals of Pope Gregory IX, a textbook in every school of canon law, help us to understand the difference between the habitual outlook of clergy and people and the standards by which they were expected to direct their lives and social relationships.[1] The opening words of c. 27, 'Cum sit ars artium regimen animarum', give the clue to the main purpose of this legislation. The government of souls is the art of arts. A vivid picture of clerks, even prelates, who spend half their nights in riotous companionships and are too sleepy for their morning office; and of others who celebrate mass barely four times in the year, and if they condescend to attend mass, avoid the silence of the choir to chatter with laymen outside it (c. 17), suggests an indifference to the decencies of behaviour strangely out of keeping with the standard defined for the guidance of the priesthood. Unless by inference, nothing is said in the canons about the large floating population of clerks in minor orders who were not actively concerned with the cure of souls. The intention was to provide a body of disciplined, educated clergy, armed with an orthodox creed against the heretical tendencies of the time (cc. 1, 2) and qualified, by character and training, to instruct their parishioners and to hear their confessions at least once a year. To this end their superiors were required to bend their energies. Every metropolitan or archbishop was to hold a provincial council once a year, whose decisions were to be

[1] The most convenient text is in Hefele-Leclercq, *Histoire des Conciles*, v. ii (1913), 1323–98, with summaries and notes. The best introduction to the canons of 1215 as applied in England is in Marion Gibbs and Jane Lang, *Bishops and Reform, 1215–1272* (1934), pp. 94–179.

published in annual diocesan synods held by each bishop. Suitable
persons were to be appointed in each diocese to investigate matters which needed correction and to report their findings to the
next provincial council, where, in particular, inquiry was to be
made into recent appointments to benefices by the diocesans
and by the metropolitan himself. A teacher or *scholasticus* for
clergy and others was to be attached to every cathedral church,
and a theologian to the metropolitan church. Several canons
dealt with the moral discipline of the parish clergy and with
abuses incompatible with the effective cure of souls; others lay
stress upon their duty to keep themselves free from worldly entanglements; just as they are protected from lay interference, so,
as men with a sacred vocation they should refuse secular office,
refrain from secular amusements, and, rendering to Caesar the
things which are Caesar's, respect the jurisdiction proper to the
lay power.

The Lateran decrees covered wider ground than this. They
were oecumenical, not local. Some of them hardly applied to
English conditions, and as a whole they were not widely known
in England; but many English prelates had attended the council
and its legislation intensified the sense of authority and purpose
of Stephen Langton and his suffragans in their own legislative
work, whether or not they explicitly referred to them. The
council had been assembled soon after King John's surrender to
the pope and his recognition of ecclesiastical liberties. It rallied
ecclesiastical energies; its decrees gave effective expression to
the sense of unity in the Church and to Christian obligations
under papal leadership.

It would be wrong, however, to ascribe a revolutionary character to the ecclesiastical activity which followed the restoration
of peace in England and the return of Stephen Langton. The
Lateran decrees themselves were the culmination of a long process of theological and legislative definition, in which English
experience and English needs had been very prominent indeed.[1]
Hence, when we study the reforming activities of the English
prelates we must not expect to find, however violently they
expressed themselves, the ardour of missionaries prepared for
any sacrifices in an alien land, but rather the varying moods of
decent men trying to improve matters in a society in which each
of them had his own life to live. Even Grosseteste, the great

[1] Cf. F. M. Powicke, *Stephen Langton* (1928), pp. 150–3.

bishop of Lincoln, the most indefatigable reformer of them all, was a many-sided and genial man, always ready to check the extravagances of impulsive persons, and ready, like the good countryman he was, with shrewd advice about everyday affairs. The same conditions prevailed in every other kingdom of the west, however much local traditions might vary.

Provincial assemblies of the kind prescribed by the Lateran decree were rarely held in England. Archbishop Stephen Langton held one at Osney abbey, outside the walls of Oxford, in 1222, and Archbishop John Pecham held two, one at Reading in 1279 and one at Lambeth in 1281. Both Langton and Pecham issued constitutions inspired by great councils of the Church, for the former had attended the Lateran council in 1215 and the latter had received papal instructions to enforce the relevant canons of the council of Lyons held in 1274. Pecham also had before him the constitutions issued by the legates Otto and Ottobuono in the councils which they had held during their respective legations in 1237 and 1268, the most important and authoritative legislation of its kind issued in medieval England; hence his constitutions were a more compact body of law than were those of his predecessor in 1222. Another difference between the provincial constitutions of 1222 and 1279–81 is suggested by the greater emphasis laid by Pecham upon the duty to resist lay interference with ecclesiastical liberties; he put the constitutions of Archbishop Boniface, which will concern us shortly, in a wider setting. The controversy which he revived added intensity to his period of office, and was continued in a fitful manner until the Reformation.

The bishop himself was, in his pastoral capacity, especially concerned with his clergy, whom he gathered together once, if not twice, a year in synods.[1] As law and administration, both secular and ecclesiastical, became more professionalized, and more care was given to clerical organization, the synod ceased to reflect the life of the diocese as a whole, though it is likely that all kinds of informal business were always done in a time of synod, if not in synod. Little, in truth, is known about the normal proceedings of the synod, where rural deans, rectors, vicars, and chaplains met in their synodal robes or habits; but it is known that they were the most active and continuous occasions of ecclesiastical legislation, whose somewhat confusing records

[1] C. R. Cheney, *English Synodalia of the Thirteenth Century* (1941).

survive in the numerous texts, generally unofficial, of episcopal constitutions. These were injunctions, which the bishop considered to be required by his clergy, defining for their guidance the law of the Church, as the legatine and provincial constitutions legislated for the English Church as a whole or for one of the two provinces of Canterbury and York. C. R. Cheney's investigations into the chaotic manuscript evidence show that the bishops —including Archbishop Stephen himself (1222)—were at first especially influenced by the statutes or constitutions of Richard Poore (1217–21), issued when he was bishop of Salisbury, and that, later in the century, the statutes of Walter Cantilupe (1240), bishop of Worcester, and Robert Grosseteste (1240–3), bishop of Lincoln, were also copied or adapted by episcopal legislators.[1] Since every parson or vicar was expected to have his copy of his bishop's constitutions and to guide himself by them, some idea of the law of the Church, however slight this may have been in many minds, was spread wide among the clergy. The enforcement of it accentuated the difficulties with which we are at present concerned.

The situation was fully realized and faced by Grosseteste. His constitutions are brief and practical, addressed solely to the parochial clergy, 'with strict attention to immediate problems'. They take the body of canon law, now better known through Pope Gregory's official compilation, for granted, and impose no penalties, though they end with Langton's excommunications. In Cheney's view 'they circulated far more freely in the Middle Ages than did any other series of English episcopal statutes'.[2] They begin with what every parish priest should know—the ten commandments, the seven deadly sins, the seven sacraments, the creed—and go on to remind him, in simple detail, of his duties, how he should behave and what he should not do. He should allow no woman, whose presence might cause suspicion of evil, to live in his house, nor frequent taverns, nor engage in merchandise, nor act as a bailiff, nor make profit of the goods entrusted to him, nor attend plays, nor game with dice, nor carry arms. The cemetery should be enclosed, no markets or games or lawsuits should be allowed in holy places, clandestine marriages should be forbidden, no laymen, except perhaps the

---

[1] Op. cit., *passim*.

[2] Op. cit., p. 110; also pp. 118–19. The best text of the *constitutiones* may be found in Grosseteste's *Epistolae*, ed. Luard (1861), pp. 154–64.

patron, should be with the clerks in the chancel during divine service.

At first sight, such instructions of a bishop to his clergy have little to do with the relations between the powers of Church and state, and in fact most of Grosseteste's colleagues, though aware of the difficulties inherent in their administration, tended to face each problem as it arose as a matter incidental to the conditions under which they lived. The bishop of Lincoln did not interpret his duties in this way. He meant his constitutions to be observed. He was a reasonable man, no fanatic, but he was more than a counsellor of his clergy. His conception of the pastoral office literally subordinated everything to the salvation of souls. The daily exercise of this office implied that 'the sacerdotal power is greater and more dignified than all secular power'. A king who made ecclesiastical persons account to him for their personal behaviour acted, in Grosseteste's view, in defiance of divine and natural law, and turned the head into the tail.[1] Grosseteste made his position clear from the first days of his episcopate (1235), and always with an immediate practical application. In 1236 he fought against the decision of the barons and judges to maintain the common law of England against the common law of the Church, when they refused to admit that subsequent marriage legitimated bastards. In 1237 he was one of those who urged the legate Otto, so far as he could, to induce the king to correct a long list of practices prejudicial to ecclesiastical liberties, and doubtless had a hand in the compilation of this first series of grievances.[2] They reappeared in substance on at least two occasions during the next twenty years, once at a great council in January 1240, and again during the discussions of 1253, when the king with papal support begged to be allowed to use crusading taxation to meet the expenses of his Gascon expedition, and the Charters of liberty were solemnly confirmed.[3] On this occasion Grosseteste, then a dying man, was especially to the fore. At some time during these years he prepared the list of grievances

---

[1] *Ann. monast.* i. 422.

[2] This interesting document was copied into the annals of Burton (*Ann. monast.* i. 254-7). In this year the legate held his famous council at St. Paul's. Grosseteste was to have preached the opening sermon, which survives, but was too ill to do so. See Dorothy M. Williamson's important paper on 'Some Aspects of the Legation of Cardinal Otto in England, 1233-41', in *E.H.R.* lxiv (1949), 145-73.

[3] Matthew Paris, *Chronica majora*, iv. 3 (Jan. 1240); Annals of Burton (*Ann. monast.* i. 305) for the revival in 1253 of the grievances of 1237.

which are definitely ascribed to him by the Burton annalist, while his official, Robert Marsh, compiled for him from the canon law a systematic statement of clerical privileges,[1] documents of peculiar interest because they were the main source of Archbishop Boniface's constitutions, which took definitive shape between the years 1257 and 1261.[2] In fact, continuity can be traced between the grievances of 1237, the constitutions of Boniface, the stand taken by Pecham in 1279, the successive lists of *gravamina* presented to King Edward and his successor between 1280 and 1316, and the practice of associating grants of clerical subsidies in convocation with a request for the redress of clerical grievances.[3]

A detailed study of the problems revealed by the *gravamina* cannot be made here; but two passages[4] from the list ascribed to Grosseteste may be quoted. The first states succinctly cases which led to the conflicts of law between the secular and ecclesiastical courts:

Under colour of a prohibition of any plea concerning money in the court Christian (unless in a testamentary or matrimonial case), the king impedes and perturbs ecclesiastical process about breach of faith, perjury, tithes and money sought as a debt by an ecclesiastical person, to the great detriment of souls.

Writs of prohibition of this kind disturbed the minds of Pecham and his suffragans in Edward I's time. The second passage illustrates the connexion between ecclesiastical legislation and the troubles which often followed attempts to enforce it:

Bishops and archdeacons have the pastoral care not only of the clergy but also of the people, and for this reason are required *ex officio pastorali* to visit both clergy and people; the duty of visitation cannot properly be performed without precise investigations, in the course of which a sacred oath (*sacramentum*) is often required of them by the inquirers; yet none the less the king prohibits the laity to give sworn testimony at the command of bishops or archdeacons and even

---

[1] *Ann. monast.* i. 422–5, 425–9.

[2] The articles published by Henry Cole, *Documents Illustrative of English History in the Thirteenth and Fourteenth Centuries* (1844), pp. 354–7, were almost certainly presented, not in 1245, as their context suggests, but *c.* 1258. They often repeat the constitutions of this year verbatim. This is the first document of its kind to which royal replies are given after each article. See G. B. Flahiff's paper on the writ of prohibition in *Mediaeval Studies*, vi (Toronto, 1944), 299–301.

[3] The sequence of *gravamina* has been explained in detail by Miss U. R. Q. Henriques in an unpublished dissertation.

[4] *Ann. monast.* i. 423.

forbids the bishops themselves to exact sworn testimony from their layfolk, to the subversion of the pastoral office and the eternal damnation of souls.

Here Grosseteste was writing from personal experience. In 1246 and the next two years he undertook a visitation of his diocese, basing his inquiries into the moral and spiritual condition of his clergy and laity upon his constitutions. His investigations, in which he associated his diocesan officials with him, were very minute, and, according to Matthew Paris, caused much scandal and complaint, especially among the laity. The king and his council were disturbed. Mandates were sent to all the sheriffs whose counties lay within the widespread diocese, that henceforward they should not allow the laymen in their bailiwick to gather together in any place on the summons of the archdeacons, officials, or rural deans of the bishop of Lincoln to make recognitions or attestations on oath, save in matrimonial and testamentary cases only.[1] The bishop persisted and in May 1249 was summoned to appear in person before the king to show cause for his distraint of unwilling men and women, under pain of ecclesiastical censure, to come before him to give evidence under oath, to the grievous prejudice of the Crown.[2] His example was infectious, for in 1252 the bishop of Coventry made a similar visitation in his diocese, and, under the year 1253, the Burton annalist inserted a very long and detailed list of questions into the life and behaviour of clerks and laymen, which, he says, were used by all the bishops.[3] One of the questions in the latter inquisition was 'whether any layman is notoriously proud or envious or avaricious or liable to the sin of slothful depression (*accidiosus*) or rancorous or gluttonous or lecherous'. In the grievances presented to the king a few years later, the bishops protested against royal interference with the practice, required as it was, in the due exercise of their office, for inquiry into the sins and errors of their subjects. The king replied to this complaint that, while he

[1] *Close Rolls*, 1242–7, p. 543, undated, but probably issued between November 1246 and March 1247. Matthew Paris gives the writ to the sheriff of Hertfordshire (*Chron. Maj.* iv. 580) and says that the bishop ascribed the king's action to the example of French baronial conspiracies against the Church (ibid., pp. 591–2).

[2] *Close Rolls*, 1247–51, pp. 221–2.

[3] *Ann. monast.* i. 296–8, 307–10. A. T. Bannister discovered an inquisition, based on these documents, in the Hereford diocese as late as 1397 and refers to a partial record of the same kind in the register of Bishop Grandisson of Exeter, earlier in the fourteenth century. See *The Nineteenth Century*, cii (Sept. 1927), 399–404.

recognized the bishops' right to investigate any one well-attested case, he objected to assemblies of people summoned for a general inquiry on oath, for such gatherings interrupted the lawful activities and duties of his subjects.[1]

The next step in the ventilation of clerical grievances came when, under the leadership of the queen's uncle, Archbishop Boniface, they were revised, strengthened, and issued with ecclesiastical sanctions against their infringement, as provincial constitutions. Archbishop Pecham later asserted that these constitutions had been given papal authority. It is doubtful, however, whether any of his successors went further than Pope Urban IV went in 1263 when he said that he could see nothing objectionable in them, though at the king's request he would not confirm them.[2] Yet historically they are very important. They originated in the discussions which followed the demands for financial aid made by Pope Alexander IV in aid of the king's Sicilian enterprise.[3] The bishops and clergy, led by the queen's uncle, Archbishop Boniface, required the king, in return for their concessions, to remedy the grievances which they formulated and debated in provincial councils in the years 1257–8. The preparation of these grievances seems to have been independent of the baronial movement for a reconstruction of the royal administration and to have had little or no connexion with the undefined ideas of the baronial leaders about the reform of the Church in England. They were first formulated in 1257 and later discussed in a council or *convocatio* at London in August of that year, in spite of the king's request for delay and a prohibition addressed to the prelates.[4] Next year, when the pope was insistent and the barons in April refused to come to the king's aid unless reforms were made, the archbishop and bishops decided to continue on their own course of action. Boniface naturally preferred to act independently, for, however sceptical he might be about the success of the Sicilian adventure, he was more concerned to secure ecclesiastical liberties than to identify

[1] Cole, op. cit., p. 356 (art. 13).

[2] The later canonists 'regarded them as of equal authority with other provincial legislation': Cheney in *E.H.R.* l (1935), 404, quoting Lyndwood who included them in his *Provinciale* and showed how they harmonized with the common law of the Church.

[3] Above, pp. 120–3; below, pp. 503–4.

[4] Annals of Burton, in *Ann. monast.* i. 404–5. The documents relating to the years 1256–8 were copied into these annals, pp. 384–92, 401–22 *passim*.

himself with a baronial opposition. Early in June a provincial council met at Merton and there the evils which oppressed the Church and the remedies required to deal with them were defined with more elaboration in the form of articles. The writs of summons to this council had stressed the importance of common deliberation and coherence. The archdeacons were required to come with proctorial powers, as representatives of their clergy, as well as in their own right. Later in the summer the articles were presented to a national assembly of ecclesiastics at Oxford, where such momentous things were happening, but no effective action was taken. The articles were not yet framed in a mandatory form. The archbishop had to wait his time.

He chose to act during the king's temporary recovery of power in 1261, when Henry and he were in political sympathy and the outlook was still uncertain. A papal legate had arrived to seek help against the Mongol menace in Syria and Palestine, and the prelates of both provinces were summoned to hear and consider the papal mandate. Boniface and his suffragans, without any notification to the king, and 'under colour of their obedience to this mandate', met in a provincial council at Lambeth on 13 May and promulgated a series of canons based upon those approved at Merton three years before.[1] The ecclesiastical penalties added to each canon may have been suggested to Boniface by the practice of the French bishops. The king and his council were made aware of the proceedings. A royal proctor duly appeared, to protest and declare that an appeal would be made to the Holy See against them as subversions of royal rights and the well-established laws and liberties of the realm. One chronicler states that Edward, the king's son, and Peter of Savoy, the archbishop's brother, also came and protested. If they did, it was a piquant scene: on the one side a Savoyard archbishop, the queen's uncle, promulgating a series of canons which contained in every chapter a 'plain-spoken reproof of the secular power' and an elaborate exposition of the rights and liberties of the Church in England; on the other his brother and grand-nephew denouncing the canons as a defiance of the accepted customs of the realm. It should also be noted that the king and his advisers

---

[1] Royal letters to the pope state that the archbishop called together his suffragans, abbots, priors, deans, and other prelates, and add 'quod a tempore consecracionis sue ante non fecerat' (*Close Rolls, 1259–61*, pp. 481–2). The king may have meant that the omission of any notification to him was unprecedented.

felt no hesitation in appealing to the pope for protection against this spirited assertion of canonical principles.

Grosseteste, it is clear, had done much to stiffen the backs of the rulers of the Church in England; but it should not be supposed that his habitual appeal to first principles was generally followed. The pious king with his powerful clerks, many of whom were canonists, did not live at constant variance with his bishops, nor did the growing emphasis upon the rights and duties of the clerical body imply a deep social cleavage between the clerk and the layman. Indeed the conception so dear to Grosseteste himself of the unity of all men, lay and clerical, as members of one Church was, for good or evil, better realized in the daily intercourse of a naughty world than it could have been if the great bishop had had his way.

There has always been some truth in the saying used by Pope Boniface VIII as the opening words of a famous bull, that laymen are notoriously hostile to clerks,[1] but the social results of the prejudice can easily be exaggerated. Nearly every membrane of the chancery and judicial records shows that the lay majority lived in close contact with the clerical minority. The history of nearly every family would reveal the existence within it of a clerical element. Hugh Giffard, for example, whom King Henry made the keeper of his first-born son, was the father of an archbishop, a bishop, and three nuns, two of whom became abbesses. Throughout England the relations between the families of their founders or patrons with monastic houses, and between patrons and rectors of churches were much more intimate than is usually supposed. Moreover, the clerks were not a compact class of men. In dignity and employment and manner of life they differed as much as the villagers, burgesses, country gentlemen, courtiers, and barons differed from each other. Half the parish clergy were paid vicars, whose independence had to be constantly safeguarded by the hierarchy against the religious establishments which had acquired the impropriation of the churches which they served. Very many rectors, in spite of the canonical requirements about age, learning, residence, and status, were privileged absentees. Some were clerks in the service of the king, magnates, bishops, and abbots, engaged in all kinds of duties, generally in low orders, often licensed (or unlicensed) pluralists who enjoyed as rectors the revenues of several benefices. These men were

[1] For the bull *Clericis laicos* see below, p. 674.

useful members of the community of the realm, civil servants, bailiffs, business agents, whose interests were not parochial at all. Others were young men who were not yet qualified to serve their benefices. The spiritual duties of these pluralists and absentees were left to the parish priests or curates,[1] one or more of whom was supposed to be attached to every parish church, whether the rector resided or not. Beneath this more stable element of paid parish priests was the floating element of un-beneficed clerks in casual employment. Lowest of all were the 'vagabonds' who caused some trouble both to secular and to ecclesiastical authorities through their fraternization with disorderly lay-folk like themselves.

If we add to this sketch the picture presented by the cathedral, conventual, and collegiate establishments, owning complexes of land and scattered manors, with their double existence as secular tenants and as centres of religious, intellectual, and artistic life, or by the cathedral and collegiate clergy, divided between those who remained in residence and those whose prebends were rewards for services rendered to the Crown, we can easily understand the violent contrast between Grosseteste's ideal and the more mundane outlook of the clerical body as a whole. We can see why regard for, if not full acquiescence in, the 'customs of the realm' competed in the minds of prelates, canons, and clerks with the impulse to reform, and we may sympathize with those who, like that excellent man, Walter de Cantilupe, bishop of Worcester, defended pluralism as a way of providing for ecclesiastics of birth and breeding,[2] or who felt that an office at court, as a minister of state, a judge, king's clerk, or royal physician, was a perfectly legitimate object of ambition to any clever young man in the Oxford schools. Naturally enough the clerks took the colour of their surroundings. They mingled with the knights of the king's household, they went on embassies with earls and barons, they upheld the claims of the common law, they wrote the letters which expounded the policy or contained the mandates of the king and his advisers. The king's clerks, for

[1] Hence the distinction between parsons (or rectors), vicars, and curates. If no vicarage had been ordained in an appropriated church, the proprietors might commit the entire cure of souls to the curate; a practice which gave rise to the 'perpetual curate', now indistinguishable from a vicar.

[2] Bishop Walter protested against the Cardinal Otto's proposed legislation on flesh-eating and pluralities during the legatine council in 1237; see *E.H.R.* lxiv (1949), 163, 164.

example, exulted in the fact that they would be protected from ecclesiastical censure in the service of their master; and fiercely resented the interference of a Grosseteste or a Pecham in the transaction of public business, or process in the courts. They regarded themselves as the true mediators of peace and order in a Church threatened alike by the presumption of the laity and the intolerable constitutions of the prelates.[1]

The high church doctrine was expounded with force and clarity by Grosseteste as early as 1236 or 1237 in a long letter to Archbishop Edmund[2] and was set out by the prelates in the statements of grievances to which we have referred. The standpoint of the royal court must be deduced from the more casual but voluminous evidence of royal letters, and from the opportunities given to litigants by the steady increase in the number of royal writs of prohibition addressed to ecclesiastical judges and devised to meet new problems raised in the course of judicial experience. King Henry, like his son after him, acted on the conviction that, as the source of law and order and in virtue of his sworn obligation to maintain the rights and peace of the Church as well as his own, he and his advisers and judges alone could decide in the end where the right lay. He was king by the grace of God and was probably never persuaded that an anointed king had not, in the anointing, acquired a sacramental 'character'.[3] Hence, even when the legatine council of 1237 met, his proctors made a formal request that nothing should be done to infringe his rights. When he heard that Archbishop Boniface was holding a council in 1261, his proctors protested against its constitutions, both before and after they were promulgated. When King Edward's council appointed proctors to represent the king at the council of Lyons in 1274, it instructed them to supplicate the pope that nothing should be done to the prejudice

[1] See the curious *apologia* for them printed in Cole, op. cit., p. 369 (apparently written in 1279 after the council of Reading) and compare the remarks about them by Pope Nicholas IV some years later (above, p. 265; cf. his letters to the king in *Cal. Papal Letters*, i. 526, 527). The 'sons of Belial' excommunicated by Pecham in October 1279 for their obstruction of the work of the council would seem from the context to have been king's clerks (Cole, p. 368).

[2] *Epistolae*, pp. 205–34. This letter, with its admirable summing up and its appendix of royal writs which illustrate its argument is much the best introduction to the whole matter from the ecclesiastical point of view.

[3] See Grosseteste's letter to Henry on this subject (*Epistolae*, pp. 348–51, no. 124) and cf. F. M. Powicke, *Stephen Langton*, pp. 108–9, for earlier discussions of the subject.

of royal rights, and defined certain customary rights which should be defended.[1] King Edward took action against Pecham in 1279–81 with a similar intention.

The king, in fact, regarded himself at the very least as the patron of the Church, just as the barons and laity laid stress on their responsibility no less than on their rights as the source of parochial and monastic endowments. It is significant that the only step towards church reform which the magnates are known to have taken in 1258–9 (though other measures may have been discussed) was a letter to Pope Alexander ¡IV in which they deplored the extensive appropriation of churches by monastic houses, a development which they had, as they confessed, frequently assisted in the past by their own gifts. They asserted, with an extravagance which the pope very rightly rebuked, that England was in consequence sadly lacking in a learned clergy, and urged that in their view the remedy lay in the restoration to them of the right of patronage and the nomination of rectors. They pointed out that monastic impropriation and the substitution of vicars for rectors led not only to an impoverished clergy but to an unhappy increase in papal provisions.[2] This argument bore fruit later in the statutes of mortmain and provisors. The king was in a much stronger position, for it lay with him to intervene in ecclesiastical matters in the interests of order and justice.

Grosseteste wished to withdraw ecclesiastics from secular office, and to close the ecclesiastical courts to all secular interference. In his view royal judges sinned grievously whenever they brought ecclesiastical persons before them in a personal action, or presumed to determine whether a case should go before a secular or ecclesiastical court or required a bishop to explain and justify his ecclesiastical acts. He was able to carry his colleagues with him in protests against particular practices but he could not combine them in a resolute stand on principle; and this for the simple reason that neither they nor the clergy could live without royal protection, even if they did not seek a career in the royal service. This becomes clear if we look at three matters in which secular and clerical interests were inextricably combined, the trial of criminous clerks, disputes about advowsons and tithes, and excommunications.

[1] Cole, pp. 358–9.
[2] This letter is known only from the pope's long reply; see *Ann. monast.* i. 487–91.

The secular courts never disputed the right of the diocesan to claim and deal with the criminous clerk. The *privilegium fori* had been acquired, with a few exceptions, in the twelfth century.[1] But the royal courts were more than clearing-stations. 'The clerk must have proved his clergy.' A clerk who fled from justice and was outlawed, or who voluntarily abjured the realm, had no benefit of clergy. If he did not flee and pleaded his clergy the judges went into the case, and frequently brought the trial to the point of conviction before handing him over. Moreover, in their scepticism about the value of the process of 'purgation' used in the ecclesiastical courts, the judges might require the bishop to keep the clerk in prison as a notorious criminal. The accused person did not always appear before the court in clerical habit. He might prefer to stand or fall on the judgement of his neighbours. Although before the end of the thirteenth century the reading test was occasionally used to prove or disprove the literacy of a man who had claimed his clergy, it was not a conclusive, still less an automatic test. When the accused man, who had been claimed by his ordinary, had been convicted and degraded in the ecclesiastical court, he was henceforward regarded as a layman. Finally, 'while it admits unreservedly the Church's jurisdiction over the persons of clerks, the Crown (at least by the time of Edward I), is vindicating its rights over the property of clerks found guilty in the lay court, just as it had established its jurisdiction in all ordinary civil actions concerning clerks'.[2] At the same time, a tendency can be seen to make ecclesiastical trials more of a reality by the use of the inquest in preference to purgation.

The records do not suggest that the tension between clerks and laymen about this matter was particularly hot or violent. A report found in one manuscript of a year book of cases in 1301–2 gives a lively account of the genial discussion which might prevail in a royal court. The itinerant justices had before them, possibly in Cornwall, a man named Hugh, who was accused of rape. Hugh began by pleading privilege of clergy, for he had been a rector. The representative of the bishop claimed him as a clerk. The judges pointed out that he had lost his

---

[1] See Leona C. Gabel, *Benefit of Clergy in England in the Later Middle Ages*, Smith College Studies in History, xiv (1928–9); A. L. Poole, 'Outlawry as a Punishment of Criminous Clerks', in *Historical Essays in Honour of James Tait* (1933), pp. 239–46; C. R. Cheney, 'The Punishment of Felonious Clerks', *E.H.R.* li (1936), 215–36.

[2] Cheney, op. cit., p. 321.

privilege, for he was known to have married a widow, and so was a bigamist. (Canon law regarded a clerk's marriage to a widow as bigamous, and a canon of the council of Lyons of 1274 had deprived a bigamist of benefit of clergy.) This point the judge determined must be decided at once by the jury (*patria*). Was his wife a widow or a virgin when he married her? Hugh pleaded that she was a virgin. The jury, mindful of their oath, said that his wife was a widow. 'You must be tried as a layman,' said the judge. 'We know that this jury of twelve will not lie, and you must submit to their verdict.' 'I will not,' replied Hugh, 'I am a knight and should be judged only by my peers.' The judge agreed to this, but Hugh became obstinate and refused to agree to any jury. The judge then gave him a long lecture on the foolishness of his behaviour, and on the penalty of imprisonment with an alternate daily diet of bread and water which followed a refusal to plead. Hugh gave in and decided to assert his right to challenge the fitness of particular jurors. This eventuality had been foreseen, for he had with him in writing objections which he begged the judge to read. 'No,' replied the judge, 'you must say them.' 'But I cannot read them.' 'How is this? You wished to plead your clergy and now you cannot read your own objections.' Hugh stood still in confusion. 'Don't be abashed (*stupefacti*); now is the time to speak,' and with these words the judge turned to one of Hugh's friends and told him to read them to him in a whisper, for the prisoner [counsel having been refused him] must speak his objections in person. This was done. The challenges against certain jurors were upheld and they were removed. The judge then charged the jury to give its verdict. The jury declared that Hugh had not been concerned in the crime. The judge dismissed him with the words: 'My lord Hugh, because these men acquit you, we acquit you.'[1]

Legal problems about advowsons and tithes were even more complicated. They generally resulted from the fact that both the Crown and the Church had an interest, which might be a vital interest, in the presentation to a benefice.[2] The Crown's interest lay in the advowson as a property whose lawful ownership had to be protected, the Church's in the lawful admission of an

---

[1] *Year Books, 30–31 Edward I*, edited A. J. Horwood (1863), pp. 529–62.
[2] On this important and neglected aspect of ecclesiastical jurisdiction see J. W. Gray, 'The *jus praesentandi* in England from the constitutions of Clarendon to Bracton', in *E.H.R.* lxvii (1952), 481–509.

incumbent. The bishop made sure that the church was really vacant, that the right of the patron to present was valid, and that the person presented was suitable. Any number of difficulties might arise, for example, if a bishop admitted a clerk to a benefice while the right to the advowson was *sub judice* in the lay court, or if the right of the patron to present was later called in question. Similarly, the jurisdiction of the court Christian over tithe disputes and disputes about pensions paid in lieu of tithe led to conflicts of law which had not been decided when Edward I died.[1] Many cases were settled by agreement between the lay and ecclesiastical authorities; and the general tendency of the royal judges was to extend the control of the Crown over tithes whose value mainly determined the value of the advowson, or which were bought or sold and thus became like any other chattel.[2]

In the legal battle, one weapon was always to hand, in ready reserve—the sentence of excommunication. So easily and so variously was it pronounced that the problems of its use and abuse gradually produced a complicated section of the canon law. A condemnation which a pope could thunder against an emperor, or a diocesan official impose upon a recalcitrant sinner, had become part of the daily give and take of casual controversy. 'The law's last and most terrible weapon against the obstinate offender' could also be used in temper or in righteous indignation against a litigious adversary or be 'regarded as a normal process for compelling the appearance in court of those who were accused'.[3] It is in the light of this development that we should regard the reaction of the English kings to the fate which threatened any royal official who failed to respect the constitutions of Archbishop Boniface or of Archbishop Pecham. The ecclesiastical authorities, since the end of the twelfth century, had enjoyed the help of the secular arm against the sinner who had remained under sentence of excommunication for forty days or more without seeking to be reconciled to the Church.

[1] See Norma Adams, 'The Judicial Conflict over Tithes', in *E.H.R.* lii (1937), 1–22.

[2] A patron, under some circumstances, might acquire the right to 'present to tithes'. See *Rotuli* of Richard Gravesend, bishop of Lincoln (C. & Y. Soc., 1925), p. 143. If a dispute about tithes involved a dispute about the boundaries of parishes, the patron was empowered by statute (Westminster II, 1285, c. 5) to take the claim about the boundary to the king's court; and if he succeeded the claim to the tithe could then proceed in the church court.

[3] Adapted from Pollock and Maitland, *The History of English Law*, i. 478.

The king, whose co-operation was regarded as so proper, naturally assumed some responsibility for the operation of the penalty and gave his protection to those of his subjects and servants who seemed to him to require it.

In the course of ecclesiastical jurisdiction excommunication of the offender was a way of bringing him to submission. He was expected to seek absolution and to expiate his offence at once. The obdurate offender gave most difficulty, and in England the Church had a way of dealing with him which was not generally available elsewhere. Pope Innocent III had approved it in 1203,[1] and Pope Clement V a century later referred to it as a pious and laudable custom.[2] This way was to seek a royal writ *de excommunicato capiendo*, which, though the king regarded it as an act of grace, appears in early registers of writs which could be sued out of the chancery. The writ ordered the arrest and imprisonment of the offender until he should satisfy the Church for contempt and injury, and its enforcement must have helped considerably to give employment to the keepers of royal and episcopal prisons.[3] 'Significations', letters patent seeking the remedy and giving particulars, were issued only by bishops and the abbots of certain privileged monasteries; and the power to issue orders for arrest was carefully safeguarded; but although the prelates from time to time complained that the secular power discriminated in favour of certain kinds of persons, the writ seems on the whole to have been enforced as a matter of course. On the other hand, the king, who was thus associated with the bishops in the maintenance of spiritual discipline, and was also well aware of the continuous recourse to excommunication by excited litigants, could not be expected to limit the exercise of his royal discretion. He had to see that justice was done to all parties. If a bishop refused to release a prisoner who had frequently declared his willingness to obey the mandates of the Church, and to provide lawful pledges for his appearance,[4] the king might

---

[1] *Corpus Juris Canonici*, ed. Friedberg, ii. 904.

[2] Wilkins, *Concilia*, ii. 323.

[3] See R. C. Fowler on secular aid for excommunication in *Trans. Royal Hist. Society*, 3rd series, viii (1914), 113–17. In the Public Record Office there are 217 files containing more than 10,000 requests for aid between 1216 and 1812. It has been estimated that they averaged some 150 a year during the last half of the thirteenth century.

[4] In such a case the king ordered the bishop to release the prisoner *caucione recepta*, and threatened to take action himself if this were not done (*Close Rolls, 1254–6*, p. 211 (July 1255)).

take action. On the other hand, when John Baliol, because the bishop of Durham had excommunicated and in due course imprisoned some of his men, retaliated by carrying off some of the bishop's men to Castle Barnard, King Henry ordered the constable of the castle to release them.[1] Indeed, the king's intervention might go far, as when he wrote from Bordeaux in July 1243 instructing his regents that they should not allow any monk of Bardney to be arrested by reason of his excommunication by the bishop of Lincoln or any other suffragan of the church of Canterbury, while an appeal was pending for the protection of the court of Canterbury. He added that they must find excuses to defer the caption of any other persons excommunicated by the suffragans until his own return to England.[2] Now the appeal of the monks of Bardney to the court of Canterbury was made during a vacancy in the archiepiscopal see. Grosseteste, the bishop of Lincoln against whom the monks appealed, held very strong views about any appeal of this kind and especially when there was no archbishop. He rallied his fellow bishops in opposition to the pretension of the prior and monks of Christ Church, the cathedral monastery at Canterbury, to hear this and similar appeals; and in the course of the dispute the prior and monks excommunicated him, and also complained to the king that the bishops were infringing the 'liberties of the churches'. The king could not allow so serious a quarrel to proceed. It affected the welfare of the realm. He called a halt and wrote that he would deal with the whole matter in full council after his return, and try to bring about an agreement.[3]

King Henry and his professional advisers expounded their view of the king's legal position on several occasions. A good example is contained in an order to the sheriff of Warwickshire in 1246. In the course of a complicated dispute in which the king was concerned, the bishop of Coventry excommunicated a local rector, one of the king's clerks. The defence of churches against aggression was, the king wrote, a duty of the power given to him by the divine clemency. The sentences of excommunication

[1] *Close Rolls, 1254–6*, p. 217. The bishop of Durham excommunicated John's men in virtue of his episcopal powers, and imprisoned them in virtue of his regality. This is the dispute which is said to have led to the foundation of Balliol College in Oxford.

[2] *Close Rolls, 1242–7*, pp. 66–67. For such appeals for the protection (*tuitio*) of Canterbury pending the result of an appeal to the pope see below, pp. 492–4.

[3] M. M. Morgan, on the excommunication of Grosseteste in 1243, in *E.H.R.* lvii (1942), 244–50; cf. *King Henry III and the Lord Edward*, i. 339.

were laid by the bishop to the prejudice of the royal dignity and still more of ecclesiastical freedom. The sheriff was ordered as quickly as possible to persuade the bishop to revoke the sentences. 'If he refuses let him know,—and tell this to him— that we will stretch our hand over his barony, for as its tenant he is bound by oath to maintain the earthly honours of the royal dignity. He could not possibly do worse than seek by his excommunications to seduce our faithful subjects from the execution of our commands; for our jurisdiction depends upon obedience to them. As for his breach of oath he must await the supreme avenger.'[1]

One important factor in establishing the claims of the lay courts was the widespread preference of clerical litigants for their jurisdiction. The bishops frequently found that writs of prohibition had been bought by clerks and they had reason to suspect that 'third parties' who procured such writs were or acted in the interest of clerks. Grosseteste, whose eyes seem to have been everywhere, called attention in 1236 to the scandalous abuse of writs of prohibition by clerks who sued out such writs in order to bring personal actions against them in an ecclesiastical court to a standstill, and the grievances of 1237 urged that clerks who did this should be punished. A long section in the canons drafted in 1258 was concerned with both laymen and clerks who sought in this way to evade their sworn obligations or contracts, which, as good faith and perjury were involved, were matters for the church courts, and it proceeds to impose a series of penalties on laymen and clerks guilty of the deceit. The bishops, of course, did not deny that writs of prohibition were right and proper if a church court presumed to deal with a clear case of land or res immobilis. They were protesting against fraudulent attempts to take shelter unlawfully and by misrepresentation behind the writs. None the less, their indignation testifies to the fact that the clerical body was by no means united in its hostility to the increase in the number of writs. Many were glad to avail themselves of the opportunities presented by them. As time went on, clerks, to avoid the penalties which publicity might incur (for the person in whose behalf the writ was issued could be summoned to explain his action before an ecclesiastical judge), were able to avail themselves of a form of words which became

---

[1] *Close Rolls, 1242–7*, pp. 477–8. The sheriff was instructed to take no action on writs of caption against the rector and others concerned (p. 461).

increasingly general in writs of prohibition. Such royal writs began with the words *rex relatu plurimorum, intelleximus*, &c. The bishops frequently protested against this form of writ, but in vain.[1]

Clerks and laymen might or might not come to dislike each other as the difference between them in legal status became more marked under two distinct systems of law; but none the less they lived together under the protection of the Crown and were well aware of their social companionship. This brings us back to the attitude of the Crown. The king, even if he had wished to do so, could not regard ecclesiastical administration with indifference. His rights and duties impinged upon it at every turn; and he was *king*. He had an interest in episcopal and abbatial elections, for the bishops and many abbots were his barons. He insisted on his right to give permission to elect, used his influence upon the electors, co-operated with or appealed to the pope in disputed cases, and took charge of the lands and other temporalities during vacancies.[2] He might direct the course of procedure in the election of a prioress of a royal foundation,[3] or define the computation of the six months, after which the episcopal right to provide to a living took effect if the patron had failed to present.[4] He might intervene to protect his own claims during the administration of a will by the executors. Royal concern with ecclesiastical affairs knew few limits.

Any idea that the Church in the thirteenth century was a united and efficient force, smoothly concentrated like a machine on a single purposeful effort, is soon dispelled by the records of litigation. In these it appears as a sensitive and quarrelsome organism of vested interests and of rights rooted in custom and privilege. The archbishops were frequently at variance with each other and with their suffragans, bishops with their chapters and the religious houses, monasteries with their neighbours, whether towns, country landholders, or other monasteries, the secular clergy with the friars. They fought about material possessions, about tithes and burial fees, about rights of prece-

---

[1] For all this see G. B. Flahiff, 'The Use of Prohibitions by Clerics against Ecclesiastical Courts in England', in *Mediaeval Studies*, iii (Toronto, 1941), 101–16.

[2] Gibbs and Lang, op. cit., pp. 85–92; *King Henry III and the Lord Edward*, i. 266–73; W. Ullmann, 'The Disputed Election of Hugh Balsham, Bishop of Ely', in the *Cambridge Historical Journal*, ix (1949), 259–68.

[3] Cf. the interesting situation at Shaftesbury in 1242 (*Close Rolls, 1242–7*, pp. 75–77.   [4] *Rotuli* of Richard Gravesend, pp. 80–81 (1278).

dence. They fought in lay courts, ecclesiastical courts, and the papal court. When a legal decision or mutual agreement had been reached on one point, controversy began again on another. Some of these disputes lasted for centuries.[1] Some are still matters of sedate disagreement.[2]

The intricate web of lay and clerical activities in English society becomes clearer in the days of Archbishop John Pecham. Pecham, as the head of a province which covered the greater part of England and the whole of Wales, took his duties very seriously; and he left behind him in his big register a detailed picture of his intensely busy life. His is the first Canterbury register to have survived, a fact which gives a misleading impression of novelty to his energy, and its quality probably owed much to his staff of trained notaries; but it reveals both the force of the man and his garrulous frankness. Hitherto he had been known as a distinguished English scholar at Paris, a leader in defence of the rule of poverty as enjoined in his order, and a theological controversialist. He had come back to Oxford in 1270 and about 1275 been elected provincial minister of the Franciscans in England; then in 1277 he had been called to the papal schools at Rome as lector in theology. A few months later (April 1278) Robert Kilwardby, the Dominican scholar and provincial who had been archbishop of Canterbury since 1272, was made cardinal bishop of Porto by Pope Nicholas III. In June he resigned his see. The monks of Canterbury, knowing the king's wishes, elected Robert Burnell, bishop of Bath and Wells, and Edward's chancellor, as archbishop. Strong representations on the chancellor's behalf were made by a royal mission to Rome, headed by the well-known Italian civilian, Franciscus Accursius.[3] The pope, however, refused to postulate Burnell

---

[1] Tithe disputes are especially long-lived. Litigation about tithes claimed by the priory of Lenton continued from John's reign till the dissolution of the monasteries. Tithes in dispute in the forest of Dean in 1309 were still in dispute in 1731. See E.H.R. lii (1937), pp. 3, note 4, and 17, note 1.

[2] The claim of the prior and convent, and later of the dean and chapter, of Durham to administer the spiritualities of the diocese during a vacancy in the see grew fierce in the days of Archbishop Wickwane of York (1283) and smouldered till Elizabeth's reign and then again until 1672. It flared up once more in 1890. In 1920 Archbishop Lang declined to assert his metropolitical rights; his successor, in 1939, appointed the dean as guardian of the spiritualities of Durham, 'without prejudice to the general question'. See York Metropolitan Jurisdiction (1959), pp. 145-7.

[3] Accursius delivered an harangue (arenga) in the form of a sermon which made

from his see at Bath to Canterbury. In January 1279 he appointed Pecham and on 26 February consecrated him as archbishop. Pecham had been in correspondence with the king about Burnell and, though he was doubtful of the chancellor's suitability, does not seem to have had either expectation or desire to become archbishop himself. He was cordially received by Edward, who received him at Amiens during the Anglo-French negotiations in May, and, as Pecham wrote to the pope, immediately admitted him to his innermost council. So the first Franciscan succeeded his friend the first Dominican archbishop.[1]

The reasons for Kilwardby's elevation are unknown. The general view is that Pope Nicholas was dissatisfied with him, but there are grounds for thinking that while the pope recognized that a change might be advantageous, the archbishop himself sought relief from his cares. He had been an acceptable primate. He was moderate in temper and had a keen sense of justice. He administered his province with credit and his widespread estates with ability; but his sense of vocation, unlike Pecham's, does not seem to have seen a challenge in the problems of office. He was a scientific thinker and a friend of saints; yet his most tiresome preoccupation as archbishop was the sense of grievance stirred in the clergy by the collection of the crusading tenth imposed upon the Church by Pope Gregory X at the council of Lyons. Nothing so severe as this sexennial tenth, based on a new assessment, had ever been exacted from the Church. Feeling ran high; the collectors were always harassed and often tactless; the penalty of excommunication for defaults of payment was ruthlessly enforced.[2] The archbishop was in a spiritual quandary, inclined to sympathy with the clergy while insisting upon the duty to pay the tax in spite of the injustice or venality of particular collectors. His troubles came to a head, however, when the resident papal nuncio or general collector, Geoffrey of Vezzano, who was not concerned directly with the crusading tax, began to interfere with the administration of wills without due regard to episcopal

a deep impression, as a rhetorical exercise, upon the pope and his other hearers. See G. L. Haskins and E. Kantorowicz in *E.H.R.* lviii (1943), 424–47; the text is edited on pp. 440–7.

[1] On Kilwardby see Ellen M. F. Sommer-Seckendorff, *Studies in the Life of Robert Kilwardby* (Rome, 1937); on Pecham, D. L. Douie, *Archbishop Pecham* (Oxford, 1952).

[2] Lunt, *Financial Relations of the Papacy with England to 1327* (1939), pp. 320–30. Pecham found the monks of Canterbury under excommunication, and one of his first tasks was to effect their release.

rights and to English ecclesiastical procedure.[1] The bishops, in congregation at Northampton, appointed proctors who, after reciting their grievances in the presence of the nuncio, appealed to the pope in the name of the whole clerical community. The prosecution of the appeal to Rome was the business of the provincial council or convocation summoned by the archbishop to meet in London on 14 January 1278.[2] Proctors of the whole clergy in each diocese were summoned to meet with bishops, leading members of cathedral chapters, and the archdeacons, and they were required to meet in order to appeal to the pope against the practices of the papal nuncio. In April the pope made Kilwardby a cardinal, and it is hard not to connect the archbishop's action against the nuncio with this abrupt and unusual elevation. Moreover, if a homily on the parable of the prodigal son which survives in a group of documents relating to the appeal and to clerical grievances against the collectors of the tenth can safely be ascribed to him, the archbishop regarded his departure for Rome as a return home to his spiritual father—and a return also to which he was impelled by compassion for 'the endangered clergy of England'. 'I will arise and go to my father, and I will arise in confidence, for I know that my return and my concern for the clergy of England are joined together.'[3] He died at Viterbo in September 1279, shortly after his successor held his provincial council at Reading.

Pecham faced his task with purposeful and far-ranging energy. He had not sought a responsibility so alien to his habitual way of life. He was always a friar at heart, inclined to do little jobs for himself in happy freedom from the oppressive state and splendour of his new surroundings; but his letters show that he was consumed by the same zest whatever he was doing, as a humble

[1] Cf. Lunt, op. cit., p. 510.

[2] The purpose of the summons (which is printed in the *Select Charters*, 9th edition, p. 447) is made clear by Kilwardby's letter of 13 December 1277 to his proctors in Rome, one of a group of documents relating to the clerical opposition to the tenth and to the dispute with Geoffrey of Vezzano later inserted in the register of John de Pontissara, bishop of Winchester, between documents of the years 1293 and 1294. In 1276 the future bishop was one of the proctors of the clergy appointed to take a petition to the pope against the working of the new assessment. This accounts for his possession of a copy of the petition and also of Kilwardby's letter of 13 December 1277. The documents are printed in the register of Pontissara, edited by Cecil Deedes for the Canterbury and York Society, i (1915), 356–66.

[3] Op. cit., pp. 359–60. Here we may perhaps find some explanation of Kilwardby's unprecedented action in taking with him his register and records with a large sum of money and other valuables of his see to the papal court.

follower of St. Francis and a servant of Christ and His Church. He was natural and simple in artless and extravagant revelations of himself. If he felt tired or ill, he said so. He was outspoken and argumentative, yet constantly surprised by the hostility which he so easily aroused, for, though inclined to be pompous and fretful, he was essentially friendly and kind-hearted. He had no patience with the malevolent sons of Belial whom he found everywhere, but that he should sever his ties with his surroundings was inconceivable. The king and queen, the chancellor, the earl of Gloucester and his other great vassals in Kent, his episcopal colleagues, and the whole Church in England and Wales were part of his life. Whatever storms he might arouse he always remained the king's faithful adviser.

After his arrival in England the disputes about the papal tenth and the administration of wills sank to their proper level. The archbishop, although he had countless things to do and did them before his enthronement on 8 October—a great social event—made a provincial council his immediate business. He had been instructed by Pope Nicholas to see that the canons enacted at the council of Lyons five years before were enforced in England. He summoned the bishops to meet him at Reading on 29 July and prepared the business of the council carefully in the light of previous legislation since the time of Archbishop Langton. He was careful to fit the constitutions of Archbishop Boniface into his survey of canonical reform,[1] and gave particular attention to the constitutions of the legate Ottobuono. He had been in England nearly all the time between Ottobuono's departure in 1268 and his own call to Rome in 1277, and was no stranger to men and events during the previous ten years.

An account of the proceedings or *acta* of the council of Reading has been preserved in some half-dozen manuscripts.[2] The archbishop spoke of the importance of the canons issued in the four councils of Stephen, Otto, Boniface, and Ottobuono, and the requirement to observe them, and to make sure that they were generally known. Stephen had ordered his canons to be 'published' annually in cathedral and lesser churches; Ottobuono had instructed the archbishops and bishops to have his canons

[1] Above, pp. 456–7.
[2] Cheney in *E.H.R.* (1935), 407–8. This record of proceedings, though the order is not quite clear, makes better sense of the text of the canons printed by Wilkins in his *Concilia*. I am indebted to Professor Cheney for the loan of his transcript of the text in Trinity College, Cambridge, MS. 1245, fols. 124ᴸ–127.

recited, word for word, every year in their synods. It was equally necessary to make Boniface's constitutions public, for they were a shield against the dangers and oppressions which, if they were ignorant of them, might quickly afflict the clergy. Pecham then defined the order of proceedings in the council. Since Ottobuono depended on Otto as Otto upon Stephen, 'like a rivulet on a limpid spring', it would suffice to concentrate on his constitutions, especially as he had imposed penalties, and then to go through Boniface's, adding such new chapters as were advisable. Then the great charter of liberties—that expression of the general agreement of clergy and people, later confirmed by the pope— with the archiepiscopal excommunication of its violators, would be recited. Finally, the various sentences of excommunication contained in the canons of all four councils would be recited and confirmed. This course was followed.[1] As the canons of Otto-buono and Boniface were read, additions were made. Here it is important to note the careful instructions about publication. For example, in order to strengthen the canon on clerical con-cubinage, the archdeacons were commanded, under pain of suspension, to have Ottobuono's canon read to their assembled clergy (laity being excluded) in the four principal rural chapters (that is, in each rural deanery) every year, so that ignorance could not be pleaded by anyone concerned. The royal charter of liberties, well and clearly written, was to be affixed in a public place within every cathedral and collegiate church, and a new copy was to be substituted for the existing copy 'at the end of the year on the vigil of Easter'. Eleven articles, extracted from the canons of the four councils, in which sentences of excommunica-tion were imposed, were to be publicly expounded by every priest in the province of Canterbury to the people committed to his care on every Sunday following the meeting of the local rural chapter. Pecham was determined not to let sleeping dogs lie. The revival of Boniface's canons with their series of penalties which King Henry had repudiated at the time, the officious posting of the Great Charter for all to see, and the attempt to make every local congregation familiar with the dire penalties incurred by those who obstructed the free course of ecclesiastical justice aroused the anger of royal clerks and officials. That some of these sentences of excommunication dated from Stephen

---

[1] In addition, two canons of the council of Lyons (1274) about the qualifications of clerks collated to benefices were read.

Langton's time was not to the point. The archbishop's offence lay in his public assertion that the Church was in danger from wanton attack by hostile and irresponsible men and in his declaration of war against them.

The most important addition made at Reading to previous legislation was intended to put an end to pluralism or the possession of more than one benefice with cure of souls. In fact not much could be done, for no legislation could touch the pluralist who had secured a papal licence to hold a number of benefices, and for good reasons or bad, as the case might be, such licences were frequent. Pecham had reason to believe, however, that unlicensed disregard of the canon law on this matter, with the consequent evil of absenteeism, was more widespread than ever; and he had so horrified Pope Nicholas by what he told him that the pope in personal interview had enjoined upon him a speedy extirpation of the nuisance. At Reading the archbishop spoke at some length about pluralism, beginning with an historical retrospect and a summary of Ottobuono's constitution on the subject. He pointed out that pluralism was so rampant that one might well think that there had never been any legislation against it. Ottobuono had decreed that anyone who held two or more benefices without dispensation must lose all but the first. The conciliar decree of 1274 permitted him to keep the last. Pecham applied the conciliar decree to existing pluralists, except in the case of the contumacious; these were to lose all. The bishops were instructed to declare such persons incapable of holding office until their vice was purged, and confessors were straitly enjoined, in the archbishop's most florid style, to impose penance upon them and, under pain of excommunication, to absolve them only after careful deliberation; for those who retained ecclesiastical benefices of this kind were criminals in contumacy. Pecham then dealt with the future. Henceforward, those who retained more than one benefice contrary to the conciliar decree were declared to be deprived of all *ipso iure* and to be *ipso facto* excommunicated. Only the archbishop or the apostolic see could absolve the offenders.[1] Finally, the bishops

---

[1] In the fifteenth century William Lyndwood argued that Pecham had gone beyond his brief in his legislation on pluralities. He had made his own canon law; cf. Maitland, *Canon Law in England*, pp. 20 ff. W. T. Waugh discussed the problem and defended Pecham in *E.H.R.* xxviii (1913), 625–35. That Pecham did not intend to make law independently is clear from a document in Pontissara's Register (i. 201–2), where it is wrongly ascribed by the editor to the next archbishop,

were required to institute a thorough inquiry, through their officials, archdeacons, and rural deans, in their dioceses. The returns, which were to be sent to the archbishop in time for a new assembly in January, were to state the names and number of the churches in each deanery, the names of the rectors in full, the dates of their collation to their benefices by whatever title, their age, and, if they were pluralists, in what order they had acquired their cures, and whether they had dispensations or not. The names of the patrons of all such cures and the value of the livings according to the assessment made by the bishop of Norwich and his colleagues in 1254 were also to be given.

The archbishop had thought out a plan. He would collect all the evidence and enlist all the forces and agents of discipline. On his diocesan visitations he would see that his plan was put into effect. He did his best, but in fact he could do little to extirpate a practice so deeply rooted, so useful and so natural to the social structure. In any case, papal dispensations could be obtained so easily and often on such plausible grounds. Some of Pecham's own colleagues had laid the foundations of their careers in reliance on their pluralities; for example, his former pupil at Paris, Thomas Cantilupe.[1] The investigations were doomed from the start by the forces of active or passive resistance, evasion, scepticism, and mockery. It was clear that this overbearing and bustling reformer must be watched. One conspicuous pluralist, Bogo de Clare, the brother of the earl of Gloucester, Pecham's friend and vassal in Kent, caused the archbishop peculiar pain. He might have been so outstanding among the noble clerks of the realm, worthy of his brother, to whom the Church of Canterbury could always turn as to a place of refuge; but the pestilent dilettante, luxuriating on the proceeds of his neglected benefices, was openly hostile and wagged his scurrilous tongue without restraint.[2]

The archbishop could find more support from the episcopate in the stand which he made against royal writs of prohibition.[3]

Robert Winchelsey. This seeks papal confirmation of certain of the Reading articles and asks how the decree of the General Council of Lyons (1274) about pluralities should be applied.

[1] See below, p. 488. Cf. above, p. 459, for the attitude of Walter Cantilupe, bishop of Worcester; also, on the pluralists, J. R. H. Moorman, *Church Life in England in the Thirteenth Century*, pp. 26–30.

[2] *Epistolae Johannis Peckham*, i. 371–2. For Bogo de Clare see Moorman, pp. 26–29.

[3] On the earlier history of writs of prohibition see Norma Adams in *Minnesota Law Review*, xx. 272–93 (Feb. 1936), and, especially, G. B. Flahiff, in *Mediaeval*

Here he was resuming Boniface of Savoy's defence of ecclesiastical jurisdiction and liberties. He could lead the clergy in the assertion of their grievances, and in so doing he emphasized their coherence at a time when the king was becoming increasingly dependent upon their financial aid.

As early as 24 October, a fortnight after his solemn enthronement, the archbishop issued a general sentence of excommunication against the sons of Belial who had begun to act against him in various ways. He sat in full consistory as an ecclesiastical judge in his hall at Lambeth. He declared that he was bound so to act by a triple cord of obligation: his position as primate, the injunctions of the pope, and his oath of office.[1] Another fortnight passed and he was required to appear before the king and council in parliament at Westminster—the parliament in which, about this time, the famous statute of mortmain or *de religiosis* was issued. Here he was brought to withdraw, as though not pronounced, three of the general sentences of excommunication issued at Reading, also to order the removal of the texts of *Magna Carta* which had been exposed on the doors of churches, and to grant that no prejudice should arise to the king or the realm from any other articles issued at Reading.[2] The three excommunications withdrawn were (1) the clause in the first sentence which explained the excommunication of those who infringed the liberties of the Church as directed in particular against all who procured letters from any lay court whereby ecclesiastical judges were impeded in the trial of cases known to belong by canon law to the ecclesiastical forum; (2) the sentence against a king's minister who did not obey the royal writ requiring him to arrest and detain an excommunicated person;[3] (3) the sentence, taken from Ottobuono's constitutions, against those who, against the will of the owner or his custodian, carried goods away from manors, houses, granges, &c., of an ecclesiastical person; for, as was pointed out to Pecham, the penalty imposed by the king for such offences was sufficient.

In Pecham's eyes the most important of the three articles was

---

Studies, issued by the Institute of Mediaeval Studies in Toronto, vi (1944), 261–313, and vii (1945), 229–90. Cf. above, pp. 467–8.

[1] Cole, *Documents*, p. 368.

[2] Memorandum printed from the Close Roll by William Ryley in his *Placita parliamentaria* (1661), p. 442, and William Prynne in his *Chronological Vindication* [or *Records*], iii (1670), 236. See *Cal. Close Rolls, 1272–9*, p. 582.

[3] Above, p. 466.

the first. As a contemporary memorandum[1] explains, ecclesiastics owed respect and obedience to prohibitions intended to impede the trial by ecclesiastical judges of actions which belonged to the king, but it was their duty to reject notoriously abusive prohibitions procured, with the connivance of the chancery officials, to impede spiritual actions; while there was a third type of prohibition, proper in itself and presumably issued out of chancery in good faith, which was procured by misrepresentation of the true nature of the case by one of the parties, who, as we have already seen,[2] was as often as not a clerk. The difficulties created by the conflict of jurisdictions were increased by the gradually growing complexity of the judicial system, the addition of new writs devised to meet new situations or problems, and, though the ecclesiastics rarely admitted this fact, the activity of the church courts, as greedy of business as any lay tribunal could be. The royal commissioners appointed in 1274 had occasion to report usurpations by ecclesiastical judges. One report expressed the view that, in Norfolk, rural deans and other officials collected more money fines from lay persons than the royal officials in the county did.[3] If a practice recommended by Bracton had been systematically adopted, as it was in 1290 in the statute of Consultation, more orderly habits of co-operation between royal and ecclesiastical judges would have been formed in the period when the king's judges were nearly always clerks and the two systems of law were less rigidly defined. This practice was an appeal against a writ of prohibition taking the form of a consultation of the royal by the ecclesiastical judges. 'A favourable reply to their inquiry, made in the king's name or in that of the justices, allowed the case to proceed in courts christian notwithstanding the prohibition'.[4] The implication that the final decision rested with the king's judges—a claim abhorrent to churchmen like Grosseteste—may have prevented the adoption of the device. In Edward I's reign acquiescence in the claim of the royal power to the last word was more general; both in fact and in theory, it was a necessary outcome of political developments, however inconsistent it might be with high church

[1] Cole, op. cit., pp. 367–8; summarized and printed by Flahiff, op. cit. vi. 287, 310–12. [2] Above, p. 467.

[3] Flahiff, op. cit. vi. 301, referring to *Rotuli Hundredorum*, i. 452.

[4] Norma Adams, op. cit., pp. 291–2. The statute of 1290 is printed in *Statutes of the Realm*, i. 108. Bracton gives three writs of consultation, but they were not included in the registers of writs and seem to have been rarely used.

doctrine. Indeed, in 1285 the king's council 'conceded' the right of access to the royal justices in cases of illegal or doubtful prohibitions.[1]

In one strong protest, addressed to King Edward on 2 November 1281, after the provincial council at Lambeth (7–10 October), Pecham did expound his views on the duty of the king to remove the causes of the bitter discord which had so long endangered the realm through the oppression of the Church contrary to the decrees of popes, the statutes of councils, and the teaching of the fathers, the sources respectively of the highest authority, the highest truth, and the highest sanctity. He followed a biblical defence of this threefold obligation with an historical retrospect. The respect which prevailed in Wales for the liberties which he sought in England showed, he said, that the British kings had maintained them. The period of oppression had really begun in the days of Henry II's controversy with the martyred St. Thomas of Canterbury.[2] Pecham had returned to England prepared to follow in the steps of St. Thomas, 'who suffers martyrdom all day so long as the causes of his martyrdom are daily renewed',[3] but he must soon have realized that times had changed. His protest to the king kept clear of fundamental principles, and he made no threats. He begged Edward's help in the removal of the causes of conflict. The scene was not set on a dramatic stage but in courts and markets where the issues were inextricably interlocked, and it was hard to separate friends from foes. The archbishop's humiliation in parliament in November 1279 had been a sharp reminder from a friendly king that he must mind his steps. At the same time, he was no coward, and he was not alone. The bishops and clergy had behind them a long tradition of corporate action, and the king's need for money was great.

The first opportunity had already come. The facts reveal another side of Pecham at the very time of his surrender in parliament. The laity granted a tax in this parliament and the king, in view of his necessities and the protection which the clergy shared with the laity under his rule, urged that the clergy should do the same.[4] Pecham, on 6 November 1279, summoned the bishops to hold diocesan meetings of their clergy and to

---

[1] *E.H.R.* lii (1937), 232.   [2] *Epistolae*, i. 239–44.
[3] Op. cit. i. 22, in a letter of 12 July 1279, written to the bishop of Tusculum before the council of Reading met.   [4] Below, p. 505.

report the outcome to him in a *congregatio* to be held the following January. He represented that all gratitude was due to the king; the period of the papal tenth or crusading tax was ending (*elapso tempore decimae*) and their timely assistance would stir the royal favour. What happened in the January convocation is not clear, but, after numerous gatherings of clergy throughout the country, a grant of a fifteenth for three years was made by the province of Canterbury. Pecham's order for the appointment of collectors was issued on 3 November 1280,[1] and on the same day the king gave provisional and verbal replies to a series of petitions or grievances which the bishops had presented to him and on which his and their representatives had held frequent discussions.[2] While the grant to the king was under consideration in the dioceses and by Pecham and his colleagues, the latter had prepared a list of grievances for presentation in parliament, and these had been examined on several occasions. With the exception of a protest against the recent statute of mortmain, the grievances dealt with familiar types of interferences with ecclesiastical order and procedure. A tradition had been revived.

Pecham was not discouraged. In 1281 he summoned a provincial council to meet at Lambeth in October to continue the work begun at Reading. Here, in spite of the usual royal warnings against interference with the king's rights and, if the Osney chroniclers can be trusted, the threatening intervention of royal proctors, the sentences of excommunication were repeated with slight modifications;[3] and, to make his position clear, the archbishop wrote to Edward the letter already described. The king wisely refrained from reprisals. Probably he had taken the

---

[1] *Epistolae*, i. 78–80, 87–88, 145. The usual royal letters of warning were issued before the January convocation; see *Cal. Pat. Rolls, 1272–81*, p. 359, where 'J. archbishop of York' should obviously read 'J. archbishop of Canterbury'.

[2] For the *gravamina* of 1280 and the part which they and the *memoriale* embodying the king's verbal replies 'played in moulding the law which defined the bounds of ecclesiastical and secular jurisdiction' see E. B. Graves in *E.H.R.* xliii (1928), 12–14, and Richardson and Sayles, ibid. lii (1937), 229–30. Lambeth MS. 1213, fol. 137ᵛ (from St. Augustine's, Canterbury) should be added to the list of copies of the introduction, text, and *memoriale*.

[3] On the council of Lambeth see Hilda Johnstone in *Essays in Medieval History presented to Thomas Frederick Tout* (1925), pp. 174–87. Pecham, as she points out, stressed the condemnation of unjust prohibitions by inserting the word *precipue*, but, it should be added, he also clarified the definition by limiting it to interference with processes 'quae *ita* ad ecclesiam pertinere noscuntur *quod nullatenus possunt nec consueverunt per seculare judicium terminari*' (Wilkins, *Concilia*, ii. 56). Pecham also omitted the order to affix Magna Carta to church doors.

archbishop's measure and realized both the value of his goodwill and the advantages of a conciliatory attitude towards
clerical grievances. After all, in any particular issue the last
word lay with the Crown. Three months later the energies of all
classes in the community, lay and clerical alike, were concentrated upon the second Welsh war. The disputes between the
two systems of law and administration should not be so isolated
as to suggest a state of perpetual tension or ill feeling.

A number of discussions in the Easter parliament of 1285 give
an unusually clear impression of the recurrent debate.[1] It was
a great occasion, for it marked Edward's return to Westminster
after an absence of more than three years and all the anxieties
and triumphs of the conquest and settlement of Wales. The
fragment of the true cross venerated by the Welsh was borne in
procession through the streets of London. Parliament opened on
4 May and lasted for two months. On 28 June the long series of
enactments known as the second statute of Westminster were
read out in Westminster Hall. During these weeks the prelates
compiled and presented three distinct sets of articles; first,
petitions of a general kind, then objections to certain details in
the new statutes,[2] and lastly, protests against usurpations of
clerical rights in the royal courts. Neither the king nor the
archbishop, who was hurrying on with his diocesan visitations,
took part in the discussions to which these *gravamina* gave rise.
The replies to the first series were given by Burnell the chancellor, himself a bishop, and other members of the king's council,
to the second and third series by persons assigned for the purpose, who presumably were counsellors. The discussions ranged
over details of procedure rather than first principles. Points
were refused or allowed or deferred; partial concessions were
made on a few, explanations were given about other articles.
With one exception the seventeen articles of the third series

[1] *Concilia*, ii. 115–19 (from the register of Godfrey Giffard, bishop of Worcester),
explained in their true order and setting by Richardson and Sayles, *E.H.R.* lii
(1937), 220–34, in the light of documents from the memoranda book of Bury St.
Edmunds, known as Kempe's Register (B.M. Harl. MS. 645).

[2] Objection was made to the following clauses, in whole or in certain details:
Stat. West. II, cc. 5 (revision of procedure in cases of advowson), 19 (administration of goods of intestates), 23 (executors to have a writ of account), 25 (extension
of writs of disseisin, so far as corrodies were concerned), 32 (collusive actions
brought by monks and other ecclesiastical persons to evade the statute of mortmain), 34 (abduction of nuns), 41 (alienations of tenements or of alms attached to
such by religious foundations).

were not answered, but they led indirectly to the famous writ *Circumspecte agatis* issued by the king at Paris in the following summer.

When they commented on the royal replies to their first series of grievances, the prelates complained of a public edict, now lost, in which the bishops were instructed to take cognizance only of testamentary and matrimonial cases. On 1 July this edict was followed up by writs addressed to the prelates, archdeacons, officials, and other ecclesiastics in various dioceses.[1] In this writ the Crown took more positive action: it claimed jurisdiction over a long list of pleas and prohibited the clergy to take cognizance of them, as they were said to be doing. The third series of petitions presented by the prelates in the parliament of 1285 was compiled in protest against the writ, and also enlarged on the malpractices and usurpations of judges, sheriffs, and other royal officers in the course of judicial proceedings. The protest was given new force by the disturbances which occurred in the diocese of Norwich, if it was not actually provoked by them. Norwich at this time was the stronghold of clerical intransigence. The bishop, William Middleton (1278–88), was a trained canon lawyer who had formerly been the official of the court of Canterbury. The dean, sub-dean, and Gregory of Pontefract, official of Lynn, were active disciplinarians and upholders of ecclesiastical rights. A commission to a royal judge and to the sheriff of Norfolk and Suffolk was appointed to search out all in the diocese who disobeyed the order of July and to cite them to appear before the justices of the king's bench. In January 1286 the commission of inquiry was replaced by a Norfolk eyre which, as the prelates had urged in their petition, would hear and determine pleas and complaints on the spot. Pleas were heard at intervals in Norwich and Lynn until the end of September 1286. Judges in ecclesiastical courts and clerks charged with trespasses injurious to the Crown were kept in custody or put on bail. A list of grievances which was probably the agenda for a provincial council summoned to meet at the New Temple in London on 13 October included 'the new oppressions of the Church especially in the parts of Norwich,

---

[1] *Statutes of the Realm*, i. 209. The printed writ is addressed to the clergy of the diocese of Norwich, but there is evidence that it was sent also to other dioceses, if not to all. See E. B. Graves in *E.H.R.* xliii (1928), 2–4, and the criticisms by Richardson and Sayles (lii. 222, 226).

and the indifferent arrests of clerks and ecclesiastical persons'.[1] Then, suddenly, on 6 October, before the convocation could meet, proceedings were stayed. A royal writ was issued to the justices on eyre in Norfolk. It stated that the bishop had offered a fine—the sum was 1,000 marks—on behalf of the clerks indicted before the commissioners and afterwards convicted before the justices, on the understanding that they should not be imprisoned or vilely treated and that amercements owing to the Crown should be covered. The king had accepted the fine on condition that complainants should receive satisfaction. No further action against the offenders would be taken.[2]

Feeling had run high in Norfolk; the bishop had acted wisely, and all the more so because the drastic behaviour of the commissioners and judges had caused some searchings of heart in the royal councils. The sharp distinction drawn between testamentary and matrimonial cases on the one hand and the claims of the Crown on the other had caused practical difficulties for a century, and the time had come for closer definition. In June 1286 the council decided to give the itinerant justices, then busy in Norwich, more precise guidance. Instructions were drafted and submitted to King Edward, who was then negotiating about Gascon problems in Paris.[3] The outcome was the writ *Circumspecte agatis*. It begins, 'Be circumspect in your dealing with the bishop of Norwich and his clergy. Do not punish them if they hold pleas on purely spiritual matters', and then it gives a list of the kinds of case which should be left to the courts Christian; moral offences, for which a financial penalty is in order, particularly if the offender is a freeman; the neglect of churches and cemeteries, for which only a financial penalty may be imposed; customary mortuary dues; local disputes between rectors or bishop and rector about tithes, provided that their value is not more than a fourth of the annual value of the church concerned; pensions due to the bishop from rectors, where the bishop has the advowson. Moreover, as had been conceded already (*alias*), cases of violence and defamation against clerks, provided that

[1] Graves, p. 7, connects the list of grievances in Giffard's Register (ed. Willis-Bund, ii. 298) with the summons to this convocation (*Concilia*, ii. 125).

[2] Printed by Graves (p. 7, note) from the assize roll. Geoffrey of Pontefract, who had expressed his contempt for royal prohibitions by casting them against the wall, was excepted from the amnesty.

[3] Above, p. 291. The text and addendum have been critically edited by Graves in his article 'Circumspecte agatis', above mentioned, *E.H.R.* xliii (1928), 15–16. See also Richardson and Sayles, in *Law Quarterly Review*, l (1934), 565.

no financial penalty is exacted, and breach of faith, though only as a sin to be corrected, might, with similar matters, be pleaded in the courts Christian. The writ was so precise and so important that it survived its occasion. By the end of Edward's reign it was cited in the royal courts as a statute; and an addendum which some legal collector of such documents may have made to it came to be regarded as part of the statute. The addition, though rather clumsily torn from its context, was apposite and certainly justified, for it might well have been given official currency six years before the date of the writ. It was the episcopal version of one of the oral replies made by King Edward to the *gravamina* of 1280;[1] and it dealt, in more detail, with the same kinds of cases as were defined in the writ of 1286—cases where the royal prohibition, if certain conditions were observed, did not lie.

So far as is known, the ventilation of clerical grievances was not resumed until 1299, in the days of Archbishop Winchelsey, though it would be hazardous to assert that no discussions took place in the interval.[2] It is probable that the writ of 1286 gave prominence to the articles of 1280 and helped to make them the standard expression of the clerical point of view. Both the royal and the ecclesiastical disputants in 1299–1301 had before them the articles of 1280 and the *memoriale* of the king's verbal replies to these articles. The *antiqua gravamina* of 1299, as they were later described, were probably prepared in convocation in November 1299. They were presented in the Easter parliament in 1300 and answered in a famous Lincoln parliament in January 1301. The replies to at least eight of the thirty-four articles were taken from the memorial of 1280. Archbishop Winchelsey resumed the attack two years after Edward I's death, in more favourable circumstances. The *gravamina* of 1309 were the most comprehensive series since that of the provincial council of 1257. They were compiled in a long and representative convocation, in which the clergy of each diocese were required to discuss all manner of grievances. The material so collected was then conflated and put into juristic form by a body of skilled clerks. Some articles were for the information of Pope Clement V, who was

[1] Above, p. 479.

[2] A comprehensive list of petitions of the prelates 'for the recovery of the liberty of the English church', inserted in Pontissara's Register (ii. 771–8) under the year 1295, may have been prepared in the convocation of this year in the New Temple: see the writ in Cotton, *Historia anglicana* (ed. Luard), pp. 293–4.

collecting material for the projected council at Vienne (1311), others for presentation to the Crown. The latter comprised the *gravamina* of 1280, 1301 (with the royal replies to each set) and some new articles, four of which were based on grievances relating to the caption of excommunicated persons, said to have been presented by the archbishop to Edward I.[1] This was the body of material available to Archbishop Reynolds in 1316, when a long list of clerical articles and royal replies (apart from some on which full satisfaction had been given) were issued in letters patent, which became known as the statute *Articuli cleri*.[2] *Articuli cleri* ended the first stage in the long movement started by Grosseteste eighty years before, and defined the issue between Church and state in the century to come.

Archbishop Pecham died at the end of 1292. After he had shot his bolt at Lambeth in 1281 and written his protest to the king he seems to have taken little part in these developments.[3] His activities during the rest of his short but crowded tenure of office were directed by his concern for order, discipline, and the well-being of souls. As pastor, friend, and judge he intervened everywhere in the affairs of high and low, and especially in the doings of his episcopal colleagues; and it is but just to add that both in the ordering of his own diocese and in the careful administration of his estates he set a high standard. He visited the dioceses of his province in England and Wales, taking great trouble with monastic houses, frequently rebuked, and not without success, pluralism in high places, and, while he welcomed co-operation with his suffragans, insisted on his supremacy as metropolitan.[4] While he maintained friendly relations with the king, he asserted his right, even in the face of royal resistance, to visit the royal

[1] Inserted in the register of John Halton, bishop of Carlisle (ed. W. N. Thompson, p. 172) under the year 1301.

[2] Ursula Henriques, in her unpublished work on the articles of grievances of the English clergy in the thirteenth and early fourteenth centuries, has dealt fully with the articles of 1309 in the light of previous lists. See also Richardson and Sayles in *E.H.R.* lii. 229–30, and cf. Makower, *Constitutional History of the Church of England* (Eng. trans., 1895), pp. 39–40 and notes.

[3] It may have significance that, as early as February 1281, he was moved by local reports to order the bishop of Norwich to put a stop to the extortions and vexations with which the bishop's officers afflicted the burgesses of Dunwich (*Epistolae*, i. 177–8).

[4] See generally D. L. Douie's biography; also C. R. Cheney, *Episcopal Visitation of Monasteries in the Thirteenth Century* (1931), especially pp. 142–8; David Knowles, in *E.H.R.* lvii (1942), 1–18; and, for estate administration, Dorothy Sutcliffe, in *Speculum*, x (1935), 53–68.

chapels or to vindicate the superiority of Canterbury to York. Yet, if the archbishop's concentration on his duties was exceptional, most of his activities were not peculiar to his administration. In the rest of this chapter we may confine our attention to wider themes suggested by Pecham's activities, and say something about the episcopate as a whole and the development of convocation.

On the whole the English bishops in the thirteenth century were able and respectable. As leaders, administrators, visitors, builders, and patrons of learning and the arts they have never been excelled. While it is convenient to distinguish them in the light of their origin or experience, as royal servants or men who had made their mark as scholars or in their localities, the groups so formed tend to dissolve into each other.[1] The monk occasionally elected by a Benedictine chapter at Durham or Ely or Rochester was not always only a *simplex claustralis* and occasionally became a very good bishop; but under the exacting conditions of a career which became more and more 'professionalized', the election of monks as bishops was not encouraged, though it is easy to think of abbots or priors, like the great Henry of Eastry, prior of Christ Church, Canterbury (1285–1331), whose worldly wisdom would have brought new strength to any episcopal bench.[2] The non-monastic bishops certainly elude exact classification. Some, like Walter Bronescombe, bishop of Exeter (1258–80), trained in the royal service, settled down to become assiduous and notable diocesans; others, like John de Pontissara, who had acquired repute as active ecclesiastics with minds of their own, won the confidence and shared the labours of the king after they had been appointed to their sees. Robert Burnell, though he could not be described as a model bishop, ruled his diocese with energy and distinction while he served King Edward

---

[1] See Gibbs and Lang, *Bishops and Reform, 1215–1272* (1934), pp. 1–93 *passim*.

[2] Richard Crockesley, abbot of Westminster (d. 1258) was a friend and servant of Henry III. One of his successors, Richard Ware, was treasurer of the exchequer from 1280 to 1283. The monastic chapters, in the constant defence or enlargement of their rights and liberties, had perforce to acquire a stock of worldly wisdom and acquaintance with both common and canon law. Commenting upon the maintenance by the prior of Durham of a number of monks as students at Oxford, the chronicler Robert de Graystanes added, with thoughts of later lawsuits, 'inde fuit occasio redemptionis nostrae': see *Camden Miscellany*, xiii (1924), p. vi. Contrast the perplexities of Odo, Abbot of Battle, in 1176, and his regret that he had never applied his mind to the study of the laws (*Chronicon monasterii de Bello* (1846), p. 173).

as chancellor and helped Archbishop Pecham out of many a tiresome situation. The career of a bishop was not directed by the royal influence, or the papal provision or the capitular preference to which he might owe his exaltation, just as, on the other hand, no bishop could dissociate himself from the limitations imposed upon his actions by the royal prerogative, the Holy See, and the corporate or personal feuds which prevailed in his diocese.

The really effective influences which gave coherence to the episcopal body were life in the schools, family connexions, patronage, and licensed or legitimate pluralism. They were, indeed, interrelated influences. A boy of parts goes to Oxford, let us say, with the help of a bishop or abbot or local landholder, or, as happened more frequently than is generally supposed, because he belongs to a family which can support him there. He makes good, and in due course incepts as master of arts. An influential teacher may open the way to a career, as the Franciscan, Adam Marsh, seems to have done for Walter de Merton, the future chancellor, bishop of Rochester, and founder of Merton College.[1] If he belongs to a well-to-do local family, the scholar's future is safe. Thus, another pupil of Adam Marsh, Oliver Sutton, whose father was a landholder in Nottinghamshire at Sutton-on-Trent, was related through his mother to the Lexington family, one of whom, Henry, was bishop of Lincoln for three years while Oliver was studying law and theology. In 1275 he was made dean of Lincoln, and in 1280 was elected bishop by a unanimous chapter, 'by the way of inspiration', or, as we now say, by acclamation. His register reveals him, during his rule of nearly twenty years, as one of the best bishops of his time.[2] Or again, a scholar bishop of good repute and knightly family, like Richard Gravesend, bishop of Lincoln, Sutton's predecessor (1258–79), might, directly or indirectly, be the means of advancing his kinsmen. Bishop Richard's nephew, another Richard, who began his career in his uncle's household, advanced in the church and diocese of London to rule that great see from 1280 to 1303, and in due course his nephews, Richard and Stephen, became respectively treasurer of St. Paul's and bishop

---

[1] Cf. *Monumenta Franciscana*, i (1858), 405, a letter to a Franciscan physician then living with Grosseteste.

[2] Cf. ibid., p. 405; Rosalind M. T. Hill, *Oliver Sutton* (Lincoln Minster Pamphlets, no. 4, 1950); and her edition of the Register, now in progress (Lincoln Record Soc., 1948–).

of London. Here the chapters clearly were influenced in their elections by local connexions and reputations. Similarly, family traditions affected the careers of the Cantilupes, and the inter-related Giffards, Byttons, and Greenfields in the west.

Episcopal influence, of course, was not confined to advancing the interests of kinsmen; for episcopal households were the nurseries of talent and, occasionally, of sanctity. Richard Wych, bishop of Chichester (1245–53), who had studied at all three of the famous *studia*, Oxford, Paris, and Bologna, and whose ser-vices had been sought by Grosseteste, attached himself to Arch-bishop Edmund of Canterbury and was with him when he died. He owed his appointment to Chichester, in face of royal oppo-sition, to the active support of Archbishop Boniface and his suffragans and to Pope Innocent IV (1245).[1] Simon Berksted, of saintly reputation, who also was a bishop of Chichester (1262–88), had been St. Richard's chaplain and familiar. Richard Swinfield, bishop of Hereford (1283–1317), a very active diocesan, had been in the service of his predecessor, St. Thomas Cantilupe. William Middleton, the canonist, bishop of Norwich (1278–88), was a friend of Archbishop Kilwardby.

Most of these bishops, who had been to the schools or had been trained in episcopal households, had been established in life by the enjoyment of benefices held in plurality;[2] and in general this recognition of their learning and practical ability was well deserved. As we have seen, the system was riddled with abuses, and it was not always clear to the conscientious in-quirer where the line between licit and illicit pluralism was to be drawn, unless a papal dispensation had settled the question,[3] but these emoluments certainly had far-reaching social results. They paved the way of poor students, maintained promising men in the standard of comfort to which they had been accus-tomed, rewarded the services of clerks, officials, family physi-cians, and others employed in royal and episcopal households; and, most important of all, by strengthening the ties between the local gentry, the schools, and the great households, they gave more coherence to English society as a whole. They added

[1] See E. F. Jacob on St. Richard in *Journal of Ecclesiastical History*, vii (1956), 174–88.
[2] See A. Hamilton Thompson's introduction to the *Rotuli Ricardi Gravesend* (Canterbury and York Soc., 1925), pp. xxiv–xxvii.
[3] See Adam Marsh's letters: *Monumenta Franciscana*, i. 185–9, 224–5; cf. Hamilton Thompson in *Rot. Ric. Gravesend*, pp. vi–vii.

a new sanction to a mingled secular and ecclesiastical structure which could look only to the Crown as its head and as the symbol of its unity.

As we review the story of the English bishops in the thirteenth century we are conscious of a gradual change in the social context of these men from the schools. The days when, under the guidance of Stephen Langton and St. Edmund, they seem to stand apart to guide public affairs, or when they divide for and against the leadership of Simon de Montfort, pass away. There is no successor to Grosseteste. Pecham is but a half-hearted embodiment of St. Thomas of Canterbury. The terrors or the inconveniences of interdict and excommunication can be brushed aside or disregarded in the interests of the common good and the royal prerogative. The king retains the loyalty, and often the friendship, of prelates, friars, and clerks, and the right to the last word. Of the distinguished masters in the Oxford schools, only Archbishop Robert Winchelsey is strong enough and sure enough of his cause to temper his loyalty with resistance, and, for a short time, to stir the old fires; and he stands almost alone.

Archbishop Pecham's most bitter experience was his quarrel with the former Montfortian and future saint, Thomas Cantilupe, bishop of Hereford. The two men present a contrast in sanctity, Cantilupe being of the more conventional and acceptable type, an austere and cultivated aristocrat, lavish and courtly. His father William (d. 1251) had been steward of the royal household, and the favour which King Henry had shown to the father was never entirely withdrawn from the son, in spite of Thomas's adherence to the cause of Earl Simon and of his uncle Walter Cantilupe, bishop of Worcester. Thomas attended both the general councils at Lyons; at the former Pope Innocent IV made him a papal chaplain and licensed him to hold benefices in plurality, at the latter Pope Gregory X again made him a papal chaplain. In the years between the two councils (1245–75) he established his worldly position on the foundation of his licensed pluralities. He studied civil law at Orleans and canon law at his old university of Paris, taught canon law at Oxford, where in 1262 he became chancellor of the University, and, after the collapse of the Montfortians at Evesham, returned to study and lecture in theology in Paris. When he was elected bishop of Hereford (1275) he was again settled in Oxford. His inception in 1273 under the presidency of his former master and friend, Archbishop Kilwardby, was one of the social events of the year. Witnesses to his sanctity during the process of canonization recalled how he had turned the enjoyment of his pluralities into a gracious ministry. He is said to have been most scrupulous in the appointment of his vicars, to have made frequent visitation of his cures, preached to his various flocks, built and repaired churches, shown hospitality, and showered alms upon the poor. If all this is true, he made his benefices a training ground in the episcopal duties which awaited him.[1]

Pecham and Cantilupe were like oil and water. The archbishop regarded the bishop of Hereford as his enemy, 'the chief obstacle to our proceedings both in and outside council';[2] as a man who 'excogitated malice under the demeanour of a dove'.[3] The exasperation of the impulsive reformer embittered the first three years of his rule; he felt the malign influence of Cantilupe's well-mannered obstinacy everywhere. In February 1282 he excommunicated the bishop, who appealed to the pope, and quietly withdrew to Italy, to die at Orvieto on 25 August. The two men must have felt an instinctive antipathy to each other, as good men can. The canonist was safely moored in a courtly tradition; the theologian was in too great a hurry. The bishop felt that he must resist the metropolitan in the interests of the ecclesiastical community which he so well understood; the primate did not see that in essentials the bishop was ordering his diocese in the light of the principles and injunctions which they both wished to see obeyed.[4] There were two occasions of offence, each of which originated in particular cases. The bishop objected to direct appeals to the court of Canterbury in London before his own court had dealt with the subject of appeal; the primate objected to the administration of wills by a local official

---

[1] See the excellent life of Thomas Cantilupe by T. F. Tout in *D.N.B.*; and, further, for his episcopal activity, his register, edited by R. G. Griffiths (Canterbury and York Soc., 1907); cf. Moorman, op. cit., pp. 22, 26 n., 222–3 and *passim*.

[2] *Epistolae*, ii. 394.

[3] Ibid. i. 319.

[4] The characters of the two men are illustrated by incidents at Leominster priory in Herefordshire. The prior had locked the door of the priory church, and Cantilupe, because it was also the parish church, ordered the door to be removed. When Pecham visited Leominster after the bishop's death he was horrified to find the monks exposed to public intervention, ordered the door to be restored, and a chapel, dedicated to St. Thomas of Canterbury, to be erected for the use of parishioners within a year (*Epistolae*, ii. 505–7).

when the testator had left property by will in more than one diocese. He claimed jurisdiction in such cases.[1]

Disputes about Canterbury jurisdiction had often arisen before. The occasions of difference were not new, nor confined to the diocese of Hereford. Pecham returned to England as archbishop at a time when, after the period of disturbance, the canonical system was in full and daily operation. It was invigorated by the diffusion of legal learning, the experience of judges, and the guidance of conciliar and episcopal constitutions, and at the same time confronted by difficulties of procedure and the necessity to resolve the problems of the relations between custom and authority.[2] Practice in the courts naturally produced a skilled body of officials, pleaders, notaries, and clerks whose local loyalties and professional jealousies were always at the service of their superiors. The new archbishop soon showed that, as a metropolitan armed with legatine powers, he would permit no diocesan interests to impede him in the exercise of his duty. He brought Italian notaries with him[3] and found skilled lawyers in England ready to serve him. His suffragans were as able as he was to protect themselves. Early in 1282 he was presented with a series of twenty-one articles in which his conduct of diocesan visitations and the indiscriminate reception of appeals,

[1] See W. W. Capes's introduction to Cantilupe's register and I. J. Churchill, *Canterbury Administration* (1933), i. 472–5.

[2] Most of the available material is still unedited and awaits systematic criticism. Some of it is hardly known to exist, e.g. the so-called ES rolls of the dean and chapter of Canterbury, containing the *acta* and processes of suits in the *Curia Cantuariensis*, before this became fully articulated. The unpublished records of judicial proceedings during the vacancies in the see after the deaths of St. Edmund, Boniface of Savoy, and Pecham are especially important. Dr. Churchill's *Canterbury Administration* (1933) laid a solid foundation; see also M. M. Morgan, 'Early Canterbury Jurisdiction', in *E.H.R.* lx (1945), 392–9; and Brian Woodcock, *Medieval Ecclesiastical Courts in the Diocese of Canterbury* (1952). On the development of episcopal secretarial organization see C. R. Cheney, *English Bishops' Chanceries, 1100–1250* (1950), and Rosalind Hill, 'Bishop Sutton and his Archives', in *Journal of Ecclesiastical History* for April 1951 (ii. 43–53). Norma Adams has in preparation for the Selden Society a volume of ecclesiastical cases. Robert Brentano has described *York Metropolitan Jurisdiction, 1279–96* (1959). Archbishop Wickwane (1279–85) on one occasion gave an excellent analysis of his powers: see his *Register*, ed. W. Brown (Surtees Soc., 1907), pp. 168–9. C. M. Fraser, *A History of Antony Bek* (Oxford, 1957), should be studied for relations between York and Durham.

[3] Notably John of Bologna, who had a great reputation as a master of his art, and whose style, with its use of the *cursus*, can be traced in some of Pecham's letters. Cf. Denholm-Young, *Collected Papers*, pp. 27, 40, 50; and C. Haskins and E. Kantorowicz in *E.H.R.* lviii (1943), 426. John's *Summa notarie*, which is dedicated to Pecham, would, he hoped, be used in the court of Canterbury and do something to extend the use and keeping of official documents in England.

especially in the comparatively new 'court of Canterbury' established at the church of St. Mary of the Arches in London, were
called in question. His first replies were couched in terms strangely reminiscent of the royal replies to clerical lists of grievances.
He asserted a custom or declared that his intentions had been
misconstrued; but he was not so firmly entrenched or so sure of
his ground as were the advisers of the Crown. He wisely referred
the episcopal case for inquiry to Bishop William Middleton and
four other ecclesiastics well versed in 'the customs and rights of
the church of Canterbury'. Their report, in five articles, defined
the appellate jurisdiction of the official of the court of Canterbury and the nature of the archbishop's legatine powers. Its
findings about the official's powers were confirmed and, in a
redrafted form, published by the archbishop on 25 April 1282.[1]

The minds of both parties had been confused about the
authority derived by the archbishop from his legatine powers.
Some bishops seem to have denied that the primate had any
power whatever to receive appeals in cases which had not been
before them or their official,[2] thus reducing him, as Pecham was
wont to complain, to the position of a 'mere metropolitan'.
Pecham, on the other hand, had tended to assume that he could
delegate his legatine authority. His commissioners drew a clear
distinction between the two sources of power. They admitted
that 'in virtue of his legation' the archbishop could hear complaints (*querelae*) from a subject of a suffragan, but they ruled
that the right did not extend to the 'ordinary jurisdiction' of the
official. Thus the jurisdiction of the official in the court of Canterbury was given precision and developed apart from the archbishop's personal jurisdiction in his court of audience. One
reason for the doubts thus removed was the fact that until
recently the judge or official had tried cases in an undifferen-
tiated court. As late as 1270–3, during the vacancy after Archbishop Boniface's death, the prior and chapter had dealt,
through the official, both with provincial appeals and with

---

[1] *Epistolae*, i. 328–9. The commission consisted of the bishop of Norwich; the
archdeacon of Canterbury; Gilbert de Sancto Leofardo, treasurer and later (1288)
bishop of Chichester, who in this year became official of Canterbury; Adam de
Hales, a former official; and Reginald de Brandon, who was active in 1300, as
Antony Bek's clerk, in the visitation of the church of Durham (below, p. 496). The
articles are discussed by Dr. Churchill, op. cit., i. 427–30.

[2] See Pecham's letter to Godfrey Giffard, bishop of Worcester, in May 1282
(*Epistolae*, i. 355–6).

cases which had arisen in the city and diocese of Canterbury. During the next vacancy (1278–9) they appointed a separate commissary to deal with the latter. In the interval provincial appellate jurisdiction had been separated from diocesan juris- diction. The existence of a provincial 'court of Canterbury' in London, held by the official or by the dean of St. Mary-le-Bow as his commissary, is first clearly observable in these years.[1] Naturally enough, its proceedings were closely watched by the bishops. In 1282 it was forbidden to 'rescribe to', that is to say, to deal with complaints or appeals from the subjects of suffra- gans in cases of which the diocesans had not had cognizance (*omissis ordinariis mediis*).

An important function of the provincial court of Canterbury was the reception of what were called tuitorial appeals, or ap- peals for the protection or *tuitio* of the court from parties which had appealed to the court of Rome and, during the inevitable delays, needed some defence against their local adversaries. Recourse to this form of appeal, a natural result of the growth in the number of appeals to the Pope, had become familiar many years before the establishment of the court of the Arches.[2] Its history is obscure and the technicalities of its procedure and development still await authoritative treatment by legal histo- rians.[3] Doubtless it was as much required in the south as it was under the more violent conditions which prevailed in the pro- vince of York; but Pecham's episcopal colleagues were equally alive to the dangers which might prejudice their own authority from an over-zealous interpretation of its protective powers by the court of Canterbury. The appellant might avail himself of the appeal to escape penalites of sequestration or excommuni- cation which he had justly incurred. In 1282 the commission appointed by Pecham ruled that, if suspension was the occasion of the appeal to the papal court, it could not be relaxed until

[1] Cf. Morgan, op. cit., p. 397; Woodcock, pp. 6–14. For diocesan commissions of 1282 and 1292 see Churchill, ii. 13. In 1273 Archbishop Kilwardby issued regula- tions about the court of Canterbury, which are preserved in the Black Book of the Arches, a compilation of various dates still in the custody of the dean of the Arches (Churchill, i. 426; ii. 207). The dean of St. Mary-le-Bow or 'the Arches' ruled a London peculiar of eleven parishes, directly subject to the archbishop, and was associated with the official as judge of the new provincial court (p. 442). In 1278–9 the diocesan commissary also was apparently regarded as commissary of the official, but his separate standing was made clear in 1292.

[2] Cf. above, p. 466.

[3] Churchill, i. 427–9, 460–7; Woodcock, pp. 64–67, 126–31.

THE PROBLEM OF APPEALS

the main case had been decided by the papal delegates, and that absolution from sentences of excommunication must be subject to guarantees (*ad cautelam*) and must be published, if it were made public, as so conditioned.

In the year 1284 the warden and scholars of Merton College, Oxford, appealed for the protection of the archbishop of York during their appeal to the pope against the redoubtable Antony Bek, who had refused to acknowledge the appropriation to them of the church of Ponteland in Northumberland. The bishop was very indignant. The archbishop of York, he declared, had never been wont to exercise such rights of protection against Durham.[1] This may well have been the case, and helps to explain the bishop's persistent refusal to respect the claim of the college to the distant church. The dispute adds point also to the spirited account given by the author of the *Gesta Dunelmensia* of the proceedings at York in 1300, when the prior and monks of Durham made a tuitorial appeal against the bishop during a famous controversy. The prior's proctors at York had obtained an archiepiscopal citation to the bishop. When the bishop's proctors appeared in York to defend his case, the disputation between the parties lasted for three days before the official of York pronounced judgement, issued the decree of protection, and appointed executors to administer it. It was, the reporter wrote, a lovely disputation—*pulcherrima fuit igitur disputacio*.[2]

At least one attempt was made to appeal to Canterbury for protection against York. This was in 1283–4 during the controversy between the prior and convent of Durham and the archbishop of York about the claim of the former to administer the spiritualities of the bishopric during a vacancy in the see. On 12 January 1284 Pecham, who was unable to be present in person, appointed commissioners to hear the appeal, 'which pends or is hoped to pend in our court of Canterbury'.[3] The archbishop

---

[1] Merton College Records, no. 578. The appeal, dated 10 October 1284, is in no. 5971. I am indebted to Mr. Roger Highfield for these references. Pope Boniface VIII's mandate of January 1302 summarized the long history of the dispute since the gift of Ponteland to the college by Peter de Montfort (*Cal. Papal Letters*, i. 605–6).

[2] *Camden Miscellany*, xiii. 9–10, 22–23. For the case see below, pp. 495–6.

[3] *Epistolae*, ii. 645; cf. Churchill, i. 461–2. Pecham's letter of 7 December 1283 to his commissaries ordering them to cite the archbishop of York to appear in London, and their reply, give a lively impression of this complicated case and the strong feeling which it aroused in York. See Robert Brentano, *York Metropolitan Jurisdiction*, pp. 136–7, 185 ff.

strengthened the provincial court to try so novel and important a case, if, in fact, action should be joined at all.

Conditions of life, while at bottom common to north and south, were more stark and tended to be more bitter in the province of York, where the archbishop and the bishop of Durham maintained an equal state, in a frequent rivalry which only the king could control. The contrast with the south may be seen in the careers of John Romanus or Romeyn, archbishop of York (1286–96), and Antony Bek, bishop of Durham (1284–1311). The archbishop was the natural son of one of the unpopular 'Romans', an Italian who had settled in England and rose to be treasurer of the cathedral church of York;[1] the bishop was the son of a Lincolnshire baron, and a close friend of Edward, whom he accompanied on his crusade, and later served at court. Both were educated at Oxford and both were pluralists,[2] but while the one under the cover of papal dispensations was elected archbishop by a friendly chapter as a local man and a teacher in theology at Paris, the other was chosen by the monks of Durham at the instance of a grateful king. The archbishop took little part in public affairs, the bishop emerged as a great baron and magnificent prelate, who astonished the world by his extravagance. The two prelates soon came into conflict about the relations between their sees. The king in vain tried to reconcile them in 1290, when they attended the funeral of the queen, and the archbishop took his cause to the papal court. Then, hearing that Bek had excommunicated two of his officials, he excommunicated him (April 1292). This brought Edward into the fray on the side of his friend, for Bek was a great temporal magnate, the lord of a palatinate, and his excommunication was regarded as a breach of the royal prerogative. After his return to England the archbishop was imprisoned in the Tower and was forced to pay an enormous fine, 4,000 marks, for his restoration to the royal favour.

---

[1] The tower and transepts of York Minster were begun in his time, and he is said to have been responsible for the north transept, famous for its window of the Five Sisters and for the tower, which was given its present form in the fifteenth century.

[2] Romanus received papal licences and a dispensation from the canonical results of his illegitimacy. A letter from Archbishop Pecham to Bek (1281) implies that Bek had not troubled to get dispensation for his pluralities (*Epistolae*, i. 244–5). Previously (in 1280) Bek had surrendered three of the five benefices with cure of souls which he held in the province of Canterbury (Pecham to Pope Nicholas III; ibid. 137–8).

Bek's turn was to come. In 1300 he broke the good relations which had persisted between bishop and chapter since the understanding reached, seventy years before, by Bishop Poore. He stirred the prior and monks to opposition by his refusal to adapt his proposed visitation of the monastery to the canonical limits which their legal advisers prescribed. The exciting story of the contest which ensued has survived in a vivid piece of contemporary narrative.[1] King Edward was on his way north to Scotland, and, as he drew nearer, the bishop sent to beg Edward not to intervene in the dispute but to leave him to deal with the offenders. The prior, on the other hand, begged for his intervention, and Edward, not willing to be warned off the ground, sent forward Otto of Granson and three clerics, including his confessor, to make a preliminary investigation. They met the monks, inspected the records of the case, and reported that the monks were anxious to submit their cause to the royal decision. The king accordingly came to Durham on 18 June:

The lord king, after making alms and devotion at the shrine of St. Cuthbert, descended to the vestry with his sworn counsellors and the monks. After some diligent discussion with his council, he called the prior and monks to him. He said that he much desired to make peace between them and the bishop, for he could not be unmindful of his obligations either to the bishop's great services to him or to St. Cuthbert. Hence he had prepared a form of peace which seemed just and honourable. 'If you are willing to agree to it, it is well; if not, let each do as seems good to him.' The prior replied that they were prepared to accept the king's ordinance in every way. The reply pleased the king who at once called his notary, John of Caen[2] and ordered him to write down the form of peace as he himself dictated it.

Edward went on to Evenwood, where on 20 June the prior and twelve of the monks and the bishop with his clerks came to him. The king explained the form of peace to the bishop, who at first hotly protested against it, but was at last brought to give it a grudging acquiescence. The form was then read aloud by one of

[1] Gesta Dunelmensia, A.D. MCCC, edit. R. K. Richardson in the Camden Miscellany, xiii. 1–52. For the king's part in the affair see pp. 15–18, 21–22, 27; cf. 44, 49, 51. See C. M. Fraser on Edward I and the regalian franchise of Durham in Speculum, xxxi (1956), 329–42.

[2] 'Johannes de Cambe' of the text (p. 17) is a misspelling, I think, of 'Johannes de Cadomo', the king's chief notary, who frequently appears as the writer of important documents. I have summarized part of the passage translated in the text.

Bek's clerks, Reginald de Brandon, the bishop received the prior's kiss of peace, and the prior received the same from the dissident monks who had adhered to the bishop's side. The king 'with all alacrity of mind' served drink to prior and monks with his own hands. He gave orders that clerks of each party should come together on the morrow to give the agreement public form 'so that by cirograph and authentic seals it could in the future be preserved inviolable'. All was in vain. The bishop refused to abide by the agreement, which required him to make his visitation with only three or four clerks and always (*semper*) to maintain the state of the prior and the liberties of the church of Durham in future visitations.[1] His bad faith led to his discomfiture in parliament at Lincoln and in 1302 to the seizure of his temporalities by the Crown. Richard de Hoton, the intrepid prior, had been the means of the temporary overthrow of one of the most powerful barons and prelates in the land.

In the previous pages we have observed the life of the Church in the light of legatine and provincial councils, diocesan synods and the constitutions, and the grievances to which these gave expression; but many other ecclesiastical councils met in England after the accession of King Henry III. Most of them were summoned to consider demands for papal or royal subsidies. Some were legatine, some national, some provincial; some consisted only of bishops, others were more or less representative of monastic and diocesan interests. The inevitable outcome of a series of assemblies faced by financial demands or requests was a growing sense of clerical coherence in council. In these occasions, more than in periodic scrutinies of the state of the Church, are to be found the origins of the later 'convocation', a representative body which usually met by the king's desire but was summoned, conducted, and dismissed by archiepiscopal authority in accordance with its own writs and procedure. This generalization, however, covers a long, uneven, and complicated piece of history. The understandings, for they can hardly be described as constitutional principles, that it was the duty of the clergy to grant subsidies to the Crown and that, on the

---

[1] The Evenwood compact was enrolled on the Coram rege roll, and is also to be found in the Pontificalia and the Cartularium Primum among the muniments of the dean and chapter of Durham (op. cit., p. 18, note). The bishop continued to disregard it even after the king and the convent had agreed, in view of his objection, to the deletion of the word *semper* (pp. 21-22).

other hand, the clergy would tax themselves only 'in their own provincial assembly convened before the archbishop for this particular purpose in pursuance of a royal writ',[1] were not fully established until the reign of Edward III. They had been formulated by Pecham, but their general recognition was postponed for several decades by the king's attempt to associate lay and clerical elements in parliament and by the imposition of mandatory taxation by the pope on the king's behalf in the last years of Edward I and throughout the reign of Edward II. Moreover, there was never any clear-cut distinction between a 'convocation' for purposes of taxation and a provincial assembly of the clergy. The archbishop frequently summoned a provincial assembly on his own initiative to consider the affairs of the Church without any order from the king;[2] an assembly for purposes of taxation might turn to other business, an assembly summoned to deal with purely ecclesiastical matters might make a grant to the Crown. Nor had the word 'convocation' a precise implication. It was a covering word, not a formal title, and did not acquire official usage as an alternative to 'provincial council' until the fifteenth century.

All the same, such solidarity as the clerical 'estate' came to possess in England was mainly due to its constant preoccupation with demands upon its revenues. Paradoxically enough, in our period, ecclesiastical assemblies earned their experience and acquired their representative character especially in disputes over papal taxation which they could rarely evade.[3] Between 1239 and 1259 and again between 1266 and 1296 the papal collectors were continuously at work on papal subsidies and income taxes—the subsidies of 1239, 1244, 1246, 1272, the taxes to which King Henry's Sicilian adventure gave rise, the triennial tenth imposed by papal authority to relieve the Crown after the barons' wars, and the two great sexennial tenths

[1] J. Armitage Robinson, 'Convocation of Canterbury: its Early History', in *Church Quarterly Review* for October 1915 (lxxxi. 81–137), p. 131. The formal royal writ does not appear until the reign of Edward II, and caused much criticism (ibid., pp. 110, 117 ff.).

[2] Archbishop Mepham in 1332 and Archbishop Stratford in 1341 went back to the Lateran Council of 1215 and, in summoning a provincial council, referred to the obligation to hold such a council once a year (op. cit., pp. 127, 128).

[3] They refused to agree to Gregory IX's suggestion for the endowment of the Holy See (1225), to Innocent IV's request on behalf of the king (1244), and to requests for papal subsidies in 1238 and 1263. These were not strictly mandatory demands.

imposed to finance projected crusades in 1274 and 1291.[1] The collectors, sometimes foreign but generally English ecclesiastics, had to organize their labours in accordance with instructions; in 1254, 1266, 1276, and 1291 they were required to make new valuations of ecclesiastical sources of income subject to the tax, both spiritualities—tithes, offerings, the annual value of glebelands and other lands—and temporalities, or lands whose proceeds did not form part of a benefice.[2] They had to deal with endless difficulties incidental to the valuations and payments and try to rake in the arrears of one tax long after the collection of another had begun. The papal bulls which directed the processes of collection and valuation, and all the subsequent papal and local rulings about complaints and exemptions, convey an impression such as we might get from the records of modern income-tax commissioners if they had to face a running fire of criticism, protests, and hostility from parliament, the church assembly, and county organizations, as well as of particular taxpayers. Nor was this all; for, about the middle of the century, the court of Rome had begun to maintain a central office in England under the direction of a permanent collector responsible for miscellaneous revenues and their arrears.

Although these taxes were levied by papal authority, it should not be supposed that they were all levied to meet papal needs, or that all roused equal opposition; still less that the king did not benefit from them. In 1217 Pope Honorius III ordered the bishops and prelates to give a subsidy to the boy-king in proportion to their resources. In 1226 a clerical subsidy was granted to the king by the clergy in obedience to a papal mandate.[3] In

---

[1] W. E. Lunt, *Financial Relations of the Papacy with England to 1327* (1939), is of fundamental authority for everything relating to papal taxation. See also his earlier work, *The Valuation of Norwich* (1926); also Rose Graham on the taxation of Pope Nicholas IV in her *English Ecclesiastical Studies* (1929), pp. 271–301, and T. F. Tout on the work of John Halton, bishop of Carlisle, as a collector in Scotland, *Collected Papers*, ii (1934), 106–23. The valuation made under the direction of the bishop of Norwich and his colleagues in 1254 onwards survives in part; it was often used later as a basis of taxation, but from 1291 the valuation, known as the *Taxatio Papae Nicholai*, published by the Record Commission in 1802, became the basis for clerical grants to the Crown. It is the most precious survey of ecclesiastical property in the middle ages.

[2] Temporalities were first included in the subsidy offered by the clergy to Innocent IV in 1251. This was the only subsidy freely granted to the pope and was intended to buy the removal of grievances occasioned by Archbishop Boniface's attempts to meet the financial embarrassments of the see of Canterbury.

[3] The king's advisers issued a royal letter to the bishops, &c., calling attention to the papal injunction (*Rotuli litterarum clausarum*, ii. 152).

1272, at the instance of Gregory X, a biennial tenth was granted by the prelates, possibly with the consent of the lower clergy, towards the expenses incurred by Edward and his brother on their passage to the Holy Land.[1] The mandatory taxes of 1250–5, originally levied to pay for Henry III's projected crusade, were afterwards applied to meet the expenses incurred by the pope after the crown of Sicily had been granted to the Lord Edmund. The triennial tenth of 1266–9 was granted by Pope Clement IV at the request of the king to remedy the damage caused by the recent disturbances, and was given effect by the legate Otto-buono. The crusading taxes of 1276 and 1291 were earmarked for King Edward's expenses on his projected crusade, and the proceeds, though retained by the papal agents, were not permitted to leave the country. Only the papal subsidies levied between 1239 and 1247 as contributions to the needs of the pope during his conflict with the emperor brought no profit to the Crown or the realm, and naturally it was these which aroused the most widespread hostility and for a time (1244–6) united king, baronage, and clergy in a common resistance. All combined to insist that papal taxation without the previous acquiescence of the king was contrary to custom.[2] Laity and clergy were at one in the defence of the rights of patronage and the local obligations of clergy to their flocks or of monasteries to their spiritual undertakings. King Henry III, however, was compelled to desist when the pope threatened him with an interdict; opposition crumbled, and the subsidies were collected. A few years later the king took the cross, and welcomed papal aid. He found, it is true, that his Sicilian enterprise, to the pursuit of which his crusading vow was converted, would cost him far more than he could recover from the papal taxes, and was compelled to come to terms with his barons in 1258; but once relieved of the Sicilian incubus he turned to the pope as his deliverer. Henceforward, until the death of Edward II, the king was the immediate or ultimate beneficiary from papal mandatory taxation.

Until 1291, apart from the tax of 1266, this was, indeed, taxa-

[1] This was the last papal subsidy, as distinct from mandatory taxation, in our period.

[2] Cf. the royal letters forbidding the Cluniacs to exact, by papal grant, a tenth from the rectors of their English churches without the king's consent (*Close Rolls, 1237–42*, p. 174 (2 Feb. 1240)). For the joint action against papal demands in 1244–6 see the summary in *King Henry III and the Lord Edward*, i. 355–60.

tion for the benefit of a crusader; but when the Scottish troubles
had led to war in Scotland and across the Channel, and it became clear that King Edward could not fulfil his vow, Pope
Boniface VIII divided the proceeds of the crusading taxes with
him. The pope went farther. In 1301 he used his mandatory
powers to impose upon the English clergy a tenth for three years
for the joint benefit of the English realm and the Holy See. His
successors Clement V and John XXII continued this policy. At
first the papal intention was not given explicit form. In 1301
Boniface VIII described his tax as an aid to the Holy See in its
Italian difficulties; Clement V defined his first exaction (1305)
as a contribution to the needs of the Holy Land, whose rescue
was still the enterprise dearest to the old king's heart;[1] but no
conditions were imposed. In 1301–2 Edward I made sure of his
interest in the proceeds by asserting an artificial claim to the
exclusive control of the taxation of the temporalities of the
clergy. The papal subterfuges were not long maintained. Edward got two-thirds of the triennial tenth levied in 1301—some
£42,000. His son received 92 per cent. of the taxes levied in his
reign—nearly £180,000.[2] These transactions surely provide the
most striking example of papal and royal co-operation in
English history. They evaded the legal objections to taxation.
The pope recognized that the king could not pay his way without the aid of the clergy, the king took full advantage of the
acquiescence of the clergy in the mandatory power of the pope
to tax them; but the king got much the best of the bargain. He
avoided the necessity to consult the clergy, who had caused him
so much trouble between 1294 and 1297; he left to the papal
organization the main burden and much of the odium caused
by the taxation; and he got the lion's share of the proceeds.
The papacy paid dearly for the plenitude of its power.

Under these circumstances papal finances during the two
centuries which preceded the Reformation naturally tended to
depend in England upon other sources of revenue, notably
annates. The right to tax had been too hardly won in the reigns
of Henry III and Edward I, as opposition gave way to obstruction and obstruction to passive resistance; indeed, it could hardly
have been established without the approval of kings who had
taken the cross. The prolonged resistance of the clergy between

[1] Lunt, *Financial Relations*, pp. 367, 383.
[2] Lunt, in *Haskins Anniversary Essays* (1929), p. 182.

1239 and 1247 had stayed the growing demand by the pope for subsidies, though they were granted in the end. The taxes levied for the Sicilian enterprise had brought the clergy together in frequent convocations as they had never been before. The development of clerical representative assemblies was a reaction to papal as much as to royal demands; hence we cannot, until Edward's reign, distinguish between these demands in our consideration of it. Henry III asked for clerical grants from spiritualities without seeking papal consent only in 1254 and 1269;[1] Edward I got six grants of this kind.[2]

The lines of development in Henry III's reign can be discerned in general, in spite of much confusion and many gaps in the evidence. The bishops and prelates, present in the great council of the king, might be asked to contribute to his needs from their spiritual as well as their temporal possessions and to comprise the whole clergy in their grant; or a mandate from the pope might be announced in a great council. Preliminary discussions of this kind can be discerned as late as 1267 and 1269; but by this time they were no more than preliminary. Discussion was referred to the dioceses and provincial assemblies. King John had consulted diocesan assemblies of clergy,[3] and in 1226 Henry III and Archbishop Langton contemplated the use of such assemblies in the enforcement of the papal mandate of February 1225, which required the clergy to provide the king with a subsidy.[4] They appear to have intended to leave the amount of the grant to local decision. Earlier in the year, however, a national church council, to which, in addition to bishops, non-exempted abbots, priors, deans of cathedral and prebendal churches and archdeacons, proctors of cathedral and prebendal chapters and of religious houses had been summoned, had rejected the proposal of Pope Honorius III that permanent

[1] See Powicke, op. cit., ii. 483, and Lunt, 'The Consent of the English Lower Clergy to Taxation during the Reign of Henry III', in *Persecution and Liberty*, essays in honour of George Lincoln Burr (New York, 1932), pp. 152, 158–9, and notes. A tenth levied in 1264, granted by the Montfortian bishops and prelates to meet the danger of invasion, and a twentieth arranged in 1267 by the legate and prelates to provide aid for the disinherited, were exceptional, and on neither occasion does the clergy as a whole seem to have been consulted.

[2] Six, if calculated on a national and not a provincial basis: in 1279–80, 1283–6, 1290, 1294, 1295, 1297. In addition he exacted a fine, equivalent to a fifth, earlier in 1297.

[3] Reply of the bishop of Salisbury to a letter from Archbishop Hubert Walter: Hist. MSS. Commission, *Report on MSS. in Various Collections*, i (1901), 233–4; *Rotuli litterarum patentium*, i. 71, 72.   [4] *Rotuli litterarum clausarum*, ii. 152.

provision should be made for the maintenance of the Roman Church.[1] The unprecedented summons of proctors had probably been suggested by the constitution of a French assembly which had met at Bourges in the previous year to consider the papal request; for, as the main demand was for the reservation of a prebend in every cathedral and collegiate church, the chapters were the parties most nearly concerned. The Salisbury chapter, a particularly learned and alert body of men, well aware of these facts, pressed for a similarly constituted council to reply to the papal request for a subsidy to meet the needs of the king. Archbishop Langton acted on the suggestion. A provincial council was convoked for 13 October in London; the proctors came with their instructions; and a grant of a sixteenth of the revenues of all churches was made, on the condition that the tax, a free gift, should not become a precedent.[2]

'Here we have the earliest example of a provincial council called, at the instance of the clergy themselves, for the sole purpose of considering the grant of a subsidy',[3] and further, in striking contrast to the incoherence of outlook which generally prevailed, the procedure adopted was due to a purposeful clarity of thought. The Salisbury chapter, in its deliberations, stressed the connexion between consent and the concern which required it, and the importance of provincial agreement rather than of diocesan variety in the answer to the papal and royal demand. Later developments, tortuous though they were, were in line with the advance made in 1226. They resulted in the comprehension within the conciliar system of the diocesan clergy, first through the archdeacons as their proctors, then through proctors of their own. Local consultations in decanal, archidiaconal, and diocesan gatherings gradually led to the representative system. It is true that the legate Otto met groups of rectors in 1240 and that proctors of the clergy appeared before the great council in 1254,[4] but this sort of consultation soon became as casual as

[1] For this see Powicke, op. cit. i. 346–8.

[2] The authority here is the documents in the *Register of St. Osmund* (Rolls Series, 1883–4), ii. 46 f., 55 ff. This is a Salisbury register. See also Armitage Robinson, op. cit., pp. 86–89; Lunt, *Consent*, pp. 120–3.

[3] Armitage Robinson, p. 89.

[4] Lunt, *Consent*, pp. 141–4. This was the occasion when the regents in England summoned knights of the shire and discreet men from each diocese (proctors appointed in diocesan assemblies) to appear before the king's council. The church was asked to agree to the diversion of a crusading tenth to meet the needs of the king in Gascony. A Durham memorandum, cited by Lunt (from B.M. Stowe MS. 930)

Henry III's financial tour of the monasteries in 1235.[1] The bishops, if they did not always assert their duty to take diocesan opinion before pledging it to contribute to a subsidy, developed a sense of their moral obligation to do so;[2] while the clergy themselves learnt, in their synods, how to give forcible expression to their rights.

Hence the next step forward was made in 1256, during the discussions with the papal collector Rostand about the taxes, graces, and other revenues with which the church was charged to pay for the Sicilian enterprise. Rostand met the prelates in October 1255; the discussion was adjourned and another council was summoned for 18 January 1256. During the interval meetings of the lower clergy met in each archdeaconry, elected proctors, and gave them instructions. Probably they also drew up the local lists of grievances addressed to the pope, of which those from the diocese of Lichfield and the archdeaconry of Lincoln are preserved in the Burton annals. The convocation of January comprised bishops, abbots, priors, archdeacons, deans of cathedral churches, proctors of cathedral chapters, and proctors of the lower clergy from each archdeaconry. 'Thus the representatives of the lower clergy came to a provincial or national convocation for the first time of which we have record.' A delegation, headed by the dean of St. Paul's, was appointed to act on behalf of the whole church in England in an appeal to the pope. The complaint by the beneficed clergy of the archdeaconry of Lincoln that the pope had granted a tenth of their benefices to the lord king without summoning those whose obligations to pay required their consent states the underlying justification of the appeal.[3]

There were many men with grievances in these critical years, the years of Archbishop Boniface's constitutions and the petitions of the barons. Reform was in the air; political reflection was stirred. The lower clergy, it is true, were represented by the archdeacons, if at all, during the next ten years;[4] but their

---

shows that 'representatives of the lower clergy met with the king's council and leaves little doubt that they exercised true representative functions' (Lunt, p. 144).

[1] Powicke, op. cit. i. 306–7.

[2] As in 1247; see Matthew Paris, *Chronica majora*, vi. 144 (in the Liber Additamentorum).

[3] Here the conclusions reached by Lunt are followed (*Consent*, pp. 144–7). For the lists of grievances of the lower clergy see *Ann. monast.* i. 360–3 (annals of Burton).

[4] In 1257 local discussions were continued and the archdeacons were required to

proctors were probably at Bury St. Edmunds in February 1267, and were certainly active during the negotiations about a clerical aid in 1269–70. However they were represented the practice of local consultation of the clergy as part of the discussion of a tax was almost as firmly established by 1272 as was the power of the pope to impose taxation. In the face of papal authority clerical debate had been 'merely exercise in dialectic',[1] but it prepared the way for the representative assemblies which discussed the aids granted directly to the king in the time of Pecham and Winchelsey; and so for the last stage of development in the history of convocation, reached in the later fourteenth century—namely, the presence of clerical proctors in all provincial councils, and the formation of a 'lower house' of convocation.

Archbishop Kilwardby is sometimes supposed to have summoned proctors of the parochial clergy to provincial assemblies for the first time, and not on financial business, but to deal with the spiritual needs of the Church.[2] This opinion rests on a misconception. As we have seen, clerical proctors were summoned in 1256 and 1269, if not on other occasions. Moreover, Kilwardby's first assembly in 1273, summoned to deal with the state of the Church, was attended not by clerical proctors but by three or four leading clerics of each diocese chosen by the bishop who brought them; and for the simple reason that the purpose of the council was almost certainly to respond to Pope Gregory's request to the archbishops of Canterbury and York for reports about the moral state of their clergy and the best ways to improve it. As is well known the pope circulated requests at this time in preparation for the forthcoming General Council at Lyons. The papal bulls were issued in March 1273 and Kilwardby sent out his writ on 7 September.[3] His second council, summoned for 14 January 1278, was called together to deal with the exactions of the papal nuncio and general collector, Geoffrey of Vezzano, who had a papal commission to collect the goods of intestate clerks. This was a financial matter directly affecting

treat with their clergy and come to the convocations of this year with procuratorial powers (*Ann. monast.* i, pp. 389, 401–5).   [1] Lunt, *Consent*, p. 149.

[2] Armitage Robinson, p. 96. The writs are printed in the *Select Charters* (9th ed.), pp. 446–7.

[3] *Registres de Gregoire X*, ed. Guiraud (fasc. i; 1892), no. 220, p. 91. The writ of summons does not refer to the papal letter, but its contents and date are consonant with it.

the local clergy. No peculiar significance need be seen in the summons of proctors of the whole clergy of each diocese to this council.[1]

Archbishop Pecham was required to consider the king's financial needs in the Michaelmas parliament of 1279.[2] A grant from the clergy had been mooted four years earlier, and the new archbishop, in view of the Welsh war, now actively supported the king's request. It was discussed in diocesan assemblies, convoked by the bishops in both provinces. Since the northern dioceses granted a tenth for two years and the clergy of the southern province a fifteenth for three years, some guidance in the matter had presumably been given and some joint action taken by the bishops before the grants were made. Two conditions were attached to the grants: the valuation of Norwich, not the new assessment for the papal tenth of 1274, was to be followed; and the clergy who were paying the current lay subsidy granted in parliament were not to be required to contribute from the same temporalities to the clerical subsidy. The collection of the subsidy was made by collectors who were appointed by the bishops, and were required to put the proceeds in safe places, whence they were collected by the king at Carlisle and London for delivery to the wardrobe, the administrators with the armies in Wales, or the king's agents, the merchants of Lucca, as the case might be.[3] The evidence gives the first clear picture of the way in which a clerical subsidy granted to the king, without papal intervention, was collected, stored, and distributed. Indeed, this was the first effective tax of its kind.

While the fifteenth was still being collected, the Welsh rebellion of 1282 put an unexpected strain on the royal finances. Edward was desperately engaged, and he took desperate measures. In June 1282 he sent out John Kirkby on his famous

[1] Above, p. 471.

[2] Above, p. 478. See H. S. Deighton's paper on clerical taxation by consent, 1279–1301, in *E.H.R.* lxviii (1953), 161–92. This paper is part of an unpublished thesis which I was allowed to see.

[3] The grant was discussed in a provincial congregation in January 1280, and generally granted before 3 November, when Pecham ordered the appointment of the diocesan collectors (*Epistolae*, i. 79–80, 145). In May 1282 he ordered the collectors to implement a royal mandate for the concentration of the proceeds in London under the supervision of John of Berwick, the king's clerk, or his agents, there to be delivered to the merchants of Lucca (i. 359–60). Of course, much money had been paid over to the king before this date, and the collection went on till 1285.

begging tour for gifts and loans to be reckoned against a future subsidy. Kirkby scraped together some £16,500.[1] In 1283 the king laid hands on sacrosanct treasure, some £40,000 of the crusading tenth which still lay in churches and monasteries and had not been handed over to the Italian bankers for safe custody.[2] This he was brought to return, not without expressions of penitence, after he had received a strong letter from Pope Martin IV and had a straight talk with the archbishop.[3] His action may have been due to the opposition of the clergy to a new demand for money. In the crisis of the war, on 24 November 1282 he had issued writs of summons to two assemblies, which were to meet him or his commissioners at York and Northampton on 20 January 1283. His intention was to gather in a practical and convenient way the military element (*ad arma potentes et aptos*) not yet called up, with representatives of shires, cities, and boroughs empowered to grant an aid, and, alongside these, the bishops, abbots, priors, and proctors of collegiate churches and of the lower clergy. The clerical body was to be summoned by the archbishops 'to hear and do what would be explained to them in the public interest'.[4] The writ to the two archbishops reveals remarkable indifference to ecclesiastical traditions. The clergy were to appear before the king's officials, they were given no opportunity to discuss the royal requirements in their dioceses, they had no full powers, and they were to do what they were told. Edward's action, in fact, shows how grave a view he took of the situation in Wales and how determined he was to crush the rebellion. Pecham, who had recently been negotiating with the Welsh, was well aware of the king's position, though when he received the royal writ at Hereford he also knew of Llywelyn's defeat and death near Builth.[5] He reluctantly circulated the writ through the bishop of London (28 December); but no adequate response to the demand for aid was given at Northampton. Only a small number of the clergy appeared, the writ of summons was clearly irregular, and all who were present agreed that the business must be referred to an assembly of the whole province after

---

[1] King Edward, in letters of acknowledgement, pointed out that the withdrawal of the army from Wales because of lack of funds must be avoided at all costs (*Select Charters*, p. 457).

[2] Lunt, *Financial Relations*, pp. 330–6. In May 1282 a sum of about £60,000 was deposited with the Italian bankers.   [3] *Epistolae*, i. 548, 635–9.

[4] *Select Charters*, pp. 457–9.   [5] Above, pp. 427–8, and note.

formal consultations in the dioceses. So, on 21 January 1283, the archbishop at Northampton summoned a council in due form. This summons formulated 'the type of such provincial assemblies as were in after times called at the king's desire . . . for the grant of subsidies'.[1]

While David of Wales was being hunted down in the Welsh hills, the clergy met in the dioceses, chose their proctors, and drew up their objections to the king's demand—a tenth for three years—just as had been done in 1256. When the 'congregation' met at Lambeth in May the grant was refused, and a new demand was adjourned to a second assembly, to meet five months later, after Michaelmas. The clerical proctors had argued that their powers, which were limited, did not extend to the new royal *petitio*. There were new diocesan meetings and new appointments of 'sufficiently instructed' proctors of the clergy.[2] At last, after the Welsh war was over, the king got an aid—a twentieth for three years. The three dioceses of the province of York were much more dilatory, and did not fulfil their promises until 1286.[3] The clergy in both provinces had plausible grounds for hesitation. They were still paying the taxes granted in 1280 and had not ceased to be worried by the arrears still due of the sexennial crusading tenth. They realized, as never before, that the king asked their help to meet the cost of a war in which Christian blood would be shed. And they knew enough about the papal part in the conflict between Charles of Anjou and Peter of Aragon to fear, or to profess to fear, that new papal demands might be made upon them; hence, they urged, they dared not grant a subsidy without consultation with the pope.[4] As events were soon to show, their fears of being caught between the claims upon them of the royal needs and of papal authority were more justified than they could have

---

[1] *Epistolae*, i. 486–8, 508–9; Armitage Robinson, op. cit., pp. 99–102. The royal commissioners at Northampton were the king's cousin, Edmund of Cornwall, the abbot of Westminster, who was the treasurer, and John Kirkby (*Epistolae*, i. 501–2).

[2] Ibid. i. 536–7, 594–5. The second letter shows that the May congregation, as Pecham describes it, met at Lambeth, not, as originally intended, at the New Temple (p. 537).

[3] The York convocation, to which Durham adhered later, granted a triennial thirtieth in reply to a letter from the king, reminding the archbishop of its earlier promise (*Foedera*, i. ii. 673; *The Records of the Northern Convocation* (Surtees Soc.), pp. 11–17; *Concilia*, ii. 127).

[4] The proctors gave the replies at Lambeth *in scriptis* (*Epistolae*, p. 536). These survive in the annals of Dunstable, *Annales monastici*, iii. 295–6.

realized in 1283. In September 1294, some months before the new archbishop, Winchelsey, had arrived in England, the king summoned the clergy to an assembly by royal writ, and made his startling demand for a half of their revenues. In 1295 he elaborated in formal and systematic fashion his idea of associating clergy and laity in parliament for purposes of taxation; and in February 1296 Boniface VIII issued the famous bull, *Clericis laicos*, which brought the archbishop and clergy into the violent political crisis of 1297. Pecham had to face nothing like this. In 1283, without any strains or difficulties, and with no sense of novelty, he relaid the foundations of convocation. In 1290, after the king's return from Gascony, he arranged, in accordance with the procedure of 1283, the diocesan and provincial consideration of a subsidy which, as contemporary evidence is sufficient to show, was granted in cheerful gratitude for the expulsion of the Jews. He died in December 1292.

The ecclesiastical crises of 1294–7 are inseparable from the history of those stormy years, which will concern us later. We may notice here that in Edward I's reign clerical insistence upon the grant and collection of clerical subsidies on a diocesan basis was not inconsistent with, but, on the contrary, was given greater effect by royal control. When convocation had granted the tax, the bishop of each diocese took charge; until 1290, if not later, he appointed the collectors, and henceforth co-operated with the royal administration, which, in all its dealings with him or the collectors, referred to the subsidy as granted by the diocese.[1] There was no centralized control under chief collectors such as existed in the case of papal taxes, which, however much the secular authorities might intervene, were subject to papal authority. This procedure, while it retained its ecclesiastical character, naturally led to increasingly close supervision by the exchequer, and especially after 1290, when lay subsidies and other royal revenues were brought under the more systematic cognizance of the exchequer.[2] The king began to nominate the sub-collectors, often appointing the heads of monastic houses who could provide strong-rooms for the proceeds of the tax; they were required to keep careful records, report regularly to the exchequer, and finally to submit their accounts for audit.

---

[1] This paragraph is based upon Deighton's evidence, drawn from the Exchequer and other records in the Public Record Office (above, p. 505, n. 2).

[2] See below, pp. 523–4.

On the other hand, the exchequer only once conducted the audit, which was entrusted to special auditors, and handled little of the actual cash. It was a court of record, always on the alert to check and inspect the work of the collectors, to provide assistance, and to see that the king got what was due to him, to dispose of as he wished and when he wished. Diocesan and local authorities worked together under the direction of the exchequer. Defaulters were distrained sometimes by the sheriffs and bailiffs, sometimes by ecclesiastical authorities. The experience acquired during decades of papal taxation was combined with the experience of traditional co-operation between diocesan and county authorities, until in due course, without any sacrifice of its diocesan organization, clerical subsidies became as normal an element in the national revenues as the lay subsidies were. The main difference between the two forms of subsidy was that whereas the goods of the laity were reassessed whenever a lay subsidy was granted, it became the practice after 1291 to base clerical grants upon the valuation of Pope Nicholas IV. The position of the clergy was clearly defined in 1307. Whenever lay subsidies were granted, the clergy were to pay on movables upon or issuing from lands acquired since 1291 or not taxed when clerical subsidies were levied.[1] In short, the clergy, as subjects of the Crown, became ordinary taxpayers under an assessment made at the instance of a pope to raise funds for the crusade on which King Edward had never been able to embark.

[1] *Rotuli parliamentorum*, i. 443. J. F. Willard, *Parliamentary Taxes on Personal Property, 1290 to 1334* (1934), pp. 96–102, has described the confusion which preceded this instruction.

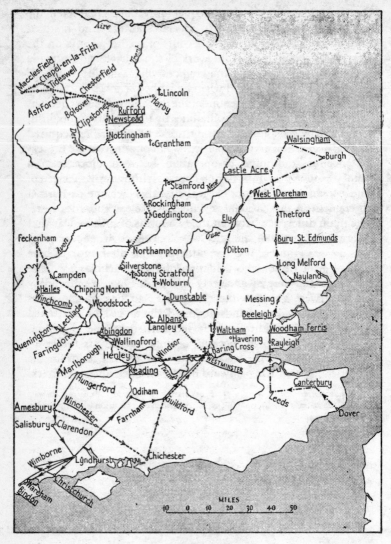

ENGLAND

SHOWING KING EDWARD'S MOVEMENTS IN 1289 AND 1290

i. Dover, Walsingham, Westminster (12 Aug. to 12 Oct. 1289). ii. Westminster, Amesbury, Salisbury, Bindon, Odiham, Westminster (15 Oct.–22 Dec.). iii. Westminster, Abingdon, Quenington, Feckenham, Woodstock, Amesbury, Winchester, Chichester, Westminster (20 Feb.–28 April, 1290). iv. Westminster, Northampton, Geddington, Macclesfield, Clipstone, Harby, where Queen Eleanor died (21 July–28 Nov.). Eleanor crosses, Lincoln–Charing Cross marked †. Monastic houses underlined.

XI

THE COMMUNITY OF THE REALM
AND TAXATION

KING EDWARD came back to England in 1289 in the height
of his fame and the maturity of his powers. He was fifty-
one years old. For the first time since his coronation he
could expatiate, move freely about, settle down to business in
long periods of parliament, and make plans for his crusade and
the future of his family and his realm. A study of his movements
between his landing at Dover in August 1289 and his parliament
at Clipstone in October 1290 suggests that these months, with
their strenuous mingling of oblations, business, and sport, were
the happiest in his reign. The death of the Maid of Norway, 'the
child of so many hopes', in September 1290 made vain his well-
ordered plans, and the death of his wife two months later
brought his happiness to an end.

The king had been anxiously awaited and was eager to return.
His cousin Edmund of Cornwall and his treasurer, John Kirkby,
now bishop of Ely,[1] had maintained the peace in England, and
rallied its military strength to crush the Welsh rebellion of 1287;
but by 1288 a restless tendency among the magnates and others
to gather in arms had caused anxiety. There had been widespread complaints of local and judicial malpractice, and the
magnates had refused to consider the grant of a much-needed
subsidy in Edward's absence. Arrears of business which required
the king's attention in parliament had been mounting up. A
settlement of Scottish affairs with English co-operation was
under active consideration. Yet there was no crisis. The king
could go to work steadily. He could divide his time between
parliaments in Westminster and a tour of his demesne, recapturing former delights in Clarendon and Lyndhurst, Quenning-
ton and Feckenham and Woodstock, Geddington and Clipstone
and Macclesfield, where he had hunted or hawked. He could

---

[1] He is said to have hurried back to his duties at the exchequer immediately after
his consecration in September 1286 (*Ann. monast.* iii. 326). He died in March 1290,
seven months after the king's return.

slip away for a fortnight to Havering, where he had gone fowling by Essex streams as a boy.[1] His court went with him: suitors and commissioners and couriers could always find him 'wherever he might be in England'. He could hold a parliament, if need be, in the heart of Sherwood forest. In 1289–90 he did all these things; but first of all he had made a pilgrimage. He had visited the shrines of saints, beginning immediately after his landing with St. Thomas at Canterbury. He had gone the rounds in East Anglia, to Bury St. Edmunds, Walsingham, Ely, and the rest. Then, when all was done, he had at last come to Westminster, in time for the feast of St. Edward the Confessor on 13 October.

It is worth while to summarize Edward's movements after his return to Westminster. In October 1289 he completed the arrangements for the hearing of complaints against judges and officials.[2] He then went to Clarendon, visiting his mother at Amesbury on his way, and stayed there for a fortnight, during which, on 6 November, the Norwegian, Scottish, and English commissioners who had been at work on the transfer from Norway to Scotland of his grandniece, the little queen of the Scots, met at Salisbury, near Clarendon, to set their seals to the agreement later confirmed by the Scots at Brigham, near Berwick (14 March 1290).[3] After a month in the New Forest and its neighbourhood Edward returned to Westminster for Christmas and the Hilary parliament, which lasted till the end of February 1290. He passed most of Lent in the upper valley of the Thames, then made a detour by Winchcombe, Hailes, Feckenham (a royal manor in Worcestershire), and Campden to Woodstock, where he spent Easter (2 April). Thence he went to Amesbury for an important family conference on the succession to the kingdom.[4] This was necessary in view of his arrangements for the marriage of his daughter Joan to Gilbert de Clare, and of his daughter Margaret to the young son and heir of the duke of Brabant, also in the event of his own death on crusade. Joan was married on 30 April, the day after the king's return to Westminster for the Easter parliament. The long Easter parliament

[1] Edward was at or near Havering for the fortnight before his daughter Margaret's wedding on 8 July 1290, during the long Easter parliament (*Itinerary*, ed. H. Gough (1900), ii. 70–71). There may have been a family gathering in the king's house there.   [2] Above, p. 362.

[3] *Documents illustrative of the History of Scotland, 1276–1306*, ed. Joseph Stevenson (1870), i. 105–11, 129–30.

[4] *Foedera*, I. ii. 742; cf. Powicke, *King Henry III and the Lord Edward*, ii. 732–3.

lasted for nearly three months, for a great many judicial cases had to be tried and settled. In this parliament Edward, on Whit Sunday (21 May), issued the so-called statute of *Quo Warranto* and, on the day of Margaret's marriage to John of Brabant (8 July), the statute *Quia Emptores*.[1] In these enactments he was at pains to satisfy the wishes of his tenants-in-chief. It is probable that he asked for a subsidy, for in June the sheriffs were ordered to send two or three knights from each shire to Westminster by 15 July to give counsel and consent to certain matters which had been under discussion; indeed, it is hard to see at what other time the fifteenth of lay movables and of the temporalities of the clergy could have been agreed upon. Moreover, the time at which the knights were to arrive coincided with that of the royal edict of 18 July for the expulsion of the Jews from the kingdom; an act of royal grace for which the grants in parliament and, later, in convocation at Ely were regarded as a thank offering.[2] Soon after this Edward set out on his third visitation of his demesne, this time to the forests of Whittlewood, Rockingham, Sherwood, the Peak, and Macclesfield. He stayed for some days at Northampton to ratify the elaborate treaty for the future marriage between his son Edward and Margaret of Scotland.[3] Two months later, towards the close of his hunting tour, he formally agreed to the plan for his crusade set out in bulls from Pope Nicholas IV.[4] This was at his hunting-lodge at Clipstone, while he was holding a Michaelmas parliament. Here he must have received a letter written on 7 October by the bishop of St. Andrews, telling him of the rumour that the queen of Scots was dead.[5]

Then, in the middle of November, came the news that his wife was ill at Harby, near Lincoln, where Edward may have left her some weeks earlier. He was with her when she died on 25 November and followed her bier for most of the way on its slow progress to Westminster.

The appointed time for the king's departure on crusade was

[1] Above, pp. 342, n., 379; for *Quo Warranto* cf. *E.H.R.* lxv (1951), 109. On the date of Margaret's marriage see J. de Sturler, *Les Relations politiques et les échanges commerciaux entre le duché de Brabant et l'Angleterre au moyen âge* (1936), p. 144 and notes.

[2] Above, p. 508. The writs for the collection of the lay subsidy were issued on 22 September from Clipstone, not in the parliament which met a month or so later, but on the king's way north.

[3] Stevenson, op. cit. i. 162–73 (28 August); below, p. 600.

[4] *Foedera*, I. ii. 747 (25 October).

[5] Ibid., p. 741.

midsummer 1293. As the problems created by the interregnum in Scotland revealed themselves he could not concentrate on his preparations and by 1294 he was too deep in difficulty to think of them. His good fortune, once praised by the poets of the Midi, deserted him. He was dogged my mischance: dark forces which no judgements in parliaments, no rapid campaigns followed by conciliatory measures could overcome, gradually beset him. At one time he was driven to fall back on the law of necessity, at another to turn to the pope for absolution from his sworn undertakings. He had no comprehension of what we call nationalism, but thought in terms of law and rights and obligation to maintain the 'state' of Crown and realm. The French, in his view, had tricked him, the Scottish lords and prelates betrayed him, the archbishop and earls deserted him. His mood hardened. He coped with the English recalcitrants, came to terms with Philip the Fair, crushed William Wallace, and drove Archbishop Winchelsey into exile, but in Robert Bruce, whose grandfather had fought on his side at Lewes, he found a new kind of enemy. He faced him and his followers, men and women alike, in a spirit of savage and ruthless exaltation.

When this arch-traitor and murderer, as he was in his lord's eyes, was crowned at Scone on 25 March 1306, Edward was a sick and lonely man. Of his old friends and advisers, only the earl of Lincoln and the ever willing Otto of Granson remained. He had able ministers, led by Walter Langton the treasurer, but none with whom he could feel the old intimacy. In this time of his weakness and emergency he turned to the young. He was well aware of the irresponsible levity of his son Edward, yet in whom could he hope if not his son and heir? Since December 1305 he had been in Dorset and Hampshire—from 1 March at Winchester. There he made arrangements for the knighthood of his son at Westminster on Whit Sunday (22 May 1306). He was carried there on a litter. It was the most splendid occasion of its kind since, in 1260, his father had knighted the young John of Brittany, who had lately died at Lyons,[1] and Edward himself had knighted the two elder sons of Simon de Montfort. Nearly 300 young men appeared to be knighted.[2] The prince held his

---

[1] On 14 November 1305, when he was killed by the fall of a wall while he was attending the coronation of Pope Clement V. His son, John of Brittany the younger (born 1266), succeeded him as earl of Richmond by royal grant in October 1306.

[2] Guisborough says 297. The list in Elias Ashmole's *Institution, Laws and Cere-*

vigils in the abbey and was knighted by the king privately and
invested with the duchy of Gascony, then knighted the rest at the
high altar in the abbey. At the feast the old king informed the
proceedings of chivalry with political significance. Two swans
were brought in and laid on the table. Edward rose and swore
'before God and the swans' to avenge the death of Comyn and
the insult to the Church; and, that done, to fight only with
infidels in the Holy Land. His son, in the general enthusiasm,
swore not to sleep more than one night in the same place till he
had reached Scotland.

The 'Feast of the Swans' has been regarded as a piece of
Arthurianism. Edward, it is said, was 'prepared to carry the
cult of Arthur to the same sort of extremes that his father had
accorded to the Confessor's memory'.[1] The 'best lance in the
world', as a southern poet had described him in 1272, had
certainly not been indifferent to the fashions and literature of
chivalry, nor to the political significance of the British history
which Geoffrey of Monmouth had given to a receptive world.
He had patronized 'round tables' and, indeed, celebrated the
conquest of Wales by a 'spectacle' of the kind at Nefyn in
Caernarvonshire, to which knights had come from far and near.
His fame as a jouster, his feasts, and especially his exploits in
Wales naturally lent themselves to romantic treatment,[2] so that
his struggle with Llywelyn, like his scrap with Adam of Gurdon
in the pass of Alton, became legendary, and was caught up and
transfigured in the courtly or popular mind.[3] How far Edward
allowed himself to live in this world of fancy and surrendered to

---

monies of the Order of the Garter (edition of 1693), pp. 38–39, gives 267 names, taken
from a roll of the great wardrobe.
    [1] N. Denholm-Young in Studies in Medieval History presented to F. M. Powicke,
(1948), p. 266. Cf. R. S. Loomis, 'Edward I, Arthurian Enthusiast', in Speculum,
xxviii (1953), 114–27. See now A. R. Wagner in Archaeologia, xcvii (1959), 127–8.
    [2] See R. S. Loomis, 'Chivalric and Dramatic Imitations of Arthurian Romance',
in Mediaeval Studies in Memory of A. Kingsley Porter (Harvard Univ. Press, 1939).
pp. 81, 92–93. Lodewijk van Velthem's fanciful narrative of Edward's wedding
feast, with round table, banquet, and play (spel), may have been suggested by the
celebrations at Canterbury in September 1299 after his marriage to Margaret of
France. It is most significant that the apparently authentic account of these in the
Annales Angliae et Scotiae (Rishanger, Chronica, ed. Riley, 1865, pp. 395–7) is copied
verbatim, with a few omissions and slight variations, from Geoffrey of Monmouth's
description of King Arthur's coronation feast in Historia regum Britanniae, c. 157,
This needs further discussion.
    [3] Edward became a Brabançon hero after 1290. Lodewijk van Velthem, the
continuator of the Flemish translation of Vincent of Beauvais's Speculum Historiale
devotes much attention to him and his Welsh wars. See Th. M. Chotzen, in the

the glamour of contemporary epic and Arthurian romance it is impossible to say. He doubtless believed in the story of Arthur, and had opened the tomb at Glastonbury in all good faith. He saw more than a symbol in his Welsh trophy, the crown of Arthur, just as he did in the cross of Neath or later in the stone of Scone. His appeal to history, when he carried back his claims to Scotland to the conquests of Brutus and his sons, was probably as sincere as his feudal interpretation of it. Yet Edward was a political realist. He lived in an age of historical propaganda and knew the value of it.[1] He was conscious of the danger latent in the mingling of the passion for tournaments with the disorderly impulses to self-help, for in his time he had drunk the heady mixture himself.[2] In his later years the danger was serious. The extravagances of Nicholas Segrave were an example of it.[3] Edward had done his best to regulate tournaments and to put down illicit assemblies of men in arms, but without much success. They could not be civilized by order. Indeed, closer inquiry might well establish the fact that in the younger generation which came to power in political immaturity after his death, the seeds of later evils were sown; and that the Scottish wars had hastened their growth. It is probable that at the feast of the swans the king sought to divert this undisciplined energy into the channels cut by his own wrath, just as, more than forty years before, he had rallied the Marcher lords against Earl Simon. Unhappily the knights who sat with him in Westminster Hall in 1306 had no strong leader, for the prince of Wales was the most unreliable of the lot.

In structure and routine the English administrative system was much the same in 1307 as it had been in 1290; yet the contrast between the group of men whom Edward had with him in Gascony and brought back with him in 1289 and the factions which began to form immediately after his death is very striking. In 1307 three earldoms had lately lapsed,[4] Devon was in suspense, eight of the rest were held by close relatives of the king.

Bulletin of the Board of Celtic Studies, vii (1933), 42–54; also G. Huet in *Moyen Age*, xvii (1913), 173–97. His narratives are nonsense, but significant, with some historical basis.

[1] This is too big a subject for discussion here; but cf. J. T. T. Brown on the origin of the House of Stewart, in *Scottish Hist. Rev.* xxiv. 265–79 (July 1927).

[2] Denholm-Young, op. cit., pp. 257–68.

[3] Above, p. 331; also Sayles, as noted above, p. 346 note.

[4] Aumale (1296), Cornwall (1300), Norfolk (1306). Salisbury, Huntingdon, and

Thomas of Lancaster, Leicester, and Derby, and the earls of
Pembroke and Richmond were Edward I's nephews, the earl of
Hereford was his son-in-law, the earl of Gloucester his grandson,
the earl of Surrey his grandson by marriage. Only the earls of
Lincoln, Oxford, Warwick, and Arundel were outside the royal
circle, and of these Edmund fitzAlan, earl of Arundel, had
married the sister of the earl of Surrey, John de Warenne.
Except the earls of Lincoln, Oxford, Pembroke, and Ulster, all
these natural leaders and hopes of the state were young men.
John of Brittany, earl of Richmond, the oldest of them, was 41,
Humphrey of Hereford was 31, Thomas of Lancaster and Guy
of Warwick were 29, the new king and his favourite Piers
Gaveston, whom he created earl of Cornwall, were 23, Edmund
fitzAlan was 22, John de Warenne 21, Gilbert de Clare, earl of
Gloucester and Hertford, 16. In the background was Roger
Mortimer of Wigmore and, through his wife, of Ludlow, a youth
of 20, already the most important lord in the Welsh Marches,
with great expectations in Ireland.[1] He was to be the first earl of
March, and the ancestor of the house of York. When Edward II
deprived the first commissions of reform of any prospect of success, and divided these hot-blooded kinsmen and advisers of his
in fluctuating party strife, he broke away from every principle of
his father's rule. He lost the leadership.

Edward I had succeeded to the throne in his absence without
difficulty. The serious situation which the earl of Lincoln and
Walter Langton had to face after his death obviously requires
some explanation. The immediate causes, especially the political
unrest between 1297 and 1307, and the conflict between the
exiled archbishop and the unpopular treasurer, will appear later.
Here we are concerned with facts more deeply rooted in Edward's
methods of government. One obvious fact is the danger latent
in the relationships between Edward and the earls. In 1274
these ties had added strength to the king: they were, indeed,
symbolic expressions of his greatness;[2] but they led to civil war

---

Winchester had lapsed in Henry III's reign; Chester had come to the Lord
Edward.

[1] Roger succeeded his father, Edmund, in 1304. He married (1306) Joan
daughter of Edward I's friend and companion Geoffrey de Geneville, who, in right
of his wife, Matilda de Lacy, had Ludlow in Shropshire and half of Meath (the
liberty of Trim). Geoffrey gave Roger seisin in 1308. Cf. the genealogical table in
Orpen, *Ireland under the Normans*, iii. 286–7.

[2] *King Henry III and the Lord Edward*, ii. 702–3.

and the deposition of his son. They neither survived personal loyalties and respect nor provided a stable basis of government, for they were dynastic rather than 'constitutional'. Henry III had begun to weave the texture when he arranged marriages in England for his half-brother William of Valence and the ladies of the house of Lusignan, established his son-in-law, John of Brittany, in the honour of Richmond, and endowed his son Edmund with three earldoms. Edward continued the process when he linked the earldoms and lands of Gloucester and Hereford by marriage and entail with the royal house, and bought the succession to the earl of Norfolk. His grandson, Edward III, followed his lead. Henceforward, until the traditions of half the great families of England were embodied in King Henry VIII, the baronage formed kaleidoscopic factions around competing members of the royal house. Its successors, continuously refreshed from the squires, merchants, and lawyers of England, produced ministers of state and, for a time, a governing aristocracy, but never again did it represent the community of the realm as it did for some twenty years under the leadership of Edward I.

Edward, apart from a watchful eye on Gilbert of Clare, does not seem to have pursued any political policy in his dealings with the baronage. The only great apanage in England was that of his brother, Edmund of Lancaster, who, like his cousin Edmund of Cornwall, served him well. His son did not become prince of Wales and earl of Chester till 1301, nor lord of Gascony till 1306, and had no independent following. Edward I's acquisitions were part of a general practice of land-jobbing, encouraged by developments in land management and access to ready money. Except in their complexity, they did not differ from the transactions of any pushing freeman in a rural manor. In short, he was trying to increase his demesne and to facilitate reversions to the Crown. His eagerness to secure the Isle of Wight before Isabella de Fors died (1293) was doubtless strengthened by strategic considerations, but the hurried sale by the dying countess was not such sharp practice as it seemed to be.[1] In some cases the king applied to his own advantage the principle of the statute *De donis conditionalibus*,[2] in others he relieved the needs of

[1] Op. cit. ii, 707–12.
[2] As originally intended; cf. Plucknett, *Legislation of Edward I*, pp. 131–2. The re-grant to Hubert de Burgh and his wife in 1239 of some of their lands is a good

a landholder who was in debt in return for part of his lands or in new enfeoffment for the tenant's life. Banstead in Surrey, Leeds castle in Kent, Bosham in Sussex, and Ellesmere in Shropshire came to him in one or other of these ways.[1] Once legal claims were ousted by prescriptive right; this was when in 1276 Gilbert de Clare's claim to the castle, town, and barton of Bristol, detained by the Crown since King John's time, was overruled by an unusually strong body of council in parliament on the ground that so long a seisin by his father and grandfather relieved the king of any obligation to reply.[2] The great port and stronghold could never be allowed to revert to private hands, and least of all to the earl of Gloucester's.

Transactions in land were, of course, not confined to the king; they were general. The money market was open to all owing to the activities of the Italian merchant companies whose operations were more fluid, more widespread, and more independent[3] than those of the Jews, 'the king's chattels'. The powerful landholder, as Edward's legislation shows, had a more mobile way of life than he had earlier in the century, more precarious if he were badly served by his stewards and agents and ran into debt, but also more dangerous to the community if he diverted his loyalties in joint ambitious enterprise. The baronial co-operation with the Crown, maintained by Edward's strong rule and immense prestige, concealed the possibilities latent in households which were supported by grants of robes, equipment, and salaries on a cash basis and which had been adapted to military ends by the king's preference for trained paid troops. Edward had provided local reserves, from which levies and volunteers could be drawn,

instance of a conditional gift, though in this the ultimate right of Hubert's son by a former wife is secured. This son, John, did not secure his own son's right when, in return for a royal grant, he surrendered his lands to the king and received them back for life.

[1] *King Henry III*, &c., ii. 703–6 for details.

[2] Palgrave, *Parliamentary Writs*, i. 6. The Clare claim to Bristol had frequently embittered Edward's relations with Earl Richard, e.g. in 1254 and 1259, and, after his death, with his son, e.g. 1262–4. In 1269 Gilbert got permission to sue his right (*Cal. Pat. Rolls, 1266–72*, p. 373).

[3] A fortnight before his death Edward was disturbed by the delay in the work on the church of the Dominicans at Leicester, founded by his dead brother Edmund, earl of Leicester. Hugh de Vienne, a king's clerk who had acted as Edmund's man of business, had left a large sum of money for this work, but his executors depended on sums held by citizens and merchants of Brabant and Lucca. The king ordered the chancellor to approach the duchess of Brabant and the *podesta* and commonalty of Lucca (*Cal. Chancery Warrants, 1244–1326*, p. 264; for Hugh of Vienne cf. *Cal. Pat. Rolls, 1273–81*, pp. 163, 436, 458).

by the military organization of the shires; and he had created the opportunity for civil disturbance when he arranged his cavalry in squadrons raised by important captains, in companies composed of a leader or banneret, knights, and squires or mounted men-at-arms. The great lord who raised a squadron for service in the Welsh and Scottish wars would enter into indentures with friends or neighbours, not necessarily his own tenants, who would provide the companies. He might contract to keep the banneret and his troop in his *ménage* or household for an indefinite time in peace and war, with robes for his knights and diet at his table.[1] Now, if we recall another type of indenture, the private treaty of alliance and defence against all save the king, such as Edward himself had made with Simon de Montfort in 1259 and Llywelyn had made with Roger Mortimer in 1281;[2] if we reflect upon the illicit tournaments or on the gatherings of gentlemen-at-arms which frightened the country in 1289; and then consider how experience in war would give strength and coherence to such extra-legal traditions, we can easily see how a wealthy and powerful man, such as Thomas of Lancaster, a cousin of the king whom he despised, could, even if he relied only on his own resources, turn a political issue into domestic strife. Just as the knights of the king's household did the staff work in a campaign, so the baronial *ménage* was a potential focus of civil war. If ready money were needed it could easily be borrowed, just as the Italian merchants advanced it to the Crown on the security of the taxes or the customs.

Old dangers take new forms in a changing economy. Under the conditions which prevailed in England during the later Middle Ages an appeal to arms degenerated into personal feuds, or, if opposition to the Crown were general, the king had to submit. Resistance to a strong king who had the confidence of his subjects was short-lived; for the more mobile the potential rebel's resources became, the more closely his interests were bound up with those of the community. In Edward I's time,

[1] For a good instance see the indenture of July 1297 between Aymer of Valence and Thomas, lord of Berkeley, in J. Bain, *Cal. of Documents relating to Scotland*, ii, no. 905; cf. Morris, *Welsh Wars*, p. 71; for another see Denholm-Young, *Seignorial Administration in England* (1937), pp. 23–24, 167–8. In general, Morris's chapter on an Edwardian army and Denholm-Young's book, especially pp. 4, 13–31, repay careful study. The first indenture so far noticed between a squadron leader and a troop commander (1287) has been printed with comments by N. B. Lewis in *Bulletin of the Institute of Historical Research*, xiii (1935), 85–89.

[2] Above, pp. 154, 427, n. 2.

though political thinkers were well aware of past and present varieties of form in the state, and of the different kinds of rule possible in kingdoms, no practical alternative to the authority of king in council could strike root. The half-hearted and transitory conception that the barons were the king's peers, or, in a more precise form, that the earls, as his *comites* or companions, had the right to meet regularly to control the king, confirms this. This doctrine, which may have had some vogue in 1258–9 and, later, among the opponents of Edward II, seems to have found literary expression in the years after 1285, the period when the investigation into franchises under writs of *Quo Warranto* aroused agitated discussion and when, in the king's absence, illicit assemblies caused anxiety, and, after the king's return, a rather unusual royal commission was hearing complaints against judges and others. It was connected with an historical fancy that when the English came to Britain a district (*comitatus*) had been given to each companion of the king, and with the more respectable claim that the followers of the Conqueror acquired independent rights in their baronies, a view taken some centuries later by the sectaries in the New Model army in their attacks on the house of lords.[1] Edward's insistence that private rights, though inviolably protected by prescription or charters, had to be legally warranted and were ultimately derived from the Crown, may well have given rise to such talk in some quarters, especially in Richard of Clare's circle. It lies behind the well-known story of John de Warenne's response to the demand 'by what warrant?', how he produced a rusty sword and exclaimed: 'The king (William the Conqueror) did not by himself subject the land: our progenitors were his partners.'[2]

The distinguished scholar and courtier Walter Burley put the argument on ground common to both king and magnates in his sensible commentary upon Aristotle's *Politics* (*c.* 1340). Burley meets the difficulty that when the prince appoints his helpers, as

[1] C. H. Firth, *The House of Lords during the Civil War* (1910), pp. 166–7.

[2] See the collected studies of G. T. Lapsley, published under the title *Crown, Community and Parliament* (1951), p. 23 and note, and, for the Warenne story, to which he gave undue credence, pp. 35–62; Helen Cam, *Liberties and Communities* (1944), pp. 173–82; Powicke, *Henry III*, &c., i. 390–1 and note; ii. 701–2, where I venture upon a possible interpretation of the disputed text, now generally regarded as an interpolation, in Bracton (cf. Lapsley, in *E.H.R.* lxii (1947), 1–19). The literary texts mentioned above are *The Mirror of Justices* and *Fleta*. Both the authors of these tracts may possibly have written them while they were in prison; see Denholm-Young, *Collected Papers*, pp. 73–74, 79, note.

political perplexities which cannot be determined by law require that he should, he naturally chooses experts as competent as himself. He makes them fellow rulers, by stressing their joint devotion to the government (*principatus*), shown in the king by his concern for the common good, and in his ministers by their devotion to him as prince, not simply as man (*talis homo*). On the principle that two eyes are better than one, government implies a number of rulers. In a kingdom this number (*multitudo*) consists of king, magnates (*proceres*), and the wise men of the kingdom, and these do as much as or even more than the king does alone (*solus*). 'This is why the king convokes parliament to deal with hard matters.' And elsewhere, in a little eulogy of Edward III, Burley states that, through the king's pre-eminence in virtue 'there is the greatest concord in the English people, because each man is content in his station (*gradu suo*) under the king'.[1] This simple exposition is closer to the facts than the conception of the state as an organism, put forward rather lightly by the baronial council in 1258, and the royalist defence of the king's rights as analogous to the rights of barons and freemen.[2] It has behind it a long and general development of thought about the criteria which should be applied by kings in council to their decisions on doubtful cases or in an emergency. Since the twelfth century theologians, civilians, and canonists had emphasized the tests of equity, necessity, and the common good as ultimate guides in political conduct. They might or might not identify these with public law. They drew no sharp distinction between judicial, legislative, and executive matters, for every kind of decision was a judgement by a court. Thus one famous civilian, Odofredo (d. 1265), treated extraordinary taxation as a legislative act, only to be resorted to if evident utility justified departure from the normal equitable standards. Others argued from the rules of law that in such circumstances private and public interests are identical, so that special privileges and immunities, which are based on agree-

---

[1] The passages summarized are quoted by S. Harrison Thomson in his paper on Burley's commentary contributed to *Mélanges Auguste Pelzer* (Louvain, 1947), pp. 556–78. See pp. 570–8 *passim*. They are comments on *Politics*, bk. iii, especially chapter 16 (*ad* 1287b), on the vexed question whether the best law or the best man should rule, a problem relevant to any discussion of Edward I's statesmanship. For Burley and other commentators on the *Politics* see Conor Martin in *History*, xxxvi (1951), 29–44, especially p. 39.

[2] Powicke, op. cit. i. 389–90; ii. 470.

ments of a contractual nature, may have to be disregarded. Edward I, indeed, had high authority for his actions in and after 1297. In his bull *Noveritis nos* (31 July 1297), Pope Boniface VIII allowed that in a state of dangerous necessity, King Philip the Fair might, if he were supported by a majority of his counsellors and were satisfied *in foro conscientiae* of its gravity, proceed to demand a subsidy from clergy and laity alike, but only for the period of emergency. Archbishop Winchelsey made this rule his guide in his relations with King Edward.[1]

Taxation, indeed, was the crucial problem. We have already seen how, by way of understandings between pope and king, the clergy were brought into the fold to be shorn.[2] The lay subsidies became a normal source of revenue in a more domestic way. They were an expression of a social unity which they did much to create. They were taxes, not on land, but on the goods or movables of all members of the community except the king at one end and those whose goods were valued at less than a certain minimum at the other end of the social scale. Other exemptions were due to particular reasons or special favour; thus the men of the Cinque Ports and other ports would be exempted because they contributed to the building of the king's ships; and active service in the army was a natural ground of exemption. The tax levied on the value of the goods assessed varied in Edward's reign from a ninth in 1297 to a thirtieth in 1283 and 1306–7. There were nine such taxes in the thirty-five years of the reign, two before 1290, seven between 1290 and 1307. In 1290 a most important change, suggesting, though not due to, an intention that this extraordinary levy had come to stay, was made in the process of collection. Hitherto a tax of this kind had come only casually within the purview of the exchequer. Its proceeds had generally been set aside for a special purpose. It had been collected in various places, and paid out, as required, to those concerned or into the king's wardrobe or to his foreign bankers, only occasionally into the treasury.[3] In 1290, after

---

[1] See Gaines Post, 'The Theory of Public Law and the State in the Thirteenth Century', in *Seminar*, an annual extraordinary number of *The Jurist*, vi (Washington, D.C., 1948), 42–59; and C. C. Bayley, on the political philosophy of William of Ockham, in *The History of Ideas*, x (New York, 1949), 199–218. Ockham, like Burley, had grown up in England in the later years of Edward I and had known England in Edward II's reign.

[2] Above, pp. 505–9. In 1290 and 1301 the goods on all temporalities of the clergy were assessed for the lay subsidy.

[3] Above, p. 32. Henry III's non-observance of the conditions of levy and

Kirkby's successor, William March (*de Marchia*), had become treasurer, the tax granted in this year was placed under the direct control of the exchequer. This was part of a larger plan. While he was in Aquitaine the king had realized the need for a financial organization of the duchy independent of the seneschal, centralized at Bordeaux; and his decision, after his return to England, to make the exchequer in Westminster responsible for all the income of the Crown was doubtless influenced by his experience in the south.[1] The new policy was not always effective but its results in the case of taxation were both immediate and lasting. Henceforth the proceeds of the lay subsidies were paid into the treasury either in cash or receipts for cash which had been paid elsewhere in accordance with writs of assignment or other writs; records of receipts and expenditure were kept by the officers of the lower exchequer on their receipt and issue rolls; the final audit was made in the upper exchequer. The subsidies became the most important of the 'foreign' accounts administered by the exchequer.[2]

The most striking fact revealed by a general survey is the absence of local opposition to the assessment and collection of these subsidies. Here and there a steward tried to prevent the intrusion of the taxers into the lands of his lord; now and then minor disturbances are recorded; but there would seem to have been no serious resistance. On the other hand, as the subsidies became more frequent, the proceeds decreased. While the fifteenth of 1290 brought in nearly £117,000, the ninth of 1297, a much heavier tax, brought in only £34,419. Of course, there was a great difference between the grateful mood in which the fifteenth

---

expenditure of the thirtieth granted in 1237 was long remembered against him. He himself had the proceeds centred in various places, including the Tower of London, Nottingham, Bristol, for delivery to his officials as he should determine (*Close Rolls, 1237–42*, pp. 116–18). [1] Above, p. 300.

[2] J. F. Willard, 'An Exchequer Reform under Edward I' in *The Crusades and Other Historical Studies presented to Dana C. Munro* (New York, 1928), pp. 225–44. On the whole subject Willard's book, *Personal Taxes on Personal Property, 1290–1334* (1934), is fundamental. Earlier he had published a celar and helpful summary in the *Annual Report of the American Historical Association for 1917* (Washington, 1920), pp. 281–92. The reform of 1290 gave necessary oversight to the practice of diverting and assigning expenditure before the proceeds of taxation could reach the exchequer, just as the audit there dealt with all the revenue for which the sheriffs had to account, however it was expended. During the Scottish wars, the sheriffs paid largely into the wardrobe or, in the north, spent much themselves under royal writs; but the exchequer audit continued to be thorough; see Mabel Mills, 'Adventus vicecomitum, 1272–1307', in *E.H.R.* xxxviii (1923), especially pp. 350–4.

of 1290 was granted and the war-weariness and impatience with which the ninth—the heaviest and last of four annual taxes—was received. Moreover, in 1297 the method of assessment was changed. The valuation was made by sworn men of each vill, not, as had previously been the practice, by twelve men of the hundred who valued the goods of every tenant in every vill with the assistance of the reeve and four men of the vill. With one exception, in 1306, this easier method continued until the process of assessment ceased in 1334, to be replaced by a fixed payment, and, as time passed, multiples of payment, from each unit of assessment, that is, each vill and borough. The change made in 1334 was a temporary expedient to avoid corrupt practices; but the careful allocation made by collective agreement in this year between officials of the exchequer and the localities endured for nearly three hundred years.[1] It is easy to imagine the state of things which made the adoption of a fixed and unchangeable sum such a relief to the central authority. Between 1275 and 1332 the country had been subjected eighteen times to a searching visitation. Chief taxers in each shire had had to arrange for the assessment of the goods of every householder, in every grade of society. They had been provided with detailed but variable and perplexing instructions about taxable goods and the goods exempt from taxation, instructions which they must interpret as best they could in the light of customary regard for the maintenance of life and for standards of living.[2] Most of the local assessments, made by neighbours, were beyond the cognizance of the chief taxers. Their writs and returns, priceless to the social historian, are also so full of anomalies that only rough-and-ready principles can be deduced from their precise details. Behind the scenes, where peasants and burgesses wrangled about what should or should not be taxed of their stores and clothes and household utensils, peace can only have been preserved by timely concessions and convenient oversights. Yet, in the course of Edward's reign, over £400,000 were raised from lay subsidies.[3] How was it done?

[1] Willard, *Personal taxes*, pp. 5, 57–58. The last grant of tenths and fifteenths on the assessment of 1334 was made in 1624.
[2] Willard, op. cit., pp. 72–86, where the importance of maintaining *contenementum*, the means of livelihood or social position, is stressed, as a probable guide to interpreting the instructions to taxers.
[3] This is J. H. Ramsay's total, which should be regarded as indicative, not as exact (*Revenues of the Kings of England, 1066–1399* (1925), ii. 87). Willard compiled

There can be no doubt that, beneath all their grumbling and evasions, these lords, knights, burgesses, and peasants had become aware of a common obligation. Their acquiescence was certainly not a form of inertia; its roots lay deeper than any respect for the constitutional niceties which may perplex the historian, for very few of them could have had even the vaguest ideas about such matters. They inherited the silent garnered experience of centuries in the common life of home, village, parish church, market, hundred, and shire; they had learned that the natural and ordered activities in which they shared, in the fields, in the courts, on juries and commissions, in watch and ward, on hue and cry, were but parts of a greater whole and subject to a wider loyalty, to whose calls they must respond, as they responded when their landmarks were removed or a felon was at large. They were susceptible to propaganda as they were to the influence of local loyalties, feuds, and passions. And when, through sheriffs and tax collectors, the king took them into his confidence, he had this in mind. Neither he nor those whom he addressed had any precise conceptions of representation or consent, in the sense foreshadowed by the canons of Salisbury in 1225[1] and emphasized by later historians. That the talk in and after the meetings of the courts in which the representatives of shires and boroughs were selected was important in the history of political education nobody should deny; but the primary intention of the royal writs was to state how and why something was to be done, to associate the future taxpayers with the government and, as far as possible, to enlist loyal support in the interests of the common good. The widespread application throughout western Europe of the legal principle that those concerned in a matter should concur in what was done had meant this, though, especially in ecclesiastical quarters, it might mean a good deal more. The representatives who came to parliament with full powers came to 'hear and do what was necessary for the common convenience of the realm' (1300) or, as in 1295, 'to do what then should be ordained *de communi consilio*' to meet the dangers which threatened the realm. We do not know exactly how they did this, or to what extent they were given or took the opportunity to make themselves better informed and to express their opinions, short of formal sessions and

detailed tables of shires, without totals; 'The Taxes upon Movables in the Reign of Edward I', in *E.H.R.* xxviii (1913), 317–21.   [1] Above, p. 502.

votes.[1] They did enough to justify the statement that they had
granted an aid. Then in the writs appointing tax collectors and
the writs ordering the sheriffs to help the collectors, the consent
of the various classes of the community to a 'gracious' or
'courteous' subsidy was described, 'as if to remind a reluctant
population that they are committed by their representatives to
the payment of the tax'.[2]

It is essential to bear in mind the intense activity of contemporary political thought and propaganda about the state.[3]
Court circles in England did not move in dignified seclusion,
adorning their speech and parchments with stray tags of rhetoric
picked up from casual acquaintances. They were no more in-
venting institutions unknown elsewhere than the masters of
Oxford were imbibing an insular learning. The independence
which gave peculiar qualities to English scholarship, art, architecture, and, most of all, to English law was grounded in ever-
changing traditions always responsive to the wider world of
which England was a part; it is all the more significant just because Englishmen shared a cosmopolitan experience. Edward's
propaganda, for example, was mainly confined to his writs;
whereas in the France of Philip the Fair we find sermons and
manifestoes. Both he and his cousin of France, however, understood the use of local negotiations to create opinion favourable
to taxation, or rather, in his case, to greater efforts in the
common interest.[4] Philip or his agents encouraged appeals to
patriotism and the will to die for a 'mystical body' of which all
clerks and laymen were living members; Edward hammered
away about necessity and the common good, or the dangers
which lurked in treacherous Welsh and disloyal Scots; though he
did at times talk about Philip's alleged intention to wipe out

[1] As intelligent and experienced men, they talked, and after they reached home
talked more. Such phrases as 'congregati et super premissis tractatum habentes,
unanimiter concesserunt' must mean something more than silent concurrence.

[2] R. S. Hoyt in *Speculum*, xxiii (1948), 60.

[3] The literature is too extensive to be noted here. Some idea of it may be got in
a suggestive paper by E. Kantorowicz '*Pro patria mori* in Medieval Political Thought',
in *American Hist. Rev.* lvi (April 1951), 472–92; and cf. J. R. Strayer, on the laicization of French and English society, in *Speculum*, xv (1940), 76–86.

[4] The difficulties of Philip the Fair and his successors were greater than those
which Edward had to meet. See J. R. Strayer and C. H. Taylor, *Studies in Early
French Taxation* (1939), pp. 56, 151 ff., and *passim*. Edward had no need to summon
assemblies from his towns to be harangued and cajoled. When negotiations were
required he began with London as in 1294 and 1297 and the others followed
(Willard, *Personal Taxes*, p. 15).

the English tongue. England, indeed, was already organized sufficiently under the guidance of the common law and the co-operation in council of king and magnates; talk about a mystical body was not needed and might be dangerous, just as the idea of a higher public law, favoured by Llywelyn of Wales and, at one time, by Robert Bruce the claimant in Scotland, was altogether repugnant to the legal mind.[1] Yet the belief in a higher moral law, defined in terms of equity, necessity, and the common good, and implying a royal power superior to baronial claims, was as strongly held in England as it was in France. In the crisis of 1297 Edward, in his writs to the sheriffs ordering a military levy, asserted his duty to represent the community, and to act on such counsel as was available: 'the emergency', he continued, 'is so great and affects all and each in the realm so nearly that it is possible to wait for no man' ('ita communiter omnes et singulos de dicto regno nostro tangit quod in hoc nemini deferri potest').[2] Much can be said for the view that, as the common law had welded what is called the feudal system into the community, so, under the stress of war and taxation, the community was enlarged to comprehend the people as a whole.[3] The first signs of change can be traced in Henry III's minority;[4] but it was in Edward's reign that nationalism was born. Edward himself was no nationalist; he would probably have been shocked by the idea; but he made war with paid levies, stressed the duty of all to defend the realm, and largely relied for funds on taxes which were national in scope and incidence, and on customs on wool and wine which, so far as they fell upon English producers or consumers, were paid by the community.

Here we are brought face to face with the change which war and taxation made or, as some would prefer to say, defined in the political standing of the knights of the shire and the cities

[1] Above, p. 381; below, p. 602. The use of manifestoes to the shires by Henry III between 1260 and 1264, and by the government of 1264–5, was the result of internal dissensions and the threat of invasion from the Continent after the battle of Lewes. See *King Henry III and the Lord Edward*, ii. 421, 427, 476, 498. It is significant that the theory of the state as an organism was advanced by the baronial council of 1258 in its letter to the pope. Academic influences may have been at work (ibid. i. 387; ii. 469).

[2] *Parliamentary Writs*, i. 281, no. 4 (5 May 1297).

[3] Barnaby C. Keeney, 'Military Service and the Development of Nationalism in England, 1272–1307', in *Speculum*, xxii (1947), 534–49; R. S. Hoyt, 'Royal Taxation and the Growth of the Realm in Mediaeval England', ibid. xxv (1950), 36–48.

[4] Above, pp. 29–31.

and boroughs of the royal demesne. The latter present the easier problem.

The change in the position of the cities and boroughs is to be considered in the light of their connexion with the royal demesne and the meaning of the levy known as tallage. The most significant evidence of the change lies in the fact that, whereas tallages on cities, boroughs, and the demesne were frequent in Henry III's reign, there was only one tax of this kind in Edward I's reign (1304). Apart from this late exception Edward did what his father could not have done; he gave a more compelling force to taxation by consent. Without surrendering his right to impose a tallage on his boroughs and demesne, he merged it in a request for general subsidies which required consent. He made the subsidy on movables a normal source of revenue, and so prepared the way for parliamentary taxation granted by lords and commons. This is not to say that he and his competent advisers created parliament, as we used to be told, or deliberately forecast the future. In a time of need they adjusted circumstance to existing methods by a series of expedients. They exploited, on the one hand, the negotiable element in the compulsory tallage and on the other hand invested the ancient right of the magnates to consent to or refuse taxation with the dignity of an obligation, common to all, to serve the common good by providing the means for the defence of the realm.

Before the end of King John's reign the old boroughs, with their heterogeneous tenures, and the new Anglo-Norman royal boroughs had become part of the royal demesne and a 'mature system of taxation', under the guidance and control of exchequer, itinerant judges, and the administrative machinery of the shires, had been established. This taxation was known as tallage, once a general word interchangeable with *auxilium*, but now mainly used to describe levies on the demesne, including the royal boroughs. The attempt of the barons in 1215 to bring the taxation at least of London under the control of the common council of the realm[1] had no success, though the objection of the Londoners to be tallaged caused some trouble as late as 1255, when it was firmly overruled.[2] During Henry III's reign, when

[1] Articles of the Barons, c. 32; Magna Carta, c. 12, omitted in 1216 (*Select Charters*, pp. 288, 294, 337).

[2] For this and the value of the tallages of Henry III see *King Henry III and the Lord Edward*, i. 307–9. The king and council proved that London had paid six tallages since the relaxation of the interdict in John's reign.

general taxation was more often refused than granted by the great council and taxes on movables were rare, the right to tallage the royal cities and boroughs as part of the demesne was very valuable. It was frequently exercised as part of the continuous and strenuous policy of the Crown to make the most of the demesne by good management, inquiries into unwarranted alienation and rigorous resumption; a policy expressed in the instructions to the judges on a general eyre, in the counsellor's oath of 1257 and most emphatically in the Dictum of Kenilworth in 1266.[1]

The Dictum speaks of 'the places, rights, properties (res) and other things pertaining to the royal crown', and the last words reflect contemporary ideas and practice. Gascony, Ireland, the Channel Islands, and Cheshire were inalienable from the *Crown*; other demesnes at least pertained to the Crown and, though alienable and even marketable, were to be jealously guarded. They tended to be amalgamated with the rights and liberties which the king, so his coronation oath was interpreted, could not surrender save in the most deliberate and formal way. The word *crown* implies the king as a king, responsible for his charge, not as a private person. This idea is implicit in the king's natural desire to safeguard the interests of his demesne manors and to protect his tenants, both as sources of revenue and, increasingly, as objects under his care; as persons and lands lying outside local jurisdiction and subject only to him and his justices, so that the villeins, as his villeins, gradually acquired special privileges as villein-socmen.[2] Now, this relationship of tempered and responsible exploitation was even more important in the case of the cities and boroughs, for, as the history of many royal boroughs shows, they were agents of the Crown, as important, especially in ports like Bristol and Southampton, as were the royal sheriffs and bailiffs. Merely to exploit them, and not to

---

[1] *Select Charters*, p. 408, c. 6. On the whole subject of the exploitation and preservation of the demesne see the study of R. S. Hoyt, *The Royal Demesne in English Constitutional History: 1066–1272* (Cornell Univ. Press, 1950) especially pp. 117–22, 143–6, 156–71.

[2] Hoyt has shown that these developments began through the courts in the first half of the thirteenth century, and were not Anglo-Saxon survivals on a mythical 'ancient demesne'. The phrase 'ancient demesne' came into use later still, to describe the *terra regis* of Domesday Book and so supply a test of old demesne apart from later escheats and acquisitions. Much of this, of course, was in private hands, but the king maintained his right to tallage it or to allow its lords to do so when a tallage was levied. See Hoyt, op. cit., pp. 171–207.

recognize their citizens and burgesses as responsible human beings would have been as foolish as it would have been inequitable. Hence tallage was more than an imposition, it was a matter for negotiation, and could become a transaction, though still a charge which could not be refused. And, as a public charge subject to discussion, it could be extended to other towns, whether they were royal towns or not, as part of a general tax granted in parliament. This was what happened in the reign of Edward I.

The collectors of tallage taxed each householder separately or, more frequently, took a lump sum whose incidence was distributed by the borough authorities or the farmers of manors. In any case the process required some negotiation, evidence of which goes back into the twelfth century. The assessments for the last tallage of Henry III, in 1267–8, went on for a long time. The escheator south of the Trent, for example, was instructed to supervise the allocation of the tax in places which compounded for it in gross, lest the rich should get off lightly at the expense of the poor. The summonses issued to twenty-seven cities and boroughs to send representatives to London seem to have been issued for the purpose of consultation about the tallage.[1] The only precedent for so general a gathering of borough representatives was the summons to selected cities to attend the parliament of 1265, when the short-lived reconciliation between the baronial government and the Lord Edward was proclaimed; but the Cinque Ports and particular boroughs had, of course, occasionally been ordered to send leading burgesses to the king's court when business affecting them had to be decided.

King Edward, from the first, showed an appreciation of the cities and boroughs as elements in the community, apart from their liability to immediate taxation. In 1266 he had been entrusted with the Cinque Ports and the protection, with power to exact new customs, of the foreign merchants.[2] He had a firsthand knowledge of the Gascon cities and towns and, as an observant man, may well have realized the use made of the representative assemblies in Italy and the Latin kingdoms in the east.[3] However this may be, in his first parliament after his

---

[1] *King Henry III*, &c. ii. 503 and note. [2] Below, p. 619.
[3] In 1267 Charles of Anjou, the conqueror of the kingdom of Sicily and south Italy, was advised by Pope Clement IV to convoke the prelates and barons and local communities; and later, in a letter of rebuke for his financial levies, to call

return (Easter, 1275), when the new duty on wool was granted 'at the request of the communities of merchants', probably more cities, boroughs, and merchant towns (*villae mercatoriae*) were represented 'than in any subsequent parliament before 1500'.[1] This parliament, however, had more than the mercantile purpose, which explains the presence of persons from little market centres which never or rarely were represented again; it was intended as a demonstration of Edward's good intentions, and in this aspect reveals a new interest in the organs of corporate activity in the realm, not an intention to link the boroughs in parliament with grants of taxation.[2] This view is confirmed by the fact that while cities and boroughs were summoned by the sheriffs to send representatives to four of the latest parliaments when no subsidy was exacted, and to the assemblies of 1283 and the parliaments of 1295, 1296, 1301, and 1306, when aid *was* granted, they were not represented in the Michaelmas parliament of 1275, nor in the parliaments of 1290, 1294, and 1297, although a subsidy was granted in these years also, and was levied on the cities and boroughs as well as on the rest of the community.[3]

During the years when the need for money began to be exceptionally great (1294–7), the government wavered between direct negotiations with the boroughs and their comprehension in parliament. After 1297, though they were twice at least approached or employed separately as parts of the demesne,[4] their representation in parliament for all purposes was assured. Yet for some time after Edward died the lists of boroughs and market towns selected by the sheriffs for parliamentary repre-

together barons, prelates, and *personae egregiae* of cities and *loci salubres*, that 'tractetur forma competens, ut sciatur in quibus casibus in tuis vel alienis nominibus collecta levare valeas'. The bulls of February and July are cited by Antonio Marongiu in an article on the *curie generali* of the kingdom of Sicily, 1194–1266, in the *Archivio storico per la Calabria e la Lucania* (1950), offprint, p. 33. Manfred had summoned such assemblies in 1258 and 1265 and they were frequent in the papal states.

[1] May McKisack, *The Parliamentary Representation of the English Boroughs during the Middle Ages* (1932), p. 5. On the subject as a whole in Edward I's reign see pp. 1–23; also Willard, op. cit., pp. 9–18, and R. S. Hoyt, 'Royal Demesne, Parliamentary Taxation and the Realm, 1294–1322', in *Speculum*, xxiii (1948), 58–64.

[2] Above, p. 343.

[3] The evidence of this for the tax of 1290 is conclusive; below, p. 534.

[4] The mission of John of Droxford in 1301 (mentioned below, p. 534) and the summons to twenty-four cities and towns, including Chester, to send two men from each who were qualified to help in the organization of a new town (Berwick). They were to meet at Bury St. Edmunds on 2 November 1296; below, p. 636.

sentation and of those assessed by the taxers did not entirely coincide.[1] The crucial year was 1294, when the subsidy was, for the first time, levied at a twofold rate, a tenth from the shires and a sixth from the cities and towns of the demesne. The tenth was granted in parliament by the magnates and knights: the sixth was negotiated with the city of London, which was both a shire incorporate and the greatest town in the kingdom, and, on the strength of its example, extended to the other demesne cities and vills. It is clear that the sixth was imposed as a negotiated tallage, just as the ninth granted, under the very unusual conditions which prevailed in 1297, by the magnates and knights, was extended to the rest of the demesne after similar negotiations with London. But in the three years' interval another important change had occurred. The double rating had been extended to the whole demesne, rural as well as urban, and also to the boroughs which were held of other lords than the king. This was probably done in the full parliament of 1295, if not in 1294; it was certainly done in the full parliament of 1296. The terms of the writ announcing the taxes of 1296 state unequivocally that

the earls, barons, knights and others of our realm have conceded a twelfth of all their movable goods in aid of the war; and the citizens, burgesses and other good men of all and every city and borough of our kingdom, of the tenures and liberties of whomsoever they may be, and of all our demesnes have conceded an eighth of all their movable goods.[2]

The record of the parliament of 1306, when the fourth double subsidy of the reign was granted, goes still further. The prelates, magnates, and knights, after discussion, conceded a thirtieth; 'the citizens and burgesses and others of the king's demesne, being assembled, discussed and unanimously conceded a twentieth'. The writ for the collection of these taxes describes the grantors of the twentieth as citizens, burgesses, communities of all the

---

[1] Willard has proved and illustrated the discrepancies in his paper on taxation boroughs and parliamentary boroughs (1294–1336), in *Historical Essays in Honour of James Tait* (1937), pp. 417–35; see, e.g., his reference to Thatcham in Berkshire, p. 425.

[2] *Select Charters*, p. 431 (from the Patent Roll). Hoyt (in *Speculum*, xxiii. 60 ff.) argues, as against D. Pasquet, *An Essay on the Origins of the House of Commons* (Eng. trans., 1925), pp. 97, 219, that from 1294, when double rating first appears, the private boroughs and rural demesne were taxed with the royal cities and boroughs. His argument is not quite conclusive.

cities and boroughs of the realm and also the tenants of the demesnes.

In Edward II's reign the process of including all subsidies at both rates in parliamentary grants was completed. The final stage was reached in 1322 when the rural 'ancient demesne', which paid at the higher rate, whoever held it, was joined with the rest of the shire for representative purposes, so that the tax on it was granted not by the civic element but by 'the earls, barons, knights, free men and communities of the shires'.[1] This does not mean that the grants of subsidies in parliament had been torn from royal control, though later developments might seem to justify this view. It means rather that the Crown, which had developed the principles of representation and consent, had gradually implanted a general system of taxation upon the whole realm, as Henry II and his sons, a century earlier, had imposed tallage on the royal boroughs and demesne. It had transcended feudal distinctions.

King Edward tallaged his cities, boroughs, and demesne in 1304 in the traditional way. Royal commissions arranged the assessment with the inhabitants.[2] The cities and boroughs had not yet acquired the right to refuse a tax. Their half-way position is revealed by a series of royal writs issued from Peebles on 2 August 1301. A single levy of a fifteenth on all taxpayers had been granted in the Lincoln parliament in January, but the assessment and collection had not yet begun. The king in his necessity set on foot a local campaign of persuasion to anticipate the grant. He appointed five commissions to visit the cities and boroughs of England, and sent writs also to each place. The commissioners were given instructions how to approach the towns, also schedules containing the sums paid as contributions to the fifteenth granted in 1290, 'when the Jews were exiled'. They were told to get at least as much and more if possible. If the fifteenth of the current year (1301) were not levied, these compositions would be repaid. The royal towns were to be visited first.[3] This visitation may be contrasted with events in Ireland in the previous year, where consent, which established no precedent, was sought from all to a request for aid. In

[1] Hoyt, op. cit., pp. 63–69.

[2] *Select Charters*, pp. 497–8. The tallage brought in £2,862: Ramsay, *Revenues*, ii. 71. For disputes about tallage and the document *de tallagio non concedendo* see below, pp. 681, n. 3, 682, n. 3.

[3] *Cal. Close Rolls, 1296–1302*, pp. 461–3; Willard, op. cit., pp. 23–24, 131–2.

January 1300 Edward sought help against the 'rebels' of Scotland from the earls, barons, knights, and people of Ireland. The justiciar of Ireland, John Wogan, summoned a general parliament to meet after Easter; but, although this was to include their representatives with power to act, he decided in the meantime 'to speak with the mayors and good men of the cities and boroughs about the subsidy'. He got promises of definite sums from twenty-two towns, beginning with Drogheda, where he exhibited letters to the mayor and community from the king himself and held diligent converse with them. Yet the later discussions in parliament were unsatisfactory, for the barons and representatives of shires and liberties showed themselves very reluctant to take action. They advised the justiciar to make another tour, this time to the districts (*patriae*). They would assist him, and the magnates would then contribute with the communities. So the justiciar set out again, passing from shire to shire, and liberty to liberty. The tenants of Munster made it quite clear that their contribution was a free gift. It was not a charge on their tenements (*non occasione alicujus tenementi*) and must not be made the excuse for a custom: and this was conceded to them.[1]

Parliamentary taxation was more developed in England in 1300 than it was in Ireland. The latest English parallel to John Wogan's tours, apart from John Kirkby's travels in search of gifts in 1282, was the local activity which preceded Henry III's last subsidy (1268–70), and this was due to the fact that no tax of the kind had been levied since 1237.[2] In Ireland the formal possession by representatives of full power to act for their communities obviously might mean little; in England it was both necessary and effective. Edward, from the outset, joined knights of the shire with prelates and barons in consent to a grant of a tax on movables. He took the lead in the establishment of a principle which had been more casually recognized in 1270, when Henry's last subsidy was finally granted.[3] Moreover, every

---

[1] *Statutes and Ordinances and Acts of the Parliament of Ireland*, edit. H. F. Berry (1907), pp. 228–36. It will be noted that no assessment is mentioned. In 1292 a request for a free grant of a fifteenth had been more successful, though it was not granted without much altercation; see the document published by Richardson and Sayles in *Proc. Irish Academy*, xxxviii, Section C (1929), 144–5.

[2] *King Henry III and the Lord Edward*, ii. 564–5.

[3] Ibid., pp. 565–6.

grant but one in Edward's reign was made in a parliament to which knights of the shire were called, and, except in 1290 and 1294,[1] when they were summoned later, were comprised in the first writs of summons. The unusual assemblies summoned to York and Northampton in January 1283 consisted only of knights and burgesses armed with full powers to agree to a tax. Edward was strong enough to meet the difficulty latent in the grants of extraordinary taxation early in Henry III's reign. The prelates and magnates in a great council in 1225, 1232, and 1237 made the grants on behalf of all the tenants and subtenants on their lands, whether freemen or villeins. This concentration of consent was convenient to the Crown and enhanced the prestige of the baronial community,[2] but with the result that it empha-sized the political, non-feudal, character of the latter. It invited the co-operation, in the grant of non-feudal taxation, of free elements which owed a wider allegiance than that defined by feudal law and custom and were increasingly conscious of an independent life.

In Edward's time the magnates still spoke for all in the sense that, as counsellors of the king in parliament, they discussed requests for taxation and, in the two times of crisis (1297 and 1301), took the lead in requiring royal concessions as conditions of a grant. They alone were powerful enough to draw out the contractual understanding implied by taxation, just as in 1225 they had combined with the prelates to get a confirmation of the Charters and in 1237 and 1270 to secure formal reaffirmation of them.[3] All the same, the magnates in Edward's time were primarily the king's advisers, co-operating with him in parlia-ment, rather than feudal critics, and the knights of the shires were needed to acquiesce in their financial decisions. The events of 1297 showed that the rules must be observed by all parties to the grant—king, magnates, and knights. A tax granted by an

[1] The argument of Richardson and Sayles that the grant of a tenth in 1294 was not made in parliament (*Bull. Inst. Hist. Research*, v. 149, note) is not convincing. The circumstances were similar to those of 1290. On the development and signifi-cance of the stipulation that representatives should have full powers see J. G. Edwards's paper in *Oxford Essays in Medieval History presented to H. E. Salter* (1934), pp. 141–54.

[2] Thus, the aids for the knighting of the king's eldest son and for the first marriage of his eldest daughter, which were reserved by King John in the original Magna Carta (c. 12), became matters for bargaining in the great council.

[3] Cf. *King Henry III and the Lord Edward*, i. 35–38, 154, 298, 368; ii. 566; and above, pp. 28, 31, 222.

informal body of men in the royal chamber was resisted as invalid and its collection was stayed. The magnates in parliament insisted on the issue of Magna Carta and additional articles, and a ninth was granted in a parliament attended by magnates and knights.[1]

Historians have rightly emphasized the importance of a duly constituted parliament and have regarded the assemblies of 1283 as an exception which proves the rule; but, in doing so, some scholars have concentrated on the judicial functions as the essence of parliamentary activity, and have treated the grant of taxation as a secondary act which could be done equally well in non-parliamentary assemblies. In their view, the pleas and petitions recorded on the authentic parliament rolls compiled at the time give the measure of parliament. Parliament could function even in the absence of the barons.[2] This is true enough in the sense that in a time of parliament, for which difficult cases, petitions, and peculiarly important pleas were reserved to be decided by the king in council,[3] the transaction of business— and the most frequent kind of business—did not necessarily require the presence of any but those who were competent to attend to it; but this was not what Edward I had in mind when he used the word 'parliament'; as when, for example, he wrote about the practice of holding parliaments to Pope Gregory X in 1275 or systematized the hearing of petitions in parliament in order that he might have more time for more serious business,[4] or so frequently laid stress on his obligation to consult in parliament those who were as much concerned as he was. When he spoke like this he was thinking of the prelates and magnates whose duty it was to obey the summons to give him their counsel; and, when he summoned knights and burgesses to parliament, he did so because he wished the men of the shires and boroughs to be cognisant of some great act, like the trial of David of Wales at Shrewsbury,[5] or to give to a projected tax the authority which

---

[1] Below, p. 683. The ninth was also paid by the boroughs and demesne after negotiations with the Londoners (above, p. 533).

[2] Richardson and Sayles, 'The King's Ministers in Parliament, 1272-1377', in *E.H.R.* xlvi, xlvii, referring to the time of Edward I: 'neither taxation nor legislation is at this period normal parliamentary business' (xlvi (1931), 549); and, 'there seems no obvious reason why parliament should not function, save in exceptional circumstances, without the assistance of the baronage' (xlvii (1932), 397).

[3] Above, pp. 345 ff.

[4] Above, pp. 342, 348.

[5] Edward went so far as to say, in his writs, that he wished to discuss with his

their 'full powers' conveyed in the name of those who would
have to pay the tax.[1] We should not restrict but extend, and
extend indefinitely, the conception of proceedings in parliament
as proceedings in the king's court, and the kernel of this conception is the legal doctrine or rule that what concerns all must be
approved by all, a rule implicit in the development of the 'community of the realm'. This does not mean that the growth of
parliament was only made possible by the reception of a rule of
private Roman law, any more than that the doctors of Roman
law created the kingdoms and city-states of Europe, or the
hierarchy of ecclesiastical courts or the representative system. It
means that, in an age when legal reflection was widespread and
legal influences penetrated everywhere, certain civilized conceptions had a common currency, far more far-reaching than the
ambit of their original use; and that these conceptions expressed
and justified tendencies in thirteenth-century society. They gave
to growing institutions such as parliament and to ancient and
natural practices, like that of using a few persons to act on behalf
of a large number, a legal imprimatur and a moral sanction.[2]

The election or nomination of a few men to serve the interests
of their community goes back very far. It can be seen in the
reeve and four men of the vill, the twelve knights of the shire, the
electoral system of a borough,[3] and in the intercourse which
linked the central to local administrations; it made possible the
organization of monastic orders and of the orders of friars. These
processes, if the element of agency required emphasis, appropriated the legal idea of the proctor, the representative who, in

subjects ('cum fidelibus nostris volumus habere colloquium') what to do about
David (*Select Charters*, pp. 460–1 (June 1283)).

[1] Even the assemblies at York and Northampton in January 1283 might with
some justification be described as stages in a distributed parliament, for the writ of
summons of November 1282 reminds the shires and boroughs that the Welsh war
had been begun by the counsel of the magnates and indeed the whole community
of the realm (ibid., p. 457). The magnates were at the war and their consent to a
tax could be taken for granted. I make this suggestion to illustrate the argument,
not as a contribution to 'constitutional history'.

[2] A good instance is the doctrine best expounded by Pope Innocent IV, of the
unitas actus, that which gives validity to an act beyond fear of appeal, so that defaulters and absentees cannot hold up proceedings. The electoral body, provided
that this has been duly constituted, can proceed without the defaulters. To avoid
injustice or absurdity this doctrine had to be limited by rules about a quorum and
a legal majority if votes were taken. Cf. H. Mitteis, *Die deutsche Königswahl* (1938),
pp. 166–74.

[3] Cf. for example, the election of the portmen of Ipswich in 1200 (C. Gross, *The
Gild Merchant* (1890), ii. 117).

lawsuits, embassies, and all forms of public and private business, acted, with full or limited powers, on behalf of his employer. The knights and burgesses who represented their shires and boroughs in parliament, especially as financial agents, were required, as were local representatives sent to similar assemblies in other countries, to come to court with this proctorial power or *plena potestas*.[1] Far from making an alien intrusion, they were summoned to extend, in their humble way, the activities of the king in council in parliament. A declaration of war, an intricate piece of negotiation with a view to a treaty, the promulgation of a statute, the trial of a great man for treason, the hearing of a petition—each was an act within the jurisdiction of the *curia regis*, and so was the grant of a subsidy.[2]

The knights in the shires were most useful people. They were the mainstay of local administration, the link in judicial procedure between central and local authority, and the leading tenants of land in the community of the shire. For a few years, during the episodes of baronial control (1258–63), they had acquired political importance as local commissioners and even as sheriffs.[3] They were kept so busy in the tasks which they might legally be required to perform that many local landholders, who preferred a quieter life on their manors or holdings, shirked the responsibilities of knighthood so far as they could or did not become knights at all—a fact which gave more influence to the wealthier and more energetic knights, who tended to acquire permanent prominence in the activities of the local courts and as royal agents.[4] We still know too little about the distribution of local groups and the relations between them and the very

---

[1] Gaines Post, 'Roman Law and Early Representation in Spain and Portugal', in *Speculum*, xviii (1943), 211–32 (pp. 229–31 deal with Italian assemblies); the same, '*Plena Potestas* and Consent in Medieval Assemblies', in *Traditio*, i (1943), 355–408. Professor Post, it should be needless to say, is concerned with the influence of legal conceptions; he is not trying to make civil and canon law the parents of our institutions. The rule *quod omnes tangit*, for example, was not a 'root' of popular sovereignty, but a principle of judicial process capable of far-flung application.

[2] The story of the justiciar's financial tours to Irish towns and communities before and after the Easter parliament at Dublin in 1300 (above p. 535), is recorded on the justiciary roll under the heading *placita de parliamento* (*Statutes*, p. 228).

[3] Above, pp. 143–6, 150, 167.

[4] See Lapsley, *Crown, Community and Parliament*, pp. 9–10, and the study of a Gloucestershire group of knights early in the century, pp. 64–83. For the knights in administration see A. B. White, *Self-government at the King's Command* (Minneapolis, 1933), and A. L. Poole, *Obligation of Society in the XII and XIII Centuries* (1946), pp. 53–56.

important knights of the king's household or the growing professional class of lay estate agents, monastic stewards, and the like. We should expect to find that the summons of elected knights to parliament gave opportunities to the more active knights of the shire; and that the elections in the shire court would reflect neither the will of the sheriff nor the spontaneous desires of the body of suitors, but, rather, the interplay of local prestige, influential connexions, and a willingness to go to the king's court at the community's expense.[1] A statute of 1275 declared that elections—including presumably such elections as these—should be free from disturbance by the great;[2] while the writs to the sheriffs stipulated that those sent to this same parliament must be chosen from the more discreet and law-worthy knights of the shire. Some responsible method of election seems to be implied. In London, which was a shire with hustings as a shire court, elections from 1296 onwards, if not earlier, were made indirectly, that is, by the aldermen and deputations from the wards, acting probably on behalf of the hustings.[3] Shire elections, of which nothing seems to be known for this period, may have been conducted in a similar but less formal way. A knight of the type required was certainly not a nonentity.[4]

The summons of knights of the shire to parliament, though a significant step forward, was not so important in Edward's reign as his efforts to restore their military contribution to the life of the community. Their share in parliamentary activities was slight and casual, symbolic rather than practical, and would depend for its growth on the increasing emphasis laid upon the independence of the squirarchy of the shires. They belonged to a landholding class which represented much greater financial resources than the burgesses did[5] but had no coherent political

[1] The studies of J. G. Edwards and G. T. Lapsley on the persons elected in the reigns of Edward I and Edward II go to support the view expressed in the text: see *Essays presented to T. F. Tout*, pp. 197–214, and Lapsley, op. cit., pp. 111–45.

[2] Stat. Westminster I, c. 5.

[3] See McKisack, op. cit., pp. 14–16.

[4] In 1259, when the knights of the shires were especially prominent, the earl of Gloucester's steward, who was holding the earl's court at Clare in Essex, was unwilling, without taking counsel, to assess damages for an assault upon a knight, because he *was* a knight (*Select Cases of Procedure without Writ*, p. 96; cf. the editors' remarks, pp. clxxi–clxxii).

[5] This is indicated by the returns of taxation, as tabulated by Willard in *E.H.R.* xxviii (1913), 519–21. For example, in 1294 the proceeds of the tenth in rural Norfolk were £7,186, and of the sixth on Norfolk boroughs £1,417 (just less than 5 : 1); in 1295 in the same shire the proceeds of the eleventh were £4,716, of the seventh

power. The prospect which the baronial reformers of 1258–9 had opened to this class had soon been clouded, nor had Edward I any idea of reopening it. But Edward did realize the value of the lower gentry as a source of military strength which could be used by the Crown whether the knights and freeholders held their lands of the king or of other lords. In his forthright way he responded to social changes more effectively than his father had been able to do. As a military organizer he gave a realistic impulse to the claim that every freeholder was immediately dependent upon the Crown and shared the obligation to defend the realm. He based the claim on the plea of necessity; and unconsciously strengthened social and political tendencies which later turned the community of the realm into a national state.

A study of the distribution of land held by knight service in England in the later thirteenth century suggests that, owing to the break up and shaping of tenements, the number of persons who were knights or held lands whose value put their holders in the social class of the knights was about 3,000, or less than half the number of 'knights fees'. Of these 3,000, about half were tenants who were 'potential' knights, that is to say, might be distrained to knighthood by the sheriffs when royal policy so enjoined. Of the 1,500 actual knights, only about 500 were warriors available at any time for service in the army.[1] Since many of the 1,500 were in constant attendance upon the king as his household knights, or were attached to baronial households, the number of knights available for duty in the shires and also physically fit must, if this analysis is approximately correct, have been very small—let us say about 1,200, scattered about the shires in a population of between two and three million people. A knight who held lands in more than one shire (and there were many such holders of scattered tenements) would normally be busiest in the shire where he lived. For example, out of 101 knights who had land in Essex in 1295, only thirty-six, of whom eleven were old or ill, were available for coast-guard duty.[2] Moreover, exemption from jury service, as from other sorts of obligation, was frequently granted by the king as a favour, so that, as the barons complained in their petition in 1258, sufficient

£647 (more than 7 : 1). The parliamentary subsidies levied in Edward I's reign amounted to £400,000 (Ransay, *Revenues*, ii. 87) of which the rural contribution was probably well over £300,000. This is indirect, but illuminating, evidence.

[1] See Denholm-Young, essay on the knights in his *Collected Papers*, pp. 56–67. His estimates are, of course, tentative. [2] Ibid., pp. 62–63.

knights were sometimes not available to form a 'grand assize' in the king's court. From our point of view the obvious way to meet the difficulties of shortage was to make a property qualification, not military rank, the ground of public service and this was sometimes explicitly enjoined upon, and, we may suspect, more often attempted by, judges and sheriffs, just as the knights of the shires in parliament in the fourteenth century were not all 'girded with the sword'.[1] The standing of this small group of leaders in 'county society' will, it would seem, tend to be measured by their local activities and relationships rather than by prowess in war or intermarriage with the great families of the land. Their feudal obligations, apart from their duty to the Crown, will be confined to rents and a few suits of court and occasional aids.[2] They will be merged in the larger body of the gentry like the knights of parliament from Bedfordshire in the fourteenth century, conspicuous only for the amount of time they devoted to local administration 'as justices of the peace and of array and of *oyer et terminer*, and as assessors and collectors of taxes. . . . Living and working in the country, they knew thoroughly its needs and the temper of its inhabitants and were the best intermediaries between the crown and the people they represented.'[3] All this is true, but it is not the whole truth. The knights of the shires were still regarded as warriors.

The social developments which combined to break down the graded system of knight service in return for the tenure of lands —a system which was never so neat as its apparent artifice suggests—cannot be separated from the military changes which gradually produced the Edwardian armies. The two movements affected each other. Legally the system remained intact: the royal licence was required for alienations of lands held in chief of the Crown if the services due to the Crown by the donor would be affected.[4] When the king granted a manor with its appurtenances he normally retained the knight service due to

---

[1] Stubbs, *Const. Hist.* iii. 410–16. In Edward II's reign 'fifty per cent. of the knights of the shire sent to parliament were not knights at all': Denholm-Young (p. 63), summarizing Lapsley's evidence (op. cit., pp. 111–45). I doubt this.

[2] e.g. aid from the tenant of a knight's fee to his lord on the marriage of the lord's daughter.

[3] Margery Fletcher in *Bulletin of the Institute of Historical Research*, xii (1934), 54, 55.

[4] For example an escheator took lands and knights' fees held by a tenant in Northamptonshire 'eo quod dicebatur quod terras illas vendidisse voluerit' (*Close Rolls, 1253–4*, p. 81). Cf. Hoyt's comments on King John's writ of 1212 printed in *Book of Fees*, i. 52 (*The Royal Demesne*, p. 152).

himself. When the feudal host was summoned, the service due—
though now, as often as not, very different from the *servitium
debitum* of the twelfth century—was forthcoming, unless the
tenant was allowed or required to compound for it by payment
of a fine. A favoured vassal might be allowed to remain at home
if he preferred to do so and to pay scutage instead;[1] an abbey
might scrape together its quota of knights or men-at-arms and
send them to be marshalled at headquarters. Conservative
opinion and the dignity of established rights, it has been suggested, maintained a preference in 1282 for the feudal host with
a period of voluntary service, and a suspicion of paid armies
collected in new ways.[2] Yet, just as the barons outside the Welsh
Marches could no longer rely upon the capacity of their tenants
to spring to arms and had to make their own arrangements, so
the king was no longer content to rely upon the feudal host. He
needed longer and more competent service; he wished to combine cavalry with crossbowmen and archers, and sometimes with
masses of infantry, under trained and trusted captains. He had
to plan in terms of campaigns, not of martial demonstrations.
The strenuous administrative services of enlistment, convoys,
commissariat, and the strain of endurance in difficult and hostile
country called for more flexible instruments—household troops,
retainers, a pool of reserves in the shires, both cavalry and foot.

These military needs had been realized during the Norman
wars and when, after his conquest of Normandy, King Philip
Augustus of France had threatened England with invasion. They
explain the attempts to translate military obligations into a
system of long service quotas, the substitution of compositions
and fines for actual service, the employment of bands of mercenaries or *ruptarii* under professional leaders, and the growth of
money-fiefs or retaining fees in return for homage and military
aid. They explain also the periodic reassertion and definition of
the ancient obligations of local defence, revived by Henry II's
assize of arms, and emphasized in our period by writs of watch
and ward, culminating in the statute of Winchester (1285). And,
finally, they led to the paid armies, centred in the royal household, and raised by indentures between selected leaders and
knights, and by the enlistment of companies of infantry in the
shires. How did this development affect the knights of the shires?

[1] Cf. charter for Geoffrey de Crowcombe, 3 July 1233 (*Cal, Charter Rolls*, i. 165).
[2] Morris, *Welsh Wars*, pp. 156–8.

The question leads us first to the money-fief.[1] The retaining fee should not be identified with the engagement of professional landless mercenaries, wandering about, like the later free companies in France and Italy, from one employer to another. Even Richard I's mercenary leader Mercadier, and John's military adventurers from Touraine were less free of local ties than these. The most remarkable feature in the careers of men like Engelard of Cigogné is their local tenacity as landholders and castellans. Wandering and landless knights existed, as wandering poets and scholars did, and especially in times of war. They presented a little problem to the framers of the Dictum of Kenilworth after the defeat of Simon de Montfort;[2] but they were not numerous. The knight-errantry of the literature of chivalry, which has not always been understood, caught none of its romantic lustre from actual life in England. The numerous money-fiefs given by King John and his successors might indeed be in lieu of land, or aids to younger sons, or temporary payments to vassals deprived of their land, but generally they were given to landed men, to 'law worthy' men, and under a definite obligation. The largest fiefs were paid to foreign princes as a guarantee that these would either provide troops or, when the occasion arose, act as recruiting agents to raise troops for service with the king of England. Numerous payments were made to men who lived in various parts of southern France, from Poitou to Provence, and became Henry III's or Edward I's men for a definite purpose. In return for an annual pension these men, great and small, became vassals sworn to give military aid. Moreover the money fee was not a stipend paid for actual service: it was a retainer, the daily pay was given to those who actually served when called upon, though these might be, and generally were, the pensioners.

The counts of Guisnes and other foreign lords who crossed the Channel to help Henry III in 1233 and on several occasions between 1260 and 1267 had money-fiefs; some had lands also in England. The king's relatives, the counts of Savoy, had money-fiefs and were careful to reserve their duty to King Edward

---

[1] See Bryce D. Lyon, 'The Money Fief under the English Kings', in *E.H.R.* lxvi (1951), 161 ff. For what seems to me to be a just criticism of Lyon's general view, see J. Prestwich, review of Lyon's later work, *From Fief to Indenture* (Harvard, 1957), in *History*, xliv (1959), 48–50.

[2] Cf. *King Henry III and the Lord Edward*, ii. 555–6.

when they entered into similar obligations with King Philip of France. English earls and barons might receive them. But the most important, because constant, retainers were the knights of the household, most of whom were men of well-established English families. And some of these grew rich in landed possessions, just as the king's clerks throve on benefices.[1] They were the core of the royal armies in Wales and Scotland, they were employed upon duties of various kinds, and the more competent among them were invaluable when an expedition was in course of preparation, whether in Britain or to Gascony. They were often young men, who were knighted on the great feasts, notably in Henry's time on St. Edward's day, and received from the king's wardrobe the costly equipment and robes of a new knight. They were soldiers and courtiers, responsive to the call to adventure and, possibly, to the appeal of the religious symbolism in the ceremony of knighthood. They would help to spread the spirit of *militia* which King Henry, especially when he undertook to send an army to assist in the conquest of Sicily,[2] was anxious to encourage in England, for they were known in their shires. Tournaments became increasingly popular in England in Edward's reign; the necessity to regulate them itself reveals an appreciation of their value as exercises in the use of arms. By the end of the century the use of coats of arms was widespread among others than earls and barons, as the 1,100 names on one roll of arms testify.[3] These imponderable tendencies, however, cannot be measured. It is more prudent to regard the household knights as a factor in the process of military organization. King Henry is said to have increased his household after the battle of Evesham

[1] Enguerrand de Fiennes (Ingram de Fenes), a protégé of Henry III, is a distinguished example. He was descended from the son and daughter of two lords of the Boulonnais whose combined fiefs (*temp.* Henry II) lay in England and the county of Boulogne. In 1247 he was pardoned his own relief and his father's debts; and at the Christmas feast had robes, as a knight of the royal household. He received wages. In 1249 he did homage as tenant-in-chief for the lands of Robert of Guines, who had sold him all his lands and the lands of the count of Guines and the advocate of Arras in England. The sale was confirmed by royal charter. His new homagers, who held tenements in these lands, included a bishop, an earl, two countesses, and other important folk. In 1253 Enguerrand was engaged in the selection of men at arms to be sent to Gascony, and was ordered to provide forty of his own, 'good strong men, well equipped with horses and arms'. He was also to send his brother Baldwin well equipped and his son William who would be maintained with the Lord Edward (*Close Rolls, 1242–7*, p. 501; ibid., *1247–51*, pp. 11, 18, 143; ibid., *1251–3*, pp. 125, 229, 486). One of his descendants built Hurstmonceaux, another succeeded to the barony of Say and Sele (*Complete Peerage*, xi. 479).

[2] Above, p. 120. [3] Below, p. 552, note.

because he had such vivid memories of his shameful experience since the disaster at Lewes.[1] Edward had a more resolute and fearless intention. He had expert knowledge of the matter. He was concerned to increase the number of knights, but he was still more concerned to turn the country gentlemen who could afford the equipment into competent cavalry, whether they were knights or not; and this meant that they should become reserves immediately dependent upon himself, responsive to their obligations and, above all, enlisted and marshalled under men on whose ability he could rely. Distraint of knighthood was important, but the liability to active service was more important, for this liability was part of a wider obligation which comprehended the male population of the land. To explain this more fully we must go back to his father's reign.

Distraint of knighthood has been described as primarily a financial measure, like the 'arrentation' of the peculiar tenures known as 'serjeanties'.[2] New knights meant more reliefs, wardships, and marriages. A second reason for the distraint was the need to increase the number of men available for the 'administrative functions which were restricted to the knightly class'.[3] Distraint would certainly have these results, so far as it was effective, and the tenants who bought or were allowed exemption by the Crown, or bribed officials to leave them alone,[4] may well have wished to avoid an increase in their local duties and liabilities; but the circumstances under which orders for distraint were made strongly suggest that the intention was to counteract the results of the fragmentation in the knights' fees, and to reassert the military obligations of the service due from them in terms both of men and money. The drive of distraints was most active in 1241–2 and 1252–4 when Poitevin and Gascon expeditions were under consideration or in execution; other orders can be associated with Llywelyn's assertions of power in Wales and with critical occasions in 1262 and 1265. The movement was connected, notably in 1241, with the inquiries into those

[1] This seems to be the implication of the words, 'qui quasi in custodia nuper fuerat', in the passage from the continuation of Florence of Worcester quoted by Denholm-Young (Collected Papers, p. 58, note).

[2] On 'arrentation' as a part of demesne policy see Hoyt, Royal Demesne, p. 148 and note. It was a valuation of demesne held by particular kinds of service, not necessarily an immediate change of service into annual rents, though this generally happened.

[3] A. L. Poole, Obligations of Society, p. 4.

[4] Cf. the articles of inquiry in 1274, c. 24, printed in Cam, The Hundred, p. 252.

who owed knight service and the services owed by tenants-in-chief and with the various revisions of the assize of arms.[1]

From the first, distraint of knighthood was especially related to oversea expeditions, for it gave a more profitable background to the dispatch of forces which, in the nature of the case, had to be wholly or mainly paid. The first distraint in Henry III's reign was ordered in November 1224, shortly before the expedition of a small paid force to Gascony in 1225. This or a later order held good in 1230, for, on the pipe roll for that year, the fines levied in lieu of service from those who, though summoned, did not cross the sea (*ne transfretet cum rege*) on the expedition to Brittany are linked with the fines for exemption from knighthood (*ne fiat miles*). The distraint of 1241 was intimately connected with the expedition of 1242. In May 1242 the king ordered that those who had not obeyed the order should be summoned to appear before the king's council, and that a list of the defaulters be sent to him together with the names of the tenants-in-chief who had not answered the summons to serve in Gascony. In other words Henry would exploit the disobedient in both kinds in order to help him to pay the money-fiefs of his recruits in the Midi. Moreover, the distraint of 1241 seems to have covered all those who held lands in knight's fee and socage to the annual value of £20, of whomsoever they had them, not only those who held of him in chief.[2] The available evidence suggests also that in 1242 he summoned to serve abroad some of the tenants-in-chief who had been newly distrained. In 1254 his regents went further. They ordered all the tenants-in-chief with lands of the annual value of £20 or more to prepare for service in Gascony.[3]

[1] M. R. Powicke, 'Distraint of Knighthood and Military Obligation under Henry III', in *Speculum*, xxv (1950), 457–70. Note W. Kienast on military service in England in the thirteenth century, in *Historische Zeitschrift*, clxxxiii (1957), 569–78.

[2] The writ of 10 December 1241 (*Close Rolls, 1237–42*, p. 428) is not so explicit as one would wish, but the absence of reference to tenures-in-chief suggests this interpretation. A distraint of 1245 clearly distinguishes between tenants-in-chief and tenants of others: the former are to be knighted in Westminster at Whitsuntide, the latter to receive arms from whomsoever they wish (*Close Rolls, 1242–7*, p. 354). Similarly in 1260 (*Close Rolls, 1259–61*, p. 171). It should be remembered that most tenants of this class held land of more than one lord, and might do actual military service to none.

[3] *Close Rolls, 1253–4*, p. 112 (5 February 1254). The statement of the Tewkesbury annalist (*Ann. monast.* i. 154) that *all* tenants paying £10 in rent were to be ready to sail, though accepted by Denholm-Young (*Collected Papers*, p. 64, note) and M. R. Powicke (op. cit., p. 463), seems to be due to a confusion between this writ and, possibly, some earlier reports.

This drastic measure came to nothing. The forces already in Gascony sufficed to subdue rebellion, and the alleged danger from King Alfonso was turned into rejoicing. The Lord Edward was knighted at Burgos and married to Eleanor of Castile. The king instead summoned to Gascony all the young tenants-in-chief whose lands were worth £60 a year, to be knighted at Burgos with the prince.[1] In England, a still more significant step had been taken. The knights not comprised in the summons of February to serve abroad—and these were not tenants-in-chief, but sub-tenants—were ordered to send representatives, two from each shire, to appear before council to say what financial aid their constituents were willing to give to the king.[2] The extension of distraint of knighthood to *all* wealthier tenants had prepared the way for political recognition of the knights of the shires of whomsoever they held their lands.

Distraint of knighthood thus made it possible for the king to revive the waning military strength of his tenants-in-chief, many of whom had not been knighted, and to call upon the new knights for service in the army. The danger in Gascony and the knighting of the Lord Edward in 1254 were used to stimulate military ardour. Distraint within the baronies brought the Crown in closer touch with the knightly class as a whole. If it were enforced, it increased the number of knights available at home: if it were not, it provided additional revenue in fines for exemption. The inducement to enforce it was greater than is often supposed. The disparity between the knight service actually given and the number of integrated knights' fees and estates now usually regarded as equivalent to the knight's fee—twenty librates of land[3] —raised serious problems. The marshal's register of 1277, when the first Welsh war of Edward I's reign began, 'shows an official record of 228 knights and 294 *servientes*', or mounted men-at-arms, of whom two were reckoned as the equivalent of a knight; that is, a total of 375 knights.[4] In Henry II's reign the total service due, though, of course, never fully available, was about 5,000 knights, and the potential strength of the country,

---

[1] *Close Rolls, 1253–4*, pp. 154–5. The king's letters did not reach the chancellor till 30 August, too late to be acted upon. Sub-tenants of the necessary standing were also pressed, not commanded, to join the others 'for love of the king's son'.

[2] Ibid., pp. 114–15, about 9 February 1254.

[3] Stenton, *English Feudalism, 1066–1166*, pp. 164–74, discusses the emergence of this and other valuations, and shows that it was by no means general in the twelfth century.   [4] Morris, *Welsh Wars*, p. 45.

reckoned in knights' fees, was nearer 6,500.[1] By the end of the thirteenth century the number of fighting knights was about 500 and, after all the systematic distraints of knighthood, probably there were only about 700 more knights scattered about the shires.[2] Obviously a social revolution had occurred; and military organization had to be put on a new basis.

Several attempts have been made to explain the drastic reductions of the *servitium debitum*. No method can be deduced from the process, which was uneven, casual, and full of anomalies and apparent injustice. One writer sees in it 'a magnificent baronial victory in a struggle the details of which have been lost to us',[3] but, as no conscious plan can be discerned, this conclusion merely restates the problem. Two considerations make useful starting-points: one is the change in the cost of knightly service, the other the contrast between the artificiality of the system imposed by the Conqueror and Henry II and the more natural complexity of English social conditions by the end of the twelfth century.

The Norman *miles* was a mounted soldier. He wore a conical iron helmet, was clad in a hauberk or mail shirt, and rode an unprotected horse. The knight of Richard I's time—in the early age of chivalry—wore a *lorica* or coat of mail over a padded garment (*gambeson*), mail hose and mittens, and a heavy pot-helmet, and his horse carried armour under its trapper of linen or silk. A hundred years later plate armour had become normal, and the horse's housings had become more elaborate affairs of mail or quilted textiles and body plates;[4] a fully equipped knight was like a moving castle, remote from his neighbours in ordinary life. His great warhorse or *dextrarius*, worth anything from £40 to £80, was his most precious possession, a source of pride and anxiety, as well known by name and qualities as he was himself, worth, indeed, his own daily wages for from seven to fourteen months or more. Obviously an army could no longer comprise an indefinite number of knights. The cost of 500 knights for two years, undertaken by Saint Louis under the terms of the treaty of Paris in 1259, became a matter of arduous

[1] Ibid.   [2] Above, p. 541.
[3] S. Painter, *Studies in the History of the English Feudal Barony* (Baltimore, 1943), p. 44, in the course of a discussion, pp. 37–45. See also H. M. Chew, *The English Ecclesiastical Tenants-in-chief and Knight Service* (1932), chap. i, especially pp. 29–30, and A. L. Poole, *Obligations of Society*, pp. 35–56, for other discussions.
[4] See the summary of these changes in Chew, op. cit., pp. 89–90.

negotiation and was fixed in 1263 at 134,000 *livres* of Tours, or some £33,000 sterling, well over King Henry's annual normal revenue.[1]

The cost of chivalry inevitably put a strain upon the Norman system; but even if costs had not risen, the structure of Anglo-Norman society was ill suited to its neat articulation. 'The feudal levy must very soon after its institution have revealed its weak points.'[2] The royal favour which might mar feudal symmetry by grants of lands for nominal services was merely one instance of a king's capacity of indiscriminate giving and went back to Anglo-Saxon times.[3] Other tendencies were more deep-seated and impersonal; especially the urge to attach particular services (or contributions to such services) to pieces of land, with the result that as the knights' fees were split into fractions, their services were turned into money payments. Tenants of an integral knight's fee were rare even in the twelfth century. Most of the tenants who owed knight service, or rather fractions of knight service, 'were not knights or capable of becoming knights'.[4] They were tenants in free socage. Many who were knights were avoiding the responsibilities of knighthood. Others were not sure what services they owed. Lords found it very difficult to enforce the service required of them by the king. Hence the tendencies, both local and central, which favoured the commutation and reduction of military service into money payments, had free play. They were assisted by the practice of the quota, which was developed not only within the baronies—for example, in the liberty of St. Albans[5]—but also in the feudal host as a whole, especially when the host was summoned for service across the Channel. It is significant that this last practice was given a form by Richard I more systematic than it was ever given in later reigns, and that it was rigorously extended by King John to home defence. The knights, in the former's reign, 'had ceased to form the rank and file of the army' in Normandy. 'The king required only a few of them to act as officers in com-

[1] Gavrilovitch, *Étude sur le traité de Paris de 1259*, pp. 54–66.

[2] Poole, op. cit., p. 39.

[3] The continuance of Anglo-Saxon elements beneath the Norman system has been emphasized by Marjory Hollings in a paper on the survival of the five-hide unit in the western Midlands (*E.H.R.* lxiii (1948), 453–87. For reductions of assessment see p. 463). [4] Poole, p. 36.

[5] Chew, op. cit., pp. 124–31; for the local muster generally and the relations between lords and sub-tenants in the thirteenth century, especially in ecclesiastical fiefs, the whole book should be studied.

mand of hired men at arms' and these few were long-service knights, paid from the proceeds of the fines levied from the lords of those who remained in England in lieu of actual service (*pro passagio*).[1]

King John's defence measures in 1205[2] are still more significant. He went behind the feudal host to the knight himself, when he arranged the knights in each shire in groups of ten, of whom nine were to equip and pay the tenth; the local knight was linked with the military organization of the male population in communities of shire, hundred, and borough, sworn to defend the kingdom as a public duty. This measure of public safety was an exercise of royal authority which was far more deeply rooted than the military system which the Conqueror had established, and revealed, in a time of crisis, a direct dependence of the sub-tenant upon the king, a dependence whose history began long before the 'oath of Salisbury'.[3] With a closer regard to 'feudal' values, John's successors maintained the tradition as the source of a more responsible communal life. Indeed, the use of the knight, as the most responsible and best-endowed freeman in the shire, for administrative and judicial purposes and in military organization, prepared the way for the later history of the country gentleman.

In the thirteenth century the social development was twofold, to a knightly class and to the higher military grade in the shires. The heavily armed horse soldier was still as much needed as before, but for several reasons—the cost of equipment, the conditions of warfare required by foreign service, and the gradual emergence of a more efficient army on a paid basis—he could no longer be mainly regarded as a unit in the *servitium debitum*. As a warrior he tended to become a member of a loosely definable social class, susceptible to the glamour of a code of chivalry. He was a landholder, for, whether he was attached to the king's household or to a baronial household, or lived on his manors, his social dignity depended on his local wealth as much as on his martial prestige; but he could become more than a local figure. He might win the favour of the great, or renown in tournaments, or fame as a banneret in command of a troop of knights and men-at-arms. He would be in the fashion and assume a coat of

---

[1] Poole, op. cit., pp. 41–43.
[2] A. L. Poole, *From Domesday Book to Magna Carta*, pp. 439–40.
[3] Cf. M. Hollings in *E.H.R.* lxiii (1948), 486–7.

arms.[1] He might, if he prospered, become a member of the baronial circle in which he moved and in due course receive a special writ of summons to parliament. Attempts to define a barony in legal terms were not very successful in the thirteenth century; the king could summon whom he wished, and a way was being prepared for a new conception of 'peerage', dependent on royal grace and recognition. On the other hand, there was no rigidity in English social distinctions, although in actual life the reality of these distinctions could be embarrassing enough. The 'poor' knight, for example, pestered at tournaments by wandering heralds whom he could not afford to employ, was a pathetic figure in the literature of chivalry. Twenty librates of land might impose an obligation of knighthood, but did not provide the means for a knightly career. At one time Edward I, mindful perhaps of courtly realities, decreed that the obligations of knighthood need not be assumed by anybody who did not possess 100 librates of land.[2] Yet, all the same, the landholding gentry of the shires, careerists, stay-at-home knights, potential knights, tenants of fifteen librates, and other substantial freeholders, were not sharply differentiated: each grade shaded off into the next. Here we come to the second line of development, the emergence of the wealthiest tenants as a military grade in the shire.

From this point of view distraint of knighthood was an addition of another obligation to the Assize of Arms. The stipulation that holders of fifteen, ten, and five librates of land must have appropriate military equipment, defined in 1242 and in the Statute of Winchester in 1285, was reinforced by the liability of the holders of twenty librates to be distrained to knighthood. The sheriff was given another task.[3] Emphasis was laid on the

[1] The earliest roll of arms, dated c. 1254, the year of Edward's knighthood, contains 218 coats of arms, of 20 earls and of lords and knights from all parts of England. A roll of c. 1312 contains 1,110 coats of arms, of which 941 are of knights from the shires. See A. R. Wagner, *Heralds and Heraldry in the Middle Ages* (1939), pp. 18, 52. A study of the 941 knights, e.g. of the origin, standing, and activities of their fathers and grandfathers as well as of their own, might be illuminating. The lists of c. 1312 are printed in *Parliamentary Writs*, i. 410–20.

[2] In 1285 (ibid. i. 249). In 1293 Edward fixed the liability to distraint at the tenure of forty librates (ibid., p. 258). In 1254 Henry III had ordered or invited those who had sixty librates to go to be knighted with his son in Spain (above, p. 548).

[3] In 1231 Henry III had summoned the *jurati ad arma* of certain shires to join him in Wales, an order later limited to the *jurati ad ferrum* or higher grades and a quota from the others. Other examples of the use made of the *jurati* outside their shires could be given.

wealth required to maintain a knight, not—as in earlier distraints—upon the tenure of a knight's fee. The effect was to
make the holders of more than twenty librates liable to be called
upon, not as members of the fifteen-librate class, but as the best-
equipped group in the county militia, whether they had been
knighted or not. From Rhuddlan on 24 November 1282, King
Edward ordered the sheriffs to enforce the appearance in January
1283 before him or his deputies at Northampton (or, from the
northern shires, at York) of all fit and suitable men (*ad arma
potentes et aptos*) in their areas who had more than twenty librates
of land and were not already engaged in the Welsh campaign.
The king realized that cavalry levies from the shires must be
efficient. The costs of horses and armour were rising. The daily
wage of a cavalry man was merely a payment to meet his expenses on actual service. The wealthier men were the more useful. Earlier in 1282 Edward had issued a proclamation through
the sheriffs requiring every tenant of thirty librates of land in
the kingdom to meet the scarcity of big war-horses (*magnis et
competentibus ad arma*) by procuring such a horse, together with
the appropriate horse-armour, so that, as often as occasion arose,
the owner would have it ready for use.[1] In 1295 all knights and
others who had £40 a year were ordered to be ready to serve
the king in Scotland at his wages as men-at-arms.[2] Two years
later Edward pushed this obligation to its logical extreme and
provoked the first political crisis of his reign. He included in his
call to foreign service the gentry of the shires—this time from
the *twenty*-librate men upwards—and also associated with
them the whole baronial class. In his writs to the barons he gave
as his justification for what amounted to the absorption of the
feudal host in the general levy the obligation of every baron to
share the duty imposed upon the wealthier landholders of the
shires, of whomsoever they held (*infra libertates et extra*).[3]

As we shall see, Edward went too far in 1297. He alienated
barons and gentry alike, the men on whom he depended for

[1] Ibid. i. 226, no. 8 (26 May 1282). The sheriffs were to make it known that those
tenants who had no horse would be allowed, on their appearance at Rhuddlan, to
make fine in lieu of service (ibid., no. 9; writs of 22 June). For the general obligation
to cavalry service under Edward I see M. R. Powicke in *Speculum*, xxviii (1953),
814–33.

[2] *Parliamentary Writs*, i. 267, no. 3.

[3] Ibid. i. 282–5. The writs sent to the barons in Ireland and Scotland omitted
the reference to the county levies and provided for explanation and discussion.

detailed help in the enlistment and organization of his armies. He had reached, in his relations with the knights and other tenants of the shires, the stage which implied conscious co-operation in the service of the realm. Behind the façade of the feudal levy hard work was required to raise paid troops of knights and men-at-arms; within the organization of hundred and shire the call to arms by the sheriffs had to be followed up by the activities of tried and well-established commissioners of array, who picked their men, both foot and horse, and arranged them in constabularies of light cavalry and infantry battalions each of a thousand, subdivided into companies of a hundred and platoons of twenty foot. The Scottish wars caused a professionalized development of the methods used in the Welsh wars, the enlistment of Welsh foot and archers, the more intense organization of the northern shires of England. Persuasion and cajoling were brought to bear in negotiations with the local communities. For work of this kind the help of the knights of the shire and other local landlords was invaluable, but they had first to be responsive to the need. There were not many of them.

The change in the military system between 1216 and 1307 is sharply revealed by the fact that, whereas in the first forty-one years of Henry III's reign the feudal host was summoned, in whole or in part, a dozen times, in Edward's reign it was summoned only six times.[1] In broad terms, Henry III's armies until 1257 were based upon the feudal levy, whose components served at their own cost for forty days, and then either returned or continued in royal pay, while other forms of service, such as that of the household knights, of bodies of crossbowmen and engineers, and of county levies raised by the sheriffs, were fitted into the organization of the host; whereas in Edward's time the feudal levy became subsidiary to the paid forces or was not summoned at all. Thus in 1282 it was summoned after the organized concentration of troops against Llywelyn and David of Wales had begun; it was not summoned to deal with the rebellions of 1287 and 1295. During the Scottish wars it was summoned in full to meet at Carlisle in June 1300, at Berwick in May 1302, and at Carlisle in July 1306; but the armies raised for the earlier Scottish campaigns contained only a few who preferred to serve without pay. The summonses to serve in the Gascon expedition

[1] 1277, 1282 (Wales); 1294 (Gascony); 1299 (for 1300), 1302 (for 1303), 1306 (Scotland).

in 1294 were formal, but owing to the Welsh rebellion no full muster was possible. The direct call to all knights and feudal tenants, whose revenues were above a certain standard, to serve for pay, was simpler than the calling of the feudal host, and more consistent with an efficient system of enrolment, both of men and horses, in the royal army.[1]

The general levy of 1294 was an important factor in the long and incoherent history of the substitution of paid forces, raised by trusted tenants-in-chief, tried bannerets, and others, for the feudal host. It was called for service against the king of France in Gascony, and the king's intention was probably to collect fines at the high rate of 100 marks the fee from those willing to compound, rather than to ship the host to the duchy.[2] In spite of the fiasco which ensued the exchequer continued to exact the fines assessed at the ports in lieu of service; but as Edward was unable to lead those who did sail, the exaction of fines raised the old problem whether feudal military service, or its equivalent in fines, was due across the sea in the absence of the king. Resistance was widespread and continuous, for in 1305 the exchequer was still threatening distraint on the lands and chattels of defaulters. Early in Edward II's reign all the fines assessed in 1294 were remitted on the grounds that the king had not been personally engaged in the war and that general service had not been done—in other words, that the feudal host had not 'functioned' at all. There can be no doubt that the famous refusal of the earl of Norfolk and others to serve in Gascony in 1297 was partly inspired by this current controversy. Edward had intended to go to Gascony in person in 1294; he had been very angry when the Welsh rebellion prevented his passage; in his necessity he needed every penny that he could get; but the fact remained that neither he nor the host had gone. The Crown had already given an automatic character to the fine proffered in commutation of military service by fixing the rate instead of making individual bargains with tenants-in-chief who did not wish to serve. It had also fined those who did not appear at the muster at double the rate.[3] But the proffer of a fine and the penalty for non-appearance still implied that the king's object

[1] For the inventories of the horses of household and stipendiary troops, compensation for loss, &c., cf. Morris, *Welsh Wars*, pp. 78–83 *passim*; and, for instances, *Cal. of Docs. relating to Scotland*, ii, nos. 1007, 1010–11, 1190.

[2] Morris, pp. 77–78, 276, corrected in part by Chew, op. cit., pp. 98–101.

[3] Cf. Chew in *E.H.R.* xxxvii (1922), 326, 330 (especially note 5), 332, 333.

in gathering the host was to use the host for military purposes under his leadership. The feudal levy could not be turned into a money-making device. The summons to military service had been for a century as precise an expression of the relations between the king and his vassals as the summons to the great council with which it had frequently been combined; but just as the great council was giving way to a co-ordinated parliament, so the feudal host was giving way to a paid army.

This development was reflected in the history of scutage,[1] or charge on the knight's fee made towards the cost of a military campaign. Scutage was closely integrated with the muster. It was a feudal aid and in a famous clause of Magna Carta was included among the 'extraordinary' aids which could only be levied by the common counsel of the realm. Although this clause was omitted from later issues of the charter, scutage in Henry III's reign was, until 1257, put in charge with the assent of the great council when the decision to summon the feudal levy was made or when the host came together. Although the sheriffs supervised the collection and accounted at the exchequer, they did not themselves collect the aid within the liberties, unless a request for their help or some unusual circumstance required their intervention. As a rule they had no direct relations with the sub-tenants who held fees or fractions of fees. As collectors, they were concerned with the minor tenants-in-chief, escheats, wardships, and other fees in the king's hands. If writs for the collection of scutage were issued, the tenants-in-chief who had obeyed the personal summons for service or had proffered fines for excuse from service were given writs *de habendo scutagio*. If a tenant-in-chief had not been summoned, he was required to pay the scutage collected from his fees into the exchequer; if he had defaulted he paid scutage as well as the penalty for default; if he had a writ of quittance, he kept the scutage-money himself. Scutage went to meet his expenses or the payment of his fine. Such seems to have been the essential idea in a system which was riddled with incoherencies and practical difficulties.

Two obvious difficulties were the division of so many fees into fractions, distributed among numerous tenants, from which

---

[1] Chew, 'Scutage under Edward I', in *E.H.R.* xxxvii (1922), 321–36. See also her book, already cited, *passim*, especially pp. 103–12, for the system generally and the chief texts and authorities. Cf. A. L. Poole, *Obligations of Society*, pp. 41–42.

scutage had to be collected, and the disparity between the service due from a tenant-in-chief and his actual resources in lands
and men. The lord of the honour of Okehampton, for example,
'recognized' that he owed the service of three knights, but his
traditional *servitium* was for ninety-two and three-quarter knights'
fees. In spite of rising costs of equipment, it would always be in
his interest to provide the three knights, or, if need be, to proffer
a fine for his and their service, rather than shirk his obligations,
for he could collect scutage from over ninety fees, though he
might find the process very tiresome and the proceeds less than
he might wish. On the other hand, if he had to pay scutage to
the Crown, did he pass on the whole sum or only the scutage on
three fees? Service and fees bore no relation to each other, and
the so-called 'fees' were represented by a tangled network of
tenements whose rights and liabilities were the easy prey of
endless litigation.

In 1258 the baronial troubles began. Between 1264 and 1267,
though several calls were made upon feudal service, any attempt
to levy scutage was out of the question. Between 1267 and 1276
there was peace in the land. Scutage had not been collected for
twenty years. King Edward did not put one in charge during
the first Welsh war, but the matter was raised after Llywelyn's
submission. The instructions to the exchequer stated that scutage
was to be levied as had been done 'for other armies of Wales in
like case'.[1] This order must have set the officials to work on their
rolls; and to some purpose. The exchequer rolls show clearly
that a deliberate attempt was made to collect scutage for the
Crown irrespective of service and to collect it, not on the number of fees for which service was recognized, but on the total
number of fees liable to payment within the fief. It is possible
that the treasurer and barons of the exchequer were affected by
an ineffectual attempt made in 1242 to increase this source of
revenue.[2] When a scutage was again granted in 1285 for the army
in Wales in 1282 and, in 1305, for the armies in Scotland in

---

[1] *E.H.R.* xxxvii. 327.

[2] In 1242, by successive writs, exhaustive inquiries into knight service due from
tenants-in-chief, and its location, were instituted with the object of collecting
scutage, *through* the *sheriffs*, on fees of the old and new enfeoffments, that is, on all
fees. The sheriffs were ordered to send in the names of all who resisted the inquiry
and the scutage. On the other hand, the interests of tenants-in-chief who had
proffered service or fines for the Gascon campaign were safeguarded. More than
100 earls and barons, &c., got writs of scutage. See *Book of Fees*, ii. 637–9; and
Madox, *History and Antiquities of the Exchequer* (edition of 1769), i. 680–2.

1300 and 1303, the same procedure was adopted. As in 1279, the scutage lists on the pipe roll were not subdivided, as they had been from 1194 to 1257, 'into tenants owing scutage and tenants quit *per breve regis*', but 'were drawn up as if for an aid, and made no allowance either for the performance of service or the payment of fines'.[1] The attempt, which lasted far into the next reign, to collect the scutages through the sheriffs had little result and was interrupted more than once by delays for further consideration. Passive resistance was general. None the less the exchequer persisted; the debts were carried over, with other debts, from year to year, until they had to be wiped off. Gradually the general feudal levy and the grant of scutage, though they were not abolished, came to an end.

King Edward has been made responsible for this development. He is said to have made scutage a tax. His new policy, we are told, 'seems gradually to have paralysed the entire feudal military system'. It would be nearer the truth to say that the action of the Crown reflected the reaction of exchequer officials to the incoherence between the traditional and existing military systems. Scutage had not been levied for over twenty years. Its revival was probably due not to the Crown but to those who wished to have writs *de scutagio* in recognition of their service or of the fines which they proffered for service. In 1279 it is said by a chronicler to have been 'conceded' by the king; in 1285 and 1305 it was apparently granted by the king in parliament. When the exchequer dealt with the matter the expeditions were events of the past. No systematic returns of service and fines had been sent in, no recent precedent could be followed. The administrators, well aware how much the wars cost the Crown, decided to put the collection of scutage into the hands of the sheriffs, to collect all they could and to consider every petition for relief on its merits, after an examination of their records. In fact the collection of scutage became a strange tug-of-war between the exchequer and such influences as the aggrieved tenants-in-chief could bring to bear. It became involved with the other grievances which absence on the king's service was always sure to create.[2] In any case it was a long-drawn

[1] Chew, in *E.H.R.* xxxvii. 327.

[2] The letters to the chancellor, Burnell, noted by J. G. Edwards in the *Calendar of Ancient Correspondence concerning Wales*, show this clearly. Thus Robert de Chandos, whom the sheriff of Hereford was distraining for scutage (*c.* 1285), asks for a writ stating that he had fulfilled his service, as recorded on the marshal's roll and the

exasperating process, whose financial returns were hardly worth the labour of investigation. When, as happened in 1292 and 1297 and 1305, tenants-in-chief presented their case in parliament and claimed to be quit of scutage upon all their fees, in virtue of their service, their petition met with sympathy: the exchequer was required to search the pipe rolls or, on the evidence of the marshal's rolls, give a respite or relief from payment. The whole story suggests that the busy king took little part in the controversy. Its value for the historian is to be found in the light which it throws upon the hard lot of an outworn institution in a changing world. Scutages and fines for a time caused much annoyance to all concerned, but they were merely troublesome incidents in the developments which gave the Crown an average income of some £80,000 a year, and united prelates and barons, knights and burgesses and merchants in a common service.

roll of Roger Mortimer (p. 114). Other letters complain of unjustified distraint of military service (pp. 127–8), of John Kirkby's unfair exactions at Shrewsbury on his financial tour (p. 125), and of various other hardships and distraints during war-time.

XII

IRELAND AND SCOTLAND
1217–1297

Taxes granted in parliament in England were not levied in other lands attached to the Crown, namely Ireland, Gascony, and Wales, nor in the county of Chester. Subsidies were granted in 1292 by the lords marcher and communities in Wales and by the magnates, both Anglo-Irish and Irish, of Ireland; also, after much discussion in the liberties, shires, and boroughs, by the Anglo-Irish in 1300, but only as acts of grace.[1] On the other hand, the king's writs ran in all lands attached to the Crown, and petitions and, with some limitations, appeals from them were considered by the king in council.[2] After the union of the kingdoms, though not of the crowns, of England and Scotland in 1291,[3] the legal relations between the two crowns were a matter of much delicacy.

Since the twelfth century the kingdom of Scotland had, more or less effectively, comprised Highlands and Lowlands alike, and in the thirteenth century its rulers displaced the authority of the king of Norway everywhere except in the Orkneys and Shetlands. Henceforward the kingdom of Scotland and the lordship of Ireland were closer neighbours than they had been before. The problem of Scotland may perhaps be studied in better proportion if in the first instance we approach it by way of Ireland.[4]

---

[1] For the grants of 1292 and 1300 see above, pp. 443, 535.

[2] Richardson and Sayles in *Proc. Irish Academy*, xxxviii, Section C (1929), p. 133, on appeals from a parliament held by the justiciar in Ireland to the king's court in England. For the system of original writs in Wales and Ireland see W. Waters, *The Edwardian Settlement of North Wales*, pp. 160–5; and Maitland, *Collected Papers*, ii. 81–83. The mingling of regard for Irish procedure and the right of appeal to the king against Irish ministers and others is illustrated by the case of Agnes of Valence against John fitzThomas in 1304–5 (Richardson and Sayles, op. cit., p. 136 and note).

[3] *Foedera*, i. ii. 757, Berwick, 3 July 1291. In view of the union of the realms *ratione superioris dominii*, the justices of the bench are ordered to admit 'brevia regis, coram eis porrecta vel retornata, de data dierum et locorum infra idem regnum Scotiae mentionem facientia'.

[4] A good brief outline is given by E. Curtis, *A History of Ireland* (3rd ed., 1947), pp. 75–94.

Ireland had no high king, though the title was occasionally assumed, as by Brian O'Neill of Tir Owen in Ulster (1260), or by some scion of the five kingly families which survived on unconquered lands or as vassals of Anglo-Irish lords. There was no such continuous native authority, as the Welsh had in Snowdonia. The most independent clan was the O'Donnells of Tirconnell, in the remote parts of Ulster; but, as one young O'Donnell, who had been fostered by the Lord of the Isles in Scotland, declared, in the words of a Scottish proverb, 'every man should have his own world'.[1] The Irish fought among themselves just as did the Anglo-Irish lords. They changed sides easily and quickly, one chieftain sometimes fighting on the side of the government against another of his own clan. Their restless desire to enlarge the boundaries allotted to them was held in check if their lands lay within Anglo-Irish shires or liberties, but it smouldered all the more fiercely even there, for the Irish were still outside the scope of the common law and the chief was generally nominated to a life tenure by agents of the Crown or by the lord of the liberty.[2] They and their conquerors were in a continuous state of private warfare, latent or open; in spite of the king's peace, and friendly intercourse, the foreign settlers thought of future conquests and the Irish of future revolt. Hence, by the end of our period, clan centres of potential resistance survived from Antrim to county Cork, most strong in the large county of Connaught (the land of the O'Conors), in Desmond in county Cork, where the MacCarthys ruled, and in Thomond, south of Galway bay, where the O'Briens opposed the Clares, whom King Edward had sent to hold them down. In the southeast the descendants of King Dermot had begun an Irish revival which permanently displaced some of the Anglo-Irish families of Leinster. To the west of the lordship of Ulster semi-independent Irish lords still ruled in lands which had never been divided into shires—in Tirconnell, Tir Owen, Fermanagh, Uriel, and Breffay, stretching from the encircling sea to the borders of Meath.[3] This is the converse of the fact that three-quarters of

[1] Orpen, *Ireland under the Normans*, iv. 274.
[2] Jocelyn Otway-Ruthven, 'The Native Irish and English Law in Medieval Ireland' in *Irish Historical Studies*, vii (1950), 1–16, at p. 3.
[3] See the map at the end of the fourth volume of G. H. Orpen's *Ireland under the Normans*. This book and E. Curtis's *History of Mediaeval Ireland, 1110–1313* (1st ed., 1923) are the best guides to the subject. They are written from somewhat different points of view and should be studied together.

Ireland was under the control of the government at Dublin, in shires or liberties, and that in King Edward's time this control was more widespread and effective than it had ever been before.

The position in Ireland was, indeed, more evenly balanced in the middle of King Edward's reign than appears at first sight. Under more favourable circumstances than were possible during the Scottish and French wars the tendency to maintain racial rivalry might have given way before more co-operative influences. Local separatism affected feudal and clannish pride alike. The family of De Burgh, for example, which had profited most from the conquest of Connaught in the early years of Henry III, was by no means always ready to support the Anglo-Irish against their Irish neighbours. The Bigods who had inherited Carlow in Leinster were kinsmen as well as lords of the descendants of Dermot and resented external interference with them. The over-riding tradition of unity against the Irish was easily forgotten by lords equally affected by the desire to maintain their local claims against local rivals and against interfering justiciars and officials. Moreover, in the interests of sound and profitable estate management the lords were disposed to grant to their Irish free tenants, or, as the Crown took greater control, to ask the Crown to grant, the privilege of subjection to the common law instead of to the personal Brehon law, still kept alive by the Irish jurists. The results of recent investigation suggest that this privilege, as it was regarded, was given more freely, and was sought more eagerly by the Irish than has been supposed. After his return to England in 1274 King Edward was strongly disposed to encourage this movement. He regarded the Irish law as detestable and he realized the advantages of extending common law to the Irish people. He welcomed the petition put forward by the archbishop of Cashel and his suffragans in 1277 that English law should be extended to the Irish and in 1280 he pressed the Irish parliament to consider the proposal carefully. Although no general action was taken, Edward decreed in council in 1290 that any Irishman who demanded the right to be under the common law should have it.[1] Legislation in the English parliament in 1321 and 1331 was passed to safeguard the Irish admitted

[1] Otway-Ruthven in *Irish Historical Studies*, vii. 1-16, and, for the attitude of Edward I to the Cashel petition, a previous article (vi. 261-70) and Aubrey Gwynn in *Trans. of Royal Hist. Society*, 5th ser. x (1960), 111-27. Cf. the memoranda of the Irish parliament of 1280 edited by H. G. Richardson and G. O. Sayles in *Proc. of Royal Irish Academy*, xxxviii, section C (1929), 142.

COMMON LAW AND IRISH LAW

to English law in their rights to enjoy it fully, provided that the lords of the *nativi* or *betaghs* should still have their ancient right over the goods and chattels of these tenants, even if they had been admitted to English law.[1]

The admission to the common law of groups of Irishmen or individuals who desired it was only the first step towards the union of the races. Even if all the inhabitants in areas controlled by the government were brought under one law, union would not follow so long as the social distinction between the *hibernici* and their conquerors continued to threaten the peace. A second step towards union might have followed if Edward had been able to give as much attention to Irish as he gave to Gascon and Welsh affairs, but this he could never do. Like his father he never set foot in Ireland. King Henry had planned an expedition in 1233. He summoned his vassals and collected a fleet of ships for the passage, but he did not go.[2] In 1255, after he had granted Ireland to his son, he arranged, on the advice of Peter of Savoy, that Edward should go from Gascony to settle the state of Ireland, but the scheme came to nothing.[3] As king, Edward was apparently content to rely on his representatives in Dublin, and they were preoccupied by the problems of every day and satisfied if they could hold their own.

On the whole they did hold their own. They had at their disposal a system of government which was a replica of that which prevailed in England. The justiciar was in fact a viceroy. He administered a body of common law based upon English custom and statutes which allowed variations of local usage. He was in frequent touch with the English administration, had his council, held parliaments,[4] supervised the business of chancery, exchequer, the judiciary, and the counties. On occasion he made judicial progresses through the counties from one side of the land to the other. By Edward's time his rule was shared by the lords of only a few liberties, for the feudal division of Leinster between the families of the five daughters of the great marshal, after the

[1] Berry, *Statutes*, pp. 292, 325. The statute of 1331 is phrased in more general terms; 'una et eadem lex fiat tam Hibernicis quam Anglicis, excepta servitute betagiorum penes dominos suos eodem modo quo usitatum est in Anglia de villanis'. The *betaghs* were the Irish peasantry of unfree status who tilled the lands.

[2] Above, p. 54.

[3] *Close Rolls, 1254–6*, p. 219 (letters of August 1255). The prince was urged to go unless he found that the voyage would be dangerous on account of the winter.

[4] On the Irish parliaments of Edward I and the earlier history of parliament see Richardson and Sayles in *Proc. Irish Academy*, xxxviii, section C (1929), 128–47.

death of their last brother in 1245, had been so minute that only the liberties of Wexford (Valence), Kilkenny (Clare), Kildare, and Carlow remained, and of these Kildare was surrendered to the Crown in 1297 by William de Vescy, and the honour of Carlow reverted to the Crown in 1306 on the death of Roger Bigod, earl of Norfolk.[1] Similarly the former Lacy liberty in Meath had been divided between the liberty of Trim and the lands of the Verdons and became a separate county in 1297, as did the liberty of Ulster, now held by Richard de Burgh of Connaught, the chief mainstay in Ireland of royal power.

As a result of these partitions the liberties which survived in Leinster and at Trim in Meath had less independence than their larger predecessors, and more responsibility was thrown upon the sheriffs and their officials. The administrative changes made in 1297 were intended to strengthen the county organization by dividing the county of Dublin, dispersed in Ulster, Meath, and Leinster, 'whereby it is remiss in obedience to the king's precepts and those of his court, and his people is insufficiently ruled or governed'.[2] Local sheriffs in the liberty of Ulster, in Meath, and in Kildare would intervene more effectively in the liberties, where they were expected to execute royal writs when default was found in the baronial seneschals, to see that the other Anglo-Irish lords did due suit in the county court, and to have better control generally of the crosslands[3] and other responsibilities and rights of the Crown. But nothing is said in the statute about the position in the other shires—Waterford, Cork, Kerry, Limerick, Connaught, Tipperary, and the royal cantrefs west of the Shannon.[4]

From the king's point of view Ireland was, or should have

---

[1] See Orpen's chapter on the partition of Leinster (iii. 79 ff.). In 1297 Kildare was made a separate county instead of a liberty attached to (*intendens*) the county of Dublin. Carlow had been given a shire organization by the marshals.

[2] Berry, *Statutes*, pp. 196–8. See generally Jocelyn Otway-Ruthven, 'Anglo-Irish Shire Government in the Thirteenth Century', in *Irish Hist. Studies*, v (1947), 1–28.

[3] Crosslands were lands held by the prelates, monasteries, and churches of the Crown, which, if they lay within the borders of liberties, were regarded as parts of the county, not of the liberty.

[4] The invaders of Ireland, many of whom were Norman lords from Wales, seem to have used this Welsh name for local divisions, old or new. The cantref could become the area of a rural deanery, when the Church was organized on Roman lines, or of a barony; cf. Orpen's account of the Fitzmaurice barons of Kerry (with a map) in *E.H.R.* xxix (1914), 304–6. The five 'king's cantrefs' retained by the Crown when the conquest of Connaught was planned (1227) comprised nearly all Roscommon and parts of Sligo and Galway.

been, a source of military and economic strength, a western
bastion enclosing the domestic waters of the Irish sea. For purposes of trade and defence the long line of ports from Drogheda
to Waterford and Cork were linked with Chester and Bristol.
The relations between Bristol and Dublin had been close since
the eleventh century and particularly close since Henry II had
given Dublin the liberties of the port on the Avon, and put
garrisons there and in the other ports created by the Norwegian
settlers or Ostmen. By King Edward's time the Ostmen had
ceased to be significant as centres of local trade and political life.
Though still numerous they were, as Ostmen, a dying race,
mingling with the English and Irish. Dispersed through the
southern half of Ireland, in town and country, they found it hard
in their equivocal position to maintain their freedom.[1] Their
ports were no longer theirs, but chartered sources of supplies of
corn, meat, wine, fish, and cloth, essential to the Crown in times
of war. Behind them lay the fiefs of the Anglo-Irish lords, partly
consolidated in a few liberties, but more generally scattered in
intricate patterns about their numerous castles, and often separated by hilly pockets of semi-independent Irish clans. These
lordships comprised a strange medley of feudal tenures, a growing complexity of peasant and small burghal holdings, and lands
of Irish 'satellites' who paid rents and were at the will of their
English lords in time of war.[2] The king looked to these arsenals
of knights and Irish troops for help against Welsh and Scots and
even against his enemies across the English Channel. In 1301,
for example, he issued 184 personal writs of summons to the war
in Scotland. The list includes several Irish names, from O'Neill
of Tir Owen to MacCarthy of Desmond.[3] Edward used Ireland
to the full in the last decade of his reign, just as he had used Irish
contingents and stores against Llywelyn of Wales.

---

[1] See Curtis, *Hist. of Mediaeval Ireland* (1923), pp. 195–200; and, on the Norse in
Ireland generally, Jean I. Young in *History*, xxxv (1950), 11–33.

[2] For the distribution of knight service in Ireland (generally with money values)
and royal rents see the documents from the Irish exchequer edited by Mary Bateson in *E.H.R.* xviii (1903), 501–7 (no. 4), 509–12 (no. 8). The varieties of services,
including those of tiny boroughs, the *betaghs*, &c., is revealed by the surviving
manorial extents and rentals; cf. Maude Clarke's review of Newport White's
edition of the Red Book of Ormond, in *E.H.R.* xlix (1934), 329. Orpen (iv. 148)
describes the relations between Richard de Burgh, earl of Ulster, and the satellite
Irish chieftains of the province of Ulster; also the difficulties in making agreements
for military service by Anglo-Irish lords outside Ireland (pp. 144–5).

[3] *Foedera*, i. ii. 938.

There was another side to this impressive picture of the resources and loyalty of Ireland. The government certainly held
its own, but only by living from day to day with little or no
thought of the future. The preoccupations of the king and a
remorseless tradition of social cleavage made the second step
towards unity impossible; and, as events were to show in the
next century, it was dangerous, if not fatal, merely to mark time.
All the tendencies which produced the statutes of Kilkenny in
1366 were already at work in the thirteenth century: the distinction between the 'land of peace' and the disturbed areas which
was to divide Ireland into the Pale or 'obedient shires' where the
use of English law, custom, and speech was enforced, and the
rest of the country; the movement to exclude *Hibernici* from
office and from cathedrals, monasteries, and even benefices; the
recognition that a state of peace was in fact a state of uneasy
truce, in which reliance must be placed upon the local Anglo-
Irish lords at the risk of leaving them to mingle with their
ancestral enemies and to intensify their independence of government control by surrender to Irish fashions and ways of life; last
and most significant of all, the resurgence of the Irish themselves,
expressed not only by the renewed vigour of their native sense of
law, poetry, and history, but also by their connexions in Scotland and Wales, their employment of mercenaries drawn to
Ireland from the west Highlands, and their reception, through
the medium of the Church, of continental learning. The English, as one historian has said, had to cut their losses;[1] but, on the
other hand, they could not be ejected. 'Irish law and custom
were unfavourable to soldiering as a profession', just as their
persistent diffusion neither required nor promoted an overruling
centre of administrative power.[2]

The story has never been fully told in one authoritative book.
Its beginnings in the thirteenth century, so significantly suggested, on the one hand, by the employment of troops of mercenary bands or gallowglasses, and on the other hand, by the
activities of the Franciscans, can probably not be told. The
gallowglasses, who fought on foot, were the followers of Highland captains whose families later became well known in Ireland,

---

[1] See E. Curtis, *A History of Ireland* (3rd ed. 1937), pp. 112-14.
[2] Eoin MacNeill, *Early Irish Laws and Institutions* (1935), p. 98; D. A. Binchy, on
the historical value of the Irish law tracts, in *Proc. British Academy*, xxix (1943),
215-16.

for example, the MacSweeneys, the MacDowells, the Mac-
Donalds, the Macruaries. They lost their Scottish roots mainly
in the Scottish wars of independence, but bands of gallowglasses appeared in Ireland in the second half of the thirteenth
century, and in the service of their employers, notably the
O'Donnells of Tirconnell and the O'Conors of Connaught,
showed the promise of the strength which they were to bring
to the Irish resistance.[1]

In a very different tradition, the Franciscans brought strength
to the Irish resistance. Their influence was most penetrating in
the fourteenth and later centuries, but their eager activity after
their first arrival at Youghal in 1231 certainly intensified the
sympathetic relations which, in spite of all attempts to repress
them, existed between the native Irish and the Church, for the
disciples of St. Francis, in their artless and unprejudiced attitude
to life, both appealed and responded to qualities in the Irish
finer and deeper than the sense of oppression.[2] During the
thirteenth century, however, the Franciscans did not take that
outstanding part in the encouragement of a national life, with
a new awareness of the riches of its heritage in the western
world, which they were to take later. They came to a land in
which the Church, so recently reorganized on Roman lines, was
torn between its desire for canonical freedom and the obligation
which the alien government imposed upon it to train the Irish in
obedience. Naturally enough, the leaders of resistance to secular
interference, though they were engaged in a struggle which as
such was not racial at all, tended to align themselves with the
Irish, and, as most of them were Irish themselves, to regard
their protests against lay interference as inseparable from the
right of the Irish to enter religious houses, to enjoy prebends
attached to stalls in cathedral churches, and to be ruled by Irish
bishops. The 'government' view, on the other hand, strongly
maintained, early in the century, by Henry of London, the archbishop of Dublin (1213–28), was that a reorganized Church in a

---

[1] Gallowglass is the anglicized form of the Gaelic *gallóclach*, 'foreign youth or
servant'. On their Highland background and later history see A. McKerral, 'West
Highland Mercenaries in Scotland', in *Scottish Historical Review*, xxx (1951), 1–14.
For their early appearances in Ireland cf. Curtis, *Hist. of Mediaeval Ireland* (1923),
pp. 161, 165, 227.

[2] See the introduction to *Materials for the History of the Franciscan Province of Ire-
land*, edit. by E. B. Fitzmaurice and A. G. Little for the British Soc. of Franciscan
Studies (vol. ix, 1920); also, Robin Flower, 'Ireland and Medieval Europe', in *Proc.
British Academy*, xiii (1927), 271–97.

barbarous island must be under English or, rather, non-Irish leadership.[1] Other springs of Irish feeling in the Church were the Cistercian monasteries and, in their early days, the Dominicans, who had first established themselves in 1224. By the end of the twelfth century thirty-six Cistercian abbeys, distributed over twenty-one dioceses, had been established in Ireland. Though, like the friars in the thirteenth century, the followers of St. Bernard had been welcomed both by the conquerors and by the Irish kings, they inevitably became more Irish in race and sympathy, especially if they relied on the protection of Irish founders and patrons. Mellifont, near Drogheda, the oldest Cistercian abbey in Ireland (1142), was founded by a prince of Uriel, and from the first was a purely Irish house. More than half the Cistercian houses in Ireland were daughters of Mellifont and shared the strong native tradition of their mother. Cathel O'Connor, the king of Connaught, founded Knockmoy abbey, near Tuam, in 1190, on the site of a victory over an English army, and died there in 1224 'in the habit of a monk after triumphing over the world and the devil.'[2] The friars, more mobile and active than the monks, soon provided vigorous Irish bishops and archbishops, able to take the lead in defence of canonical rights and racial claims. After all, the clergy were required to be able to speak the language of their flocks. The attempt to impose an alien hierarchy, never whole-heartedly approved by the papacy, met with little success. On the other hand, as we have seen, bishops took the lead in the campaign for the admission of the Irish to the rule of the common law.

A turning-point, indicating the later policy of rigid division between the English Pale and the rest of Ireland, was reached at the time of the Welsh wars of Edward I. Irish sympathy with

[1] The best introduction to this aspect of Irish history is Aubrey Gwynn's paper on Henry of London in *Studies* (September and December 1949), pp. 297–306, 389–402, especially the account of the efforts of Donnchad Ua Longargain, archbishop of Cashel, against Archbishop Henry's campaign for an English hierarchy in Ireland. The archbishop of Cashel's complaints of abuses from which the Church and the Irish suffered, and the English defence sent to Pope Honorius III, give a good picture of the situation (pp. 393–7). The complaints were frequently repeated later in the reign.

[2] A. Hamilton Thompson, A. W. Clapham, and H. G. Leask, 'The Cistercian Order in Ireland', in *Archaeological Journal*, lxxxviii (1932), reprint of 28 pages. Cf. also Orpen in *E.H.R.* xxviii (1913), 306. The condition of the Cistercian foundations in 1228 is vividly revealed in the record of the official visitation by Stephen of Lexington, abbot of Stanley, later abbot of Clairvaux; see A. Gwynn's review of Stephen's register, edited by B. Griesser (Rome, 1950) in *Studies*, xl (1951), 368–70.

the Welsh was widespread. The differences of outlook within the Irish Church could no longer lie dormant. In 1285 we read of complaints against the favours shown to Dominicans and Franciscans at the exchequer and of suggestions that no Irishman should ever be an archbishop or bishop, 'because they always preach against the king', and 'provide their (cathedral) churches with Irishmen, so that an election of bishops might be made of Irishmen, to maintain their language'. The Franciscan province itself was rent into hostile factions. Nicholas Cusack, the Franciscan bishop of Kildare, of an Anglo-Irish family, reported to the king how he had been told in Dublin about poisonous colloquies held with the Irish and their kings by Irish religious (i.e. monks and friars) of various orders, who instigated them to rebellion as a fight justified by human and divine law. The bishop advised the removal from the convents in dangerous districts of religious with Irish sympathies, and that only good picked Englishmen with English companions should be sent among the Irish in future.[1]

The words 'dangerous districts' are significant. Before long, the policy would not be to send Englishmen into these, but to keep Irish out of religious houses and ecclesiastical office in the 'land of peace', the future Pale. The state of Ireland when King Edward's influence was at its height was revealed in the legislation of the Irish parliament, which would seem to have met early in 1297,[2] the year in which King Edward was hoping for large reinforcements from Ireland in his efforts to concentrate the military resources of England against the king of France.[3] The justiciar summoned to a general parliament prelates, barons, and two knights to be elected with full powers in each county and liberty. After describing the creation of the new counties separated from the unwieldy county of Dublin,[4] the record sets out a long series of provisions designed to maintain the peace in Ireland. These provisions imply that the areas at peace were bounded by marches in which the normal condition was one of

[1] *Materials for the History of the Franciscan Province*, pp. xxii–xxiii, 52–53, and for quarrels in 1291 between the English and Irish friars in the provincial chapter at Cork, pp. 63–64.

[2] The record of this council or parliament survives only in the Black Book of Christ Church, Dublin. It is printed in Berry, *Statutes*, pp. 194–212.

[3] See writs of May 1297 addressed to the justiciar and to the earl of Ulster and thirty other Anglo-Irish lords (*Parl. Writs*, i. 280, 283). Cf. above, p. 553, note 4.

[4] Above, p. 564.

war and truce. Great persons and others who had lands in the
marches were wont to leave them waste and unguarded, and so
to invite depredation in the peaceful manors by Irish felons who
came and went without arrest, hue and cry, or hindrance. The
men of the districts (*compatriotae*) had no armed horses for the
pursuit of felons, and often allowed them to pass with their spoil,
as though they rejoiced in the ruin of their neighbours. Absentee
lords withdrew all the profits of their lands to England or elsewhere and left no provision for their defence. Great men who
resided were too prone to lead armed hosts without warrant
through lands at peace and marches at truce to the grievance of
the community, or to surround themselves with kerns (*kaernias*)
or idlers who battened on the community. Truces were too local
and unregulated, so that the Irish at war entered into them to
suit their temporary convenience, going on to attack others and
sometimes returning to destroy the forts (*forceletta*) and manors
of those with whom they had pretended to make friends. The
English, on their part, were apt to attack and spoil Irish who
were at peace or protected by a general truce or armistice, and
so to provoke them, in their light-mindedness (*cum leves sint*), to
instant and indiscriminate warfare, all the more devastating
because, if the justiciar were not near to take charge, few or none
could be found to resist them. The highways, in this country of
thick woods and deep bogs, were overgrown; bridges and cause-
ways were in need of repair or reconstruction, whereby the Irish
were made more confident in the pursuit of mischief. Finally,
there were English so degenerate as to wear Irish dress and let
the hair grow down from the back of their half-shaven heads in
what the Irish call the *culan*, so that they were regarded as Irishmen and slain, whence feuds among kindred arose, and the
administration of the law which required different ways of
punishment for the killing of an Irishman and an Englishman
(a frequent ground of complaint by the Irish) was confused.

Such is the picture so vividly described in the provisions of
parliament. The appropriate remedies are enjoined, with penalties of distraint and other punishment for non-observance. They
include measures on the lines of the Statute of Winchester (1285)
—local corporate action, to be backed if need be by central support, and, it is interesting to find, the duty of holders of twenty
librates of land or more to be ready with a horse and weapons for
instant resistance to attack. The picture suggests a harassed

justiciar responsible for a lax and diffused administration, officials easily corrupted by power and as easily weakened by fear, indifference, or isolation.[1] We see a land of large counties, in which the operation of the law is supplemented by the traditions of self-help, under the cover of innumerable forts, in a constant state of local strife which, as the history of the previous decades had shown, easily flared up into racial war. Intermarriage, the mingling of Irish and English fashions, and religious influences were bringing about new ways of Anglo-Irish life. The Irish looked for a deliverer, and for a time Robert Bruce seemed to have provided one, when, in the year after his victory at Bannockburn (1314), he sent his brother to Ireland.

The Scots of the fourteenth and fifteenth centuries looked back upon the reigns of Alexander II (1214–49) and Alexander III (1249–86) as a golden age. 'Our gold was changyd into lede.' The child Margaret, who was whisked away from her brother Edward and her companions in Windsor castle to become queen of Scotland in 1251 at the age of eleven and died in 1275, thought Scotland a most uncomfortable land.[2] In fact, life in the 'governed' parts of Scotland was happier and safer, on the whole, in the thirteenth century than it was to be for centuries. The wars of independence created a watershed in Scottish experience as stern as the Grampians. Yet it is always easy to exaggerate the prosperity of the time to which one looks back with regret. The tragic element in Scottish history lies in the broken promise of better things latent in a growing society; broken, as the more fragile promises of unity in Ireland were broken by the social stalemate which led to the statutes of Kilkenny.

In some ways, indeed, Scotland was like Ireland. It also was divided between lands of peace and difficult lands, or rather, into more sharply defined governed and ungoverned areas. This division lasted until the eighteenth century, in spite of the military progresses into the Highlands of the kings in the twelfth and

[1] The impression is confirmed by the *Calendar of the Justiciary Rolls of Proceedings in the Court of the Justiciar of Ireland*, edit. J. Mills (1905), which covers the regnal years 23–31 Edward I (1294–1303). Cf. Mary Bateson in *E.H.R.* xxii (1907), 158–60; and Richardson and Sayles, op. cit., pp. 132–8 *passim*.

[2] Her experiences in the castle at Edinburgh (*castrum puellarum*) were detestable. In May 1258, after the *coup d'état* of the Comyns (below, p. 592), Malise, earl of Strathearn, who had been an ally of King Henry's, undertook to do his best to see that she was not taken against her wish to any place *menti sue tediosa* (*Foedera*, i. i. 371). For details of her life see *D.N.B.*

thirteenth centuries, the surrender of the western Isles and of his hold on the mainland by the king of Norway in 1266, and the resettlements in the sixteenth and seventeenth centuries.[1] In so far as they suggest a united country, maps of medieval Scotland divided into dioceses and shires are misleading. The burghs and castles erected on the edge of the ungoverned lands were strong-points for the defence of their districts, not centres of an ordered administration. Such at first were Inverness and Dumbarton. Centuries later, in the reign of James VI, a suggestion was made to build burghs in Kintyre, Lochaber, and Lewis, as 'colonizing' agencies to hold these areas.[2] The independence of the High-lands was more complete than that of Ireland outside the Pale. This was not due to race. Scotland as a whole was not Anglo-Saxon or Norman-French. The Highland clans grew out of the kinships or *progenies* which in the Lowlands, for example in Fife and Tweeddale, gave coherence and character to feudal rela-tionships. A lord might be described as head of the kindred (*caput progeniei*). The Scot in the twelfth and thirteenth centuries was more conscious of the ties of kindred than English society was, yet more easily adaptable, in the 'governed' parts, than the Irishman to a changing system of land tenure. The sense of personal relations naturally flourished in the Highlands and un-governed parts, and tended to be more relaxed in the governed parts, but in a sparsely inhabited and still primitive country it was always there, for the *nativi* were always there, not to be lumped together as 'Celtic', but as the 'native' population, whether Picts, Scots, British, Angles, or any other folk whom the Normanized kings and lords had introduced to new ways of life and administration. The outcome was the English-speaking Scot with his pungent virility, the verse of Gavin Douglas and Dun-bar, the prose of John Knox, and the patriotic legacy of William Wallace.

The population of Scotland in 1300 has been estimated as about 400,000, of whom nearly half were in the two large dioceses

[1] Cf. J. Hill Burton, *Hist. of Scotland*, vi (1870), 306–13; also A. McKerral, 'The Tacksman and his Holding in the South-west Highlands', in *Scot. Hist. Rev.* xxvi (1947), 10–25.

[2] Here and elsewhere in this brief account of Scotland in the thirteenth century I have been greatly assisted by Professor W. C. Dickinson. For what follows see especially his introductions to *The Sheriff Court Book of Fife, 1515–1522* (1928) and *The Baron Court Book of the Barony of Carnwath, 1523–1542* (1937), both published by the Scottish Historical Society.

of St. Andrews, stretching from Brechin southwards round the estuaries of the Tay and the Forth to the lower Tweed, and Glasgow, embracing the whole of the southern area except the diocese of Whithorn or Galloway, from Dunblane to the Solway and the Cheviots. The bulk of the people 'live in or near lands that can be farmed or coasts that can be fished'. This would indicate, in such a country as Scotland then was, a concentration 'along the shores of the Moray Firth and in Aberdeenshire, Angus, Fife and Strathearn' north of the Forth, and south of the Forth, in Lothian, Tweeddale, and on the shores of the Solway.[1] Only a fraction of the 100,000 people scattered over the diocese of Glasgow can have lived in the large area covered by Ettrick Forest and the hills of the Border. Scotland, it is true, enjoyed, comparatively speaking, much prosperity in Alexander III's time. Connexions with England were continuous, overseas trade was growing, the wealthier landholders, both lay and ecclesiastical, and the burghers in the towns seem to have lived well, some even luxuriously. The intelligent reception of architectural influences can be traced in cathedrals, abbeys, and castles.[2] The income derived from the lands and tithes of the Church, if compared with the population, was nearly as great as that of the Church in England.[3] The Scottish penny was supposed to be equal to the penny sterling, and the currencies of England and Scotland were interchangeable.[4] All the same, a wild country of

[1] T. M. Cooper, in *Scot. Hist. Rev.* xxvi (1947), 2–9, with a sketch-map of the dioceses and tentative tables.

[2] The choir of Glasgow cathedral was built in this period; and cf. W. Douglas Simpson on the influence of Coucy on castle-building in his article on Dirleton castle (ibid. xxvii (1948), 48–56). Alexander II's second wife came from Coucy, and her seneschal was lord of Dirleton.

[3] By 1287 the total sums actually levied from the papal tenth (for six years) of 1274 were £128,388 in England and £17,884 in Scotland, roughly 7 : 1 (Lunt, *Financial Relations*, p. 341). The annual ecclesiastical revenues of England and Scotland as assessed for the next papal tax (1291) were roughly £210,000 in England and £40,000 in Scotland (the sums to be levied being one-tenth of these for each year of the tax). The ratio here is nearer 5 : 1. The Scottish total is given in the report of the collector, John Halton, bishop of Carlisle (*Register* (Canterbury and York Soc., 1913), p. 153), viz. £39,479. 16s. 8d. The total sum collected for the first four years of the tax before the outbreak of war was about £2,000 less than the £15,788 due (ibid., p. 155, where the total due includes in addition the net sum due for the fifth and sixth years from the Isle of Man). For the texts cf. below, p. 583, note.

[4] Cf. *Close Rolls, 1253–4*, p. 2 (letters of 1 November 1253). The regents in England tell Alexander III that the new money in Scotland has been found to 'lack' eightpence in the pound instead of sixpence as in the new English coinage. He is desired to remedy the defect and conform Scottish to English coins *in lacta*; otherwise Scottish money will not be allowed to run in England.

400,000 inhabitants separated in local self-sufficiency by mountains and moorland, forests and bogs, and diverse in outlook and traditions, could not assert itself as though it were Flanders or Provence. In spite of its desolate Border and the comparative isolation of the northern English shires from the lands south of the Trent, its coastal areas could easily be overrun by a resolute foe.

During the two centuries before the death of William the Lion the Scottish kings had generally looked south of the later Border. The alliance with the royal house of Wessex had intensified their ambition to add Northumbria and Cumbria to their kingdom. King John had arrested the claim to the three northern shires and it was formally abandoned in 1237 in the treaty of York. The attempt to assert it should be regarded not as the act of a united Scotland but as a southern development (based on traditions of a Northumbria stretching from the Forth to the Trent) in the formation of a Scottish state. The establishment of the existing Border in 1237 was an incident in a process which was continued in the Highlands by the campaigns of Alexander II and his son. The importance of the southern phase in the process lies in its effects upon the state. For a time the administrative centre was moved from *Scotia* proper, north of the Forth (*ultra mare Scotie*), to the Lowlands. King David frequently held court at Roxburgh and Carlisle; the bounds of his kingdom were, in his view, the river Tees and, in the west, the hills beyond Appleby and Brough, where the Rere Cross in Stainmore marked the frontier.[1] He applied to the defence and administration of Scotland the energy which his English mother, St. Margaret, had shown in religious reform. The unity of Scotland in the governed lands was gradually achieved by his successors on the Anglo-Norman lines which he adopted. Bit by bit the system was applied, first in Lothian, then along the east coast, 'Stirling having been secured as the nodal point', then in the western Lowlands and the central lands from the Clyde to Inverness.[2] The inclusion of Moray in the governed area as a

---

[1] David, when still earl of Cumbria, revived the bishopric of Glasgow. When in 1133 Henry I created the see of Carlisle, the bishop of Glasgow resented the intrusion. A later bishop of Glasgow, John de Cheam, an Englishman (1259–67), claimed the right to extend the boundaries of his see to the Rere Cross of Stainmore. See E. W. M. Balfour-Melville in *Scot. Hist. Rev.* xxvii (1948), 182–4.

[2] Dickinson, *Sheriff Court Book of Fife*, p. 368. See also G. W. S. Barrow on the beginnings of feudalism in Scotland, in *Bulletin of the Institute of Historical Research*, xxix (1956), 1–31.

shire, with its *caput* at Inverness, was an important step in the process.

The earliest sheriffdoms, centred at Roxburgh, Berwick, Edinburgh, Haddington, and Linlithgow,[1] were primarily defence measures against England; but the system as a whole was an assertion of royal authority in the interests of peace and order. King David and his successors, in a word, created a new monarchy, and at the outset depended largely upon feudal vassals of English, Norman, Flemish, and Breton extraction. Unlike the Conqueror in England they could not adopt an existing organization of shire and hundred as the basis of their administration. They did not divide Scotland into clearly defined areas. They used or built primitive castles, to which burghs were generally attached as market centres, under the military control of *vicecomites* or sheriffs, just as the dukes of Normandy and other French princes had done and as, at first, the Norman and Angevin kings did in Wales and Ireland. Their leading vassals often administered their lands as *constabulariae* or, in some cases, hereditary sheriffdoms, in the same way. Indeed, in Selkirk from the time of William the Lion and, later, in Cromarty the king had his own hereditary sheriff.[2] The history of the sheriffdoms, naturally enough, is perplexing, for the formation of the modern shires as definite areas, like the baillages which were established in Normandy and later in France, was a slow and intermittent process, in which king, earls, and barons took part. Although in Alexander III's time the sheriff had his financial, judicial, and administrative duties, he was still primarily the head of a military district, in which castle guard was the main service due from the landholders. The royal and mediated burghs probably owed their early communal character to the share which they had in this administrative system.[3] King David had even linked the abbeys to this system by the grant of additional or 'second' tithes of the proceeds of sheriffdoms to these powerful social communities.[4]

[1] The earliest exchequer accounts (1263) show Haddington and Linlithgow as *constabulariae* of Edinburgh.

[2] Dickinson, *Sheriff Court Book of Fife*, pp. 357, 362. For Cromarty, over the ferry from William the Lion's castle at Dunscaith, and the Norman family of Montalt (Scottish Mowat) see *Scot. Hist. Rev.* xxvi (1947), 171–2.

[3] On the relation between castle and burgh cf. the reviews of W. Murray Mackenzie's important book on the Scottish Burghs (1949) by G. S. Pryde (*Scot. Hist. Rev.* xxviii. 156) and Dickinson (*E.H.R.* lxiv. 513–16).

[4] Dickinson, *Sheriff Court Book*, pp. 386–8.

The new monarchy inevitably roused local opposition. The king ruled rather like a Norman earl of Chester. He had his justiciar, constable, steward, and chancellor. His exchequer was controlled by a chamberlain. He had his household knights and clerks.[1] The population regarded him as a frenchified lord, surrounded by aliens in a court given to foreign ways of life.[2] Local disturbances—for they were no more than local—were followed by grants of land in feudal form. But this phase was over by the time that Moray had been made a shire in the north and Alexander II had given burghal status to Dumbarton, on the north of the Clyde, in return for its defence of the Lennox against the men of the mountains. Behind the line from Cromarty to the Clyde the government was generally accepted. Acceptance was, indeed, as inevitable as sporadic resistance had been, for the veneer of foreigners spread over the land was thin, and the 'native' element of freemen, especially the thanes, rapidly mingled with it in a common social and administrative life. There was no clearly defined 'baronage' in thirteenth-century Scotland. Barons, thanes, and knights shade into each other in the more anglicized areas which had once been part of Northumbria. Distinctions became clearer in the following centuries, when tenures in free barony appear, and the 'free tenants' of king and lords become respectively lairds and 'gudemen'. Rents and services of all kinds existed but not an articulated system of knight service. The Anglo-Norman barons and knights who acquired lands in Scotland had to adapt themselves to a pre-existing economy, in which the 'native' free tenants (as distinct from the *nativi* proper, who were not serfs though probably tied to the land, and the servile element beneath them) were an important class of men. William Wallace, a tenant of the king's steward in Renfrew, then in the sheriffdom of Lanark, was a free tenant in this sense. In later days he would have been styled a 'gudeman' holding of the house of Stewart in its barony of Renfrew.

Hence the system of government in Scotland was much less rigid than that of England. The Norman feudal structure was more susceptible, from top to bottom, to continuous Scottish

---

[1] Cf. the writs issued by the guardians of Scotland to the chamberlain for the payment of fees due to knights, as in King Alexander's time; also the receipts, in I. Stevenson, *Documents illustrative of the History of Scotland*, i (1870), 39–128 *passim* (1286–90).

[2] Cf. Walter of Coventry, ii. 206 (*s.a.* 1212).

practices of every kind. Alexander III, who had very little Scottish blood in his veins, was recognized as king in the traditional Irish manner of the Scots, when he was installed on the stone of Scone, and acclaimed.[1] His earls, who by this time were of very mixed stock, were conscious that they represented the seven Scottish *mormaers* who had ruled ancient provinces and whose successors still claimed an authoritative voice. They and other lords of regalities, including some of the abbeys, were independent of the sheriffs and held their courts with little interference from the Crown. The sheriff, as he came to administer new law, was superseding the local *judex* who declared the law of the province, but the *judex* still survived and became the dempster who declared the judgement of the court.[2] The practices of land tenure were rooted in ancient custom. At the same time, though the social landscape of the thirteenth century is largely hidden in mist, it is possible to discern in it, in simpler and looser form, a lively and vigorous replica of the system which prevailed in England. The mist is certainly there. The laws ascribed to the early feudal kings from King David onwards still await thorough critical investigation in the light of recorded fact, the law books *Regiam majestatem*, based on Glanvill, and *Leges Burgorum* are unsafe as practical guides, the earliest registers of writs were compiled in the fourteenth century, the official records, inventoried in 1282 and also in 1291, are lost, the administrative and legal activities in Scotland of Edward I may tend to hide as much as they reveal, the practices of later times may often suggest a false archaism, unjust to the earlier royal administration just because they seem so primitive and disorderly[3]—all this is true, yet something substantial remains.

---

[1] Schramm, *The English Coronation*, pp. 13, 243–5.

[2] Dickinson, op. cit., pp. lxvi–lxix.

[3] For example, one would like to know how far exemption from the jurisdiction of a sheriff on the ground of his 'deadly enmity and feud', and enactments to limit 'followings' of friends and retainers, and the procedure of repledging, whereby a lord could recall an action, as within his lawful or chartered jurisdiction, under pledge to do justice in his court—all well-known later practices—prevailed in the period before 1286. (For these see Dickinson, pp. xxvii–xxx, 344–6.) See also for Scottish law in the thirteenth century the introduction to Lord Cooper's *Select Scottish Cases* (1944) and his edition of *Regiam Majestatem* (Stair Soc., 1947). Now that more is known about the growth of procedure under royal writs in England, and the great activity of the English shire courts in the thirteenth century, it is easier to realize at what stage judicial administration had arrived in Scotland, where there was no central bench of common pleas. Cf. G. J. Turner, *Brevia Placitata* (Selden Soc., 1951).

There was a coherent system of justice controlled by the justiciars and by the king in council. The lesser landholders owed
suit to the shire courts. Appeal of neglect of justice from their
courts could be made to the sheriff and from the sheriff to the
Crown. The new law was growing and taking hold. Commissions of inquiry to establish the facts by local juries were used.
Self-help was restrained by frequent resort to special commissions, arbitral awards and compositions roughly corresponding
to the English final concord in its early and less fictitious form.

In Alexander III's reign government was controlled by the
king, magnates, the justiciar of Scotland, the justiciar of Lothian,
the steward, the chamberlain at the exchequer, and the sheriffs.
During the king's minority (1249-62) the country had got used
to a group of governors, who reappear after his death. Assemblies or parliaments of prelates and magnates seem to have met
at intervals and, later in the reign, perhaps more regularly.
Judicial business of special importance might be decided in
parliament, and though it is unlikely that parliament had 'as its
primary purpose the dispensing of justice', a regular succession
of assemblies, in which cases were tried 'before the king and his
council in parliament', appears in John Baliol's brief reign.[1] The
sheriffs were given more freedom than they possessed in contemporary England. They collected all the ordinary revenue
and accounted to the exchequer for the proceeds of Crown lands,
thanages, feudal dues, escheats, profits of justice and on merchandise; they assessed lands and rents for purposes of occasional
taxation and collected the tax.[2] They co-operated with the
justiciar when he was on eyre, and were responsible for gathering and leading the men of their shires in time of war, including
probably the tenants of monastic liberties.[3] But to an extent
unknown in England the leadership in both war and peace lay
with the prelates, earls, and magnates. Only when these were
hopelessly divided, as they were in 1296-7, after Edward I's
first great campaign, did the free tenants of the king and lords
begin to display their latent power of resilient independence.

[1] For the minority of Alexander III see below, pp. 589-91; on the early parliaments see Richardson and Sayles, 'The Scottish Parliaments of Edward I', in *Scot.
Hist. Rev.* xxv (July 1928), 300-4. They seem to me to strain the evidence of continuity between 1255 and the reign of Robert Bruce.

[2] Dickinson, op. cit., pp. xlvii-xlviii. A grant of the 'tenth penny' to King Robert
in 1326 was based upon a valuation made in Alexander III's reign.

[3] Cf. ibid., p. xlii.

Normally the lords of regalities in the 'governed' lands shared the responsibility of war and administration with the Crown, as leaders in war, as counsellors or, if need be, as governors, and often as justiciars and sheriffs. It is advisable, at this point, to look at their ties with England.

First let us consider the lay lords. Anglo-Scottish social relationships after King David's time were not like those of the lords of the Isles, Argyll (*Ergadia*) and Galloway, with the native lords of Ulster, and the kings of Man. In this sphere of social awareness, age-long traditions and proximity to a common sea, under the distant protection of the kings of Norway, fostered understandings and led to family unions, but they could achieve little more. In 'governed' Scotland, on the other hand, the new monarchy, by its very nature, seemed to seek and provide closer ties with England, so that the prospect of a more formal union was always open. During the century before the settlement of the frontiers in 1237, the integration of Scottish, English, and Norman-French lordships in a single aristocratic society proceeded rapidly on the basis laid by the Norman, Flemish, and English vassals of King David and his successors. The history of the English and Scottish peerage culled from royal records, private charters, and chroniclers reveals the process at every turn. In the reign of Alexander III most of the earls and magnates held honors or manors in England of the English king; some of them were more active in England as vassals of Henry III than they were in Scotland. They were summoned to the feudal hosts, fought in Wales and Gascony, held office as judges, castellans, and sheriffs, and appeared constantly as litigants in the English courts. A younger branch of the house of Baliol was early settled at Cavers in Roxburghshire. Alexander Baliol of Cavers, the chamberlain of Alexander III, whose brother Guy had borne Simon de Montfort's standard at Evesham and been killed with his leader, was regarded as a Scot in England; but he belonged to a group of Anglo-Scottish families, and, after service with King Edward, retired to a Kentish manor.[1] The house of Stewart, which gloried later in its fictitious Scottish ancestry, was descended from a young member of the Breton family of FitzAlan,

[1] *Complete Peerage*, ed. Vicary Gibbs, i. 386; and the lives of Alexander and his father Henry in *D.N.B.* They intermarried with the houses of Berkeley and Valognes. Alexander acquired Chilham in Kent through his wife. His grandson sold Cavers to the earl of Douglas in 1368, and was the last of the Baliols in the Scottish records.

so famous in Shropshire and Sussex and, indeed, in English history. Walter FitzAlan was established by King David, after his arrival from Oswestry, at Renfrew among the Welsh of Strathclyde. He was the first of the hereditary lay stewards. He founded the Cluniac priory at Paisley with monks from Wenlock, 'for the souls of King Henry of England, King David and King Malcolm'. His family flourished, intermarried with other great Anglo-Scottish families, and in due course became the royal house of Stewart.[1]

In the twelfth century, it has been said, the ruling class in Scotland was almost exclusively recruited from the Norman element, to which the Breton and Flemish should be added. The house of Moray (*Moravia*) was of Flemish origin. Alexander Pilche, who joined Andrew of Moray in the first resistance to King Edward, was a Fleming. In the thirteenth century such descendants of the ancient Scottish families as were earls were closely intermingled with the new families from the south. So were the English earls of Dunbar; so were the new earls of Ross, son and grandson of the native Highlander Ferquhard Mac-Taggart, who had received his earldom in 1225 after strenuous service to William the Lion and Alexander II.[2] The earldom of Angus passed by marriage to the house of Umfraville, of Buchan to the Comyns, of Monteith to the Stewards. After a turbulent history, the lordship of Galloway was divided between John Baliol and Roger de Quincy, earl of Winchester, one of the most widespread landholders in England and Scotland; but before this happened the lords of Galloway had become firmly embedded in the new order.[3] The Baliols of Castle Barnard and

---

[1] J. T. T. Brown, 'The Origin of the House of Stewart', in *Scot. Hist. Rev.* xxiv (July 1927), 265–79. It is possible that Walter was the knight who troubled Ailred, later abbot of Rievaulx, when Ailred was King David's *dapifer*, for he is said to have been given high office later. In fact he became steward to David and Malcolm. See Powicke, *Ailred of Rievaulx* (1950), p. 9, n.; and for King Malcolm's famous charter, granting him the hereditary stewardship with Renfrew and Paisley, &c., see Brown, pp. 273–4. As Brown shows (p. 267, n.) the English fitzAlans were well aware of their connexion with the Scottish family. In 1334 Richard fitzAlan claimed to be high steward of Scotland.

[2] *Complete Peerage*, xi. 142–3. Ferquhard is said to have been lay priest of Apple-cross; his ancestral lands in the north of the province of Argyll were added to his earldom. His son William Ros, earl from 1251 to 1274, married a daughter of William Comyn, afterwards earl of Buchan in right of his Scottish wife, and justiciar. His grandson the third earl served King Edward from 1303 and was made warden of Scotland beyond Spey in 1305. The second son of this third earl was a scholar at Cambridge in 1306–7 (Bain, *Calendar*, ii, no. 1937).

[3] Roland, who died at Northampton in 1200, had been justiciar and, in right of

Galloway, and the Bruces of Yorkshire, who had long been lords of Annandale on the Scottish side of the Solway, were at first less firmly rooted in Scottish affairs than were the Comyns, who claimed descent from Donald Bane, the eleventh-century king of Scots. The founder of the fortunes of this family was a clerk, William Cumin, who had probably come north with Henry I's chancellor Godfrey in 1133, when the latter became bishop of Durham, and when King David and his son Henry were so powerful in Northumbria. William became King David's chancellor. 'The Scottish king had taken the chancellor straight from the English chancery'.[1] The chancellor's nephew Richard, who married into a well-established English family in Northumberland, was the first of the Scottish family of Cumin or Comyn, the Comyns of Badenoch.[2] It was his descendant, William Comyn (d. 1233) who, in right of his wife, became earl of Buchan and was succeeded in the earldom by his son Alexander (d. 1289). It was Alexander's brother Walter of Badenoch, earl of Menteith[3] (d. 1258), who was the mainstay of King Alexander II and who, during the minority of Alexander III, with Alexander and others was ejected from the council of regency in 1255 by King Henry III, and made the *coup d'état* of 1257.[4] Walter was succeeded in Badenoch by John Comyn (d. 1274), the father of the claimant to the throne, and the grandfather of the John Comyn of Badenoch (the Red) who led the Scottish resistance on behalf of King John Baliol, and was slain in Dumfries by Robert Bruce in 1306. In the course of time these men had added to their influence by marriage. Earl Alexander had married a coheiress of Roger de Quinci, so that his son succeeded

his wife, held the lands in Scotland and England of William de Morville, the constable of Scotland, whom he succeeded. (For this Morville family, the first of whom had founded Dryburgh abbey, and its Norman and English connexions, see Lewis C. Lloyd, *The Origins of some Anglo-Norman Families* (Harleian Soc., 1951), pp. 49–50, 70. The Haigs of Bemersyde, near Dryburgh, probably came with this Hugh de Morville to Scotland in King David's time.) Roland of Galloway's successor, Alan, married a daughter of David, earl of Huntingdon, and Devorguilla, wife of John Baliol, lord of east Galloway *jure uxoris*, was his daughter. Hence came the claim of their son to be king of Scotland.

[1] J. H. Round, 'The Origin of the Comyns', in *The Ancestor*, x (July 1904), 104–19, at p. 108.

[2] Round disentangled the story of Richard Cumin's relations in Northumberland. The later claim to descent from Donald Bane was traced through Richard's wife Hextilda.

[3] The earldom ultimately went to the Stewards.

[4] See below, p. 592.

to lands in west Galloway. John Comyn the claimant married a
daughter of John Baliol. John the Red married a sister of King
Edward's lieutenant Aymer de Valence, earl of Pembroke.

The confederates who seized power in 1257-8 under the
leadership of Walter of Badenoch, earl of Menteith, and his
brother Alexander, earl of Buchan, the justiciar of Scotland,
comprised five members of the Comyn family, the earls of Mar
and Ross, members of the Montalt, Berkeley, and Moray families, and three or four more, including the chamberlain.[1] They
were, in the main, a court party, opposed to those who had
taken action with King Henry on behalf of his daughter the
queen. They resented Henry's masterful intervention in the administration of Scotland, but they resented equally the rise of
another party which had driven the Comyns from power in
1255. The events of 1255-8, to be described later, are prophetic
of the kind of trouble which would arise when the succession to
the throne was in doubt, but they do not reveal the existence of a
national party. After Alexander III came of age (1262) the relations of the court and magnates, including earl Alexander and
John Comyn of Badenoch, with the English court were friendly
and intimate for thirty years. The earl was especially concerned
to secure in England the rights, disputed in the court of Henry
III by her sister, of his wife, a daughter and coheiress of the earl
of Winchester. John Comyn, as a vassal of Henry for his lands in
Northumberland, was summoned with other northern barons
to serve against the Welsh early in 1264, and later in the year
fought in the royalist army at Northampton and Lewes, where
he was taken prisoner. Later he was handsomely rewarded by the
king and was frequently in England.[2] William Comyn of Kilbride, another member of the family, was disinherited of his
English lands as a partisan of Earl Simon, then pardoned at the
instance of King Alexander.[3] Other magnates of Scotland were

[1] The list of names is taken from the parties to the agreement with the Welsh
princes early in 1258 (J. G. Edwards, *Littere Wallie*, p. 184). It should be noted that
until Queen Margaret began to complain the Comyns had co-operated in council
with John Baliol and Robert de Ros, kinsmen of King Alexander, whom King
Henry had made governors of the royal pair, and whom he dismissed with the rest
of the council of regency (below, pp. 589-90).

[2] For the summons see *Close Rolls, 1261-4*, pp. 381-2; for King Henry's lavish
promise of 300 librates of land and the 'foretaste of more abundant grace' which
marked his inability to fulfil it see *Cal. Pat. Rolls, 1266-72*, pp. 175, 535; with
Edward I's confirmation (1275), ibid., *1272-81*, p. 90.

[3] *Close Rolls, 1264-8*, p. 437.

still more involved in English interests than were the Comyns. Indeed, if King Alexander had not had a fatal accident in 1286 at the early age of forty-five, the social connexion between the two kingdoms might well have become stronger.

The outlook of the bishops, religious houses, and clergy of Scotland was more parochial. Even the friars, in spite of their far-flung organization, seem to have shared it.[1] The Church in Scotland was self-contained, always on the alert against inter-ference from the province of York, and determined to maintain its direct dependence upon the Holy See. The popes had not confirmed William the Lion's recognition, forced on him by Henry II, that the Scottish bishops were dependent upon York. They had declared the Church in Scotland to be immediately subject to the Holy See as its *filia specialis*. Pope Honorius III, who confirmed the bulls of his predecessors in 1218, defined the relationship when in 1225, refusing to give Scotland provincial status by the creation of an archbishopric, he allowed the bishops to hold councils under the presidency of a *conservator* to be chosen by them from among themselves.[2] His successor, Gregory IX, extended the legatine authority of the Cardinal Otto in 1237 to Scotland, and, in spite of King Alexander II's reluctance to receive him, Otto, in the autumn of 1239, held a council in the monastery of Holyrood, issued constitutions based upon those issued in London, did a good deal to strengthen the reforming element in the Scottish Church, and, it would seem, arranged for the collection of a subsidy for the papal crusade against the emperor.[3] It was not, however, through legatine commissions and papal taxation[4] that Scotland was welded to the Holy See

[1] Cf. W. Mackay Mackenzie on the grey friars in *Scot. Hist. Rev.* xxvii (October 1948), 105–13, where the argument is rather forced. On the Scottish Church gener-ally see John Dowden, *The Medieval Church in Scotland* (1910), also his *Bishops of Scotland* (1912); and A. R. MacEwen, *History of the Church in Scotland*, i. 174–251.

[2] The outcome in provincial and diocesan constitutions, though encouraged by the legate Otto, was not considerable. See next note.

[3] See Dorothy M. Williamson, in *Scot. Hist. Rev.* xxviii (April 1949), pp. 20–26, and the texts and literature there used.

[4] The earliest record of papal taxation in Scotland is the incomplete return of the crusading tenth ordered at Lyons in 1274 for six years. This was made by Baia-mundus de Vitia, the papal collector. In later versions it was known in Scotland as Bagimond's Roll. The original record, which survives in a Vatican manuscript, was partly printed by Theiner, *Vetera monumenta Hibernorum et Scotorum historiam illu-strantia* (1864), pp. 109–16, and partly by W. E. Lunt in *E.H.R.* xxxii (1917), 59–61 (with other documents from the same volume in the Vatican). The whole state-ment has been re-edited, with an introduction, by Annie I. Dunlop in *Miscellany of the Scottish History Society*, vi (1939), 77 pages. The relations between his assessment

and that the Scottish bishops and clergy acquired, in their reliance upon it, their sense of confident independence, but through the constant oversight of the Curia and its use of episcopal authority and local judges delegate. Pope Gregory might feel in 1237 that the Scottish Church did not recognize the Roman Church as its sole mother and metropolitan,[1] but he and his successors certainly acted as though it did. They took the place of an archbishop. Since they had perforce to rely on local knowledge and to delegate much authority, they indirectly widened the experience and gave purpose to the activity of their subjects. The influence of this discipline was especially marked in the conduct of elections and the administration of justice. The general level of ability and character maintained by the Scottish episcopate was higher than might be expected; and this must be attributed to the care with which the popes, working through commissions of bishops, supervised the conduct of elections.[2] The use of judges delegate, generally denizens of Scotland, has been regarded by jurists as the most remarkable legal feature of Scottish history in the early thirteenth century. Conflict between lay and ecclesiastical jurisdiction, compared to the developments in England, was so casual as to make it insignificant; in cases which affected the interests of the Church, 'parties chose the tribunal which they preferred, . . . even for the decision of disputes not falling within the proper jurisdiction of the Courts Christian'—about claims to land, rights of patronage, dower (or terce), tithes, and other matters; and most of the cases came before judges delegated by the pope to hear them.[3] Knowledge of legal principles and procedure, the study of canon law, and the growth of a legal profession were promoted where they were most needed.

The strength which papal guidance gave to the Scottish Church was certainly needed. Without it the impetus given by St. Margaret might well have died for lack of direction. The lavish endowment of abbeys and the formation of parishes, deaneries, archdeaconries, and dioceses did not ensure the

---

and that of John Halton, bishop of Carlisle, the collector of the tenth for six years ordered by Pope Nicholas IV in 1291, were examined by T. F. Tout, in his introduction to Halton's register, reprinted in his *Collected Papers*, ii (1934), 107–23, and by Mrs. Dunlop in her introduction.   [1] *Cal. Papal Letters*, i. 161.

[2] Ibid., *passim*, for numerous examples.

[3] Cooper, *Select Scottish Cases*, pp. xxvii–xxxix. The quotation in the text is from p. xxxv.

continuation of religious fervour or the canonical growth of an
orderly ecclesiasticism.[1] The records of the new foundations are
themselves the best witness to the perplexing way in which
geographical and social forces seemed, as though of set purpose,
to shape them and adjust them to the influence of the old Scottish life and the new feudalism. This is part of Scottish history,
too intricate to be considered here. The leaders of the Scottish
Reformation in the sixteenth and seventeenth centuries were
themselves forced to compromise with the obstinate persistence
of traditions which the wars for independence had done much
to revive. In the thirteenth century, however, a practical concordat between the lay and ecclesiastical systems was reached.
Bishops and abbots worked with earls and magnates as guardians of social order and as advisers of the king; and, whether he
realized it or not, King Edward had more reason to fear the ecclesiastics than the barons.[2] The ecclesiastics were both more rooted
in the land and wider in their outlook; more alert to meet any
danger to their independence and better able to rally the lairds
and gudemen of the country-side in resistance to English claims.

The prosperity enjoyed by the Scottish kingdom during the
reigns of Alexander II and his son, and their successful re-establishment of royal authority, at least in name, over the western
Highlands were largely due to their relations with the English
Crown. Apart from two or three military demonstrations from
each side, the high road was open,[3] the borders were free from
unusual disturbance, and peace prevailed between the two
countries. In 1221 Alexander II (1214–49) married Joan, the
young sister of King Henry; in 1251 Alexander III, his son by
his second wife, Marie de Coucy, was married at the age of ten
to Henry's daughter Margaret, a child of eleven. These domestic
ties maintained frequent intercourse between the two courts,

[1] See M. Morgan's paper, 'The Organization of the Scottish Church in the
Twelfth Century', in *Trans. Royal Hist. Soc.*, 4th series, xxix (1947), 135–49; also
Annie Dunlop's introduction to *Bagimond's Roll* (noted above, p. 585, n.). Mrs.
Dunlop has kindly discussed problems of Scottish history with me.
[2] When Queen Margaret was dying at Cupar castle in February 1275, she
received the last sacraments from her Franciscan confessor, and refused the bishops
and abbots admission to her chamber (*Lanercost Chronicle*, ed. J. Stevenson (1839),
p. 97).
[3] Cf., for example, the papal provision in 1255 for the Cluniac priory of Pontefract, 'on the high road from England to Scotland', where travellers were received
(*Cal. Papal Letters*, i. 314).

and raised hopes, not in England only, of still closer relations in the future. At the same time, as the political and ecclesiastical administrations in the northern kingdom became more stable and intricate, its relations with other lands grew in intimacy, notably with the lands stretching from Scandinavia to France, while friendly and tactful supervision of Scottish affairs by the popes was continuous. When Alexander III died in 1286 Scotland seemed to be well established as one of the smaller states of the west.

The first important step towards the establishment of good relations between Alexander II and his brother-in-law was made in 1237, under the guidance of the legate Otto. From the first Alexander had complained with some justice that King John's treaty with his father William the Lion (1212) had not been observed, and pressed for the return at least of £10,000 exacted under the treaty from the Scots. He also revived the claim to the northern counties.[1] The difficulties which beset the minority of King Henry and his own connexions with baronial parties in England had encouraged Alexander to maintain his claims, in spite of the failure of his former ally Louis of France to establish himself in England.[2] In the spring of 1237 relations between the two kings were very strained, but the arrival of the legate in July, armed with a papal mandate to reconcile their differences, eased the tension.[3] Under his guidance the kings came to an agreement at York in September. Alexander abandoned his claim to the northern counties and the demand for the money paid under the treaty of 1212 and agreed to the cancellation of this treaty; in return he was granted lands in the two northern shires, outside boroughs and castles, of the annual value of £200, to be held of the king of England with full regalian rights and exemption from taxation, but subject to the jurisdiction by English justices on eyre of the pleas of the Crown.[4] The alloca-

---

[1] A. L. Poole, *From Domesday Book to Magna Carta*, pp. 281–3. The arrangements, so far as they went, made at the time of his marriage (1221) and at a meeting between the two kings in September 1236, had not satisfied Alexander.

[2] King Henry regarded Alexander with much suspicion because of his activities on the Border, his reception of persons regarded as traitors, the growth of piracy in the Irish Sea, and the alleged disregard of Alexander's oath of allegiance. He objected to the election of the prior of Durham as bishop of the see, as an enemy who had taken an oath of fealty to the king of Scots: papal mandate to the legate Otto in October 1239 (*Cal. Papal Letters*, i. 183).

[3] Dorothy M. Williamson, 'The Legate Otto in Scotland and Ireland', in *Scot. Hist. Rev.* xxviii (1949), 14–20.   [4] *Foedera*, i. i. 233–4.

tion of these lands in Northumberland and Cumberland was made by sworn men from both sides, under the arbitration of the legate and his clerks. Ultimately the king of Scots was granted the honor of Tyndale in Northumberland (at one time held by his ancestors) and the manor of Penrith with other lands and rights in Cumberland.[1] The honor, in fact, remained geographically part of England, and the settlement of 1237 maintained the borders between England and Scotland as they had been established in the days of Henry II and John.

King Alexander was not satisfied, and King Henry was still suspicious. The death of Joan, wife of the one and sister of the other, on 9 March 1238 broke a close tie and, as she left no children, made the succession to Scotland uncertain. It must have been at this time that Alexander put forward the young Robert Bruce, son of his niece Isabel, as his heir and, if the story is true, got him recognized as such by the earls and magnates of the kingdom.[2] In May 1239, however, the king married Marie de Coucy, the daughter of a great French house. The birth of a son and heir in September 1241 restored his confidence, while his new relation with France must have disturbed King Henry, still longing, as he was, to recover Poitou and to win a name for himself on the continent. Then, hard on Henry's failure in the French war of 1242–3, came the threat of trouble in Wales and the outbreak of 1244.[3] Alexander was building forts near the Border, Scottish pirates were active in the Irish Sea. Henry's complaints were fruitless, and, before turning against David of Snowdonia, he decided to make a great demonstration of strength. He closed the ports of England and Ireland to Scottish trade and shipping and the roads to Scotland to aliens, summoned the feudal host to meet at Newcastle on 1 August 1244, collected ships and supplies, and ordered his Irish vassals, including the Irish chiefs, to be ready to come to his aid, in case the king of Scots should refuse to give him satisfaction.[4] King Alexander came to Newcastle in force. The expected happened.

---

[1] Bain, *Calendar of Docs. relating to Scotland*, i. no. 1575. For the negotiations cf. *Close Rolls, 1237–42*, pp. 121, 141. The king of Scots' lands in Tyndale comprised west Northumberland in the valleys and uplands of the north and south Tyne. The administrative centre was the manor of Wark, to be distinguished from the castle of Wark-on-Tweed. See Margaret M. Moore, *The Lands of the Scottish Kings in England* (1915), *passim*.

[2] Below, p. 602.   [3] Above, p. 399.

[4] See *Close Rolls, 1242–7*, pp. 142–3, 253–7, and *passim*; Shirley, *Royal Letters*, ii. 37–38.

A new treaty was made; the king of Scots, in terms less sub-
missive than those imposed on William the Lion by King John
(1212), solemnly promised not to enter into any alliance hostile
to his liege-lord or his heirs, provided that the settlement of 1237
were observed and that the marriage arranged between his son
Alexander and King Henry's daughter were made.[1]

Alexander died, on an expedition through the west Highlands,
in June 1249, before the marriage of his son. A new phase in
Anglo-Scottish relations opened when the boy, eight years of
age, was set as king on the stone at Scone. Alexander III was
brought to York, did homage for his lands in England, was
knighted, and was married to Henry's daughter Margaret.
Henry had already taken steps, immediately after Alexander II's
death, to settle the delimitation of the Border, a problem which
had been investigated in local disputes and discussed in 1222 and,
again, in 1246-8. The sheriffs of Northumberland, Berwick, and
Roxburgh were required to perambulate the March, and to
establish its customs or law with the aid of local recognitors. The
findings were set out in a definite treaty.[2] The importance of this
treaty does not lie in the actual details of demarcation, for, as
late as the sixteenth century, the actual frontier both in east and
west was still disputed in certain areas,[3] but in the fact that it
was an attempt to deal with the whole situation. Until the end
of the century, when the state of war required a special military
and administrative system under wardens of the March, the
responsibility for maintaining the peace and dealing with cases
'according to the custom of the March' was the sheriff's, and, it
would seem, the earl of Dunbar's.[4] It would not be easy to say
what exactly the range of the March was, for cattle-lifting, illicit
dealings in stolen cattle, forays, and robberies might have to be

[1] *Foedera*, I. i. 257. Richard of Cornwall, for King Henry, and four Scottish barons,
for King Alexander, swore observance of the settlement at Newcastle. Later, Scottish bishops, seven earls, and others, who had also made oath, appended their seals
to the terms, as sent by Alexander to Henry.

[2] R. R. Reid in *E.H.R.* xxxii (1917), 479-82, where the texts and literature on
the subject are noted.

[3] See W. Mackay Mackenzie in *Scot. Hist. Rev.* xxx (1951), 109-25, on the
'debatable' land, especially between the rivers Esk and Sark in the west March.

[4] The earl of Dunbar held his lands in Northumberland for an annual payment
of thirty shillings and, say the jurors of an inquisition in 1292, 'shall be *inborwe* and
uteborwe', on the March (Bain, *Calendar*, ii, no. 632). His duties, as described by Miss
Reid, were to grant safe-conducts to men crossing the border in search of justice
and to distrain breakers of the law of the Marches (op. cit., p. 481). For the duties
of the sheriff see a case of 1249 in *Close Rolls, 1247-51*, pp. 345, 356.

traced over a wide area in wild and desolate country. The customs of the March, with their realistic practices,[1] suggest a vague area, where escape to or raids into a land under an alien jurisdiction were easy. There was certainly no systematic fortification of the Border,[2] which in this respect differed from the Welsh March or even the chaotic marches distributed through Ireland. The long peace between England and Scotland in the thirteenth century was not an 'armed' peace. Barons like the Baliols and Bruces enjoyed their lands and rents in both kingdoms and served each king with little embarrassment; and when war came the freemen of the northern shires had to be drilled and cajoled into the service of the Crown.

King Henry regarded himself as responsible, in a way never clearly defined, for the well-being of the realm of Scotland and the fortunes of his son-in-law and daughter. He attached two members of the Scottish council of regency, John Baliol and Robert de Ros, to their household as guardians.[3] The domestic solicitude and characters of Henry and Queen Eleanor would make them continuously attentive to news from Scotland. Difficulties began in 1254, when Henry was in Gascony. At the end of December 1253 the queen and the earl of Cornwall in Henry's name urgently required Alexander to convoke the prelates and magnates of Scotland at Edinburgh castle where he and Margaret lived, to hear what royal messengers from Gascony would expound to them and to beg their counsel and aid. The royal letters justify this request on the ground that the close ties between the two kingdoms required mutual consideration between them of urgent and difficult matters affecting the interests of both or either of them; and it would seem that King Henry wished to have Scottish help against Alfonso of Castile.[4] If this

[1] Cf. T. Hodgkin in *Pol. Hist. of England*, edit. Hunt and Poole, i. 424–5. The *Leges*, as described in 1249, are printed in *Acts of the Parliament of Scotland*, i. 413–16.
[2] See especially the interesting discussion of the so-called 'peels', erroneously associated with the Border, by W. Mackay Mackenzie, *The Medieval Castle in Scotland* (1927), pp. 18–21, 196–202. Edward I's timbered enclosures at Lochmaben (outside Bruce's castle) and Selkirk were called 'peels'.
[3] Baliol of Castle Barnard was lord of half Galloway; Ros of Wark-on-Tweed also had lands in Scotland. Both were descended from kings of the Scots. The young king and queen grew very impatient of their interference (*Chron. maj.* v. 272, 501–6; cf. *Ann. monast.* i. 337). Their discharge of their duties led to the amercement of Baliol and the temporary downfall of Robert de Ros; see *Complete Peerage*, xi. 120.
[4] *Close Rolls, 1253–4*, p. 108. This view is not certain, but is suggested by the request for counsel and aid (*auxilium*).

were so, the demand would certainly meet with opposition in Scotland and would help to explain later developments. The crisis in Gascony passed, and was succeeded by a domestic crisis at the Scottish court, complicated by the resistance of Alexander and his wife to their guardians. In August Baliol and Ros were ordered to withdraw from Alexander's council pending its reconstruction, and in September the archbishop of York and Simon de Montfort were sent to the king and his council on business affecting the honour of both kings.[1] After his return to England in 1255 Henry negotiated busily with his friends at the Scottish court. He had decided to go north himself.

The king combined what he described as the fulfilment of his long-felt desire to see his beloved daughter with a military demonstration. Not only the tenants-in-chief but also the *vavassores* who held of them were summoned by the sheriffs to join him in arms. He made Ros's castle of Wark-on-Tweed his headquarters (8–21 August) and there awaited the arrival of Alexander and Margaret, for whom he had previously issued safe-conducts.[2] In the meantime his agents in Edinburgh, the earl of Gloucester and John Mansel, had combined with Henry's chief ally, Alan the Durward (*ostiarius*), to bring the king and queen to Roxburgh. There a body of important persons, including the earls of Fife, Dunbar, Strathearn, and Carrick, established a new council of regency, to hold office for the next seven years, until Alexander came of age. The new counsellors displaced the two Comyns, earls of Menteith and Buchan, John Baliol, Robert de Ros, and other counsellors of whom Alexander and Margaret had complained. In the document in which they described their *coup d'état*, the young king is made to declare that King Henry had come to the March at his and their request and that the new government had been established in co-operation with him. Henry, on the same day, took them under his protection and promised not to have any relations with 'the rebels'. He stated explicitly that the earl of Gloucester and John Mansel had enlisted the support of the new leaders (*ad se attraxissent*) and that the former counsellors had resisted his orders (*rebelles mandato nostro*). He promised that, after the expiry of the seven years, no prejudice to the liberties of the Scottish realm should arise and that the statement (*scriptum*) submitted to him should

---

[1] *Close Rolls, 1253–4*, pp. 266, 272–3.
[2] *Close Rolls, 1254–6*, pp. 216, 218.

then become null and void. The new counsellors did not intend to create a precedent for interference with their king.[1]

This is not quite the whole story. Three of the Scottish earls and most of the new counsellors had been in communication with Henry some weeks before he reached Wark. Letters of assurance and protection were issued for them at Cawood in Yorkshire early in August. The earl of Gloucester and his colleagues found the ground prepared. Moreover, it is clear from these letters that Henry's action was due to his anxiety about his daughter. He denied that he had any intention to seek a dissolution of her marriage, or to attempt to procure the disinheritance of the king. Also both sides already had in view a settlement for the next seven years, until Alexander was twenty-one years of age.[2] Henry regarded the settlement as a responsibility which bound both parties to it. The new council in Scotland had been appointed by himself (*posuimus*). Its opponents were rebels, against whom he would defend the king and queen with all the military strength of the northern shires of England. Alexander, until he came of age, had submitted himself to Henry's counsel and protection. The alliance between them justified Henry's intention to bring 'wholesome counsel and aid to the reform of your (Alexander's) state, to the honour and advantage of yourself and your realm'. In 1256 he sent John Mansel to treat between Alexander and the 'rebels' and provided for armed support, should this be required. When, in 1257, the queen mother returned to Scotland with her second husband, John of Acre, the butler of France, Henry, as the condition attached to their safe-conduct, required from them a sworn undertaking that they would do nothing to disturb the settlement.[3] In 1260 Queen Margaret was brought to England to give birth to her first child. Even in 1263, a year after Alexander came of age, Henry and his council urged him, in the interests of his family, not to run the risks attached to the

---

[1] *Foedera*, I. i. 327, 329. The statement of 20 September with the king's assurances of 21 September were afterwards, according to a note on the patent roll, combined in letters patent by the earl of Gloucester and other English barons at Carlisle. Henry himself returned to Westminster for the feast of St. Edward (13 October).

[2] Ibid., pp. 325, 326. At Wark, Queen Eleanor fell ill, and wished her daughter to stay on with her after Henry had left. This was allowed on Henry's assurances for her restoration to her husband (p. 328).

[3] *Close Rolls, 1256–9*, p. 134; see also pp. 290, 329, where Henry expounds his position. For the mission of John Mansel in 1256, *Foedera*, I. i. 347.

expedition to the west Highlands and Islands which is the most famous incident in his reign.[1]

Henry's pertinacity was not entirely fruitless, in spite of the distractions which prevented the resolute action which he was prepared to take in 1258. What happened is well known. In 1257 the opposing party, led by the Comyns, got possession of King Alexander at Kinross and seized power. In March 1258, while Henry was still holding in reserve the northern barons and knights whom he had called up against them, the Comyns made a convention with Llywelyn of Wales and his leading followers, and undertook to protect Welsh interests.[2] Although Henry's first attempts at mediation had failed, and military action was prevented, first by the Welsh war and then by the new order in England, the influence of the queen mother and her husband and the political sense of Gamelin, the bishop of St. Andrews, combined with the good offices of English intermediaries to effect a compromise which was formally accepted by King Henry and his council in November 1258. The bishop of St. Andrews, the queen mother, John of Acre, Alexander Comyn, earl of Buchan, the earl of Mar, and four more, including Alan Durward, undertook the 'care of the king'.[3] In 1262 Alexander came of age. He maintained cordial relations with Henry and Edward I until his death in 1286, and ruled his kingdom with spirit and independence.

King Henry's supervision of Scottish affairs between the death of Alexander II and 1257 was more significant than historians have supposed. It anticipated in some respects the situation in 1286 after the death of Alexander III. It would live in the memory of the young Edward, who in 1286 laid stress, in letters

[1] *Royal Letters*, ii. 246-7. The latter is undated and may possibly have been written in objection to a previous plan; but this is not likely.

[2] *Littere Wallie*, ed. J. G. Edwards, pp. 184-5. This document gives the names of the Scottish leaders in revolt. It shows that they were not sure of their position and anticipated possible changes, in which case they would do what they could to help the Welsh.

[3] Henry's military preparations in 1257-8 and subsequent attempt at negotiation with the Scots in parliament at Edinburgh may be studied in the *Close Rolls, 1256-9*, pp. 168, 290-1, 296-9; 207-8, 310-11, 329 (when, on 27 August, he expresses surprise on hearing of developments, no doubt those which led to the new government). For the recognition of the new body of rulers in November, and a suggested draft of assurances to be made by it, see ibid., pp. 461-2. A good account of the career of Alan Durward, Henry's chief ally in Scottish affairs, may be read in the *D.N.B.*, s.v. Durward. He appears in the records as *ostiarius* or Usser, i.e. usher.

to the pope, on his practical experience of the country.[1] It
showed that the magnates, so persistent in party feeling, could
be counted upon to provide a pro-English element in Scottish
society, so long as Scottish susceptibilities were not outraged:
but it also revealed the existence in Scotland of a feeling which
made any attempt to define the peculiar interest of the English
king in precise terms of lordship very imprudent. Matthew Paris
was not altogether wrong in seeing in the events of 1257 a revolt
of the 'native and natural' counsellors of the Scottish king
against the court circle created by King Henry.[2] It was not a
racial movement, for Scottish earls and lords did not hesitate to
ally themselves with King Henry; but it is significant that in
October 1257 Pope Alexander IV was persuaded to confirm to
the king of Scots the privileges granted by the Apostolic See to
him and his ancestors and the ancient and reasonable customs
of his realm,[3] and that in May 1259 Alexander, still a minor,
asked for the return of the document confirming the settlement
of 1255 and begged King Henry would put no obstacle in the
way of his coronation.[4] In Henry's eyes a royal coronation,
especially if the king were anointed, was inconsistent with his
conviction that the king of Scots should be his liegeman, not
only for his lands in England, but for his kingdom also. On this
point Henry could depend upon papal neutrality. In 1221
Honorius III had forbidden his legate in Scotland to crown
Alexander II: the king of Scots, he reminded the legate, was
said to be subject to the king of England, and he should have
nothing to do with the matter without the consent of King
Henry and his counsellors.[5] He refused the Scots permission to
have their king anointed, and his successor repeated the refusal

[1] *Cal. Papal Letters*, i. 479–80. Edward had asked leave to choose the Scottish
crusaders who would join him and be paid from the proceeds of the papal tenth of
1274. From childhood Edward and his sister Margaret had much affection for each
other.

[2] *Chron. maj.* v. 325. The chronicler compares the objection with the action of the
Emperor Frederick II in sending home the companions of his wife, Henry III's sister
(ibid. iii. 325). He was not thinking in terms of Picts and Scots, as some writers have
supposed, e.g. Sir Herbert Maxwell, *The Early Chronicles relating to Scotland* (1912),
p. 232.

[3] *Cal. Papal Letters*, i. 271. It is likely that the bishop of St. Andrews was concerned
with this bull. He had been forced to leave Scotland in 1256 and on assurances was
given a safe conduct to return through England in 1258 (*Close Rolls, 1256–9*, p. 293).

[4] Ibid., p. 477 (Henry's reply, in which Alexander is advised to wait for a time).

[5] *Cal. Papal Letters*, i. 83; Marc Bloch, in *Scot. Hist. Rev.* xxiii (1926), 105; P.
Schramm, *A History of the English Coronation* (Eng. trans., 1937), pp. 13, 130, 243–4.

in 1237. Innocent IV, in his turn, refused to grant King Henry's request in 1251 that the king of Scots as his liegeman should not be anointed or crowned without his consent;[1] but this did not imply that the pope would allow Alexander III to be anointed. Papal permission for this was first given in 1329.

So we come to the problem of the homage due from the king of Scots to the king of England. This had been discussed on and off since the accession of Henry III. There is unhappily no record of the terms in which Alexander II did homage to the boy-king at Christmas 1217, but, as the marshal and Guala the papal legate were working for quiet and order everywhere, it is unlikely that there was any reference to the Scottish crown. Alexander was enfeoffed with the earldom of Huntingdon, then held of him by his brother David, and after David's death in 1219 was allowed, as he afterwards alleged, the custody of his heir, John the Scot.[2] In the meanwhile Alexander had sent to Pope Honorius a copy of the treaty of Norham made in 1212 between his father William the Lion and King John. The pope sent this to the new legate Pandulf and asked him to provide an answer to Alexander's request that it should either be ratified or annulled. Pandulf's negotiations with Alexander in 1219 were successful (*laudabiliter expeditis*)[3] and the marriage of the king with Joan two years later was the outcome; but they left such important matters as Alexander's claim to the northern counties undecided until 1237, when, under the treaty of that year, the conventions of 1212 were declared null and void, and the records of them were destroyed. Hence the terms of the transaction in 1212 can be reconstructed only in part; we do not know the precise words in which the relations between the two kings were defined in that year. This would not matter if the treaty of 1237

[1] *Cal. Papal Letters*, i. 271.

[2] The grant of the honor of Huntingdon in 1217-18 confirmed an arrangement made by William the Lion, father of Alexander and David. It implied tenure of the English Crown, but it was apparently disregarded, for in 1237, when Alexander claimed the *comitatus* as overlord and former guardian of John the Scot after the latter's death in June, the king's council overruled the claim on the ground that, if founded on fact, it was due to illegal action by Hubert de Burgh during Henry III's minority. Alexander was given the fee of Huntingdon, but as this was divided between John's co-heiresses, the concession meant nothing. See R. Stewart-Brown's comments on the case in Bracton's Note Book, no. 1221, in *E.H.R.* xxxv (1920), 47. In 1256 Henry granted the honor with wardships and other rights to Alexander III (*Royal Letters*, ii. 120).

[3] Letters of the pope and Pandulf in *Foedera*, i. i. 157; K. Norgate, *Minority of Henry III*, pp. 126-7.

did not contain the significant reservation that, if the records of the treaty of 1212 contained any clauses affecting the interests of the two kingdoms which had not been dealt with in 1237, these should be gone into again (*innovari*).[1] The two confirmatory letters of King William which did survive in the English archives certainly suggest that, in leaving the marriage of his son and heir, as King John's liege vassal, in the hands of the king of England, he acknowledged a relationship of dependence more far-reaching than homage as the tenant of lands in England.[2] Pope Honorius, who had read the treaty of 1212, wrote in 1221 that the king of Scots seemed to be subject to the king of England; and thirty years later Henry III, though he did not press the point, is said to have demanded homage for Scotland from Alexander III. So, when Alexander came to England in 1279 to do homage to Edward I, Edward was careful to reserve the right to talk about the homage for the kingdom of Scotland when he wished.[3]

At this point some record of Edward's talk with his father and later discussions with his closest advisers about the realm of Scotland would be invaluable. That he believed in his right is certain, but whether he would ever have tried to realize it if the line of succession had not been broken is a matter of opinion. Temperamentally a legalist, he does not appear, until the end of his reign, to have been attracted by the argument from 'British history', and he was always unwilling to adopt the 'imperial' attitude which had prevailed in the eleventh century.[4] The probability is that he saw no reason to create difficulties for himself so long as the cordial relations between the two courts were maintained. That he, one of the busiest of our kings, who deliberately dedicated himself to the pursuit of the Crusade,

---

[1] *Foedera*, p. 234.   [2] Ibid. 103, 104 (King William's confirmations).

[3] Ibid. I. ii. 563. A good account in Ramsay, *Dawn of the Constitution*, pp. 322–4. Alexander did homage with the words: 'I become liege man of the lord Edward king of England *contra omnes gentes*.' Edward accepted this subject to the reservation noted above. Robert Bruce, earl of Carrick (son of the future claimant), swore fealty in Alexander's name with the duty of service for lands *quae teneo de rege*. Edward had written to his chancellor (March 1278) that Alexander had promised to come and do the homage due from him *absque conditione aliqua* (ibid., p. 554). Ramsay interprets this as 'an unrestricted, i.e. an indeterminate recognition of superiority'; and, though he claimed homage for the kingdom, Edward left the matter thus for the time being.

[4] On the implications of the titles *Basileus* and *Imperator* in the eleventh century see Schramm, *Hist. of the English Coronation*, pp. 30–31, 246, with references. For Edward's attitude see Powicke, *King Henry III and the Lord Edward*, ii. 663–9.

planned a conquest of Scotland from the outset of his reign is a
fantastic view, as unreasonable as the belief that his efforts to
compose his difficulties with Llywelyn of Wales were riddled by
hypocrisy. Edward was an able, but short-sighted opportunist.
He did not suddenly invent his claim to be overlord of Scotland;
he welcomed an opportunity to act upon it with Scottish consent; then, being the man he was, he would not withdraw.
Everybody in England, and many people in Scotland, approved
his obstinacy. His reputation throughout the west would have
suffered if he had given way.

King Alexander III, as the lord of a united and prospering
land, won much distinction at the age of twenty-five, for in 1266
Magnus IV, king of Norway, ceded to him the Isle of Man and
all the western isles.[1] This success ended the last stage in the
growth of the new monarchy of Scotland. William the Lion and
his son Alexander II had won the recognition, at least in name,
of their claims to the lordship of Argyll and the western mainland. Alexander II had died on the island of Kerrera in the
course of an expedition to the west (1249). In 1263 the old king
Hakon of Norway had sailed with a great fleet from Bergen to
reassert his rights in the threatened islands, and had joined
forces with his son-in-law, the king of Man. After some demonstrations on the coasts of the mainland, his ships were harassed
by violent storms. A force landed by Hakon on the Ayrshire
coast to defend some stranded galleys was overwhelmed by the
local Scottish levies at Largs on 2 October 1263. The fleet,
broken by the foul weather, made its way back to Orkney where
Hakon died. King Alexander III was free to assert himself in the
inner and even the outer Hebrides. This was the only military
enterprise of his reign.[2] In 1281 his eldest child, Margaret—the

---

[1] The expulsion of the Norse was a slow process which should not be made too
dramatic; see A. A. M. Duncan and A. L. Brown on Argyle and the Isles, in *Proc.
of Society of Antiquaries of Scotland*, xc (session 1956-7), 192-220, especially 215-16.

[2] The Isle of Man and the western isles of Scotland had been comprised in the
Norwegian system of defence known as 'leding'. One of the conditions of the grant
of the Isle of Man by King Robert Bruce to the first earl of Moray (1313) was that
the new lord should place six ships, each of twenty-six oars, annually at the king's
disposal. See, for naval defence in Norse Scotland, H. Marwick in *Scot. Hist. Rev.*
xxviii (April 1949), 1-11. Man was occupied by Edward I in 1291 and for a time
was held of him by Antony Bek, bishop of Durham (1298-1310). It was held again
for a few years by the Scottish kings from 1313 to 1333. From 1333 until 1765, when
it was revested in the Crown, it was under the suzerainty of the English kings. The
bishopric of Sodor and Man continued in the ecclesiastical province of Nidaros in

child who had been born in England in 1261—was married to Eric, the young king of Norway. She died in April 1283, when her daughter, Margaret, the 'Maid of Norway', was born.

King Alexander lost all his children before he died. His second son David died when he was nine (1281), his elder son and heir Alexander died in January 1284 in his twentieth year without issue of his marriage with a daughter of the count of Flanders. Unless the king should marry again and have male issue, the child Margaret was now the heir to the throne. She was formally accepted as such a week after the young Alexander's death by the earls and barons of Scotland in a solemn gathering at Scone.[1] In October 1285 the king did marry again. He chose Yolande, a daughter of the court of Dreux. In the following March he insisted on riding from Edinburgh to his wife at Kinghorn in Fife in wild weather. As he was nearing Kinghorn after night-fall his horse stumbled and fell. The king was killed. He was forty-four years old, in full vigour.

The community of the kingdom of Scotland, presumably the body of prelates and magnates which assembled at Dunfermline for the king's funeral (29 March 1286), appointed six guardians of the realm. They were the bishops of St. Andrews and Glasgow, the earls of Fife and Buchan, John Comyn of Badenoch, and James the Steward. After the deaths of the two earls the other four continued to act alone until in June 1291 King Edward added his knight Brian fitzAlan of Bedale to their number.[2] The guardians remained in office until the accession of John Baliol to the throne, though for some time they had been overshadowed by the authority of Edward, as 'superior lord of Scotland'.

Margaret was only three years old when her grandfather died and no effective attempt was made to bring her to Scotland till 1289, not long before King Edward's return from Gascony. Scotland was quiet under the regency. The steward of Scotland, one of the regents, and others of his family combined in September 1286, with the earl of Dunbar and his sons and Robert Bruce

Norway until the fifteenth century, when Man came in practice to the province of York (by law in 1542), while the Sudreys or Western Isles continued as a Scottish see. The bishopric of Orkney became a Scottish see when the Orkneys and Shetlands were annexed by the Scottish Crown in 1472. See *Handbook of British Chronology* (1939), pp. 61–63, 208, 227–8. The see of Whithorn or Galloway remained suffragan to York, though regarded as one of the Scottish sees, until the time of the Great Schism (ibid., pp. 208, 225).   [1] *Foedera*, I. ii. 638.

[2] Norham, 13 June 1291 (*Foedera*, I. ii. 768). At the same time the four surviving guardians took an oath of office to Edward as deputed to the custody of the realm.

and his son, the earl of Carrick, to enter into an obligation to adhere to two great Anglo-Irish lords, the young earl of Ulster and Thomas de Clare, and their allies, but whether this pact, which no doubt was mutual, related to Scottish or to Irish affairs is not stated in the document issued by them at Turnberry castle.[1] One phrase does imply that, in spite of the oaths of adherence given to Margaret in 1284, the succession to the Scottish throne was still regarded as uncertain: the usual saving clause runs, 'saving faith to the lord king of England and to the person (*illius*) who, by reason of the blood of the late king Alexander, shall obtain the realm of Scotland in accordance with the ancient customs hitherto approved and applied (*usitatas*) in the realm of Scotland'; but the careful words 'ratione sanguinis ... Alexandri, regis Scotiae, qui ultimo obiit' might imply a possibility that Queen Yolande might bear a son, just as in 1284 the possibility that the widow of the young Alexander might have a child had been explicitly taken into account. Queen Yolande, however, is never mentioned in the surviving records of this period after her husband's death. In 1294 she married Arthur the elder son and heir of Duke John of Brittany.[2]

In 1289 the Maid of Norway was regarded by all as the rightful queen, and in October of that year three of the guardians, the bishops of St. Andrews and Glasgow and John Comyn of Badenoch, were sent with Robert Bruce to treat with the commissioners of Norway and England about her return. The report of the three groups of commissioners was presented at Salisbury on 9 November and received their formal agreement in King Edward's presence.[3] The queen was to reach Scotland or England before the day of All Saints (1 November) in 1290. She was to come free of any marriage contract. King Edward was to

[1] Stevenson, *Documents*, i. 22–23. In 1286 Richard de Burgh led an expedition into Connaught, no doubt connected with a royal commission given to Thomas de Clare and others to deal with the king's waste lands there (cf. Orpen, iv. 74–75, 112, 139–40); the two men had obviously entered into an agreement to further their interests and may have enlisted support in Scotland. It is possible that the pact referred to activity in Scotland itself, prophetic of future rivalries, and reminiscent of events in 1253–8 (above, pp. 589–92). If this were so, nothing came of it all. I am inclined to think that some Irish enterprise was the occasion of the pact.

[2] Through her mother, Beatrice of Montfort l'Amauri, Yolande inherited Montfort. John de Montfort, her son by Arthur, thus originated the Montfort claim to the duchy of Brittany in 1341. Arthur, duke from 1305 to 1312, was succeeded by his son by a former wife.

[3] Above, p. 512. That Edward was present at Salisbury is stated in the later confirmation at Brigham.

receive adequate assurances, first, that she would not be married save by his ordinance, will, and counsel; and secondly, that the land of Scotland was in a safe and peaceful condition, so that she might live there willingly 'as its true lady, queen and heir'; but, mindful of troubles of a previous minority, the Scots asserted their right to remove any undesirable guardians or servants sent from Norway and to substitute Scots who were to be approved by men of both countries and by King Edward's agents. In this and, indeed, in all matters affecting the welfare of the realm, on which disputes arose, the mediation and counsel of the king of England were to be sought. The agreement was to be confirmed by the people of Scotland (*gens Scotiae*) in Mid-Lent next.[1] Accordingly, on 14 March 1290, a singularly impressive and complete body of Scottish bishops, earls, abbots, priors, and barons set their seals at Brigham to a formal confirmation of the settlement made at Salisbury.[2] On the same day the four surviving guardians and the community of Scotland sent letters to the kings of England and Norway which show that discussions about a marriage between Margaret and Edward's son and heir had made much progress. King Edward, indeed, before he left Gascony[3] had opened negotiations with Pope Nicholas IV and a papal bull had been issued in the previous November granting dispensation for a union between the two cousins.[4] As its contents make clear, Edward had laid stress on the dangerous discord which might arise if Margaret were betrothed to anybody else, especially if the king was on crusade. In their letters of March 1290 the Scots welcomed the proposed match; they asked King Eric to agree to it and informed King Edward that they were sending representatives to conclude the discussion in the English parliament.[5]

As the powers of the envoys were found to be insufficient to enable a settlement to be completed in parliament, negotiations were continued with the Scots by Antony Bek, bishop of Durham, and others. A draft treaty was made at Brigham in July. King

---

[1] Stevenson, i. 105–11. [2] Ibid. i. 129–31.

[3] Edward had asked the senior guardian, William Fraser, bishop of St. Andrews to come to him in Gascony early in 1289. The bishop and his companions had been arrested and ill treated in Yorkshire on their way (ibid. i. 79, 121).

[4] Ibid. i. 111–13. The Scots had no official knowledge of this bull and refer to it in March 1290 only as joyful news, 'ke mult le gent parlent' (*Foedera*, i. ii. 730). It is addressed to the young Edward in reply to letters sent in his name.

[5] *Foedera*, i. ii. 730–1.

Edward was disposed at first to combine his confirmation of it with far-reaching demands. In August he asked the guardians to recognize the bishop of Durham as the lieutenant in Scotland of Margaret and her husband and to defer to him in all matters 'which are required for the governance and peaceful state of the realm'.[1] He had also instructed his commissioners to demand that the castles and forts of Scotland should be put under his control, but this had been refused. The Scots on their side had required that no additions should be allowed to the English fortifications in the March of Scotland, a stipulation which was repudiated in the treaty as one-sided. At last on 28 August, Edward confirmed the Brigham terms, while the Scots undertook that the Scottish castles should be restored to the queen and to the young Edward at the time when they took the oath to observe the customs of the land. Each party was anxious about the future during the dangerous period of the queen's minority; and each decided to take risks. The kingdom of Scotland was to remain separate from England, 'free in itself without subjection' under its own liberties and customs. No Scottish parliament was to be held outside Scotland for the discussion of matters affecting the kingdom; acts of homage and fealty to the Crown and judicial proceedings were to be transacted only within its bounds. The line of the Border was to be maintained.[2]

On the Sunday after Michaelmas the magnates of Scotland were assembled at Perth to meet the bishop of Durham and the Earl Warenne and hear messages from King Edward. After the meeting the envoys with the bishop of St. Andrews and others set out to receive Queen Margaret in the Orkneys; but rumours came that the queen had died. The bishop of St. Andrews, on 9 October, wrote to Edward from Leuchars: Robert Bruce had

[1] The bishop had been Edward's chief agent in Scottish and Norwegian affairs. In February 1290 Edward made him guardian of the king of Scotland's lands in Tyndale and Penrith, and in June empowered him to admit to the king's peace the men of the Isles of Scotland 'who were in war and discord'. The bishop had gone surety for pensions to Norwegians, to last until Queen Margaret reached the age of fifteen; and in return was given the manors of Wark, Penrith, and other lands north of the Trent until her twentieth year, to the amount of the pensions (£400). The bishop was also authorized to borrow money for the king's service to the amount of £5,000 (see Stevenson, i. 122, 161-2; 178-9; cf. 113, 181). Indeed, King Edward seems to have borne the financial burden for the Scots and King Eric in addition to his own.

[2] *Foedera*, i. ii. 735-8 *passim*. The best text of the treaty, as confirmed at Northampton, is in Stevenson, i. 162-73. There was constant disturbance in the March at this time.

gone to Perth in force; what his intentions were the bishop did not know; but the earls of Mar and Athol were raising an army, and the country was in danger. A later report said that the queen was better but still weak. The party would wait to hear more before proceeding north. If John Baliol came to Edward the bishop advised the king to come to an arrangement with him; and if the queen died to come to the March, to be a consolation to the people, to prevent bloodshed, and enable the rightful heir to succeed, provided, adds the bishop, 'that he is willing to abide (*adherere*) by your counsel'.[1] The queen, in fact, had died on 26 September, but, by the time the truth reached him, Edward had thoughts only for his dying wife and, then, for his own grief. In Scotland the unity, so impressively displayed at Brigham a few months earlier, was broken at once. Bishop Fraser's hopes of Baliol's quiet succession were in vain. Disturbance was rife in Moray and Mar. Old rivalries sprang to life again, every latent ambition was roused. Before the end of the year a strong body of earls and magnates had rallied to the cause of Robert Bruce. The bishop of St. Andrews and John Comyn of Badenoch were the objects of almost hysterical abuse. Yet all, earls, magnates, and claimants alike, turned to Edward, sought for protection and begged for his presence.[2] Scotland was in turmoil, torn asunder, and anything might happen.

The anger of the Bruce party was due to the attempt of the bishop of St. Andrews and John Comyn to anticipate the issue by trying to make John Baliol king. The earls, as representing the 'seven earls' who were alleged to possess the ancient right to institute the king, refused to be brushed aside, while Baliol, who was in close touch with the bishop of Durham, declared himself to be 'heir of the kingdom of Scotland'.[3] Neither they nor Bruce meant to suggest that they would refuse to abide by Edward's decision. Bruce, indeed, seems to have been prepared, in virtue of the authority of the seven earls, to deny the validity of King Richard's surrender of the right of the lordship acknowledged by William the Lion in the treaty of Falaise with Henry II.

[1] *Foedera*, i. ii. 741.

[2] See the violent protest of the 'seven earls' addressed to the two guardians, probably towards the end of the year, in Palgrave, pp. 14–21. The seven earls were presumably Angus, Athol, Lennox, Mar, Menteith, Ross, and Strathearn, but they are not enumerated.

[3] So styled in his letters patent of a grant to the bishop of Durham, issued at Gateshead on 15 November (Stevenson, i. 203–4).

Richard had 'sold' the kingdom.[1] He sought Edward's recognition of the ancient law of succession, which it was the privilege and duty of the seven earls to declare in the institution of a new king at Scone. Later, as the case went against him, he changed ground, but in the autumn of 1290 his position was stronger than his rival's. He was eighty years of age with a long record of service to the kings of both realms. He had held his lands in Annandale north of the Solway and in Cleveland in Yorkshire since his father's death in 1245. In 1238 Alexander II, when a childless widower, had had him recognized as his heir in case he should not return from an expedition to the western Isles.[2] In England Bruce had served King Henry as a judge for nearly twenty years, and had retired in 1269 as the first chief justice of the king's bench. No layman can have had his experience or been so familiar with the practice of the law as he had been in his prime. John Baliol, on the contrary, was little known in Scotland, though, after his mother Devorguilla's death in January 1290, he was better endowed than Bruce.[3] He had been a younger son and owed his vast estates in Northumberland, Durham, and Galloway to the deaths of his brothers in his father's lifetime. His wife was a daughter of King Edward's close friend and ally, the earl Warenne. He did not belong to Bruce's generation, and though descended, as Bruce was, from Scottish kings, was more at home in English than Scottish circles. Moreover, he had not the strength of character which distinguished Bruce and his young grandson, the future king, who in 1290 was a lad of sixteen.

And so we come to the great case.[4] Edward was determined

[1] See the puzzling document in Palgrave (pp. 21-22) who ascribes it to Bruce.

[2] Ibid., pp. 19-20; and Bruce's petition, pp. 29-30. The protest of the earls states that Alexander II put Bruce forward because he had come *fere ad senilem etatem* (p. 19). In 1238 King Alexander was only 40 years of age and Bruce was 28. The reason given in the petition is to be preferred.

[3] Hodgson, *A History of Northumberland*, vi (1902), 52-53 and notes, for his lands. The relief to be paid for Devorguilla's lands was no less than £3,829. 14s. 1½d. Edward pardoned him £3,000 of this after he became king (*Cal. Pat. Rolls, 1292-1301*, p. 12).

[4] Some of the original documents are in the official *Rotuli Scotiae*, a series of enrolments in the English Chancery which begins in 1291; vol. i (1814); many more are in Palgrave's collection of documents (1837). The official record of proceedings was written by the papal notary John Arthur of Caen, who had served Edward in a similar capacity during the negotiations with the king of Aragon in 1288-9 (above, p. 283): see *Foedera*, i. ii. 762-84. Another and in some respects more complete record, obviously based on John's materials, is edited in annals of the kingdom of Scotland, in Rishanger, *Chronica* (ed. Riley, 1865), pp. 243-368. Rishanger's own

to deal with the competitors for the crown of Scotland as the judge of a court with authority to enforce its decisions; and this implied general recognition of his right to do so. His claim to be the superior or direct lord of the kingdom must be admitted without equivocation. Hence he began by instituting a comprehensive historical survey of the evidence contained in chronicles of the relations between the two realms throughout the centuries. Most of this inconclusive material still survives.[1] The Scots met the king in a joint assembly in the parish church of Norham, hard by the bishop of Durham's castle, seven miles from Berwick, on 10 May 1291. Roger Brabazon, in a carefully prepared statement, said by one chronicler to have been drafted by the provincial of the Dominicans, William of Hotham,[2] explained the necessity for an acknowledgement by the competitors of King Edward's superiority. Discussion was deferred to the next day, when the evidence for the claim was expounded and the Scots were allowed a period for deliberation. The meetings were resumed on 2 June. This adjournment had obviously been anticipated, for in April royal writs had summoned the king's brother Edmund, a few earls and prelates, many of the barons who held lands in the north of England and, through the sheriffs, those who owed him service as tenants in the northern counties, to meet in arms on 3 June at Norham.[3]

chronicle shows knowledge of some of the documents; e.g. (pp. 124–5) the petition of the community of Scotland, presented at Norham about 2 June 1291, the text of which has recently been discovered by Professor Stones in a collection of documents relating to Scotland, formerly in Wrest Park, now in the Glasgow University Library. The medieval compiler of this manuscript used the exchequer documents, edited by Palgrave, and copied a few which did not survive into modern times. Mr. Stones has kindly allowed me to refer to these. The latest analysis of the proceedings is B. C. Keeney's study 'The Medieval Idea of the State: the Great Cause, 1291–2', in the *University of Toronto Law Journal*, viii (1949), 48–71.

[1] Palgrave, pp. 56–137: cf. Rishanger, *Chronica*, pp. 123–4. In some religious houses this search was naturally regarded as a step towards the 'subjugation' of Scotland. The annalist of Waverley adds a bit of gossip that Edward had declared his intention to subjugate Scotland as he had subjugated Wales; but the context suggests that he confused events (*Ann. monast.* ii. 409). Sir James Ramsay, in his excellent summary, unfortunately laid stress on this casual and isolated passage, as clear proof of Edward's intentions (*Dawn of the Constitution*, p. 380). He was followed by E. M. Barron, *The Scottish War of Independence* (1914), p. 89, as also in his charge of deliberate falsification by Edward of the words of submission made by the competitors, by the addition, in the official record, of the words *seu directus* to *superior dominus* (Ramsay, pp. 382, n., 385).

[2] Guisborough, ed. Rothwell, p. 235. For the provincial, much in Edward's service, cf. above, pp. 261, 265.

[3] *Parliamentary Writs*, i. 256. How large this force actually was does not seem to have been worked out.

The adjourned assembly held nine sessions (2-13 June), the larger gatherings in the open air, on a green in the village of Upsetlington on the Tweed, opposite the castle, others in Norham church, two (one of which was adjourned from the village) in the king's chamber in the castle.[1] The outcome was that the competitors swore and repeated their oaths publicly to accept Edward as superior lord of Scotland, with lawful cognizance of the case, and that the custody of Scotland was granted to Edward, on his solemn guarantee to restore the realm, within two months of the award, to him 'who shall gain the right, by judgement, of royalty', and to demand on the death of a Scots king nothing but homage and the rights incident to homage.[2] In a joint letter they declared that cognizance implies judgement, judgement execution, execution the possession and seisin of the land and castles. Here, indeed, was recognition of direct lordship, during the vacancy of the throne, in their sovereign lord. The realm was resigned into Edward's hands. He reappointed the four guardians, who swore fealty to him. He added Brian fitzAlan to their number and also made him castellan of Roxburgh, Jedburgh, Dundee, and Forfar. He appointed a new chancellor, and gave a colleague to the chamberlain. The guardians, officers, and magnates of Scotland swore to obey him and he swore to govern the realm in accordance with its laws and customs. Public proclamation was made in the name of the guardians and the magnates. Edward made it quite clear that his new responsibilities as lord of Scotland in no way prejudiced his position as lord. At Norham (3 June) he reserved his freedom to maintain, if he wished, his hereditary right to the kingdom *quoad proprietatem*. A month later, in the chapel of Berwick castle (3 July), he protested before the chief men of Scotland and the English prelates and magnates in his company that by his grace to those who had sought his judgement he did not intend and never had intended to prejudice his right and the rights of his heirs to the free exercise of his lawful powers as sovereign lord of Scotland.[3] In the meantime the treasurer at Westminster had been ordered to send to the cathedral churches and principal

---

[1] *Annales* (in Rishanger), pp. 252-3, with the names of those present.

[2] The text of this important undertaking, which was known to Rishanger (p. 128), is preserved in the unpublished Glasgow University manuscript, noted above, p. 603, n. The king reissued part of it at Newcastle on 4 January 1293, to justify his right to hear appeals (*Rotuli Scotiae*, i. 15-16; below, p. 609, n.).

[3] *Foedera*, i. ii. 766, 774.

monasteries of England, for inclusion in their chronicles, transcripts (from the originals in the treasury) of the personal submissions of the competitors and their letter agreeing to the submission of the realm and castles of Scotland to the king's custody. Several of these writs dated 9 July still survive.[1]

. According to the official record, neither the guardians, earls, prelates, and barons of Scotland nor the competitors had disputed King Edward's claim. One petition, it was true, had been presented in the name of the community of Scotland; but it contained nothing to the purpose ('nihil tamen efficax fuit per communitatem eandem propositum').[2] This report was literally correct, but did injustice to a very significant document. The petition had been presented in the name of the community as soon as the Scottish leaders and competitors had reassembled in Norham. It expressed the mind of those whom they had been able to consult during the brief interval allowed them. It stated that the community knew of no previous demand by a king of England for recognition as supreme lord, that only their own lord could reply to such a demand and that, as they had no king, they could not reply without great risk to themselves. They were bound by oaths taken after the death of Alexander III and by the terms of the treaty of Northampton in the previous year, and they begged king Edward to trust their loyal intentions and sense of obligation to him, without pressing his claim.[3] Edward and his advisers, on the contrary, regarded the treaty of Northampton as void. It had been Margaret of Norway's marriage contract, and Margaret was dead; and, without more ado, the Scottish leaders and competitors agreed to Edward's terms; but there can be no doubt that the petition of the community expresses the feeling that the king of England should act as an arbitrator, not as a judge in the court of a lord.

At Norham it had been agreed to submit the pleas of the competitors to the judgement of twenty-four of Edward's council, assisted by eighty assessors, forty chosen by Bruce and forty by

---

[1] e.g. to Lewes, Ely, dean and chapter of York (Palgrave, pp. 137–8); St. Mary's, York (Bain, ii, no. 503); dean and chapter of Salisbury (Hist. MSS. Com., *Various Collections*, i. 379). The treasurer was instructed by writs of privy seal, and sent the transcripts under the seal of the exchequer.

[2] *Annales* (in Rishanger), pp. 244–5. This passage was omitted in the final official record, or Great Roll, printed in the *Foedera*.

[3] The text survives in the Glasgow University manuscript. It was summarized by Rishanger, pp. 124–5.

Baliol: these latter were to give their opinions on questions of law and to approve the judgements. This court of 104 auditors was copied, it has been suggested,[1] from the *judicium centumvirale* of Roman procedure. Hearings were to begin at Berwick on 3 August. Edward left Berwick on 5 July on his first tour of Scotland. He proceeded to St. Andrews and came back by way of Perth. At Stirling, on his way north, he issued an ordinance requiring all persons who normally made oaths of fealty to a king of Scotland to make them to him or to one of the guardians.[2] On 3 August the twelve competitors appeared before the king and auditors at Berwick. Their petitions were lodged. On 12 August the documents were sewn up in a sack sealed with the seals of the bishop of St. Andrews and Glasgow and the earls of Buchan and Mar. The sack was deposited in the castle. Edward, who had much business to do in England, adjourned the hearing of the petitions until 2 June in the following year.[3]

The parties met on 2 June 1292, but were adjourned until 14 October to allow the eighty assessors to consider their reply to the question by what laws and customs the right of succession should be determined. The hearings lasted from 14 October to 17 November, the day on which King Edward declared the judgement in favour of John Baliol. The choice really lay between the three descendants of David, earl of Huntingdon, the brother of William the Lion, for David had been William's heir and it was decided at Berwick that his descendants, through his three daughters, had the better claim, as against that of Florence, count of Holland, who was descended from a sister of William.[4] The three descendants were Baliol, Bruce, and John Hastings or Abergavenny. Baliol was grandson of the eldest,[5] Bruce son of the second, Hastings grandson of the third daughter of David. Bruce, in fact, could remember how after the death of David's son, John the Scot, earl of Chester and Huntingdon, the three families had disputed about the succession to the two earldoms in 1237, when King Henry had bought out the claimants to the

---

[1] George Neilson, in *Scot. Hist. Rev.* xv (1918), 1 ff.

[2] *Foedera*, i. ii. 774. Lists of oaths of fealty on pp. 772-4.

[3] Palgrave, pp. 35-36. The petitions of the twelve, to which was later added one from Eric, king of Sweden, in *Foedera*, pp. 775-7.

[4] G. G. Simpson has edited, in a paper on Florence's claim (*Scottish Hist. Rev.* xxxvi (1957), 124), two confirmations made in 1291 of an alleged surrender by Earl David of his rights to the Scottish crown. The Scottish annals (Rishanger, pp. 268-9) mention this document.

[5] Margaret, Devorguilla of Galloway's mother.

county of Chester and had divided the honor of Huntingdon between Bruce's father, Baliol's grandfather, and Hastings's grandfather, leaving only the empty shell to King Alexander II of Scotland.[1] Now, similar but more difficult questions had to be faced. Was a kingdom partible, as an English barony was? If it was impartible, did not Scottish custom and the custom of other lands allow the son of a younger daughter a better claim to succeed than a grandson of an elder daughter? In any case did common law suffice to settle so important a matter as the succession to a kingdom, when there was a conflict of law or custom, and especially when one of the claimants had, at one time, been accepted as heir in an identical situation? Edward had defined the rules of succession by seniority to the indivisible kingdom of England in April 1290; but he does not seem to have had a decided preference for Baliol or Bruce; and he could hardly have withstood the unanimous opinion of the eighty; but the eighty could not agree about Scottish law, were uncertain whether the same law of succession applied in both England and Scotland, or a new law should be made.[2] They threw back the decision upon the king's counsellors, at this time (November) a mixed body of earls, barons, ecclesiastics, and lawyers.[3] The first decision taken was between Bruce and Baliol. The counsellors were asked whether, according to the customs of the kingdoms of England and Scotland, Bruce, as the son of a younger sister, or Baliol, as the grandson of an elder sister, had the better right. They answered, one by one, in favour of Baliol. The eighty were then interrogated with the same result, the bishop of Glasgow, James the steward, and one or two more explaining that, though they had at first supported Bruce, they had been convinced by the arguments. The king, on 6 November, declared judgement for Baliol as against Bruce. The claims of the other competitors were then argued as against those of Baliol. The crux came when Hastings, here supported by Bruce, pleaded that Scotland was held of the king of England as any other barony was held at common law, and was partible between the descendants of David's three daughters. The argument turned on the status of a kingdom as distinct from an earldom or a barony. Finally the

---

[1] Cf. above, p. 197, n.; and see R. Stewart-Brown in *E.H.R.* xxxv (1920), 26–54.

[2] *Annales*, p. 258.

[3] It is significant that the adjournment from June to October was made to the time of Edward's next parliament (*in proximo parliamento suo*) ·(*Foedera*, p. 777). The last sessions of the trial were held in a Michaelmas parliament.

decision was in favour of Baliol on the ground that Scotland was an impartible kingdom. On 17 November Roger Brabazon gave judgement in the king's name. On 19 November the constables of Berwick and twenty-two other castles throughout Scotland were ordered to surrender their charges to Baliol; and the seal of the governors, used since the death of Alexander III, was broken. On the next day in Norham castle Baliol swore fealty to Edward for the realm of Scotland, held of him as superior lord.[1] On 30 November he was installed on the stone at Scone by John de St. John, who acted for the earl of Fife, then a child. On 26 December, at Newcastle after the Christmas feast, he did homage.

Immediately, the meaning of Edward's undertaking to exercise no authority in the realm of Scotland except what was implied in the oath of homage and pertained to him as superior lord was brought in question by the bishop of St. Andrews, the earl of Buchan, and two other Scottish lords. It so happened that at Newcastle, a few days before (22 December), Edward in council had decided, after inquiry into Scottish law, an appeal by a burgess of Berwick against the action of the justiciars and auditors whom Edward, after the kingdom had been entrusted to him, had appointed to deal with Scottish cases.[2] As we have seen, Edward had formally reserved his rights as superior lord before the proceedings at Berwick. The protesters again appealed to the clause in the treaty of Northampton which ensured the right of the Scots to plead or answer for offences only in their own country and not outside the kingdom. The king of England at once made his position clear, first through his justice Roger Brabazon, then in a speech in his chamber to the king of Scotland and the prelates and lords of England and Scotland who were in Newcastle for the feast. He regarded the accession of Baliol as the opening of a new chapter in Anglo-Scottish relations. The right to hear appeals in England belonged to him as sovereign lord. (He doubtless had in mind his relations as duke of Aquitaine with the king of France.) He swept aside as irrelevant obligations into which he had entered during the interregnum, except his undertaking to respect the rights of the new king in Scotland. If he wished to do so, he would summon the king of Scotland to appear before him in person. On 2 January Baliol formally acquitted Edward of these obligations, including the obsolete

[1] *Annales* (in Rishanger), pp. 361-8.
[2] For the case see Stevenson, i. 377-89.

treaty of Northampton, and promised to respect the validity of
the acts done by Edward as lord while the kingdom was in his
hands. This last promise was required, of course, to maintain in
the interests of all the continuity of justice, finance, and government generally.[1]

The English king's right to hear appeals from the king of
Scotland sitting and judging in parliament—for later appeals in
1293-4 were at this high level[2]—should be considered not only
as implied by his superior lordship, but also in the light of events.
For thirty years King Alexander III had lived on friendly terms
with his English relatives. Social and economic relations between Scots and English, indeed between Scots, Irish, and
Gascons also, had become closer. The Scots had welcomed with
relief the re-establishment of a family settlement after the tragic
deaths of their king and his children. Perplexed by a disunion
which might easily have degenerated into civil war all parties
had applied to King Edward, who had seen his hopes of averting
future danger from Scotland frustrated, and now welcomed the
opportunity to unite the two realms under his lordship. The
Scots had accepted his lordship and, pending the succession
of a new king, had submitted the kingdom to his direct rule. The
new king was his vassal and Edward had made it clear that his
superiority was to continue. His court had decided that as a
kingdom Scotland was impartible, but not that it was independent. The records of the years 1293-6 show that Edward as lord
of Scotland maintained close, if casual, relations with individual
Scottish bishops, lords, and boroughs. As the mayor, reeves, and
burgesses of Berwick described him in a petition (1294) he was by
divine providence ruling the three realms of England, Scotland,

---

[1] *Foedera*, i. ii. 783-5. On 4 January the late guardians were ordered to surrender
to the new king all rolls of judicial proceedings during their period of office. On
6 January the Isle of Man was surrendered to him by Edward. Letters patent of
4 January embody a transcript of a clause in Edward's promise at Norham to hand
over the kingdom to the successful candidate. Edward apparently cited it to prove
that from the first he had retained the right to hear appeals.

[2] Edward heard appeals from Scotland before the king's bench as well as in
parliament, but there is no evidence that he heard appeals from any lower court in
Scotland than the king in parliament, although he may have received petitions
from Scottish parties. The statement that there was 'a regular stream of citations on
appeals to the court of the king of England' is not borne out by the evidence cited
by Richardson and Sayles in *Scot. Hist. Rev.* xxv. 309; these refer to the Berwick case
(*sub judice* before as well as after Baliol did homage), the Mason and Macduff cases,
and an appeal from the abbot of Reading (*Cal. Chanc. Warrants*, p. 38), all from the
king of Scotland in parliament.

and Ireland.[1] The two realms were interlocked, for they were in so many ways bound to each other by common interests. Like the new king himself, lords and merchants had on occasion the desire to consult with their friends and relations in England.[2] Hence Edward received appeals from the court of the Scottish king on several occasions in 1293; from Macduff of Fife, from a Gascon merchant, from a claimant to the Isle of Man, and others.[3] And when Baliol failed to appear either in person or through his representatives to defend his actions, the royal court in England compiled a series of rules, based on common-law procedure, designed to control and penalize his disobedience. If, for example, when a warden (*custos*) had been appointed to protect the appellant's interests, family, and lands in Scotland pending the appeal, injury were done within the *custodia*, and its protection were imperilled, the king of Scotland would lose his homage and lordship, and these would lapse to the overlord.[4]

King Edward had no exalted ideas about the nature of Scottish kingship, and no illusions about the state of the kingdom. He respected without question the customs and institutions of Scotland. He maintained the king both as king and as an English baron in all his rights;[5] but he was also determined, as sovereign lord, to maintain order and justice in Scotland as in England. Although his attitude may seem strange to us, he was convinced of his rights, not seeking by subterfuge things which he knew were not his to claim. The Anglo-Scottish lords, in

[1] Bain, *Calendar*, ii, no. 696: They complained of the seizure of their ships in English waters, but also against the chamberlain of Scotland, Alexander Baliol. Bain's date (1294) appears to be confirmed by a petition forwarded to Edward by the king of Scotland in July 1294 (Stevenson, i. 426-7).

[2] See the record of the parliament at Stirling in August 1293, when the Flemish case for the payment of the dower of the young Alexander's widow—much discussed since his death in 1284 (above, p. 597)—was deferred because the king was going into England to consult his friends and kinsmen (*Foedera*, i. ii. 791).

[3] Macduff, younger son of a previous earl of Fife who had died in 1266, claimed lands in Fife. His case had been tried by the guardians of Scotland, but was later rejected in Baliol's court. John le Mazon, or Mason, a merchant of Bordeaux, claimed large sums as due to him from the executors of Alexander III. This complicated case was interrupted by Mason's death (Palgrave, p. 140) after going on for many years, but his and Macduff's appeals caused the trouble in 1293 (*Foedera*, i. ii. 787-9).

[4] *Rotuli parliamentorum*, i. 110-11, record of proceedings in Edward's parliament in Easter term, 1293.

[5] For example, Baliol's rights in Tyndale, Penrith, &c., under the treaty of 1237, were examined and confirmed while the dispute about appeals was at its height (*Foedera*, i. ii. 792). The relief due for his mother's lands in Galloway, &c., was pardoned earlier in the year (Palgrave, p. 138).

turn, must have learned much during the debates in Norham
and Berwick. They had heard Bruce's attorneys discuss the law
of nature and the law of Rome and the lessons to be drawn from
Scottish history. His defence of the age-long traditions of a
united Scotland had impressed them more than his later plea
that the kingdom, if judged as a barony, should be divided as a
barony.[1] Gradually the legend grew that Edward, a foe in the
guise of a friend, had struck down a trustful and defenceless
people.[2]

The king of Scotland appeared at Westminster in parliament
after Michaelmas to answer to the appeal of Macduff from the
judgement of imprisonment imposed upon him in the previous
February in the Scottish parliament at Scone.[3] He was in a
difficult position. Although one chronicler, writing after the
events of his reign, probably went too far when he pictured the
king in Scotland as friendless, 'a lamb among wolves',[4] he certainly did not come to England with his hands free. He refused to
answer to Macduff's appeal. He was king of Scotland, and he
dared not reply on any matter affecting it without the counsel of
the good men of his realm. To the obvious retort that in that case
he must ask for an adjournment (and so recognize the competence
of the court) he answered that he would admit no adjournment.
Edward was in no mood to dally with this 'evasion and inerva-
tion' of his superior jurisdiction.

[1] Bruce had urged his claim as, at one time, Alexander II's tanist, or accepted
successor, and on Scottish custom and the duty of the court to transcend English
common law. In his view his most formidable rival was the count of Holland, not
Baliol. This is clear from his indenture with Florence, count of Holland, as early as
14 June 1292, i.e. before the real trial took place. The two claimants agreed that if
either were successful he should enfeoff the other with a third part of the kingdom
(Stevenson, i. 318–21). After the trial Bruce retired to his castle of Lochmaben in
Annandale and died there in 1295. His son, on 7 November 1292 (the day after the
first judgement (above, p. 607)), resigned his earldom of Carrick to his son, the future
king, as heir of his mother, Margery of Carrick, who had died. This was regularized
in parliament at Stirling in August 1293 (*Foedera*, i. ii. 791). In this year he took his
daughter Isabel to Norway to become King Eric's second wife. King Edward sent
her fine presents of robes, &c. (Bain, ii, no. 675).

[2] Declaration of 6 April 1320 to Pope John XXII, described by Lord Cooper 'as
one of the masterpieces of political rhetoric of all time'. See his address in his little
book *Supra crepidam* (1951), pp. 48–71 (with text and translation).

[3] *Rot. parl.* i. 112–13. For the Scottish parliaments at Scone and Stirling in 1293 and
the chronology of the Macduff case see Richardson and Sayles in *Scot. Hist. Rev.* xxv
(1928), 303–4, 306, n., 309, n.; cf. *Foedera*, i. ii. 786, 791, and Palgrave, pp. 141–51.

[4] See the opening of the so-called annals of England and Scotland which follow
the annals of Scotland in Cotton MS. Claudius D. vi, and are printed with them
in Rishanger, p. 371. They cover the years 1293–1300.

The council in parliament at Westminster decided that Baliol was in mercy and must deliver three of his strongest castles to remain in Edward's hands until the disobedient vassal had given satisfaction for his act of contempt. At this point Baliol's relatives and friends at court may well have persuaded him to submit: for before judgement was given he uttered a supplication in person and gave it in writing; as Edward's man for the realm of Scotland ('Sire, jeo suy vostre homme de realme de Escoce') he asked for a day and promised to reply in the next parliament after taking counsel. This was granted. The Welsh and French wars of 1294-5 prevented a final decision in the case before Baliol had become the ally of the French king.[1]

In 1294 Edward was involved in war for Gascony. In June he forbade the ports of England to allow any outward sailings across the seas and ordered the king of Scotland to proclaim the same prohibition in the Scottish ports. On 29 June he included the king, eight earls, the steward, and a dozen barons of Scotland in his summons to the host to assemble in London by 1 September.[2] His plans were upset by the outbreak of the Welsh rebellion in this year. Before this had been crushed the king's council in Scotland had decided to seek allies in France.[3] Early in July 1295, in parliament at Stirling, Baliol was given a council of twelve advisers—four bishops, four earls, and four barons; and the bishops of St. Andrews and Dunkeld and two barons were accredited to the French with powers to arrange a marriage between Edward, Baliol's son and heir, and Jeanne of Valois, Philip's niece. The king, who had already been persuaded to dismiss the English element in his household, was, in general esteem, deprived of leadership. 'He opened not his mouth.'[4] King Philip and his counsellors were busily concerned to secure diversions from the north and to make alliances in reply to Edward's alliance with the king of Germany and the princes of the Rhineland. Negotiations with the Scots were closely combined with negotiations

---

[1] *Rot. Parl.* i. 113; Palgrave, pp. 145-51; with the critical comments in *Scot. Hist. Rev.* xxv. 309 and note.   [2] *Foedera*, I. ii. 801, 804.

[3] King Philip's letters to the count of Flanders (Stevenson, ii. 2-3; cf. his open letters of protection, p. 5) show that good relations had been established in the spring of 1295, for Scottish merchants trading with Flanders were given his protection, as his friends. The traitor, Thomas Turberville, released by King Philip after capture in Gascony to spy in England, reported in August 1295 that if the Scots made war the Welsh would rise yet again (Cotton, *Hist. anglic.* (ed. Luard), p. 305). For this traitor see J. G. Edwards in *Studies in Medieval History presented to F. M. Powicke*, pp. 296-309.   [4] Rishanger, p. 372.

with King Eric of Norway, who, in spite of his recent marriage to Isabel Bruce, was easily persuaded, in return for an annual payment of £50,000 sterling, to equip a fleet of 100 great ships to be used for four months each year so long as the war against the king of England lasted, and in the meanwhile to submit his claims on the king of Scotland to Philip's arbitration or at least enter into a mutual undertaking with the Scots to defer his disputes with them. A series of agreements to this effect was made at Paris on 22 October 1295, when the French treaties with Norway and Scotland and the marriage contract were approved. The king of Scotland bound himself to invade and harry England if Edward left the country or sent large forces to make war on Philip. Philip undertook to give aid to Scotland in case of need.[1]

King Edward must have been made aware of the secret negotiations before the treaties were made. On 5 October he appointed the bishop of Durham and Earl Warenne, Baliol's father-in-law, custodians of the shires north of the Trent; also Warenne as castellan of Bamborough and Robert Bruce, who lately had succeeded to Annandale, as castellan of Carlisle.[2] He ordered Baliol to surrender, for the period of the war with France, the castles and boroughs of Berwick, Roxburgh, and Jedburgh, and on 16 October he issued writs to all the sheriffs in England for the seizure of the English lands, goods, and chattels of John Baliol and all their tenants who dwelt in Scotland.[3] He decided, as his father had decided in 1244 and 1255, on a military demonstration. On 16 December 1295, he issued writs to over 200 of his tenants to appear at Newcastle in March 1296 with horses and arms. He intended, he wrote, to seek a remedy against Baliol for his infringement of his sworn obligations.[4] In February he collected a fleet of ships from the eastern ports north of Lynn.[5] By the time he reached Newcastle he knew that the Scots would fight. The Scottish earls, leaving Baliol behind, gathered their forces on the Border. Some of them made an abortive raid on Wark castle. Edward moved north to Wark, where he was met by the earls of Dunbar and Angus and Robert Bruce and his son,

[1] *Foedera*, i. ii. 822, 830–2; Stevenson, ii. 8–15. On these treaties see now Ranald Nicholson in *Scottish Hist. Rev.* xxxviii (1959), 114–32.

[2] *Cal. Pat. Rolls, 1292–1301*, pp. 147, 152; Stevenson, ii. 6–7.

[3] *Foedera*, i. ii. 829; Stevenson, pp. 7–8; cf. pp. 22–23. Baliol had been summoned to appear at Newcastle.

[4] *Parl. Writs.* pp. 275–7.

[5] Stevenson, ii. 23–24.

the future king, who did fealty and homage for their lands in Scotland.[1] On 28 March the English crossed the Tweed, and, after trying in vain to parley with the burgesses of Berwick, stormed and sacked the town. On 5 April Edward was given in Berwick castle Baliol's formal *diffidatio* or renunciation of homage and fealty.[2]

Just as on the threshold of Wales in 1277 the king had made the building of castles and towns at Rhuddlan and Flint one of his first tasks, so in April 1296 he paused to make a new Berwick on the threshold of Scotland. He collected as many ditchers, masons, carpenters, and smiths as could be found in Northumberland and himself took a hand, like St. Louis of France at the abbey of Royaumont, in the first labours of reconstruction. During the year the flimsy outworks of Berwick were replaced by a deep ditch and broad, high earthworks. In January 1297 a committee of experts was called upon to advise on the planning of a new town under the direction of his treasurer of Scotland. Edward designed Berwick to be the financial capital of the country with an exchequer based on the model of the exchequer in Westminster, as well as a centre of trade and stores settled by men who would displace the burgesses who had resisted him.[3] By this time he thought that he had conquered Scotland. After some savage raids into Northumberland and Cumberland and their defeat at Dunbar by the Earl Warenne on 27 April, the Scots had made little resistance. Their leaders, including the earls of Athol, Ross, and Menteith, the son of John Comyn of Badenoch, and some six or seven more, had been captured in the battle of Dunbar or in Dunbar castle and distributed among the castles of England. The steward of Scotland surrendered Roxburgh, Lothian was overrun, Edinburgh castle subdued by the king's engines. Here the Scottish regalia and a mass of state records were seized. From Stirling, where Edward was joined by the earl of Ulster and a contingent from Ireland, the king's march was more like a procession, punctuated by submissions, than a campaign. At Montrose John Baliol's abdication was completed. Thence Edward made a sweep round the north-eastern coasts to

---

[1] Chronicle of Walter of Guisborough, ed. Rothwell, pp. 283-4 (25 March). For the story of the campaign, briefly summarized in the text, see Ramsay, op. cit., pp. 423-34.   [2] *Foedera*, I. ii. 836-7.

[3] Stevenson, ii. 37-38, 149-51, 152-6; cf. below, p. 636. For the exchequer at Berwick see the interesting letter from the barons of the exchequer of England to Hugh Cressingham, Edward's treasurer in Scotland, 6 March 1297 (ibid., pp. 163-4).

Elgin, the bishop of Durham going ahead to prepare his way. On his return journey he took possession of the stone of Scone. On 22 August he came back to Berwick, where he proceeded to hold a Scottish parliament and order the affairs of his realm.[1]

John Baliol had already made his submission and left Scotland, never to return. On 2 July, at Kincardine, he confessed his offence in making terms with the king of France and in renouncing his homage, and surrendered his kingdom to Edward.[2] On 7 July, in the cemetery at Stracathro, he publicly denounced his errors and confirmed his reconciliation with the king of England. On 10 July at Brechin he made to the bishop of Durham the formal act of surrender by enfeoffment and on the same day at Montrose repeated it to Edward himself. He and his young son Edward were taken by sea to England and allowed for a time to live in freedom at Hertford. When in 1297 William Wallace rose in Baliol's name, they were transferred to the Tower. In 1299 they were allowed to leave England under papal safeguards. Baliol died in Normandy in 1315, the year after the battle of Bannockburn.

What happened in the parliament at Berwick is best told in the words of the anonymous journal of King Edward's movements in Scotland:

At Berwick he held his parliament; and there were all the bishops, earls, barons, abbots and priors, and the 'sovereigns' of all the common people; and there he received the homages of all, and their oaths that they would be good and loyal to him. To the well regulated people he forthwith gave up all their own goods and those of their tenants; the earls, barons and bishops he permitted to enjoy their lands, provided they came at All Saints to the parliament at St. Edmunds. Then he appointed the Earl Warren to be guardian of the land, and sir Hugh de Cressingham treasurer, sir Walter of Amersham chancellor. Then he tarried at Berwick three weeks and three days,

---

[1] Edward's progress through Scotland is described in detail in an anonymous journal, edited from a fourteenth-century manuscript in the Bibliothèque Nationale, Paris, by Stevenson, ii. 25–32. An indenture of military service between the king and Robert Clifford (2 April 1296) illustrates the way in which Edward arranged for the pacification of the country (in this case the forest of Selkirk and south-west Scotland) and the giving of hostages (ibid. ii. 36–37). For order and justice maintained in the king's army during its march see the cases from the army plea roll in Bain, ii. 189–92, no. 882.

[2] *Foedera*, i. ii. 841–2, from the original letters sealed with the great seal of Scotland. The great seal was afterwards broken; for details and references to the proceedings of 7 and 10 July see Stevenson, ii. 59–62.

arranging his affairs, and set out on his road to England on the
Sunday after the feast of the Holy Cross[1] (16 September 1296).

The memorial of the main proceedings at Berwick, on 28
August, is the record known as the Ragman Roll, thirty-five
pieces of parchment on which Andrew, apostolic notary, who
was present during the execution of the various instruments of
homage and fealty, copied them word for word.[2] If all the persons and communities who did homage and gave in their bonds
under their seals actually gathered together to make sworn
allegiance on one day, it was a very busy day indeed. Many earls
and magnates and lesser folk had sworn fealty already, but everybody was expected to take part in one impressive demonstration
of loyalty to Edward and of repudiation of all dealings with the
king of France. Local clergy, burgesses, and men of the shires
had flocked to Berwick to join the bishops, earls, and barons in
parliament in a common act of fealty, not to a new king of Scotland but to the king of England.

Robert Bruce of Annandale, the son of the competitor and the
father of the king, was believed by the Scottish chroniclers to
have put forward a claim to the throne. Edward, the story continues, replied, 'Have I nought else to do, but win a kingdom for
you?' Here, it may well be, Edward made the biggest mistake in
his life. He had Scotland at his feet. It would have been unwise
to incur the risks of exalting Bruce; but he could have established
a body of Scottish guardians and appointed Scottish ministers of
state, sheriffs, and castellans to administer the kingdom under
his superior lordship, leaving the throne vacant for a time.
Familiar as he was with the problems of his own obligations to
King Philip he could have regulated the procedure of appeals as
it had been regulated by the *parlement* of Paris for Gascony in
1286, when the seneschal and other high officials were exempted
from penalties when appeals from them were sustained.[3] Doubt-

---

[1] Stevenson, ii. 31–32. Of course, much more was done in completion of acts
taken during the king's tour of Scotland; e.g. the disposition of castles and local
government. Not all the bishops, earls, and barons were present at Berwick. Bishop
Fraser of St. Andrews, who died in France in 1297, the earls and barons in English
prisons, and others were absent.

[2] Printed in *Instrumenta publica sive processus super fidelitatibus et homagiis Scotorum
domino regi Anglie factis, 1291–6*, edited T. Thomson (Bannatyne Club, 1834), and
summarized from the original roll in Bain, ii. 193–215, no. 823. The notary, who
describes himself as 'Andreas quondam Guillelmi de Tange clericus' was also responsible for the accounts of Baliol's relations with Edward from December 1292 to
his surrender in July 1296.   [3] Above, p. 314.

less Edward understood the position of affairs in 1296 better than we can. His clemency, he may have felt, had been more than generous; but he could not see the clouds gathering in the west. Not all the substantial free tenants of Scotland went to Berwick to do homage; some never did homage; one of these was biding his time near Paisley; and there were others in Moray.

XIII

THE CROWN AND THE MERCHANTS

THE submission of the Scots at Berwick in September 1296 was the culminating point in Edward I's reign. He tried, in a supreme effort, to bring all the resources of his kingdom and his lordship of Ireland to bear upon his conflict with King Philip of France. The strain was too great. In 1297 the incoherences and diffusion of interests peculiar to the medieval state system in western Europe were revealed in a tangle of crises, and not even Edward's splendid energy could control them. He was fifty-seven years old when he left Berwick; he died ten years later, valiant and determined as ever, but a broken man. These last ten years of his reign are the first ten years of a new age in our history. Perhaps the most significant factor in later developments was Edward's effort, during these years, to rally, on the plea of necessity, the financial and military resources of the country. In the attempt he found himself forced to stress the prerogative of the Crown, and to resist the baronial desire to subject his claims to the principles of the Great Charter and the Forest Charter in an enlarged form. The king had to scrape together every penny that he could find and to exploit every kind of wealth available to him—wool and the customs, prises and purveyance, the forests, and the man-power of the shires, and the ports. His enlargement of the principle of consent to taxation in parliament, his realization of the growing importance of the wool trade, his far-reaching employment, as agents and creditors, of the merchant community were positive contributions to the national life; but they were interlocked with the problems of law and prerogative. They led to new adjustments between the secular and spiritual powers, to the displacement of the great council and high appeals to the Great Charter by parliaments and statutes, of the old local system by justices of the peace, of the feudal levy by commissions of array; but they led also to the long-drawn disputes about customs, prises, purveyance, forest rights, and the prerogative generally. So the social order in church and state was refashioned.

When the expedition to the north was under preparation in 1295–6, the keeper of the royal household authorized the exchequer to send £10,000 and more by 1 March to Newcastle, to be ready for the king's business, also to pay £1,000 a week at Newcastle on 1 March and in each succeeding week for the payment of 1,000 men-at-arms and 60,000 foot 'and for other expenses of the household'.[1] War meant money and still more money. War, and especially foreign war and foreign alliances, involved the household and exchequer in a network of international finance. It submitted leisurely experience to the grip of statute law and the control of the Crown; and it created the conditions under which the future commercial and industrial strength of the land was to develop until the era of free trade.

The story begins after the battle of Evesham, when the Lord Edward was given control of the foreign merchants in England, made warden of the Cinque Ports, and, it should be added, resumed his personal interest in the city of London. The control of the foreign merchants was granted in April 1266 after consultation with merchants. Edward had the right to grant or withhold licences to enter and trade in England, and to levy a general customs duty on imports and exports. He levied the tax and appointed collectors throughout the country. In the next year he farmed out the 'new aid' to Italian merchants for 6,000 marks a year.[2] Henceforward Edward, as duke of Aquitaine as well as king of England, was the patron and also the exploiter of commerce. He maintained a close oversight over the English exporters and importers no less than over the foreign merchants. The political utility of the customs system centralized in Bordeaux was already appreciated; money could be raised on its security.[3] The Italian merchant and financial companies became the chief agents of the royal finances both in England and Gascony. In Gascony the wealth latent in the wine trade, in England the highly organized export trade in wool could be manipulated. And, if trade was to be encouraged, the traders must be protected. The coinage must be sound, and more attention must be

[1] Stevenson, *Hist. Docs.* ii. 20–21: 23 January 1296, from the memoranda roll.
[2] *Foedera*, i. i. 468; for opposition to the collectors, *Cal. Pat. Rolls, 1266–72*, pp. 1, 2. For the farming of the customs and the exemption of the protesting Londoners from contribution in 1267, *Liber in antiquis legibus* (ed. Stapleton, 1846), pp. 109–10. King Louis of France also protested and was invited to send ten merchants to the fair at Winchester to advise the king (*Cal. Pat. Rolls*, p. 141, June 1267).
[3] Above, pp. 281, 304.

paid to the central control of standard weights and measures and to the use of them.[1] Royal control must be exercised in a constructive way, not as it had been in King Henry's time, when a vendetta against the hated foreign merchants and usurers expressed itself in edicts of expulsion tempered by a species of blackmail.[2] The merchants must be welcomed as well as controlled. Local monopoly and prejudice must not be allowed to hamper their activities and make it so hard for them to collect their debts. The law merchant and the allied maritime law—the law of Oléron, that important island off the Poitevin coast which since 1254 had been attached to the Crown[3]—must be observed and given full play in the courts of London and other trading centres. A concordat between merchant law and the common law of England must be reached, and the king's council, judges, and barons of the exchequer must be ready to further the interests of speedy justice. The statutes of Acton Burnell (1283) and of merchants (1285) and the *Carta Mercatoria* (1303) were inspired by this policy.

National developments could do little to regulate the crude methods of force which were the sanctions of order and disorder in wider disputes between the subjects of different states. Yet, here also, the reign of Edward I brought some change. The statutes of 1275, which (c. 4) alleviated the savagery of the custom of wreck, also gave wider authority to the tendency to limit the custom of reprisal by the provision (c. 23) that no foreigner could be distrained for debt, unless he were the debtor

---

[1] See the useful paper by Grace Faulkner Ward on the early history of the Merchant Staplers in *E.H.R.* xxxiii (1918), 297 ff., where an attempt is made to trace a continuity between the Lord Edward's responsibility in 1266 and fourteenth-century developments. References to work on coinage, weights and measures, and the law of Oléron are given in the discussions on pp. 303–6. The undated assize or ordinance of weights and measures (*Statutes*, i. 204), re-edited by Hubert Hall and Frieda J. Nicholas in their 'Tracts and Table Books of English Weights and Measures', pp. 9–10 (*Camden Miscellany*, xv, 1929), may belong to the last years of Henry III. For the control of local standard weights and measures and the foreign way of using the balance see two cases printed in *Select Cases on the Law Merchant*, ii. 52–53 (no. 23); 76–78 (no. 32).

[2] *Henry III and the Lord Edward*, i. 313–16.

[3] Sea law of Oléron was a variant of the customs of the sea, used in this important port of call, and was connected with the customs of the island. It was the type adopted all along the coasts from Spain to the Low Countries and in England. Several English copies from 1266 onwards are extant, but the law became known from the evidence of merchants on the custom of the sea by which the disputes of these 'migratory litigants' were tried in local courts. 'The ships', it has been suggested, 'carried the law with them as part of their cargo': C. G. Crump's review

or a pledge for the debt.[1] Membership of a privileged society,
like the *hansa* of German merchants in London, might save a
foreigner from spoliation as the fellow citizen of a body of pirates.[2]
The fierce conflicts between Norman, Gascon, and English
mariners which led to the war with France in 1294 led also to
lengthy processes of arbitration on mutual claims for damages.[3]

The Lord Edward was involved as early as 1270 in a dispute
which had serious consequences in Anglo-Flemish relations. In
the thirteenth century Flemish trade with England was strongly
organized in another London *hansa*, membership of which was
confined to an association of local guilds of merchants in Flanders,
a burghal aristocracy. An artisan of Bruges, for example, could
not reach municipal office unless he had renounced his craft and
gained a footing in the *hansa* of London.[4] The Flemings imported wool to Flanders and exported cloth. Edward on his way
to join King Louis on crusade, heard that the aged countess,
Margaret of Flanders, always one of the storm-centres of her
time, had, early in September 1270, seized the goods of many
English, Welsh, Irish, and Gascon merchants in payment of
arrears of pension which were owed to her by King Henry, and
had ejected the merchants from Flanders.[5] She had done this
kind of thing before, as early as 1230 and again during the
baronial troubles;[6] it was the usual form of reprisal in times of
dispute; but her action in 1270 was flagrant and it is hard not to
see in it some resentment against the new customs policy in
England. Edward wrote fiercely about the matter, and the
English government immediately seized all Flemish merchandise

---

of Bémont's essay on the custumal of the isle of Oléron (1917) in *E.H.R.* xxxiv
(1919), 599. In general see Holdsworth, *A History of English Law*, 3rd ed., i (1922),
526 ff., and Bémont's review of P. Studer's edition of the Oak Book of Southampton, ii (1911), in *Rev. historique*, cix (1912), 393–6, where the literary history of the
subject is summarized.

[1] In 1282 the seneschal of Gascony applied this principle to reprisals or arrests in
disputes between the sailors of Normandy and Bayonne: see P. Chaplais, 'Règle-
ment des conflits internationaux franco-anglais au XIVᵉ siècle', in *Le Moyen Âge*
for 1951, p. 277 and note.

[2] See the interesting case of 1309–10, printed in *Select Cases on the Law Merchant*,
ii, p. xci.   [3] Below, p. 657.

[4] See H. Pirenne in *Bull. de l'Acad. de Belgique*, Classe des lettres (1899); also his
Belgian Democracy (Eng. trans., 1915), pp. 113, 117.

[5] *Cal. Pat. Rolls, 1266–72*, pp. 456–7, 462; *Liber de antiquis legibus* (FitzThedmar's
London chronicle), pp. 126–7.

[6] See a case in *Select Pleas in Manorial Courts*, ed. Maitland (1888), p. 10, for a
result of the seizure in 1230; cf. *Royal Letters*, ii. 305–6, and *Foedera*, i. i. 468 (letters
of Edward and Henry III to Margaret, 1266).

and imposed an embargo on all exports of wool to Flanders. The merchants in England were sworn to respect the embargo.

Two results of administrative significance followed. The first was the introduction of a licensing system on exports of wool and rigid control over the operations of merchants. The record of licences on the Patent Rolls has enabled scholars to compose a most valuable survey of the extent and nature of English exports of wool during the next decade, for, although a truce with Flanders was made in 1274 the prohibition was not finally withdrawn until February 1278. During the year 1273 the export licences covered 32,743 sacks of wool, of which English merchants exported about a third. The average price was 10 marks a sack. The Italian merchants handled 37 per cent. of the wool exported by foreigners, the merchants of northern France 24 per cent., the merchants of Brabant—whose economic and political relations with England were to become very close—17 per cent. Three Italian firms invested capital to the amount of 41,000 marks. Most of the wool went to the Low Countries and France, whether exported by Italians or not; and a large sum was paid in fines for exports to the Flemish cities.[1] Such was the profitable source of wealth which Edward was later to seize when he was forming his alliances. It increased the operations of English and foreign capitalists, established English mercantile families whose original capital came from rents, and helped to elaborate the modern instruments of credit.[2]

The second result of the trouble with Flanders followed the truce made by Edward at Montreuil-sur-mer on his way home for his coronation in 1274. He was met there by the son of the Countess Margaret, Guy of Dampierre, who succeeded his mother in Flanders in 1280.[3] Guy promised to pay the difference between the value of the countess's seizures, which the London chronicler says were worth 40,000 marks, and of the goods taken in reprisal in England; also to find hostages, liable to imprison-

---

[1] A. Schaube, on English wool exports in 1273 in *Vierteljahrsschrift für Sozial- und Wirtschaftsgeschichte*, vi (1908), 39–72, 159–85; J. de Sturler, *Les Relations politiques et les échanges commerciaux entre le duché de Brabant et l'Angleterre au moyen âge* (Paris, 1936), pp. 126–34, on the Brabant trade of the period.

[2] G. Unwin noted in his review of Schaube's paper, *E.H.R.* xxiv (1909), 399, that the leading London exporters were aldermen and sheriffs who derived much of their income from rents in London and other cities.

[3] The contested succession had been settled by the arbitration of St. Louis in 1256; cf. Ch.-V. Langlois in Lavisse, *Hist. de France*, iii. ii. 89–91. Guy's nephew, John d'Avesnes, succeeded to Hainault.

ment, if the sums owing were not paid by a fixed date. The bill came to £4,755 and the date of payment was deferred later to 1277; but some money was still owing as late as 1285. An arrangement was finally reached in 1286. Further difficulty was caused by the indifference of the Flemish mariners to the truce. During the period of embargo they had apparently run riot in informal warfare at sea. Even after 1286 they resumed their attacks on English and Gascon shipping, and reprisals were again made in England. By this time, however, Count Guy was on friendly terms with King Edward. In 1279 he was given an annual money fee of 500 marks and did homage for it. In 1282, with Edward's approval, he married his daughter to the heir of Alexander III of Scotland. Political tension at home and abroad drew the two men together; and in 1292 peace was made between them.[1] Now during the first years of this long period the tedious investigations required by the truce of Montreuil had proceeded. The account between the two countries had to be balanced. In October 1274 Edward had appointed a body of auditors who were required, with the aid of Flemish assessors, to hear pleas of chattels and debts of Flemish merchants in England, occasioned by the treaty of Montreuil.[2] The auditors took a wide view of their duties. It would be difficult to separate such cases from other cases of debt under the law merchant.

One case which, for a time, came within the cognizance of the auditors, may well have been one of the immediate causes of the statute of Acton Burnell and the statute of merchants.[3] It shows the need of an official recognizance and registration of debts, especially between widely separated parties. Towards the end of Henry III's reign James le Roy, a merchant of Dixmude, entered into a contract of partnership with a Lincolnshire landholder, John de Redmere, of the manor of Appleby. The former was to ship cloth, spices, and other wares from Flanders, the latter wool from England, each to have or incur a fourth part of the gain or loss resulting from the sale of the goods which he transmitted.

---

[1] H. Berben, in *Études d'histoire dédiées à la mémoire de Henri Pirenne* (Brussels, 1937), 1–17. The narrative in the text is based upon *Foedera*, i. ii. 513–14, 555, 613, 659, 759; *Cal. Pat. Rolls, 1272–81*, p. 331 (Count Guy's money fief); Bartholomew Cotton, *Hist. Anglicana*, pp. 178–9.

[2] *Cal. Pat. Rolls, 1272–81*, p. 60. The auditors were John Bek and Fulk Lovel, with four English and four Flemish merchants. They sat at St. Martin's le Grand in London (*Select Cases on the Law Merchant*, ii. 18, n.).

[3] The case of *James le Roy of Dixmude v. John de Redmere of Appleby* (Lincs.) (*Select Cases*, ii. 18–27; cf. pp. xxxii–xxxiv and vol. iii, p. xxi).

The Fleming impleaded John in the shire court at Lincoln for default, claiming a large sum due to him, and agreed with John in writing for a payment of 200 marks. This was in Henry III's time; and the matter was no doubt interrupted by the Flemish troubles in 1270–4. The claim was renewed before the auditors of Flemish debts after the truce of 1274. Here John produced a deed sealed by James and his nephew, quitclaiming all debts and contracts made between them. James and his nephew, after inspecting the document, declared it to be a forgery, but when it was submitted by the court of auditors to the inspection of the king's justices 'sworn of the council of the lord king', the latter, after comparing the seals with those attached to the original contract of partnership, concluded that it was authentic. Whereupon the auditors committed James to prison, to be redeemed at the king's will. He was able to bring a complaint of error to the notice of the king who in pity ordered John Bek, the chief auditor of Flemish cases, to release him and in February 1278[1] ordered William of Norbury to re-examine the case and to do justice according to law merchant. The new judge associated with himself five others, including the mayor and two other merchants of Lincoln. The alleged forgery was the main point at issue. The Lincoln merchants, asked 'whether it was the law merchant that anyone might prove the seal of one writing by collation with the seal attached to another', emphatically denied that he ought to do so, for it was easy to use a lost seal or to take a seal by force or steal it in the night. John de Redmere was allowed, on payment of forty shillings, to make terms with James le Roy, in accordance with the earlier agreement that he should pay 200 marks. In full county court at Lincoln he found pledges for the payment of the debt.

This, however, was by no means the end of the matter, for James le Roy was unable to get payment at the periods fixed. The sheriff of Lincoln, a friend of John de Redmere, asserted that John had nothing on which he could be distrained; his pledges, on the other hand, insisted that he could well afford to pay without making them responsible. The case lingered on till 1284, and thrice the king had again to intervene; on the last occasion, it is interesting to note, at Acton Burnell, the home of Robert Burnell, the chancellor, when he seems to have referred the tiresome affair to his judges sitting at Shrewsbury. It was at this same time that,

[1] See *Cal. Pat. Rolls*, *1272–81*, pp. 287–8.

in a Michaelmas parliament, the statute of Acton Burnell was issued. Its second edition, the statute of Merchants, was issued in 1285, not long after James le Roy's troubles came, we may hope, to an end. This second statute revised the first, provided drastic ways of repayment of debts of which the debtors had made official recognizance, and extended the system, established at Acton Burnell, of making and sealing recognizances before local wardens and clerks assigned by the Crown. As soon as the bond was in default the debtor was to be committed to prison until his affairs were settled, and repayment was to be made from chattels and, if need be, from lands, to which the creditor obtained a right of freehold. In the same parliament of 1285, in the statute of Westminster II (c. 18), the common law of debt was altered to give the creditor an alternative and speedier process (*elegit*) analogous to that prescribed in the statute of Merchants.[1]

The aims of the statutes of 1283 and 1285 were clearly set out. They were the speedier payment of debts, encouragement to foreign merchants to come to trade in England, and more control over sheriffs and other local and municipal officers whose familiarity with the law merchant had by no means modified their parochial prejudices against the alien. The merchants, whether alien or English, got statutory access, in fairs and all centres of trade, as in Bordeaux and elsewhere abroad, to official registries of deeds of recognizance. They could even become freeholders of English land, while their debtors rotted in prison. Above all, they came more directly under the law of the land and the king's courts, including the exchequer. The statutes were enforced,[2] though their enforcement was not always so speedy as the merchants may have hoped. In course of time the law and courts of the realm would reduce the value of the courts of law merchant; but in Edward's reign justice in the courts of piepowder in the fairs and in the local tribunals which administered law merchant in ports and market towns was probably more effective than it had ever been.[3]

[1] Plucknett, *Legislation of Edward I*, pp. 135–50. The Jews, who came under another well-established procedure, were excluded from the operation of the statute of Merchants. They were expelled five years later.

[2] See specimens of writs in *Select Cases*, iii, pp. liii ff. Alice Beardwood has written a helpful account of the investigation, under a writ of 1307, into Walter Langton's use of merchant recognizances, in *Mediaevalia et Humanistica*, ix (Boulder, Colorado, 1955), 54–70.

[3] On the law merchant see generally W. Mitchell, *Early History of the Law Merchant* (1904) and C. Gross's introduction to the *Select Cases*, i. The most useful

It was essential to retain a system which associated merchants, either as judges or, as in London, as assessors in mercantile cases, for they alone could be depended upon to know the body of custom by which good faith was maintained and technical practices were regulated throughout the trading world. As the case of James le Roy shows, even the king's judges in council could err. In another case (1291) the barons of the exchequer found, when a dispute between a merchant of Lucca and his agent had been sent to them on a complaint of error, that they could not understand the books and accounts presented to them; they did not know the language (*idioma*) and technicalities and the common law did not apply. They referred the matter back to the auditors and finally the decision was left by agreement to a body of arbitrators.[1] Even in international cases resort to law was not regarded as altogether vain. In 1281 a merchant known to the king sought redress because the Florentines had destroyed his palace and towers in Florence during their party strife and it was only after much dispute, in which the great Accursius was invoked, that an attempt to get redress from Florentine merchants dwelling in London was given up as hopeless.[2] Such matters, indeed, could be considered only at a high political level. As some 'men of England' complained to the king in 1306, Florentine merchant companies, like the Pulci, belonged to a community which had no sovereign like a king or a prince, who could be required to do right in such cases.[3]

King Edward was certainly a sovereign. He was ready for action at home and abroad, as his relations with the Londoners show. In 1285 he took the city into his own hands and ruled it through a warden for thirteen years. Some rioting and jail breaking had occurred and John Kirkby, the treasurer, and others were appointed to make judicial investigations in the Tower. The mayor, Gregory of Rokesley, led the aldermen in a protest. He appeared to make his protest without his official insignia and the seal of the community. Kirkby took the opportunity to

---

text is preserved in the *Little Red Book of Bristol* (ed. F. B. Bickley, 1900), a treatise composed about 1280. See H. G. Richardson, 'Law Merchant in London in 1292', in *E.H.R.* xxxvii (1922), 242–9, at 243, n.

[1] This very interesting case of *Gettus Honesti* v. *Pelegrin* is in *Select Cases*, ii. 53–62.

[2] *Select Cases*, ii. 34–39. Here we have a lively picture of Florentine life and politics.

[3] P.R.O. Anc. Pet. 3936, to which Professor George Haskins has called my attention. Cf. above, p. 519, n. 3.

declare that London was without a mayor, and formally took
the city into the king's hands (28 June). The offenders were
summoned to appear before the king at Westminster. Ralph of
Sandwich was made constable of the Tower and warden of the
city, with a house on Cornhill. A series of ordinances was made
and published for the administration of London.[1] There can be
no doubt that this action was taken and maintained of set purpose, not merely as a penalty for a discourteous demonstration.
The king did not intend to interrupt the normal government of
the city. The London courts continued to act, with the warden
in place of the mayor; the customary rights of the city were maintained; but London was put under firmer control. The new
'establishments' or ordinances were largely directed to the ends
which inspired the contemporary statutes of Westminster and
Winchester, including the statute of Merchants: order, watch
and ward, legal procedure, so that merchants, whether English
or alien, might go about their business without interference and
anxieties. They included clauses about the accessibility and use
of the king's balances, the safe harbourage of all merchants, the
expulsion of disreputable, and the welcome, with the status of
citizens in their dealings, of good and sufficient merchant
strangers, and the regular holding of the customary daily court
to try cases in which foreign merchants might obtain or suffer
speedy justice. In 1289 the exchequer—the department most
closely connected with the financial activities of the city, including the exchange—was transferred, though possibly only as a
court, to the place of the London hustings.[2] The treasurer, now
within the city, seems to have assumed increasing control of
affairs, a control far more irksome to the citizens than that of the
warden, who, as administrator and in his court, was really a
more responsible mayor.[3] This was too much for the Londoners

[1] M. Weinbaum, *London unter Eduard I und II*, i (Stuttgart, 1933), 91–100; *Select
Cases before the King's Council*, ed. I. S. Leadam and J. F. Baldwin (Selden Soc., 1918),
pp. li–lvi. The 'establishments' or ordinances of 1285 were copied into the London
Liber custumarum in the fourteenth century, and thence in the *Liber Albus* of the
fifteenth century; they are printed in the Rolls Series edition of the latter (*Munimenta Gildhalliae Londoniensis*, i (1859), 280–97).

[2] Madox, *Hist. of the Exchequer* (1769), ii. 9. When, in 1298, the exchequer was
removed to York as a whole, with its records, the great hall and the tower of York
castle were prepared to receive it; it is unlikely that everything was removed in
1289 to the London Hustings.

[3] Kirkby died in 1290 and was succeeded by William March who bore the brunt
of the Londoners' indignation.

to bear. They felt humiliated. They voiced their grievances to the king's council in 1295.[1] By this time, Edward's necessities were incompatible with the danger of a hostile London. The treasurer, William March, was removed, the liberties of London were restored,[2] and in 1298, while Edward was in Flanders, the mayoralty was resumed.

The conclusion to be drawn from the previous discussion is that, during the twenty years after 1266 Edward had brought the merchants in England, both English and foreign, under protection and control. Although it is unlikely that the community of English merchants had gone far to establish common interests, still less an organization like the later staple system of Edward III's reign,[3] they had acquired by 1285 a standing wider than that implied by occasional consultations with the king or at the exchequer or in the local courts of law merchant. The fact that the customs on wool, wool-fells, and hides of 1275 were imposed in a full parliament at the request of the merchants shows that a period had begun of contractual understandings between them and the Crown on a more national basis.

The development of the customs system was the outstanding contribution to English finance in Edward's time.[4] After King John's short-lived attempt to impose a national system,[5] no general system, except the 'semi-national' export duties or last-age on wine levied in certain places, and the import duties or scavage levied at London and perhaps in other seaports, existed in England until 1266. All over the country local customs were collected by lords of liberties and town officials, and their levy was directed by ancient practices or limited by charters of local or general exemption;[6] but, except indirectly through the rents or farms paid annually to the king by the boroughs of his demesne, these did not increase the royal revenue. In 1266, as we

[1] *Select Cases before the King's Council*, pp. 8–18: *Citizens of London* v. *Bishop of Bath*. March had been bishop of Bath and Wells since 1293.

[2] See a note in the list of sheriffs and mayors in the *Liber Custumarum* (*Munimenta Gildhalliae*, II. i. (1860), 293).

[3] The English merchants at Antwerp, where foreign trade was concentrated in 1296, had a corporate organization which anticipates the later system in England. Cf. Sturler, op. cit., pp. 208, 214; below, p. 663.

[4] N. C. B. Gras, *The Early English Customs System* (1918); cf. J. Tait in *E.H.R.* xxxiv (1919), 251–3; Eileen Power, *The Wool Trade in English Medieval History* (1941), pp. 63–85.

[5] The fifteenth on imports and exports of 1203 (Gras, pp. 48–53).

[6] See the interesting documents from Torksey (1228), Ipswich, Berwick, and Sandwich (1303–4) in Gras, pp. 155–72.

have seen, Edward was allowed by his father to levy customs on the merchandise of all merchants; but this 'new custom', so important as a precedent, aroused such widespread opposition that it was discontinued, probably in 1274. It seems to have comprised duties on all imports and exports, and its general incidence was inconsistent with the rights and privileges and exemptions with which it conflicted. The customs levied in 1275, which died away only in the sixteenth century, mark a new departure in our economic history. They were not, as used to be thought, a development of the royal practice of prise.[1] They were not subject to local variations, traditions, and ownership, as were the customs on wine, lastage, and scavage. They were not imposed on all sorts of merchandise, imported or exported, nor liable to local and personal exemptions. They were export duties on wool, wool-fells, and leather or hides, payable at London and thirteen other ports to local officials under the supervision of controllers (who kept the counter rolls of shipments). The chief collectors were Luke of Lucca and other foreign merchants, who were thus the financial agents of the king in all matters affecting the levy and its expenditure. The decision to confine the levy to half a mark on the sack of wool (26 stone, or 364 lb.) and on 300 wool-fells, and a mark (13s. 4d.) on the last of leather, may be ascribed to the need to provide a more satisfactory substitute for the 'new custom' of 1266.[2]

The decision must have followed much deliberation between the king's advisers and the merchants. Duties which were few and precise, not too hard to collect, and which could be passed on to the foreign buyers, were the most advisable. Wool in England, like wine in Gascony, was obviously the best merchandise to choose. Moreover, the duty would protect the merchants against the inclusion of their wares in the list of movables liable to royal taxation, and there had been some danger that this might happen. Indeed, during the previous five years, the export trade in wool had been a political preoccupation, owing to the embargo on

[1] The prise of wine was the king's right to buy two casks, one on each side of the mast of the ship. It was a tax only so far as the ordinary purchase price exceeded the price given for wine taken in prise. In 1302 the merchants of Bordeaux were allowed to commute prise for a custom of two shillings per tun. In 1303 this permission was extended to all foreign importers of wine, in the *Carta Mercatoria*. See Gras, pp. 37–46, 67–68, 262 (14).

[2] See Gras, pp. 223–4 for the text. The average purchase price of a sack of wool was about £6 sterling; prices varied from about £9. 7s. 6d. to £2. 10s. 0d. The prices on the Flemish market were twice as much (Power, p. 23).

trade with Flanders. It had been subjected, as never before, to government control; and quite naturally it was chosen, by the king and the merchants alike, as the subject of the new deal. They were justified. The return from the custom for the nine years 1278–87 averaged £8,800, and for the last four years of the reign about £13,000 a year.[1] Apart from the *maltote* of 1294–7 and the royal seizure of wool stocks which will require our notice later, the next step—indeed the only step of permanent importance—was taken in 1303, when the king on 1 February issued at Windsor a far-reaching charter to all alien merchants trading in England.[2]

The *Carta Mercatoria* was an assertion of prerogative following discussion with the merchants. It did not comprise English merchants, nor affect the 'great custom' of 1275 and local and 'semi-national' customs. It confirmed or granted rights and privileges to the foreigner in return for additional dues at half the rate of the existing customs on wool, wool-fells, and leather, dues on wine, cloth, and wax, and an *ad valorem* duty of three-pence in the pound sterling on all other exports and imports. This general duty was 'the model for the later subsidy of pound-age', just as the new custom on wine or composition for prise, at two shillings on the tun, 'was a prototype of the subsidy of tun-nage'. The new or, as it came to be called, 'petty' custom, added an average sum of from £9,000 to £10,000 a year during the last four years of the reign. The returns in Boston, Bristol, and other ports give a good idea of the nature and extent of English trade, particularly of the exports and imports in the miscellaneous goods on which the *ad valorem* duty was paid, and of the variety of places from which the foreign merchants came.[3]

From the contemporary point of view, the status allowed to the foreign merchants by the *Carta Mercatoria* in 1303 was as significant as the new duties. The charter defines the position attained by the merchants during the previous thirty years and generalizes the London ordinances of 1285. They were placed under the king's special care and protection. They were free of payments for walls, bridges, and paving, could sell freely in cities, towns, and market centres to all, whether in large or

[1] Ramsay, *Dawn of the Constitution*, pp. 533–4.
[2] The best text, from the Fine Roll, is in Gras, pp. 259–64: for an analysis and comments, pp. 65–71, 136–8, 257–9.
[3] Gras, pp. 264–360, for some accounts in detail. As he shows (p. 258 and note) the duty of 3d. per pound was on the pound value, not on the pound weight.

small quantities. They could come in and go out, import or export goods (except to the king's enemies), and had the right of quiet lodging where they wished. Their contracts were to be firmly respected and disputes about them to be settled according to the uses and customs of the fairs and towns where they were made. Their merchandise was to be free of prises, arrests, delays, and interference by officials. In fairs, cities, boroughs, and market centres the bailiffs were to do speedy justice to all complainants from day to day according to merchant law, and if they did not were liable to penalties imposed by the Crown as well as to compensation to the aggrieved party. A special justice for the merchants was to be appointed in London to remedy delays and defects in the daily courts of the sheriffs and mayor. All civil and criminal pleas, except those which might lead to the death penalty, were to be tried with the aid of a mixed jury or inquisition in places where foreign merchants could be found to do their part. Standard weights and balances were to be available in each market town and fair. Finally, no merchant was to be required, as he moved about the country, to pay the new customs more than once. The result of these 'concessions' was to put foreign merchants from Germany, Lombardy, Tuscany, and the west of Europe on the same footing as the home merchants, for they could buy and sell to all as they pleased and were free of tolls of passage. In return they had to pay, over and above local customs, the great custom of 1275 and any semi-national duties of lastage and scavage, the additional duties on wool, and the new import and export duties from which the home merchants were exempt. Resentment against the freedom of trade granted to the foreigners and the fear that the new duties would affect prices account for the refusal of the home merchants to allow a general extension of the new duties.[1]

King Edward had advisers and experts among the merchants, both home and foreign. The former helped him to plan new towns and to carry through his manipulations in wool, the latter

---

[1] Gras, p. 70. Except the new duties on wool, wool-fells, and leather, the new custom was suspended in 1309 because of petitions against it, but it was restored in 1310 when it was found that 'no utility resulted to the king and people in the better price of such merchandise' from the cessation (*Cal. Fine Rolls, 1307–10*, pp. 67–68). The ordainers abolished the whole custom in 1311, but it was restored again in 1322, to remain for centuries. Both wool customs died because exports were forbidden in Tudor times; the export duties ceased in 1672, the additional import duty on wine in lieu of the king's right of prise came to an end in 1809 (Gras, p. 71).

controlled the administration of the customs, acted as bankers, advanced loans, and, generally with English colleagues, directed the mints and exchange. Among the English were Laurence of Ludlow, Gilbert of Chesterton, and other wool merchants whose names become familiar to students of the financial records of the king's relations with the duke of Brabant and neighbouring allies. These and some London merchants, notably Henry le Waleys and Gregory of Rokesley (until his fall in 1285) had grown rich and bought up many houses and manors in town and country, whose rents provided capital for wider business. The English fortunes of the great foreign houses of merchants, the Riccardi of Lucca and later the Frescobaldi of Florence, were bound up with their papal, Italian, and west European business. Until 1279[1] Luke of Lucca, who had been prominent in England for a quarter of a century, seems to have been in closest relations with the king; then followed Orlandino de Podio and, when the Riccardi company collapsed, the leading partners in England of the Frescobaldi.

England needed a new coinage; Henry III's money was becoming debased, a new king should have his own money, and—perhaps the most important consideration of all—foreign trade required that the coin presented at the exchanges, at home and abroad, should be in good repute. Debasement of the coinage was an expedient to which only the king might resort, as his moneyers did to a slight extent in 1300, when he was trying to extirpate the false and debased *ballards*, *pollards*, and other coins which had been brought into England and Ireland from German and Rhenish ports, the aftermath of Edward's operations oversea in 1297–8.[2]

---

[1] Luke was alive in July 1279, but dead before 8 November (*Cal. Close Rolls, 1272–81*, pp. 532, 544).

[2] After an earlier drive in 1294 (see below, p. 670), Edward had permitted such money if the depreciation was only two shillings in the pound, but his expedients on campaign had apparently let loose on the British Isles a flow of bad and false money. In 1299 he allowed currency to some of this—e.g. when money nominally worth a pound was assayed at a mark (13s. 4d.). Also, when he forbade all export of money in the same year, he allowed outgoing and incoming merchants to exchange at Dover and other ports as much as was required for expenses. In April 1300 he condemned all the bad money, allowed currency only to sterling, and forbade, except under licence, the export of all silver, in coin or in any other form. See the ordinances in Berry, *Early Statutes of Ireland*, pp. 213–14, 221–7, 239; *Foedera*, I. ii. 919; and the writs to the Londoners and proclamation in London, 1299–1300, in *Munimenta Gildhalliae*, II. i. 187, 189–93. For the slightly depreciated coinage of 1300 see Ramsay, op. cit., p. 540.

In the brighter days which followed the first Welsh war a good new currency had been planned. The way was prepared by a drive against speculation in silver by clippers of coin and collectors of silver bullion and plate. Jews and merchants in particular were suspect. Judicial commissions were appointed to seek out offenders; and the export of silver was prohibited.[1] A new coinage required the collection of spare silver and the calling in of the old money for exchange with the new. The new dies were made and entrusted to Gregory of Rokesley and Orlandino de Podio as wardens of the mint and exchange. The three masters of the mint were an expert from Marseilles, William Turnemire, and his brother, and an Italian from Asti. In December 1279 technical and financial arrangements for minting were concluded with William Turnemire and the assayer, a Florentine. Furnaces were set to work in London, Canterbury, York, and Exeter. Two changes were made in the coinage. In addition to the penny sterling, round farthings (the more difficult minting of which was concentrated in London) and a gross fourpenny piece (the groat) were produced, and, rather later, the halfpenny piece or *maille* was added. The distribution of mints and exchanges, reorganized in Henry III's time when his new coinage was issued (1247–8),[2] was revised.

An ordinance of 1300 shows that by this year the furnaces for minting and the exchanges were confined to the Tower of London, Canterbury, Kingston-on-Hull, Newcastle-upon-Tyne, Bristol, Exeter, and Dublin. Later an exchange was established in Chester. The English mints were under the direction of John Porcher, master of the money of England, the exchanges were supervised by John Sandal, warden of the king's exchanges. The exchanges of Canterbury and Bristol were under the exchange at London. The exchanges at Kingston-on-Hull, Newcastle, Exeter, and Dublin were held by the Frescobaldi of Florence, who were empowered to exchange the bad money, withdrawn in this year 1300, for good. In Dublin an Italian from Lucca had the mint and was responsible to the Irish exchequer. The close connexion between the exchanges and trade is emphasized by

[1] For the commissions of 1278–9 cf. *Cal. Pat. Rolls, 1272–81*, p. 297; *Cal. Close Rolls, 1272–9*, p. 529; export was forbidden in December 1278 (*Foedera*, i. ii. 564). The Jews suffered atrociously, and very many were hanged.

[2] For Henry III's coinage see especially the document printed as an appendix to the *Red Book of the Exchequer* (edit. Hubert Hall), iii. 1072–81; also Powicke, op. cit. i. 316–21; and Denholm-Young, *Richard of Cornwall*, pp. 58–65.

the responsibilities given to the Frescobaldi. The geographical distribution of the exchanges prepared the way for the later establishment of centres of foreign trade in the towns of the Staple.[1]

The new coinage rapidly gained currency. It has been estimated that by the end of 1284 nearly £37,000 was paid into the king's wardrobe from the profits due to the Crown from the mints.[2]

The ordinance of 1300 includes the name of Kingston-on-Hull as one of the seven centres of minting and exchange. Hull, previously Wyke-on-Hull or simply Hull, but now dignified as a royal creation, was not a new town founded by Edward I on the site of a village, as used to be supposed. It had contributed £345, or nearly half as much as Boston did, to King John's custom, the fifteenth; and in the first ten months of payment of the new custom of 1275 merchants there, including members of the firms of Riccardi and Frescobaldi, paid no less than £1,431.[3] What Edward did was to realize the possibilities of the place. He was direct lord of Holderness in succession to the earl of Aumâle, and a good port was needed to replace Ravenser, now encroached on by the sea. Wyke or Hull, where the Hull flows into the Humber, was the obvious place. Hence in 1293 he exchanged the rights of the monks of Meaux in Hull for lands elsewhere, changed the name to Kingston-on-Hull, proclaimed the creation of two markets a week, and set to work. The course of the Hull was diverted to give better protection and facilities, and new roads were made to the place. William de la Pole of Ravenser, founder of the great merchant family of Pole, was given the manor of Myton near by and made Kingston his headquarters. In 1299 the town received its first royal charter, and was granted liberties as a free borough based in part on those of Scarborough. Edward did not lay out the town, which was already well inhabited; its careful plan is the work of the next century; but he established its mint and exchange, and was the founder of Hull's later importance as a centre of trade.[4]

---

[1] *Red Book of the Exchequer*, iii. 980–3, 985–90. The farthing had been current in London under the name 'Londoner' (*Lundrensis*) before 1279 (p. 986). The halfpenny piece is mentioned in a note of payments to William Turnemire in 1284 (p. 983). It had been a common practice to break the earlier penny into two or four parts to provide half and quarter pennies. The sequence of events in Ramsay's account of the new coinage in his *Revenues of the Kings of England*, ii. 13–14, is not quite correct.

[2] Ramsay, op. cit., p. 14.   [3] Gras, pp. 222, 225–44.

[4] See J. Bilson, *Wyke-upon-Hull in 1293* (1928); T. F. Tout, 'Medieval Town Plan-

Since his boyhood Edward had been familiar with such town-planning as there was in his time in western Europe. The royal hunting-lodge or palace of Clarendon overlooked the new town of Salisbury, which had been laid out around the new cathedral and in 1227 was given the liberties of Winchester. Edward must often have been there. Later, as lord of the town and castle of Bristol, he would be aware of the engineering feats done there between 1240 and 1250, when the Avon was diverted into its new cut to provide for town extension, and Redcliff and the manor of the Templars were enclosed by wall and ditch.[1] As duke of Aquitaine he knew all about the extensive foundations of bastides in Languedoc by Saint Louis, Alphonse of Poitiers, and other lords, and had encouraged the extension of the movement to Gascony in the time of his seneschal John de Grilly. Indeed, some of his companions were commemorated by the new towns. The new port of Libourne on the Dordogne (1269) bears the name of his seneschal Roger Leyburn, the later bastide of Baa did honour to the great chancellor, Robert Burnel, bishop of Bath.[2] The bastides were usually market towns, but some of the new foundations were strongly combined with new castles, as they were also in Savoy; and, as we have already seen, Edward's castle- and town-building in Wales took the same course.[3] Then, in 1280, while his first Welsh foundations were proceeding at Rhuddlan and Flint, Edward turned his attention to Winchelsea, the busiest of the Cinque Ports, that turbulent federation which in war and peace had for many years been a special object of his care and in his reign reached the peak of its activity under the direction of his judges at the Shepway.[4] The situation at Winchelsea is tersely described in the terms of a commission given in 1284, four years after he had bought the site overlooking the estuary of the river Brede near the sea and had begun his operations: the warden of the Cinque Ports, Henry le Waleys, the great London merchant, and Gregory of Rokesley, then

ning', in his *Collected Papers*, iii. 80–81, with the notes correcting the text of the original article (1917–18).

[1] S. Seyer, *Memoirs of Bristol* (1821–3) for a full description. Cf. Carl Stephenson, *Borough and Town* (1933), pp. 203–4, and plan.

[2] See above, pp. 308–10, for the Gascon bastides.

[3] Above, pp. 430–3; and J. G. Edwards on the building of Flint in *Flintshire Hist. Soc. Publications*, xii (1951–2), 5–20.

[4] K. M. E. Murray, *The Constitutional History of the Cinque Ports* (1935), especially chaps. 3 and 5. Cf. J. A. Williamson, in *History*, July 1926 (xi. 97–115), on the changes in the coastline in the district of the Cinque Ports.

mayor of London, were appointed 'to plan and assess the new town of Iham, which the king is ordering to be built there for the barons of Winchelsea, as that town is already in great part submerged by the sea and is in danger of total submersion'. So New Winchelsea gradually came into being with its plots and streets, churches, walls and moats, and wharves. It was Edward's most ambitious and successful piece of town-planning, for it was completed in his lifetime, soon enough, indeed, for him to make it the port of departure on his expedition to Flanders in 1297.[1] Unhappily the treacherous sea turned back, and the town was left high and dry on its hill above its silted harbour. Winchelsea wasted while Hull grew and prospered.

Edward's last adventure in town-planning was at Berwick. Here he had less to do, for a busy port, with ancient practices of its own, was already in being when, on the eve of his first Scottish conquest in 1296, the king began its new fortifications.[2] Berwick was certainly less wasted and depopulated by the English troops than is usually supposed, though many burgesses were deprived of their holdings and new-comers were settled there to give the town a more English character. The interest of Edward's plans for Berwick lies not in what he did but in the elaborate measures which he took to gratify an ambitious but, so far as is known, an unformulated desire. At Winchelsea he had been compelled by local hesitations to use one set of experts after another, leaving the work at last to his practical treasurer, John Kirkby, and to the burgesses. He decided to seek the advice of the boroughs about his projects for Berwick. In the end of August 1296, before he left Berwick, he had summoned a full parliament to meet at Bury St. Edmunds in November.[3] A few days later, on his way south, he ordered experts in town-planning to be elected in London and twenty-four other specified boroughs, to appear at Bury. In the discussions at Bury he was apparently given the names of the most suitable experts, for he summoned Henry le Waleys of London, Thomas Alard of Winchelsea (the warden

[1] See the excellent story in Tout, op. cit. iii. 81–84. Henry le Waleys was, in his time, mayor both of London and Bordeaux; see his life in *D.N.B.*

[2] Above, p. 614. That there was little breach of continuity at Berwick is suggested by the list of local customs and practices drawn up by a Berwick jury in November 1303 (Gras, op. cit. pp. 164–7).

[3] *Parl. Writs*, pp. 47–49. The Scottish magnates had undertaken to appear in this parliament (above, p. 615). A financial subsidy was granted (Rishanger, p. 165).

and chief merchant of the port),[1] and twenty-seven others by name from various cities and boroughs. The conference seems to have taken place at Harwich in January, for there, once again, Edward sent mandates to a new set of men to appear at Berwick. This was the body by which anything that was done was done; but the sequence of summonses suggests that Edward found it impossible to get any satisfactory results by such means.[2] The story is significant as a witness to a growing concern for the co-operation of a community reluctant or unable to co-operate. The merchants of the Staple were yet to come upon the political stage.

Edward, in fact, found his most helpful servants among the Italian merchants, who dominated the scene and kept him in touch with the wider world of affairs.[3] Several of the large companies of Lombardy and Tuscany had their offices in London. As wool merchants they still shipped little direct to the Mediterranean; the Genoese galleys were only beginning to appear in the English Channel in the last decade of the thirteenth century.[4] The English wool which reached Florence and other Italian cities was, in the main, sent overland through France and Germany, and most of the wool handled by the Italians went to the weavers of France, Flanders, and Brabant. Italian merchants were, indeed, well acquainted with the English sources of supply. Francesco Pegolotti, who from 1318 to 1321 represented the Florentine firm of the Bardi in England, used earlier statistics to compile a list of wool-producing English religious houses; the value of their wool on the Flemish market, graded from 28 marks a sack of Tintern wool down to inferior wool at 7 marks, was

[1] The 'matchless series of Alard tombs' in the church of St. Thomas (Tout, p. 84) perpetuate the memory of the days when New Winchelsea flourished.

[2] *Parl. Writs*, pp. 49–51. Cf. Tout, pp. 84–86.

[3] W. E. Rhodes, 'The Italian Bankers in England and their Loans to Edward I and Edward II', in *Historical Essays*, by members of the Owens College (1902, reissued 1907), pp. 137–67; R. J. Whitwell, in *Trans. Royal Hist. Soc.*, N.S., xvii (1903), 175–233; Emilio Re, 'La Compagnia dei Riccardi in Inghilterra', from *Archivio della R. Società romana di storia patria*, xxxvi (1913), 87–138; A. Sapori, *Studi di storia economica medievale* (2nd ed., Florence, 1946), especially the long essay on the Frescobaldi in England, pp. 579–646. On Italian merchants and the wool trade see C. Bigwood, in *Annales de l'hist. écon. et sociale* for April 1930 (li. 193–209).

[4] R. Doehaerd in *Bulletin de l'Institut belge de Rome*, xix (1938), 1–76; A. A. Ruddock, *Italian Merchants and Shipping in Southampton, 1270–1600* (1951), chap. 1. Genoese fleets were organized for Flanders in 1277 and England in 1278, but progressive development began in 1298. The first recorded visit of the Venetian state fleet was in 1319.

about twice the prices paid to the wool growers.[1] Pegolotti inserted his list in a big book; the title and contents of his compilation remind us of some important truths. He was not only interested in wool, and he spent the greater part of his life as an agent of the Bardi in Cyprus. In fact, the multifarious activities of the Italian merchant bankers in England must be regarded in a setting of world trade and international, especially papal, finance, and as part of a commercial revolution which was as momentous in history as the industrial revolution in modern times.[2] They exemplify the beginnings of a system of exchange whereby purchasing power could be maintained without the transport of coin, and a regular balance of payments over long distances could be secured by the use of the pen, not by elaborate agreements to send particular sums of money over sea and land. This development led to, or was at least connected with, the use of gold as the most reliable and acceptable basis of international commerce and exchange. Pegolotti, for example, was surprised to find no gold coinage in England.[3] In short, the local industrial systems with their local currencies became distinct from the commercial and financial operations of a new society which tended to bring them together on the basis of money, and was

[1] See Allan Evans's edition of Pegolotti's *La Pratica della Mercatura* (Mediaeval Academy of America, 1936), p. 392. Pegolotti himself called it 'a book of descriptions of countries and of measures of merchandise'. He died in 1340. Cf. Eileen Power, op. cit., pp. 22–23. See also R. J. Whitwell on the English monasteries and the wool trade, in *Vierteljarhschrift für Sozial- und Wirtschaftsgeschichte*, ii (1904), 1–33.

[2] Sapori's paper on international commerce, op. cit., pp. 665–703; R. de Roover, *Money, Banking and Credit in Mediaeval Bruges* (Med. Acad. of America, 1948); cf. R. Mols in *Rev. d'hist. ecclés.*, xlvi (1951), 265–72.

[3] Henry III, like St. Louis and other western princes, had issued a gold coin in 1257 worth twenty silver pennies and with the weight of two pennies. The London merchants reported that it was useless as currency and that since its appearance the price of gold had fallen (*Liber de antiquis legibus*, pp. 29–30). Obviously they had not yet found gold to be specially convenient in large operations. What was required was a larger silver coin like Edward I's groat (above, p. 633), the French *gros tournois* or shilling (about 3d. sterling) issued in 1266, and similar coins equal to 12d. in Italian and other currencies. Edward III's florin (1344) was the first English gold coin to acquire currency, as the Florentine 'florin' (1252), the Venetian ducat (1284), and other gold coins had done before. Gold money was not yet a 'supraregional instrument' or guarantee of credit and the means of exchange by bills. On the history of gold in Europe since Merovingian days see Marc Bloch's classic paper, 'Le Problème de l'or au moyen âge', in *Annales de l'histoire économique et sociale*, v (1933), 1–34. Robert-Henri Bautier has analysed the movement of gold and silver in the light of world trade from the end of the thirteenth century to the Hundred Years War in a communication to the Académie des Inscriptions et Belles-lettres, *Comptes-rendus* (1951), pp. 169–74.

more aware of what it was doing than it has generally been supposed to have been.

The foundations of the modern commercial system had long been laid in Italy, where compact urban communities had developed methods of trade which involved less distinction between industry and commerce. The north can show no counterpart to the cash-books of a house in Siena (1277–82), a survival of numerous account books and ledgers, but sufficient to suggest the busy scene.[1] There was no commander in northern seas like the Genoese admiral and merchant Benedetto Zaccaria, who helped to conquer Gibraltar from the Moors, drew up for Philip the Fair a plan for the blockade of English trade, commanded the French fleet which sailed for Flanders in 1299, and ended his life as lord of Chios, with its profitable alum mines.[2] England became the hunting-ground of Italian merchant houses early, partly because of its monopoly in wool but also because of the royal need of ready money in England and Gascony after the baronial wars, and again during Edward's crusade and the Welsh, French, and Scottish wars, and, not least, as a result of the importance of the new-comers as papal bankers. They busied themselves upon the periphery of events mainly as papal and royal agents until other instruments were ready to do their work, but, all the same, they brought with them and applied the resources and technique of Italian experience. They were much more than alien money-lenders settled in England like the Jews, whose continental affiliations had been confined to cultural and learned relations with their co-religionists. They looked to their partners in Lucca or Florence or Piacenza or wherever their headquarters were, and many of them were in close and constant touch with the papal curia. King Edward found them indispensable. In the first decade of the fourteenth century the leading members of the Frescobaldi firm lived in England as privileged citizens, with a freedom greater than that granted by the *Carta mercatoria*. They were exempted from aids, tallages, and local services, and controlled most of the income of the realm. They lived as grand seignors. Amerigo dei Frescobaldi, their chief representative, described by Edward I as his 'yeoman', was by 1308 warden of the English exchanges, constable of Bordeaux

[1] Cf. Florence Edler on G. Astuti's edition of this text (Turin, 1934) in *Speculum*, xi (1936–7), 390–3.

[2] Roberto Lopez, *Benedetto Zaccaria, ammiraglio e mercante* (1933).

and receiver in Gascony, and a Lincolnshire landholder. His kinsmen were granted prebends and benefices.[1] But the lot of an Italian merchant in England was precarious. The fall of the Frescobaldi was coming near. A poetic member of the family wrote a sonnet of counsel for merchants going to England: 'Wear no bright colours, be humble; appear stupid but be subtle in act. Spend freely and do not show yourself mean. Pay as you go; collect your debts courteously, pleading your need; do not be too inquisitive; buy as good occasion offers, but have no dealings with men of the court. Be obedient to the powerful, keep on good terms with your fellow country men, and bolt your door early.'[2]

Details about the transactions of the Italian merchants in England could be collected *ad infinitum*, but no coherent history of them has been written. The account books and ledgers which would reveal their operations with Italian thoroughness do not seem to exist; and if they did exist they would have to be studied in the light of the records of the papacy, of the local and cameral merchants in Italy, and of the records, day by day, of administration in England, local and central, from port-books to the records of high affairs of state and of relations with the papal curia and foreign princes and communities. Some attention has been given to the two greatest societies, the Riccardi and the Frescobaldi, yet any exact picture of their personnel and activities eludes us; and they were only the most outstanding in a big group of firms and merchants whose presence in England is known from casual references to their dealings with the Crown. The Lombards or money-lenders, who were given a separate legal status in Flanders as licensed usurers, do not seem to have become a distinct class in England. Another class, of exchangers, who formed a distinct group in fourteenth-century Flanders, could not have existed in a land where the exchanges were kept under government control, or were only granted to Italian merchants as royal agents or when security was required for large loans to the king. It is, indeed, impossible at present either to distinguish clearly the personnel of the societies founded in England or to disentangle their activities as merchants, money-lenders, brokers, bankers on deposit, and papal or royal agents.

[1] Sapori, op. cit., pp. 601–8.
[2] Adapted from Rhodes, op. cit., pp. 151–2; the text of the sonnet is printed on p. 152, n.

Some dozen firms appear, mainly from Lucca and Florence, but, with a few exceptions, their *socii* or agents came and went—as one would expect in societies constituted as theirs were[1]—and it would be hard to say precisely how some of the Italians busy in England at any one time were related to particular societies. However, a few points may be made before we leave the subject.

In June 1277 seven societies were entrusted on deposit with some of the proceeds of the first year of the papal tenth imposed at the Council of Lyons in 1274. They were the Riccardi of Lucca, the Scoti of Piacenza, the Ammanati of Pistoia, the Pulci and Rembertini of Florence, the Mozzi of Florence, the Scala of Florence, and the Bonsignori of Siena. The total sum collected in the first year was 22,586 marks, of which about 9,200 marks were divided between the seven firms and handed over in the treasury of the New Temple at London in seventy-seven big sacks, one small sack, and a leathern purse. Some of the sacks contained £30 or 7,200 little silver pennies. This measure, which seems to have been suggested by Pope John XXI, was adopted after a discussion between the chief collectors, a number of bishops, deans, and other clergy, and the merchants themselves. The reasons given were that it would be safer than the usual practice of storing the money in cathedrals and abbeys or even the Temple, especially during the king's absence on the Welsh war, and that the cash would be more easily available when it was needed.[2] The practice became common. By 1280 the Riccardi had more than £13,000 on deposit, and the Frescobaldi, a new arrival, had received a modest deposit of 500 marks.[3] The receivers undertook all responsibility for repayment at any place or time required, provided that the requisition was made at their house or place of business in London.[4] To what extent they were free to use the money is not clear. Italian merchant firms

---

[1] See Sapori's paper on the Tuscan mercantile companies of the thirteenth and fourteenth centuries, op. cit., pp. 327–70; cf. 689–93. They were not corporations like modern joint-stock companies, though they gradually outgrew their patriarchal character; they made periodic general settlements of profits.

[2] See the documents in the appendix to Ré's monograph, pp. 125–32; also Lunt, *Financial Relations*, pp. 331–4; and 641–65 for a full statement of deposits as they stood in 1283. For examples of the wider activities of papal merchants on the business of the tenths, especially during the final render of their accounts by collectors, see Halton's Register (pp. 150–61 *passim*) and the documents printed by Lunt in *E.H.R.* xxxi (1916), 112, 113, 119.

[3] Cf. undertaking of the Riccardi on receiving £11,935 on deposit from numerous dioceses in March 1279 (Ré, pp. 132–5).   [4] Ré, op. cit., p. 96. n.

were not primarily bankers; they treated deposits as additions to capital and the depositors as creditors; but the crusading tenth was in another category. Though under papal control it was earmarked for Edward's expenses as a crusader. All the same the deposits steadied the business of the Riccardi. When, in accordance with Pope Nicholas IV's agreement of 1290–1 with Edward, they were required, as papal and royal merchants, to find 100,000 marks for Edward from the deposits in their and other merchants' chests, a member of the society of Cerchi observed that the result would be that money would be dearer.[1]

By this time the Riccardi had acquired a predominance among the merchants. They were, until 1290, the collectors of the custom and had made large advances or loans to the Crown, as Lucas of Lucca had done earlier.[2] They charged no interest on these loans, but, apart from such repayments as were made (either direct or on some source of royal revenue) and occasional gifts, they benefited by their prestige, enhanced by royal protection, and their freedom to pursue their normal business as merchants and financiers. They ran grave risks, and by the end of the century were so discredited that they did not long survive. They suffered from internal disputes within their house in Italy at a time when the papacy was particularly exacting and the war between the kings of France and England had cut them off from co-operation with their *socii* in the west of Europe. From about 1293 they had been gradually displaced by the Frescobaldi, who would seem to have been better able to cope with the dangers of this difficult time, and to cover their enormous loans to the Crown more thoroughly. They controlled more sources of revenue—customs, exchanges, mines, proceeds of Ponthieu and Gascony, were granted more assignments on revenue and more gifts—e.g. £13,000 in the years 1300–2—in return for their services and in recognition of delays in repayment. But the less discriminating favours of Edward II hastened their downfall and left the field open to the Bardi and Peruzzi.[3]

---

[1] Ré, p. 101; cf. above, p. 266; Lunt, *Financial Relations*, pp. 340, 346.

[2] Above, p. 632.

[3] According to Sapori their advances to the Crown had reached the total of £122,373 by 1310 (op. cit., p. 591), but one cannot but feel doubtful about this unless it is accompanied by a clear balance-sheet. What exactly did the Crown mean when it said that the Riccardi or the Frescobaldi were in its debt? To what extent was their gamble worth while? For the latter part of the story in Edward II's

In his years of difficulty and frustration Edward I was strangely entangled with the Florentines, whose 'sudden riches' their fellow citizen Dante so bitterly deplored.[1]

reign see Charles Johnson, 'An Italian Financial House', in the *Transactions* of the St. Albans and Hertfordshire Architectural and Archaeological Society, N.S. i (1903), 320–4.

[1] 'La gente nuova e i subiti guadagni' (*Inferno*, xvi. 73).

Additional Note. Reference should be made to J. de Sturler's papers on the payment of allies in the Low Countries (1294–7). In addition to the entries on pp. 622 n., 661 n., 662 n., 663 n., see his paper on payments in May 1297, printed in *Cahiers Bruxellois*, v (1960), 18–37, and cf. p. 679 n. below. Since this book was published, a good deal of work on Edward's debts to merchants and others has been done in England, and this work throws light on the king's sense of frustration during his later years; but it does not change the impression of him which I have tried to give. Contemporary accounts of Edward, shortly after his death, tend to picture him as a great warrior, in France, Wales, and Scotland, rather than as the saddened crusader, but I should combine both elements in my own view of his character between 1290 and 1307.

The short account, on pp. 626–8 above, of Edward's action in London should now be revised in the light of G. A. Williams' essay, 'London and Edward I', printed in *Trans. of the Royal Hist. Society*, 5th ser. xi (1961), 81–99.

XIV

THE YEARS OF EMERGENCY

Eᴅᴡᴀʀᴅ's last years, passed under the heavy cloud of
'necessity', are the most familiar period of his reign. A
great book has yet to be written about them, both as a
complicated series of dramatic events and as part of the history
of the west of Europe. They may be regarded as the opening
phase of a new era. In this book they may with equal justice be
treated as an epilogue to all that precedes them.

When King Edward left Berwick for the south in 1296 he was
at war with King Philip in Gascony. The trouble which had led
to this breach of friendly relations had come to a head on 15 May
1293 when the fleet of the Cinque Ports defeated a Norman fleet
off Cap Saint-Mathieu in Brittany and afterwards sacked La
Rochelle in Poitou.[1] The Portsmen declared during later inquiry
that they had been assailed by the Normans, whose ships flew
bausons or streamers of red sendal 'which everywhere amongst
mariners mean death without quarter and war to the knife'.
Whenever the *bauson* was flown, neither side, according to the
custom and law of the sea, was required to make restitution for
losses of any kind.[2] This naval battle was by no means a solitary
incident. The English fleet had almost certainly been collected
to make reprisals on the Normans in a bitter warfare between
the subjects of the king of France and of the king of England, the
outcome, with or without official cognizance, of frequent acts of
lawless passion and piracy from the North Sea to the coasts of
Spain and Portugal.[3] The development has never been explained.

---

[1] According to Cotton, p. 227, the fight was between a superior Norman fleet
and a mixed fleet of ships from England and Bayonne.

[2] K. M. E. Murray, *Constitutional History of the Cinque Ports* (Manchester, 1935),
p. 32. Mr. Charles Johnson, in a letter of 5 Sept. 1954, suggests that, philologically,
bauson implies 'black and white', like the 'Jolly Roger'.

[3] Ramsay, *Dawn of the Constitution*, pp. 401–3, for various incidents. Add the
disputes between Breton and Gascon fishermen and the resort to reprisals against
Castilian and Portuguese merchants by the men of Bayonne; see the case presented
to a court of auditors in parliament at Canterbury (Easter, 1293) in *Select Cases on
the Law Merchant*, vol. ii, pp. xciii–civ. King Sancho of Castile is said here to have
ordered the decapitation of Bayonne merchants who landed in Spain. In June a
truce was made. The Portuguese quarrel was settled in the spring of 1294.

The mariners of the Cinque Ports had shown no national prefer-
ences: they were a terror to the English ports in the Channel
and to the Irish ports; they had a perennial quarrel with the
men of Yarmouth; their feuds with the sailors of Bayonne had,
in this very year, led to royal intervention.[1] It is probable that
the effects of the Flemish embargo twenty years before had never
died away, and that King Philip's determination to protect his
coasts and to organize a fleet had already begun to affect the
Norman sailors.[2] Whatever the reason for the concentrated
passions of 1293 may have been, the French king decided to
take action, and to take action in Gascony.

King Philip and his legists had shown their minds before the
battle at sea in May. Each king had issued orders that no subject of the other should be molested, but the French king had
also proclaimed in Bordeaux that he would not tolerate attacks
on his subjects. After the Norman defeat and the sack of Rochelle
he required the delivery to him of Gascon offenders and restitution for damages, and sent troops to the frontiers. He extended
his right to hear appeals from the subjects of the duke to a right
to direct interference; whereas Edward, who had the Gascons
behind him, regarded the complaints and offences of mariners
on each side as matters for adjudication under the law of Oléron
(the custom of the sea) and by joint commissions of inquiry.
Hence Edward in July 1293 made three alternative proposals to
the French king—adjudication on the grievances of the French
sailors in the English court, or by four commissioners, two English and two French, or by reference to papal arbitration. His
envoys were told that the French king could not accept any of
the suggestions; the matter was too serious; as sovereign lord
of Gascony he would exercise his ordinary authority (*cognicio
ordinaria*). Philip ordered the mayor, jurats, and a hundred leading citizens of Bayonne to be delivered to him for imprisonment
at Perigueux 'on account of the damage done to Normans on
the coast of Brittany'. The Gascons appealed to the customs
which had prevailed in Gascony and elsewhere in disputes between states: to the settlement by arbitrators on the marches of
complaints between them and inhabitants of France not subject

---

[1] Murray, op. cit., pp. 32–33; and, for the incessant trouble with Yarmouth
about the herring fair there, the important study of the origin of the Ports' court of
Brodhull, pp. 146–53. Such disputes were never localized; they led to fights on the
high seas and in distant places. [2] Below, p. 646.

to the king of England, and to the law of Oléron on disputes arising at sea.[1] Philip ordered the surrender of Bordeaux and the Agenais; his commands were resisted. On 27 October he formally summoned Edward to appear in person at Paris in January 1294 to answer the charges against him.[2] French feeling, especially in the followers of Charles of Valois, the king's brother, had been deeply stirred by the events at sea. The legists welcomed the opportunity to follow up the legal penetration of the duchy of Aquitaine in the *parlement* of Paris by its annexation to the French Crown. In the exercise of sovereign authority it is hard not to see a malicious parody of Edward's conduct of Scottish affairs. King Philip was for the time being carried along the stream of angry resolution. He had already made his plan for the building of a great fleet of galleys in the Mediterranean and the blockade of English ports.[3]

Edward did not want war. As is generally agreed, he was eager to come to an arrangement which would both be consistent with his point of view and show his respect for his duty as Philip's vassal. He was gradually forced into a position from which war was the only escape.[4] His brother Edmund had charge of the negotiations in Paris. He was provided with Edward's letters patent, dated 1 January 1294, ordering obedience in Gascony to such mandates as were necessary, but, as his own account of events shows,[5] he was to issue no orders until he was

---

[1] The course of negotiations from 1292 to 1307 is conveniently summarized by Mary Salt, 'Embassies to France, 1272–1307', in *E.H.R.* xliv (1929), 270–8. As early as August 1292 Stephen de Pencestre, constable of Dover and warden of the Cinque Ports, was ordered to inquire into the grievances of the men of Bayonne and of English and French sailors. In May 1293 (before the fight at sea) Edmund of Lancaster was in Paris to arrange a truce with a view to a settlement on maritime disputes. It is significant that in January Stephen had made his well-known report to the exchequer on the Ports and their services, 'the Domesday of the Ports' (Murray, pp. 43, 241). The Gascons' view survives in documents copied in Edward III's time: these are printed by P. Chaplais, in his paper in *Le moyen âge* (1951), 273, n., 295–6.   [2] *Foedera*, I. ii. 793.

[3] For an account of French naval activity, in co-operation with the Genoese and the royal house of Anjou in Provence and Naples, see the important essay of Ch. de la Roncière, 'Le Blocus continental de l'Angleterre sous Philippe le Bel', in *Rev. des questions historiques*, ix (1896), 402–41.

[4] On Anglo-French relations (1293–1303) see a masterly summary in R. Fawtier, in *Hist. du moyen âge*, edit. G. Glotz, VI. i. 314–25. On the war in Gascony see Bémont's introduction to his edition of the Gascon Rolls, iii (1906), pp. cxxiv–clxxxii, with full bibliography and references.

[5] *Foedera*, I. ii. 794. This remarkable document, which rings true, is the chief authority on the negotiations. See the story in W. E. Rhodes's paper on Edmund (*E.H.R.* x (1895), 227–31).

satisfied that a surrender to Philip as sovereign lord would be followed by a speedy reconciliation. Indeed, as his wife, who was with him in Paris, was the mother of Queen Jeanne of France, and as King Edward was seeking Philip's sister Margaret in marriage, Edmund, and perhaps the great ladies themselves, were easily deluded to regard the negotiations as a pleasant domestic discussion. Even the queen dowager, that gay in-triguer Mary of Brabant, who took a leading part, may have been deceived.[1] However this may be, Edmund and his wife were duped. A stately marriage treaty was drafted with careful clauses about the succession to the duchy of Aquitaine and a revised statement about the process and penalties in cases of appeal.[2] Secret agreements, to which King Philip in person solemnly gave his approval, were made, defining exactly how the citation of Edward to appear in Paris should be withdrawn, and a settlement be reached in joint conference between the kings at Amiens, and how the surrender of Bordeaux, ten border towns in the Agenais and Saintonge, and Gascon hostages, re-quired to satisfy Philip's outraged dignity, should be revoked after a decent interval (apparently forty days). The private talks between the queens and the English ambassadors were easy, friendly, and confidential, the king intervening now and then with solemn assurances that all was well. On 3 February Edmund of Lancaster, thoroughly satisfied, ordered John St. John, Edward's lieutenant in Gascony, to transfer the seisin of the duchy as King Philip's letters patent would prescribe. The news spread through the south that peace had been made. Gentlemen of Aragon who had offered their services against the king of France stayed at home. In March the constable of France took control. John St. John broke off his preparations for de-fence and returned to England through Paris. Yet nothing happened in Paris. At last, in April, Edmund begged the queens to seek the withdrawal of the citation, the relief which King Edward had most at heart. Philip again appeared to explain

---

[1] At this time the friendship between the house of Brabant and Edward I was close.

[2] *Foedera*, I. ii. 795. Though the draft treaty is dated February, it must have been the result of long and careful work by the lawyers on each side and deserves more attention as an indication of feudal principles than it has received. In some quarters in England Edward was criticized for his desire for this marriage; it shows at any rate his eagerness to strengthen the domestic ties with the French court which had persisted for thirty-five years.

that there was some opposition and a hard answer would be made, but he need not be alarmed. The royal counsellors made it clear that there was to be no withdrawal from the duchy; and on 21 April, in the king's presence in the *parlement* chamber, Edward was again cited to appear in Paris. No safe-conduct was granted, no delay allowed. On 19 May Edward was condemned as a defaulter and his duchy was declared to be confiscated.[1]

The effect in England was immediate. Edward's feverish activity is still reflected in the entries on the Gascon rolls compiled day by day in his chancery. The first letter recorded was a regretful communication to the count of Flanders that, as his negotiations with the king of France had not gone as the king expected, Flemish merchants could no longer be received. All passages of ships to the continent from the British isles were stopped. Proclamations in the shires invited persons charged with felony, whether detained in prisons or at large, to volunteer for paid service in Gascony.[2] The prelates and barons of Gascony were besought individually to rally to the defence of their country in answer to the 'malicious deception' of the French. A great council of prelates, magnates, and barons, hurriedly gathered early in June—there was no time for formal summons to a parliament—gave the king authority to seize all the wool, fells, and hides in England, and eagerly agreed to military action in Gascony. Collectors of the wool were appointed all over the land. Letters of 18 June addressed to every bishop, the provincials of the Dominicans and Franciscans, and the chancellor of the university of Oxford, explained how the king had been forced into war, and begged that the people be urged to pray in every church in the land for the help so much needed from the King of Kings. Six days later Edward sent an embassy to France with the king's formal renunciation of homage. He had already

[1] Edmund closes his narrative with the failure of the royal proctors (*les sages*), who acted for King Edward in the *parlement*, to obtain the slightest adjournment, 'denied to no man, rich or poor, however small his cause'. The refusal was certainly at variance with the practice of courts in England, e.g. the adjournments allowed to John Baliol.

[2] *Rôles gascons*, nos. 3032, 3033, and *passim* (12 June). It is wrong to say that the prisons were searched for scoundrels. Many of the three hundred and more persons who appeared before the royal commissioners and, if fit for service, got letters to the chancery, and were given the king's peace, had evaded justice or been outlawed. They were required to find pledges and, after return, to present themselves to answer to any charge which might be brought against them. Cf. Bémont, pp. cxxxvi–cxxxix. Later, similar action was taken in the north of England before Edward's first Scottish campaign in 1296 (Stevenson, *Hist. Documents*, ii. 38–39).

begun to issue the writs of summons demanding the presence of the feudal host at Portsmouth by 1 September for service with him in Gascony. He organized his fleet and sought foreign alliances. The tiresome dispute about petitions from Scotland became of secondary importance. King John Baliol had himself attended the great council in June.

As we know, Edward's fierce concentration was distracted into another quarter by the Welsh rebellion. The king had planned to send troops and supplies to Gascony in three stages. The first force was to sail in July under his new lieutenant or *capitaneus*, his nephew John of Brittany, son of the count of Brittany, with whom John St. John was associated as seneschal of Gascony, and Robert Tybetot, justice of south Wales, as director of finance. John of Brittany was empowered to make alliances in Spain and in southern France, from which many lords and knights were in any case hastening to fight for Edward. A second force was to be led by Edmund of Lancaster and Henry de Lacy, earl of Lincoln. Finally, so Edward had announced to the Gascons, he hoped to follow himself.[1] John of Brittany had sailed but, for some reason, had been compelled to return to port. The first expeditionary force in fact did not get away until 9 October, some time after the Welsh rising had begun. Reinforcements on foot were sent in the summer of 1295; but Edmund of Lancaster and the earl of Lincoln did not sail from Plymouth with the second main expedition until January 1296. Edmund, a sick man, died in June, and the earl of Lincoln was left in command to co-operate with John of Brittany and the seneschal. He held on, almost deserted, while Edward was dealing with the Scots and preparing his allies for a major attack on King Philip in Flanders, until the truce of 9 October 1297. The truce, made in Flanders, included operations in Aquitaine until Epiphany (6 January 1298), but it was renewed from time to time until the definitive treaty of Paris on 20 May 1303, by which Gascony was restored to Edward.

The French armies under Charles of Valois in 1295 and Robert of Artois in 1296 had more than held their ground in Gascony. During the years of truce Bordeaux and the greater part of the

---

[1] See especially the *littera excusatoria* to the Gascons (Portsmouth, 1 July) in *Rôles gascons*, no. 2934. The various commissions are nos. 2932-3, 2934-8. Tybetot returned to Wales in 1298; his military were probably more important than his financial duties.

duchy proper, as well as the Agenais and the outlying provinces of Aquitaine, remained subject to Philip the Fair. Edward's authority was confined to Blaye and Bourg on the eastern shore of the Gironde in the north of the duchy, and to Bayonne and the lower valley of the Adour in the south. The French occupation inevitably threw the cost of the defence of the duchy, so far as it was retained by Edward and his allies, upon the English. The citizens of Bayonne, indeed, were able to lend large sums, amounting to nearly £45,800 sterling, but this money was repaid between 1299 and 1304 from the proceeds of the English custom on wool, wool-fells, and leather,[1] and to it must be added the vast total of £359,288 for which the two king's clerks responsible for the finances of the war made their final account in 1314–15. The account reveals the payment of £137,595 to Gascon, and £37,000 to English knights and men-at-arms, £17,928 to foot-soldiers, £16,869 to mariners. Expenses on services, including the cost of transport from England, doctors, surgeons, engines of war, stores, &c., amounted to £13,778. No less than £30,690 had been paid to Gascons during the period of truce (*vadia de tempore sufferencie*), and, it is interesting to note, nearly as much—£25,816—in compensation for war-horses lost during the war.[2] The cost of saving and keeping Gascony was about half the estimated total of receipts from all the lay subsidies of Edward I's reign.

The struggle for Gascony naturally brought under review the status of the duchy. This problem was raised when, during the truce in 1298, the two kings submitted their causes to Pope Boniface, who agreed to arbitrate between them in his private capacity as Benedetto Gaetani.[3] Before the formal act of *com-*

[1] Bémont, *Rôles gascons*, iii, pp. clxx–ii, based on the *computus* in the Pipe Roll, 35 Edward I (1306). The citizens of Bayonne appointed delegates to reside in England and receive the proceeds of the custom in London and the chief ports of England and in Dublin.

[2] Op. cit., pp. clxvii–clxix, from the Pipe Roll, 8 Edward II. The period covered was Michaelmas 1293 to 24 June 1314, but the payment of wages to troops in war-time was reckoned from 11 November 1294 to 24 March 1298, and in the time of truce from the latter date to 14 August 1303. [Bémont's reading of the year, xxvii, should probably be corrected to xxxi (1302–3) or xxxii.] The wages included payments to disinherited persons. Of the total sum, about £300,000 had been received from the exchequer or wardrobe.

[3] Both kings wrote to Boniface, expressing their wish to submit the matter to him as pope, Edward in February, Philip in March 1298 (*Foedera*, i. ii. 887, 888–9, where the dating is in the French style). The reference to him as a private person appears in the papal award on 30 June and the official record of proceedings

promissum, accepting Boniface as arbitrator, Edward's representatives, William of Hotham, now archbishop of Dublin, the bishop of Winchester, and others, put forward suggestions which apparently were intended to clear the air. They proposed that some of the lands of the duchy should go to France in recognition of the status of the duchy, either as an independent lordship, free from French sovereignty, or as a fief free from any exercise of French jurisdiction, or as a fief subject to mitigated and clearly defined French right to receive appeals; or finally as a fief held of the Roman Church.[1] These suggestions came to nothing, and, after the act of compromission, the envoys presented terms of a more realistic kind. They demanded full restitution, compensation for damages inflicted by the French, the release of hostages as the truce required, rejection of the French demand that the Scots should be included in any treaty, and the annulment of all gifts, privileges, and liberties granted by the king of France during the period of war, in lands held by the king of England.[2] In support of this demand a more detailed statement of legal rights and grievances had been prepared. The legal argument was to the effect that Gascony had always been and, in spite of the treaty of 1259, still was an allod, free of all external obligation; or, alternatively, if it were now a fief held of the French Crown, that the failure of the French king to fulfil the conditions of the treaty and his infringement of the feudal contract had deprived him of any rights or claims to sovereignty. A long list of grievances followed, from the seizure of Limoges more than twenty years before to the trick which King Philip had played on Edward in 1293–4. The main object of the English case was to controvert the French claim that Aquitaine had been forfeited.[3]

The significance of these arguments lies in their later develop-

(pp. 894–5, 896). The king of France certainly recognized no superior *in temporalibus*; and probably was responsible for the change, but the pope, who had been trying to make peace, with Edward's concurrence, since 1295, seems to have raised no objection. Mary Salt gives an impressive summary of the peace movement from 1295 in *E.H.R.* xliv (1929), 271–4.

[1] Pierre Chaplais on English arguments concerning the feudal status of Aquitaine in the fourteenth century, in *Bulletin of the Institute of Hist. Research* (1948), pp. 203–13, at p. 211. The interpretation of the documents suggested above depends upon a distinction between the *intencio* submitted *ante compromissum* (p. 211) and that presented later (pp. 210–11). [2] Ibid., pp. 210–11.

[3] For this document see H. Rothwell, 'Edward I's Case against Philip the Fair over Gascony in 1298', in *E.H.R.* xlii (1927), 572–82. The formal proceedings at Rome seem to have lasted only a fortnight (14–30 June): cf. *Foedera,* i. ii. 896.

ments,[1] not in any immediate effect. Pope Boniface was not prepared to define the feudal status of the duchy nor to stress the
high church doctrine—dogmatically expressed four years later
in the famous bull *Unam Sanctam*—of papal supremacy over
temporal as well as spiritual affairs. To do either would have
involved him in endless controversy.[2] His sympathies seem to
have lain with Edward, of whose aid when he was in the suite of
Cardinal Ottobuono in England in 1267 he had appreciative
memories; but, at the same time, he deplored the fact that
Edward had not confined his opposition to King Philip to the
defence of Gascony, but had entangled himself in Scotland and
Flanders. He thought that Edward should have put his duchy
under papal protection and appealed to Rome on moral grounds
against the king of France.[3] Now it was too late to do anything
except to strengthen the truce by arranging marriages between
Edward and Philip's sister and between the boy Edward of
Caernarvon and Philip's daughter Isabella; also to suggest that
both kings should submit lands in dispute to him until outstanding questions about the duchy and the claims of each party to
reparations had been settled, preferably by the parties themselves, but if not in this way, by the pope in his personal capacity,
as arbitrator. An award to this effect was proclaimed by the
pope in public consistory, and sealed on 30 June 1298.[4] A dispensation for the marriage between Edward and Margaret was
issued on the next day.[5] After much coming and going by English
and French envoys, an understanding was reached at Montreuil-

[1] The arguments and 'exceptions' of the case—perhaps compiled by Philip
Martel (on whom see above, p. 278) and drawn in part from the *Libri feudorum*, a
collection of Lombard feudal law made in the twelfth century and studied with the
Corpus juris civilis—were known to Edward III's advisers. The claim that Gascony
was alodial reappears during the negotiations at Avignon in 1344. See E. Déprez on
the conference of Avignon in *Essays in Medieval History presented to T. F. Tout* (1925),
pp. 301–20.

[2] For example, with King Philip in his relations with Edward's recent ally, the
count of Flanders, who appealed to Boniface as lord *in temporalibus*, when it seemed
that Edward would leave Flanders to Philip's mercy. Count Guy's sons in Rome
wrote pathetic reports of their discussions with the archbishop of Dublin and their
interviews with the pope. See their letters in Migne, *Patrologia Latina*, clxxxv, cols.
1867–74, where Kervyn de Lettenhove's study and texts are reprinted (cols.
1834–1920) from the *Mémoires* of the Royal Academy of Brussels, xxvii (1853).

[3] These points are brought out in the report of discussions near Anagni in August
1300 between Pope Boniface and Edward's envoys appointed for the completion of
peace. The report, discovered by C. Johnson, was printed by J. G. Black in his note
on 'Edward I and Gascony in 1300', in *E.H.R.* xvii (1902), 518–27.

[4] *Foedera*, I. ii. 894–5.   [5] Ibid., p. 897.

sur-mer in June 1299, and was confirmed by King Philip in August at the abbey of l'Aumône in the diocese of Chartres. The pope, in the meanwhile, had agreed to the retention for the time being by each king of the lands held by him in Aquitaine. On 4 September Margaret of France was married to Edward by Archbishop Winchelsey at Canterbury. John Baliol had been released to the papal envoy in July on the condition that no papal pronouncement affecting the status of Scotland should be made on the late king's behalf.[1]

Pope Boniface had achieved his main purpose. He had helped to bring about an Anglo-French alliance, and to make provision for a peaceful settlement of the disputes about Gascony and the losses incurred at sea; but whether the alliance would stand the strain of unresolved difficulties was still in doubt. Edward had deserted the count of Flanders and acquiesced in the dissolution of his fragile system of alliances with Rhenish princes. He had kept the Scots outside the terms of settlement, but he had not regained anything in Gascony. Disorder was still rife at sea, adding claim to claim. King Philip had refused to submit the lands which he held in Aquitaine in bail to the pope, and Edward, though he had been prepared to bail his holdings, had naturally not gone farther in view of Philip's refusal.[2] The Scots, with such aid as John Baliol was able to give them in France, kept in touch with the papal and French courts and did their best to prevent a settlement in which they were not included. Uncertainty prevailed for four more weary years of fitful negotiation. Edward's cousin, Amadeus of Savoy, John de Pontissara, bishop of Winchester, Otto of Granson, Geoffrey de Joinville, Henry Lacy, earl of Lincoln, and other trusted diplomats of Edward were sent to and fro to the papal court and to meetings with French commissioners, in the effort 'to settle all disputes'. The truce was renewed again and again.

Philip's defeat at the hands of the Flemings at Courtrai in 1302, and the danger of a new alliance between the pope and the emperor-elect, Albert of Austria, ended the stalemate. At last peace was made at Paris on 20 May 1303,[3] when Henry Lacy in

---

[1] The texts supporting this narrative are noted by M. Salt, *E.H.R.* xliv. 272–3.

[2] *Foedera*, I. ii. 905: Edward's arrangement in June 1299 for delivery of Gascony into the hands of the bishop of Vicenza in accordance with papal instructions (p. 904). For the non-fulfilment of this clause of the award cf. the discussions with the pope in 1300 (*E.H.R.* xvii. 524).

[3] An interesting discussion at Edward's court turned on the position of the

the king's name made the oath of fealty to King Philip for Gascony; and, through his proctors, the count of Savoy and the earl of Lincoln, the young Edward was affianced to Isabella, King Philip's daughter. On 10 June King Edward ratified the treaty at Perth, and a month later ordered its proclamation throughout England, Wales, and Ireland. King Philip made his ratification in August. Commissioners set to work on the restoration of Edward's authority in Aquitaine. King Edward was free to deal with the Scots; but it was impossible to break with the past. The status of Gascony had become involved in a network of juristic learning; the boundaries were not clearly fixed; old disputes had not been settled. In Edward II's reign all sorts of thorny difficulties survived to become still more complicated in the processes of Périgueux and the Agenais. The duty of the duke to take the oath of fealty as well as to do homage in person was disputed. The marriage between Edward II and Isabella of France raised the great problem of the French succession. The treaty of 1303 was but an incident, a breathing-space in the interminable wrangle which the treaty of 1259 had produced.[1]

The complexity of the issues raised by King Philip, the wide range of Edward's activity, and the concentration upon the problem of Aquitaine, not only in the duchy but at the papal court and indirectly in negotiations with German and Rhenish princes, give this period (1293-1346) much importance in the history of diplomatic practice. The long and tenacious efforts to reach a settlement on claims for reparation for losses at sea before the naval war, and then as a result of infractions of the

emperor-elect, Albert of Austria. Supplementary conditions of the treaty required Edward and Philip to assist each other as allies (Edward later sent troops to join the French in Flanders), but while Philip excepted Albert and the count of Hainault from his obligation, Edward excepted the duke of Brabant, and (in July) had wished to except Albert also. By the end of July he had been persuaded to change his mind (*Cal. Chancery Warrants*, i. 185); and in August Philip undertook, in spite of his exception, to give aid to Edward, if required, against Albert (*Foedera*, i. ii. 958). In 1303 neither king, after Albert's agreement with Pope Boniface, could feel sure about the position of the emperor-elect; cf. Alfred Hessel, *Jahrbücher des deutschen Reichs unter König Albrecht I. von Habsburg* (1931), pp. 128-33. In fact there was no need for alarm.

[1] Salt, op. cit., pp. 274-8; Rothwell in *E.H.R.* xlii. 374-6; P. Chaplais in *Le Moyen Âge* (1951), pp. 279-91; G. Cuttino, *English Diplomatic Administration, 1259-1339* (1940), pp. 12-18, and passim. The alleged act of homage by the young Edward, acting for his father, to Philip at Amiens is inconsistent with the document of 1304 edited by C. Johnson in *E.H.R.* xxiii (1908), 728-9.

terms of truce (1297–1303), put the seafaring and mercantile
population from the Bay of Biscay to the North Sea in the forefront of the political scene. Although no serious raids were made
upon English or French soil,[1] the operations both of Philip's
fleet under a Genoese admiral, Reyner Grimaud or Grimaldi,
and of the English ships raised thorny problems about damages
incurred in time of war.

King Edward had realized from the first that the equipment
of large fleets for Gascony, as later for Flanders, and the protection of the coasts from Cornwall to Berwick, called for more substantial and extended measures of control than those of his
father and grandfather and Simon de Montfort. He tightened
the loose organization of the Cinque Ports, with their traditional
obligation to provide for a short period each year fifty-seven
ships manned by 1,254 men, and made them the core of a naval
command under a single captain or admiral, a title first officially
used in England about 1295. The first captain, William Leyburn, had command of the seamen, not only of the English
ports but of all places 'where ships ply within the kingdom and
our authority (*potestas*), including Bayonne, Ireland and Wales'.[2]
Three years later (8 March 1297) he could be described as
'admiral of the sea of the king of England', in command of a
disciplined fleet, every ship of which was to carry the 'signal of
the arms of the king'.[3] In the equivocal phrase *amiral de la mer* we
can trace the origin of an assertion later made in a general petition of the various 'commonalties of subjects' against Grimaldi's
claim to exercise, in the king of France's name, the sovereignty
of the English sea: from time out of mind, the petition protested,
the king of England had possessed this sovereignty of the sea of
England, and its exercise was delegated to the admiral of the
fleet, with full powers of jurisdiction. In this last statement the
petition reflected the wide range of the admiral's authority,
from which in the middle of the fourteenth century the hearing
of cases before the admiral and the establishment of the court of
admiralty were derived.[4]

[1] Cf. the attack upon Dover, by a great galley in 1294 (*Flores Historiarum*, iii. 94,
280), and the grant of four French ships to their captors, the bailiffs of Yarmouth
(*Rôles gascons*, iii, no. 3047).

[2] Commission of 7 June 1294 in *Rôles gascons*, iii, no. 3006.

[3] *Foedera*, i. ii. 861, in the indenture between the count of Flanders and Edward's
agents about the maintenance of peace and justice between the English and
Flemish fleets.

[4] The petition is 'part of the memorable *Fasciculus de superioritate maris* [P.R.O.,

The first admiral, a member of the well-known Kentish family of Leyburn, was primarily an administrator with no defined jurisdiction, but with wide powers to supervise the knights and soldiers levied to sail on the ships, the collection and building of ships, and the purchase of stores. Local officials, notably the foresters who provided the timber for the two hundred new ships ordered by the king, were required to satisfy his demands.[1] He had lieutenants, whom he was empowered to appoint to keep the eastern and south-western coasts of England. The next admiral, Gervase Alard of Winchelsea, who appears in 1300, was an important baron of the Cinque Ports, sailor, merchant, and pirate in one. By this time the need for a united command from Berwick to Bayonne had disappeared. The control of ships and the custody of the coasts was regarded as an extension of the duty of the Cinque Ports. Alard was admiral of the fleet of the Cinque Ports from Dover to Cornwall. In 1306 he had a colleague, Edward Charles, 'captain and admiral of the fleet of the Cinque Ports from the Thames to Berwick-on-Tweed'. The attempt of 1294 to build a big royal fleet was not maintained, though the building of large galleys was continued. A galley cost from £200 to £500, and might take from 44 to 18 weeks to build, according to the capacity of the shipbuilding yard.[2] When the king arranged his return from Flanders in 1298 his son, in his father's name, sent letters to the keeper of the wardrobe and to each Cinque Port, Yarmouth, and Portsmouth for the provision of the hundred and more ships required. When in 1301 he wished to collect a fleet at Berwick, instructions were sent direct to the ports of England and Ireland. The development of an

D.D.C. 32/19/1] which fired the minds of Selden, Coke and Prynne' in the seventeenth century (Cuttino, p. 54). See also R. G. Marsden's introduction to *Select Pleas in the Court of Admiralty*, i (1894), and T. W. Fulton, *The Sovereignty of the Sea* (1911), pp. 25–56.

[1] *Rôles gascons*, nos. 3281–5, and Bémont's introduction, pp. cxlv–cxlvi. Care was taken to provide means for the safe passage of horses, including wooden bridges for their embarkment and landing.

[2] N. Harris Nicolas, *A History of the Royal Navy*, i (1847), 264 ff., 436–7; and, for the ships, the still valuable chapter, pp. 284–315, notably the story of Edward's attempt to get the men of Bayonne to provide ships to aid Alfonso of Castile against the Moors (1276–80; cf. *Foedera*, I. ii. 531, 552, 580). On ships generally, in peace and war, see F. W. Brookes, *The English Naval Forces, 1199–1272* (n.d.), pp. 1–78; for the galleys cf. Nicolas, p. 304 (galley of 120 oars ordered at York in 1295); for details of construction Whitwell and Johnson in *Archaeologia Aeliana*, 4th series, ii (1926), 142–93; C. Johnson in *Antiquaries Journal*, vii (1927), 424–37, and articles by Brookes and R. C. Anderson in *The Mariner's Mirror*, xiv, xv, xix.

admiralty was to be a slow and tentative process, a child of circumstance.[1]

The strange contrasts of traditions, customs, and jurisdictions which frustrated for centuries the attempts to comprehend within the political framework the men who go down to the sea in ships are vividly revealed in the story of the arbitrations about damages required under the treaty of 1303. The customs of the sea combined an ordered savagery, rules of reprisal, the quick decisions needed in a turbulent element where surprises must be met by instant responsibilities, and the more sedate practices which gave to age-long experience the first effective system of international law. The piratical habits of wreckers and fisher-men were entangled with the careful code of merchants who entrusted their precious wares to the captains and crews of cargo boats. And now, since there were no maritime courts in each country, exercising a jurisdiction under definite rules and principles of law, the damages and losses incurred before the outbreak of war and during the periods of truce had to be re-ferred to a special joint tribunal. King Edward was dead before the desultory 'process of Montreuil-sur-mer' had effectively established itself, so far as it was ever effective, but before he died the difficulties and cross-purposes which revealed its futility had become clear.

The negotiations begun on King Philip's complaints in 1293 —when Edward had proposed alternative ways of settlement[2]— had been resumed in 1297 and 1298 and led to the clauses com-prised in the treaty of Paris in 1303; but the court of claims— claims now indefinitely widened—was not set up until 1305–6 under an ordinance of the Gascon pope Clement V.[3] Four auditors, two from each side, were appointed to hear the cases submitted by each side at Montreuil. The chief English auditor was Philip Martel, the keeper of Gascon processes, who was familiar with civil and canon law. The reports of this experienced agent give the best account of the difficulties which beset the

[1] *Foedera*, I. ii. 886–7, 928; cf. the list of thirty ships of the Cinque Ports, with their names and the numbers of their crews for service in the Scottish war, 1299–1300, in Nicolas, pp. 293–8; contrast the order to the admiral of the fleet of the Cinque Ports to receive into the king's peace Alexander of Argyll and the lesser folk of the Scottish Isles (Bain, *Calendar*, ii, no. 307, June 1301).

[2] Above, p. 645.

[3] For what follows see Cuttino's chapter on the process of Montreuil, op. cit. pp. 49–72.

process. He died at the papal court at Bordeaux on 21 September 1306 on a mission to seek a revision of the commission. Even if the auditors could have confined themselves, as the articles prescribed, to summary process in accordance with rules of equity to be agreed upon between them, they would have had more than enough to do. The long delays had brought new cases from the years of peace, and as Martel once pointed out, there was no body of law to guide them. When a rule existed, such as the distinction between acts done in war by royal command and other acts, the ascertainment of facts might be almost impossible. But the auditors could not confine their attention to maritime cases; they were also expected to decide cases which arose out of alleged damages and losses to merchants on land and often on lands whose allegiance was still in dispute.[1] It became clear in 1306 that King Philip's advisers, and his auditors themselves, were by no means prepared to allow the court at Montreuil to decide cases impartially by rules of equity. The French legists were in their element. They regarded the process as an outwork of the *parlement* of Paris. They used all the familiar arts of juristic finesse. They wished for a roving commission which would visit the coasts of Normandy, Brittany, and Poitou; and even to review the feudal relationships and conflicts of administration which, since 1259, had been so often discussed in Paris. Martel, on the contrary, wished to deal quickly at Montreuil, and in the friendly spirit which the new alliance should have evoked, first with the later cases and then with the more difficult pre-war disputes. No clear-cut policy was adopted. After 1311 nothing was done at Montreuil. Matters were allowed to drift 'within the purview of the Parlement of Paris', until the outbreak of the Hundred Years War brought discussions about them to an end.

The preceding survey of the problems raised by the violence at sea and the French seizure of Gascony has carried us far beyond the events of 1293–4. We must now return to study the efforts of King Edward to range the princes of the Rhineland and Netherlands against King Philip, and the political and ecclesiastical resistance which he had to face in England and,

[1] Cuttino (p. 54) associates with the 'process' a common petition by 'proctors of the commonalties of subjects of the king of England' everywhere, demanding compensation for damages inflicted by the Scots after the truce of 1297 and the peace of 1303, and for crimes committed by Scots living in France during the years 1303–6. The claims reached the fantastic total of £1,500,000.

after his annexation of Scotland in 1296, in the lands north of the Border. The king's necessities and resentments carried him far in the spring and summer of 1294. He took the wool trade of the land into his own hands, imposed a new tax on exports of wool and hides, and, without any regard for the independence of the Church, exploited the clergy. For the expedition to Gascony he ordered the building of a large fleet, heavy prises of food and goods, and the levy of knights, men-at-arms, and foot-soldiers for service across the sea, by precept or entreaty or local engagement, as the case might be. These measures, though they were approved by the magnates at the time, produced political trouble later; in the meanwhile they provided men and means, stopped trade with the dominions of King Philip, and by con-centrating the market in wool in Holland or Brabant enabled Edward to establish a war department of supply and finance in close touch with his allies. Reinforcements to the Gironde and Bayonne continued to be sent from Plymouth; but the main bases at home were the ports of East Anglia.

Edward soon realized that he could not gratify his wish to join his friends in Gascony. He had for some time fostered relations with the Low Countries. Since 1292 he had been on friendly terms with Count Guy of Flanders. A marriage alliance between the children, Edward of Caernarvon and Philippe of Flanders, had been under consideration. Although the trade in wool be-tween the two lands had been again cut off—for Flanders was a fief of France—the negotiations were pressed on and the marriage treaty was made by the end of August 1294; but Count Guy was in no position to break with his lord King Philip. Philip's grip upon Flanders had been tightened by his support of the closed patriciates of the Flemish towns, especially Ghent, on whose belfry the royal banner flew. In October the count was forced to come to heel at Paris and to leave his little daughter in French care. Not until 1297 was Guy driven in mingled hope and desperation to defy his suzerain and become Edward's ally and pensioner, only to be left in the lurch a year later. Edward, on his part, had by no means pinned his hopes upon the count of Flanders. He had what seemed firmer allies in Henry III, count of Bar, Florence V, count of Holland, John, duke of Brabant, and, above all, Adolf of Nassau, who in May 1292 had been elected king of Germany in succession to Rudolf of Habs-burg and was determined to bring to a halt, and, if possible, to undo, French penetration of the imperial lands which separated the French fiefs from Germany proper. King Adolf may or may not have made advances to Edward through the count of Holland and the archbishop of Cologne, but in any case he needed little solicitation to join forces with him. An understanding was reached before the end of June 1294; an alliance was made at Nuremberg in August and confirmed by Edward in October. The terms set out the conditions of a joint war with Philip of France but left the time and place of meeting in arms to be decided by their agents.[1] King Adolf sent a curt and insulting letter to King Philip without delay (31 August): he had endured French usurpations on his rights and territories long enough; he warned Philip that he was going to reveal his might ('disponimus contra vos vires nostre potentie exercire'). The official historiographer of France tells a story that, when Philip referred this letter to his advisers for advice, the count of Artois and the great council sent back to him a massive parchment; when Philip broke the seal he found nothing but the two words 'Troup Alemant', a jibe which had been current in Paris for more than a hundred years.[2]

Adolf of Nassau was a doughty prince, of headstrong temper and savage in warfare. He had been elected by the three ecclesiastical electors, the archbishops of Mainz, Cologne, and Trier, and other princes in opposition to Albert of Austria, King Rudolf's son and heir, who was bitterly incensed by the failure of his candidature. The new king soon lost support. He was too independent in his desire to recover imperial domains, especially in Thuringia, too brutal in his methods. His supporters had expected to find in him a pupil, not a turbulent force; and in 1298 he was destroyed by a coalition led by Albert of Austria. In 1294, with his lands and fortresses on the east of the Rhine

---

[1] *Foedera*, I. ii. 812. The most thorough and comprehensive study of the political situation in this period is F. Kern's *Die Anfänge der französischen Ausdehnungspolitik bis zum Jahr 1308* (1908), especially pp. 161–89. The extensive literature on Adolf's policy and character has been discussed and criticized by G. Barraclough in the *Cambridge Hist. Journal*, vi (1940), 225–62. R. Fawtier's narrative, op. cit., pp. 347–78, provides a healthy corrective to the view that King Philip and his contemporaries acted throughout on preconceived plans (cf. p. 361).

[2] R. Fawtier in *Annuaire-Bulletin de la société de l'histoire de France* for 1946–7 (1949): 12 pages on 'Un Incident diplomatique franco-allemand au temps de Philippe le Bel'. The phrase, in a reply to an earlier imperial threat, was used by King Louis VI, according to Walter Map, *De nugis curialium* (ed. M. R. James, pp. 228–9), cited by Fawtier. It might be rendered, 'The German again, worse than ever'.

and his powerful friends in Cologne and Holland, he may well have seemed to be a helpful ally, worth the 100,000 marks which he required as a financial aid; for, though his dominions were small, and he could not bring to King Edward the strength of a united Empire,[1] he showed purpose. His co-operation undoubtedly helped Edward, harassed though he was by the Welsh war, to turn his friendships with Holland, Brabant, Bar, Guelders, and other lordships into a coherent system of military alliances in 1294 and 1295. Some of the most important agreements, it is worthy of note, were concluded at Conway and at Llanfaes in Anglesey in the spring of 1295.[2]

Edward's system of alliances, resting partly on King Adolf but probably more on his sons-in-law in Bar and Brabant, maintained a watch upon King Philip for nearly three years. Adolf would have preferred immediate action, but neither Edward nor Philip was ready for a great campaign like that of Bouvines sixty years earlier. Philip could afford to wait; he was free from entanglements elsewhere, for King James of Aragon had made peace with the pope and Charles of Naples; and he could, through the *parlement* of Paris, keep his enemies in check on his eastern frontiers by a policy of penetration. He satisfied himself for the time being with a reply to King Adolf's challenge, though he waited for six months before he sent it; if Adolf persisted in his *diffidatio*, Philip was quite ready for him. It was the new pope, Boniface VIII, and King Edward who wanted a speedy peace. The pope had finally brought to conclusion, in the treaty of Anagni, the struggle between Aragon and the house of Anjou for Sicily, and, hardly had he done this, when the Sicilians refused to receive back their rightful king, Charles II, and turned to Frederick, the brother of James of Aragon. Papal plans for the control of Italy and, less wholeheartedly, for the long-heralded Crusade in Syria, had been embarrassed by the treacherous islanders. Sympathies in Italy were divided. It was essential to concentrate upon a crusade against the Sicilians, and therefore

[1] In January 1295 Adolf invited Edward to send his representatives to a German parliament in mid-Lent (Cotton, Appendix, p. 434, wrongly dated 1294) but he could not have given an imperial status to the alliance, as Lewis of Bavaria did in 1338, at a diet attended by his vicar, Edward III; cf. H. S. Offler in *E.H.R.* liv (1939), 617. Adolf was not 'bribed' to fight for Edward I, but he took money as the richer duke of Brabant and other allies did.

[2] *Foedera*, I. ii. 818–21. In August 1294 Adolf, at Edward's instance, had urged John of Brabant to join the alliance; J. de Sturler in *Revue belge de philologie et d'histoire*, xi (1932), 635.

to have peace in France and Germany. And so, during the years 1295-7, the cardinal legates of Albano and Preneste were hard at work, in France and England, trying to reconcile Philip and Edward. Edward's desire for peace was due to other considerations. He was spending enormous sums on the defence of Gascony and the financing of allies; his hopes of a quick success had been destroyed by the Welsh and the Scots. Hence he co-operated with the papal legates in their endeavours to arrange a peace; but until Philip agreed he could not withdraw from his commitments with his allies nor relax his vigilance at Bayonne; and Philip would not give anything away.

English activity in these years (1294-8) was intense from Savoy to the Low Countries. At home the whole administration of war and alliances was centred in the king's wardrobe, whose staff, under the keeper John Droxford,[1] 'paid, horsed and equipped the armies, purchased and distributed supplies, financed the king's allies and the king's fleet at Plymouth, issued letters both of great and privy seal, went on diplomatic missions'.[2] Abroad the king's agents in Holland and Brabant were the king's clerk Robert de Segre, 'receiver of the king's moneys', William Wake, Elias Russell, a citizen of London, Gilbert Chesterton of Stamford, and others concerned in the wool trade. In the chief English ports merchants were elected and assigned to collect, export, and sell the king's wool and hides.[3] The accounts of Segre, Russell, and Chesterton reveal the way in which the proceeds of wool and hides were used to supplement the king's treasure in forming alliances and preparing for war on King Philip's eastern flank; and how these men co-operated day by day with royal agents, diplomats, local princes, and Italian and local merchants in the cities and towns of Brabant and, rather later, of Flanders. The expenditure in these parts was as great as that in Gascony and in Spain and the south of France, where royal officials recruited the recipients of money-fiefs and military stipends. In 1294-5 the wardrobe account alone showed a receipt of nearly £125,000 and an expenditure of over £138,000, and the accounts of succeeding years not much less.

One interesting result of the concentration of effort in the Low

[1] Droxford succeeded Walter Langton, who became treasurer in 1295.

[2] Tout, *Chapters in Medieval Administrative History*, ii. 118-19 and *passim*.

[3] Sturler, *Relations politiques*, &c., pp. 165-221; also on the accounts of Robert de Segre, in *Bulletin de la Commission Royale d'Histoire*, cxxv (1960), 561-612.

Countries was an anticipation of the foreign staple established in 1313. This 'preinstitutional stage', as it has been called, was the natural result of Edward's policy. He may have intended in June 1294 to turn the wool trade into a royal monopoly, but more probably he wished to confine it to certain channels and exploit his control of it by the imposition of a high additional export duty which could be the basis of a war fund. According to the Dunstable annalist he was advised by the merchant Laurence of Ludlow.[1] The wool was first collected in certain ports. Though the king kept some, seized from owners who would later be compensated, most of it had been bought by merchants who were expected, though apparently not compelled, to export it by way of Dordrecht, and, in any case, to pay the old and new custom on it. The new custom was ultimately fixed at five marks on the last of leather and three marks on each sack of wool and on each parcel of 300 wool-fells, five or six times the rate of the custom of 1275. The incidence of this heavy tax or *maltote*, as it was commonly called, has not been and possibly cannot be clearly shown; presumably the exporters divided the burden with their customers in the Low Countries during the three years of the levy's existence; but the anger which it aroused in England was one of the causes of the crisis in 1297. The duty would also enable the king, who would not pay it himself, to profit by his own operations in wool and hides and to make gifts to the duke of Brabant and others. In 1297 Edward, after a fresh seizure of wool, reserved to himself stocks of more than five sacks, allowing lower quantities to be exported. By this time he had moved the staple from Dordrecht to Brabant, first in the summer of 1295 to Malines, then, a year later, to the growing port of Antwerp, where henceforth a community of English merchants may be traced.[2]

The relations between King Edward and his son-in-law the

---

[1] A levy of this kind was suggested, together with sumptuary taxation and duties on internal sales, in a project of taxation presented about this time to Edward I: see Ch.-V. Langlois in *E.H.R.* iv (1891), 321–3.

[2] The chronology was established by J. de Sturler in 1932 in a paper, presented to the congress at Liège of the Belgian archaeological and historical federation, on the Anglo-Brabançon trade and the origins of the English staple (offprint). See also his *Relations politiques*, &c. (1936), pp. 186–9, 212–19. On the ordinances for the seizure of wool in 1297 see G. O. Sayles in *E.H.R.* lxvii (1952), 543–7. Robert L. Baker has described the nature of a change in the wool staple in a paper on the establishment of the staple in 1313, in *Speculum*, xxxi (1956), 444–53.

duke of Brabant became very close after Duke John entered into a military alliance at Llanfaes in April 1295, and engaged himself, in return for a payment of 160,000 *livres* tournois (or about £40,000 sterling), to serve him with 2,000 mounted knights and men-at-arms.[1] Brabant became the base of English influence across the Channel. Antwerp was a more convenient centre than Dordrecht, which had been chosen in 1294 when the count of Holland conducted the last stages of the treaty between Edward and King Adolf.[2] Edward's reliance on John II of Brabant involved him at once in difficulties with the count. Whether the removal of the staple from Dordrecht to Malines was a cause of Count Florence's defection or a precaution taken in fear of it is not clear; but undoubtedly Florence, in the later part of 1295, was persuaded by King Philip's emissary, John of Hainault, to desert the Anglo-German alliance. At the very time when Edward was accrediting Walter Langton and other envoys to strengthen his alliance with Holland,[3] the count was on his way to Paris where, on 9 January, he became King Philip's pensioner and formally promised to support him in war against all princes, except his lord King Adolf, who were pensioners and allies of the English king. The news stirred the duke of Brabant to instant action. His vassal, John, lord of Cuyck, who was one of Edward's most faithful pensioners and acted as liaison officer between him and the duke, arranged, with the aid of some lords of the princebishopric of Utrecht, for the capture of Count Florence on his way home. The intention had been to send the count to England and to install his son in Holland; but his captors murdered him (27 January 1296).[4] Holland was no longer one of the keystones of the alliance, though it remained a friendly state.

The next defection from the alliance was more serious. In 1297 King Adolf at last came to an understanding with King Philip. This development must be considered in the light of events in 1296–7. As we have seen, Count Guy, in the face of

[1] *Foedera*, I. ii. 820. John II, who had married Edward's daughter Margaret on 8 July 1290, and had lived much in England, succeeded his father John I, who was killed in a tournament at Bar-le-Duc, in May 1294.

[2] Cotton, pp. 244–5; Sturler, *Relations*, pp. 182–4.

[3] *Foedera*, I. ii. 835 (St. Albans, 1 January 1296).

[4] For the treaty of 9 January and the death of the count see Kern, *Acta Imperii, Angliae et Franciae* (1911), nos. 111, 112, 132, 309; and his *Ausdehnungspolitik*, p. 176; Sturler, *Relations*, pp. 160–2 (for the lord of Cuyck). For poems about the murder see H. S. Lucas in *Speculum*, xxxii (1957), 283–98.

Philip's opposition, had not been able to implement the alliance of 1294 with Edward[1] and until the end of 1296 he was restlessly subservient to his suzerain, who played him and John of Avesnes, count of Hainault, off against each other.[2] Guy, however, had not ceased to maintain good relations with King Edward and to receive money from him, and, as John of Avesnes became increasingly active as the friend and agent of King Philip, and the easy subjection of Scotland in 1296 set Edward free to turn his mind to a renewed military effort both in Gascony and in the Low Countries, Guy decided to throw in his lot with Edward, and to defy his lord. The alliance of January 1297, concluded after Edward's return from Scotland, has rightly been described as a 'turning point in the diplomatic war' which had existed throughout the west of Europe since the middle of 1294.[3] It was a perpetual defensive alliance against France, accompanied by a marriage treaty between Edward of Caernarvon and one of Guy's daughters; it was followed by the adhesion of the nobles of Flanders and terms of co-operation between the English and Flemish fleets.[4] A few days before, after the Christmas feast at Ipswich, John, the young count of Holland, married Edward's daughter Elizabeth, to whom he had been affianced since 1281, and entrusted Edward with the task of a settlement of disputes between Holland and Brabant.[5] Yet although negotiations proceeded busily with these and other princes, Edward still hoped for peace. On 6 February, while he was on a pilgrimage to Walsingham, he authorized Amadeus of Savoy, Otto of Granson, and Walter Langton to arrange, with the two cardinal legates, terms of a truce between King Adolf and himself on the one side and King Philip on the other.[6] This was four days after Count Guy's representatives had sworn adhesion to the Flemish treaty 'in the chapel of Our Lady at Walsingham upon the Holy Gospels'.[7]

On 30 January, at Castle Acre, Edward had been informed by the bishop of Hereford of the decision of the clergy in convo-

[1] Above, p. 659. [2] Fawtier, op. cit., pp. 361–4.
[3] Barraclough, op. cit., p. 244. This article contains the best and clearest account of the circumstances in which King Adolf came to terms with Philip of France.
[4] *Foedera*, I. ii. 850–3, 856–8, 861–3, where the various agreements from January to April are printed.
[5] Ibid., pp. 850 (notification of the marriage at Ipswich, 7 January), 853 (on settlement with Brabant). Count Guy had already submitted his own quarrels with the count of Holland to Edward's settlement, p. 851.
[6] Ibid., p. 859. [7] Ibid., p. 856.

cation to make no grant without the consent of the pope, and he had promptly deprived them of royal protection. Having put the clergy outside the law of the land he had proceeded to Walsingham to make his devotions, seek a truce, and, at the same time, secure religious sanction for the loyalty of the count of Flanders to a military alliance. He was not conscious of any incoherence; it was his duty, now that he had dealt with the Scots, to be ready both for war and peace across the Channel. On 26 January he had summoned his magnates to confer with him on his military plans in parliament at Salisbury. He met them there in the first week of March.[1] By then he would have heard from Gascony that the earl of Lincoln had suffered the biggest defeat in the war. A large body of horse and foot was conveying supplies to hard-pressed garrisons in St. Sever and the *bastide* of Bellegarde. As it approached the latter place, it was overwhelmed by the count of Artois on 30 January—the day, as monastic chroniclers did not fail to note, on which the king had outlawed the clergy. The seneschal of Gascony, John of St. John, and many others were captured.[2] The news roused Edward to hasten his arrangements to send another expedition to Gascony; but at Salisbury he met with unexpected resistance from the earl of Norfolk, the marshal. The earl and others flatly refused to go to Gascony unless the king went with them; and Edward intended to go to Flanders. The parliament dispersed in confusion. A political crisis was added to the ecclesiastical *impasse* created by the papal bull *Clericis laicos*.

Apart from the revictualling of Blaye and Bourg on the Gironde, little or no aid could be sent to Gascony;[3] but, crisis or no crisis, Edward concentrated on his plan for a massive enterprise in Flanders. By the end of April he was satisfied that King Philip was planning an invasion of Flanders. Early in May he sent out those urgent writs, to which reference has already been made,[4] for the gathering of the national forces in London on 7 July. Food and other supplies were requisitioned in unprecedented use of the prerogative of prise. A royal ordinance authorized seizure by royal pre-emption of all the wool in the country, to be sent abroad for the use of the ambassador in the

---

[1] *Parl. Writs*, i. 51; summons of 26 January to meet on 24 February. In fact Edward was at Salisbury from 1 to 8 March.

[2] Bémont in *Rôles gascons*, iii, pp. cliv–clv; Cotton, pp. 318–19, on the coincidence of dates, *quasi vindicta Dei*. [3] Bémont, op. cit., pp. cliv–clv and note.

[4] Above, p. 553.

Low Countries, Walter Langton, in negotiations with the king's allies. Langton also had the power to pledge the tin of Cornwall and Devon and to contract loans with merchants and cities.[1] In June thirty-six barrels of money were shipped to Ghent for payment of the subsidies granted by treaty to the counts of Flanders and Bar.[2] On 17 May Edward informed King Adolf of his intention to sail for Flanders in July and begged him to hasten to join forces with him,[3] but the letter crossed one from Adolf which reached Edward on 2 June. This letter brought an earnest invitation to Edward to meet the king of Germany in Holland, preferably without an armed force, for a discussion. He could not, he said, nor ought he to raise his hand against the king of France until he and Edward had talked together.[4] Edward replied at once on 4 June: joint armed action in defence of the count of Flanders was essential; the plans were made; even if he shipped his army to Dordrecht, he would have to march through Holland and Brabant, whereas the ports of Flanders were easily accessible.[5]

In fact Adolf had already begun to listen to the suggestions of King Philip. Both kings had good reasons to come to terms. Philip wished to consolidate his acquisition of the Free County of Burgundy in the face of local resistance; and to have his way clear in Flanders.[6] For three years Adolf had had to wait on Edward's necessities and to acquiesce in the negotiations for a truce in which the pope and Edward himself had urged him to join. He had lost the confidence of the German princes and knew that Albert of Austria was waiting to strike. In view of the feeling in England and the restlessness in Scotland, and also of

[1] Langton, treasurer since 1295 and elected bishop of Coventry and Lichfield in 1296, was active on his embassy for nearly eighteen months (June 1296–November 1297). His *computus* or financial account, which was rendered in the king's wardrobe at York in July 1298, gives a valuable impression of relations with legates, princes, cities, merchants, &c. It has been edited by G. Cuttino in a volume of *Studies in British History* by various writers (University of Iowa, 1941), pp. 147–83: cf. also Cuttino, *English Diplomatic Administration*, pp. 128–33.

[2] Cuttino, in notes to his edition of Langton's account, p. 182. In 1296–7 Guy of Flanders received in all £36,526 sterling.   [3] *Foedera*, I. ii. 865.

[4] See, for this letter, Barraclough, op. cit., pp. 245–6.

[5] *Foedera*, I. ii. 866–7.

[6] On Philip's gradual reduction of the Free County under the suzerainty of France, with the willing support of its Francophil count, Otto IV, see Fawtier, op. cit., pp. 367–9. The feudatories who resisted him in favour of the overlord, King Adolf, were subvented by King Edward in 1295–7. Adolf deserted them in 1297, but they were comprehended in the terms of truce between Philip and Edward later in the year. For Count Otto cf. above, p. 248.

Edward's propensity to use his allies to display his strength in negotiations for a truce, he could not feel sure that Edward could wage effective war in Flanders. And so he was ready to listen to the skilful and persuasive tongue of Philip's agent, a certain Muscitto, known in France as 'Monseigneur Mouche'. The evidence strongly suggests that, in addition to a promise to pay 80,000 *livres* tournois, or £20,000 sterling, in three instalments, King Philip offered a settlement of boundary disputes on the imperial and French frontiers, with some indication that he would consider the restoration of lands already occupied. With the goodwill of Pope Boniface, negotiations proceeded throughout the summer, probably until autumn. A joint commission empowered to settle boundary disputes was discussed and on 30 July was definitely authorized by Philip to act. Adolf did not denounce his alliance with Edward and retained his freedom of action, but he disengaged himself from the war. As late as 31 August he wrote to Guy of Flanders promising so far as possible to safeguard Flemish interests in any 'final settlement' with King Philip. His detachment from Anglo-French relations is clearly revealed in the truce made between the kings of France and England at Vyve-Saint-Bavon on the river Lys on the day of St. Denis (9 October). Each party undertook to announce the truce to his allies, and Edward's list of allies was headed by the name of the king of Germany; but each agreed that Adolf was at liberty to 'break the truce' (*ceste souffrance roumpre*) if he wished to do so.[1] Nine months later, on 2 July 1298, King Adolf met Albert of Austria in battle and was slain.

Edward had made a supreme effort to raise a great army for Flanders, and, as we shall see shortly, had overreached himself. His passage from Winchelsea to Sluys was delayed until 22 August. His force was not big enough to drive King Philip out of Flanders.[2] His allies, even his loyal son-in-law, Henry of Bar,[3] were slow or unable to move, either too watchful of events or kept in check, as in the Free County and Bar, by the threat of French operations. In west and southern Flanders, since early in July, King Philip had established himself as easily as his

---

[1] *Foedera*, i. ii. 878–9. Barraclough's reconstruction of events seems to me convincing, as against the view that Adolf was bribed to make peace in July 1297. He discusses the texts and recent discussions of the evidence by Kern, Böck, and other scholars. [2] Below, p. 679.

[3] Henry had married Edward's eldest daughter Eleanor in 1293. On his difficult relations with King Philip see Fawtier, op. cit., pp. 365–6.

lieutenants had overrun Gascony. On 20 August the Flemish forces had been defeated at Veurne, and on 25 August the long-beleaguered garrison of Lille was compelled to promise that it would capitulate unless relieved, as it was not, by the end of the month. The capital town of Bruges was dominated by the rich burghers, nicknamed the 'men of the lily' (*leliants*), who for years had been partisans of Philip, so that Edward was forced to make his headquarters at Ghent, where he hired a local labour corps of diggers and sappers to strengthen the defences. Relations between his troops in and outside the walls and the population soon became strained in this static warfare. Even the sea was not safe from the coastal sweeps of Philip's fleet of galleys. In September the news came that William Wallace had broken the Earl Warenne's army at Stirling.

Philip was quick to see that he could gain no more advantage in an uncertain war in Flanders than he already possessed. So the first truce was made on 9 October, and after its renewal Edward returned to England. He landed at Sandwich on 14 March 1298. The story of the truce and of the peace of 1303 has already been told.[1] It is not a glorious story, but it is very revealing. It shows that Edward, in spite of his desertion of the Flemings, had helped to implant in the counts and the lesser *bourgeoisie* of the towns the spirit of resistance to which their unexpected victory at Courtrai in 1302 gave the strength of determination. In 1328, after incessant intervention, the kings of France were no nearer to the subjugation of Flanders than they were in 1303; and English wool was no less a necessity to the well-being of its citizens.[2] Edward, in his turn, recovered Aquitaine[3] and was left free by Philip the Fair to deal with the Scots.

The difficulties which had delayed Edward's passage to Flanders and pursued him across the Channel were due to his exactions from the clergy, his prises of food and stores, his seizure of wool and hides, the *maltote* of 1294–7, and his attempt to enlist military aid, paid and unpaid, on an unprecedented

[1] Above, pp. 649–54. Ramsay, op. cit., pp. 456–8, has summarized the history of the Flemish campaign.

[2] Cf. Langlois in Lavisse, *Hist. de France*, III. ii. 302–11. Hence the co-operation of Edward III and Jacques von Arteveldt.

[3] At the end of Edward's reign, from one-fourth to a fifth of the exports of wine from Bordeaux and Libourne came annually to England, i.e. about 20,000 of a total export of 90,000 to 100,000 tuns: see Margery K. James in *Economic History Review*, 2nd series, iv (1951), 175–6.

scale for foreign service. The resistance to foreign service did not endure, as Edward III's large contract armies show, but it was one, and not the least, cause of the domestic crisis of 1297.

One of Edward's concerns in the summer of 1294 was a debased currency and the amount of coin out of circulation. He would be required to send more money out of the country to pay his allies and soldiers than he had ever done before, and it must be good money, worth its face value. Three years before, he had issued a proclamation to be read in every shire court, city, and market town forbidding the currency of debased or false coins, but he knew that much bad money was still in circulation among merchants and others. On 16 June 1294 he announced the appointment in each shire of persons who should co-operate with the sheriff to scrutinize the deposits in churches, religious houses, and elsewhere, take a careful record of them and, though this is implied rather than enjoined, separate and return the bad coins to the exchanges. This was not all. At the same time, using some list of deposits of the crusading tenths in cathedral and monastic churches, he ordered the surrender, through the local sheriffs, of these and any additional deposits to the treasury in London.[1] Since the date of his passage on crusade had passed, he feared lest the pope might withdraw from England the proceeds of the crusading tenths, which, as we have seen,[2] tended to be centralized in the care of the Frescobaldi and other foreign merchants. He was determined to prevent this both by negotiations at the Roman Curia and by seizing the much larger sum still deposited in local churches. About £33,000 passed into his hands in addition to £10,000 which the collectors of the tenth had lent to Italian merchants in May 1293 for the expenses of Edmund of Lancaster in the king's service abroad.[3] Finally, all alien priories subject to religious houses within the power of the king of France were entrusted to wardens who made a survey of their possessions and revenues; this was done to prevent the export of revenues to the mother houses.[4]

---

[1] *Rôles gascons*, iii, nos. 2679–82; Lunt, *Financial Relations*, pp. 361–5, where the evidence is interpreted rather differently. The money seized in 1294 was later comprised in the settlement in 1300 between Boniface VIII and Edward for a division of the proceeds of the papal tenths.　　　　[2] Above, pp. 641–2.

[3] *Foedera*, I. ii. 788. The claim for repayment of this loan as a separate debt to the papal camera was disputed by Edward in 1302; he considered that it was comprised in the concessions of 1300. It was still regarded as a debt to the camera as late as 1362–70 (Lunt, pp. 364–5).　　　　[4] Cotton, pp. 299–302.

These various measures have been sometimes described as flagrant acts of expropriation. This judgement is too sweeping. It is clear from the writs and the lively account of the Norwich chronicler that the scrutiny of deposits was intended to stop short with a record in duplicate and the sealing up of the deposits. Although, as Edward later admitted, his instructions had sometimes been exceeded, his object was to secure the observation of the ordinances against bad money.[1] The seizure of the proceeds of the papal tenth was a high-handed forced loan. The monks in alien priories were in general allowed to manage their affairs as before on condition of passing to the Crown the money which would otherwise have gone to the enemy. All the same, such drastic action, following on the seizure of wool, by which the monasteries must have been especially embarrassed, brought with it much hardship and sharp practice; but the worst had yet to come.

Edward, more forcefully than his father, regarded himself as the patron and protector of the clergy, with the right to insist that they should fulfil their obligations as vassals and subjects of the Crown. In Archbishop Pecham's time the provinces of Canterbury and York had thrice come to his assistance, in 1279, 1283–6, and 1290, and Pecham, on his side, had successfully defined the independent structure of convocation.[2] In 1294 the clergy were still paying arrears of these three subsidies, in addition to the crusading tenth imposed by Pope Nicholas IV for six years; but in his necessity Edward was determined that they should make a new and heavy contribution. Owing to the long vacancy in the papal see, ended by the elections of the hermit-pope Celestine V (July 1294), and, after his quick resignation, of Boniface VIII (December), Pecham's successor, Robert Winchelsey, though elected by the monks of Canterbury in February 1293, was still in Italy awaiting papal approval and consecration.[3] The king decided to summon the clergy himself without regard to the formal niceties. In August he issued writs

[1] Cotton, pp. 237–8; Guisborough's account of Edward's discussion with the clergy in September, ed. Rothwell, pp. 249–50.

[2] Above, pp. 507–8.

[3] Rose Graham, 'Archbishop Winchelsey: from his Election to his Enthronement', in *Church Quarterly Review*, cxlviii (1949), 161–75. The process of the election and other documents are printed as Appendix I to her edition of Winchelsey's *Register* (Cant. and York Soc.), pp. 1257–88. The archbishop was consecrated at Aquila on 12 September 1294 and took the oath to Pope Celestine on receiving the pallium (17 September).

to the archbishop of York, the warden of the spiritualties of Canterbury, the bishops and numerous abbots, ordering them to appear at Westminster on 21 September.[1] The writs to the bishops in most particulars observed the forms used by Pecham in 1283, and also anticipated in wording the well-known summons of the clergy to parliament in 1295 and, as a rule, to later parliaments.[2] The assembly in fact was a convocation summoned by the king, who expounded his needs and allowed it three days for consideration. An offer of two tenths was rejected. Edward, through his proctors, demanded one-half of clerical revenues, as recently assessed for the tenth of Pope Nicholas. The scene in the refectory at Westminster must have been a painful one. The bishops were apparently willing to agree, but some of the clergy refused. They were told that all who resisted would be deprived of the king's protection. The subsidy was granted and was collected in three instalments by diocesan collectors under constant pressure and warnings. By September 1295, it has been estimated, about £80,000 had been collected. In return the king had agreed to exempt from the tax benefices of less than the annual value of ten marks (the sum regarded as an adequate stipend for a vicar or perpetual curate), and had issued both general letters of protection for the clergy against the prises of corn and other goods which were being taken for the ships, and particular writs of protection to those who paid the tax.[3]

The new archbishop returned by way of Germany and sailed from Dordrecht, reaching Yarmouth on 1 January 1295. His election had cost the monks of his cathedral more than £3,000, and he himself was embarrassed by his debts to Italian merchants. He went to the king, who was at Conway—for the last Welsh war was now being fought—and, after taking the oath of fealty in the terms used by his predecessors, was given control

---

[1] *Parl. Writs*, i. 25–26.

[2] J. Armitage Robinson, in *Church Quarterly Rev.* lxxxi (1915), 104–6 and note.

[3] *Flores Historiarum*, iii. 90–91 (here a Westminster chronicle); Cotton, pp. 248–50, with writs of protection and collection); Guisborough, pp. 249–50. I have omitted in the text the story that the dean of St. Paul's died of fright when he heard the royal demand for a half of clerical revenues. The Westminster account (*Flores*, iii. 90) implies that the dean, sent by the assembly to ask for information, had a stroke and died; also it states that the demand for the moiety was made later in the refectory. What caused the shock is not stated. The dean, William de Montfort, was an elderly man, the son of the important baron Peter de Montfort of Beaudesert. He was a papal chaplain and was much employed by King Edward. Earlier in 1294 he had escorted the king's daughter, Eleanor of Bar, to the Continent (*Cal. Chancery Warrants*, i. 42).

of his temporalities (4 February).[1] Winchelsey was widely known and respected. His election had been welcomed, for he was able and had been the most distinguished secular clerk and master in the Oxford schools. He was determined to maintain the dignity and rights of his great office, but he was also eager to help the king in his difficulties. His enthronement at Canterbury in October was a great occasion, attended by the king and the royal family, eight bishops, and five earls.

Edward was in greater need of money than ever. The Gascon expeditions, the Welsh rebellion, the subventions to his allies, the danger latent in the Franco-Scottish alliance, and the more immediate danger of a French invasion involved him in heavy expenditure. More taxation was essential. In November 1294 a grant of a tenth had been made in parliament and a sixth had been levied on the boroughs. In November 1295 new demands were made.[2] This was the most comprehensive assembly yet summoned in England, for in addition to the earls, barons, prelates, knights, and burgesses, it included, on the ground that common dangers needed general remedies (for what affects all should justly be approved of by all), the same clerical elements as had been summoned to Westminster in September 1294.[3] The lords and shires gave an eleventh, the boroughs a seventh, and the clergy a tenth. The clergy were expected to give more, and undertook to do so if the need arose. They were aware that negotiations for a truce were on foot; indeed they were painfully aware of this, for the two cardinal legates who had come to England in this year 1295 had been levying procurations for their expenses.[4] When King Philip refused a truce, Edward reminded the archbishop of the clerical promise. He summoned

[1] Graham, op. cit., pp. 173-5. The archbishop did not take the oath in the form demanded by the king, and confined his obligation to his temporalities. His first responsibility was to St. Peter, Holy Church, and the pope (cf. his oath of 17 September 1294, p. 172).

[2] *Parl. Writs*, i. 29-31; Cotton, pp. 297-9. An earlier parliament which met in August 1295 consisted of magnates, prelates, judges, and members of council, and was concerned with discussions with the papal legates about a truce, and important judicial business, including the complaint of a Dutch merchant. See *Parl. Writs*, i. 28-29; *Foedera*, i. ii. 824-6; *Rot. Parl.* i. 132-42.

[3] In the writ to the archbishop and bishops about the representation of the clergy, the operative word *praemunientes* took the place of the words *vocantes prius* used in the writ of 1294.

[4] See the documents copied in Cotton's narrative, pp. 282-93, and the clerical petition of August 1297 to the pope in Winchelsey's *Registrum*, pp. 533-4, with Rose Graham's discussion of it in her *English Ecclesiastical Studies* (1929), pp. 302-16.

the clergy to another full parliament to meet at Bury St. Edmunds early in November 1296.[1] The comprehension of the clergy in parliament as a simple way of uniting all elements of society in the grant of taxation might well have become permanent if the archbishop and his colleagues had not been compelled in 1296 to take account of Pope Boniface's bull *Clericis laicos*. The future history of clerical assemblies would, in that case, have been very different from that of the later medieval convocation.

In *Clericis laicos*, issued at the end of February 1296, Pope Boniface carefully defined the law of the Church, expressed in 1215, that lay taxation of the clergy required the authority of the Holy See and declared all concerned in unauthorized taxation to be *ipso facto* excommunicated.[2] He was an astute man of the world and, as he soon showed, was ready to admit modifications of the principle, but recent events, especially in France and England, made him insist that papal approval was normally required. That he had Edward's action in 1294 in mind is clear from the references to a moiety and to the seizure of treasure deposited in churches. In some ways King Philip had been a greater offender; on the other hand, Boniface, who deplored Edward's policy in Scotland and his alliances with King Adolf and other princes, seems to have felt that Philip could put in the stronger plea of necessity. If Edward could talk about the danger of invasion by sea, Philip, with more reason, was soon able to talk about the danger of invasion by land, and to carry not only his magnates but his bishops and the pope himself with him. In his bull *Etsi de statu* of 31 July 1297 Boniface followed up previous admissions with a full acceptance of much current thought when he declared that *Clericis laicos* did not apply to a period of admitted emergency and that the prince and his advisers could decide when such a situation had arisen.[3]

[1] *Parl. Writs*, i. 47–48, for writs sent from Berwick in August 1296; cf. above, pp. 615, 636. The financial details of the lay subsidies levied in 1294, 1295, and 1296 are tabulated in *E.H.R.* xxviii (1913), 519–20.

[2] *Foedera*, ii. i. 836.

[3] For the French story see G. Digard, *Philippe le Bel et le Saint Siège* (Paris, 1936), i. 246–345. A good survey of the taxation of the French clergy is in *Studies in Early French Taxation*, by J. R. Strayer and C. H. Taylor (Harvard Univ. Press, 1939), pp. 23–43; and for the doctrine of necessity see H. Rothwell in *E.H.R.* lx (1945), 16–27. Rothwell seems to me to exaggerate what he describes as the pope's 'political humiliation' in July 1297 (p. 19). *Etsi de statu* can be read in the *Registres de Boniface VIII*, no. 2354.

Although *Clericis laicos* had not yet been published throughout England,[1] the archbishop had, of course, received it when the king, in parliament at Bury St. Edmunds, asked the clergy to contribute a fifth. A Bury annalist asserts that he 'published' the bull in parliament.[2] He was allowed a delay until January, and at once summoned the clergy to a great congregation at St. Paul's, London, on 13 January,[3] the first of four such meetings in the year 1297. In fact the arena of discussion was henceforth to be in convocation and not in parliament. Issue was joined when, after hearing the refusal of the clergy to grant a subsidy, Edward withdrew his protection from them and exposed them to the losses and suffering of outlawry (30 January).[4] Any ecclesiastic who did not pay the fifth and receive a royal writ of protection was liable to seizure of his lands and manors and might be imprisoned.[5] This drastic action broke the unity of the clergy. The debates in a second convocation in March lasted for eight days, the leader of the opposition to the archbishop being a Dominican, possibly the king's redoubtable henchman, William of Hotham, the provincial, who later, as archbishop of Dublin, was to be one of the chief agents in the negotiations for the truce with King Philip and in the discussions at Rome. Convocation agreed that no way out of the dilemma in which it was placed could be found; the archbishop left the solution to each man's conscience. He himself was torn by it, as his long writ of summons to the convocation of January had shown. Nowhere were the perils to which the realm was exposed by a 'perfidious enemy' so fiercely and eloquently described as they had been in that writ. He could sympathize with those who paid the fifth and received royal protection; yet he felt that it was wrong to disregard the papal inhibition. In February he had repeated his injunction for its publication and reproved those who neglected

[1] Winchelsey ordered its publication in the dioceses on 5 January 1297, in a mandate reciting the bull and the pope's order to the cardinal legates, then in France, for its promulgation in France and England. These had been sent by the legates to the archbishop in October (*Registrum*, pp. 159–62).

[2] Edited by V. H. Galbraith in *E.H.R.* lviii (1943), 64.

[3] *Registrum*, pp. 144–7.

[4] Above, p. 665.

[5] The sheriff and a knight appointed in each shire were authorized, by an ordinance of 1 March, not only to give the king's protection to those who submitted, but to imprison those who, by sentences of excommunication, propaganda, and any other way impeded the national effort. See the long instruction printed in the appendix to *Parl. Writs*, i. 393–4 (from the Patent Roll). Cf. the Bury annalist in *E.H.R.* lviii. 65–66. The monastery of Bury suffered from both sides.

it. It should be expounded to the people in their native tongue (*lingua materna*).[1]

Some relief came to him in the summer. It became known in England that the French bishops had petitioned the pope to allow them to grant a subsidy to King Philip, and that the pope accepted the plea of necessity.[2] What could be done in France could be done in England. Moreover King Edward was prepared to confirm the charters of liberty and the forests. The archbishop came to an understanding with the king. On 11 July Edward restored his lands, on 16 July the archbishop issued writs for another convocation to meet on 10 August. The assembly met, decided to approach the pope, and informed the king that it expected to get leave to grant a subsidy without any trouble.[3] At the same time, the archbishop and his colleagues refused in any way to relax resistance to the widespread infringements of the bull *Clericis laicos*: to the seizure of ecclesiastical goods and lands and deposits, to the heavy prises on wool and corn and other provision for the use of the king, and to invasion on the sanctity of churches and the freedom of the clergy, all of which were explicitly condemned by Pope Boniface. Minute and stringent instructions for the issue of sentences of excommunication against offenders in general and obdurate offenders by name were prepared for publication on 1 September.

The bishops who conveyed the decisions of convocation found Edward at Winchelsea, a few days before he sailed for Flanders. He treated them with calm courtesy, but made no concessions. He forbade the issue of the sentences of excommunication, and sent to the exchequer an ordinance in council ordering the collection forthwith of a third of the temporalities of the clergy, or, if they should prefer, a fifth of their assessed revenues; that is to say, he enforced by royal authority the demand for money which he had made at Bury. He explained in his ordinance that he could not defend the realm and sustain his allies abroad without the help of all, both clergy and laity. He anticipated the obvious retort that an invasion of France from Flanders could

---

[1] *Registrum*, pp. 154–9.

[2] Ibid., pp. 174–9, for correspondence between the French bishops and the pope, significantly inserted just before the summons to the convocation of August, issued on 16 July.

[3] Ibid., pp. 179–80, 189–90. For what follows see Rothwell in *E.H.R.* lx. 32–34, and H. S. Deighton, who has collected more evidence in his paper on clerical taxation in the reign of Edward I, ibid. lxviii (1953), 161–92.

not be described as an act of dire necessity by the argument that to act from a distance was the safer course ('plus seurement de loing qe de pres').[1] Then he set sail. To what extent the proclamations on either side were effective is not clear. The archbishop's sentences of excommunication were probably held in reserve in some dioceses. The levy on the clergy was allowed to lapse when a clerical tenth was granted in the southern and a fifth in the northern province later in the year. Yet it is doubtful if such drastic action was ever taken on either side in the history of the relations between Crown and Church as was taken in England in August 1297; and taken, it should be remarked, in an atmosphere of mingled discomfort and goodwill. When, in view of the general rising in Scotland, the archbishop summoned the fourth convocation of the year to meet in November, goodwill prevailed. A truce had been made with France, the Charters had been confirmed with vital additions, the bull *Etsi de statu* had become a matter of common knowledge. The king was still abroad; his son and the earls, now reconciled with the Crown, had to meet a Scottish invasion. Winchelsey agreed that the plea of necessity might be adopted without previous reference to the pope, on the understanding that clerical aid should not be used to assist the pursuit of the Scots across the border and that the levy should cease as soon as the time of emergency had passed.[2]

So, after all, a clerical subsidy was granted; but it was the last clerical subsidy of the reign to be freely granted in convocation, nor did Edward again try to tax the clergy by royal decree. The plea of necessity was double-edged, and he found it easier to turn to the pope himself than to an archbishop fenced in by canon law. Relying on the precise reservations made by Pope Boniface in the summer of 1297, and following the example of the French clergy in March 1297, Winchelsey kept the collection of the tenth in clerical hands, deposited the proceeds in the New Temple, and, after the emergency was over, used the residue for ecclesiastical purposes.[3] Edward accepted the position

---

[1] Cotton, pp. 327–30, 335–6; *Foedera*, I. ii. 875 (royal prohibition of excommunications, 19 August); *Parl. Writs*, i. 395 (ordinance of 20 August).

[2] *Registrum*, pp. 198–200; and for the collection, pp. 212–15; see also Winchelsey's explanatory letter to the pope, pp. 528–31. The account given by the Bury annalist, op. cit., p. 70, shows that the reason for the change of front was well understood in England.

[3] See especially Rose Graham on this tenth for national defence, in her *English Ecclesiastical Studies* (1929), pp. 317–23.

when, in April 1298, after his return to England, he asked the
archbishop to summon another convocation, and when this met
in June expressed the hope that, if necessity arose, more clerical
aid would be given, and requested that in the meanwhile the
residue of the tenth should be released to him. To the first
suggestion Winchelsey replied that no subsidy should be hoped
for without papal consent, to the second that a similar situation
might lead to the concession of the residue. Processions and
prayers for the king's success in Scotland were gladly promised;
but the excommunication of those who invaded the rights,
goods, and persons of the clergy was renewed, and this time
with impunity.[1] In Archbishop Winchelsey Edward had met his
match; and he was never generous enough to forgive him.

The archbishop was sworn to a double allegiance, to the pope
and the king, and he took both obligations very seriously.
When the opportunity to co-operate with the king came in July,
and again in November, 1297 he welcomed it; but *Clericis laicos*
was still part of the law of the Church and stiffened clerical
resistance to the seizures and prises which did so much to alienate the laity. Hence clergy and laity came together in an appeal
to the Charters of liberty.

The opposition which the earl of Norfolk, the marshal, had
expressed at Salisbury in March 1297[2] came to a head in July,
when the military strength of the land was concentrated in
London. In spite of all that happened there, the king, with the
archbishop's aid, proceeded with his plans and sailed to Flanders
on 22 August; but he did not sail with the army which he had
expected to have. Instead of an impressive galaxy of English,
Irish, and Scottish earls and barons marshalled in a flexible
host of some two thousand cavalry comprising the flower of the
knights and squires or men-at-arms (*armigeri*) who had lands in
their shires of the annual value of £20 and more, Edward left
Winchelsea with 100 knights and bannerets and 570 squires.
He never had more than 140 knights and bannerets and 755
squires with him from the British Isles. About two-thirds of
these, until the Scottish prisoners released on condition of service and an Irish contingent arrived in September, were household troops. 'The maximum cavalry force supplied by the

---

[1] *Registrum*, pp. 250–2, 260–2, 268–72; also Winchelsey's letter to the archbishop
of Dublin at Rome, pp. 536–8, and the lively account in the Bury annals, op. cit.,
p. 71.   [2] Above, p. 666.

general body of his subjects', in addition to the 195 who went with the king, 'barely amounted to 200'.[1] In addition he had in his pay 7,810 archers on foot, of whom about 5,300 were from Wales and the rest from the English shires and the marches. The army was sufficient to hold Philip in check and to induce him to agree to a truce, but, in the absence of most of the allies upon whom he had squandered several hundred thousand pounds, it was unable to do more.[2] The great army raised for service in the Scottish campaign which culminated in the battle of Falkirk less than a year later (July 1298) was nearly three times as large.[3]

In his stress upon necessity, Edward had let his anger and ambition carry him too far. He could not convince his barons that the emergency justified an appeal for a great voluntary effort, in which the normal ways of raising a force were merged in a demand for the aid of every freeholder, whether knight or not, whether tenant-in-chief or not, whose income from land enabled him or her to give or provide unpaid service on horse-back across the Channel.[4] As barons they had been affection-ately begged to join this motley throng in London on 7 July. Some of them, if the sheriffs really acted on their returns to the king's writ, had even been enjoined to appear as landholders in particular shires, along with knights, squires, the heads of religious houses, and women who possessed twenty librates or more. Most of the local knights and freeholders who had obeyed the sheriffs' injunction were as reluctant as the barons and much worse prepared to go across the sea. They must have had little money and often no war-horses. Neither they nor the barons had been able to make bargains for high payments like the lord of Offaly in Ireland. The earl of Norfolk and his supporters, after the protest at Salisbury in March, had already met for conference in the forest of Wyre in the Welsh March and had,

[1] N. B. Lewis in *Studies in Medieval History presented to F. M. Powicke* (1948), pp. 310–19.

[2] Above, p. 668; what part the duke of Brabant, who received more than any-body between 1295 and 1297, would have taken is not very clear. He provided the economic base and in March 1298, by an arrangement like that between Henry III and the count of Savoy in the Alps (above, p. 250), gave over and received back Antwerp as a fief held of Edward (J. de Sturler, op. cit., pp. 152–3, 157–9).

[3] Morris, *Welsh Wars*, pp. 284–92, 313–14.

[4] *Parl. Writs*, i. 284–96. It is hard to disengage the knights and squires in the sheriffs' lists, but the sheriff of Northampton classified his returns, giving 41 *armigeri* (p. 289).

then or later, been joined by the constable, the earl of Hereford.[1] Hence, when on 8 July the two earls were required, in accordance with their customary duties, to enrol the names and the number of horses of those who were willing to serve, they refused.[2] They had been asked to come, they wrote, as volunteers, and could not enter on their office as though the feudal host had been summoned in due form. They and their companions withdrew from court, after confirming their action in interview with Geoffrey de Geneville and other important persons sent by the king; and, although the archbishop, now restored to royal favour, tried to mediate, they remained obdurate and elusive until Edward left to join his fleet.

In the meantime Edward completed his arrangements. He moved with great rapidity. He appointed Geoffrey de Geneville marshal and Thomas de Berkeley constable. On 14 July he appeared with the archbishop on a platform erected in front of Westminster Hall, made a moving and persuasive speech, and called upon the bishops and magnates present to take the oath of fealty to his son Edward and to swear to take him for king and lord after his father. They did so, the archbishop first, then the bishops, followed by the earl of Warwick and other magnates faithful to the king throughout this critical time. The two earls and many more took the oath two days later, with the aldermen and citizens of London. They were not traitors; they were preparing their case. Later in the month, when or where is not certain, the king got the approval of his companions, at a meeting held in his chamber, to the levy of an eighth from the laity and a fifth from the towns, and at the same time 'in order to foster unity', as the Westminster chronicler puts it, declared his intention to confirm the Charters, a step which he had already promised the archbishop to take. On 30 July commissions were issued for the collection of this subsidy and for a prise of 8,000

[1] *Flores*, iii. 101, 294. The constable had been one of the escort of the king's daughters, the duchess of Brabant and the countess of Holland, to Brabant earlier in the year and was not present at Salisbury, as the Guisborough chronicler states; cf. Sturler, p. 147, n., and Rothwell, in *E.H.R.* lx. 25, n. Rothwell's criticism of the reliability of Guisborough (generally known as Hemingburgh) should be studied in his edition, pp. xxv–xxxi.

[2] For what follows and for the political events in England during the king's absence see especially H. Rothwell, in *E.H.R.* lx. 24–35, 177–191, 300–15; also J. G. Edwards's searching survey of the texts in the same *Review*, lviii (1943), 147–71, 273–300. Some of the texts have been translated and discussed by B. Wilkinson, *The Constitutional History of England*, i (1948), 187–232.

sacks of wool, to be paid for from the proceeds of the tax. On his way to the coast he ordered the barons of the exchequer to hasten the collection and to prepare an ordinance to guide a campaign of propaganda by the assessors of the subsidy. On 12 August, at Udimore, near Winchelsea, he issued a manifesto to be published by the sheriffs, in which he gave his version—very fairly, on the whole—of events since 8 July. He had heard, he wrote, that the earls had prepared articles of remonstrance, but he had not received them. He would make amends for the hardships of his people when he had put an end to the business which had caused them such loss and anguish. He was not sparing himself. Disturbers of the peace and trouble-makers of all kinds would fall, he declared, under the excommunication pronounced on such by Pope Clement IV, which was in the royal possession.[1] Edward then, as we have seen, received the bishops, fresh from convocation, and issued the writs for the collection of the third and fifth from the clergy. Finally, on board his ship he received the great seal from the chancellor, John Langton. Three days later his son Edward, as his lieutenant, entrusted the chancellor with the seal of absence which had been used in England during the king's long absence in Gascony ten years before.[2]

Edward is sometimes said to have won over the barons and knights as a whole in July 1297; but the evidence does not support this view. The men who supported him at Westminster when he spoke so feelingly from a platform, and who gathered in his chamber to approve a lay subsidy and at Winchelsea to approve a clerical subsidy, were the men who went or had been willing to go with him to Flanders—his cousin Aymer of Valence, his friend Geoffrey de Geneville, Thomas of Berkeley and a dozen or so more, and the officers and members of his household. Most of the knights and squires so carefully summoned to join him held aloof, and those who went or joined him later were, like those of the household, paid wages.[3] The two earls

---

[1] This was the bull authorizing action by the legate Ottobuono in May 1265, and acted on in 1267. Cf. *Cal. Papal Letters*, i. 427, 435.

[2] *Foedera*, I. ii. 876.

[3] Cotton (p. 327) lays stress on two concessions made by the king in 1297, the confirmation of the Charters and the decision, after much altercation in parliament, i.e. of Michaelmas, that service in Flanders was not obligatory by those who owed service, nor by the holders of twenty librates of land, 'nisi ad vadia et pro stipendia'. These local landholders were comprised also in the indemnity requested in the document 'de tallagio non concedendo' and granted by the regent in October and

who led the opposition rapidly gained strength and confidence. Their articles of grievance were sent to the king and probably reached him at Winchelsea.[1] In the name of the whole community the earls protested against the irregularity of the king's writs and his supposed intention to cross to Flanders, where service had never been done. In any case those who owed service were worn down by all the recent tallages and prises and could not afford to go. Public business was not being transacted according to the law and customs of the land; the Great Charter and the Charter of the Forest were not observed; the tax on wool, whose value was half that of all the land, was intolerably high. Finally the expedition to Flanders was advantageous to nobody, so long as support there was not assured; the Scots were moving and their rebellion would grow worse as soon as the king had crossed the sea. The document reveals a state of opinion far removed from the general enthusiasm in 1294, when a common enterprise was undertaken in legal form, elastic enough to comprehend the service of gentry of the shires, and the host was summoned to go to Gascony, only to be diverted by a Welsh rising.

The remonstrance was put out of date by Edward's persistence. The earls now proceeded to action. On the morning of the king's departure they entered the exchequer and forbade the collection of the eighth and fifth, of which they and those whose consent was required had not been told. The officials—and, the earls professed to believe, without any royal authority—were acting as though England was full of serfs who paid merchet and were tallaged at will.[2] Edward met the gesture by proclaiming that the tax was not to be regarded as a precedent and that those who paid could ask for letters to this effect; but both he and the advisers of the regent—his guardian Reginald Grey, recently justiciar of Chester, with the earls of Cornwall, Warwick, and Oxford, and the permanent official element—were determined to resist any attempt by the opposition to seize

the king on 5 November (cf. Edwards, p. 166). On *De tallagio*, probably compiled as a basis for discussion in parliament, see Rothwell, pp. 309–13; also V. H. Galbraith, *Studies in the Public Records* (1948), pp. 146–50. Edwards takes a more sceptical view.

[1] Best edited by Edwards, pp. 170–1; translated by Wilkinson, pp. 220–2.

[2] Documents relating to this incident will be found in *Trans. Royal Hist. Soc.*, new series, iii (1886), 281–91; see Edwards (pp. 154–7) on the reference to serfdom and the loose sense in which the word 'tallage' was often used, and the sinister suggestion which it could be made to imply; also cf. Rothwell, pp. 34–35.

power. For a time the danger of civil war must have seemed real to a terrified people. Even before he sailed the king, on 20 August, had issued writs to a large number of knights to go to his son at Rochester by 8 September, and the regent's council added other precautions in readiness for a parliament which was summoned to meet the day after Michaelmas (30 September) in London. Each side was manœuvring for advantage. Then came the news of Wallace's victory at Stirling on 11 September.

The result is well known. The promise to issue a confirmation of the Charters was enlarged to an agreement in which the influence of all alike—of the regency, the earls, and the archbishop—had effect. On 10 October the Charters were confirmed with the addition of important promises which recall the articles and declarations of the earls. The recent aids and prises would not be turned into a servile obligation. No appeal could be made to the record of them. Henceforth all such aids, mises, and prises would be taken only 'with the common consent of the whole kingdom and for the common benefit of the same kingdom, saving the ancient aids and prises due and accustomed'. The maltote on wool was abolished, not to be renewed without common consent and goodwill, though the custom granted in 1275 was to remain. The king was induced to confirm and issue these articles on 5 November at Ghent. About the same time he confirmed the pardon of the earls and all others who had refused to come to his aid in Flanders. In view of the emergency in Scotland and in consideration of the agreements in parliament, the prelates, barons, and knights had already granted, to take the place of the irregular and contested eighth and fifth, a new subsidy of a ninth, which was afterwards extended to the boroughs. In November the clergy granted their tenth. Action was taken to defend the marches in the north and the enlistment of large forces for the reconquest of Scotland was begun.[1] For the rest of the reign the struggle for Scotland dominated the political scene.

The brooding discontent which King Edward left behind him in Scotland burst out in May 1297 into widespread disorder.[2]

[1] The close connexion between movements in England and Scotland in 1297–8 is shown by Morris, *Welsh Wars*, pp. 280–5.

[2] Ramsay, *Dawn of the Constitution* (1908), pp. 449–520 *passim*, is the best general

On 4 June he gave powers to Henry Percy and Robert Clifford, two foremost barons in the border shires, to deal with the disturbances with the aid of local levies from Cumberland, Westmorland, and Northumberland, and the officials and castellans in Scotland. The first open move had been made by William Wallace, and began with a dispute in the court of the English sheriff of Lanark. He murdered the sheriff and, shortly afterwards, forced the justiciar of Scotland to flee from his court at Scone, and, after further forays, established himself for the time in Ettrick Forest. In the meanwhile Andrew of Moray had rebelled in the north and soon, wrote the treasurer, the land was in such turmoil that no issues or writs could be collected; indeed the shires were 'void of guardians', and in many of them the Scots had set up bailiffs of their own.[1] The worst news, however, in Edward's eyes was that the earl of Carrick, Robert Bruce the younger, had risen with James the steward and John his brother, Alexander Lindsay, and William Douglas of Douglas and had collected a force in Ayrshire, for this meant the revival of baronial faction. They had with them Robert Wishart, the bishop of Glasgow, who was generally regarded as the main fomenter of popular discontent and was certainly in later years to be, with Wallace's friend William Lamberton, bishop of St. Andrews, a mainstay of clerical resistance.[2] Bruce at first seems to have hesitated, and is said to have attacked the lands of his neighbour William Douglas, the first Scottish baron to desert the king.[3] The reason which the confederates gave for their action was their fear that Edward, who had sought extensive aid from the Scottish lords and summoned them to London with his other subjects, was planning to denude the country of its

guide on Scottish history and relations between 1297 and 1307. The most interesting and provocative book on the war in detail is E. M. Barron's critical study, *The Scottish War of Independence* (1914), pp. 1–275. Bain's *Calendar*, vol. ii (1884), is essential for the record evidence.

[1] Stevenson, *Documents*, ii. 206–7; treasurer's report of 24 July.

[2] Wishart's part is hard to follow, and he seems to have got frightened. In one letter he told the treasurer that the tumult would not have arisen if he (the treasurer) had been in Scotland (ibid. ii. 220). Lamberton, the chancellor of Glasgow, was elected on 5 November 1297—the king later said at Wallace's instance, and was consecrated in Italy in June 1298. His political activities in Scotland began in 1299; see John Dowden, *Bishops of Scotland* (1912), pp. 21–22; and Palgrave, *Documents and Records*, pp. 331–2 (Edward's articles against him, addressed in 1306 to Pope Clement V). Ramsay (p. 465) is wrong in saying that the bishop did homage to Edward in 1298. He was in France.

[3] See the story in Guisborough, ed. Rothwell, p. 295.

manhood;[1] but obviously the defection of Bruce was open to a more sinister explanation.

Percy and Clifford at once turned their attention to this group and to such effect that they submitted to the king's will at Irvine on 9 July.[2] Douglas, whose lands in England had been seized nearly a month before, was set apart from the others. He was an old offender. He failed to produce his hostages, as he had promised Percy to do, on the appointed day and was imprisoned in Berwick castle, where he was reported to be 'very savage and abusive'. Next year he was transferred to the Tower of London, where he died. His son James, a child of three or four at this time, became a protégé of Bishop Lamberton, and later, as Bruce's devoted friend, one of the most famous figures in Scottish legend and history.[3] Bruce and the others were more fortunate. They were given certain promises at Irvine, including an undertaking that they should not be sent to serve in Gascony against their will. The bishop, the steward, and Lindsay became sureties for Bruce, liable for life and lands, until he surrendered his daughter Margery as a hostage. Bruce, the bishop, and the steward were awaited at Berwick as late as 8 August to complete the covenant. The covenant was not completed. Bruce and the steward remained at large, deprived of their lands, Lindsay made his own peace and was restored to favour, the bishop was imprisoned at Roxburgh and possibly was not released until 1299. For the time being, the lead in the resistance came to Andrew of Moray and William Wallace, who fought in Baliol's name; but the future lay with Bruce and the house of Stewart.[4]

It was most unfortunate from the English standpoint that at a critical time in June neither the warden John de Warenne, earl

[1] Stevenson, ii. 198–200. Bruce and his companions are all named in the list of Scottish barons to whom Edward wrote from Portsmouth in May 1297 (ibid., pp. 167–9).

[2] See the texts in Palgrave, pp. 197–200, and Stevenson, pp. 198–227 *passim*. Guisborough, p. 334, refers to Wishart's imprisonment, and Pope Boniface's well-known protest of 27 June 1299 shows that he was still believed to be in prison then: see the text in Guisborough, p. 337.

[3] Douglas was in rebellion before 12 June, and probably in May (Stevenson, ii. 176–7). He had been in trouble some years before on account of his unlicensed marriage with the widow of William Ferrers, but had been pardoned, and had done homage with other Scots in 1296. For his imprisonment at Berwick see Stevenson, pp. 205, 218. For his son James as a child cf. Bain, ii. 175 and the *D.N.B.*

[4] The son of James the steward, Walter III, married Bruce's daughter Margery (1315). Their son Robert was the first Scottish king of the house of Stewart.

of Surrey, nor the treasurer, Hugh Cressingham, was in Scotland. The former had been ordered to return on 14 June but did not appear until the end of July. The latter was back early in July and, to do him justice, bestirred himself. He realized, as treasurer, that the position was serious, collected a fleet at Berwick and a considerable force on land. He had planned to strike hard at once, either north of the Forth or at Wallace in Ettrick forest, but unwillingly acquiesced in delay when Percy and Clifford came to Roxburgh with the news that Bruce had submitted.[1] The general mood in official circles was optimistic, almost care-free; indeed Warenne had arranged to join the king in Flanders and a successor, Brian fitz Alan of Bedale, who was familiar with Scottish affairs, had been appointed by the king (14 August), but on 7 September, four days before the battle of Stirling, the regents ordered the earl to remain in Scotland, and, after the news of the disaster, ordered fitz Alan, Percy, and Clifford to serve under him.[2] During this long period of delay, the influence of Andrew of Moray and William Wallace had grown. The two leaders joined forces, and were waiting across the Forth a mile from the old bridge when Warenne reached Stirling on 10 September. Their position was well chosen; a swampy meadow lay between them and the bridge; cavalry could not freely deploy. After a tardy and reluctant start on the 11th, Warenne's van was cut off by a body of Scottish spearmen at the bridge. Thereafter all was confusion. The earl rode back to Berwick; Cressingham was killed. Only the garrisons of Stirling, Edinburgh, Roxburgh, and Berwick held out. In October the Scots overran Northumberland and much of Cumberland. All had to be done again.[3]

Throughout the disturbance King Edward retained the support of many bishops, earls, and lords and had released some of the leaders whom he had taken prisoner at Dunbar in 1296 or

[1] Cressingham's important letter to the king, 23 July, in Stevenson, ii. 200–3.

[2] For the discussions with fitz Alan at Berwick and his stipulation that, as a baron of small means, he must at least have Warenne's stipend to keep the land to the king's honour and provide fifty armed horses see the letters of 4–5 August from Berwick, ibid., pp. 221–7. Fitz Alan's own lands, he says, were worth only £1,000 (i.e. were about 100 librates on the usual estimate of value). He was appointed by Edward on 14 August at Udimore and could hardly have taken over from Warenne before the battle of Stirling. See *Foedera*, i. ii. 874 and Stevenson, pp. 230–2.

[3] Ramsay, pp. 453–6; for the raids Guisborough, pp. 303–8, who cites writs of Moray and Wallace on behalf of the canons of Hexham. On this period as 'a turning-point in the history of Northumbria', cf. B. Wilkinson in *E.H.R.* lxiii (1948), 5.

sent to live in England; but Andrew of Moray's successful resistance in the north, followed by Wallace's triumphant emergence
with him at Stirling Bridge, reduced them to impotence. Bruce
and the steward, though they seem to have remained aloof,
were now able to move freely in Ayr and Renfrew where they
seem to have awaited events.[1] The government of Scotland for
ten months was in the hands of Wallace. Moray was severely
wounded in the battle, and died in November, but until then
he and Wallace issued writs as joint leaders (*duces*) of the army
of the kingdom of Scotland. One interesting writ, which survives among the records of the German Hansa, invited the
friendly merchants of Lubeck and Hamburg to pursue trade in
a safe Scotland which 'had been recovered by war from the
power of the English'.[2] Moray's death was a real misfortune,
for he was young and influential and probably had better judgement than his famous colleague,[3] who now had to maintain
unity and prepare to meet the English.

The unexpected disaster at Stirling Bridge put an end to the
crisis in England. The preparations for civil war were interrupted, and on 10 October the regent and his council submitted
to a reconciliation with the earls. While the king continued to
enlist new forces for Flanders, a mightier effort was made to
raise an army against the Scots. The earls, barons, and other
magnates of the realm were summoned to meet at Newcastle by

[1] Barron, whose survey of the division of interests in 1297–8 is valuable, has
shown that, owing to a misdating of documents, Bruce has wrongly been accused of
treachery to both sides during the years 1297–1300 (pp. 124–31).

[2] Hill Burton, *History of Scotland*, ii (1877), 296. The writ is printed in the *Han-
sisches Urkundenbuch*, i (Halle, 1876), no. 1251. For its significance cf. J. W. Dilley
in *Scottish Hist. Rev.* xxvii (1948), 142–3. On trade and Scottish independence see
W. S. Reid in *Speculum*, xxix (1954), 198–209.

[3] Andrew of Moray *junior* was the son of Sir Andrew, who died in the Tower, and
the nephew of Sir William of Moray, lord of Bothwell (d. 1300). For the lands of
Sir Andrew in Moray and the exploits of his son in the north of Scotland see Barron,
passim. Andrew *junior* had been imprisoned in Chester in 1296, but when and how
he got into Moray is not known. That he was 'killed at Stirling *contra dominum
Regem*' is stated precisely in a Berwick inquisition *post mortem* (November 1300)
after his uncle's death; and Bain sees a contradiction between this evidence and his
survival as *dux* for a time (*Calendar*, ii, pp. xxix–xxx and note, on no. 1178). Ramsay
appears to solve the difficulty by saying that Andrew was killed at Falkirk in 1298
(p. 464). A more likely solution would be that he was killed at Stirling, but not in
the battle of Stirling Bridge. I assume with Barron (p. 69) that he was wounded in
the battle and died later. His posthumous son, another Andrew (born 1298), was the
heir of William Moray of Bothwell and was destined to play an important part
during and after the reign of Robert Bruce, whose sister Christina he married as her
third husband.

6 December, to march with the young prince.[1] Later writs issued on 8 January 1298 state that the king would shortly return to aid his faithful people.[2] The prince did not, in fact, go north, nor did the king immediately return; the date of the rendezvous at Newcastle was postponed until the end of January under the captaincy of the Earl Warenne; the feudal host was organized, not in customary form, but as a paid force of some 750 cavalry, the cost of which was partly drawn from the clerical subsidy lately granted by the province of Canterbury.[3] In the meantime local officials and special commissioners had been ordered to raise fixed quotas of suitable foot in the king's pay from Yorkshire, Westmorland, and other shires and from Wales. Before proceeding to Newcastle, Warenne, the earl of Gloucester, the marshal, constable, and others met at York, where the Scottish magnates had been summoned to appear. They did not appear. Warenne's orders were to secure the Borders. This he did. The Scots withdrew, on his approach, from the towns of Roxburgh and Berwick, where they had been investing the castles. Berwick was the army headquarters until the king arrived at Roxburgh in June. The town, which the late treasurer had neglected or been unable to surround with a stone wall, was strengthened. Open warfare was not easy during the winter; and Edward forbade operations on a large scale until he came.[4]

The king landed at Sandwich on 14 March. He had a *colloquium* at Westminster, where important business was done, some of which will be noticed later. He decided to make York his administrative centre. The exchequer and the bench were transferred and stayed there until Christmas 1304.[5] Writs were issued for a parliament (*colloquium speciale*) of magnates and representatives of shires and boroughs to meet there at Pentecost

[1] *Parl. Writs*, i. 304 (4) of 23 October, addressed to William Ormesby and describing the orders made to raise infantry, states this clearly. The army was numbered, i.e. marshalled, at Newcastle. This suggests that the marshal and constable, although they served at the king's cost and the summons was not in strict feudal form, were satisfied.

[2] *Parl. Writs*, i. 309 (26).

[3] Morris, *Welsh Wars*, pp. 285–6.

[4] Guisborough, pp. 314–15; and cf. below, p. 697. Rothwell (p. xxx) requires corroboration of the explicit passage in Guisborough about the summons of the Scottish leaders to a conference (*parliamentum*) at York on 14 January 1298, but the royal letters referred to do not necessarily imply a parliamentary writ. On the fortification of Berwick and border castles, see Stevenson, ii. 160, and *passim*.

[5] *Rot. Parl.* i. 143; Guisborough, p. 358.

(25 May). Edward ordered Warenne to come secretly from
Berwick (so that his departure might not be generally known)
and also summoned from Berwick the earls of Norfolk, Hereford,
Arundel, and Angus. He wished to complete his reconciliation
with the marshal and constable, and indeed at York he gave
them the kiss of peace. The Scottish magnates were again
straitly ordered to come or to face the consequences as public
enemies.[1] Finally military writs of summons to join the host at
York were sent in all directions, including Ireland, and arrangements were made for the enlistment and paid service of battalions
and companies of foot, this time almost entirely from Wales
and the Welsh Marches. A Gascon corp of lords, knights, and
mounted crossbowmen was probably already on the way to
England. In all, when the field army was marshalled at Roxburgh at the end of June, it must have contained some 2,400
horse, of whom about 1,300 were paid by the Crown, and 10,500
paid Welsh archers.[2] How many of these were actually engaged
in battle at Falkirk it is impossible to say.

The king marched north from Roxburgh, crossing the Tweed
at Kelso, and on 15 July reached Kirkliston, on the road from
Edinburgh to Stirling, some eight miles east of Linlithgow. The
bishop of Durham in the meanwhile was sent to clear the coast-
lands south of the Forth, where the Scots held Dirleton and
other castles. He joined the king at Kirkliston. Wallace's main
force had withdrawn, the land was wasted, the ships carrying
stores were delayed, hunger and disease began to work havoc on
the Welsh archers, who, after they had been revived by wine
which had arrived, quarrelled with the English, were attacked
by men-at-arms, and became mutinous. Edward was about to
retire on Edinburgh to wait for stores when he learned that the
Scottish army was near Falkirk, twenty miles away, prepared to
follow him up if he retreated. The news settled his doubts. He

---

[1] *Parl. Writs*, i. 65–77; Guisborough, pp. 323–4. It is not easy to see why Richardson and Sayles accept the *colloquium* of Easter as a parliament, and deny the description to the much bigger and formally constituted *colloquium speciale* of Pentecost
(*Bull. of Institute of Hist. Research*, v (1928), 149).

[2] *Parl. Writs*, i. 312–16; Morris, op. cit., pp. 286–93, 313–14. Cotton (p. 343)
states definitely that both knights who held of the king and those who did not
owe him service were summoned; Guisborough that foot-soldiers were not called
[from the English shires] though volunteers were received. The northern shires had
suffered, and also the levies raised there in 1297 were half-hearted; cf. the assurance of 24 June 1297 that the voluntary service of the men of Cumberland would
not be made a precedent (Stevenson, ii. 186–7).

immediately marched on, and with his men slept that night (21 July) on the Burgh Muir of Linlithgow. Before sunrise the army set out again and early in the day came in sight of the Scots. It was the feast of St. Mary Magdalen. A tent was pitched and mass was celebrated. Wallace had grouped the Scots—foot armed with pikes or lances—behind a swamp in four circles or *schiltrons*. Companies of archers from Ettrick Forest, under the command of the steward's brother John, were placed between the circles. The pikemen stood, kneeled, and sat in ordered rings, closely packed behind a fence of stakes and ropes. 'I have brought you to the ring,' Wallace is said to have exclaimed, 'hop if ye can.' The English cavalry was in four brigades, perhaps of three or four hundred each—the van under the earl of Lincoln and the earls of Norfolk and Hereford; the second under the bishop of Durham; the third with the king, who had with him his nephews, the two young sons of Edmund of Lancaster and John of Brittany, his pensioner John of Bar, the earl of Warwick, and some Gascons. The fourth was in reserve, under the four earls of Gloucester, Arundel, Oxford, and Pembroke. The first brigade, unaware of the marsh, was held up for a time in attack and had to divert to the left round to the rear of the Scots; the second did the same, on the right. According to the detailed report used by the chronicler Guisborough, the two battalions met, scattered the smaller cavalry force of the Scots, and overwhelmed the archers under John Steward, who was killed. The *schiltrons* were exposed, immobile; the English archers, who also carried slings, broke the rings of pikemen, first with arrows, then with stones. It is unlikely, however, that the battle was so simple an affair as Guisborough makes it appear to be. The bishop of Durham at one point tried in vain to get his brigade to wait for Edward; there was obviously at first some haste and disorder; and the victory may well have owed much to the cooler and better-timed use made by the king both of his Welsh archers and of the Gascons and others under his direct command. What is certain is that the Scots had not yet mastered the use of infantry. Wallace, who had chosen his own ground, and need not have joined battle at all, must have relied on numbers and may have hoped that the English would repeat their errors at Stirling Bridge.[1]

[1] Guisborough, pp. 325-8, for the campaign and battle; used by Ramsay, op. cit., pp. 460-4; Rishanger, p. 187. Morris lays stress on the importance of Edward's

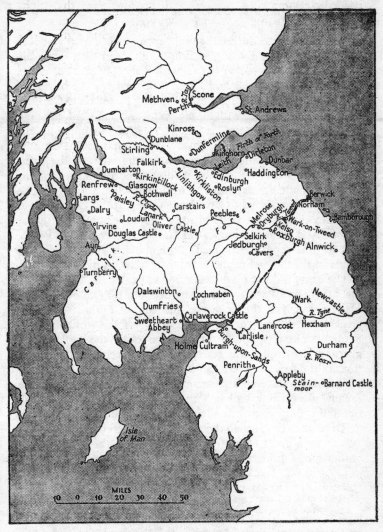

MILES
10   0   10 20 30 40   50

SOUTH SCOTLAND AND THE NORTH OF ENGLAND

Edward was not able to follow up his victory. After a fortnight at Stirling, where he recovered at the Dominican priory from a kick from his horse during the night spent on Linlithgow moor, he encamped by the castle at Edinburgh,[1] and then made his way across country to Ayr to deal with Robert Bruce; but Bruce had fled, and after he had seized Lochmaben, the ancestral castle of the Bruces in Annandale, the king passed on to Carlisle, where he took counsel with his magnates and endowed, in name rather than fact, some of his followers with lands in Scotland.[2] He had wished to occupy Galloway, but the state of the country and lack of provisions prevented a continuation of the campaign. Everywhere south of St. Andrews and Perth his captains found or made desolation. The tenants-in-chief who had done unpaid service wished to have leave to depart. So Edward, late in September, issued writs of summons to a number of earls, barons, and knights to appear at Carlisle on the vigil of Pentecost (6 June 1299).[3] He stayed in the marches and the north of England till the end of the year, then went south.

The army did not meet at Carlisle at Pentecost. The order to meet there or elsewhere was postponed four times, now because negotiations with the pope and the king of France were in a critical stage, now for other reasons. A force summoned in September for a campaign, probably to relieve the hard-pressed garrison at Stirling, was got together in December, but desertions of the foot were serious, the military tenants of the bishop of Durham had refused to serve beyond their shire, and in the meanwhile Stirling had fallen.[4] Edward decided to fall back upon the fully and formally constituted feudal levy and on 30 December 1299 issued the necessary writs from Berwick. This was to be a great effort from Carlisle where the army was to gather by 24 June.[5] A fleet of fifty-eight ships, thirty of which

leadership and the value of the Welsh archers, points not revealed clearly in Guisborough's source (op. cit., pp. 67–68, 96–97, 104, 292–3; for the four battalions, p. 314).

[1] A reply to the ambassadors of King Philip about breaches of truce, &c., ends, 'Actum in castris seu tentoriis dicti regis Anglie, prope castrum Puellarum in Scotia, quod vulgariter nuncupatur Edenbourgh', &c. (Foedera, 1. ii. 899).

[2] Guisborough, pp. 328–9. Trivet, ed. Hog, p. 373.

[3] Parl. Writs, i. 317–18 (to earls and barons).   [4] Morris, p. 298.

[5] Parl. Writs, i. 327 ff.; Morris, pp. 298–303, for details of numbers and composition of the army. Apart from the army to go to Gascony (1294), which was diverted, this was the first feudal host of the traditional type since that summoned in 1282. It comprised also the newer elements, e.g. holders of forty librates of land, and contract forces as well as unpaid tenants-in-chief.

came from the Cinque Ports, was moored in the Solway.[1] The outcome was another fiasco. The total force in cavalry and foot was comparable with that which Edward had at Falkirk, but nothing happened except the fall of Carlaverock castle and some marching to and fro in Galloway. The foot, nearly all drawn this time from the northern shires, and those of Nottingham and Derby, not from Wales, were again troublesome.[2]

The king lingered in the district north and south of the Solway till November. Late in August the archbishop of Canterbury found him, after much search and waiting, at Sweetheart abbey and presented him with the famous exhortation, compiled more than a year before (27 June 1299), in which Pope Boniface, after an historical survey, bade Edward cease to afflict the Scots and to withdraw from a land held in feof of the Holy See. Edward deferred his answer until the matter had been considered in parliament.[3] On 30 October at Dumfries he announced that, at the request of King Philip, he had agreed to a truce with the Scots, to last until Pentecost 1301;[4] but he neither wished nor expected that it would be renewed, and when negotiations about the Scots with the French envoys broke down in the spring[5] he proceeded with his plans for a campaign. At the Lincoln parliament in February 1301 he had already issued writs to earls and barons and to the gentry of the shires, each by name, summoning them to appear at Berwick on 24 June.[6] Rather later he

---

[1] See G. Neilson, 'Annals of the Solway until 1307', in *Trans. Glasgow Arch. Soc.*, n.s. iii (1899), 246–308, with a map; especially pp. 297–301.

[2] Morris, pp. 298–303. The brief siege of Carlaverock has given this campaign an undeserved prominence in history, owing to the publication by Harris Nicolas in 1828 of the text of the poem written about it, with arms of the earls, barons, and knights present and memoirs of the personages commemorated by the poet. This is an important contribution to the history of heraldry.

[3] See below, p. 702. Winchelsey wrote a vivid account to the pope of the chaotic state of Galloway and of his reception by the king: for the text see the London annals in *Chronicles of Edward I and II*, i (1882), 104–8. Sweetheart abbey had been founded not long before by Devorguilla, in memory of her husband, John Baliol, the father of the exiled king of Scotland.

[4] Palgrave, pp. 247–9, a writ sent to his various wardens, sheriffs, and castellans in Scotland individually by name. Edward insists that he has made the truce at the instance of Philip as his friend and 'amiable compositeur', not as an ally of the Scots. The document calendared by Bain (ii, no. 1164) obviously belongs to a later time of partial truce. It refers to Bothwell (captured in September 1301) as one of the castles in English hands, also to Perth and Banff. Barron accepts Bain's wrong date, but rightly is surprised (p. 189).

[5] Bain, ii, no. 1198, Edward to the chancellor, 25 April 1301.

[6] *Parl. Writs*, i. 346–60. The long lists of knights and other forty-librate land-

decided that under the guidance of the veteran earl of Lincoln, his son, created prince of Wales at Lincoln, should operate separately from Carlisle[1] and get a closer knowledge of war than he had been permitted to acquire during the Galloway campaign in the previous year. The forces which met at Berwick and Carlisle, though not so impressive as had been planned in February, were considerable and included about 6,800 foot, mainly archers from Wales and some English shires.[2]

The campaign lasted actively till October, when the king went to winter at Linlithgow. Here he strengthened the castle and was in touch with his ships in the Forth. During the campaign Edward had occupied Peebles in the wild central district of hills and forest, gone on to Glasgow—his western fleet had been busy in Bute and the estuary of the Clyde—and captured the important castle of Bothwell, the inheritance of the infant son of Andrew of Moray.[3] The most serious threat from the Scots had been in the south-west, where Lochmaben, Turnberry-in-Carrick and the new castle of Ayr had been in danger. On 26 January 1302 at Linlithgow, another truce, to last till St. Andrew's day, was ratified. This was an outcome of the Anglo-French negotiations which culminated in the peace of 1302–3, and Edward again made it clear that, although Philip still regarded John Baliol and the Scots as his allies, he did not admit the validity of this alliance nor in any way recognize Baliol's claims.[4] The proviso would be welcome to Robert Bruce who was at last becoming convinced of the inability of the Scots to control the south of the country. After the battle of Falkirk and Wallace's loss of power, he had for a time become joint guardian with John Comyn of Badenoch. He had ceased to be a guardian by 10 May 1300, when in a parliament at Rutherglen, near Glasgow, Ingram de Umfraville was chosen to succeed him. He took no part with the guardians in their resistance to Edward in the Galloway campaign of 1300, and made his peace before

holders are based upon the sheriffs' lists of 1300, and show that mesne tenants were included.

[1] Cf. the letter to the earl of Lincoln of 1 March (Bain, no. 1191) and the writs about Welsh recruits to the earl of Hereford and others, *Parl. Writs*, i. 357, 359.

[2] Cf. Morris, op. cit., p. 303, where the importance of the campaign is unduly depreciated. See the map in Gough's *Itinerary*.

[3] Above, p. 687, n. See Bain, ii, pp. xxxiv–xxxviii for the main facts and the distribution of castles, &c.

[4] Bain, no. 1282, and the much corrected draft of King Philip's proposals in Palgrave, pp. 241–7.

16 February 1302,[1] possibly after it became known that Baliol had retired to his castle in Picardy.[2]

Although, for reasons which will be considered later, Edward was unable to touch Scotland north of the Forth or to exercise full control anywhere except in Lothian during the four years which succeeded his victory at Falkirk, he was by no means immobile in the south of the country. York remained his administrative capital, where his professional captains, John of St. John, Robert Clifford, William Latimer, the earl of Dunbar, and others, could, on occasions, consult together. The marches east and west of Roxburgh were carefully organized for the first time under wardens who had as colleagues the military governors of districts in the north of England and the castellans in the Lowlands of Scotland. A special clerk was assigned to act as paymaster of the Scottish garrisons from Berwick to Linlithgow and round the west to Ayr, Turnberry, and Lochmaben; and, at least in the more settled areas, the garrisons were paid from the proceeds of local rents, dues, and amercements. The wild country enclosed by these fortresses was not impenetrable. Raids were frequently planned. Indeed, at one time, Patrick, earl of Dunbar or March, was warden of the whole of Scotland south of the Forth. The area was administered as though it were an extension of the north of England. If their writs, financial accounts, and correspondence survived we should doubtless find that the guardians of Scotland regarded much of this land in the same way, as annexed to Scotland north of the Forth and their recaptured fortress at Stirling.[3]

---

[1] As Barron shows (pp. 132–8), King Philip's letter to Bruce and Comyn as guardians should be dated April 1299, not 1302 (see text in Bain on pp. 535–6). They first appear together in a writ of 2 December 1298, and last appear as colleagues, with Bishop Lamberton, on 13 November 1299, in a letter to Edward accepting King Philip's plan for a truce (*Foedera*, i. ii. 915). For the parliament at Rutherglen and the relations between the guardians see Sayles, *Scot. Hist. Rev.* xxiv (1927), 245–50. The pardon issued by Edward on 16 February 1302 at the instance of Bruce shows that he had already made his peace.

[2] See E. L. G. Stones, 'The submission of Robert Bruce to Edward I, *c.* 1301–2', in *Scottish Hist. Rev.* xxxiv (1955) 122–34. This corrects my interpretation in the first edition of this book of the rhyming chronicler Langtoft's account of the presence of the Bruce at Lincoln in 1301. The relations between Bruce and parliament mentioned by Richard Siward (Bain, ii, no. 1334) and Langtoft are confusing, but the problem of Bruce's peace with Edward is more serious. W. C. Dickinson in *A New History of Scotland*, i (1961), 160, suggests that the rival claim of Comyn was the cause.

[3] This paragraph is based upon the documents edited by Stevenson and noted in Bain's *Calendar*. What evidence exists on the holding of parliaments and on adminis-

The difference between the two administrations was that, while Edward, in spite of his embarrassments, was master of his own household and acted through well-tried and loyal friends and Scots—notably Alexander Baliol of Cavers and, until his desertion in 1300, Simon Fraser of Oliver castle—the Scottish leaders were not thoroughly united. A story told by a spy sent out by the sheriff of Roxburgh has, perhaps, been given undue credit, but is illuminating. The man reported a raid into Selkirk forest by the Scots and a meeting there at Peebles of the Scottish leaders, including the guardians, in August 1299, with a view to an attack on Roxburgh. A dispute arose about the disposition of Wallace's lands. Some, it would seem, regarded the patriot's intention to leave Scotland at that time as desertion, because he had not sought leave to go, others upheld his rights. At one point John Comyn took Bruce by the throat, and his namesake and cousin, the earl of Buchan, laid hands on the bishop of St. Andrews. In the end the magnates decided that the bishop should be principal warden, with control of castles, as the colleague of Bruce and Comyn. The company then dispersed to various parts, after arranging for raids on the English march from the forest.[1] Much that was unknown to the spy must have lain behind this strange report, and much that he had heard was probably garbled; but it suggests that Wallace, who about this time did go to France and possibly on to the papal court,[2] was a cause of controversy, and that the bishop, who had lately arrived in Scotland with messages from King Philip, was given precedence as a guardian in the interests of peace.

The outlook on Scottish affairs, from Edward's standpoint, was more promising when he left Linlithgow in 1302 than it

tration has been collected by Richardson and Sayles in the *Scot. Hist. Rev.* xxv (1928), 314-16.

[1] Bain, ii, Addenda, p. 525. Bishop Lamberton was known in July to be embarking from Flanders with another future guardian John of Soules and efforts were made to intercept him (Bain, no. 1071). It has not been noted that a letter of 9 August, wrongly attributed by Stevenson (ii. 301-4) to the previous year, obviously refers to this inroad south of the Forth by the Scottish magnates, including the bishop. The writer, who was castellan of Edinburgh, suggests that Simon Fraser, warden of the forest, was in league with them. Simon's loyalty to Edward may have been shaken then. Fraser, lord of the barony of Oliver castle in Peeblesshire, was held in high regard by the king. See Bain's *Calendar*, index, p. 621; cf. Barron, pp. 144-5 and *passim*. He probably deserted in 1300. In September 1301 he was a leader on the Scottish side in the neighbourhood of Lochmaben (Stevenson, p. 431).

[2] The evidence is discussed in the *D.N.B.*, s.v. Waleys, William.

had been since he left Berwick in 1296. Hitherto he had been hampered at every turn. The reluctance, outside the range of his household troops, to serve in his armies beyond England had reduced him to cajolery in the shires to persuade men to serve, and to savage punishment of those who took their wages only to desert. The king of France had urged the Scots to rally round their absent king, to maintain their constancy, and depend upon his determination to support them.[1] The guardians, in their turn, had welcomed the suggestion of a truce because it came from him[2] and might lead to a settlement in their favour. Even when the negotiations for peace between France and England had resulted in the treaty of 1303, from which the Scots were excluded, the Scottish envoys in Paris wrote confidently about Philip's assurances.[3] Edward could not feel secure until this danger was removed, and after Philip's defeat by the Flemings in 1302 at Courtrai and the peace, it was, for a time, removed; just as in the parliament of Lincoln, when the barons combined with their king to repudiate the papal claim to order the affairs of Scotland, the prospect of greater unity at home seemed to be clearer.

Until the compromise reached in this parliament the opposition voiced in 1297 by Roger Bigod, earl of Norfolk, the marshal, and Humphrey de Bohun, earl of Hereford, the constable,[4] continued to express itself in demands for the firm observance of the Charters, and of the new articles in particular. At York, in January 1298, before joining the army at Newcastle, the magnates insisted on a public proclamation of the charters and of the sentence of excommunication against all who infringed them. At Roxburgh, six months later, the two earls required the king, as a proof of good faith, to swear, through the bishop of Durham, and the earls of Surrey, Gloucester, and Lincoln, that he would order a perambulation of the forests and observe other articles.

---

[1] See especially the letter to Bruce and Comyn of 6 April 1299 in Bain, ii, no. 1301 and pp. 535–6, where it is wrongly dated 1302.

[2] *Foedera*, II. i. 915.

[3] Ibid., pp. 955–6, May 1303: to Comyn as guardian from the bishops of St. Andrews and Dunkeld, John, earl of Buchan, James, the steward, John of Soules, Ingram de Umfraville, William Baliol, in Paris. The kings of England and France would meet, 'in quo tractatu rex Francie pacem nostram faciet, utilem pro regno nostro, ut idem rex nobis promisit firmissime'.

[4] The earl of Hereford died at the end of 1298; the earl of Norfolk was relieved by Edward from financial embarrassment in 1302, much to the king's advantage; see Guisborough, p. 352; and *King Henry III and the Lord Edward*, ii. 705–6.

At Carlisle, after the Falkirk campaign, the two earls, who had served at their own cost, were said to have expressed annoyance with the king's disposal of lands in Scotland and received licence to depart. The winter campaign of 1299, says the chronicler, was interrupted at Berwick because the magnates objected to the weather and did not wish to labour in vain unless the king observed his promises.[1] Indeed the postponements of the summons for June 1299 from one date to another had been partly due to this clamour for certainty. The king was distrusted. Here we must turn to events in England between his return in 1298 and the parliament of Lincoln in January 1301.

Edward in 1298 was determined on two things. He would fulfil his independent promises, made the previous year, to relieve the sufferings and grievances of his people, a congenial duty in line with his inquiries after his return to England in 1274 and again in 1289; and he would live on his own without resort to taxation either of clergy or laity, a decision which was compatible only with the reservation that at every turn he would exploit his prerogative and restrict to the utmost the operation of the additional articles contained in his confirmation of the Charters, a concession which had been wrung from him in the height of his necessity.[2] He combined a searching inquiry into malpractices—which was sorely needed[3]—with an assertion of his right to maintain strict supervision over any tendency to encroach upon his forests. After an arduous reign as a sovereign entrusted by God with the welfare of his people, a reign which would culminate in a great crusade, Edward felt that he had been tricked by his cousin of France, treacherously attacked by the Scots, and stabbed in the back by men at home to whom he looked for friendship and counsel. He would give these men the kiss of peace, and would seek an understanding with King Philip and, if they would respect their ties of allegiance, with the Scottish magnates, but he would not surrender his rights in Gascony and Scotland, and, rather than submit to the humiliations

[1] Guisborough, pp. 314, 324, 329, 332; cf. the editorial remarks, p. xxx.

[2] The narrative in Stubbs, *Const. Hist.* ii. 152–65, should be re-read in the light of H. Rothwell's paper in *Studies presented to Powicke*, pp. 319–32.

[3] Two cases are well worth study. One is of a corrupt chamberlain of the exchequer and supervisor of prise in Kent in 1297: see H. Rothwell, 'The Disgrace of Richard of Louth 1297', in *E.H.R.* xlviii (1933), 259–64. The other is the burglary of the great wardrobe, so far as it was deposited under the chapter-house of Westminster Abbey, in 1303, when the exchequer was still at York. This exciting and illuminating story can be read in full in Tout, *Collected Papers*, iii. 93–116.

endured by his father, he would rely, as long as possible, on his own resources. The orderly proceedings in his great parliament in 1305, when Scots and Gascons presented their petitions, were the measure of his fugitive success.

Edward, during the meeting of council after his return to England in 1298, began with an order for an account of the customs collected on wool since the declaration of war with France in 1294, and with writs for a general inquiry into the administration of the prises taken since the same date. At Newcastle, after the Falkirk campaign, he appointed a strong commission of bishops, earls, and barons, seven in all, to investigate the conduct of forest officials throughout England. The most significant of these ordinances was that for an inquiry into grievances connected with prise.[1] The rolls of the inquiry give a picture of the way in which the system of prise operated and of the co-operation between the local officials and the ports from which the goods seized were sent; but they do much more; they reveal, even more glaringly than the returns to the investigation of 1274, the extent of malpractices open to venal and unprincipled agents of the Crown. The commissioners, sitting with local juries, were especially required to distinguish between goods taken with and without guarantees of repayment; in the former cases payment would be made, in the latter compensation should be awarded the owner and punishment be meted out to the official concerned. They did not and could not distinguish between customary and excessive prises, just as the commissioners into forest abuses did not deal with the problems of forest extents.[2] Legislation on these matters came two years later in the Easter parliament of 1300.

In 1299 at an Easter parliament the magnates reminded the king of the sworn assurances which had been given on his behalf at Roxburgh.[3] By this time there was open talk in wider circles that he did not intend to keep his promises to observe the Charters. Even the Bury chronicler speaks of the exasperation

---

[1] See W. S. Thomson, *A Lincolnshire Assize Roll for 1298* (Lincoln Record Soc., 1944) for this inquiry; cf. my observations in *E.H.R.* lxi (1946), 261–4, on the importance of this edition of one of the returns. The ordinance is printed on p. 136; the orders to the commissioners in groups of shires in *Foedera*, i. ii. 891.

[2] During Edward's absence, on 26 November 1297 (*Parl. Writs*, i. 396), the council of regency had ordered a perambulation of the forests in accordance with the Charter of the Forest; but little was done until the orders of September 1299 and April 1300. On the whole matter see Petit-Dutaillis, *Studies supplementary to Stubbs*, ii (1915), 218–27.   [3] Above, p. 697; Rishanger, p. 190.

which his verbose ambiguities aroused among the barons.[1] The reference is to statements contained in a miscellaneous statute issued on 2 April in which, without any reference to the additions of 1297, Edward confirmed the Charters of Henry III, but omitted the clauses (1–5) of the Forest Charter about the deforestation of earlier encroachments. Edward here declared that he was determined to observe the Charters and to hurry on a perambulation as soon as the very important negotiations with France and at the Roman court were completed and his counsellors were more at liberty; but, he stated, the reports of the commissioners must be submitted to him for scrutiny before any execution of them. He must safeguard his oath to maintain the rights of the Crown and his interests and those of others.[2] When the confirmation was read with these reservations at the cross of St. Paul's, the gratification of the crowd 'turned to curses'. The indignant barons were pacified by fair words at a later meeting, and in September a start was made with the perambulation of the forests; but Edward had revealed his mind, and suspicion was rife. After the fall of Stirling and during his frustration on the border at the turn of the year (1299–1300), he realized that he must clear the air. He issued writs from Berwick for a fully constituted parliament of all sections of the community to meet in Lent; and also ordered writs to be made 'as strong as possible' for the levy of the feudal host, the army which gathered for the Galloway campaign in the summer.[3]

In the parliament of Westminster in March 1300 there was much debate among the barons. Heads of proposals were presented, and the outcome was fresh articles *super cartas* in which the grievances about prises, forests, and other matters were met, so that the sufferings of the people caused by the wars might be allayed.[4] The Charters, as granted by Henry III, were again confirmed, that of the Forest this time in full, and in charter form, not by letters patent; that is to say, the copies, as inspected and confirmed by the king on 28 March, were attested under their seals by a crowd of bishops, earls, barons, and others. 'The long lists of witnesses are convincing proof of the importance

---

[1] *E.H.R.* lviii (1943), 72; Guisborough, pp. 329–31, and Trivet, pp. 375–6.

[2] In the statute *de finibus levatis* (*Statutes*, i. 126 ff. of 2 April). On the diplomatic activity in this year see Mary Salt in *E.H.R.* xliv (1929), 273; cf. above, p. 653.

[3] Cf. an order to the chancery dated 1 January, *Cal. Chancery Warrants*, i. 106.

[4] Draft articles survive in the Acland-Hood collection (*Hist. MSS. Commission, Sixth Report* (1877), App., pp. 344–52). See Rothwell, op. cit., p. 327.

attached to the occasion.'¹ The safeguards for the observance of the Charters, in spirit as well as letter, were issued in a separate list of concessions. The first of these, made by request of parliament, took the form of sanctions of the kind so often required by the clergy or familiar to the baronial governments of 1258–9 and 1265. The Charters were to be published in full county court four times a year, and infringements of them were to be heard, determined, and punished by three good men, elected in each shire. The other articles were issued as acts of royal grace so that the people might be more willing and better able to give the king their service and aid. They provided remedies for the maladministration of the king's right of prise, dealt with the jurisdiction in the courts of the marshal, constable, and the constable of Dover castle, restricted the use of the king's privy seal and a few other matters; but they did not meet a demand that the king should punish his ministers and judges who infringed the Charters in the course of their normal official duties. The responsibility here, as he had shown after his return from Gascony, was his; there could be no tampering with his control, no return to the schemes of the previous reign. Edward, in fact, had not conceded much that he had not shown himself ready to do in earlier years. A clause saving the right and lordship of his crown was inserted in the ordinance announcing the *articuli super cartas*; and, while the perambulation of the forests was hurried on, no decisions about the reports would be made until the next parliament.

Parliament was summoned to meet at Lincoln on 20 January 1301. The writs are dated Rose Castle (the home of the bishop of Carlisle), 26 September 1300. Those addressed to the bishops and abbots refer to the business of the forests, those to the earls and barons refer to no special business, those to the sheriffs order them to send the knights and burgesses who had attended the last parliament and have others elected only when the death or incapacity of the former members made this necessary; but other writs, addressed to groups of canonists, judges, and to the chancellors of the universities of Oxford and Cambridge, refer to business of another kind, namely the doubt expressed in some quarters concerning the rights of the king in Scotland and the desire of the council to hold 'special colloquy' with them and with four or five scholars learned in the law from each university.

¹ Rothwell, l.c. Cf. V. H. Galbraith, *Studies in the Public Records*, p. 148.

In November the prior provincial of the Dominicans and the minister provincial of the Franciscans were summoned to appear at Lincoln, each with two or three of the wiser brethren of his order. Moreover the official 'remembrances' about the Scottish business and the chronicles and archives of deans and chapters, the cathedral monasteries, and some thirty-three more religious houses were searched for evidence.[1] All this preparation was required because it was intended at Lincoln to reply to the letter of Pope Boniface, brought by the archbishop of Canterbury to the king at Sweetheart abbey a month before the date of the parliamentary writs.[2] The king and his advisers had welcomed a chance of relaxing political tension in a combined resistance to the papal claims.

It would be hard to say whether the king felt more strongly about the forests or about the papal intervention in Scotland. There had been no urgent reason why perambulation of the forests should have become the test of royal good faith. Disputes about forest boundaries had always been tiresome since in 1217 the great marshal and his colleagues had definitely decided to fix them as they had been when King Henry II was first crowned. Edward was quite prepared to restrain abuses and maladministration in the forests; certainly he was not more indifferent to them than were baronial lords of parks and woodlands. The truth seems to be that the imagination of both king and barons had been fired by this example, affecting the resources and amenities of each, of the issue raised in the name of the Charters. Some attempt seems to have been made during the Galloway campaign to come to a settlement before parliament met. The whole chancery was required to appear at Holme Cultram abbey in Cumberland on 11 September 1299, a fortnight before the writs for parliament were ordered, and to summon the justices appointed to make the perambulation to meet there 'the earls, barons and other great lords according to agreement'.[3] If this conference was held it effected nothing. In writs issued to the local commissioners in the shires Edward, requiring their attendance with their returns at Lincoln, explained that the whole business could only be matured there, after due consideration of the reasons (*rationes*) for their findings in the presence of those bound by oath, as the king was himself, to maintain the

---

[1] *Parl. Writs*, i. 88 ff.   [2] Above, p. 693.
[3] *Cal. Chancery Warrants*, i. 114.

rights of the realm and the Crown.[1] Edward was determined that the reports of the commissioners should provide material for examination, not verdicts to be enforced.[2] And at Lincoln he was compelled to give way on this precise point as a condition of the grant of a subsidy. In the Lent parliament of 1300 a twentieth had been granted under the same condition. Now it was raised to a fifteenth, to be collected after the perambulation had been enforced. The consequent delay compelled the king, as we have already seen, to anticipate by local persuasion the levies from the boroughs.[3] He never forgave this humiliation. In 1305 he reduced the effect of the perambulation by denying to persons who lived outside the new bounds of the forests the privilege of rights of common pasture within the bounds and by maintaining his rights of chase and warren on his demesne. In 1306, after Pope Clement V had absolved him from the oath, taken under duress in Flanders in 1297 and renewed by force of 'presumptuous instance' after his return to England, he annulled the disafforestations altogether, although he was careful to renew his orders for the relief of those oppressed by corrupt forest officials.

The papal bull of 29 December 1305, though it released Edward from his various concessions, did not affect the Charters as such. They were and remained part of the law of the land. The *inspeximus* of 1300 became the standard text, frequently confirmed, and 'most commonly included in the manuscript and printed volumes of the statutes'.[4] The view that political controversy ceased after Edward's time to revolve round the Charters is true just because they were part of the law and only incidentally affected current problems in parliament. Edward had resented not his duty to observe the Charters but the attempt to take advantage of his difficulties. From the first he had reserved his obligation to scrutinize with his advisers the results of the perambulations, just as the king in parliament today has the right to legislate or not on the findings of a royal commission. He was the sovereign. He used the papal dispensation to maintain this right, and he seems to have used it for little else. The

---

[1] *Parl. Writs*, i. 88 (writs of 25 September 1300).

[2] How carefully he prepared for this appears from his orders for the searching of records, including Domesday Book, in both York and London (*Cal. Chancery Warrants*, i. 120 (November 1300).   [3] Above, p. 534.

[4] Faith Thompson, *Magna Carta: its Role in the making of the English Constitution, 1300–1629* (1948), p. 5.

charge on which he has stood at the bar of historical judgement is that he made use of a friendly Gascon pope to seek relief at all. His reply might be that whatever a pope could or could not do he could and should relieve a man from an oath taken unwillingly under the stress of circumstance. That papal duty was part of the law of the Church. His was the only tribunal to which the victim of such an oath could appeal.

To return to the parliament in Lincoln, Edward's sense of outrage—his own word—was intensified by the way in which the prelates, led by Archbishop Winchelsey, and the magnates drove their success home. Through Henry of Keighley, one of the knights of the shire for Lancashire, they presented a bill on behalf of the whole community, a form of procedure hitherto unknown. When, five years later, the king identified the knight, he sent him to the treasurer to be kept in honourable captivity in the Tower of London.[1] The twelve petitions contained in the bill were, in the main, such as the king could freely grant (*placet expresse*). They asked for the observance of the Charters and of the article of 1300 about prises, for a declaration that statutes contrary to the Charters were null and void,[2] for the speedy completion of the perambulation and the postponement of the collection of the subsidy meanwhile. A request that the powers of the justices elected in 1300 to enforce the Charters should be more clearly defined after the advice of the prelates and magnates had been taken was granted (*placet tacite*) with a gesture of silent consent, while a suggestion that any proceedings against the king's ministers should be taken by auditors acceptable to the prelates and magnates was refused—the king would find his

[1] Madox, *Hist. of the Exchequer*, 2nd ed. ii (1769), 108, prints the order to the treasurer, dated from Finedon, 5 June [1306], where the king was on that day (see Itinerary). Under another privy seal writ Keighley was released shortly afterwards on his oath not to offend against king or Crown. Stubbs, who copied the first writ (ii. 158, n.) wrongly, ascribed it to the year 1301. Keighley had been one of the knights first summoned by the regents to London in September 1297 but ordered to go north to join Warenne. At the same time he was elected one of the knights to attend parliament; again for the parliament at York in 1298. He was one of the justices elected under the *Articuli super cartas* to enforce the Charters (1300), and appeared at Lincoln in this capacity as well as in his capacity as knight of the shire. In April 1303 he was a commissioner of array in Lancashire. See the references in *Parl. Writs* (i. 686).

[2] Rothwell, op. cit., p. 330, n., points out that the so-called confirmation of the Charters of 14 February is in fact an assertion of this principle (see *Foedera*, i. ii. 927). Edward could hardly have been expected to issue another confirmation so soon after the stately document of 1300 (above, p. 700).

own remedy. The last article, a reminder that the prelates could not agree to the taxation of their temporalities as part of the lay subsidy without papal approval, was repudiated outright, although the magnates endorsed it.[1] The bishops and other ecclesiastics held baronies and lands of the king, and the king was sure that Winchelsey was the instigator of the impertinent persecution to which the bill had subjected him. He turned with relief to answer the pope's letter about Scotland.

The answer was twofold—a declaration dated 12 February bearing the names and seals of seven earls and ninety-seven barons in the name of the whole community, and an historical argument in the name of the king dated three months later (17 May) from Kempsey, during an Easter holiday in the valley of the Severn. The letter of the barons stated their resolution, after diligent deliberation (no doubt with the judges and others learned in the law) to maintain the rights of the Crown, even if the king were prepared to comply with the papal mandate. No king of England had been or should be responsible to any judge in matters affecting his temporal rights; the royal state and ancient custom required him to maintain his independence. The sealing of this document, of which many copies must have been made, took some time. The king's son, who had been created prince of Wales at Lincoln, and some lords of the Welsh Marches and elsewhere had gone home after the parliament, which presumably ended when the king left Lincoln on 1 March; and a responsible clerk of the wardrobe, Alexander le Convers, was sent to divers magnates of England with copies of the letter 'which was to be sent by the king to the supreme pontiff so that the seals of the same magnates might be imposed by their own hands'.[2] Edward's historical survey, submitted courteously to Pope Boniface for his earnest consideration, took longer to prepare. It begins with the coming to Britain of Brutus of Troy in the time of Samuel and Eli and continues until John Baliol's

[1] *Parl. Writs*, i. 104-5.

[2] In *Parl. Writs*, i. 102-4, two surviving sealed copies, then in the chapter-house of Westminster Abbey, are printed separately. For the seals see the lists, descriptions, and facsimiles in the *Ancestor* (1903-4), no. vi, 190-6; no. vii, 248-59; no. viii, 100-9. H. Maxwell-Lyte printed entries from the wardrobe account about the journeys of Alexander le Convers, ibid., no. vi, 189-90, at the end of a note by J. H. Round (pp. 184-9) on the admissibility of the barons' letter as proof of sitting in parliament. Some of those whose seals were sought may not, it is suggested, have been at Lincoln. Alexander le Convers had been sent to collect transport vessels between Hartlepool and Berwick in November 1299 (Bain, ii, no. 1112).

surrender of his kingdom and the submission of the prelates, magnates, and others of Scotland to Edward as their immediate lord. The conclusion to be drawn from the facts, says the king, is as clear as it is notorious. 'The kingdom of Scotland belongs to us *pleno jure*, by reason of *proprietas* no less than of possession.' His right and duty to repress the insolence of his rebellious subjects is unquestionable, and he will do or write nothing which could derogate from it in any way.[1]

After he had taken a well-earned rest in Worcestershire, mainly at Evesham and at his manor of Feckenham, where he spent Easter, the king proceeded to the north for the double campaign, described earlier in this chapter, from Carlisle under the new prince of Wales and the earl of Lincoln, and from Berwick under his own command. While he secured the inner country south of the Forth, his fleet made some impression from the Clyde on the lords of the isles. Edward and his son wintered at Linlithgow, and early in 1302 he renewed the truce with the Scots while the last important negotiations for a definitive peace with France were continued. In spite of the activities of their embassy in Paris, the Scots were excluded from the terms of peace.[2] Edward decided, after the expiry of the truce in December, to strike again, and this time, to use his own words, to make an end of the business. In November he again summoned the feudal host to meet at Berwick at the end of May 1303. Although his arrangements were minute he did not intend to take a great force but to depend on those tenants-in-chief who did not make fines with him for non-appearance, and on county levies of horse and foot. Local commissioners rather than the sheriffs were appointed to seek recruits, and doubtless troops of horse were raised in some cases by contract. Numerous entreaties were sent to the king's vassals in Ireland.[3]

Edward's incessant correspondence during the twelve months before he set out on his last Scottish campaign reveals the care with which the organization of the Marches was combined with the administration of Scotland south of the Forth. It was, indeed, a preparation for a future control of the whole country. In July 1302 he promoted his trusted friend, John of St. John, his captain in the north-west from the Mersey to Roxburgh, to be his lieutenant in Scotland, with powers over the three wardens

[1] *Foedera*, i. ii. 932–3.   [2] Above, pp. 654, 697.
[3] *Parl. Writs*, i. 361–73 *passim*.

of the March.[1] There seems to have been a council of high officials, with the cofferer of the wardrobe, Ralph de Manton, as its link with the king. John of St. John died in September, and was succeeded by John Segrave, the head of a distinguished English family, who had a position in Scotland comparable to that held so long by John de Warenne, earl of Surrey, now too old for service and near his end.[2] In the meanwhile, Ralph the cofferer, as paymaster and political missioner for the king, continued to organize the Scottish castles and sheriffdoms and to recruit the English gentry and other folk, especially in Durham and Northumberland. Indentures were made with the earl of Dunbar for the keeping of the castle and sheriffdom of Ayr, and with other castellans and sheriffs for Kirkintilloch, Linlithgow (shire and castle), Lanark (shire and Carstairs castle), Roxburgh, and Jedburgh, and with William Latimer and other leaders of troops stationed at Roxburgh.[3] A notable result of the king's campaign in 1301 had been the appointment of a sheriff at Peebles and the building of a new castle or 'peel' at Selkirk entrusted to Alexander of Baliol, the new warden of Selkirk forest.[4] Another result was the presence in the garrisons of the castles of men who served for lands held in Scotland; in September 1302, out of 508 officers, bannerets, knights, men-at-arms, crossbowmen, and archers, 113 served for lands, and 395 were in the king's pay. The castles were stocked with weapons and stores from Newcastle and Berwick, either directly or through the port of Leith. These arrangements may be regarded as typical of the way in which Scotland was held, so far as it was held, in the years to come.

Local forays from Berwick, Roxburgh, and Lochmaben were now followed by a more ambitious enterprise pending the king's arrival with his army. Segrave was to be the leader of this. In August he had been made warden of Berwick and at the end of

---

[1] Ibid. i. 364. In 1300 his great services had been recognized by a grant of lands in Galloway, for which, as the issues could not be collected, tenure for life of Cockermouth and Skipton castles and other lands in England to the annual value of 1,000 marks was substituted (Bain, ii, no. 1153).

[2] In 1300 Segrave had acted as lieutenant for the earl marshal in the Galloway campaign, and his brother Nicholas as lieutenant for the constable. He received the fee (*du veierage*) of £100 in 1302 (Bain, nos, 1145, 1146, 1323). Like Roger Bigod, John de Warenne was dropping out of the war; he died in 1304.

[3] Bain, nos. 1321, 1324.

[4] Bain, no. 1321, items 7 and 8; a report of progress in no. 1324. Cf. above, p 694.

September had been given general charge of the defence of the country. Then orders came in October from England that he and the cofferer should arrange an expedition as far as Stirling—still held by the Scots—and report upon the 'condition and news' of Scotland.[1] The expedition was probably not found to be feasible, for a more ambitious plan was prepared for January. Segrave was appointed the king's lieutenant. The cofferer was ordered to use his persuasive arts in Northumberland, where a local force of cavalry, to serve for eight days at its own charges and later for pay, was assembled at Wark-on-Tweed.[2] The result was not successful; indeed disgrace was narrowly averted. Segrave and Manton by 23 February had reached Roslin, a few miles south of Edinburgh. Whether Segrave intended to go farther south into the forest or west, by Linlithgow, to the area of Stirling is not known; in any case his forces, arranged in three divisions, were not prepared for the sudden attack which John Comyn and Simon Fraser, dashing north from the wild district between Lanark and Peebles, delivered on the following day, a Sunday. Segrave, his brother Nicholas, and sixteen other knights were captured; Manton was killed. Fortunately for Segrave, some of his force was not engaged; its leader was hearing mass not far away when he heard of the fight and was able to rescue him.[3] The English south of the Forth had still to keep to burghs and castles and be content with local raids.

Edward punctually left Roxburgh with his army in May, crossed the Forth on two wooden bridges which had been constructed at King's Lynn and sent by sea with a large escort of ships, and arrived at Perth on 11 June.[4] Here he heard of the peace arranged at Paris on 20 May, and, not without careful deliberation about its terms, triumphantly announced his ratification of it on 10 July.[5] The story of the next few months, until the king, in March 1304, held a Scottish parliament at St. Andrews, is rather like that of his progress before his last parliament, the great gathering at Berwick in August 1296. His

---

[1] Stevenson, ii. 444, 445, 448.   [2] Parl. Writs, i. 368–9.
[3] Guisborough, p. 352, gives Robert Nevill as the name of the rescuer—there is no official reference to him. He would be the elder son of Ralph Neville of Raby, and doubtless had been enlisted by Manton to come with the knights of Durham. He became famous in story as the 'peacock of the North', and was killed in a border fray by James Douglas in 1318. His father died in 1333.
[4] For what follows see especially Bain, ii, pp. xxxix–xlv.
[5] Foedera, I. ii. 958; cf. above, p. 654.

marches were punctuated by the siege of Brechin in August 1303, a long pause near Kinloss abbey in Moray to strengthen his hold on the north and receive submissions, and a still longer stay in Dunfermline abbey, where he resided from October to February with his son and, after her arrival at the end of January, with his French wife. Here, and in other parts of Scotland, men and communities, as in 1296, flocked to submit. John Comyn of Badenoch, the guardian who had taken the lead since 1298, capitulated with eleven companions on 9 February at Strathorde in Perthshire. The settlement reached in parliament at St. Andrews in March, when 'practically every man of note in Scotland seems to have been present',[1] was, indeed, wise and indulgent. Oaths of fealty and homage were to be renewed and fines of redemption were to be arranged; no lands were to be forfeited, no hostages given, no judicial action taken on past offences. The Scottish leaders might be required, however, to go into exile for a time. Only William Wallace and the garrison in Stirling castle, who had refused to surrender, were excluded from the terms. They were judged in parliament, according to rightful process and by the law of Scotland, to be outside the law.[2]

As later traditions and contemporary reports combine to show, the country was seething with the will to resist, especially in Moray;[3] but Edward had regained to his allegiance the Scottish leaders and could hope, through them, to start afresh with a new form of government. In the south a fierce local outburst on the western borders had tested the organization of the Marches, but in that part of the land the energies of Bruce, now, after his father's death, full lord of Annandale as well as of Carrick, could be depended upon. He and Segrave and the contingents from Ireland led by the earl of Ulster had earned the thanks of the king. For the prince of Wales and his companions the campaign had been a pleasure trip rather than a stern lesson in the art of war. Yet Edward's easy triumph was due as much to the change in the political atmosphere of the west of Europe as to the might of his knights and engineers. In August 1302 Pope Boniface, in letters to the Scottish bishops and to Robert

---

[1] *Scot. Hist. Rev.* xxv. 311.

[2] The records of the negotiations with Comyn and others are printed in Palgrave, pp. 272–8; cf. Bain for the dates, nos. 1419 (30 December 1303), 1444–63, 1473 (on exchange of prisoners). The best account of the parliament is in one of the manuscripts of Trivet's *Annales*, p. 402 n.

[3] Barron, op. cit., pp. 191–208, analyses the evidence for this statement.

Wishart, bishop of Glasgow in particular, had revealed a complete change of front. The bishops were rebuked as sowers of discord, deliberately leading their flocks astray, Wishart as a rock of offence; they were exhorted to compose all differences with the king.[1] The pope, now engaged in a new conflict with King Philip, was anxious to have Edward on his side.[2] King Philip also had ceased to urge on the Scots to resistance and was now confining his goodwill to bland assurances that he would make all well with them in discussions with his brother-in-law of England. When the bishop of St. Andrews and his colleagues returned to Scotland from their mission to Paris, where things had seemed so hopeful, they realized that they had been living in a fool's paradise. They joined Comyn and the rest of the Scottish lords in the renewal of their allegiance. The king could afford, he thought, to be generous.[3] He forgave the bishop of Glasgow, and even Simon Fraser.[4]

The campaign ended with the long siege of Stirling castle. The king settled down before the fortress from the end of April until its surrender towards the end of July 1304. The garrison in the castle was a small one, only some thirty persons. The siege was not hurried but, rather, turned into a social and military occasion with a display of twelve siege engines, each of which had its own name. A wardrobe account records payment for the construction in the king's house in the town of an oriole from which the queen and her ladies could watch the engines in action; a private letter, written on the day of surrender (20 July), states

---

[1] *Foedera*, I. ii. 942

[2] Trivet, p. 396, who was familiar with gossip in high quarters, goes so far as to say that the pope urged Edward to make war on Philip, but that Edward preferred to recover his rights by other means. Edward's hesitations about the new king of Germany, Albert of Austria (above, p. 654), suggest that discussions with him and his ally the pope had been going on. The pope in 1300 had made his financial deal with Edward (above, pp. 500, 670 n).

[3] The Scottish embassy had gone to Paris during the truce, under Philip's auspices (see his letter to Edward, 25 July 1302, in Palgrave, pp. 261–2). As late as May 1303 the ambassadors were urging their friends in Scotland to resist if Pharaoh hardened his heart (*Foedera*, I. ii. 955–6). Their optimistic letter when Philip ratified the peace with England is noted above, p. 697 n. Lamberton renewed his oath to Edward and got possession of his lands in May 1304 (Palgrave, p. 201; Bain, nos. 1455, 1529–31). Wishart, who had sworn fealty in October 1300, then rejoined the Scottish leaders, now sought forgiveness from Edward in March 1303 and took the oath to him at St. Andrews at Easter; see *Foedera*, p. 924, and the later account of his tergiversations in Palgrave, pp. 340–50.

[4] That Simon Fraser sought peace has been denied; but he was associated with Comyn as one of those who were to go into exile (Palgrave, p. 276); cf. below, p. 711.

that the king was permitting no man to enter the castle until it had been struck by the 'warwolf' (*loup de guerre*), a new engine which apparently had not yet been employed.[1] On the morrow Edward announced to the barons and knights assembled at Stirling that he proposed to issue an ordinance about the rewards to be made to them and to others who had served him on campaign. He begged them to make their requests at once; but after much consultation the warriors asked that the matter should be deferred to the next parliament in England. The king agreed.[2] He appointed John Segrave his justice and captain south of the Forth, and the earl of Athol north of the Forth. He tried to make sure that Wallace, now an outlaw at large, would be captured by the promise of leniency towards those who, like John Comyn and Simon Fraser, might be required to go into exile, and in the settlement of ransoms, if the outlaw were caught and handed over to him. Three ex-guardians, the steward, Ingram d'Umfraville, and John of Soules, would remain 'outside the power of the king' until this was done. The bishop of Glasgow was required to live south of the Trent so long as the king should ordain.[3] Edward began his return to England in mid-August. The exchequer and other branches of the administration established at York since 1298 were sent back to London.[4]

All the evidence available about Edward's plans suggests that he intended the government of Scotland to be similar to that of Ireland.[5] The magnates of Scotland, assembled in parliament at Scone or elsewhere, would deal with affairs and matters referred to them from England.[6] The official element would be derived in part from England but mainly from Scotland. Scottish, like Irish and Gascon petitions would be received in parliament in England, to be answered there by the triers or sent with instructions to the king's lieutenant and other high officials in Scotland.[7]

---

[1] Bain, ii, pp. xlii–xliii and notes; and particularly nos. 1560, 1599. For a list of the barons and knights present at the siege see Palgrave, pp. 267–74.

[2] Palgrave, pp. 274–5. They expressed a general wish to have wardships of marriages, offices (*baillie*), and franchises.

[3] Ibid., pp. 275–7.   [4] Above, p. 688.

[5] See Richardson and Sayles in *Scot. Hist. Rev.* xxv. 311–13.

[6] The lieutenant seems to have held a parliament at Scone after Lent in 1305, for a petition that the statute of merchants should run in Scotland was referred to the decision of the magnates of Scotland in parliament at Scone (*Memoranda de parliamento, 1305*, ed. Maitland, pp. 178–9).

[7] See the replies to the Scottish petitions received in the Lent parliament at Westminster 1305, ibid., pp. 168–232. Cf. pp. lix–lx.

Statutes made in England might be enforced, if the king wished, in Scotland as they were in Wales and Ireland.[1] The king began preparations for a 'form of peace' in Scotland in the full parliament which he summoned in November 1304 to meet in the following February. The rich records of this assembly, as we have already seen, give a remarkably clear idea of what an English parliament was like at the end of Edward's reign.[2] Much business was done; and one of the king's first acts was to consult three leading Scottish magnates who were available about the way to proceed. These were the bishop of Glasgow, Robert Bruce, and John Mowbray. They reported that in their view a meeting of the *communa* of Scotland should be summoned to elect ten persons who should represent it at a parliament in England. The king accepted the suggestion.[3] The Scots met at Perth in May to elect their representatives; ordinances for the settlement of Scotland were made in parliament in September. By this time William Wallace had met his fate. He was betrayed and captured in or near Glasgow in May, taken to London, tried in Westminster Hall on 23 August, condemned and, with no delay, dragged by a horse from the Hall to the Tower and thence to the Elms in Smithfield, where he was hanged and quartered. His head was impaled on London Bridge.

The ordinances of September were clear and precise. Scotland was to be governed by a lieutenant, a chancellor, and a chamberlain, the last-named with a department of finance at Berwick. The lieutenant was to have a council which, as first constituted, was composed of the officers and ministers of the Crown and twenty-two others—four bishops, four abbots, five earls, and nine magnates of Scotland. Justices were to be assigned to Lothian, Galloway, the land between the Forth and the mountains, and the mountain area. Sheriffs and escheators were to be appointed. The laws of King David, as amended and extended in later reigns, were to be revised in a Scottish assembly in accordance with 'God and reason', and the new code, with those hard matters for which the royal decision was required, was to be presented to the king by the lieutenant and elected Scottish

---

[1] A statute made in the Lent parliament 1305 against the levy of rents and other dues by foreign abbeys from their English houses and the export of the proceeds from England was deferred and finally issued in the Carlisle parliament of 1307, when it was applied to England, Wales, Ireland, and Scotland (see *Early Statutes*, ed: Berry, p. 240).

[2] Above, pp. 349–50.   [3] *Memoranda*, pp. 14–16.

commissioners three weeks after Easter 1306.[1] The king was so
pleased with the plan that in October he rescinded the decrees
of banishment, even of Simon Fraser, and let the Scottish leaders
off with ransoms of three or four years' issues of their lands. The
lay followers of Comyn were required to pay the annual value
for two years, the clerics for one year, except the bishop of Glasgow, who was to pay for three years.[2] John of Brittany was
appointed lieutenant, John de Sandale treasurer. Lamberton
acted as chief warden until the lieutenant could arrive. Both
Earl Robert Bruce and John Comyn were among the new
counsellors.[3]

The new government was settling down to work when, on 10
February 1306, all was thrown into confusion by the murder of
John Comyn at Dumfries and by the coronation of Bruce at
Scone a few weeks later (25 March). The secrets of this dark
story can never be fully known. The Red Comyn and the Bruce
had always been rivals. Yet as neighbours at Lochmaben and
Dalswinton, they may well have arranged to meet at Dumfries
while the royal justices were in session there and to withdraw to
the church of the Greyfriars for conference. The future was uncertain. The king was known to be in bad health, and in fact had
already been stricken by the disease from which he died. It may
be true that Bruce, remembering his grandfather's compact
with his fellow competitor the count of Holland,[4] suggested
something similar to Comyn—that if either should obtain the
kingdom he should give his own lands to the other—and that
Comyn had threatened to betray the suggestion to the king.
Whatever the reason was, the story runs that Bruce stabbed
Comyn, Comyn's uncle Robert attacked Bruce, and Bruce's
brother-in-law Christopher Seton cut Robert down. Comyn
was dispatched by Bruce's squires by the high altar or after he

[1] *Parl. Writs*, i. 160-2, including the names of the ten Scots and twenty English
commissioners. A tract on the Scottish king's household, edited and translated by
Mary Bateson in the *Miscellany of the Scot. Hist. Soc.*, ii (1904), 31-43, has been
ascribed to this period, but the argument is not altogether convincing.

[2] *Foedera*, II. i. 974-5. The decisions about banishment, &c., had undergone
some changes, in parliament at St. Andrews and after the fall of Stirling, since the
first agreement at Strathorde in February 1304, printed in *Rot. Parl.* i. 212-13.

[3] For these and other appointments see *Foedera*, II. i. 975; Palgrave, pp. 292-3. As
the lieutenant could not go to Scotland for some time, the bishop of St. Andrews,
the treasurer, and two others were made wardens. At first the bishop and Brian
fitz Alan were chosen, but Brian, who died later in this year, did not take office.

[4] Above, p. 611 n.

had been taken into the cloister.[1] That Bruce had not expected
the fatal result of the interview may be believed, but that he had
already planned a *coup d'état* seems to be clear from the rapid
sequence of events. He seized the castle of Dumfries and imprisoned the justices in session; his coronation in March was
attended by the bishop of St. Andrews, the senior of the four
wardens of Scotland, the bishop of Glasgow, the earl of Athol,
recently warden north of the Forth, the earl of Lennox, and
many more. The countess of Buchan, though she had married
John Comyn's cousin, set Bruce in the seat of royalty as the
representative of her brother the earl of Fife. Few of those present
could have had cognizance of the tragedy at Dumfries until they
got Bruce's version of it; but Bishop Lamberton was later accused
of hurrying to Scone on the very day on which the council was
discussing at Berwick what action was to be taken about Comyn's
violent death.[2] Indeed, nearly two years earlier, in June 1304,
during the siege of Stirling, Lamberton and Bruce had entered
into a mutual compact of defence against any who should
threaten danger to them, a compact which, whatever it meant
in 1304, shows that the two men had renewed their friendship
while they were in Edward's court.[3] Finally, it is clear that before
and after his coronation Bruce gathered a considerable following. The bishop of Moray is said to have agitated on his behalf
as for a crusade.[4] King Edward had declared in October 1305
that he was prepared to confide in the Scottish leaders; and his
illusion was the measure of his fury against Bruce, the earl of
Athol, Simon Fraser, the bishops, and all the other traitors
whom he had trusted so recently with power and responsibility. This time he had to deal not so much with the 'middle

[1] The detailed story told by Thomas Gray in his *Scalacronica*, ed. Stevenson
(1836), p. 129, is translated, to be ridiculed, by Barron (pp. 179–80), but should
not be dismissed so lightly, in spite of Gray's embroideries. The story told to
Edward at the time was certainly that Bruce killed Comyn because the latter refused to aid him in an act of treason (Palgrave, p. 335).

[2] So in the charges against the bishop sent to Pope Clement (Palgrave, pp. 335–6).

[3] The indenture, dated 11 June 1304 at Cambuskennath near Stirling, was
copied and carefully described from Bruce's part of the cirograph, after identification by Lamberton himself, at Newcastle in August 1306. It does not in itself go
further than other documents of its kind. It is merely a pledge of mutual protection; but it omits the usual clause saving the faith of the parties to the king. See
ibid., pp. 323–5.

[4] He preached that those who fought for Bruce would acquire as much merit
'quam si in Terram Sanctam contra Paganos et Saracenos proficisserent' (ibid.,
p. 330). Barron (pp. 224–35) gives a useful list, with comments, of Bruce's supporters.

folk', whom he bore no ill will, but with greater men who had recently co-operated with him in the drafting of a new Scottish government.[1]

The news of disturbances in Scotland reached the king at Winchester at the end of February, and he at once began to order stores to be collected with a view to military operations in the summer; but it was only later that he learned the facts. Early in April he created two commands, one under his cousin Aymer de Valence in Yorkshire, Northumberland, and Lothian, the other under Henry Percy in the north-western shires of England and Galloway. In May he was carried to Westminster and rallied the young knighthood of England at the great feast which has already been described in a previous chapter.[2] The tournaments which had been arranged since the return of the barons and knights from the siege of Stirling were prohibited throughout England, and a more serious gathering of barons, knights, and foot, especially from the northern shires, was summoned to meet at Carlisle early in July.[3] In a parliament held in June, a light subsidy of a twentieth and thirtieth was granted and the king annulled the results of the perambulation of the forests.[4] In the same parliament two papal bulls were proclaimed, the one absolving the king from his oath to observe the articles of 1297, the other anathematizing Bruce.[5] In the meanwhile the prince of Wales and his company were hastening north. They entered Scotland from Carlisle, took Bruce's castle of Lochmaben on 11 July, and pushed on to join Aymer de Valence at Perth.[6]

The prince arrived in Scotland to share in the aftermath of victory, for in June Bruce's rising had collapsed. His force of earls and landholders was too small, his resources too casual, to overcome the efficient system created in Scotland between 1301 and 1305. The system held firm. Aymer de Valence had made Perth his headquarters, and on 20 June routed Bruce at Methven, six miles away. Bruce tried to rally in the west, but was again

---

[1] Edward authorized his officials to bring the middle folk to the king's peace, unless they had been concerned in Bruce's activities, and is said to have rebuked his son for maltreating them. Cf. the ordinance in *Foedera*, I. ii. 995–6.

[2] Above, p. 514.

[3] *Parl. Writs*, i. 374–7.

[4] Ibid., i. 164–7. The subsidy was granted as an aid for the prince's knighthood.

[5] The bull excommunicating Bruce was issued at Bordeaux, 18 May (*Foedera*, I. ii. 987).

[6] For the war in 1306–7 see Bain, ii, pp. xlv–lii; Barron, pp. 236–78.

defeated at Dalry by John of Argyll, the lord of Lorne.[1] His brief effort had been broken by the Scots themselves rather than by the English, but by Scots who could rely on a competent military administration and an organized commissariat on land and sea.

Edward showed no mercy to the insurgents. Twelve knights captured at Methven were hanged at Berwick on various charges. The bishop of Glasgow, captured in Fife before the battle, was sent to Porchester castle, to be kept there in irons. The bishop of St. Andrews, who had surrendered himself to Aymer de Valence, was sent, after an examination at Newcastle, to Winchester castle, to be kept in irons. The abbot of Scone was kept in irons in the castle of Mere in Wiltshire. The earl of Athol and Simon Fraser suffered Wallace's fate in London, Christopher Seton was executed at Dumfries. Bruce eluded capture, but the members of his family and the countess of Buchan were rounded up. One brother was executed at Berwick, two others at Carlisle. His wife, sisters, and daughter were taken by the earl of Ross from sanctuary at Tain, far to the north. Elizabeth de Burgh, Bruce's second wife, whom he had married in 1302, was a daughter of his friend the earl of Ulster, always a staunch vassal of the English king; she disapproved of her husband's behaviour and was treated by Edward with consideration in her captivity at Burstwick in Holderness.[2] Bruce's sisters, Elizabeth Siward and Christina Seton, were imprisoned in England, and his daughter by his first wife was sent to the Gilbertine house at Watton. Another sister, Mary, and the countess of Buchan, whose political sympathies were so different from those of her husband, were treated with peculiar ferocity. Wooden cages were constructed in turrets in the castles of Roxburgh and Berwick, one for Mary, the other for the countess. There they were confined, served only by Englishwomen, and debarred from all other contact with the world.

The king superintended these and innumerable other things during his slow progress northwards in a litter, first to the eastern

---

[1] Probably Dalry in Ayr. John of Argyll held Ayr and the district in 1307 (Bain, no. 1957).

[2] She complained to Edward that his bailiffs were not giving her and her attendants the honourable sustenance promised (Bain, no. 1963). The provision made for her comfort was honourable, if the royal orders were observed (Palgrave, pp. 357–8). She is said to have compared Bruce and herself to children playing at being kings and queens.

Marches, then across to Lanercost priory, not far from Carlisle, where he lay ill for five months (29 September 1306 to 4 March 1307).[1] Before he left Winchester for the celebrations at Westminster he had decided the fate of Archbishop Winchelsey, whom he regarded, with the perversity of a sick man, as the main cause of his troubles.[2] The archbishop's highly meritorious career shows how important co-operation between king and primate was. Since the days of Becket every archbishop except St. Edmund, even Pecham, had been able to maintain it through good times and bad. Winchelsey could not do this, however hard he tried. He was the victim partly of a rigid conscience but probably more of the strains and stresses at court after the outbreak of the war with France. Even the unity of his province was threatened; it became the fashion for a bishop in the service of the Crown to seek relief from his metropolitan by appealing to the curia. In February 1297 the bishop of Winchester obtained from Pope Boniface exemption for his life-time from the jurisdiction of Canterbury. In 1298 Walter Langton, bishop of Coventry and Lichfield, the treasurer of the exchequer and the king's right-hand man, sought the same exemption, though in vain. In 1302 Winchelsey wrote to several cardinals that even the monks of Ely, because he had refused to confirm the election of their bishop, were conspiring to follow the same course.[3] Moreover, in this period of intense diplomatic activity, when embassies passed to and fro and English proctors were as busy in the curia as papal agents and merchants were in the English court, the archbishop, himself familiar with the papal entourage, tended to lose something of his traditional prestige in England unless he could retain the royal confidence.

If he had not enjoyed good relations with his cathedral church and its prior, the great Henry Eastry, Winchelsey would have been a lonely man indeed. His visitation[4] and disciplinary work were hampered, especially when he tried to control the treas-

[1] J. R. H. Moorman has compiled from the wardrobe accounts and other records a most interesting story of the king's long and unintended stay at Lanercost (*E.H.R.* lxvii (1952), 161–74). The accounts of expenditure on drugs are especially noteworthy.

[2] His petulant imprisonment of Henry of Keighley in July, on his way north, gives an indication of his state of mind; it was due to his hostility to the archbishop (above, p. 704). For what follows see Rose Graham's introduction to Winchelsey's *Register*, pp. xx–xxvii.   [3] Graham, op. cit., pp. xiv–xv.

[4] His visitation articles have been printed from a Cottonian manuscript in the *Registrum*, pp. 1289–1303.

urer's behaviour and to exercise jurisdiction over the royal chapels and to enforce residence in their benefices upon royal clerks. His anxieties were increased by his debts to merchants and a long controversy with the abbey of St. Augustine at Canterbury. The king was embittered by the archbishop's refusal to realize the need, as it seemed to him, for consideration for his difficulties in time of war. He was especially angered by Winchelsey's attitude to the Scottish question in its later phases, by his demand for Langton's dismissal from office, and by the articles presented, under his guidance, in the parliament of Lincoln. Edward's opportunity came when his subject Bertrand Got was elected pope as Clement V in 1305. Langton, sent as one of his representatives at the papal coronation at Lyons, was charged to explain to the pope the royal grievances against Winchelsey. In February 1306 Pope Clement suspended the archbishop and summoned him to answer the charges brought against him. Winchelsey went to see Edward at Winchester but with no avail. The king, reporting the interview to the pope, repeated his complaints: the archbishop had brought the kingdom to the edge of rebellion, 'he was spiteful and perverse'. On 19 May the archbishop left England from Dover. He never saw Edward again. The province and diocese of Canterbury were entrusted to papal commissioners, including the new collector William Testa, whose exactions of first-fruits and other measures helped to excite the protests of the laity in the last parliament of the reign, at Carlisle.[1]

This full parliament had been summoned in November to meet at Carlisle in January 1307 for the consideration of a Scottish settlement (*stabilimentum*), but owing to the king's illness nothing seems to have been done.[2] The lead was taken by the clergy and laity in other kinds of business. Since the flight of Bruce Scotland had been comparatively quiet. The English and Scots who had served the king during the last three years began to reap their reward in the lands and rents of the insurgents.[3] Then, in February, the news came that Bruce had reappeared not far away, in Carrick. Bodies of foot were raised in various parts of England and in the Lowlands to help to hunt him

[1] See W. E. Lunt, *Financial Relations*, pp. 487–90, for a discussion of the pope's order to collect annates and the reaction of the clergy and laity at Carlisle.

[2] *Parl. Writs*, i. 181–91. See Richardson and Sayles in *E.H.R.* liii (1938), 425–37.

[3] Cf. the list of demands made to the king in 1304 and later, with notes of some of the grants made up to this time (Palgrave, pp. 301–18).

down.[1] Aymer de Valence encircled him in the neighbourhood of Glentrool, but he evaded his pursuers and, in May, some time later, defeated them in a fight at Loudun in Ayrshire. He was at large when the king died on 7 July.

Before he moved on to Carlisle in March Edward had begun to show more energy. He had been incensed by the departure from Scotland without leave of some of the knights in his service, including Piers Gaveston, whom on 26 February he again dismissed, under oath to leave England. The reappearance of Bruce and his success at Loudun roused the old warrior to fresh efforts. A report of affairs at Carlisle written on 15 May speaks of Edward's rage at the news of the retreat of the guardian and his force before 'King Hobbe', and refers to the coming campaign to be led by the king in person.[2] Another letter, written from Forfar on the same day, gives a very different impression, and shows how everything depended on the king's life. If Bruce appears in the north and help against him is not forthcoming, loyal men will become desperate, for, says the writer, the earl never had so much goodwill at his service as he has now. The preachers are spreading a prophecy of Merlin, how after the death of 'Le Roi Coueytous', the Scots and Welsh would unite and have everything as they willed.[3]

Edward, during the weary months at Lanercost and Carlisle, had fought for life. He had devoted physicians, and was grateful to them. Four or five days before he died at Burgh-upon-the-Sands on the Solway, he had set out, slowly and painfully, to lead his forces against his enemy. He had worked on the business of his realm up to the last.

[1] *Parl. Writs*, i. 379–80. On Bruce's adventures and return see Barron, pp. 248–79. [2] *Bain*, ii, no. 1979.
[3] Ibid., no. 1926, and text on pp. 536–7. For a literary expression of this prophecy see M. O. Anderson in *Scot. Hist. Rev.* xxviii (1949), 33–34.

BIBLIOGRAPHY

Note. The following list of authorities follows in general the arrangement of the bibliography contained in the preceding volume of this History, written by Dr. A. L. Poole. Articles and books on special points referred to in the footnotes are generally not included. *E.H.R.* = *English Historical Review.*

1. Bibliographies and Books of Reference.
2. Charters, Records, and Other Documents.
3. Narrative Sources.
4. Ecclesiastical Records, Letters, and Wills.
5. General and English Political History.
6. Law and Institutions in England.
7. Scotland.
8. Wales.
9. Ireland.
10. The Church in England.
11. The Social Order.
12. Literature and Art.

1. BIBLIOGRAPHIES AND BOOKS OF REFERENCE

See Poole, pp. 487–8.

2. CHARTERS, RECORDS, AND OTHER DOCUMENTS

Magna Carta in its revised confirmations and the Charter of the Forest of 1217 are printed in C. Bémont, *Chartes des libertés anglaises* (Collection de Textes, 1902). See also Faith Thompson's books, *The First Century of Magna Carta* (Minneapolis, 1925) and *Magna Carta, its Role in the Making of the English Constitution, 1300–1629* (Minneapolis, 1948). Royal charters and confirmations, so far as they were enrolled in the chancery, have been calendared for the period 1226 (when Henry III began to use his seal) to 1307 in the first three volumes of the *Calendar of Charter Rolls* (1903–8). Of the collections of texts and facsimiles mentioned by Poole (pp. 489–90) F. M. Stenton's *Transcripts of Charters relating to Gilbertine Houses* (Lincoln Record Society, 1922) is of special value for the introductory discussion on the private charter in the thirteenth century. Kathleen Major has set a standard for the collection of episcopal *acta* in her *Acta of Stephen Langton* (Canterbury and York Society, vol. l

(1950)). The editions and calendars published by local societies of the deeds of religious houses, honors, and manors and boroughs are too numerous to mention here. References to some of them can be found in Gross's *Sources*. On the great collection of Ancient Deeds in the Public Record Office, cf. the introduction to the first volume of the published *Calendar of Ancient Deeds* (1890). Cf. the *Index to the Charters and Rolls in the British Museum* (1900–   ) and similar catalogues of other libraries. The consolidated index to the ten volumes of Farrer and Clay, *Early Yorkshire Charters* (vol. x, 1955) should be noted; also G. R. C. Davis, *Medieval Cartularies of Great Britain: a short catalogue* (1958), especially valuable as a guide to the monastic cartularies mentioned below (p. 737, top).

The Public Records become more complicated and numerous as the thirteenth century proceeds. They should be regarded as part of history, helping to explain the structure of society, not merely as sources of information, though as sources their technical peculiarities have to be understood, e.g. the dating by the regnal year and the way in which the entries on the *dorso* or back of the membranes of a chancery roll fit chronologically into the entries on the *recto* or the front. In general see H. Maxwell Lyte, *Historical Notes on the Great Seal* (H.M. Stationery Office, 1926) and V. H. Galbraith, *An Introduction to the Use of the Public Records* (Oxford, 1934) with the bibliography, pp. 89–99; also the *Handbook of Dates*, ed. C. R. Cheney (Royal Historical Society, 1945).

Officers of the household, chancery, and exchequer, judges and local officials had to co-operate, and their dependence on each other is reflected in the records and in the repositories where they were kept. Judicial records and many documents of special importance were kept in the treasury of the exchequer. The records of chancery and exchequer dovetailed into each other. For example the scutage rolls, in which the names of those entitled to collect their scutage after a campaign because they had served or agreed to a fine in lieu of service, were derived from the office of the Earl Marshal in the army, were chancery rolls, and were transmitted to the exchequer for the guidance of the treasurer and barons of the exchequer. The scutage rolls of 1285–1324 are summarized in the *Calendar of Various Chancery Rolls, 1277–1326* (Stationery Office, 1912) alongside a calendar of the Welsh Rolls for 1279–94. See on this J. H. Round in *E.H.R.* xxviii (1913), 358–60. The early antiquaries, working as they did in several different places (e.g. Westminster Abbey and the Tower of London), did not draw distinctions so sharply as they have to be drawn by modern editors. Note, e.g., Henry Cole's *Documents Illustrative of English History in the Thirteenth and Fourteenth Centuries, from the Records of the Queen's Remembrancer* (Record Commission, 1844). The transition to order and method can be traced in the reports of the Record Commission and the annual *Reports of the Deputy Keeper* after the Public Record Office Act (1838). See Galbraith, op. cit., pp. 69–71.

CHANCERY. The Patent Rolls for 1216–32 have been printed in the Latin text in two volumes, those for 1232–1307 are summarized in the *Calendar of Patent Rolls* (9 vols.). The Latin text of the Close Rolls of Henry III is printed for 1216–27 in the *Rotuli litterarum clausarum*, 2 vols. (Rec. Com., 1833, 1844), continued in the twelve volumes of *Close Rolls*, Henry III from 1227 to 1272. The Close Rolls of Edward I are calendared in five volumes. An important volume, illustrating the use of the king's privy seal in instructions to the chancery, is the *Calendar of Chancery Warrants, 1244–1326* (Stationery Office, 1927). For the history of the privy seal and the business done in the king's wardrobe see T. F. Tout, *Chapters in the Administrative History of Medieval England*, vols. i–ii (Manchester, 1920). See also, with reference especially to pp. 336–7 and 662 above, P. Chaplais on drafts, rolls, and registers of privy seal in the time of Edward I and Edward II, in *E.H.R.* lxxiii (1958), 270–4. Types of documents which come under the heading of chancery are the Liberate Rolls (orders for payments), the Fine Rolls (records of payments due in return for grants of licences, pardons, &c., part of the quantity of 'fines' promised to the king in agreements about all sorts of things, e.g. in lieu of service on a military campaign), and the collections of records of negotiations and affairs in Gascony, Wales, Scotland, &c. The *Liberate Rolls* for the years 1226–51 have been published in three volumes (1916–37). For the Fine Rolls see *Excerpta e rotulis finium, 1216–72* (2 vols., Rec. Com., 1835–6) and *Calendar of Fine Rolls, 1272–1337* (4 vols., 1911–13). The rolls, registers, and files of documents relating to public business which was not recorded on the Patent and Close Rolls have not been edited or calendared, with the exception of the Gascon Rolls[1] and the Welsh and Scottish Rolls noted in later sections of this Bibliography; they are used freely, however, in the edition of Rymer's *Foedera* prepared for the Record Commission, vol. i, in two parts (1816). The *Foedera* draws much on the class of ancient correspondence, which comprises many letters written in a familiar and personal way, in Latin or French. A 'special collection' of documents formerly contained in the archives of the chancery and exchequer, it now consists of sixty-two volumes of which the first fifty-eight are briefly described in the *List of Ancient Correspondence* (P.R.O. Lists and Indexes, no. xv, 1902). Its value has long been recognized by British and foreign scholars: cf. Ch.-V. Langlois in *Journal des Savants*, new series, ii (1904), 446–53, and the preface to J. G. Edwards's useful *Calendar of Ancient Correspondence concerning Wales* (Board of Celtic Studies, Cardiff, 1935). W. W. Shirley's *Royal and other Historical Letters Illustrative of the Reign of Henry III*, 2 vols. (Roll Series, 1862–6) still valuable, is mainly derived from the Ancient Correspondence, and the Patent and Close Rolls. Recently the systematic publication of original diplomatic documents and the so-called 'treaty rolls' has begun. The first volume of diplomatic documents (chancery and exchequer), 1101–1307, is in the press. The first volume of the treaty rolls, containing ten rolls of earlier date than the French and German rolls, and covering the period 1234–1325, has been edited by P. Chaplais (H.M. Stationery Office, 1955).

EXCHEQUER. The records of the Exchequer become numerous in the thirteenth century, though the annual account or Pipe Roll is the main guide to the finances. The treatise of Thomas Madox, *The History and Antiquities of the Exchequer of England*, in the second edition, 2 vols. (1769), is still fundamental, both as a commentary and, in the absence of continuous series of printed texts, as a collection of extracts from the Pipe Rolls and other records. One Pipe Roll, that for 14 Henry III (1229–30), has been edited for the Pipe Roll Society by Chalfont Robinson (1927), another, for 26 Henry III (1241–2), by H. L. Cannon (New Haven, 1918). A few extracts or translations from the Pipe Rolls relating to particular counties for certain years have been published, e.g. for Northumberland. The annual Memoranda Rolls mainly prepare to advance the business before the Barons

---

[1] *Rôles Gascons*, ed. Ch. Bémont (Doc. inédits sur l'hist. de France, 1896–1906).

of the Exchequer and to record decisions made by them, contain matter of historical importance and have been constantly used by historical scholars, e.g. for the negotiations preceding the confirmation of the Charters in 1297 (above, p. 682, n. 2). For the roll of the king's remembrancer of 3 Henry III see *Proceedings of his Majesty's Commissioners on the Public Records, 1832–3*, ed. C. P. Cooper (Rec. Com., 1833). Another roll, for 14 Henry III (1229–30), has been edited by Chalfont Robinson (Pipe Roll Society, 1933). The range of returns of others than the sheriffs was greatly extended as the duties of keepers of the royal demesne, escheators, clerks, and commissioners responsible for wages of soldiers and labourers in the army, the building of castles, and towns, embassies, &c., were defined. Some of these have been edited or summarized by writers on various subjects. On the relations between these accounts and the exchequer and wardrobe see especially Tout's *Chapters* noted above. The normal financial co-operation between the Crown, chancery, judges, and exchequer, as expressed in the Originalia and estreat rolls, giving details of payments due to the king, is described by Mabel Mills in a long introduction to her edition of *The Pipe Roll for 1295, Surrey Membrane* (Surrey Record Society, 1924). This is the best exposition of exchequer procedure at the end of our period.

Few of the other rolls and of the great quantity of original accounts (on the king's remembrancer side of the exchequer) have been printed. The receipt and issue rolls have been used by students of the royal revenue (cf. J. H. Ramsay's *Revenues of the Kings of England*, 2 vols., Oxford, 1925, and Gross, pp. 423–4). Some for Edward I's reign are given in the *Calendar of Documents relating to Ireland*, ed. H. S. Sweetman (1875–86). For the rolls of receipts from Jewish sources, recorded in a department of the exchequer of receipt, see Hilary Jenkinson in the *Transactions* of the Jewish Historical Society, viii (1915–17).

One of the most valuable sources of information about the finances and the movements of the king is the series of wardrobe accounts preserved in the exchequer. Unfortunately the series as a whole has not been calendared. The earliest surviving wardrobe account (Jan. 1224–Apr. 1227) has been edited by Tout, op. cit. i. 233–8. The account of the controller of the wardrobe for 28 Edward I (1299–1300), in the Library of the Society of Antiquaries, was printed by the society in 1787 under the title *Liber quotidianus contrarotulatoris garderobe*. On the financial relations between the wardrobe, the exchequer, and other sources of revenue see Tout, ii. 85–130. For a good example of the interest and value of such records see the summary of the household roll of Edward, prince of Wales, for 1302–3 in Bain's *Calendar of Documents relating to Scotland*, ii. 364–70. Finally, the records of taxation should be noted. The proceeds of the lay subsidies granted to Henry III were not, like tallages and scutages, entered on the Pipe Roll, but accounted for by special commissioners. The totals of the earlier subsidies, to 1237, were entered in the *Red Book of the Exchequer* (iii. 1064). The various records which mark the stages in the assessment, collection, audit, and final account of a lay subsidy in Edward I's reign have been described by J. F. Willard, *Parliamentary Taxes on Personal Property, 1290 to 1334* (Mediaeval Academy of America, 1934), pp. 64–72, 313–21. They are (*a*) Local assessment rolls, mainly surviving in local possession; some of the few survivors from Edward's reign have been published or summarized in the proceedings of local societies, &c.; e.g. Lynn, 5 Edw. I, Dartford, 29 Edw. I (Gross, nos. 1962, 1955*a*). Two Colchester rolls of 24 and 29 Edw. I were, oddly enough, printed from a local source in *Rotuli parliamentorum*, i. 228–38, 243–65; (*b*) County rolls, summarizing for the exchequer account the local assessments in the shire (cf. Gross, nos. 1975*a*, 1978, 1983–4); see for these the introduction to the edition of the only surviving Surrey roll (assessment of 1332) in *Surrey Record Society*, No. xviii (1922); (*c*) The records of accounts of chief collectors, the audit and final account, culminating in the L.T.R. Enrolled Accounts, Subsidies. J. A. C. Vincent's *Lancashire Lay Subsidies*, i (1216–1307), published by the *Record Society for Lancashire and Cheshire* (1893), is a valuable examination of the subject, with texts. Eilert Ekwall, *Two Early London Subsidy Rolls* (Lund, 1951) contains the text of a London assessment made in 1292, arising out of the subsidy granted in 1290, but suggesting a tax higher than a fifteenth. The introduction is important for the social history of London.

In the year 1302 an assessment of knights' fees liable to an aid for the marriage of Edward I's oldest daughter was preceded by a collection of existing precedents in the exchequer in a handy form. The outcome was the *Liber Feodorum* in two volumes, commonly known from a name previously given to part of its contents as the *Testa de Nevill*. A faulty publication of this book by the Record Commission in 1807 has been superseded by the fine work *The Book of Fees* in three volumes (1920–31), the third volume entirely devoted to an invaluable index. The preface to the first volume, an illuminating essay, and the introductions to the various sections, explain the nature of the documents, which are generally edited from the original manuscripts still preserved in the Public Record Office. The famous *Red Book of the Exchequer*, ed. H. Hall (R.S., 1896), in three volumes, was begun with a similar intention about 1230 by Alexander Swereford, an exchequer official who later became one of the first 'expert' barons of the Exchequer. It contains some valuable material, added later, e.g. on Edward I's new coinage (above, pp. 632–4), but most of its contents relate to the twelfth century. See Gross, no. 1917.

LEGAL. As a link with the section on the exchequer the development of the exchequer as a court should first be noticed. Although always, as one of the expressions of the *curia regis*, a judicial body, its operations and records as a court began to be expressed about the time when Alexander Swereford and others were appointed to reside at the exchequer as barons (1234). For the history, records, and nature of the court see *Select Cases in the Exchequer of Pleas*, ed. H. Jenkinson and Beryl Fermoy for the Selden Society (1932); cf. *Select Pleas, Starrs and other Records from the Rolls of the Exchequer of the Jews, 1220–84*, ed. J. M. Rigg (Selden Society, 1902) and *Calendar of the Plea Rolls of the Exchequer of the Jews*, 3 vols. (Jewish Historical Society, 1905–29, vol. iii, ed. H. Jenkinson). It should be noted that public business was often done at the exchequer, e.g. an important case about the treasurership of York Minster, heard by the council of Edward I in the last year of the king's life, is recorded in the K.R. Memoranda Roll: see *Select Cases Before the King's Council*, ed. L. G. Leadam and J. F. Baldwin (Selden Soc., 1918), pp. 18–27.

Royal jurisdiction. For the records of cases in council, and in council in parliament, see *Rotuli parliamentorum* (1707) and above, pp. 344 n., 347 n. The series of Curia Regis Rolls (Poole, p. 492) has been continued for the years 1219–22 (vols. viii–x, 1938–49). The plea rolls of cases *corum rege*, and of common pleas in the Bench, have not been printed in full. An abstract of pleas made in the time of Elizabeth and James I and printed in *Placitorum abbreviatio*, Richard I–Edward II, published by the Record Commission in 1811, is still of much value in spite of the splendid labours of the Selden Society in their volumes of select cases; notably *Select Cases in the Court of King's Bench, Edward I*, ed. G. O. Sayles, 3 vols. (1916–19), where the emergence of this court is described; but see a revised view, in vol. iv (1957), p. xxx, and his Selden Society Lecture on the Court of King's Bench (1959), pp. 9–12. For merchant law cases which came before royal courts see *Select Cases concerning the Law Merchant*, vols. ii, iii, ed. H. Hall (1930–2); vol. i, ed. C. Gross (1908), deals with local courts of Piepowder. Three volumes contain the full texts of early rolls of justices in eyre: these are the rolls of pleas and assizes for Lincolnshire, 1218–19, Worcestershire, 1221 (1934), Yorkshire, 1218 (1927), Gloucestershire, Warwickshire, and Staffordshire, 1221–2 (1940). Lady Stenton's introductions are important contributions to the history of English common law in the time of the judges whose rolls were used by Bracton when he compiled his *Note Book* (ed. F. W. Maitland, 3 vols., 1887): see especially the volume for Lincolnshire and Worcestershire, with its study of Bracton and his predecessors. For Bracton and his famous treatise *De legibus et consuetudinibus Angliae* (ed. G. G. Woodbine, 1915–22) see also H. Kantorowicz, *Bractonian Problems* (Glasgow, 1941), and the literature to which it has given rise: C. H. McIlwain in *Harvard Law Rev.* lvii (1943), 220–40; F. Schulz in *Law Quarterly Rev.* lix (Apr. 1943), 172–80, and *E.H.R.* lx (1945), 236–76; H. G. Richardson in *E.H.R.* lix (1944), 22–47, 376–84. F. W. Maitland's early classic, *Pleas of the Crown for the County of Gloucester, 1221* (1884), should always be read.

On the records of the office of the coroners, so closely connected with the eyre, see *Select Pleas from the Coroners' Rolls, 1265–1413*, ed. C. Gross (Selden Soc., 1896). Pleas before itinerant justices and the final concords before royal justices provide essential material for the local historian; local societies have done much to edit, calendar, and catalogue such records of this kind as concern their shires and towns, e.g. *Three Early Assize Rolls for Northumberland*, ed. W. Page (Surtees Society, 1891), rolls of 1256, 1269, and 1279, with abstract of Feet of Fines; *Oxford City Documents*, ed. J. E. Thorold Rogers (Oxford Historical Society, 1891), containing pleas before the justices at Oxford in 1285, and coroners' inquests, &c., from 1297; *A Calendar of Feet of Fines relating to the County of Huntingdon, 1194–1603*, ed. J. G. Turner (Cambridge Antiquarian Society, 1913), with a good diplomatic survey of the nature, history, and study of final concords. A list of similar texts and calendars, which vary in merit, is given in Gross, pp. 457–63.

The Patent and Close Rolls contain much information about cases heard under special commissions, including assizes of novel disseision, &c. Record publications of special value are *Placita de quo warranto* (Rec. Com., 1818), *Rotuli selecti*, ed. J. Hunter (Rec. Com., 1834), including (pp. 105–265) pleas in four counties under the Dictum of Kenilworth; *State Trials under Edward I* (Royal Historical Society, 1906), see above, pp. 361–5; and *The Welsh Assize Roll, 1277–84*, ed. J. Conway Davies (Cardiff, 1940). Forest proceedings are illustrated in *Select Pleas of the Forest, 1209–1334*, ed. J. G. Turner (Selden Soc., 1901), with an important introduction. The returns to inquisitions which often preceded special commissions provide invaluable material, especially the *Rotuli Hundredorum*, 2 vols. (Rec. Com., 1812–18) on which see above, p. 359, n. 1; *Inquisitions and Assessments relating to Feudal Aids*, vol. i (1899), for Kirkby's Quest, &c. (above, p. 359, n. 2); *Calendar of Inquisitions, Miscellaneous*, vol. i (1916), containing, *inter alia*, a calendar of 'Inquisitiones de rebellibus', after the fall of Earl Simon; J. H. Round's review of this book is illuminating (*E.H.R.* xxxiii. 395 ff.); *Calendar of Inquisitions post mortem*, Henry III–Edward I, vols. i–iv (1898–1913), with the material in *Calendarium Genealogicum*, ed. C. Roberts, 2 vols. (1865). For calendars, abstracts, and translations of inquisitions *post mortem* relating to particular counties see Gross, pp. 484–91. These inquisitions by the escheators generally, but not always, saved the heirs and widows of the deceased from litigation. Cf. for the escheators F. M. Powicke, *King Henry III and the Lord Edward*, i. 105–8.

At this point the collections of texts and the legal treatises (apart from Bracton's), which deal with the administration of the law, may be noted. The most important are the *Summae* of the justice Ralph de Hengham, ed. W. H. Dunham, Jr. (Cambridge, 1932); cf. *Four Thirteenth Century Law Tracts*, ed. G. E. Woodbine (New Haven, 1910); *Select Cases in Procedure without Writ under Henry III*, ed. H. G. Richardson and G. O. Sayles (Selden Soc., 1941), illustrating procedure by petition in the royal courts; and cf. *Select Bills in Eyre, 1292–1333*, ed. W. C. Bolland (Selden Soc., 1914). Maitland's view that the Year Books or professional reports of cases have their origin in such works as the *Brevia placitata*, now in print, ed. G. J. Turner and F. T. Plucknett (Selden Soc., 1951), and the *Casus Placitorum*, now in print, ed. W. H. Dunham, Jr., together with *Reports of Cases in the King's Courts, 1272–8* (Selden Soc., 1952), has been confirmed by Dunham, whose introduction is the best guide to the history of the literature about the origin and nature of the Year Books. The Year Books which report cases of 20–22, 30–35 Edward I were edited in the Rolls Series by A. J. Horwood in 5 vols. (1866–79). Turner has ascribed the *Brevia placitata* to the judge John le Breton, who became Bishop of Hereford in 1269, and is inclined to rehabilitate him as the author of the French treatise *Britton*, ed. F. H. Nichols, 2 vols. (Oxford, 1865). For the legal treatise *Fleta*, ed. J. Selden (2nd ed., 1685), cf. above, p. 521 n. The text has been re-edited by the Selden Society, lxxii (1955); cf. C. A. F. Meekings in *E.H.R.* lxxiii (1958), 672–5, and, for the prologue, E. Kantorowicz in *Speculum*, xxxii (1957), 231–49. On collections of statutes, see above, p. 370.

Local Courts. In the introduction to the *Brevia placitata* Turner breaks new ground when he treats of the history of the register of writs and the writ of right and the importance, greater than has been supposed, of the county court. Very few records of the county court survive, except for those of Chester; see R. Stewart-Brown, *Calendar of County Court, City Court and Eyre Rolls of Chester, 1259–97* (Chetham Soc., 1926); and below, p. 750. Strangely, few legal records of the honour courts of lords survive. Maitland edited the rolls of the Abbot of Ramsey's court at Broughton (1255–60) in his *Select Pleas in Manorial and other Seignorial Courts* (Selden Soc., 1889), pp. 48–83; see also W. D. Ault, *Court Rolls of the Abbey of Ramsey and of the Manor of Clare* (New Haven, 1928) and A. J. Taylor, *Records of the Barony and Honour of Lewes* (Sussex Record Society, xliv, 1939), pp. 1–49, rolls of the Earl Warenne's court of the rape of Lewes (1265–6).

Rolls of manorial courts have survived in great number, especially when the manors with their records were held by or passed to corporate bodies like colleges or to the Duchy of Lancaster (*Report of the Deputy Keeper of Public Records*, xliii, Appendix i (1882), 206–362) though fewer have survived from the thirteenth century than one might have expected. The

following are the more important printed texts: Rolls of the
Bishop of Ely's court at Littleport, ed. in *The Court Baron* (Selden
Soc., 1891), 107–47; of the Prior and Convent of Durham's
court, extracted in *Helmota prioratus Dunelmensis* (Surtees Soc.,
1889); of some manors of Ramsey, Battle, and Romsey abbeys,
edited in *Select Pleas in Manorial and other Seignorial Courts*, ed.
Maitland, (Selden Soc., 1889), 86–183; of Ingoldmells, Lincs.,
translated by W. O. Massingberd (1902); of Alrewass, Staffs.,
ed. W. N. Landor in *Collections* of the William Salt Archaeological Society, new series, x, pt. i (1907), 245–93, and xiii (1910),
87–137; of Hayles, Worcs., from 1272 to 1307, ed. J. Amplelett
and S. G. Hamilton, 2 vols. in Worcestershire Historical Society
(1910–12); of Wakefield for 1274–1309, 2 vols. ed. W. P.
Baildon in Yorkshire Archaeological Society Rec. Series, xxix
(1901), xxxvi (1906). Other rolls have been edited in monographs, e.g. Frances M. Page, *The Estates of Crowland Abbey*
(Cambridge, 1934), pp. 331–40.

Some thirteenth-century tracts, composed as guides to precedents and procedure in manorial courts, were edited by F. W.
Maitland and W. P. Baildon in *The Court Baron* (Selden Soc.,
1891). The tract, *La court de baron* (pp. 19–67) was probably
compiled about 1268 by Robert Carpenter of Hareslade, for
whom see N. Denholm-Young, *Collected Papers* (1946), 96–110.
For other manorial records, ecclesiastical sources, and borough
records see later sections.

3. NARRATIVE SOURCES

The fullest narrative history was written in St. Albans in the
chronicle of Roger of Wendover to 1235, ed. H. O. Coxe, 5 vols.
(English Historical Society, 1841–4), and, not so well, by H. G.
Hewlett, 3 vols. (R.S., 1886–9), copied, enlarged, and continued by Matthew Paris till 1259 in his *Chronica Majora*, ed.
H. R. Luard, 7 vols. (R.S., 1872–83), and in the *Flores His-
toriorum*, ed. Luard, 3 vols. (R.S., 1890), first at St. Albans, till
1265, then at Westminster, till 1306. Matthew Paris's *Historia
Anglorum*, ed. F. H. Madden, 3 vols. (R.S., 1866–9), has independent value. The *Chronica* ascribed to William Rishanger,
a monk of St. Albans, ed. H. T. Riley (R.S., 1865) may have
been compiled in Edward I's reign for the years 1259–72 by
Rishanger, but the rest (1272–1306) is later still and probably
not his work. It shows knowledge of the official material in the

so-called *Annales regni Scotiae* (above, p. 602, n. 3) and of the *Annales Angliae et Scotiae* (1292–1300). A definitive study of the relation between the *Flores* and other chronicles and of the value of Rishanger is still needed. Wendover, Paris, and the Flores have been critically studied by F. Duffus Hardy in his *Calendar of Materials relating to the History of Great Britain and Ireland*, iii (R.S., 1871), pp. xxxii–lxxxv, by Luard in his fine prefaces, and by F. Liebermann in his edition of portions of the chronicle literature of England in the *Monumenta Germaniae Historica*, Scriptores, xxviii (cf. Gross, nos. 1774, 1830, 1864 for bibliographical notes). W. H. Stevenson's review of Hewlett's edition of Wendover in *E.H.R.* iii (1888), 353–60, is an important and characteristic piece of criticism. See also C. Jenkins, *The monastic chronicles and the early school of St. Albans* (1923), V. H. Galbraith, *Roger of Wendover and Matthew Paris* (Glasgow, 1844), and F. M. Powicke, in the *Proceedings of the British Academy*, xxx (1944), 147–60, where the view that Wendover continued a work of John de Cella, abbot of St. Albans, is controverted, and the chronology and method of Matthew Paris's historical work is discussed. For Matthew's *Vitae abbatum* and artistic work cf. below, pp. 739, 778. The most comprehensive study on the various aspects of Matthew's life and work is now Richard Vaughan, *Matthew Paris* (Cambridge, 1958); see *E.H.R.* lxxiv (1959), 482–5.

Next comes the Bury St. Edmunds and Norwich group. Putting aside a late chronicle (1020–1346), printed with other historical pieces in *Memorials of St. Edmund's Abbey*, vol. iii, ed. T. Arnold (R.S., 1896), 1–73, the historical interest here was maintained by John Tayster, to 1265, and by two successors (1265–95, 1296–1301). Their chronicle from 1152 to 1295 was edited by B. Thorpe as a 'continuation' of the chronicle of 'Florence of Worcester' (English Hist. Soc.), ii (1849), 136–96. The third part (1296–1301) has been edited by V. H. Galbraith, with a critical introduction on the Bury tradition, in *E.H.R.* lviii (1943), 51–78. A composite Norwich chronicle is an independent source for the years 1263–79 and 1285–91. In its present form it was put together and continued from 1291 to 1298 by a monk of Norwich, Bartholomew Cotton, whose name has been given to the whole. See the introduction to *Bartholomei de Cotton Historia Anglicana*, ed. Luard (R.S., 1859). In his part of the work Cotton copied a large number of documents.

It is significant that Cotton, if it was he, prefixed to the chronicle Geoffrey of Monmouth's British History (Luard, p. xix) in accordance with the prevailing fashion of interest (above, p. 515, and Laura Keeler in *Speculum*, xxi (1946), 27 ff.). The metrical chronicle in English of Robert of Gloucester, to 1270, useful for the later part of Henry III's reign, also begins with the story of Brutus; see W. A. Wright's edition, 2 vols. (R.S., 1887), and the authorities noted by Gross (no. 1783). Gross notes an unpublished metrical chronicle by T. Castleford.

The other main authorities, apart from the numerous annals, are the Life of William the Marshal, the Canterbury and Dover Chronicles, Walter of Hemingburgh, Nicholas Trevet or Trivet, and the chronicle of Lanercost. The metrical *Histoire de Guillaume le Maréchal*, ed. Paul Meyer, 3 vols. (Soc. de l'Hist. de France, 1891–1901), is of fundamental value for the years 1216–19. (Cf. for the war with Louis of France, the *Hist. des ducs de Normandie*, ed. F. Michel, Soc. de l'Hist. de France, 1840, the chronicle by an anonymous writer of Béthune in *Recueil des historiens de France*, xxiv. 750–75, and the similar work printed, with part of the Merton chronicle, by Petit-Dutaillis in his book on Louis VIII.)

The chronicles of Canterbury and Dover are represented by the continuations of the *Gesta regum* of Gervase of Canterbury, ed. Stubbs, in *The Historical Works of Gervase of Canterbury*, ii (1880), 106–324. That for the years 1242–79 (pp. 201–91) is a Dover chronicle. Stubbs gives a masterly appreciation of the value of the continuations and their relation to the Canterbury material. The annals from 1227 to 1241 are largely based on records and other texts, some of which are not found elsewhere.

The chronicle of Walter, a canon of Guisborough priory, Yorkshire, until recently known as Walter of Hemingburgh, ed. H. C. Hamilton, 2 vols. (Eng. Hist. Soc., 1848–9) is particularly valuable for the later years of Edward I and the Scottish wars. A new edition, much needed, has now appeared in the Camden Series, lxxxix (1957), by H. Rothwell under the title, 'The Chronicle of Walter of Guisborough'. This edition, containing a careful introduction and revised text, should be preferred to Hamilton's edition. The *Annales* of Nicholas Trevet to 1307, ed. T. Hog (Eng. Hist. Soc., 1845), was written after 1320, possibly for Edward II. Trevet was familiar with Edward I's court: see Ruth J. Dean in *Studies in Philology*, lxv (1948), 541–64. The Lanercost chronicle, 1201–1346, ed. J. Stevenson (Bannatyne

Club, 1839), and translated for the years 1272–1346 by Herbert Maxwell, with an introduction by James Wilson (1913), is based on a chronicle, now lost, by a northern Franciscan, Richard of Durham (to 1297), and continued by another Franciscan. This chronicle was extant and known to the Greyfriars of London in the early sixteenth century. Its gist survives in an altered, abbreviated, and interpolated version, made at the priory of Lanercost in Cumberland. See A. G. Little's paper in *E.H.R.* xxxi (1916), 269–79, reprinted in his *Franciscan Papers, Lists and Documents* (Manchester, 1943), pp. 42–54.

Peter Langtoft, a canon of Bridlington, wrote a chronicle in French verse from Brutus to 1307, ed. W. A. Wright, 2 vols. (R.S., 1846–8). For Edward I's reign this has contemporary value. A later translation in English verse by Robert Mannying of Bourne, a Gilbertine, was edited by T. Hearne, 2 vols. (Oxford, 1725). The translator inserted interesting local matter of his own; see Gross, no. 1816, for modern critical studies. *Political Songs of England from the Reign of John to that of Edward II*, ed. T. Wright (Camden Soc., 1839), includes poems on Simon de Montfort and Edward I, among them a famous tract, better edited by C. L. Kingsford, *The Song of Lewes* (Oxford, 1890). For other poems on Earl Simon see J. O. Halliwell's edition of the *De bellis*, which also contains the miracles of Simon, G. W. Prothero, *The Life of Simon de Montfort* (1877), Appendix iv, and Maitland, *Collected Papers*, iii. 43–49. For the hagiography of Simon see Bémont's *Simon de Montfort* (Paris, 1884), pp. xv–xix. A rhythmical tract against the 'Romans', *De humana miseria*, was printed by M. Esposito in *E.H.R.* xxxii (1917), 400–5.

Monastic and London chronicles are particularly important as material for English history in the thirteenth century. Annalistic notes form the basis of chronicles, great or small. The best known are those edited by Luard in the *Annales monasticae*, i–iv, with an index, vol. v (R.S., 1864–9). Those of Margam in Glamorgan, to 1232, Tewkesbury, to 1263, and Burton-on-Trent, to 1262, are printed in vol. i; of Winchester to 1277, and Waverley, to 1291, in vol. ii; of Dunstable (till 1242 by the prior, Richard de Morins, then to 1297), in vol. iii; of Osney, Thomas Wykes (to 1289) and Worcester and Bermondsey in vol. iv. Three London works are of more than local importance: the annals of St. Paul's, ed. Liebermann in *Mon. Germ. Hist.*, *Scriptores*, xxviii. 548–51, useful for the barons' war in Henry

III's reign; Arnold fitz Thedmar's 'Chronica majorum et vicecomitum Londoniarum', 1188–1274, ed. T. Stapleton in *Liber de Antiquis Legibus* (Camden Soc., 1846), a city chronicle valuable for its notes on general history and the relations between the Crown and the city; *Annales Londonienses*, ed. Stubbs in *Chronicles of the Reigns of Edward I and Edward II* (R.S., 1882), i. 1–251, based till 1301 on the *Flores* but independent and general for the last years of Edward I's reign. Other monastic annals and chronicles tend to be concerned mainly with local and domestic matters and often throw much light on monastic customs, manorial and economic history, e.g. the trade in wool, and lawsuits, though at least two short texts, the *Annales Cestrienses*, a chronicle of the abbey of St. Werburgh, Chester, ed. R. C. Christie, in *Record Society for Lancashire and Cheshire* (1887), and the *Annales Stanleienses* (on which the annals of Furness are based), ed. R. Howlett, *Chronicles of the Reigns of Stephen, etc.* ii (R.S., 1885) are mainly concerned with general affairs. The following also deal with our period: Robert de Graystanes, *Historia de statu ecclesiae Dunelmensis*, ed. J. Raine in *Historiae Dunelmensis Scriptores Tres* (Surtees Soc., 1839, pp. 33–123), depends in part on the Durham annals, 1207–86, ed. F. Barlow in *Durham Annals and Documents of the Thirteenth Century* (Surtees Soc., 1945, pp. 1–84). Cf. the *Gesta Dunelmensia* described above (p. 495 n.). Robert Swapham, continued by Walter de Whitlesey, compiled a Peterborough chronicle, 1177–1321, ed. with other Peterborough chronicles by J. Sparke in *Historiae Anglicanae Scriptores*, part iii (London, 1723), pp. 97–216; see W. T. Mellowes, *The Peterborough Chronicle of Hugh Candidus* (1948). A *Chronicon Petroburgense*, ed. T. Stapleton (Camden Soc., 1849), contains detailed accounts of lawsuits in Edward I's time, when it was compiled. Adam of Domerham wrote a similar history of Glastonbury, ed. in T. Hearne's *Adami de Domerham Historia de rebus gestis Glastoniensibus* (Oxford, 1727), ii. 303–96. Similarly the chronicle of Evesham, ed. W. D. Macray (R.S., 1863), the chronicle of Meaux compiled by Thomas Burton (d. 1437), ed. E. A. Bond, *Chronica monasterii de Melsa*, 3 vols. (R.S., 1866–8) and William Thorne's Chronicle (to 1397) of St. Augustine's Abbey, Canterbury, printed in Roger Twysden's *Historiae Anglicanae Scriptores Decem* (1652) and in translation by A. H. Davis (Oxford, 1934),[1] give faithful accounts of monastic life and economy. *The Chronicle*

---

[1] On this see the critical review in *Speculum*, ix (1934), 330–2.

of St. Mary's Abbey, York, ed. H. E. Craster and M. E. Thornton
(Surtees Soc., 1933), followed by the consuetudinal, is also
mainly concerned with domestic affairs at York and in the
daughter house at St. Bees. The Pershore annals, in Leland,
Collectanea, ed. Hearne (edition of 1774), i. 245, were continued
from 1265 at Evesham; cf. *E.H.R.* li (1936), 108–13, for an
important entry about the visit to England of Archbishop Odo
Rigaud of Rouen (1260). A short Battle Abbey chronicle, entitled *Brutus abbreviatus*, ends with the battle of Evesham; the
last part (1258–65) was printed by Ch. Bémont in his *Simon de
Montfort* (Paris, 1884), pp. 373–80. The chronicle *De Bellis*, ed.
J. O. Halliwell (Camden Soc., 1840), is probably a late production, written to glorify the baronial party and Simon de
Montfort. It is written with knowledge of Rishanger's chronicle
and contains some traditional information of significance.

A precious work, unique of its kind, is Thomas of Eccleston's
De adventu Fratrum Minorum in Angliam, ed. A. G. Little (Paris,
1904), revised in second edition (Manchester, 1951).

The monastic annals which are mainly concerned with
general affairs must be appreciated in the light of their relations with each other. They are not separate works of equal
value. Critical study was given great impetus by F. Liebermann,
Ungedruckte Anglo-normanische Geschichtsquellen (Strasbourg, 1879);
cf. his 'Annals of Lewes Priory' in *E.H.R.* xvii (1901), 83;
and M. Tyson on the annals of Southwark and Merton in
Surrey Archaeological Collections, xxxvi (1926), 24–57, with extracts. For the later part of our period N. Denholm-Young on
the Winchester–Hyde Chronicles in his *Collected Papers*, pp. 86–
95, and on Thomas Wykes and his chronicle, *E.H.R.* lxi (1946),
157–79 are especially valuable. The latter paper gives significance to an obscure canon of Osney Abbey as a well-informed
admirer of Richard, earl of Cornwall.

4. ECCLESIASTICAL RECORDS, LETTERS, WILLS

The archives of cathedral and monastic churches in the
middle ages held registers, volumes of memoranda, liturgical and
administrative customaries, letter books and miscellanea. Some
are still *in situ*, more scattered in libraries, probably most were
lost. These contain much of general historical interest, as well
as valuable material on the history of ecclesiastical institutions.
The writing in history could not be so regulated as a Worcester

annalist would have wished (*Annales monastici*, iv. 355). The annals of Rochester (Wharton, *Anglia Sacra*, i. 341–55) seem to have originated in notes written by a monk, Edward of Haden-ham (*c.* 1307) in a copy of the *Flores*; a monk of Abingdon made additions to a copy of Hemingburgh, which still survives (Gross, no. 1741) and so compiled a local chronicle from 1218 to 1304; but, indeed, the whole body of the material now to be reviewed reveals a preoccupation with the past.

The reports of the Historical Manuscripts Commission contain articles on most of the archives of the bishops, deans, and chapters. The most important for this period are on Canterbury in v (1876), 426–62, viii (1881), 315–55, ix, pt. i (1883), 72–129, and the first report on Various Collections (1901), 205–81, with texts of letters, &c.; on Salisbury, in the same report on Various Collections, 338–88; on Wells in i. 106–8, viii. 351–65, x, pt. iii (1885, reprinted 1906), 1–373, and in a separate report on the manuscripts (1906).

A great deal of the material in diocesan and cathedral archives still needs systematic classification and indexing, though much work has been done and is being done in this direction, notably at Lincoln, where the late Canon C. W. Foster set a fine example. The similar records of great monastic houses were of course scattered, but important volumes and registers survive. The central interest was the *opus Dei*, the liturgical life in the church and choir, and the cult of patron saints. The publications since 1890 of the Henry Bradshaw Society illustrate the litera-ture of this kind, e.g. *The Customary of the Monasteries of St. Augustine, Canterbury and Westminster*, 2 vols. (1902–4). Cf. the *Barnwell Observances*, ed. J. W. Clark (Cambridge, 1897). A study of Bradshaw's *Lincoln Cathedral Statutes*, ed. Chr. Words-worth, 3 vols. (Cambridge, 1892–7), especially the introduction to the Liber Albus in vol. i, reveals the diffusion of liturgical uses, and the connexion between these and other customs and cathedral statutes, e.g. at Salisbury; see the *Register of St. Osmund*, ed. W. H. R. Jones, 2 vols. (R.S., 1883–4), the *Statuta et consuetudines*, ed. E. A. Dayman and W. H. R. Jones (Bath, 1883), and the Salisbury *Ceremonies and Processions*, ed. Chr. Wordsworth from a fifteenth-century text (Cambridge, 1901). The *Worcester Liber Albus*, ed. J. M. Wilson (Worc. Hist. Soc., 1920), gives a good idea of a more general register. The *Liber memorandorum Ecclesie de Bernewelle*, ed. J. W. Clark (Cambridge, 1907) is of special value. Then come the monastic cartularies or collections of charters and other evidences relating to the lands and offices of a religious house. These are too numerous to be mentioned separately here. A useful list of the more important of them will be found in J. H. R. Moorman, *Church Life in England in the Thirteenth Century* (Cambridge, 1945), pp. xvi–xxi.

Ecclesiastical legislation, national, provincial, and diocesan (cf. above, pp. 451 ff.), is to be found sometimes in separate, sometimes in miscellaneous manuscripts. Most of it, in an uncritical form, is in the collection *Concilia Magnae Britanniae et Hiberniae*, ed. David Wilkins, a Prussian who began to work under the patronage of Archbishop Wake, four volumes (1737), vols. i, ii. For Wales (to 1295) this work has been superseded by the first volume of *Councils and Ecclesiastical Documents relating to Great Britain and Ireland*, ed. A. W. Haddan and W. Stubbs (Oxford, 1869). *The Records of the Northern Convocation*, ed. G. W. Kitchin (Surtees Soc., 1907) is not authoritative.

Monastic history centres on William Dugdale's *Monasticon Anglicanum*, first published 1655–73 and based on the collections of Roger Dodsworth. The edition of 1817–30 (reprinted 1846), six volumes in eight, contains much additional material from original sources. The legislation and *acta* of the Benedictine provincial chapters have been collected by W. A. Pantin in *Chapters of the English Black Monks, 1215–1540*, 3 vols. (Royal Hist. Soc., 1931–7); of the Augustinians by H. E. Salter in *Chapters of the Augustinian Canons* (Cant. and York Soc., 1921–2). The procedings of the Cistercian general chapters, which abbots from all parts were expected to attend, in *Statuta capitulorum generalium ordinis Cisterciensis*, ed. J. M. Cannivez (Louvain, 1931–), contain some English material; see also J. T. Fowler, *Cistercian Statutes, 1256–88* (1890, from *Yorks. Archaeol. Journal*). For the Cluniac priories cf. G. F. Duckett, *Visitations and Chapters-general of the Order of Cluni* (Lewes, 1893), pp. 207–317; and his *Charters and Records among the Archives of the Abbey of Cluni, 1077–1534, Illustrative of the Acts of our Early Kings and all the Abbey's English Foundations*, 2 vols. (Lewes, 1888). F. A. Gasquet, *Collectanea Anglo-premonstratensia*, 3 vols. (Royal Hist. Soc., 1901–6), deals mostly with the Premonstratensians in the fourteenth and fifteenth centuries. The *Cartulaire général de l'ordre des hospitaliers de S. Jean de Jérusalem, 1100–1310*, ed. J. Delaville le Roulx, 4 vols.

(Paris, 1894–1906), contains documents relating to the Hospitallers in England and Ireland; see also the survey of 1338 in L. B. Larking, *The Hospitallers in England* (Camden Soc., 1857). The returns to the inquiry of Geoffrey fitz Stephen, Master of the Temple in England (1185), ed. Beatrice Lees, *Records of the Templars in England in the Twelfth Century* (British Academy, 1935), seem to have had no later equivalent until the royal inquiry when the Order was suppressed in Edward II's reign.

On the taxation of the clergy by the Pope, the outstanding memorial is the *Taxatio Ecclesiastica Angliae et Walliae auctoritate P. Nicolai IV circa A.D. 1291* (Rec. Comm., 1802), on which cf. Rose Graham, *English Ecclesiastical Studies* (1929), pp. 271–301. The extant returns to this and earlier assessments of ecclesiastical property, and the record evidence relating to them have been analysed, but not edited, except as illustrative documents, by W. E. Lunt in his books and papers, notably *The Valuation of Norwich* (Oxford, 1926), and *Financial Relations of the Papacy with England to 1327* (The Mediaeval Academy of America, 1939). His articles are listed in the bibliography to the latter (pp. 706–7). Cf. the translation of illustrative documents in his *Papal Revenues in the Middle Ages*, 2 vols. (Columbia Univ. Press, 1934), vol. ii, *passim*.

Biographical literature is best studied in the collection of texts compiled by Henry Wharton, *Anglia Sacra*, 2 parts (1691). Lives of thirteenth-century archbishops and bishops include those of the Archbishops of Canterbury (i. 1–48) wrongly attributed by Wharton to the monk Stephen of Birchington; see J. Tait, *Chronica Johannis de Reading* (Manchester, 1914), pp. 63–68; of the bishops of Coventry and Lichfield by Thomas of Chesterfield (i. 421–59); of the bishops of Bath and Wells (i. 551–71); Richard of Bardney's life of Robert Grosseteste (ii. 325–41), verse; for this work (1503) see J. C. Russell in *Medievalia et Humanistica*, no. 2 (Boulder, 1944), 45–54, and D. A. Callus in *Oxoniensia* (1945), x. 44–45. *Chronica pontificum ecclesiae Eboracensis*, a composite work, written for the period 1147–1373 by Thomas Stubbs, is edited in the second volume of Raine's *Historians of the church of York* (R.S.). Three canonized saints were commemorated in extensive literature: (1) Archbishop Edmund of Abingdon, canonized 1246–7; see Martene and Durand, *Thesaurus novus anecdotorum* (1717), iii, cols. 1751 ff.;

also for other texts, Wilfred Wallace, *St. Edmund of Canterbury* (1893), and H. W. C. Davis in *E.H.R.* xxii (1907), 84–92. (2) Richard Wyck, bishop of Chichester, canonized 1262; see *Acta Sanctorum*, April, vol. i, pp. 277 ff. (3) Thomas de Cantilupe, bishop of Hereford, canonized 1320, ibid. Oct., vol. i, pp. 539–705. Bartholomew Cotton's *Tractatus de archiepiscopis et episcopis Angliae*, edited by Luard in his edition of the *Historia Anglicana* (pp. 345–418), is based on William of Malmesbury, but is interesting in conception and useful for the short accounts of the thirteenth-century bishops of Norwich.

Monastic biography, as an historical source, is happily exemplified by Matthew Paris in his *Vitae Abbatum*, continued from 1255 to 1307 by an anonymous writer. It was again continued by Thomas Walsingham, who incorporated it in his *Gesta abbatum monasterii S. Albani*, ed. H. T. Riley, 3 vols. (R.S., 1867–9).

When all else has been said, narrative history depends especially upon letters, which express opinions and directions at the time of writing. Papal bulls, episcopal registers, the chancery rolls, the 'ancient correspondence' noted above, collections of letters, miscellaneous letters in cathedral and monastic archives, and the formulary books or guides to letter-writing based upon actual letters, all belong to the same class of historical material and remain the chief source of evidence.

Many papal bulls were treasured in the royal and other archives in England, as in other countries, and many were copied into chronicles and registers. Cf. H. I. Bell, 'List of original papal bulls and briefs in the British Museum', in *E.H.R.* xxxvi (1921), 393 ff., 556 ff., especially pp. 400–11, and the index, pp. 576–83; C. Johnson, on the keeper of papal bulls (*c.* 1269) in *Essays in Mediaeval History presented to T. F. Tout* (Manchester, 1925), pp. 135–8, and the texts in Cotton, *Hist. Anglicana*, pp. 259–81. By no means all of these bulls were copied into the papal registers; the lasting value of A. Potthast's *Regesta Pontificum Romanorum*, 1198–1304, 2 vols. (Berlin, 1874–5), is largely due to the fact that Potthast included in his chronological calendar the papal bulls already printed in learned historical works, e.g. in A. Theiner's *Vetera monumenta Hibernorum et Scotorum historiam illustrantia*, 1216–1547 (Rome, 1864), in Rymer's *Foedera*, the *Bullaria*, and other collections bearing on the history of the various orders of monks and friars, and so on. The complete edition of the papal registers of the successors of Innocent III began with P. Pressutti's *Regesta Honorii Papae III*, 1216–27 (Rome, 1888–95), and the series of the registers of thirteenth-century popes, from Gregory IX to Boniface VIII, issued by the Écoles françaises d'Athènes et de Rome (1884–). The registers of all the popes —except the short-lived Innocent V (the theologian Peter of Tarantaise) and Adrian V (the legate Ottobuono)—are now entirely in print or in progress. They abound in material for British and Irish history. An essential guide to this material is still the *Calendar of entries in the papal registers relating to Great Britain and Ireland; Papal Letters*, i, ed. W. H. Bliss (1893).

The surviving registers of English archbishops and bishops are now for the most part in print. (Cf. A. C. Fowler, *Episcopal Registers of England and Wales*, Helps for students of history, no. 1 : S.P.C.K.) *Canterbury*: most of Pecham's Register (1279–92) was published in the *Registrum epistolarum Fratris Johannis Peckham*, ed. C. T. Martin, 3 vols. (R.S., 1882–5). For the rest see the *Registrum*, ed. C. Jenkins (Cant. and York Soc., 1908–). The Register of Robert Winchelsey (1294–1308) ed. Rose Graham (Cant. and York Soc., 1917–). *York*: The register or rolls of Walter Gray (1216–55) with illustrative documents, ed. James Raine (Surtees Soc., 1870),[1] contains a calendar of rolls from 1225 to 1255, with documents from the *Registrum Magnum Album* of the Dean and Chapter and other sources. The Registers of Walter Giffard (1266–79), William Wickwane (1279–85), John Le Romeyn (1286–96), all edited by W. Brown, and of Thomas Corbridge (1300–4), ed. W. Brown and A. Hamilton Thompson, have also been published by the Surtees Society (1904–28). See also *Historical Papers and Letters from the Northern Registers*, ed. James Raine (R.S., 1873). *Carlisle*: Register of John de Halton (1292–1324), ed. W. N. Thompson, with an introduction by T. F. Tout (Cant. and York Soc., 1913). *Exeter*: Registers of Walter Bronescombe (1257–80), Peter Quivil (1280–91), with records of Thomas de Bytton's episcopate (1292–1307), ed. F. L. Hingeston-Randolph (London, 1889). *Hereford*: Register of Thomas de Cantilupe (1275–82) and Richard de Swinfield (1283–1317), both edited by W. W. Capes (Cant. and York Soc., 1907 and 1909). *A*

---

[1] 'The first attempt at an edition of an English episcopal register'; see A. Hamilton Thompson, *The Surtees Society* (Surtees Soc. 1939), p. 153.

Roll of the Household Expenses of Richard de Swinfield, 1289–90, ed. J. Webb, 2 vols. (Camden Soc., 1854–5), gives an excellent idea of a bishop on a visitation. *Lincoln*: Hugh of Wells (1209–35), *Rotuli*, ed. W. P. W. Phillimore (Cant. and York Soc., 1907–9) and the *Liber Antiquus*, ed. A. Gibbons (1888), containing his arrangement for vicars in appropriated benefices; *Rotuli* of Robert Grosseteste (1235–53), ed. F. N. Davis (Cant. and York Soc., 1913); also of Richard of Gravesend (1258–79), ed. F. N. Davis, C. W. Foster, and A. Hamilton Thompson (Cant. and York Soc., 1925); Register of Oliver Sutton (1279–99), ed. Rosalind Hill (Cant. and York Soc., in progress). *Salisbury*: Register of Simon de Gandavo (1279–1313), ed. C. T. Flower and M. C. B. Dawes (Cant. and York Soc., 1914–32). *Winchester*: Register of John de Pontissara (1282–1304), ed. C. Deedes (Cant. and York Soc., 1913–24). *Worcester*: Registers of Godfrey Giffard (1268–1301) and William de Geynsburgh (1302–7), ed. J. Willis Bund (Worc. Hist. Soc., 1898–1902, and 1907–29).

The monastic register proper was primarily a letter-book, 'analogous to the episcopal and papal registers'; see W. A. Pantin, 'English Monastic Letter-Books', in *Historical Essays in Honour of James Tait* (Manchester, 1933), pp. 201–12, with a list, pp. 213–22. Calendars of some of these, with many texts, have been made by Rosalind Hill, *Ecclesiastical Letter-Books of the Thirteenth Century* (privately printed, no place or date). The value of these collections deserves wider appreciation.

There was constant correspondence between the king, bishops, &c., and cardinals, and many letters survive. Some can be found in the 'Ancient correspondence', episcopal registers, and other sources. For letters written by Ottobuono while he was legate in England (1265–8) see Rose Graham in *E.H.R.* xv (1900), 87–120, and K. Hampe in *Neues Archiv*, xxii (1897), 337–72. For the rich store of letters preserved at Canterbury see the reports of the Hist. MSS. Commission, also *Literae Cantuarienses*, ed. J. B. Sheppard, 2 vols. (R.S., 1887–9). Letters to Ralph Nevill, bishop of Chichester, Henry III's chancellor, were printed by W. H. Blaauw in *Sussex Archaeol. Collections*, iii (1850), 35–76; J. Boussard in a paper on Nevill in the *Revue Historique*, clxxvi (1935), 217–33, and C. A. F. Meekings on letters from a judge to Nevill in *E.H.R.* lxv (1950), 492–504, have shown the value of the 'ancient correspondence' as an historical source. The *Epistolae* of Robert Grosseteste, ed. H. R. Luard (R.S., 1861) and of his friend Adam Marsh, an Oxford Franciscan, ed. J. S. Brewer in *Monumenta Franciscana*, i (R.S., 1858), 77–489, are of outstanding importance. Some interesting letters written by W. de Bernham, a Scottish master of arts at Paris and Oxford *c.* 1250, were copied, apparently by the writer, on the lower margin of a manuscript (All Souls MS. 35); they have been edited by N. R. Ker and W. A. Pantin in *Oxford Formularies*, ii (Oxford Hist. Soc., 1942), 472–91. A valuable series of letters has been edited from three Durham formularies by F. Barlow in *Durham Annals and Documents of the Thirteenth Century* (Surtees Soc., 1940), 88–202; cf. pp. ix–xix (a list) and 233–45. Richard de Bury's large formulary, *Liber Epistolaris*, ed. N. Denholm-Young (Roxburghe Club, 1950), though of later date (*c.* 1324) contains many thirteenth-century letters, including letters of Edward I, as was shown in the report on the Ormsby-Gore MSS. in the *Fourth Report* of the Hist. MSS. Commission (1874), pp. 379–97. On Bury's work and on formularies in general see Denholm-Young, *Collected Papers*, pp. 5–7, 26–54. H. G. Richardson has noted the study of *Dictamen* at Oxford in the thirteenth century, *Bulletin of John Rylands Library*, xxiii (1939–40), 445–52. C. R. Cheney has edited 32 letters of William Wickwane, written 1266–8 when he was chancellor of York—'a humble attempt at a letter-book' —in *E.H.R.* xlvii (1932), 626–42; and has written on the letters of Gervase, abbot of Prémontré, some of which concern English affairs early in the century, in *Bull. John Rylands Library*, xxxiii (1950–1), 25–56, including an appendix of texts. In the same *Bulletin*, xxiii. 487 ff., F. J. Tanqueray published some private letters (1302–5) from Edward I about his falcons to Robert de Bavent. Finally, Hilda Johnstone's important volume, *Letters of Edward, Prince of Wales, 1304–5* (Roxburghe Club, 1931) should be noted.

WILLS. For the legal history and its outcome in the administration of wills by the Church, the limitation of testamentary powers to chattels, except in the case of burgage tenure, and the rules for dealing with intestacy, see Pollock and Maitland, ii. 323–63. Wills are valuable social documents, though not so many survive from the thirteenth as from later centuries. See J. Nichols, *A Collection of Wills of the Kings and Queens of England from William the Conqueror to Henry VII* (1780). For bishops' wills see *E.H.R.* xv (1900), 523–8 (Nicholas Longespee, of Salisbury, 1296); and *Camden Miscellany*, xiv (Royal Hist. Soc., 1926), the will of Peter of Aigueblanche, bishop of Hereford, 1268. For the wills of knights cf. Hist. MSS. Comm., *Report on Duke of Rutland's MSS.*, iv (1905), 14, 27; and H. E. Salter's text of an Oxfordshire will 1230–1, in *E.H.R.* xx (1905), 291. For the wills of villeins see A. E. Levett, *Studies in Manorial History* (1938), 20 ff. In general, N. Harris Nicolas, *Testamenta Vetusta*, 2 vols. (1826).

5. GENERAL AND ENGLISH POLITICAL HISTORY

English history is more involved in general history in the thirteenth than it is even in the twelfth century. The most comprehensive general history is L. Halphen, *L'Essor de l'Europe* (*XIe–XIIIe siècles*) in the series 'Peuples et civilisations', vi (2nd ed., Paris, 1941); cf. H. Pirenne, and others, *Le fin du moyen âge* in the same series, vol. vii, pt. i (1931), pp. 5–70, for the period, 1285–1314; also the *Cambridge Medieval History*, vi and vii (1929–32). R. Fawtier, *L'Europe occidentale de 1270 à 1380*, pt. i (1270–1328), in the *Histoire général* directed by G. Glotz, vi. i (Paris, 1940), is especially useful for the time of Edward I. The introductions to the various papal registers, directed by the French school at Rome (above, p. 740) are sometimes valuable for contemporary history; notably those of E. Berger on the pontificate of Innocent IV. There are numerous histories of the Church of variable value. W. Moeller, *History of the Christian Church*, trans. A. Rutherford, ii (2nd ed., 1910), is good. G. Schnürer, *Kirche und Kultur im Mittelalter*, 3 vols. (Paderborn, 1924–9) is an able and suggestive book. The narrative sections in the French translation of Hefele's *Histoire des Conciles*, by H. Leclercq, vi. i (Paris, 1913–14), are very useful. On Pope Boniface VIII see Digard's book (above, p. 674 n.) and T. S. R. Boase, *Boniface VIII* (1933).

The following books deal generally with the feudal states most in touch with England: A. Cartellieri, *Philip II August*, vol. iv (Leipsic, 1922), C. Petit-Dutaillis, *Louis VIII* (Paris, 1894), and *La Monarchie féodale en France et en Angleterre, Xe–XIIIe siècles* (Paris, 1933); Ch.-V. Langlois, covering the period 1226–1328 in E. Lavisse, *Histoire de France*, iii. ii (Paris, 1911); E. Berger, *Blanche de Castille, reine de France* (Paris, 1895),

H. Wallon, *Saint Louis et son temps*, 2 vols. (Paris, 1876); Ch.-V. Langlois, *Le règne de Philippe le Hardi* (Paris, 1887); H. Pirenne, *Histoire de Belgique*, i (3ᵉ ed., Brussels, 1909); F. Funck-Brentano, *Philippe le Bel en Flandre* (Paris, 1896); V.-L. Bourilly and R. Busquet, *La Provence au Moyen Âge* (Paris, 1924); P. Fournier, *Le Royaume d'Arles et de Vienne* (Paris, 1891); E. Jordan, *Les origines de la domination angevine en Italie* (Paris, 1939); O. Redlich, *Rudolf von Hapsburg* (Innsbruck, 1903). Guides to the foreign relations of Henry III and Edward I, in addition to the texts and other authorities noted in the chapters of this book, will be found in Langlois, Halphen, Fawtier, the bibliography in the *Cambridge Medieval History*, e.g. vi. 908; vii. 869–70, and especially in the long bibliography in Fritz Kern, *Die Anfänge der französischen Ausdehnungspolitik bis zum Jahre 1308* (Tübingen, 1910), pp. viii–xxvii. Cf. Yves Renouard on the role of the Angevin empire in the formation of France and French civilization in the twelfth and thirteenth centuries, in *Revue Historique*, cxcv (1945), 289–304; and his paper 'Ce que l'Angleterre doit à l'Aquitaine' in *Conférences de Lundi* (1945–6), publication of the University of Bordeaux, no. 7, pp. 113–24.

England. See, for earlier work, Gross, pp. 618–32. J. H. Ramsay, *Dawn of the Constitution* (1908) covers the whole period, F. M. Powicke, *King Henry III and the Lord Edward*, 2 vols. (Oxford, 1947), the reign of Henry III and a study of Edward I. Henry's minority is described or discussed in Kate Norgate, *The Minority of Henry III* (1912); S. Painter, *William Marshal* (Baltimore, 1933); G. J. Turner in *Trans. R. Hist. Soc.*, n.s., xviii (1904), 245–95, and 3rd s., i (1907), 205–62; F. M. Powicke in *E.H.R.* xxiii (1908), 220–35; Mabel Mills on exchequer procedure in *Trans. R. Hist. Soc.*, 4th s., viii (1925), 151–70. For the period 1227–58 see Mills on exchequer reform (1232–42), ibid. x (1927), 111–34; R. F. Treharne, *The Baronial Plan of Reform, 1258–63* (Manchester, 1932); N. Denholm-Young, *Richard of Cornwall* (Oxford, 1947); Ch. Bémont, *Simon de Montfort* (Paris, 1884), with appendixes of documents omitted from the English edition (Oxford, 1930). For the period 1258–67 see in addition to the works of Bémont and Treharne, E. F. Jacob, *Studies in the Period of Baronial Reform and Rebellion, 1258–67* (Oxford, 1925), with new documents; also his edition of the king's complaints in 1261, in *E.H.R.* xli (1926), 559–71; H. G. Richardson and G. O. Sayles on the Provisions of Oxford and John Selden's abridgement of a lost text in *Bulletin of the John Rylands Library* (July 1933); F. M. Powicke on the baronial council (1258–60) in *Essays . . . presented to T. F. Tout* (Manchester, 1925), pp. 119–34; Denholm-Young on negotiations after the battle of Lewes, in his *Collected Papers*, pp. 111–29; W. H. Blaauw, *The Barons' War* (2nd ed., 1871); Mabel Mills, '*Adventus vicecomitum*, 1258–72', in *E.H.R.* xxvi (1921), 481–96 (for royal finances); H. S. Snellgrove, *The Lusignans in England* (Univ. of New Mexico Press, 1950); F. R. Lewis on William of Valence in *Aberystwyth Studies*, xiii. 11–35, xiv. 69–92 (1934–5); F. Mugnier, *Les Savoyards en Angleterre au XIIIᵉ siècle et Pierre d'Aigueblanche, évêque d'Hereford* (Chambery, 1890). For the end of the reign and Edward's crusade and return to England in 1274 see Powicke, *King Henry III*, &c., ii. 551–617. The authorities on Edward I's reign are noted in the text and in other sections of this bibliography. H. Gough, *Itinerary of Edward I*, 2 vols. (Paisley, 1900), is inadequate, but still essential. How a revised edition should be done is shown by J. B. Trabut-Cussac in his itinerary of Edward in France, 1286–9, in *Bulletin of the Institute of Hist. Research*, xxv (1952), 160–203. Three biographies should be noted: C. L. Kingsford on Otto de Grandison or Granson (d. 1328), Edward's closest companion, in *Trans. R. Hist. Soc.*, 3rd ser., iii (1909), 125–95; Inna Lubimenko, *Jean de Bretagne, comte de Richmond* (Lille, 1908), on Edward's nephew (1269–1334); Hilda Johnstone, *Edward of Carnarvon, 1284–1307* (Manchester, 1947), on the early years of the future Edward II.

FOREIGN RELATIONS AND GASCONY. In addition to the general works and monographs noted above, P. Boissonade, *Histoire de Poitou* (Paris, 1915); C. Farcinet, *Hugues IX de Lusignan et les comtes de la Marche* (Vannes, 1896); H. J. Chaytor; *Savaric de Mauléon* (Cambridge, 1939); S. Painter, *The Scourge of the Clergy* (Baltimore, 1937), on Peter of Dreux; E. Berger on Henry III's invasion of Brittany (1229–30) in *Bibliothèque de l'école des chartes*, liv (1893), 5–44; E. Boutaric, *Saint Louis et Alphonse de Poitiers* (Paris, 1870); L. Delisle, on a letter from a citizen of Rochelle to Queen Blanche, in *Bibl. école des Chartes*, xvii (1856), 513–55, Ch. Bémont on King Henry's campaign of 1242–3 in *Annales du Midi* (1893), pp. 289–314; M. Gavrilovitch, *Étude sur le traité de Paris de 1259* (Paris, 1899), and the authorities on

Edward's continental activities noted in the text (chapters vi, vii, xiv). A slight but scholarly introduction to Gascon history by Eleanor C. Lodge, *Gascony under English Rule* (1926) contains useful maps and bibliography; see also her paper on Edward I and his Gascon tenants-in-chief in *Trans. R. Hist. Soc.*, 4th ser., vii (1924), 1–26. J. de Jaurgain, *La Vasconie*, 2 vols. (Paris, 1898–1902), is a good general book, and P. de Marca, *Histoire de Béarn* (1640) still stands out among local histories. For the bastides see A. Curie Seimbres, *Essais sur les villes fondées dans le Sud-Ouest de la France au XIIIᵉ et XIVᵉ siècles* (Toulouse, 1880). and above, pp. 308–9. Recent concentration on Gascon history is noteworthy in the work of Boutruche, Chaplais, Cuttino, Trabut-Cussac, and others. The studies of Gascony's allodial character are especially important; see above, pp. 120, 297–8, 300, 313, 651, 654 and notes. A. G. Little made a list of alms given by Edward I in 1289 to mendicant orders: *Revue d'hist. franciscaine*, ii (1925), 178–85.

6. LAW AND INSTITUTIONS IN ENGLAND

The fundamental books are Stubbs, *Constitutional History of England*, vol. ii (cf. for studies and literature about him, J. G. Edwards, *William Stubbs*, Hist. Association, 1952), Pollock and Maitland, *The History of English Law before the time of Edward I*, 2 vols. (Cambridge, 1898), and Maitland's *Collected Papers*, 3 vols. (Cambridge, 1911). Later work comprises W. S. Holdsworth, *History of English Law*, especially the vols. i–iii in the third edition and subsequent reprints; F. T. Plucknett, *Legislation of Edward I* (Oxford, 1949); *Select Essays on Anglo-American Legal History*, 3 vols. (Boston, 1907–9; listed in Gross, p. 127), and *Magna Carta Commemoration Essays* (Royal Hist. Soc., 1917). More recent books have probably been influenced, directly or indirectly, by C. H. McIlwain, *The High Court of Parliament* (New Haven, 1920), an essay 'on the boundaries between legislation and adjudication', cf. A. F. Pollard, *The Evolution of Parliament* (2nd ed., 1926), J. E. A. Jolliffe, *The Constitutional History of Medieval England* (1937) and G. O. Sayles, *The Medieval Foundations of England* (1948), pp. 409–65. Other influential books have been L. Riess, *Geschichte des Wahlrechts zum englischen Parlament* (Leipsic, 1885); D. Pasquet, *An Essay on the Origins of the House of Commons* (Eng. trans., Cambridge, 1925); J. F. Baldwin, *The King's Council* (Oxford, 1913); A. B.

White, *Self-government by the King's Command* (Minneapolis, 1933); H. M. Cam, *Studies in the Hundred Rolls* (Oxford, 1921), important for the development of the great eyre; and, as a forceful presentation of the tract, *Modus tenendi parliamentum*, M. V. Clarke, *Representation and Consent* (1936).

The best starting-point in the recent discussions on parliament and council are Maitland's edition of the *Memoranda de Parliamento* (R.S., 1893) and G. O. Sayles, *Select Cases in the Court of King's Bench*, 3 vols. (Selden Soc., 1936–9). The papers of Richardson and Sayles and their joint books and papers are noted above (Ch. VIII), as are the papers by Edwards and others which discuss the disputes of 1297–1301 (Ch. XIV). B. Wilkinson has dealt with various problems in his *Constitutional History of England*, i (1948), and, more minutely, in his *Studies in the Constitutional History of England in the Thirteenth and Fourteenth Centuries* (Manchester, 1937). On the continental background see H. G. Richardson on the origin of parliament in *Trans. R. Hist. Soc.*, 4th ser., xi (1928), 137–83, and the reports presented to the 'Commission internationale pour l'histoire des assemblés des états' in the *Bulletin of the International Committee of Historical Sciences*, ix (1937), 409–73, and in *Recueil des travaux* published by the University of Louvain (Louvain, 1937 and 1939); cf. also the number of *Speculum* (xxix (1954), 347–476) consisting of articles by Cam, Post, and other scholars. See also Gaines Post in the articles noted above (p. 539 n.) and A. Marongiu, *L'Istituto parlamentare in Italia* (Rome, 1949). On Germany cf. A. Brackmann's essay in G. Barraclough's *Medieval Germany* (Oxford, 1938), ii. 281–99; and H. Spangenberg, *Vom Lehnstaat zum Standestaat* (Munich, 1912). On France cf. J. R. Strayer and C. H. Taylor, *Studies in early French taxation* (Harvard Univ. Press, 1939).

Articles to be noted are J. E. A. Jolliffe, on the beginning of the English parliament, in *Trans. R. Hist. Soc.*, 4th ser., xxii (1940), 101–39; R. F. Treharne on the nature of parliament in the reign of Henry III, in *E.H.R.* lxxiv (1959), 590–610; W. A. Morris on the term 'community of the realm' in *Medievalia et Humanistica*, i (Boulder, Colorado, 1943), 58–94.

The history of taxation in thirteenth-century England has been discussed by S. K. Mitchell, *Studies in Taxation under John and Henry III* (New Haven, 1914), and in his posthumous work, *Taxation in Medieval England*, ed. S. Painter (New Haven, 1951), which appeared too late to be used in this book; and by J. F. Willard, *Parliamentary Taxes on Personal Property, 1290 to 1334* (Medieval Academy of America, 1934). J. H. Ramsay calculated the royal revenue from year to year in *A History of the Revenues of the Kings of England, 1066–1399*, 2 vols. (Oxford, 1925), see i. 262–368; ii. 1–90. Also, on scutage, see H. M. Chew, 'Scutage under Edward I', in *E.H.R.* xxxvii (1922), 321–66, and her *Ecclesiastical Tenants in Chief and Knight-Service* (Oxford, 1932). Cf. J. H. Round in *E.H.R.* xxviii (1913), 358 on the scutage rolls.

For the administrative system T. F. Tout, *Chapters in Medieval Administrative History*, 6 vols. (Manchester, 1923–35), is essential; see vols. i–ii, the chapter on the great wardrobe (iv. 349–437) and the valuable lists of officials and index in vol. vi. On the great offices see J. H. Round, *The King's Serjeants and Officers of State* (1911) and L. W. Vernon-Harcourt, *His Grace the Steward and Trial of Peers* (1907) with Round's review in *E.H.R.* xxii (1907), 778–82. On serjeants generally Elizabeth Kimball, *Serjeant Tenure in Medieval England* (New Haven, 1936); and on *Judgement by Peers*, B. C. Keeney (Harvard Univ. Press, 1949). For the exchequer see above, p. 744, and the memoranda, including an estimate of revenue, 'on the machinery required to give effect to the statute of Rhuddlan (1284)', edited by M. H. Mills in *E.H.R.* xl (1925), 229–34. C. A. F. Meekings on 'The Pipe Roll Order of 12 February 1270', in *Studies presented to Sir Hilary Jenkinson* (1957), is suggestive. Payments into the king's household are illustrated by ordinances for the guidance of a deputy treasurer during Walter Langton's absence (1305), edited by J. F. Willard, *E.H.R.* xlviii (1933), 84–89; see also his notes on the treasurer's clerk and the issue roll in *Bulletin of the Inst. of Hist. Research*, viii (1931), 129–35, and on the observance of Sundays and vacations in the Lower exchequer, in *University of Colorado Studies*, xxii (1935), 281–9. On the chancery see Tout, op cit., *passim*, L. A. Dibben, *E.H.R.* xxvii (1912), 39–51, B. Wilkinson, *The Chancery under Edward III* (Manchester, 1929), pp. 1–10.

On law and procedure in royal justice see Turner's *Brevia Placitata* (above, p. 729); cf. also C. T. Flower, *Introduction to the Curia Regis Rolls, 1189–1230* (Selden Soc., 1944), J. Goebel, *Felony and Misdemeanor* (New York, 1937), and Elsa de Haas, *Antiquities of Bail* (New York, 1940). On the statutes see H. G. Richardson and G. O. Sayles in the *Law Quarterly Review*, l

(1934), 201–23 and Sayles on the statute of Gloucester (1278) in *E.H.R.* lii (1937), 467–74. W. C. Bolland's useful *Manual of Year Book Studies* (Cambridge, 1925) should be read in the light of Dunham's introduction to the *Casus Placitorum* (above p. 729). On the relative values of Year Books and Plea Rolls cf. H. G. Richardson in *Trans. R. Hist. Soc.*, 4th ser., v (1922), 28–51. In several most suggestive papers S. E. Thorne has illustrated the interplay of law and social conditions, of the English and canon law and of law and custom: e.g. '*Statuti* in the Post-glossators', in *Speculum*, xi (1936), 453–61; 'The assize *Utrum* and canon law', in *Columbia Law Rev.* xxxiii (1933), 428–50; 'Livery of Seisin', in *Law Quarterly Rev.* lii (1936), 345–64.

The best account of *local government* is H. M. Cam's *The Hundred and the Hundred Rolls* (1930), supplemented by the papers included in her *Liberties and Communities in Medieval England* (Cambridge, 1944). W. A. Morris's books, *The Frankpledge System* (New York, 1910), *The Early English County Court* (Berkeley, Cal., 1926), and *The Medieval English Sheriff* (Manchester, 1927) are scholarly and helpful, but the first should be used in the light of R. Stewart-Brown's *The Serjeants of the Peace in Medieval England and Wales* (Manchester, 1936), where several current generalizations are modified (pp. 99–104) and a widespread police system, common to border districts where local military obligations, mainly enforced by local lords, prevailed, is revealed as a natural alternative to the system of frankpledge and tithing. A good example of the difference between the two areas is provided by the avowries of Cheshire, a system of protection described by Stewart-Brown in *E.H.R.* xxix (1914), 41–55. The administration of the palatinates and franchises and their part in the king's government are described in G. T. Lapsley, *The County Palatine of Durham* (New York, 1900), J. Tait, *Cartulary of St. Werburgh's, Chester* (Chetham Soc., 1920–3), vol. i, pp. xliv–l and 101–9 (the *Magna Carta of Cheshire*, 1215–16), the books and articles of Stewart-Brown, *Cheshire Chamberlain's Accounts*, 1301–60 (Record Society of Lancashire and Cheshire, 1910), *Chester County Court Rolls* (Chetham Soc., 1925) of the years 1259–97, with an inquest of military service (1288), 'The Exchequer of Chester' in *E.H.R.* lvii (1942), 289–97, on the financial organization under the chamberlain; and A. Cantle, *Pleas of Quo Warranto for the County of Lancaster* (Chetham Soc., 1951), proceedings in 1292. In general see

N. Denholm-Young, *Seignorial Administration in England* (Oxford, 1937); S. Painter, *Studies in the History of the English Feudal Barony* (Baltimore, 1943), especially chapters iii and iv. On the ecclesiastical liberties see the books noted below (p. 762).

The great part played by the shire court until it gave way to commissions of justice and the peace is now being realized. G. J. Turner, in his edition of *Brevia Placitata* (pp. lvi–lix), has shown how slowly its jurisdiction was encroached upon by original writs issued by chancery. As, in one aspect, a function of the *Curia Regis* and a court of record, it has been obscured by the disappearance, except in Chester and for a few surviving fragments elsewhere, of the rolls and writs passed on by sheriff to sheriff with the shire and castle; cf. *Rotuli de Liberate* (Rec. Com., 1844) of John's reign, p. 7. See S. E. Thorne on courts of record in *West Virginia Law Quarterly*, xl (Morgantown, West Virginia, 1934), 347–59, and cf. G. B. Adams in *American Hist. Rev.* xxi (1915), 91–92, and G. T. Lapsley in *Law Quarterly Rev.* li (1935), 299–325. H. Jenkinson and Mabel Mills have discussed the sheriffs' records in their description of some Bedfordshire survivals (1329–34), in *E.H.R.* xliii (1928), 21–32; these rolls were later edited by G. H. Fowler for the Bedfordshire Historical and Record Society, Quarto memoir (Apsley Guise, 1929). On the other hand G. O. Sayles has dispelled an illusion that local branches of the royal chancery existed: *Bull. of Inst. of Hist. Research*, xv (1937–8), 69–70. J. H. Round explains the relation of the castle and 'shire-house' in its area with the county and town, in *E.H.R.* xxxvi (1921), 210–14; see also Mabel Mills in *Studies presented to Sir Hilary Jenkinson* (1957).

7. SCOTLAND

The loss of records makes the history of Scotland particularly difficult. We have to depend too much on the English records. M. Livingstone, *Guide to the Public Records of Scotland* (Edinburgh, 1905) and J. Maitland Thompson, *The Public Records of Scotland* (Glasgow, 1922) comment on the documents regarding the Scottish muniments (1282–96) which are printed in *Acts of the Parliaments of Scotland*, i (1814), 107–18 (in red), and on other texts. In view of the process at Berwick in 1291–2 the keeper of the rolls and other persons transferred the muniments in the treasury at Edinburgh to Berwick Castle. An indenture of 1292 contains a detailed list of the records to be restored to the Scots after John Baliol's accession to the throne. In 1296 the records again fell under King Edward's control. Divers writings and memoranda found in Edinburgh castle were transferred, together with jewels and relics, to the wardrobe at Westminster in one large and two small coffers. These may have been those mentioned without details in Bishop Stapledon's calendar of the exchequer records (1323); see F. Palgrave, *Antient Kalendars and Inventories* (Rec. Com., 1836), i. 137.[1] It is certain that records required by the Anglo-Scottish parliament, including account rolls, royal charters, and patent rolls were still in Scotland in 1306 at the chamberlain's disposal (cf. Livingston, pp. x–xii, Thompson, p. 6). It is apparently impossible to determine the extent to which the disappearance of the Scottish muniments (with a few exceptions) was due to the action of King Edward in 1296 or on what principles, if any, the documents transferred to England in that year were selected.

In the absence of other records the numerous collections of charters and monastic chartularies have been the main original source of early Scottish history. A list is contained in W. Angus, *Sources and Literature of Scots Law* (Stair Society, Edinburgh, 1936), pp. 259–64. Many chartularies have been edited. This material is the basis of the valuable *Origines Parochiales Scotiae*, by W. Anderson and others, edited by C. Innes, 2 vols. in 3 (Bannatyne Club, Edinburgh, 1850–5) and of such books as J. F. S. Gordon's *Monasticon*, the third volume of his *Ecclesiastical Chronicle for Scotland* (London and Dumfries, 1875), S. R. Macphaile's *Religious House of Pluscardyn* (Edinburgh, 1881) and later works of this kind.

For some of the surviving documents see *Facsimiles of National Manuscripts of Scotland* (Southampton, 1867–71).

The English records, so far as they refer to Scottish affairs, including the documents printed in the *Foedera* and elsewhere, were calendared by J. Bain, *Calendar of Documents relating to Scotland*, vols. i, ii (Edinburgh, 1881–4), covering the period 1108–1307. His dating is not always correct. For the series of texts edited by F. Palgrave, *Documents and Records illustrating the*

---

[1] The entries in detail under the heading *Scocia* in Stapledon's Calendar (pp. 127–36) do not refer to documents brought from Scotland but to documents dealing with Scotland, as in the later lists under the headings, Holland, Bar, Brabant, Sicily, Ponthieu, Flanders, Norway, Castile, Aragon, and Burgundy.

History of Scotland (Rec. Com., 1837), J. Stevenson, *Historical Documents*, 2 vols. (Edinburgh, 1870), and in Riley's edition of Rishanger, see above (p. 602 n., and *passim*). The official *Rotuli Scotiae*, i (Rec. Com., 1814) supplement the texts in the *Foedera*, Palgrave, and Rishanger from the year 1291. The acts of homage by the Scots to King Edward (1291–6), the so-called Ragman Rolls, were edited by G. T. Thomson for the Bannatyne Club (Edinburgh, 1834). Cf. also J. Anderson, *Selectus diplomatum et numismatum Scotiae thesaurus* (Edinburgh, 1739) and J. Stevenson, *Documents illustrative of Sir William Wallace* (Maitland Club, Edinburgh, 1841).

Chronicles. On the English chronicles see above, and A. O. Anderson, *Scottish Annals from English Chronicles, 500–1286*, also his more general *Early Sources of Scottish History, 500–1286*. 2 vols. (Edinburgh, 1922), with a full bibliography in vol. i, pp. xxii–ci. Owing to its Franciscan origin in the Franciscan Anglo-Scottish custody of Newcastle, the Lanercost chronicle, ed. J. Stevenson (Bannatyne Club, 1839), can be regarded as a Scottish as well as an English source. Apart from the brief notes in the Holyrood Chronicle, ed. M. O. Anderson (Scottish Historical Society, 1938), the only contemporary Scottish chronicle is that of Melrose, J. Stevenson's edition of which (Bannatyne Club, 1835) has been superseded by the facsimile edition of A. O. Anderson, M. O. Anderson, and W. C. Dickinson (London, 1936). Scottish annalistic literature is, in fact, mainly represented by later chronicles: Thomas Gray's *Scalacronica* (Maitland Club, 1836), translated by H. Maxwell (Glasgow, 1907); *Scotichronicon*, or John of Fordun's chronicle, ed. W. Goodall, 3 vols. (Edinburgh, 1759); and Andrew of Wynton's chronicle, a Scots poem, ed. D. Laing in *Historians of Scotland*, 3 vols. (Edinburgh, 1872–9). See the notes in Gross, nos. 1784, 1775, 1869. These three chronicles contain much traditional information, but naturally should be used with caution, as must the political poems *Barbour's Bruce*, ed. W. M. Mackenzie (1909) and *Blind Harry's Wallace*, ed. J. Moir (Scottish Text Society, 1889).

The best-known histories of Scotland, still helpful, are Lord Hailes, *Annals of Scotland*, 3rd ed., 3 vols.(Edinburgh, 1819), W. F. Skene, *Celtic Scotland*, 2nd ed., 3 vols. (Edinburgh, 1886–90), which does not confine itself entirely to early times, and the histories of Scotland by P. F. Tytler (from 1249 to 1603) in 9 vols. (Edinburgh, 1841–3), J. H. Burton, new ed., 8 vols. (Edinburgh, 1897), A. Lang, 4 vols. (Edinburgh, 1900–7), and P. Hume Brown, 3 vols. (Cambridge, 1911). For various works on Anglo-Scottish relations, now somewhat outdated, see Gross, no. 2807 (pp. 612–13), and A. H. Dunbar, *Scottish Kings* (Edinburgh, 1906). E. M. Barron, *The Scottish War of Independence* (1914) had a second edition in 1924. There are two good maps of medieval Scotland in the *Oxford Historical Atlas*.

For social, legal, and administrative history see the works of Lord Cooper, W. M. Mackenzie, and W. C. Dickinson cited above (pp. 572–85) with the references to articles in the *Scottish Hist. Rev.* and other periodicals there noted. Add W. C. Dickinson's paper on the administration of justice in medieval Scotland, in *Aberdeen University Rev.* xxxiv (1952), 338–51. Cosmo Innes's *Scotland in the Middle Ages* (Edinburgh, 1860), *Sketches of Early Scotch History and Social Progress*, and *Lectures on Scotch Legal Antiquity* (Edinburgh, 1872) were the work of a remarkable scholar. R. S. Rait, *The Parliament of Scotland* (Glasgow, 1924)—cf. T. F. Tout in *Scottish Hist. Rev.* xxii. 95 —I. F. Grant, *Social and Economic Development of Scotland before 1603* (Edinburgh, 1931), and G. G. Coulton, *Scottish Abbeys and Social Life* (Cambridge, 1933) should be noted.

The papal registers, Theiner's *Vetera monumenta* and the *Calendar of Papal Letters*, vol. i, noted above, are essential for the history of the Scottish Church, as is the *Statuta Ecclesiae Scoticanae*, ed. J. Robertson, 2 vols. (Bannatyne Club, 1866). A. R. MacEwen, *History of the Church in Scotland*, vol. i (1913), and J. Dowden, *The Medieval Church in Scotland, its Constitution, Organisation, and Law* (Glasgow, 1910), are the best guides to the subject; see also for biographical summaries, E. Dowden, *The Bishops of Scotland* (Glasgow, 1912). Add W. Stanford Reid on the papacy and the war of independence in *Catholic Hist. Rev.* xxxi (1945), 282–301, and Annie I. Cameron on documents relating to John Baliol in the Vatican Archives in *Papers of the British School of Rome*, xii (1933).

On architecture see W. M. Mackenzie, *The Medieval Castle in Scotland* (1927), and the works of D. MacGibbon and T. Ross, *Castellated and Domestic Architecture of Scotland*, 5 vols. (Edinburgh, 1887–92), and *Ecclesiastical Architecture of Scotland*, 3 vols. (Edinburgh, 1896–7).

8. WALES

A good introduction to the bibliography is given in the *Cambridge Med. Hist.* vii (1932), 908–10.

Welsh records before the statute of Wales are scanty and scattered, though much charter evidence survives from ecclesiastical and monastic sources and the marcher lordships. Many documents have been printed by the Cymmrodorion Society in *Y Cymmrodor* and its *Transactions*, by the Powysland Club in its *Montgomeryshire Collections*, by the Board of Celtic studies in its History and Law series and its *Bulletin*, by the National Library of Wales in its *Bulletin*, and by other societies. A grant of Llewelyn ap Gruffydd, later recognized as the first Prince of Wales (1267), is of special interest, for it reveals him as a powerful man as early as 1243; see J. Conway Davies in the *National Library of Wales Bulletin*, iii (1944), 158–62, with a facsimile. The English chancery kept Welsh rolls from 1277 to 1294, calendared in a *Calendar of Various Chancery Rolls* (1912), pp. 157–362. On the public records removed to the Public Record Office see Lists and Indexes, xi (1914) and R. A. Roberts in *Y Cymmrodor*, x (1890), 157–206. The most useful publications from English records are the three volumes published in the History and Law series of the Board of Celtic Studies (nos. ii, v, vii; Cardiff, 1935, 1940), *Calendar of Ancient Correspondence concerning Wales*, ed. J. G. Edwards, *Littere Wallie* by the same editor, and *The Welsh Assize Roll, 1277–84*, ed. J. Conway Davies. For these and for the various sources and later writers, bearing on Anglo-Welsh relations between 1217 and 1307, see Chapter IX above.

The two most important chronicles are the *Annales Cambriae* ed. John Williams ab Ithel (R.S., 1860), continued, probably at Strata Florida, from 954 to 1288 with additions from other sources: and the *Brut y Tywysogion*, ed. with translation by the same (R.S., 1860) from 681 to 1282, but much better by J. Rhys and J. G. Evans in *The Red Book of Hergest*, ii (Oxford, 1890), 257–384. On these two chronicles see *Y Cymmrodor*, xi (1892), 133–75, and for a continuation in the Peniarth MS. 20, to 1332, Hist. MSS. Comm. *Report on Welsh Manuscripts*, i, pt. ii (1899), 341–6, and T. Jones's edition (Board of Celtic Studies, 1941). On the Welsh chronicles generally see J. E. Lloyd, in *Proc. of the British Academy*, xiv (1928), 369–91.

J. E. Lloyd described the MSS. and editions of the Welsh

Laws in his *History of Wales to the Edwardian Conquest*, 2 vols. (3rd ed., 1939), i. 354–6. See also F. Seebohm, *The Tribal System of Wales* (2nd ed., 1904) with its appendix of documents, and T. P. Ellis, *Welsh Tribal Law and Customs*, 2 vols. (Oxford, 1926), and the *Survey of the Honour of Denbigh*, ed. P. Vinogradoff and F. Morgan (British Academy, 1914).

The main authorities for the political, social, and ecclesiastical history of Wales, the conquest and settlement, boroughs and castles, are noted in Chapter IX. Cf. also, for local history, surveys, accounts, &c., Gross, pp. 192–6, 580–5. Add J. Conway Davies in the *Montgomeryshire Collections*, xlix, pt. 1 (1945), 1–78, on lordships and manors in this county; A. J. Roderick on feudal relations between the English Crown and the Welsh princes, in *History*, xxxvii (1952), 201–12, and A. J. Taylor on the birth of Edward of Caernarvon and the beginnings of Caernarvon castle in *History*, xxxv (1950), 256–61.

Except W. Rees, *South Wales and the March*, 1284–1415 (Oxford, 1924), which deals mainly with a later period, as does his fine map of parts of the same area, there is no full study of the Marches. On their relation to early Welsh principalities see especially J. G. Edwards in the *Proceedings of the British Academy* for 1956, 155–77; on local history notably Eyton's *Antiquities of Shropshire*, 12 vols. (1854–60), and C. T. Clark's *Cartae et munimenta*, new edn., 6 vols. (Cardiff, 1910). Other books are noted in Gross, e.g. pp. 580–5 *passim*.

9. IRELAND

The bibliography in *Cambridge Med. Hist.* vii (1932), 911–14, is particularly valuable.

The destruction, on 3 June 1922, of the Irish records in Dublin, makes H. Wood's *Guide* (Dublin, 1919), the Reports of the Irish Record Commissioners (1815–25), especially the *Eighth Report* (London, 1819), and the annual *Reports of the Deputy Keeper of the Public Records, Ireland* (Dublin, 1869–) doubly precious. Thus, the Report of 1819, pp. 125–36, contains an inventory of the pipe rolls of the Irish Exchequer, the D.K. Report, xxiv (1892), a table of the contents of the Red Book of this exchequer, and the D.K. Reports, xxxv and xxxvi (1903–4), catalogues of accounts on Pipe Rolls in the reign of Henry III and the years 1–12 Edward I. A *Calendar of the Justiciary Rolls of Ireland, 23–31 Edward I*, ed. J. Mills, 2 parts, had also been published (Dublin, 1905–14). The memorial of the Irish Chancery rolls is the *Rotulorum patentium et clausorum cancellariae Hiberniae Calendarium*, ed. E. Tresham (Irish Record Commission, 1828). Still more valuable is *Chartae Privilegia et Immunitates* (Irish Rec. Com., 1889), for this contains transcripts of original grants to cities, towns, colleges, &c., now destroyed.

Entries in the English public records relating to Ireland are summarized in the *Calendar of Documents relating to Ireland (1171–1307)*, ed. H. S. Sweetman, 5 vols. (1875–86). Vol. v (pp. 202–323) contains the taxation of the Irish dioceses in 1306. For the text, with a translation, of the taxation relating to three northern dioceses see *Ecclesiastical Antiquities of Down, Conner and Dromore*, ed. W. Reeves (Dublin, 1847). For legislation see *Statutes and Ordinances and Acts of the Parliament of Ireland*, ed. H. F. Berry, i (1204–1421), taken mainly from the Red Book (R.S., Dublin, 1907).

Registers, chartularies, collections of town muniments, &c., are noted in Gross, pp. 539–42, and some private collections of deeds, &c., in the reports of the Hist. MSS. Commission. The *Liber niger Alani*, a register compiled by Archbishop Alen of Dublin (d. 1534), calendared by G. T. Stokes in the *Journal* of the Royal Society of Antiquaries of Ireland (1893–8; see Gross, no. 2412) has since been made more, but not entirely, available in *Calendar of Archbishop Alen's Register, circa 1172–1534*, ed. C. McNeil (Dublin, 1950, for the Society). The most valuable private collection available is the *Ormond Deeds*, 2 vols. (Dublin, 1932), comprising the text of the *Red Book of Ormond*, ed. Newport B. White, and *Calendar of Ormond Deeds, 1172–1350*, ed. E. Curtis.

A convenient list of editions of Irish laws, Irish annals, and Latin annals can be found in the *Cambridge Med. Hist.*, vii. 911, 913; cf. Gross, nos. 1707–13.

The historical literature on Irish political, ecclesiastical, and administrative history is noted above, in the first part of Chapter XII. For the purposes of the present work, the books of Orpen and Curtis and the articles of Jocelyn Otway-Ruthven, Aubrey Gwynn and Richardson and Sayles are especially helpful.

10. THE CHURCH IN ENGLAND

As a massive collection of extracts from the records, &c., William Prynne's *An Exact Chronological Vindication of Our King's Supreme Ecclesiastical Jurisdiction on All Religious Affairs*, vol. iii

(1668, reissued 1670, 1672), covering the reigns of John, Henry III, and Edward I, is still valuable. The different view, given classical expression by F. W. Maitland, *Roman Canon Law in the Church of England* (Cambridge, 1898), while generally accepted, must be interpreted in the light of the accommodation, as well as by the disputes, between royal and ecclesiastical jurisdiction. In general see H. R. Luard, *On the Relations between England and Rome during the Early Portion of the Reign of Henry III* (Cambridge, 1877), F. A. Gasquet, *Henry III and the Church* (1905 and 1910), A. L. Smith, *Church and State in the Middle Ages* (Oxford, 1913), L. Dehio, *Innozenz IV und England* (Berlin, 1924), and W. E. Lunt, *Financial Relations of the Papacy with England to 1327* (Med. Academy of America, 1939). Cf. J. T. Ellis, *Anti-Papal Legislation in Medieval England* (Washington, 1930) and Ann Deeley on legal provisions and royal right of patronage in *E.H.R.* xliii (1928), 497 ff. Parts of Maude V. Clarke's *Medieval Representation and Consent* (1936) lay stress on the influence of ecclesiastical practices and theories upon the growth of parliament (pp. 246–347); cf. E. Barker, *The Dominican Order and Convocation* (Oxford, 1913). Ecclesiastical organization is described in F. Makower, *The Constitutional History and Constitution of the Church of England* (Eng. trans., London, 1895), Irene J. Churchill, *Canterbury Administration*, 2 vols. (1933), R. Brentano, *York Metropolitan Jurisdiction and Papal Judges Delegate (1279–1296)* (Univ. of California Press, 1959), and A. Hamilton Thompson, *The English Clergy and their Organization in the Later Middle Ages* (Oxford, 1947); cf. his 'Diocesan Organization in the Middle Ages' in *Proc. of the British Academy*, xxix (1943), 153–94, his papers on pluralism, and other papers in the list of his writings (Oxford, 1948, privately printed).

Ecclesiastical legislation, discussed above (Ch. X), was papal, legatine, provincial, and diocesan. The texts and authorities already noted above should be studied in the light of C. R. Cheney's works: 'Legislation of the English medieval Church' in *E.H.R.* l (1935), 193–224, 385–417, and *English Synodalia of the Thirteenth Century* (Oxford, 1941), and of the chief books and papers on the history of Convocation. The background in the Western Church is considered by E. Kemp in a paper on the origins of the Canterbury Convocation in the *Journal of Ecclesiastical History*, iii (1952), 132–43. J. A. Robinson's paper on Convocation in the *Church Quarterly Rev.*, lxxxi (1915), 81–137, is fundamental. Dorothy B. Weske's *Convocation of the Clergy* (1937) is a good study with useful lists; cf. her essay on the attitude of the English clergy to the obligation to attend convocation and parliament in *Essays in History and Political Theory in Honour of C. H. McIlwain* (Harvard Univ. Press, 1936), pp. 77–108.

On the episcopate and higher clergy see Le Neve, *Fasti ecclesiae Anglicanae*, corrected, &c., by T. D. Hardy, 3 vols. (Oxford, 1854), and W. Stubbs, *Registrum sacrum Anglicanum*, 2nd ed., Oxford, 1897). On Wharton's *Anglia Sacra* see above, p. 738. G. Oliver, *Lives of the Bishops of Exeter, and a History of the Cathedral* (Exeter, 1861) is a good example of the numerous books, which vary in merit, on episcopal and diocesan history. The published episcopal registers (above, pp. 740–1) contain useful biographies, sometimes (e.g. A. H. Thompson on Bishop Gravesend of Lincoln) of much value. The best account of the episcopate in Henry III's reign is in M. Gibbs and Jane Lang, *Bishops and Reform, 1215–72* (Oxford, 1934). W. F. Hook, *Lives of the Archbishops of Canterbury* (1860–76), vol. iii, is now outdated. C. H. Lawrence, *St. Edmund of Abingdon* (Oxford, 1960) is the best study of this archbishop. Decima Douie's *Archbishop Pecham* (Oxford, 1952) deals with him fully as a scholar and as a metropolitan. A life of Boniface of Savoy is needed; on Robert Winchelsey see above (pp. 671, 673) for Rose Graham's essays. Ellen M. F. Sommer-Seckendorff, *Studies in the Life of Robert Kilwardby, O.P.* (Rome, 1937) is a competent book, with the texts of a sermon and fourteen letters (pp. 162–85). F. S. Stevenson's *Robert Grosseteste* (1899) should now be supplemented by the commemorative volume, edited by D. A. Callus, *Robert Grosseteste, Scholar and Bishop* (Oxford, 1955). Constance M. Fraser, *A History of Antony Bek* (Oxford, 1957) is a good guide to the political and ecclesiastical activities of King Edward's famous counsellor. Much work has been done on diocesan life, and the episcopal visitation of religious houses and of the secular clergy: see especially J. R. H. Moorman, *Church Life in England in the Thirteenth Century* (Cambridge, 1945) with a good bibliography, C. R. Cheney, *Episcopal Visitation of Monasteries in the Thirteenth Century* (Manchester, 1931), David Knowles, *The Religious Orders in England* (Cambridge, 1948), pp. 78–114, Douie, op. cit., pp. 142–91, Rose Graham, *English Ecclesiastical Studies* (1929), pp. 330–59 (Winchelsey's visitation of the diocese of Worcester in 1301). On the household, staff, and records of the bishops see C. R. Cheney, *English Bishops' Chanceries 1100–1250* (Manchester, 1950), C. Jenkins on some thirteenth-century registers in *Church Quarterly Rev.*, xcix (1933), 69–115, and Rosalind Hill's study of Bishop Sutton and his archives in the *Journal of Ecclesiastical History*, ii (1951), 43–53. Miss Hill's introduction to the *Rolls and Register of Bishop Oliver Sutton of Lincoln 1280–1299*, i (Lincoln Record Soc., 1948) is a useful short account of the work of a bishop. Her paper on public penance in *History*, xxxvi (1951), 213–26, should be noted. Cf. C. J. Offer, *The Bishop's Register* (1929).

The history of canon law, the legal profession, and ecclesiastical courts is still in the making. In addition to the works of Churchill, Woodcock, and the authorities noted above (Ch. X) may be noted an introductory study on the Anglo-Norman canonists of the twelfth century, by S. Kuttner and Eleanor Rathbone in *Traditio*, vii (1949–51), 279–358, especially for Ricardus Anglicus (d. 1242), F. de Zulueta on the Oxford canonist, William of Drogheda and his *summa aurea* in *Mélanges de droit romain dédiés à Georges Cornil* (Ghent, 1926), pp. 641–57, and N. Denholm-Young on *dictamen* and the notarial art in his *Collected Papers*, pp. 26–54. J. W. Gray 'The Jus praesentandi in England from the constitution of Clarendon to Bracton' in *E.H.R.* lxvii (1952), 481–509, is an important study in the mutual relations between the English common law and the canonical procedure in the appointment to benefices. On two other matters, episcopal election and provisions, see Powicke, *King Henry III* in ch. 7 (pp. 259 ff.) and the works there cited, also, as a sketch of a canonist in episcopal service, the life of Lawrence of Somercote, the author of a treatise on canonical elections, in J. C. Russell, *Dictionary of Writers of Thirteenth-century England* (1936), pp. 81–82. Miss Norma Adams has in preparation a volume of cases in the ecclesiastical court of Canterbury, mainly in the periods of vacancy after the deaths of archbishops Edmund, Boniface, and John Pecham.

The cathedral and the organization of the chapter (secular or monastic) have been described by A. Hamilton-Thompson, *The Cathedral Churches of England* (1925), including a chapter (pp. 31–97) on their architectural development, and by Kathleen Edwards, *The English Secular Cathedrals in the Middle Ages* (Manchester, 1949), a valuable study with a most helpful bibliography of texts, treatises, and monographs. The cult of saints and veneration of relics as influences on structure are emphasized by C. R. Cheney in a paper on church building in the *Bulletin of the John Rylands Library*, xxxiv (1951–2), 20–36. For the liturgical life see Daniel Rock, *The Church of Our Fathers*, 2nd ed., 4 vols. (1903–4).

The parish and the parish church. A. Hamilton Thompson, *The Historical Growth of the English Parish Church* (Cambridge, 1911); *The Ground Plan of the English Parish Church* (Cambridge, 1911); *Parish History and Records* (Helps to studies of history, 1919); F. A. Gasquet, *Parish Life in Medieval England* (1906); J. C. Cox, *The English Parish Church* (1914); F. L. Cutts, *Parish Priests and Their People in the Middle Ages in England* (1898); H. G. Richardson, on the parish clergy in the thirteenth and fourteenth centuries in *Trans. R. Hist. Soc.*, 3rd ser. vi (1912); M. Deanesly, 'Village mass', in *The Listener* for 20 March 1942. For preaching see below (p. 765). On the husbandman's year and his church cf. G. C. Homans, *English Villagers of the Thirteenth Century* (Harvard Univ. Press, 1941), pp. 353–401; and on the whole subject, Moorman, op. cit., chapters vi, vii, xi. For penances imposed (or paid in money) on those who had taken the cross and could not go on crusade (above, p. 81) cf. *Hist. Papers and Letters from the Northern Registers* (R.S., 1873), pp. 46–56 (1276) and the documents noted in Hist. MSS. Comm., *5th Report*, Appendix (1876), 462, *Var. Coll.* i (1901), 235–6, and *8th Report* Appendix, pt. i (1881): lists of crusaders in Cornwall and Lincoln of various ways of life (late twelfth century) and articles of inquiry, apparently about 1292.

The best books on the dedication of churches are Frances Arnold-Forster, *Studies in Church Dedications*, 3 vols. (1899) and F. Bond, *Dedications and Parish Saints of English Churches, Ecclesiastical Symbols, &c.* (1914).

The authorization and supervision of the appointment of vicars to parish churches 'appropriated' by monastic bodies was an important duty of the bishops in the thirteenth century. It was a difficult duty, especially when it conflicted with orders of canons which appointed vicar-canons and were protected by papal privilege. See R. A. R. Hartridge, *A History of Vicarages in The Middle Ages* (Cambridge, 1930), H. M. Colvin, *The White Canons in England* (Oxford, 1951), pp. 272–88, and A. H. Sweet on papal indults, in *Speculum*, xxxi (1956), 602–10.

David Knowles has followed up his *Monastic Order in England*

(Cambridge, 1940), with his *Religious Orders in England* (Cambridge, 1948), which deals especially with monks and friars in the thirteenth century, with a bibliography. E. M. Thompson, *The Carthusian Order in England* (1930), Eileen Power, *Medieval English Nunneries* (Cambridge, 1922), and Rose Graham, *S. Gilbert of Sempringham and the Gilbertines* (1901), with the paper on the order of Grandmont (pp. 209–46) and other papers in her *English Ecclesiastical Studies* (1929), should also be noted; also H. M. Colvin's important book on the Premonstratensians cited above. W. A. Hinnebusch, *The Early English Friars Preachers* (Rome, 1951) supersedes, though with due acknowledgements and appreciation of its predecessors, all that has been written about the Dominican Order in England; it contains a full bibliography. A. G. Little's *Studies in English Franciscan History* (Manchester, 1917) is the best introduction both to the subject and to the other work of the distinguished scholar who did so much to revive learned and popular interest in the followers of St. Francis; see Knowles, *Religious Orders*, pp. 335–6, for a select list of his writings. A few additions to Knowles's discussion (pp. 194–204) and bibliography of the other friars and lesser orders may be given; on the Victorine houses, notably at Bristol and Wigmore, see Rosalind Hill, *Ecclesiastical Letter-Books* (privately printed), pp. 285–7, and B. Smalley's chapter on Andrew of St. Victor, Abbot of Wigmore, in her *Study of the Bible in the Middle Ages* (2nd ed., Blackwell, Oxford, 1952), pp. 112–19. The text of acts in a general chapter printed by H. E. Salter in *E.H.R.* lii (1937), 267–74, may be Victorine, not Arrouasian, as Salter decides. Richard W. Emery, in *Speculum*, xxiv (1949), 228–38, throws light on the Friars of the Blessed Mary or Pied Friars, sometimes confused with the Carmelites. The Templars are discussed by C. Perkins in *E.H.R.* xxv (1910), 209–30; Egerton Beck, ibid. xxvi (1911), 498–501, shows that North Ferriby was a cell of the Austin Canons of the 'Templum Domini' in Jerusalem, not a house of the Templars, who took their name from the Temple of Solomon. The financial and administrative importance of the New Temple in London was discussed by the late Agnes Sandys (Mrs. K. Leys) in *Essays . . . presented to T. F. Tout* (1925), pp. 147–62. For the Hospitallers see above, and J. H. Round on the order in Essex, in *Essex Archaeological Society's Transactions*, viii (1901), 182–6.

The monastic custumals of the regular life, of meetings in chapter, and of the administration and accounts of obedientiaries (the holders of offices, sacrist, cellarer, &c.) should not be separated too sharply from the registers of title deeds, charters, and lawsuits and the court rolls and accounts of monastic manors. All this mass of material was, at least in theory, subservient to the purpose of the *opus Dei*. Monastic economic administration, as the records of visitations show, was only one aspect of a great responsibility. Cf. the chapter ordinances and the statutes and injunctions of the bishops at Ely (1241–1307), printed by S. S. A. Evans in *Camden Miscellany*, xvii (Royal Hist. Soc., 1940), 1–35, or W. W. Hudson on the *camera* roll of the prior of Norwich (1283) in *Norfolk and Norwich Archaeol. Society*, xix, 268–313. Important recent studies of administration are R. A. L. Smith, *Canterbury Cathedral Priory* (Cambridge, 1943), and his *Collected Papers* (1947); H. M. Cam, 'The King's government as administered by the greater abbots of East Anglia', in her *Liberties and Communities*, pp. 183–204; A. E. Levett, 'Studies in the manorial organisation of St. Alban's Abbey' in her *Studies in Manorial History*, ed. H. M. Cam and L. S. Sutherland (Oxford, 1938), pp. 74–247; Marjorie Morgan, *The English Lands of the Abbey of Bec* (Oxford, 1946); F. Barlow, *Durham Jurisdictional Peculiars* (Oxford, 1950), Edward Miller, *The Abbey and Bishopric of Ely* (Cambridge, 1951); H. P. R. Finberg, *Tavistock Abbey* (Cambridge, 1951). See also, for monastic expenditure, A. Watkin on a fragment of a receiver's roll from Winchester Cathedral priory, in *E.H.R.* lxi (1946), 89–105, and, on the financial relationships between a lord and his officials in charge of manors (cf. above, pp. 366–8), J. S. Drew on the financial account of the same priory, ibid. lxii (1947), 20–40.

Susan Wood, in *English Monasteries and Their Patrons in the Thirteenth Century* (Oxford, 1955), deals with a subject of much social and religious importance too long neglected in England. Cf. H. M. Colvin, *The White Canons*, pp. 291–306. When William Ralegh, bishop of Winchester, discovered that the prior and convent of Mottisfont (Hants) had no temporal patron to whom they could turn, he took them under his protection; Hist. MSS. Comm., *Report on Various Collections*, iv, (1907), 144. More work on this subject is needed.

Schools and Universities. M. Deanesly on medieval schools to *c.* 1300 in *Cambridge Med. Hist.* v (1926), 765–79, and the bibliography;[1] R. W. Hunt on English Learning in the late twelfth century, in *Trans. R. Hist. Soc.*, 4th ser., xix (1936), 19–42; A. G. Little, on theological schools in medieval England, in *E.H.R.* lv (1940), 624–30; K. Edwards, The *English Secular Cathedrals* (Manchester, 1949), pp. 187–208. For the Universities see H. Rashdall, *The Universities of Europe in the Middle Ages*, 2nd ed. by F. M. Powicke and A. B. Emden (Oxford, 1936), vol. iii; A. B. Emden's massive *Biographical Register of the University of Oxford to 1500* (3 vols., Oxford, 1957–9); A. G. Little on the friars and the foundation of the faculty of theology at Cambridge, in *Mélanges Mandonnet* (Paris, 1930), ii. 389–401. On the statutes and curriculum of Oxford see the introduction to Strickland Gibson, *Statuta antiqua Universitatis Oxoniensis* (Oxford, 1931), and A. G. Little and F. Pelster, *Oxford Theology and Theologians* (Oxford Hist. Soc., 1934). The Dominican and Franciscan schools are discussed by Knowles, *The Religious Orders*, pp. 163–253 *passim*; Hinnebusch, *The Early English Friars Preachers*, pp. 332–419; and A. G. Little in *The Grey Friars in Oxford* (Oxford Hist. Soc., 1892), and his later study of the Franciscan school at Oxford in the thirteenth century, *Archivum Franciscanum Historicum*, xix (1926); cf. his introduction on Roger Bacon's life and works to *Roger Bacon Commemoration Essays* (Oxford, 1914) and his lecture on Bacon in *Proc. of the British Academy*, xiv (1928), 265–96; J. R. H. Moorman, *The Grey Friars in Cambridge* (Cambridge, 1951).

On early developments see A. B. Emden, *An Oxford Hall in the Middle Ages* (Oxford, 1927); H. E. Salter, *Medieval Oxford* (1936), pp. 90–102; D. A. Callus on Grosseteste, *Oxoniensia*, x (1945), 42–72. On the chancellors and their relations with the bishop of Lincoln see *Snappe's Formulary and Other Records* (Oxford Hist. Soc., 1924), pp. 318–36; Strickland Gibson in *E.H.R.* xxvi (1911), 501–12; and Rosalind Hill on Oliver Sutton and the University in *Trans. R. Hist. Soc.*, 4th ser., xxxi (1949), 1–16. J. F. Willard, *The Royal Authority and the Early English Universities* (Philadelphia, 1902); F. Pegues on royal support of students, in *Speculum*, xxxi (1956), 454–62, and G. L. Haskins on the *Jus ubique docendi* in *E.H.R.* lvi (1941), 281–92, illustrate other points. Graduates play a large part in J. C. Russell's *Dictionary of Writers*

[1] On A. F. Leach, *The Schools of Medieval England* (1915), see A. G. Little in *E.H.R.* xxx (1915), 525–9.

of Thirteenth Century England (Institute of Historical Research, 1936).

For the development of thought in the medieval universities, the history of science (in which Oxford took the lead in the thirteenth century), and the disputes which led to Pecham's intervention as archbishop in Oxford, see the book on Grosseteste noted above (p. 758), D. A. Callus on Aristotelian learning in Oxford in *Proc. of the British Academy*, xxix (1943), 229–81; D. L. Douie, *Archbishop Pecham*, pp. 272–301 (with full references to the literature on the dispute about forms). The introduction in this period to later scientific thought may be studied in the writings of several scholars, e.g. A. C. Crombie, *Robert Grosseteste and the origins of experimental science, 1100–1700* (Oxford, 1953); M.-D. Chenu in *Rev. des sciences philos. et theol.* xxix (1940), 206–17 (on Kilwardby's scientific acumen); and the bibliography in the books of Hinnebusch and Knowles.

The range of learning open to a scholar is well shown by Grosseteste's writings: see S. Harrison Thomson, *The Writings of Robert Grosseteste* (Cambridge, 1940). Here it is sufficient to emphasize the practical bearing of an academic training in theology, for the 'art of arts' was the cure of souls and the intention of the Lateran decrees of 1215 could best be put into effect by men trained in Biblical studies and the art of preaching, and by the provision of books for the guidance of priests, as well as by the instruction of the clergy generally through episcopal injunctions, visitation, and local inquiries by archdeacons, &c. A good survey of the literature is given by E. J. Arnould in his edition of one of the guides, *Le Manuel des Péchés* (Paris, 1940), an anonymous work written *c.* 1260, and in his bibliography (pp. 437–48); cf. for the interaction of these influences in Wales, Idris Foster, 'The Book of the Anchorite', in *Proc. of the British Academy*, xxxvi (1950), 197–226. A tradition had been set early in the twelfth century by Honorius, called Augustodunensis (see Eva M. Sanford in *Speculum*, xxiii (1947), 397–425), but form was given by the Lateran decrees of 1215, the compilation of the Gregorian decretals, on which Raymond de Pennaforte worked and Raymond's own *summa de casibus* (*c.* 1236). For the impetus of biblical study and commentaries see Beryl Smalley, *The Study of the Bible in the Middle Ages* (2nd ed., Oxford, 1952), where both scientific studies and the connexion between commentaries and preaching are illustrated. Preaching itself might reflect academic discipline according to rules or become homely and vivid exhortation abundantly illustrated by stories or *exempla*, just as painting was applied to mural pictorial teaching in churches: see D. W. Robertson on frequency of preaching in thirteenth-century England, in *Speculum*, xxiv (1949), 376 ff. For handbooks on preaching see the lists in H. Caplan, *Medieval Artes praedicandi* (Cornell Studies in Classical Philology, nos. 24, 25, 1934-6), and his paper on 'Classical rhetoric and mediaeval theory of preaching', in *Classical Philology*, xxviii (1933), 73-96; and especially Th. M. Charland, *Artes praedicandi* (Paris and Ottawa, 1936), with texts of the guides to preaching by Robert of Basingwork and Thomas Walys, who had several English predecessors; of H. G. Pfander in *Medium Ævum*, iii (1934), 19-29, for the alphabetical reference books for preachers; also Arnould, op. cit., p. 114. For collections of *exempla* see J. Th. Welter, *L'Exemplum dans la littérature religieuse et didactique du moyen âge* (Paris, 1927); the *Liber exemplorum* compiled for the use of preachers by a Franciscan in Ireland, ed. A. G. Little in *Brit. Soc. for Franciscan Studies*, i (1908), and the *Speculum laicorum*, ed. Welter (Paris, 1914). On sermons and their authorship see Jennifer Sweet in *Journal of Ecclesiastical History*, iv (1953), 27-36. One popular and lively English preacher was Odo of Cheriton (d. 1247), whose *exempla* were printed by L. Hervieux, *Les Fabulistes latins*, iv (Paris, 1899); on him, his writings, and his activities in the west of Europe in general, see A. C. Friend in *Speculum*, xxiii (1948), 641-58. For two sermons by St. Dominic's successor as master-general of his order, preached at Oxford in 1229, see A. G. Little, *E.H.R.* liv (1939), 1-19; for two sermons by the Franciscan minister-general, preached at Oxford in 1291, A. G. Little in *Collectanea Franciscana*, iv (Assisi, 1934), 161-74. In a well-known sermon Grosseteste advised a priest who knew no Latin to get a neighbour to expound to him the gospel for the coming Sunday, so that he could preach about it to his flock; this bit was quoted in an English Lollard tract long afterwards; see C. T. Buhler's edition of the tract in *Medium Ævum*, vii (1938), 167-83.

Recluses, men and women, were often more influential in spiritual matters than is usually supposed. Some had belonged to the same society as that for whose great ladies Matthew Paris wrote lives of saints in French verse. See F. M. Powicke on

Loretta, Countess of Leicester, in *Historical Essays in Honour of James Tait* (Manchester, 1933), 247–71, especially pp. 268–70; also, for the spiritual tradition, C. H. Talbot's edition of Ailred of Rievaulx, *De institutis inclusarum*, in *Analecta sacri ordinis Cisterciensis*, vii (1951), 167–217. On the recluses generally see R. M. Clay, *The Hermits and Anchorites of England* (1914).

Miscellaneous. J. L. Cate on the Church and market reform in the reign of Henry III, in *Essays in Honour of James Westfall Thompson* (Chicago, 1938), pp. 27–65; H. MacKenzie on the anti-foreign movement in England, 1231–2 (against the 'Italians') in *Haskins Anniversary Essays* (Boston, 1929), pp. 183–203; J. C. Russell on the canonization of opposition to the king in Angevin times, ibid., pp. 279–90.

11. THE SOCIAL ORDER

A. L. Poole, in the previous volume of this History (pp. 1–96) and in his *Obligations of Society in the Twelfth and Thirteenth Centuries* (Oxford, 1946), deals to some extent with this period; and the two volumes, edited by him, of the rewritten *Medieval England* (Oxford, 1958) keep alive an old book first edited by F. P. Barnard and published in 1902. Mary Bateson's *Medieval England* (1903), L. F. Salzman's *English Life in the Middle Ages* (1927), and Doris M. Stenton's *English Society in the Early Middle Ages* (1952) are good books.

The King and his Demesne. P. E. Schramm, *A History of the English Coronation* (Eng. trans., Oxford, 1937), especially pp. 71–73, 235; for the jewels and regalia used in 1220 (only a few were lost by King John in the Wash) see *History*, viii (1922), 161–8.[1] For the services claimed at the Coronation, officers of state, &c., see J. H. Round, *The King's Serjeants* (1911). E. H. Kantorowicz, *Laudes Regiae* (Univ. of California Press, 1946), pp. 171–9, throws light on the royal chapel and singers, and on Henry III's cult of the Confessor as the occasion for the more frequent singing of *Christus vincit*. Henry's artistic and favourite themes are brought out by Tancred Borenius, 'The cycle of images in the palaces and castles of Henry III' in *Journal of the*

---

[1] For the coronation chair (1300–1) and the stone brought from Scone (1296) see L. Tanner and C. F. Davidson in *The Times*, 11 May 1937. Hemingburgh describes the stone on which John Baliol was set at Scone in 1292 quite differently as 'lapis pergrandis in ecclesia Dei juxta majus altare, concavus quidem et admodum rotundae cathedrae confectus' (ed. Hamilton, ii. 38).

BIBLIOGRAPHY

Warburg and Courtauld Institutes, vi (1943), 40–50. One favourite story was the parable of Dives and Lazarus; and on the distribution of alms on special occasions in the royal households see Hilda Johnstone in *Speculum*, iv (1929), 149–67. Henry, in youth and again later (*c.* 1244–62), had a *versificator* or rhymer, the poet Henry of Avranches, on whom see J. C. Russell and J. P. Heironimus, *The Shorter Latin Poems of Master Henry of Avranches relating to England* (Med. Acad. of America, 1935). Mary C. Hill has described the King's messenger service and its relation to the King's wardrobe in *E.H.R.* lxi (1946), 315–28.

The financial system and records of the royal household of the king, queen, and royal children are most clearly described by C. Johnson in the *Trans. R. Hist. Soc.*, 4th ser., vi (1923), 50–72. This paper gives an excellent picture of the household and its financial department, the wardrobe, from surviving records, as developed from the time of the *Constitutio Domus Regis* of Henry I. G. H. White, *Antiquaries Journal*, xxx (1950), 52–63, takes this tract as the basis for a description of the king's sport, dogs, hawks, &c.; cf. Round, op. cit., pp. 268–317. The best detailed guides to the whole subject of royal and baronial households are Tout's *Chapters* (see especially the classified index, vi. 278–90, s.v. Household) and Denholm-Young's *Seignorial Administration*, pp. 6–31, where Edward's household from 1254 is described (pp. 8–11). The introduction to the printed bishops' registers generally give some account of episcopal households. See also, for Eleanor, countess of Leicester and Queen Eleanor of Castile, T. H. Turner, *Manners and Household Expenses of England* (Roxburghe Club, 1841) and cf. Hilda Johnstone on the Queen's Exchequer under the three Edwards in *Historical Essays in Honour of James Tait*, pp. 143–6.

The royal domain comprised not only lands, palaces, castles, and houses, but many of the boroughs, most of the forests, and most of the Jews. On the domain see R. S. Hoyt, *The Royal Demesne in English Constitutional History* (Cornell Univ. Press, 1950, London, 1951). For the boroughs and castles, &c., see below. A. L. Poole's pages on the forests, *From Domesday Book to Magna Carta* (pp. 28–35), and the essential work of Turner, Petit-Dutaillis, and Bazeley (noted by Poole, p. 503), may be supplemented by E. C. Wright, 'Common Law in the thirteenth century English royal forest', in *Speculum*, iii (1928), 166 ff., and M. L. Bazeley on the Forest of Dean and its relation with the Crown in the *Trans. of Bristol and Gloucestershire Archaeol. Soc.* xxxiii. 153–285. Cf., for much relevant to this period, N. Neilson's chapter on the forests in *The English Government at Work, 1327–36*, i (Med. Acad. of America, 1940), 394–467.

The Jews. The Jews were royal chattels, both exploited and protected by the Crown, but they were also members of a widespread community with relatives in other countries, and knit together by their religion and their learning, and by traditions to which the Christian Church owed more than respect; cf. Margaret Schlauch in *Speculum*, xiv (1939), 448–64. J. Parkes on 'The Church and the Synagogue in the Middle Ages' in *Trans. of the Jewish Hist. Soc. of England*, xvi. 25–33, is an address (1949) on the subject of his larger book (1934). See also S. Grayzel, *The Church and the Jews in the Thirteenth Century* (Philadelphia, 1933), C. Roth, *The Intellectual Activities of Medieval English Jewry* (Brit. Academy, Supplemental Papers, no. viii, 1949), and his *The Jews of Medieval Oxford* (Oxford Hist. Soc., 1951), ch. vi; and B. Smalley, *The Study of the Bible in the Middle Ages* (2nd ed., 1952), pp. 156–72, 338–55. Roth's *History of the Jews in England* (Oxford, 1941), pp. 18–131, refers to the records of the organization of the Jews in the English exchequer, gives a list of the chief modern books, and summarizes the history of the Jews and their expulsion in 1290. Cf. also G. Caro, *Sozial- und Wirtschaftsgeschichte der Juden im Mittelalter und in der Neuzeit*, ii (Leipzig, 1919) ch. 1; Alicia C. Cramer on the Jewish exchequer in *American Hist. Rev.* xlv (Jan. 1940), 327 ff.; and P. Elman, on the economic causes of the expulsion, in *Econ. Hist. Rev.* vii (1937), 145–54.

Barons and Knights. The history of these orders and their lands is intensely complicated, as new baronial complexes formed and parcels of knights' fees dissolved and were reshuffled and single fees were split up. The difficulties are increased by the lax use in records and annals of the words honour, baron, barony, and tenure *per baroniam*. Dugdale's *Baronage* (1675–6), Madox's *Baronia Anglica* (1736 and 1841), the *Complete Peerage* and W. Farrer's *Honors and Knights' Fees* (Manchester, 1923–5) grapple with the problems and trace particular developments. J. H. Round devoted several books and numerous scattered papers to the subject. See also a paper on the survival of the honour of Eudo Dapifer and its court at

Walbrook in London by N. Denholm-Young, in his *Collected Papers*, pp. 154–61; S. H. F. Johnston on the lands of Hubert de Burgh, *E.H.R.* l (1935), 418–32, and W. H. Stevenson on the ways in which the archives of half a dozen important families were comprised in the muniments of the Willoughbys at Wollaton: Hist. MSS. Comm., *Report on the MSS. of Lord Middleton* (1911), p. vi.

The terms baronage and peerage, from the early days when a baron was a tenant-in-chief, a king's man, however great or small, or a great lord's man (Stenton, *First Century of English Feudalism*, pp. 83–113), were discussed by Round in his peerage cases, and in articles in periodicals, some collected in his *Studies in Peerage* (1901) and *Peerage and Pedigree*, 2 vols. (1910). See the bibliography in the posthumous collection, *Family Origins and Other Studies* (1930), edited by W. Page, pp. xlix–lxxiv. His most important papers from a general point of view are 'The House of Lords and the Model Parliament' (*E.H.R.* xxx, 1915, 385–97), 'Barons and Peers' (ibid. xxxiii, 1918, 453–71), and 'Barons and Knights in the Great Charter' (*Magna Carta Commemoration Essays*, pp. 46–77). In these papers he explains why the peerage lawyer is bound to believe what the critical historian may have to reject, and also how the exchequer and other royal courts, in particular cases in the thirteenth century, tried to decide between tenure by barony and tenure by knight's service in the assessment of feudal reliefs. Rachel R. Reid made a gallant attempt in the *E.H.R.* xxxv (1920), 161–99, to get behind these problems and, in the light of Anglo-Saxon, Scottish, and Norman evidence, to define 'barony' in terms of its judicial liberties and obligations and to identify the greater barons with those tenants who had castles. Here we come to seignorial jurisdiction and household administration, discussed by Denholm-Young in his valuable book *Seignorial Administration in England* (Oxford, 1937), and previously by J. F. Baldwin in the *E.H.R.* xlii (1927), 180–9, on the household system of Henry Lacy, Earl of Lincoln (1295–1305). See also L. M. Midgley, *Ministers' Accounts of the Earldom of Cornwall*, 2 vols. (Royal Hist. Soc., 1942–5). Cf. Hist. MSS. Comm., *Report on Lord Middleton's MSS.* (1911), pp. 324–7, on Henry de Grey; and M. S. Giuseppi, *Archaeologia*, lxx (1920), on Bogo de Clare. S. Painter, *Studies in the History of the English Feudal Barony* (Baltimore, 1943), attempts a survey of wide range which is useful and suggestive.

For the administration of ecclesiastical liberties see above p. 762. On heraldry and coats of arms see A. R. Wagner, *Heralds and Heraldry in the Middle Ages* (Oxford, 1939).

The social distinctions within the knightly class and the changes in its essentially military character are discussed above (Ch. XI). Denholm-Young's paper on the tournament, in *Studies . . . presented to F. M. Powicke*, pp. 240–68, is essential, and add to the other references given above (p. 515), Mary E. Giffin on the Mortimers and the Wigmore MS. now in Chicago, in *Speculum*, xvi (1941), 109–20, R. W. Ackerman on the ceremonies of knighting in the Middle English Romances, ibid. xix (1944), 285–313 and R. S. Loomis, 'Edward I, Arthurian Enthusiast', ibid. xxviii (1953), 114–27. The mingling of military and more domesticated influences in the century is illustrated by contrast with the more active survival, in the border districts in west and north, of local military services attached to parcels of land, and of castle guard; see Painter, *English Feudal Barony*, pp. 130–5, Stewart-Brown, *Serjeants of the Peace*, and Una Apps on the *muntatores* or mounted soldiers who appear especially in Shropshire, *E.H.R.* lxiii (1948), 528–33, and cf. (for service due in Wales) Hist. MSS. Comm., *Rep. on Duke of Rutland's MSS.* iv (1905), 37, 38. The local commission of array which, like the use of military indentures at a higher social grade, reflects the gradual breakdown of traditional services, had its counterpart in police measures like watch and ward; cf. B. Lees on the *villa integra* in *E.H.R.* xli (1926), 98–103.

The royal palaces, baronial houses and domestic architecture generally, especially in quieter areas, supplemented, but never displaced, castle building. See A. Hamilton-Thompson, *Military Architecture in England during the Middle Ages* (London, 1912), and the bibliography in *Cambridge Med. Hist.* vi. 969–70. Add A. J. Taylor on the career of the carpenter and engineer, Thomas de Houghton (1290–c. 1312), in *Antiquaries Journal*, xxx (1950). For the Welsh castles and towns see W. Rees, *Caerphilly Castle* (Cardiff, 1937) and the works noted above (p. 430 n.). On the features common to military and domestic buildings and the development of the latter see Hamilton-Thompson, *The English House* (Hist. Association Pamphlet, 1936); cf. J. N. L. Myres on Hamstead Marshall in *Transactions of the Newbury District Field Club*, vi (1932), reprint of sixteen pages. Henry III's buildings and artistic interests and the services of Edward, son of Odo, goldsmith, painter, and royal agent, are discussed in H. F. Westlake, *Westminster Abbey*, 2 vols. (1923), W. R. Lethaby, *Westminster Abbey and the King's Craftsmen* (1906), and *Westminster Abbey Re-examined* (1925), H. Jenkinson, on Edward son of Odo, in *Archaeologia*, xxiv (1925), 322–4; J. G. Noppen in *Antiquaries Journal*, xxviii (1948), 138–48 and xxix (1949), 13–25; and, for Clarendon, &c., by T. Borenius and J. Charlton in *Antiquaries Journal*, xvi (1935), 55–84, and T. Borenius in his paper 'The cycle of images in the palaces and castles of Henry III', *Journal of the Warburg and Courtauld Institutes*, vi (1943), 40–50, with references, plan of Clarendon and lists of buildings. See generally T. Hudson Turner, *Some Account of Domestic Architecture in England*, 3 vols. in 4 (Oxford, 1851–9). For particular houses cf. E. Clive Rouse on Longthorpe Tower, near Peterborough (*Country Life*, 4 Apr. 1948); an article on The Mounts, Pachesham, near Leatherhead in *The Times*, 31 August 1949, and, for a town house in London of Philip Marmion (1269–73), Hist. MSS. Comm., *Report on Lord Middleton's MSS.* (1911), 73–75. A good idea of the development of farm buildings and the management of a manor can be got from *Henry of Bray's Estate Book*, or Harleston register (Royal Hist. Soc., 1916), valuable for the interests, official life, and independence of a country gentleman.

The whole subject of the masonic craft is explained in D. Knoop and G. P. Jones, *The Medieval Mason* (Manchester, 1933), and in the full and elaborate survey of L. F. Salzman, *Building in England down to 1540* (Oxford, 1952).

Municipal, Industrial, and Commercial History. C. Gross, *The Gild Merchant*, 2 vols. (Oxford, 1890) made a fresh start in English municipal history. The bibliography (i. 301–32) lists the literature up to 1890. More convenient bibliographies, brought up to date, can be found in A. Ballard and James Tait, *British Borough Charters, 1216–1307* (Cambridge, 1923), and J. Tait, *The Medieval English Borough* (Manchester, 1936), books essential to study of the subject. Cf. a useful review of the former by C. Johnson, in *E.H.R.* xxxix (1924), 119–21, where the difficulty in defining a borough, e.g. the difference between a borough and a market town (above, pp. 532–3), is discussed. Cf. J. H. Clapham on a thirteenth-century market town: Linton, Cambs., in the *Cambridge Hist. Journal*, iv (1933), 194–202. W. Savage, *The Making of our Towns* (1952), is a suggestive and pleasant little book. Recent additions to local histories include Gladys A. Thornton, *A History of Clare, Suffolk* (Cambridge, Heffer, 1930), a market town, M. D. Lobel, *The Borough of Bury St. Edmunds* (Oxford, 1935), a good account of a town ruled by a great abbey, H. E. Salter, *Medieval Oxford* (Oxford Hist. Soc., 1936), and J. W. F. Hill, *Medieval Lincoln* (Cambridge, 1948), an excellent book. Royal and seignorial boroughs were regarded as demesne and only gradually acquired self-government under mayor and council. To an important extent royal towns acted, through their officials, as royal agents, like knights of the shire, especially in ports like Bristol and Southampton. Even London was taken at will into the king's hands (cf. above, pp. 626–8). On the legal status of markets see L. F. Salzman in *Cambridge Hist. Journal*, ii (1928), 205–12.

The government of London is discussed by Tait (see the index to his book on the borough, s.v. London) and by A. H. Thomas, *Calendar of Early Mayors' Court Rolls, 1298–1307* (Cambridge, 1924); cf. also the introductions to *Munimenta Gildhallae Londoniensis*, 3 vols. (R.S., 1859–62). The chief history is M. Weinbaum, *Verfassungsgeschichte Londons, 1066–1268* (Stuttgart, 1929), continued in *London unter Eduard I und II*, 2 vols., the second a volume of texts (Stuttgart, 1933). G. Unwin wrote a description of London *c.* 1250, and an essay on London tradesmen and their creditors: see *Studies in Economic History: the Collected Papers of George Unwin*, ed. R. H. Tawney (1927), pp. 76–91, 100–16; cf. Vincent B. and Lilian J. Redstone on the Heyrons of London (1290 onwards) and the origins of the Chaucer family, in *Speculum*, xii (1937), 182–95. E. Ekwall, *Two Early London Subsidy Rolls* (Lund, 1951), has given a minute analysis of the London population, its origin, trades, &c., at the turn of the century. E. L. Sabine's papers on sanitation and the need for it, in *Speculum*, viii. 335–52; ix. 303–21; xii. 19–42 (1933–7) reveal the less savoury side of London life.

The Cinque Ports and the development of English naval forces (see above, Ch. XIII) have been studied by K. M. E. Murray, *The Constitutional History of the Cinque Ports* (Manchester, 1935), also a paper on Faversham and the Cinque Ports in *Trans. R. Hist. Soc.*, 4th ser., xviii (1935), 53–84; and by F. W. Brookes in a paper on the Cinque Ports in *The Mariner's Mirror*, xv (1929), 142–91, and his book *The English Naval Forces, 1199–1272* (Hull, 1932).

Towns, industries, commerce, and the manorial system are dealt with in the general works on economic history, W. A. Ashley, *An Introduction to English Economic History and Theory*, 2 vols. (1888–93, 3rd ed. of vol. i, 1894); W. Cunningham, *The Growth of English Industry and Commerce*, i (5th ed., Cambridge, 1910); G. Brodnitz, *Englische Wirtschaftsgeschichte*, i (Jena, 1918), and E. Lipson. *The Economic History of England*, i (revised ed., 1937); cf. also L. F. Salzman, *English Industries of the Middle Ages* (new ed., Oxford, 1923), and, for trade and special industries, *Cambridge Economic History of Europe*, ii (Cambridge, 1952); G. R. Lewis, *The Stannaries: a Study of the English Tin Miner* (Harvard Univ. Press, 1908), N. S. B. Gras, *The Evolution of the English Corn Market* (Harvard Univ. Press, 1915), E. M. Carus-Wilson on the cloth industry in late twelfth and early thirteenth centuries, in *Econ. Hist. Rev.* xiv (1944), 32–50; also ibid. xi (1941), 39–60, on the introduction of fulling-mills in the thirteenth century. The appropriate sections in the various Victoria County Histories are helpful for local industries. A good local county survey is H. J. Hewitt, *Medieval Cheshire* (Chetham Soc., 1929), e.g. on the wiches or salt workings, pp. 108–21. On wool, the wool trade, and the home and foreign merchants see the references above, pp. 622, 628, 662 ff., notably, J. de Sturler, *Les Relations politiques et les échanges commerciaux entre le duché de Brabant et l'Angleterre au moyen âge* (Paris, 1936); cf., for useful local details, L. V. G. Owen on Lincolnshire and the wool trade in the *Reports and Papers* of the associated architectural and archaeological societies, xxxix, pt. 2 (1929), 259–63; also J. Conway Davies, 'The Wool Customs accounts for Newcastle-upon-Tyne for the reign of Edward I', in *Archaeologia Aeliana*, 4th ser., xxxii (1954), 220–308. On north European trade see H. G. Leach, *Angevin Britain and Scandinavia* (1921), O. A. Johnsen on Norwegian trade in *Revue Historique*, clxxviii (1936), 385–410, and H. S. Lucas in *Speculum*, xii (1937), 167–81.

Agrarian Society. The best introduction to recent discussions and the voluminous literature on this subject is by Nellie Neilson in the *Cambridge Economic History of Europe*, i (Cambridge, 1941), 438–66, with its valuable bibliography (pp. 665–70). The original sources range from the lawbooks, statutes, Curia Regis, eyre, and other plea rolls, to ministers' accounts (of lands temporarily in royal hands), collections of charters, surveys, extents, court rolls, accounts, and treatises on husbandry, &c. Much of this material, e.g. the registers and other records of monastic houses noted above (p. 737), has been published, calendared[1] and used in articles. Good examples, easily overlooked, are the Reports of the Hist. MSS. Comm., notably on the *MSS. of the Duke of Rutland*, iv (1905), and the scattered papers of J. H. Round, particularly in the *Transactions of the Essex Archaeological Society*, e.g. *The Making of Brentwood* (xvii. 69): see the list in *Family Origins*, ed. W. Page (1930), pp. lxi–lxv.

Good histories are G. C. Homans, *The English Villagers of the Thirteenth Century* (Harvard Univ. Press, 1941), H. S. Bennett, *Life on the English Manor, 1150–1400* (Cambridge, 1937); also C. S. and C. S. Orwin, *The Open Fields* (Oxford, 1938), H. L. Gray, *English Field Systems* (Harvard Univ. Press, 1915), and N. C. B. and C. C. Gras, *The Economic and Social History of an English Village* (Harvard Univ. Press, 1930) on the history of Crawley in Hampshire; cf. C. W. Foster, *A History of the Village of Aisthorpe and Thorpe in the Fallows* (Lincoln, 1927), and R. W. Jeffery, *Thornton-le-Dale* (Wakefield, 1931). P. Vinogradoff, *Villeinage in England* (Oxford, 1892) and *The Growth of the Manor* (3rd ed., 1920) are classics, though sometimes disputable, and F. Seebohm's famous *English Village Community* (1883, re-issued 1913), is still valuable (cf. especially ch. ii). G. G. Coulton, in his discursive way, discussed many features of village life in his books, *The Medieval Village* (Cambridge, 1925) and *Medieval Panorama* (Cambridge, 1938). On corn and prices see W. Ashley, *The Bread of our Forefathers* (Oxford, 1928), and W. H. Beveridge (on the Winchester rolls) in *Econ. Hist. Rev.* ii (1929), 93–113, and in a supplement to the *Economic Journal* (May 1927, pp. 155–67). These are complementary to the great work of J. E. Thorold Rogers, *History of Agriculture and Prices*, vols. i and ii (Oxford, 1866–92). To the bibliography in the *Cambridge Econ. Hist.* add *Surrey Manorial Accounts*, ed. H. M. Briggs (Surrey Rec. Soc., 1935), including a catalogue of the rolls before 1300.

In recent years scholars have tended to concentrate upon a

---

[1] e.g. *East Kent Records: Calendar of Unpublished Deeds and Court Rolls in Lambeth Palace*, ed. Irene Churchill (Kent Archaeological Society, 1922); H. Hall and Frieda J. Nicholas, 'Manorial accounts of the priory of Canterbury, 1260–1420' in *Bulletin of the Institute of Historical Research*, viii (1931), 137–55; also J. A. Raftis, *The Estates of Ramsey Abbey* (Toronto, 1957).

series of related forces which faced lords and stewards and bailiffs and affected the prosperity of the free and unfree tenants and the growth of the free element in the population. These were the tendency to a rise in prices, the growth of population, rent values, and the profits of demesne farming, none of which was so powerful as to prevent the landholder from such changes of course in estate management as circumstances suggested. See E. A. Kosminsky, *Studies in the Agrarian History of England in the Thirteenth Century* (Eng. Trans., Oxford, 1956), the work of R. A. L. Smith noted above (p. 762), Denholm-Young's *Seignorial Administration*, and the articles of T. A. M. Bishop, H. L. Gray, E. A. Kosminsky, R. Lennard, S. A. Moore, N. Neilson, and M. Postan noted in the *Cambridge Econ. Hist.*; also R. H. Hilton's *Social Structure of Rural Warwickshire in the Middle Ages* (Dugdale Society occasional papers, no. 9, 1950) and his articles on peasant movements in *Econ. Hist. Rev.*, 2nd ser., ii (1949), 117–36, and on a thirteenth-century poem on disputed villein services in *E.H.R.* lvi (1941), 90–97. Cf. F. M. Powicke on the English freeholder in *Wirtschaft und Kultur: Festschrift zum 70. Geburtstag von Alfons Dopsch* (Baden-bei-Wien, 1938), pp. 382–93, Joan Wake on the *communitas villae* at Harleston, Northants., *E.H.R.* xxxvii (1922), 406–13; W. O. Ault on village by-laws, ibid. xlv (1930), 208–31; Eileen Power's comments on work by Frances M. Page and Helen Briggs in *History*, xxii (1937), 264–7. For drainage operations, marsh embankments, essarts, &c., see R. A. L. Smith in *Econ. Hist. Rev.*, x (1940), 29–37 (Kent), and the books of J. W. F. Hill on Lincoln and E. Miller on Ely, already noted; cf. Kathleen Major's paper on Conan, son of Ellis, for activities at Holbeach early in the century, in *Reports and Papers* of the Associated Architectural and Archaeological Societies, xlii, pt. 1 (1934), 1–28; and see also H. C. Darby, *The Medieval Fenland* (Cambridge, 1940). The Reports of the Hist. MSS. Comm. contain material on manorial customs, &c.: e.g. *Report on MSS. of Marquess of Lothian* (1905), pp. 6–10, 22–24, 33–39; *Report on MSS. of the Dean and Chapter of Wells*, i (1907), 332–6, on a manor held in ancient demesne, Curry Norton; *Reports on Various Collections*, iv (1907), 74, an inquiry by two stewards of the exchequer of St. Peter's cathedral church, Exeter, into amercements imposed by mistake upon *nativi* at Stoke Canon whose local speech had been misunderstood (*de stipite in stipitem, anglice* 'stok after stok') as a claim to hold in socage. J. F. Willard, in *The Bodleian Quarterly Record*, vii (1932), 33–39, examined in the light of illuminated calendars in the library the occupations of the months in medieval times.

Communications. F. M. Stenton 'The road system in medieval England', in *Econ. Hist. Rev.* vii (1930), 1–21; Dorothy Broome, 'Exchequer Migrations to York in the thirteenth and fourteenth centuries', in *Essays . . . presented to T. F. Tout* (1925), pp. 291–300, with a map; Hill, *Medieval Lincoln*, ch. xv, on communications and trade (pp. 304–27; cf. pp. 9–14); Hewitt, *Medieval Cheshire*, pp. 112–13. An average day's journey in medieval France seems to have been from 20 to 30 miles; see Marjorie N. Boyer in *Speculum*, xxvi (1951), 597–608. Much attention has been given lately to this subject.

12. LITERATURE AND ART

Literature. J. E. Wells, *A Manual of the Writings in Middle English*, 1050–1400 (New Haven, 1918) with supplements, 1919–; R. M. Wilson, *Early Middle English Literature, 1066–1300* (1939); J. Vising, *Anglo-Norman Language and Literature* (1923); H. D. L. Ward, *Catalogue of Romances in the Department of MSS. of the British Museum*, 3 vols. (1883–1910, vol. iii by J. A. Herbert); also M. D. Legge, *Anglo-Norman in the Cloisters* (Edinburgh, 1950) and her essay in *Medieval Studies presented to Rose Graham* (Oxford, 1950), pp. 146–62. The best introduction to the discussion about the languages spoken in England is R. M. Wilson's paper 'English and French in England 1100–1300', in *History*, xxviii (1943), 37–60; cf. J. R. Hulbert, 'English in manorial documents of the 13th to 14th centuries', in *Modern Philology*, xxxiv (Aug. 1936), 37–61; and, more generally, J. Westfall Thompson, *The Literacy of the Laity in the Middle Ages* (Berkeley, Cal., 1939), especially pp. 166–95. On plays see E. K. Chambers, *The Medieval Stage*, 2 vols. (Oxford, 1903), and for the liturgical background the fine work of Karl Young, *The Drama of the Medieval Church*, 2 vols. (Oxford, 1933), though this is not primarily concerned with England nor with our period. A petition of the prioress of Clerkenwell (1300–1) shows that 'miracles' were not necessarily devout and quiet performances: see W. O. Hassall in *Modern Language Rev.* xxxiii (1938), 564–7.

A few books and articles may be noted to indicate kinds of literature and its loss through lack of written record: R. W.

Chambers, 'The lost literature of medieval England', in *The Library*, 4th ser., v (1924–5), 293–321; Carleton Brown's selection in *English Lyrics in the XIIIth century* (Oxford, 1932); J. Murray's edition of Grosseteste's *Le Château d'amour* (Paris, 1948): L. Brandin's edition of *Fouke Fitz Warin* (Paris, 1930) and his paper on the romance of Fulk fitzWarin, in *Romania*, lv (1929), 17–44; J. W. Ashton, 'Rymes of Randolph, Erl of Chester', in *Eng. Lit. Hist.* v (1938), 195–206; and four volumes published by the Anglo-Norman Text Society (Oxford, Blackwell), viz. *La Seinte Resureccion*, a play ed. T. Atkinson Jenkins and others (1943); *Le secre de secrez*, ed. O. A. Beckerlegge (1944), by Pierre d'Abernon of Fetcham; *An Anglo-Norman Rhymed Apocalypse with Commentary*, ed. Olwen Rhys (1946); and *St. Modwenna*, ed. A. T. Baker and A. Bell (1947).

Art. The development of the arts was influenced by and, in its turn, influenced social change and technological advance. Thus the diffusion of the Roman breviary, especially by the friars, both reflected the reaction against long-drawn-out and difficult musical services in monastic churches and led to the canonical obligation to say the office day by day, while, on the other hand, it left the monks and canons free to develop their musical modes: cf. S. A. van Dijk, 'Historical Liturgy and Liturgical History', in *Dominican Studies*, ii (1949), 161–82. Again, technical inventions, e.g. in the manufacture of textiles, in hull-design, rig, and rudder in ships, the processes of reckoning, exchange, and minting, the invention of spectacles, affected society and, therefore, interest in science and the arts profoundly; see a suggestive paper by Lynn White, Jr., on technology and invention in the Middle Ages, in *Speculum*, xv (1940), 141–59, and, for technical processes of the exchange, C. G. Crump and A. Hughes on the tract in the Red Book of the Exchequer (iii. 979–1010), in *Economic Journal*, v (1895), 50–67.

In addition to Peter Brieger's volume on the thirteenth century in the Oxford History of English Art (1957), the relevant chapters in *Medieval England*, ed. A. L. Poole (Oxford, 1958), and books and articles noted above (pp. 770–1), note the following.[1]

Architecture. E. S. Prior, *A History of Gothic Art in England* (1900); F. Bond, *An Introduction to English Church Architecture*, 2 vols. (Oxford, 1913); a pamphlet of Geoffrey Webb, *Gothic*

[1] I am indebted to Mr. T. S. R. Boase for a list on which what follows is based.

Architecture in England (1951), a summary of the latest views; M. E. Wood on 'Thirteenth-century domestic architecture in England', a supplement to *Archaeological Journal*, cv (1950). Cf. J. Harvey, *Gothic England* (1947). Work on medieval architecture is, indeed, proceeding busily.

Sculpture. E. S. Prior and A. Gardner, *An Account of Medieval Figure Sculpture in England* (Cambridge, 1912). An important discussion of English thirteenth-century sculpture is contained in A. Andersson's *English Influence in Norwegian and Swedish Sculpture in Wood, 1220–70* (Stockholm, 1940). See also W. H. St. John Hope and W. R. Lethaby on the imagery and sculpture on the west front of Wells Cathedral, in *Archaeologia*, lix (1904), 165 ff., and N. Pevsner, *The Leaves of Southwell* (1945).

Wall-painting. E. W. Tristram, *English Medieval Wall Painting: the Thirteenth Century*, 2 vols. (Oxford, 1950).

Illumination. E. G. Millar, *English Illuminated Manuscripts from the 10th to the 13th Century* (Paris and Brussels, 1926); O. E. Saunders, *English Illumination*, 2 vols. (Florence and Paris, 1928); M. R. James, on the drawings of Matthew Paris, in *Walpole Society*, xiv (1925–6), and on *The Apocalypse in Art* (1931); A. Hollander on pictorial work in the Chetham MS. of the *Flores Historiarum*, in the *Bulletin of the John Rylands Library*, xxviii (1944), 361–81; G. Haseloff, *Die Psalter Illustration im 13. Jahrhundert* (1938); D. D. Egbert, *The Tickhill Psalter and related Manuscripts* (New York, 1940).

INDEX

Abbeville, 235.

Aberconway, Cistercian monastery, burial place of princes, 389.
— abbot of (1248), 389–90.
— *See* Conway.

Aberffraw (Anglesey), 387, 392 n.; prince of, origin of title, 393.

Abergavenny, lordship and castle of, 172, 395 & n., 396, 402 & n., 443 n.; parliament in (1291), 346.

Abermoyl, market town, 387.

Aberystwyth, castle, or Llanbadarn, 394; a centre of administration, 410; restoration of, 430, 432; borough of, 433; in the revolt of 1294–5, 441, 442.

Abingdon, St. Edmund of, *see* Edmund.

Accursius, Franciscus, 286, 469 & n., 626.

Acre, fall of (1291), 267.
— John of, *see* Brienne.

Acton Burnell, 337, 338, 339, 624; statute of, 625, *and see* Statutes.

Adams, G. B., note on shire courts, &c., as of record, 750.

Adams, Norma, on the judicial conflict over tithes, 464 n., 469 n.; on writs of prohibition, 475 n.

Admiral of the fleet, first, powers and jurisdiction of, 655 & n., 656; *see* Leyburn, William; Alard, Gervase.

Admiralty, 655–7; court of, 655 & n.

Adolf of Nassau, king of Germany (1292–8), 659–68 *passim*.

Adour, lower valley of, 650.

Advowsons, in English and canon law, 463–4.

Aedh, king of Connaught, 42.

Agen, 291, 292–3; Edward I at (1286), 256 n.
— bishop of (1279), 292–3.
— diocese of, 292 n.

Agenais, rights in the, 127, 128; the succession to the, 272, 273; transferred to Edward I, 289, 291–3; ordinance for administration of (1289), 298, 302–3. *See also* 647, 650, 654.

Aids, feudal, in Henry III's time, 32–33.

Aigueblanche, Peter of, bishop of Hereford (1240–68), on a mission to western princes (1242–3), 104; and treaty of Toledo (1254), 118; during barons' war, 175, 199.

Aigues Mortes, 224, 255.

Ailred, abbot of Rievaulx, previously *dapifer* of King David I, 580 n.

Aire, bishop of, 295 n.

Alan the Red, count of Brittany, 236 n.

Alard, family of, 637 n.
— Gervase, admiral (1300), 656.
— Thomas, of Winchelsea, 636–7.

Alba, battle of, 225.

Albert, king of Germany and emperor-elect, 653, 660, 667, 710 n.; and treaty of 1303, 653–4 n.

Alençon, count of, 248.

Alexander IV, Pope (1254–61), and the Sicilian business, 106, 120 & nn., 122–5 *passim*; and the English baronial leaders, 131 & n., 135–6, 461; releases Henry III from his oath to the Provisions of Oxford, 163–5 *passim*; his nuncios in England, 159 n., 167 & n.; and the customs and privileges of Scotland, 593 & n.
— II, king of the Scots (1214–49), 16, 73, 89; his homage to Henry III (1217), 594; papal refusal to allow coronation of (1221), 593; his relations with England, 585–8; Henry III's claim to his homage for Scotland, 594–5; and the earldom of Huntingdon, 594 & n.; his marriages, *see* Joan, sister of Henry III, and Coucy, Marie de; his sisters, *see* Isabella, Margaret, Marjorie.
— — his clerk, Robert of St. Germain, 12.
— III, king of Scots (1249–86), acclaimed, 577; does homage for English lands and married to Margaret, d. of Henry III (1251), 581; his minority, 138, 582 & n., 589–92; desires to be crowned, 593, 594; Henry III's attempt to get his homage for Scotland, 595; terms of his homage to Edward I (1279), 595 & n.; his second marriage (1285), and death (1286), 597; his administration of Scotland, 577–8, cf. 198; the appeal of his creditor, John le Mason, 610 n. *See* Margaret, Yolande.
— elder son of Alexander III, king of Scots, marries d. of Guy, count of Flanders, 597, 623; his early death (1284), 597; later dispute about his wife's dowry, 610 n.

Alfonso X, the Wise, king of Castile (1252–85), his relations with Navarre, Gascony, and Henry III (1252–4), 116–18; his projected crusade in

Africa, 118; his later relations with Henry III, 119–20, 122 n.; his election as king of the Romans and claim to the Empire, 119, 232; and Navarre (1275), 241–2 & n.; his quarrel with Philip III of France and the problem of the succession, 242–4; his relations with Edward I, 226, 242–5 & nn., 656 n.

Alfonso king of Aragon (1285–91), 252; his negotiations with Edward I on the release of Charles of Salerno (1286–91), 256–7, 259–63, 282–4, 305; his projected marriage with Eleanor, d. of Edward I, 257–8 & nn., 259, 263–4; his death (June 1291), 264.

— third son of Edward I (1273–84), 226 n., 238 n., 429.

Alliances, of Edward I with continental princes, 1294–1303, 658–70; cost of, as revealed by *computus* of Walter Langton (1298), 667 & n.

Allods and allodial tenure in Gascony, 108 & n., 297–8; claim that Gascony was itself an allod, 313, 651, 652 n.

Almain, Henry of, son of Richard of Cornwall, 41 n., 152; in the Lord Edward's circle, 153, 154; joins the baronial party of 1262–3, 173, 178; rejoins Edward, 177; a hostage after his capture at Lewes, 190; allowed to go to the French court as mediator, 194 n.; released (1265), 198; at Chesterfield, 209; his part in the Dictum of Kenilworth, 209; mediator in 1267, 214; takes the cross (1268), 219; murdered at Viterbo by Guy de Montfort (March 1271), 226. *See* Béarn, Constance of.

Alnwick, the Lord Edward at (1267), 214.

Alphonse of Poitiers, brother of Louis IX, count of Poitou and, in right of his wife, of Toulouse, 100–3 *passim*, 127, 184 n.; bastides of, 273, 293; his death (1271), 272; problems of succession to his lands, 273–4, 289–91. *See* Toulouse, Jeanne of.

Amadeus IV, count of Savoy (1233–53), uncle of Eleanor of Provence and father-in-law of Manfred, 123 n., 247 n.; becomes vassal of Henry III, 250, 679 n.

— V, count of Savoy, disputes about succession of (1285), 250–1 & nn.; relations with Edward I and Philip the Fair, 251 & n., 653, 665.

Amersham, Walter of, chancellor of Scotland (1296), 615.

Amesbury, nunnery of, Queen Eleanor (of Provence) retires to, 73; Mary,

d. of Edward I, a nun there, 268 n.; a family settlement about succession to the Crown made at (1290), 268, 512.

Amiens, award or mise of (1264), 130, 182–4; treaty of (1279), 235; proposed conference of kings at (1294), 647.

Amiral de la mer, 655 & n.

Anagui, 652 n., 661.

Ancient demesne, growth of the phrase, 530 n.

Anderson, M. O., on a prophecy of Merlin, 719 n.

Andrew the notary, 616 & n.

Angers, 93.

Angevin party at the French court, 245.

Anglesey, ravaged from Ireland (1245), 399; occupied (1277), 412; under treaty of Conway, 412–13; in the war of 1282–3, 426–7, 428; Beaumaris founded in (1295), 443 & n.

Angoulême, county of, 89; *see* Isabella.

Anian, bishop of Bangor (1267–1305), 390–1.

— I, bishop of St. Asaph's (1249–66), 390–1.

— II, bishop of St. Asaph's (1268–93), 390–1, 434–5.

Anjou, county of, 93; and treaty of Paris (1259), 126.

— house of, in Provence, Naples, and Sicily; *see* Charles I; Charles II; Robert, king of Naples.

Annandale, 692, 709.

Annates, papal, 500.

Anointing of Scottish kings, papacy and, 593–4.

Antwerp, English merchants at, 628 n., 663 & n., 664; held as fief of Edward I by duke of Brabant (1298), 679 n.

Appeals: to the *parlement* of Paris, 311–15, 647; from Gascony to the king of England, 307–8, 315–18; to judges of appeal in Gascony, 314–15 & n., 317; Nicholas Segrave's attempt to appeal from English to French court, 332–3; from Scottish court to English king, 608–12, 616; regulations in parliament for, 610; tuitorial, 466 & n., 492–4.

Applecross, lay priest of, later first earl of Ross, 580 n.

Apps, Una, on the *muntatores*, 770.

Aquitaine, extent of in Edward I's time, 273–4, 291–2; administration of, 273–80 *passim*; temporary sale to Louis IX of King Henry's rights in the bishoprics of Limoges, Cahors, and Périgueux, in 280–1, and their surrender by Edward I (1279), 289; the 'privileged' in, 290–1, 298; *recognitiones* in, 295–6 & nn.; ordinance of Condom and, 298–304, 524; discussions on status of, 647 & n., 650–1; and the process of Périgueux (1310–11), 291, 292 n.

Aragon, kingdom of, a fief of the Holy See, 252; connexion of, with Provence and Toulouse, 100, 101, 252; liberties of and the royal needs (1283), 255; Edward I and nobles of, 269 & n.

— kings of, *see* Alfonso, James.

— Sanchia of, wife of Raymond VII of Toulouse, 99, 100.

Arbitrators, boards of, suggested in 1264, 194.

Archdeacons and archdeaconries, 445, 454; of Berkshire, 448; publication of canons of councils by, 473; inquiries ordered by Pecham in, 475; and clerical taxation, 502 and *passim*.

Archers, 422 & n.

Arches, court of the, at St. Mary-le-Bow, London, as the Court of Canterbury, 492 & n.

— Black Book of, 492 n.

Architecture, military and domestic, bibliographical notes on, 753, 770–1.

Arghun, khan of Persia, 252 & n., 265.

Argyll, Alexander of, 657 n.

— John of, 716 & n.

Aristotle, medieval commentaries on his *Politics*, 521–2 & n.

Arles, kingdom of, 98–99; plans for the restoration of, 246–7 & n.

Armagnac, 291, 292 n.

— count of, 293.

Armour, development of, 549, 553.

Arms, coats and roll of, 551–2 & n.

Army, Edward I's, 409–11, 422, 428 n., 439–40, 441–3, 445, 519–20, 603, 612, 613, 649, 666, 668–9, 678–82 *passim*, 686, 687, 688–94, 700, 706, 708–11 *passim*, 715; development of a paid army as a reflection of social change, 542–56 *passim*, 669–70, 681 n. *See* Feudal host; Knights; Money fief; Service, military.

— feudal, summoned against Welsh (1263), then directed against the Lord Edward in Windsor (1263), 175, 176; the general levy of 1264, 192–3.

Arnould, E. J., on guides for the clergy, 764.

Arras, constable of, 11.

Array, commissions of, 554.

Arrentation, 546 n.

Arteveldt, Jacques von, 669 n.

Arthur, King, and Arthurianism, 515–16 & nn.

— crown of, 429 n., 516.

Articles in opposition to Edward I's Flemish campaign, 682 & n.

— of bill presented to Edward I at Lincoln (1301), 704–5.

Articuli super cartas (1300), 697, 698, 700–1, 704 n.

— *cleri*, statute (1316), 484.

Artois, county of, 12.

— Robert of, 239, 240, 241, 242; in command of French forces in Gascony (1296–7), 649, 666.

Arundel, earls of, *see* FitzAlan.

Arwystli, cantref of west Powys, claimed by Llywelyn ap Gruffydd (1278–82), 417–20.

Ashford, manor of (Derbyshire), 326.

Ashmole, Elias, edits list of knights made in 1306, 514 n.

Assessments of clerical revenue, 221, 498 & n., 505, 509.

Assignment of revenue, 524 n.; of English customs to citizens of Bayonne, 650 & n.

Assize of Arms, and distraint of knighthood, 552–3.

Athée, Gerard of, 22.

Athol, earl of, appointed warden of Scotland north of Forth (1304), 711; at Bruce's coronation (1306), 714; hanged in London, 716.

atillator, 303.

Auch, city and ecclesiastical province of, 292 n.

Auditors, of bailiffs' accounts, 366–7; of Flemish cases under treaty of Montreuil (1274), 623 & n.; of Spanish and Portuguese complaints against merchants of Bayonne (1293), 644 n.; of cases at Montreuil (1305–6), 657, 658 & n.; the 104 auditors, in parliament, of Scottish succession case (1292), 605–8.

Audley, Hugh of, 283.

— James of, 190, 196.

Avesnes, John of, count of Hainault, 622 n.; and Philip IV of France, 664, 665.

Avignon, imperial city, united under Charles II of Sicily, later acquired by the papacy, 99, 272–3 n.; negotiations at (1344), 652 n.

Axholme, Isle of, rebels in (1265–6), 206, 208 n., 210.

Ayr, castle of, 694, 707; garrison of, 695.

Baa, bastide near Bordeaux, 309–10 & n.

Babwell, Franciscan friary at, 363.

Babylon, name for Cairo, 82.

Bachelors, 152, 153–4 & n.

bachinator, 303.

Bacon, Robert, Dominican, 55.

— Roger, 230.

Badenoch, the caput of the senior branch of the house of Comyn, 581.

Bagimond's Roll, 585 n.

Baiamundus de Vitia, papal collector in Scotland, 583 n.

Bailiffs, their lords and the law, 366–8; auditors of their accounts, 366–7.

Balearic Isles, and Aragon, 256, 257, 260, 262. *See* James, king of Majorca.

Balfour-Melville, E. W. M., on John de Cheam, bishop of Glasgow, 574 n.

Baliol, house of, in Scotland, its two branches, 579 & n., 580–1.

— Alexander, of Cavers, chamberlain, 579 & n., 610 n., 695, 707; his brother Guy, 579.

— Edward, son of John, king of Scots, 612–13, 615.

— John, of Barnard Castle, m. Devorguilla, heiress of part of Galloway, 581 n., 693 n.; a guardian of Alexander III in his minority, 582 n., 589 & n., 590; other references to, 190, 197, 466 & n.

— John, son of John and Devorguilla, king of Scots (1292–6), m. Isabella, d. of John de Warenne, 138 n.; describes himself as heir to the kingdom of Scotland (1291), 601; his position as a Scottish magnate, 602; his claim examined and approved at Berwick, 327, 606–8; does fealty to Edward I, is installed at Scone, and does homage at Newcastle, 608; his reign and relationships, 608–9 & n., 610 & n. 3, 611, 613; renounces his homage, 614; his abdication, 615; his later life, 615; references to, 648 n., 653, 685, 694, 697; his seneschal, 366.

— William, one of Scottish embassy in France (1302–4), 697 n.

Bamborough castle, in the settlement of 1265, 198, 199.

Banff castle, 693 n.

Bangor, 428; alleged attempt on Llywelyn's life at, 427 n.; Edward I at (1294–5), 442, 443; liberties of diocese of, confirmed by Edward I, 434.

— bishops of, 390–1. *See* Anian, Richard.

Bannister, A. T., on episcopal inquisition of 1253, 455 n.

Banstead, John of, king's clerk, 337.

Bar, Henry III, count of, marries Eleanor, eldest daughter of Edward I, 1293, 264, 668 n.; relations of with Edward I, 659, 668.

— John de, 690.

Bardi of Florence, 637, 638. *See* Pegolotti.

Bardney, the case of the monks of, and their appeal to Canterbury against Grosseteste, 466.

Bardolf, Doon, 23 n.

Barham Down, Montfortian camp on, 193.

Bar-le-Duc, tournament at (1294), 664 n.

Barlow, F., edition of Durham annals and documents, 734, 742.

Barnard castle, 465, 580.

Baronage: in Scotland and its Scottish and English affiliations, 579–83.

— literature on, 768–9.

Baronial committees, 78–79.

— leaders' sworn agreement in 1258, 130–1 & nn.; later developments of, 135 & n., 140, 146 & n.

— reform, plans of (1238–58), 77–79.

Baronies and Knights' Fees, 550.

Barons and baronage; Edward I and, 516–19 *passim*, 521; political thought about status of, 520–3; and the Crown, 542–3; households and military aspect of, 519–20. *See* Seignorial administration.

Barons' War in 1264, begins in the Marches, 185; dated from attack on Northampton or from *diffidatio* at Lewes, 187, 209; end of, 204, 209; ordinances for peace and restoration of order, 204–5; restoration of peace (1266–7), 206–15.

Barraclough, G., on Adolf of Nassau and Edward I, 660 n.

Barrow, G. W. S., on feudalism in Scotland, 574 n.

Basingwerk, Cistercian abbey, 412.

Basset, Fulk, bishop of London (1244–59), 125, 133, 150 n.

— Gilbert, 53–54, 60, 66, 150 n.

— Philip (d. 1271), justiciar, 150 n., 153, 157–9 *passim*, 161, 162, 164, 165, 166, 171, 190, 204, 214, 225.

— Ralph, of Drayton, 202.

Bassingburn, Warin de, 153.

Bastardy, law of, 70–71, 453.

Bastides, 308–10, 431 n., 635.

Bateson, Mary, on Irish exchequer documents, 565 n.; on Irish justiciary rolls, 571 n.; on a tract about the Scottish king's household, 713 n.

Battle, Odo abbot of, 485 n.

bauson, 644.

Bautier, Robert-Henri, on the movement of gold and silver, 638 n.

Bayley, C. C., on Ockham, 523 n.

Bayonne, 244; and barons' war, 281; in treaty of Paris (1259), 126; meeting between kings of France and Castile at (1290), 262; ship-building at, 656 n.; court of mayor and jurats of, appeals from, 316, 317; and the Channel Islands, 318; feuds, of men of with sailors of the Cinque Ports, Spain, Portugal, and Normandy, 644 n., 646 n.; Philip IV demands punishment for damages done by, 645; citizens of, during the war of 1294–1303, 650 & n., 659, 662.

Bazas, court at, 109, 285, 301; bishop, chapter, and commune of, 275.

Beardwood, Alice, on Walter Langton's operation of recognizances, 625.

Béarn, Constance of, countess of Marsan, d. of Gaston, wife of Henry of Almain, 284, 287 n., 316.

— Gaston, viscount of, 108, 109, 112, 284; his family relationships, 112 n.; and Simon de Montfort, 112–13; and Alfonso X of Castile, 116, 118; his rebellion against Edward I and reconciliation (1273–8), 285–7; and treaty of Canfran (1288), 282, 283; and the succession to Bigorre, 287 n.; sent to help Alfonso X, 245.

Beatrice of Provence, wife of Charles of Anjou, 119, 234.

— of Savoy, wife of Raymond-Berenger of Provence, 74, 107, 119.

— d. of Amadeus of Savoy, wife of Manfred, 247 n.

— d. of Henry III (d. 1275), wife of John of Brittany (1260), 97, 159 & n., 235.

Beauchamp, William de, 26 & n.

— William, earl of Warwick, 409; defeats Madog ap Llywelyn at Maes Moydog, 442–3 & n.

Beaumaris, castle, 431, 432, 443 & n.; borough, 432–3.

Beaumont, Robert de, earl of Leicester (d. 1190), 75 & n.; his daughters Amicia and Margaret, 75 n.

Beck, Egerton, on the Austin canons of the Temple of the Lord, 761.

Becket, *see* Thomas, St.

Beckley (Oxon.), 160.

Bedford, castle, and Fawkes de Breauté, 26 & n.; siege of (1224), 27.

Beeston castle (Cheshire), 202.

Bek, Antony, bishop of Durham (1284–1311), 290, 493–6; his mission to Aragon (1282), 257 n., 294; and the Isle of Man, 596 n.; and Scottish affairs, 599–600 & n., 613, 615, 689, 690, 697.

Bek, John, 623 n., 624.

— Thomas, bishop of St. Davids (1280–93), 418, 435.

Bell, H. I., on papal bulls in the British Museum, 739.

Bellegarde, bastide, defeat at (1297), 666.

Bellême, 93, 94 & n.

Bemersyde, Haigs of, 580 n.

Bémont, Ch., and the baronial compact of 1258, 130 n.; on the law of Oléron, 621 n.; on Henry III's campaign of 1242–3, 745.

Benauges, 288.

— viscount of, *see* Grilly, John de.

Bench, King's, and the king's council, 326–8, 334; rolls of, 334 & n.; judges of, 341; and state trials, 362 & n.

Benefice, 446.

Benevento, 120 n.

Bennett, Josephine W., on the medieval loveday, 39.

Berben, H., on the quarrel with Flanders, 623 n.

Bere, castle and borough, 429, 432 n., 441.

Bereford, Chief Justice, 373.

Berger, E., on Henry III's Breton campaign (1230), 94 n., 745.

Bergerac, 292, 293; lord of, 293.

Berkeley, Thomas de, appointed constable (1297), 680, 681.

Berkhamsted, manor and castle, 9, 40 & n., 160.

Berksted, Stephen, bishop of Chichester (1262–87), 176 n., 186, 487; as a Montfortian, 189, 191–2, 208 n.

Bermondsey, Cluniac priory, prior of and Adam de Stratton, 365.

Bernham, W. de, a Scottish scholar, his letters, 742.

Berwick, castle, burgh, and shire: Edward I at (1291–2), 604, 606; appeal of burgess of, to Edward I, 608; petition of burgesses of, 609–10 & n.; captured (1296), 614; parliament in, 615–17; centre of Edward's Scottish administration and exchequer, 614, 686, 712; new town planned at, 614, 636–7; in war time (1297–1305), 656, 686, 688, 692–5 *passim*, 706; other references to, 685, 687 n., 700, 716.

— John of, king's clerk, 268 n., 505 n.

Betaghs, 563 & n., 565 n.

Beziers, 99.

— viscount of, 99.

Bibars, sultan of Egypt, 186.

Bibury, King Edward at (1282), 331 n.

Bigod, Hugh, earl of Norfolk (d. 1225), m. Matilda, d. of the Marshal, 41 n.
— Hugh (d. 1266), son of earl Hugh; justiciar (1258–60), 41 n., 54, 124, 125; his political and judicial activity, 130–1 & nn., 135, 137, 140, 146 & n., 148, 151, 156; during royal absence (1259–60), 150, 156–8; ceases to be justiciar, 162, 163; later history of, 164, 165, 174 n., 175, 190.
— Roger (d. 1270), eldest son of Earl Hugh; and his successor as earl of Norfolk, 41 n.; as a baronial leader, 130 n., 140, 150 & n., 156, 174 n., 175, 204.
— Roger, earl of Norfolk and earl marshal (d. 1306), leader of opposition to the king's policy (1297), 666, 678–83 passim; later references to, 518, 689, 690, 697 n., 707 n.
Bigorre, county of, 112 & n., claimed by Constance of Béarn, 287 n.; count of, 293; seneschal of, 292, 294 n.
Bigwood, G., on Italian merchants and the wool trade, 637 n.
Bill, or written petition, 352.
Bills, 355; in eyre, 355.
Bilson, J., on Wyke-upon-Hull, 634 n.
Binchy, D. A., on Irish law, 566 n.
Bingham, Robert, bishop of Salisbury (1228–46), 60.
Bishops, English, 340–1, 485–8; Welsh, 390–1; Scottish, see Church, Scotland; elections of, 468; as rulers in their dioceses, 451–6, 474–5; monastic, 485 & n.; family connexions of, 486–7; jurisdiction of and the metropolitan, 489–93; and clerical taxation, 501–9 passim; in English political life, 23–24, 46–47, 55–60 passim; used to inquire into charges against Simon de Montfort (1260), 161; the Montfortian (1263–5), 176 & n., 186, 189, 192, 193, 194–5, 208.
Blaauw, W. H., on letters to Ralph Nevill, 741.
Black, J. G., on Edward I and Gascony in 1300, 652 n.
Blanche of Artois, wife (1) of Henry, count of Champagne and King of Navarre, and (2) of Edward of Lancaster, 236, 238–41 passim.
— of Castile, queen of France, mother of Louis IX, 8, 12, 88 n., 91–94 passim, 97, 102; death of (Nov. 1252), 114.
Blanquefort, near Bordeaux, 264 n.
Blaye, on the Gironde, 103, 650, 666.
Bloch, Marc, on coronation and unction of Scottish kings, 593 n.; on the problem of gold, 638 n.

Blund, John, 56.
Blundevill, Ranulf de, earl of Chester, 2, 3, 11; his position in England, 20 & n.; his charter of liberties, 20 n.; and the royal castles, 24–25; and Fawkes de Breauté, 27; and Richard of Cornwall (1227), 40; and Llywelyn ab Iorwerth, 45, 392; and Hubert de Burgh, 51 n.; in Normandy, 96; his death and successors, 51 n., 197 & n.
Bohun, Humphrey de, earl of Hereford (d. 1275), captured at Lewes, 190.
— Humphrey de, junior, his son, a Montfortian, 182, 185; on council of nine (1264), 192; captured at Evesham and dies of his wounds, 202.
— Humphrey de, grandson of previous earl, earl of Hereford (d. 1298), constable, recovers Brecon (1277), 409, 411; on trial in 1290, 329; in 1294, 441; not present in parliament at Salisbury (1297) but joins the earl marshal in opposition to Edward I's policy, 680 & n., 681–3; dies (1298), 697 n.; other references, 689, 690, 698.
Bologna, John of, and his summa notarie, 490 n.
Boniface VIII, Pope (1294–1303), 233; his attitude to the Anglo-French war of 1294–8 and his efforts for peace, 661–2, 668; his arbitration in his private capacity (1298), 650–3 & n.; his bull Clericis laicos, 666, 674–6, and its gloss in the bull Etsi de statu (1297), 674 & n., 677, cf. 523; his intervention in the Scottish war, 228–9, 685 n., 693, 701–2; replies to him from Edward I and the barons of England, 697, 702, 705–6 & n.; his financial arrangement with Edward I and his change of attitude to Scottish affairs, 500, 709, 710 & n.
— count of Savoy (1253–63), 249, 250 n.
— of Savoy, uncle of Queen Eleanor (of Provence), archbishop of Canterbury (d. 1270), 74, 79, 118, 143, 145 n., 150 n.; papal injunctions to, about the Provisions of Oxford, 165; his provincial councils and constitutions, 165 n., 167, 451, 454, 456–7, 472–3; leaves England (1263), 175, 178; at Boulogne, 179; the baronial council orders his return, 199; his death, 225 n.
Bonluc, near Bayonne, 238 n.
Bonnegarde, Edward I's Christmas at (1288), 284.
Bordeaux, 90, 91, 92 n., 95, 103; and Simon de Montfort, 111, 112; in

treaty of Paris (1259), 126; and the Baron's War, 281; as an international meeting place, 254 & n., 256, 293; Philip IV demands surrender of, 646–7; subject to Philip during truces (1297–1303), 649–50; general court at, 295, 297; appeal of citizens of to Paris (1289), 312 & n.

Bordeaux, ecclesiastical province of, 292 n.

— court of, one of four courts of Gascony, 109, 285, 301; constable of, 109, 292 n., 298, 300–1, 304–6; castle of, and archives, 298, 300, 301; money of, 306; customs on wine of, 281–2 & n., 305–7; exports of wine from, 669 n.

— tenure and rights of citizens of, 108; parties in, 109; mayoralty of, 280.

Border, the Scottish, 574, 588–9, 600.

Boreham, Essex, 339.

Borenius, Tancred, on cycle of images in Henry III's palaces and castles, 766–7, 771.

Borenius, T., and *Charlton, J.*, on Clarendon palace, 771.

Boroughs and market towns, literature on, 771–2.

— representation of selected cities and, in 1265, 197; in 1273, 225; development of, and taxation, 529–34; Welsh, 432–3.

Bothwell castle, 693 n., 694.

Boulogne, county of, 12; *émigrés* and conferences at (1263–5), 178, 179 & n., 181 & n., 193–5 *passim*.

Bourg, 650, 666.

Bourges, assembly of French clergy at (1225), 502; assembly at (1283), 254; ecclesiastical province of, 292 n.

Boussard, J., on Ralph Nevill, 741.

Boyer, Marjorie N., on a day's journey in medieval France, 776.

Brabant, Edward I and, 647 n., 661, 664, 665; merchants of, 519 n.; wool trade with, 622 & n., 637, 659, 662; beginnings of English staple in, 663 & n., 679 n.

— dukes of, *see* John I; John II.

— Marie of, queen of France, *see* Marie.

Brabazon, Roger, judge, spokesman of King Edward's demands in Scotish case, 603, 608; pronounces judgement in favour of Baliol, 608.

Brackley (Northants.), negotiations at (1264), 186.

Bracton, Henry de, judge, 212 n., 374; and writs of consultation, 477 n.; on kingship, 512 n.

Brandon, Reginald de, 491 n., 496.

Braose, Eva de, d. of William the Marshal, and wife of William, son of Reginald de Braose, 395.

Braose, Graeca de, d. of William Brewer, first wife of Reginald de Braose and mother of William, 395 n.

— Isabella de, d. of William de Braose (hanged 1230) and wife of David, son of Llywelyn the Great, 395–6.

— John de, lord of Bramber and Gower (d. 1232), 396 & n.

— Matilda de, 201.

— Reginald de, lord of Abergavenny (d. 1227), 394, 395 & n., 396 n.

— William de (d. 1211), father of William junior (d. 1210) and Reginald, and grandfather of John; lord of Gower, 396 n.

— William de, son of Reginald, lord of Abergavenny, 45; hanged by Llywelyn the Great (1230), 395–6 & n.; succession to his lands, 396–7 & nn.

Bray, Henry of, king's clerk, 415.

Breauté, Fawkes de, 3 & n., 4, 9, 11, 22, 25–27, 52 n., 81 n., 85.

— William de, 27.

Brechin, John Baliol's formal surrender of enfeoffment of Scotland at, 615; siege of (1303), 709.

Brecon, Bohun lordship in, 402, 406, 409, 439, 441.

Brentwood (Essex), 50.

Breton, John le, judge, bishop of Hereford (1269), and the treatise Britton, 729.

Brewer, William, 3, 4, 28; his daughter Graeca, 395 n.

Brienne, John de, butler of France, (1) second husband of Marie de Coucy, queen of Scots, in Scotland (1257–9), 591, 592; (2) appointed to administer Champagne for Edmund of Lancaster, 240.

Bridgnorth castle, 20, 200.

Bridport, Giles of, bishop of Salisbury (1257–62), 156.

Brigham, near Berwick, Scots agree to settlement of English, Scottish, and Norwegian commissions about Margaret of Norway at (March 1290), 599; draft treaty about her marriage at (July), 599–600.

Brindisi, 107.

Bristol, castle, town, and barton, and Dublin, 565; the Clare claim to, 173 n., 519 & n.; town development in, 635; and service to the Crown, 530; confirmation of Charter of Liberties at (1216), 4; centre of the Lord Edward's household administration (1254), 118, 159, 401; feudal army summoned to meet at (1257), 138; Edward fails to hold (1263), 176 n.; held by his friends (1264), 196; ceded to Simon de Montfort, 197, 198; burgesses support earl Simon, but make terms with Henry III after Evesham, 200, 202, 203; parliament of magnates and Christmas feast at (1284), 430; as a military and naval base, 422, 442; castellans of, 3 n., 22; the *Little Red Book* of, 626 n.

Brittany, succession to, 92 n.; Peter of Dreux and, 92–94, 96; Henry III's expedition to and its results (1230–4), 94–97; its dynastic relations with Champagne and Navarre, 236–8; origin of the Montfort claim to, 598 n. *See* Dreux, Peter of.

— Alice of, 92 & n.

— Arthur of, 92 n., 116, 242.

— Arthur, duke of (1305–12), 598 n.

— Eleanor of, 92 n.

— John, duke of, son of Peter of Dreux (d. 1285), 159 n., 235–6 n.

— John, duke of (1285–1305), m. Beatrice, d. of Henry III (1260), 97, 159, 235–6 & nn., 514 & n.

— John of, second son of the preceding, earl of Richmond (d. 1334), 236 n., 283, 514 n., 649, 713 n.

— Yolande of, d. of Peter of Dreux, 93.

Brodhull, Cinque Ports' court of, 645 n.

Bromfield (Maelor), 410 & n., 424.

Bromholm priory (Norfolk), 49.

Bronescombe, Walter, bishop of Exeter, 485.

Brookes, F. W., on the Cinque Ports, 772; on ships, 656 n.

Broome, Dorothy, on exchequer migrations (and routes by land and water), 776,

Brown, J. T. T., on origin of the Stuarts, 516 n.

Bruce, Christina de, sister of Robert, king of Scots, wife of Christopher Seton and, later, of Andrew, son of Andrew of Moray junior, 687 n., 716.

— Isabel, sister of Robert, king of Scots, m. Eric, king of Norway, 611 n., 613.

— Margery, infant d. of Robert, king of Scots, demanded as hostage (1297), 685; later the wife of Walter the Steward, and mother of the first Stuart king, 685 n.

— Mary, sister of Robert, imprisoned in a cage (1306), 716.

— Robert, the claimant, lord of Annandale from 1245 to 1295, recognized as his heir by Alexander II in 1238, 587, 602; captured at Lewes (1264), 190; a judge in England before 1269, 190; his compact with Richard de Burgh and Thomas de Clare (1286), 597–8; one of commissioners appointed to arrange for the succession of Margaret of Norway (1289), 598; his action after her death, 600–2; his claims to the throne, 606–7, 611 & n.; his indenture with Florence, count of Holland, 611 n.; his death at Lochmaben (1295), 611 n.

Bruce, Robert, earl of Carrick, son of the claimant, 595 n., 598, 611 n., 613, 616, 695 n.

— Robert, earl of Carrick, grandson of the claimant, the future King Robert II, 602, 611 n.; his fealty and homage, for his Scottish lands, to Edward I (March 1296), 613–14; in revolt (1297–8), 684–5, 687, 692; one of guardians of Scotland (1299–1300), 694, 696, 697 n.; his return to King Edward I, 694–5 & nn.; in the campaign of 1303–4, 709; advises the king in 1305 and becomes a counsellor in Scotland, 712, 713; his insurrection in 1306, 514–15, 713–16 *passim*; flight and return of (1306–7), 718–19 & n.

Bruges, capital town of Flanders, partisans of Philip IV in (1297), 669.

Buchan, countess of, sister of the earl of Fife, and installation of Robert Bruce at Scone, 714, 716.

— earls of, *see* Comyn.

Buhler, C. T., on a sermon by Grosseteste, 765.

Builth, district and castle of, 155, 394–6, 397, 401, 402, 404, 406, 409; rebuilt (1277), 403 n., 410–11 & n., 430, 432; in war of 1282, 422, 428; John Giffard in, 438; attacked in 1294, 441.

— borough of, 433.

— constable of (1277), *see* Hywel ap Meurig.

Burgesses and merchants, in conference with Edward I on town planning, 635–7.

Burgh (Norfolk), 369 n.; Henry III's compact with his ministers (1232) made at, 49.

Burgh-upon-the-Sands, Edward I dies at, 719.

Burgh, family of, in Connaught and Ulster, 562, 564.

— Elizabeth de, d. of earl of Ulster, second wife of King Robert Bruce, 716 & n.

Burgh, Hubert de, justiciar, earl of Kent, 2, 4, 9, 18, 20; deals with William of Aumâle, 21; his character, ambitions, and rule as justiciar, 23–28 *passim*, 39–45 *passim*, 93, 394–7; his fall, 45–51; rescued from Devizes, 60; his administration and its influence on later policy, 61, 65 and *passim*; his death (1243), 61; his marriages, 23 n., 41; his daughter Megotta, 43 & n.; his clerks and his relations with the bishops, 46–47; his ship, 13; other references to, 519 n., 594 n.

— John de, 519 n.; his son, 188.

— Margaret de, d. of William the Lion, and third wife of Hubert de Burgh, 23 & n., 41, 43 & n., 73 n.

— Richard de, nephew of Hubert, and justiciar of Ireland (1228–32), 42–43, 54, 58.

— Richard de, earl of Ulster, 564, 565 n.

— Richard de, earl of Ulster, 564, 565 n.; his compact with Robert Bruce, the later claimant (1286), 597–8 & n.; serves with Edward I in Scotland, 614, 709.

— Walter de, earl of Ulster, 43.

— William de, brother of Hubert, 43.

Burghs, Scottish, 572, 575 & n.

Burgos, 118.

Burgum Regine, bastide, 310.

Burgundy [Hugh IV], duke of, and countess Eleanor's claims, 164.

— Robert II, duke of, 248; his daughters, 250 n.

— free country of, and Philip IV, 667 & n., 668.

— Otto IV, count of, 667 n.

Burley, Walter, 523 n.; his commentary on Aristotle's *Politics* and his views on kings and magnates, 521–2 & n.

Burnell, Philip, 339.

— Robert, king's clerk, chancellor, bishop of Bath and Wells (1275–92), 225 & n.; life and character of, 338–9; his lands and barony, 339; as chancellor, 335–8, 558 n.; as bishop, 485–6; elected archbishop of Canterbury (1278) but rejected by Pope Nicholas III, 469–70 & n.; his Gascon mission (1278), 287–9, 297, 338; at Paris (1286), 290–1; and the state-trials of 1289, 362; and the bastide of Baa, 309 n.

Burstwick, in Holderness, 716.

Burton, annals of, and documents contained in, 125, 136 n., 453 n., 454–5, 456 n., 503 & n.

Bury St. Edmunds, parliament at (1267), 213, 221; parliament at (1296), 636 & n., 674 & n., 675, 676; ecclesiastical council at (1267), 504.

Bycarrs Dyke, convention made at, 206.

Bytham castle, 21, 22.

Caen, John Arthur of, notary, 283, 495 & n., 602 n.

Caerleon, 397.

Caernarvon, 429; castle and borough, 430–2, destroyed and rebuilt (1294–5), 441, 443 n.

— Edward II born at, 429.

Caerphilly castle, 406.

Caerwys, borough of, 433.

Caetani, Benedetto, *see* Boniface VIII, Pope, Gaetani.

Cahors, bishopric of, in treaty of Paris, (1259), 127, 128, 280–1, 289, 292 n.; merchants of, 281 nn. *See* Quercy.

Cairo, 82.

Callus, D. A., on the early life of Grosseteste, 738; on learning in Oxford, 764.

Cam, Helen, on the knights reporting to parliament in 1258, 144 n.; on 'quo warranto', 377 n.; on abbatial administration of royal government, 762.

Cambridge, castle, 9; chancellor of university of, 701; son of earl of Ross, a scholar at (1306–7), 580 n.

Cameron, Annie I., on documents in Vatican archives relating to John Baliol, 753. *See* Dunlop, Annie I.

Canfran, treaty of (1288), 260, 269 n., 282–4.

Cannon, H. L., Pipe Roll 26 Henry III, 723.

Canon law, 450, 452, 462–6; study and practice of, 485 n., 489–92; its importance in Scotland, 584–5. *See* Law; Legislation.

Canterbury, a royal Christmas at (1262), 171; meeting of bishops at (1263), 176 n.; peace of (1264), and discussions and plans arising therefrom, 194–6 & n., Henry III awaits arrival of queen and legate at (1265), 206; trial of case between foreign and Gascon merchants at (1293), 644 n.

— archbishops of, *see* Thomas (St.) Becket; Walter (Hubert); Langton (Stephen); Grant (Richard); Edmund (St.) of Abingdon; Boniface of Savoy; Kilwardby (Robert); Pecham (John); Winchelsey (Robert).

— courts of archbishop of, provincial and diocesan, 490–3 & nn.; appeals to provincial court of, 466, 491–4; *see* Appeals, tuitorial; and Wales, 406.

Canterbury, Christ Church, prior of, see Eastry.
— Henry of, and the Gascon records, 278 n.
Cantilupe, George de, heir to Abergavenny, 172, 402 n.
— Thomas de (St.), chancellor of the university of Oxford, bishop of Hereford (1275–82), 475, 488–90; at Amiens (1264), 182; chancellor of king under baronial rule (Feb. 1265), 198; withdraws from court (May), 200.
Cantilupe, Walter de, bishop of Worcester (1237–66), constitutions of (1240), 452; and pluralism, 459 & n.; his political career as a reformer and Montfortian, 113 n., 124, 125, 150 n., 164, 176, 178, 185, 186, 189, 192, 193, 194, 200; death of, 208.
Cantle, A., on quo warranto pleas in Lancashire, 749.
Cantref Mawr, 436, 438, 440.
Cap Saint-Mathieu, Brittany, fleet of Cinque Ports defeats Norman fleet at (1293), 644 & n.
Capitaneus, 173, 649.
Capitula itineris, 16, 39 & n., 353–4 & nn.
Caplan, H., on medieval theory of preaching, 765.
Carcassonne, 99.
— viscount of, 99.
Cardigan, castle and honour of, 42, 43, 44, 52, 393, 394, 396, 397; shire of, 397–8 & n.; granted to the Lord Edward (1254), 401; a centre of royal administration, 406, 410; attacked (1294), 441.
Carlaverock castle, siege of (1300), 693, and poem on, 693 n.
Carlisle, and the Scots, 574; in Scottish wars, 613, 692, 698, 715–19 passim; parliament of (1307), 712 n., 718 & n.
— see of, 574 n.; election of a bishop of and proceedings in parliament (1279), 347.
— bishops of, see Mauclerc, Halton.
Carmarthen, honour and castle of, 42, 43, 44, 52, 393, 394, 396, 397; shire of, 397–8 & n.; granted to the Lord Edward (1254), 401; a centre of royal administration, 406, 410; Welsh victory near (1257), 137; shire court of, 439 & n.
Carpenter, Robert, and his legal collections, 150 n., 366 n., 370; and the tract, La court de baron, 730.
Carreg Cennen castle, 410, 414, 419, 437 n., 439.
Carrick, earls of, see Bruce.
Carstairs castle, 707.

Carta mercatoria (1303), 620, 630–1.
Carucage, 27, 29, 31.
Carus-Wilson, E. M., on the cloth industry and fulling mills, 773.
Cashel, archbishop and suffragans of, 562 & n. See also Donnchad.
Castile, problem of the succession to (1275–89), 242–5, 262.
— kings of, see Ferdinand III; Alfonso X; Sancho.
— see also Blanche, Eleanor.
Castillon-sur-Dordogne, castle, 112, 288.
— viscount of, see Grilly, John de.
Castle Acre, 665.
— Cornet, Guernsey, 319.
— Gorey, Jersey, 319.
— Holgate, barony of, 339.
Castles, in warfare, 8–9; royal and private, 20; resumption of control over royal, 21–25; Hubert de Burgh and, 48, 50; royal castles in 1232, 52; in 1258, 137; in 1261, 164–5; in 1263, 176, 181; in 1264–5, 190, 191, 196, 198–9; building of, in Wales, 430–2; in Aquitaine, 292, 300, 303.
— in Scotland, 575 & n., 589 n., 600, 604, 608, 613, 616 n., 686, 689, 692, 694–6 passim; garrisons of, 707.
Castro, Philip de, 269 n.
Catalonia and the war of 1285, 255.
Cate, J. L., on the church and market reform, 766.
Catesby (Northants.) nunnery, 182 n.
Caux, John of, abbot of Peterborough, treasurer (1260–3), 162.
Cavalry, see Knights, Men-at-arms.
Caversham, 17.
Cawood, 591.
Celestine V, Pope (July–Dec. 1294), 671 & n.
Cerdagne, province, 255.
Ceredigion, 398, 401, 410.
Ceri, 44, 45.
Chaceporc, Peter, king's clerk, 113 n.
Châlon, tournament at, 226, 233.
Chamber, the royal, 323–4.
Champagne, county of, 236–41 passim; its administration by Edmund of Lancaster, 240; survey of (1276–8), 241 n.
— counts of, see Theobald IV, V; Henry; Blanche of Artois; Jeanne, queen of France.
— Blanche of, marries John, later duke of Brittany, 236, 237.
Chanceaux, Andrew of, 22.
Chancellor, the position of, in Edward I's reign, 335–9.
Chancery and the wardrobe, 336–8. See Writs.

Channel, the English, in war of 1216–17, 9–10.

—Islands, the, 9, 10, 14, 31; social and administrative developments in, 318–21; granted to the Lord Edward, 118, 318; inquiry into state of (1274), 320, 358; and Norman ecclesiastical courts, 350 n.

Chapels, king's, and diocesan rights, 326 n.

Chaplais, P., on treaty of Paris, (1259), 120 n., 126 n.; on the allodial status of Gascony, 120 n.; on Gascon problems, 300, 313 n., 315 n., 651 n.; on reprisals, settlement of local disputes between states, &c., 621 n., 646 n., 654 n.; on privy seal records, 722.

Charente, river, border between French and Aquitanian areas in Saintonge, 102–3, 127.

Charles the Simple, king of France (d. 929), imprisoned (923–9), Simon de Montfort's reference to (1242), 104.

—of Anjou, count of Provence, king of Sicily (d. 1285), 119, 121, 231, 232, 531 n; his relations with Edward I, 234, 248; and Guy de Montfort, 225–6; his party in the French court, 245, 248; his dealings with Rudolf of Habsburg and resistance to claims of Margaret of Provence, 247–9; at feud with Aragon, 252; Sicilian revolt against, 249, 253; his proposed duel with Peter of Aragon, 254; the Venaissin and, 272 & n.; his death, 255.

—of Salerno, count of Provence, king of Sicily, son and successor of Charles of Anjou; his friendship with Edward I, 234, 247, 248; Alfonso X of Castile and (1280), 243–4 & nn.; defends Provence (1282), 249; captured in naval battle off Naples (1284), 253; the negotiations for his release, 256–7, 258–63, 283 & n.; acquires the whole of Avignon (1290), 272 n.; Pope Boniface VIII and, 661.

—of Valois, son of Philip III of France, invested by the pope with Aragon, 254–5; receives Anjou and Maine instead, 262.

Charles, Edward, admiral of part of English fleet (1306), 656.

Charter of Liberties, the Great, 142; significance of its reissue in 1216, 4–5; second reissue, 1217, 15 (*see* Forests); confirmation of 1225, 28–30; and taxation, 31; appeal to, in 1233–4, 53, 55, 59–60; and legislation, 67–70; confirmation of 1237, 75, 78, 536; of 1253, 79, 453; of 1297, 536–7, 683; of 1300, 700–1; excommunication of infringers of, 75, 198, 217, 222, 473, 476, 697; in 1264–5, 194, 198, 217; in 1267, 216–18; emphasis on statutory nature of, in 1267 and 1300, 217–18; during the years 1297–1307, 676, 682, 683, 697, 701, 703–4; in pleadings in the king's courts, 326, 329–30; copies of, affixed in churches, 473, 476; local justices elected in shire courts to deal with infringements of (1300), 701, 704; statutes contrary to, declared invalid (1301), 704 & n.

Charters, royal and private, 38–39; interpretation of royal, by the courts, 328.

Chartley, 212 n.

Chartres, Henry III in, 119.

Chaworth, Pain de, lord of Kidwelly, 196, 409, 410, 415 & n.

Cheam, John de, bishop of Glasgow (1259–67), and his claims for his see, 574 n.

Cheney, C. R., on baronial plans of reform, 79; on provincial councils and diocesan synods, 447 n., 451 n., 452; on criminous clerks, 462 n.; on letters of Gervase of Prémontré and of William Wickwane, 742; on the cult of saints and church building, 759–60.

Chenu, M.-D., on Kilwardby as a scientific thinker, 764.

Cheriton, Odo of (d. 1247), and his sermons, 765.

Chester, shire, castle, and honour of, succession to, in 1232 and 1237, 197 n., 606–7; rights in shire acquired by and annexed to the Crown, 197 n.; shire and city of, granted to the Lord Edward (1254), 118; acquired in exchange by Simon de Montfort, 197–8; recovered by Edward, 203; as a base in war, 138, 411, 422, 441; exchequer of, 412, 414; justice of, 414; legislation in county court of (1260), 379 n.; taxation of community of (1291), 443; bibliographical note on justice and administration in the county of, 749.

—earls of, *see* Blundeville; John the Scot.

Chesterfield, defeat of disinherited at, 208, 210.

Chesterton, Gilbert of, wool merchant, 632, 662.

Chew, Helena M., on scutage, 35 n.; on scutage under Edward I, 556 n.

Chichester, bishop of, and the chapel in Hastings castle, 326 n.
— bishops of, *see* Berksted; Nevill; Poor; Wych.
Chinon, 23; truce of (1214), 84, 88; its renewals before the treaty of Paris (1259), *see* Ch. III *passim*.
Chirk, Mortimer lordship of, 424.
Chotzen, Th. M., on Lodewijk van Velthem, 515–16 n.
Christus vincit, 59.
Chronicles and Arthurianism, 515 n.
Church, attempt to unite Greek and Latin, 231–2.
— and state, relations between powers of, 453–69, 473, 475–85.
— in Ireland, the, and its problems, 567–9.
— in Scotland, the, 583–5; papal taxation of (1274 and 1291), 573 n., 583 & n.
Churchyards, markets and fairs in, 369.
Cigogné, Engelard of, 22 & n., 25, 544.
Cilgerran, 443 n.
Cinque Ports, the, in 1216–17, 9–10; in Welsh wars, 138, 409, 411, 422; during the years 1263–5, 175, 187, 193, 200; Edward I and, 207, 531, 619, 635, 655; in the Scottish war, 657 n., 692–3; and the Crown, 158, 523, 531, 646 n., 655–6; in war and piracy, 644 & n., 645; the Shipway, 86 n.; Brodhull court, 645 n.
Cippenham, near Windsor, 170.
Circumspecte agatis, 482–3.
Cistercians, the, in Wales, 389–90; in Ireland, 568; Pecham's opinion of, 434 n.
Citeaux, abbot of, 12.
Claims, court of, at Montreuil-sur-mer, 1305–11, 657, 658 & n.
Clairvaux, abbot of, 12.
Clapham, J. H., on a thirteenth-century market town, 771.
Clare, court of, 540 n.; family of, 519 & n., 561.
— Bogo de, 475.
— Gilbert of, earl of Gloucester and Hertford (d. 1230), 41; his son and heir, *see* Clare, Richard de.
— Gilbert of, earl of Gloucester and Hertford, son of Richard, his difficult succession (1262–3), 173 & n., 175, 181 & n.; as a baronial leader (1264), 184, 187; knighted by Simon de Montfort, 188; one of the three in 1264–5, 191, 194, 196; his defection (1265), 199–201; his intervention on behalf of the disinherited (1267), 213–15; takes the cross, 219; his co-operation in council during Edward's

absence, 225; builds Caerphilly castle, 406; defeated at Llandeilo (1282), 420, 422; joins in suppression of Rhys ap Mareddud (1287), 439; and writs of *quo warranto*, 378; marries Joan, d. of Edward I, 268, 329, 512; and the liberties of the Marches, 329–30; rebellion in Glamorgan against, 440, 443; his son Gilbert, 517; other references to, 152, 327, 519 n.
Clare, Richard of, earl of Gloucester and Hertford (d. 1262), 41, 43, 44; and Scottish affairs (1255), 590, 591 & n.; and the baronial movement (1258–60), 130, 140, 147–8, 150 n., 154–8 *passim*; his bachelors, 152; his relations with Simon de Montfort, 147; his compact with the Lord Edward, 152; his royalism in 1260, 161; his brief reaction in 1261, 164, 166; his death, 171; succession to, 173 n.
— Thomas of, and Edward's escape from Hereford (1265), 200–1; his compact with Robert Bruce the claimant (1286), 598 & n.
Clarel, John, king's clerk, 136 n.
Clarendon, 512.
Clarke, Maude, on tenurial complexity in Ireland, 565 n.
Clement IV, Pope (1265–8), former cardinal legate to England, 180; and Charles of Anjou, 121, 531 n.; and Simon de Montfort, 199; his excommunication of disturbers of the realm, 681 & n. *See* Gui Foulquois.
— V, Pope, coronation of (Nov. 1305), 514 n., taxes English clergy (1305), 500; and the court of claims at Montreuil, 657; absolves Edward I from his oath to observe the articles of 1297, 703–4; suspends archbishop Winchelsey, 718; and the clerical *gravamina* of 1309, 483–4; on the writ of caption, 465; as castle-builder, 444.
Clergy, works written for guidance of, as priests and preachers, 764–5.
— English, numbers of, 445–6; types of, 458–9; and laity, 86; and Hubert de Burgh, 46–47; in war-time (1264), 193, 195; views of, on a crusade (1291–2), 267 & n.; representation of (1254), 117 n.; taxation of, during years 1266–73, 220–4; and during years 1294–8, 672 & n., 673, 675 & n., 676–7, 678, 681, 688; Edward I and, 666, 671–5 *passim*; and Pope Boniface VIII, 673 n., 676.
— *See* Clerks; Convocation; Dioceses;

Gravamina; Representation; Taxation.

Clergy, French, 267 & n., 674 & n., 676 & n., 677.

Clericis laicos, Bull of Boniface VIII (1296), 458 & n., 666; 674 & n.; Edward I and, 675 & n.; 676–7; infringements of in England, Archbishop Winchelsey and, 676.

Clerks, beneficed, Adam Marsh on, 445; status of, 447–9, 458–9; confessions of, 447; discipline of, 449, 451–3; problem of criminous, 462–3; resort to king's courts by, 467–8.

— king's, 278–9, 340–1, 458–60 & n.

Clifford, Robert, 615 n., 684–5, 686, 688 n., 695.

Clifford, Roger, of Eardisley, 153, 172–5 *passim*, 185, 190, 197.

— Roger, junior, 419, 420.

— Walter, 428 n.

Clipstone (Notts.), royal hunting lodge, parliament at, 266, 513 & n.; Edward I ratifies papal plans for his crusade at (1290), 266, 268.

Cockermouth, honour and castle, 21, 364, 707 n.

Cognac, 124.

Coinage, Edward I's new (1279–80), 632–4; in Gascony, 306; *see* Morlaas, sterling, Tours, &c.; debased and false coins, judicial action against, 632 & n., 633.

Coins; groat, maille (or halfpenny), farthing, 633, 634 n.

Coke, Sir Edward, his manuscripts of the Provisions of Oxford, 147.

Colchester castle, 9.

Coleville, William de, 21, 22.

Colloquium speciale, 688, 689 & n., 701.

Cologne, archbishop of, 660; (Engelbert), 73.

Colon, family of in Bordeaux, 109, 111.

— Gaillard, 109.

Communa of Scotland, 605, 712.

Communitas, proctors of, at the papal court (1245), 133, 150 n.

'Community of the realm', 67, 131–7 *passim*, 141–2 & n., 146 & n., 192, 528.

— of the vill, 143.

Compromissio, compromissum, 182–4 *passim*, 650–1.

Comyn, family of, its origin and genealogy in Scotland, 581–3.

— Alexander, earl of Buchan (1233–89), 581, 582, 589, 592.

— John, of Badenoch (d. 1274), 190, 581, 582.

— John, of Badenoch, the claimant, 582; one of guardians of Scotland

(1286), 597, 598; supports John Baliol, 601.

Comyn, John, the Red, of Badenoch (slain 1306), 581; captured at Dunbar (1296), 614; one of guardians of Scotland (1300–5), 694, 695 n., 696 & n., 697 & n., 708, 709 & n., 711, 713; murdered at Dumfries, 713–14.

— John, earl of Buchan (d. 1308), 581–2, 606, 608, 696, 697 n.; his wife, 714, 716.

— Richard, 581.

— Walter, of Badenoch, earl of Menteith (d. 1258), 581, 582, 589, 592.

— William, clerk, chancellor of David I, 581.

— William, earl of Buchan (d. 1233), 581.

— William, of Kilbride, 582.

Condat, near Livourne, ordinance for the Agenais issued at (1289), 298, 302–3.

Condom, in the Agenais, 298 n.; ordinances of (1289), 298–301, 303–4; *paréage* at, 308.

Condover, 339.

Connaught, conquest of, 42, 43, 54; shire and cantrefs of, 564 & n.; expedition in (1286), 598 n.

Conrad of Hohenstaufen, son of Frederick II, 107 n., 121–2.

Conradin, son of Conrad of Hohenstaufen, 122.

Consent to taxation and the sense of obligation, 526–7. *See* Representation.

Conservator of the Church in Scotland, 583.

Conservators of liberties, demand for, 77–78.

Conspiracy, writ and ordinance of, 354 n.

Constabulariae, in Scotland, 575 & n.

Constabularies of burghers (1265), 200.

Constance, queen of Aragon, d. of Manfred, and wife of Peter of Aragon, her claim to Sicily, 252, 253.

Constantine, donation of, 98.

Constantinople, conquest of, by the Latins (1204), and its results, 82.

Consultation, writs and statute of, 477–8 & nn.

contenementum, 6.

Contis, Arnold de, of Bayonne, warden of the Channel Islands (1271), 318.

Contracts, seals of, *see* Seals.

Convers, Alexander le, clerk, 705 & n.

Convocation, 479, 483 n., 496–508, 665, 674; of 1295, 483 n.; of 1297, 675–7; of 1298, 678; of 1299–1316, 483–4.

Conway, castle and borough, 430–3 *passim*; mayor of, 433; Cistercian abbey moved from, to Maenen (1284), 434–5. *See* Aberconway.
— treaty of (1277), 412–13, 415, 416; in the Welsh revolt (1294–5), 442 & n.; agreements with continental princes concluded at (1295), 661 & n.; archbishop Winchelsey takes oath of fealty at, 672, 673 n.
Cooper, T. M., on Scottish population, 573 n.; *Select Scottish Cases,* 577 n.; his edition of *Regiam Majestatem,* 577 n.
Corbeil, treaty of (1258), 253.
Corfe castle, 1, 22, 23, 53, 198, 331.
Corner, William de la, bishop of Salisbury, his letter to Henry Eastry, 262.
Cornwall, tin of, pledged (1297), 667.
— Edmund, earl of, 57, 344 n., 507 n., 511, 519.
— Richard, earl of, *see* Richard.
Coronation oath, 1, 7, 75; and the award of Amiens, 183.
— of Scottish kings and the papacy, 593–4.
Cortenuova, battle of, 98.
Cosenza, 240 n.
Coucy, Marie de, second wife of Alexander II, king of Scots, 573 n., 585, 587; as queen-mother in Scotland, 591, 592. *See* Brienne, John de.
Council, the Great, 66–67; and the king, 74–79; and legislation, 67 ff.; and taxation, 29 ff., 536; in 1258–62, 131–7; Edward I and, 331 & n., 382; of June 1294, 648, 649.
— the king's, 3, 30, 66, 74–75 & n.; oath taken by members of, 74 n., 125, 133; the king's right to appoint members of, 77–78, 130, 132–4, 180, 183, 186; as reformed in 1258, 136–7, 139, 147; committees of, 150; the Three and the Nine (1264), 191 ff., 192 n.; suggested compromises on appointments to, 194–5; directed by the guardians of Edward's children and lands during his absence (1270–4), 224–5; as a court, 326–8, 334; in parliament, 328–30, 331–4, 346 ff.; and Gascon affairs, 275; records of proceedings in, 346 & n.
— of Scottish king, 578; John Baliol forced to accept twelve advisers (1295), 612; and the alliance with Philip IV of France, 612–13; for Scotland, 707, 712, 714.
Councils, legatine and provincial, in English church, 451, 453, 456–8, 471, 472–5, 479–80, 481–2, 497 & n., 502. *See* Convocation.
— and officials of lords of liberties, 367.

Courtenai, Robert de, 13.
Courtrai, Flemish defeat of Philip IV at (1302), 653, 669, 697.
Courts, ecclesiastical and the Crown, 454, 462–9, 477–8, 481–4; alleged usurpations by, 477, 481–2, 484 n. *See* Canterbury, York.
— of the marshal, the constable, and the constable of Dover castle (1300), 701; of admiralty, 655 & n.
— royal, *see* Bench; Exchequer; King's Bench, &c.
Coutances, bishop of, in Channel Islands, 350 n.; diocese of, 318.
Coventry, plan of Dictum of Kenilworth worked out at, 209.
Coventry and Lichfield, bishops of, *see* Stavensby; Patteshall; Weseham; Longespée.
Craon, Maurice de, 243, 244 & n., 283; Edward's lieutenant in Gascony, 279, 317.
Cressingham, Hugh de, treasurer of Scotland, 614 n., 615; killed at Stirling (1297), 686.
Criccieth castle, 430–2 *passim*, 441, 442.
Crockesley, Richard, abbot of Westminster, 485 n.
Cromwell, John, his quarrel with Nicholas Segrave, 332.
Cross of Neath, *see* Neath.
Crossbowmen, 422 & n.
Crown, the state, rights and duties of the, 5–8, 16, 28, 38–39, 48, 53, 67–68, 144–5, 150–1, 530; in relation with the lords of liberties, 368, 376–9; and public safety, 551, 701; succession to, 1, 225, 268; Gascony, Isle of Oléron, and other lands inalienable from the Crown, 274–5, 381, 530; and Ireland, 562, 564 *and passim*; and feudal relations with Scotland, 381; and with Wales, 381–2; and the ecclesiastical system, 453–69, 475–85; and the boroughs, 530–1; and knight service, 542, 546.
Crump, C. G., on law of Oléron, 620–1 n.
Crusade, the, in the thirteenth century, 80–83; of 1236, 105, 107; of Louis IX, 110, 114; *see* Louis IX; Henry III and, 106; the Lord Edward's, 221–4; 264–7, 281–2 & n.; against Aragon (1284), 254; against Sicily, 660–1; Alfonso X and, 118; preaching of, 219, 231–2; English clergy on, 267. *See* Taxation, papal.
Crusaders, on commutation of vows of, 760.
Cumberland, local levies in, to deal with Scottish disturbances (1297),

684, 689 n.; much of, overrun by Scots, 686.

Curates, temporary and perpetual, 459 & n.

Cure of souls, 449 *and passim*.

Curragh, the (Kildare), 58.

Currency, debased, 670, 671; in Scotland, 573 & n. *See also* Coinage.

Cusack, Nicholas, bishop of Kildare, 569 n.

Custodes pacis, in the shires, 176, 182.

Customs on trade, 619, 628–31; the 'new aid', of 1266, 619, 629–38; the 'great custom' on wool and leather (1275), 629–30; the maltote of 1294–7, 630, 659, 663, 683; the 'petty' custom dues and *ad valorem* duties of 1303, 630–1 & nn. *See* Wool.

Cuttino, G., on the records relating to Gascony, 276–8 nn.; on the king's clerks, 340 n.; on Walter Langton's accounts, 667 n.

Cuyck, John, lord of, 664.

Cwm Hir, Cistercian abbey, burial-place of Llywelyn ap Gruffydd, 428.

Dafydd Benfras, the peot, 386, 390.

Dalry, Bruce defeated at (1306), 716.

Damages, in naval warfare, 1294–1303, 657; court of claims for, at Montreuil-sur-mer, 1305–11, 657–8; claims for, against Scots, 658 n.

Damietta, crusaders at, 90.

Dammartin, Simon de, count of Ponthieu, 73 & n.

Dampierre, Guy of, count of Flanders (1280–1305), son of the countess Margaret; his relations with Edward I from 1274 to 1292, 622–3, 648, 659; Philip IV and his treaty for marriage of Edward of Caernarvon with his daughter (1294), 659; his position, 1294–7, 659, 664–5; becomes Edward's ally and is deserted, 665 & n., 667–9 *passim*; his appeal to Boniface VIII, 652 n.; Philip IV and, 612 n., 659, 668–9.

Danegeld, 31.

Dante, 85 n., 230, 232–3, 643.

Darlington, John of, Dominican, royal confessor, 156, 176 n.; his oath of fealty as archbishop of Dublin, 348.

Daubeny, Philip, 9–10, 13, 40, 91.

David I, king of the Scots, 574 & n., 575, 577; laws of, 712; and his steward, 579–80 & n.; his chancellor, 581.

— earl of Huntingdon (d. 1219), brother of William the Lion, king of Scots, 581 n., 594 & n.

David, son of Alexander III, king of Scots; his early death (1281), 597.

— prince of Snowdonia (d. 1203), 385.

— lord of Snowdonia, son of Llywelyn the Great and Joan (d. 1246), 393 & n., 395, 398–400.

— ap Gruffydd, brother of Llywelyn, 400, 403 n.; his treachery (1274) against his brother, 406–7; plans for a provision made for in north Wales, 413–14; grievances of, 414–16; revolt of (1282), 419–20; refuses conditions of peace, 425–6; his last stand, capture, and execution, 428–9; his seal, 429 n.

Davies, J. Conway, on a charter of Llywelyn ap Gruffydd, 754; on lordships and manors of Montgomery, 755; on Newcastle wool customs accounts, 773.

Davis, A. H., translation of Thorne's chronicle, 734 & n.

— H. W. C., on St. Edmund of Abingdon, 739; on the survey of Champagne (1276–8), 241 n.

Dax, court at, 109, 285, 287 n., 301.

Dean, forest of, 199, 409.

Dean, Ruth J., on Trevet, 732.

Deanesly, Margaret, on the village mass, 760.

Deans, rural and rural deaneries, 445, 475, 477; recitation of canons in chapters of, 473; and taxation, 502.

Debt, law of, 624–5.

Debts, and creditors, 373–4 & n., 375–6.

De donis (1 Westminster II), 373, 518 & n.

Deeley, Ann, on royal patronage and provisions, 757.

Defensores of ducal rights in Aquitaine, 303–4.

Deganwy, Degannwy, castle, 137, 172, 178 n., 398, 399, 423; rebuilt by Henry III, 399, 400, 402, 404; in Welsh war (1277), 412.

Deheubarth, kingdom of, 386, 393.

Dehio, L., on Innocent IV and England, 757.

Deighton, H. S., on clerical taxation by consent in Edward I's reign, 505 n., 508 n., 676 n.

Delisle, L., on letter from a citizen of Rochelle, 745.

Delsoler, family of Bordeaux, 109, 111, 171.

Demesne, royal, and the boroughs, 529–34; farming of, 63 & n.

Denbigh, centre of David of Wales's barony, 419, 423; creation of honour of, 424; later shire of (1536), 424 n.; castle of, 430, 441.

Denholm-Young, N., on the Winchester-Hyde chronicles, and on Thomas Wykes, 735; on formularies, 724; on baronial plans of reform, 79; on the Mise of Lewes and later documents, 190 n.; on Fleta, 356 n.; on Robert Carpenter, 370 n.; on the feast of the Swans, 515 n.; on tournaments, 515–16 nn., 770; on the number of knights in England, 541 n.

Déprez, E., on the conference of Avignon (1344), 652 n.

Derby, earls of, *see* Ferrers, Lancaster (Henry of).

Derbyshire, footsoldiers from, on Scottish campaign (1300), 693.

Dereham, Elias of, 8, 12, 14.

Dermot, king of Leinster, descendants of, 561, 562.

Despenser, Hugh, justiciar (1260–1), 162, 163; again in 1263, 176, 194, 198 & n., 200; slain at Evesham, 202.

Devizes, castle, 1, 9, 331, 422; Hubert de Burgh in, 51, 53, 60.

Devon, tin of, pledged (1297), 667.

— earldom of, Fawkes de Breauté and lands of, 26; *see also* Fors, Isabella de.

Devorguilla, d. of Alan of Galloway and Margaret, d. of David of Huntingdon, brings part of Galloway to her husband, John Baliol, 581 n., 606 n.; her death (1290) and relief of her lands, 602 & n., 610 n.; founder of Sweetheart Abbey, 693 n.

Dibben, L. A., on the chancery, 748.

Dickinson, W. C., on Scottish administration and social grades, 572 n.; on Scottish burghs, 575 n.; on administration of justice in medieval Scotland, 753.

dictatores, of Simon de Montfort's Gascon accounts, 113.

Dictum of Kenilworth, 209–13, 370, 530; King Edward's conditions for enforcement of (1276), 209–10.

diffidatio, 55 & n., 189, 203 n., 614, 661.

Diffinitores, 86–87 & n.

Dilley, J. W., on William Wallace's letter to German merchants, 687 n.

Dinas Bran castle, 410 n., 424.

Dinefwr castle, 391; a centre of administration, 410 & n., 420, 438; capture and recovery of (1287), 439, 440.

Dioceses, 445; assemblies of clergy in, 448 & n., 478–9, 501–9; archives of, 490 & n.

Dirleton castle, 573 n., 689.

Diserth castle, 137, 172, 178 n., 399, 400; destroyed by Llywelyn ap Gruffydd (1263), 402, 403 n., 404.

Disinherited, the, action against (1265–7), 206–9, 213–15. *See also* Dictum of Kenilworth.

Distraint, 368, 372 & n.

Distraint of knighthood, 546–8, 552–3; and the investigations of 1279, 359.

Districciones Scaccarii, statute, 325 n.

Doehaerd, R., on Genoese shipping, 637n.

Dolforwyn castle, 387, 406, 409.

Dolwyddelan castle, 428, 441 n.

Domesday Book, 6, 530 n., 703 n.

'Domesday of the Ports', 646 n.

Dominicans, 24; provincial of, letter of Edward I to, 1294, on outbreak of Gascon war, 648; summoned (1300) to Lincoln parliament of 1301, 702. *See also* Hotham, William of.

Donald Bane, ancestor of the Comyns, through Hextilde, wife of Richard Comyn, 581 & n.

Donnchad Ua Longargain, archbishop of Cashel, 568 n.

Dordrecht, 663, 664, 667.

Douglas, James, son of William Douglas, 685 & n., 708 n.

— William, 684, 685 & n. 3.

Dover castle, besieged (1216–17), 1, 4, 9, 10, 12; held by justiciar, 48; and by Peter de Rivaux, 52; in the baronial disturbances, 163, 165, 176, 181, 187, 198; the Lord Edward and (1265–6), 206, 207; constable of, and Nicholas Segrave, 332; attacked by French galley (1294), 655 n.; court of constable of, 701.

Dower, law of, 326.

Dreux, Peter of, count of Brittany, 15 n., 73; his relations with Blanche of Castile and Henry III, 91, 92–97 *passim*; fights for Louis IX (1242), 103; his descendants in Brittany, 159 n., 235–6 n.; his attempt to secure the succession to Navarre for his son, 237. *See* Brittany.

Drew, J. S., on Winchester priory and its manorial officials, 762.

Droxford, John, keeper of wardrobe, 662 & n.

Dryslwyn castle, 410, 421, 438; siege of, 439–40; under a royal castellan, 440.

Dublin, its connexion with Bristol, 565; division of county of, 564, 569; shipping of, 442; mint and exchange of, 633; collection of customs at, 650 n., archbishops of, *see* London (Henry); Darlington (John); Hotham (William).

Dubois, Pierre, 82–83.

Duel, challenge of Gaston of Béarn to Edward I, 285 & n.; the fiasco of the duel arranged between Charles of

Anjou and Peter of Aragon, 254; canon law and the, 254 n.

Dumfries, castle and burgh, truce with Scots announced at (1300), 693 & n.; meeting of Bruce and Comyn at (1306), 713, 714 & n.; execution of Christopher Seton at, 716.

Dunbar, castle, battle near (1296), 614; release of prisoners taken at, 686.
— earl of, his duties in the Marches, 588 & n.
— Patrick, earl of, 695, 707.

Dunfermline abbey, 709.

Dunham, W. H., Jr., on origin of the Year Books, 729; on Hengham's dismissal, 363 n.

Dunkeld, bishop of, on Scottish embassy to France, 1302–4, 697 n.

Dunlop, Annie I., 585 n.; edition of Bagamond's Roll, 583 n.

Dunstable, justices of assize at, 27.

Dunwich, burgesses of, 484 n.

Durham, cathedral church of, 495; prior and convent of, dispute with archbishop of York about rights during a vacancy in the see of Durham, 469 n., 493–4; and the bishop of, 493, 495–6; prior of, and Alexander II, king of Scots (1239), 586 n.; bishop of, and John Baliol, 266; monks of, at Oxford, 485 n.
— bishops of, *see* Marsh; Poor; Kirkham; Bek.

Durward, Alan (*ostiarius*), 590, 592 n.

Dyffryn Clwyd, one of the Four Cantrefs, 400 n.; granted by Edward I to David of Wales, 414; the later barony of Ruthin, 424.

Dynefor, *see* Dinefwr.

Eardisley castle, 172, 175.

Earls, English, 40–41, 50–51; personnel of, in 1306, 516–17 & n.; relations of Edward I and Edward II with, 517–19; theory of earls (*comites*) as peers and companions of the King, 521.
— Scottish, 577, 578–82 *passim*; during Alexander III's minority, 590–2; claim authority during interregnum (1291), 601–2 & nn.; in 1296, 613, 614.

East Anglia, ports of, 659.

Eastry, Henry, prior of Canterbury, 485, 717; letters to, 261–2, 262 n.

Eckhart, Meister, 230.

Edinburgh, castle (*Castrum Puellarum*), 571 n., 589, 590, 614, 686, 692 & n.; parliament in (1258), 592 n.

Edler, Florence, on a merchant house of Siena, 639 n.

Edmund, St., of Abingdon, archbishop of Canterbury, 47, 56–60 *passim*, 68, 71, 76; his sisters at the nunnery of Catesby, 182 n.; his shrine at Pontigny visited by Henry III (1254), 119, and by Edward I (1286), 256 n.
— second son of Henry III, later earl of Lancaster; crown of Sicily offered to by the pope and accepted for him by Henry III, 121–3 & nn.; released by pope Alexander IV from his obligations (1258), 136; later history of claim, 167, 168; sent to England from Paris as *capitaneus* (1262), 171, 172 n., 173; surrenders Dover, 176; with his mother in France (1263–5), 280; created earl of Leicester and seneschal of England (1265), 206; receives lands of earl of Derby, 212 & n.; takes the cross, 219; his career, character, lands, &c., and loyalty to Edward I, 235–6 & nn., 239, 240, 518; his marriage to Blanche of Artois, countess of Champagne, and his position as vassal of Philip III, 236–41 *passim*; joins the league of Mâcon, 248; in west Wales, 406, 410, 414; with Edward I in Paris (1286), 290; regent in England (1286–9); puts down rebellion of Rhys ap Mareddud, 439 & nn.; his negotiations in Paris (1293–4), 646–8; leads expedition to Gascony and dies (1296), 649; acquired Peter of Sovoy's house in the Strand, 250 n.; founder of Dominican priory at Leicester, 519 n.

Ednyfed Fychan, seneschal of prince of Snowdonia, 391.

Edward the Confessor, king and saint, 18; Henry III and his annual feast of (13 Oct.), 159 & n., 161, 205; his translation in 1269, 224.

Edward, I, King of England: *before 1258*: knighted by Alfonso X, 548; as future lord of Gascony, 113, 115; negotiations for his marriage to Eleanor of Castile, 116, 118; his establishment and marriage (1254), 118–19, 318, 401; plan for a visit to Ireland of (1255), 563.

From 1258 to 1274: during the changes in 1258, 129–30, 135 & n., 139–40; his interest in general complaints, 145, 149, 153–4; his compact with Richard of Clare (1259), 152, and with Simon de Montfort, 154; his group of friends, 153–4; his estrangement from his father, reconciliation and withdrawal from England (1260–3), 156–60 *passim*, 164,

171, 172 & n.; and the ecclesiastical council of 1261, 457; and Llywelyn of Wales, 172, 404; takes the lead, 173, 176, 177; his success in the west (1264), 185; his conduct of the war, from Oxford to Lewes, 186–90; a hostage, 190; his status under the peace of Canterbury, the pact of Worcester, and the settlement of 1265, 194, 197–8; his escape, successes, and victory at Evesham, 200–3; his share in the restoration of peace, 206–7, 208, 213–15; takes the cross (1268), 219; as a crusader, 82, 223–4; his immediate succession to the throne in his absence (1272), 225; his slow return, 225–6; his coronation (19 August 1274) and coronation oath, 7, 226; his control of merchants, Cinque Ports, and his new duty on exports and imports (1266–74), 619, 620 n.; his dispute with Flanders and its aftermath (1270–85), 621–3.

As King in England and Wales: in council and parliament, Ch. VIII *passim*; his relations with his lords and barons, 516–19; his development of cavalry from gentry of the shires, 546, 548, 551–6 *passim*, 678–81 & n.; and foreign merchants, 619, 626, 630–2 *passim*, 637, 639–40; new coinage of (1279–80), 633–4; London in his hands (1285–98), 626–8; as a town-planner, 634–7; and the boroughs, 531–2 & nn.; his relations with Archbishop Pecham, 476, 478–80, and Antony Bek, 494–6; his taxation of the clergy, 501, 505–8, 675–7; his use of papal aid, 500, 506; his relations with Llywelyn of Wales and point of view, 381–2, 407–8, 416–18, 420–1; his leadership in the Welsh wars and Welsh administration, 408–43 *passim*; his return to Westminster from the Welsh settlement (1285), 369 & n.; his return to England from his long absence in Gascony (1289), and his reliance upon his former companions in Gascony, 268, 362, 510–13; his policy in Ireland, 562–3, 565; as a hero of legend and Arthurian chivalry, 515–16 & nn.; his later difficulties (1294–1301), 669–83, 697–705; a study of his personality in the light of his times, 227–31; his last days, after hearing of Bruce's rising, 514–15, 716–19.

As a continental statesman (1273–91): his relationships and outlook, 234–5,

236–7, 241–4 & nn., 258, 270–1; his treaty with Henry, king of Navarre (1273), 238; his interests in Navarre, 240, 241 n.; his efforts to make peace between France and Castile (1276–80), 242–4: helps Alfonso X of Castile against Sancho (q.v.), 244–5; as a statesman and arbitrator (1276–91), 245–64 *passim*; Margaret of France seeks his aid, 246–8; his marriage treaty with Rudolph of Habsburg, 246–7; mediates between Rudolph and his relatives in Savoy, 249–51; seeks peace between Alfonso of Aragon and Charles of Salerno (1286–91), 255–61, 263, 282–4; expenses of this activity, 305; his marriage treaty with Alfonso of Aragon (1273–91), 257–8, 259, 263–4; his plans for a crusade, 252, 264–7.

As duke of Aquitaine: his status, seal, and style before his succession to the duchy (1272) and afterwards, 274–5 & n., 280–1 & n., 311; his administration of Gascony in 1273–4, 293–4; concludes the treaty of Amiens (1279) and Paris (1286), 289–91; does homage to Philip IV, 290; on his military obligations to the king of France, 311 & n.; his qualities and policy as duke, 287, 294–8, 307–8, 310–18.

Edward I's dispute about Gascony with Philip IV (1293–1303), 644–69.

The Gascon phase, 644–58, 666; the period of alliances (1294–7), 658–69; the period of truce (1297–1303), 649, 650–4; his attempts at compromise with Philip IV's claim to exercise ordinary authority (*cognicio ordinaria*) as sovereign lord of the duchy of Aquitaine, 645–8; his alternative suggestions about the status of the duchy during the arbitration of Pope Boniface VIII (1298), 650–2; concludes the treaty of marriage between himself and Margaret of France (1299), 652–3; makes definite peace and marriage treaty between his son and Isabella of France and confirms the treaty of Paris (May 1303) at Perth (June 1303), 653–4; his later discussions about damages at sea and breaches of truce of 1297–1303, 657–8.

Edward and Scotland: his knowledge of the Scots, 592–3; his relations with Alexander III, 595; negotiates Anglo-Scottish marriage and future Scottish relations (1290), 598–600; administers Scotland as supreme lord until John Baliol's succession, 604–8; insists on his appellate jurisdiction as Baliol's overlord in Scotland, 608–12; hears of Scottish alliance with Philip IV, forces Baliol's abdication, and adds the kingdom of Scotland to his own (1296), 613–17; his leadership in the Scottish wars (1297–1307), 688–97, 706–16, 718–19.

Henry III on Edward's character, 171; Edward's description of parliament in a letter to Pope Gregory X, 537; his remark on the duel projected between Charles of Anjou and Peter of Aragon, 254 n.; Edward and Eleanor's children, 268 n.; *see* John; Henry; Alfonso; Edward of Caernarvon; Eleanor; Joan; Margaret; Mary.

Edward of Caernarvon, Edward II, 517, 518; born (1284), 429; betrothed to Margaret of Scotland (1290), 265, 268 & n., 599–600; treaty for his marriage with a daughter of Guy, count of Flanders (1297), 659, 665; oath of fealty to (1297), 680; regency of, during his father's absence in Flanders, 681–3 *passim*, 687–8; created Prince of Wales (1301), 436–7, 694, 705; affianced to Isabella, d. of Philip IV (1303) and alleged homage for his father to Philip, 654; on Scottish campaign of 1301–2, 694, 706; of 1303–4, 709; of 1306, 515, 715; knighted and invested with Gascony (1306), 514–15.

— son of Amadeus V, 251 n.

Edwards, J. G., on the Welsh Laws, 388 n.; on the name Flint, 412 n.; on the building of Flint, 635 n.; on Edward I's castle-building, 430 n.; on Thomas Turberville, 440 n.; on Madog ap Llywelyn, 440 n.; on Sir Gruffyd Llwyd, 441 n.; on the battle of Maes Moydog, 442 n.; on 'full powers', 536 n.; on persons elected to attend parliament, 540 n.; on the crisis of 1297, 680 n., 682 n.; on William Stubbs, 746; on the Welsh Marches, 755.

Egypt, sultan of (1239–40), 105, 110; Mamlūks of, 167 n.

Ekwall, E., London subsidy rolls, 725.

Eleanor of Aquitaine, queen of England, 73, 126.

— sister of Henry III, married (1) William the Marshal junior, (2) Simon de Montfort, 41; *see* Montfort, Eleanor de.

— of Provence, queen of England (d.

1291), 73–74, 112; in Gascony and Paris (1254), 118, 119; molested by Londoners (1263), 176; in France (1263–5), 178, 180, 192; debts incurred by her on behalf of Henry III, 220, 280–1, 305; her claims in Provence, 234, 246, 247 nn.; her rights in the honour of Richmond, 159 n., 249 n.; commutation of her rights in the Agenais, 305; her bastide of Monségur, 308; the succession to Savoy and, 250–1; gives Peter of Savoy's house in London to Edmund of Lancaster, 250 n.; at Amesbury, 268, 512; and her daughter Margaret, queen of Scots, 589, 591 n.

Eleanor of Castile, queen of England (d. 1290), half-sister of Alfonso X, king of Castile, 73 n.; married to Edward (1254), 116, 118; her dower, 118; visits Alfonso X in Spain (1273), 226; her succession to Ponthieu (1279), 235; as arbitrator, 312; death of, 268, 511, 513; her children, 268 n.

— d. of Edward I, 118 n.; betrothed to Alfonso, king of Aragon, 257–8, 263–4; married Henry III of Bar (Sept. 1293), 264, 668 n., 672 n.

Elections, and conditions of validity, 538–40.

Elections, episcopal, 347, 468; in Scotland, 584.

Elfael, campaign in (1231), 44, 45, 393, 397; Llywelyn ap Gruffydd and, 406.

Elizabeth, d. of Edward I, marries John, count of Holland (1297), 665, 680 n.

Ellesmere, 399.

Ellis, J. T., on anti-papal legislation, 757.

Elman, P., on economic causes of the expulsion of the Jews, 768.

Ely, disinherited in Isle of (1266–7), 208, 210, 213–15, 331; their episcopal exemplars, 57; convocation of clergy at (1290), 513.

— Nicholas of, chancellor, 176, 181 n.

— William of, treasurer, 65.

Emery, R. W., on the Pied Friars, 761.

Emlyn, and new castle of, 439, 440.

Enclosure of common pasture, 69.

Englefield (Tegeingl), one of the Four Cantrefs, 400 n., 414.

Epidemic in Paris (1262), 171.

Equity, 328 & n.

Eric, king of Norway, 599, 606 n.; marries Isabel Bruce, 611 n.; his treaty with Philip IV of France, and understanding with the Scots (1295), 613.

Escheats and escheators, 63–64.

Esposito, M., on rhythmical tract against the 'Romans', 733.

Estella, castle, in Navarre, 238, 239, 241.

Etsi de statu, papal bull, 674, 677.

Ettrick forest, William Wallace established in (1297), 684, 686, 690.

Eustace the Monk, and his brothers, 10, 12–13, 14.

Evans, S. S. A., on monastic chapter ordinances and episcopal statutes at Ely, 762.

Evenwood, compact between bishop and monks of Durham made at, 494–5 & n.

Evesham, battle of, 178, 202–3; Edward I at, in 1301, 706.

— Eustace of, bishop of Worcester (d. 1218), 3.

Exchanges, the royal, 65, 207, 663–4; in Flanders, 640.

Exchequer, the royal, reopened (1217), 16; and the investigation of rights, 39, 62–63; developments in functions and records of, 62–65; in 1259, 150; in 1263, 181 & n.; state of, 1264–8, 220; transferred to London (1287), 627; and to York (1298–1304), 627 n., 686, 711; and the collection and audit of lay subsidies, *temp.* Edward I, 323–4 & n.; its intervention in collection of clerical subsidies, 508–9; and fines and scutages when feudal levy summoned, 555, 557–9; and audits of bailiffs' accounts, 366; and return of writs, 378; Irish and Gascon accounts at, 306 & n.; enrolment and deposition of a papal bull in, 268 n.; a chamberlainship of, in fee, 364; a corrupt chamberlain of, 698 n.

— and Chamberlain of Scotland, 578, 604; established by Edward I at Berwick, 614 & n.

Excommunication, 464–7; general sentences of, 75, 421, 473, 476, 674–7 *passim*, 681 & n.: *see* Charter of Liberties; and writs of caption, 476, 484.

Exempla, bibliographical note on, 765.

Exeter, the 'statute' of (1286), 359–60 & n.

Extenta or survey of Champagne (1276–8), possible English influence on, 241 n.

Eyvill, John d', 208, 213–15.

Fair pleading, 217.

Falkirk, battle of (1298), 443, 689–90 & n., 694, 695.

Familia, royal, duty of members of, 151 n.

Farm, the sheriff's, 62–63 & n.

Fasciculus de superioritate maris, 655–6 n.

Fauconberg, Eustace de, treasurer, later bishop of London (1221–28), 16.

fautores of Simon de Montfort, treatment of, 204. *See* Dictum of Kenilworth.

Faversham, Eustace of, chaplain and biographer of St. Edmund, 57 n.

Fawtier, R., on a diplomatic incident (1294), 660 n.

Feckenham (Worcs.), royal manor, 512, 706.

Felony, persons charged with, invited to volunteer for service in Gascony (1294), 648 & n.; and Scotland (1296), 648 n.

Ferdinand III, king of Castile, 102, 116, 235.

— de la Cerda (d. 1275), elder son of Alfonso X, king of Castile, his widow a sister of Philip III of France, 242; his sons' rights to the succession in Castile, 242–4, 253, 262.

Ferre, Gui, ducal lieutenant in Gascony (1300), 317.

Ferréol, Stephen of, 294.

— William of, his letter to Edward I (1282), 294 & n.

Ferrers, Robert, earl of Derby (1260–6; d. 1279), 42 n.; 181, 184, 185, 187, 188, 199, 208 & n., 212 n.

— William, earl of Derby (d. 1247), 3, 4, 11, 42 n.

— William, 685 n.

Feudal host, in royal levies, 543, 547–8, 553–9.

Fezenac, 291.

Fiennes, Enguerrand de, household knight of Henry III, 545 n.

Final concords, 39 & n.

Finance, war: Henry III's, 32, 121 (Sicily); Edward's crusade, 224, 281 & n.; Edward I's wars in Wales, 413, 422 (1282–4), 432 (castles); arrangements for costs of Scottish expedition in 1296, 619; expenditure in the Low Countries (1294–8), 662, 666–7, 673–4; accounts for expenses in Gascony (1294–1303), 650 & nn.

Finedon, 704 n.

Fines in lieu of military service, 547–8, 556; the exchequer and fines of 1294, 555.

Fishponds, private, 69, 367.

Fitz Alan, Brian, of Bedale, appointed one of guardians of Scotland by Edward I (1291), 597 & n., 604; later appointments of, in Scotland, 686 & n., 713 n.

— John, lord of Arundel, capture at Lewes, 190.

Fitz Alan, Walter, steward of David I, king of Scots, 580 & n.

Fitz Geoffrey, John, 130 n., 173–4 n.

Fitzgerald, Maurice, justiciar of Ireland, 58.

Fitz John, John, son of John fitz Geoffrey, joins Simon de Montfort (1263), 174 n.; knighted at Lewes, 188.

— Robert, 323.

Fitzmaurices, in their barony in Kerry, 564 n.

FitzNicholas, Ralph, 95.

FitzOtto, Hugh, 323.

FitzPeter, Geoffrey, 23 n.

FitzThomas, Thomas, mayor of London, 186.

FitzWalter, Robert, 8, 11.

Flahiff, G. B., on writs of prohibition, 454 n., 475–6 n.; on the use of writs of prohibition by clerks, 468 n.; on critics of the crusade, 80 n.

Flanders, in 1127, 132 n.; Henry III and, 621; the break with Edward I and the embargo on English wool to (1270–8), 621–3, 645; hold of Philip IV as suzerain on, 648, 659, 669; Edward I in (1297), *see* Edward I; French invasion and defeat at Courtrai in (1302), 653, 669, 697; later relations with France of, 669; hansa in London, 621; exports of wool to, 637.

Flanders, counts of, *see* Dampierre (Guy); Margaret.

— Philippe of, d. of count Guy, 659.

Fleet prison, the, 356 n., 364, 366.

Fleta, 356 n., 521 n.

Flint, the royal headquarters (1277), castle built at, 412, 430–2; new town founded at, 412, 432; county of, 435.

Florence, city of, its life, reflected in a lawsuit, 626; merchants of, 641. *See* Bardi, Frescobaldi.

Florence, count of Holland, claimant of kingdom of Scotland, 606; his compact with Robert Bruce, 611 n.; as pensioner of Edward I and Philip IV, 659, 664; murdered (1296), 664.

Flower, Robin, on Ireland and medieval Europe, 567 n.

Foggia, Charles of Anjou dies at, 253.

Fontevrault, prioress and convent of, 268 n.; Isabella of Angoulême's last years at, 103; Henry III at (1254), 119; Edward I at (1286), 256 n.

Forcalquier, county of, 112 n., 246, 247 n; Garsenda of and her d. Garsenda, mother of Gaston of Béarn, 112 n.

Forests, royal, 767–8; charter of (1217),

15, 40; confirmations of, in whole or in part (1297–1300), 683, 700 & n.; disputes about perambulation of, 40, 697, 699 & n., 700–3; Edward I's inquiries into malpractices in, 698, 699, 702, 703; his hunting tours in (1290), 512–13.

Form of government of June 1264, 191–4, 198. *See* Canterbury, peace of.

Forma pacis of 1263, 176 & n.

Forz, Isabella de (d. 1293), countess of Aumâle and lady of the Isle of Wight, 518; and Adam de Stratton, 364–5.

— William de (d. 1241), count of Aumâle, 21–22.

— William de (d. 1260), count of Aumâle, 155, 156 n.; and the succession to the earldom of Chester, 197 n.

Foster, Idris, on the 'book of the anchorite', 764.

Fountains abbey, 21.

Four Cantrefs of Perfeddwlad, north Wales, surrendered to Henry III (1247), 400 & n.; allotted to the Lord Edward (1254), 401; overrun and held by Llywelyn (1256), 401 n., 402; lost by Llywelyn (1277), 412; Edward's administration in, 414; rising in, reconquest and redistribution of (1282), 419–20, 423–4.

Fowler, G. H., editor of Bedfordshire survivals of sheriff's records, 750.

France, barons of, their alleged influence on English opposition to episcopal discipline, 455 n.; bishops and clergy of, action of, adopted by English bishops (1225, 1261, 1297), 502, 457, 676; peers of, 55–56; Henry III becomes a peer of (1259), 84, 126, 313; Edward I as peer of, 243 & n.; increase of royal domain in, after death of Alphonse of Poitiers, 272–3 & n.; patriotic propaganda in, 527 & nn.

Francis, St., extreme followers of, 233.

Franciscans, in Ireland, 567, 569.

— provincial of, in England, royal letters to (1294), on outbreak of Gascon war, 648; summoned (1300) to Lincoln parliament, 1301, 702.

Fraser, C. M., on regalia franchise of Durham, 495 n.

Fraser, Simon, of Oliver castle, his desertion of Edward I and later career in Scotland (1300–6), 696 & n., 708, 710 & n., 711, 713, 714, 716.

— William, bishop of St. Andrews (1280–97), one of the guardians of Scotland (1286), 597, 598, 599 n., 606; his letter to King Edward (Oct. 1290), 268 n., 600–1; supports John

Baliol, 601; queries Edward's right to receive appeals from Scotland, 608; one of the Scottish plenipotentiaries in France, 612; dies in France (1297), 616 n.

Frederick II, Emperor (d. 1250), 233; as a crusader and in his relations with the papacy, 48, 83, 88; marries Isabella, sister of Henry III (1235), 59, 72, 593 n.; Henry III's letter to, 59, 132; his relations with Henry III, 97, 98, 103; his break with the papacy and policy in the Arelate, 98–99, 247 & n.; and Richard of Cornwall, 105, 106; and Simon de Montfort, 107 & n.; and the kingdom of Jerusalem, 107 & n.; regarded as Anti-Christ, in league with Tartars, 110 n.

— of Aragon, brother of James II, king of Aragon, elected king of Sicily, 661.

Free County of Burgundy, see Burgundy.

Freising, Otto of, 85.

Frescobaldi of Florence, 632, 639–42 passim; control of local exchanges in England by, 633–4.

Frescobaldi, Amerigo dei, Edward I's yeoman, 639–40.

Friend, A. C., on Odo of Cheriton, 765.

Fronsac, viscount of, and the parlement of Paris, 311–12.

Furnes, see Veurne.

Gabaston, in Béarn, 276 n.

Gabel, Laura C., on benefit of clergy, 462 n.

Gaetani, Benedict, cardinal, later Pope Boniface VIII, 263 & n.; arbitrates between Edward I and Philip IV, when pope, in his private capacity, 650 & n.

galanas, 389.

Galbraith, V. H., on the 'statute' of Exeter, 360 n.; on annals of Bury St. Edmunds, 675 n.; on De tallagio non concedendo, 682 n.; on the confirmation of the Charters in 1300, 701 n.; on the Tower as a record office, 277 n.; on Roger of Wendover and Matthew Paris, 731; on the chronicle tradition at Bury, 731.

Galloway, Roland of, and his successors, 580–1 n.

— Edward I in, 692–4 & n., 707 n.

gallowglasses, mercenaries from Scotland, in Ireland, 566–7.

Gamelin, bishop of St. Andrews (1255–71), 592, 593 n.

Gannoc, campaign of (1245), 399; see Degannwy.

Gaol delivery, 361.

Gascony, duchy of, attacked by Louis VIII and saved (1224–6), 90–91; Henry III and (1227–30), 94–95; Henry III in (1242–3), 100, 103, 557 n.; conditions in and administration of, 108–10, 274–80, 295–318 passim; Simon de Montfort as custos of (1248–52), 110–13; Henry's plans for Edward in, 115; Henry's expedition to (1253–4), 116–19, Edward's establishment in, 118–19; Henry's lordship over recognized in treaty of Paris (1259), 126, 128; affairs of, in 1262, 170–1; in the settlement of 1265, 198; status of, as attached to the Crown, before Henry III's death, 274–5; Edward I in (1273–4), 226, 295–6; conference of kings of France and Castile in (1280), 243–4 & nn.; contingents from in Welsh war (1282), 421 & n., 422 n., 427; hostages and pledges of barons and towns of, under treaty of Canfran, 260–1; King Edward in (1286–9), 295, 298 and passim; close relations between England and, 276, 280–4, 294; Philip IV claims immediate jurisdiction over Gascon disturbers of his peace, is allowed temporary occupation of parts of, and (May 1294) declares the duchy confiscated, 645–8 passim; war and truce in (1294–1303), and discussions of status of, 648–58; cf. 297–8, 313; Channel Islands and, 318; contingent from at Falkirk (1298), 689, 690.

Gascony, administrative division of, 301; allods in, 297–8; coinages in, 305; court of, 297 & n.; dioceses of, 292 n.; exchequer of, 300; finances of, 296, 304 ff.; homages of vassals in, 295; lieutenants of duke in, 275, 279; paréages and bastides in, 308–10; seneschal of, 300–1, 312; wine exports of, 669 n.

Gaveston, Piers, 276 n., 324, 719.

Gaza, battle of (1239), 105.

Geneville, Geoffrey de, lord of Ludlow and Trim, 201, 517 n.; as Edward I's agent in Paris (1280), 244 & n.; appointed marshal (1297), 680, 681; one of Edward's commissioners, 653.

Genoa, galleys of, 637 & n.; and Philip IV's naval activity (1293–4), 646 n.

Gentry, country, Edward I and the military development of, 546, 548, 551–6 passim, 678–81.

Geoffrey, husband of Constance of Brittany, 92.

Gerald of Wales on Welsh, Normans, and English, 384 n., 385.

Germany, the double election of king in (1257), 119; merchants of, invited by Scottish leaders to pursue trade with a 'safe Scotland', 687.
— hansa of, *see* Hansa, of Germany.
— kings of, *see* Adolf of Nassau; Albert of Austria; Richard of Cornwall; Rudolf of Habsburg.
Gerona, 255.
Gervais, John, bishop of Winchester (1262–8), 186, 194, 195, 208 n.
Gesta Dunelmensia, 494–5.
Ghent, closed patriciate of, supported by Philip IV, 659; thirty-six barrels of money shipped to (1297), 667 & n.; headquarters of Edward I (1297), 384 & n.; Charters confirmed at, 683.
Giffard, Hugh, guardian of Edward, son of Henry III; father of bishops and abbesses, 458.
— John, of Brimpsfield, 172–3, 199, 428 & n., 438, 441; his wife, Maud Longespée, a granddaughter of Llywelyn the Great, 428 n.
— Walter, a son of Hugh Giffard, chancellor and bishop of Bath and Wells (1265–6), archbishop of York (1266–79), 203, 225.
Giotto, 230.
Glamorgan, honour of the house of Clare, 406; Hubert de Burgh and, 43, 44, 396; revolt in (1294), 440; King Edward in (1295), 443.
Glasgow, 694, 712; cathedral of, 573 n.; see of, 573, 574; bishops of, *see* Cheam, Wishart.
Glendower, Owen, ancestry of, 424.
Glentrool, 719.
Gloucester, Henry III's first coronation at, 1; discussion about regency at, 2; great councils at (1233–4), 53, 58; cf. 54, 55; peace of (1240), 398; in war of 1263–5, 175, 185, 200, 201–2; parliament in (1278), 345; statute of, *see* Statutes.
— earls of, *see* Clare.
Glyn Dyfrdwy, district of, gave name to Owen Glendower, 424.
Gold, and gold currencies, 638 & n.
Goronwy ab Ednyfed, seneschal of prince of Snowdonia, ancestor of Owen Tudor and the royal house of Tudor, 391 & n.
— ap Heilyn, seneschal of Llywelyn ap Gruffydd and David of Wales, 416, 417, 429 n.
Got, Bernard, *see* Clement V, Pope.
Gower, 396 & n.; Edward I in (1284), 437 n.
Graham, Rose, on assessment of Nicholas

IV, 498 n.; on Archbishop Winchelsey, 671 n.; 673 nn., 717; on clerical tenth of 1297, 677 n.; on letters of Ottobuono, 741.
Granson, Otto of, Burgundian friend and counsellor of Edward I, 514; as lord of the Channel Islands, 319–21 *passim*; his mission to France and Gascony (1278), 287–9, 297, 338; sent to Savoy (1282), 250; in command in Anglesey (1282–3), 427, 428; occupies coast castles of Snowdonia, 428–9; justice of Wales, 435–6; as hostage for observance of treaty of Canfran (1288), 283; on mission at Rome (1289), 261, 265; as royal commissioner during negotiations of 1297–1303, 653, 665; and the quarrels at Durham (1300), 495.
Grant, Richard, archbishop of Canterbury (d. 1231), 47.
Grantham, granted to the Lord Edward, part of dower of Eleanor of Castile, 118.
Gravamina, ecclesiastical, 453–4, 456, 479, 480–4; and taxation, 456; of the English clergy, addressed to the pope (1255–6), 503.
Graves, E. B., on the writ *Circumspecte agatis*, 479 n., 481 n., 482 n.
Gravesend, Richard, bishop of London (1258–79), 176 & n.; 208 n.; 486–7; and the problem of pluralities, 487 n.
— Richard, treasurer of St. Paul's, 486.
— Stephen, bishop of London (1280–1303), 486–7.
Gray, J. W., on the *jus praesentandi*, 463 n.
Gray, Walter, archbishop of York, regent in 1242, 102.
Great St. Bernard pass, 250; hospice of, 250 n.
Greenfield, William of, king's clerk, 266.
Gregory IX, Pope (1227–41), 45, 46, 89 n., 92 n.; and Frederick II, 48, 59, 98, 106; letter to, from Henry III, on Peter of Dreux, 97; sends the legate Otto to England and Scotland, 74, 583, 584; and Raymond of Toulouse, 100; and Richard of Cornwall, 106; decretals of, 449, 453; dies, 100.
— X, Pope (1271–6), policy of, 231–2; and the council of Lyons (1274), 232–3; and the crusade, 264; and taxation of the clergy, 266, 499; and Edward I, 233; and the problem of Provence, 247; his appointment of

Kilwardby as archbishop of Canterbury, 225 & n.; and Welsh problems, 406, 407 n.

Grey, John de, 402 n.

— Reginald de, justiciar of Chester, 336, 436, 441; on commission of inquiry into Welsh precedents, 418; granted Duffryn Clwyd (later barony of Ruthin), 424, 430; and Edward of Caernarvon (1297), 682.

— Richard de, castellan of Dover (1264), 187.

Grierson, P., on the Norman duke's homage to the king of France, 382 n.

Griesser, B., on Stephen of Lexington's register, 568 n.

Grievances, lists of ecclesiastical, see Gravamina.

Grilly, in Savoy, 288 & n.

— John de, 243 & n., 244 n., 279; seneschal of Gascony, first in 1266, 281 n., later in 1278–87, 254, 288–9, 306, 309; his part in the transfer of the Agenais, 292–3; seneschal of all Edward's lands in Aquitaine (1279), 293–4; his disgrace and later life (1287–1301), 289.

Grimaud (Grimaldi), Reyner, Genoese admiral in service of Philip IV, 655.

Grosmont castle, 43.

Grosseteste, Robert, bishop of Lincoln (1235–53), 47, 57, 70, 78, 450–1; on law of bastardy, 70–72, 453; constitutions of, 452–3; and the legate Otto, 453; and the gravamina of the clergy, 453–6, 460 & n.; on the anointing of kings, 460 & n.; on secular office held by ecclesiastics, 461; his attack on the court of Canterbury (sede vacante), 466; his relations with Simon de Montfort, 107, 113; at Lyons (1250), 114; his tract on kingship, 114; his advice on preaching, 765.

Gruffydd, natural son of Llewelyn the Great, 390; disinherited, 393; Henry III and, 398–9; death of, 399.

— ap Gwenwynwyn, lord of South Powys, 398, 403 & n.; his conspiracy against Llywelyn (1274), 406–7; as a baron of Wales, 414, 417–19, 421, 427 n., 428; his wife, 326 n.

— Fychan, ancestor of Owen Glendower, 424 & n.

— ap Madog, of Bromfield, 382 n., 409–10 & n., 424.

— ap Rhys ('Sir Gruffydd Llwyd'), 441 & n.

— ap Tudur, son of the last Welsh seneschal, in Edward's service, 441 & n.

Guala, cardinal-priest of St. Martin, papal legate; his part in the government of England (1216–18), 1, 2, 3, 11, 12, 16; seals the first reissue of the Great Charter, 4; and Wales, 393.

Guardians of Scotland, in Alexander III's minority, 578, 582, 590–2; their agreement with the Welsh princes (1258), 582, 592; after death of Alexander III (1286), 597 & n., 599, 604, 609; their seal broken (1292) on Baliol's succession, 609; their court of justice, 610 n.; during the period 1298–1304, 694, 695 n., 696, 697, 709.

'Gudemen' of Scotland, 576.

Guernsey, see Channel Islands.

Gui, Foulquois, legate, 180; his correspondence with the English baronial leaders (1264); issues sentence against upholders of the Provisions of Oxford, 195; recalled to become pope, 195. See Clement IV.

Guines, count of, 54, 214, 544, 545 n.

— Robert of, 545 n.

Gurdon, Adam of, 207, 208, 515.

Gwent, the three castles of, 20, 43, 52, 396, 401.

Gwerthrynion, district of, 406.

Gwladus Ddu, d. of Llywelyn the Great, wife (1) of Reginald de Braose, (2) of Ralph Mortimer, 395 & n., 403 n.

Gwynn, Aubrey, on Edward I and the archbishop of Cashel, 562 n.; on Henry of London, 568 n.; on Stephen of Lexington in Ireland, 568 n.

Gwynedd, or Snowdonia, primacy of princes of, 386 and Ch. IX passim; see Owain; Llywelyn the Great; David; Llywelyn ap Gruffydd.

hafod, hafota, 384 n. 4.

Haifa, lord of, see Valenciennes, John de.

Hainault, county of, 622 n.

—count of, see Avesnes, John of.

Hakon, King of Norway, his expedition to the west of Scotland (1263), 596.

Hall, H., and Nicholas, Frieda J., on weights and measures, 620 n.

Halnaker, 279.

Halton, John, bishop of Carlisle (1292–1334), as papal collector in Scotland, 573 n., 584 n.

Hampe, K., on Ottobuono's letters, 741.

Hampton Wyck, manor of (Dorset), 327 & n.

Hansa, the, records of, 687; German, in London, 621; London, of Flemish merchants, 621.

Harlech, 429; castle, 430–2 passim; borough of, 433; and the Welsh revolt of 1294–5, 442 & n.

Hartlebury (Worcestershire), 356 n.

Hartlepool, 705 n.

Hartmann, son of Rudolf of Habsburg, and his betrothal to Joan of Acre, 246, 247, 249.

Haskins, G. L., on petitions of representatives, 350 n.; on jus ubique docendi, 763.

Haskins, G. L., and Kantorowicz, E., on Accursius, 470 n.

Hastings, king's chapel in castle of, 326 n.

— Henry of, defender of Kenilworth, 208, 212 n.

— John, lord of Abergavenny, &c., 438; his sister Ada, wife of Rhys ap Mareddud, 438, 440; claimant of the Scottish kingdom, 606, 607; in Gascony, 279.

Havering (Essex), 512 & n.

— John of, justiciar of Wales and seneschal of Gascony, 279–80, 312, 436, 442–3.

Hawarden castle, 419.

Hay, Nicolas de la, castellan of Lincoln, 11.

Hedingham castle, 9.

hendref, hendrefa, 384 n. 4.

Hengham, Ralph, chief justice of the King's Bench, 347, 356 n., 363 & n., 373; investigates the grievances of Rhys ap Mareddud, 438.

Henriques, U. R. Q., on ecclesiastical grievances, 454 n., 484 n.

Henry II, king of England, his relations with Wales, 385, 386, 391.

— III, king of England (1216–72); succession and first coronation, 1; and the treaty of Kingston, 14; his second coronation (1220), minority and character, 18–19, 21, 38, 59; his patron saint, Edward the Confessor and the feast on 13 October, 18, and see Edward (St.) the Confessor, Westminster abbey; in control of his seal (1223), 24–25; declares himself of age, 38; quarrels with his brother Richard, 40–41; disappointed in Wales and Brittany (1228–31), 45, 92–97 passim, 397; his bid for a papal legate (1230), 46; asks for a papal legate (1230), 46; his political readjustment, 59–63; marriage plans end in marriage to Eleanor of Provence (1236), 72–73; his relations with the great council (1236–58), 74–79, 132–4; his relations with Ireland, 54, 57–58, 563; with Scotland, 138, 585–

95; and with Welsh princes, 382, 393 n., 397–404 passim; his period of hostility to the papacy (1244–5), 133, 150 n., 499; his financial tour of monasteries (1235), 503; his disregard of conditions attached to grant of the lay subsidy of 1237, 523 & n.; his ecclesiastical relations, 460–1, 465–7, 468, 501; his administration of the royal demesne and boroughs, 529–31 passim.

Foreign affairs: see Ch. III passim: claims Normandy (1223), 87; defends Gascony (1224–30), 90–91, 94–95; his expedition in 1242–3, 97–105 passim; his relations with Frederick II, 97–98, 103; becomes friendlier with Louis IX, 104, 106, 119–20; takes the cross (1250), 106, 116; and Gascon affairs (1248–54), 107–8, 110–18; see Alfonso X; returns to England through Paris, 119; involved in affairs of Sicily, 106, 120–3 passim, 124, 125, 134–6; makes peace with Louis IX (1257–9), 84, 120, 122–8; his new seal and style, 126 n.; as vassal of king of France (1259), 126–8.

The baronial movement: Henry's sworn agreement to change (1258), 134–5; his absence in France (1259–60) and the council of regency, 150 & n., 154–9; fears Edward's disloyalty, 156–9 passim; his uncertain relations with Simon de Montfort, 154, 156–61; reasserts his independence (1261), 161–6; released by the pope from his oath to the Provisions of Oxford, 163, 165, 168; his breach with Simon de Montfort (1262–3), 168–71, 174–5; in Paris (1262), 170–1, 173; his serious illness, 171; surrenders to a new movement (1263), 172–7 passim; holds his own during references of difficulties to Louis IX, 178–84 passim; from Oxford to Lewes (1264), 185–90; in honourable captivity, 191, 193–4, 198, 200–2; during the restoration of peace, 203–15 passim; his debts in 1268, 220; seeks papal aid, 220; his last days, 224–5.

Henry, second son and (1271–4) heir of Edward I, plans for his future (1273), 238 & n.; death of (Oct. 1274), 238.

— count of Champagne and king of Navarre (1270–74), m. to Blanche of Artois, 238; see Artois, Blanche of, and Jeanne; his relations with Edward I, 238.

Hereford, castle, 22; baronial headquarters (1265), 200–1, 202; liberties of borough of, copied in Wales, 433; earls of, *see* Bohun.

Hereford, Walter of, mason and master of works, 431.

Hertford, castle, 9; earls of, *see* Clare.

Hewitt, H. J., Medieval Cheshire, 773.

Hexham, Scottish writs on behalf of canons of (1297), 686 n.

Hill, Mary C., on the king's messengers, 767.

Hill, Rosalind, various essays on Bishop Sutton, 486 n., 758–9, 763; on the Victorines, 761; on Lincoln diocesan archives, 490; on ecclesiastical letter-books, 741.

Hilton, R. H., on social structure of rural communities, 359 n., 775.

Hobregge, Gervase, 8, 12, 14.

Holderness, 21, 634, 716.

Holland, merchants of, 348; English trade in wool through, organized by Edward I, 659, 662–4 *passim*; counts of, *see* Florence, John.

Hollings, Marjorie, on Anglo-Saxon precedents for reduction of service and the dependence of the under-tenants on the king, 550 n., 551 n.

Holme Cultram, abbey, the chancery required to appear there (1299), 702.

Honorius III, Pope (1216–27), and the Albigensian crusade, 87–88 & n., 91; and Henry III, 16, 24; and Fawkes de Breauté, 26; and taxation of the clergy, 498, 501–2; and Ireland, 568 n.; allows election of a *conservator* of the Church of Scotland, 583; forbids coronation and unction of Alexander II, king of Scots, 593; on feudal relations between kings of England and the Scots, 594–5; on the rights of David of Snowdonia, 393 & n.

Honorius IV, Pope (1285–7), on conditions of peace with Aragon, 256, 257; renews papal prohibition of Anglo-Aragonese marriage, 258; and the crusade, 265.

Hopton, Walter de, president of Welsh judicial commission (1278), 415, 416, 417–18, 440; on commission of inquiry into precedents in Wales, 418.

Horses, the war horse (*dextrarius*), value of, 549–50, 553.

Hospitallers, the, 82.

Hostages, 190, 193–4, 282–4, 647.

Hotham, William of, Dominican, prior provincial in England, later arch-bishop of Dublin, 261 n., 269, 675; his letters to Henry Eastry, 261–2; Edward I's agent at the papal court

(1289), 261–2, 265–6, 340 n.; and the Scottish case, 603; Edward I's representative during arbitration at Rome (1298), 651, 652 n., 678 n.

Household, royal, 767; as centre of administration, 48, 60, 323–4, 662; steward of, 323; knights of, 545–6.

Hoyt, R. S., on the coronation oath, 7 n.; on taxation and growth of the realm, 528 n.; on borough representation, 532 n.

Hudson, W. W., on the *camera* roll of the prior of Norwich, 762.

Hugh, St., of Lincoln, 56; canonization of, 24.

Hughes, Ursula, on Robert Burnell, 339 n.

Hull, river, *see* Kingston, Wyke.

Hundred, court, 68; private, 67 & n., 366; rolls, 359 n., 360 & n.

Hunt, R. W., on English learning in late twelfth century, 763.

Huntingdon, honour and earldom of, 594 & n., 606–7.

Hurstmonceaux, 545 n.

Hywel Dda, laws of, 388, 390, 416.

— ap Meurig, constable of Builth, career of, 411, 415.

Impropriation of churches, 458–9; the magnates of England's letter to Alexander IV on, 461.

Indentures, military, 520 & n.

Ingram, H., on Edward I as a foreign statesman, 246 n.

Innocent III, Pope, 17, 24, 87; and the Lateran Council, 449; on the writ of caption, 465.

— IV, Pope (1241–54), 110; and Frederick II, 98, 448; and the Sicilian business, 106, 121–2 & n.; and Simon de Montfort, 115; on coronation and anointing of the king of Scots, 594; on *unitas actus*, 538 n.

Inquiry, commissions of, in England, 322, 353, 355–61 *passim*, 481, 633, 698–9 & n., 702, 703 & n.; archi-episcopal, into diocesan rights, 491–3; in Gascony, 295–6 & n.; in Wales, 329, 415–16, 418; in Channel Islands, 320, 322, 358; in Champagne, 240–1 n., 322.

Ipswich, Christmas feast and marriage at (1296–7), 665 & n.; the election of portmen at, 538 n.

Ireland, Hubert de Burgh made justiciar of, 49; Henry III's plan to go to, 54; the war of the marshal in, 54, 57–8; vassals and chiefs of, summoned to aid Henry III (1231, 1244), 392, 587; revenues of, applied to Gascony (1249), 111; and the

Lord Edward (1254), 118; suggested visit of Edward to (1255), 563; in the settlement of 1265, 198; trouble in (1276–7), 242, 243 n.; volunteers from Ireland invited for service with Edward I in wars against Philip IV and the Scots, 553 n., 565 & n., 678, 689, 706, 709; Edward I's desire to extend the English common law to all native Irish, 562–3; parliament of 1297 in, 564, 569–71.

Social, ecclesiastical, and political condition of Ireland in the thirteenth century, 561–71; appeals to Crown from, 560 & n., 711 n.; English writs and statutes in, 69–70, 357 & n., 560 & n.; exchequer and justiciary records of, 357 n., 565 n., 571 n.; treasurer of and the English exchequer, 306 n; justiciar of, 535, 560, 563, 569; shires and liberties in, 561, 563–4, 569–71; parliament in, 535, 560, 562 n., 563; taxation in, 535 & n., 560; the Irish subjects of Crown and liberties in, 561–2, 565; problem of Church in, 564 & n., 567–8.

Irvine, agreement with Bruce at (1297), 685.

Isabella, first wife of King John, her later marriages, 23 n., 40 n.

— of Angoulême, widow of King John, and wife of Hugh de Lusignan, count of La Marche, 89–91, 92 n., 95; and the French war of 1242–3, 97, 102–3; dies (1246), 103; her tomb at Fontevrault, 119.

— sister of Henry III, m. Frederick II, 72.

— of Aragon, first wife of Philip III of France, mother of Philip IV, 239–40 & n.

— d. of Peter of Aragon, 257.

— d. of Philip IV, 652; affianced to Edward of Caernarvon (1303), 654.

— of Scotland, wife of Roger Bigod, earl of Norfolk, 73 n.

Isgenen, district of, 438, 440.

Isleworth, Richard of Cornwall's manor of, 175; attacked by Londoners (1264), 186.

Italian merchants, see Merchants.

'Italians', movement against (1231–2), 45, 46, 766. See also 'Romans'.

Italy, representation of cities in, 531 & n.

Jacob, E. F., on St. Richard Wych, 487.

James I, king of Aragon, 99–100, 102, 116, 252.

— II, king of Aragon, 263 & n., 661.

— king of Majorca, 253, 255, 256, 260, 263.

James, Margery K., on exports of wine from Gascony, 669 n.

Jarnac, 124.

Jeanne, queen of France, daughter and heiress of Henry, count of Champagne and king of Navarre, 238–41 passim, 647.

Jedburgh castle, 707.

Jenkins, C., on thirteenth-century episcopal registers, 758.

Jenkinson. H., on the fifteenth of 1225, 32; on Edward I's second parliament, 343 n.; on receipts from Jewish sources, 724.

Jenkinson, H., and Mills, Mabel, on the sheriff's records, 750.

Jersey, 319, 320; see Channel Islands.

Jerusalem, capture of (1244), 110; Latin kingdom of, 107 & n., 134 & n., 137.

Jews, the, 36, 102, 768; attacks on, in 1264, 184, 186, 191; statute of (1275), 322; excluded from the operation of the statute of merchants, 625 n.; sufferings of, during the drive of 1278–9 against speculation in silver and debasement of the coinage, 633 & nn.; expulsion of (1290), 513.

Joan, wife of Llywelyn the Great and natural daughter of King John, 45, 391, 393; declared legitimate, 393 n.; her intrigue with William de Braose, 395.

— sister of Henry III and wife of Alexander II, King of Scots, 89, 585; death of (1238), 587.

— of Acre, daughter of Edward I, m. to Gilbert of Clare (1290), 268, 512.

— of Ponthieu, affianced to Henry III, later second wife of Ferdinand III of Castile, and mother of Eleanor of Castile, 73 & n., 235.

John XXI, Pope, 641.

— king of England: his death, burial, and executors, 1–3; his castellans and mercenary leaders during Henry III's minority, 20–27 passim; and the sheriffs, 62; his tax on exports and imports (1203), 628 & n.; and national defence, 550–1; and diocesan assemblies, 501.

— eldest son of Edward I, 224; dies (1271), 226 n.

— brother of Louis IX, King of France, 93.

— I, duke of Brabant, killed at tournament in Bar-le-Duc (1294), 664 n.

— II, duke of Brabant (1294), m. Margaret, d. of Edward I (1290), 268, 512 & n., 513 & n., 664 n.; his military alliance with Edward I (1295), 661 n., 663–4, 679 n.

John, count of Holland, m. Elizabeth, d. of Edward I (Jan. 1297), 665; Edward I entrusted with settlement of his disputes with Flanders and Brabant, 665 & n.

— the Scot, earl of Chester and Huntingdon (d. 1237), son of David, earl of Huntingdon, 197 n., 594 & n., 606.

— of Wales, Franciscan scholar, with Pecham in Wales, 424 & n., 425.

Johnsen, O. A., on Norwegian trade, 773.

Johnson, C., on the royal household and wardrobe, 767; on the keeper of papal bulls, 739; on boroughs and market towns, 771; on the Frescobaldi, 642–3 n.; on the building of galleys, 656 n.

Johnstone, Hilda, on the county of Ponthieu, 235 n.; on the council of Lambeth (1281), 479 n.; on royal alms, 767; on the queen's exchequer, 767.

Jolliffe, J. E. A., on the beginnings of parliament, 747.

Jones, F., on bonds made by Welsh freemen to keep the peace, 421 n.; on Welsh and Marcher subsidy of 1291–2, 443 n.

Jones-Pierce, T., on Welsh social developments, 384 n., 387–9 & nn.

Joneston, Elias, 278.

Judges, the, in council and parliament, 334–5, 341, 355–6; and the baronial government of 1259, 150; and the law merchant, 624, 626; on eyre, 16, 22, 39, 68, 335; Hugh Bigod and his colleagues on eyre, 146, 150–1; on general eyre again, 162, 357 n.; under Dictum of Kenilworth, 212–13 & n.; on eyre in 1278, 352 ff., 357 n., 358; in diocese of Norwich (1286), 481–2. See *Capitula itineris.*

— delegate, papal, in Scotland, 584.

Judicaturae of the Agenais, 302–3.

Junquera, Charles of Salerno meets Alfonso of Aragon near, 262.

Jurati ad arma, 551–3.

Jurats, 321.

Justices, local, to enforce observance of the Charters of Liberties (1300, 1301), 218, 701, 704 & n.; of the peace, 218 n.

Kantorowicz, E. H., on alienation, 7 n.; his *Laudes regiae,* 59 n.; on Stephen of St. George, 421 n.; on 'pro patria mori', 527 n.

Kantorowicz, H., on Bracton, 727.

Keeler, Laura, on Arthurian fashions, 732.

Keeney, B. C., on military service and nationalism, 528 n.; on the great Scottish case, 603 n.

Keepers of the peace, 218 n.

Keighley, Henry of, 704 & n., 717 n.

Kelso, 689.

Kemp, E., on the origins of convocation, 757.

Kempsey (Worcs.), 202, 705.

Kenilworth, castle, home of Simon and Eleanor de Montfort, 107; Earl Simon at (1263–4), 181, 182, 184, 185; hostages at, 194; Edward agrees to pact of Worcester at, 197; Edward surprises the younger Simon de Montfort at (July 1265), 202; operations against (1265–6), 206, 208, 213; issue of papal bull for taxation of the clergy at (1266), 221. See Dictum of Kenilworth.

Kensham, William of, 10.

Ker, N. R., and *Pantin, W. A.,* on the letters of a scholar at Paris and Oxford, 752.

Kern, F., on Rudolf of Habsburg's foreign policy, 248 n.; on Edward I and Peter of Aragon, 258 n.

Kerrera, island of, 596.

Kerry (Ceri), district in Wales, campaign of, 395. See Ceri.

Khorasmians, 110.

Kienast, W., on military service in England, 547 n.

Kidwelly, 409 n., 410.

Kilkenny, statutes of (1366), 566.

Kilwardby, Robert, Dominican, archbishop of Canterbury (1272–8), and cardinal: appointed archbishop by Gregory X, 225; and Edward I's succession, 225; and the court of Canterbury, 492 n.; his friendship with Thomas of Cantilupe, 489; his provincial assemblies, 504–5; and Llywelyn of Wales, 408; his difficulties, elevation to the cardinalate and death, 469, 470–1; his register, 471 n.

Kincardine, John Baliol surrenders the kingdom of Scotland at, 615.

Kinghorn (Fife), 597.

Kingsford, C. L., on Otto of Granson, 745.

King's Lynn, 708.

Kingship, bibliographical notes on, in action, 766–8; nature and theories of, 7, 59, 68, 129, 131–4, 145, 179, 192, 216, 520–3; Grosseteste on, 453 & n.; Walter Burley on, 521–2; and local law, 281–2; compared, in a petition, with civic republics, 626. See Crown.

Kingship, Scottish, and the papacy, 593–5, 693, 702, 705–6, 709–10; in the succession case (1291–2), 601–2, 605, 607–8, 610–11 & n., 706.

Kingston-on-Hull, new town of Wyke-upon-Hull, or Hull, 634.

Kingston-on-Thames, conferences at, 76, 166; treaty of (1217), 13–15.

Kinloss abbey, 709.

Kinross, Alexander III taken at (1257), 592.

Kirkby, John, king's clerk, deputy chancellor, treasurer (1284), bishop of Ely (1286–90), 335, 507 n.; financial tour of, 505–6 & n., 559 n.; his 'quest' (1285), 359 & n.; his judicial inquiry at the Tower of London (1285), 626; during Edward I's absence (1286–9), 511 n.; death of (1290), 627 n.

Kirkham, Walter of, bishop of Durham (1249–60), and John Baliol, 466.

Kirkintilloch, castle, 707.

Kirkliston, 689.

Knaresborough castle, 52 n.

Knights, 770; and knight service, inquiry into (1242), 102; changes in military aspects of, 542–3, 549–53; valuation of knight's fee, 548 & n., 552; break-up of knights' fees, 550; number of fighting knights, 548–9; cost of maintenance and equipment of, 549–50; distraint of knighthood, see Distraint; growth of a knightly class, 551–2, cf. 545, 547 n.; also 514–15 & n.; household knights, see Household; landless knights, 545; knight-service in Ireland, 565; growth of principle of paid forces during crisis of 1297–8, 678–9, 681, 689 & n.

— of the shires, their local importance and number, 539–42; in 1254, 117 & n., 141, 548; in administrative system of 1258–62, 142–6, 150, 166, 167; their reports to council in parliament (1258), 144 & n., 145; in parliaments of 1264–5 and 1273, 191, 197, 225; on their representation in parliament, 535–40.

Knockmoy, Cistercian abbey, 568.

Knoop, D., and Jones, G. P., on Beaumaris and Caernarvon, 430 n.

Knoville, Bogo de, justiciar of West Wales, 414–15.

Knowles, D., on archbishop Pecham, 484 n.

Kuttner, S., and Rathbone, Eleanor, on the Anglo-Norman canonists, 759.

Lacy, Henry de, earl of Lincoln (1272–

1311), 514, 517, 653; in Welsh wars, 409, 411, 421 n., 441; granted Rhos and Rhufoniog (later honour of Denbigh), 424; with King Edward in Paris and Gascony (1286–9), 283, 290, 362; at Tarascon (1291), 263; leader of forces in Gascony (1296–7), 649; on Scottish expeditions, 690, 694 & n., cf. 697; proctor for the King and Prince Edward in 1303, 653–4.

Lacy, John de, earl of Lincoln (1232–40), 51 & n.

— Matilda de, heiress of Ludlow and Trim, 517 n.

— Walter de, lord of Ludlow and Meath, 3, 4.

Laity, ecclesiastical discipline of, 454–6; and clerks, 458; views of, on the state of the Church (1258), 461.

La Marche, county of, 89–90, 97; counts of, see Lusignan.

Lamberton, Willam of, bishop of St. Andrews, election of (1297), 684 & n.; returns to Scotland and becomes chief guardian (1299), 695 n., 696 & n.; in Paris (1302–4), 697 n., 710 & n.; takes oath to King Edward (1304), 710 & n.; compact with Bruce (1304), 714 & n.; appointed chief warden of Scotland by Edward I (1305), 713 & n.; joins Bruce, surrenders himself, and is confined in irons at Winchester, 714, 716.

Lambeth, provincial council at (1261), 457–8; consistory at (Oct. 1279), 476; provincial council at (1281), 478; convocation at (1283), 507 & nn.

Lanark, shire and castle of, 707; sheriff of, slain by Wallace (1297), 684.

Lancaster, honour of, and Denbigh, 421 n.; Henry, earl of, 212 n. See Edmund.

Land, transactions in, 518–19.

Lanercost, priory, Edward I at (1306–7), 717 & n., 719.

Langley, Geoffrey of, 401 n.

Langlois, Ch.-V., on a scheme of taxation suggested to Edward I, 663 n.; on the Ancient Correspondence, 723.

Langtoft, on Bruce and parliament of Lincoln (1301), 695 n.

Langton, John, chancellor (1297), 681.

— Simon, brother of Archbishop Stephen, chancellor of Louis of France, 8, 12, 14.

— Stephen, archbishop of Canterbury, in Rome (1216), 1, 3, 17; procures Pandulf's withdrawal, 18; his co-operation with Hubert de Burgh, 23–28 passim, 47; his constitutions,

24, 421, 450–2 *passim*, 472, 472; and Wales, 393 n.; and clerical taxation, 501–2; death of (1228), 47.

Langton, Walter, treasurer (1295), bishop of Coventry and Lichfield, 335, 514, 517, 662 n.; his mission to Edward's allies, 664, 665, 667 n.; and Archbishop Winchelsey, 717, 718.

Lapsley, G. T., on *quo warranto*, 521 n.; on shire courts and their records, 750.

Largs, Norse defeat at (1263), 596.

Lastage, 628, 631.

Lateran council (1215), 447, 449–50; and clerical taxation, 222–3, 497 n., 507.

Latimer, William, 362 & n., 695.

Lauds, Henry III and, 59.

L'Aumône, abbey of, 653.

Law, the rule of, 84–87, 216–18, 522–3, 526–9, 538 & n.; common and natural, 327, 381–2, 528; common and Brehon law in Ireland, 562–3, 566; common and canon, 70–72, 463–8; common and statute, 369–80 *passim*; Roman, rules of, in political thought and practice, 538–9 & nn.; Scottish, 577, 601, 607, 608, 712; Welsh, 388–9, 398, 415–19 *passim*; study of, 485 n. *See* Canon law; Maritime law; Merchant law; Statutes.

Lawrence, C. H., on St. Edmund of Abingdon, 57 n.

Laymen as judges, 341 & n. *See* Bruce, Robert, the claimant.

Lees, B., on *villa integra*, 770.

Legate, papal, Henry III asks for (1230), 46; baronial council's request for (1258), 135, 136; in France (1283–4), 254–5; archbishop of Canterbury's authority as, 18, 491–2. *See* Guala; Pandulf; Otto; Gui; Ottobuono.

Legates, cardinal, work of, for peace between Edward I and Philip IV, 662, 665, 673 n.; procurations of, 673.

Legenda, 447 n.

Leges Burgorum, Scottish law book, 577.

Legists, French, 646, 648 & n., 651 & n., 654, 658.

Leicester, Dominican priory at, 519 n.
— earldom and honour of, 11, 20 n., 75 n.; earls of, *see* Beaumont; Montfort; Edmund of Lancaster.

Leinster, the Marshal's honour in, 53, 58, 561, 562, 563–4.

Leith, 707.

Leliants, the 'men of the lily' at Bruges, 669.

Lemarignier, J. F., and feudal frontiers, 382 n.

Lennox, earl of, 714.

Leominster, priory of, as a parish church, 489 n.

Leopold VI, duke of Austria, 73.

Le Patourel, J., on St. Peter Port, 318 n.

Lestrange, Hamo, 153, 173.
— Hawise, 326 & n.
— Roger, in Welsh war (1282), 422, 427, 428.

Levett, A. E., on wills of villeins, 743; on manorial organization of St. Albans, 762.

Levies, local (1297–1307), 684, 689 n., 703, 708.

Lewes, honour and castle of, 187; battle of (1264), 55 n., 188–90; Mise of, 190, 191; 'Song' of, 192.

Lewis IV, king of Germany and emperor, 661 n.

Lewis, F. R., on William of Valence, 745.

Lewis, N. B., on early military indentures, 520 n.; on Edward I's army in Flanders (1297), 679 n.

Leyburn, Roger, in the Lord Edward's circle, 153, 154, 157; his quarrel with Edward and political opposition (1262–3), 172, 173; made steward of royal household, 177; and the pact of Worcester (1264), 197; rescues the king at Evesham, 202; Edward's lieutenant in Kent (1266), 207, 208, 422 n.; his activity in 1267, 214; Edward's lieutenant in Gascony and death (1271), 275 & n., 279, 635.

Leyburn, William, first admiral of English fleet, 655–6.

Leys, Agnes, see Sandys.

Liberties, Charter of, *see* Charter; royal and seignorial, *see* Crown; Inquiries, &c.

Libourne, 635, 669 n.

libri feudorum, 313, 652 n.

Lichfield, bishops of, *see* Coventry.

Liebermann, F., on the monastic annals, 735.

Lille, siege of (1297), 669.

Limoges, bishopric of, 292 n.; in treaty of Paris (1259), 126, 128, 280–1, 289; castle of, 305 n.; Edward I's intervention in troubles of city and viscountess at (1273–4), 285, 305 & n.; viscount of, 5, 157, 160 n.

Lincoln, castle and city of, 11; battle of, 11–12; crusade preached at (1267), 219; a case of law merchant in shire court of, 624; parliament in (1301), 693, 695 & n., 697, 701–5 *passim*.

Lincoln, bishop of, his castles, 21. *See* Hugh (St.); Grosseteste; Gravesend; Sutton.

— earldom of, 20 n.; earls of, *see* Blundeville, Lacy.

Lindsay, Alexander, 684, 685.

Linlithgow, 689, 690, 692; castle of, 431, 694, 695, 701; Edward I winters in (1301–2), 694, 706.

Lisle, Baldwin de, 153; Brian de, 51, 52 n., 58.

litera excusatoria of Edward I to the Gascons (1294), 649 n.

Little, A. G., on the Lanercost chronicle, 732–3; on Edward I's alms, 746; on theological schools, 763; on friars and universities, 763, 765; on Leach, *Schools of medieval England*, 763 & n.

Llanbadarn castle, *see* Aberystwyth.

Llandeilo Fawr, Welsh victory at (1282), 420, 422.

Llandovery castle, 410, 428 n., 439.

Llanfaes (Anglesey), 661 n., 664.

Llanfyllin, in Powys, borough of, 433.

Lleyn, 443 n.

Lloyd, J. E., on Welsh dwellings, 385 n.; on Ceredigion, 398 n.; on the Welsh chronicles, 754.

Lloyd-Jones, J., on the Welsh court poets, 390 n.

Llywelyn ab Iorwerth, the great, prince of Aberffraw and lord of Snowdonia (d. 1240), 1, 20, 391–8 *passim*; makes peace at Worcester (1218), 16, 393; his sympathy with Fawkes de Breauté, 27, 85; Hubert de Burgh and, 44–45, 394–7 *passim*; Richard Marshal and, 53, 55–56, 57, 397; makes truce at Middle (1234), 60, 397; his wife Joan, *see* Joan.

— ap Gruffydd, first 'prince of Wales', 392, 404; his career to 1267, 137–8, 155–6, 161, 163, 171–4 *passim*, 177, 185, 201, 400–5; and the treaty of Montgomery (1267), 215, 406–7; his views on his relations with the Crown, 381–3, 416–19; Edward I declares war on, 242, 243 n., 408; submission of (1277), 412–13; his marriage, 331, 414; assents to David's rebellion, 419; his movements, negotiations, and death, 420, 424–8 & nn.

— ap Mareddud, a royal pensioner, career of, 440 & n.

Lochmaben, castle of the Bruces at, in Annandale, 692, 694, 695 & n., 696 n., 707, 715; Edward I's 'peel' at, 589 n.

Lodge, Eleanor C., on Gascon tenants-in-chief, 746.

Lombards, their league against Frederick II, 98; or money-lenders, in Flanders, 640.

London, city and shire of, bibliographical note on history of, 772; controlled by Louis of France (1216–17), 1, 8, 10–11, 14; and Hubert de Burgh, 50; provincial council at (1257), 456; and the provisions of Oxford, 135 n.; and the Lord Edward (1260), 157–8; citizens of required to swear fealty to the king and his son (1263), 175; in the wars of 1263–5, 176, 178, 181–2, 184; military organization of, in the battle of Lewes, 189, 190; their fine (1265), 205, 281 n.; restored to king's peace (1266), 205 & n.; and the new duties on trade (1266), 619 n.; commune formed in and royalist investment of (1267), 214; restoration of civic liberties in (1268–70), 218; convocation of clergy at (1278), 471; in royal hands and under royal ordinances (1285–98), 626–8, 630; forces for Flanders summoned to (1297), 666, 678, 679.

Elections to parliament in, 540; taxation on movables and, 527 n., 529 & n., 533; exchequer and, 65, 627; exchange and mints of, 633, 634 n.; hansas of foreign merchants in, 621; hustings of, 627; mayor and aldermen of, 135 n., *see* Rokesley; Waleys; warden of, *see* Sandwich, Ralph of.

— Holy Trinity, Aldgate, 214; New Temple, 17, 136, 147–8; St. Martin's-le-Grand, 623 n.; St. Mary-le-Bow, dean of, 492 & n., *see* Arches, court of; St. Paul's, 129, 176, 177, 191, 219; Tower of, *see* Tower.

— bishop of, 50; *see* Fauconberg; Niger; Basset (Fulk); Wingham; Sandwich (Henry); Gravesend (Richard).

— Henry of, archbishop of Dublin (1213–28), 567–8 & n.

'Londoner', term for a farthing, 634 n.

Longespée, Roger, bishop of Coventry and Lichfield (1257–95), 156, 176, 186.

— Stephen, 153.

— William, earl of Salisbury, deserts Louis of France, 10; seeks a palatinate, 20; and William de Forz, 21; and Fawkes de Breauté, 26; in Gascony, 40, 91,

Loomis, R. S., on Arthurianism, 515 n., 770.

Lopez, R., on Benedetto Zaccaria, 639 n.

Loria, Roger, admiral, 253, 255.

Lorris, treaty of (1243), 103.

Lothian, 695; justices for, 712.

Loudun (Ayrshire), Bruce's success at (1307), 719.

Louis VIII, king of France (1223–6), 73; his previous occupation of part of England, 1, 3–4, 8–15 *passim*; makes peace at Kingston, 13–14; returns to France, 15; accession of, 87; maintains his rights in Normandy, 87; overruns Poitou (1224), 88, 90–91; his Albigensian crusade, 87–88, 91; death of, 91.

— IX (St.), king of France (1226–70), marries Margaret of Provence, 73; and Peter of Dreux, 94, 96, 103; and southern politics (1241–3), 97–103 *passim*; his relations with Henry III (1243–58), 104, 106, 119; on crusade, 110, 114; and the treaty of Paris (1259), 84, 123–8, 135, 549–50; and English affairs (1258–65), 130, 155, 157, 161, 164, 170–1, 178–9, 181–4, 186, 191, 193–5 *passim*, 280–1; and the children of Simon de Montfort, 212 n.; protests against new English duties on trade (1267), 619 n.; his crusade in Tunis, and death, 224, 226 n.; and Edward's crusade, 281; his position in history, 143, 229–30, 231, 245.

— (St.) of Toulouse, son of Charles of Salerno, as a child hostage for his father, 283.

— of Savoy, 251.

Louth, Richard of, chamberlain of the exchequer, 698 n.

— William of, keeper of the wardrobe, 280, 305, 362.

Lucas, H. S., 664 n.; on north European trade, 773.

Lucca, *podesta* and commonalty of, 519 n.; merchants of, 505 & n., 633, 639, 641. *See* Riccardi.

— Luke of, 629, 632 & n., 642.

Luci, Richard de, justiciar, 71.

Ludlow, castle, 201; lords of, *see* Geneville, Lacy.

— Laurence of, wool merchant, 632, 663.

Luna, Petrus Martini de, 269 & n.

Lunt, W. E., on consent of clergy to taxation, 501 n.

Lusignan, castle, 89, 102; house of, 89, 97; and the Provisions of Oxford, 135, 138–40. *See* Valence, William of.

— Aymer de, bishop-elect of Winchester, 139, 140 & n., 141, 159, 162 nn., 327.

— Geoffrey de, lord of Jarnac, 124, 138–40; 157, 159, 162 n., 274–5.

Lusignan, Guy de, lord of Cognac, 124, 138–40, 157, 159, 162 n., 190, 274–5, 283.

— Margaret of, 100.

Lyndwood, *Provinciale*, 456 n., 474 n.

Lynn, 481.

Lyon, Bryce D., on the money fief, 544 n.

Lyons, council of (1274), 232–3; local reports for, discussed by English clergy (1273), 504; Edward I's proctors at, 460; Archbishop Pecham and, 451, 472–5 *passim*; canon of, on bigamy, 463.

— archbishop of, joins league of Mâcon, 248.

MacCarthys of Desmond, 561, 565.

Macclesfield, forest of, 513.

— archers from, 411.

Macduff of Fife, his appeal from Scottish to English king (1293), 610 & n.

McIlwain, C. H., on Bracton, 727.

MacKenzie, H., on the anti-foreign movement in England (1231–2), 766.

Mackenzie, W. M., on the 'debatable' land in the Scottish Marches, 588 n.; on 'peels', 589 n.

McKerral, A., on the gallowglasses, 567 n.; on the tacksmen in the southwest Highlands, 572 n.

Mâcon, conference at (1281), 248, 288 & n.

MacTaggart, Ferquhard, first earl of Ross, 580 & n.

Madog ap Llywelyn, rebel leader in 1294–5, 440–3.

Maefienydd, district of, 394, 406.

Magna Carta, *see* Charter of Liberties.

Magnus IV, king of Norway, cedes the western Isles and Man to the king of Scots (1266), 596.

Maine, county of, 93; and treaty of Paris (1259), 126.

Mainpast, 151 & n.

Maintenance, baronial, in the courts and in mainpast, 151–2.

Major, Kathleen, Acta of Stephen Langton, 720.

Majorca, king of, *see* James.

Malcolm, king of Scots (1153–65), and the stewardship, 580 & n.

Malden (Surrey), 157.

Malines, English staple at (1295), 663, 664.

Maltote, on wool, of 1294–7, 630, 663, 669, 682, 683.

Man, Isle of, as part of the Norwegian system in war and administration, 596 n.; its later history (1266–1765), 596 n., 609 n.

Manfred, natural son of Frederick II, and king of Sicily (1258), 121, 122,

123 & n., 532 n.; marries Beatrice, d. of Amadeus of Savoy, 247 n.; their d. Constance marries Peter of Aragon, 252.

Manorial life, villages and villagers, bibliographical notes on, 773–6.

Mansel, John, king's clerk, 113 n., 116, 145 n., 154, 162, 164, 339; and Scottish affairs (1255–6), 590, 591; at the papal court (1261), 163 & n.; in Paris with King Henry (1262), 170–1; leaves England (1263), 175, 178; an authority on Spanish affairs, 278.

Mansourah, battle of (1250), 114.

Mansuetus, papal penitentiary, legate in France, 120 n., 124.

Mantle-children, 70.

Manton, Ralph de, cofferer of the wardrobe, acts on behalf of Edward in Scotland and north of England, 707–8 & n.; killed at Roslin (1303), 708.

March, earl of, see Dunbar.

— (Marchia), William de, treasurer, 524; and the Londoners (1289–95), 627–8.

— homage on the, 382 & n.; arbitration on the, e.g. of Gascony, 645.

Marches of Wales, lords of, during the period 1262–7, 171–2, 175, 178, 190, 196–202 passim; and the royal prerogative, 329–30. See Wales.

— of Scotland, see Border.

Marden, denns in hundred of, 10.

Mareddud ap Rhys Gryg (d. 1271), 406.

Margaret of Provence, queen of France, wife of Louis IX, 73, 119; and English affairs (1261–5), 164, 178, 184 & n.; and Edward I, 244, 248–9; her claims in Provence, 234, 239, 246, 248–9; invested by Rudolf of Habsburg, 247 n.; forms the league of Mâcon (1281), 248; her concern for her relatives in Savoy, 249–50; in the case of Gaston de Béarn, 286; and John de Grilly, 288 & n.

— queen of England, sister of Philip IV of France, draft treaty (1294) for her marriage with Edward I, 647 & n.; papal dispensation for marriage of, 652; treaty for marriage of, and marriage of (1299), 653; resides at Dunfermline Abbey (1304), 709; watches the siege of Stirling (1304), 710.

— (St.), queen of Scots, 574, 584.

— queen of Scots, d. of Henry III (d. 1275), 571 & n., 582 n., 585 & n., 588, 589–91 passim, 593 n.

Margaret queen of Scots, the 'maid of Norway', 512, 597; betrothed to Edward of Caernarvon, 265, 268 & n., 598–600; her death in Orkney, 268 & n., 511, 513, 600–1.

— d. of Alexander III, king of Scots, wife of Eric, king of Norway (1281–3), 596–7.

— d. of Edward I, wife of John II of Brabant, 268, 511, 512 & n., 664 n., 680 n.

— countess of Flanders, 621, 622.

— d. of William the Lion, see Burgh, Margaret de.

— d. of Charles of Salerno, m. Charles of Valois, 272 n.

Marie of Brabant, second wife of Philip III of France (1274), 239, 240 n., 647.

Marisco, de, see Marsh.

Maritime law, 620; and disputes at sea, 644–6 & nn., 654–5. See Oléron.

Marjorie of Scotland, wife of Gilbert the Marshal, 73 & n.

Mark, Philip, 21.

Markets, the Church and, 369, 766; legal status of, 772.

Market towns, represented in parliament of Easter 1275, 532; assessment for taxation did not imply representation in parliament, 532–3 & n.

Marlborough, castle, 9, 40; statute of (1267), 69, 147, 216–18, 356, 368, 369, 371 n., 372 n. See also Statutes.

Marmande, castle of, 302; customs collected at, 304.

Marongiu, A., on curie generali in kingdom of Sicily, 532 n.

Marriages, general dispensation granted by the Pope for those of Edward I's daughters, 258 n.

Marsan, viscountess of, see Béarn, Constance of.

Marseilles, 99, 100, 255.

Marsh, Adam, Oxford Franciscan, 73, 115, 445, 446, 486; and Simon de Montfort, 107, 113 & n.

— Geoffrey, 58.

— Richard, chancellor, bishop of Durham (1217–26), 16.

— Robert, 454.

— William, 58, 362.

Marshal, the lord, and the feudal host, 548; rolls of, 548, 558 n., 559. See Bigod.

— John, 26.

— Richard the, earl of Pembroke, and Hubert de Burgh, 51 & n.; his war against Henry III and his death, 53–55, 57–58.

— William the, earl of Pembroke, rector

regni, 2–4, 6–17 *passim*, his death, 17; division of Irish lands of, after death of his last son (1245), 564.

Marshal, William the, junior, earl of Pembroke, 10, 15, 26, 40, 76; marries Eleanor, sister of Henry III, 41; in Ireland and Wales, 42–43, 394–6 *passim*; in command in Brittany (1230), 95; dies (1231), 96.

Martel, Philip, 278, 313, 652 n., 657–8.

Martin, Conor, on medieval commentaries on Aristotle's *Politics*, 522 n.

Martin IV, Pope (1281–5), 248; and Peter of Aragon, 251, 253–5 *passim*, 258 & n.; issues general absolution for sacrilege in baronial and Welsh wars, 434; on Edward I's seizure of proceeds of papal taxes (1283), 506.

Marwick, H., on Norwegian naval defence, 596 n.

Mary, d. of Edward I, a nun at Amesbury, 268 n.

— of Hungary, wife of Charles of Salerno, 283.

Mason or Mazon, John le, merchant of Bordeaux, his appeal to Edward I from the king of Scots, 610 n.

Matthew Paris, on the years 1201–50, 114; on St. Edmund of Abingdon, 57, 58 n.; his interest in the exchequer, 65; on kingship, 72; on the crises of 1238 and 1244, 76–79 *passim*; on Grosseteste's inquisitions into the morals of the laity, 455 & n.; on the Tartars, 110 n.; on Henry III and the Scots, 593 & n.; on the dispute between the earls of Leicester and Gloucester (1259), 147; on the success of Llywelyn ap Gruffydd, 401.

Mauclerc, *see* Dreux, Peter of.

— Walter, bishop of Carlisle, treasurer, 48, 51.

Mauléon (Poitou), 90.

— Savari de, 3 & n.; seneschal of Poitou, 90, 91.

Mauley, Peter de, 22 n., 23.

Maxton (Roxburghshire), 230.

Measures, of cloth, 347.

Meaux, Cistercian abbey, 634.

Meekings, C. A. F., on some letters from a judge to Ralph Nevill, 741–2; on Robert Carpenter, 370 n.; on the Pipe Roll order of 1270, 748.

Mellifont, Cistercian abbey in Ireland, and its daughter houses, 568.

Men-at-arms, mounted, 547, 548–9, 553, 554 *and passim*.

Menteith, earldom of, 581 n.

Mercadier, 544.

Mercenary troops in England, 12–13; in 1233, 54; in 1260, 156, 157, 158;

in 1261, 163, 166 & n.; in 1262, 171, 176, 181; in 1265, 199; in 1267, 214. *See* Artois; Boulogne; St. Pol; Money fiefs.

Merchant law, 620, 623, 625 & n., 627, 630–2; and the common law, 620, 625, 626; in London, 626 n., 627.

Merchants, home and foreign, Ch. XIII *passim*, and also 191, 207, 347, 348, 505 & n., 506, 519 & n., 648; English, at Antwerp, 663 & n.; German, and Scots, 687 & n.; Italian, 304–5, 662, 670, 672; Spanish and Portuguese, 644 & n.

Merchet, 682.

Mere castle (Wilts.), 716.

Merlin, prophecy of, 719.

Merton, priory, 50; legislation in council at (1236), 69–71, 367, 370; provincial council at (1258), 457.

— Walter de, king's clerk, chancellor, bishop of Rochester (1274–7), 157, 165, 176 n., 225, 486.

— College, Oxford, 486, 493 & n.

Messengers, the king's, 767.

Methven, Bruce routed at (1306), 715, 716.

Michael Palaeologus, emperor, 231, 232, 253.

Middle, truce of (1234), 60, 397.

Middleton, William, bishop of Norwich (1278–88), 481–2, 487, 491.

Milford Haven, 54.

Mills, Mabel, on exchequer procedure and reform, 724, 744; on royal finances (1258–72), 745; on an exchequer estimate of revenue, 748; on the shire-house, 750.

Milton (Kent), manor of, 10.

Mint and exchange, 65. *See* Exchanges.

Mirror of Justices, the, 521 n.

Moissac, wine merchants of, 306.

Mold, 399.

Molis, Roger de, 442.

Mols, R., on R. de Roover's *Money, Banking and Credit in Medieval Bruges*, 638 n.

Monasteries, books and articles on the administration and economy of, 762; patrons of, 762; and legal studies, 485 n.; abuses of hospitality in, 375; in Wales, 389–90.

Money, exchange equivalents of, 282 n.; of Bordeaux, Morlaas, and Tours, 306.

— fiefs, 544–6.

Mongols, 110 & n. *See* Tartars.

Monmouth, 201.

— Geoffrey of, 515 & n.

— John of, 3, 4.

Monségur, bastide, 309, 310.

Monseigneur Mouche ('Muscitto'), agent of Philip IV, 668.

Montalt (Mowat), family of, and Cromarty, 575 n.

Montauban, wine merchants of, 306.

Montfort l'Amaury, home of house of Montfort, lords of; Amaury, constable of France, elder brother of Earl Simon, 75 n., 88, 105, 114; Simon II, grandfather of Earl Simon, 75 n.; Simon III, the crusader, father of Earl Simon, 75 n., 88, 115; Beatrice de (mother of Yolande duchess of Brittany, formerly queen of Scots), heiress of Montfort, and the claim of her grandson, John, to Brittany (1341), 598 n.

— Amauri de, clerk, son of Earl Simon, 206, 212 n., 330–1 & n., 408.

— Eleanor de, sister of King Henry III, widow of William the Marshal *junior*, marries Simon de Montfort, Earl of Leicester (1238), 76, 107; dispute about dowry of, 107, 125, 126 & n., 164, 169, 170, 194 n.; after the battle of Evesham, 204, 206.

— Eleanor de, d. of Earl Simon, wife of Llywelyn ap Gruffydd (Oct. 1278), 331, 408, 441.

— Guy de, son of Earl Simon, captured at Evesham, 202; his later career in Tuscany, 225–6; murders Henry of Almain at Viterbo (1271), 226.

— Henry de, eldest son of Earl Simon, knighted by the Lord Edward, 159; at Amiens, 182; begins war in the Marches, 185; in charge of Edward (1264–5), 98, 201; slain at Evesham, 202.

— Peter de, of Beaudesert, head of the English family of Montfort, 113 n., 150 n., 164; defends Abergavenny, 172, 174 n., 179, 402 & n.; at Amiens, 182; captured at Northampton, 186; released after the victory at Lewes, 190; on the council of nine, 192, 193, 194; slain at Evesham, 202; his son, Peter, 173; his son William, *see below*.

— Philip de, lord of Toron in Syria, 107.

— Simon de, earl of Leicester, his succession and marriage, 41, 75–76 & n.; his relations with King Henry, 103–4, 106–7; his crusade (1240–2) and settlement in England, 79, 107–8; intends to join Louis IX on crusade, 110; his command in Gascony (1248–52), 110–13; his character, 114–15; esteem for, in France, 114; during the scare in 1254, 117 & n.; on mission to Scot-land (1255), 590; and the treaty of Paris (1257–9), 124–6 *passim*, 135–6; and the 'common enterprise', 129 n., 130, 134, 140, 145 n., 147–8, 151; his compact with Edward (Oct. 1259), 154 and n.; his independent role and influence on Edward in 1260, 154–61 *passim*; episcopal inquiry into charges against, 161; discussion renewed about his wife's dowry, 164, 170; disillusioned, 166, 171; heads a new opposition and takes control (1263), 174–7; his dilemma, 179–81 *passim*; kept at Kenilworth by an injury, 182, 184, 185, 187 n., his military operations (1264), 187–90; his rule in 1264–5, 191–201; his isolation and treaty with Llywelyn, last campaign and death at Evesham, 201–3, 403; felon and saint, 203, 206, 733; and the office of steward, 192 n., 200; his accomplices (*fautores*), 16, 104; his episcopal exemplars, 57; his views on the English, 72; in the *De bellis*, 735.

Montfort, Simon de, son of Earl Simon, 159, 185, 186, 190; his movements in 1265, 201–2; at Kenilworth and in Axholme, 204, 206; escapes abroad, 206, 208, 213; King Louis IX and, 212 n.; in service of Charles of Anjou, 225–6.

— William de, son of Peter, dean of St. Paul's; his sudden death (1294), 612 n.

Montgomery, new castle and honour of, 20, 43, 44, 394–5, 401, 442; ford of, 382; truce at (1259), 402; submission of Marcher lords at (1264), 196; treaty of (1267), 215, 383, 404–5, 412; pleadings in Arwystli case at, 418.

Montpellier, 99.

Montreuil-sur-mer, 178; treaty of, between Edward I and Flanders (1274), 622–4; treaty of (1299), 652–3; court of claims in (1305–6), 657–8.

Montrose, John Baliol's abdication completed at, 614, 615.

Moore, Margaret M., on lands of Scottish kings in England, 587 n.

Moorman, J. R. H., on Edward I at Lanercost (1306–7), 717 n.

Moray, district and shire of, 574–5, 576; rising in (1297), 580, 684; in 1304, 709; bishop of, his crusade on behalf of Robert Bruce (1306), 714 & n.; family of, 580, 687 n.

— Andrew of, 687 n.; his son, Andrew (d. 1297 or 1298), leader in the risings of 1297, 580, 684–7 *passim*, 687 n.;

his grandson, Andrew, heir of Bothwell, career of, 687 n., 694.

Moray, William of, Lord of Bothwell, 687 n.

Morgan, rebel in Glamorgan (1294), 440 & n.

Morgan, M. M., on the Scottish Church in twelfth century, 585 n.; on the excommunication of Grosseteste (1243), 466 n.; on early Canterbury jurisdiction, 490 n.; on English lands of Bec abbey, 762.

Morlaas (Béarn), 108; money of, 108.

Mormaers, 577, 601–2.

Morocco, crusade to, 118.

Morris, W. A., on the community of the realm, 142 n.

Mortimer, Edmund (d. 1304), son of Roger, 427 n., 428, 517 n.

— Roger (d. 1282), lord of Wigmore, Weobley and Radnor &c., grandson of Llywelyn the great, 403 n., 404; a regent during Henry III's absence (1259–60), 150 n.; and the castle of Builth (1260), 155, 404 n.; his resistance to and relations with Llywelyn ap Gruffydd, 402, 403 n., 404, 406; his support of Edward during 1264–5, 185, 190, 191, 196–7, 199, 200–1, 202; his hostility to Gilbert of Clare (1266–7), 213; one of guardians of Edward's lands during his absence (1270–4), 225; during Welsh wars, 409, 411, 422; additional lordships granted to, 414, 424; his pact with Llywelyn (1281), 427 n.; death, 427 & n.; roll of, 559 n.; his son, Roger, 428.

— Roger, son of Edmund, later earl of March, 517 n.

Mortmain, statute of (*de religiosis*), 325. *See* Statutes.

Morville, family of, in Scotland, 581 n.

Mountsorel, castle, 9, 11.

Movables, taxation of, 28–32 *passim*, 222–4, 323–5. *See* Taxation, s.v. Lay subsidies.

Mowbray, John, 712.

Muntchenesy, Joan de, daughter of William the Marshal and mother of Joan, wife of William of Valence, 139 & n.

— Warin de, 139 & n.

Murray, K. M. E., on Faversham and the Cinque Ports, 772.

Muscitto, agent of Philip IV, 668.

Myres, J. N. L., on Hamstead Marshall, 770.

Nantes, 90, 95.

Naples, naval battle off (1284), 253.

Nativi, various meanings of word in Scottish usage, 576.

Naval warfare, 644–5, 655–7. *See* Navy.

Navarre, kingdom of, 111, 116, 118, 237, 242 & n., 257; kings of, *see* Sancho VII, Theobald, Henry, Blanche of Artois, Jeanne, Philip IV, King of France.

— Berengaria of, 109 n.

— Blanche of, wife of Theobald IV of Champagne, 109 n.

Navy, English, and development of, 655–6 & nn., 659, 662, 665 & n., 692–3, 694; French, 645, 646 & n., 655 & n., 669.

Neath, Cross of, captured in Wales, 369.

Necessity, the doctrine of moral and political, 522–3 & n., 528, 679, 704.

Nefyn, 'spectacle' and 'round table' at, 429, 515; princely residence at, 392 n.

Neilson, G., on the 104 auditors in the Scottish case, 606 n.; on the Solway, 693.

Nesle, lord of, 194 n.

Neston, in Dee estuary, 422.

Nevill, Ralph, chancellor, bishop of Chichester (1224–44), 16–17, 47, 50 n., 60, 66, 75; granted office for life, 48; elected archbishop, but rejected by the pope, 56; compared with Burnell, 335 n.

— Ralph, of Raby, 708 n.

— Robert, in Scottish war (1303), 708 n.

Nevyn, *see* Nefyn.

New Model army, on the House of Lords, 521.

Newark castle, 11, 21.

Newborough (Newport), in Anglesey, 433.

Newcastle-under-Lyme castle, 198.

Newcastle-upon-Tyne, Anglo-Scottish treaty of, 1244, 587–8 & n.; John Baliol does homage for Scotland at, 608; a base of war finance (1296), 619; feudal host summoned to gather at (1297–8), 687, 688 n.; Edward I at (1298), 699; Bishop Lamberton examined at (1306), 716.

Newport (Monmouth), 202.

Nicaea, Greek empire of, 233.

Nicholas III, Pope (1277–81), and Peter of Aragon, 253; his relations with Kilwardby and Pecham, 469–71, 474 & n.

— IV, Pope (1288–92), denounces treaty of Oloron, 260; refuses to honour Charles of Salerno's engagements, 261; grants dispensation for marriage of Edward of Caernarvon to Margaret of Scotland, 265, 268 n., 599 & n.; on the king's clerks and the Church in England, 261, 265–6, 340 n., 460 n.; plans a crusade, 265–7, 513; the assessment of English clergy for the tax imposed by him (1291), 498 n., 509.

Nicholson, R., on the Franco-Scottish and Franco-Norwegian treaties of 1295, 613 n.

Niger, Ralph, critic of the third Crusade, 80 n.

— Roger, bishop of London, 50, 55, 60.

Noaillan, Gilles de, 285 n.

Noppen, J. G., on Edward, son of Odo the goldsmith, &c., 771.

Norbury, William of, justice, 624.

Norfolk, Adam of, king's clerk, 309 n.

Norfolk, archdeacon of, 186.

Norham, treaty of (1212), 586, 594–5; Anglo-Scottish discussions and agreements at (1291), 603–4; John Baliol swears fealty to Edward I at, 608.

Normandy, duchy of, homage of dukes of, on the border, 382 & n.; demand for restoration of, to Henry III, 14, 15, 84, 87, 93–5; Henry III surrenders his claim to (1259), 126, 127; fleet and sailors of, and the war with the Cinque Ports, 644–5; the Channel Islands and, 319, 320; 'lands of the Normans' in England, 15.

Northampton, 11; captured by the Lord Edward (1264), 186–7, 190; court and baronial government at (1265), 200; crusade preached at (1268), 219; congregation of bishops at (1277), 471; assemblies of laymen and clergy at (1283), 506, 507; treaty of (August 1290), 513, 600, 605, 608.

Northumberland, local levies in (1297), 684; overrun by Scots (1297), 686; levies in (1302), 708.

Norway, kings of, and their hold on Scotland before 1266, 572, 574, 579, 596–7. *See* Hakon; Magnus IV; Eric.

Norwich, castle, 9; disturbances in diocese of (1285–6), 481–2; cathedral archives of, 267 n.; assessment of ecclesiastical revenues made under direction of Bishop Suffield, papal collector, known as 'valuation' of, 498 n., 505; bishops of, *see* Pandulf; Ralegh; Middleton.

Notaries, 490 & n.

Nottingham castle, 11, 198.

Nottinghamshire, footsoldiers from, on Scottish campaign (1300), 693.

Novel disseisin, writ and assizes of, 361 & n.

Nuremberg, alliance between Edward I and Adolf of Nassau made at (1294), 660.

Oaths sworn to maintain the Provisions of Oxford by king, barons, and freemen, 135 & n., 140, 146 & n., 152; the crucial clause, 161–2; papal dispensation from, 163, 165, 168 & n. Oaths to settlement of May 1265, 198. Oath sworn by Edward I to observe the concessions of 1297, 697, 703; papal absolution from (Dec. 1305), 703. Oaths of fealty sworn by the Scots to Edward I in 1291, 606, and 1296, 615–16. Oaths sworn to Edward's son and heir (1297), 680.

O'Briens of Thomond, 561.

Ockham, William of, 523 n.

O'Conors in Connaught, 561; Cathel (d. 1224), 568.

Odiham, castle, 22 & n., 25, 48.

Odofredo (d. 1265) on utility, necessity, and taxation, 322.

O'Donnells of Tirconnell, 561.

Offaly, the lord of, 679.

Official of archbishop and the Court of Canterbury, 491–2 & n.

Offer, C. J., on the bishop's register, 759.

Offler, H. S., on Lewis of Bavaria and Edward III, 661 n.

Okehampton, honour of, military service of, 557.

Oléron, Isle of, 88, 90, 92 n., 95, 97, 103, 127; granted to the Lord Edward, 118; Edward's attempt to grant it away (1258), 275; law of, 620 & nn., 645–6.

Oloron, in Béarn, treaty of (1287), 259, 260; Edward I at (1288–9), 283–4.

Ombrière, near Bordeaux, provost of, 304.

O'Neills of Tir Owen, 561, 565; Brian, 561.

Orewin bridge, fight at, 428.

Orford, castle, 9.

Organism, theory of the body politic as an, 522, 527, 528 n.

Orkneys and Shetlands, the, 596, 597 n.

Orléans, treaty of (1275), 239.

Ormesby, William, 688 n.

Orpen, G. H., on the Fitzmaurice barons in Kerry, 564 n.

Orthez, in Béarn, 285.

Orvieto, Pope Gregory X and Edward I at, 225, 226.

Ostmen, the, decay of, in Ireland, 565.

Oswestry, pleadings at, 417, 418.

Otto, cardinal deacon of St. Nicola,

papal legate in England, Scotland, and Ireland, 74, 76, 398, 583, 586; council and constitutions of (1237), 451, 453, 473; and clerical taxation, 502.

Otto IV, count of the Free County of Burgundy, fief of the Empire, 248, 667 n.

Ottobuono Fieschi, cardinal legate, later Pope Adrian VI (1276), 180; commission to, 199, 207; in England (1265–8), 206, 207–8, 209; his success as peacemaker, 213–15, 218; and the treaty of Montgomery, 215, 383; and the statute of Marlborough, 216; preaches a crusade and holds a legatine council, 219; his constitutions, 451, 472–4 *passim*; importance of his legation, 219, 220.

Otway-Ruthven, Jocelyn, on native Irish and English law, 561 n., 562 n.; on shire-government in Ireland, 564 n.

Outlawry, law of, 60.

Owain ap Gruffydd, elder brother of prince Llywelyn, 400, 413.

— Gwynedd, prince of North Wales (d. 1170), 391, 392 n.

Owen, L. V. G., on Lincolnshire and the wool trade, 773.

Oxford, provincial council at Osney, near (1222), 24, 421, 451; ecclesiastical council at (1258), 457; parliament in (June 1258), 123, 135 & n., 136–8, 140–5; royal headquarters in 1264, 185–6; Marcher lords summoned to by baronial government (1264), 196.

— Provisions of, 136–7; and subsequent provisions, 147–8 & n., 149–51; Henry III's protests against, 163, 168; papal action against, 168; action against opponents of (1263), 174, 177; joint reference to Louis IX as an arbitrator on, 179–84 *passim*; compared with Aragonese limitations on the Crown, 255. *See* Oaths.

— University of, 56, 57, 70; dispersion from (1264), 186; chancellor of, summoned to parliament of Lincoln, 701; inception of Thomas de Cantilupe at (1273), 489–90; as a training ground of ecclesiastics, 486–8 *passim*; Durham monks as students of law at, 485 n.; bibliography, 763–4.

Padua, Amauri de Montfort a student of, 212 n.

Painscastle, 45, 397.

Paisley, Cluniac priory of, 580.

Palermo, 121.

Pampeluna, 238.

Pandulf, bishop-elect of Norwich and papal legate, 16–18 & n.; and the claim to Normandy (1223), 86; and Wales, 393 n.; and Alexander II, king of Scots, 594.

Pantin, W. A., on monastic letter books, 741.

Papacy, *see* Crusade; Scotland; Sicily; Taxation; Wales, &c.

Pardon, the royal, 330 & n. 372 n.

paréages, in Gascony, 308.

Paris, Henry III in (1254), 119; negotiations in (1257–9) and treaty of (1259), 84, 122, 123–8, 124 n., 135; later discussions, execution of and changes in the treaty of, 170, 186 & n., 273, 289–91; Henry III in (1262), 170–1; Edward I in (1273), 226; truce between Philip III and Alfonso X of Castile made at (1280), 243; Edward I's second visit to and treaty of, 1286, 255–6, 290–1; negotiations of Edmund of Lancaster at (1293–4), 646 & n., 647; Scottish embassy in. 1302–4, 697 & n., 710 & n.; peace of (1303), 653–4, 708.

— the Louvre, 255; Saint-Germain-des-Prés, abbey, 255; Sainte-Chapelle, 119; Temple, 82, 126, 281.

— *parlement* of, *see* Parlement of Paris.

— Matthew, *see* Matthew Paris.

Parishes, number of English, 445; and boundary disputes, 464 n.

Parks, private, malefactors in, 69, 367.

Parlement of Paris, Edward I's relations to, 245 & n.; its *arresta* on the rights of the French Crown to the lands of Alphonse of Poitiers and his wife, Jeanne of Toulouse, 272–3; and the affairs of Aquitaine, 273, 276, 285–6, 291, 298, 305 & n., 306, 310–15, 646–8, 658.

Parliament, in Henry III's reign, 341–2; in Edward I's reign, 342–50, 356, 526–40; in the Provisions of Oxford, 155, 159 n.; Edward I's conceptions of, 343, 348–9; 'general', 343 & n.; kinds of business done in, 347–8; petitions in, 348–9; records of, 346 ff.; judicial proceedings in, on Llywelyn's claims (1280), 417–18, on right to Scottish throne (1292), 606 & n., and on petitions from Scottish court, 610 & n. *See* Council; Ireland; Prerogative; Scotland; Statutes; Taxation, &c.

— in 1258–9, *see* Oxford, Temple, Westminster; in 1260, 156–7; in London (Oct. 1263), 177, 179, 180; in June, 1264, 191–2: in 1265, 197–9; in 1269–70, 222; in 1275 342–3,

531–2; in Shrewsbury (1283), 537 & n.; in 1285, 369; in 1290, 342 n., 379 n., 513; in 1294–6, 615, 636, 673–4 & nn.; in 1297, 681, 683; in 1298, 688 & n.; in 1299–1301, 699–705; in 1305, 308, 332–4, 345–6, 349 n., 350, 712; in 1306, 715; in 1307, 712 n., 718.

Parson, 458. *See* Rectors.

Parthenay, lord of, 90, 91.

Partibility, rules of, 197 n.; a kingdom not partible, 607–8.

Passelewe, Robert, 51, 52 n., 58.

Patronage of monastic houses, 762.

Patteshall, Hugh, treasurer, bishop of Coventry (1240–1), 60.

— Martin, judge, 17, 68.

Peace, wardens of, in the shires, 176, 182, 354 & n.

— proclamation of, 190, 204–5, 214, 708.

Peak, the, castle of, 118, 198; forest of, 513.

Pecham, John, Franciscan, archbishop of Canterbury (1279–92), career and papal appointment of, 469–70; his provincial councils and constitutions, 451, 472–5, 479–80; gives shape to convocation, 505–8, 671, 672; summons council to express views on the crusade (1291–2), 267; and Thomas de Cantilupe, 489–90 & nn.; the criticism and grievances of his suffragans about his exercise of his authority, 490–3; his relations with, the king, 476, 478–80; and the Welsh, 383, 384 n., 391, 415, 418, 421 & n., 424–6, 427 n.; and the Church in Wales, 430, 433–5; at Westminster in 1285, 369; and the case of Amauri de Montfort, 331 & n.; his last years and death (1292), 484–5.

Peebles, 694, 696 & n., 707.

Peers, Peter des Roches on, 55; of France, 243 & n.

Pegolotti, Francesco, of the Bardi company, and his book on mercantile practice, 637–8 & n.

Pegues, F., on *clerici*, 445 n.; on royal support of students, 763.

Pennaforte, St. Raymond de, 764.

Pen-y-Castell, 395.

Pencestre, Stephen de, warden of Cinque Ports, 646 n.

Perambulation of the forests, 1297–1305, 699 & n., 700–3 *passim*, 715. *See* Forests.

Perche, count of, 11, 12.

Percy, Henry, 138 n., 684–6 *passim*, 715.

— Richard, 66.

Perfeddwlad, 400 & n. *See* Four Cantrefs.

Périgord, 291–2; French and Aquitanian administration in, 300, 301, 303.

Périgueux, 645; city and diocese of, 291, 292 n., 309; diocese of, in treaty of Paris (1259), 126, 128, 280–1, 289; process of (1310–11), 291, 292 n., 654.

Perpignan, death of Philip III at (1285), 255; Charles of Salerno at, 262.

Persia, khan of, *see* Arghun.

Perth, assemblies at, 600, 712; Edward I at (June 1303), 708; castle, 693 n.

pes finis, 39 n.

Peter, king of Aragon (1276–85), 239, 242; and Navarre, 241 n.; and the Castilian dispute, 244; as the successor to the Hohenstaufen, 245, 252–3; accepts crown of Sicily and goes to war with Charles of Anjou and Philip III of France, 252–5; at Bordeaux for a duel with Charles (1283), 254; his difficulties, success, and death, 254–5.

— count of Savoy (1263–8), uncle of Eleanor of Provence, queen of England, 74, 174 n., 177, 179, 294 & n., 250 & n.; and the honour of Richmond, 97, 159 n.; and the negotiations for peace with France (1257–9), 123–5 *passim*; as a baronial leader in England, 130, 134–5, 140; his relations with Simon de Montfort, 113 n., 156 & nn., 171; and the council of Lambeth (1261), 457; his castle and town at Yverdon, 431.

— the chamberlain of France, 164, 194 n.

Peterborough, abbot of, *see* Caux, John of.

Petitions, 348–55 *passim*, 658 n.; procedure of, in parliament, 348–9, and in papal and other courts, 351 & n. *See* Plaint; Gascony; Ireland; Scotland.

Pevensey, 190.

Pfander, H. G., on reference books for preachers, 765.

Philip Augustus, king of France (1180–1223), 8, 10, 12; and the duchy of Gascony, 84; and the succession to Brittany, 92 & n.; death, 87.

Philip III, king of France (1270–85), 226 & n.; Edward I's homage to (1273), 226, 234; his relations with Edward, 236, 285–6; makes treaty of Amiens (1279), 289; and Eleanor of Castile's succession to Ponthieu, 235, 244 n.; his quarrel with Alfonso X of Castile, 242–4; arbitrates about his mother's claims in Provence, 249;

as executor of crusade against Peter of Aragon, 251, 253–5; his death, 255; increase of royal domain in his reign, 237–41 *passim*, 272–3.

Philip IV, the Fair, king of France (1285–1315), his relations with Edward I, 236–7, 271, 290–1; his succession to Champagne and Navarre, 240–1; and Amadeus V of Savoy, 251 & n.; and negotiations with Aragon for the release of Charles of Salerno, 256, 260; his meeting with Sancho of Castile at Bayonne, 262; his dispute with Edward I about Gascon and English sailors (1293), the development of the breach with him, and his occupation of Gascony, 644–54; his alliance with the Scots and Eric of Norway (1295), 612–13 & n.; his naval plans, 646 & n.; his relations with Guy of Flanders, 652 n.; 653, 659, 668–9, 697; and with Adolf of Nassau, 660, 661, 668; truces and peace with Edward I, 649, 650 & n., 653–4; and the Scottish wars, 653, 669, 693–7 *passim*, 710 & nn.; and Boniface VIII, 523, 650–3, 661–2, 668, 675 n., 676, 710 & nn.; his propaganda, 527.

— count of Savoy (d. 1285), 248, 249, 250–1.

Pickering castle, 165.

Piepowder, court of, 625.

Pilche, Alexander, 580.

Pilgrimages, royal, to shrines and relics, 49, 57, 59, 369 n., 512. *See* Pontigny.

Pipton, treaty of, 201, 403.

Plaint (*querela*), 143, 350–5 *passim*; in 1258–60, 142, 144–8.

plena potestas of proctors and representatives, 536 & n., 538–9 & n.

Pleshey, castle, 9.

Pluralism and pluralities, 458–9 & n., 474–5, 487–8; Hengham's, 356 n.

Plymouth, expedition to Gascony from, 649, 659, 662.

Plympton, 26.

Podio, Orlandino de, 632, 633.

Poitevins, outcry against (1232–4), 52.

Poitiers, 96, 100; Alphonse of, brother of Louis IX, count of Poitou, *see* Alphonse.

Poitou, county of, claims to, 84; occupied by Louis VIII and retained by Blanche of Castile for Louis IX, 88–93; Henry III's march through, 95; Henry's last bid for, 97, 100–4; Alphonse of Poitiers installed as count, 100; claim to, surrendered by Henry III (1259), 126. *See* Alphonse of Poitiers.

Pole, William de la, 634.

Pontefract, Cluniac priory at, 'on the road from England to Scotland', 585 n.

— Gregory of, official of Lynn, 481, 482 n.

Ponteland, church, 493 & n.

Ponthieu, county of, 73 n., 235, 244 & n.; seneschal of, 280. *See* Dammartin (Simon de); Eleanor of Castile; Joan.

Pontigny, shrine of St. Edmund of Abingdon at, 57; Henry III at, 119; Edward I at, 256 n.; abbot of, 12.

Pontissara, John de, bishop of Winchester (1282–1304), 362 & n., 471 n., 485, 651, 653; exempted (1297) by Boniface VIII from the jurisdiction of Canterbury, 717.

Pool castle, 421, 438. *See* Welshpool.

Poole, A. L., on criminous clerks, 462 n.

Poore, Richard le, bishop successively of Chichester, Salisbury, and Durham, 3, 495; constitutions of, 452.

Popes: *see* Innocent III; Honorius III; Gregory IX; Innocent IV; Alexander IV; Urban IV; Clement IV; Gregory X; John XXI; Nicholas III; Martin IV; Honorius IV; Nicholas IV; Celestine V; Boniface VIII; Clement V; their registers, 740.

Porcher, John, master of the king's money (1300), 633.

Porchester castle, 716.

Portfangos, Catalonia, 253.

Portland, case of manor of, 327 & n.

Ports, Cinque, *see* Cinque Ports.

Portsmouth, 45, 117, 649; ship of, 656.

Portugal, merchants of, 644 n.

Post, Gaines, on law and the state, 523 n.; on Roman law and representation, and on *plena potestas*, 539 n.

Powicke, F. M., on the freeholder, 379 n., 775; on Matthew Paris, 731; on Henry III's minority, 744; on Edward I, 230 n.; on the baronial council (1258–60), 745; on recluses, 765–6.

Powicke, M. R., on distraint of knighthood, 547 n.; on cavalry service, 553 n.

Powys, 393 & nn., 398, 402, 403 n., 409–10, 417, 423–4, 442.

— lords of, *see* Gruffydd ap Gwenwynwyn; Gruffydd ap Madog; Gruffydd Fychan.

Pozzi of Lucca, 305.

Preaching, guides to, and literature about, 765.

Prerogative, the royal, 324–33 *passim*.

Prise, royal exercise of, in war of 1294–7, 659, 662, 666; of wool, 680–1; and the confirmation of the Charters (1297), 683; inquiry into grievances of collection of (1298), 699 & n.; and the *articuli super cartas* (1300), 700, 704; of wine, and its commutation (1302–3), 629 n., 631 n.; a corrupt supervisor of, in Kent, 698 n.

Prisoners of war, in 1264–5, 190, 191.

privilegium fori, 462–3.

Process of Montreuil-sur-mer, 657, 658 & n.

Processes, keeper of, 278.

Proclamations, royal (1258–65), 145–6, 158, 163, 165–6, 181 n., 182, 201; to persons charged with felony, 648 & n.; concerning debased currency (1291), 670; in Scotland, 604. *See* Excommunication; Peace.

Procurations, of papal legates (1295), 673.

Prohibition, writs of, 454, 467–8, 474–8, 479 n., 482 n.

Propaganda, 8, 174, 200, 526–8 & nn.; in the boroughs, 527 n., 534; in Ireland, 534–5. *See* Proclamations.

Provence, the house of, 73; its problems (1239–43), 98–100, 103; effects of succession of Charles of Anjou to, 246, 250, 252; fleet of (1285), 255; in treaty of Oloron, 259; marquisate of, *see* Venaissin; Alfonso II, count of, 112 n. *See* Beatrice; Eleanor; Margaret; Raymond-Berengar; Sanchia.

Provins, 240.

Provisions, papal, movement in England against (1231), 45–46.

Pryde, G. S., on Scottish burghs, 575 n.

Pugeys, Imbert, 143.

Putnam, B. H., on evolution of justices of the peace, 218 n.

Quarr abbey, Isle of Wight, abbot of, and Adam de Stratton, 365.

Quercy, French and English rights in, 127, 272, 273, 289, 291; ducal administration in, 302, 309. *See* Cahors.

querela, see Plaint.

Quincy, Roger de, earl of Winchester, Scottish lands of, 580.

—Saer de, earl of Winchester, 8, 11, 51 n., 75 n.

Quo warranto, writs and pleas of, 39, 376–9, 521.

Rabastans, wine merchants of, 306.

Rabban Cauma, emissary of khan of Persia, 252.

Radnor, lordship and castle of, 185, 397, 404.

'Ragman' rolls, 358 & n.; the Ragman Roll, or copy of the separate instruments of fealty and homage to Edward I by the Scots (1296), 616 & n.

Ralegh, William, judge, later bishop of Norwich (1239) and Winchester (1244–50), 68, 70, 71, 75; and monastic patronage, 762.

Ranulf the Breton, treasurer of the chamber, 48.

Ravenser, 634.

Raymond VII, count of Toulouse, 87–88 & n.; his treaty with the king of France (1227), 92; his wavering ambitions (1239–43), 99–103; makes peace at Lorris, 103; dies (1246) 103; inheritance to lands and rights of, 127; his daughter Jeanne, *see* Toulouse, Jeanne of.

Raymond-Berengar, count of Provence, 98–100, 103, 112 n.

Ré, island of, 103.

Re, Emilio, on the Riccardi, 637 n.

Reading, provincial council at (1279), 472–5.

receptoria of the Agenais, 302.

Recluses, 765–6.

Recognitiones feodorum in Aquitaine, 295–6 & n.

Record, courts of, 334; the king as a, 330.

Records, English, 277; register of foreign, Gascon and other affairs, 277 n.

Rectors, 458–9 & n.; and the legate Otto, 448 & n., 502.

Red Book of the Exchequer, 65.

Redmere, John de, of Appleby (Lincs.), his suit with James le Roy of Dixmude, 623–5.

Redstone, V. B. and *L. J.*, on the Heyron family in London, 772.

Rees, W., on the Welsh marches, 755; on Caerphilly castle, 770.

Regiam majestatem, Scottish law book, 577.

Registers, archiepiscopal, 469, 471 n.; Pontissara's, 471 n., 474 n.

Regna, the age of the, 233; and sovereignty, 381–2.

Reid, Rachel R., on the barony, 769; on the organization of the Scottish March, 588 n.

Reid, W. Stanford, on trade and Scottish independence, 687 n.; on the war of Scottish independence and the papacy, 753.

Renouard, Yves, on the Angevin empire, 744.

Replevin, 368, 377.

Representation and taxation, 30 n.; of cities and boroughs to discuss tallage in council (1268), 222 & n.; and consent, 117 & n., 222–3, 501–8 passim, 526–40 passim, 675–8.

Reprisal, custom of, 620–1 & n., 626, 644 & n.

Reversi, the, and their lands (1217), 15–16.

Rhodes, W. E., on Edmund of Lancaster, 239 n., 646 n.; on Italian bankers in England, 637 n.

Rhos, one of the Four Cantrefs, 400 n., 414; part of new honour of Denbigh, 421 n., 424.

Rhuddlan, new castle of, 403 n., 412, 413, 423, 430, 431; as army head-quarters, 422–6 passim, 428, 429, 441; borough of, 432 n.; statute of (1284), 65, 359; see Statutes; statute of Wales issued at, 429.

Rhuvoniog, one of the Four Cantrefs, 400 n., 414; part of the new honour of Denbigh, 421 n., 424.

Rhys, the Lord, prince of Deheubarth (d. 1197), 385, 386, 390 n., 391, 392, 393; his descendants, 393, 398, 402, 410–11, 419, 421, 438.
— ap Maredudd, of Dryslwyn, 410 & n., 491, 421; as a baron of Wales, 438; his rebellion and end, 438–40.
— Fychan (d. 1271), 411.
— Wyndod, descendant of the Lord Rhys, 410, 438.

Riccardi, the, of Lucca, 266, 632, 634, 641 & n., 642.

Richard I, king of England, accession of, as limit of legal memory, 379; and the feudal quota, 550; and Quercy, 127; ransom of, 31; validity of his surrender of his lordship over Scotland discussed (1291), 601–2 & n.
— bishop of Bangor, 390–1.
— natural son of King John, 13.
— earl of Cornwall, later king of the Romans, brother of Henry III, 40; his expedition to Poitou and Gascony (1225–7), 40, 91–92; his quarrel with Henry (1227), 40–41; in Brittany (1230), 95; marries Isabella, d. of the Marshal and widow of Gilbert of Clare (1231), 41; his lordships in England, 40, & n., and the fall of Hubert de Burgh, 44, 51; his objection to Simon de Montfort's marriage to his sister and opposition, 76–77; his crusade, share in the Poitevin expedition of 1242, and marriage to Sanchia of Provence (1243), 104–6; and the new coinage (1247), 105; regent in England (1253–5), 116–17, 119; refuses the crown of Sicily, 121; elected king of the Romans (1257),

106, 119; his letter to Llywelyn ap Gruffydd, 401 n.; and the treaty of Paris, 124, 125; and the crisis in 1260, 158, 160 & n.; his four visits to Germany, 160 & n.; arbitrates on the appointment of sheriffs (1261–2), 166–7; his vacillations in 1262–3, 170, 174, 175, 181; and the war in the Marches, 185; captured at Lewes (1264), 189, 190; released on conditions by Simon de Montfort, the younger, after the battle of Evesham (1265), 204; his moderation, 206, 214; guardian of Edward's children during their father's absence (1270–2), 224; his death (April 1272), 231; his devotion to St. Edmund of Abingdon, 57; his sons, see Almain, Henry of; Cornwall, Edmund of.

Richardson, H. G., on the coronation oath, 7 n.; on the counts of La Marche, 89 n.; on the legislation of 1234–6, 68 n.; on collections of statutes, 370 n.; on law merchant in London, 626 n.; on Bracton, 727; on dictamen at Oxford, 742; on the origin of parliament, 747; on Year Books and Plea Rolls, 749; on the parish clergy, 760
— — and Sayles, G. O., on the early statutes, 370 n.; on the texts of the Provisions of Oxford, 147 n.; on the parliaments of Edward I, 344 n., 718 n.; on ministers in parliament, 537 n., on Edward's parliaments in Ireland, 560 n., 562 n., 563 n.; on Scottish parliaments, 578 n.; on ecclesiastical gravamina, 479 n.; on circumspecte agatis, 482 n.

Richmond, honour of, and Brittany, 15 n., 93, 96, 97, 159 n., 236 n.

Rigaud, Odo, archbishop of Rouen, 125 n.; in England (1260), 161, 735; suggested as arbitrator on English affairs (1264), 194 n.

Rivaux, Peter de, and his rise to power, 48–49, 51–52; dismissed, 58; nature of his administration, 60–65 passim.

Robert II, king of Scots, see Bruce.
— III, king of Scots, 685 n.

Robert, king of Naples, a hostage in childhood, 283.

Robertson, D. W., on preaching, 765.

Robinson, J. A., on convocation, 497 n.

Rochelle, La, 88, 90, 96, 102, 103, 644, 645.

Roches, Peter des, bishop of Winchester, crowns Henry III (1216), 1, 2; his charge of the king, 2; at Lincoln, 11–12; his political position, 17, 24, 26; his return to England from the crusade, &c., 45, 47; mediates in France (1231), 96; his influence on Henry III (1231-4), 47-49, 51, 53-59 *passim*, 72; death of (1238), 74.

Rochester, 187, 191, 683; bishops of, *see* Sandford; Merton.

Roderick, A. J., on the feudal relations between the Crown and the Welsh princes, 755; on the Four Cantrefs, 410 n.

Rokesley, Gregory of, mayor of London, 626, 632; warden of the mint, 633; and the new town of Winchelsea, 635.

'Romans', 494; tract against, 733. *See also* 'Italians'.

Romeyn, John, archbishop of York (1286-96), 494, 672.

Roncière, Ch. de la, on the naval activity of Philip IV, 646 n.

Ros, Robert de, of Wark-on-Tweed, one of guardians of Alexander III and Margaret, 582 n., 589 & n., 590.

Rosas (Catalonia), Philip III's base in 1285, 255.

Rose Castle, 701.

Roslin, fight at (1303), 708 & n.

Rosponte, Wexford, 442.

Ross, earldom and earls of, 580 & n.

Rostand, Master, papal nuncio and collector, 122 n., 136, 503.

Rothbury, Gilbert of, judge, clerk of council and parliament, 334, 356 & n., 372.

Rothwell, H., on Edward I's case against Philip the Fair (1298), 313 n., 651 n., 654.; on the crisis of 1297, 674 n., 676 n., 680 n., 682 n.; on Edward I and the struggle for the Charters, 698 n., 700 n.; on the disgrace of Richard of Louth, 698 n.

Rouergue, 272.

Round, J. H., on his papers, &c., on the baronage, 768-9; on various Chancery Rolls, 721; on miscellaneous inquisitions, 728; on the scutage rolls, 748; on the 'shire house', 750; on the Hospitallers in Essex, 761; on local history, 774; on the origin of the Comyns, 581 n.

—— and *Maxwell-Lyte, H.*, on the barons' letter to the Pope (1301), 705 n.

Roussillon province, 255, 262.

Roxburgh castle, David I and, 574; Bishop Wishart of Glasgow imprisoned in, 685 & n.; in Scottish wars (1297-1303), 686, 688, 689, 695, 707, 708; Edward I's oath to the Charters renewed at (1298), 697, 699.

Roy, James le, of Dixmude, his suit against John de Redmere, 623-5, 626.

Ruddock, A. A., on Italian shipping at Southampton, 637 n.

Rudolf of Habsburg, elected king of the Romans, 232; his relations with Edward I and Charles of Anjou, 246-50; his form of peace with Charles of Anjou, 247 & n. *See* Arles; Margaret of France; Philip of Savoy.

Russell, Elias, citizen of London, 662.

Russell, J. C., on clerical population, 445 n.; on Bardney's life of Grosseteste, 738; on the canonization of opposition to the king, 776.

—— and *Hieronimus, J. P.*, on Henry of Avranches, court poet, 767.

Rutherglen, Scottish parliament at (1300), 694, 695 n.

Ruthin, barony of, 424; castle of, 431.

Rye, 10.

Sabine, E. L., on sanitation of medieval London, 772.

Sacrilege, acts of, in wartime, 434.

St. Albans abbey, in war of 1216-17, 9; military service from liberty of, 550; knights of shire summoned to (1261), 166.

St. Andrews, bishopric of, 572-3; parliament in (1304), 709 & n., 713 n.; bishops of, *see* Gamelin; Fraser; Lamberton.

St. Asaph, diocese of, liberties of, 434; proposed transfer of cathedral of, to Rhuddlan, 434-5; bishops of, 390-1; *see* Anian I and II.

St. Briavell, 409.

Saint-Denis, 159 n.; abbot of, 311, 314.

Saint-Ferme, abbot of, 309 n., 310.

St. George, Master James of, mason and master of works, 431-2, 444.

—— Master Stephen of, king's clerk, 263 n., 421 n., 431 n.

Saint-Georges-d'Espéranche, Edward I at (1273), 431.

St. Germain, Robert of, 12.

Saint Gildas, 94.

Saint James-de-Beuvron castle, 93, 96.

St. John, John of (d. 1302), 280, 283, 290, 362, 695; Edward I's lieutenant in Gascony (1293), 279 & n., 647; seneschal of Gascony, captured at Bellegarde, 666; Edward's lieutenant in Scotland, 706-7 & n.

Saint Malo, 94, 96.

Saint Maur-des-Fossés, 170.

St. Omer, Henry III at (1260), 155-7; merchants of, 14.

St. Peter Port, Guernsey, 218.

St. Pol, count of, 157, 214.

Saint Quentin, Master Bonet of, 290 & n., 298.

Saint Sever, 301, 666; court of, 109, 285, 301; *paréage* at, 308.

St. Victor, order of, 761; Andrew of, 761.

Saintes, 90, 92 n.; Henry III at (1242), 103, 104; castle of, 301.

Saintonge, southern, 88, 647; Henry III's failure in (1242), 101–2; French and English rights in, 127, 272, 273, 289, 291; administration of, 301, 303.

Salisbury, new cathedral and city of, 14, 635; agreement about Margaret of Scotland sealed at (Nov. 1289), 512, 598 & n., 599; parliament in (1297), 666, 678, 680 n.

— dean and chapter of, and clerical taxation, 502; bishops of, *see* Bingham; Bridport; Poore; earl of, *see* Longespée (William).

Salt, Mary, on embassies in France (1272–1307), 646 n., 651 n., 654 n., 700 n.

Salter, H. E., the acts of a general chapter, Arrouasian or Victorine, 761.

Salzman, L. F., on building, 771; on the legal status of markets, 772.

Sanchia of Provence, first betrothed to Raymond of Toulouse (1241), then m. Richard of Cornwall (1243), 100, 104, 105, 107, 119.

Sancho, king of Castile, 242, 244–5, 262, 644 n.

— VII, king of Navarre, 109 n.

Sancto Leofardo, Gilbert de, bishop of Chichester (1288–1305), 491 n.

Sanctuary, 50, 60.

Sandal, John de, warden of the exchanges (1300), 633; treasurer of Scotland (1305), 713.

Sanders, I. J., on treaty of Paris, 120 n.

Sandford, Henry, bishop of Rochester (1227–35), 60.

Sandwich, 156, 207, 669, 688; naval battle off, 13; hospital of St. Bartholomew at, 13.

— Henry of, bishop of London (1263–73), Montfortian, 176 & n., 189, 192, 194, 195, 208 n.

— Ralph of, constable of the Tower and warden of London, 627.

— Thomas of, seneschal of Ponthieu, 280.

Sandys, Agnes, on the New Temple at London, 761.

Sanford, Eva M., on Honorius Augustodunensis, 764.

San Germano, treaty of (1235), 48.

Sapori, A., on the Frescobaldi, 637 n.; on international commerce, 638 n., on Tuscan mercantile companies, 641 n.

Saragossa, coronation of Peter of Aragon at, 252.

Sauveterre-de-Guyenne, bastide, 309 & n., 310.

Sauveterre-en-Béarn, 242.

Savoy, castles in, 431; county of, and its neighbours, 249–51; customs of, 374; palace of, in the Strand, 249 & n., ruling house of, 74, 98; Edward I in, 226; counts of, *see* Amadeus; Boniface; Peter; Philip; Thomas; *see also* Beatrice; Boniface (archbishop); William.

Say and Sele, barony of, 545 n.

Sayles, G. O., on administrative changes in 1234, 61 n., 727; on the change in social attitudes, 1286–1304, 346 n., 516 n.; on writ to boroughs (1268), 222 n.; on the statute of Gloucester, 749; on ordinances for seizure of wool (1297), 663 n.; on the Scottish parliament at Rutherglen (1300), 695 n.; on alleged local branches of the chancery, 750.

Scaccario, Matthew de, 356 n.

Scarborough castle, 165, 198.

Scavage, 628, 631.

Schaube, A., on English wool exports (1273), 622 n.

Schiltrons, at Falkirk (1298), 690.

Schools, for clergy, in cathedral churches, 450; and universities, as training-ground of ecclesiastics, 485 n., 486–8 *passim*; literature on history of, 763–5.

Schulz, F., on Bracton, 752.

Scone, abbey, stone of, 615, 766 n.; recognition of Margaret as heir to Scottish throne at (1284), 597; Wallace and the justiciar of Scotland at (1297), 684; parliament in (1305), 711 & n.; Robert Bruce installed king at (1306), 713; abbot of, 716.

Scot, John the, *see* John.

Scotia and *mare Scotiae* (the Firth of Forth), 574.

Scotland:

Before Alexander III's death (1286): 571–85; geography, races, and population, 571–5, 579; currency of, 573 & n.; formation of the state, 574–8; administration, 575–9; barons, thanes, and free tenants, 576; justice, 577–8 & n., 584; taxation, 578 & n.; Church in, 583–5; the Border, 588–9; Henry III's request for an aid from (1253), 589; council and guardians of (1255–61), 590–2; parties in, 593–4; treaty with Llywelyn ap Gruffydd (1258), 138, 592 & n.; the papacy and the king and state of, 593–5; the problem of homage, 381, 594–6. *See* Alexander II; Alexander III; Castles; Henry III; Edward I.

From 1286 to 1296: 512, 597–617; disturbances in (1290), 600 n., 601; Edward I as supreme lord of, 560 & n., 597 n., 604–5; the great case of, and the documents in the case, 602–8 & nn.; reign of John Baliol in, 609–13; Edward I insists on his right to hear Scottish petitions, 608–12; surrender of kingdom of, and its union with England, 613–16; pacification of (1296), 615 n.; records and regalia of, 614; great seal of, broken (1296), 615 n.; loss of public records of, 750–1. *See* Council; Guardians; Edward I; Philip IV.

From 1297 to 1307: risings in, 1297, 669, 677, 678, 683–7; Andrew of Moray and William Wallace, *duces* of the Scottish army, 687; Edward I's first campaigns (1298–1300) and truce with Scots, 689–93; his campaign in 1301–2 and control of the Lowlands of, 693–4, 706; his subjection of, in the campaign of 1303–4, 708–11; defence and administration of, by the Scottish guardians (1298–1304), 694, 696, and by Edward I in the Lowlands (1298–1303), 695, 706–7; plan for government of (1305), 711–13; the emergence, defeat, and reappearance of Robert Bruce in (1306–7), 713–16, 718–19; claims for damages from, 658 n.; *communa* of (1305), 712; petitions to king in parliament from (1305), 699. *See* Boniface VIII; Edward I; Philip IV.

Scotus, Duns, 230.

Scutage, 33–36, 556–9.

Seagrave (Leics.), 50 n. *See* Segrave.

Seals: the great seal, of Henry III, 16, 24–25; his new seal (1259), 126 n., 157 n., 274; control of, in 1263, 181 n.; other royal seals. 157, 181 n., 681; the Lord Edward's seal, 274; Edward I's seals, 662, 681, 701; privy seal and writs of, 336–7, 662; dates of letters under great seal, authorized by privy seal, 337 n.; secret use of great seal, 337–8; of Scotland, 615 n.; on the use of seals to forged mercantile instruments, 624; seals of contracts, 297 n., 302, 320–1.

secretarii, king's, 334.

Segrave, John, son of Nicholas, lieutenant of Edward I in Scotland (1302), 707 & n.; 708 & n., justice and captain south of the Forth (1304–5), 332, 711.

— Nicholas, son of Nicholas, 332–3, 516, 707 n.

— Nicholas, son of Stephen, 331–2.

Segrave, Stephen, justiciar (1232), 50 & n., 51, 52, 57, 58, 60 & n., 62, 331.

'Segrave', name of a siege-engine, 332.

Segre, Robert de, king's clerk, agent in Holland and Brabant, 662.

Seignorial administration, bibliographical note on, 769; royal inquiries in (1259), 146–8; jurisdiction, 328, 368, 377–8; land management, 366–7; liberties and *quo warranto* proceedings, 376–9.

Seisin and conveyance of land, written evidence of, 38–39.

Selden, John, his abridgement of the Provisions of Oxford, &c., 147 n.

Selkirk, new castle of, 589 n., 707; forest of, 696, 707; Simon Fraser, warden of forest of, 696; Alexander Baliol, castellan of, and warden of forest of, 707; sheriffdom of, 575.

Sempringham, order of, liberties of, 328.

Senghenydd, district of, 406.

Serjeanties, and arrentation of, 546 & n.

Sermons, *see* Preaching.

servitium debitum, 549–51, 556–7.

Seton, Christina, sister of Robert Bruce, 716; her husband, Christopher Seton, 713, 716.

Sheep, as objects of distraint, 372 & n.

Sheriffs: and castles, 20 ff.; and inquiries into royal rights (1223), 28; and taxation, 29, 33, 524 n., 527; their relations with the exchequer, 62–65 *passim*; and bailiffs of hundreds, 366, 368; and the *jurati ad arma*, 551–2 & n.; and scutage, 33–34, 556–8; chosen from the vavassors (1258–61), 144, 146, 150, 162; Henry III appoints new sheriffs (1261), 164, 165; arbitration about appointment of, 166–7; decrease of payments into exchequer of (1264–8), 220; and shires in Ireland, 563–4; in Scotland, 574–9; in Wales, 435–7.

Shepway, Shipway, *see* Cinque Ports.

Sherwood forest, 513; bands of the disinherited in, 215.

Ships and shipping, 13; capacity of, 94; building of, 656 & n.; Norwegian organization of, 596 n., 613; Edward I's organization of, in wartime, 442, 613. *See* Cinque Ports.

Shires, levies in, 551–4; wardens of (1261), 166, 167; records of, 750. *See* Sheriffs.

Shrewsbury, 20, 407; constabulary of burgesses in (1265), 200; negotiations at (1267), 215; parliament in (1283), 344, 429.

Shrines, royal visits to, *see* Pilgrimages.

Siberston, Siberton (Kent), 143.

Sicilian vespers, 253.

Sicily, kingdom of, succession to, 106, 120 ff., 131, 134–6, 167–8, 497, 499, 503; Aragonese intervention and its consequences, 252–64 passim, 661–2.

Siege-engines, 439, 440, 614, 710.

Silver, speculation in, 632 n., 633.

Simpson, W. D., on Dirleton castle, 573 n.

sirventés, 95.

Siward, Elizabeth, sister of Robert Bruce, 716.

— Richard, leader in war of 1233–4, 54, 60.

— or Syward, Richard, in Edward I's service, 695 n.

Skenfrith castle, 43.

Skipton castle, 21, 364, 707 n.

Sleaford castle, 11, 21.

Sluys, 668.

Smith, R. A. L., writings of, 762.

Smithfield, Elms at, 712.

Snellgrove, H. S., on the Lusignans, 140 n.

Snowdonia, as defined in 1277, 413 n., 417.

Sodor and Man, bishopric, 396–7 n.

Solway, 693 & n.

Soules, John de, a guardian of Scotland, 696 n., 697 n., 711, 713.

Southampton, and service to the Crown, 530.

Southwark, 182, 213, 214.

Sovereignty, in Scotland and Wales, 381–2; of the sea, 655 & n.

Spain, merchants of, 644 n. See Aragon; Castile; Navarre.

Spiritualities, 498, 509.

spoliatores, 177.

Sproemberg, H., on political conceptions in Flanders (1127), 132 n.

Squibes, Richard, case of, 330.

Stainmore, Rere Cross of, 574 & n.

Stamford, 40, 118.

Standard, the royal, 186.

Stapledon, Walter, treasurer (1320), bishop of Exeter, and the classification of archives, 278 n., 751.

'State of the king and the realm', 6, 67, 514.

State trials of 1289–93, 361–6 passim.

Statutes, private collections of, 70, 370. See Dictum; Marlborough; Merton; Westminster, provisions of.

— of Edward I, 355–80 passim; background of, 352–5; Acton Burnell (1283), 356, 375, 620, 625; *de finibus levatis*, 700 & n.; *de justiciis assignatis*, 352, 358; *Districciones Scaccarii* (1275), 325 n., 372 & n.; Gloucester (1278),

328 n., 330 n., 353, 357, 372 n., 376, 377; Jews (1275), 322; merchants (1285), 356, 357 & n., 367, 375, 620, 625, 627, 711 n.; Mortmain (*de religiosis*, 1279), 325, 476, 479; *Quia emptores* (1290), 357, 376, 379–80; *Quo Warranto* (1290), 357, 372, 376–9, 513 & n.; Rhuddlan (1284), 356, 357 n.; Wales (1284), 322, 429, 435–7 passim; Westminster I (1275), 353, 356, 357, 361 & n., 368, 371 n., 372 n., 375, 377, 540, 620; Westminster II (1285), 357, 361 n., 366, 369, 371 n., 373–4, 377, 379 n., 464 n., 480 & n. (clerical objections to), 625, 627; Winchester (1285), 357 & n., 369, 374, 543, 570, 627.

Stavensby, Alexander, bishop of Coventry (1224–40), 60.

Stenton, D. M., on Bracton, 727.

Stenton, F. M., on the road system, 776.

Stevenson, W. H., on Hewlett's edition of Wendover, 731.

Steward of the royal household, 50, 323.

— Stewart, Stuart, family of, in Scotland, and the stewardship, 576, 579–80 & n., 685 & n.; James the, one of the guardians (1286), 597, 607, 612; in Scottish wars, 684, 687, 697 n., 711; his brother John, killed at Falkirk, 690; his son Walter, husband of Margery Bruce and father of King Robert III, 685 n. See FitzAlan (Walter) for the first hereditary steward.

Stewart-Brown, R., on the succession to the honour and county of Chester, 197 n.; on serjeants of the peace and Cheshire administration, 749.

Stirling Bridge, battle at (1297), 669, 683, 686, 687, 690.

— castle, 574, 614, 686; captured by the Scots (1299), 692; held till 1304, 695, 708, 711; siege of and surrender of (1304), 710–11; pact of Bruce and Lamberton at (1304), 714 & n.; parliament in (1295), 612; Dominican priory of, 692.

Stones, E. L. G., 603 n.; on the submission of Robert Bruce to Edward I, 695 n.

Strata Florida, Cistercian abbey in Ceredigion, 389, 393; abbot of (1248), 389–90.

Stratford Langthorne, royalist headquarters at (1267), 214.

Strathcathro, 615.

Strathorde, 709, 713 n.

Stratton, Adam de, career and downfall of, 364–5, 366.

Strayer, J. B., on Norman administration, 320 n.; on laicization, 527 n.

Sturler, J. de, writings of, 643 n.

Subsidies, *see* Taxation.

Suit of Court, 67–68, 147, 149.

Susa, 250; Henry de, archbishop of Embrun, 135–6.

Sutcliffe, Dorothy, on administration of Pecham's estates, 484 n.

Sutton, Oliver, bishop of Lincoln (1280–99), 486, 490 n.

Swans, feast of the (1306), 515–16 & nn.

Sweet, A. H., on papal indults, 760.

Sweet, Jennifer, on preaching, 765.

Sweetheart abbey, 229, 693 & n., 702.

Swereford, Alexander, and the exchequer, 65.

Swift, F. D., on the marriage alliance between Edward and Peter of Aragon, 258 n.

Swinfield, Richard, bishop of Hereford (1283–1317), 487.

Synods, diocesan, and constitutions, 451–2.

Syria, cross-currents in (1260), 167 n.

Syward, *see* Siward.

Taillebourg, 103, 105.

Tain, 716.

Tait, J., on Wharton's attribution of the lives of the archbishops of Canterbury, 738.

Talbot, C. H. on recluses, 766.

Tallage, 529–31; in Henry III's time, 36; in 1268, 221–2 & n.; in 1304, 534; use of term in 1297, 682 & n.; *de tallagio non concedendo*, 681–2 n.

Talley church, 390 n.

Talmont, 90.

Tanqueray, F. J., letters of Edward I, 742.

Tany, Luke de, seneschal of Gascony (1272–8), his career, 279; and Gaston of Béarn, 284–5; replaced by John de Grilly, 288; his operations and death in Anglesey (1282), 426–7 & n.

Tarascon, treaty of (1291), 261, 262.

Tarragona, archbishop of, 252, 258.

Tartars, 110 n., 167 & n. *See* Mongols.

Taxatio papae Nicholai, 498 n., 509.

Taxation, in Henry III's reign, 28–37, 75, 78, 221–4, 281 n., 535–6; proposed in 1258, 135, 142; in Edward I's reign, 37, 343–4, 513, 523–8, 534–6, 673, 674 n., 680–1, 703, 715; of Chester, Wales and the Marches (1290–2), 259, 443, 560; of Ireland, 535 & n., 560. *See* Parliament, Representation.

— of the clergy, 478–9, 500–9, 675–7; in parliament, 673–4; by the pope, for the king, 220–1, 497, 498–500.

— of the clergy for and by the pope,

as subsidies, 448, 497 & n. 3, 499 n., 501; as mandatory, 264–7, 470 & n., 472, 496 ff., 641–2 & n.; in Scotland, 573 & n., 583 & n., in provinces of Gaul for crusade against Aragon, 254 & n.

Taylor, A. J., on James of St. George, 430 n.; on Caernarvon castle and town well, 430 n.; on rolls of court of rape of Lewes, 729; on the birth of Edward of Caernarvon, 755; on Thomas of Houghton, engineer, 770.

Tegeingl, *see* Englefield.

Templars, 27, 82, 761.

Temple, the new, London, 17, 82, 136, 147–8, 641, 677; in Paris, 14, 126; Master of the, in England, 3, 17, 112.

Temporalities, 498 & n., 509, 513, 523 n.

Testa, William, 718 & n.

teste me ipso, 25.

Thatcham (Berks.), 535 n.

Theobald IV, count of Champagne, king of Navarre (d. 1253), 104, 105, 109 & n., 111, 116, 237.

— V, count of Champagne; king of Navarre (1253–70), 237–8.

Thomas, St., Aquinas, 230.

— St., Becket, of Canterbury, new shrine of, 14, 24; Pecham on his martyrdom, 478; cf. 489 n.

— count of Savoy (d. 1233), 73, 250 n.

Thompson, A. Hamilton, on diocesan organization, 445 n.; on the Welsh dioceses, 390 n.

Thomson, S. Harrison, on Burley's commentary on the *Politics*, 522 n.

Thomson, W. S., on the history of prise, and an assize roll of 1298, 699 n.; cf. 218 n.

Thorne, S. E., various articles on the interplay of law and custom, 749; on courts of record, 750.

Thouars, 91; family of, 87, 90, 91.

— Guy, count of, 92 n.

— later name of the bastide of Baa, 310.

Throop, P. A., on criticism of the crusade, 83 n.

Thuringia, 660.

Thurkelby, Roger, judge, 150 & n.

Tickhill, 118.

Tithes, 464 & n., 469 n.

Toledo, treaty of (1254), 118, 120.

Tonbridge castle, 187.

Tonneins, 294.

Toron, 107.

Toulouse, county of, 87–88; wine merchants of, 306; conference at (1280), 253.

— Jeanne of, wife of Alphonse of Poitiers (d. 1271), 272 & n.

— Raymond, count of, *see* Raymond.

Tourn, sheriff's, 68.

Tournaments, 515 and n., 516, 770; the Lord Edward and, 159.

Tours, 91.

Tout, T. F., on Wales and the March, 400 n.; on Bishop Halton as a papal collector, 498 n.; on medieval town-planning, 634 n.; on the burglary of the great wardrobe (1303) 698 n.; on the Scottish parliament, 753.

Tower of London, 20, 24, 25, 48, 50, 52, 65, 76, 369, 399, 685, 687 n., 704, 712, 716; during the years 1258–67, 137, 163, 165, 176, 180, 187, 188, 203, 213, 214; John and Edward Baliol in (1297–9), 615; records in, 277.

Town-planning, 634–7.

Toynbee, Margaret, on the sons of Charles of Salerno, 283 n.

Trabut-Cussac, J.-C., on Edward I and Gascony, 274 n., 746, and Ch. VII *passim*; on Edward I's itinerary (1286–9), 745; on the bastides, 308 n.; on the foundation of Sauveterre, 309 n.

Trade, and credit on a gold basis, beginnings of, 638–9; bibliographical note on, 773.

Trailbaston, 345–6.

Trajan, story of, 143.

Trapani, 232, 253.

Treaties and sworn compacts, 49, 152.

Treharne, R. F., on Henry III's *gravamina* (1263–4), 179–80 n.; on the battle of Northampton, 187 n.; on Henry III's parliaments, 747.

Trim, liberty of, 517 n., 564.

Troubadours and politics, 95–96, 99, 100, 102.

Trubleville, Henry de, 98, 318.

— Hugh de, 275.

Truces and treaties, 84–87.

Tudor, Owen, and the royal house of, 391 n.

Tudur ab Ednyfed, seneschal of Llywelyn ap Gruffydd, 391.

tuitio, 466 n., 492–4.

Turberville, Thomas, the traitor, 440 n., 612 n.

Turnberry castle, 598, 694, 695.

Turnemire, William of, master of the mint (1279), 633, 634 n.

Turner, G. J., on final concords, 728; on John le Breton, 729; on Henry III's minority, 744.

Tutbury (Staffs.), 184.

Tweng, Robert, 45–46.

Tybetot, Robert, 196; justiciar of west Wales (1281), 415, 422, 436; and Rhys ap Maredudd, 438–40; sent to Gascony (1294), 441, 649 & n.

Tyndale, honour of, 587 & n., 600 n., 610 n.

Tyre, archbishop of, 12.

Tyson, M., on the annals of Southwark and Merton, 735.

Udimore, 681, 686 n.

Ullmann, W., on kingship, 381 n.; on a disputed episcopal election, 468 n.

Ulster, Anglo-Irish liberty in, and shire of, 564; earl of, *see* Burgh, Richard de.

Umfraville, family of, 580; Ingram d', a guardian (1300), 694; in France (1302–4), 697; King Edward and, 711.

Unam Sanctam, 652.

Unwin, G., on London wool exporters, 622 n.

Urban IV, Pope (1261–5), and the Sicilian business, 121, 123, 168; annuls Provisions of Oxford, 168; and Richard of Cornwall, 173–4; sends cardinal legate (Nov. 1263), 180; on the constitutions of Archbishop Boniface, 456.

Usk castle, 54, 55.

Utrecht, prince-bishopric of, 664.

Vale Royal, abbey of, 230; foundation stones laid at (1277), 412; building accounts of, 432.

Valencia, bishop of, 258.

Valence, bishop-elect of, *see* William of Savoy.

— (Saintonge), 139 n.

— Aymer de, son of William, 681; in Scotland, 1306–7, 715, 719.

— William de, eldest son of Isabella of Angoulême and Hugh of La Marche, lord of Pembroke in right of his wife, 133 n., 171; his actions in 1285, 137–40 *passim*; returns to England (1261), 162; escapes abroad after the battle of Lewes, 190; lands in Pembroke (1265), 200; takes the cross (1268), 219; presides over the transfer of the Agenais (1279), 292; with Edward in Gascony, 290; and Wales, 406 & n., 422, 441.

Valenciennes, John de, lord of Haifa, in England (1264), 186.

Valery, Érard de, 285 n., 312.

Valle Crucis, Cistercian monastery in Powys, 389, 410 n.

Valois, Charles of, second son of Philip III, declared king of Aragon by the pope, 254–5; receives Anjou and Maine, 272 n.; and the Gascon trouble, 646; commands French troops in Gascony (1295), 649.

INDEX

827

Valois, Jeanne de, treaty for her marriage with Edward Baliol (1295), 612, 613.

Vaud, 251.

Vaux, John de, 153.

Velthem, Lodewyk van, on the Welsh soldiers in Flanders, 384 & n.; on Edward I, 515 & nn.

Venaissin, 99, 272 & n.

Vendôme, treaties of (1227), 91–92 & n., 93.

Vere, Robert de, earl of Oxford, knighted at Lewes, 188.

Vescy, John de, of Alnwick, 173, 214, 257 n., 283.

Veurne (Furnes), defeat of Flemings at (1297), 669.

Vezzano, Geoffrey of, papal collector, and the administration of wills, 470–1, 504.

Vicars, 458–9, 760.

Vienne, council of (1311), material collected for use in, 483–4.

— Hugh de, king's clerk, 519 n.

Villandraut (Gironde), castle built by Pope Clement V, 444 (add. note).

Villefranche-de-Belvès, 302; castle of, 301.

Vincent, J. A. C., Lancashire lay subsidies, 725.

Vinea, Peter de, in England, 72.

Vipont, Robert de, of Appleby, 173.

Visconti, Tedaldo, *see* Gregory X.

Viterbo, murder of Henry of Almain at, 226.

Vyve-Saint-Bavon, truce of (1297) between Edward I and Philip IV, 644, 668.

Wagner, A. R., on the symbolism of the swans, 515 n.

Wake, Baldwin, 208.

— *Joan*, on the *communitas villae*, 775.

— William, 662.

Waleran the German, 40.

Walerand, Robert, 153, 163, 167, 196.

Wales, and the Crown, 381–2; English and foreign descriptions of the inhabitants of, 383–4; in the twelfth and thirteenth centuries, 384–91; changes in princely nomenclature in, 385, 392 n., 393; the Church in, 388–91, 406, 433–5; relations of Henry III with (1216–47), 20, 43–45, 54–55, 57, 60, 392–400; military geography in Marches of, 394, 406, 410–11; princes of and the Scots, 138, 582 & n., 592; how divided and administered between the first two Welsh wars (1277–82), 412–19 *passim*; centre and west overrun by David and Llywelyn, and reoccupied, 419–23;

absolution of and bonds made by Welsh to keep the peace, 421 n.; castles and boroughs of, 430–3; statute of, and administration of (1284–1307), 322, 429, 435–8, 443; last risings in, 438–43, 649.

Wales, barons of, royal vassals in so styled, 398, 413, 417, 418, 420, 421, 424 & n.

— Marches of, 368; social complexities in, 403 n., 409–10 & n., 437 & n., 443–4.

— 'friendly' Welsh in, 411, 421; archers and foot soldiers of, in Flanders, 384, 679; in Scotland, 689, 690, 694 & n.

Waleys, Henry, merchant of London, mayor of London and Bordeaux, 632, 635, 636 & n.

Wallace, William, 332, 333, 572, 576; his rise to power (1297–8), 669, 683, 684, 686 & n., 687; his defeat at Falkirk, 689, 690; his later years (1299–1305), 694, 696 & n., 709, 711, 712.

Wallingford castle, 40 & n., 160, 170, 196; mayor of, 366.

Walne, P., on the baronial grievances, 183.

Walsingham abbey, Edward I at, 665, 666.

Ward, Grace F., on early history of the Merchant Staplers, 620 n.

Wardrobe, the king's, 767; as centre of administration, 337–8, 524 n., 662, 667 n.; keepers of, *see* Droxford, Langton (Walter); the great, 698 n.

Ware, Richard, abbot of Westminster, treasurer (1280–3), 485 n.

Warenne, family of, 23 & n., 51.

— John de, earl of Surrey (d. 1304), 153, 154; marries Alesia de Lusignan (1247), 138 n.; and the Provisions of Oxford, 138, 140; views of, in 1261, 164; joins the new baronial party (1262–3), 173; rejoins Edward, 177; in war of 1264, 187, 190; lands in Pembroke (1265), 200; at Chesterfield, 209; takes the cross (1268), 219; granted Bromford and Yale, 424; and the legend of *quo warranto*, 521 & n.; father-in-law of John Baliol, king of Scots, 602 n.; custodian of northern shires (1295), 613; defeats Scots at Dunbar (1296), 614; warden of Scotland, 615, 685, 686 & n., 688, 689, 704 n., 707; defeated at Stirling bridge, 669, 686; his death, 707 n.

— John de, earl of Surrey, grandson and heir of John, m. Joan of Bar (1306), 138 n., 517; his father, William, 138 n.

Wark, manor, in Tyndale, 587 n., 600 n.

Wark-onTweed, castle, 20, 613; Henry III at (1255), 590, 591 n.

'Warwolf', siege engine, 711.

Watch and ward, 53–54, 69 n.

Watkin, A., on a Winchester priory receiver's roll, 762.

Watton, 716.

Waugh, W. T., on Pecham and pluralities, 474 n.

Wayland, Thomas de, chief justice of common pleas, 363.

Weald, the, 10; archers of, 422 n.; men of, 187.

Weights and measures, ordinance of, 620 n.

Weiss, R., on some letters of Benedict Gaetani, 263 n.

Wells, hall of bishop at, 339.

Welshpool, borough, 433.

Westminster, great councils at (1293–4), 55, 57; in 1237, 75; parliaments in 1258 and 1259, 144–6, 148–50; Llywelyn ap Gruffydd does homage at (1277), 412; archbishop Pecham and parliament in (1279), 476; Edward I's return to (1285), 480; Provisions of (1259), 146, 147–9, 174, 194, 216, 217, 370; statutes of, see Statutes.

— Abbey, 18, 119, 222, 224; burglary in (1303), 689 n.; chapel of St. Katherine, 75 (solemn excommunication of offenders against the Charters, 1237); refectory, 78, 113, 672 (discussions of 1244, trial of Simon de Montfort in 1252, 'Convocation' of 1294); records in, 277; abbots of, see Crockesley; Ware.

— Hall, Provisions of Westminster read in (1259), 148; settlement of March 1265 proclaimed in, 198; William Wallace tried in (1305), 712; Feast of Swans in (1306), 514–15, 715; proclamations about petitions in, 350.

Westmorland, local levies in (1297–8), 684, 688.

White, G. H., on the royal household and king's sport, 767.

White castle, 43.

Whithorn, see of, 597 n.

Whitland, Cistercian abbey, and its daughter houses, 389.

Whitwell, R. J., on Italian merchants, 637 n.; on monastic wool trade, 638 n.

— and C. Johnson, on galley building, 656 n.

Whorlton castle (Yorks.), 203.

Wickwane, William, archbishop of York (1279–85), his dispute with the prior and convent of Durham, 469 n.; on the duties of a metropolitan, 490 n.

Wieruszowski, Helene, on the background of the Sicilian Vespers, 253 n.

Wight, Isle of, acquired by Edward I, 518. See Forz; Quarr.

Wigmore, 185, 201, 203.

Wilkinson, B., on the crisis of 1297, 680 nn.; on the Scottish raids into Northumbria, 686 n.

Willard, J. F., on taxation and parliamentary boroughs, 533 n.; on exchequer reform (1290), 524 n.; his tables of taxes on movables, 526 n.; on an ordinance for the guidance of a deputy treasurer, 748; on the treasurer's clerk and the issue roll, 748; on the observance of Sundays in the lower exchequer, 748; on the agricultural year, 776.

William the Lion, king of Scots, 23 n., 574, 575, 585; his treaty with King John (1212), 586, 594–5; and Richard I, 601.

— of Savoy, bishop-elect of Valence, uncle of Eleanor of Provence, 74–75.

Williams, G. A., on Edward I and London, 643 n.

Williamson, Dorothy M., on Cardinal Otto's legation in England, 453 n.; and in Scotland, 585 n.

Williamson, J. A., on changes in the southern coast-line, 635 n.

Willikin of the Weald, see Kensham, William of.

Wills, administration of, 470–1, 490–1.

Wilton, William of, judge, 176 n.

Winchelsea, 10, 207; new town of, 635–7 & n.; Edward I's port of departure for Flanders (1297), 636, 668, 676, 678.

Winchelsey, Robert of, archbishop of Canterbury, 488; his character, 673, 678, 717–18; his election and arrival in England, 671–3 passim; his debts, 672, 718; his dilemma in regard to clerical taxation by the king, 523, 672–8 passim, 680; takes papal letters about Scotland to the king (1300), 229, 693 & n., 702; his action in parliament of Lincoln (1301), 704, 705; his strained relations with Edward I, suspension and departure from England, 717–18.

Winchester, 10; castle, 716; fair of, 619 n.; Christmas feast of 1231 at, 48; declaration of peace and ordinance against Montfortians issued at (1265), 203, 204, 209, 213; statute of (1285), 54, see Statutes.

— bishops of, see Roches; Ralegh; Lusignan (Aymer); Gervase (John); Pontissara.

Winchester, earls of, *see* Quincy.

Windsor castle, 22, 25, 48, 63 n., 118 n.; council at (1236), 74 n.; knights of shire summoned to (1261), 166; the Lord Edward surrenders (1263), 176, 180, 181; restored to King Henry, 203; ordinances issued at (1265), 204–5.

Wine, prise of, 629 n., 631 n.; trade with Gascony in, 276, 669 n. *See* Bordeaux, customs of; Gascony.

Wingham, Henry of, king's clerk, chancellor (1255–60), bishop of London (1260–2), 112, 162.

Wishart, Robert, bishop of Glasgow (1273–1316), one of the guardians of Scotland (1286), 597, 598, 606; his vote in succession case, 607; and the rising of 1297, 684 & n.; imprisoned (1297–9), 685 & n.; swears fealty to Edward (1300), 710 n.; his defection, rebuked by Pope Boniface, 709–10; his later tergiversations and imprisonment (1303–6), 710 n., 711–14 *passim*, 716.

Wither, William, 46; *see* Tweng.

Wogan, John, justiciar of Ireland, 535.

Wolverhampton, 339.

Wolvesey, castle of bishop of Winchester, 140.

Woodstock, treaty of (1247), 400 & n., 412.

Wool, fells, and hides, continental trade in English and Welsh, 637–8 & nn.; customs on, 532, 628, 629–31 & nn.; receipts from, 630; embargo on export of, to Flanders (1270–8) and value of licensed exports, 621–2; maltote on (1294–7), 630, 663, 669, 682, 683; prices of, 629 n., 637–8; seizures and royal control of sales of, as a war measure (1294–7), 648, 662–3, 666, 671; centralized control of exports to Holland and Brabant and beginnings of the staple, first in Dordrecht, then in Antwerp, 663–4; prises of, 659, 680–1, and inquiries into, 699; assignation of customs on, to men of Bayonne (1299–1304), 650 & n.

Worcester, King John buried in cathedral church of, 1; treaty of (1218), 16, 393; stormed in 1264, 185; pact of (1264), 196–8, 199; headquarters of the Lord Edward (1265), 202; King Edward's armies at, 408, 441.

— bishops of, *see* Evesham, Sylvester of; Cantilupe, Walter de.

Wreck, law of, 375, 620.

Wright, E. C., on common law and the forests, 767.

Writs, royal, control of new, 78; of expenses, 144 n.; return of, 366, 377–8; special, 327, 330, cases without, 218; register of original, in Ireland and Wales, 560 & n.; dated in Scotland to be admitted in England (1291), 560 n.

Writs, of caption, 465 & n., 467; *de tali saisina habenda*, 15–16, 205; *rex relatu plurimorum*, 468.

Wulfstan, St., shrine of, 1.

Wych, St. Richard, bishop of Chichester (d. 1253), 57, 487.

Wycombe, Bucks., 53.

Wyke-on-Hull, 634.

Wykes, Thomas, on the crisis of 1260, 156, 158, 159, 162.

Wyle, Walter de la, bishop of Salisbury (1263–71), 176 n.

Wyre, forest of, baronial meeting in (1297), 679–80.

Yale (Ial), 410 n., 424.

Yarmouth, disputes between men of and men of Cinque Ports, 645 & n.; ships of, in war time, 655 n., 656.

Yolande, d. of John of Brienne and heiress of kingdom of Jerusalem, second wife of Frederick II, 107 n.

— of Dreux, second wife of Alexander III, king of Scots (1285), 597, 598; marries Arthur, later duke of Brittany (1294); transmits the Montfort claim to Brittany, 598 & n.

York, treaty of (1237), 574, 579, 586, 593–4; Henry III writes to archbishop and citizens of (1260), 158; assemblies of laymen and clergy at (1283), 506; transfer of exchequer and bench to (1298–1304), 627 n., 688; administrative centre during Scottish wars, 688, 695, 704 n., 711; summons to parliament in (1298), 688; royal council to meet in (1301), 316.

— ecclesiastical province of; archbishop's claim over Scottish bishoprics, 583; court of archbishop of, 493–4; convocations of clergy of, 506, 507 & n. *See* Gray; Giffard; Romeyn; Wickwane.

— castle, 627 n.; great hall of, 627 n.; minster, 494 n.; St. Mary's abbey, abbot of, 165.

Young, Jean I., on the Ostmen, 565 n.

Yverdon, castle and town, 431.

Zaccaria, Benedetto, admiral and merchant, 639.

Zuche, William de la, 153.

Zulueta, F. de, on William of Drogheda, 759.